Encyclopedia of
JAPAN

Japanese History and Culture, From Abacus to Zori

Dorothy Perkins

A Roundtable Press Book

Facts On File
New York • Oxford

Encyclopedia of Japan: Japanese History and Culture, from Abacus to Zori
Copyright © 1991 by Roundtable Press and Dorothy J. Perkins

Facts On File, Inc.   Facts On File Limited
460 Park Avenue South   Collins Street
New York NY 10016   Oxford OX4 1XJ
USA   United Kingdom

Library of Congress Cataloging-in-Publication Data

Perkins, Dorothy.
   Encyclopedia of Japan: Japanese History and Culture, from Abacus to Zori /
   Dorothy Perkins.
      p.   cm.
   Includes bibliographical references.
   ISBN 0-8160-1934-7
   1. Japan—Dictionaries and encyclopedias. I. Title.
DS805.P47 1991
952'.003—dc20   89-71499

A British CIP catalogue record for this book is available from the British Library.

Facts On File books are available at special discounts when purchased in
bulk quantities for businesses, associations, institutions or sales
promotions. Please call our Special Sales Department in New York at
212/683-2244 (dial 800/322-8755 except in NY, AK or HI) or in Oxford at
865/728399.

Jacket design by Ed Atkeson
Composition by Facts On File
Manufactured by The Maple-Vail Book Manufacturing Group
Printed in the United States of America

10 9 8 7 6 5 4 3 2 1

This book is printed on acid-free paper.

For Herman

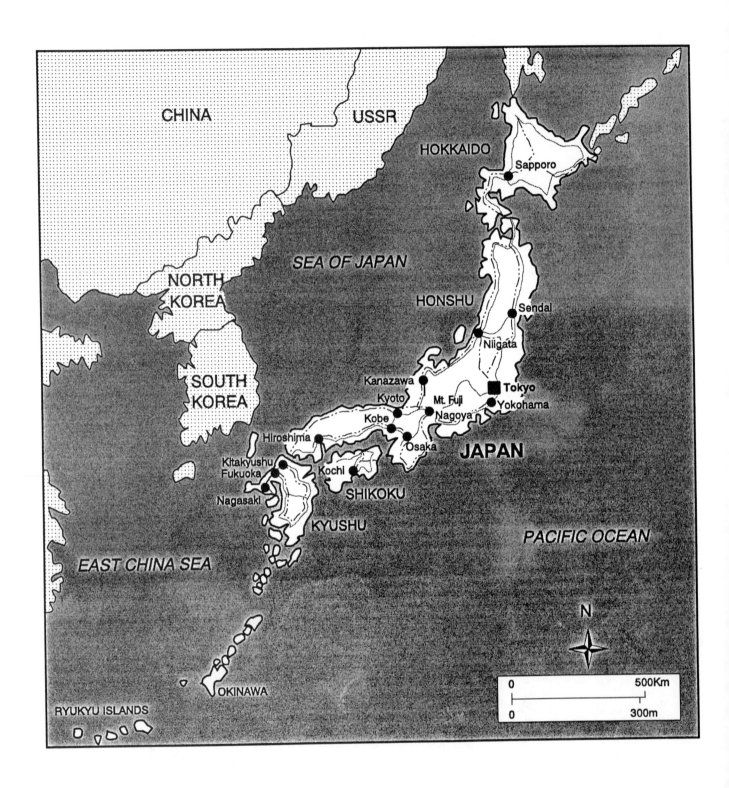

CHINA

USSR

HOKKAIDO

Sapporo

SEA OF JAPAN

NORTH
KOREA

HONSHU

Sendai

Niigata

SOUTH
KOREA

Kanazawa

Kyoto

Mt. Fuji

Tokyo

Kobe

Nagoya

Yokohama

Hiroshima

Osaka

JAPAN

Kitakyushu
Fukuoka

Kochi

Nagasaki

SHIKOKU

PACIFIC OCEAN

KYUSHU

EAST CHINA SEA

N

OKINAWA

0	500Km
0	300m

RYUKYU ISLANDS

CONTENTS

PREFACE

Japan is perhaps the most homogeneous yet most complex, the most ancient yet most modern country in the world. This book is intended to serve as an introduction to the history and culture of this fascinating nation. Toward this end, we have presented alphabetical entries covering the following categories:

major cities
geography and climate
animals, birds, vegetation
historical eras and figures—ancient, feucal and modern
government and politics
business and economics
religion—sects, leaders, shrines and temples, festivals
language and writing system
literature
fine arts
crafts and architecture
customs and etiquette
family life
food and clothing
daily life and popular culture
sports and martial arts
important Westerners in Japan

Copious cross-references lead the reader to related terms, and a bibliography is included for readers who want further detail.

All Japanese, Chinese and Korean personal names are given in the customary East Asian order, with family name first followed by the given name (for example, Kaifu Toshiki), except for Japanese-Americans, whose names are given in the Western manner (e.g., George Nakashima). The romanization of Japanese words has created numerous and often confusing variations in spelling; this book attempts to follow common usage in this area. A Japanese word can be both singular and plural; therefore an *s* is not added to Japanese words; *geisha* and *kimono*, for example, are either singular or plural, depending on the context. Some Japanese words have long, or double, vowels, which are usually indicated by macrons; for example, *ryokan* is a traditional Japanese inn, while Ryōkan is a famous 18–19th century poet. However, macrons have not been used in this text, with the Western reader in mind. Pronunciation of Japanese words is explained in the entry ''Language, Japanese.''

Japanese words familiar to Western readers, such as samurai, shogun, and sushi have not been italicized. These entries, and those for which there is no ready English equivalent, are listed under their Japanese term. Most entries, however, are listed under their English name. Some words are commonly preceded by the honorific *o-* in Japanese, such as *o-bento* (lunch box); entries have been listed without the use of *o-* for the reader's convenience.

The information in this book was current as of press date. In consideration of the rapid rate of change in Japan—and the world—particularly in the economic and political spheres, we will make every effort to revise the text in subsequent editions.

A

ABACUS *(soroban)* A traditional device for performing addition and other mathematical calculations. Invented in China, the abacus was brought to Japan in the 14th century by Chinese merchants. An abacus has a rectangular frame with vertical rods divided by a central bar into two sections. Each rod has one bead in the upper section and four or five beads in the lower section. The upper beads across the abacus represent 5, 50, 500, etc. from right to left. The lower beads represent 1s, 10s, 100s, etc., also from right to left. Addition, subtraction, multiplication and division are performed by moving the appropriate beads toward the central bar. The abacus is cleared to zero by moving the beads away from the central bar. Although electronic calculators are now commonly used in Japan, learning to use the abacus is still popular and many private schools offer lessons. From six months to one year of training is required to learn basic mathematical calculations. The Japan Chamber of Commerce and Industry holds annual nationwide abacus tests and competitions. See also EDUCATION SYSTEM; JAPAN CHAMBER OF COMMERCE AND INDUSTRY.

ABALONE *(awabi)* Large marine snails; a type of seafood. Ten species of abalone, three of which are commonly eaten, live in the waters off Japan's coasts. They are also cultivated by shellfish farmers. The Japanese eat abalone boiled or raw and served with a soy sauce dip. Since ancient times, the abalone has been used by Japanese poets to symbolize unrequited love because, unlike clams, e.g., it has only one shell. The abalone also has religious significance. Strips of abalone were dried and flattened, then attached to offerings made to *kami,* or divine spirits in the Shinto religion. Today, gifts given in Japan for auspicious occasions are decorated with specially folded paper strips, known as *noshi,* which represent dried abalone. See also KAMI; SEAFOOD; SHINTO; SOY SAUCE; WRAPPING.

ABE KOBO (1924–) A prominent contemporary Japanese novelist and playwright. Abe was born in Tokyo to a family originally from the northernmost island of Hokkaido, but he was raised in the town of Mukden (Shenyang) in northern China. In 1941, during World War II, Abe was sent to Tokyo for military training and higher education. He studied medicine at Tokyo University because of family pressure to go into his father's profession, but he did not become a doctor. He married an artist and stage designer named Machi while still in school. She has illustrated many of his books. Abe began writing stories and plays in medical school, many of which were published in the late 1940s and 1950s. He went on to write novels that portray the alienation of modern human beings and their loss of personal identity in urban, industrial society.

Abe's concern with these universal contemporary issues has led critics to characterize him as an existentialist writer. His style is often described as "absurd." Characters are trapped in what he portrays as the "labyrinth"—the modern, impersonal city—with no escape and no higher meaning.

A theatrical group headed by Abe produces his plays. Many of Abe's novels and plays have been translated into English, including *The Woman in the Dunes* (*Suna no onna,* 1962; translated in 1964; also made into a movie), *The Face of Another* (*Tanin no kao,* 1964; translated 1966), *The Ruined Map* (*Moetsukita chizu,* 1967; translated 1969), *Friends* (*Tomodachi,* 1967; translated 1971), *The Man Who Turned into a Stick* (*Bo ni natta otoko,* 1969; translated 1975), *The Box Man* (*Hato otoko,* 1973; translated 1974), *The Secret Rendezvous* (*Mikkai,* 1977; translated 1979), and *The Ark Sakura* (*Sakura no Bune;* translated 1987). See also FILMS; NOVELS.

ABE MASAHIRO (1819–1857) A *daimyo* (feudal lord) of Fukuyama (part of modern Hiroshima Prefecture) who was forced by U.S. Commodore Matthew Calbraith Perry to sign a treaty of friendship between Japan and the United States. This ended Japan's isolation from Western countries, which had been imposed by the Tokugawa Shogunate, or military regime (1603–1867), in A.D. 1639. Abe was a senior councillor *(roju)* in the Tokugawa government from 1843 to 1857 and served as chief senior councillor *(roju shuseki)* between 1845 and 1855. In 1853 Perry confronted Japan with a fleet of American warships and demanded that Japan end its isolation. Abe wanted to ensure that the Tokugawa Shogunate's reply to Perry would maintain Japanese unity, so he consulted the country's *daimyo,* political scholars, and the imperial court in Kyoto. This proved unwise, as Abe received no direct replies indicating support for any decision by the shogunate. Moreover, opening up the decision-making process to powerful *daimyo* and the imperial court eventually caused them to work for the downfall of the Tokugawa Shogunate and the restoration of imperial power under Emperor Meiji in 1868. When Abe decided to sign the agreement between Japan and the United States, known as the Kanagawa Treaty, he reversed the shogunate's policy toward Western countries. This angered many in Japan, who adopted the slogan "Expel the Barbarians." The treaty with the United States also provided a model for the so-called Ansei Commercial Treaties between Japan and other Western nations, which the Japanese considered unfair. In 1855 Abe was forced by political opponents to resign as chief senior councillor, although he retained influence with the shogunate until his death. See also ANSEI COMMERCIAL TREATIES; DAIMYO; ISOLATION OF JAPAN; MEIJI RESTORATION OF 1868; PERRY, MATTHEW

1

CALBRAITH; "REVERE THE EMPEROR, EXPEL THE BARBARIANS"; TO-
KUGAWA SHOGUNATE.

ACUPUNCTURE   See MEDICINE, TRADITIONAL; SHIATSU.

ADAMS, WILLIAM (1564–1620)   A ship navigator and
the first Englishman to reside in Japan. Adams was navi-
gating the Dutch ship *Die Liefde* to the East Indies when it
was wrecked in a storm off the Japanese coast. The Japanese first saw his ship near the town of Funai (modern
Oita) off the coast of Kyushu Island on April 19, 1600.
Adams became the few surviving sailors' leader because
he spoke Portuguese, a language with which the Japanese
were familiar from Portuguese Jesuit missionaries active in
Japan. Adams was taken to the city of Osaka three times
in May and June of that year to meet the powerful warlord
Tokugawa Ieyasu. Tokugawa took control of Japan after
winning the Battle of Sekigahara a few months later and
established the Tokugawa Shogunate, the government that
ruled a unified Japan until the Meiji Restoration of 1868.
Valuing the information that Adams could provide about
Western technology, government, trade, religious affairs,
and maritime navigation, he made Adams one of his official
foreign advisors and gave him an estate with about 100
retainers in the village of Hemimura (now part of the naval
port of Yokosuka) on the Miura Peninsula. Adams also
had a house in Edo (modern Tokyo), the city chosen by
Tokugawa Ieyasu to supersede Kyoto as the new capital of
Japan. The house survived until the 1930s, and the street
on which it was located, in the Nihonbashi district, used
to be known as Anjin-cho, The Navigator Street. Adams
was known to the Japanese by the name Miura Anjin, for
the peninsula where he had his estate (Miura) and for his
vocation as a ship navigator *(anjin)*.

Adams had left a wife and daughter in England, but
Tokugawa refused permission for him to return there. Six
of the letters Adams wrote to his wife describing his experiences in Japan are preserved in the records of the
British East India Company, and have been published. His
ship's log remains as well. Letters and diaries written by
other Englishmen in Japan 1613–20 provide a few more
details about Adams, as do some Japanese records. He
wore Japanese clothing, became fluent in the language and
married a Japanese woman who bore him two children,
Joseph and Susan. When England and Japan signed their
first commercial treaty in 1613, Adams helped to establish
an English trading station in Hirado on Kyushu Island and
acquired trading privileges in Japan for the London East
India Company. He could have returned home on an
English ship then, but he chose to stay in Japan, partly
because of his many conflicts with the English traders. He
also navigated a Japanese trading ship to Thailand and
back in 1615–16.

After Tokugawa Ieyasu died in 1615, his son and successor, Tokugawa Hidetada, began to persecute foreigners
in Japan. Adams became ill in 1619 and died at Hirado at
the age of 57 on May 16, 1620. His Japanese son Joseph
inherited the estate in Hemimura. He, too, became a ship's
pilot and navigated several trading ships to Southeast Asia.

Adams had continued to send money to his English family,
and his will provided for them and his Japanese family
alike. The town of Ito on the Izu Peninsula holds an annual
festival to honor Miura Anjin. The district of Hemimura
outside Yokosuka holds occasional celebrations for him.
William Adams became a romantic figure to Westerners
and the subject of more than half a dozen novels and
biographies. The best-known, based on Adams' experience, is *Shogun* (1975) by James Clavell, about a pilot named
Blackthorne. The book was turned into an acclaimed television mini-series by a joint Japanese and American production starring Richard Chamberlain and into a Broadway
musical. See also DUTCH IN JAPAN; EDO ERA; FOREIGN TRADE;
FOREIGNERS IN JAPAN; IZU PENINSULA; KYUSHU ISLAND; PORTUGUESE
IN JAPAN; SHOGUN; TOKUGAWA IEYASU.

ADULTS' DAY (Seijin-no-hi, "Coming-of-Age Day")   A
national holiday on January 15th to honor individuals
reaching their 20th birthday in the year up to and including
this date. In Japan, 20 is the age of majority. At this age,
Japanese are allowed to vote, drink and smoke. Each city
and village has a celebration for Adults' Day. In Tokyo,
new adults visit Meiji Shrine to give thanks and to pray
for a long life. Unmarried women put on a kimono called
a *furisode* with long sleeves and colorful designs. Adults'
Day was first celebrated on January 15, 1949. See also
BIRTHDAYS; HOLIDAYS, NATIONAL; KIMONO; MEIJI SHRINE.

ADVANCED MATERIALS   Japanese scientists have played
a leading role in developing advanced or new materials,
particularly plastics, ceramics and metal alloys, for industrial purposes. Industrial advanced ceramics, called fine
ceramics in Japan, are used for electronics, construction
and medical equipment. Created by reaction-bonding cal-
cination of chemically synthesized inorganic compounds,
they are harder, stronger and longer-lasting than metal,
and they can withstand high temperatures and heavy im-
pacts and do not rust. Examples of advanced ceramics are
almina-ceramic, used to make integrated circuit boards for
computers; silicon carbide, silicon nitride, and partially
stabilized zirconia. In 1990 Honda Motor Corporation introduced a sports car with a body made largely of plastic
and titanium alloy. Fine ceramic parts are also utilized in
automobile engines. Nissan Motor Co. sells six automobile
models that employ a ceramic turbocharger rotor. Composite materials are made by embedding metal fibers or
ceramics in plastics, and are used to manufacture aircraft
that are lighter, longer-range, and more fuel-efficient. The
United States–Japan cooperative project to develop the
FS-X fighter plane will utilize composite materials to construct one-piece wings. Advanced plastics and composites
are usually lighter, stronger and less expensive than metal,
and they decrease friction, vibration and noise and do not
corrode. However, they do not withstand high temperatures and the equipment for manufacturing them is extremely expensive. New materials are also used to make
microelectronic devices. These include silicon, an element
found in sand and used to etch electronic circuits on tiny
microprocessors, and gallium arsenide, made from gallium

and arsenic, to build semiconductors for satellites that consume less power and perform better than silicon devices. Japanese researchers are developing thin-film superconductors that offer no resistance to electricity and thus can be used for magnetic levitation trains and superefficient electric power lines. Telecommunications have been revolutionized by replacing copper wires with optical fibers, strands of glass the width of a human hair that carry thousands of telephone calls or digitized data in the form of light. Optical telecommunications cables are even being laid under oceans. Strong, long-lasting superglues have begun to replace welding as the means of bonding plastics, metal and ceramics. Cement for highways and buildings is made stronger and lighter by blending it with ceramics, plastics and metals. See also AUTOMOBILE INDUSTRY; COMPUTER INDUSTRY; ELECTRONICS INDUSTRY; RESEARCH AND DEVELOPMENT; SEMICONDUCTOR INDUSTRY; TELECOMMUNICATIONS SYSTEM.

ADVERTISING (senden) The Japanese advertising industry spent $34.5 billion in 1988, making it the second largest in the world after that of the United States. Advertising appears in newspapers and magazines and on television and radio.

Newspaper advertising began with the development of Westernized mass media during the Meiji Era (1868–1912). The first Japanese advertising agency (kokoku dairiten) was founded in 1873. Agencies developed as sales representatives for the media, rather than as marketers for corporate clients, as is the case in the United States. Commercial broadcasting, which began in Japan in 1951, stimulated the growth of postwar advertising, and as the Japanese economy grew rapidly starting in the 1960s, advertising agencies have flourished and copied many techniques from American advertisers.

At present there are around 4,000 Japanese advertising agencies, many of them small, which are mostly located in Tokyo or Osaka. Dentsu, Inc., is the largest advertising agency in Japan and one of the largest in the world. With around 6,000 employees, in 1987 Dentsu had billings of more than US$7 billion. It handles advertising for most large Japanese companies and public relations for the Japanese government. Dentsu was established in 1901 by Mitsunaga Hoshio, who also founded a telegraph company and news agency; the companies were merged in 1907. Dentsu maintains offices in the United States, Europe, and Southeast Asia.

Shop signs or signboards (kamban) were in use by the ninth century A.D., and traditional shop signs have become collectible folk art objects. Today, shopping and entertainment districts of Japanese cities, such as the Ginza in Tokyo, are brightly lit with colorful and imaginative neon signs. Divided curtains (noren), traditionally hung over shop entrances, are also decorated with symbols of the shops' products. Noren became popular in Japanese cities during the Edo Era (1600–1868), as did printed advertisements such as handbills. Woodblock prints (hanga) were largely used as advertisements for actors in the Kabuki theater. Today, posters remain an important Japanese form of advertising and are hung in subways, rail stations, and other public places. In fact, the French critic Roland Barthes has termed Japan "the empire of signs." Even department-store shopping bags, bento (food boxes), and wrapped sweets (kashi) are decorated with attractive calligraphy and graphic designs. Advertisements on Japanese television and in magazines aim to create a mood rather than simply describe a product. Their beauty and creativity have won them many international awards. See also BROADCASTING SYSTEM; CALLIGRAPHY; CAMERAS AND PHOTOGRAPHY; DEPARTMENT STORES; GINZA; MAGAZINES; NEWSPAPERS; SIGNBOARDS; STATIONS; WOODBLOCK PRINTS; WRITING SYSTEM, JAPANESE.

AESTHETIC CONCEPTS See HISAMATSU SHIN'ICHI; MA; MONO NO AWARE; SABI AND WABI; SEN NO RIKYU; SHIBUI; ZEAMI; YUGEN.

AGENCY FOR CULTURAL AFFAIRS See MINISTRY OF EDUCATION, SCIENCE, AND CULTURE; MUSEUMS IN JAPAN; NATIONAL TREASURES.

AGENCY OF INDUSTRIAL SCIENCE AND TECHNOLOGY (AIST) See MINISTRY OF INDUSTRIAL SCIENCE AND TECHNOLOGY; TSUKUBA ACADEMIC NEW TOWN.

AGRICULTURE Short-grain rice has long been the basic agricultural product in Japan. The traditional Japanese diet consists of rice, vegetables (often pickled), and fish. Many Japanese religious rituals and festivals are associated with the cycle of rice planting and harvesting. Today, Japanese farmers produce 10–13 million tons of rice annually, a volume far in excess of Japanese consumption. Output increased greatly in the 1960s, with improvements in rice varieties, mechanization of farming and government incentives to increase production, such as crop subsidies and price supports that have raised the price of domestic rice to 10 times the international market rate. Bread made with imported flour has become popular in Japan, contributing to a steady decrease in rice consumption. Except for rice, most of the agricultural products consumed by the Japanese have to be imported, especially other grains and soybeans. The Japanese government has restricted imports of rice, beef and oranges to protect domestic producers, but countries exporting these products have been lobbying to get these restrictions lifted.

Since Japan is a nation of small, mountainous islands, the amount of arable land is very limited and the soil is not very fertile. However, there is an abundance of rainfall, and a relatively mild climate and long growing season. The southern half of the country can grow two crops a year. Most agricultural products are grown by farm families who own less than 2 hectares (5 acres) of land but who get a high yield per acre. The Japanese quickly adopted advanced agricultural techniques from the West, such as mechanization and chemical fertilizers and pesticides.

Vegetables grown in Japan include potatoes, sweet potatoes, cabbage, cucumbers, eggplants, and daikon (Japanese radish), and fruits include persimmons, apples, pears, and, in southern regions, citrus fruits. There are large dairy farms, on the American model, on the cool northern island of Hokkaido. The Japanese have traditionally consumed little meat, and raised cows and horses mainly as draft animals. Today increasing amounts of meat are eaten. Chicken and pork breeding have increased, and meat imports increased 3.8 times between 1970 and 1983.

Local agricultural cooperative associations (nogyo kyodo kumiai, abbreviated nokyo) were established in 1900, disbanded in 1943, and revived throughout Japan with the land reforms during the postwar occupation. Tenant farming was abolished, and farm families were given 10–20 acres from the large estates, which were broken up. Today there are more than 10,000 agricultural cooperatives with a total membership of about 6 million. The cooperatives purchase fertilizer, seed and equipment in bulk, coordinate marketing of members' products and provide credit and other financial services. They have close ties with other local associations and with prefectural and national federations. The Central Union of Agricultural Cooperatives (Nokyo), organized in 1947, is the national federation of local cooperatives. It has persuaded the government to keep price supports for rice and other crops and prevent cheaper agricultural imports. Farmers demonstrate in Tokyo every year to pressure members of the Diet (parliament) to include generous farm supports in the national budget. Nokyo has made large contributions to campaign funds of the dominant Liberal Democratic Party (LDP), and farmers have been a major LDP constituency. They claim that agriculture is integral to the spirit of Japan and that self-sufficiency in food production is crucial to Japan's security. Other agricultural interest groups include the National Federation of Agricultural Cooperative Purchasing Associations and the National Federation of Agricultural Cooperative Marketing Associations.

With economic development, there has been a rapid decrease in the number of farm workers, and the farm labor force is aging, as young people move to the cities to attend universities and get good jobs. Most farm households have a source of income in addition to agriculture. By 1984, 4.5 million, or 12%, of Japanese households were engaged in farming, but only 13.5% of those households were exclusively engaged in agriculture. 71.1% had a larger proportion of their income from non-agricultural activities, such as factory work. The ratio of cultivated land in 1984 was 14.5% of the total land area, or 5.4 million hectares. The average area of cultivated land per farm household was 1.2 hectares. See also CITRUS FRUIT; CLIMATE OF JAPAN; COOKING, JAPANESE; DAIKON; EXPORTS AND IMPORTS; FAMILY; FARMHOUSE; FISH AND FISHING INDUSTRY; GEOGRAPHY OF JAPAN; PERSIMMON; PICKLES; RICE; RICE PLANTING AND HARVESTING FESTIVALS; SEASONS OF THE YEAR; SHINTO; SWEET POTATO.

AIKIDO "The Way of Harmony with Universal Energy"; a martial art of self-defense that emphasizes the relation of the person to ki (chi in Chinese; universal energy or power). Aikido was developed in Japan by Ueshiba Morihei (1883–1969) on the basis of ancient Chinese techniques for unarmed combat, known as jujutsu, which in modern times have become the sport of judo. Ueshiba adapted techniques for restraining attackers by flowing with their attacks and

turning their ki back against them. Manipulation of pressure points on the attackers' shoulders, elbows, wrists and other joints can lead to their being thrown or pinned down. Aikido students also learn special breathing and meditation techniques. The non-aggressive philosophy of aikido teaches how to overcome an opponent without harming him. Many women and elderly people have been attracted to the study of aikido. The Aikido Association was founded in Japan in 1948, and now has member groups throughout the world. See also JUDO; MARTIAL ARTS.

AINU A group of indigenous people who live on the northern island of Hokkaido and form one of Japan's three main minority groups, along with Koreans and a people of Japanese stock called burakumin ("people of the hamlets"). Formerly, the Ainu were a number of nomadic tribes spread over northern Japan who lived by hunting and fishing. They were gradually pushed out of their homeland by ethnic Japanese settlers moving north. By 1878 the Ainu tribes joined together in a common identity in opposition to the Japanese, who called the Ainu kyudojin ("former indigenous people"). The Ainu were finally forced to leave Honshu Island and move north to the less hospitable climate of Hokkaido and the Kuril Islands. Many placenames in northern Honshu are of Ainu origin.

It used to be thought that the Ainu belonged to the Caucasian race because of their light skin, facial and body hair, and lack of Mongoloid features that characterize the Japanese people. Recent genetic studies relate the Ainu to the Uralic, Altaic and Tungusic populations of Russian Siberia. Few Ainu of pure racial stock exist today because most Ainu have intermarried with Japanese. Almost no one speaks Ainu as their primary language. In addition to the Japanese language, the Ainu have taken up Japanese customs in food and housing, clothing, and ways of making a living. They have turned from nomadic hunting, fishing and plant gathering to agriculture, commercial deepsea fishing and seafood gathering. Traditional Ainu homes were rectangular buildings made with pole frames, thatched roofs and walls, and dirt floors. A raised wooden area covered with mats was used for sleeping. Fires were built in an open pit in the center for cooking, heating and religious ceremonies.

The Ainu believe in a remote world where the spirits of the ancestors live. These spirits control everything in the material world, so they must be given offerings to secure their blessings. Religious leaders called shamans communicate with the spirits by persuading spirit animals, especially bears, foxes and weasels, to deliver their messages. One of the most sacred Ainu rituals was the Bear Festival, at which they sacrificed a bear that they had raised from a cub. The bear is a god of the mountains having great power for the Ainu. At the festival the bear was led to an altar and given sake (rice wine) to drink. The women sang and danced for the bear. Then it was killed so that its spirit could return to the spirit world. The festival still takes place in the winter but the bear is no longer sacrificed. During the festival the Ainu wear their unique traditional clothing. A man dresses in a calf-length robe similar to a coat woven

An Ainu ceremony. The Ainu, a minority group racially distinct from the Japanese, are members of an indigenous tribe now living on the northern island of Hokkaido.

of fibers made from the bark of elm trees, and also a woven belt and deerskin vest. A woman wears a longer robe made in the same way and a cloth head covering. Clothing for special ceremonies is highly decorated with cotton appliques in bold abstract designs that originated in prehistoric times. Women also were heavily tattooed around the mouth, and on the backs of the hands and forearms, before they married. The Hyokeikan Gallery of the Tokyo National Museum in Ueno Park has a room displaying objects used by the Ainu in their daily life. Although the Ainu, not unlike Native Americans, have been discriminated against, the Japanese young Ainu have recently taken interest in their culture's art, rich folklore and way of life. The Hokkaido Utari Kyokai (Utari Association) was formed to represent the interests of the Ainu people. See also BURAKUMIN; FISH AND FISHING INDUSTRY; HOKKAIDO ISLAND; HONSHU ISLAND; KURIL ISLANDS; MINORITIES IN JAPAN; SAKE; SHAMANS AND SHAMANISM; UENO PARK.

AIR DEFENSE COMMAND See SELF-DEFENSE FORCES.

AIRLINES AND AIRPORTS Japan has three airline companies, three international airports and a nationwide network of domestic airports. The largest airport, New Tokyo International Airport, was opened in 1978 in Narita, north of the city of Tokyo. The airport was built in the middle of a rice-growing area, and its opening was delayed due to violent protests by radical students and farmers against the government taking their property. Narita Airport handles about 200 international flights every day by over three-dozen airlines from all over the world and is being expanded, despite opposition, with two new runways and a new passenger terminal. It has supplanted the Tokyo International Airport at Haneda as the major international airport, but Haneda is still used for domestic flights and some foreign flights. It too is being expanded. Osaka International Airport (Itami Airport) handles around 50 international flights daily. The noise from the airplanes caused Osaka residents to go to court to limit the airport's operations and to gain financial compensation for people who were affected by the noise. Similar actions were taken at Haneda. The Kansai International Airport is being constructed in Osaka Bay, after delay by strong local opposition.

The Japan Ministry of Transport administers these three "Class 1" airports, and also the "Class 2" airports that are located in 24 major cities, some of which also handle international flights. The main routes within Japan connect Tokyo with Osaka to the west, Sapporo to the north, and Fukuoka to the south. Local prefectures administer 46 additional "Class 3" airports that are located in less urbanized areas. Moreover, there are six airports that are shared by commercial airlines and the military—both Japan's Defense Agency and the U.S. military. In 1952 Japan passed the Airport Law, which governs the operations of its airports according to the regulations of the International Civil Aviation Organization.

The primary Japanese international airline, Japan Air Lines Co., Ltd. (JAL), is renowned for its world-class service and reliability. JAL began as a joint-stock company in 1951, but was reorganized as a government-affiliated company in 1953, giving it exclusive rights at the time to fly international routes. The first JAL trans-Pacific flight took place in 1954. In 1967 JAL became the third international airline to fly around the world, and in 1970 it was the first non-Soviet airline permitted to fly regularly over Siberia. JAL has an automated freight-handling operation, called JALTOS, based at Narita Airport. The airline also operates a chain of hotels around the world under the name JAL Hotel System International, and offers package tours under the names of JALPACK and ZERO. In 1987 the Japanese government sold its controlling shares in JAL and the company was privatized.

All Nippon Airways Co., Ltd. (ANA; Zen Nippon Kuyu) carries more than half of Japan's domestic passengers. ANA's parent company was Nippon Helicopter Transport Co., which began in 1952. ANA merged with Far East Airlines in 1958 under the name All Nippon Airways. The company started flying internationally in 1971 by offering flights to Hong Kong. A few years later ANA began trans-Pacific flights to the United States. By 1989, ANA surpassed JAL as Japan's largest airline company. TOA Domestic Airlines Co., Ltd. (Toa Kokunai Koku; TDA), Japan's third major airline company, started as the Japan Domestic Airlines Co. in 1964. When it merged with Toa Airways Co. in 1971, TDA began using its present name. See also JAPAN AIR LINES CO., LTD.; TOKYO.

AKASAKA A district of Tokyo west of the Imperial Palace with government and diplomatic buildings and an entertainment area. Prominent in this area is the Akasaka Detached Palace (Akasaka Rikyu), the residence of the crown prince. It was designed by Japanese architect Katayama Otokuma to resemble the Palace of Versailles and the Louvre Museum and was built between 1909 and 1919. The Meiji government was eager to show that Japan equalled the West, and spent enormous sums to import building materials and furnishings for the palace. It was restored in 1974 and turned into the official state guesthouse for foreign dignitaries visiting Japan. Also in Akasaka is the Diet building, which houses Japan's parliament, with the House of Councillors (upper house) on one side and the House of Representatives (lower house) on the other. Completed in 1936, the building has a central tower 65.5 meters (215 feet) high that is a well-known Tokyo landmark. Other government buildings in Akasaka include the Ministry of Foreign Affairs, the Metropolitan Police Department and the embassies of the United States, Canada and Mexico. A number of hotels are also located in this area, as are the

Suntory and Nezu art museums, and Hie Shrine, which holds its annual festival in June. By night, part of Akasaka becomes an entertainment district, along with its neighboring district of Roppongi. Their restaurants, bars and discos are especially popular with foreign residents and tourists. See also CROWN PRINCE; DIET; HIE' SHRINE; IMPERIAL PALACE (TOKYO); MEIJI RESTORATION OF 1868; TOKYO.

AKIHABARA A section of Tokyo with the largest discount center for electric and home appliances, audio and video equipment, cameras, computers, and other electronic items. This area around a convenient railroad station is packed with hundreds of small and medium-sized stores and stalls on the street, brightly decorated with flashing neon signs and playing loud music. Prices are about one-quarter less than in other districts of Tokyo, but special sales offer bigger discounts. Electronic parts and equipment are sold along the side streets and alleys. As much as 10% of all Japanese sales of electronic and electrical products take place in Akihabara. As many as 50,000 shoppers come here on weekdays and 100,000 come on the weekend. The larger stores have tax-free export sections that sell products designed to be used overseas. See also CAMERAS AND PHOTOGRAPHY; COMPUTER INDUSTRY; ELECTRONICS INDUSTRY; TOKYO.

AKIHITO, EMPEROR (1933–) The reigning emperor *(tenno)* of Japan and the 125th emperor in the traditional count. Akihito's reign is named Heisei, "Achieving [or Accomplishing] Peace," or "Peace and Concord." Akihito was the crown prince during the reign of his father, Emperor Hirohito (1901–1989), now known as Emperor Showa ("Enlightened Peace") because his reign was named the Showa Era (1926–1989).

From the age of three, Akihito was raised apart from his father and mother, Empress Nagako (1903–), and trained by the Imperial Household Agency (Kunaicho) to become the next emperor. He was moved from Tokyo to a mountain resort town during World War II. After Japan surrendered in 1945, Akihito returned to Tokyo and was educated at Gakushuin High School (Peers' School) and Gakushuin University, where he studied marine biology. He was also tutored in English and Western culture by an American woman, Elizabeth Gray Vining (1902–), who has written several books about her friendship with Akihito.

In 1952 Akihito celebrated his coming-of-age and was invested as heir to the Japanese imperial throne. In 1959 he married Shoda Michiko (1934–), after a much celebrated courtship which began on the tennis courts. She was a commoner whose father was president of a flour-manufacturing company. This was the first time in Japanese history that an heir to the throne married someone who was not from a family belonging to the traditional court nobility. Prince Akihito and Princess Michiko lived in Togu Palace in Tokyo until they became emperor and empress in 1989. They have two sons and one daughter. Their oldest son is Crown Prince Naruhito (Hiro no Miya Naruhito, 1960–), who will become the next emperor of Japan. Their other children are Prince Aya (Aya no Miya Fumihito; 1965–) and Princess Nori (Nori no Miya Say-

A store with consumer electronics for sale at discount prices in the Akihabara district of Tokyo.

ako, 1969–   ). Prince Aya was married in 1990 to a commoner, Kawashima Kiko (1966–   ), and he was given the new name Prince Akishino.

As Crown Prince, Akihito made numerous state visits to foreign countries. In 1989, shortly after his father died and he became emperor, Akihito was presented with the imperial and state seals, and with wrapped replicas of the sacred sword and curved jade jewels, two of the three so-called Imperial Regalia that symbolize the Japanese imperial family. A replica of the third object, a sacred mirror, is kept in a shrine on the grounds of the Imperial Palace in Tokyo. Emperor Akihito and Empress Michiko presided over the funeral of his father, which was attended by 10,000 dignitaries from all over the world.

Akihito's official enthronement ceremony will be held in November 1990 at the time of the rice harvesting festival. His birthday, on December 23, is a national holiday. Emperor Akihito has one younger brother, Prince Hitachi (1935–   ). His four sisters gave up the title of princess when they married commoners and took their husband's family names: Higashikuni Shigeko, Takatsukasa Kazuko, Ikeda Atsuko, and Shimazu Takako. See also EMPEROR; CROWN PRINCE; HEISEI ERA; HIROHITO, EMPEROR; IMPERIAL HOUSEHOLD; IMPERIAL HOUSEHOLD AGENCY; IMPERIAL PALACE (TOKYO); IMPERIAL REGALIA; RICE PLANTING AND HARVESTING FESTIVALS; VINING, ELIZABETH GRAY.

AKITA DOG   See DOG.

AKIYAMA SANEYUKI (1868–1918)   An officer in the Imperial Japanese Navy and architect of the pre–World War II Japanese navy. Akiyama was born into a samurai family in Matsuyama. In 1890 he graduated from the Japanese Naval Academy, where he had a reputation as a brilliant naval analyst. The Japanese government sent him to study in the United States from 1897 to 1899, where he was allowed to be a foreign observer with the U.S. naval squadron of Admiral Sampson in the Spanish-American War. In this capacity, he observed the American landings in Cuba and the destruction of the Spanish fleet, and sent intelligence reports back to Japan, providing valuable information about the American navy. Akiyama then served as an instructor at the Japanese Naval Imperial Staff College three times (1902–03, 1905–08 and 1912–14), where he combined Japanese and Western tactics to revolutionize the organization and defense strategy of the Japanese Imperial Navy. During the Russo-Japanese War of 1904–05, Akiyama was a senior staff member of the First Fleet under Togo Heihachiro, and he drew up the battle plan that enabled Togo to destroy the Russian fleet in the decisive Battle of Tsushima. Akiyama rose to the rank of rear admiral. See also IMPERIAL JAPANESE ARMY AND NAVY; MEIJI RESTORATION OF 1868; RUSSO-JAPANESE WAR; TOGO HEIHACHIRO.

AKIYOSHI TOSHIKO (1929–) A Japanese-born jazz pianist, composer and leader of her own 16-member Toshiko Akiyoshi Jazz Orchestra. Akiyoshi was born in Manchuria, at that time controlled by Japan, and later moved to Japan. She was trained as a classical pianist, but her interest in jazz was stimulated by the American pianist Hampton Hawes, who was stationed in Japan following World War II. Akiyoshi had her own quartet by 1952 in Tokyo, where she was discovered by the famous Canada-born pianist Oscar Peterson. In 1956 she won a scholarship to the Berklee College of Music in Boston. After graduation she moved to California and married fellow jazz musician Lew Tabackin. Since forming the Toshiko Akiyoshi/Lew Tabackin Big Band, they have won international acclaim. The American jazz magazine *downbeat* four times named her best jazz composer and arranger, and five times named the Toshiko Akiyoshi Jazz Orchestra best jazz band. She has also received more than a dozen nominations for Grammy awards. Some of her finest works include "Kogun" ("One Who Fights Alone") and "Long Yellow Road." Akiyoshi was the first Asian jazz musician, composer and arranger to gain wide acceptance in the United States and Europe. She paved the way for many other Japanese artists who came on the jazz scene in the 1970s.

AKO INCIDENT   See FORTY-SEVEN RONIN INCIDENT.

AKUTAGAWA RYUNOSUKE (1892–1927) A modern Japanese writer of short stories, poetry, and critical essays. The Akutagawa Prize, the most important literary award in Japan, comparable to the Pulitzer Prize in the United States, is named for him. Akutagawa was born in Tokyo and graduated from Tokyo University with a degree in English literature. He was familiar with the classics of Japanese, Chinese, and Western literature, and the modern Japanese novelists Mori Ogai (1862–1922) and Natsume Soseki (1867–1916) also influenced his writing. Many of Akutagawa's approximately 100 stories were modern interpretations of folktales from medieval Japanese collections. His most famous story from the early period of his career is "Hell Screen" ("Jigokuhen," 1918; translated 1948), about the bizarre suffering of an artist painting the tortures of hell on a folding screen. Another story, "In a Grove" ("Yabu no naka," 1922; translated 1952), was adapted by the Japanese movie director Kurosawa Akira (1910–) for his acclaimed movie *Rashomon* (1950). "In a Grove" is about the murder of a nobleman and rape of his wife by a bandit, as told by several different characters whose versions do not agree. The story is disturbing in the way it denies absolute truth. Affected by ill health in the final period of his career, Akutagawa turned from storytelling to autobiographical writing that was the apparent expression of mental illness. He committed suicide in 1927 when he was only 35 years old. The Akutagawa Prize was established eight years after his death to honor talented new Japanese writers. See also KUROSAWA AKIRA; NATSUME SOSEKI; POETRY; RASHOMON.

ALCOHOLIC BEVERAGES   The drinking of alcoholic beverages, especially sake (rice wine), has been popular in Japan since ancient times. Sake was the only alcoholic beverage in Japan until the modern era. Rice is the Japanese staple, and rice and sake are both sacred to the *kami* (sacred spirits) of Shinto, the indigenous Japanese religion. The Japanese drink sake on all ceremonial occasions, including weddings, funerals and religious festivals. Sake is shared with the *kami* at festivals and is then drunk by the worshippers in a banquet known as *naorai*. In a wedding ceremony, the bride and groom exchange three cups of sake three times in a row. This ceremony is called *sansankudo*, or "three-three-nine times." The eighth-century A.D. chronicle *Nihon Shoki* records that Omiwa no Kami was worshipped as the *kami* of sake. Sake *kami* known as the "Three Wine Deities" (Sanshujin) are still worshipped at the Omiwa Shrine in Nara Prefecture and the Matsuo and Umemiya shrines in Kyoto. Round designs made from leaves of the sacred cryptomeria tree at Omiwa Shrine have been used as trademarks by sake brewers. Similar balls are still hung in breweries during the production of new sake. In the seventh century A.D., the imperial court established a Sake Production Bureau (Sake no Tsukasa) where special women designated as *ietoji* pounded the rice from which the sake was brewed. Buddhist temples and farmers brewed sake as well. During the Edo Era (1600–1868), commercial breweries began to produce sake. Drinking became a popular form of social entertainment and usually took place at so-called teahouses, or *chaya*.

Beer, which was first brewed in Japan in 1873, has also become a popular alcoholic beverage. Asahi Breweries, Ltd., Kirin Breweries, Ltd., and Sapporo Breweries, Ltd. are the largest Japanese brewers and exporters of beer. Whiskey is another popular drink in Japan, especially among modern urban office workers known as salarymen, who spend week nights drinking with their colleagues after office hours.

Businessmen have generous expense accounts because they often make important connections and business deals during such drinking sessions. Suntory, Ltd. is the third-largest whiskey distilling company in the world, and Old Suntory is the world's best-selling whiskey. Foreign brands such as Johnny Walker and Remy Martin are also popular in Japan. There are many kinds of places to drink, ranging from small, cozy bars to large so-called hostess bars where clients pay women to sit and talk with them. The hostesses are a modern variation of the traditional geisha (female entertainer). Japanese also enjoy drinking while eating traditional inexpensive snack foods such as *yakitori* (grilled pieces of chicken) at portable food stalls (*yatai*) on the street. Women did not drink socially before World War II, except for geisha and other women of the "water trade" (*mizu shobai*), or world of nighttime entertainment. The Japanese believe it is polite to pour drinks for each other. When everyone has full glasses, they raise them and shout the toast, "*kampai!* (to your health)." Alcoholism is a rising problem in Japan, and there are an estimated 2.5 million alcoholics, whose problems are often hidden by families and office colleagues. See also EXPENSE ACCOUNTS; FESTIVALS; FOOD STALLS; GEISHA; KAMI; KAMPAI; RICE; SAKE; SALARYMAN; SHINTO; TEAHOUSE; WATER TRADE; WEDDINGS; YAKITORI.

ALIEN REGISTRATION   See FOREIGNERS IN JAPAN; MINORITIES IN JAPAN.

ALL NIPPON AIRWAYS CO., LTD. (ANA)   See AIRLINES AND AIRPORTS.

ALPS OF JAPAN   See JAPAN ALPS; SNOW COUNTRY.

ALTARS IN HOMES (*butsudan; kamidana*)   Small shrines established in Japanese homes so that the family can worship the deities (*kami*) of Shinto, the native Japanese religion, and keep memorial tablets for ancestors according to the practices of Buddhism, the religion introduced into Japan from China in the sixth century A.D. In Japan, Shinto and Buddhism exist together. The Shinto altar, or *kamidana* (god shelf), is usually placed above a door in the most formal room of the home. Talismans of deities that are worshiped in the local area, or of deities from major shrines such as Ise, are kept on the *kamidana*, along with candles and offerings of food and sake (rice wine). A sprig of pine or the sacred tree known as *sakaki* is often placed on the *kamidana*, as the gods like to dwell in these trees. The altar may be located in the kitchen if it is dedicated to a deity of the kitchen or of good fortune, such as Daikoku or Ebisu. Temporary altars may also be set during the two most important festivals of the year: New Year in the winter, when the gods come to visit; and Bon in the summer, when the spirits of ancestors visit their families.

The *butsudan* (Buddha shelf) is kept in a small wooden cabinet with doors that open outward. A statue of Buddha stands in the center, in front of which are placed the ancestral memorial tablets (*ihai*), a flower vase and an incense holder. Family members pray to the ancestors with heads bowed and hands together. Regular offerings of food and flowers are made to the ancestors on the *butsudan*, while incense is burned and Buddhist scriptures are read. See also BON FESTIVAL; BUDDHISM; DAIKOKU; EBISU; FAMILY; FUNERALS; HOMES AND HOUSING; INCENSE; KAMI; NEW YEAR FESTIVAL; SAKAI TREE; SCRIPTURES, RELIGIOUS; SHINTO; TALISMANS.

ALTERNATE ATTENDANCE (*sankin kotai*)   A policy of the Tokugawa Shogunate (1603–1867) requiring the *daimyo* (feudal lords over the Japanese provinces) to spend alternate years or six months each year residing in the capital city of Edo (modern Tokyo). *Sankin* literally means "reporting to one's lord to render service." The families of feudal lords had to reside permanently in Edo. The shogunate devised this system, which was in fact a way of keeping the lords and their families hostage, to maintain strict control over the *daimyo*, half of whom opposed the shogunate. While half of the *daimyo* were in Edo, the other half would be living in their own domains. When one group reported to the capital, the other half would *kotai* or "rotate" back home. Each *daimyo* spent up to 80% of his

income (which was measured in volumes of rice known as *koku*) traveling back and forth with his retinue and in maintaining two residences and offering valuable gifts to the shogun. The wives and children of *daimyo* were forced to live permanently in their *yashiki* or mansions in Edo as virtual hostages to ensure the loyalty of the *daimyo*.

The custom of requiring vassals to report to their lords for service had been practiced throughout the feudal era in Japan (12th–16th centuries). The third Tokugawa shogun, Iemitsu (1604–1651), formalized and enforced this system, which remained in effect until 1862. Although the alternate attendance system placed a great financial burden on the *daimyo*, it did serve to centralize the government and economy and to unify the country, which helped Japan make the transition from the feudal to the modern era when the Tokugawa Shogunate was replaced by the Meiji Restoration of 1868. It also stimulated the growth of Japanese cities and the communication of ideas and information. See also DAIMYO; EDO ERA; FEUDALISM; KOKU; MEIJI RESTORATION OF 1868; TOKUGAWA IEMITSU; TOKUGAWA SHOGUNATE.

AMAMI ISLANDS (Amami Shoto)   A group of islands lying between Kyushu, the southernmost of the four main islands of Japan, and the Ryukyu Islands (Okinawa Prefecture) to the very south. The Amami Islands cover a total of 477 square miles and include five main islands. The largest is Amami Oshima, with an area of 274 square miles. Its major city is Naze. The Amami Islands are surrounded by coral reefs and have a subtropical climate. They belonged to Ryukyu kingdom, centered on Okinawa Island, until the Shimazu clan on southern Kyushu took control of the Ryukyus in 1609. Since the Meiji Era (1868–1912), the Amami Islands have been administered by Kagoshima Prefecture on Kyushu, except during a period of rule by the American military from 1946 to 1953. The main products of the Amami Islands are sugar, sweet potatoes, pineapples and a type of silk known as Oshima *tsumugi*. See also KAGOSHIMA; KYUSHU; OKINAWA ISLAND; RYUKYU ISLANDS; SHIMAZU CLAN; SILK.

AMANOHASHIDATE   "Bridge of Heaven"; a sandbar covered with gnarled pine trees that is one of the Three Famous Views of Japan (*Nihon sankei*), along with Matsushima and Miyajima (Itsukushima Shrine). Amanohashidate, part of the Wakasa Bay Quasi-National Park, is located on the western coast of central Honshu Island, facing the Sea of Japan, north of the city of Kyoto. The sandbar is about 2 miles long, and its width ranges from about 65 to 558 feet. Tradition says that if one views Amanohashidate upside down through one's legs, the sandbar looks like a bridge to heaven. Most people view the sandbar from nearby Kusamatsu Park. See also MATSUSHIMA; MIYAJIMA; NATIONAL PARKS; PINE TREE; SEA OF JAPAN.

AMATERASU O MIKAMI   "Great Divinity Illuminating Heaven"; the Sun Goddess, who is considered the supreme deity (*kami*) of Shinto, the indigenous Japanese religion. Amaterasu is the divine mythical ancestor of the imperial family. Legends about Amaterasu are recorded in the official chronicles *Kojiki* (A.D. 712) and *Nihon Shoki* (or *Nihongi*, A.D. 720). They claim that she was born from the original creator gods, Izanagi and Izanami, and was made the ruler of the High Plain of Heaven (Takamagahara). Amaterasu's younger brother Susanoo no Mikoto acted so badly, even defiling her throne, that she angrily withdrew into a cave and left the universe in darkness. She was finally lured out of the cave by the raucous dancing of another goddess, a crowing rooster and a mirror. Amaterasu gave this sacred mirror, along with a sacred sword and curved jewels (*magatama*), to her grandson Ninigi no Mikoto when she sent him down to earth to rule the islands of Japan. These three treasures, known as the Imperial Regalia, were tokens of his divine right to rule. They were handed down to Ninigi's grandson Jimmu Tenno, the legendary first emperor of Japan, and to successive emperors to legitimize their reigns. Amaterasu is worshipped at the Inner Shrine (Naiku) of Ise Shrine, the main Shinto shrine, on east-central Honshu Island. Ise Shrine houses the sacred mirror of Amaterasu, which was supposedly enshrined there by the 10th Japanese emperor, Sujin. A princess of the imperial family has always served as high priestess (*saishu*) at Ise Shrine, except for the years 1868–1946. During the medieval era (12th–16th centuries), the Kegon and Shingon sects of the Buddhist religion attempted to associate their chief deity, Dainichi, with Amaterasu. Dainichi's name was written with characters that mean great sun. Since the 17th century, the Japanese have made pilgrimages to Ise Shrine in large groups, a practice known as *okage mairi*. On New Year's Day, a million people visit Ise. See also IMPERIAL HOUSEHOLD; IMPERIAL REGALIA; ISE SHRINE; IZANAGI AND IZANAMI; JIMMU TENNO; KAMI; KOJIKI; NIHON SHOKI; NINIGI NO MIKOTO; SHINTO; SUN; SUSANOO NO MIKOTO; TENNO.

AMERICA AND JAPAN See EXPORTS AND IMPORTS; EXPOSITIONS, INTERNATIONAL; HARRIS, TOWNSEND; IMMIGRANTS, JAPANESE; INVESTMENTS OVERSEAS, JAPANESE; JAPANESE-AMERICAN CITIZENS LEAGUE; MACARTHUR, DOUGLAS; OCCUPATION OF JAPAN; OKINAWA ISLAND; PEACE TREATY OF 1952; PEARL HARBOR, JAPANESE ATTACK ON; PERRY, MATTHEW CALBRAITH; REISCHAUER, EDWIN OLDFATHER; SUPREME COMMANDER FOR THE ALLIED POWERS; WAR CRIMES TRIALS; WASHINGTON CONFERENCE AND NAVAL TREATY OF 1922; WORLD WAR II.

AMIDA One of the most important deities in the Mahayana branch of Buddhism, the religion introduced into Japan from China in the sixth century A.D. The name Amida, or Amita, derives from the Indian Sanskrit name Amitabha, "Immeasurable Light," or Amitayus, "Immeasurable Life." Amida is believed to have made a Great Vow to help all suffering beings, and when this was fulfilled, he became a Buddha (Enlightened Being) and created a paradise in the west known as the "Pure Land." Amida was worshipped by other sects of Buddhism in Japan, but he became the central figure in the Pure Land sect of Buddhism. This sect took root in Japan during the Heian Era (794–1185), but it spread rapidly among the common people in the 12th century A.D. The religious leaders Honen

and Shinran taught that anyone could be blissfully reborn in the Pure Land by having sincere faith in Amida and repeating his name with a prayer known as the *nembutsu*. This is an abbreviation of Namu Amida Butsu, meaning "I place my faith in Amida Buddha." Many buildings, known as *amidado*, were built throughout Japan for the worship of Amida. Statues and paintings of Amida show him accompanied by two bodhisattvas (enlightened beings), Seishi and Kannon (Goddess of Mercy). In Japan, there have always been more statues of Amida than of any other deity. See also BUDDHISM; DAIBUTSU; HONEN; KANNON; NEMBUTSU; PURE LAND SECT OF BUDDHISM; SHINRAN; SCULPTURE; TEMPLES, BUDDHIST.

AMULETS (*omamori*) Small objects that serve as good-luck charms. Amulets are commonly sold at Shinto shrines and Buddhist temples, especially during festivals, and have been blessed by the gods. A variety of cloth, wood, paper and plastic charms are sold as sacred souvenirs. Small brocade bags on cords, with the name of the shrine or temple and a prayer, are the most popular type. The Japanese often hang amulets in their car windows or doorways. Popular inscriptions on amulets are *josai shofuku* (away with misfortune, welcome to good luck), *gakugyo seikyo* (success in examinations), or *kotsu anzen* (traffic safety). *Gofu* are rectangular pieces of paper (or sometimes wood) sold or given out at Shinto shrines and Buddhist temples. A deity's name is written on the *gofu*. *Gofu* are thought to bring positive benefits, such as good health, money or protection from accidents. People carry the *gofu* with them, attach them to a doorway or place them on the small Shinto altars (*kamidana*) in their homes. These amulets belong to a category of protective talismans known as *omamori* or *ofuda*. Large talismans such as arrows and wooden plaques (*ema*) are also thought to bring good fortune. Small animal figures are commonly used for protection in Japan. *Inuhariko* is a papier-mache dog charm to protect women giving birth and raising children. *Wara-uma* is a straw horse that helps bring a good harvest. *Akabeko* is a red papier-mache ox that keeps misfortune away. Red is a popular color for amulets because the color is believed to protect against smallpox and other diseases. The Daruma doll is supposed to help make a wish come true. A figure of a beckoning cat (*maneki-neko*) attracts customers into a restaurant. Local communities throughout Japan often have their own special protective amulets. Various objects, such as sea shells, mushrooms or ladles, may be hung from gates or eaves of homes to keep away evil spirits, disease and natural disasters, a practice known as *mayoke*. Children are believed to require special protection from evil spirits that cause illness. Traditional *mayoke* to protect them include embroidering colorful symbols on the back of their kimono or writing the Chinese character for dog on their foreheads with ash. See also ALTARS IN HOMES; BUDDHISM; CAT; DARUMA; DOG; HORSE; NEW YEAR FESTIVAL; SHINTO; TALISMANS.

ANA (All Nippon Airways Co., Ltd.) See AIRLINES AND AIRPORTS.

ANCESTORS AND ANCESTOR WORSHIP   See ALTARS IN HOMES; BON FESTIVAL; FAMILY; FUNERALS; SHINTO.

ANGLO-JAPANESE ALLIANCE, 1902 (Nichiei Domei)   An agreement signed by Great Britain and Japan on January 30, 1902, which was the first equal diplomatic and military alliance between Japan and a powerful Western nation. The alliance was meant to forestall Russian expansion into China, where both countries sought to promote their own political and economic interests. The terms guaranteed joint military action against any Russian encroachment. The treaty stipulated British acceptance of Japan's special interests in Korea in exchange for the strengthening of British naval power by joint operations with the Japanese fleet.

The term of the alliance was five years. In August, 1905, it was extended for 10 more years. Britain and Japan also held talks on military and naval issues in 1906–07. In July 1911, Britain agreed to renew the alliance for another 10 years, despite misgivings about aggressive Japanese actions in China. The Russian threat was diminished by this time, and the United States was beginning to oppose Japan's aggression in China and its naval expansion in the Pacific. Thus, the renewed Anglo-Japanese Alliance excused Britain from giving aid to Japan in the event of war against the United States. Japan decided to enter World War I, even though the alliance did not require it to do so, and quickly captured Germany's holdings in China and the Pacific Islands. Japan also sent ships to aid the British Navy in the Indian Ocean and the Mediterranean Sea. Despite this, many British saw Japanese activities as a threat to British interests in China and British markets in the Far East and India. Japan for its part distrusted the closeness between Britain and the United States and resented American criticism of Japanese expansion in China and of the Japanese naval buildup in the Pacific. Yet Japan and Britain both had to accept the crucial role the United States played as a major power in maintaining the security of the Pacific, with bases in the Philippine Islands. These issues were discussed at the Washington Conference of 1921, at which Britain, Japan, the United States, and France signed the Four-Power Treaty on December 13, agreeing to respect one another's territorial holdings in the Pacific and to consult together if they were threatened by other powers. When this treaty took effect on August 17, 1923, it canceled the Anglo-Japanese Alliance. See also ANSEI COMMERCIAL TREATIES; IMPERIAL JAPANESE ARMY AND NAVY; PACIFIC OCEAN; RUSSO-JAPANESE WAR; SINO-JAPANESE WAR OF 1894–95; WASHINGTON CONFERENCE AND WASHINGTON NAVAL TREATY OF 1922; WORLD WAR I.

ANIMALS   See BADGER; CAT; DEER; DOG; DRAGON; HORSE; LION; MONKEY; OX; RABBIT; RAT AND MOUSE; SNAKE; TIGER; TORTOISE.

ANSEI COMMERCIAL TREATIES (Ansei gokakoku jo-yaku)   Also known as the "Unequal Treaties"; commercial agreements made in 1858 between the Tokugawa Shogunate that governed Japan from 1603 to 1867 and five Western nations: the United States, Great Britain, the Netherlands, France and Russia. The treaty between the United States and Japan was negotiated by Townsend Harris (1804–1878), the first U.S. consul to Japan, and is known as the Harris Treaty. This was only five years after U.S. Commodore Matthew Perry opened Japan to the outside world after more than two centuries of self-imposed isolation. The Harris Treaty paved the way for the four other treaties. The five treaties were named for Ansei 5, Japanese for 1858. One of their major provisions was the opening of the Japanese cities of Hakodate, Nagasaki, Osaka, Edo (modern Tokyo), Niigata, Hyogo (modern Kobe) and Kanagawa to foreign trade. Yokohama later replaced Kanagawa, and many Western traders and government representatives were allowed to settle there with autonomy over their communities. Japanese opponents of the treaties considered them "unequal" because they gave many benefits to Western nations, such as the right to determine tariff rates on trade. The radical Japanese pro-imperial faction opposed any dealings between Japan and Western nations. Ii Naosuke (1815–1860), who held the position of Great Elder (tairo) in the Tokugawa government, signed the treaties without the agreement of the Japanese emperor. He purged many opponents of the Tokugawa government from 1858 until 1860, when he was assassinated. The Western nations were not able to fully implement the commercial treaties until 1865, when they sailed nine warships into Hyogo Bay and demanded that the imperial court ratify the treaties. The emperor had no choice but to comply. However, lingering opposition to the treaties contributed to the downfall of the Tokugawa Shogunate and the Meiji Restoration of 1868. The Meiji government attempted to revise the treaties in the late 19th century, and finally concluded new agreements in 1911 that gave back to Japan the autonomy to set tariffs. See also HARRIS, TOWNSEND; MEIJI RESTORATION OF 1868; PERRY, MATTHEW CALBRAITH; SECLUSION, NATIONAL; TOKUGAWA SHOGUNATE; UNITED STATES AND JAPAN; YOKOHAMA.

ANTI-COMINTERM PACT   See IMPERIAL JAPANESE ARMY AND NAVY; TRI-PARTITE PACT; WORLD WAR II.

ANTOKU, EMPEROR   See DANNOURA, BATTLE OF; MINAMOTO NO YORITOMO; TAIRA CLAN; TAIRA-MINAMOTO WAR.

APARTMENT HOUSE (danchi)   A housing complex with a large number of compact, inexpensive apartments. Many danchi have been built by the Japan Housing Corporation (JHC), which was established in 1955 to deal with the pressing postwar demand for housing. Before the war, apartment buildings were constructed of wood, the same as single homes. Since the war, most buildings have been constructed of reinforced concrete, due to a shortage of wood. Concrete also better withstands earthquakes, which occur frequently in Japan. A typical danchi apartment (apato) has two or three small rooms, plus a dining-kitchen room ("DK"), a room for bathing and a toilet. The DK apartment is usually about 86 square feet. An enlarged DK is called a living room-dining-kitchen room ("LDK"). Danchi recently built by the JHC usually have three DK or three LDK units.

Danchi residents tend to be families of young white-collar workers, known as "salarymen," who live in *danchi* until they can afford to buy their own home. However, three-quarters of the population now live in urban areas, and real-estate prices have become so high that many Japanese have to postpone or forego buying their own homes and remain in *danchi*. The Japanese use the term *manshon* for more expensive apartment buildings with individual units that are purchased by residents, similar to condominiums in the United States. See also EARTHQUAKES; FAMILY; HOMES AND HOUSING; SALARYMAN.

APPRENTICE SYSTEM (*totei seido*) A traditional system of apprenticeship for young people seeking to learn a craft whereby they become assistants (*totei*) to a master of the craft. Apprentices were generally male, although women sometimes served apprenticeships as well, notably *geisha*.

A master-apprentice relationship existed in medieval guilds (*za*), but became formalized when merchant guilds (*kabunakama*) were organized and regulated during the Edo Era (1600–1868). It was a contractual relationship that mutually bound the master (*shokunin*, artisan; also called *oyakata*, literally "father person") and the apprentice. A young man became an apprentice by first paying a formal visit (*memie*) to the master of a particular craft, who then paid "advance money" (*tetsuke*) to the boy's parents. A formal agreement (*shomon*) was drawn up specifying the length of time and duties the apprentice was required to serve. The term of indenture was originally 10 years, although in later years this time was shortened. A boy usually became indentured between the ages of 10 and 12. He was not paid for his work, but lived with the master as a member of his family. The apprentice performed household chores in addition to learning the craft. The system was subject to abuse, and many boys ran away after being treated as slaves. In order to ensure that a boy fulfilled his contract, a master could threaten *kagyo-gamo*, a legal barrier that would prevent the apprentice, even if he was qualified, from practicing the trade the master taught him.

When the apprentice completed his term of service, he received a set of tools from the master and could set up his own shop. He could even become a master himself if he gained admittance to the artisan's guild for his particular craft. Eventually the membership in guilds became limited, and craftsmen found it very hard to become masters in their own right. Many had to travel to find work, or remain in their masters' shops to earn a living.

The merchant guilds were disbanded during the Meiji Era (1868–1912), which caused a decline in the apprentice system. However, it survived until recently in some crafts, such as ironcasting. Many young men still learn traditional crafts, such as pottery, carpentry, metalwork and lacquer ware, by working with masters in a close father-son relationship. The Japanese government protects and encourages traditional crafts by designating highly skilled artisans as Living National Treasures. Also, some young women still enter formal relationships with geisha "mothers" to become *maiko*, apprentice geisha, and study traditional Japanese music, dance, and other arts. See also FAMILY; FATHER; GEISHA; LIVING NATIONAL TREASURES.

ARCHERY (*kyudo*) The martial art and competitive sport of shooting arrows with a bow (*kyu*). Archery in Japan was known as "the technique of the bow" (*kyujutsu*) until the 19th century, when the term "the Way of the Bow" (*kyudo*) came into use. Mounted archery (*yabusame*) dates back at least to the third century A.D. in Japan but became prominent in the 12th and 13th centuries, as a result of the Taira-Minamoto War (1180–1185), which initiated military government in Japan. Archery in a standing position was introduced from China in the sixth century A.D. There is also a third form of archery in a sitting position.

A samurai was characterized as "he who carries a bow and arrow." Archery was also known as "the way of the bow and the horse." Training in archery became formalized into different schools, each with its own rules for handling the bow and arrows. During the feudal era governed by the Ashikaga Shogunate (1338–1573), the family of Ogasawara Sadamune (1292–1347) was foremost, and it remains one of the three major kyudo schools in modern Japan. The other two are the Heki school of archery founded by Heki Danjo Masatsugu (d. 1502) and the Honda school founded by Honda Toshizane (1836–1917).

A bow is about 7 to 9 feet long and made of laminated strips of bamboo and mulberry or cherry wood. Length of the bow depends on whether it is used for target practice, for a ceremonial occasion, or, in the past, for battle. Such a long bow is unique to Japan and was very difficult to handle in combat. The hand grip on the bow is two-thirds of the way down from the top. The bowstring is made of twisted hemp coated with resin and glue. The arrows are made in sets of four from reed bamboo with metal tips and eagle or falcon feathers. They are slightly less than 3 feet long. When drawing the bowstring and arrow, an archer wears a reinforced three-fingered glove (*yugake*) with a groove at the base of the thumb to hold the bowstring.

Targets 14 inches in diameter are placed at a distance of 92 feet from the archer. In competition, an archer shoots two arrows in a turn for a total of 20 arrows. As in all Japanese martial arts, form (*kata*) is the most important aspect of *kyudo*. A student must learn how to perform each action according to prescribed form, including the way to position the feet, steady the body, hold the bow, raise the bow, draw the bowstring, and release the arrow. In the standing form of archery, a student learns *kyu-jitsu*, or physical training, in order to hit the target, and *shado*, spiritual training. Archery has about half a million students in Japan. It is regulated by the Japanese Kyudo Federation, which sponsors competitions, including an archery competition that has been held in the Sanjusangendo, a Buddhist temple in Kyoto, since 1606.

Archery has been greatly influenced by the religious philosophy of the Zen sect of Buddhism. The goal of the Way of Archery is to learn how to shoot an arrow without being concerned about hitting the target. In Shinto, the indigenous Japanese religion, arrows are regarded as a means of purification. Many shrines sell arrows to worshippers, particularly at the New Year, and they are kept in homes to absorb impurity and evil. The arrows are then burned during ceremonies to mark the end of the year. Arrows with white eagle feathers are shot in traditional archery ceremonies to eradicate evil forces. A *yabusame* festival and ceremony is held at the Hachiman Shinto temple in Kamakura every September 15th and 16th. See also ASHIKAGA SHOGUNATE; BAMBOO; HORSE; MARTIAL ARTS; SAMURAI; SHINTO; TAIRA-MINAMOTO WAR; ZEN BUDDHISM.

ARCHITECTURE See APARTMENT HOUSE; CASTLE; FARMHOUSE; HOMES AND HOUSING; IMPERIAL HOTEL; IMPERIAL PALACE (KYOTO); IMPERIAL PALACE (TOKYO); ROOF TILES; SHOIN STYLE OF ARCHITECTURE; SHRINES, SHINTO; STOREHOUSE; TEAHOUSE; TEMPLE, BUDDHIST; WOODWORKING.

ARIGATO (GOZAIMASU) An informal Japanese word for thank you. A recent survey revealed that the Japanese regard 'arigato' as the most beautiful word in their language. A more formal way of saying thank you is *domo arigato*. The most formal expression for thank you is *arigato gozaimasu, gozaimasu* being a formal form of the verb "to be." Expressing gratitude is an important aspect of Japanese culture and is related to the concepts of duty (*giri*) and indebtedness (*on*). Saying thank you is so important in Japan that there are two gift-giving seasons, in midsummer and at the end of the year, when people give presents to thank social superiors who have assisted them, such as employers or go-betweens at their weddings. The Japanese always express their gratitude for any gift or kindness, either in person or in a letter. See also DUTY AND FEELINGS; ETIQUETTE; GIFTS; INDEBTEDNESS.

ARITA WARE (*arita-yaki*) A type of porcelain made in the Arita region in Hizen Province (modern Saga Prefecture) on the southern Japanese island of Kyushu. Arita ware is also known as Imari ware for the port of Imari, from which the porcelain was exported to other countries. The name Arita ware is applied as well to two other types of porcelain made in the Arita region, Kakiemon ware (*kakiemon-yaki*) and Nabeshima ware (*nabeshima-yaki*). Ri Sampei (Yi Samp'yong in Korean), a Korean potter who had been brought to Arita in 1616 following the second invasion of Korea by the Japanese warlord Toyotomi Hideyoshi (1536–1598) in 1592, found that clay in the Arita region was well-suited for making delicate porcelain. The earliest porcelain objects produced at Arita had pure white bodies with decorative motifs in a blue underglaze, in imitation of Chinese Ming dynasty porcelain, which had long been imported through the nearby town of Hirado. Multicolored pieces were produced after the technique of red enamel overglazing was created by Sakaida Kakiemon (1596–1666) in the 1640s. Designs on Arita ware gradually became quite colorful and adapted more Japanese motifs, especially bird-and-flower designs and patterns taken from textiles. The Nabeshima clan controlled the development and production of Arita ware, which reached its height during the Genroku Era

(1688–1704). It was made in great quantities for use by all classes in Japan, and was exported to Europe by the Dutch East India Company from the mid-17th to mid-18th centuries. After that time, the quality of Arita ware lessened, and its production was moved to factories during the Meiji Era (1868–1912). Arita continues to be a major Japanese porcelain center. The Arita Ceramics Museum, Kyushu Ceramic Museum, and Historical Museum display old Arita ware and give the history of its production. Many family operated kilns make and sell porcelain in the Arita area. A ceramic fair, the largest of its kind in Japan, is held in the town of Arita May 1–5 each year. See also DUTCH IN JAPAN; GENROKU ERA; KAKIEMON WARE; NABESHIMA WARE; PORCELAIN; TOYOTOMI HIDEYOSHI.

ARMED FORCES See IMPERIAL JAPANESE ARMY AND NAVY; SELF-DEFENSE FORCES.

ARMOR (*yoroi, domaru*) Japanese armor known as *yoroi* was developed in the ninth century A.D. and worn by samurai archers, spearmen and leaders. Japanese armor is flexible because it is constructed mainly of leather and small iron plates bound together in overlapping horizontal tiers. The plates are coated with lacquer to make them stronger, and then laced together with braided silk cords (*kumihimo*) to create larger sections, which are in turn fastened to leather or solid iron pieces. The upper portion of a *yoroi* suit of armor includes a solid armor chest plate (*munaita*) and tiers of plates (*tateage*) in the front and back. On the lower portion is the tiered *kabukido*, which protects the front, back, and left side of the lower part of the trunk, and the separate tiered *waidate*, which protects the right side of the body. A protective skirt (*kusazuri*), made from large vertical sections of lacquered iron tiers, is hung from the upper section of the suit of armor. There are also tiered upper-arm guards (*osode*), and two small iron plates that hang from the shoulders over each side of the chest. The lacquered tiers that hang over the chest have a leather cover (*tsurubashiri*) that provides a smooth surface across which the archer draws his bow. The armor is hung on the body with shoulder straps.

A large helmet (*kabuto*) is worn with a suit of armor. The bowl of the helmet is made from iron plates coated with black lacquer, and a neck guard (*shikoro*), made of laced tiers of lacquered iron plates, flares out from the bottom of the bowl. There is a peak on the front of the helmet where a piece of iron (*kuwagata*) that resembles horns or some other design is attached to give the samurai a menacing appearance. The helmet is tied on the head with thick cords.

A type of armor known as *domaru*, originally worn by common foot soldiers from the ninth century on, was adapted in the 14th century by high-ranking samurai and worn into the 16th century. The *domaru* is similar to the *yoroi* but easier to put on and less bulky. It has one continuous upper portion of tiered pieces of lacquer-coated leather, and is wrapped around the wearer's body and fastened on the right side. Some iron tiers are interspersed with leather ones to protect certain parts of the body. This type of armor also has a tiered skirt and upper arm guards. A similar type of armor known as *haramaki* is fastened in the back. Shin guards (*suneate*) made of curved plates of lacquered iron were also worn with suits of armor.

Armor was decorated with various techniques, such as openwork, high relief, application of gold or silver inlay (*iro-e*), and metalwork to create a raised-dot surface (*nanako*). The *iro-e* technique was often used to work a family crest (*mon*) into the metal.

A type of armor known as *tosei gusoku*, "modern equipment," was developed in the second half of the 16th century to give samurai mobility in battle, especially on foot, and to protect against Western firearms, which had recently been introduced. It was first worn by the warlord Toyotomi Hideyoshi (1536–1598), one of the three unifiers of Japan. This type of armor was made either from large sheets of iron or long horizontal laced tiers of small lacquered panels. Special pieces of armor, such as sleeves and an apron, protect important parts of the body and are connected with chain mail that has a cloth backing. This type of armor was influenced by European-style armor that was introduced into Japan during the 16th century, and provided greater protection against firearms. The Tokugawa shoguns who ruled Japan from 1603 to 1867 wore suits of *tosei gusoku* armor as symbols of their power. See also ARCHERY; CORDS, BRAIDED; FEUDALISM; FIREARMS, INTRODUCTION OF; LACQUER WARE; SAMURAI; TOKUGAWA SHOGUNATE; TOYOTOMI HIDEYOSHI.

ARMS See ARCHERY; ARMOR; FIREARMS, INTRODUCTION OF MARTIAL ARTS; NAGINATA; SAMURAI; SWORD.

ART See BIRD-AND-FLOWER PAINTING; BUDDHISM; CALLIGRAPHY; FIGURE PAINTING; FISH PRINTING; INK PAINTING; LANDSCAPE PAINTING; LACQUER WARE; MUSEUMS IN JAPAN; NATIONAL TREASURE; PAINTING; SCROLLS; SCREENS; SCULPTURE; SEALS AND SIGNATURES; SHOSOIN; WOODBLOCK PRINTS.

ARTIFICIAL INTELLIGENCE (AI) See COMPUTER INDUSTRY; FIFTH-GENERATION ADVANCED COMPUTER SYSTEMS; SEMICONDUCTOR INDUSTRY.

ASAHI BREWERIES, LTD. See ALCOHOLIC BEVERAGES

ASAHI OPTICAL CO., LTD. See CAMERAS AND PHOTOGRAPHY.

ASAHI SHIMBUN See NEWSPAPERS.

ASAKUSA A district of Tokyo that was the old downtown (Shitamachi) section settled by merchants during the Edo Era (1600–1868). Asakusa is best known for Sensoji Temple, the oldest Buddhist temple in Tokyo. Dedicated to Kannon, the Buddhist Goddess of Mercy, Sensoji is popularly known as Asakusa Kannon Temple. It is claimed to have been established in the seventh century when local fishermen discovered a statue of Kannon in their nets. The gate at the main entrance to the temple is the Kaminari-

mon, the Gate of the God of Thunder, and has a huge red paper lantern. A large bronze incense container stands in front of the temple. Worshippers wave the billowing incense smoke over themselves to heal or prevent illness. A smaller gate called Hozo-mon leads to a five-story pagoda, the main temple building, and Asakusa Jinja, a Shinto shrine. The main hall of the temple, destroyed during World War II, was rebuilt as a replica of the hall built in 1651. It houses the statue of Kannon, which is never seen by the public. Two major festivals held by Sensoji Temple every year are the Sanja Festival May 16–18 and the Hagoita Festival December 17–19. A *hagoita* is a paddle (or battledore) decorated with a colorful picture. The paddle is used with a shuttlecock to play a traditional game similar to badminton during the New Year Festival. Nakamise Street, the central street leading to the temple, is lined with stalls selling traditional Japanese items and souvenirs. The covered passageways and side streets of Asakusa contain many shops, restaurants and teahouses, as well as a great variety of nighttime entertainment. Stores in the restaurant supply area on Kappabashi Street sell the plastic models of food that are displayed in restaurant windows all over Japan. The new Kokugikan sumo wrestling stadium is also located in the district. See also BUDDHISM; FOOD MODELS, PLASTIC; KANNON; NEW YEAR FESTIVAL; SHITAMACHI; TEMPLES, BUDDHIST; TOKYO.

ASANUMA INEJIRO (1898–1960) A prominent leftist politician who was stabbed to death by a right-wing reactionary youth at a political rally. Asanuma joined the Japan Communist Party while he was a student and graduated from Waseda University in Tokyo in 1923. The next year he was sentenced to five months of hard labor for his part in a violent demonstration during a labor dispute. He then became active in forming several socialist parties prior to World War II. In 1936 he was elected to the House of Representatives, the lower house of Japan's Diet (Parliament), on the Socialist Masses Party (Shaikai Taishuto) ticket. He served in this capacity nine times over a period of 20 years. After the war, he helped form the Japan Socialist Party and soon became its secretary-general and chairman. In 1959, while on a trip to the People's Republic of China, he denounced what he considered U.S. imperialism as a common threat to Japan and China. This "Asanuma Statement" created a political controversy in Japan. See also DIET; ELECTIONS; JAPAN COMMUNIST PARTY; JAPAN SOCIALIST PARTY; POLITICAL PARTIES.

ASHIKAGA SHOGUNATE (1338–1573) Also known as the Muromachi Shogunate; the second of three military governments (*bakufu*, usually translated as shogunate) that ruled Japan over a period of seven centuries. Muromachi is the district in Kyoto near the Imperial Palace where the third Ashikaga shogun, Ashikaga Yoshimitsu (1358–1408), built his "Palace of Flowers" (Hana no Gosho) and administrative headquarters in 1378.

The first military government in Japan was the Kamakura Shogunate (1192–1333) and the third was the Tokugawa Shogunate (1603–1867). The Ashikaga Shogunate was founded by Ashikaga Takauji (1305–1358), a military commander sent by the Kamakura Shogunate to thwart Emperor Go-Daigo's attempt to restore imperial power in 1333. Takauji switched briefly to the emperor's side, but in 1336 defeated Go-Daigo's supporters and took control of Kyoto. Go-Daigo (1288–1339; r. 1318–1339) fled south of Kyoto, and Takauji put Emperor Komyo (1322–1380; r. 1336–1348) on the throne as the Ashikaga puppet. This created a split in the imperial throne known as the Nambokucho, or Southern and Northern Courts (1336–1392), Era. The third shogun, Ashikaga Yoshimitsu, ended the southern imperial line in 1392.

In 1338 Takauji took the title that Minamoto no Yoritomo had taken upon founding the Kamakura Shogunate: *seii tai shogun* ("barbarian–subduing generalissimo"), abbreviated as *shogun*. Although the Ashikaga shoguns extended their political and military rule over much of Japan, they never had complete control. Under a system established by the Kamakura Shogunate, the provinces were governed by provincial commanders (*shugo*) and military land stewards (*jito*). During the Ashikaga Shogunate, the *shugo* combined their military power with the administrative power formerly held by civil provincial governors (*kokushi*). A balance of power was established between the shoguns and the *shugo* or *shugo daimyo* (feudal lords). Powerful *shugo* families, such as the Hosokawa, Shiba and Hatakeyama, controlled the office of shogunal deputy (*kanrei*) and the shogun's senior councils. The Ashikaga shoguns in Kyoto had secure control of central Japan, but provinces in the eastern Kanto region and the southern island of Kyushu retained a measure of autonomy. This balance of power broke down under the eighth shogun, Ashikaga Yoshimasa (1436–1490), causing the Onin War (1467–1477) between *shugo daimyo* factions. This war initiated a century of military conflict, known as the Sengoku Era (Warring States Era; 1467–1568), and ended the power of the Ashikaga Shogunate outside of Kyoto. The warlord Oda Nobunaga (1534–1582) captured Kyoto in 1568 and drove the last Ashikaga shogun, Ashikaga Yoshiaki (1537–1597), out of the city in 1573. Yoshiaki tried to remain the shogun in exile, but finally resigned in 1588.

Altogether there were 15 Ashikaga shoguns. Since the title of shogun was conferred by the emperor, who continued to be revered, the Ashikaga shoguns assimilated into the ranks of the aristocracy and became increasingly removed from the warrior class. They also enhanced their status by patronizing the arts. Noh drama was developed by Kan'ami and his son Zeami (1363–1443), and painting, poetry and gardening flourished. The beautiful Gold and Silver pavilions, Kinkakuji and Ginkakuji, were built by Yoshimitsu and Yoshimasa respectively. The new culture synthesized aristocratic and warrior aesthetics, and was especially associated with the religion of Zen Buddhism, which had been introduced from China in the 12th century A.D. See also ASHIKAGA TAKAUJI; ASHIKAGA YOSHIMASA; ASHIKAGA YOSHIMITSU; BAKUFU; DAIMYO; GINKAKUJI; GO-DAIGO, EMPEROR; HOSOKOWA CLAN; KAMAKURA SHOGUNATE; KINKAKUJI; KYOTO; NAMBOKUCHO ERA; NOH DRAMA; ODA NOBUNAGA; ONIN WAR; PAINTING; POETRY; SENGOKU ERA; SHOGUN; ZEAMI; ZEN SECT OF BUDDHISM.

ASHIKAGA TAKAUJI (1305–1358) A military leader who founded the second military government (*bakufu*) in medieval Japan, known as the Ashikaga Shogunate (also known as the Muromachi Shogunate; 1338–1573). Takauji was born into the Seiwa Genji, a branch of the Minamoto family, which had been powerful for several centuries. He served Japan's first military government, the Kamakura Shogunate (1192–1333), named for the city of Kamakura on eastern Honshu Island where its headquarters were located. The Kamakura Shogunate had many opponents in Kyoto, the imperial capital on western Honshu, who supported Emperor Go-Daigo (1288–1339; r. 1318–39). In 1333 the shogunate sent an army led by Ashikaga Takauji against the imperialist faction in Kyoto. But Takauji switched sides, declared his support for Go-Daigo, and took control of Kyoto. General Nitta Yoshisada dealt the final blow to the shogunate's headquarters in Kamakura. Emperor Go-Daigo attempted to restore imperial rule in Japan, but Takauji began unifying samurai (warriors) in Kyoto who were dissatisfied with the emperor's policies. In 1335 Takauji began a rebellion against Go-Daigo, leading an army to Kamakura and preparing there to attack Kyoto. Go-Daigo sent an army to Kamakura, but was pushed back to Kyoto. Other imperial forces drove Takauji's army to the southern island of Kyushu. He built up his forces and attacked Kyoto in 1336, only three years after the emperor's so-called Kemmu Restoration, and Go-Daigo fled south to Yoshino in Nara Prefecture. Takauji put a prince from the senior branch of the imperial family on the throne as Emperor Komyo (1322–80; r. 1336–48). The court remained divided, with one emperor in Kyoto and one in Yoshino, for half a century, known as the Nambokucho (Southern and Northern Courts) Era (1336–92). In 1338 Takauji had the Northern Court in Kyoto grant him the title of shogun (*seii tai shogun*; "great barbarian-subduing generalissimo"), and founded the Ashikaga Shogunate. As shogun, Takauji had to deal with military conflicts caused by supporters of the Southern Court and within the shogunate. Takauji sided with two military vassals of the Ko family against his own brother, Ashikaga Tadayoshi. This conflict ended when Tadayoshi was murdered in 1352. Takauji died six years later, and his son Yoshiakira (1330–68; ruled 1359–68) became the next Ashikaga Shogun. Japanese historians, especially just before World War II, tended to regard Ashikaga Takauji as a traitor for mistreating the rightful emperor of Japan. See also ASHIKAGA SHOGUNATE; GO-DAIGO, EMPEROR; KAMAKURA SHOGUNATE; NAMBOKUCHO ERA; SAMURAI; SHOGUN.

ASHIKAGA YOSHIAKI See ASHIKAGA SHOGUNATE; ODA NOBUNAGA.

ASHIKAGA YOSHIMASA (1436–1490) The eighth shogun (military ruler) of the Ashikaga Shogunate (also known as the Muromachi Shogunate; 1338–1573); ruled 1449–1474. Yoshimasa was the son of the sixth Ashikaga shogun, Ashikaga Yoshinori, who was assassinated in 1441. Yoshimasa's oldest brother, Yoshikatsu (1434–1443), became the seventh Ashikaga shogun. He died two years later, and Yoshimasa succeeded him as shogun.

Despite his title, Yoshimasa was not interested in being a military ruler, but preferred the elegant, aesthetic life of the imperial court. He was unable to cope with the political and economic problems that were overwhelming the capital city of Kyoto, including famine, disease and rebellions. The *daimyo* (feudal lords) who governed the provinces for the Ashikaga Shogunate were also engaging in civil warfare. Yoshimasa decided to retire as shogun. In 1464 he designated his brother Yoshimi (1439–1491) as his successor.

The following year, however, Yoshimasa's wife, Hino Tomiko, gave birth to a son, Yoshihisa (1465–1489), and demanded that he become his father's successor. Political and military factions took sides in this dispute, and it escalated into the Onin War (1467–1477), which devastated Kyoto, abolished the power of the Ashikaga Shogunate outside Kyoto and initiated a century of military struggle known as the Sengoku Era or the Era of Warring States (1467–1568). In 1474, Yoshimasa abdicated the title of shogun to his son Yoshihisa. Yoshimasa followed the example of his grandfather, Ashikaga Yoshimitsu (1358–1408), who had erected a magnificent retreat known as Kinkakuji (Golden Pavilion), and built the retirement retreat Ginkakuji (Silver Pavilion) on East Hill (Higashiyama) in Kyoto.

Despite the bitter struggles during his time, Yoshimasa patronized the fine arts and enabled them to flourish, especially poetry, ink painting, Noh drama and the tea ceremony. These arts were closely related to Zen Buddhism, which had been introduced from China in the 13th century A.D. The Zen concepts of restraint and simplicity were particularly influential on these arts. See also ASHIKAGA SHOGUNATE; ASHIKAGA YOSHIMITSU; GINKAKUJI; INK PAINTING; KYOTO; KINKAKUJI; NOH DRAMA; ONIN WAR; POETRY; SENGOKU ERA; SHOGUN; TEA CEREMONY; ZEN BUDDHISM.

ASHIKAGA YOSHIMITSU (1358–1408) The third shogun (military commander) of the Ashikaga Shogunate (1338–1573; also known as the Muromachi Shogunate). Only 10 years old when he became shogun, Yoshimitsu and his deputy Hosokawa Yoriyuki (1329–92) increased the power of the shogunate until it controlled most of Japan. He also ended the division into two branches of the imperial court, known as the Southern and Northern Courts (Nambokucho) Era. This division has great historical significance because it belied the traditional belief that the emperors descended in an unbroken line from the Sun Goddess Amaterasu o Mikami. The so-called northern emperor was controlled by the Ashikagas in the capital city of Kyoto. The southern emperor continued the line of Emperor Go-Daigo (1288–1339), who overthrew the Kamakura Shogunate (1192–1333), but was in turn ousted by the Ashikaga Shogunate. Yoshimitsu convinced the southern emperor to return to Kyoto by promising him that the two lines of imperial descendants would alternate. But he broke this promise and the northern line continued to hold the throne. Yoshimitsu had to put down several uprisings led by military governors in the Japanese provinces. He handed the title of shogun to his son Yoshimochi (1386–1428) in 1395, but in fact Yoshimitsu kept control of the govern-

ment. He resided in an opulent Buddhist temple compound known as the Golden Pavilion (Kinkakuji) and awarded himself the highest ranks in Japan. Yoshimitsu acquired a great fortune by opening up diplomatic and trade relations between Japan and China, which was then ruled by the Ming dynasty (1368–1644). See also ASHIKAGA SHOGUNATE; BAKUFU; CHINA AND JAPAN; GO-DAIGO, EMPEROR; KINKAKUJI; NAMBOKUCHO ERA; SHOGUN.

ASHIKAGA YOSHINORI See ASHIKAGA SHOGUNATE; ASHIKAGA YOSHIMASA; ZEAMI.

ASO, MOUNT (Asosan) A volcano on central Kyushu Island that has the largest crater (caldera) in the world, 15 miles long, 11 miles wide, and 50 miles in circumference. The rim of the crater actually consists of five mountains. Four are extinct, but Nakadake (4,986 feet high) is still the most active volcano in the world and constantly rumbles and pours out steam and ash that periodically destroy crops in the area. Lava has flowed out from Mount Aso in a radius of 62 miles, covering much of Kyushu and killing area residents; the latest eruption was in 1979.

Mount Aso is part of Aso National Park (Aso Kokuritsu Koen). Because of the volcanic activity, there are many hot spring resorts (*onsen*) in the region. Visitors are allowed to climb up to the rim of the volcano to view the steaming green lake at the bottom of the crater. The Volcano Museum has screens on which visitors can watch eruptions photographed by cameras trained on the active crater. The Sacred Fire Ritual (Hirubi-Shinjio) is held at Aso Shrine every March 3rd. See also HOT SPRING; KYUSHU ISLAND; NATIONAL PARKS; VOLCANO.

ASTROLOGY See BIRTHDAYS; ZODIAC.

ASUKA A region about 15 miles south of the city of Nara on western Honshu Island; the cultural and political center of Japan during the sixth and seventh centuries; also, an era in Japanese art history dating from 552, when the Buddhist religion was introduced into Japan from China, until the Taika Reform of 645. The Aya clan, which emigrated from Korea, settled in the Asuka region beginning about A.D. 400. Korean and Chinese artists also moved into this region, and created Buddhist sculptures, paintings, and temples in the style of Chinese art of the Six Dynasties Era (220–589). Horyuji Temple, located to the north of Asuka, is an example of this style. Most of the rulers of Japan before the eighth century A.D., including the legendary first emperor of Japan, Jimmu Tenno, supposedly had residences in or near Asuka. Only the foundations of these ancient palaces remain. The *Nihon Shoki* (*Chronicles of Japan*; A.D. 720, Japan's first official history) records events that took place in the Asuka region. The Soga clan, whose territorial seat was at Nara, became the most powerful group in Japan in the late sixth century A.D. They established their court at Asuka, but moved it to the newly constructed capital of Nara in A.D. 710. Asakudera (also known as Angoin, Hokoji or Moto Gangoji) was the first complete Buddhist temple complex in Japan, built to house a gift of Buddhist relics sent by the Korean kingdom of Paekche in A.D. 588. Korean monks and craftsmen also went to Japan to help construct the buildings. A plan of the temple compound, excavated in 1956–57, shows that within the walls were three halls situated around a central pagoda. A lecture hall behind the temple reflects Asakudera's role as a center for Buddhist knowledge in Japan at that time. A 13-foot-high bronze statue of the Buddha, founder of the Buddhist religion, all that remains from the original temple, is the oldest extant Buddhist sculpture made in Japan. Asakudera fell into neglect after the capital moved to Nara in A.D. 710. See also AYA CLAN; BUDDHISM; CHINA AND JAPAN; HORYUJI; JIMMU TENNO; KOREA AND JAPAN; NARA; NARA ERA; NIHON SHOKI; SOGA CLAN; TEMPLES, BUDDHIST.

ATAMI The largest and most famous hot spring (onsen) resort in Japan. Part of Fuji-Hakone-Izu National Park, Atami, with a population of 50,000, is located on Sagami Bay on the northeast coast of the Izu Peninsula, one hour south of Tokyo on the Pacific (east) coast of Honshu Island, and is easily reached by the "Bullet Train" (Shinkansen). Because of its numerous hot springs, Atami was a resort town as early as the eighth century A.D. Visitors walk around town wearing yukata, cotton robes similar to kimono but worn as bathrobes. There are hundreds of geisha (traditional female entertainers) in Atami who sing and dance at parties for rowdy groups of businessmen or workers on company-sponsored vacations.

The MOA Museum of Art (MOA Bijutsukan), located in Atami, was opened in 1982 by a religious organization founded by Mokichi Okada (1882–1955) that also operates the Hakone Museum of Art. The MOA museum has an excellent collection of Japanese, Chinese and European art collected by the religion's founder. Many of the art objects have been designated as National Treasures or Important Cultural Properties by the Japanese government. The museum also has a garden, tea ceremony room and theater for Noh drama.

Atami holds a plum festival in January, a fireworks display in early August and a fall festival honoring Ozaki Koyo (1867–1903), who wrote a novel set in Atami. See also BULLET TRAIN; GEISHA; FUJI-HAKONE-IZU NATIONAL PARK; HOT SPRING; IZU PENINSULA; MUSEUMS IN JAPAN; YUKATA.

ATOMIC BOMB A bomb with highly explosive power caused by chain reactions based on nuclear fission. Japan is the only country to have been attacked with atomic weapons. The United States dropped atomic bombs on the cities of Hiroshima and Nagasaki to hasten the end of World War II and force Japan to surrender. The first, dropped on Hiroshima at 8:15 A.M. on August 6, 1945, was a uranium-235 bomb that released energy equivalent to 12.5 kilotons of TNT. As many as 145,000 people died in Hiroshima within five years, from burns, severe injuries, shock and radiation illness. The second atomic bomb was dropped at 11:02 A.M. over Nagasaki on August 9, 1945. This was a plutonium-239 bomb that had even greater power than the first. Up to 140,000 people there had died by 1950. The atomic bombs forced Japan's surrender and

eliminated the need for an invasion of the archipelago. Survivors of the blasts, called hibakusha, have been prone to a wide range of physical and psychological problems, and are socially and economically discriminated against in Japan even today. Atomic-bomb-related disease is called gembakusho.

The U.S.–Japan Joint Commission was appointed in October 1945 to study long-term effects of radiation. In 1947 the Atomic Bomb Casualty Commission (ABCC) was established in conjunction with the Japan National Institute of Health. In 1975 this commission became the joint Japan-U.S. Radiation Effects Research Foundation (RERF).

Most of the buildings near the epicenter of the Hiroshima blast were destroyed. A Peace Memorial Park in the city has been laid out around the skeleton of a domed building that was partially destroyed in the blast. The Hiroshima Peace Memorial Museum displays information about destruction caused by the bomb. Visiting schoolchildren leave origami (folded paper) cranes to commemorate the victims.

Nagasaki, hilly and less easily destroyed, lost slightly fewer than half its buildings. A Peace Park there houses a similar museum. Emperor Hirohito (1901–1989; now known as Emperor Showa) announced Japan's surrender on August 9, 1945. A Japanese movement against nuclear weapons became strong in the mid-1950s but has lessened in recent decades. See also CRANE; HIROSHIMA; NAGASAKI; ORIGAMI; SURRENDER OF JAPAN; WORLD WAR II.

ATSUTA SHRINE (Atsuta Jingu) An important Shinto shrine in Atsuta Ward in the city of Nagoya that draws many pilgrims. Atsuta Shrine is believed to hold the sacred sword, one of the three Imperial Regalia or sacred treasures that legitimize the rule of the Japanese emperors. The other regalia are the sacred mirror, housed at Ise Shrine, and the sacred jewels, kept at the Imperial Palace in Tokyo.

Tradition claims that Atsuta Shrine was built prior to the ninth century A.D. by a consort of Prince Yamato Takeru, a legendary war hero who extended the territory ruled by the Yamato clan. The sword, which supposedly saved Prince Yamatotakeru's life during a military campaign, bears the name "Grass-Cutting Sword" (Kusanagi no Tsurugi). The sword got this name because when Yamatotakeru was attacked by bandits in a prairie fire, he used the sword to cut the grass down around him and then started his own fire to drive away the bandits. The Yamato originated the rule of the Japanese emperors, and their court was centered around the region of Asuka and Nara in western Honshu, the main island of Japan. In A.D. 808 the imperial court, responding to a complaint that Atsuta Shrine was being neglected, awarded the shrine a large tract of land and promoted it to the highest rank of Shinto shrines. Patronage of the shrine was continued by the military regimes of Japan, the Ashikaga Shogunate (1338–1573) and Tokugawa Shogunate (1603–1867). When imperial rule was restored with the Meiji Era (1868–1912), Atsuta Shrine was honored for its special status, making it equal to the main Shinto shrine at Ise.

Atsuta Shrine celebrates its annual festival on June 5th. See also IMPERIAL PALACE, TOKYO; IMPERIAL REGALIA; ISE SHRINE;

MIRROR; NAGOYA; PILGRIMAGE; SHINTO; SHRINES, SHINTO; SWORD; YAMATO.

AUTOMOBILE INDUSTRY (*jidosha sangyo*)

In 1980 Japan became the world's largest producer of motor vehicles and largest exporter of automobiles and trucks. The industry is represented by the Japan Automobile Manufacturers Association (JAMA). Motor vehicles are Japan's largest single export item, accounting for nearly 20% of total Japanese exports. In 1989 Japan produced 13.03 million vehicles. The Toyota Motor Corporation produces the most Japanese vehicles, closely followed by its rival, Nissan Motor Co., Ltd. Other Japanese automobile manufacturers include Honda Motor Co., Ltd., Mitsubishi Motors Corporation, Toyo Kogyo Co., Ltd. (Mazda), Isuzu Motors Ltd., Fuji Heavy Industries, Ltd. (Subaru), Suzuki Motor Co., Ltd. and Daihatsu Motor Co., Ltd.

The Japanese automobile industry developed very quickly after 1965, and with less government assistance than has been typical for the development of other Japanese industries. Auto manufacturers were able to take advantage of the oil crises and high gasoline prices in the early 1970s because they were already producing small, fuel-efficient vehicles that appealed to consumers over large, fuel-inefficient cars. Japanese automakers were also among the first to use robots in the assembly line production, which lowered manufacturing costs and increased product reliability, all factors in growing sales. They have emphasized research in new technology to create automobiles with complex electronics systems, turbo-charged engines, and lighter, more durable materials such as ceramics for engine parts.

There is some foreign investment in Japan, with Ford owning 25% of Toyo Kogyo, General Motors Corporation 34% of Isuzu, and Chrysler 15% of Mitsubishi. In 1981, Japanese automakers agreed to abide by voluntary restraint agreements reducing the number of cars they exported to the United States and Canada. Japanese companies have established subsidiaries or joint manufacturing plants in the U.S. and many other countries. Japanese automakers belong to the Japan Automobile Manufacturers Association. Japanese car makers built eight assembly plants in the United States during the 1980s. In 1989 the Honda Accord was the best-selling car in the United States. That year Japan manufactured 13.03 million vehicles, making it the world's largest automobile maker. See also CORPORATIONS; EXPORTS AND IMPORTS; MITSUBISHI; MOTORCYCLE INDUSTRY; NISSAN MOTOR CO., LTD.; ROBOT; TOYOTA MOTOR CORPORATION.

AUTUMN

See AUTUMN FLOWERS AND GRASSES; CHRYSANTHEMUM; CLIMATE OF JAPAN; MAPLE TREE; MOON-VIEWING FESTIVAL; RICE PLANTING AND HARVESTING FESTIVALS; TYPHOONS.

AUTUMN FLOWERS AND GRASSES (*akigusa*)

Also known as the seven flowering herbs of autumn, which parallel the seven herbs of spring (*nanakusa*), these are plants and flowers appearing in August and September that are admired by the Japanese for their natural, unpretentious beauty. They include the Japanese bush clover (*hagi*), pampas grass (*susuki*), kudzu vine (*kuzu*), fringed pink (*nadeshiko*), valerian (*ominaeshi*), ague weed (*fujibakama*), and balloon flower (*kikyo*). The Japanese display these flowers and grasses in arrangements during the autumn months, placing them in woven bamboo baskets that complement their simple beauty. A famous Japanese poem composed during the Nara Era (710–794) counts seven flowers blooming in the fields of autumn. The Japanese have a strong identification with nature and are deeply moved by the beauty of the changing seasons. They admire the forms of plants rather than their colors and scents, and appreciate beauty that is natural and imperfect or irregular. For example, the valerian (maiden flower) has a disagreeable odor that the Chinese find offensive, but Japanese poets have praised it as one of the most beautiful flowers of autumn. Other autumn vegetation admired by the Japanese includes the chrysanthemum (*kiku*) and autumnal maple leaves (*momiji*) that turn color. *Akigusa* have been a popular design motif in Japan since the Heian Era (794–1185) for such crafts as textiles, lacquerware writing boxes, and handmade paper, especially for sheets on which poetry is written. Akigusa are often shown with the moon (*tsuki*), which is also associated with autumn, when the Moon-Viewing Festival is celebrated. Akigusa motifs were especially used to decorate articles used by women, such as lacquerware cosmetic boxes. See also BASKETS; BOXES; CHRYSANTHEMUM; CLIMATE OF JAPAN; FLOWERS; LACQUER WARE; MAPLE TREE; MOON; MOON VIEWING FESTIVAL; PAPER; SEVEN HERBS OF SPRING; TEXTILES.

AWARDS, GOVERNMENT

See DECORATIONS, CIVILIAN.

AYA CLAN

A wealthy and powerful group whose members became prominent in ancient Japanese government and religious institutions. The Aya clan consisted of eight families that emigrated to Japan from Korea around A.D. 400 under the leadership of Achi no Omi, and their descendants. Later groups who were influenced by Achi to emigrate from Korea were called *ayahito*, or *imaki no* (newly arrived) *ayahito*. They may have been descendants of Chinese who had earlier moved to Korea. Several other large groups emigrated to Japan from Korea at that time, such as the Hata clan.

The character for the name Aya, the same as that used to write the name of the Chinese Han dynasty (206 B.C.–220 B.C.), may actually relate to the place name Ara (also pronounced Aya) in southeast Korea. The Yamato no Aya became the dominant branch of the Aya clan in early Japan and settled in Yamato Province (modern Nara Prefecture), particularly the Asuka region. Family members held important positions in the imperial government, military and hierarchy of the Buddhist religion. In the seventh century, the Yamato no Aya became allied with the powerful Soga clan. The most important branch of the Aya clan was the Sakanoue family, whose members held high government and military positions in Japan from the sixth through 14th centuries. This family was distinguished for its mastery of archery and horsemanship.

Sakanoue no Tamuramaro (758–811), who led the military forces that conquered the indigenous Ezo people of northeastern Japan, was admired for a thousand years in Japan as the ideal warrior. He was the first to be awarded the title *seii tai shogun* ("barbarian-subduing generalissimo") by the emperor. This title, abbreviated as *shogun*, was taken up by warriors who founded the military governments *(bakufu)* that ruled Japan from the 12th through 19th centuries. See also ARCHERY; ASUKA; BAKUFU; HATA CLAN; HORSE; KOREA AND JAPAN; SHOGUN; SOGA CLAN; YAMATO.

AZUCHI-MOMOYAMA ERA (1568–1600) Also known as the Momoyama Era; the period in Japanese history when the country was unified by three powerful warlords: Oda Nobunaga (1534–1582), Toyotomi Hideyoshi (1536–1598), and Tokugawa Ieyasu (1543–1616). This era is regarded as the time when Japan made the transition from the medieval to the early modern era.

The Azuchi-Momoyama Era is named for Azuchi Castle, which Nobunaga built in Omi Province (modern Shiga Prefecture), and the place where Hideyoshi built Fushimi Castle in Yamashiro Province (part of modern Kyoto Prefecture). This era began in 1568 when Nobunaga entered the capital city of Kyoto and took control of the Ashikaga Shogunate (also known as the Muromachi Shogunate; 1338–1573). In 1573 he brought down the shogunate by driving Shogun Ashikaga Yoshiaki (1537–1597) from Kyoto. The Azuchi-Momoyama Era was preceded by a century of civil warfare known as the Sengoku (Warring States) Era (1467–1568), and followed by more than two centuries of peace during the Tokugawa Shogunate (1603–1867), a military government founded by Tokugawa Ieyasu after he defeated his rivals in 1600 at the Battle of Sekigahara. Some historians date the end of the Azuchi-Momoyama Era in 1598, when Hideyoshi died, or in 1603, when Ieyasu took the title of shogun.

The Azuchi-Momoyama Era was a period of great castle building by *daimyo* (feudal lords) and the rise of an urban merchant and artisan class in towns that rapidly grew up around the castles. The most famous castle that remains from this time is Himeji Castle, built by the *daimyo* Ikeda Terumasa (1564–1613) in Hyogo Prefecture. Castles were not only military fortifications; their gorgeously decorated interiors reflected the power and wealth of the *daimyo* who erected them.

Free trade was encouraged at this time; silver and gold mines were developed; and Western influences were brought into Japan. The so-called Namban (Southern Barbarian) culture appeared during this era, brought by Roman Catholic Jesuit missionaries and Portuguese traders. However, Hideyoshi and Ieyasu decided to suppress the Christian religion in Japan. Japanese arts flourished, particularly painting, much of it on screens, as well as poetry and drama. The tea ceremony was patronized by the warlords as a means of displaying their wealth and cultural attainments. Sen no Rikyu (1522–1591), the great tea master who formalized the tea ceremony, was a retainer of Nobunaga and Hideyoshi. See also ASHIKAGA SHOGUNATE; CASTLES; CHRISTIANITY IN JAPAN; DAIMYO; HIMEJI CASTLE; MUROMACHI ERA; NAMBAN; ODA NOBUNAGA; POETRY; PORTUGUESE IN JAPAN; SCREENS; SEKIGAHARA, BATTLE OF; SEN NO RIKYU; SENGOKU ERA; SHOGUN; TEA CEREMONY; TOYOTOMI HIDEYOSHI; TOKUGAWA IEYASU; TOKUGAWA SHOGUNATE.

AZUKI BEANS See BEANS; SWEETS.

B

BABIES IN JAPAN See BIRTHDAY; CHILDREN IN JAPAN; DEPENDENCY; FAMILY; MOTHER.

BADGER *(tanuki)* A small animal that appears frequently in Japanese folk tales and songs. Actually, the tanuki is not really a badger, even though it is usually translated as such, but a raccoon dog similar to the North American raccoon without rings on its tail. The badger is thought to have supernatural powers. Supposedly able to transform itself into human form, it is often depicted as a Buddhist monk. The Japanese compare a crafty person to the tanuki. The fox is another animal that is thought to transform itself, and both the badger and fox are cunning tricksters; unlike the fox, however, the badger is not frightening but comical. Folk-art pottery statues of badgers are common in Japan and are often placed in gardens. Many of these statues show the animal in a standing position with a lotus-leaf hat and a large belly. Badgers are believed to beat their bodies like drums with their forepaws or, when they disguise themselves in human form, their hands. Japanese eat the meat of the tanuki and use its fur to make brushes. There is a saying that if a tanuki is freed from a trap, it repays the kindness of its liberator. See also BRUSHES; FOX.

BAKUFU "Tent government"; the term for three military governments, usually translated into English as "shogunates," that ruled Japan from the late 12th through the late 19th centuries: the Kamakura Shogunate (1192–1333), Ashikaga Shogunate (also known as the Muromachi Shogunate; 1338–1573) and Tokugawa Shogunate (1603–1867). The Japanese term *bakufu* comes from the Chinese term *mufu*, which means the field headquarters of an army general. In Japan, *bakufu* was used to designate the headquarters of the Inner Palace Gaurds (Konoefu), who guarded the emperor; the residence of the guards' commander; or the commander himself *(konoe no taisho)*. The term *bakufu* became applied to Minamoto no Yoritomo (1147–1199), who established the first military regime in Japan after the Minamoto clan under his leadership defeated the Taira clan in the Taira-Minamoto War (1180–1185). In 1192 Yoritomo persuaded the imperial court in Kyoto in western Japan to award him the title *shogun*, or commander in chief of the country. He had built up a power base with many vassals in Kamakura in eastern Japan. Yoritomo's headquarters there were thus called the *bakufu*, or shogunate. The *bakufu* did not replace the imperial dynasty located in the capital city of Kyoto. Rather, all three shogunates used the imperial throne to legitimize their own military rule. However, the feudal system of lords and vassals developed by the *bakufu* did gradually replace the civil bureaucracy of the imperial court. See also ASHIKAGA SHOGUNATE; FEUDALISM; KAMAKURA SHOGUNATE; SHOGUN; TOKUGAWA SHOGUNATE; MINAMOTO NO YORITOMO.

BAMBOO *(take)* A perennial plant that grows wild in Japan and many other tropical and subtropical countries and is used in numerous ways. About 1,250 species of bamboo have been classified, and between 400 and 500 of these can be found in Japan. Bamboo is also cultivated. Although it is often called a tree, bamboo is a unique plant that some botanists classify as a grass.

The varieties of bamboo known as *take* in Japan grow very rapidly and very tall and are put to many uses. The hollow trunk, properly called a culm, grows tall and straight, with many joints. Along with roots, bamboo sends out rhizomes, underground shoots that sprout to form new plants. Fronds of delicate leaves appear high up on bamboo culms. Bamboo is very hardy, although most types can grow only in climates where the temperature does not drop below zero degrees Fahrenheit. Species of *take* bloom only once every 60 years or even less frequently, and when a species blooms, most of the plants of that species die all over Japan; it takes them a decade to return to their former numbers. A species with long joints known as the *madake*, which includes almost three-quarters of all Japanese *take* bamboo, bloomed in the late 1960s, the first time in over a century.

Bamboo has traditionally been used in every aspect of daily life in Japan. Young shoots *(take-no-ko,* or "bamboo children") are cooked and eaten. Strong yet pliable, bamboo is used for pillars, roof beams, window lattices, fences, rakes, ladders, fishing poles, umbrellas, spoons, plates, writing brushes, toys, fans, flutes, bows for archery, woven baskets, storage containers and flower vases. The Japanese tea ceremony employs bamboo for tea scoops, tea whisks, water ladles and vases. These objects are simple, at times even rustic in design, yet have an appealing natural beauty.

Bamboo motifs are common in Japanese family crests, and the word for bamboo is included in many Japanese names. Bamboo is widely planted in Japanese gardens and even outside urban homes. The Three Friends of Winter is a popular decorative motif combining bamboo, pine *(matsu)* and plum *(ume)* blossoms, all of which are sturdy and remain fresh in the winter. A *kadomatsu* (gate pine), made of three pieces of green bamboo and pine branches tied together, decorates the entrance to every Japanese home at the New Year Festival.

Sasa is a type of bamboo that is closely related to grass. It is shorter than other types of bamboo, on average no more than 7 inches high, and sometimes growing only a few inches. Most Japanese bamboo is *sasa*. It grows wild over much of the northernmost Japanese island of Hok-

Bamboo grass (sasa), the most common type of bamboo plant in Japan.

kaido. *Sasa* is used mainly as a decorative plant in gardens. Japanese also use green and white *sasa* leaves to decorate *sashimi* (raw fish). See also ARCHERY; BASKETS; BRUSHES; CREST; FANS; FLOWER ARRANGING; FLUTES; GARDENS; HOMES AND HOUSING; PINE TREE; PLUM TREE; NEW YEAR FESTIVAL; SHAKUHACHI; TEA CEREMONY; THREE FRIENDS OF WINTER; TOYS, TRADITIONAL.

BAMBOO CUTTER, THE TALE OF THE (*Taketori Monogatari*)   A tale dating from the ninth or 10th century A.D. about an old man who finds a beautiful divine princess when he cuts a bamboo stalk. He takes her home, and he and his wife raise her as their daughter. When Kaguyahime, "The Shining Princess," comes of age, her now-wealthy human father pleads with her to marry one of the five aristocrats who have proposed, but she gives each one a task that he is unable to fulfill. Kaguyahime even refuses the emperor's marriage proposal. She finally tells her parents that she is from the Palace of the Moon, and that she must return there with messengers who are coming to accompany her. Kaguyahime is very sad that she must leave, but her human family is powerless to keep her on earth. She puts on a robe of feathers that erases her memories of this world and flies back to the moon.

The Japanese term *monogatari*, "tale," was later applied to various types of prose fiction, but it originally meant supernatural stories that were based on two sources: folk legends handed down orally, and miracle stories in the Buddhist religion that were recorded in Chinese and intro-duced into Japan. *The Tale of the Bamboo Cutter* is the earliest surviving *monogatari* of this type. Murasaki Shikibu (fl. c. A.D. 1000), author of the first Japanese novel, *The Tale of Genji (Genji Monogatari)*, described *Taketori Monogatari* as the "archetype" of Japanese romance fiction. It was translated into English as *The Tale of the Bamboo Cutter* in 1956. See also BAMBOO; BUDDHISM; GENJI, THE TALE OF; MOON; MURASAKI SHIKIBU; NOVELS.

BAMBOO SHOOT TRIBE (Takenokozoku)   The name for a large group of Japanese teenagers who gather on Sunday afternoons in the Harajuku district of Tokyo. They dress in colorful costumes, wear elaborate makeup and perform well-rehearsed dance routines to American rock-and-roll music from the 1950s. Males and females usually dance separately in lines that face each other. The name "Bamboo Shoot Tribe" comes from Takenoko, a popular clothing boutique in the district and suggests youth. Members of another gorup called the Wild Driving Tribe (or hot rod gang; Bosozoku) dress in black leather jackets and wear their hair slicked back to imitate American motorcycle gangs. They also perform elaborately choreographed dance routines to rock music, and ride their motorcycles in close formations while noisily honking their horns. The Bosozoku have a bad reputation, although most Wild Drivers hold jobs or go to school. Similar recent trendy groups in Japan have included the Sun Tribe, whose members wear Hawaiian shirts and dark sunglasses, and the Harajuku tribes. These teenaged "tribes" appear shocking and rebellious to conventional Japanese. Foreigners who watch them perform generally find them comparatively wholesome and entertaining. See also HARAJUKU.

BANCHA   See TEA.

BANK OF JAPAN (Nihon Ginko or Nippon Ginko)   The central government bank of Japan, which is directed by the Ministry of Finance and is responsible for implementing the Japanese government's monetary policy. The Bank of Japan has its head office in Tokyo, and has several dozen domestic branches and offices, and a number of foreign offices.

The Bank of Japan was established in 1882 by finance minister Matsukata Masayoshi (1835–1924) to stabilize the *yen* (Japanese currency) and provide funds for the growth of Japanese business and industry. Its monetary policy was to prevent inflation and to maintain the value of the yen, as was done following the oil crisis of 1973 and the fluctuating value of the yen in the 1970s. The policy board of the Bank of Japan includes the bank governor, representatives from the Economic Planning Agency and the Ministry of Finance, and appointees from private banks, with the Banking Bureau of the Ministry of Finance providing major administrative guidance. The Japanese banking system combines government and private banking institutions, with the Bank of Japan at the head of the system. Through the Bank of Japan, the Ministry of Finance sets minimum lending rates and the amount of deposits other banks have to make, which makes large private Japanese banks dependent on the Bank of Japan. The Ministry of International Trade and Industry (MITI) controls the lending of money to commercial banks by the Bank of Japan. The Bank of Japan controls credit expansion on individual commercial banks by so-called "window guidance," whereby it sets for each public and private bank a quarterly ceiling on the amount of credit increase during each financial quarter. See also BANKING SYSTEM; MINISTRY OF FINANCE; MINISTRY OF INTERNATIONAL TRADE AND INDUSTRY; OIL CRISIS OF 1973; YEN.

BANKING SYSTEM The earliest bankers in Japan were *ryogaesho* (money changers), who originated in the 13th century and became prominent in the Edo Era (1600–1868). They were especially active in Edo (modern Tokyo), Kyoto and Osaka, the commercial center of Japan during the Edo Era. *Ryogaesho* exchanged gold and silver, accepted deposits, made loans and remitted funds. Large money changers also acted as agents of the Tokugawa Shogunate (1603–1867) and *daimyo* (feudal lords). After the Meiji Restoration of 1868, the *ryogaesho* were replaced by exchange companies *(kawase kaisha)*, which functioned as modern commercial banks.

These did not succeed for long, and were replaced in the 1870s by a new system of government-chartered national banks. Finance minister Matsukata Masayoshi (1835–1924) established the Bank of Japan (Nippon Ginko) as the central bank in 1882, and the national banks were reorganized into ordinary banks. Savings banks, specialized banks for dealing in foreign exchange and long-term financing, and long-term credit banks for lending money to industry and agriculture were also organized at this time. Many banks failed or were forced to merge during the financial crisis of 1927.

The present Japanese banking system was organized after World War II. The Bank of Japan remains as the central bank, and its major functions include issuing currency *(yen)* and carrying out the monetary policy of the Ministry of Finance, such as setting the interest rate paid on deposits. There are four main categories of banks in Japan. The largest comprises the 13 city banks *(toshi ginko)*, such as the Bank of Tokyo, which control more than 40% of all bank deposits. These banks are based in large cities but have networks of national and foreign branch offices. They have a large consumer and corporate deposit base and specialize in extending short-term loans to industry. The second category is the 70 regional banks *(chiho ginko)*, which are similar to city banks but operate in a local economic area. The third category consists of the seven trust banks *(shintaku ginko)*, which extend long-term loans to industry. The fourth category is public long-term credit banks, which offer long-term corporate bonds (debentures) or time deposits to other financial institutions, in order to fund long-term loans to Japanese corporations. These banks include the Nippon Credit Bank, the Long-term Credit Bank of Japan and the Industrial Bank of Japan. The Export-Import Bank finances overseas investments and expensive exports such as assembly plants or major manufacturing equipment. The Japan Development Bank provides funds for industrial development. Ten public corporations engage in finance *(koko)* by extending loans to special sectors, such as house buyers or small business.

Large Japanese banks are members of *keiretsu*, industrial groups of many interconnected companies. The bank owns stock in companies belonging to its *keiretsu*, and makes loans to them. Foreign banks have also established branches in Japan. Similarly, 25% of Japanese bank assets are now in overseas branches. The top 10 banks in the world are Japanese; the four largest are Dai-Ichi Kangyo, Fuji, Sumitomo and Mitsubishi. Japanese banks have grown rapidly due to the rising value of the yen in the 1980s and an individual savings rate of around 20% of income, the highest of any industrialized country.

Around one-third of personal savings are deposited in the savings system of the Japanese postal system, the largest savings institution in the world. An individual depositor can deposit a large sum of money tax free, and Japanese often open many different postal savings accounts to evade taxes.

The Japanese usually pay cash for retail purchases. Checks and credit cards are not widely used in Japan, although credit card companies have recently begun to expand there. Many Japanese have their wages paid by a direct-deposit system to their individual bank accounts. They can send money to family members and pay for mail-order purchases by having their banks transfer money to branch offices through a nationwide online system. Until recently, Japanese banks have not widely made loans to individuals, so many Japanese borrowed from moneylenders *(sarakin)* at interest rates as high as 100%. The government has been attempting to reform this system. See also BANK OF JAPAN; MATSUKATA MASAYOSHI; MINISTRY OF FINANCE; YEN.

BANNERS See FLAGS AND BANNERS.

BANZAI "Ten thousand years"; an enthusiastic shout that is equivalent to "three cheers" or "hip hip hurrah." One traditional usage has been to wish long life to the emperor. The Japanese shout *"banzai"* three times, with their arms raised straight above their heads, at the climax of a celebration. Groups often do this to wish a good trip to a colleague or company executive at an airport or railroad platform. In place of *"banzai,"* the Japanese may now conclude a celebration or special meeting with the practice of *tejime*, in which they clap their hands a total of ten times in a 3-3-3-1 rhythm.

BARS See ALCOHOLIC BEVERAGES; EXPENSE ACCOUNTS; KARAOKE; WATER TRADE.

BASEBALL *(yakyu)* The most popular team sport in Japan on both amateur and professional levels, baseball was first taught to Japanese students at Kaisei Gakko (now Tokyo University) in 1873 by an American named Horace Wilson, and was soon played at other schools. By 1880 there was a regular team at the Shimbashi Athletic Club. Games were played from 1890 to 1902 between students of a Tokyo high school and Americans living in the port city of Yokohama. Baseball became so popular that by 1900 most Japanese schools and universities had teams that held intramural competitions. Today Japanese school teams enter several national competitions that are televised live nationwide: the National Invitational High School Baseball Championship, which was first held in 1924; the All-Japan High School Baseball Championship Tournament, which dates back to 1915; and the Japan Collegiate Baseball Championship. There are now more than 250 college baseball teams; the Tokyo Big Six University Baseball League has the favorite clubs. There are also many non-student amateur teams that compete in the Intercity Baseball Championship Tournament and the Japan Amateur Baseball Championship Tournament. School and amateur teams are governed by the Japan Amateur Baseball Federation. About 50 high school teams qualify for the Koshun Tournament held every spring and autumn at Koshien Stadium in Kobe. The whole nation enthusiastically follows this tournament.

Professional baseball, which began in 1934, has a very strong following in Japan. The professional season runs from April through October, during which time every team plays 130 games. There are two leagues, which were formed in 1950, with six teams each. The Central League includes the Chunichi Dragons, Hanshin Tigers, Hiroshima Toyo Carp, Taiyo Whales, Yakult Swallows and Yomiuri Giants; the Pacific League includes the Hankyu Braves, Kintetsu Buffaloes, Lotte Orions, Nankai Hawks, Nippon-Ham Fighters and Seibu Lions. Each professional team can have two American players. The best known, Randy Bass, left Japan in 1988. The top team from each league plays a final seven-game championship series in October, called the Japan Series. Millions of Japanese fans attend professional baseball games each year and chant organized cheers in a way similar to football fans in the United States. Oh Saduharu, the greatest Japanese player, hit 868 home runs in his 22-year career (1959–1980).

Exhibitions have been held between Japanese and American teams since 1905. Since 1972, a Japan-United States College Baseball Championship has been held every other year between college all-star teams, with the game alternating between countries. On the professional level, American major-league teams have played teams in Japan since 1949, and more than 200 American baseball players have been signed up to play on Japanese professional teams.

BASHO (1644–1694)   Also known as Matsuo Basho; the finest Japanese poet of the form known as *haiku*, a short poem having three lines with 17 syllables in a 5-7-5 pattern. Basho was born to a samurai family in Iga Province and learned to write poetry while in the service of Lord Todo Yoshitada. His adult name was Matsuo Munefusa; he took the name Basho in 1681 from a type of banana tree growing next to his home. In 1666 Basho went to the old capital city of Kyoto, where he continued to write poems and published a book of commentaries on other poets. He moved to the new capital city of Edo (now Tokyo) in 1672, where he gained a reputation as a poet and teacher. Yet Basho felt deep anxiety about life and he began studying the religion of Zen Buddhism, although he did not become

a monk. His strong urge to travel led him to make many journeys throughout Japan in the years 1684–1691. The travel sketches he published from the journals and poems he wrote on his trips indicate that his journeys were in fact pilgrimages that gave him a broad understanding of life that enhanced his poetry. His most famous travel sketch has been translated into English as *The Narrow Road to the Deep North* (*Oku no hosomichi*, 1694). After his travels, Basho remained in Edo for a while, but became depressed. In 1694 he decided to visit the southern island of Kyushu, and on the way he died in the city of Osaka.

Basho's volumes of poetry and commentaries have had a lasting effect on poets in both Japan and foreign countries, where the haiku form has become popular. Basho wrote many poems about nature, identifying the self with the creative spirit of nature. His most famous haiku is about a frog jumping into a pond:

Furuike ya	The old pond
Kawazu tobikomu	A frog jumps in
Mizu no oto	The water's sound!

See also HAIKU; PILGRIMAGE; POETRY; ZEN SECT OF BUDDHISM.

BASHOFU   See RYUKYU ISLANDS; TEXTILES; YUZEN DYEING.

BASKETS (*kago*)   Containers woven from strips of plant materials such as bamboo or wisteria vines. The bark of cherry and birch trees, willow branches, wheat and rice straw, rush, other vines and imported cane or rattan are also used. Baskets are occasionally woven from wire or leather strips.

Basket making belongs to the category of functional yet beautiful objects known as *mingei* or folk crafts, which have always played an important role in Japanese culture. Techniques for softening plants and cutting them into thin strips for weaving baskets were known in Japan as far back as the Jomon Era (c. 10,000–300 B.C.). Korean and Chinese artisans who emigrated to Japan starting in the third century A.D., and particularly after Buddhism was introduced in the sixth century, brought sophisticated techniques for weaving bamboo. Usually plants have to be soaked in water, dried in the sun or smoked until their bark is soft enough to be cut into strips.

Japanese baskets range from coarse to fine weave and have been put to a great variety of uses. Farmers use large, heavy baskets to carry and store things. Kitchen utensils include sieves, vegetable containers and strainers. A type of wide, flat-bottom woven basket, known as a *mi*, or winnower, is traditionally used to separate rice grains from chaff. A *mi* is also used to separate chopped mulberry leaves from their stems so the leaves can be fed to silkworms. Large and small containers of all sorts play an important role in Japanese culture. Boxes tightly woven from flat strips of bamboo have been used to carry food and to store kimono (traditional clothing) and other household goods. Various methods of twining baskets have traditionally been applied to making fences as well. Bamboo baskets have been popular containers for flower arrangements (*ikebana*), especially in the summer. Simple flower arrangements for the tea ceremony (*chanoyu*), known as *chabana,* are often placed in open-weave baskets that have a rustic but appealing beauty. The great tea master Sen no Rikyu (1522–1591) brought many everyday bamboo objects into the tea ceremony. His emphasis on the aesthetic principles of *sabi* and *wabi,* meaning beauty having a rustic simplicity, has had a major influence on Japanese culture.

The finest baskets are still made on Kyushu, the southernmost of the four main islands of Japan. The contemporary bamboo basket maker Shono Shounsai has been honored by the Japanese government with the designation Living National Treasure *(ningen kokuho).* See also BAMBOO; FLOWER ARRANGING; LIVING NATIONAL TREASURES; MINGEI; MULBERRY BUSH; RICE; SABI AND WABI; SEN NO RIKYU; STRAW WARE; TEA CEREMONY; WISTERIA; WOODWORKING.

BATH *(furo* or *o-furo)*   A deep square tub of very hot water in which a bather sits or squats. The word *furo* refers to the wood or charcoal fire underneath a traditional bathtub that heated the water. Today the bathtub is usually filled with cold water and heated by gas. The tub is called a *yubune,* or "hot-water ship." Although traditional tubs made of wood such as cypress, cryptomeria, chestnut or black pine are valued, most tubs are now made of tile, plastic or other synthetic materials. A bather washes the entire body with soap and water outside the tub and rinses thoroughly before entering the bathtub. Dirty water runs down a drain in the tiled floor. The clean hot water in the tub is for long soaking and relaxation. The bath, the place of purification, is located in the room called a *furoba,* which is always separate from the toilet.

While homes today often have their own baths, public bathhouses *(sento)* have played an important role in Japanese life since the Edo Era (1600–1868). Although becoming more scarce, they still operate in cities, where people may still live in small apartments without baths. Customers enter the men's section *(otokoyu)* or women's section *(onnayu)* and leave their clothes in a basket or locker. Large tiled areas for washing have water spigots and mirrors. Bathers use a wooden pail *(oke)* or plastic or metal pan *(senmeki)* to pour water over their bodies, and a small cotton towel *(tenugui)* for both washing and drying. A *hechima,* or sponge gourd plant, was traditionally used for scrubbing. A *sento* is usually open 3–11 P.M. and places no limit on the time a customer can spend in the bath. In Edo times, people could spend many hours eating, drinking and playing games in a *sento.* One type of bathhouse associated with the "floating world," or licensed pleasure quarters, also offered sexual services, which the Tokugawa government (1603–1867) unsuccessfully tried to ban.

The Japanese enjoy bathing as a social custom and like to vacation at hot spring resorts *(onsen).* The practice of men and women bathing together *(konyoku)* was abolished by the Meiji government (1868–1912) because Westerners in Japan were shocked by public nudity, although it still occurs at a few hot springs. Until the Edo Era, hot water for bathing was plentiful only at hot springs, and steam baths were the most common way of bathing. Large public steam baths were maintained by large Buddhist temples as

far back as the Nara Era (710–794). Bathing has always had a religious aspect in Japan. Ancient myths of Shinto, the native Japanese religion, note that the *kami* (sacred spirits) bathed or purified themselves with water when they created the universe. The main *kami,* including those of the sun, moon and agricultural fertility, were born when the creator deity Izanagi washed himself. Shinto associates evil and immorality with impurity, and goodness with cleanliness. The Shinto concepts of purity and simplicity have affected all aspects of Japanese life, including architecture, arts and crafts, food preparation and social organization. Bathing has a strong connection with ancient Shinto rites of purification and exorcism *(misogi, yuami, harai).* See also EDO ERA; FLOATING WORLD; HOMES; HOT SPRING; IZANAGI AND IZANAMI; KAMI; PURIFICATION; SHINTO; TENUGUI; WATER.

BATTLEDORE AND SHUTTLECOCK   See ASAKUSA; FAIR DAY; GAMES; NEW YEAR FESTIVAL; TOYS.

BEAN CURD   See SOYBEANS; TOFU.

BEANS *(mame)*   One of the most important foods in the Japanese diet. Soybeans are widely used to make foods eaten by people every day in Japan. The beans are cooked and mixed with a coagulant to make tofu (bean curd), soft white blocks that are high in protein. Cooked soybeans are also fermented to make *miso* (soybean paste), which is used in soups and other dishes, and soy sauce *(shoyu).* Soybeans can also be eaten fresh when boiled in their shells.

Azuki are small dried red beans that are prepared in a variety of ways. Cooked *azuki* beans are mixed with rice to make *sekihan,* or "red rice," served on auspicious occasions. The beans are also boiled with sugar, mashed and pureed to make a sweet bean paste called *azuki an,* which is used in many Japanese sweets *(kashi).* Sweet bean paste can be smooth *(koshi an)* or contain partially crushed beans *(tsubushi an).* The paste can be bought ready-made in cans and in instant powdered form *(sarashi-an).* *Yokan,* which can also be bought in ready-made packages, is a popular sweet made by mixing sweet bean paste with a thickener called agar-agar *(kanten).* The Japanese enjoy a great variety of sweets that are beautifully prepared to reflect the season of the year. In Japan, sweets are not usually eaten after a meal, but served between meals with tea. Sweets made with bean paste also play an important role in the Japanese tea ceremony. See also BEAN-THROWING FESTIVAL; MISO; SOY SAUCE; SOYBEANS; SWEETS; TEA CEREMONY; TOFU.

BEAN-THROWING FESTIVAL *(Setsubun)*   A festival that takes place on February 3, the last day of winter and the day before Rishun, the first day of spring and the new year according to the lunar calendar. To celebrate, roasted soybeans are scattered in and around homes, shrines and temples to chase away the demons of illness and misfortune. The term for this ceremony is "bean-scattering" *mamemaki.* While the beans are being tossed, people call out, *Oni wa soto, fuku wa uchi!* (Go out, demons! Welcome, good fortune!). Celebrities such as actors and sumo wrestlers are invited to throw beans into the crowd at shrines and temples as good luck charms. Those chosen *(toshiotoko)* were born under the same animal year in the twelve-year zodiac cycle as the new year that is being celebrated. In Tokyo, the most popular temples for the Bean-Throwing Festival are Asakusa Kannon Temple and Zojoji Temple. In Kyoto, many people make a pilgrimage to four shrines representing each of the four compass points to celebrate the transition from the old to the new year; these shrines are Yoshida, Kitano, Akiba, and Mibu. Gion Shrine in Kyoto is especially famous for its celebration of Setsubun. Young geisha and *maiko* (women training to be geisha) dance to honor the gods on an outdoor stage and then toss soybeans into the crowd of onlookers. *Shogozake*, a sweet, fermented rice drink flavored with ginger, is sold from wooden vats only at this festival. The day of Setsubun used to be celebrated by dressing up in costumes that often symbolized role reversals; for example, young girls and married women might put on each other's clothes. Skits and dances were also performed by bands of traveling entertainers who wore masks to scare away demons. As the meeting point of the old year and the new year, the day of Setsubun was thought to be a time when the world of the spirits was very close to ordinary human life. In private homes, on the afternoon of February 3, a square wooden box used for measuring rice is filled with cooked soybeans and placed on the family altar as an offering to the gods. After sunset, the head of the family takes the beans and tosses them at the door and the dark corners of each room while shouting to chase away demons. The children scramble to get the beans, then eat as many beans as their age to remind themselves that they are one year older. See also ALTARS IN HOMES; CALENDAR; DEMONS; GEISHA; NEW YEAR FESTIVAL; SOYBEANS; ZODIAC.

BEAR See AINU.

BEARERS OF INTANGIBLE CULTURAL PROPERTIES
See LIVING NATIONAL TREASURES.

BEDDING See FUTON.

BEER See ALCOHOLIC BEVERAGES.

BELLS Various types of bells have been produced in Japan over the centuries for religious and decorative purposes.

Cylindrical bronze objects known as *dotaku* discovered from the Yayoi Era (c. 300 B.C.–c. A.D. 300) are shaped like bells, although their actual function is uncertain. They may have been symbols of wealth and power, as were other bronze and iron objects introduced into Japan from China and Korea, such as mirrors, weapons and large bowls. They may also have been musical instruments or ceremonial objects. *Dotaku* range in size from several inches to more than 4 feet tall. Linear designs were cast on them to create geometric patterns such as square blocks, and to represent animals, hunters and fisherman, dwellings, and other scenes.

Bronze bells are used for religious functions in shrines of Shinto, the indigenous Japanese religion, and temples of Buddhism, the religion that was introduced from China in the sixth century A.D. At many Shinto shrines, a metal bell with a rope attached hangs above the offering box in front of the sanctuary housing the *kami* (sacred spirit) of the shrine. A worshiper jangles the bell to get the *kami's* attention, drive away evil spirits and produce a calm feeling with the sound. Buddhist temples often have large hanging cylindrical bronze bells known as *tsurigane* or *bonsho*. This type of bell has no clapper and is struck on the outside with a long wooden post to produce a low, resonating tone.

The oldest temple bell in Japan, cast in A.D. 689, is at Myoshinji Temple in Kyoto. The largest bell, at Chion-in Temple in Kyoto, weighs 74 tons. Temple bells are struck to sound the hours of the day, and on New Year's Eve to mark the end of the old year and the beginning of the new, a custom known as Joya-no-kane. There are also small Buddhist hand bells *(rin)* and resting bells *(kin)*. Various types of bells, gongs and other struck instruments are used in Japanese religious, court and festival music. A small gong *(shoko)* is played in classical court music *(gagaku)*. The Japanese hang wind bells or chimes *(furin)* outside their homes in the summer. See also BUDDHISM; GAGAKU; NEW YEAR FESTIVAL; SHINTO; SHRINES, SHINTO; TEMPLES, BUDDHIST; YAYOI ERA.

"BELLY LANGUAGE" *(haragei)* The art of sensing another's thoughts and feelings intuitively. Silent or nonverbal communication, literally "speaking from the belly," is very important for the Japanese. This kind of unspoken communication, which relies on shared cultural understanding, can make Westerners very uncomfortable, and businessmen, for example, can be thrown off guard in negotiations where Japanese businessmen keep silent for long intervals.

Hara means belly, abdomen, gut, but not just the physical center of the body; it is the place where one's soul dwells, and the source of one's will, motivation, thoughts and emotions. *Hara* figures in numerous Japanese proverbs and idiomatic expressions. If a person is angry, his "belly stands up" *(hara ga tatsu)*. A person who is generous has a "broad belly" *(hara ga futoi)*. An evil person's belly is "dirty" *(hara ga kitanai)*. Two people who cooperate or have a private understanding "put their hara together" *(hara o awaseru)*. Harakiri, "belly slitting," is the impolite term for *seppuku*, ritual suicide by slashing the stomach. *Hara* can also mean a woman's womb. The notion that a woman "lends" her womb to her husband's family is expressed in the proverb, "The womb is a borrowed thing" *(hara wa karimono)*. See also SUICIDE.

BENEDICT, RUTH   See DEPENDENCY; SHAME.

BENKEI (?–1189) A legendary warrior-monk who is the hero of several plays in the repertoire of Noh drama and Kabuki theater. The best known is the Kabuki play *Kanjincho*, which was written in 1840 and translated into English in 1966 as *The Subscription Lost*.

Stories describe Benkei as a shrewd and strong master

of the martial arts. He became a retainer of Minamoto no Yoshitsune (1159–1189) during the Taira-Minamoto War (Gempei no Soran) of 1180–1185. Legends tell how Yoshitsune, when only a boy, was attacked on Gojo Bridge in the city of Kyoto by Benkei and defeated him. Benkei, remained loyal to Yoshitsune when his brother Minamoto no Yoritomo (1147–1199), founder of the Kamakura Shogunate (1192–1333), later turned against him out of jealousy; he single-handedly fought off their enemies to give Yoshitsune time to commit suicide in the ritual manner before being killed himself. While there was a historical person named Benkei recorded in the 13th-century text *Azuma Kagami (The Mirror of Eastern Japan)*, later stories about Benkei made him an almost superhuman figure. See also KABUKI; KAMAKURA SHOGUNATE; MARTIAL ARTS; MINAMOTO NO YORITOMO; MINAMOTO NO YOSHITSUNE; NOH DRAMA; SUICIDE; TAIRA-MINAMOTO WAR.

BENTEN (Benzaiten) The Goddess of music, water and wisdom, and the only female deity among the Seven Gods of Good Fortune. Benten, or Benzaiten, was adopted from a goddess of the Hindu pantheon in India whose Sanskrit name is Sarasvati. In Japan Benten is always depicted playing the *biwa*, a musical instrument similar to a mandolin. Shrines dedicated to Benten are usually placed on islands in ponds, often within the compounds of Buddhist temples. There is an island with a temple devoted to Benten in Shinobazu Pond in Ueno, a large park in north Tokyo. See also BIWA; BUDDHISM; SEVEN GODS OF GOOD FORTUNE; UENO.

BENTO (or *o-bento*; meal in a box) A portable box, usually disposable, filled with small portions of various types of food that can be eaten at lunchtime, outdoors, on trains, at the theater or any other place where food is eaten quickly and conveniently. The word *bento* is usually preceeded by the honorific *o-*. Many stores (*bento-ya*) sell a wide variety of take-out foods as *o-bento*. About half the box is filled with rice in easily handled compressed portions or balls (*onigiri*). Other basic ingredients include cooked or raw fish (*sakana*), fish cakes (*kamoboko*) made of steamed fish paste, sweet egg omelette (*tamagoyaki*), and pickles (*tsukemono*). A pair of chopsticks is included. A typical box lunch called *makunouchi-bento*, or "between the curtains," is still sold in Kabuki theaters to be eaten quickly during intermission. *Eki-ben* are *o-bento* sold in railroad stations and on trains. These boxes, made in different shapes and covered with paper decorated with designs and calligraphy, contain food specialties of the regions in which they are sold. *Bento* originated in the lacquer boxes holding food delicacies that were taken on picnics and sightseeing trips by upper-class Japanese during the Edo Era (1600–1868). Such boxes are still used today. For example, *hanami-bento* are food boxes taken to cherry blossom-viewing parties. See also BOXES; CHERRY BLOSSOM; CHOPSTICKS; FISH AND FISHING INDUSTRY; FISH CAKES AND FISH PASTE; KABUKI; O-; PICKLES; RICE; STATION; SUSHI.

BENZAITEN See BENTEN.

BEPPU A city on the east coast of Kyushu Island, the southernmost of Japan's four main islands, which is Japan's most famous hot-spring (*onsen*) resort. Beppu has more than 3,000 hot springs that pour forth 220,000 million gallons of hot water a day. Each year 12 million people come to Beppu to relax by bathing in public bathhouses, which number close to 200. Many hot springs and baths are rich in minerals, such as sulfur, iron, radium, salt, and acid and alkaline elements that are thought to heal various physical ailments. Baths in mud and hot sand are also available. The temperature of the hot springs in Beppu averages 136°F, but some springs register over 200°F and have to be cooled for bathers. Steam is vented into the air through pipes all around the city. The hottest spring in Beppu is also one of Japan's largest geysers, Tatsumaki Jigoku. Kyushu University runs an Institute of Balneotherapeutics in Beppu to study the benefits of mineral bath therapy. Kyoto University also maintains a Geophysical Research Station. One of Beppu's oldest public baths, the Takegawa Bath House, was built in 1879. The most spectacular baths are in the Suginoi Palace run by the Suginoi Hotel, where bathing areas for men, women, and mixed bathing, along with smaller pools having different water temperatures, replicate a lush tropical garden. Eight of Beppu's hot springs are known as Jigoku, the Hell Pools, because volcanic activity causes the water in them to boil. The name of one of these pools, Blood-Pond Hell (Chinoike Jigoku), comes from the red clay dissolved in the water. The port of Beppu is a center for shipping and commercial fishing because ships can easily sail from Beppu Bay through Bungo Channel to the Pacific Ocean. See also BATH; GEOGRAPHY OF JAPAN; HOT SPRING; KYUSHU ISLAND.

BEVERAGES See ALCOHOLIC BEVERAGES; KAMPAI; SAKE; TEA; TEA CEREMONY; VENDING MACHINES.

BINGATA See RYUKYU ISLANDS; TEXTILES; YUZEN DYEING.

BIOTECHNOLOGY INDUSTRY By 1986, more than 200 Japanese companies were engaged in biotechnological research and development (R&D) in such areas as pharmaceuticals, foods, chemicals and fiber electronics. Other major areas of research in this field include medical treatments (especially for cancer), livestock breeding, agricultural chemicals and bioelectronics. Japanese pharmaceutical firms have many joint ventures and licensing agreements with foreign companies, primarily in the United States. Two major concerns of Japanese biotechnological research are recombinant DNA and cell fusion. Biotechnology is one of three high-technology industries currently being given special impetus in Japan, along with microelectronics and materials research. National government agencies and prefectural governments actively promote R&D in biotechnology. They appropriated about US$17.6 million for biotechnology for fiscal year 1986, and Japan is currently rivaling the U.S., the present leader in the industrialization of biotechnology.

In fiscal year 1989 the Ministry of Agriculture, Forestry

and Fisheries budgeted $27 million for biotechnology and related research, and the Ministry of International Trade and Industry (MITI) budgeted about $45.7 million for this purpose. The Science and Technology Agency provided $57.2 million for cancer research and $10.4 million for the Human Frontiers Science Program, to which MITI also allocated $6.7 million. The Ministry of Education supports basic biotechnology research in the national university system and scientific exchange programs; in fiscal year 1989 it also provided $1.4 million for the National Gene Laboratory. For centuries the Japanese have been skilled in fermentation technology using microorganisms, particularly for soy sauce, *miso* (soybean paste), and sake (rice wine), basic elements of the Japanese diet, and Japanese companies now have a virtual monopoly on the production of amino acids by fermentation. See also AGRICULTURE; ELECTRONICS INDUSTRY; MISO; SAKE; RESEARCH AND DEVELOPMENT; SOY SAUCE.

BIRD-AND-FLOWER PAINTING (*kachoga*)

One of the three general categories of Japanese and East Asian painting, along with landscape painting (*sansuiga*) and figure painting (*jimbutsuga*). Paintings are traditionally executed on horizontal rolling scrolls (*emakimono*) or vertical hanging scrolls (*kakemono*). Birds and flowers are portrayed through conventional motifs that usually pair certain birds and flowers together for seasonal representation, such as the bush warbler (nightingale) and plum. In Japan, the most popular subjects for paintings of this style have been birds such as ducks, geese, cranes, crows, hawks, and bush warblers and a wide variety of flowering trees (*kaboku*), flowering plants (*kaki*), and flowering grasses (*soka*). Related elements of nature are also included in this category, such as fruits and vegetables, insects and grasses, and even fish and seaweed. Paintings of animals (*sojuga*), including tigers, monkeys and horses, are often classified in this style as well.

Flowers have been a popular subject in Japanese art beginning with the colorful Heian Era (794–1185) *Yamato-e* (native Japanese style of painting). However, the depiction of birds and flowers as a separate theme developed in the Muromachi Era (1333–1568), when Japanese Zen Buddhist priest-painters adapted the monochrome style of ink painting (*sumi-e* or *suibokuga*) from China. Bamboo groves and plum trees, or river reeds and geese, were typical subjects depicted by sparse black lines on white backgrounds. In the 15th and 16th centuries, Japanese artists began painting birds and flowers in bright colors. Sesshu Toyo (1420–1506) combined bird-and-flower themes with landscape paintings, especially on large decorative screens. Painters of the Kano school depicted birds and flowers in gorgeous colors on goldleaf backgrounds on screens to decorate castles during the Azuchi-Momoyama Era (1568–1600). Artists during the Edo Era (1600–1868) employed all of the above styles of bird-and-flower painting. Tawaraya Sotatsu (d. 1643?) and artists of the Rimpa School became known for depicting *shiki soka*, flowering plants or grasses of the four seasons, which is a standard Japanese motif with classical literary associations. In the 18th century, realistic sketches of birds and flowers from nature (*shaseiga*) were executed by a number of Kano and Rimpa artists, such as Ogata Korin (1658–1716). See also FIGURE PAINTING; FLOWERS; INK PAINTING; KANO SCHOOL OF PAINTING; KORIN; LANDSCAPE PAINTING; MUROMACHI ERA; RIMPA SCHOOL OF PAINTING; SCREENS; SCROLLS; SESSHU TOYO; SOTATSU; ZEN BUDDHISM.

BIRDS

See BUSH WARBLER; CHICKEN AND ROOSTER; CRANE; CROW; PLOVER.

BIRTHDAYS (*tanjobi*)

Birthdays are traditionally celebrated by many special occasions throughout the life of a Japanese person. *Sekihan,* an auspicious dish of red beans and rice, is often served at these celebrations. The Japanese consider a person to be one year old at birth. A baby is named seven days after birth (Shichi-ya, "Seventh Night") at a family feast. A baby boy is taken to the local Shinto Shrine 32 days after birth, and a girl at 33 days, for a ceremony called Miya Mairi (Shrine Worship) with prayers for its healthy growth. The baby is then taken to visit relatives and friends. At the First Meal (Tabe-zome) 100 or 120 days after birth, the baby is given rice for the first time. A child's first birthday is a special occasion. All these ceremonies developed in a traditional society where the infant mortality rate was high. Subsequent birthdays are celebrated much as in the West, with birthday gifts and dinner parties. Children ages seven, five and three are taken to Shinto shrines for the Seven-Five-Three Festival (Shichi-Go-San) every year on November 15 to pray for their continued health. All Japanese young people who turn 20 in any year preceding January 15th are honored that day by the Adults' Day Festival (Seijin-no-hi).

The traditional Japanese zodiac assigns an animal to each year in a 12-year cycle, starting with the rat and ending with the boar. A person is characterized by his or her animal. There are five sets of 12-year cycles that total a complete cycle of 60 years. Anyone who turns 60 is said to have completed the entire cycle and returned to a "second childhood." To celebrate the 60th birthday (*kanreki*), a person wears something red, an auspicious color also used to dress babies. A man at 60 was traditionally expected to resign from his positions, hand over leadership of the family to his oldest son, and become a retired person (*inkyo*). A person's 70th, 77th, 80th, and 88th birthdays are also significant, and are celebrated with banquets and mementoes. The character *ki,* meaning happiness, looks similar to the characters with which the number 77 is written. The three characters used to write the number 88 are similar to the character for rice, the most important food in the Japanese diet. See also ADULTS' DAY; CHILDREN'S DAY; FAMILY; RETIREMENT; SEVEN-FIVE-THREE FESTIVAL; ZODIAC.

BISHAMON

The God of Fortune and War, and one of the Seven Gods of Good Fortune (Shichifukujin) in Shinto. Bishamon, also known as Bishamonten, was originally a Buddhist deity called Tamonten, guardian King of the North. He is depicted wearing a suit of armor and standing over a vanquished evil demon, holding a small pagoda in his left hand and a spear in his right. See also ARMOR; BUDDHISM; DEMONS; PAGODA; SEVEN GODS OF GOOD FORTUNE; SHINTO.

BIWA A stringed musical instrument similar to a mandolin or lute. It is named for the loquat fruit (*biwa*), which is round and has a short, thin neck. The *biwa* derives from a Chinese instrument called the *pipa*, which in turn came from the Turkish *barbat*, which itself was taken from the ancient Greek *barbatos*. The pipa was brought to Japan from China in the eighth century, during the Nara Era (710–794). The *biwa* played in Japanese court performances was of two types, with either four or five strings. A variety of shapes and sizes of *biwa*, with differing numbers of strings, were used over the centuries. Four strings became standard, but three and five strings were also common. The strings have four to six frets. The *biwa*, which was a solo instrument in China, was incorporated into musical ensembles (*gagaku*) in Japan, and was used to accompany chants performed by singers. Different versions of *biwa* music developed on the Island of Kyushu, where it was frequently played by blind monks, and in the City of Kyoto, where it was associated with the Tendai sect of Buddhism. The most popular style of *biwa* music was developed in the 16th century by Shimazu Nisshinsai, a feudal lord who created songs to inspire his soldiers in battle. Prior to this time, the *biwa* had been played for recitations of military epics in the 13th and 14th centuries. This style, called Hei-Kyoku, came to influence popular vocal music in the 16th and 17th centuries, which was often accompanied by a musical instrument, newly introduced into Japan, known as the *shamisen*. The *biwa* has been played very little in recent times. See also GAGAKU; SHAMISEN; SHIMAZU CLAN; SINGING; TENDAI SECT OF BUDDHISM.

BIWA, LAKE The largest freshwater lake in Japan, with an area of 260 square miles, a circumference of 117 miles and a deepest point of 340 feet. Lake Biwa is situated in central Honshu Island northeast of the city of Kyoto. The natural scenery of Lake Biwa has been enjoyed over the centuries at the Eight Scenic Places of Omi (Omi Hakkei). The lake was named Biwa because its shape resembles the *biwa*, a Japanese musical instrument similar to a mandolin or lute. Lake Biwa has been designated by the government as a "quasi-National Park." Since the Heian Era (794–1185), the lake has been a major route for transportation and the shipping of rice and other agricultural products. More recently, Lake Biwa has provided electric power and water for industries in the Keihanshin Industrial Belt (cities of Kyoto, Osaka, and Kobe). Freshwater fishing and freshwater pearl cultivation also take place here. In 1964 the cities of Otsu and Moriyama were connected by the Great Bridge of Lake Biwa. See also BIWA; NATIONAL PARKS; PEARL; WATER.

BIZEN WARE (*bizen-yaki*) A type of pottery made in Bizen Province (modern Okayama Prefecture) on the southeast coast of Honshu Island. Bizen ware is rough, unglazed stoneware that is fired for up to 30 days at high temperatures in wood-burning kilns. The wood ash glazes the stoneware orange, gold or blue-green, or creates irregular dark spots on the surface. Red streaks are also created when straw wrapped around Bizen pots burns away in the kiln. These effects are called *higawari* (fire-change) and *hidasuki* (fire-cord), respectively. Bizen potters traditionally specialized in making dynamic and strong-shaped vases, sake (rice wine) bottles, large storage jars and water jars for the tea ceremony. Bizen is classified as one of the six oldest pottery kilns in Japan, dating back to the Kamakura Era (1192–1333) or earlier. It may have originated with a similar unglazed, high-fired type of pottery known as Sue ware, which dates back over a thousand years. Early Bizen (*ko-bizen*) objects were made from gray, rough clay from mountains and fired in underground kilns. Tea ceremony masters in the 15th and 16th centuries encouraged Bizen potters to use smoother clay from rice paddies. The finest Bizen ware was made during the Azuchi-Momoyama Era (1568–1600) with encouragement from the great tea masters Sen no Rikyu and Furuta Oribe. Bizen potters came from six families that were organized into three guilds under the patronage of the feudal lords of the Ikeda clan, who controlled Bizen Province. Today around 200 potters still produce Bizen ware, making functional items such as tiles and bricks along with traditional objects. Contemporary Bizen potters Kaneshige Toyo and Fujiwara Kei were named Living National Treasures. Collections of Bizen ware are displayed at the Bizen Ancient Ceramics Art Museum (Bizen Koto Bijutsukan), the Bizen Pottery Traditional and Contemporary Art Museum (Bizen Togei Kaikan) and the Fujiwara Kei Memorial Hall. See also FURUTA ORIBE; KILN; LIVING NATIONAL TREASURES; POTTERY; SEN NO RIKYU; TEA CEREMONY.

BLACK CURRENT (*Kuroshio*) See CLIMATE OF JAPAN; GEOGRAPHY OF JAPAN; SEA OF JAPAN.

BLACK SHIPS See PERRY, MATTHEW CALBRAITH.

BLOWFISH (*fugu*) A spiny marine fish that swells up when it is threatened by predators. It is also called the pufferfish, globefish and swellfish. Highly poisonous if prepared improperly, the blowfish is considered a delicacy in Japan because of its tastiness, its supposed aphrodisiac powers, and its potential danger. Blowfish, or *fugu*, must be prepared by a professional chef who has undergone intensive training and acquired a special license awarded by the Japanese Ministry of Health and Welfare (Koseisho). The chef carefully removes the liver and ovaries, where the poison is concentrated, and then slices the meat for serving. People who try to prepare *fugu* at home can make fatal mistakes. The poison in the fish immediately attacks the motor-nervous system, and within 20 minutes overwhelms the respiratory system. Since the Japanese government began regulating *fugu* preparation in 1949, only one person has died from eating it in a restaurant. In 1975 the Kabuki actor Mitsugoro Bando persuaded a chef to serve him the liver, which killed him. The chef was fined, and in 1984 the government made it illegal to serve *fugu* liver.

The emperor and the imperial family are forbidden by law to eat any *fugu*. Authorized *fugu* restaurants serve the fish in several courses. First the fins are toasted and warm sake is poured over them and drunk. The *fugusashi*, the meat of the fish, is then served raw, sliced very thin and arranged in a pattern resembling a crane or a round flower such as a peony or chrysanthemum. The slices of fish are dipped into a sauce made of soy sauce, daikon (Japanese radish), chopped scallions, *sudachi* (bitter orange), and red pepper. Next, a one-pot dish called *fuguchiri* is served, made with fugu and vegetables. A concluding dish of rice porridge made with remains of the *fuguchiri* may end the meal. *Fugu* is eaten in colder months when it is thought to be less toxic, and is considered at its best from January to March. Most *fugu* are caught near Shimonoseki on the southern part of Honshu Island, where annual Shinto funeral rites are held for the souls of the *fugu* that are caught. An island in Shinobazu Pond in Ueno, a district of Tokyo, has a stone tablet carved with a *fugu* that commemorates all of the fish that have been savored by Japanese connoisseurs. See also COOKING; FISH AND FISHING INDUSTRY; SASHIMI; SHIMONOSEKI; SHINTO; UENO.

BLUESTOCKING SOCIETY (Seitosha)   The first feminist organization in Japan, founded in 1911 by Hiratsuka Raicho (1886–1971) with "the development of women's talent" as its goal. She and four other young single women of the upper middle class, who had been schoolmates, organized the group as a feminist literary circle, and began publishing a literary magazine for and by women, named *Bluestocking (Seito)*. The magazine was published until 1916. Raicho wrote a poetic manifesto for the first issue titled "In the Ancient Time Woman Was the Sun" (*Genshi josei wa taiyo de atta*), identifying women with Sun Goddess Amaterasu o Mikami. During the first year of the magazine's publication, it was concerned with the problems of Japanese women in marriage and society. The editors then began publishing essays and translations dealing with issues addressed by the feminist movement, such as women's suffrage.

Japanese women were beginning to enter public life for the first time in the early 20th century, in such positions as teacher, nurse and artist. Several hundred women became active in the Bluestocking Society. However, the organization began to decline in 1914, due partly to public criticism of the controversial life-style of the "new women" who were its members. Raicho began openly living with a painter, by whom she had a daughter and son. Her economic difficulties led her to join several other women in 1920 to found the New Woman's Association (Shin Fujin Kyokai), to fight for political, economic, social and legal reforms that would benefit Japanese women. This group succeeded in having the Public Order and Police Law passed in 1922, giving women some legal rights of participation in political activities. The Universal Manhood Suffrage Act was passed in Japan in 1925 but did not extend the vote to women. In the 1930s other women's groups campaigned for women's suffrage and civil rights, but the Diet (Parliament) never passed these measures. Japanese

women finally received the vote in 1946 during the postwar Allied Occupation of Japan (1945–52), and 39 women were elected to the House of Representatives (lower house of the Diet) that year. Women still do not play a major role in Japanese politics but do exercise political influence through various women's organizations and consumer groups. See also AMATERASU O MIKAMI; DIET; ELECTIONS; FEMINIST MOVEMENTS; OCCUPATION OF JAPAN; WOMEN'S ASSOCIATIONS.

BOARD GAMES   See GO; SHOGI.

BOARD OF AUDIT   See CABINET, PRIME MINISTER'S.

BODAI DARUMA   See DARUMA.

BODHI DHARMA   See DARUMA.

BODHISATTVA (*bosatsu*)   Deities of the Mahayana branch of Buddhism, the religion introduced into Japan through China from India in the sixth century A.D. Bodhisattva is the Sanskrit term (*bosatsu* in Japanese) for a compassionate being who has reached a great spiritual height and is ready to attain enlightenment, but has vowed to defer enlightenment in order to help save all other beings. Mahayana Buddhism is characterized by this universal emphasis on the attainment of Buddhahood by all beings. A bodhisattva is ranked just below the Buddha himself. Some of the most revered bodhisattvas in Japan are Amida, God of the Pure Land or Western Paradise; Kannon, the Goddess of Mercy; Miroku, the Buddha to come in the future; and Jizo, the guardian saint of children. See also AMIDA; BUDDHISM; JIZO; KANNON; MIROKU.

BOKUSEKI   See CALLIGRAPHY.

BON FESTIVAL (Urabon'e or O-Bon)   A Buddhist festival that honors the spirits of the dead, who are believed to return to their homes during the feast. Bon is known as the Festival of the Dead or the Feast of Lanterns. Bon, usually preceeded by the honorific suffix *O-*, has been traditionally celebrated in the seventh month of the lunar calendar. Today it is held July 13–15, although some areas of Japan celebrate it August 13–15.

The term *Urabon* traces back to a memorial ceremony in India, called *ullambana* in Sanskrit, intended to rescue dead souls from hell. The custom was introduced through the Buddhist religion from China into Japan in the seventh century A.D., where it was practiced by the aristocracy at first. Bon was gradually combined with native Japanese religious ceremonies to welcome the souls of ancestors in the summer and with agricultural ceremonies, until it became one of the two most important Japanese festivals, along with the New Year Festival.

For Bon, each family cleans the graves of its ancestors and sets up a special "spirit altar" (*shoryodana*) for the ancestors in front of the Buddhist family altar (*butsudan*) in the home. Offerings of flowers, sake, and food such as *somen* noodles, fruits, vegetables and rice dumplings are placed on the altar, and a Buddhist priest may read a *sutra*, or religious scripture, in front of it. The spirits are welcomed on the 13th day of the month by bonfires known as *mukaebi* (welcoming fires), and on the 15th or 16th day, they are shown the way back to their world by fires known as *okuribi* (sendoff fires). In Kyoto on the evening of August 16th, an enormous bonfire is lit on Mount Daimonji in the eastern part of the city. Tourists flock to see the fire, which forms the shape of the character *dai*, or "big," for which the mountain is named. In many places in Japan, candles are placed in paper lanterns *(toro)* and floated down rivers to guide the spirits away from human dwellings and back to their world. The spirits may also be sent away in little boats made of paper or straw. A highlight of the Bon Festival is Bon *odori* (dance), outdoor dancing and singing at night in which everyone participates, including children. The large groups of dancers, many wearing *yukata* (informal cotton robes) and straw hats, move in large circles around the musicians or a small stage while singing and clapping in time to the music. See also ALTARS IN HOMES; BUDDHISM; DANCE, TRADITIONAL; FAMILY; FESTIVALS; FUNERALS; KYOTO; LANTERNS; YUKATA.

BONIN ISLANDS (Ogasawara Shoto)   Also known as the Ogasawara Islands; a small archipelago in the Pacific Ocean 600 miles south of Tokyo. This group also includes the Volcano Islands (Io Islands), one of which is Iwo Jima, site of the major battle in World War II.

The name Ogasawara was given to the island group in honor of Ogasawara Sadayori, who supposedly discovered them in 1593. The Tokugawa Shogunate (1603–1867) conducted an official survey of the islands in 1675. They were known to American and British sailors in the early 1800s. Commodore Matthew Perry, the American who opened Japan to Western nations, raised the American flag in the Bonin Islands in 1853. In 1862 the Tokugawa Shogunate claimed them for Japan. The Meiji government (1868–1912) officially declared them to be Japanese territory in 1876. The sparsely inhabited Bonin Islands proved to have strategic importance during World War II, when the Japanese built naval and air force bases on them. Captured by American forces in 1945, the Bonin Islands were administered by the U.S. during the Occupation of Japan after the war. The entire Bonin Island group was returned to Japanese rule in 1968. Today there are fewer than a thousand people, mostly farmers, living on the islands. See also IWO JIMA; MEIJI RESTORATION OF 1868; OCCUPATION OF JAPAN; PACIFIC OCEAN; PERRY, MATTHEW CALBRAITH; TOKUGAWA SHOGUNATE; WORLD WAR II.

BONITO *(katsuo)*   A processed fish product that is used to make a soup stock called *dashi*, a basic ingredient of Japanese cooking. The bonito, which belong to the mackerel family, are cut into four fillets apiece and put through a six-month process of steaming, wood-smoking and drying that makes them hard and dry. The dried brown slabs of bonito are called *katsuo bushi*. Fresh *dashi* is made by shaving a piece of dried bonito with a special bladed instrument and cooking the flakes with water and kelp *(kombu)*, an edible seaweed. Dried bonito flakes are sold in packages.

However, *dashi* made with bonito flakes that are shaved from a fillet just before cooking is more flavorful. The bonito-flavored stock is used to make soups and broths for noodles, and to simmer root vegetables that require long cooking. Dried bonito flakes are also used as a garnish or topping for some Japanese dishes. See also COOKING; FISH AND FISHING INDUSTRY; GARNISHES FOR FOOD; NOODLES; SOUP.

BONKEI   See BONSAI.

BONSAI   "Tray planting"; the art of cultivating miniature trees and other plants in containers. Small trees and other plants have been cultivated in Japan since these methods were introduced from China in the 13th century A.D. as one of the many cultural activities connected with the Zen sect of Buddhism. The effects of natural conditions such as wind, snow and dry soil are reproduced by techniques that control the size and shape of the plants. These include pruning branches and roots with special shears, changing pots and wrapping wires around branches and trunks. There are specific categories of style in bonsai, and their names describe the way the trees look: upright, slanting, cascading, weeping-cascade, twisting-trunk, twin-trunk or clumped. There are even miniature landscapes created by the forest style with several trees in one container, and a rock-planting style in which a plant grows upon or up out of a rock, with the roots covered by moss. Bonsai trees and plants are grown in wide, flat ceramic containers which are most often unglazed and dark-colored. In Japan, they are kept outdoors much of the year. Some of the trees commonly found in bonsai are pine, cypress, maple, oak, plum and cherry, which produce their flowers or fruits even in their miniature state. In the plant category, technically considered "grasses" in bonsai, can be found bamboo, shrubs such as azaleas, and mosses, as well as chrysanthemums. The most valuable bonsai have been cultivated for hundreds of years, often handed down within the same family. They exemplify the Japanese appreciation of nature, which is the central principle of Shinto. Bonsaido, the "Way of Bonsai," which follows the motto "Heaven and earth in one container," is also practiced today in many other countries. Bonsai clubs and collections have been established in many countries. In the United States, there are excellent bonsai collections at the Brooklyn (N.Y.) Botanic Garden and the National Arboretum in Washington, D.C. A related art form known as *bonkei* ("tray scenery") uses plants, moss, pebbles and so forth to create whole miniature landscapes on lacquer trays. See also MOSS; SHINTO; ZEN SECT OF BUDDHISM; NAMES OF INDIVIDUAL PLANTS AND TREES.

BONUSES   See GIFTS; INCOME.

BOOKBINDING, TRADITIONAL   The oldest printed materials in Japan are small pieces of paper printed with Buddhist spells *(dharani)* that were placed in temples in the Nara region in A.D. 770. The copying of religious scriptures has been regarded as an act of merit in the Buddhist religion, which was introduced into Japan from India through

China in the sixth century A.D. Starting in A.D. 1009 in Japan, Buddhist scriptures were printed in large quantities by various temples. Movable type was introduced from the West and from Korea in the late 16th century, and its use flourished with the rapid growth of urban culture during the Edo Era (1600–1868). However, popular books were commonly printed using woodblocks (hanga) until metal movable type was introduced in the late 19th century. The earliest Japanese books were horizontal scrolls, introduced in the sixth century, which were unrolled and read from right to left. Known as kansubon, they were made by pasting sheets of paper together to make a single long strip that could be rolled up and tied to secure it. Folding or "accordion" books (orihon) were developed around the ninth century and were especially used for reciting Buddhist scriptures. Rather than being rolled, a long strip of paper was folded into rectangles like an accordion, and given heavy covers. Such books pulled apart easily and did not survive much handling. Three new types of bookbinding were developed in the 12th century. The "butterfly" style (kochoso) was made by folding sheets of paper with the written or printed text facing inward, and joining them together with paste on both sides of the fold. This meant that there were two blank sheets after every two written or printed sheets. To solve this problem, sheets were folded in half to form a signature, and signatures were sewn together at folded edges, similar to modern books. Another style of binding, known as yamatotoji, entailed folding the sheets in half with the writing surface on the outside, stacking the sheets, and tying them together with string at two points on the right margin. A similar type of bookbinding known as fukurotoji, introduced from China by the 14th century, came to replace all of these styles in Japan. Sheets of paper were folded as in the yamatotoji style but tightly sewn together with thread through four holes on the right margin. Much thinner paper could be used for this style, but the inside surfaces of the double leaves of paper could not be written on. Blank books are still frequently bound this way in Japan for calligraphy and poetry writing. See also BOOKS AND BOOKSTORES; BUDDHISM; CALLIGRAPHY; PAPER, HANDMADE; SCRIPTURES, RELIGIOUS; SCROLLS; WOODBLOCK PRINTS.

BOOK OF TEA, THE   See OKAKURA KAKUZO.

BOOKS AND BOOKSTORES   The Japanese have a literacy rate of virtually 100% and are avid readers of books, magazines and newspapers. Books illustrated with woodblock prints were printed during the Edo Era (1600–1868), and Western printing techniques were adopted during the Meiji Era (1868–1912). Today, approximately 50,000 new books are published in Japan each year, about the same number as in the United States and the United Kingdom. The majority are in the areas of literature and the social sciences. Small, inexpensive paperbacks (bunkobon) are widely sold. The Japanese read many translations of Western books. The largest Japanese publisher is Kodansha, Ltd., which also publishes many books about Japan in English. Kinokuniya Shoten operates many bookstores in Tokyo

and other Japanese cities, and has established branch stores in New York, Los Angeles and other foreign cities. Maruzen Company is another large Japanese bookstore with several branches. The American publisher Charles E. Tuttle, which specializes in books about Japan, operates bookstores throughout Japan. Kanda, the student district of Tokyo, is filled with secondhand bookstores. See also BOOKBINDING, TRADITIONAL; EDUCATION SYSTEM; KANDA; KODANSHA, LTD.; MAGAZINES; NEWSPAPERS; NOVELS.

BOSHIN CIVIL WAR (1868–1869) (Boshin Senso)   The name given to a number of battles that helped bring about the overthrow of the Tokugawa Shogunate (1603–1867) and the return of power to the emperor in the Meiji Restoration of 1868. The Tokugawa Shogunate had become weak and in 1858 capitulated to the demands of Western powers to open Japan to foreign trade after more than two centuries of national seclusion. A faction of samurai (warriors) from Choshu, Satsuma and several other domains in southern Japan opposed the Tokugawa military government and favored imperial rule; its slogan was Sonno Joi, "Revere the Emperor, Expel the Barbarians." Shogun Tokugawa Yoshinobu (1837–1913) realized that his forces could not withstand the pro-imperial forces. In November 1867 he agreed to a compromise in which he would return political power to the emperor, and in return he would lead a council of daimyo (feudal lords). However, Satsuma and Choshu had already decided to overthrow the shogunate. On January 3, 1868 their forces seized the imperial palace in Kyoto and declared the imperial restoration (osei fukko). Yoshinobu moved from Edo (modern Tokyo) to Osaka Castle, and his forces lost a battle with pro-imperial forces on January 27, 1868 at Toba and Fushimi, near Kyoto, after which Yoshinobu returned to Edo. Saigo Takamori (1827–1877), the leader from Satsuma, negotiated the surrender of Edo with Katsu Kaishu (1823–1899), the shogun's retainer. A number of pro-Tokugawa troops continued to resist, however, and 2,000 were defeated by pro-imperial troops in the Ueno district of Edo. A league of daimyo domains in northern Honshu Island also resisted but surrendered on November 6 after their defeat in the Battle of Aizu. The closing battle of the Boshin Civil War ended with the surrender of a fleet of pro-Tokugawa ships off Hokkaido Island in northern Japan in June 1869. The new Meiji government (1868–1912) moved its capital from Kyoto to Edo and renamed it Tokyo (Eastern Capital). Leaders from Satsuma and Choshu became dominant figures in the Meiji government and guided Japan from centralized feudalism into a modern nation state. See also ANSEI COMMERCIAL TREATIES; CHOSHU PROVINCE; EDO; EMPEROR; KATSU KAISHU; KYOTO; MEIJI RESTORATION OF 1868; OSAKA; SAIGO TAKAMORI; SATSUMA PROVINCE; SHOGUN; TOKUGAWA SHOGUNATE; UENO.

BOW AND ARROW   See ARCHERY.

BOWING (ojigi)   A custom that Japanese people follow when meeting and saying goodbye to each other, expressing thanks or apologies, and paying respect. Bowing can be done in a standing position or when kneeling on straw floor mats called *tatami*. A person performs a bow by bending from the waist while keeping the back straight and lowering the head. When bowing while standing, men hold their arms straight at the sides and women place the palms of their hands on their knees. In a kneeling position, the palms are placed on the floor in front of the body. A bow can range from informal to very formal, depending on the relationship between the person bowing and the person being bowed to, as well as the nature of the occasion. The Japanese are very conscious of social rank. The person with a lower rank bows more deeply to his or her superior and holds the bow longer. When Japanese people are introduced to other people, they often exchange *meishi*, or name cards that indicate a person's position, so they can determine who is higher and who is lower in rank. Close friends may just bow to each other lightly by bending the body at a slight angle. Young people in Japan do not practice the custom of bowing as formally as previous generations did. However, students and teachers still bow to each other at the beginning of a class. See also ETIQUETTE; MEISHI; TATAMI.

BOXES (*hako*) Boxes have played an important role in Japanese culture since ancient times. They have been made of many different materials, including bamboo, porcelain and metal, but they are most commonly made of wood, which is often decorated with lacquer. The general term for boxes is *hako*, but this changes to *bako* when combined with another character, such as *bentobako* (portable food box). Boxes were used in the Buddhist religion for storing religious scriptures and priests' robes (*suebako*). Portable shrines and home altars in boxes have also been produced.

The use of beautiful and functional boxes became widespread in the Edo Era (1600–1868) when the growth of cities during two centuries of peace created a great demand for luxury goods. Wealthy merchants and *daimyo* (feudal lords) required lavish objects to furnish their mansions, and Japanese artisans developed the finest lacquer-ware techniques in the world.

Jubako (literally, "stacked-up boxes") are small lacquered food boxes stacked on top of each other in groups of two, three or five and covered with a lid. They are usually decorated with black lacquer on the outside and red lacquer on the inside, and can be richly decorated with sprinkled gold lacquer (*maki-e* technique) or inlay. *Jubako* came into common use in the Edo Era at elegant picnics, theatrical performances and flower-viewing parties (*hanami*). Such picnic boxes are also known as *kochu* (portable kitchen), *sageju* (portable tiered box with matching flask and cups for sake), or *hanami bento* (food box for flower viewing). They are also traditionally used for giving presents of rice cakes or *sekihan* (red beans and rice for auspicious occasions), to serve food at weddings and the New Year Festival, and to serve red-bean-paste sweets at a tea ceremony.

Plain wooden portable lunch boxes are known as *bento* or *o-bento*. A *suzuribako* is a shallow, rectangular box with a matching cover for storing writing utensils, including an inkstone, ink stick, water dropper and calligraphy brushes. The interior is divided into four sections with trays to hold the utensils. A *suzuribako* may be decorated to match a low rectangular writing table (*bundai*). A *ryoshibako* or *bunko* is a similar box for writing paper or documents. These boxes are also usually covered with decorative lacquer both outside and inside. Writing boxes designed by artists such as Hon'ami Koetsu (1558–1637) and Korin (1658–1716) have been designated Japanese National Treasures.

A *kobako* or *kogo* is a small decorative lidded box, frequently round, to hold incense. A *natsume* is a deeper round lidded black lacquer container for *matcha* (powdered green tea leaves) used in the tea ceremony. A *kishidai* (comb stand) is a decorative lacquered stand that holds *kushibako* (boxes for combs and brushes) and *tebako* (boxes of powder and oils). A *zushidana* is a large decorative box containing smaller boxes of cosmetics. Lacquered cosmetic boxes and mirror stands traditionally formed part of a Japanese bride's dowry, as did a *haribako* or sewing box, and often included a family crest (*mon*) as part of the decoration. Beautiful lacquered boxes have also been made to store painted seashells used in the shell-matching game known as *kai-awase*. Other decorative boxes include *chabako* (for tea), *obibako* (for *obi* sashes worn with kimono), *tantobako* (for swords), and *hashibako* (for chopsticks). *Inro* are small containers with several sections for carrying medicine, tobacco and so forth, which are attached to *obi* with carved figures known as *netsuke*. See also BASKETS; BENTO; CALLIGRAPHY; COSMETICS; CREST; FLOWERS; HON'AMI KOETSU; INCENSE; INRO; KORIN; LACQUER WARE; MIRROR; NETSUKE; SHELLS; SWEETS; TEA CEREMONY; TRAYS.

BOXWOOD   See COMBS AND HAIR ORNAMENTS; WOODWORKING.

BOYS' DAY FESTIVAL   See CHILDREN'S DAY FESTIVAL.

BREWING AND FERMENTING METHODS   See ALCOHOLIC BEVERAGES; BIOTECHNOLOGY INDUSTRY; MISO; PICKLES; SAKE; SOY SAUCE.

BRIDGES (*hashi*) Bridge-building techniques were introduced into Japan from China and Korea in the seventh century A.D. This style of bridge was built from wood and had handrails with ornamental covers. Until the mid-19th century, Japanese bridges were usually constructed of wooden foundations and piers that supported arched walkways made of wooden boards. People walking across bridges over rivers in Edo (modern Tokyo) and other places in Japan are depicted in woodblock prints (*hanga*) by famous artists such as Hokusai (1760–1849) and Hiroshige (1797–1858).

European techniques for building stone and steel bridges were introduced during the Meiji Era (1868–1912). Numerous stone arch bridges were built on Kyushu Island in the 19th century. The first Japanese steel bridge was built in Nagasaki Prefecture on Kyushu in 1869, and steel truss or arch bridges were soon completed in the cities of Yokohama, Osaka and Tokyo. The first reinforced concrete bridge in Japan was constructed over a canal near Lake Biwa, Japan's largest lake, in 1903.

Three rivers flow through the capital city of Tokyo, the Edogawa, Sumidagawa and Arakawa. After much of Tokyo was destroyed in the Great Earthquake of 1923, modern bridges using Japanese-developed technology were built over the Sumida River in Tokyo. More bridges were built after the city was destroyed again in World War II, but districts of Tokyo are still known by the names of old bridges, such as Shimbashi and Nihombashi. The four main islands of Japan are connected by bridges and tunnels. The Kammon Bridge, one of the world's longest suspension bridges, was built in 1973 to link Honshu and Kyushu Islands. The Seto-Ohashi Bridge, built over the Inland Sea to connect Honshu and Shikoku Islands, was completed in 1988. It is actually six bridges connecting small islands in the sea.

Many bridges have historical associations for the Japanese. The tragic heroic figure Minamoto no Yoshitsune (1159–89) defeated the legendary warrior-monk Benkei, who attacked him on Gosho Bridge, after which Benkei became the loyal lifetime companion of Yoshitsune. Uji Bridge near Kyoto figures in many scenes of the great 11th-century novel *The Tale of Genji (Genji Monogatari)*. Important battles of the Taira-Minamoto War (1180–85) were fought on the bridge. A ceremony is held on the bridge to commemorate the dipping of water for tea by the national unifier Toyotomi Hideyoshi (1536–1598).

The hill or pond style of garden, known as *tsukiyama*, contains ponds and streams that are connected by bridges for viewers to stroll over. The most popular style of tying a woman's *obi* (kimono sash) into a bow is known as the *taiko* or "drum style." It was created by geisha to celebrate the opening of a drum-shaped arched bridge *(taiko-bashi)* at Tenjin Shrine in Tokyo. See also BENKEI; BIWA, LAKE; GARDENS; GENJI, THE TALE OF; HIROSHIGE; HOKUSAI; INLAND SEA; OBI; SHIKOKU ISLAND; TAIRA-MINAMOTO WAR; TOKYO; UJI; WOODBLOCK PRINTS.

BROADCASTING SYSTEM Radio broadcasting began in Japan in 1925 through government-controlled stations in Tokyo, Osaka and Nagoya. In 1926 the government established the Japan Broadcasting Corporation (Nippon Hoyo Kyokai; NHK), which acts as the official public station and carries no advertising. Half of all Japanese households owned radio receivers by 1944. Commercial broadcast began in 1951 with two privately owned stations in Osaka and Nagoya. The two main commercial radio broadcasting networks are the Japan Radio Network (JRN) and the Nippon Radio Network (NRN). There are about 318 AM and 58 FM radio stations in Japan in addition to NHK, although there are few FM stations because Japan has strict broadcast laws. The English-language U.S. military service Far East Network (FEN) broadcasts a wide range of news, sports, music and dramatic programs in Japan. Many Japanese listen to FEN to learn English and follow American trends.

Television broadcasting began in Japan in 1953 and surged in popularity with the broadcasts of the wedding of Crown Prince Akihito in 1959 and the Tokyo Olympic Games in 1964, which the development of satellite hook-ups enabled to be broadcast to 21 countries for the first time. Regular Japanese color television broadcasts began in 1960. Today television watching is a major leisure activity in Japan. In Tokyo there are seven VHF television channels and several UHF stations. The government-sponsored broadcasting authority, NHK, charges an annual reception fee from all viewers. The more than 12,000 other stations are private and receive their funds from advertising. Television is the largest medium for advertising revenue in Japan. The four commercial television broadcasting networks are the Tokyo Broadcasting System, Inc., Nippon Television Network Corporation, Fuji Telecasting Co., Ltd., and Asahi National Broadcasting Co., Ltd. Each network has a news network: the Japan News Network (JNN), the Nippon News Network (NNN), the Fuji News Network (FNN), and the Asahi News Network (ANN). Local stations around the country are free to broadcast their own programs in addition to network productions. Domestic communication satellites were opened in 1988 and cable television is also becoming popular. Nearly all Japanese households have one television set, and more than half have two or more sets. The Broadcast College (Hoso Daigaku) offers university-level courses on radio and television. Japanese researchers developed technology for stereo and dual language broadcasts, and are leading in the development of the new High-Definition Television (HDTV) technology. See also ELECTRONICS INDUSTRY; JAPAN BROADCASTING CORPORATION.

BROCADE *(nishiki)* A general term for multicolored silk textiles woven with supplementary patterns in gold or silver thread, or thick, shiny silk threads, sometimes resembling embroidery. Brocade is used for kimono (robes), *obi* (sashes), costumes for Noh drama, scroll mountings, *shifuku* (pouches to store tea ceremony objects such as tea containers), Buddhist priests' robes, temple hangings, altar cloths, and modern purses, hats and shoes.

Brocade was imported to Japan from China by the third century A.D. The Japanese also wove their own brocade for the court aristocracy, achieving great refinement in the Nara Era (710–794). Common brocade patterns have been flowers of the four seasons, dragons, phoenixes, *kirin* (mythical Chinese unicorns), vine scrolls and arabesques. Tapestry weave, known as *tsuzuri-ori* ("vine weaving") or *tsuzure nishiki,* is the oldest type of brocade in Japan. Brocade weaving declined during the military government of the Kamakura Shogunate (1192–1333) bur revived with the patronage of the Noh drama by the Ashikaga Shogunate (1338–1573). A type of plain-weave silk brocade known as *kinran* (gold brocade) was imported to Japan from China during the Kamakura Shogunate and was used for ceremonial purposes. *Kinran* uses fine strips of gilded paper *(kinshi)* instead of colored threads. *Ginran* is a similar technique using strips of silver paper.

The Japanese learned how to make *kinran* themselves in

the 16th century. Japanese weavers had fled Kyoto, which was largely destroyed in the Onin War of 1467–77 and in turmoil during the century of civil war known as the Sengoku (Warring States) Era (1467–1568). Many weavers settled in the wealthy port city of Sakai near modern Osaka, which was also a center of the tea ceremony. Looms imported from China were set up at Sakai, and the technique of making gold-paper thread, gold or silver leaf pasted into paper and wrapped around narrow strips of silk, was learned from Chinese weavers fleeing political turmoil in Ming China.

National unifier Toyotomi Hideyoshi set up a special quarter for weavers in Kyoto in 1582. Known as Nishijin, this district is still the center for brocade weaving in Japan. Gold thread came into widespread use for garments in the 17th century and is still used today for Noh drama costumes. Stiff but gorgeous, shiny brocade textiles are known as *karaori*, "Chinese weave," even when produced in Japan. Japanese weaving techniques reached their height in the Edo Era (1600–1868), largely due to Noh. *Karaori* costumes are stiff and angular and are worn as outer garments by actors playing female roles. *Karaori* Noh costumes are frequently decorated with patterns of grasses and flowers, which are female motifs, or with motifs related to poetry that suggest court ladies. Male and demon-god roles are played by actors in *atsuita* costumes. *Atsuita* is another type of heavy brocade with designs woven in colored, gold and silver threads. Such robes have strong designs such as lions, lightning or clouds. Pottery and porcelain are sometimes decorated with an overglaze design known as brocade style (*nishiki-de*) in transparent green, yellow, bluish purple, gold, silver and other colors. See also FLOWERS; KIMONO; NISHIJIN; NOH DRAMA; OBI; SAKAI; SCROLLS; SILK; TEA CEREMONY; TEXTILES.

BRONZE See BELLS; SCULPTURE.

BRUSHES (*fude, hake*) The Japanese traditionally use brushes made of bamboo or wood handles with tips of animal hair. Tubular brushes known as *fude* are used for writing the Japanese language with black ink (*sumi; shodo* is calligraphy or the "art of writing"), painting, applying makeup, and decorating pottery, lacquerware and other objects; flat brushes known as *hake* are used for applying paste or starch, such as in repairing shoji (sliding screens). Writing brushes were introduced to Japan from China with the system of writing characters or ideographs in the eighth century A.D. Seventeen brushes housed in the eighth-century Shosoin (Imperial Storehouse) in Nara are so highly valued that they have been designated National Treasures. There are over 300 kinds of writing and painting brushes, which range from thick (*futofude*) to thin (*hosofude*), depending on their specific use. More than 200 kinds of hair are used for making the tips, which are conical and narrow down to a point, including squirrel, deer, dog, raccoon, horse and even human hair. Light brown weasel hair is used for brushes for fine writing. Brushes made of cat hair, which is wider at the tip and holds ink well, are used for painting faces on dolls and designs on lacquerware. Brushes

can be hung with the tip down on a small bamboo rack known as a *fude-kake*. Brushes are flexible and absorbent, and a writer or painter can create many kinds of brushstrokes through slight variations in pressure, speed and the angle at which the brush is held. An upright brush creates a strong, hard line, whereas a brush held at a slant produces a softer line. The Japanese believe that one's brushstrokes reveal one's personality. Japanese potters often decorate their wares with *hakeme*, "brush-grain decoration," using broom-like brushes made from fibers such as straw and pounded palm. See also CALLIGRAPHY; INK PAINTING; LACQUER WARE; MAKEUP; PAINTING; POTTERY; SCREENS; SHOJI; WRITING SYSTEM, JAPANESE.

BUDDHA See BUDDHISM.

BUDDHISM A religion founded in northern India by Siddhartha Gautama, called The Buddha, Enlightened One, in the fifth century B.C. and introduced to Japan in the sixth century A.D. Buddhism, which became the major religion of Asia, divided into two main branches: Theravada or Hinayana Buddhism, which spread through South and Southeast Asia, and has a monastic emphasis; and Mahayana Buddhism, which spread through Central Asia to China, Korea and Japan, and emphasizes universal salvation. Mahayana further divided into various sects that have a large body of religious scriptures and worship a pantheon of deities that are represented by sculptures in Buddhist temples.

In A.D. 604 the Japanese imperial court officially adopted Buddhism, and the religion became the means by which a writing system, architectural forms and many other aspects of Chinese civilization were transmitted to Japan. The court patronized the copying of scriptures and the building of temples. When the imperial court moved to the new capital city of Nara (Nara Era, 710–794), six main Buddhist sects took hold, dominated by the Hosso sect. The court build Todaiji (Great Eastern Temple), the largest wooden building in the world, which houses the world's largest bronze sculpture, a 53-ft.-high Daibutsu (great sculpture of Dainichi Buddha), to symbolize its authority.

To escape the influence of Buddhist monks in Nara, the court moved in A.D. 794 to another new capital city, Heiankyo (Kyoto), which remained the imperial capital until 1868 and became the headquarters of new Buddhist sects founded by Japanese monks. The Tendai sect founded by Saicho (767–822) and the Shingon sect founded by Kukai (774–835) became dominant during the Heian Era (794–1185). Saicho built Enryakuji, the main Tendai center, on Mount Hiei. Many Japanese religious leaders studied at Enryakuji, and the monastery's monks exerted great political power during the medieval era (12th–16th centuries). Kukai built the main Shingon monastic center on Mount Koya. Buddhism did not displace Shinto, the native Japanese religion, but coexisted and even intermingled with it. Some Shinto deities came to be regarded as manifestations of Buddhist deities. The Pure Land sect taught by Honen (1133–1212) and Shinran (1173–1263) spread Buddhism to the Japanese masses. Emphasizing simple faith in Amida Buddha, god

A thousand gilded wooden sculptures of Kannon, the Buddhist Goddess of Mercy, in Sanjusangendo Hall of the Rengeoin, affiliated with Myohoin Temple in Kyoto. They surround a large "thousand-handed" sculpture of Kannon that was carved in A.D. 1254.

of the Western Paradise, where believers would be reborn after death, Pure Land thrived during the military government of Japan under the Kamakura Shogunate (1192–1333). Believers recite a simple phrase known as the Nembutsu that proclaims their faith in salvation by Amida. Nichiren (1222–1282) taught a militant form of Buddhism based on faith in the saving power of one Buddhist scripture, specifically the Lotus Sutra. The Ashikaga Shogunate (1338–1573) patronized the Zen sect of Buddhism, introduced from China, which emphasizes self-discipline and meditation as means of realizing *satori* (enlightenment). The Rinzai school of Zen was founded in Japan by Eisai (1141–1215) and the Soto school by Dogen (1200–1253). The tea ceremony *(chanoyu)* and ink painting *(sumi-e)* have a close connection with Zen Buddhism, and Zen has had a widespread influence on Japanese culture as a whole. Important Zen temples in Kyoto include Kinkakuji, Ginkakuji and Daitokuji. Modern Zen thinkers Suzuki Daisetz Teitaro (1870–1966) and Hisamatsu Shin'ichi (1889–1980) have been responsible for introducing Zen-Buddhism to the West.

After a century of warfare during the Sengoku Era (1467–1568), the warlord Oda Nobunaga (1534–1582) helped unify Japan by destroying Enryakuji and other powerful Buddhist temples. However, the Tokugawa Shogunate (1603–1867) used Buddhism to help administer the country by requiring all Japanese to register with local Buddhist temples. Leaders of the Meiji government (1868–1912), which restored political authority to the emperor, suppressed Buddhism and promoted militant nationalism through the cult of State Shinto. This policy was continued by 20th-century leaders, but after Japan was defeated in World War II, authorities of the Allied Occupation abolished State Shinto. Some Buddhist sects have been growing in popularity, notably the Nichiren sect. Many historic Buddhist temples throughout Japan have become pilgrimage centers and tourist attractions. The midsummer Bon Festival, one of the two main annual festivals in Japan, is a Buddhist celebration to welcome spirits of visiting ancestors. Many Japanese families have Buddhist altars *(butsudan)* in their homes which contain memorial tablets *(ihai)* of their ancestors. See also ALTARS IN HOMES; BODHISATTVA; BON FESTIVAL; LOTUS SUTRA; MEDITATION; MONASTICISM, BUDDHIST; NEMBUTSU; PAGODA; PILGRIMAGE; SATORI; SCRIPTURES, RELIGIOUS; SCULPTURE; SHINTO; STATE SHINTO; SHRINE; NAMES OF INDIVIDUAL DEITIES, SECTS, TEACHERS, TEMPLES.

BUGAKU "Elegant dance"; the traditional dance form associated with the Japanese imperial court. *Bugaku* was introduced from China in the seventh and eighth centuries A.D. It is accompanied by *gagaku* (elegant music), traditional Chinese court music performed by an orchestra of bells, flutes, drums and other instruments. *Bugaku* and *gagaku* are still performed today by the Imperial Court orchestra in Tokyo, making them the world's oldest continuously performed arts. *Bugaku* derives from ritual dances performed in ancient China, which in turn were influenced by dances from the Buddhist cultures of Korea and Central Asia. *Bugaku* is very slow, majestic and ritualistic. Dancers in gorgeous silk robes in the style of the Heian Era (794–1185) perform on a square platform. *Gagaku* musicians, also in costume, sit behind the platform. There are two types of dance in the *bugaku* repertoire, termed dances of the left (*saho no mai*), which are danced in red costumes, and dances of the right (*uho samai no mai* or *umai*), which are danced in blue or green costumes. Left and right indicate the ranks held by courtiers on each side of the emperor. The dances are further categorized as military dances (*bu no mai*) or civil dances (*bun no mai*); the latter are also known as level, or even, dances (*hira-mai*). There is also a special category of dances, called *dobu*, danced by children. See also DANCE, TRADITIONAL; GAGAKU; HEIAN ERA.

BULLET TRAIN (Shinkansen) A popular name for the high-speed electric railroad line that is part of the system operated by Japan Railways (JR). It is called the Bullet Train in English because its cars are sleek and rapid, but in Japan it is referred to as Shinkansen, New Trunk Line. The Railway Technical Research Institute of the JR began developing a high-speed railroad system in the 1950s. The first branch of the Shinkansen line, the New Tokaido Line, opened in time for the Olympic Games held in Tokyo in 1964. It was the world's fastest train, with a maximum speed of 130 miles per hour. The 345-mile trip between Tokyo and Osaka, Japan's most highly industrialized corridor, takes three hours and 10 minutes by express train. In 1975, the Shinkansen line was extended south to Hakata on Kyushu Island, through the Kammon undersea tunnel between Honshu Island and Kyushu; this route, termed the Tokaido-San'yo Shinkansen Line, totals 664 miles. Trains make the trip in six hours and 30 minutes. There are several other, shorter routes in the Shinkansen system.

Two types of Bullet Trains are in operation. The Hikari (Light) stops only at major stations, such as Nagoya, Osaka and Kyoto, while the Kodama (Echo) makes more stops. Each train has 16 cars, including reserved (green cars) and regular class and dining cars. Up to 100 Bullet Trains are in operation at peak times, and a central control room at Tokyo Station, employing computerized systems to monitor and control the trains, is responsible for monitoring the system's excellent safety record.

A high-speed Bullet Train (Shinkansen) passing Mount Fuji, the highest mountain in Japan and a symbol of the country. Bullet Trains run between major Japanese cities.

The success of the Japanese Shinkansen has spurred other countries to revitalize their own railways. However, the Bullet Trains run at an enormous deficit even though Japan Railways, formerly state-subsidized as Japanese National Railways, was privatized in 1987 to offset its losses. See also JAPAN RAILWAYS; RAILROADS.

BUNRAKU Puppet theater, which is also called *ningyo joruri*, or *ayatsu joruri*. The term *Bunraku* is commonly used for various types of puppet theater in Japan. Puppet shows were performed by itinerant entertainers as far back as the 11th century A.D. Some of the puppeteers settled in Sanjo

A puppet of the Bunraku traditional theater. A Bunraku puppet is two-thirds life size and is manipulated by three men.

A master puppeteer and two assistants manipulating a puppet in a traditional Bunraku performance.

on Awaji Island, now considered the birthplace of professional Japanese puppetry. In the strictest sense, Bunraku refers to the puppet theater in Osaka City founded by Uemura Bunrakken (or Bunrakuken) around 150 years ago. Bunraku evolved from Joruri, the chanting of narrative ballads in the 16th century. Puppets were later added to enhance the narration. Bunraku and Kabuki were the two popular forms of theater in the Edo Era (1600–1868). After a fire destroyed much of Edo (modern Tokyo) in 1657, the puppet chanters moved to the Osaka-Kyoto region. In 1684 the chanter Takemoto Gidayu (1651–1714) opened a puppet theater named the Takemoto-za in Osaka and employed the great dramatist Chikamatsu Monzaemon (1653–1724). His plays, both historical dramas and stories of urban life, comic as well as serious, still form the basic Bunraku repertoire.

Bunraku puppets are about one-half to two-thirds life size. Each puppet playing a major character is handled by three puppeteers (sanninzukai) dressed in black, with their lower bodies concealed by a screen. The chief puppeteer (omozukai) manipulates the puppet's head, eyes, mouth, and right arm and hand. He often leaves his face uncovered. One assistant manipulates the puppet's left arm and hand, and another the legs and feet. The audience soon concentrates only on the puppets and forgets the puppe-

teers' presence. The puppets are dressed in costumes of the Edo Era. Their heads, which can be changed by different wigs, are classified by character types according to their age, sex and personality. A chanter or narrator (tayu) sits on a revolving dais to the right of the puppet stage and is accompanied by a musician (tayutsuke) who plays the shamisen, a stringed instrument similar to a banjo. Narrative shamisen music for Bunraku, called gidayu-bushi, was also developed by Takemoto Gidayu. One singer chants the dialogue for all puppets on the stage, although for large scenes, several chanters may perform together. Today Bunraku performances are given at the Asahiza Theater in Osaka and the National Theater in Tokyo, as well as at smaller regional theaters. See also CHIKAMATSU MONZAEMON; EDO ERA; KABUKI.

BURAKUMIN The largest minority group in Japan, numbering around 3 million. Burakumin literally means "hamlet people" or "people of special hamlets." They are descendants of Edo Era (1600–1868) outcastes who butchered animals, worked with leather and took care of the dead. These hereditary occupations are all considered impure since handling dead animals is taboo in the Buddhist religion. Burakumin still work with leather, making such things as baseball gloves and drums.

Although the burakumin do not differ physically or culturally from other Japanese, they still live in 6,000 segregated communities (buraku) scattered around Japan but concentrated around Osaka, Kobe and Kyoto in central Japan. In 1871 the Meiji government (1868–1912) decreed that burakumin should not be treated as outcastes, and should be referred to as "new common people" (shin heimin), but to little avail. They are still not integrated into the Japanese education system, and are prevented from getting good jobs. Some burakumin cut their family ties and try to pass as regular Japanese, but it is nearly impossible for them to hide their backgrounds, because of the household register system (koseki) in which all Japanese citizens are listed. Nevertheless, conditions are slowly improving for burakumin, due to the efforts of the Buraku Liberation League (BLL), a private organization formed after World War II to improve living conditions and fight discrimination. Today the BLL has 2,000 branches throughout Japan. The Buraku Liberation Research Institute at Osaka City University studies the causes of prejudice against burakumin and suggests remedies. See also EDUCATION SYSTEM; HOUSEHOLD REGISTER; MINORITIES IN JAPAN.

BURDOCK (gobo) A long, thin root vegetable eaten by the Japanese. Burdock roots are about 1 or 2 feet long and ½ to 1 inch in diameter. They are sliced diagonally and blanched in hot water to soften them before cooking. Burdock may have been used as a medicine in ancient China. By the 10th century, burdock was being eaten in Japan for its supposed ability to help a person recover from illness and to provide energy. Burdock has an earthy but mild flavor, and it absorbs the flavors of other foods with which it is simmered or sauteed. Slices of burdock are often served rolled up with other ingredients such as beef or eel.

It can also be served alone with a marinade of vinegar, soy sauce, *mirin* (sweet rice wine for cooking) and toasted sesame seeds. This dish is often served at the New Year holiday. See also EEL; MIRIN; NEW YEAR FESTIVAL; SOY SAUCE.

BUREAUCRACY   See CABINET, PRIME MINISTER'S; CORPORATIONS.

BUSH WARBLER (NIGHTINGALE) *(uguisu)*   A small bird that makes a beautiful whistling sound like a European nightingale. Bush warblers are about 6 inches long and have olive-brown bodies with white chests. Females lay their eggs in nests, which they build in bamboo grass *(sasa)* that grows in mountainous regions of Japan, Korea, northeastern China and the Philippine Islands. Bush warblers come down from the mountains in autumn and winter and are commonly found in parks and gardens. Starting in February or March, the traditional beginning of spring in the Japanese lunar calendar, the birds can be heard singing in farm fields and towns. Hence the bush warbler is also known by the poetic names "spring bird" *(harudori)*, "spring-announcing bird" *(harutsugedori)*, "first song" *(hatsune)* and "flower-viewing bird" *(hanamidori)*. Hearing the bird's song, sounded *ho-ho-kekyo* by the Japanese, is a sign of good luck and happiness.

Bush warblers are often mentioned in Japanese poetry. A popular artistic motif pairs bush warblers with plum blossoms, bamboo, or cherry, pine or willow trees. Bush warblers have also been raised as pets in Japan for many centuries. A station on the Yamanote Line, the railway line that circles the central area of Tokyo, is called Uguisudani, "Nightingale Valley." Nijo Castle in Kyoto was built with so-called "nightingale floors" because the boards squeak to warn that someone is approaching. Japanese women have long used nightingale droppings *(uguisu no fun)* as a beauty treatment. See also BAMBOO; NIJO CASTLE.

BUSHIDO   The "way *[do]* of the warrior *[bushi]*"; a code of chivalry that guided members of the ruling samurai (military) class in Japan. *Bushido* required honor, bravery, self-sacrifice and discipline, duty, and above all, loyalty to one's feudal lord *(daimyo)*, as well as skill in the use of weapons and the martial arts.

Basic principles of *bushido* developed during the military conflicts of the late Heian Era (794–1185), especially the Taira-Minamoto War (1180–85), which resulted in the Kamakura Shogunate (1192–1333), the first of three military governments *(bakufu)* that ruled Japan for nearly seven centuries. However, *bushido* was not codified until the Tokugawa Shogunate (1603–1867), when warfare was forbidden and the ethical teachings of Confucianism were widespread. In medieval Japan the warrior's code was known by such terms as the "way of the horse and the bow" or "customs of those who bear bows and arrows" *(yumiya toru mi no narai)*. Samurai leaders wrote guides, known as *kakun*, detailing the ideals of samurai behavior, which emphasized absolute loyalty and willingness to fight to one's death for one's *daimyo*. This ideal was not always

practiced, and many independent samurai *(ronin)* sold their services to the highest bidder, often changing allegiance.

The austere philosophy and practices of the Zen sect of Buddhism, a religion favored by the Ashikaga Shogunate (1338–1573), contributed to the concept of *bushido* and the development of the martial arts.

In the late 16th century, after a hundred years of civil warfare in Japan, the great warlords Toyotomi Hideyoshi (1536–1598) and Tokugawa Ieyasu (1543–1616) and the *daimyo* who were their vassals began transforming the samurai from fighters into bureaucratic administrators. Peasants were disarmed, and samurai were brought into the castle towns that quickly grew into cities and were given stipends based on measures of rice *(koku)* rather than money, which was considered crass. (Rice was exchanged for necessary commodities.) Samurai helped *daimyo* administer their domains and fulfill their required alternate-year attendance *(sankin kotai)* in Edo (modern Tokyo), capital of the Tokugawa Shogunate. The shogunate borrowed the Chinese model of the administrative elite, known as the *shi (shih)*, and Neo-Confucian teachings to create the ethical and martial code of *bushido* to guide the samurai in their new role. Confucian ethics stress personal relationships and the fulfillment of the requirements of one's position in society. But while family relationships are most important in Confucianism, in feudal Japan the relationship between lords and vassals held the highest place. Many stories tell of husbands sacrificing wives, parents sacrificing children, or vice versa, in the service of feudal lords.

The first systematic presentation of *bushido* was made by Yamaga Soko (1622–1685), who wrote in great detail about *bukyo*, or "the warrior's creed," and *shido*, "the way of the samurai." He emphasized that samurai must know literature and history along with martial arts and military science, and that such knowledge would help them set the moral example for other social classes in Japan. Yamamoto Tsunetomo's treatise, *Hagakure* (1716), promoted self-effacing service to one's lord, even if the samurai were dismissed from service or required to commit suicide. Samurai carried two swords, a long one for killing an enemy by cutting off his head or slicing him down the middle, and a short one for committing suicide by disemboweling oneself *(seppuku,* vulgarly known as *hara-kiri)* after being defeated. *Bushido* motivated the so-called 47 Ronin who avenged the murder of their lord and were ordered to commit suicide for their actions. The code also influenced the samurai of Satsuma and Choshu provinces who helped overthrow the Tokugawa Shogunate, restore imperial power in the Meiji Restoration of 1868, and lead Japan from the feudal into the modern era.

Nitobe Inazo explained the principles of *bushido* to the Western world in a book translated into English in 1900 as *Bushido: The Soul of Japan.* As Nitobe explained, *bushido* had come to influence Japanese of all social classes. Schoolchildren were taught the values of *bushido*, such as honor, loyalty and bravery, until the end of World War II. The postwar Japanese novelist Mishima Yukio (1925–1970) wanted Japan to "purify" itself by returning to *bushido*, and made his point by committing suicide in the traditional manner. See also ALTERNATE ATTENDANCE; ARCHERY; ASHIKAGA SHOGUNATE; BAKUFU; CASTLES; CHOSHU PROVINCE; CONFUCIANISM; DAIMYO; FEUDALISM; FORTY-SEVEN RONIN; KAMAKURA SHOGUNATE; MARTIAL ARTS; MEIJI RESTORATION OF 1868; MISHIMA YUKIO; RICE; SAMURAI; SATSUMA PROVINCE; SUICIDE; SWORD; TAIRA-MINAMOTO WAR; TOKUGAWA SHOGUNATE; TOYOTOMI HIDEYOSHI; WORLD WAR II; ZEN SECT OF BUDDHISM.

BUSINESS See BANKS AND BANKING; CORPORATIONS; EMPLOYMENT; EXPORTS AND IMPORTS; FEDERATION OF JAPANESE ECONOMIC ORGANIZATIONS; JOINT-VENTURE CORPORATION; MEISHI; SECURITIES COMPANIES; STOCK MARKET; TRADING COMPANIES, GENERAL.

BUSINESS CARDS See MEISHI.

BUTOH A unique form of avant-garde dance originated in the 1950s that aims to shock and disturb the audience. The two characters in the word *butoh* mean "dance" *(bu)* and "step" *(toh)*. Hijikata Tatsumi (1928–1986), an originator of the Butoh dance form, called his performance style *ankoku butoh*, "dance of darkness and gloom." Hijikata and his collaborator, Ohno Kazuo (b. 1906), now known as the Father of Butoh, were influenced by the devastation of Japan during World War II. Ohno was a well-known performer of modern Japanese dance. He and Hijikata turned away from Western dance forms popular in postwar Japan and sought to create a new expressive form of movement inspired by Noh, Japanese folk traditions and such European movements as Dada. They created a dance style in which performers wear white face and body paint, grotesque makeup and costumes, and move in ways that express terror and anguish. Yet Butoh is also concerned with such themes as birth and the resolution of suffering. Hijikata drew upon gestures and body movements in Japanese folk dances and was also inspired by European experimental theater, Dadaism, and Surrealism. Butoh is starkly modern yet is also related to the traditional Japanese theatrical form known as Noh drama, which consists of restrained dances that express powerful emotions.

Kasai Akira (b. 1943) and Maro Akaji (b. 1943) became active in Butoh during the 1970s. Maro founded the Dai Rakudakan troupe in 1972 and brought an element of spectacle into Butoh performances. Recent well-known Butoh performers include Uno Man, Ashikawa Yoko and Tanaka Min. The most famous Butoh troup of the 1980s was Sankaijuku, founded in 1975 by Amagatsu Ushio (b. 1949), a member of Dai Rakudakan. The Sankaijuku troupe, whose members perform with shaved heads and nude bodies painted white, have appeared in many foreign cities. While performing their most famous number in Seattle in 1987, in which four dancers are lowered from a building by ropes tied to their ankles, a rope broke and a dancer fell to his death. After a year, the troupe began performing again but no longer does this number. See also DANCE, TRADITIONAL; MAKEUP; NOH DRAMA.

BUTTERFLY *(cho)* In Japan there are 265 species belonging to nine families of butterflies. Since these insects metamorphose from larvae into butterflies in early summer, they are associated with flowers and transformation. The butterfly has been a design motif in Japan since the Nara Era (710–794), as shown by objects in the eighth-century Shosoin (Imperial Storehouse) in Nara. For example, a round bronze mirror is decorated on the reverse side with stylized butterflies, flowers, birds and clouds.

The famous Heian Era (794–1185) writer Sei Shonagon portrayed butterflies as lovable. Murasaki Shikibu, author of the important 11th-century novel *The Tale of Genji (Genji Monogatari)*, describes butterflies as ornamenting Rokujoin, Genji's palace. Delicate butterfly motifs decorate many handmade papers on which classical poems were written. The powerful Taira clan used the "armored butterfly" *(yoroi cho)* for its crest. Starting in the Muromachi Era (1333–1568), butterflies became a popular decorative motif for Japanese furniture, ornate lacquer ware, and armor.

Today, butterfly bows are displayed as auspicious symbols at weddings. There are several ways of tying women's formal and informal *obi* (sashes) into decorative butterfly bows at the back of kimono.

Westerners associate butterflies with Japanese women because of *Madama Butterfly*, an opera by Giacomo Puccini about the tragic love affair between a Japanese girl named Cho-Cho-san and an American naval officer named Lieutenant Pinkerton. Puccini based his opera on a play produced in America by David Belasco. Belasco had adapted the play from a story, "Madam Butterfly," written in 1898 by John Luther Long, an American lawyer who had never been to Japan. Long had taken his story from *Madame Chrysanthemum*, a novel by French author Pierre Loti about his temporary "marriage" in 1885 to a teenage Japanese girl while he was in Nagasaki with the French navy. Loti's book romanticizes teahouse parties, lantern processions, paper parasols and long-sleeved silk kimono. See also ARMOR; FLOWERS; FURNITURE, TRADITIONAL; GENJI, THE TALE OF; KIMONO; LACQUER WARE; MIRRORS; OBI; SEI SHONAGON; SHOSOIN; WEDDINGS.

C

CABINET, PRIME MINISTER'S (Naikaku) An administrative body of the Japanese government, composed of the prime minister and ministers of national agencies, in which executive power is vested by the Constitution of 1947. The prime minister is head of the cabinet and presides at its meetings. He has the power to appoint and dismiss other cabinet ministers, and he represents the cabinet in the Diet (Parliament). The constitution requires that the majority of cabinet ministers be members of the Diet. In addition to the Prime Minister's Office (Sorifu), the cabinet includes 12 ministries: Justice; Foreign Affairs; Finance; Education, Culture and Science; Health and Welfare; Agriculture, Forestry and Fisheries; Construction; Transport; Posts and Telecommunications; Labor; International Trade and Industry (MITI); and Home Affairs. There are also ministers without portfolio, who are appointed to head the commissions and agencies within the Office of the Prime Minister. One such agency is the Defense Agency, which is comparable to a department of defense, although it does not have the status of a ministry because Article 9 of the constitution renounces war. Other agencies include the Fair Trade Commission, the Economic Planning Agency, the Science and Technology Agency, the Environmental Disputes Coordination Commission and the Hokkaido and Okinawa Development Agencies. The Imperial Household Agency, which administers the affairs of the imperial family, also belongs to the Office of the Prime Minister. The Cabinet Secretariat coordinates the activities of the ministries and prepares material for policies that are discussed at cabinet meetings. The chief cabinet secretary *(kambo chokan)* functions as the prime minister's chief of staff. The Cabinet Legislative Bureau aids the drafting of legislation the cabinet proposes to the Diet, which constitute the majority of bills introduced into the body. The Board of Audit keeps track of how the government spends money. There are also a National Defense Council and a Ministerial Council on Overall Security Problems. See also CONSTITUTION OF 1947; DIET; HOKKAIDO ISLAND; IMPERIAL HOUSEHOLD AGENCY; MINISTRY OF INTERNATIONAL TRADE AND INDUSTRY; OKINAWA ISLAND; PRIME MINISTER; SCIENCE AND TECHNOLOGY AGENCY.

CALENDAR *(reik)* Several different calendrical systems have been used in Japan. The Japanese officially followed a lunar calendar until January 1, 1873, when the country converted to the solar-based Gregorian calendar that is used in the West. A solar calendar counts one year as the time the earth takes to revolve once around the sun, or 365 days, and is divided into 12 months. Every four years an extra day is added (Leap Year) to keep the calendar accurate. The traditional lunar calendar follows the phases of the moon from full to new moon to full again, with one phase taking about 29 days. The Japanese lunar calendar, which was introduced from China, placed the new moon on the first day of every month. In some years, a 13th month had to be added so that the calendar would properly correspond to the season of the year. Japanese farmers also followed an old solar calendar, used in China as well, which marked the times for planting and harvesting crops based on the changing seasons.

Traditional calendars still play a role in Japanese culture. They place the New Year at the beginning of the spring season in Japan, which usually falls in the beginning of February in the Gregorian calendar. Today the traditional New Year (Risshun) is celebrated on February 4th or 5th. The day before that, the last day of the old year, is regarded as "dividing the seasons" of winter and spring and is celebrated by the Bean-throwing Festival (Setsubun). Many Japanese festivals, particularly those for planting in late spring or early summer and harvesting in autumn, are determined by traditional ways of counting the year. *Setsu* is the term for the 12 divisions, or months, of the traditional year. The beginning *(sekki)* and midpoint *(chuki)* of each *setsu*, which total 24 in one year (nijushisekki), have a special name that reflects seasonal and climatic conditions, such as "Frost falls" at the end of October, or agricultural developments, such as "The lesser ripening," or sprouting of seeds around May 21.

Various charts have been published that match up traditional and solar dates in Japanese history with the corresponding dates in the Gregorian calendar. Several complicated systems for reckoning the years of Japanese history have also been used. In A.D. 645, the Japanese adopted the Chinese system of applying special names *(nengo)* to historical eras. For example, that year is referred to as Great Reform (Taika), based on the many changes made in the Japanese government. *Nengo* do not always correspond with the reign years of Japanese emperors. A system to identify imperial reign years was begun during the Meiji Era (1868–1912). The reign of Emperor Meiji's son is called the Taisho Era (1912–26) and that of his grandson, Hirohito, is the Showa Era (1926–1988). The current reign of Akihito, son of Hirohito, is called Heisei, "Achieving [or accomplishing] Peace."

Yet another calendrical system used in Japan is a zodiac consisting of 12 animal signs which recur in a five-cycle system totaling 60 years. The animal zodiac is also used to denote the times of day. See also AGRICULTURE; FESTIVALS; HIROHITO, EMPEROR; MEIJI RESTORATION OF 1868; NEW YEAR FESTIVAL; RICE PLANTING AND HARVESTING FESTIVALS; SHOWA ERA; TAIKA REFORM; TAISHO ERA; ZODIAC.

CALLIGRAPHY (*shodo*) The "Way of Writing"; the most highly regarded art form in Japan. Calligraphy is the artistic writing of Chinese and Japanese characters (*kanji* and *kana*) on handmade paper (*washi*) using a brush (*fude*) and black india ink (*sumi*). Calligraphers write on large pieces of paper (*hanshi*), large square writing cards (*shikishi*), or long, narrow cards on which poems are written (*tanzaku*).

Sumi is ink made from lampblack or soot mixed with hide or fishbone glue, then dried and compressed into sticks. The stick is rubbed with water on an inkstone (*suzuri*) to make liquid ink. Water is added slowly from a water dropper (*suiteki*). Today, ink can also be bought premixed. Calligraphy brushes, which are made in different sizes and thicknesses, have bamboo handles and tips made of animal hair. These utensils are stored in a writing-equipment box (*suzuribako*) that is frequently made of beautifully decorated lacquer. Calligraphy is difficult because the brush tips are flexible and hard to control. Also, the paper soaks up the ink, making it impossible to correct mistakes.

Recognizing the importance of written records, historical documents and poetry, the Japanese began adapting the Chinese system of writing with characters or ideographs (*kanji*) in the fifth century A.D. Calligraphy was also connected to Buddhism, which was introduced into Japan from China in the sixth century A.D., and copying Buddhist religious scriptures was an important religious and cultural activity. Calligraphy became a major art form in Japan starting in the ninth century A.D. The Japanese Buddhist monk Kukai (774–835), is credited with developing native Japanese phonetic scripts (*kana*) that were combined with Chinese characters. Writing in *kana* was stimulated by great literary works such as the *Kokinshu*, a 10th-century anthology of *waka*, or Japanese poetry, and *The Tale of Genji (Genji Monogatari)*, a novel written c. A.D. 1000 by Murasaki Shikibu. *Wayo* is the term for the Japanese art form of calligraphy written in *kana* that became established in the 10th and 11th centuries. During the Heian Era (794–1185), a person was judged by the beauty of his or her writing. The artistic appreciation and collection of calligraphy became an important activity during the Edo Era (1600–1868). Calligraphy works dating from the eighth to the 14th century, known as *kohitsugire* ("old brush fragment"), are the rarest and most highly valued art objects in Japan.

Five basic scripts are employed in calligraphy. A stylized ancient Chinese script (*tensho*) is used for official stamps and signature seals. Another ancient script called *reisho* or clerical script was used for writing official documents. Block script (*kaisho*) is a popular style with easily identifiable characters that is used in typeset publications as well as brush writing. "Running-style" script (*gyosho*) is a less formal style written quickly with a brush. It runs together and abbreviates some of the strokes that make up the characters. "Grass writing" (*sosho*), an informal, flowing and curved style that elongates characters and runs them together, is the most dynamic and artistic style of calligraphy. Another important calligraphy style is "traces of ink" (*bokuseki*), done by Zen Buddhist monks and often used for scrolls hung during a tea ceremony. Ink painting (*sumi-e*), monochrome paintings of scenes from nature, is a related art form also introduced from China and practiced especially by Zen monks. During the late Edo Era and the Meiji Era (1868–1912), a Chinese style known as *karayo* was also used by Japanese artists and scholars, especially for educational texts. Modern Japanese artists have developed an abstract, avant-garde calligraphy style known as *zen'ei shodo*.

Students learn the five basic styles by copying the works of great calligraphers from the past. The act of learning to write characters, known as *shuji*, is only a preliminary to the art form of calligraphy, or *shodo*. The beauty of the characters lies in their shape and position, the gradation of the ink, and the force of the brushstrokes. The characters can be admired as abstract forms or designs for their own sake. The Japanese have always believed that calligraphy represents the character and state of mind of the calligrapher. The Japanese government sponsors annual exhibitions of calligraphy, painting and sculpture, as well as calligraphy competitions for school children at the start of the New Year. See also BOXES; BRUSHES; BUDDHISM; CHINA AND JAPAN; GENJI, THE TALE OF; HIRAGANA; INK PAINTING; KANA; KATAKANA; KANJI; KOKINSHU; KUKAI; LACQUER WARE; NEW YEAR FESTIVAL; PAPER, HANDMADE; POETRY; SCRIPTURES, RELIGIOUS; SCROLLS; WRITING SYSTEM, JAPANESE; ZEN SECT OF BUDDHISM.

CAMELLIA (*tsubaki*) Flowering evergreen trees belonging to the tea family. Camellias are found throughout Japan except the northern island of Hokkaido. There are several hundred varieties, with flowers that range in color from white to pink, dark red, and streaked types. Some varieties are introduced from China. Two common types of camellia are native to Japan, the *yabutsubaki* (or *yamatsubaki*, "mountain camellia") and the *yukitsubaki* ("snow camellia"). The *yabutsubaki*, found in coastal areas, grows more than 30 ft. high, with a grayish white bark and thick, glossy leaves in pointed oval shapes. Its flowers are red and cylindrical, with five petals, and bloom in winter or early spring. The *yukitsubaki* is a shrub that grows to a height of 3–7 ft. in snowy regions along the western coast of northern Honshu Island. Its red flowers bloom in late spring after the snow thaws.

Camellias were cultivated by the Japanese as ornamental garden trees starting in the Edo Era (1600–1868). Some varieties of camellia with small leaves are used for miniature bonsai plantings. Camellia flowers are usually not displayed on festive occasions in Japan because the flower drops to the ground suddenly, suggesting sudden death, or decapitation by a samurai sword. However, a camellia bud is often displayed as a winter flower arrangement for a tea ceremony.

In ancient Japan, camellia stems and leaves were burned to produce a type of purple dye for textiles known as *murasaki-zome*. Camellia wood is hard and has been used for making household objects. Oil pressed from camellia seeds and fruits has been used for cooking and as hair oil. Dried camellia leaves can be burned to repel mosquitoes.

The leaves can also be soaked in salt water and wrapped around Japanese-style sweets. See also BONSAI; FLOWER ARRANGING; SWEETS; TEA CEREMONY.

CAMERAS AND PHOTOGRAPHY   Japanese companies benefited from advanced optical technology developed during World War II, and Japan has been the world's largest exporter of cameras since 1967. Major Japanese camera manufacturers include Asahi Optical Co., Ltd. (Asahi Pentax); Canon, Inc.; Minolta Camera Co., Ltd.; Olympus Optical Co., Ltd.; Ricoh Co., Ltd.; and Yashica Co., Ltd. Fuji Photo Film Co., Ltd. is the largest Japanese producer of photosensitive material, and the second largest in the world after the U.S. company Eastman Kodak. Founded in 1934, Fuji began commercializing color films in 1946 and manufacturing cameras in 1948. In 1962 it established Fuji Xerox Co., Ltd., a joint venture with the British company Rank Xerox. Konishiroku Photo Industry Co., Ltd., is the second largest Japanese manufacturer of photo film, under the brand name Sakura, and also manufactures Konica cameras. Japanese camera companies also manufacture and export photocopying machines and related equipment.

During the late Tokugawa Era (1603–1867), Japanese interested in the West learned how to use the daguerreotype and other photographic techniques soon after they were introduced into Japan. Photographs of Japanese and their daily lives were taken by 19th-century Western photographers such as Felix Beato, A. Farsari & Co., and Baron von Stillfried. Eliphalet Brown, the official photographer of U.S. Commodore Perry's naval expedition to Japan (1853–1854), published lithographs in 1856. Uchida Kuichi (fl. 1859–1875) and Ueno Hikoma (fl. 1862–1890) were the first indigenous professional photographers in Japan. In the 20th century, photography became an established art form; a movie industry quickly developed, and amateur photography groups and exhibitions became popular. Early in the century, Japanese men who emigrated to other countries married "picture brides," women in Japan who exchanged photographs with the men, married them in absentia, and then traveled to live with their new husbands. Japanese photographers documented their country's efforts during World War II. After the war, young Japanese art photographers began experimenting with new techniques and strove to develop their own personal image (eizo). The Japanese advertising industry has become renowned for photographs that are both beautiful and technically advanced. Numerous camera magazines are published for amateurs and professionals alike. Today camera-toting Japanese tour groups are famous around the world, and every group has to have its "souvenir picture" (kinenshashin) taken in front of major sites. See also ADVERTISING; ELECTRONICS INDUSTRY; EXPORTS AND IMPORTS; PERRY, MATTHEW CALBRAITH; PICTURE BRIDE.

CANDY   See SWEETS.

CANON, INC.   See CAMERAS AND PHOTOGRAPHY.

"CAPSULE," OR MODULE, HOTEL   An inexpensive hotel consisting of plastic modules stacked two or three high in horizontal rows. Each module is about 6 feet long and 3 feet high, just large enough for an overnight patron to crawl in and lie down. It contains a television, radio and intercom, and has a curtain for privacy. The hotel also has a lounge, refreshment area, and bathing facilities. Capsule hotels have been built primarily around Japanese train stations to accommodate businessmen who miss the last train home, usually because they have been out with co-workers or clients. See also EXPENSE ACCOUNTS; SALARYMAN.

CARD GAMES   There are several popular Japanese games that use playing cards. The Japanese word for cards is karuta, from the Portuguese word for card, carta. Western-style card games were introduced by the Portuguese into Japan in the 16th century, but they quickly became associated with gambling, and the Tokugawa Shogunate (1603–1867) banned card playing and gambling in 1697. The word still used in Japan for gangsters, yakuza, was taken from a card game of this type. Western-style cards are now called torampu.

Popular Japanese-style card games played today entail the matching of poems or pictures that are printed on the cards. The game of uta karuta, also known as hyakunin isshu or ogura hyakunin isshu, uses cards printed with classical poems written in the waka form by one hundred famous poets. Most of the poems are taken from a poetry anthology, Single Poems by 100 Poets (Hyakunin isshu), systematized by Fujiwara no Teika (1162–1241), and many Japanese memorize the poems in this anthology so they can become expert at the game. It requires two sets of cards. Each card in one set has either the first three lines (17 syllables) or all 31 syllables of a poem. Cards in the second set have the final two lines (14 syllables) of the same poems. The second set is spread out in front of the players. One player reads the lines of a poem on a card from the first set, and the other players pick out the matching card. This game, which became popular in the Edo Era (1600–1868), is played by many Japanese as part of New Year's celebrations. It derived from a traditional Japanese game known as kai-awase, in which halves of clamshells painted with famous episodes from classical literature or lines of poetry are matched. Irota karuta is a similar card game in which the matching cards are decorated with proverbs and pictures that illustrate them. Each proverb begins with a different character from the Japanese syllabic writing system (kana).

The game of hanafuda uses 48 cards decorated with flowers (hana). Each of the 12 months of the year is represented by four cards that depict the flower associated with that month. Other figures added to some of the cards, such as birds or animals, assign different numerical values. Since the goal of hanafuda is to accumulate the most points, it is a popular gambling game. See also FLOWERS; FUJIWARA NO TEIKA; KANA; NEW YEAR FESTIVAL; POETRY; SHELLS; WAKA; YAKUZA.

CARP (koi)   A freshwater fish related to the goldfish. Prized by the Japanese as the "king of river fish," carp are raised with great care. Some varieties are an important food source. Edible carp are associated with the sea bream *(tai)*, "king of sea fish," and the crane *(tsuru)*, "king of birds," as the epitome of food sources. The carp, sea bream and crane are auspicious in Japan and are often depicted in the fine arts. Other varieties of carp are bred as ornamental fish for garden ponds. Those originally bred in Niigata Prefecture, and known as *nishikigoi* (also *irogoi* or *hanagoi)*, are famous the world over for their vivid colors. As carp are powerful swimmers able to leap high into the air and jump up river rapids and small waterfalls, they are a symbol of courage and strength, traditional male virtues in Japan. At a festival held on May 5th every year, which was formerly called Boys' Day but is now called Children's Day, carp kites known as *koinobori* are hung by families on long bamboo poles. See also CHILDREN'S DAY FESTIVAL; CRANE; FISH AND FISHING INDUSTRY; GARDENS; SEA BREAM.

CARS See AUTOMOBILE INDUSTRY; NISSAN MOTOR CO., LTD.; TOYOTA MOTOR CORPORATION.

CASTLES *(shiro)* Various types of military fortifications have been constructed in Japan since ancient times. In the feudal era, lords *(daimyo)* built fortifications on high ground, where they could oversee battles. During the civil warfare that wracked Japan during the Sengoku (Warring States) Era (1467–1568), *daimyo* began erecting more permanent castles. Such architecture reached its height during the Azuchi-Momoyama Era (1568–1600). Typical castles of that era were built on low-lying plains or plateaus and were thus known as *hirajiro*, "castles on the plain," or *hirayamajiro*, or "castles on the plateau." They are designed to take advantage of terrain by careful site planning *(nawabari)*.

The central castle structure is a tower or donjon *(tenshu* or *tenshakaku)*, similar to a pagoda, with multiple levels and overhanging roofs. This was the castle headquarters and the place of final retreat in a battle. The lord of the castle lived in the *tenshu* when the castle was under siege. There were openings *(sama* or *hazama)* in the tower walls through which guns could be fired or arrows shot. Surrounding the donjon is a main compound *(hommaru)* and several smaller compounds or enclosed areas. There may also be several smaller donjons *(shotenshu)*. A castle is surrounded by concentric fortified courts, each protected by massive stone walls *(ishigaki)* and often also by outer moats. Special chambers known as *ishiotoshi* were built over the wall of a castle with floors that could be opened downward to drop rocks onto attackers scaling the walls. The front entrance *(ote)* is supplemented by a rear entrance *(karamete)*, which could be used for escape if enemies overran the castle. A castle entrance was defended by a *masugata*, a square embattlement that forced people entering the castle to make a right-angled turn before they could pass through the main gate; archers in two-story towers *(yagura)* shooting arrows could decimate invading enemies at this point.

The castle built in Azuchi between 1576 and 1579 by the powerful warlord Oda Nobunaga (1534–1582) was the first castle in Japan to be erected on a massive stone base. Its design was influenced by Western castles, knowledge of which had just been brought to Japan by Portuguese Jesuit missionaries. Nobunaga's seven-story castle was made of wood but protected with metal doors, bridges and casemates, armored openings through which guns are shot. Because Japanese castles were usually built of wood and were thus quite vulnerable to fire, outer walls came to be plastered to provide resistance to fire and firearms. Since castles were difficult to capture by frontal assault, special troops known as *ninja* were specially trained in the art of stealth *(ninujutsu)* to sneak into castles.

Castles were defensive structures but also embodied the power and wealth of their lords. Their interiors were decorated with sumptuous works of art such as brightly painted screens.

In 1615 the Tokugawa Shogunate (1603–1867) consolidated its power by ruling that each *daimyo* could keep only the central castle in his domain, and that all other castles had to be demolished. The remaining castles served as the centers of political and economic activities in each domain, and "castle towns," known as *joka machi* (city under a castle), grew up around the castles to supply the goods and services the lords and their retainers needed. Many castle towns rapidly grew into cities during the Edo Era (1600–1868).

The most famous castle in Japan was at Kumamoto, on southern Kyushu Island, but it was destroyed during the Satsuma Rebellion of 1877. It has been reconstructed, as have Osaka Castle and Nagoya Castle, among others. Remains of many other castles can be seen, such as Takamatsu Castle on Shikoku Island. Some castles that have survived in their original state are Maruoka Castle (1576), Matsumoto Castle (c. 1597), and Matsue Castle (1611). The Imperial Palace in Tokyo is located in Edo Palace, built by the Tokugawa Shogunate (1603–1867) in their new capital city of Edo. Nijo Castle was built by the Tokugawa in Kyoto. Himeji (White Heron) Castle, built from 1600 to 1609, is a beautiful large castle. See also ARCHERY; AZUCHI-MOMOYAMA ERA; DAIMYO; FEUDALISM; HIMEJI CASTLE; IMPERIAL PALACE (TOKYO); KUMAMOTO; MATSUE; NAGOYA; NIJO CASTLE; NINJA; ODA NOBUNAGA; OSAKA; PAGODA; SCREENS; SENGOKU ERA; TAKAMATSU; TOKUGAWA SHOGUNATE.

CAT *(neko)* Cats were introduced into Japan from China and Korea by the ninth century A.D. Although there is little historical documentation about cats in Japan in ancient times, records mention the gifts of a black cat from China to Emperor Koko (830–887; r. 884–887) and a cat from Korea to Emperor Ichiji (980–1011; r. 986–1011). Cats were rare enough to be highly valued in Japan during the ninth and 10th centuries, but were common by the end of the Heian Era (794–1185). The Japanese variety of cat had short white hair with brown and black spots. Cats with long tails were popular until the middle of the Edo Era (1600–1868), after which cats with stubby tails, introduced from Malaya, were preferred.

Japanese literature has many stories about cats, and there

is a category of folklore about "monster cats" (bakeneko) that have been killed and seek to avenge their murders. Such cats are also represented in woodblock prints of giant cat spectres looming behind human figures. Natsume Soseki wrote a famous novel in 1905, titled *I Am a Cat*, about a man who is afraid of cats. There is a famous carving of a sleeping cat at Nikko, the mausoleum of Shogun Tokugawa Ieyasu (1543–1616). Folk art dolls of a beckoning cat (maneki-neko) are placed in restaurants in Japan, as they are believed to attract customers and good fortune for the owners.

The southern island of Iriomote in the Ryukyu Island chain is known for a rare species of small wild cat, the "mountain cat" (yama neko). See also NATSUME SOSEKI; RESTAURANTS; RYUKYU ISLANDS; WOODBLOCK PRINTS.

CERAMICS   See ARITA WARE; KILN; PORCELAIN; POTTERY.

CERAMICS, INDUSTRIAL   See AUTOMOBILE INDUSTRY.

CHAMBER OF COMMERCE   See JAPAN CHAMBER OF COMMERCE AND INDUSTRY.

CHANOYU   See TEA CEREMONY.

CHARCOAL   See HEARTH; HIBACHI; INCENSE; KETTLE; TEA CEREMONY.

CHARMS   See AMULETS; TALISMANS.

CHERRY BLOSSOM (sakura no hana)   The most beloved flower in Japanese culture, the cherry blossom is a delicate pink or white flower with five notched petals, and is widely used as a decorative motif. It was already highly regarded in ancient Japan, as evidenced by dozens of poems in the eighth-century anthology *Manyoshu* that mention cherry blossoms. The cherry blossom symbolizes the Japanese values of simplicity, purity and fleeting beauty. Samurai (warriors) saw in the cherry blossom a symbol for the ideal of the military spirit; samurai were expected to give their lives in their prime—falling in battle like cherry blossoms blown down from the trees.

Cherry trees were planted profusely in Japan, especially in Kyoto, the former capital of Japan, and Edo (modern Tokyo). Spring outings to view the flowering trees became an annual custom as far back as the reign of Emperor Saga (r. 809–823). *Hanami*, or cherry-blossom-viewing parties, are still very popular. Areas with many trees, such as Ueno Park in Tokyo, are filled with people eating, drinking and dancing under the branches during the few short days they are in bloom. Geisha in the Gion district of Kyoto perform "cherry dances" in the spring. Cherry blossoms herald the spring season, and the Japanese eagerly follow news of the *sakura zensen*, or "cherry blossom blooming front," as it moves north through the country, starting in the southern island of Kyushu around the end of March. Japanese flowering cherry trees have been taken to many countries around the world. The best known are the 11 varieties of cherry, numbering more than a thousand trees, that were given to Washington, D.C., by the mayor of Tokyo in 1909. See also FLOWERS; GEISHA; GION; MANYOSHU; SAMURAI; UENO.

CHESS   See GO; SHOGI.

CHEST (tansu)   Japanese chests are beautifully crafted from wood and have drawers to store clothing and household items. Chests were first used in Japanese homes and shops in the 17th century. Most storage areas in traditional Japanese homes are built into the walls, but chests were useful because they could be moved if fire or earthquake struck, as they often did. Chests have different shapes and names for different uses. *Yofuku-dansu* hold Western-type clothes, while *wadansu* hold kimono, traditional Japanese garments, which are folded flat for storage. *Chadansu* are small chests used to store tea utensils and dishes. Antique chests have become popular collector's items, especially those with many small drawers used to store herbal medicine. The finest woods have been used for Japanese chests, in particular paulownia (kiri). Paulownia expands in humid weather, common in Japan, keeping dampness out of the drawers, and shrinks in cool weather, enabling air to circulate through them. Traditionally, when a daughter was born, her parents planted a paulownia tree, which was later used to make her bridal chest. See also KIMONO; PAULOWNIA; WOODWORKING.

CHIBA PREFECTURE (Chiba Ken)   A prefecture just north of the city of Tokyo on central Honshu Island. Chiba covers 1,974 square miles and has a population of nearly 5 million. Northwestern Chiba, adjoining the Tokyo-Yokohama region, is densely populated and heavily industrialized, with electronics, petrochemicals, shipbuilding and steel. With the Pacific Ocean to the east and south, Chiba is also a major recreation area, with many beaches and two quasi-national parks, Suigo-Tsukuba and Southern Boso. Commercial fishing in Tokyo Bay along the southern border of Chiba was a major industry until the water became polluted. Rice and produce farming are still important. Japan's major international airport is located in the town of Narita, where a Buddhist temple known as Shinshoji is visited by over 1 million people a year. See also AIRLINES AND AIRPORTS; PACIFIC OCEAN; PREFECTURE; TOKYO; YOKOHAMA.

CHICKEN (tori)   The chicken plays an important role in Japanese mythology and religion and is also a source of food. There are presently about 30 breeds of chicken in Japan, 16 of which have been designated by the government as specially protected animals. The ancestor of Japanese domesticated chickens was the red jungle fowl, introduced into Japan with rice cultivation in the late Jomon Era (c. 10,000–c. 300 B.C.). The elegant, long-tailed *shokoku* was introduced into Japan from China before or during the Heian Era (794–1185) and was crossbred with native Japanese varieties. *Shokoku* were regarded as sacred birds and thus kept in Shinto shrines. They were also used in cockfights (tori-awase) at the imperial court. Because roosters, or cocks (niwatori) announce the time by crowing each morning, the government office responsible for announcing the time was known as *Tori no Tsukasa.* Cocks were believed to chase away evil spirits, because they crow when the sun rises and darkness disappears. Chickens were often used as religious sacrifices or to divine the future. Many *haniwa,* or ancient clay tomb figures, depict chickens. Japanese myths about the Sun Goddess, Amaterasu o Mikami, tell how the sound of a crowing cock helped lure the goddess out of a cave where she had gone into hiding. *Torii,* the entrance gate to a Shinto shrine, means "bird perch." Shinto shrines often keep cocks in their compounds. The rooster represents courage and protection, and a rooster sleeping on a drum represents peace.

During the Edo Era (1600–1868), several new varieties of chicken were introduced into Japan. The colorful bantam (*chabo*) was imported from Indochina. The *shamo,* a delicious game bird used in cockfighting, was imported from Southeast Asia. The beautiful and highly valued long-tailed cock (*onagadori* or *chobikei*), originally introduced from Korea, was bred in the Tosa area of Japan. Its tail feathers grow as long as 15 feet. Western varieties of chicken were introduced in the 19th century and commercially crossbred with Japanese varieties to produce fine meat and eggs. Chickens have been eaten throughout Japanese history. *Yakitori,* small pieces of grilled chicken, is a popular fast food in Japan.

Many Japanese artists portrayed chickens in scroll paintings, woodblock prints or illustrated books. The cock is one of the animals in the traditional 12-year zodiacal cycle. People born in the Year of the Cock are thought to be courageous and reliable. See also AMATERASU O MIKAMI; SHINTO; SHRINES, SHINTO; TORII; YAKITORI; ZODIAC.

CHIKAMATSU MONZAEMON (1653–1724) The greatest Japanese dramatist of the Edo Era, who wrote nearly 100 plays for Bunraku (puppet theater) and collaborated on about 30 Kabuki (traditional theater) plays. His plays are still performed today.

Chikamatsu was born Sugimori Jirokichi to a samurai family that settled in the old capital city of Kyoto in the 1660s. He served a number of court nobles and was trained in Buddhist and Confucian philosophy and Japanese literature. Under the pen name Chikamatsu Monzaemon, he wrote his first Bunraku play in 1683, *The Soga Heir (Yotsugi Soga)* about a famous vendetta in Japanese history. His first Kabuki play was produced in 1684. Chikamatsu wrote many plays for Takemoto Gidayu, a famous Joruri chanter, and the Kabuki actor Sakata Tojuro I. (Joruri, storytelling by chanting to the accompaniment of a stringed instrument called the *shamisen,* is the foundation of Bunraku.) In 1705 Chikamatsu moved to the commercial city of Osaka, where he wrote for Takemotoza, the Bunraku theater operated by Gidayu. Chikamatsu wrote numerous historical dramas (*jidaimono*), but he specialized in *sewamono,* "talk of the town" plays, which dealt with conflicts between duty (*giri*) to family and society and human feelings (*ninjo*) suffered by members of the merchant class. Love often won out, especially between shop merchants and courtesans of the licensed pleasure quarters, but suicide was the only possible ending. Chikamatsu wrote 20 plays about love sui-

cides. The best known is *The Love Suicides at Sonezaki (Sonezaki shinju,* 1703; translated 1961), based on a true story, which has been adapted many times and made into a movie. His most famous historical drama is *The Battles of Coxinga (Kokusen'ya Kassen,* 1715; translated 1951) about a legendary Chinese warrior. Chikamatsu wrote parts that utilize the highly developed skills of Japanese puppeteers. The puppets even perform lively tumbling and supernatural feats that continue to thrill audiences to this day. See also BUNRAKU; DUTY AND FEELINGS; KABUKI.

CHILDREN (*kodomo*) Children are well loved in Japan, as shown by the nickname for children, *kodakara,* "child treasure." Many rituals have traditionally been conducted after the birth of a baby to protect its spirit and to introduce it to the human community. The naming ceremony is held between the 3rd and 14th day after birth. Thirty-two days after the birth of a boy or 33 days after the birth of a girl, the baby is taken to the local Shinto shrine to be introduced to the *kami* (sacred spirits) and thereby recognized as an *ujiko,* a member of the shrine and of Japanese society; this first shrine visit is known as *hatsu miya mairi.* Every November 15th, girls age 3 and 7 and boys age 5 are dressed up and taken to shrines to gain the protection of the *kami*; this is known as the Seven-Five-Three Festival (Shichi-Go-San). The Doll Festival (Hina Matsuri), also known as Girls' Day, is celebrated on March 3rd. Children's Day (Kodomo-no-hi), formerly known as Boys' Day, is celebrated on May 5th, when families hang a carp fish kite (*koi-nobori*) for each child in the family. The Japanese traditionally mark the end of childhood at age seven. Teenagers are regarded as young people (*wakamono*) or "green years" (*seinen*). There are youth associations (*seinendan*), especially in rural areas, which are modern carryovers of traditional groups for unmarried young people ages 15 to 25, known as *wakamono-bumi* (for men) and *musume-gumi* (for women). The Japanese feel a close bond with members of their same age and sex group. Young people in Japan are considered to become adults at age 20, celebrated by the Adults' Day Festival (Seijin-no-hi) on January 15th each year.

Young children are indulged and are almost never left alone or with babysitters. Mothers carry them on their backs for years, and they sleep with their parents until around age 10. Mothers and children have a relationship of dependency (*amae*), in contrast to the relative independence that is generally encouraged in Western children. Children are constantly praised for good behavior and are punished when necessary, rarely by physical punishment, but by shaming the child into realizing how his or her behavior affects the family. Married women in Japan rarely work at outside jobs while their children are young, but consider the raising of children their full-time occupation. Mothers today push their children to study hard and are often caricatured as "education mamas" (*kyoiku mama*).

Although large families were common in the past, most Japanese families now have one or two children. Grandparents customarily lived with the family, but modern homes and apartments are too small for three generations to live together. Many children rarely see their fathers, who work long hours and frequently socialize in the evening with their coworkers. Children are raised to obey and feel responsible for their parents, a Confucian concept known as filial piety (ko), and to realize that their duty (giri) to family and society must take precedence over personal feelings (ninjo). There is a fairly low rate of juvenile delinquency and crime in Japan.

Boys and girls are socialized into different roles from a very young age. Older children look after their younger brothers and sisters, who are expected to obey and respect their elder siblings. Boys are often given names that indicate their rank in the family (first son, second son, etc.). The eldest son feels a very strong responsibility as the family heir.

Japanese children usually begin nursery school at age three, although school is not compulsory until age six. They spend six years in primary school and three years in junior high school. Although it is not compulsory, 94% of all Japanese young people complete high school, which takes three years. Most children have a heavy daily schedule because they also take lessons in piano, abacus, swimming or other activities after school. They suffer intense pressure from "examination hell" (juken jigoku) to get into the best schools. Many attend juku ("cram schools") in addition to regular classes to prepare for the rigorous entrance examinations. A family will make many sacrifices in order to help a child succeed, which puts a tremendous burden on the child not to disappoint or shame the family, and some end up committing suicide.

Children are trained in origami, the art of folding paper into different shapes, which gives them manual dexterity and an understanding of plane geometry. Among the many children's games, one of the first games they learn is "Scissors-Paper-Stone" (jankenpon), a hand game used by children and adults alike to determine who is "it" or will take the first turn (known as "Rock-Scissors-Paper" in the United States). There is a wide variety of traditional toys unique to different regions of Japan, and robots, other modern toys, video games, television, sports such as baseball, and comic books (manga) are popular with Japanese children. See also ABACUS; ADULTS' DAY; BASEBALL; CHILDREN'S DAY FESTIVAL; COMIC BOOKS; DEPENDENCY; DOLL FESTIVAL; DUTY AND FEELINGS; EDUCATION SYSTEM; FAMILY; FATHER; FILIAL PIETY; GAMES; JUKU; KAMI; LOYALTY; MOTHER; ORIGAMI; SCISSORS-PAPER-STONE; SHINTO; TELEVISION; TOYS, TRADITIONAL.

CHILDREN'S DAY FESTIVAL (Kodomo-no-hi) A festival for children held on May 5, which was formerly known as Boys' Day (Tango-no-Sekku) and was celebrated on the fifth day of the fifth month in the traditional Japanese lunar calendar. In 1948 the Japanese government declared May 5 a national holiday and renamed it Children's Day. On this day, families hang large carp (koi) kites (koinobori) from bamboo poles in front of their homes, a large black carp for the father, a smaller red carp for the mother and a small blue carp for each child (formerly each son) in the family. At the top of the pole are streamers and golden ornaments. The carp represents the qualities of courage and perseverance because it is a strong fish that swims upstream against

the current. The practice of hanging carp kites was inspired by a Chinese legend about a carp that turned into a dragon after it leaped up a waterfall in the Yellow River. In the Edo Era (1600–1868), samurai families celebrated May 5 by hanging military banners in front of their homes. The flower called shobu, the Japanese iris or sweet flag, is associated with the Boys' Day Festival because during the rise of the warrior class in 12th-century Japan, the word shobu became associated with a similar-sounding word that meant "respect for the martial arts." Japanese people float iris leaves in the bath water on May 5 in accord with an old belief that the sword-shaped leaves have the power to drive away evil spirits and put out fires. They also hang iris leaves under the eaves of their homes. On Children's Day, families display a set of samurai dolls, called gogatsu ningyo, miniature armor and weapons in the tokonoma, an alcove in the main room of the home. To honor the dolls, the family eats kawashimochi, rice cakes filled with sweet bean paste and wrapped in oak leaves, and chimaki, rice cakes wrapped in bamboo leaves or cogon grass, and sake with iris petals floating in it is drunk. See also BATH; BEANS; CARP; DOLLS; IRIS; KITE; MOCHI; MONGOL INVASIONS OF JAPAN; SAMURAI; SWEETS; SWORD; TOKONOMA.

CHINA AND JAPAN The Japanese adapted many aspects of their culture from China, including their writing system, calendar, calligraphy, fine arts and crafts, social values, forms of government and the Buddhist religion. Although China and Japan developed into very different countries, the Japanese look to China as their cultural source much the same way Europeans look to ancient Greece and Rome.

The earliest mention of Japan is a reference to the rulers of Wa (Yamato, in western Japan), in the third-century A.D. Chinese historical document Wei Chih (Wei Zhi). In Yamato the powerful Soga clan, especially Empress Suiko (554–628) and her regent, Prince Shotoku (574–622), promoted the adoption of Chinese culture and government organization to enhance their power and prestige. In A.D. 607 the first Japanese embassy was sent to China. The name Nippon (or Nihon; "the place where the sun rises"), the name the Japanese use for their country, was first used by Shotoku in an official letter to China. Shotoku's Seventeen-Article Constitution drew upon the teachings of Confucius to emphasize hierarchical social and political organization, learning and respect for rulers. These developments were furthered by the Taika Reform of A.D. 645. The Buddhist religion was adopted from China in the sixth century A.D. and served as a major vehicle of culture, with its complex theology, monastic structure, written scriptures and temple architecture. Due to political turmoil in T'ang dynasty China, Japan sent its last official embassy there in A.D. 838.

Japan itself went through political upheaval with the rise of the samurai class, which took control after the Battle of Dannoura in 1185 (Kamakura Shogunate, 1192–1333), initiating seven centuries of feudalism. Unofficial trade continued with China because the Japanese desired Chinese textiles, porcelain, paintings and other luxury goods. The

Zen sect of Buddhism, introduced into Japan in the 12th century, renewed an interest in Chinese culture, including monochromatic ink painting and tea drinking, which developed into the Japanese tea ceremony. In A.D. 1325 Emperor Go-Daigo (who briefly regained power from military rulers, 1333–1336), sent an official Japanese embassy to China. The Ashikaga shoguns, who controlled much of Japan from 1336 into the 16th century, fostered diplomatic and trade relations with China. Fukuoka City on Kyushu Island was an important trading port. Very close to the Korean Peninsula, which juts out from China, Kyushu had always been the traditional point of entry for mainland Asian civilization into the Japanese islands.

Japanese trading missions to China continued during the century of civil warfare suffered by Japan from the Onin War (1467–1477) until the country was unified under the Tokugawa Shogunate (1603–1867). During this time the city of Sakai near Osaka became very wealthy as the main trading port with China. The warlord Toyotomi Hideyoshi (1536–1598) unsuccessfully invaded Korea twice, in 1592 and 1597, with the larger aim of conquering China. After Hideyoshi died suddenly, Tokugawa Ieyasu (1543–1616) was able to consolidate power and establish Tokugawa rule over the unified country. Western powers had made inroads in Japan, especially the Portuguese and Spanish, which the Tokugawa shoguns perceived as a threat to their authority. By 1641 Tokugawa Iemitsu had expelled all foreigners from Japan, forbade all Japanese to leave the country, and limited foreign trading to a small and highly regulated community of Chinese and Dutch traders in the southern port city of Nagasaki. The Shimazu clan, who ruled Satsuma Province on southern Kyushu, got around these bans by invading the southern Ryukyu Islands (modern Okinawa Prefecture) in 1609. Ryukyu was a great trading kingdom that had become a tributary state of China in 1372. Control of Ryukyu's trade with China made Satsuma very wealthy. Military men from Satsuma helped overthrow the Tokugawa Shogunate and establish the modern Japanese state with the Meiji Restoration of 1868.

In 1872 Ryukyu was made a prefecture of Japan, with no protest from China, which had been forced into a weak position by Western powers. The Japanese wanted to show their strength, and ended up going to war with China in 1894 over possession of Korea. Its defeat of China in the Sino-Japanese War of 1894–1895, and of Russia in the Russo-Japanese War (1904–1905), gave Japan an empire that included Korea, southern Manchuria, southern Sakhalin Island and the island of Taiwan. In 1911–1912 the Chinese overthrew their imperial system and established a revolutionary government, but the country broke down into factions led by warlords. Japan entered the side of the British in World War I and quickly took control of German possessions in Asia, including Shantung Province in China. In 1915 Japan presented China with the so-called Twenty-one Demands, which increased Japanese control in China. In the 1920s Japan agreed to withdraw from Shantung and limit its naval fleet. However, Japan soon embarked on a course of military conquest and sent troops into Manchuria, known as the Manchurian Incident of 1931. Japanese troops

expanded further south into China, and in 1937 met resistance from the Nationalist Government of Chiang Kai-shek. Chinese Communists and Nationalists joined forces to battle the Japanese in the Sino-Japanese War of 1937–1945. Japan also invaded Southeast Asia and was opposed by the Allied Powers. In 1945 Japan finally surrendered to the Allied Powers and was forced to give up Taiwan, Korea and its other colonies. The Ryukyu Islands were occupied by U.S. forces until 1972.

The Communists took control of China in 1949 and the Nationalists under Chiang Kai-shek fled to Taiwan. In 1952 the U.S. forced Japanese Prime Minister Yoshida Shigeru to recognize the Nationalist Government on Taiwan as the real China, despite popular Japanese opposition. Japan did have an economic and political interest in its former colony of Taiwan. In 1972, after U.S. president Richard Nixon reestablished American relations with the People's Republic of China (PRC), Japanese Prime Minister Tanaka Kakuei went to China and awarded the PRC full diplomatic recognition in place of Taiwan. In 1978 Japan and the PRC signed the China-Japan Peace and Friendship Treaty. However, Japan has continued important trade relations with both Chinas, which are primary export markets for Japanese products. See also ASUKA; BROCADE; BUDDHISM; CALLIGRAPHY; CONFUCIANISM; EXPORTS AND IMPORTS; FUKUOKA; INK PAINTING; KOREA AND JAPAN; KYUSHU ISLAND; MANCHURIAN INCIDENT; MEIJI RESTORATION OF 1868; MONASTICISM; NARA ERA; NIPPON; PAINTING; PORCELAIN; OCCUPATION OF JAPAN; OKINAWA PREFECTURE; RYUKYU ISLANDS; SAKAI; SATSUMA; SHIMAZU CLAN; SHOTOKU, PRINCE; SINO-JAPANESE WAR OF 1894–1895; SINO-JAPANESE WAR OF 1937–1945; SURRENDER OF JAPAN; TAIWAN AND JAPAN; TEA; TOYOTOMI HIDEYOSHI; TWENTY-ONE DEMANDS ON CHINA; WRITING SYSTEM, JAPANESE; ZEN SECT OF BUDDHISM.

CHINA-JAPAN PEACE AND FRIENDSHIP TREATY
See CHINA AND JAPAN; SINO-JAPANESE WAR OF 1937–1945.

CHINESE IDEOGRAPHS See KANJI; LANGUAGE, JAPANESE; WRITING SYSTEM, JAPANESE.

CHINESE IN JAPAN See MINORITIES IN JAPAN.

CHOJIRO (1516–1592) A potter in the capital city of Kyoto who originated the pottery style known as Raku (raku-yaki). Chojiro's father was a tilemaker who may have come to Japan from Korea, the place of origin for much Japanese pottery. Chojiro came to the attention of the great tea ceremony master Sen no Rikyu (1522–1591), and the two men worked together in developing the kind of tea bowl (chawan) best suited to contain frothy, bright green ceremonial tea. Their preference was a black, asymmetrical, hand-formed bowl that sat comfortably in the hand and slowly transmitted the warmth of the tea; this style was known as black Raku (kuroraku). Chojiro also produced a red Raku (akaraku) style of tea bowl, as well as some white pieces. Rikyu and Chojiro remained lifetime friends. When the warlord Toyotomi Hideyoshi gave Rikyu the surname Sen, Rikyu gave his former name, Tanaka, to Chojiro, who then called himself Tanaka Choyu. Rikyu introduced Cho-

jiro to Hideyoshi and the warlord Oda Nobunaga, another tea patron, who used both black and red Raku tea bowls. A number of Chojiro's tea bowls have been designated National Treasures (Important Cultural Properties) by the Japanese government. Raku tea bowls made by Chojiro and by the head of each generation of his descendants continue to be highly valued by tea ceremony masters. See also NATIONAL TREASURES; ODA NOBUNAGA; POTTERY; RAKU WARE; SEN NO RIKYU; TEA BOWL; TEA CEREMONY; TOYOTOMI HIDEYOSHI.

CHOPSTICKS (*hashi*) Utensils for eating, commonly made from plain wood, such as pine or cedar, bamboo, lacquered wood or plastic, but for special usage, of ivory and mother-of-pearl inlay. Each family member often has his or her own set. Japanese chopsticks were originally connected and looked like pincers. The word *hashi* may have been chosen because those chopsticks may have resembled the beaks of birds, also pronounced hashi. Restaurants provide *waribashi,* disposable wooden chopsticks. Most Japanese food is served in small pieces easily eaten with chopsticks. Long chopsticks used for cooking are 12 inches in length; most of these are wood or bamboo, but metal ones are used for deep frying.

Japanese chopsticks are smaller than those used in China and Korea, where they are also common. Chopsticks are usually held in the right hand. The lower stick rests on the fourth finger and the saddle of the thumb and does not move. The upper stick, which is moved up and down, is held between the thumb and the index and middle fingers. There are many rules of etiquette for using chopsticks—the diner should never grab them with a fist, wave them in the air or over the food, skewer the food or dig through a shared dish to find the best pieces. Nothing should be taken by chopsticks from someone else's chopsticks, as this is done only with cremated bones at funerals. Chopsticks are never stuck upright in a bowl of rice; this is how meals are offered on Buddhist altars to spirits of the dead. When taking food from a common dish, for sanitary reasons, chopsticks are turned around to use the handle ends. To lay chopsticks down, place them on the small chopstick rest (*hashioki*), a small decorative object shaped as a fish, flower and so forth, made of porcelain, pottery or bamboo. If there is no chopstick rest, place the chopsticks across the dish lowest to the table. When the Japanese pick up their chopsticks to begin a meal, they traditionally put their hands together, bow their heads and say, "*Itadakimasu*" ("I receive"). See also ALTARS IN HOMES; COOKING; RESTAURANTS.

CHOSHU PROVINCE A domain on the southwestern tip of the main island of Honshu, now known as Yamaguchi Prefecture. Samurai from Choshu played an important role in the overthrow of the Tokugawa Shogunate (1603–1867), and led the Meiji Restoration of 1868 and the modernization of Japan. These leaders included Ito Hirobumi (1841–1909), Japan's first prime minister and author of its first constitution; Kido Takayoshi (1833–1877), negotiator of the 1850s alliance between Choshu and Satsuma provinces to overthrow the shogunate who later became chief Choshu representative in the new Meiji government;

and Yamagata Aritomo (1838–1922), architect of the modern Japanese army and a prominent Meiji statesman. Choshu and Satsuma were both opposed to the Tokugawa government in Edo (modern Tokyo) and to concessions the shogunate made to Western powers under the Ansei Commercial Treaties. The two factions competed to control the imperial court in Kyoto, and Choshu forces succeeded in 1863, only to be driven out of Kyoto by Satsuma forces in a coup d'etat on September 30, 1863. Choshu forces failed in their attempt to regain Kyoto in 1864, and the shogunate sent an army against Choshu Province. Soon after, combined British, French, Dutch and American naval forces bombarded Choshu in retaliation for attacks Choshu had made on Western ships in the nearby Strait of Shimonoseki, which connects the Inland Sea and Japan Sea and divides the Choshu region on the southern tip of Honshu Island from Kyushu Island. The Western powers destroyed Choshu defenses and demanded that the shogunate pay huge reparations, which it was unable to do. Although these events discredited the anti-shogunate faction in Choshu, Choshu's modern army, which included volunteer units of peasants and townsmen who fought alongside samurai, seized the Choshu capital, and fought alongside forces from Satsuma, Tosa, and Hizen provinces to eventually overthrow the shogunate. Choshu became Yamaguchi Prefecture when the Meiji government abolished feudal domains in 1871 and created a new prefectural system (*ken*).

Today Yamaguchi Prefecture has a population of more than 1.5 million and covers an area of 2,353 square miles. Major cities include Yamaguchi, the capital of the prefecture; Shimonoseki; and the old castle town of Hagi, famous for pottery and tourism. See also ANSEI COMMERCIAL TREATIES; HAGI; ITO HIROBUMI; KIDO TAKAYOSHI; KOREA AND JAPAN; MEIJI RESTORATION OF 1868; SATSUMA PROVINCE; SHIMONOSEKI; TOKUGAWA SHOGUNATE; YAMAGATA ARITOMO.

CHRISTIANITY IN JAPAN The Christian religion was introduced into Japan by the Portuguese Roman Catholic Jesuit missionary St. Francis Xavier (1506–1552), who landed on the southern island of Kyushu in A.D. 1549. He was followed by other Jesuit missionaries, who succeeded in converting more than 200,000 Japanese, including some *daimyo* (feudal lords), mainly in the Kyushu area, who sent envoys to the pope in Rome. The Christian belief in one god and the exclusive nature of Christianity is very different from the polytheistic worship of Shinto and Buddhism, the principal religions practiced in Japan.

Christianity appealed to some Japanese because it was foreign and exotic, and because Western traders accompanied the Jesuits and brought many new items that symbolized superiority and power. The national unifier Oda Nobunaga (1534–1582) was receptive to Christianity because he was strongly opposed to the political and military power of Buddhist sects in Japan. However, the two other national unifiers, Toyotomi Hideyoshi (1536–1598) and Tokugawa Ieyasu (1543–1616), saw Christianity as an ideological and political threat to their power, in part because the Kyushu domains were not cooperative with the Tokugawa Shogunate (1603–1867). The Tokugawa Shogunate founded by Ieyasu banned Christian missionaries and actively persecuted Japanese Christians. Suspect Japanese were forced to tread on reproductions of Christian images (*fumi-e*, "pictures to step on"), something most Christians would not do, to prove that they did not follow the Christian religion. Every Japanese family was required to register with a Buddhist temple. The Shimabara Uprising of 1637–1638 by Christians on Kyushu was brutally suppressed by the shogunate.

In 1639 Japan was secluded from all Western influences, and only a handful of Dutch traders, who were Protestants and not aggressive seekers of converts, were allowed to engage in strictly controlled trade with Japan. When Japan was opened to the West in the 1850s, Protestant as well as Catholic missionaries became active. A Catholic missionary found "hidden Christians" (*kakure kirishitan*) in Nagasaki and nearby islands whose families had continued to secretly practice the religion for two centuries, eventually combining it with Shinto, Buddhist and folk religious practices. Protestant and Catholic missionaries won nearly a million converts by the end of the 19th century, when Japan was undergoing modernization. However, Christianity declined prior to World War II when State Shinto was used to promote Japanese nationalism. The devastation of the war caused some Japanese to turn to Christianity for new religious meaning.

Christians have established charitable organizations, schools, and hospitals, and have influenced the Japanese labor movement. The United Church of Christ in Japan, formed during World War II, became the largest Protestant body in the country. The number of Christians in Japan remains at around 1 million, about two-thirds of them Protestant. Many of the Buddhist "New Religions" that have became popular since the war have adapted Christian social and charitable practices. Some Japanese couples have Christian weddings while also practicing Shinto and Buddhism. See also BUDDHISM; DUTCH IN JAPAN; NAMBAN; NEW RELIGIONS; PORTUGUESE IN JAPAN; SECLUSION, NATIONAL; SHIMABARA REBELLION; SHINTO; STATE SHINTO; TOKUGAWA SHOGUNATE; TOYOTOMI HIDEYOSHI; XAVIER, ST. FRANCIS.

CHRYSANTHEMUM (*kiku*) The chyrsanthemum has been so highly regarded by the Japanese that it is used for the crest (*mon*) of the imperial family, and the emperor is said to sit on the Chrysanthemum Throne. Chrysanthemum motifs are used for many decorative purposes in Japan, but they must always have fewer or more than the 16 petals illustrated in the imperial crest.

The chrysanthemum plant was probably introduced into Japan from China during the Nara Era (710–794) or early Heian Era (794–1185). Members of the imperial court and aristocracy cultivated them in their gardens and celebrated a Chrysanthemum Festival (*Choyo-no-Sekku*) on September 9th in the traditional lunar calendar. On this day they drank chrysanthemum wine and, following the Chinese notion that the plant had magical properties, rubbed their bodies with cotton permeated with the moisture and scent of chrysanthemum. During the Edo Era (1600–1868), chry-

santhemums became popular with the general population, and many new varieties and growing techniques were developed. Public exhibits of chrysanthemums became an autumn custom that is still practiced today. For example, from mid-October through mid-November, chrysanthemums are exhibited in Tokyo at Meiji Shrine, Yasukuni Shrine and Shinjuku Imperial Gardens. There are also associations for admirers and growers of chrysanthemums that were organized during the Taisho Era (1912–1926). They had been inspired by the revival of the Chrysanthemum Festival in the imperial court during the Meiji Era (1868–1912).

The chrysanthemum plant, which can grow over 3 feet high, has many types associated with various regions of Japan. The flowers are classified by size into small, medium or large. European varieties of chrysanthemums, which are also cultivated in Japan, tend to have larger flowers. The Japanese have developed chrysanthemum varieties that bloom in different seasons, but they especially admire the noble autumn flowers that bloom despite the difficult weather conditions of the impending winter. See also CREST; FESTIVALS; FLOWERS; GARDENS; IMPERIAL HOUSEHOLD; MEIJI SHRINE; SHINJUKU; YASUKUNI SHRINE.

CHUBU REGION See GEOGRAPHIC REGIONS; JAPAN ALPS.

CHUGOKU REGION See GEOGRAPHIC REGIONS.

CHUZENJI, LAKE See KEGON WATERFALL; NIKKO NATIONAL PARK.

CITIES See FUKUOKA; HIROSHIMA; INDUSTRIAL ZONES; KAGOSHIMA; KAMAKURA; KANAZAWA; KAWASAKI; KITA KYUSHU; KOBE; KYOTO; MATSUE; NAGASAKI; NAGOYA; NAHA; OSAKA; SAKAI; SAPPORO; SENDAI; SHITAMACHI; TAKAMATSU; TOKYO; TOWNSPEOPLE; WARD; YOKOHAMA.

C. ITOH & CO., LTD. See ITOH, C., & CO., LTD.

CITRUS FRUIT Two common types of citrus fruit in Japan are the *yuzu* (citron), comparable to a grapefruit or lemon, and *mikan*, similar to a tangerine or mandarin orange. The *yuzu* is used mainly for its aromatic rind, which is often cut into decorative shapes to garnish food and subtly flavor soups, stews and other dishes. *Yuzu* rind is green in summer and autumn, then turns gold in late autumn and winter. The juice may also be used with *sashimi* (raw fish) and in soy-based dipping sauces. Japanese traditionally celebrate the winter solstice on December 23rd by adding fragrant *yuzu* slices to their bath water. Legend has it that this will warm their bodies and protect them from catching cold during the winter. The *mikan* is popular for eating and is widely available in Japanese markets. Another large citrus fruit, the *daidai*, is displayed in decorative arrangements at the New Year because it symbolizes long life. See also BATH; NEW YEAR FESTIVAL; SASHIMI; SOUP; SOY SAUCE.

CLAMS See SEAFOOD; SHELLS.

CLAN (*uji*) A group within the ruling elite of ancient Japan that consisted of a number of households sharing a common ancestry and led by a hereditary patriarchal chieftain, called the *uji no kami*. The clan system probably began in the fifth century A.D. and was centralized in the sixth century. Clan members worshipped the clan's particular god, or *ujigami*. Also attached to a clan were groups known as *be* or *tomo* (guilds or corporations), whose members were connected to the clan not by ancestry but by occupation. They made necessary objects such as utensils, weapons and textiles, performed physical labor or military service, or carried out religious rites. Members of these groups inherited their positions.

Prior to the Chinese-inspired reforms that Prince Shotoku (574–622) made to centralize government in Japan, there were a number of autonomous but loosely connected clans. The dominant Yamato, or imperial, clan claimed to be descendants of the Sun Goddess Amaterasu o Mikami. This clan included the reigning house and also several great families that were headed by *omi*, "great men." Below this clan were the divine clans, who claimed to be descendants of other divine beings. Their chieftains were called *muraji*, or "group chiefs." There were also stranger clans, whose members had immigrated from China and Korea. *Uji* chieftains were given positions in the Yamato court and were awarded the title *kabane*. Although clan heads acknowledged the supremacy of the imperial clan, they controlled the members and property belonging to their own groups. Clans often fought among themselves and even tried to overthrow the imperial clan, although no faction became strong enough to usurp imperial authority. Rather, a powerful clan would gain influence over the reigning family through marrying their daughters to imperial princes. In the sixth century the Soga clan became the most powerful clan through this method and gained control over the royal treasury. The Nakatomi clan, which later was known as the Fujiwara clan, became very powerful in the seventh century. However, the Taika Reform of A.D. 645, which created a new bureaucracy through the conferral of ranks by the imperial court, began to replace the earlier clan hierarchy, which was determined by birth. See also AMATERASU O MIKAMI; FUJIWARA CLAN; SHOTOKU, PRINCE; SOGA CLAN; TAIKA REFORM; YAMATO.

CLASS STRUCTURE The Constitution of 1947 abolished the ranks of hereditary nobility, except for the Imperial Household, and today, 90% of Japanese consider themselves as belonging to the middle class. Such social equality is a relatively recent development in Japan, however.

In the prehistoric Jomon Era (c. 10,000–c. 300 B.C.), the Japanese were nomadic hunter-gatherers. With the introduction of wet-rice cultivation and mainland Asian culture during the Yayoi Era (c. 300 B.C.–c. A.D. 300), they settled into agricultural communities. Large immigrant groups from China and Korea settled in western Japan during the Kofun Era (c. 300–710), some of whom were horse-riding nomadic tribes who became the ruling elite. Ancient Japan was dominated by powerful clans, one of which, the Yamato, gained ascendancy as the imperial clan. During the Nara

Era (710–794) and the Heian Era (794–1185), the population was divided into a small, cultured aristocracy, located in Nara and then in Heian (later known as Kyoto), and a large group of peasants who worked the land. There were also a Buddhist priesthood and a landed gentry. By the end of the Heian Era, a warrior class (samurai) had become the ruling class in the provinces. From the late 12th century, shogun became the actual rulers of Japan, although they did not replace emperors but derived their legitimacy from them. *Daimyo* (feudal lords) ruled local provinces. During nearly seven centuries of feudalism, the population was divided into the samurai, aristocratic and peasant classes. Samurai originally lived in farming villages, but in the late 15th and early 16th centuries they moved into towns around the castles of *daimyo* or shogun and became a distinct hereditary social class superior to peasants.

The Tokugawa Shogunate (1603–1867) instituted a strict system of four social classes; in descending order, they were samurai, farmer, artisan and merchant. The latter two classes, known collectively as townspeople (*chonin*), clustered in castle towns, which grew into large cities during the Tokugawa Era. At the top were the samurai, from *daimyo* down through lower levels to poor foot soldiers. Samurai comprised around 7% of the population of about 30 million. During the centuries of peace under the Tokugawa, samurai were transformed from warriors into bureaucrats. Next were the peasants, who cultivated rice, the basis of the economy, because taxes were paid in measurements of rice known as *koku*. They comprised 80% of the population. Below the peasants were the artisans, who produced beautiful and useful goods. At the bottom were the merchants, who theoretically produced nothing, but became the wealthiest class through distributing goods and food. This ranking system is known as *shi-no-ko-sho* (samurai, farmers, artisans, merchants). There were also outcastes, such as *burakumin* ("hamlet people") who were considered unclean because they handled dead animals, which was taboo in Buddhism; and Ainu, indigenous nomadic peoples in northern Japan. The Shogunate adapted the concepts of Neo-Confucianism and the samurai code of *bushido* ("way of the warrior") to reinforce the class structure. The popular culture that developed in the Edo Era (1600–1868) had as a common theme the conflict many Japanese experienced between social duty (*giri*) and human feelings (*ninjo*).

Samurai from western Japan led the revolt that overthrew the Tokugawa Shogunate and returned authority to the emperor with the Meiji Restoration of 1868. The Meiji government (1868–1912) abolished the Tokugawa four-class system. In 1869, *daimyo* and court nobles were combined into a new aristocratic class, known as peers (*kazoku*). Samurai were classified as gentry (*shizoku*), and in 1876 they were forbidden to wear two swords, the symbol of their former rank. Commoners were given more privileges, including the rights to move, to buy and sell land, to take family names and to marry with members of higher classes. In 1871 the *burakumin* and other outcaste categories were abolished, and members were designated commoners. The universal conscription law of 1873 removed the feudal distinction between samurai and commoners. Theoretically, except for the small aristocracy, all Japanese became social equals. Samurai virtues and reverence for the emperor were inculcated in the population by military leaders who gained increasing influence in Japan in the 20th century and led the country into World War II. During the postwar Allied Occupation of Japan, many social and economic reforms were enacted to give all Japanese greater equality. See also AINU; BURAKUMIN; BUSHIDO; CLANS; CONFUCIANISM; CONSTITUTION OF 1947; DAIMYO; DUTY AND FEELINGS; EMPEROR; FEUDALISM; HEIAN ERA; HORSE-RIDER THEORY; IMPERIAL HOUSEHOLD; JOMON ERA; KOFUN ERA; KOKU; MEIJI RESTORATION OF 1868; MINORITIES IN JAPAN; OCCUPATION OF JAPAN; RICE; SAMURAI; TOKUGAWA SHOGUNATE; TOWNSPEOPLE; YAMATO.

CLASSICAL LITERATURE See DIARIES; GENJI, THE TALE OF; HEIKE, THE TALE OF THE; ISE, TALES OF; KOKINSHU; MANYOSHU; MONOGATARI; NOVELS; POETRY; SEI SHONAGON; RENGA; TANKA; WAKA.

CLAVELL, JAMES (author of *Shogun*) See ADAMS, WILLIAM; HOSOKAWA GRACIA; SHOGUN.

CLEAN GOVERNMENT PARTY (Komeito) A party that originated as the political wing of Soka Gakkai (Value Creation Society), the lay organization of Nichiren Shoshu, a sect of the Buddhist religion. Soka Gakkai, one of the largest postwar religions in Japan, established a League for Clean Government in 1962. Two years later the Komeito, usually translated as Clean Government Party, became a full-scale political party. It is now the second largest opposition party in Japan, after the Japan Socialist Party (Nihon Shakaito; abbreviated JSP).

The Komeito's pragmatic social welfare platform has addressed the needs of young, lower-class urban factory workers who do not belong to the privileged labor union and salaryman groups given lifetime employment by large corporations. The Komeito supports free enterprise but calls for more equitable distribution of wealth by Japanese business. It also advocates Japanese neutrality in foreign affairs and a nuclear-free zone in the Asian-Pacific region. Although the Komeito became independent from Soka Gakkai in 1970, the general Japanese public tends to distrust the party's centralized authoritarian control. In 1979 the Komeito had 142,000 registered members. It publishes a daily newspaper, *Komei shimbun,* and two monthly journals, *Komeo gurafu* and *Komei.* See also ELECTIONS; JAPAN SOCIALIST PARTY; POLITICAL PARTIES; NICHIREN SECT OF BUDDHISM; SOKA GAKKAI.

CLIMATE OF JAPAN Japanese climatic conditions are generally temperate but vary widely between the northernmost island of Hokkaido and the southernmost Ryukyu Island chain (Okinawa Prefecture). Japan's climatic variations are roughly the same as those of the east coast of North America, from Nova Scotia to Georgia. However, Japan is very humid and has more rainfall than other countries in the temperate zone, averaging 1600 mm. (64 in.) annually. The central Japanese islands of Honshu and Shikoku experience four distinct seasons, although the Inland Sea gives Shikoku milder weather. Hokkaido and the mountainous regions of northwest Honshu have long, cold winters with heavy snowfall brought by winds from Siberia and Mongolia that pick up moisture over the Sea of Japan. The eastern, or Pacific Ocean, side of Japan enjoys a milder climate and more annual sunshine. To the south, Kyushu Island and the Ryukyu Islands are subtropical. The climate of Japan is affected by the continent of Asia to its west and by ocean currents that flow around the islands. The Black Current (Kuroshio) flows up the eastern side of the country, warming it as far north as Tokyo. A smaller branch, the Tsushima Current, flows up the Sea of Japan on the western side. The Parent Current (Oyashio) flows south along the northern Pacific side of Japan, cooling the coastal areas. These cold waters have abundant plankton, which draw fish, and the meeting point of the Black and Parent Currents is the center of Japanese commercial fishing.

Since ancient times, Japanese art and culture have been influenced by the seasonal changes. The traditional year revolves around flower viewing and planting festivals in the spring, summer festivals along riverbanks, autumn harvest festivals, and the New Year festival that marks the end of winter and the beginning of spring. Plants and trees that grow in this climate, such as bamboo, cherry, maple, pine and plum trees, are important symbols in Japanese art and religion. The rainy climate also promotes the cultivation of rice, the staple of the Japanese diet.

Spring *(haru)* in Japan brings plum and cherry blossoms, and everyone follows the "cherry blossom front" *(sakura zensen)* as it moves northward. The rainy season *(tsuyu;* also called "plum rain," *bai-u,* for the plums that ripen at this time) comes in mid-June to mid-July, followed by a hot, humid summer *(manatsu).* The period from the end of August through mid-September brings the typhoon season, when violent storms similar to hurricanes strike the Japanese islands, particularly the Ryukyus. Autumn *(aki)* has clear weather and is the favorite traveling season in Japan, especially for viewing the red maple leaves *(momiji).* Winter *(fuyu)* comes from December through March and brings much snow north of Tokyo, but little snow south of it. The temperature in Tokyo usually stays above freezing. See also AGRICULTURE; CALENDAR; FESTIVALS; GEOGRAPHY OF JAPAN; INLAND SEA; RAIN; RICE PLANTING AND HARVESTING FESTIVALS; SEA OF JAPAN; SNOW; TYPHOON.

CLIQUE *(batsu)* The *batsu* system is a continuation of traditional Japanese political and social networks. The leader of a *batsu* provides assistance to members, who repay him by their loyalty and are also obligated to assist each other. Employment, promotion, and the awarding of business and political favors are commonly controlled by *batsu.* There may also be small cliques or factions *(ha)* within larger *batsu.* A *mombatsu* is a clique based on family connections, and in addition to blood relatives, includes subordinates not related by blood. *Keibatsu,* a subcategory of *mombatsu,* are cliques formed by marriage alliances at the highest level of society in order to exercise political or economic power; this practice dates back to ancient times in Japan. For example, the Fujiwara clan became dominant by marrying its daughters to members of the imperial court in the Heian Era (794–1185). During the feudal era, marriage alliances were made among warring *daimyo* families for political and military gains. In the modern era, Japanese politicians and business leaders are often related through similar networks. *Gakubatsu* are cliques whose members attended the same university. Top Japanese universities select almost all of their faculty members from their own graduates. Tokyo University graduates, particularly those who studied with the Faculty of Law, hold the most important positions in the Japanese government, especially in the powerful ministries of Finance, Foreign Affairs and Home Affairs. *Hambatsu* are factions within political parties and trade unions organized around leading members. *Chihobatsu* or *kyodobatsu* are factions whose members come from the same prefecture or local area and who control a company or other organization. Members of *hambatsu* from Satsuma and Choshu Provinces dominated the Meiji government (1868–1912), including the Imperial Japanese Army and Navy, and brought Japan from the feudal into the modern, industrialized era. *Gumbatsu*, or military cliques, gained influence over the government and became most powerful in Japan during World War II, when the army and navy comprised competing *batsu*. *Zaibatsu*, financial conglomerates in the late 19th and early 20th centuries, were each controlled by a family, such as Mitsui. Because of their connections with the militaristic government, the *zaibatsu* were dissolved by Occupation authorities after World War II. Large corporate groupings still control the Japanese economy, but are now generally called enterprise groups. See also CLAN; CORPORATIONS; DUTY AND FEELINGS; FACTIONS, POLITICAL; FAMILY; FINANCIAL WORLD; FUJIWARA CLAN; IMPERIAL JAPANESE ARMY AND NAVY; MARRIAGE; MEIJI RESTORATION OF 1868; OBLIGATION; UNIVERSITIES; ZAIBATSU.

CLOISONNE (*shippo*, "seven precious stones") A decorative technique by which enamel is applied to a metal base and baked to create designs. The French term "cloisonne" refers to the "cells" (*cloisons*) that are made by attaching thin strips of metal or wires to a metal base. Molten colored enamels are poured into these cells. Then the decorated metal is fired in a kiln to "bake" the enamels, after which it is ground and polished to produce a smooth surface. The cells can also be created by the techniques of carving them out of solid metal (champleve), hammering them from sheet metal (repousse), or casting. In Japan, the oldest object decorated with enameled patterns, a small yellow and white plaque, was found in a tomb mound that dates back to the Asuka Era (late sixth century–710). There is also a cloisonne mirror in the Shosoin Treasure House at Nara, decorated with a lotus flower, that may date from the eighth century. Some cloisonne objects remain from the Heian Era (794–1185), but between that time and the 15th century there is no evidence of cloisonne in Japan. Only in the 17th century did cloisonne become a widely used Japanese decorative technique, and then mainly for architectural features such as doorpulls on sliding screens

and nail covers on wooden rafters. These can be seen at the Katsura Detached Palace and the Shugakuin Detached Palace. Cloisonne was also used to make fittings for swords and wooden chests, as well as objects necessary for calligraphy. One of the finest cloisonne craftsmen in Japan was Hirata Narikado (1644–1757), who ran a large studio where may apprentices learned this technique. Namikawa Sosuke (1847–1910) invented a method of creating cloisonne without separating the colored enamels by metal strips; this is called lineless cloisonne (*musen shippo*). Cloisonne continues to be produced in Japan, especially as decorative objects such as vases and plates. See also KATSURA DETACHED PALACE; METALWORK; SHOSOIN; SHUGAKUIN DETACHED PALACE; TOMB MOUND.

CLOSING OF JAPAN See CHRISTIANITY IN JAPAN; DEJIMA; DUTCH IN JAPAN; PERRY, MATTHEW CALBRAITH; PORTUGUESE IN JAPAN; SECLUSION, NATIONAL; TOKUGAWA SHOGUNATE.

CLOTHING (*wafuku*) Native Japanese clothing is termed *wafuku*, as distinct from *yofuku*, Western-style clothing. The traditional Japanese kimono, consisting of straight panels of cloth sewn together, including panels for the sleeves, is wrapped around the body and tied with an *obi* (sash). The left side is always folded over the right, except on dead bodies. Both women and men wear kimono. The word *kimono*, which originally meant "garment," consists of the words *mono*, "thing," and *ki*, from the verb *kiru*, "to wear." The type of robe commonly known as a kimono is more properly called *kosode* ("small-sleeved garment"). The kimono is practical for the traditional Japanese life-style, where people kneel on straw floor mats (*tatami*).

Japanese clothing styles and techniques for weaving and dyeing textiles were adapted from the Asian mainland, mainly China, Korea and Mongolia. Ancient Japanese garments were worn in two parts, a jacket and a divided skirt (*hakama* or *mo*). During the Heian Era (794–1185), noblemen wore an upper robe (*noshi*), a cap (*eboshi*) and divided trousers (*sashinuki*) for everyday. Ceremonial dress (*sokutai*) consisted of divided trousers, a robe (*ho*), a trailing panel of cloth (*shitagasane*) and a cap (*kammuri*). This costume is still worn by Shinto priests for religious rituals and by members of the imperial court for ceremonies at the Imperial Palace. The kimono was adapted by Nara Era (710–794) court ladies from clothing of Tang (T'ang) dynasty (618–906) China but made into a distinctly Japanese style, known as "layered robes" (*kasane-gi*). Ladies of the Heian court wore a formal kimono known as "12 unlined robes" (*juni hitoe*), that is, 12 layers of trailing robes in coordinated but contrasting colors (*kasane no irome*, "color combinations of layered robes"), tied with a narrow cord. Beneath the robes they wore an under-kimono and *hakama*.

Not all Japanese clothing consists of robes. Members of the peasant class who work the land, men and women alike, have always worn simple loose shirts or jackets (*hippari* or *happi* coat) and baggy trousers (*monpei*), made from panels of plant fibers such as hemp or cotton and usually dyed with blue indigo. In ancient times, only the aristocrats wore silk. Peasants have also traditionally worn rain capes, hats, sandals and other garments made of straw.

When the samurai class ruled Japan starting with the Kamakura Shogunate (1185–1333), samurai women did not wear 12-layered garments, but wore from one to three robes with a small *obi* around the hips. This style, known as "single-layer wear" (*hitoe-gi*) was more suited to an active life and to the samurai code of simplicity and frugality. The single-layer kimono evolved into the *kosode* (small sleeves), as a popularization of costumes from Noh drama, which originated in the 14th century. The *kosode* is worn by both women and men. It had been an undergarment, but now became the main garment, and was worn over *hakama*. Court women also wore *kosode*, but covered them with large trailing robes, known as *uchikake*, for formal occasions. These robes were later worn by women of other classes as well and are still worn by Japanese brides. While traveling, samurai women covered their faces with an umbrella-like headdress hung with cloth (*ichimegasa*).

Peasants began wearing short coats (*doboku*), which were adopted by upper-class men in the Muromachi Era (1333–1568). Samurai wore *hakama* with a short jacket, adapted from peasant work clothes, known as *hitatare* and later as *daimon*. In battle they wore lacquered suits of armor (*yoroi*). A sleeveless upper garment with large shoulders, known as a *kataginu*, was later adopted from peasants by samurai and worn over kimono, an outfit known as the *kamishimo*. This was combined with *hakama* to form the ceremonial costume for high-ranking samurai, which was later adopted by scholars and wealthy merchants.

Clothing became very colorful in the Azuchi-Momoyama Era (1568–1600) and the Edo Era (1600–1868), as the wealthy merchant class and courtesans and geisha in pleasure quarters ignored the sumptuary laws frequently passed by the Tokugawa Shogunate. The style of dress was simplified to two layers, which are still worn today, the under-kimono (*nagajuban*) and kimono. Narrow *obi* were worn until well into the Edo Era, then gradually became wider, influenced by Kabuki actors who played women's roles (*onnagata*). Bows were tied in the back in many different styles, and *obi* became as elaborate in color and design as kimono. Heavy weaves were introduced from China, such as *kinran* and *ginran* (gold and silver brocade). By the end of the Edo Era, women's kimono became tighter, more tubular in appearance, and no longer flowed on the floor. This is the style of kimono worn today. The brightly decorated, long-sleeved *furisode* (swinging sleeve) style of kimono evolved for young unmarried women; these are still worn at the New Year Festival and on Adults' Day. Hairstyles were also developed to complement the kimono. Japanese women wore long, straight hair gathered in back until the Edo Era, but then began to pile their hair elaborately on the head, keeping the neck and collar free. A kimono is worn with white split-toed socks (*tabi*) and thonged sandals (*zori*). Many sashes are used to hold the foundation layer, under-kimono, and kimono in place. Most modern Japanese women do not wear kimono except for special occasions, such as New Year and weddings. They usually have a black kimono with family crests (*mon*) that is worn on very formal occasions. Men's kimono are in solid dark colors and worn with a narrow brocade *obi* tied in a flat knot in the back. Japanese men rarely wear kimono today except at their own weddings. Cotton robes similar to kimono, known as *yukata*, are worn at home as bathrobes, and at summer festivals and resorts. The Japanese began wearing Western clothing during the Meiji Era (1868–1912) when Japan became modernized. Contemporary Japanese fashion designers have adapted traditional clothing techniques into Western styles. See also ARMOR; CLASS STRUCTURE; COURTESAN; CREST; EDO ERA; FASHION DESIGNERS; FOOTWEAR; GEISHA; HAIRSTYLES; HAKAMA; HAORI; HAPPI COAT; HEADWEAR; HEIAN ERA; HEMP; INDIGO; KABUKI; KASURI; KIMONO; NEW YEAR FESTIVAL; NISHIJIN; NOH DRAMA; OBI; SAMURAI; STRAW WARE; TEXTILES; WEDDING; YUKATA; YUZEN DYEING.

COFFEE SHOPS (*kissaten*) Cafes serving drinks and light food where people can meet with friends or conduct business. Coffee and tea in coffee shops are fairly expensive and served in single cups with no refills, but customers can stay as long as they wish. Many cafes offer a low-priced breakfast ("morning service") that includes a boiled egg, toast and butter, and coffee or tea. A coffee shop usually has a rack of newspapers, magazines and comic books, which customers are free to read as long as they want. Some even have video games built into the tables. A number of coffee shops specialize in certain types of recorded music, such as rock, classical or jazz, and will play customers' requests. Traditional tea rooms, known as *kammikissa*, serve Japanese green tea with various kinds of Japanese-style sweets (*wagashi*) and desserts of fruit, ice cream, and so forth. Women frequent traditional cafes most often. See also COMIC BOOKS; MAGAZINES; NEWSPAPERS; TEA; SWEETS.

COLLEGES See EDUCATION SYSTEM; UNIVERSITIES.

COMBS AND HAIR ORNAMENTS (*kushi* and *kanzashi*) Combs (*kushi*) were introduced into Japan from China in ancient times. They had long teeth to hold the hair in place. In Japan, combs came to be used as symbols of a woman's married status. During the medieval era (13th to 16th centuries), Japanese combs were beautifully decorated with gold lacquer and mother-of-pearl inlays. During the Edo Era (1600–1868), women's hairstyles became very elaborate, and combs were created in many materials and designs to complement hairstyles. In addition to wood, combs also were made of bamboo, ivory, tortoise shell and metal. Combs were regarded as charms that protected the honor and virtue of the women who wore them, and even today, the Japanese believe it is bad luck to pick up a comb that someone else lost or to give a comb as a gift to another person.

Women also traditionally decorated their hair with ornaments on long straight metal pins (*kanzashi*). The ornaments were made of many different materials, such as lacquer, coral, metal, cloth and gold paper, and many of them depicted flowers. Several of these pins could be placed into the hairdo in front of a decorative comb. A special type of double-sided hairpin known as a *kogai* was also worn. Styles of combs and ornaments and ways of wearing them reflected a woman's age and social position. An aristocratic Japanese woman's comb was traditionally marked with her family crest *(mon)*. Women entertainers and courtesans wore the most elaborate accessories. When Japanese women began changing to simpler Western hairstyles in the Meiji Era (1868–1912), hair ornaments became less popular. Today there are only four Japanese shops that sell traditional handmade wooden combs, two in Tokyo and two in Kyoto. Most combs are crafted of camellia wood *(tsubaki)* or boxwood *(tsuge)*, which is more expensive. Functional combs used for arranging the hair are known as *tokigushi no sashiara*. Decoratives combs, known as *sashi-gushi*, have two styles: a long comb like a hairpin, and a round comb shaped like a half moon. See also COURTESAN; CREST; HAIRSTYLES; LACQUER WARE.

COMIC BOOKS *(manga)* Comics, or *manga* ("random sketches"), go back to ancient times in Japan. Comic caricatures have been found in the Shosoin, an eighth-century treasure house, and on the walls and ceilings of Buddhist temples from the Heian Era (794–1185). Heian aristocrats liked to make comic drawings *(oko-e)*, and picture scrolls from the time satirize humans by depicting animals acting like people. The Buddhist religion spread throughout Japan during the Kamakura Era (1185–1333) with the aid of scrolls, especially those portraying human suffering and ghosts. Popular culture of the Edo Era (1600–1868) preferred works of exaggeration and humor, such as woodblock prints *(hanga)* showing Kabuki actors and amusing ink paintings *(sumi-e)* by Zen Buddhist monks Hakuin (1686–1769) and Sengai Gibon (1750–1837). Western influences starting in the Meiji Era (1868–1912) stimulated Japanese comic artists, and cartoons and comic strips were published in newspapers. During the Depression, comics took a slant toward the grotesque and erotic, and in the 1930s they reflected rising Japanese militarism. American influences during the Allied Occupation of Japan after World War II led to publication of mass-market comic magazines. Today these magazines are published weekly, biweekly and monthly for millions of readers in four markets: boys, girls, young people and adults. Women's magazines also publish comics in serial form. Many businessmen read comic books or magazines, which frequently portray violence, while commuting on trains and subways. Recently, comics have even been used to explain serious topics, such as the Japanese economy and patent laws. Contemporary serious comic artists term their work *gekiga*, "drama comics" or "dramatic pictures." See also BOOKS AND BOOKSTORES; HAKUIN; INK PAINTING; MAGAZINES; SCROLLS; SENGAI GIBON; WOODBLOCK PRINTS.

COMMUNICATIONS See BROADCASTING; JAPAN BROADCASTING COMPANY; MAGAZINES; NEWSPAPERS; NIPPON TELEGRAPH AND TELEPHONE CORPORATION; TELECOMMUNICATIONS SYSTEM.

COMMUNIST PARTY See JAPAN COMMUNIST PARTY.

COMPANIES See CORPORATIONS; EMPLOYMENT; JOINT-VENTURE CORPORATION; TRADING COMPANY, GENERAL.

COMPUTER INDUSTRY Japanese companies began manufacturing computers in the late 1950s, about a decade after American companies. IBM long had a near monopoly in the world market, and IBM Japan, a wholly owned subsidiary of the American parent, long dominated the Japanese market, which has been the world's second largest computer market, next to the United States. The Japanese computer industry developed rapidly by capturing Japan's domestic market from IBM and because of government assistance in building up the new industry. Starting in the 1960s, Japanese companies made technical assistance and licensing agreements with American companies. In the early 1970s American companies controlled 94% of the world market, and Japanese companies only 2%. By 1980 the Japanese computer industry was second only to that of the United States. The Ministry of International Trade and Industry (MITI) set the goal of increasing computer exports by 30% per year through 1985.

There are six major Japanese computer producers: Fujitsu, Ltd.; Hitachi, Ltd.; Mitsubishi Electric Corporation; Nippon Electric Company, Ltd. (NEC); Oki Electric Industry Co., Ltd.; and Toshiba Corporation. In 1979 Fujitsu, the largest Japanese computer company, surpassed IBM in the Japanese market. In 1989 Toshiba and Matsushita joined Fujitsu, NEC and Hitachi among the top 20 revenue-makers in information systems and services industries. Moreover, Fujitsu moved into second place behind the American corporation IBM by acquiring Internatijonal Computers, a British company. In the 1970s, the Japanese government organized the six largest computer companies into three groups, to fund and oversee their research and development of a high performance computer, as well as minicomputers and peripheral equipment. MITI established several priority projects, such as the VLSI (very large scale integrated) circuit research and development projects (1976–1979) and the recent Fifth–Generation artificial intelligence computer project. In 1978 the Special Measures Law Concerning Promotion of the Specialized Machine and Information Industry was passed to enhance Japanese government assistance to the computer industry. Until 1981, government procurement policy also excluded most foreign computers and software.

Japan has emphasized computers and computer technology because they are a key factor for competitiveness in many other industries. The Japanese automobile and other industries have succeeded in large part because of automated assembly lines. The computer industry, a high-tech field, does not require the importation of many raw materials, and computers are important export products.

Japanese companies have lagged in the development of software but have attempted to improve the situation by making IBM-compatible machines, and by establishing software subsidiaries and joint ventures with American companies. Japan has been extremely successful in designing and manufacturing semiconductors, silicon circuits (integrated circuits, or microchips) that are the basic components of computers. Technology for manufacturing supercomputers is still dominated by an American company, Cray Research Inc., and deemed critical to national security by the U.S. Defense Department. However, Hitachi recently signed a cross-licensing agreement with Cray in hopes of improving its marketing efforts in the United States. Rapid progress has been made in telephone switching systems, cable carrier communication, microwave communication systems and digitalization. Computer games made by Nintendo and other Japanese companies are popular worldwide. See also AUTOMOBILE INDUSTRY; ELECTRONICS INDUSTRY; FIFTH-GENERATION ADVANCED COMPUTER SYSTEMS; MINISTRY OF INTERNATIONAL TRADE AND INDUSTRY; NIPPON TELEGRAPH AND TELEPHONE CORPORATION; RESEARCH AND DEVELOPMENT; ROBOTS AND ROBOTICS; SEMICONDUCTOR INDUSTRY; TELECOMMUNICATIONS SYSTEM.

CONFUCIANISM   A set of ethical principles introduced into Japan from China with many other aspects of Chinese culture between the sixth and eighth centuries A.D. Confucianism, attributed to the Chinese philosopher Confucius (Kung Fu Tzu; c. 551–479 B.C.), was the political and ethical foundation of the Chinese bureaucratic model of government later introduced into Japan. Legal principles, a system of examinations to choose civil servants and other structures of government were all modeled on Confucian principles. The Five Classics of Confucianism were studied by members of the Japanese aristocratic class. The Seventeen-Article Constitution promulgated by Prince Shotoku (Shotoku Taishi; 574–622) took ideas from the *Analects* of Confucius.

The basic concept of Confucianism is social harmony, which is created through the loyalty of the people to their ruler, whose authority is mandated from heaven. Another basic concept is filial piety, respect for one's parents and reverence for one's ancestors. The principles of loyalty and filial piety remain fundamental in Japanese culture.

A revival and reinterpretation of Confucian thought known as Neo-Confucianism, developed in Sung (Song) dynasty (960–1272) China, was used by the Tokugawa Shogunate (1603–1867) to strictly enforce social hierarchy. Neo-Confucian thought was elaborated upon by the Japanese scholar Hayashi Razan (1583–1657) and his followers. Neo-Confucianism teaches that social harmony is created by the obedience of inferiors to superiors in all human relationships, especially those of subject and ruler, and child and parent. This ideology was combined with the traditional virtues of the ruling samurai (warrior) class to form a code of conduct known as *bushido* (the "way of the warrior"), which helped transform samurai from feudal fighters into peaceful bureaucrats based on the Chinese model of the scholar-bureaucrat. Career bureaucrats in the Tokugawa government were educated at private schools that taught Chinese classical texts through the study of Neo-Confucian commentaries. Confucian ideas were used to unify Japan and became deeply rooted in the behavior of all classes of Japanese people. Its principles were also incorporated into

State Shinto, an indeology used to inspire nationalism in the Japanese prior to World War II. See also BUSHIDO; CHINA AND JAPAN; FILIAL PIETY; HAYASHI RAZAN; LOYALTY; SAMURAI; SHOTOKU, PRINCE; STATE SHINTO; TOKUGAWA SHOGUNATE.

CONSTITUTION DAY (May 3) See HOLIDAYS, NATIONAL.

CONSTITUTION, MEIJI (1889) (Meiji Kempo)   The constitution of Japan, prepared by leaders of the Meiji government (1868–1912), which remained in effect from 1889 until the present constitution was promulgated in 1947. The Meiji Constitution, more properly known as the Constitution of the Empire of Japan (Dai Nihon Teikoku Kempo), was modeled on the Prussian constitution but incorporated many Confucian concepts. It vested sovereignty in the Japanese emperor, who was declared to be "sacred and inviolable," and was used by the Meiji elite to solidify the institutions they developed after 1868. This was influenced by the notion of *kokutai,* the unique national essence of Japan headed by the emperor who is descended from the Sun Goddess Amaterasu o Mikami. The emperor was the source of legitimacy, and the constitution sanctioned the power already being exercised by the Meiji bureaucracy. The constitution also established a centralized executive body, with powers invested in the institution of the emperor. It also established an Imperial Diet, a legislature with two houses: the appointed House of Peers (upper house) and the elected House of Representatives (lower house). The constitution also provided for a modern judicial system, a system for government financing and taxation, and a statement of the rights and duties of citizens. The greatest power was not given to the legislature, but was concentrated in the executive branch of government, which claimed to act in the name of the emperor. The most powerful institutions were the cabinet of the prime minister, the highest levels of the civil and military bureaucracy, the Privy Council and the *genro* ("elder statesmen"), a body of senior Meiji leaders. The constitution did not specify how members of these bodies were to be chosen or what their responsibilities were. Since it placed the military as well as the civil government directly under the emperor, the military was able to increase its power by claiming that is represented the emperor. Despite the limitations of the Meiji Constitution, it is significant as the first constitutional form of government adopted by an Asian country. See also CABINET; PRIME MINISTER'S; CONFUCIANISM; CONSTITUTION OF 1947; DIET; EMPEROR; GENRO; KOKUTAI; MEIJI RESTORATION OF 1868; PRIME MINISTER.

CONSTITUTION OF 1947 (Nihonkoku Kempo)   The present constitution of Japan, promulgated in May 1947, replaced the Constitution of the Empire of Japan (Dai Nihon Teikoku Kempo, also known as the Meiji Constitution, or Meiji Kempo, of 1889). The 1947 constitution was prepared and enacted during the Allied occupation of Japan (1945–1952) following Japan's defeat in World War II. Often considered a foreign constitution by Japanese, it contains elements insisted upon by U.S. General Douglas MacArthur (1880–1964), the Supreme Commander for the

Allied Powers (SCAP) during the occupation, to demilitarize Japan and reform it along the lines of Western democracies. The Japanese emperor, in whom sovereignty was vested by the Meiji Constitution, is retained by the new constitution only as "the symbol of the State and of the unity of the people." Sovereignty is transferred from the emperor to the Japanese people.

The Meiji Constitution had established a two-chamber Imperial Diet (Parliament) subordinate to the emperor, with an appointive House of Peers as the upper house. The 1947 constitution abolished the House of Peers and created a popularly elected two-chamber National Diet as the highest organ of Japanese government. The constitution entrusts executive power to a cabinet formed by the majority political party in the Diet and responsible to the Diet. The courts are made independent of other branches of government, and the Supreme Court is given the power to review the Constitution. The constitution also strengthens local government by creating local elective assemblies.

Thirty-one articles of the constitution have to do with civil liberties, which are declared "eternal and inviolate." women are given full equality with men; labor is permitted to organize; and freedom of religion is guaranteed. The constitution prohibits the Japanese government from engaging in any religious activity, a specific prohibition of the nationalistic cult of State Shinto, which had been abolished after the war.

The most controversial aspect of the 1947 constitution is Article 9, the Renunciation of War. The article's first paragraph states that the Japanese people "forever renounce war as a sovereign right of the nation" and reject the "threat or use of force as a means of settling international disputes." The second paragraph states that "land, sea, and air forces, as well as other war potential will never be maintained." However, the Japanese government was later permitted to establish a military force for internal security, known as the Self-Defense Forces (SDF; Jietai).

The constitution has been controversial in Japan ever since it was enacted. Some Japanese argue that it was an American document imposed on the defeated country and should be revised to more truly reflect Japanese values. In 1956 an Investigation Commission on the Constitution was established to consider revision of the constitution, and eight years later it concluded that Article 9 should be modified and provisions should be added to strengthen the authority of the central government. The constitution can be amended by a minimum two-thirds vote in both houses of the Diet, upon which the proposed amendment is to be voted by the Japanese people in a referendum. However, despite opposition of right-wing political groups to Article 9 and other points, the constitution has not been revised to date, largely because the majority of the Japanese people support it. See also CABINET, PRIME MINISTER'S; CONSTITUTION, MEIJI (1889); DIET; ELECTIONS; EMPEROR; OCCUPATION OF JAPAN; PRIME MINISTER; SELF-DEFENSE FORCES; SUPREME COMMANDER FOR THE ALLIED POWERS.

CONSUMER ELECTRONICS See AKIHABARA; CAMERAS AND PHOTOGRAPHY; COMPUTER INDUSTRY; ELECTRONICS INDUSTRY.

COOKING (ryori) Japanese cooking methods use fresh seasonal ingredients and prepare them lightly to preserve their original flavor as much as possible. The main ingredients in Japanese cooking are rice, seafood and vegetables. Raw fish has always been an important part of the Japanese diet. Soybeans are processed to make many staple foods, including tofu (bean curd) and the two basic flavoring agents, soy sauce and miso (fermented soybean paste). Some other popular seasonings are wasabi (a paste of Japanese horseradish), mirin (sweetened rice wine), vinegar, sake (rice wine), ginger and edible seaweeds. Foods are often simmered in dashi, a broth made with bonito fish and kelp (a kind of seaweed).

There are three types of classical Japanese cooking: honzen ryori, kaiseki ryori, and chakaiseki ryori. Honzen ryori, or formal banquet dishes, date back to aristocratic meals of the Heian Era (794–1185). They are now served only on occasions such as wedding and funeral banquets, but have widely influenced Japanese cuisine. Kaiseki ryori are special dishes served at sake parties, which originated with banquets for poets in the 19th century. Chakaiseki ryori are special dishes served at tea ceremonies, which were formalized in the 16th century, to complement the flavor of thick green ceremonial tea. There are several other types of Japanese cooking. Kyodo ryori are dishes special to particular regions of Japan. Gyoji ryori are foods served at annual events, especially at New Year, Doll Festival, Children's Day Festival, Bon Festival, and Moon Viewing Festival. Shojin ryori are vegetarian dishes developed in light of Buddhism's restrictions on consumption of animal foods. This type of cooking uses soybean products, particularly tofu, in creative ways.

The most basic Japanese meal comprises miso soup, rice and pickles. The traditional formula for cooking is "soup and three" (ichiju sansai): a soup and three main dishes prepared with various techniques, such as fresh, uncooked fish (sashimi), a grilled dish (yakimono) and a simmered dish (nimono). These are always followed by white rice (gohan), pickles (tsukemono) and tea (cha). Fresh fruit may conclude a meal.

A Japanese meal is served on a variety of dishes rather than on one patterned set. The food is prepared in many small portions that can be eaten with chopsticks. Except for formal banquets, dishes are usually set out all at once rather than in separate courses. A Japanese meal was traditionally placed on individual small low tables (zen), as many as five per person; these are still used at formal banquets. A complete Japanese banquet contains dishes prepared with all the basic methods of Japanese cooking, and is served in three sections. The first section includes small appetizers (zensai), clear soup (suimono) and fresh raw fish (sashimi). The middle section includes grilled foods (yakimono), steamed foods (mushimono), simmered or stewed foods (nimono) and deep-fried foods (agemono). Or these four dishes may be replaced by a one-pot hot dish (nabemono). Then comes a salad that has a vinegar marinade (sunomono) or a dressing (aemono). At the end are served rice, miso soup, pickles and tea. A proper Japanese meal requires a variety of ingredients and cooking techniques.

It is important to carefully mix flavors, colors and textures, and the visual appeal of Japanese food is just as important as the taste. Some foreign dishes such as noodles, fried pork and curried beef have been adapted by the Japanese, especially for quick meals. See also BON FESTIVAL; CHILDREN'S DAY FESTIVAL; CHOPSTICKS; KNIVES; DOLL FESTIVAL; FOOD STALLS; GARNISHES FOR FOOD; KAISEKI; KNIVES; MOON-VIEWING FESTIVAL; NEW YEAR FESTIVAL; RESTAURANTS; SEASONING FOR FOOD; TEA CEREMONY; NAMES OF INDIVIDUAL DISHES AND INGREDIENTS.

CORD, BRAIDED (kumihimo)

The Japanese use long, colorful cords made of four or more strands of silk or other fibers, such as gold or silver threads, for a variety of purposes. Hundreds of strands can be braided together, with each strand consisting of 20 to 200 or more threads. Kumihimo is the term for a braided cord and also for the technique of braiding. A cord is braided by unwinding fiber strands of different colors from weighted bobbins on a small wooden frame, and crossing the strands in a certain order to produce the desired pattern. This is a very time-consuming process. There are hundreds of ways to intertwine the strands to create flat or round braided cords. A short tassel of unbraided threads is left on both ends of the cord.

Braided cords have been used in Japan since ancient times. During the Jomon Era (c. 10,000–c. 300 B.C.), braided strands were pressed into pottery to make decorative patterns. Beautiful silk braided cords are preserved in Buddhist temples and in the eighth-century Shosoin (Imperial Storehouse) in Nara. Such cords have been used for decorative purposes and to indicate social status, as well as to bind, fasten and hang objects. Their beauty is enhanced by tying them into decorative knots. Braided cords were used on banners, priests' robes and cases for amulets. Samurai wore armor (yoroi) made from lacquered metal strips laced together and trimmed with braided silk cords. Cords known as sageo were used to decorate samurai swords. Cords were also attached to screens, chests, mirrors, hanging scrolls and screens, musical instruments and masks. A braided silk cord known as an obi-jime is tied around the obi (sash) of a woman's kimono. A haori-jime is a short braided silk cord that fastens haori, short jackets worn over kimono. The art of tying braids into elegant knots of various shapes is highly valued in Japan. Different knots can symbolize such things as social status, good or bad fortune, or gender. Special knots are also tied on wrapped gifts. See also ARMOR; HAORI; KIMONO; OBI; SILK; SWORD; WRAPPING.

CORMORANTS, FISHING WITH (ukai)

A unique traditional method of fishing using long-necked birds called cormorants, which dive into the water to catch fish. The cormorants are tied to ropes about 10 feet long, which are held by the fishermen. The birds dive underwater and catch the fish, which they are prevented from swallowing by neck rings. When they surface, the fishermen pull the birds back into the boat, and they release their catch. This method was practiced in Japan as far back as the seventh century A.D., as recorded in documents from that time. However, today it takes place mainly on the Nagara River (Nagaragawa) in Gifu Prefecture on central Honshu Island. Each night from May to October, except when there is a full moon or after a storm, fishermen sail up the river from Gifu City in small wooden boats. Flaming torches hanging on the front of the boats lure small sweetfish, called ayu, and other river fish such as carp and minnows. Each boat holds four men: two to pole the boat and two to work the cormorants, as many as eighteen birds to a boat. Many tourists in boats watch this colorful method of fishing while enjoying picnic meals and sake. See also FISH AND FISHING INDUSTRY; SAKE.

CORPORATIONS (kaisha)

The most common type of Japanese corporation is the joint-stock company (kabushiki kaisha). There are also unlimited partnership companies (gomei kaisha), limited partnership companies (goshu kaisha) and limited liability companies (yugen kaisha). Most small businesses are still owned by individuals but are often incorporated as joint-stock companies. A joint-stock company is formed by at least seven promoters, and is managed by a board of directors, statutory auditors and a general meeting of stockholders.

There are more than a million corporations in Japan, with most having fewer than 5,000 employees. The 300 or so largest firms account for nearly 20% of all regular employees. A large corporate conglomerate may have as many as 100 subsidiaries and even more subcontractors.

Prior to World War II, the Japanese economy was dominated by large financial combines known as zaibatsu. The government dissolved them after the war, instituted anti-monopoly legislation and permitted labor unions to organize, all in order to establish a competitive free-market system. However, large corporate groups have survived and are central to the Japanese corporate system. Known as enterprise groups (keiretsu), they include several companies that are descendants of prewar zaibatsu (such as Mitsubishi, Mitsui and Sumitomo) and companies formed around major commercial banks (Fuyo, Sanwa and Dai-Ichi Kangyo, or DKB). The large companies have general trading companies (sogo shosha) that coordinate their financing, production, sales, shipping and marketing. A third type of corporate group includes companies centered around a major industrial manufacturer, such as automobile producers. Members of such a group are often subsidiaries, affiliates or subcontractors that build components for their parent companies.

Individual stockholders hold less than a third of the assets of Japanese companies, with banks and other businesses holding more than 60%. The corporations thus have little public accountability, and their stockholder meetings are often purely formal. The typical Japanese corporate strategy is to get long-term market share for their products rather than short-term financial returns for stockholders.

Japanese management practice stresses employee participation, consensus in decision making, loyalty to the company and a hierarchical system based on seniority. The lowest level of a corporate hierarchy is the section (or occasionally, subsection), which generally has 8–20 employees, including managers and clerks or production

A unique method of catching fish at night using cormorants. The birds have rings placed on their necks to prevent them from swallowing the fish.

workers. The section functions as a team under the leadership of a section chief, who is highly respected and serves as a father figure. Several sections form a department, with large corporations grouping departments into divisions. Corporate directors above the rank of managing director form the executive committee, the main decision-making body of a corporation. However, the decision-making process often works from the bottom up, a system known as *ringi seido.* Lower-level managers in sections often take the initiative in gathering information on company problems and suggesting ways to resolve them. Interoffice memoranda *(ringisho)* from managers are sent up to departments, where they are approved or amended, and then passed on to top managers for final decisions.

There are close relationships between corporate and political and bureaucratic leaders, which have been dubbed "Japan, Inc." by foreigners. Government bureaucrats who take early retirement often assume top positions in corporations, a practice known as *amakudari,* or "descent from heaven." The Federation of Economic Organizations (Kei-

danren) represents the interest of large companies, and the Japan Chamber of Commerce and Industry speaks for medium-size and small companies.

Many books have been published in English to explain the Japanese corporate system in detail, such as *Kaisha: The Japanese Corporation,* by James C. Abegglen and George Stalk, Jr. (1985). See also EMPLOYMENT; FEDERATION OF ECONOMIC ORGANIZATIONS; JAPAN CHAMBER OF COMMERCE AND INDUSTRY; "JAPAN INC."; JOINT-VENTURE CORPORATION; LABOR UNIONS; LIFETIME EMPLOYMENT SYSTEM; OFFICE LADY; RETIREMENT; SENIORITY SYSTEM; TRADING COMPANY, GENERAL; ZAIBATSU.

COSMETICS See MAKEUP; SHISEIDO CO., LTD.

COURTESAN *(oiran* or *tayu)* The highest rank of women who sold their sexual favors in the government-licensed pleasure quarters, such as the Yoshiwara in Edo (modern Tokyo), during the Edo Era (1600–1868). These quarters, where men of the wealthy urban merchant class enjoyed parties, sex and theatrical entertainment, such as Kabuki, were known as the "floating world" (ukiyo). The women of pleasure were divided into many ranks, with the courtesan at the top. The joro or yuna, who worked in public bathhouses, held the lowest rank. Other types of women also worked in the pleasure quarters but did not engage in sex with customers, such as waitresses and geisha. Many poor families sold their daughters into prostitution in the pleasure quarters, which were surrounded by walls and strictly regulated to keep the girls from running away. Prostitutes were usually deeply in debt to the men who owned their contracts, although it was possible for wealthy men to buy them out of their contracts.

Japanese social customs differentiated between wives, who were dutiful mothers and home managers, and women who provided sensual pleasures. Men were not stigmatized for seeing prostitutes, unless they fell in love and neglected their family duties. This did happen quite often, as recounted in many songs and Kabuki dramas about tragic love suicides.

Courtesans were a popular subject in woodblock prints (ukiyo-e, "pictures of the floating world."). They wore gaudy padded kimono, heavy makeup and elaborate hairstyles and hair ornaments. They tied their obi (sashes) in the front, rather than in the back as ordinary women wore them. Courtesans were knowledgeable in techniques for giving a man sexual pleasure. They were also trained to speak with customers in a stylized manner, functioning as much like actresses as prostitutes. A man had to spend a lot of money to conduct a relationship with a courtesan, but he also had to prove himself witty, sophisticated and in the know about the intricate rules of etiquette that guided relations in the pleasure quarters. Flirtatious courtship was almost more important than sex in the "play" between courtesans and their customers.

Men could buy joro hyobanki, guidebooks to the various pleasure quarters, which provided critical reviews of individual courtesans. These manuals provided the material for popular erotic novels, known as sharebon, such as those by Ihara Saikaku (1642–1693).

Although the "floating world" is associated with the Edo Era, prostitution was legal in Japan until 1957. In the modern era the world of pleasure and entertainment continues as the so-called "water trade," conducted by beautiful young hostesses in bars and nightclubs frequented by Japanese salarymen. See also EDO ERA; FLOATING WORLD; GEISHA; HAIRSTYLES; KABUKI; KIMONO; OBI; WATER TRADE; WOODBLOCK PRINT; YOSHIWARA.

CRAB   See SEAFOOD.

CRACKERS, RICE (sembei)   A popular snack food made of glutinous rice and soy sauce. Rice crackers have been enjoyed in Japan for more than 400 years. They are eaten any time of the day or night and are often served with green tea. The crackers have an irregular shape and are very crisp. The dough is made by grinding rice, steaming and then flattening it, and cutting it into round or oblong shapes that are dried before roasting. Rice crackers can be made by machine in factories, but hand-made ones roasted over charcoal fires have more flavor. The finest quality sembei have an amber color that is compared to the color of a fox (kitsune-iro). Sembei are commonly given at the year-end exchange of gifts called seibo. See also GIFTS; RICE; SOY SAUCE; TEA.

CRAFTS   See BAMBOO; BASKETS; BOXES; DOLLS; HAMADA SHOJI; HEMP; KASURI; KITES; LACQUER WARE; LEACH, BERNARD; LIVING NATIONAL TREASURES; MASHIKO; METALWORK; MINGEI; PAPER, HANDMADE; POTTERY; TEXTILES; TOYS, TRADITIONAL; WOODWORKING; YUZEN DYEING.

CRAM SCHOOL   See JUKU.

CRANE (tsuru)   The crane is a very auspicious symbol for a long life in Japan. As such, the wading bird is often depicted with the tortoise, another symbol of longevity. There is a Japanese saying, "the crane lives for a thousand years and the tortoise for ten thousand." Jurojin, the god of longevity, is always shown with a crane, tortoise or deer to represent contented old age. The crane, with it's long, elegant legs and beak, is a common motif in family crests (mon) and trademarks. Japan Air Lines uses a crane as its company logo. Many Japanese folk stories involve a "crane wife," a crane freed from capture by a young man that turns into a woman and subsequently marries him. Therefore, the crane also represents happy marriage. The crane is the most popular shape in origami, the Japanese art of paper folding. Folding and stringing together "a thousand cranes" (semba-zuru) is thought to guarantee the fulfillment of a wish. Semba-zuru are often left by schoolchildren in the Peace Park in the city of Hiroshima that commemorates the dropping of the atomic bomb there on August 6, 1945. A young girl who was injured in the blast attempted to get well by folding a thousand cranes, but she died before she finished. The Nobel Prize–winning Japanese author Kawabata Yasunari (1899–1972) wrote a novel that has been translated into English as A Thousand Cranes. (Sembazuru, 1949–1951; tr. 1959) See also ATOMIC BOMB; CREST; DEER; HIROSHIMA; JAPAN AIR LINES, CO., LTD.; JUROJIN; KAWABATA YASUNARI; ORIGAMI; TORTOISE.

CREATION STORY   See IZANAGI AND IZANAMI; KOJIKI; NIHON SHOKI.

CREMATION   See FUNERALS.

CREST (mon)   A simple, elegant design that in more traditional times symbolically identified a family or other group. Each family had its own crest, which would be engraved on formal clothing and other possessions. Many of the motifs are based on nature, such as flowers and birds, and originated in patterns that decorated clothing and accessories of the imperial court in the Nara Era (710–794) and Heian Era (794–1185); for example, the plum blossom, maple leaf and crane. Crests became widely used by military clans that took control of Japan in the 12th century following the Taira-Minamoto War (1180–1185). Rival armies fought under colored banners bearing the

Cranes are symbols of long life and happy marriage in Japan. The cranes on this screen, *Walking Cranes,* were painted by Korin (1658–1716) in the Rimpa style.

identifying marks of their groups, which had become standardized heraldic emblems by the 14th century. Powerful lords used crests for political purposes and awarded important followers the right to use their own family crests. Aristocratic families began to utilize crests as well. In the 13th century the Japanese imperial family made the chrysanthemum and the paulownia leaf its official symbols. They later permitted major warlords to use these symbols, but even today only the imperial family is allowed to use a chrysanthemum motif with 16 petals. Branches of families began using variations on the basic designs belonging to the heads of their families. A book published in the early 16th century lists 255 crests used by families in the region, which included Kyoto, Osaka and Shikoku Island.

When Japan was unified under the Tokugawa Shogunate (1603–1867), books were published on the heraldry *(bukan)* of the ruling samurai class. The hollyhock *(aoi)* was the official crest of the Tokugawa family. The retinues of *daimyo* (great lords) required to travel between their lands and the new capital city of Edo (modern Tokyo) were identified by their crests. Ordinary Japanese citizens also began using crests during this time. Designs were standardized to fit within a circle that was about 1 to 1 ½ inches in diameter. Circular crests were stamped on kimono. The most formal kimono have five crests, placed on the back, shoulders and sleeves. Crests were even taken up by Kabuki actors and courtesans in the licensed pleasure quarters of large cities. Published catalogs showed thousands of variations that could be made on basic motifs. At present there are 4–5,000 crest patterns in Japan, based on about 250 different motifs. These include flowers, trees, birds, animals, insects and man-made objects such as arrows, wheels and *torii* (shrine gates). Crests are also used as corporate trademarks; in fact, today crests are used mostly by companies, and seldom by families. The Japan Airlines symbol of a red crane in a circle is well known around the world. See also CHRYSANTHEMUM; CLAN; FAMILY; FEUDAL ERA; FLAGS AND BANNERS; HEIAN ERA; KIMONO; NARA ERA; PAULOWNIA; SAMURAI; TAIRA-MINAMOTO WAR; TOKUGAWA SHOGUNATE; NAMES OF INDIVIDUAL ANIMALS, BIRDS, FLOWERS AND TREES.

CRICKET *(korogi)*   There are about 40 species of cricket in Japan. The Japanese have always loved the sound of crickets. The *Manyoshu,* a Japanese poetry collection from the eighth century A.D., includes seven poems about *korogi,* a general term used at that time for all insects that chirp. Since the Edo Era (1600–1868), vendors have sold crickets and similar insects in bamboo cages, as good luck charms. See also BAMBOO; INSECTS; MANYOSHU; POETRY.

CRIME AND CRIMINALS   See LEGAL SYSTEM; POLICE SYSTEM; YAKUZA.

CROW *(karasu)*   The crow has been considered a messenger of the gods in Japan. The *Kojiki,* an official chronicle written in A.D. 712, tells of a crow that served as a guide for the army of Jimmu Tenno, the legendary first emperor of Japan who supposedly began his reign in 660 B.C. Ceremonies to honor crows, in which they are offered rice cakes, are held at Atsuta Shrine in Nagoya and Taga Shrine in Shiga Prefecture. Two species of crow reside permanently in Japan: the jungle crow *(hashibuto-garasu),* which is found in many environments and even cities, and the carrion crow *(hashibo-garasu),* which lives along rivers and in agricultural areas. Migratory species of crow are also found in Japan, including the raven *(watari-garasu)* on the northern island of Hokkaido, and the rook *(miyami-garasu)* and the jackdaw *(kokumaru-garasu)* on the southern island of Kyushu. See also ATSUTA SHRINE; JIMMU TENNO; KOJIKI.

CROWN PRINCE *(kotaishi)* The oldest son of the reigning emperor and the person first in line to become the next emperor. The crown prince's oldest son comes next in the line of succession. Since the eighth century, only males have been permitted to sit on the Japanese imperial throne. The current crown prince is Prince Naruhito (formerly known as Prince Hiro no Miya Naruhito) (1960–), oldest son of Emperor Akihito (1933–) and Empress Michiko (1934–). Akihito was crown prince for more than 50 years because his father, Emperor Showa (formerly known as Hirohito; 1901–1989), had the longest reign of any Japanese emperor. After World War II, Akihito completed his education at Gakushuin High School (Peer's School) in Tokyo. He was also tutored in the English language and Western culture by an American woman, Elizabeth Gray Vining (1902–), who has written several books about her experiences with the crown prince. Akihito studied at Oxford University in Great Britain as well. In 1952 Akihito celebrated his coming-of-age (adulthood) ceremony and his investiture as heir to the imperial throne. Akihito was the first crown prince to marry a woman who was not a member of the aristocracy. Shoda Michiko, now Empress Michiko, is the daughter of a commoner named Shoda Eizaburo, who was president of a large flour company. Their first son, then called Crown Prince Hiro, celebrated his coming-of-age ceremony in 1980, and graduated from Gakushuin University two years later. He has a brother, Prince Aya no Miya Fumihito (1965–) and a sister, Princess Nori no Miya Sayako (1969–). Prince Aya was married in 1990 to a commoner, Kawashima Kiko (1966–), and given the new name Prince Akishino. Akihito had been removed from his family at age three for training to become the next emperor, but he and his wife decided to end that traditional practice and keep Crown Prince Naruhito and their other children with them. See also ADULTS' DAY; EMPEROR; IMPERIAL HOUSEHOLD; VINING, ELIZABETH GRAY.

CUISINE See COOKING; KAISEKI; RESTAURANTS; NAMES OF INDIVIDUAL DISHES AND INGREDIENTS.

CULTURAL PROPERTIES PROTECTION DIVISION See NATIONAL TREASURES.

CULTURE DAY See HOLIDAYS, NATIONAL; MEIJI SHRINE.

CURRENCY See BANKING SYSTEM; MATSUKATA MASAYOSHI; YEN.

CUSTOMS See BOWING; ETIQUETTE; FESTIVALS; FUNERALS; GIFTS; GO-BETWEEN; TEA CEREMONY; WEDDINGS; WRAPPING.

CYPRESS *(hinoki)* "Tree of fire"; a type of evergreen whose wood is put to many uses in Japan. The *hinoki* may come from the ancient Japanese method of starting a fire by rubbing sticks of cypress wood together. Sacred fires are still created this way at Ise, the holiest shrine of Shinto, the indigenous Japanese religion. A cypress tree grows over 100 feet high and has a diameter of 3–5 feet. An ornamental tree, it has thin horizontal branches with deep green leaves, and flowers that grow into brown cones. Cultivated in Japan for thousands of years, cypress trees grow on the islands of Honshu, Kyushu and Shikoku. The Japanese consider cypress the finest wood because it is delicate yet sturdy, medium hard, and has a fine grain and pleasant fragrance. Shinto shrines are always constructed of cypress, including the shrine at Ise, which is newly built every 20 years. Many parts of a traditional Japanese home are made of cypress wood, such as ceiling boards, fittings for doors and windows, and posts for the alcove known as *tokonoma* where scrolls, flower arrangements, and other decorative objects are displayed. Fine wooden bathtubs are often made of cypress, as are many utensils used in daily life, and even informal raised wooden sandals called *geta*. Cypress wood is also used to build ships, and a resilient fiber made from split cypress can be used to make rafts and anchors. The bark of cypress trees has long been used in Japan to make roofs known as *hiwadabuki*. Fragrant oil can be extracted from cypress leaves for use in perfumes. See also BATH; FOOTWEAR; HOMES AND HOUSING; ISE SHRINE; SHINTO; SHRINES; TOKONOMA; WOODWORKING.

D

DAGGER   See SWORD; SWORD GUARD.

DAIBUTSU   "Great Buddha"; a large, usually bronze, statue of The Buddha, the Indian founder of Buddhism, which was introduced into Japan from China in the sixth century A.D. The Japanese call a statue *daibutsu* if it is *joroku*, that is, higher than the traditional measurement of one *jo*, six *shaku*, (16 ft.), the traditional height of the actual Buddha. Large statues of other Buddhist deities, such as Amida, Kannon and Miroku, are also called *daibutsu*. The first Japanese *daibutsu* was made in A.D. 606 for Asakudera Temple in the Nara region. It still exists but has deteriorated badly. Three other famous *daibutsu* were cast around the same time, and were installed at Todaiji in Nara, Chishikiji in Kawachi (now part of Osaka Prefecture) and Sekidera Temple in Omi (Modern Shiga Prefecture). The Chishikiji Daibutsu of Kannon stood 59 feet high. The Nara Daibutsu at Todaiji in the ancient capital city of Nara can still be seen today. Todaiji is the world's largest wooden

The Nara Daibutsu, a 53-foot-high sculpture of the Buddhist god Dainichi, in the Todaiji, Nara. Todaiji is the largest wooden building, and the Daibutsu is the largest bronze sculpture, in the world.

building, and its *daibutsu* remains the largest in Japan, at 53 feet high. Originally completed in A.D. 752, it has been damaged and repaired many times. The second largest *daibutsu*, the Kamakura (or Hase) Daibutsu, was originally housed inside Kotokuin Temple in the city of Kamakura. This 37.7-foot seated bronze statue of Amida was completed in the mid-13th century. The statue has sat in the open air ever since the temple was destroyed by a tidal wave in 1495. Today it is a popular tourist attraction. See also AMIDA; ASUKA BUDDHISM; DAINICHI; KAMAKURA; KANNON; MIROKU; NARA; TODAIJI.

DAIEI, INC.   See DEPARTMENT STORES.

DAIEI CO., LTD.   See FILM.

DAIHATSU MOTOR CO., LTD.   See AUTOMOBILE INDUSTRY.

DAIKOKU   The God of Wealth and one of the Seven Gods of Good Fortune. Daikoku is also known as Daikokuten and as Mahakara, from the Sanskrit name for the Indian god Mahakala, who battled the forces of evil and safeguarded the Buddhist religion. The priest Saicho (767–822) introduced the worship of this god into Japan and built a shrine to the god on Mount Hiei near Kyoto. Daikoku also became associated with the god Okuninushi no Mikoto of the Shinto religion, which is native to Japan. Daikoku is portrayed wearing a black hat, carrying a bag of treasures on his shoulder and holding in his right hand a golden mallet (*uchide-no-kozuchi*), which grants wishes if it is shaken and which symbolizes wealth and prosperity. Daikoku and the god Ebisu are honored as gods of the kitchen in some parts of Japan, where the women offer tea and rice to them each morning. On the islands of Shikoku and northern Kyushu, Daikoku is also honored as a god of the rice fields (*ta no kami*) who ensures a good harvest. See also BUDDHISM; EBISU; HIEI, MOUNT; RICE; SAICHO; SEVEN GODS OF GOOD FORTUNE; SHINTO; TEA.

DAIKON   A large Japanese white radish that is usually 1–2 feet long, 2–3 inches in circumference, and often weighs up to 4 or 5 pounds. The word *daikon* means "great root." The daikon, a common ingredient in Japanese cooking, is frequently grated raw into dipping sauces and salads. Because enzymes in the daikon are said to aid digestion of oily foods, the sauce used with tempura (deep-fried seafood and vegetables) always includes grated daikon. Shredded daikon is also served with raw fish because it is believed to help in the digestion of protein. Daikon is very high in vitamin C as well. Pickled daikon (*takuan-zuke*) is another basic element of the Japanese diet. These crunchy pickles, bright yellow and with a sharp flavor, are made by drying daikon in the sun and pickling them in salt and rice bran. Daikon can also be served as a fresh vegetable by boiling them and adding a variety of sauces. Daikon are available in the markets year-round, but those found in the cooler months are of the highest quality. Daikon sprouts, each a few inches long with only two leaves, are also popular in salads and as garnishes for sushi and sashimi (raw fish). See also PICKLES; SASHIMI; SUSHI; TEMPURA.

DAIMARU, INC. See DEPARTMENT STORES.

DAIMONJI, MOUNT See BON FESTIVAL.

DAIMYO A term, loosely translated as "great names," for the feudal lords who controlled the provinces of Japan during the medieval and early modern eras (1185–1868). The term was originally used for absentee landholders, primarily aristocrats and Buddhist temples, who were awarded provincial estates by the imperial court of the Heian Era (794–1185). While these landowners remained in the capital, provincial warrior bands became increasingly powerful, and the imperial court eventually lost its ruling power to a new military government (bakufu) known as the Kamakura Shogunate (1192–1333). By the 14th century, the term daimyo was applied to military leaders who had been appointed land stewards (jito) by the shogunate and thus held local authority over provincial domains. The Ashikaga Shogunate (1338–1573), the second military government of Japan, appointed powerful leaders of warrior clans as constables (shugo) with military and civil authority over one or more provinces. These leaders became known as shugo daimyo. By the mid-15th century the shoguns had become weak, and shugo daimyo increased their power over their provinces and built up large bands of warriors who pledged their loyalty as vassals of the daimyo. The Onin War (1467–1477) broke down the alliance between shogun and shugo daimyo and initiated a century of civil war in Japan, known as the Sengoku (Warring States) Era (1467–1568). Many of the shugo daimyo were overthrown by their own vassals, and about 250 daimyo families, known as sengoku daimyo, took power over local regions of the country. The sengoku daimyo built castles around which towns grew up, and the more powerful daimyo began taking over neighboring provinces.

Three warlords, Oda Nobunaga (1534–1582), Toyotomi Hideyoshi (1536–1598) and Tokugawa Ieyasu (1543–1616), unified Japan by establishing their authority over the daimyo, who retained autonomy as vassals. Ieyasu founded the Tokugawa Shogunate (1603–1867) and rewarded loyal vassals with lands that qualified them to be daimyo. The term daimyo was officially applied to vassal military lords whose annual wealth was assessed at 10,000 koku (a measure of volume for rice and other grains that equals about 5 bushels). Ieyasu established the domain–central government or bakuhan system of government, whereby a strong central military government (bakufu) was placed above the daimyo domains (han). Daimyo were defined by three cate-

gories, shimpan, fudai and tozama. Shimpan ("related fiefs") belonged to collateral branches of the Tokugawa family, primarily the estates of Ieyasu's three sons. Fudai (hereditary vassals) were mostly in central Japan and had been allies of Ieyasu in the decisive Battle of Sekigahara (1600). Tozama (outside lords) were autonomous lords of very large provinces, such as the Maeda and Shimazu, who swore allegiance to Ieyasu only after he defeated his rivals for power. The tozama daimyo were further from the capital of Edo, and their resentment surfaced in the 19th century when they led the revolt against the shogunate and brought about the Meiji Restoration of 1868.

The Tokugawa Shogunate controlled the daimyo by requiring them to spend every other year or half year in the new capital city of Edo (modern Tokyo), a practice known as "alternate attendance" (sankin kotai). Two hundred forty-five daimyo administered around two-thirds of the lands not directly controlled by the shogunate. Daimyo were given the rights of law enforcement, taxation and maintenance of standing armies in their domains, but they owed the shogunate military services when required, and assistance in constructing castles and other public works. They were allowed to have only one castle each in their domains. The daimyo had always practiced the military arts, known as bu, but they were also great patrons of the arts and cultural activities, termed bun, such as painting, the tea ceremony, pottery, lacquer ware, poetry and calligraphy. The shogunate secluded Japan from the West in 1639, largely because Christian missionaries and traders had presented threats to its power. When U.S. Commodore Matthew Perry attempted to open Japan to Western trade in 1853, the shogunate and fudai daimyo were in favor of such trade. However, tozama and shimpan daimyo resisted foreign demands. Using the slogan Revere the Emperor, Expel the Barbarians (Sonno joi), leaders from Satsuma, Choshu and Tosa provinces successfully led the movement that overthrew the shogunate and restored imperial power. They became leaders in the new Meiji government (1868–1912), which in 1871 abolished the daimyo domains (han) and established the modern administrative system of prefectures (ken). Former daimyo received noble titles and pensions and retired to Tokyo. See also ALTERNATE ATTENDANCE; ARMOR; ASHIKAGA SHOGUNATE; BAKUFU; BUSHIDO; CASTLES; CHOSHU PROVINCE; EDO; FEUDALISM; KAMAKURA SHOGUNATE; KOKU; LANDED ESTATES SYSTEM; MAEDA CLAN; MEIJI RESTORATION OF 1868; ODA NOBUNAGA; ONIN WAR; PREFECTURE; SAMURAI; SATSUMA PROVINCE; SENGOKU ERA; SHOGUN; TOKUGAWA IEYASU; TOKUGAWA SHOGUNATE; TOYOTOMI HIDEYOSHI; NAMES OF INDIVIDUAL ARTS.

DAINICHI "Great Sun" (also known in Japanese as Dainichi Nyorai); a Buddhist deity, ranked as a Buddha (Hotoke; Butsu; Butsuda), who in Japan is the central deity of the Shingon sect and the esoteric branch of the Tendai sect. Dainichi (Mahavairocana in Sanskrit) is the supreme spiritual principle of the cosmos in Buddhism, the religion introduced into Japan from India through China in the sixth century A.D. He is the Buddha of ultimate reality, which has no beginning and no end, and all things that exist are embraced in him. Sakyamuni, the historical Buddha (also known as Siddhartha Gautama), is regarded as one of Dainichi's numerous manifestations. The symbol of Dainichi is the *vajra* (*kongo* in Japanese), an esoteric ritual implement that is considered to have the hardness of a diamond and the energy of a thunderbolt, giving it the power to destroy all delusions. Esoteric Buddhism was called Vajrayana, the "Diamond" or "Thunderbolt" Vehicle. During the medieval era (12th–16th centuries) the Sun Goddess, Amaterasu O Mikami, the central deity of Shinto, the native Japanese religion, came to be regarded as a manifestation of Dainichi. An enormous 53 foot-high bronze statue of Dainichi, which has become known as the Nara Daibutsu (Great Buddha), was placed in Todaiji in the old capital city of Nara in the eighth century A.D. Today it is a major tourist attraction. Dainichi is also the central figure in complex esoteric Buddhist paintings known as mandalas (*mandara*). See also BUDDHISM; DAIBUTSU; SHINGON SECT OF BUDDHISM; TENDAI SECT OF BUDDHISM; TODAIJI.

DAISEN-IN   See DAITOKUJI.

DAITOKUJI   "Great Virtue Temple"; a temple in the ancient capital of Kyoto belonging to the Rinzai sect of Zen Buddhism. The original building was a small monastery built in 1315 by Soho Myocho (Shuho Myocho), a Zen priest. In A.D. 1325 the retired Emperor Hanazono (1297–1348; r. 1308–1318) declared Daitokuji a place of worship for the imperial court, and a hall for religious instruction (*hodo*) and living quarters for the abbot (*hojo*) were added. A ceremony of dedication was held for Daitokuji in A.D. 1326, which is considered the real founding of the temple. In 1333 Emperor Go-Daigo ranked Daitokuji as one of the Gozan (Five Temples), the most important Zen Buddhist temples in Japan. Daitokuji lost this ranking and its close association with the Japanese government in 1386, but it was able to develop independently as an important Zen temple. Most of the buildings were destroyed twice by fire, in 1453 and during the Onin War (1467–1477). In 1474 the controversial Zen monk Ikkyu Sojun (1394–1481) was named head priest of Daitokuji and enlisted the aid of wealthy merchants to rebuild the temple. Many of Daitokuji's sub-temples (*tatchu*) were founded in the 16th century. Daitokuji was supported by the great warlord Toyotomi Hideyoshi (1537–1598), who helped complete its restoration. He also buried Oda Nobunaga (1534–1582), another great warlord, at Daitokuji. Sen no Rikyu (1522–1591), the most important master of the Japanese tea ceremony, built tearooms and gardens there, as did other famous tea masters. Rikyu rebuilt the temple's outer gate (*sammon*) and put a statue of himself on top of it. This angered Hideyoshi so much that it may be one reason why Hideyoshi commanded Rikyu to commit suicide. He supposedly died in the tearoom of Jukoin, a sub-temple in the Daitokuji complex. Rikyu and each generation of his descendants who head the main tea-ceremony schools are buried at Daitokuji. The buildings and gardens of Daitokuji cover 25 acres, and include 24 sub-temples, eight of which are open to the public. A beautiful garden belonging to Daisen-in is one of the most famous gardens in Japan. Murasaki Shikibu,

author of the great 11th-century novel *The Tale of Genji* (*Genji Monogatari*), is believed to be buried in the South Garden of Ryugen'in. Daitokuji houses many important Japanese art treasures, some of which are publicly displayed every October. See also IKKYU SOJUN; MURASAKI SHIKIBU; ODA NOBUNAGA; RINZAI SECT OF ZEN BUDDHISM; SEN NO RIKYU; TEA CEREMONY; TEMPLES, BUDDHIST; TOYOTOMI HIDEYOSHI; ZEN BUDDHISM.

DAIWA SECURITIES CO., LTD.   See SECURITIES COMPANIES.

DALBY, LIZA CRIHFIELD (1948–)   An American woman who has studied geisha, women trained in traditional Japanese arts who entertain at exclusive parties arranged through traditional tea houses. Dalby actually lived as a geisha for a year in the Pontocho district of the old capital city of Kyoto, the only foreign woman to have done so. She entered a formalized "sister" relationship with a practicing geisha named Ichiumi, and was given the geisha name Ichigiku. Dalby began her study of geisha in order to write a doctoral dissertation in anthropology at Stanford University. After she completed her dissertation, she wrote the informative book *Geisha*, which was published in 1983. Dalby's interest in geisha developed out of her study of the *shamisen*, a stringed musical instrument associated with geisha, when she was an exchange student in Japan. She also wrote a book called *Ko-uta* (*Little Songs of the Geisha World*; 1979) about traditional short songs that are sung and played by geisha. Dalby had studied *naga-uta*, or "long songs," for nine years prior to learning *ko-uta*. At present she is writing a book about kimono, traditional Japanese clothing. She has also contributed articles about Japan to numerous publications. See also GEISHA; KYOTO; PONTOCHO; SHAMISEN; SINGING.

DANCE, TRADITIONAL (*buyo, mai, odori, Nihon buyo*)   Dance, along with music and singing, has always been a major aspect of Japanese culture. Many types of traditional dance are still performed in Japan. *Mai* (the character for which can also be pronounced *bu*) is the Japanese term for ancient, elegant line and circle dances that emphasize graceful movements of the arms and hands. *Odori* (also pronounced *yo*) is the term for Edo Era (1600–1868) energetic dance forms that emphasize jumping and stamping of the feet. Ritual court dances that date back to the seventh century A.D. are known as *bugaku*, and are accompanied by court ensemble music called *gagaku*. By the 12th century, popular Japanese Buddhism, especially the Pure Land (Jodo) sect, encouraged the common people to perform dances of worship known as *nembutsu odori*. This type of dance has survived as part of the midsummer Bon Festival to worship visiting ancestral spirits. Lively regional folk dances are also performed at Shinto festivals. *Taue odori* are dances and songs performed at rice-planting festivals that developed out of ancient forms known as *dengaku*. *Kagura* is the term for ritual dances performed at Shinto shrines by priests and by special priestesses known as *miko*.

Noh drama, which developed in the 14th century, combines elements from many Japanese dance forms, including stylized court dances, Buddhist dances, earthy folk dances, popular vaudeville-type entertainment known as *sarugaku* ("monkey music") and a women's pantomime dance known as *kusemai*. *Nihon buyo* is the contemporary term for Japanese classical dance performed on a stage or at private banquets or homes; this art form is studied by many Japanese women today, especially by geisha, who put on public dance performances in the spring and autumn in the Gion and Pontocho districts of Kyoto. This type of dance developed from *shosagoto*, dance pieces within traditional Kabuki theater performed by female impersonators known as *onnagata*. Other types of dance are also performed in Kabuki, involving spectacular costume changes and stage effects.

Traditional Japanese dancers wear gorgeous kimono and elaborate face makeup or masks, and often carry fans or other stylized props. Folk and classical dances are accompanied by singing and musical instruments such as drums, flutes and a banjo-like stringed instrument called a *shamisen*.

Many dance schools originated as training centers for Kabuki actors. Geisha and Kabuki actors study with the same dance teachers. The largest *buyo* school today is Hanayagi (Hanayagiryu), which was founded in 1849 and has formed international performing troupes. Dance students who reach a high level of accomplishment are given professional "dance names" by their schools, qualifying them to be dance teachers themselves.

Western classical and modern dance forms, known collectively as *yobu*, are also popular in Japan. Butoh, a modern Japanese avant-garde dance form, has gained international attention. There are more than 4 million student and professional dancers in Japan. Traditional dance performances are frequently broadcast on nationwide television by the Japan Broadcasting Corporation (NHK). See also BON FESTIVAL; BUGAKU; BUTOH; DRUMS; FANS; FLUTES; GAGAKU; GEISHA; GION; KABUKI; KAGURA; KIMONO; MAKEUP; MASKS; NOH DRAMA; PONTOCHO; RICE PLANTING AND HARVESTING FESTIVALS; SHAMISEN; SHINTO; SINGING.

DANNOURA, BATTLE OF (1185) (Dannoura no Tatakai)

A naval conflict on April 25, 1185 in the Straits of Shimonoseki separating Honshu and Kyushu islands that ended the Taira-Minamoto War (1180–1185) and changed the course of Japanese history when the Taira (or Heike or Heishi) clan was thoroughly defeated by the Minamoto (or Genji) clan. Minamoto forces led by Minamoto no Yoshitsune (1159–1189) had won a major battle at Yashima on Shikoku Island the month before. The few thousand surviving Taira troops sailed west on the Inland Sea to escape, but Yoshitsune sailed after them and trapped them at Dannoura, where his smaller fleet managed to defeat the Taira clan by taking advantage of changing tides and currents. Admiral Taira no Tomomori and many of his samurai were drowned, along with Emperor Antoku, the seven-year-old grandson of the powerful Taira leader Taira no Kiyomori. Legends tell that the sacred jewel, one of the three Imperial Regalia that symbolize the Japanese imperial throne, disappeared into the sea with Antoku. Taira no Munemori, Kiyomori's heir, was captured and executed by the Minamoto. Small crabs native to this area of the Inland Sea are known as Heike (Taira) crabs because their shells look like scowling human faces and are thus believed to contain spirits of drowned Tairas. The Taira downfall at the Battle of Dannoura has been described in the 13th-century military saga, *The Tale of the Heike (Heike Monogatari)*. The battle ended 25 years of Taira control over the Japanese imperial court and government, enabling the head of the Minamoto clan, Yoshitsune's brother Minamoto no Yoritomo (1147–1199), to strengthen his power. He founded the Kamakura Shogunate (1192–1333), which initiated nearly seven centuries of military rule in Japan. See also HEIKE, THE TALE OF THE; IMPERIAL REGALIA; INLAND SEA; MINAMOTO CLAN; MINAMOTO NO YORITOMO; MINAMOTO NO YOSHITSUNE; SHIMONOSEKI; TAIRA CLAN; TAIRA-MINAMOTO WAR.

DARUMA

Also known as Bodai Daruma; the legendary religious teacher credited with having brought the Chan (Zen) sect of Buddhism from India to China, where he was known as Bodhidharma, in the sixth century A.D. Daruma is the pronunciation of his name in Japan, where Zen was introduced from China in the 12th century. Legend says that Daruma spent nine years meditating facing the wall of a cave, and his persistence caused him to lose the use of his arms and legs. In Japan, Daruma is portrayed by round dolls that always roll back to an upright position if they are pushed over. They are called *okiagari koboshi*, "the little priest who stands up." Such dolls first appeared in the Edo Era (1600–1868) as talismans against smallpox.

The Daruma doll market at Jindaiji, a Buddhist temple near Tokyo. Daruma dolls, named for the legendary monk who established Zen Buddhism in China, are thought to bring good fortune.

They are still considered lucky, and people often use them to help make a wish come true or a venture succeed, especially businessmen and politicians. Daruma dolls are painted bright red and have amusingly fierce faces with round, empty eyes. A person paints one of the doll's eyes in when he or she buys it, and paints the other eye in when his or her wish is fulfilled. Most Daruma dolls are made in the city of Takasaki in Gumma Prefecture, where Darumaji temple holds a Daruma fair (darumaichi) every January 6th and 7th. Around a hundred stalls are set up in the temple grounds to sell Daruma dolls. See also DOLLS; EDO ERA; TALISMANS; ZEN SECT OF BUDDHISM.

DASHI See BONITO; SOUP.

DEATH See FOUR; FUNERAL; SUICIDE.

DECORATIONS, CIVILIAN (kunsho) Awards are given by the Japanese government to honor persons who have made important contributions in their fields. These awards were based on award systems in European countries and were first given out in 1875. The highest award is the Supreme Order of the Chrysanthemum (Daikun'i Kikukasho). The chrysanthemum is associated with the Japanese imperial family. There are also the Order of the Rising Sun (Kyokujitsusho), given to men; the Order of the Precious Crown (Hokansho), given to women; and the Order of the Sacred Treasure (Zuihosho), given to both men and women. Each of these four awards has ranks from the first class to the eighth class to distinguish degrees of merit. In 1890 a new award was added, the Order of the Golden Kites (Kinshi Kunsho), to honor military personnel, but this award was abolished by the new Japanese constitution in 1947, which states that Japan shall have no armed forces. In 1937 another new award was created, the Order of Culture (Bunka Kunsho), to honor distinguished people in the arts and sciences. These awards are celebrated annually in Japan by a public holiday on November 3, Culture Day (Bunka-no-hi). Recipients of the decorations are chosen by the prime minister's cabinet. The emperor presents the awards twice annually, in the spring and fall. Some foreigners have been awarded decorations by the Japanese government for their unique contributions to the country. See also CABINET, PRIME MINISTER'S; CHRYSANTHEMUM; CONSTITUTION OF 1947; EMPEROR; HOLIDAYS, NATIONAL.

DEER (shika) The shika deer, found throughout East Asia, averages just under 6 feet in length and 90–175 pounds. The brown deer develops white spots in summer, and the male deer grows a long mane in winter. Although the deer has inhabited all four main islands of Japan, it now exists mostly within protected preserves. The best place to see deer is in Nara, northwest of the old capital city of Kyoto. Nara was the capital of Japan from A.D. 710 to 794, but today only Buddhist temples and Shinto shrines remain for tourists to visit. Tame deer wander through Nara Park because deer are considered the guardians of Kasuga Shrine, associated with the influential Fujiwara clan. The Japanese consider the deer the messenger of the gods. The deer also represents prosperity and longevity in association with the god Jurojin. Deer antlers have been carved to make netsuke and pipe cases, and ground for medicinal use. The deer is a common decorative motif. A deer among maple leaves symbolizes autumn. See also FUJIWARA CLAN; JUROJIN; KASUGA SHRINE; MAPLE TREE; NARA.

DEFENSE AGENCY See CABINET, PRIME MINISTER'S; SELF-DEFENSE FORCES.

DEJIMA A small artificial former island constructed in the harbor of Nagasaki between 1634 and 1636 to house first Portuguese and then Dutch traders. Twenty-five wealthy Japanese traders paid for the construction of Dejima. When Dejima was built, the Tokugawa Shogunate (1603–1867) moved all Portuguese who were in Japan to this island. Subsequently, Portuguese Catholic missionary activity and the Christian Shimabara Uprising of 1637 caused the shogunate to crush Christianity and expel all Portuguese from Japan. The shogunate limited Japanese trade with foreigners, and closed Japan to the West altogether in 1639. From 1639 until 1856, the Dutch, who were Protestants, were the only Westerners permitted to trade there. In 1641 the shogunate closed the Dutch trading post at Hirado (near Nagasaki) and confined the Dutch to Dejima. The island, constructed in the shape of a fan, covered only 130 acres. On this small space were housed the director and employees of the Dutch East India Company, sailors, warehouses and an office for Japanese interpreters, as well as gardens and pastures for domestic animals. Dejima was connected to Nagasaki by only one small bridge (Dejimabashi). The Nagasaki city commissioners (Machi Bugyo) administered Dejima and strictly controlled who could enter and leave the island. The Dutch were forbidden to leave except for ceremonial occasions. Japanese traders needed special permits to enter Dejima when Dutch ships were in the harbor. The only women allowed on the island were Japanese prostitutes. In spite of these regulations, Dutch traders provided the Tokugawa Shogunate with valuable information about the West. In 1720 Tokugawa Yoshimune removed the ban on Dutch books, and during the 18th century, European books supplied by the Dutch began circulating throughout Japan. Nagasaki became an open port in 1859. When Nagasaki Harbor was reconstructed in the Meiji Era (1868–1912), landfill was used to connect Dejima with the city. The Dutch warehouse was restored as a historical monument in 1957. The Nagasaki Municipal Dejima Museum displays a model of Dejima and objects from the era of Dutch trading (c. 1641–1859). See also CHRISTIANITY IN JAPAN; DUTCH IN JAPAN; ISOLATION OF JAPAN; NAGASAKI; PORTUGUESE IN JAPAN; SHIMABARA UPRISING; TOKUGAWA SHOGUNATE.

DEMING, EDWARD; DEMING PRIZE See QUALITY CONTROL CIRCLE.

DEMOCRATIC SOCIALIST PARTY (DSP; Minshu Shakaito or Minshato) A major Japanese political party that was founded on January 24, 1960 by a conservative faction that split from the Japan Socialist Party (JSP; Nihon Shakaito). The Democratic Socialist Party was known as Minshu Shakaito from 1960 until 1970, when it changed its name to Minshato. It is one of the four main opposition parties in the Japanese political system, but frequently forms coalitions with the ruling Liberal Democratic Party (LDP; Jiyu Minshuto). In 1980 the DSP held 33 seats in the House of Representatives, the lower house of the Diet (Parliament), and 12 seats in the House of Councillors (upper house). This ranked it fourth and fifth in terms of party seats in the respective houses.

The DSP is mainly supported by the Japanese Confederation of Labor (Domei), a labor union with about 2.5 million members, and by owners of small businesses and manufacturing companies. Its policies advocate progressive social welfare through increased social-security benefits and protection against unemployment. However, the party is conservative on issues of defense and economic policy. In 1975 the DSP openly supported the Security Treaty between Japan and the United States, which had been revised in 1960 and approved again in 1970. More progressive Japanese political parties strongly opposed this treaty. In the February 18, 1990 elections for the House of Representatives, the DSP won 14 out of a total of 512 seats, a loss of 12 seats. See also ELECTIONS; LABOR UNIONS; LIBERAL DEMOCRATIC PARTY; POLITICAL PARTIES; JAPAN SOCIALIST PARTY; SECURITY TREATY BETWEEN JAPAN AND THE UNITED STATES.

DEMONS AND GHOSTS (oni, tengu, yokai, yurei) These spine-chilling supernatural beings fall into two categories: yokai, the general term for monsters and demons; and yurei, ghosts of people who have died. Demons and ghosts became a popular subject in Japanese literature and art from the end of the Muromachi Era (1333–1568). In the Edo Era (1600–1868) they often came to be portrayed with long, wild hair and dangling arms, but without feet. One well-known yokai is the oni, a horned, red-face figure who commonly appears in folktales and proverbs as a demon or ogre. In traditional dramas, oni run amok violently before they are subdued, and oni have been associated with demon torturers in Buddhist hells. However, oni also have a positive aspect. For example, in many festivals (matsuri), the oni leads the procession to exorcise evil influences.

Since the Heian Era (794–1185), the Japanese traditionally believed in monomoke, spirits who possess people out of anger or jealousy and cause illness or death. Plagues and other disasters were believed to be caused by vengeful spirits (goryo), who could be pacified by religious rituals known as goryoe. The yamauba or yamamba is a vengeful female demon believed to dwell in the mountains. She is often portrayed in folktales and legends as an old hag who devours human beings. Bakemono is the general term for various monsters and goblins, such as the kappa, a type of water demon. Tengu are creatures with a human body and limbs, a long nose and wings, and glowing eyes. Tengu, often believed to be the cause of otherwise unexplainable things that occur on mountains, are usually considered keshin, or transformations of yama no kami, the guardian spirit of particular mountains. Tengu, depicted as enemies of Buddhist priests and abductors of children but also as protectors and transmitters of supernatural powers, are associated with male shamans known as yamabushi, or "mountain ascetics." Yokai can be apparitions that appear in natural forms such as fire and wind, or at twilight in certain places such as mountains or bodies of water.

Yurei, or ghosts, are the souls of the dead who appear in their original human form to family members or other persons with whom they have had close relationships. They appear for a specific purpose, such as communicating a message or exacting revenge. The Japanese traditionally believed that souls of people who died natural deaths would join their ancestral spirits, but those who died by violent means could not make the final passage into the spirit world and would roam the earth. These spirits no longer belonged to the world yet were still tied to it and reluctant to leave. Snow woman, yuki onna or yuki joro, is a type of ghost often blamed for mysterious occurrences. She appears as a woman dressed in white on snowy nights when the moon is full or at the new year. Often carrying a baby, she is believed to have died in childbirth. The yuki onna is a form of the New Year deity (toshigami) who visits human beings at the beginning or end of the year. The main characters in traditional Noh dramas are often disguised ghosts. Kabuki theater also widely uses "footless" ghosts who appear to float mysteriously across the stage because the actors wear special gray tabi (socks) that are difficult to see. The Japanese enjoy sending chills up their spines in the hot summer by telling ghost stories or looking at pictures or movies about ghosts.

Ugetsu Monogatari (Tales of Moonlight and Rain) by Akinari Ueda (1734–1809) is a famous collection of supernatural tales which was filmed in 1953 by the renowned Japanese director Mizoguchi Kenji (1898–1956). See also FESTIVALS; KABUKI; KAPPA; MIZOGUCHI KENJI; MOUNTAINS; NEW YEAR FESTIVAL; NOH DRAMA; PURIFICATION; SHAMANS AND SHAMANISM.

DENGYO DAISHI See SAICHO.

DENTSU, INC. See ADVERTISING.

DEPARTMENT STORES (hyakkaten; depato) Department stores became widespread in Japan in the early 20th century. Some developed from older dry-goods stores in major cities, or from local stores in smaller cities. Others were started by private railroad companies and built at large railroad stations. The largest department store chain in Japan in retail sales is Daiei, Inc., which was founded in 1959. Daiei has ties with the American company J. C. Penney and the French department store Au Printemps. The second largest, and the best known, is Mitsukoshi, Ltd., which was founded in 1904 but was originally a 17th-century dry-goods store. Takashimaya Co., Ltd. is another famous Japanese department store. Other major Japanese chains are Daimaru, Inc.; Hankyu Department Stores, Inc.; Isetan Co., Ltd.; Matsuzakaya Co., Ltd.; Parco; Seibu Department Stores, Ltd.; Sogo Co., Ltd.; Tokyu Department Store Co., Ltd; and Wako. Most of their flagship stores are located in the Ginza, a popular shopping and entertainment district of Tokyo. Large department stores have branches in many Japanese cities and even foreign cities. Japanese department stores, which by law must cover at least 16,000 square feet, or 32,000 square feet in larger Japanese cities, offer a vast range of domestic and imported items. Larger ones have restaurants, roof gardens and amusement parks, theaters, and art galleries. Sale items are usually on the top floor. The basement levels sell many kinds of Japanese and Western food. There is often one floor just for kimono and traditional accessories. Sales clerks are famous for their courtesy and efficiency. In some department stores, the staff line up and bow to the first customers who enter when the store opens and to the last customers to leave. Uniformed women on the elevators also bow to customers. Clerks carefully wrap purchases in the store's own beautifully decorated paper. Each department store closes one day a week. Major sales are usually held twice a year around the major summer and winter gift-giving seasons. Shopping is an important activity for many Japanese women because gift-giving is a major way of cementing social relations. They are also very fashion-conscious. See also FASHION DESIGNERS, CONTEMPORARY; GIFTS; GINZA; WRAPPING.

DEPENDENCY (*amae*) *Amae*, often translated as "dependency wishes," is the noun form of the Japanese verb *amaeru*. This verb derives from the same root as the word "sweet" (*amai*) and can be translated "to coax," "to look to others for affection," "to act like a spoiled child," or even "to play baby." *Amaeru* is used in many common Japanese phrases, such as "I am taking you up on your offer" (*goshinsetsu ni amaeru*) or "I take you at your word" (*okotoba ni amaeru*). Strictly speaking, *amae*, or dependency, denotes the feelings of dependency an infant has for his or her mother. The mother-child relationship is a much closer one in Japan than in many Western cultures. The child wishes to cling to the mother and not be separated from her; it is indulged by her but also accepts her authority. This kind of dependent relationship is carried over into many adult relationships, including wife and husband, teacher and student, and leader and follower. This last relationship, known as *oyabun-kobun*, is found even among *yakuza*, or Japanese gangsters. But a dependent relationship also gives the subordinate the right to request favors from the superior.

The concept of dependency, or *amae*, has been described by the Japanese psychiatrist Doi Takeo (1920–) as the primary way in which Japanese people interact. In contrast to Western cultures, which play down or even deny feelings that express a need for dependency, Japanese culture actually encourages dependency wishes. Doi's study, *Anatomy of Dependence* (*Amae no kozo*, 1971; translated 1973), became a best-seller in Japan. He regards dependency as the way that Japanese reconcile the conflicting demands of social obligations (*giri*) and human feelings (*ninjo*). In Japanese society people are expected to be able to "merge" (*tokekomu*) with others for social harmony and they receive social approval for conforming to the norms of their groups,

which gives them a sense of self-worth. Doi's work continues a tradition of psycho-social analysis of Japanese culture begun by the American Ruth Benedict in *The Chrysanthemum and the Sword* (1946) and also carried out by Nakane Chie in *Japanese Society* (translated 1973). See also DUTY AND FEELINGS; FAMILY; INDEBTEDNESS; MOTHER; YAKUZA.

DESHIMA See DEJIMA.

DESIGN See ADVERTISING; CALLIGRAPHY; CAMERAS AND PHOTOGRAPHY; CREST; FLOWERS; GARDENS; KANO SCHOOL OF PAINTING; LACQUER WARE; NOREN; RIMPA SCHOOL OF PAINTING; SCREENS; SIGNBOARDS; TEXTILES; TOSA SCHOOL OF PAINTING; WRAPPING.

DESSERTS See SWEETS.

DEVILS See DEMONS AND GHOSTS.

DIARIES (*nikki*) Also known as "diary literature" (*nikki bungaku*); an important traditional Japanese literary form that developed in the 10th century A.D. Prior to that time, Japanese officials wrote diaries that copied a Chinese form used to keep records of the words and actions of emperors. When the Japanese imperial court adopted the Chinese style of bureaucratic government known as the *ritsuryo* system in the seventh century A.D., official state events were recorded in Chinese characters, or *kanji*. Japanese officials in the Heian Era (794–1185) also wrote private diaries detailing court and government matters in *kanji*, a form of writing then used only by men in Japan. The development of a Japanese vernacular syllabic script known as *kana*, which was normally used by women, gave rise to the private form of literary diaries written in the first person. The first Japanese literary diary was the *Tosa Nikki* (935; translated into English in 1969 as *The Tosa Diary*). It was actually written by a male provincial governor named Ki no Tsurayuki (872?–945) but in the voice of a court lady who supposedly accompanied him on his return trip from Shikoku Island to the capital city of Kyoto upon retirement. Many court ladies wrote diaries during the 10th and 11th centuries. Fujiwara no Michitsuna no Haha (d. 995?) wrote about being a wife in *The Gossamer Years* (*Kagero Nikki*, c. 974; translated into English 1964), a diary that influenced many later Japanese women writers. The *Izumi Shikibu Diary* (*Izumi Shikibu nikki*, c. 1008; translated 1969), attributed to the lady of that name, records one of the most common themes in Japanese literary diaries, love and fleeting passion. A critique of daily life in the imperial court was recorded in the *Murasaki Shikibu nikki* (c. 1010) by Lady Murasaki, who wrote the first Japanese novel, *The Tale of Genji* (*Genji Monogatari*). Two other highly regarded Heian Era diaries are *As I Crossed a Bridge of Dreams* (*Sarashina nikki*, c. 1060; translated 1971) by Lady Sugawara no Takasue no Musume (b. 1008), and *Sanuki no Suke Nikki* (c. 1112; translated under that title 1977) by Lady Sanuki no Suke (b. 1079). Japanese literary diaries always contain numerous poems that express emotions and relate key events, as poetry is the most highly regarded literary form in Japan. Diaries often trace the subtle swings of emotion in love affairs and the exchange of poems between lovers. Diaries continued to be written in the medieval era (12th–16th centuries), during which time travel diaries became a popular form. One of the finest Japanese travel diaries is *The Narrow Road to the North* (*Oku no Hosomichi*, 1694; translated 1966) by the great *haiku* poet Matsuo Basho (1644–1694). In the modern era, many Japanese diaries have been written in a confessional form, notably those by the novelist Natsume Soseki (1867–1916).

A literary form related to the diary is known as "follow the pen" or "running brush" (*zuihutsu*) essays, in which authors record their miscellaneous impressions and opinions in a seemingly artless and spontaneous way. The first *zuihutsu*, *The Pillow Book (Makura no Soshi)*, by the court lady Sei Shonagon (fl. late 10th century A.D.), regarded as the finest of its type, records daily activities of Heian aristocrats, their love affairs and gossip. The author also expresses her frank opinions, often in lists on specific topics; for example, "Elegant Things," and "Things That Do Not Linger for a Moment." See also BASHO; GENJI, THE TALE OF; HAIKU; HEIAN ERA; IMPERIAL COURT; IZUMI SHIKIBU; KANA; KANJI; MURASAKI SHIKIBU; NATSUME SOSEKI; POETRY; SEI SHONAGON; TOSA DIARY; WRITING SYSTEM, JAPANESE.

DIET, NATIONAL (Parliament; *Kokkai*) The Japanese parliament, the legislative branch of the Japanese government. The current Diet was established by the Constitution of 1947, still in effect, which defines it as "the highest organ of state power" and "the sole lawmaking organ of the State."

An Imperial Diet was established by the Meiji Constitution of 1889, with an appointive upper house, the House of Peers, and an elected lower house, the House of Representatives. However, the Meiji Constitution stated that the emperor held legislative power, with only the "consent of the Diet," and until the 1920s the Imperial Diet was secondary in importance to the prime minister's cabinet. The Meiji Constitution also gave the Japanese military as much power and independence as the Diet, and in the 1930s the military took control of state affairs.

After World War II, Occupation authorities instituted the Constitution of 1947, which abolished the House of Peers. The current Diet consists of the House of Councillors (upper house; Sangiin) and the House of Representatives (lower house; Shugiin), both of which are elected by popular vote. The 512 members of the House of Representatives are elected from 130 constituencies, each of which has 3–5 representatives; they serve four-year terms, unless the prime minister or members of the House dissolve the government and call for a general election. The 252 members of the House of Councillors are elected for six-year terms, with one-half facing election every three years; the House of Councillors cannot be dissolved by the prime minister. Some members are elected by constituencies of the 47 Japanese prefectures (provinces or states) and municipalities, and others are elected on a nationwide basis.

The Diet selects the prime minister from among its members. The Diet is responsible for making laws, approving the budget of the national government and ratifying treaties between Japan and other nations. The Diet also has the authority to draft amendments to the constitution, which must then be voted on by the Japanese people in a referendum, but it has never passed such an amendment. The Diet has the power to impeach judges convicted of criminal or irregular conduct and may conduct investigations of the government and its ministers.

The more powerful House of Representatives can pass bills vetoed by the upper house, and has the final say in disagreements over the national budget, approval of treaties, and choice of the prime minister. The major role of the House of Councillors is to reexamine decisions handed down by the House of Representatives.

The Diet controls it own budget, and each house elects its presiding officers. Sessions of the Diet ordinarily last 150 days, although both houses can convene extraordinary sessions.

Each house in the Diet has 16 standing committees. Twelve committees correspond to the ministries in the prime minister's cabinet, and two deal with internal Diet matters. Two more committees, the Audit Commit and the Budget Committee, deal with financial and budgetary matters. Special committees can be established to deal with urgent national concerns; recent special committees have dealt with such issues as pollution, energy policy and science and technology.

A bill first goes to the Speaker of the House of Representatives, then to the appropriate committee, and then to a full session of the House of Representatives. If the bill is passed, it is sent to the Speaker of the House of Councillors, then to an appropriate committee, and finally to a full session. The House of Councillors can veto a bill or send amendments to the House of Representatives. If a bill is passed, it is signed by cabinet ministers and then is sent to the emperor for his signature, which is a formality. The bill then goes into law.

Because the Liberal Democratic Party has been the majority party since 1955, every prime minister since then has been the president of the LDP, and the Diet has mainly served to formalize LDP policies worked out by the party and the bureaucracy. Since the LDP has commanded a majority in the Diet, chaired most of the committees and prepared most of the legislation, the role of the opposition parties has been limited to obstructionist tactics in the Diet.

The Diet Building, completed in 1936, is located in the Akasaka district of Tokyo. See also AKASAKA; CABINET, PRIME MINISTER'S; CONSTITUTION, OF 1947; ELECTIONS; LIBERAL DEMOCRATIC PARTY; POLITICAL PARTIES; PRIME MINISTER.

DILIGENCE (*kimbensei*) A characteristic of the Japanese people, who take pride in working hard and persevering to succeed. In Japan diligence is related to the notion of "face" (*kao*), whereby the Japanese strive to maintain their honor and avoid bringing shame on themselves, their families and other groups to which they belong. For the Japanese, working hard in cooperation with group members is generally seen as positive and enjoyable. This attitude may have developed with the necessity for village members to work together to cultivate rice in irrigated paddy fields. Loyalty (chu) to superiors and groups, another value related to diligence, survives from the feudal era (12th–16th centuries). The feudal samurai emphasis on self-discipline has also permeated all Japanese social classes. During the Edo Era (1600–1868), members of the merchant class were excluded from government but exercised their power in the economic sphere. At the same time, the samurai made the transformation from warriors to government and corporate bureaucrats. Thus, when Japan entered the modern world during the Meiji Era (1868–1912), a popular slogan was "success in life" (shusse), which could be gained through diligence. This emphasis in Japan on hard work and economic success, part of the Confucian heritage, is often compared to the so-called "Protestant ethic" in the West. See also CONFUCIANISM; DUTY AND FEELINGS; FACE; FEUDALISM; LOYALTY.

DISTRIBUTION SYSTEM   The network in which wholesale firms function as intermediaries to distribute consumer goods and industrial products from manufacturers to retailers or other end users. Japan has many retailers and intricate delivery relationships. Large department-store chains and supermarkets account for around one-fifth of all retail sales, but most retail stores are small, family owned enterprises with two or fewer employees. The wholesale business is a major element in the Japanese economy, and there are four times as many wholesale firms as retail stores, operating in a multilayered distribution system. The majority of wholesale firms are also small, with fewer than 10 employees. The Large-Scale Retail Stores Law protects small and medium-sized retailers and restricts the big chain stores. This is a bone of contention with the United States, which is attempting to get Japan to change the law to allow more large stores. Because foreign companies wishing to distribute their products in Japan cannot break into the market unless they go through the complex and fragmented distribution system of wholesalers, foreign companies will often enter into a joint venture with Japanese companies in the same product area, to gain access to the distribution network.

Japanese wholesalers maintain inventories of goods from which they make frequent deliveries to retailers. They provide goods on credit to retailers and handle the collection of accounts from them. Most products are sold on consignment. Representatives of wholesalers visit retail stores on behalf of manufacturers, to make sure that their products are displayed and to develop personal relationships with retailers. Wholesalers also provide information to manufacturers as to whether their products are selling and what can be done to make the products more attractive to buyers. Food retailers and restaurants in large cities generally acquire their fish, produce and other products through central or regional wholesale markets. See also DEPARTMENT STORES; TOKYO CENTRAL WHOLESALE MARKET; VENDING MACHINES; WOMEN'S ASSOCIATIONS.

DIVINATION   See FORTUNE TELLING; SHAMANS AND SHAMANISM.

DIVORCE   See FAMILY; HOUSEHOLD REGISTER.

DOG   (inu)   Dogs were domesticated in Japan by emigrants to Japan during the Jomon Era (c. 10,000 B.C.–c. 300 B.C.). Written records from the Nara Era indicate the use of dogs for hunting by that time (710–794). White dogs were especially valued and were sometimes presented as gifts to emperors. Records also describe the sport of dog shooting (inuoumono) during the Kamakura Era (1192–1333), in which archers on horseback shot arrows with padded tips at dogs.

Chinese and European breeds (kara inu) were introduced into Japan through foreign trade during the Muromachi Era (1333–1568). Large foreign hounds or mastiffs were owned by warlords during the Azuchi-Momoyama Era (1568–1600) and the Tokugawa Shogunate (1603–1867). Tokugawa Tsunayoshi, the fifth Tokugawa shogun, built shelters to protect stray dogs and even created an Office of Dog Affairs. Tokugawa Tsunayoshi was born in the year of the dog, one of the animals forming a 12-year cycle in the Japanese zodiac. People born in the year of the dog are thought to be loyal, honest and champions of righteous causes.

Nihonken or nipponken is the term for indigenous breeds of strong, alert Japanese dogs, which have small ears, small slanted eyes and a bushy tail that curls or stands upright. A type of large dog bred in the Akita region of Honshu Island, the Akita inu, is famous for its fierce courage and loyalty to its master. Akita dogs were used to hunt large wild animals and also for dog fighting, although dogs are now bred for this purpose in the Tosa region of Japan.

A 20th-century dog named Hachiko is commemorated by a famous statue in front of Shibuya Station in Tokyo for being faithful to his dead master by waiting for him at the station every day for 10 years after he died. In Japanese folklore, dogs were sometimes associated with wolves in the spirit of the mountain god (yama no kami) that is believed to give protection against fire, theft, difficult childbirth and loss of crops to wild animals. A dog-shaped traditional toy called inu hariko was originally a talisman to protect babies from evil spirits. Ferocious statues called komainu stand in front of gates and main halls of numerous Shinto shrines and Buddhist temples to keep away evil spirits. Although their name translates as "dog" (inu) they are most often regarded as mythical lion-like beasts. At birth, children are given papier mache dog-shaped boxes (inubariko) as protective talismans. Dog images are pasted on houses to keep away fire, robbers, and disease. See also LION AND LION DANCE; SHIBUYA; ZODIAC.

DOGEN   (1200–1253)   Also known as Dogen Kigen or Kigen Dogen; a religious leader and philosopher who founded the Soto branch of the Zen sect of Buddhism in Japan. Dogen was born to an aristocratic family in the capital city of Kyoto and was educated in Chinese studies. The Fujiwara regents who ran the government offered to groom him to be prime minister of Japan, but Dogen wanted to live a religious life, partly because his parents had died when he was young, giving him a realization of what Buddhism calls the "impermanence of all things." Dogen studied Tendai Buddhism at Mount Hiei but was not satisfied with its teachings. He then studied the teachings of Eisai (1141–1215), who had established the Rinzai branch of Zen Buddhism in Japan in A.D. 1191. Dogen next spent six years at Kenninji temple with Eisai's disciple, Myozen (1184–1225). Still not satisfied that he had found the truth he was seeking, Dogen traveled to many other monasteries as well. In despair, he went to China, as Eisai had done, to study with Zen (Ch'an or Chan in Chinese) masters. Dogen finally became enlightened when he heard the Chinese Soto Zen master Zhangweng Rujing (Changweng Ju-ching; 1163–1228) teach that Zen means "dropping off [or transcending] both body and mind," and in 1227 Rujing certified Dogen as his successor in Soto Zen. Dogen returned to Japan and taught that meditation (zazen) is the only necessary religious practice. Under opposition from the Tendai Buddhist monks, Dogen was eventually forced to leave the Kyoto area. In 1244 he founded Daigutsuji temple, renamed Eiheiji two years later, on Mount Kichijo in Echizen Province (part of modern Fukui Prefecture) northeast of Kyoto. His disciples accompanied him, and the Soto monastic community continued to grow. He lectured on Zen to Hojo Tokoyori, the regent of the Kamakura Shogunate (1192–1333), and received patronage from the former emperor Go-Saga (r. 1242–1246). Dogen wrote numerous books explaining how to realize enlightenment through meditation. He downplayed the Rinzai Zen school's emphasis on solving koan, or religious riddles, which could become too intellectual and goal-oriented. Instead Dogen and Soto Zen advocated finding one's true Buddha nature by sitting in meditation without being concerned about enlightenment as a "thing" to be attained. Many of Dogen's writings have been translated into English. See also EISAI; KOAN; MEDITATION; RINZAI SECT OF ZEN BUDDHISM; SOTO SECT OF ZEN BUDDHISM; TENDAI SECT OF BUDDHISM; ZEN SECT OF BUDDHISM.

DOI TAKAKO (1928–) Chairperson of the Japan Socialist Party (Nihon Shakaito; abbreviated as JSP) and the first woman to ever lead a political party in Japan. The JSP is the largest Japanese opposition political party. Its major support comes from the General Council of Trade Unions of Japan (Sohyo), and the JSP advocates social welfare policies and consumer price controls. Born in Hyogo Prefecture, Doi attended Doshisha University in Tokyo and taught constitutional law there. In 1969 she was elected to the House of Representatives (Lower House) of the Japanese Diet (Parliament), representing Hyogo Prefecture for the Japan Socialist Party. She continued to be active within the party, and became its vice-chairwoman in 1983. In September 1986 Doi was selected as the party's 10th chairperson. The JSP gained 46 seats for a total of 85 seats in the July 1989 elections for the House of Councillors (upper house of the Diet), while the dominant Liberal Democratic Party (LDP; Jiyu Minshuto) lost seats due to the Recruit Scandal and the introduction of a national sales tax. After

the election the House of Councillors selected Doi as prime minister, while the House of Representatives selected Kaifu Toshiki. This was the first time in 41 years that the two houses had chosen different candidates as prime minister. Kaifu won because the Japanese constitution states that in case of difference, the decision of the lower house prevails. Doi again lost to Kaifu after the February 18, 1990 House of Representatives elections because, while the JSP jumped from 83 to 141 seats, the other opposition parties lost ground and could not unite behind Doi. But she remains a strong force in Japanese politics, and on March 9, 1990, she was reappointed for a third term as party head; her candidacy had been unopposed. See also DIET; ELECTIONS; JAPAN SOCIALIST PARTY; LIBERAL DEMOCRATIC PARTY; POLITICAL PARTIES; RECRUIT SCANDAL.

DOI TAKEO See DEPENDENCY; SHAME.

DOJO A training hall or gymnasium where a martial art, such as judo or karate, is studied. Do means "the way" and jo means "place." The dojo has a polished wooden floor on which students perform their exercises. For some martial arts, the floor is covered with mats during practice. Students must be disciplined, obey the rules of their martial art and be respectful to their teacher (sensei) while in the dojo. See also JUDO; KARATE; MARTIAL ARTS; SENSEI.

DOLL FESTIVAL (Hina Matsuri) A festival for girls, held on March 3, which is also known as the Peach Festival (Momo-no-Sekku). The peach flowers that bloom at this time of year symbolize the gentleness and grace that are ideals for young women in Japan. For the doll festival, families with girls exhibit a set of 15 hina dolls depicting the ancient imperial court. The dolls, dressed in authentic costumes and accompanied by miniature objects, are displayed on a tier of shelves covered with red cloth in the tokonoma, an alcove in the main room of the home, along with a vase of peach blossoms. On the top shelf sit the emperor and empress with gilded folding screens and

A girl in traditional kimono celebrating the Doll Festival, also known as the Peach Festival, on March 3rd. Families display sets of 15 dolls depicting the emperor and empress and other members of the ancient imperial court.

lanterns. Below them are three ladies-in-waiting, five musicians, two court ministers and three guards. Miniature household furniture, sets of lacquered dishes and trays, musical instruments, weapons and armor, and pots of artificial trees in bloom are also displayed. The complete sets, which are often family heirlooms, are kept on display for a week. Girls dress in kimono and entertain their family and friends in front of the dolls, serving small rice cakes (hishi mochi) and tiny cups of shirozake, a sweet, thick rice wine. The custom of displaying dolls in this way is nearly a thousand years old in Japan and was originally practiced by wealthy families of high social rank. In the 17th century, the shogun Tokugawa Iyenari, who had many daughters, took a special interest in the festival and had dolls of different designs made to order. By 1770 the Doll Festival had become widespread in Japan, and the workmanship for the dolls and their furniture and utensils had become very elaborate. See also DOLLS; FESTIVALS; IMPERIAL HOUSEHOLD; KIMONO; PEACH TREE; TOKONOMA.

DOLLS (ningyo) There are many kinds of dolls in Japan, which are generally regarded as works of art to be admired for their beauty. Expensive dolls are often encased in glass and displayed in the entrance (genkan) of a Japanese home or in a tokonoma (special alcove in the most formal room). Dolls can be made of wood, fabric, porcelain, papier mache or paper, and can be elaborate art objects or simple works of folk art. Since ancient times, dolls were used in Japan for religious purposes, especially for the exorcism of impurities or illness. Mothers often presented dolls symbolizing their children to shrines to secure the protection of kami (sacred spirits) for their offspring. Today, broken dolls are still brought to many temples in Japan to commit their spirits to the gods.

The written characters for the word doll, ningyo, can be read as hito-gata, "human shape." The Japanese word hina is also used for doll and is used for the Doll Festival (Hina Matsuri) or Girls' Festival on March 3rd, at which families display heirloom sets of dolls dressed in beautiful costumes of the ancient imperial court. For boys, there are also warrior dolls (musha ningyo) dressed in medieval armor.

Each region of Japan has its own type of doll. For example, the wooded Tohoku region is known for the kokeshi, a wooden doll with a simple cylindrical body and spherical head. This doll has no limbs, but it does have clothing and facial features painted on the wood in bright colors. Nagashibina are flat, angular dolls made of colored pieces of handmade paper (washi) folded to depict human bodies and traditional clothing. Edo anesama are another type of doll made from colorful handmade paper. Nihon ningyo are dolls dressed in beautiful and elaborate kimono to represent classical Japanese dancers. The Daruma doll is a popular good-luck figure named for Bodhidharma (Daruma in Japanese), the legendary monk who introduced Chan (Zen) Buddhism from India to China. This red doll is painted with a fierce bearded face, and is weighted so that if tipped over it will upright itself. The gosho is a porcelain doll shaped like a chubby child. The hakata doll is made from baked clay and is beautifully painted.

Many small figurines of animals, gods or humans are used as good-luck amulets and are sold by temples and shrines; the oldest type are made of painted clay (tsuchin-ingyo). Statues of beckoning cats (maneki-neko) are placed in restaurant windows to attract customers. Clay statues of warriors, horses, houses, and other figures, known as haniwa, were placed around tomb mounds in the Kofun Era (c. 300–710).

Also related to dolls are masks, which are often worn by traditional folk and classical dancers, and at festivals. Bunraku is a traditional puppet theater that uses human figures that are two-thirds life size to tell stories set in the Edo Era (1600–1868).

See also AMULETS; BUNRAKU; DOLL FESTIVAL; HANIWA; MASKS; ROBOTS; TOYS, TRADITIONAL.

DRAGON (ryu, tatsu) A mythical scaly beast that resembles a gigantic snake, but has claws and a fierce-looking head. The dragon flies through the sky and breathes fire. Although dragons symbolize evil in Western countries, in Japan the dragon is associated with rain and fertility, and represents the most beneficent heavenly power. A symbol of life and growth, the dragon is believed to bring the blessings of wealth, harmony, virtue and long life. The dragon was introduced from China, where it was associated with the emperor. In Japan the dragon is identified with Ryujin, the king of the sea. Legends in the Nihon Shoki (A.D. 720) relate that the god Susanoo no Mikoto killed an eight-headed dragon and found in its tail the sword that later became one of the three Imperial Regalia. In Japanese art the dragon is never fully seen, partly hidden in turbulent waves or stormy clouds. It is believed to rise into clouds, thunder and lightning at the spring equinox, and to descend into the sea with the "Tide-Ruling Jewels" at the autumn equinox. The dragon is one of the animals in the Japanese 12-year zodiac calendar, and the fortunate person born in the year of the dragon is thought to be honest, brave and energetic. It is especially propitious for a man to be born in the dragon year.

See also IMPERIAL REGALIA; SUSANOO NO MIKOTO; ZODIAC.

DRINKING See ALCOHOLIC BEVERAGES; EXPENSE ACCOUNTS; KAMPAI; KARAOKE; SAKE; SALARYMAN; VENDING MACHINES; WATER TRADE.

DRUMS There are two basic types of drum in Japan: the hourglass-shaped tsuzumi, played with the hand, and the larger, barrel-shaped taiko, played with sticks (bachi).

Tsuzumi are made from lacquered wood. On each end, leather skins are sewn onto iron rings larger in diameter than the rim of the drum and are laced onto the drum with cords. The large tsuzumi (otsuzumi) is about 11 inches long and has cowhide heads that are tightly laced. The left hand holds the drum on the left thigh while the right hand strikes the drum heads, which are heated before a performance to produce a sharp, dry sound. A drummer playing an otsuzumi wears papier-mache finger guards on the middle and ring fingers of the right hand, as well as a leather palm guard, to heighten the sharpness of the sound. The small *tsuzumi (kotsuzumi)* is about 10 inches long and has loosely laced horsehide heads. It is held on the right shoulder with the left hand, and the player alters the tone by squeezing the laces with that hand while striking the drum head with the right hand and fingers. Hourglass-shaped drums were introduced into Japan from China in the seventh century A.D. Several types played with sticks are still used in the orchestra for traditional court music known as *gagaku,* which accompanies court dances known as *bugaku.* The term *tsuzumi* is specifically used for the hourglass-shaped hand drums used in Noh and Kabuki theatrical performances.

There are several types of *taiko,* or large barrel-shaped drums. Traditional court music employs a huge laced-head drum known as *dadaiko;* a drum with its head nailed to the body, known as *tsuridaiko;* and a laced-head drum carried on a pole in processions, known as *ninaidaiko.* Large, barrel-shaped, nailed-head *taiko* are played at traditional festivals; they can be mounted on wheels for processions. A *taiko* is often played on a stage at the Bon and other festivals. People dance in large circles around the stage. Smaller *taiko* may also be hung around the necks of the players who accompany dancers, such as women transplanting rice seedlings into wet paddy fields during the rice-planting festival. In Noh and Kabuki theater the *hirazuri-daiko,* a thin, barrel-shaped drum suspended on a stand, is used to create various effects, such as the sounds of battle, rain, wind, thunder and the roar of ocean waves. The drum is also accompanied by the flute *(fue)* to give a sense of foreboding when a ghost appears on stage. Recently, groups that put on lively performances of *taiko,* Japanese village drumming rituals, have become popular in Japan and the West. The *taiko* symbolizes a rural community; boundaries of a village are determined by the farthest points the *taiko* can be heard. Members of Kodo (meaning both "heartbeat" and "children of the drum"; formerly called Ondekoza, Demon Drummers), the best known Japanese *taiko* troupe, share a spartan life on Sado Island in the Sea of Japan but perform around the world. Their largest drum, five feet across and weighing 900 pounds, produces wall-shaking vibrations.

See also BON FESTIVAL; BUGAKU; FESTIVALS; FLUTES; GAGAKU; KABUKI; NOH DRAMA.

DUTCH IN JAPAN The Dutch were the only Westerners permitted to trade with Japan during the period of Japanese seclusion from 1639 to 1854. The first Westerners in Japan, starting in 1542, had been Portuguese and Spanish Roman Catholic missionaries and traders, followed by British and Dutch traders in 1600.

William Adams, an English navigator of Dutch ships, was shipwrecked off Japan in 1600, and remained in Japan as a Western advisor to Tokugawa Ieyasu (1543–1616), founder of the Tokugawa Shogunate (1603–1867). Adams warned Ieyasu that relations with Catholic Portugal and Spain were dangerous to Japan, and requested permission for the Protestant British and Dutch to trade in Japan instead. The Dutch East India Company received permission to trade in 1609.

In the early 17th century, the shogunate persecuted and finally banned Christianity as a threat to its authority and expelled all Portuguese and Spanish, who had been successful in gaining Japanese converts to Roman Catholicism. When the British decided not to pursue trade relations, the Dutch, who were Protestants and had helped the shogunate exterminate Japanese Catholics in the Shimabara Uprising of 1637–1638, were the only Westerners permitted to engage in limited trade with Japan until U.S. Commodore Matthew C. Perry opened Japan to the West in 1854.

Beginning in 1641, fewer than 20 Dutch traders from the Dutch East India Company were allowed into Japan, where they were confined to Dejima, then an artificial island in Nagasaki harbor on southern Kyushu Island, their activities constantly monitored. Once a year the Dutch traveled the 1,300-mile round-trip overland to pay their respects to the shogun in Edo (modern Tokyo). Dutch trade, known as *Oranda boeki* (Holland trade), brought valuable merchandise to Japan, including raw silk, silk textiles, sugar and spices, tin, and Western goods, books and medicine. In exchange, the Dutch acquired camphor, lacquerware, copper and silver from the Japanese, which helped the Dutch maintain their colonies in the East Indies (now known as Indonesia).

When the shogunate relaxed the ban against the importation of foreign books in 1720, Japanese scholars went to Nagasaki to learn the Dutch language and to translate Dutch books on subjects such as anatomy, art, astronomy, botany, geography, mathematics, physics, military science and history into Japanese. Dutch studies (and in fact all Western studies) came to be called *rangaku* (*Ran* meaning Holland), and its scholars as *rangakusha.* Western medicine was termed *rampo* (Dutch laws) to distinguish it from *kampo,* traditional Chinese-style herbal medicine. Dutch traders such as Hendrik Doeff, Philipp F. von Siebold and Carl P. Thunberg helped advance Western learning in Japan. Records kept by the traders on Dejima are preserved at the National Archives in The Hague, capital of the Netherlands.

After Commodore Perry forced the shogunate to conclude a treaty in 1854 allowing the United States limited trade in Japan, other Western countries negotiated the so-called Ansei Commercial Treaties with Japan. The Treaty of Friendship and Commerce between the Netherlands and Japan was signed in 1858, and in 1860 the Dutch trading post on Dejima became the Dutch consulate. After the Meiji Restoration of 1868, the Japanese government attempted to learn as much as possible about Western government and technology. Scholars quickly realized that they would now have to learn English, by then the language of international trade and diplomacy, rather than Dutch. Competition from American and British traders sharply cut into Dutch trade in Japan.

See also ADAMS, WILLIAM; ANSEI COMMERCIAL TREATIES; CHRISTIANITY IN JAPAN; DEJIMA; MEIJI RESTORATION OF 1868; PERRY, MATTHEW CALBRAITH; PORTUGUESE IN JAPAN; SECLUSION, NATIONAL; SHIMABARA UPRISING; TOKUGAWA SHOGUNATE.

DUTY AND FEELINGS (*giri* and *ninjo*) The terms duty, or *giri* (also known today as *gimu*), and human feelings, or *ninjo,* are commonly associated together because they express the two opposing aspects of Japanese life. A high moral value is placed on fulfilling the reciprocal requirements of social relationships, even when an individual might not desire to do so. The code of the feudal samurai class obligated the warriors to faithfully serve their lord, even to die for him, as repayment for the land or money the lord had given them. *Giri* also characterizes other relationships, such as master and servant or employer and employee, as well as assistance that is expected among equals for farm labor, help with funeral services and so forth. The Japanese have traditionally felt that favors or benevolence *(on)* they have received from superiors, rulers and even parents, place a heavy burden of indebtedness on them. They have been strongly aware of the need to help others who have helped them, and to return favors to those who have done favors for them. One cannot escape the network of binding relationships in which one exists. Sometimes, however, a real conflict is created by feelings of love, which are only natural, such as those between a parent and child or between two lovers. This is related to the feelings of dependency *(amae),* which are also valued in Japan. Japanese literature is filled with the conflict between social duty and illicit love for another. Usually the only way out for the lovers was to adhere to the social order by committing suicide.

See also DEPENDENCY; FAMILY; FILIAL PIETY; INDEBTEDNESS; SAMURAI; SUICIDE.

E

EARTHQUAKES *(jishin)* More than 1,500 earthquakes a year occur in Japan, which represents nearly 10% of the world total. Minor tremors are felt almost every day in some areas of the country. At least 23 destructive earthquakes have struck Japan during the past century, including the catastrophic Great Kanto Earthquake of September 1, 1923, which struck the country's most densely populated area, including the cities of Tokyo and Yokohama. More than 100,000 people were killed, over 60,000 in Tokyo alone, mainly because of the ensuing fires. Modern building regulations aim to reduce the damage caused by earthquakes and fires, and new buildings are now designed to withstand heavy tremors. The Japanese government also conducts regular training so the population is prepared to cope with severe earthquakes and fires.

In 1965 the government also began funding research on the distortions of the earth's crust and the movement of several fault planes near Japan that cause earthquakes. A fault zone runs just off the east, or Pacific, coast of Japan, the upper layer of which is moving east and south toward the Pacific Ocean. When this fault slips, the result is an earthquake.

Two foreigners were influential in the development of seismology (the study of earthquakes) in Japan in the late 1800s, Englishman John Milne and Scotsman James Alfred Ewing. Milne helped found the Seismological Society of Japan in 1880, while Ewing invented instruments to measure the motions of the earth's crust. His student, Sekiya Kiyokage (1854–1896), contributed to the start of accurate seismic record keeping by the Tokyo Meteorological Observatory in 1885. Another Japanese scientist, Koto Bunjiro, used a severe earthquake in 1891 to prove that dislocations of the earth along fault lines cause earthquakes. The Committee for Earthquake Disaster Prevention (Shinsai Yobo Chosakai) was founded in 1892 as Japan's main organization for the study of seismology; in 1925 this became the Earthquake Research Institute of Tokyo University. The scientist most responsible for Japan's national earthquake prediction program was Imamura Akitsune, who had accurately predicted the Great Kanto Earthquake of 1923 and the severe Nankaido earthquake of 1946. Japan experiences a great deal of volcanic activity as well as earthquakes, and the two are often related.

See also GEOGRAPHY OF JAPAN; KANSAI AND KANTO; PACIFIC OCEAN; TOKYO; VOLCANO; WAVES; YOKOHAMA.

EAST CHINA SEA See GEOGRAPHY OF JAPAN; SEA OF JAPAN.

EASTERN SEA CIRCUIT See TOKAIDO ROAD.

EBISU God of wealth and patron of fishermen; one of the Seven Gods of Good Fortune. Ebisu is depicted wearing a *hakama* (man's formal divided skirt) over his kimono and a tall hat. He holds a fishing rod in his right hand, and a red fish, the sea bream, which symbolizes good luck, is tucked under his left arm. Fishermen return their first catch of the season to the sea as an offering to Ebisu in expectation of a good fishing season. Farmers also revere Ebisu as a god of the kitchen. Ebisu worship is traditionally centered in the town of Nishinomiya in Hyogo Prefecture, and puppeteers called *ebisumawashi* traveled from this town to perform stories about Ebisu all over Japan. Some regions celebrate the Festival of Ebisu in January, and others in October. Ebisu is also known as Ebisu Saburo, the third son of the creator gods Izanagi and Izanami, and Kotoshironushi no Kami, the son of the god Okuninushi no Mikoto.

See also HAKAMA; FISH AND FISHING INDUSTRY; IZANAGI AND IZANAMI; SEA BREAM; SEVEN GODS OF GOOD FORTUNE.

ECHIZEN WARE See POTTERY.

ECONOMIC PLANNING AGENCY See CABINET, PRIME MINISTER'S.

ECONOMIC SYSTEM See BANKS AND BANKING; CORPORATIONS; EMPLOYMENT; EXPORTS AND IMPORTS; INCOME; JOINT-VENTURE CORPORATION; MINISTRY OF FINANCE; TAX SYSTEM; TRADING COMPANY, GENERAL; YEN.

EDO ERA (1600–1868) The period of Japanese history that marks the transition from the medieval *(chusei)* to the early modern *(kinsei)* era, with more than two centuries of peace and prosperity as a unified country, and the rapid growth of cities and the flourishing of popular culture. Edo (modern Tokyo) was the largest city in the world during the 17th century.

The Edo Era coincided with the military government *(bakufu)* of the Tokugawa Shogunate (1603–1867), founded by Tokugawa Ieyasu (1543–1616), who consolidated power after winning the Battle of Sekigahara in 1600. Ieyasu located his headquarters at Edo Castle (also known as Chiyodajo) in the fishing village of Edo on east central Honshu Island. Edo, which means "rivergate," sat at the mouth of the Sumida River (Sumidagawa), which flows into Edo Bay (Tokyo Bay). The samurai class that formed the elite of Japan in 1600 were required to move to Edo with the shogun. *Daimyo* (feudal lords of Japanese provinces) were required to spend every other year or half year (alternate attendance, *sankin kotai*, system) in Edo, in order to ensure their loyalty.

The shogunate enforced the strict division of social classes into samurai, farmers, artisans and merchants *(shi-no-ko-sho)* and passed numerous sumptuary laws to control the increasingly wealthy merchant class. It also licensed districts of Edo and other cities, such as Kyoto and Osaka, as pleasure quarters; the best known of these was the Yoshiwara in Edo. The licensed pleasure districts are known as the "floating world" (ukiyo). Many cultural aspects now thought of as distinctly Japanese developed in these districts, such as Kabuki and Bunraku (puppet) theaters, geisha, haiku poetry, kimono styles, woodblock prints (hanga), and the Rimpa school of painting. The height of this popular culture is known as the Genroku Era (1688–1704). Arts and crafts such as pottery, lacquerwork and textiles were greatly stimulated by patronage of daimyo, who were required to present gifts to the shogunate each time they returned to Edo. A widespread system of education was also developed, which gave Japan a very high literacy rate. Two hundred and seventy regional schools and 1,500 private urban academies were established to educate samurai and others. Townspeople were educated in more than 11,200 small, private elementary schools run by Buddhist temples (terakoya), and in 600 government-sponsored schools (gogaku).

The imperial court moved from Kyoto to Edo after the Meiji Restoration of 1868, and Edo was renamed Tokyo, Eastern Capital.

See also ALTERNATE ATTENDANCE; BUNRAKU; CASTLES; CITIES; COURTESAN; DAIMYO; FLOATING WORLD; GEISHA; HAIKU; KABUKI; LACQUER WARE; MEIJI RESTORATION OF 1868; POTTERY; RIMPA SCHOOL OF PAINTING; SAMURAI; SEKIGAHARA, BATTLE OF; SUMIDA RIVER; TEXTILES; TOWNSPEOPLE; TOKUGAWA IEYASU; TOKUGAWA SHOGUNATE; YOSHIWARA.

EDUCATION SYSTEM   A system of free universal public education, based on a U.S. model, was established by the Fundamentals of Education Act of 1947 during the Allied Occupation of Japan following World War II. The Meiji government (1868–1912) attempted to modernize education in Japan through the Fundamental Code of Education of 1872, which made education universal and compulsory, and organized it into a coherent system that progressed from elementary school to university. By the early 20th century, 90% of Japanese children attended elementary school. However, the Meiji education system was very authoritarian and selective at the secondary stage. The best schools were expensive and channeled their students to the top universities. During the 1930s and 1940s, secondary education in Japan was geared to the military aims of the country. After the war, Occupation leaders felt that educational reform was crucial to instituting democratic values in Japan, and under the new system, all Japanese children are required to take six years of elementary school, beginning at age 6, and three years of junior high school. More than 90% also take three noncompulsory years of senior high school. About one-third of Japanese students go on to four years of university, and many others attend two-year or vocational colleges. Most Japanese children actually begin their education by attending noncompulsory kindergarten from ages 3 to 5. The national education system is highly centralized under the Ministry of Education, Science and Culture. All schools in the country follow the same basic curricula, which include nine subjects: Japanese language, mathematics, social studies, science, music, arts, homemaking, moral training, and special activities. Each prefecture has a five-member board of education, appointed by the governor, which administers the high school system, pays elementary and junior high school teachers' salaries, and guides municipal boards of education. The latter administer city schools from kindergarten through secondary school and control hiring and firing of teachers and selection of textbooks from the list approved by the Ministry of Education.

The Japanese have always valued education, particularly reading and writing, ever since Chinese writing was introduced into Japan through the Buddhist religion in the sixth century A.D. Today the literacy rate in Japan is nearly 100%, and the Japanese educational system is widely praised as among the best in the world.

Teaching is one of the most respected professions in Japan. Teachers are addressed by the honorific title sensei (master). There are five major nationwide teachers' unions. More than 50% of all public school teachers belong to the Japan Teachers Union (Nikkyo-so), which is the largest union in Japan and the largest of its type in the world. Most schools have Parent-Teacher Associations (PTAs).

Recently the Japanese educational system, from elementary school through university, has been criticized for relying on rote learning and for stifling creativity and individuality. Elementary and secondary students are required to wear uniforms and to obey strict rules of behavior, and a popular adage advises, "The nail that sticks out get hammered down." Competition is also a fundamental aspect of the system from the very beginning because students must take extremely difficult examinations to get into the best high schools and universities, which feed students into the best jobs after graduation. Many students attend private no-credit juku, or "cram schools," in addition to public schools, even as early as elementary school, to prepare for this so-called examination hell (juken jigoku). Japanese students who live and go to school in foreign countries because their fathers are sent there on business have a hard time fitting back into the Japanese educational system. Recently, Japanese schools have been established in the New York City area to keep students living abroad "on track" with the Japanese system and to give them a competitive capability when they return home.

All Japanese public schools are in session Monday through Friday and half a day on Saturday. The school year begins April 1, the start of the fiscal year in Japan, and is divided into three terms totaling 35 weeks: April to July, September to December, and January to March.

See also CHILDREN IN JAPAN; JUKU; MINISTRY OF EDUCATION, SCIENCE AND CULTURE; SENSEI; UNIVERSITIES; WRITING SYSTEM, JAPANESE.

EELS (unagi)   Eel is a favorite food in Japan. The Japanese farm about two-thirds of their eel consumption and import the rest. In Tokyo alone there are about 3,000 restaurants that serve eel. Eel is prepared by cooking methods that remove the oils and tenderize the white flesh. They are first steamed, then cut into fillets that are broiled or grilled while being basted with a sauce made of soy sauce and *mirin* (sweet rice wine for cooking). *Kabayaki* is the most elegant way to serve eel; the eel is grilled and served by itself in a lacquered box. When grilled eel is served over a bed of rice in a lacquered box, it is called *unaju*. Grilled eel served over rice in a large bowl is known as *unagi donburi*, or abbreviated as *unadon*. *Unadon* was first served at the most popular Kabuki theater during the Edo Era (1600–1868), the Nakamura-za, so the audience could eat quickly during intermission. *Unaju* and *unadon* are both covered with the cooking sauce and sprinkled with an herbal pepper called *sansho*. They are also served with *kimosui*, a clear soup made of eel liver. The eel liver is also broiled (it is then called *kimoyaki*) and served. Other ways of serving eel are with sauces made with a base of vinegar and soy sauce, or rolled up with burdock root, cooked egg or other ingredients. *Anago* is a type of sea eel that is cooked and served on small portions of rice as sushi. Since ancient times, the Japanese have especially like to eat eel on the two Days of the Ox (in the animal zodiac calendar) during the hot summer because it is thought to make the heat more endurable. This custom is generally attributed to the 18th-century writer Hiraga Gennai, although a poem in the eighth-century Man'yoshu collection also asserts that eating eel gives one strength in the summer heat.

See also BOXES; BURDOCK; FISH AND FISHING INDUSTRY; KABUKI; MIRIN; RESTAURANTS; SOY SAUCE; SUSHI; ZODIAC.

EIHEIJI TEMPLE   See DOGEN.

EISAI (1141–1215)   The founder of the Zen sect of Buddhism in Japan who also brought tea plants to Japan from China. Also known as Myoan Eisai or Yosai, Eisai was born in what is now Okayama Prefecture. He began studying the Buddhist religion at age seven, and at 13 he became a monk at Enryakuji Monastery on Mount Hiei near Kyoto, center of the Tendai sect of Buddhism. In 1168 Eisai made a five-month pilgrimage to Tendai monasteries in China (known as Tiantai or Tien-t'ai in Chinese). He returned to China in 1187 and studied Rinzai Zen (Linji or Lin-chi in Chinese) for four years, finding *satori* (enlightenment) through the practices of meditation and the study of *koan* (religious questioning). When Eisai went back to Japan in 1191, he taught Rinzai Zen in Fukuoka on the southern Japanese island of Kyushu and in Kyoto. He was opposed by the monks at Enryakuji, and defended himself by writing two books, *Essentials of the Monastic Life* (*Shukke taiko*; 1192) and *Promulgation of Zen as a Defense of the Nation* (*Kozen gokoku ron*; 1198). In 1199 Eisai went east to Kamakura, the new capital of the military government under the Kamakura shogunate (1192–1333), where he was supported by the Minamoto family, who had founded the shogunate. Minamoto no Yoriie appointed Eisai the abbot of the newly built Kenninji monastery in Kyoto, where he combined the practices of Zen, Tendai and Pure Word (Shingon) Buddhism. He also wrote two more books, *A Plea for the Revival of Japanese Buddhism* (*Nihon buppo chuko gammon*; 1204) and *Tea Drinking for the Cultivation of Life* (*Kissa yoji ki*; 1211). Eisai advocated the drinking of powdered green tea, the type of tea still used in the Japanese tea ceremony, as a Zen meditation practice that also has medicinal value.

See also BUDDHISM; ENRYAKUJI; HIEI, MOUNT; KAMAKURA; KOAN; MEDITATION; RINZAI SECT OF ZEN BUDDHISM; SATORI; SHINGON SECT OF BUDDHISM; TEA; TEA CEREMONY; TENDAI SECT OF BUDDHISM; ZEN SECT OF BUDDHISM.

ELECTIONS   The Meiji Constitution of 1889 established a national legislative assembly, or parliament, known as the Imperial Diet. When the first election for the House of Representatives (lower house) of the Diet was held in 1890, only male property owners age 25 or over who paid certain taxes were allowed to vote, totaling only about 1% of the population. The Universal Manhood Suffrage Law enacted in 1925 removed the tax restrictions and extended the vote to all qualified adult males. Japanese women were given the franchise in 1945 during the postwar Occupation of Japan.

The Public Office Election Law of 1950 established the current election system in Japan. All citizens age 20 or over may vote unless they are in jail or mentally incompetent. Citizens age 25 or over are eligible to serve in the House of Representatives (lower house; Shugiin) or as local government representatives. Those age 30 or over can stand for election to the House of Councillors (upper house; Sangiin) or as governors of prefectures.

Members of all legislative bodies, including the Diet and prefectural and municipal assemblies, are elected by popular vote, as are governors of prefectures and heads of local governments. However, the prime minister is elected by members of the Diet. The 512 members of the House of Representatives are elected for four-year terms, unless the House is dissolved sooner at the request of the prime minister. They are elected from 130 electoral districts, each of which has three to five representatives, based on its population. The 252 members of the House of Councillors serve six-year terms, with half of them running for election every three years. Each of the 47 prefectures chooses from two to eight councillors, depending on its population, and each voter also votes for one nationwide candidate.

Elections for prefectural and local executives and assemblies are usually held every four years. The election system is overseen by the Central Election Administrative Committee of the Ministry of Home Affairs, and by election committees at each administrative level. A voter is qualified to register to vote in a district if he or she has resided there for at least three months. Japan has strict laws regulating election campaigns, including the length of time they can be conducted, the way campaign funds are used, and advertising. In recent elections, the issue of campaign funding and expenditures has been an important factor. Scandals, tax issues and public policy changes tend to be the issues by which the Japanese vote.

See also CONSTITUTION OF 1947; DIET; LIBERAL DEMOCRATIC PARTY; POLITICAL PARTIES; PREFECTURE; PRIME MINISTER; RECRUIT SCANDAL.

ELECTRONICS INDUSTRY Electronics are a major industry in Japan, encompassing computers, robots, photocopiers and other commercial and industrial equipment, as well as a wide range of consumer electronic products, including cameras, televisions, radios, tape recorders, video cassette recorders (VCRs), calculators, microwave ovens and other kitchen appliances.

Japanese electronics engineering began with the country's first radio broadcast in 1925, and grew into a large industry prior to World War II, primarily in conjunction with the shipbuilding industry. Japan was also active in technology for television broadcasting at this time. After 1945, the Japanese government promoted technological exchange with foreign companies, which enabled the electronics industry to recover from the war and grow rapidly. In 1955 the world's first transistorized portable radio was produced in Japan. In 1958 the Ministry of International Trade and Industry (MITI) promoted cooperative research and development (R&D) projects and sponsored the formation of the Japanese Electronic Industry Development Association (JEIDA). Japanese companies led the development of such consumer products as the Trinitron color television and hand-held calculators. In the 1960s MITI realized the importance of semiconductors to the electronics industry and the Japanese economy, and funded cooperative research in semiconductor high technology.

During the 1970s Japan paid U.S. $200 million to American companies for licensing and technology, and emerged as a world leader in the manufacture of electronic equipment, machinery and consumer goods. The VCR was developed by the Japanese electronics industry, and all VCRs sold in the United States are now manufactured in Japan. Japanese companies initially developed consumer electronics technology to serve the domestic market, which sought goods that were compact in size and of high reliability. However, these goods were also highly desirable in world markets. Japan's first major success in electronic exports was with televisions. Japan began manufacturing color television sets in 1962 and was exporting nearly half of its total output by the early 1970s. In fact, it sold so many TVs in the United States, Australia and Europe that these countries required Japan to limit its exports. Japanese manufacturers countered by establishing production facilities in foreign countries, which allowed them to circumvent the quotas.

In the 1970s, Japan's electronics industry changed in emphasis from consumer products to commercial and industrial equipment, such as computer technology, communications and robotics. Today Japan's export of electronic machinery is second only to its export of automobiles. Major Japanese electronics manufacturers include Hitachi, Ltd.; Matsushita Electric Industrial Co., Ltd. (Panasonic); Mitsubishi Electric Corporation; Nippon Electric Co., Ltd. (NEC); NCR Japan, Ltd.; Oki Electric Industry Co., Ltd.; Pioneer Electronic Corporation; Ricoh Co., Ltd.; San'yo Electric Co., Ltd.; Sharp Corporation; Sony Corporation; and Toshiba Corporation.

See also AKIHABARA; BROADCASTING SYSTEM; CAMERAS AND PHOTOGRAPHY; COMPUTER INDUSTRY; EXPORTS AND IMPORTS; MINISTRY OF INTERNATIONAL TRADE AND INDUSTRY; ROBOTS AND ROBOTICS; SEMICONDUCTOR INDUSTRY; SONY CORPORATION; TELECOMMUNICATIONS SYSTEM.

EMA See HORSE; TALISMANS.

EMPEROR (*tenno*) The titular head of state in Japan. The emperor and the imperial family have had a complex and varied history over the last 1,500 years. Japan's imperial line is the oldest hereditary monarchy in the world, dating back to before the fifth century A.D. The eighth-century official chronicles *Kojiki* and *Nihon Shoki* trace the emperor's ancestry back to the Sun Goddess, Amaterasu o Mikami, through her grandson Ninigi no Mikoto and his grandson, Jimmu Tenno, the legendary first emperor of Japan. According to the legend, Amaterasu gave Ninigi a sacred mirror, sword and jewel, as the three symbols of authority when she sent him down to earth. These three sacred treasures, or Imperial Regalia, serve to legitimize imperial authority and are presented to each new emperor.

The reigning emperor is referred to as *tenno*, or "heavenly sovereign." In ancient times, there were female *tenno*, but by the eighth century only males were allowed to hold this position. An emperor is succeeded by his eldest son, the crown prince (*kotaishi*). The emperor's main role has been chief priest of Shinto, the native Japanese religion, as well as the symbol of the state. After Emperor Kammu (737–806; r. 781–806), emperors did not exercise actual power, but were manipulated by members of the imperial clan and court aristocracy, especially the Fujiwara clan. Between 1087 and 1192, emperors ruled through "cloister government" (*insei*), whereby power was wielded by a retired emperor who resided in a cloister or monastery. Ruling power was later exercised by feudal military leaders who took the title of shogun, beginning with Minamoto no Yoritomo, who founded the Kamakura Shogunate (1192–1333). Emperor Go-Daigo (1288–1339; r. 1318–1339) led a rebellion in 1333 to reassert imperial power but was soon defeated and exiled by Ashikaga Takauji, who founded the Ashikaga Shogunate and installed his own puppet emperor. The imperial line was thus divided into the Southern and Northern Courts, known as the Nambokucho Era (1336–1392), and Go-Daigo's line died out.

The third military government, the Tokugawa Shogunate (1603–1867), was overthrown by samurai who used the slogan Revere the Emperor, Expel the Barbarians (*Sonno joi*). This Meiji Restoration of 1868 restored the emperor to his position as head of state, although governing power was exercised in his name by Meiji leaders.

The cult of State Shinto was developed in 1869 to increase nationalistic fervor by promoting reverence for the emperor. The imperial family was moved from the Imperial Palace in Kyoto, the imperial capital for more than a thousand years, to a new palace on the site of Edo Castle in Tokyo (formerly Edo), whose name means "eastern capital."

At the end of World War II, Emperor Hirohito surrendered to the Allies and renounced his claim to divinity. Authorities of the postwar Allied Occupation of Japan

List of Emperors and Reigning Empresses

Number in Traditional Count	Sovereign	Birth and Death Dates	Reign Dates	Year of Enthronement[1]	Number in Traditional Count	Sovereign	Birth and Death Dates	Reign Dates	Year of Enthronement[1]
1	Jimmu[2]				66	Ichijo	980–1011	986–1011	
2	Suizei				67	Sanjo	976–1017	1011–1016	
3	Annei				68	Go-Ichijo	1008–1036	1016–1036	
4	Itoku				69	Go-Suzaku	1009–1045	1036–1045	
5	Kosho				70	Go-Reizei	1025–1068	1045–1068	
6	Koan				71	Go-Sanjo	1034–1073	1068–1073	
7	Kōrei	legendary			72	Shirakawa	1053–1129	1073–1087	
8	Kogen	emperors			73	Horikawa	1079–1107	1087–1107	
9	Kaika				74	Toba	1103–1156	1107–1123	(1108)
10	Sujin				75	Sutoku	1119–1164	1123–1142	
11	Suinin				76	Konoe	1139–1155	1142–1155	
12	Keiko				77	Go-Shirakawa	1127–1192	1155–1158	
13	Seimu				78	Nijo	1143–1165	1158–1165	(1159)
14	Chuai				79	Rokujo	1164–1176	1165–1168	
15	Ojin	late fourth to early fifth century			80	Takakura	1161–1181	1168–1180	
16	Nintoku				81	Antoku[5]	1178–1185	1180–1185	
17	Richu	first half of the fifth century			82	Go-Toba[6]	1180–1239	1183–1198	(1184)
18	Hanzei				83	Tsuchimikado	1195–1231	1198–1210	
19	Ingyo	mid-fifth century			84	Juntoku	1197–1242	1210–1221	(1211)
20	Anko				85	Chukyo	1218–1234	1221	
21	Yuryaku				86	Go-Horikawa	1212–1234	1221–1232	(1222)
22	Seinei				87	Shijo	1231–1242	1232–1242	(1233)
23	Kenzo	latter half of the fifth century			88	Go-Saga	1220–1272	1242–1246	
24	Ninken				89	Go-Fukakusa	1243–1304	1246–1260	
25	Buretsu				90	Kameyama	1249–1305	1260–1274	
26	Keitai				91	Go-Uda	1267–1324	1274–1287	
27	Ankan	first half of the sixth century			92	Fushimi	1265–1317	1287–1298	(1288)
28	Senka				93	Go-Fushimi	1288–1336	1298–1301	
29	Kimmei	509–571	531 or 539–571		94	Go-Nijo	1285–1308	1301–1308	
30	Bidatsu	538–585	572–585		95	Hanazono	1297–1348	1308–1318	
31	Yomei	?–587	585–587		96	Go-Daigo	1288–1339	1318–1339	
32	Sushun	?–592	587–592		97	Go-Murakami	1328–1368	1339–1368	
*33	Suiko	554–628	593–628		98	Chokei	1343–1394	1368–1383	
34	Jomei	593–641	629–641		99	Go-Kameyama	?–1424	1383–1392	
*35	Kogyoku[3]	594–661	642–645		N1	Kogon	1313–1364	1331–1333	(1332)
36	Kotoku	597–654	645–654		N2	Komyo	1322–1380	1336–1348	(1338)
*37	Saimei	594–661	655–661		N3	Suko	1334–1398	1348–1351	(1350)
38	Tenji	626–672	661–672	(668)	N4	Go-Kogon	1338–1374	1351–1371	(1354)
39	Kobun	648–672	672		N5	Go-En'yu	1359–1393	1371–1382	(1375)
40	Temmu	?–686	672–686	(673)	100	Go-Komatsu	1377–1433	1382–1412	(1392)
*41	Jito	645–703	686–697	(690)	101	Shoko	1401–1428	1412–1428	(1415)
42	Mommu	683–707	697–707		102	Go-Hanazono	1419–1471	1428–1464	(1430)
*43	Gemmei	661–722	707–715		103	Go-Tsuchimikado	1442–1500	1464–1500	(1466)
*44	Gensho	680–748	715–724		104	Go-Kashiwabara	1464–1526	1500–1526	(1521)
45	Shomu	701–756	724–749		105	Go-Nara	1497–1557	1526–1557	(1536)
*46	Koken[4]	718–770	749–758		106	Ogimachi	1517–1593	1557–1586	(1560)
47	Junnin	733–765	758–764		107	Go-Yozei	1572–1617	1586–1611	(1587)
*48	Shotoku	718–770	764–770		108	Go-Mizunoo	1596–1680	1611–1629	
49	Konin	709–782	770–781		*109	Meisho	1624–1696	1629–1643	(1630)
50	Kammu	737–806	781–806		110	Go-Komyo	1633–1654	1643–1654	
51	Heizei	774–824	806–809		111	Gosai	1637–1685	1655–1663	(1656)
52	Saga	786–842	809–823		112	Reigen	1654–1732	1663–1687	
53	Junna	786–840	823–833		113	Higashiyama	1675–1709	1687–1709	
54	Nimmyo	810–850	833–850		114	Nakamikado	1702–1737	1709–1735	(1710)
55	Montoku	827–858	850–858		115	Sakuramachi	1720–1750	1735–1747	
56	Seiwa	850–881	858–876		116	Momozono	1741–1762	1747–1762	
57	Yozei	869–949	876–884	(877)	*117	Go-Sakuramachi	1740–1813	1762–1771	(1763)
58	Koko	830–887	884–887		118	Go-Momozono	1758–1779	1771–1779	
59	Uda	867–931	887–897		119	Kokaku	1771–1840	1780–1817	
60	Daigo	885–930	897–930		120	Ninko	1800–1846	1817–1846	
61	Suzaku	923–952	930–946		121	Komei	1831–1867	1846–1867	(1847)
62	Murakami	926–967	946–967		122	Meiji	1852–1912	1867–1912	(1868)
63	Reizei	950–1011	967–969		123	Taisho	1879–1926	1912–1926	(1915)
64	En'yu	959–991	969–984		124	Hirohito	1901–1989	1926–1989	(1928)
65	Kazan	968–1008	984–986		125	Akihito	1933–	1989–	

*Empresses.

N: Emperors of the Northern Court during the period of the Northern and Southern Courts.

[1] Year of formal enthronement when later than first year of actual reign.

[2] The first 14 sovereigns are considered legendary rather than historical by modern scholars; traditional reign numbers are given here for convenience because they are still often used. The traditional reign dates given in the chronicle *Nihon shoki* for these sovereigns and for sovereigns 15 through 28 are rejected as impossibly early; however, the latter (15–28) are accepted as historical figures. The approximate dates given here for sovereigns 15 through 28 are based on recent archaeological evidence and on citations in Chinese and Korean sources.

[3] Kogyoku (35) later reigned as Saimei (37).

[4] Koken (46) later reigned as Shotoku (48).

[5] During the last phase of the Taira-Minamoto War, Antoku (81) fled the capital with the Taira and Go-Toba (82) was installed as rival emperor by the Minamoto; their reign dates thus overlap.

NOTE: The life and reign dates in this table have been carefully corrected for discrepancies between the Japanese lunar and Western solar calendars. In some instances they may differ from the tables in standard Japanese reference works, where the calendar conversion is often approximate. The reign dates of Suiko, for example, are often given as 592–628.

(1945–1952) allowed the imperial institution to be retained but abolished State Shinto. The Japanese constitution promulgated in 1947 and still in effect states that the emperor is the "symbol of the State and of the unity of the people" and that the emperor "shall not have powers related to government." There has been disagreement in postwar Japan about the role of the emperor as the symbolic head of the state. Some want to abolish the imperial system altogether, while others want to give the emperor a larger governing role. Shinto priests still regard the emperor as the chief priest of Shinto and the embodiment of the Japanese nation, and government funds have been used to support Ise and other Shinto shrines. The emperor leads the official rites at the most important Shinto ceremonies held at the three shrines within the Imperial Palace grounds. Nevertheless, there was much controversy about the inclusion of Shinto rites for the funeral of Emperor Hirohito (1901–1989; r. 1926–1989) in 1989.

Hirohito, known after death as the Emperor Showa, had the longest reign of any emperor in Japanese history. His eldest son, Akihito (b. 1933), is the current reigning emperor. Akihito's eldest son, Crown Prince Naruhito (b. 1960), is expected to become the next emperor of Japan. The enthronement ceremony for a new emperor is modeled on the Shinto thanksgiving festival following the new harvest.

See also AKIHITO, EMPEROR; AMATERASU O MIKAMI; CONSTITUTION OF 1947; CROWN PRINCE; FUJIWARA CLAN; GO-DAIGO, EMPEROR; HIROHITO, EMPEROR; IMPERIAL HOUSEHOLD; IMPERIAL PALACE (KYOTO); IMPERIAL PALACE (TOKYO); IMPERIAL REGALIA; ISE SHRINE; JIMMU TENNO; KOJIKI; MEIJI, EMPEROR; MEIJI RESTORATION OF 1868; NAMBOKUCHO ERA; NIHON SHOKI; NINIGO NO MIKOTO; RICE PLANTING AND HARVESTING FESTIVALS; REVERE THE EMPEROR, EXPEL THE BARBARIANS; SHINTO; STATE SHINTO; SHOWA ERA; TENNO; YAMATO.

EMPLOYMENT Around 60 million Japanese, about half of the total population, are in the work force. Throughout the 1980s, unemployment figures remained at less than 3%. In 1987 the percentage of people working in primary industries such as agriculture, fishing and forestry dropped to around 8.3%, the percentage in secondary industries such as manufacturing and construction was 33.3%, and the percentage in service industries such as distribution and retailing increased to 58.5%. Few young Japanese are now choosing to work in the primary or manufacturing industries.

Men who work full time in white-collar positions for large companies are referred to as salarymen. Hired in groups when they graduate from college, they are expected to remain with the same company throughout their working lives. Companies usually promote groups of coworkers in accordance with a seniority system. White- and blue-collar workers are expected to be loyal to the company and to work hard, but they benefit from job security. They have a close relationship with their bosses similar to that between children and parents. Groups of coworkers often spend the evening out together, eating and drinking with their bosses. Company loyalty is reinforced by company uniforms, badges, songs and sports facilities. Large bo-

nuses, home mortgages, company trips and similar benefits are commonly provided to the salarymen. Companies generally do not lay off workers unless business conditions are extremely bad. Most workers retire in their 50s. Until recently, the Japanese have worked six days a week, but the government is encouraging companies to institute a five-day work week. Most workers do not use their full vacation time, but take only about six days of vacation a year.

Young Japanese women commonly work for several years and then quit their jobs when they get married in their 20s. Japanese women traditionally did not work outside the home, but become mothers and homemakers. However, this situation is changing. The Equal Employment Opportunity Law was passed in 1986. In 1987, the number of working women in Japan rose to 16.1 million, a 38% increase since 1975. Women comprised 36.5% of the work force, and more than two-thirds of working women were married. Around 60% were more than 35 years old. The average Japanese woman has two children, and many mothers return to the work force after their children start school. Japanese working women get fourteen weeks of maternity leave. Most working women are considered part-time workers, and as such do not have the job security, benefits, income or the chance of advancement enjoyed by the salarymen, but women raising children often prefer the flexible schedules made possible by part-time employment. Young Japanese women who want to become career executives often seek employment with foreign companies that have branch offices in Japan, where they feel their chances of promotion are more favorable. Japanese women who perform clerical work are popularly referred to as "Office Ladies" or OLs. Teaching, nursing, retail sales and factory assembly work are other jobs readily available to women.

See also CORPORATIONS; GEISHA; INCOME; LABOR UNIONS; LIFETIME EMPLOYMENT SYSTEM; OFFICE LADY; RETIREMENT; SALARYMAN; SENIORITY SYSTEM.

EMPRESS See EMPEROR; IMPERIAL HOUSEHOLD; JINGU, EMPRESS; JITO, EMPRESS; SUIKO, EMPRESS.

EN See YEN.

ENAMEL, COLORED See CLOISONNE.

ENDO SHUSAKU (1923–) A well-known Japanese Roman Catholic novelist, playwright and humorist who has won every major Japanese literary award. Endo has also served as editor of an important literary journal, as chairman of the Literary Artists Association (Bungeika Kyokai) and on the selection committee for the Akutagawa Prize, Japan's most prestigious literary award. In addition, he manages Kiza, the largest Japanese amateur theatrical troupe.

Endo was born in Tokyo but lived in China until his parents divorced and his mother brought him back to Japan in 1933. His aunt convinced him to be baptized as a Roman Catholic when he was 11 years old. He studied French literature at Keio University and spent several years at the

University of Lyons in France, the first Japanese to study abroad after World War II. Endo suffered from respiratory illness, which often required him to be hospitalized, and he set many of his novels in hospitals to explore the connection he perceived between physical and spiritual ailments. His novels *White Man* (*Shiroi hito*; 1955), which won the Akutagawa Prize, and *Yellow Man* (*Kiiroi hito*; 1955) are concerned with different attitudes in Japan and the West regarding sin, guilt and the Christian religion. *Silence* (*Chimmoku*; 1966, translated 1969), which won the Tanizaki Prize, deals with the Japanese government's brutal persecution of Japanese Christians in the early 17th century. The image of Christ that he presented in this novel is developed in *By the Dead Sea* (*Shikai no hotori*; 1973) and *A Life of Jesus* (*Iesu no shogai*; 1973, translated 1978). He presents a personal view of the foreign Christian religion in his historical novel about a Japanese trade mission to the West in 1614, *Samurai* (1980), which won the Noma Prize. Other novels by Endo include *The Sea and Poison* (*Umi to dokuyaku*; 1957, translated 1972), *Wonderful Fool* (*Obakasan*; 1959, translated 1974), *Good Grief!* (*Taihen da*; 1969), *The Girl I Left Behind* (*Watashi ga suteta onna*; 1963), *When I Whistle* (*Kuchibue o fuku toki*; 1974, translated 1979) and *Scandal* (translated 1988) an autobiographical novel about a famous Japanese Catholic author. Endo's most recently translated novel is *Foreign Studies* (1965; tr. 1990), about the dislocation of three Japanese men in different eras who traveled to the West. See also AKUTAGAWA RYUNOSUKE; CHRISTIANITY IN JAPAN; NOVELS; TANIZAKI JUN'ICHIRO.

ENGLAND AND JAPAN See ADAMS, WILLIAM; ANGLO-JAPANESE ALLIANCE; EXPOSITIONS, INTERNATIONAL; WASHINGTON CONFERENCE AND NAVAL TREATY OF 1922; WORLD WAR I; WORLD WAR II.

ENLIGHTENMENT See BUDDHISM; SATORI; ZEN SECT OF BUDDHISM.

ENRYAKUJI The principal temple of the Tendai sect of Buddhism, founded by Saicho (767–822), on Mount Hiei (Hieizan) in the northeast section of the old capital city of Kyoto. Enryakuji is one of the most important religious and historical sites in Japan.

Saicho originally founded it as a small rural temple, named Heisanji or Ichijo Shikan-in, where he could live a quiet religious life. After studying Tendai (Tiantai or T'ient'ai in Chinese) Buddhism in China in A.D. 804, Saicho made this temple the Tendai center of Japan, and most of the great religious leaders in Japanese history subsequently studied on Mount Hiei. The temple was named Enryakuji by Emperor Saga in A.D. 823 for Enryaku, the official name of the year in which the temple was founded, A.D. 788. Enryakuji was believed to guard the city of Kyoto from demons who would attack from the northeast direction.

The temple complex grew to contain more than 3,000 buildings, and Tendai practices were combined with those of Shingon ("True Word" or Esoteric) Buddhism and Shinto, the indigenous Japanese religion. In the 10th and 11th centuries A.D., large factions of armed monks (*sohei*; also called *akuso*, "rowdy monks") fought each other at Enry-

akuji and threatened Kyoto. They made demands for court titles and large estates. When the warlord Oda Nobunaga (1534–1682) fought to gain control of central Japan, the warrior monks of Enryakuji refused their support. In 1571 Nobunaga attacked Mount Hiei, destroying the thousands of temple buildings and killing 3,000 monks and villagers who had sought protection there.

Some of Enryakuji's structures were restored by the warlords Toyotomi Hideyoshi (1536–1598) and Tokugawa Ieyasu (1543–1616), and can be seen today. The Kompon Chudo (also known as Ichijo Shikan-in), rebuilt in A.D. 1642, is the third-largest wooden building in Japan and a designated National Treasure. The Shakado, a building formerly called the Temborindo, is an original structure that was not destroyed during Nobunaga's attack. The Yokawa section of Enryakuji is regarded as the birthplace of the Pure Land (Jodo) sect of Buddhism because its founder, Honen (1133–1212), resided there. The precious objects in the treasure house of Enryakuji include calligraphy by Saicho and a monk's robe (*kesa*) that he acquired in China. See also BUDDHISM; HIEI, MOUNT; HONEN; KYOTO; MONASTICISM, BUDDHIST; NATIONAL TREASURES; ODA NOBUNAGA; PURE LAND SECT OF BUDDHISM; SAICHO; SHINGON SECT OF BUDDHISM; TEMPLES, BUDDHIST TENDAI SECT OF BUDDHISM; TOKUGAWA IEYASU; TOYOTOMI HIDEYOSHI.

ENTERPRISE GROUPS See CORPORATIONS.

ENVIRONMENTAL DISPUTES COORDINATION COMMISSION See CABINET, PRIME MINISTER'S; ENVIRONMENTAL ISSUES.

ENVIRONMENTAL ISSUES IN JAPAN Ever since Japan embarked on an ambitious program of modernization and industrialization a century ago, the majority of the Japanese population and industries have been crowded along the Pacific (eastern) coast, especially from Tokyo-Yokohama southwest to Nagoya and Osaka-Kobe. This region was decimated by bombing raids during World War II but was quickly rebuilt. By the 1960s, rapid economic growth created severe air pollution from automobiles, oil refineries, and iron, steel and petrochemical factories, and many people became ill. Rivers and coastal waters were also badly polluted; noise pollution, food poisoning and pollution by chemicals used in agriculture became serious problems as well.

During the 1950s and 1960s the Japanese had been shocked by cases of cadmium and mercury poisoning from wastes discharged into rivers. The most famous incident was Minamata disease, named for a city on Kyushu Island where people died, went blind or suffered brain damage from eating fish and shellfish contaminated by mercury dumped into the water. Minamata disease became a general term in Japan for pollution-caused diseases. By the 1970s, Japanese began to protest the injurious effects that rapid industrial expansion had on health and the environment. Japanese women have played a major role in the protests, through complaints issued by consumer movements and women's associations. Opposition political parties were also able to exploit health problems, such as the high incidence of asthma in the industrial city of Yokkaichi near Nagoya. Citizen's groups took legal action against companies that damaged people's health by polluting, known as "public injury" (kogai), and won many court decisions.

Another issue has been the "right to sunshine." The Japanese consider sunshine critical to their quality of life for solar heating, drying laundry etc., and have protested the blocking of sunshine by high-rise buildings. In 1971 the national government began enforcing a Waste Management and Public Cleansing Law, which over the years helped slow pollution and reverse its effects on the environment. In 1971 the government created the Environment Agency and established very strict emission standards that have been effective in cutting air pollution. Court cases between 1971 and 1973 decided that polluting companies should pay for damage they cause to the health and well-being of individuals. In 1972 Prime Minister Tanaka Kakuei announced a plan to spread industrial activity more widely around the Japanese islands, which would reduce pollution. But economic inflation and the so-called Oil Shock of 1973 prevented much of the plan from being implemented. However, air- and water-pollution control laws were passed and amended several times as necessary. Pollutants have been regulated, and offending companies have been prosecuted under the laws. Guilty companies are required to pay compensation and medical expenses for people who become ill from pollution. By the 1980s the government was awarding official compensation for victims of pollution. In 1981 70,000 Japanese were certified by the Environmental Agency as victims of pollution-related health problems. An Environmental Disputes Coordination Commission was established in the Prime Minister's Office to monitor complaints to local governments about pollution. There has been a large increase in complaints about the disposal of industrial waste. Environmental pollution will continue to be a major issue, and the Japanese are investing heavily in the development of pollution controls. The Ministry of International Trade and Industry (MITI) is responsible for resolving conflicting claims between pollution control and industrial growth and competitiveness.

Japan has been criticized by the world community for the practices of its fishing industry. Huge factory ships roam the oceans and decimate fishing grounds. Tuna fishermen in particular are denounced for killing dolphins in large numbers. Japan is also censured for commercial whaling, because whales are endangered species. Japan dissented from the 1985–1986 worldwide moratoriums on whaling, and although the United States and other nations have pressured Japan to abandon whaling, this issue is not yet settled. Japanese companies are also being criticized by the international community for such practices as cutting down vast rain forests in Malaysia, Indonesia and Brazil to produce disposable items like wooden chopsticks.

In 1988, Japan's Environment Agency issued a white paper, "Japan's Contribution toward the Conservation of the Global Environment," which offered an outline for future actions, especially through financial aid and technological expertise. In July 1989 Japan joined with the other Group of Seven industrial democracies in a call for increased attention to environmental issues. It has also participated in the work of the Intergovernmental Panel on Climate Change to help eliminate carbon dioxide and chlorofluorocarbons to prevent depletion of the ozone layer. The Japanese government allocated $2.1 billion specifically for environmental projects over FY 1989-FY 1991. The Tokyo Conference on the Global Environment and Human Response toward Sustainable Development was held in September 1989. Japan allocated $797 million for bilateral and multilateral environmental preservation projects in 1988. The Japan Federation of Economic Organizations (Keidanren) has set up a "global greenery" fund of $14.3 million to be used for such projects as irrigation. 1989 was designated Japan's "Year of Environmental Diplomacy," and saw a total ban on ivory imports there. Various coalitions of non-governmental organizations organized several conferences, notably the International People's Forum on Japan and the Global Environment. One group is the Japan Tropical Forest Action Network (JATAN); some of its major campaigns are to stop destruction of Malaysian rain forests and Southeast Asian mangrove forests.

In December 1989 the Central Council for Environmental Pollution Control, an advisory body to the Environment Agency, proposed a 38% reduction in nitrogen oxide (NO) emissions from diesel trucks and buses by the year 2000.

Beginning in the late 1960s, large corporations invested $7 billion annually for a decade to develop non-polluting, energy-efficient technology; this made Japan a world leader in pollution control. See also FISH AND FISHING INDUSTRY; INDUSTRIAL ZONES; MINAMATA DISEASE; MINISTRY OF INTERNATIONAL TRADE AND INDUSTRY; WATER; WHALING; WOMEN'S ASSOCIATIONS; NAMES OF INDIVIDUAL CITIES AND INDUSTRIES.

ESOTERIC BUDDHISM   See SHINGON SECT OF BUDDHISM.

ETHICS   See BUSHIDO; CONFUCIANISM; DILIGENCE; DUTY AND FEELINGS; ETIQUETTE; "FACE"; FAMILY; FILIAL PIETY; FEUDALISM; INDEBTEDNESS; LOYALTY; PURIFICATION; SHAME.

ETIQUETTE   The Japanese follow strict rules of etiquette in order to maintain social harmony. They bow when greeting another person, and to express humility when talking to another person. They will even bow while talking on the telephone. There are many levels of bows, from formal to informal. One bows more deeply to a person of a higher social rank.

The Japanese address each other by their family names with the honorific suffix -san (similar to Mr., Mrs., Miss, Ms.); for example, Suzuki-san. Only family members and close friends address each other by their given names. Businessmen exchange meishi (name cards) displaying their names and job titles when they meet for the first time, so they can determine which person has the higher social rank.

Japan has been described as a "vertical society" in which each person is always conscious of his or her rank in a social situation or group and behaves accordingly. Respect for seniors is considered essential. Children are trained in the virtue of filial piety (ko), or obeying and caring for one's parents. Duty (giri) to family and employer takes precedence over personal feelings (ninjo). Not doing anything to bring shame to one's family or social group is emphasized by the concept of "saving face." People who act as go-betweens (nakodo) are used, not only to bring prospective brides and grooms together, but also when a person wants to avoid direct confrontation with another.

The Japanese language is structured so that different levels of formals or informal speech are used depending on the situation and the relationship among speakers. Honorific language (keigo) is used to show respect for a person of higher status. Women use more honorific language than men.

Gift-giving is a very important aspect of Japanese culture that reinforces the network of social relationships. There are two main seasons when Japanese give gifts to thank superiors who have helped them in some way, at midsummer (chugen) and at the end of the year (seibo). Gifts are also given for weddings and other congratulatory occasions, and as souvenirs from a trip. They must be properly wrapped to reflect the occasion and the social status of the recipients.

In order to maintain social harmony and group solidarity, the Japanese practice rules of behavior based on the distinction between tatemae, the "front face" or public action, and honne, real intention, motive or substance. The terms omote (front) and ura (back) are also used to distinguish between public and private behavior. Thus one's real intentions may be hidden in a social situation to avoid conflict. The term tatemae also refers to the formal etiquette of the Japanese tea ceremony. See also BOWING; CLASS STRUCTURE; DEPENDENCY; DUTY AND FEELINGS; "FACE"; FAMILY; FILIAL PIETY; FUNERALS; GIFTS; LANGUAGE, JAPANESE, MEISHI; OBLIGATION; TEA CEREMONY; WEDDINGS; WRAPPING.

EXILE (ru) A traditional Japanese punishment for criminals and others out of political favor between the sixth century A.D. and the Meiji Era (1868–1912). Exile, or banishment, was considered only slightly less terrible than being sentenced to death. The Japanese, more than most Westerners, define themselves in terms of their familial, social and political groups, and have always found it distressing to be cut off from these groups. A legal code enacted in the seventh century A.D. specified "five punishments" (gokei) for criminals, of which exile was the fourth and death was the fifth. A criminal could be sent into exile nearby (kinru; up to 700 miles away), a medium distance away (churu; up to 1300 miles), or to a distant place (onru; about 3,000 miles away). The banished person would be carefully guarded in the place of exile, which was often an island. Sado Island in the Sea of Japan, off the coast of Niigata Prefecture on western Honshu Island, was the place where many deposed statesmen and even emperors were banished. A major episode in The Tale of Genji (Genji Monogatari, 11th century A.D.), the first and greatest classical Japanese work of fiction, tells of Prince Genji's exile by political rivals after his father abdicated the imperial

throne. The religious leader Nichiren (1222–1282) was exiled twice, the second time to Sado Island. Codes of the samurai class, which ruled Japan from the 12th century until the Meiji Restoration of 1868, included exile as a criminal punishment. During the Tokugawa Shogunate (1603–1867), exile was actually called "banishment to a distant island" (ento). Criminals were frequently banished to Hachijojima, an island off the east coast of Honshu Island south of Edo (modern Tokyo). The first modern criminal code in Japan, the Shinritsu Koryo (1870), specified that certain criminals could be exiled to the northern island of Hokkaido, for 18 months, one year or two years. The Penal Code, enacted in 1908 and still followed in Japan, dispensed with exile as a criminal punishment. See also GENJI, THE TALE OF; HOKKAIDO ISLAND; SEA OF JAPAN.

EXPENSE ACCOUNTS (kosaihi) Business entertainment is carried out on such a massive scale in Japan that annual expenditures equal $U.S. 20–30 billion, approximately the same amount as the Japanese defense budget. In 1988 total entertainment costs reached $32.5 billion, an increase of 8.3% over the previous year. This figure is nearly three times higher than in the United States and 14 times higher than in Great Britain. Until the 1970s, the Japanese government was very lenient about tax regulations for such entertainment expenses because they helped to influence foreign buyers and thus to encourage the export of Japanese products. The practice continues on a large scale despite tax reform, however, and has created an entire subculture of nighttime entertainment, particularly in the Akasaka and Ginza districts of Tokyo. Executives often take their clients to a Japanese-style restaurant (ryotei) serving 10 or more courses over several hours. Women entertainers known as geisha may also be hired to dance, sing and play the shamisen, a musical instrument similar to a banjo. The guests and hosts (who are generally all male, as women as a rule do not rise to executive positions in Japanese companies) will also sing their favorite songs. Later in the evening the party usually moves on to a bar with beautifully dressed hostesses. Karaoke bars, where customers sing to prerecorded music, are very popular with Japanese businessmen. Drinking, eating and the companionship of women who are trained to keep the conversation flowing, all help to smooth relations between buyers and sellers and pave the way for successful business transactions. See also AKASAKA; CORPORATIONS; GEISHA; GINZA; KARAOKE; RESTAURANTS; SHAMISEN; WATER TRADE.

EXPO '70 Osaka International Exposition of 1970; the first world's fair to be held in an Asian country, held from March 15 to September 13, 1970, in Osaka, Japan's second largest city. The theme of the fair was Progress and Harmony for Mankind, and its emblem was a cherry blossom, symbol of Japan, with five petals representing five continents. There were more than 100 pavilions with exhibits by 77 countries and private companies, including major Japanese corporations such as Mitsubishi, Mitsui, and Sumitomo. The fair cost about Y120 billion (U.S.$335 million) to produce. Many exhibits featured space technology, and the American spaceship Apollo and a rock brought back from the moon were popular attractions. Fifty million people visited Expo '70. Two thousand Japanese hostesses speaking a total of 29 languages greeted more than 1 million visitors from outside Japan. This was the first World's Fair that transported people by a moving sidewalk, electric cars and a monorail, and the first to use computers to provide information for visitors. Japan first participated in a world's fair in Paris in 1867. It had been scheduled to hold a world's fair in Tokyo in 1940, but the fair was canceled after the outbreak of World War II. See also EXPOSITIONS, INTERNATIONAL; OSAKA.

EXPO '85 See TSUKUBA ACADEMIC NEW TOWN.

EXPORTS AND IMPORTS Japanese exports consist of manufactured goods and services, especially autos, electronics and industrial machinery, while imports consist of raw materials, including food, oil, iron, copper, wood, wool and cotton. Because Japan has few natural resources, it has concentrated on exporting manufactured goods. In order for Japan to rebuild its economy and industries after World War II, the Japanese government heavily emphasized the export of goods, and provided tax credits, financing and guidance for industries that could produce exportable goods. The Ministry of International Trade and Industry (MITI) was created in 1949 to oversee foreign trade, which is conducted mostly through the large trading companies (sogo sosha). The Japan Export Bank, later called the Import-Export Bank, was established in 1950 to provide long-term loans for export-oriented businesses and to extend loans to developing countries so they can import Japanese products. The Japan External Trade Organization (JETRO) was established in 1951 to conduct marketing and trade research. Japan was admitted to the General Agreement on Tariffs and Trade in 1955. From 1960 to 1970, Japanese exports increased at an annual rate of 17%. Japanese companies became successful by acquiring foreign technology, engaging in research and development, and constructing new manufacturing plants, many of which were automated to increase productivity and product reliability.

As Japan's trade surplus has grown since the late 1970s, it has been accused by its trading partners of maintaining nontariff barriers to imports. These include import quotas, mainly on agricultural commodities; complicated procedures for approving imports of manufactured goods; and restrictions on imports that would affect employment or political conditions in Japan. Bowing to pressure by the United States and other countries to remove restraints on imports, Japan has agreed to some "voluntary export quotas" on products such as automobiles, television sets and textiles, and has negotiated "orderly marketing agreements." Many countries have also enacted or threatened to enact legislation to protect their own industries from Japanese imports, as well as to force Japan to open its markets to more imported goods.

The highest percentage (24%) of Japanese exports go to the United States, followed by West Germany, South Korea, Taiwan, China, Saudi Arabia and Hong Kong. The United States and Saudi Arabia have been the largest exporters to Japan, followed by Indonesia, the United Arab Emirates, Australia, Canada, Iraq, China, Iran, Malaysia and Kuwait. In 1987, Japanese exports were worth a total of U.S.$229 billion, and imports totaled U.S.$150 billion.

Japan believes it necessary to have trade surpluses with a number of countries in order to offset its trade deficits with oil-exporting countries. The oil crisis of 1973, when Arab nations placed an embargo on oil exports, shocked the Japanese into realizing their vulnerability to imports of fuel and other vital commodities. Energy-conservation measures were undertaken and manufacturing plants were modernized to maintain high productivity while decreasing Japan's dependence on imported resources. See also AUTOMOBILE INDUSTRY; BANKING SYSTEM; CORPORATIONS; COMPUTER INDUSTRY; ELECTRONICS INDUSTRY; FOREIGN TRADE; INVESTMENTS OVERSEAS, JAPANESE; JAPAN EXTERNAL TRADE ORGANIZATION; MINISTRY OF INTERNATIONAL TRADE AND INDUSTRY; OIL CRISIS OF 1973; ROBOTS AND ROBOTICS; SEMICONDUCTOR INDUSTRY; SHIPPING AND SHIPBUILDING; TRADING COMPANY, GENERAL.

EXPOSITIONS, INTERNATIONAL (EXPO) The first international exposition was held in 1851 at the Crystal Palace in Hyde Park, London, for countries to exhibit their manufactured and handmade goods and art. International expositions served as global trade fairs but also opened windows into different world cultures. When England held a second international exposition in London in 1862, hundreds of Japanese products were exhibited for the first time abroad, including porcelain and pottery, lacquer ware, inlaid woods, bronze ware, paper samples, medicines and surgical instruments. They were not sent by the Japanese government but were from the collection of Sir Rutherford Alcock, the first British minister to Japan. The items fueled Western interest in Japan, which had just been opened to the West after more than two centuries of self-imposed isolation.

In 1867 Japan accepted the invitation of Napoleon III (1808–1873) to exhibit at an international exposition in Paris. The French were already familiar with Japanese woodblock prints. The Tokugawa Shogunate (1603–1867) sent an official mission to the exposition led by Tokugawa Akitake (1853–1910). It also sent thousands of agricultural and manufactured products, crafts and art works, including 445 pieces of lacquer ware, 214 ceramic objects, 190 swords, 5,600 woodblock prints, 690 fans, and musical instruments, armor and boats. The Japanese provinces of Saga and Satsuma also sent independent exhibitions; Saga sent 60,000 ceramic objects, and Satsuma sent crafts from the southern Ryukyu Islands, which it controlled.

In 1873 another international exposition was held in Vienna. The new Meiji government (1868–1912), which had the goal of modernizing and industrializing Japan, sent an exhibition of Japanese crafts, thus gaining more attention from the Western powers.

In 1876 Japan participated in the Philadelphia Centennial Exposition in the United States. Japanese ceramics, lacquer ware and copper ware proved very popular. Some of the objects that were displayed remain in museum collections in Philadelphia and Washington, D.C.

A Japanese garden by Matsukata Masayoshi was built for the 1878 International Exposition in Paris. For the 1893 World's Columbian Exposition in Chicago, Japan built a pavilion in the style of the Phoenix Hall at Byodoin temple in Uji near Kyoto, and filled it with a wide variety of craft items and artworks. There were also international expositions in London in 1886, Paris in 1889 and Brussels in 1897. The Japanese pagoda and landscape garden built for the 1894 Midwinter Exposition in San Francisco were given to the city as a public garden, which remains open today.

For the 1900 international exposition in Paris, the Japanese pavilion displayed a massive exhibition of classical arts and crafts, including paintings, sculpture, wood carvings, ceramics, metal work, lacquer ware and Noh drama costumes. This was the first major exhibition of Japanese classical art abroad.

During the early 20th century, Japanese arts and crafts were overshadowed by industrialization and militarization. But in 1970 Japan was honored as the first Asian country to hold a world's fair, known as Expo '70, in Osaka. Japan has held several expos since then, including Expo '85 in Tsukuba and Expo '90 in Osaka. See also EXPO '70; MEIJI RESTORATION OF 1868; SECLUSION, NATIONAL; TOKUGAWA SHOGUNATE; TSUKUBA ACADEMIC NEW TOWN; NAMES OF INDIVIDUAL ARTS AND CRAFTS.

F

FABRICS See BROCADE; HEMP; KASURI; SILK; TEXTILES.

"FACE" *(kao)* The individual or personal self as seen by others in public; a person's reputation. The Japanese are concerned about keeping up a good image with other people. They want to avoid doing anything that would bring shame to themselves and, by extension, their families. Respecting and caring for one's elders, known as filial piety, is a central principle of Confucianism, which was introduced into Japan with Chinese culture in the sixth century A.D. The Japanese concept of face is also related to the principles of etiquette known as *tatemae* and *honne; tatemae* is a formal mode of public behavior and expression which masks *honne*, one's true feelings or honest opinion. The harmony of a group is maintained, and danger to social relationships is prevented, by avoiding the direct expression of *honne*. Differences of opinion may be expressed indirectly or through superiors or go-betweens. A conflict may arise between duty *(giri)* to one's group or family and personal feelings *(ninjo)*; in extreme cases, the only way to resolve the conflict and hence "save face" was traditionally to commit suicide. A common theme of popular entertainment in the Edo Era (1600–1868) was the double suicide of doomed lovers. Committing suicide to save face is also related to the feudal concept of loyalty to one's lord, which required a samurai to commit suicide to avoid defeat in battle. In Japan, "face" as a social concept is often used literally. A person has a "broad face" or reputation *(kao ga hiroi)* if he or she knows many people. The face of a person who has been shamed is "smeared with dirt" *(kao o yogosu)* or "smashed" *(kao o tsubusareru)*. On the contrary, to "save face" with others is spoken of as "making one's face stand" *(kao o tateru)*. The concept of face is also an important aspect of traditional Japanese theater. For example, Kabuki actors wear highly stylized facial makeup which expresses their character. Main characters in Noh drama cover their faces with masks which represent the essence of the figures being portrayed. Geisha also wear heavy makeup which hides their real features. Japanese women of all classes like to keep their faces carefully made up so as to present a good public image. See also CONFUCIANISM; DUTY AND FEELINGS; ETIQUETTE; FILIAL PIETY; GEISHA; KABUKI; LOYALTY; MAKEUP; NOH DRAMA; SHAME; SUICIDE.

FACTIONS, POLITICAL *(habatsu)* Competitive groups organized around individuals within political parties, especially the Liberal Democratic Party (LDP; Jiyu Minshuto), the dominant political party in Japan; close personal ties rather than a shared political ideology, characterizes the factions.

The LDP is actually a combination of various groupings, which may have protracted intraparty struggles with each other. The number of factions in the LDP has ranged from eight to 13, with some factions having as few as four members and others having more than 100. All faction members are members of the Diet, the Japanese parliament. The faction system is most entrenched in the House of Representatives (lower house) of the Diet, which has more power than the House of Councillors (upper house). Since the LDP controls the Diet, whichever faction leader becomes president of the LDP is automatically selected as prime minister. Hence if a politician wants to become prime minister of Japan, he must first become a local leader (since the vast majority of national politicians are recruited from local government) and then the leader of a party faction. Faction members are pledged to vote for their leader as prime minister, in return for assistance that furthers their own careers, such as funds for offices and staff, campaign funds, and introduction to influential industry and government leaders. In choosing a new prime minister, senior party leaders create a balance of power between the factions that support the leader and those that do not. The prime minister puts together a cabinet that carefully represents the strengths of the various LDP factions, with members of the most powerful factions chosen to head the most important ministries. Most faction leaders chosen as prime minister gain valuable experience by serving in the government bureaucracy before being elected to the Diet. They also serve in various key party positions, such as secretary-general of the LDP, and as top cabinet ministers.

Some faction leaders who have served as prime minister are Tanaka Kakuei (1972–1974), Miki Takeo (1974–1976), Fukuda Takeo (1976–1978), Ohira Masayoshi (1978–1980), Nakasone Yasuhiro (1982–1987), and Takeshita Noboru (1987–1989).

The faction system was technically abolished in 1976, but factional groups continue to operate in much the same way despite several attempts to eliminate them. Following the February 18, 1990 elections for members of the House of Representatives, the most powerful LDP factions were led by Takeshita Noboru, Abe Shintaro, Watanabe Michio (who replaced Nakasone Yasuhiro), Miyazawa Kiichi, and Komoto Toshio, whose faction includes current prime minister Kaifu Toshiki. See also CABINET, PRIME MINISTER'S; DIET; ELECTIONS; LIBERAL DEMOCRATIC PARTY; POLITICAL PARTIES; PRIME MINISTER; NAMES OF INDIVIDUAL PRIME MINISTERS.

FAIR DAY *(ennichi)* A market fair held at a Shinto shrine or Buddhist temple to honor a god. The word *ennichi* is written with the characters for "union" or "special connection" *(en)* and "day" *(nichi)*.

Fair days originated as special days in the Buddhist calendar for communion with Buddhist gods, with a particular day set aside for each god. For example, the 18th day of the month was the fair day of Kannon and the 24th that of Jizo. People who took part in religious worship on a particular fair day were thought to receive special favors from the god being honored. Merchants set up stalls on shrine or temple grounds to sell goods and snacks to large crowds attending the fair.

Fair days became popular secular amusements during the Edo Era (1600–1868), and many shrines and temples around the country continue to have regular fair days on specific dates, many of which feature the sale of special items. At the Ground Cherry Fair (Hosuki-ichi), held at Sensoji Temple in the Asakusa district of Tokyo every July 9th and 10th, more than 300 stalls sell potted ground cherry (or Chinese lantern) plants. Sensoji also holds the traditional Battledore Fair (Hagoita-ichi) December 17th–19th. Battledores are decorated paddles used to play *hanetsuki,* a game similar to badminton, especially at the New Year Festival. Morning glory plants are sold at the Morning Glory Fair (Asagao-ichi) at Iriya, in Tokyo, every July. Bamboo rakes (*kumade*), decorated with the face of a comic figure named Okame and intended to bring good fortune to their owners, are sold at the Rooster Fair (Tori-no-ichi) at Otori Shrine in Tokyo; this is held on the Day of the Rooster in November, the month associated with the rooster in the traditional zodiac calendar. Kitano Shrine in Kyoto holds a traditional public market one day every month. See also ASAKUSA; CHICKEN AND ROOSTER; FESTIVALS; GODS; JIZO; KANNON; NEW YEAR FESTIVAL; OKAME; SHRINES, SHINTO; TEMPLES, BUDDHIST; ZODIAC.

FAIR TRADE COMMISSION See CABINET, PRIME MINISTER'S; EXPORTS AND IMPORTS.

FAMILY *(ie)* The traditional Japanese family is an extended patriarchal group known as an *ie* (stem family), usually translated as "household," which often includes branch families under the authority of the main family, as well as distant relations and persons unrelated. It is often referred to as a "fictive" kinship relationship, since family members may be adopted and blood lines do not determine relationships.

The *ie* developed from the ancient system of family groups known as *uji,* similar to clans, which were economic units including people who worked for a household as well as close and distant relatives. In an *ie,* the father traditionally had absolute authority over individual members of the family. He was responsible for the family's economic well-being, conduct of family members, performance of ceremonies honoring deceased ancestors, and other matters affecting the family. The eldest son became the family head when the father retired from household responsibilities or died. If there was no son, a daughter would be married to a man who was adopted into the family to become its leader. Some Japanese men still become "adopted sons-in-law" (*mukoyoshi* or *yoshi*) to continue the family name, or inherit a family business or property. This practice is also followed if a son is not responsible enough to become head of the family, or if the family does not want to lose a daughter. Daughters usually "married out" into the families of their husbands (*yome ni iku,* "to go as a bride") and had to submit to their rules, enforced by authoritarian mothers-in-law. Sons other than the eldest son were adopted into other families or started new branch families. Sons are frequently given names that indicate their birth order. The eldest son and his wife traditionally lived with his parents to care for them and inherit the family property or business. Obedience to and respect for parents, a central concept of Confucianism known as filial piety, is a basic principle of Japanese society. This is reinforced by the Japanese concept of duty (*giri*) and obligation (*on*) to one's parents.

In Japan, marriage has been a union of two families rather than of two individuals. Each family keeps a household register (*koseki*) listing all its members. Formerly, a wife was erased from her family's register and added to that of her husband. Legal reforms enacted in 1947 require that each newlywed couple start a new household register.

Wives are called *okusan* (more formally, *okusama*), or "Mrs. Interior." Family roles have always been strictly divided. The wife traditionally stays at home and raises the children, with whom she develops an extremely close relationship, described as dependency (*amae*). Wives handle family finances and give their husbands allowances, make major decisions about purchases, investments and education of children. Women who are divorced traditionally return to their own families and are known as *demodori,* or "returnees."

From the 13th century until 1873, a woman could not request a divorce. During the Edo Era (1600–1868), a man could divorce his wife merely by sending her a note known as "three-and-a-half lines" (*mikudarihan*). Most divorces today are requested by the wife, who keeps custody of the children. The Japanese divorce rate is still low, around 10% of marriages, because divorced women cannot easily support themselves or find other husbands.

Since World War II, the traditional family system is less common. Today a typical Japanese family consists of two parents and one or two children. Most people live in urban areas where housing space is very limited, so three generations cannot always live together in one home, although they try to live near each other. Japanese children call their grandmothers *obasan,* and their grandfathers *ojisan.* Male and female grandchildren are both referred to as *mago* (child lineage). See also ALTARS IN HOMES; CHILDREN; DEPENDENCY; DUTY AND FEELINGS; FATHER; FILIAL PIETY; FUNERALS; HIGAN; HOMES AND HOUSING; HOUSEHOLD REGISTER; MOTHER; NAMES, JAPANESE; RETIREMENT; WEDDINGS.

FANS *(ogi, sensu, uchiwa)* Fans are traditionally used by men and women alike in Japan, and are usually made of bamboo and paper. The two most common types of Japanese fan are the *sensu* or *ogi,* a folding fan, and the *uchiwa,* a flat fan. The latter type was probably introduced into Japan from China in the sixth century A.D. Folding fans were invented by the Japanese in the seventh century A.D.

and were called *ogi* at that time. An *uchiwa* is made by pasting thick paper onto a long-handled frame of bamboo to make a round, flat fan that cannot be folded. The paper is decorated with a simple but brightly colored design. An *uchiwa* can be tucked into the *obi* (sash) of a *yukata*, an informal cotton robe, for use on hot summer nights. It is also used to cool hot rice to be used in sushi, and to fan charcoal on which food is being grilled. A special type of flat fan known as *gumbai* was used in the feudal era by military officers to signify their rank and to issue orders to their troops. Such a fan had an iron handle and a body made of heavy paper or leather decorated with a symbol such as a family crest. The *gumbai* is still used by referees in sumo wrestling bouts. Iron fans called *gunsen* were also used in battle, held as symbols by leaders. Samurai carried fans called *jinsen*, made of peacock or pheasant feathers. *Sensu* or *ogi*, folding fans, are used more widely today than flat fans. A *sensu* is made by connecting from three to 25 bamboo ribs at a pivot (*kaname*) at the base, and pasting a semicircular piece of paper onto the ribs. The paper is decorated with an elegant painting or calligraphy. Fans painted by famous Japanese artists have become valuable collector's items, and beautiful fans can be displayed on special stands.

In Japan, fans have served as signs of respect on religious and ceremonial occasions, as gifts on auspicious occasions, and as decorations. Large folding fans are still used as accessories in classical Japanese dance (*Nihon buyo*) and as props in storytelling (*rakugo*), Kabuki theater and Noh drama. Small folding fans are used in the closed position during formal bows in the tea ceremony. Buddhist priests and persons chanting religious scriptures (*sutras*) also use fans. See also BAMBOO; CALLIGRAPHY; DANCE, TRADITIONAL; KABUKI; NOH DRAMA; PAINTING; PAPER, HANDMADE; SUMO; TEA CEREMONY.

FARMHOUSE (*minka, noka*) *Minka* is the general term for a Japanese home of simple construction inhabited by a member of the nonruling class, prior to the introduction of Western architecture in the late 19th century. A farmhouse, while often referred to as a *minka*, is properly called a *noka*. A townhouse is known as a *machiya*, and a home in a fishing village is called a *gyoka*. *Minka* are made of wood; walls are sometimes made of bamboo plastered with clay. Grass is used to thatch the steeply pitched roof, and straw is used to make thin mats (*mushiro*) and *tatami* (thick mats) used as floor covering. Stones are used for foundations but not for walls.

Minka differ in style depending on when and where they were built, but they share certain general features that were developed in the late 16th to early 17th centuries. The structure is a framework of joined columns and beams. Walls are fitted between columns but do not bear the weight of the structure, so they can be opened to the outside by moving *shoji* (sliding screens). Sliding walls or screens (*fusuma*) can alter the size of rooms or provide privacy. There are commonly four rooms. A work area (*doma*) with an earthen floor, comprising about one-third of the floor area in a farmhouse, contains a clay stove (*kamado*) for cooking. Large pottery jars of water and food are stored in this area. Another area, raised about 20 inches off the ground and covered with *tatami* mats for sitting and sleeping, contains an open hearth (*irori*), which is the center of family life and provides the only heat for the house. A large iron kettle (*kama*) is suspended over the hearth (*irori*). The front room (*zashiki* or *dei*) is used to receive guests or for formal occasions; it has a *tokonoma* (decorative alcove) for displaying flower arrangements and scrolls. A covered narrow wooden verandah (*engawa*) runs along the side of the house. The bath and toilet are often placed in separate buildings outside the house, along with a storehouse (*kura* or *dozo*).

A townhouse has similar features but is usually long and narrow because sites in urban areas were limited. It often has a second floor. Because fires have been a constant danger in Japanese cities, exteriors of townhouses are commonly coated with clay, and roofs are usually tiled or shingled rather than thatched.

Some old *minka* have been designated National Treasures (Important Cultural Properties) by the Japanese government. Outdoor museums with collections of *minka* may be visited in several regions of the country. See also BATH; KETTLE; ROOF TILES; STOREHOUSE; STRAW WARE; TATAMI; TOILET; TOKONOMA; WOODWORKING.

FARMING See AGRICULTURE.

FASHION DESIGNERS, CONTEMPORARY JAPANESE
Western-style clothing is called *yofuku* in Japan to distinguish it from *wafuku*, or native Japanese clothing. *Wafuku* consists of kimono and other robes, such as the casual *yukata*, made from long, narrow panels of fabric and wrapped to conceal the shape of the body.

Mori Hanae (known abroad as Hanae Mori; b. 1926) became the first internationally renowned Japanese fashion designer. Her clothes are tailored in the Western style, but she follows Japanese tradition in using beautiful fabrics that are sewn together with great care and attention to detail.

Younger contemporary Japanese fashion designers have become known for incorporating Japanese elements into their Western-style clothing, using large pieces of fabric that are not fitted to the body and that are monotone in color, especially gray or black. Such strong but unstructured designs, which have a monumental, sculptural quality and allow freedom of motion, have been a major influence on Western designers.

Important Japanese designers have studied fashion in Paris, and show their collections in Paris and New York as well as Tokyo. Kawakubo Rei (known abroad as Rei Kawakubo) emphasizes freedom of the body. Her label is Comme des Garcons. Some famous male designers include Takada Kenzo (known abroad as Kenzo; b. 1939), Miyake Issei (known abroad as Issey Miyake; b. 1938), and Yamamoto Yohji (known abroad as Yohji Yamamoto). Kenzo attracted worldwide attention with his "big silhouette" designs. He is highly regarded in Japan as a pioneer who opened the way for international recognition of Japanese designers. The Council of Fashion Designers (CFD), Tokyo, headed by former New York freelance fashion writer Ota Nobuyuki, has 44 paid designers who represent the top names in the Japanese fashion world, including Mori Hanae, Miyake Issei, Yamamoto Kansai, Yamamoto Yohji, Kawakubo Rei, and newcomers such as Higa Kyoko (A Rose Is a Rose), Ota Norihisa (C'est Vrai), Abe Kensho (Kensho), and menswear designers Onozuka Akira (Odds On), Kobayahi Yukio (Monsieur Nicole), Hosokawa Shin (Shin Pashu) and Katoh Kazutaka (Tete Homme). The CFD mediates between designers and their financial backers, negotiates agreements on trademark and other important issues, and serves as an information clearing house for visiting foreign fashion writers. See also CLOTHING; KIMONO; MORI HANAE; TEXTILES.

FATHER (otosan)   Japan has a patriarchal system in which the father is the head of the family. When he retires or dies, his eldest son becomes the new head of the family. In ancient Japan, descent was through the female side of the family, but with the introduction of patriarchal Chinese culture in the sixth century A.D. and the rise of the samurai class in the feudal era (12th–16th centuries), the father became the central authority figure. An old Japanese proverb states that children are most afraid of "earthquakes, lightning, fires, and father."

Marriage in Japan has traditionally been an arranged economic relationship binding two families rather than a personal relationship between two individuals. The woman marries into the husband's family. The traditional Japanese household, known as an *ie*, could include branch families and other persons who were all placed under the authority of the head of the family. The Meiji government (1868–1912) enacted a civil code in 1898 that gave the father complete control over family property, the right to decide where the family would reside, and the right to approve or disapprove marriages and divorces by family members. Sons usually took on their fathers' social roles and trades or occupations. Boys who became apprentices to learn traditional crafts and trades entered into fictive father-child relationships with their teachers or employers.

In modern Japanese families, the husband and father supports the family and is its nominal head. The father serves as the symbol of authority and proper behavior for his children and metes out punishment when necessary. However, the wife or mother runs the home, handles the family finances and makes major decisions about the children's education. Because of this, in Japan it is commonly said that a man is a "guest" in his own home. The Japanese father projects a strong image in his public role, but modern comic books and television shows often satirize him as actually weak and helpless, another child for the wife to take care of. Many fathers, especially businessmen, do not spend much time with their children because they socialize after work with their coworkers and arrive home late at night. Sunday is often the only day fathers and children are together. Fathers who are sent to work in other cities or abroad often leave their families behind.

The primary relationship in a family is not between husband and wife, but between mother and child. The father and mother fulfill their specific duties in separate spheres. Husband and wife respectfully address each other as "mother" (okaasan or mama) and "father" (otosan or papa), a reflection of the primacy of the parenting role rather than the spouse role. See also APPRENTICE SYSTEM; CHILDREN; FAMILY; MOTHER; RETIREMENT.

FATHER-SON RELATIONSHIP   See APPRENTICE SYSTEM; DEPENDENCY; FAMILY; IEMOTO; YAKUZA.

FEBRUARY 26TH INCIDENT (1936) (Niniroku Jiken)   An attempted coup d'etat by 1,400 soldiers who belonged to the so-called Kodo faction (Kodoha, Imperial Way Faction) of the Imperial Japanese Army's 1st Division. The Kodo faction called for a return to traditional military values, devotion to the Japanese emperor and the defeat of the Soviet Union as part of its imperialist designs on the Asian mainland. The Kodo faction was a rival to the Tosei faction (Toseiha, Control faction), which supported a modern army and expansion into China rather than war with the Soviet Union. The factional conflict was heightened when General Mazaki Jinzaburo, a leader of the Kodoha, was removed from his post after he was implicated in a plot to assassinate leading Japanese politicians in 1934. A Kodo officer retaliated by murdering General Nagata Tetsuzan of the Tosei faction in 1935. During the 1930s there were many political assassinations and rebellions by members of the Japanese military. Tensions were high due to poverty and suffering caused by the Depression and by famine in rural areas, limitations on Japanese imports by foreign countries, a Russian military buildup following the Japanese takeover of Manchuria in 1931, and the ineffectiveness of Japanese politicians. The 1st Division of the Imperial Japanese Army was ordered to Manchuria in late 1935. On February 26, 1936, junior officers in the Kodo faction of the 1st Division led an occupation of the central district of Tokyo, surrounding the Imperial Palace, occupying several government buildings, including the Army Ministry, and assassinating three major government figures and shooting two others. They attempted to murder Prime Minister Okada Keisuke but instead shot his brother-in-law by mistake. Leaders of the rebellion ordered Army Minister Kawashima Yoshiyuki to set up a new governing cabinet headed by an army general who agreed with their goals. The military did not move against the rebellion immediately because a number of high-ranking officers supported it. However, the general staff of the army and navy opposed the rebellion, as did Emperor Hirohito (now known as Emperor Showa). After two days of inconclusive negotiations, martial law was declared in Tokyo on February 27th; troops were brought in; and on February 28th an imperial command ordered that the rebels be ousted. On February 29th, the army succeeded in convincing most of the soldiers to give up in exchange for a pardon, and two officers who led the rebellion committed suicide. Other officers were court-martialed in secret; 19 were executed for their role in the rebellion and 70 others were given prison terms. Senior army officers who did not participate but agreed with the rebellion were forced to resign their posts. Martial law was ended in Tokyo on July 18, 1936. See also HIROHITO, EMPEROR; IMPERIAL JAPANESE ARMY AND NAVY; MANCHURIAN INCIDENT.

FEDERATION OF JAPANESE ECONOMIC ORGANIZATIONS (Keizai Dantai Rengokai; abbreviated Keidanren)

The most important of the four main business associations in Japan, along with the Japan Chamber of Commerce and Industry, the Japan Committee for Economic Development and the Japan Federation of Employers' Associations. Founded in 1946 when Japanese business was being reorganized under the Allied Occupation following World War II, in 1952 it became very influential after it merged with the Japan Industrial Council (Nihon Sangyo Kyogikai). Representing key industries, Keidanren serves as a mediator of differences among its members and advises the Japanese government on ways to improve the economy. During the 1950s and 1960s, the Keidanren played a major role in helping the Japanese government draw up a comprehensive business plan for the country. As a representative of big business, it is influential in Japanese politics. In 1955 it was a driving force in the formation of the dominant Liberal Democratic Party (LDP) through the union of the Japan Democratic Party and the Liberal Party. It also provided much of the LDP's funding until a law was passed in 1976 regulating campaign contributions. The Keidanren has nearly 40 committees on major business issues, such as economic cooperation, foreign trade, defense production and energy sources. It also functions on the international level by working with business leaders in other countries. See also CORPORATIONS; JAPAN CHAMBER OF COMMERCE AND INDUSTRY; LIBERAL DEMOCRATIC PARTY.

FEMALE IMPERSONATORS See KABUKI; OKUNI.

FEMINIST MOVEMENTS

The first feminist organization in Japan was the Bluestocking Society (Seitosha), founded in 1911 by Hiratsuka Raicho (1886–1971) and four other women. It addressed social problems of Japanese women. The first Japanese national group for women's rights was the New Woman's Association (Shin Fujin Kyokai), founded in 1920 by Hiratsuka to fight for political, economic, social and legal reforms to benefit Japanese women. In 1922 the group gained the right for women to participate in political activities. Other important feminist leaders include Kato Shizue (1897–   ), who has been active in family planning, and the educator Kawasaki Natsu (1889–1966). Ichikawa Fusae (1893–1981) was a prominent leader of the prewar suffrage movement. The Universal Manhood Suffrage Act was passed in Japan in 1925, but did not extend to women the right to vote. Women campaigned for suffrage and other rights during the 1930s but their struggles were displaced by Japan's involvement in World War II. During the Allied Occupation of Japan, under the leadership of U.S. General Douglas MacArthur, a new Japanese constitution enacted in 1947 and still in effect gave women the right to vote and stated that women are equal under the

law and should not be discriminated against in political, economic or social relations.

In 1975 a Liaison Group was formed, under the leadership of Ichikawa Fusae, as a federation of about 50 women's organizations to implement goals of the United Nations Decade for Women. It presented the Japanese government with demands that grew out of the Japan International Women's Year Conference in 1975, particularly the end of discrimination against women. Active protests in 1980 forced the Japanese government to sign the International Convention for Eliminating All Forms of Discrimination against Women. The Equal Employment Opportunity Law for Men and Women was passed in 1985 and went into effect in April 1986. The law's intent is to eliminate discrimination against women in the workplace. It requires businesses to provide equal opportunities for women in the areas of hiring, work assignments, promotions, overtime and late-night work. However, Japanese women still do not enjoy the lifetime employment and seniority systems that men do. Most women work between graduation and marriage in their mid-20s, usually as salesclerks, waitresses, teachers, secretaries (known as office ladies or OLs) and other low-paying jobs. Japanese women put their family first, especially the education of their children; if married women work at all it is usually part time.

Ancient Japan was matriarchal and women had a great deal of power into the eighth century A.D. But the introduction of patriarchal Confucianism from China, and the long era of feudalism dominated by the samurai (warrior) class, increased the restriction of women to the roles of wife and mother. Japanese women even speak in a language system that differs from that used by men. However, they dominated the household, a trend that continues today, with women handling all the family finances and making major decisions regarding the family. They have not been drawn to Western-style women's liberation movements, because they value the power they have in their traditional roles. A split developed in women's roles between wives and mothers who stay at home and women of pleasure who entertain men, such as courtesans, prostitutes and geisha. Prostitution was licensed for centuries by the Japanese government. In 1956, due largely to protests by women, the Prostitution Prevention Law was enacted. However, unlicensed prostitution continues, and many Japanese women find employment in the nighttime pleasure world as bar hostesses and in massage parlors.

The Japan Socialist Party (JSP), the largest opposition political party in Japan, is headed by a woman, Doi Takako. In 1989 the JSP won an important election, which moved Doi closer to the possibility of becoming the first woman prime minister of Japan. Women voters and elected officials have begun playing a decisive role in Japanese elections. The majority of Japanese women belong to women's associations, which are not directly political in nature and are more concerned with consumer issues. But women have actively protested the unpopular consumption tax passed in 1988 and the political scandals associated with the ruling Liberal Democratic Party. See also BLUESTOCKING

SOCIETY; CONSTITUTION OF 1947; DOI TAKAKO; ELECTIONS; FAMILY; GEISHA; MOTHER; OFFICE LADY; PROSTITUTION; WOMEN'S ASSOCIATIONS.

FENOLLOSA, ERNEST FRANCISCO (1853–1908)

An American scholar who contributed to the Western appreciation of traditional Japanese arts and the preservation of art treasures in Japan; the first Western scholar in the field of Japanese art history. Fenollosa attended Harvard University and then studied painting at the Boston Museum of Fine Arts. In 1878, Edward S. Morse, an American teaching at the University of Tokyo, persuaded Fenollosa to take a position there teaching philosophy and related subjects. At this time, Japan was rapidly becoming Westernized following the Meiji Restoration of 1868. Fenollosa began to persuade the Japanese that their traditional art must not be destroyed, and he collected many fine objects that are now exhibited at the Boston Museum of Fine Arts. He also helped found what is now known as the Tokyo University of Fine Arts and Music. In 1886 the Ministry of Education and the imperial household gave him a contract to catalog and exhibit Japanese art and sent him to the United States and Europe in 1886–89 to study museum techniques and administration. He was accompanied by his former student Okakura Kakuzo, a Japanese art historian and curator who also helped introduce Japanese art to the West. Fenollosa became head of the Oriental Department at the Boston Museum of Fine Arts in 1890. He returned to Japan in 1897, where he lectured and taught for three years, and then took a teaching position in the United States at Columbia University. His major works include *The Masters of Ukiyoe* (1896), *Epochs of Chinese and Japanese Art* (1912), *Certain Noble Plays of Japan* (1916) and *'Noh'; or, Accomplishment, a Study of the Classical Stage of Japan* (1916), most of which were published after his death by his literary executor, Ezra Pound. See also MEIJI RESTORATION OF 1868; OKAKURA KAKUZO; MORSE, EDWARD SYLVESTER.

FERMENTING METHODS

See ALCOHOLIC BEVERAGES; BIOTECHNOLOGY INDUSTRY; MISO; PICKLES; SAKE; SOY SAUCE.

FERRIES

Japan is an archipelago of four main islands and hundreds of smaller ones, stretching for well over 2,000 miles from Hokkaido in the north to the southern Ryukyu Islands (Okinawa Prefecture), which are connected by an extensive network of ferry boats. Some are large luxury car ferries, popular with honeymooners, that travel to and from major cities such as Tokyo, Osaka and Nagoya. A ferry ride from Tokyo to southern Kyushu Island takes around 20 hours, and to northern Hokkaido around 32 hours. The trip from Tokyo to Naha (Okinawa) via Kagoshima (Kyushu) takes 60 hours. Ferries are linked at coastal cities to the extensive Japanese railway system. Two major ferry routes operated by Japan Railways are the Seikan Ferry linking Honshu Island with Hokkaido Island via Aomori and Hakodate, and the Uko Ferry linking Honshu with Shikoku via Ube and Takamatsu. The most scenic routes are on the Inland Sea. Japanese ferries also travel to neighboring countries such as Korea and Taiwan. Traveling by ferry is slower but less expensive than airline travel. Moreover, some places in Japan can only be reached by boat. See also GEOGRAPHY OF JAPAN; INLAND SEA; RAILROADS; SHIPS AND SHIPBUILDING; NAMES OF INDIVIDUAL ISLANDS AND CITIES.

FESTIVAL OF THE AGES (Jidai Matsuri)

A festival held in the city of Kyoto every year on October 22nd by Heian Shrine (Heian Jingu); a major tourist attraction. Its main event is a procession of 1,700 people dressed in colorful authentic costumes of the Japanese historical eras, starting with the Meiji Era (1868–1912) and going back in time to the Heian Era (794–1185). Many famous historical figures are represented, such as military generals, samurai and women who wrote great works of classical literature. The procession leaves the old Kyoto Imperial Palace (Gosho) around noon and arrives at Heian Shrine several hours later. The Festival of the Ages started in 1895 when Heian Shrine was built to commemorate the 1,100th anniversary of the founding of Kyoto in A.D. 794 by Emperor Kammu (737–806). Kyoto remained the imperial capital until the Meiji Restoration of 1868. See also HEIAN SHRINE; IMPERIAL PALACE (KYOTO); KYOTO; SAMURAI.

FESTIVALS (matsuri; nenju gyoji)

Matsuri are annual rituals and celebrations held by shrines of Shinto, the indigenous Japanese religion. Participants commune with *kami* (sacred spirits) through rituals of purification, dances (*kagura*), offerings and feasts (*naorai*) shared by *kami* and human beings. Festivals also feature parades in which sacred objects embodying *kami* are carried in palanquins (*mikoshi*); large decorated floats (*yamaboko*); games and contests, such as tug-of-war, kite flying, and horse or boat races. Traditionally, competitions were a means of divining the will of the *kami* and to predict the success of the annual harvest.

Matsuri are conducted by Shinto priests and a group of lay members from the community. *Matsuri* are usually local events, observed at individual shrines. They are closely related to the seasons, particularly the cycle of planting and harvesting rice and other crops. Thus many Japanese festivals are held in the spring and autumn. Some *matsuri* have become major tourists attractions, such as the Hollyhock Festival, Gion Festival, and Festival of the Ages, all held in Kyoto, and the Snow Festival in Sapporo.

The ancient Japanese adapted from China a cycle of annual events known collectively as *sekku* in Japanese. *Nenchu gyoji* (or *nenju gyoji*) are annual festivals still celebrated in Japan that have diverse origins, including the Buddhist and Christian religions, but also include some Shinto *matsuri*. *Nenchu gyoji* are celebrated by all Japanese at about the same time of year. Five of these annual festivals are *sekku*: Seven Herbs Festival on January 7, Doll Festival on March 3, Children's Day Festival on May 5, Star Festival on July 7, and Chrysanthemum Festival on September 9. Other major annual festivals include the New Year Festival, Bean-Scattering Festival, Flower Festival,

Moon-Viewing Festival and Seven-Five-Three Festival. *Higan*, a Buddhist memorial for ancestors, is held at the spring and autumn equinox. Year-end fairs (*toshi no ichi*) are held in December to purchase decorations and other supplies needed for the New Year Festival. Snow-Viewing Festivals are held in northern regions of Japan. Christmas is celebrated as a secular event in conjunction with "forget-the-year" (*bonenkai*) parties. The two most important festivals in Japan are the quasi-religious New Year Festival in January and the Buddhist Bon Festival in midsummer to welcome visiting ancestral spirits. There is also a cycle of national holidays celebrated annually throughout Japan. See also BUDDHISM; CALENDAR; FAIR DAYS; HOLIDAYS, NATIONAL; SHINTO; RICE PLANTING AND HARVESTING FESTIVALS; NAMES OF INDIVIDUAL FESTIVALS.

FEUDAL LORD   See DAIMYO.

FEUDALISM (*hoken seido*)   A traditional paramilitary political system based on strong ties between lords and their vassals. Japan had various forms of feudalism from the late 12th through the mid-19th centuries. The feudal ruling elite consisted of armored, mounted warriors known as *bushi* (from the characters for "military" and "knight" or "gentleman"). They are also known as *samurai*, which originally meant "military retainer" and comes from the Japanese verb *sabarau*, "to serve or wait upon." Feudal values emphasized obedience and loyalty to one's lord, self-control and bravery.

Nomadic mounted warriors who migrated to Japan from Asia formed an elite class during the Kofun Era (c. 300–710), and some became members of the court aristocracy in the capital city of Kyoto in western Japan during the Heian Era (794–1185). A hereditary military aristocracy arose in the Japanese provinces after the 10th century A.D., although it did not abolish the imperial Yamato clan in Kyoto. By the late Heian Era, many warriors in the provinces were small independent landholders or managers of landed estates (*shoen*) owned by Kyoto aristocrats. They received income from peasants who farmed their land, and such rights often became hereditary from father to first son. Kyoto owners of *shoen* depended on local warriors to defend their estates. Local leaders organized small warrior bands (*bushidan*), whose members were related by blood and by ties of personal loyalty and who were given rewards in the form of booty or land in return for service to their leaders.

By the 12th century, alliances had developed among large warrior clans, led by imperial descendants who moved to the provinces from the capital. The dominant clans were the Taira (or Heike) and the Minamoto (or Genji). Local warrior chieftains served as intermediaries between provinces and the capital and gave military support to factions struggling against each other in Kyoto. The Taira were defeated by the Minamoto in the Taira-Minamoto War (1180–1185), after which Minamoto no Yoritomo forced the emperor to award him the title of *shogun*, short for "barbarian-subduing generalissimo" and founded the Kamakura Shogunate (1185–1333), the first of three feudal governments (*bakufu*, "tent government"; translated as "shogunate") that ruled Japan until 1868. Under the shogunate, many vassals were appointed as land stewards (*jito*) or as provincial governors (*shugo*), that is, liaisons between the Kamakura government and local vassals.

By the early 14th century, *shugo* had enlarged their powers to become a threat to the Kamakura regime and to local imperial authority. *Shugo* leaders led a rebellion that ended the Kamakura Shogunate in 1333, and Ashikaga Takauji founded the second *bakufu*, the Ashikaga Shogunate (1338–1573). Under the second shogunate, the office of *shugo* became hereditary, and its powers were greatly extended. *Shugo* made aggressive local warriors (*kokujin* or *jizamurai*) of their vassals, although warriors sometimes rebelled against *shugo*. The Ashikaga shoguns became ineffectual as political fragmentation increased and led to the Onin War (1467–1477) and the Sengoku (Warring States) Era (1467–1568).

By the mid-16th century; the feudal system had become highly developed. The central figure was the *daimyo*, a local feudal magnate who ruled over an autonomous domain. Some *daimyo* were descendants of earlier *shugo* families, but many were local warriors who took advantage of political disruption to seize power by force. For a while there were more than a hundred *daimyo* in Japan. Their relationships with their vassals resembled those of fathers and sons, as vassals gave loyal service to their *daimyo* in exchange for land rights. A land grant, or fief, was called *chigyochi*. A *daimyo*'s vassal warrior band (*kashindan*) consisted of two main groups: fief holders, known as kinsmen (*ichimon*), hereditary retainers (*fudai*), direct followers (*jikishin*) or allies (*tozama*); and cavalrymen; foot soldiers, junior vassals and attendants. Some *daimyo* had armies with tens of thousands of warriors. Foot soldiers armed with spears and halberds (replaced later by firearms) became the primary units of *daimyo* armies by the late 16th century. Despite this shift from mounted to infantry warfare, ownership of horses and swords still distinguished higher-ranking samurai from lower ones. The *daimyo* built great castles, where samurai settled and cities developed.

Large-scale alliances of *daimyo* were made under the national unifiers Oda Nobunaga, Toyotomi Hideyoshi and Tokugawa Ieyasu, who founded the Tokugawa Shogunate (1603–1867), Japan's third and most centralized feudal government. Under centralized feudalism, *daimyo* were considered direct vassals of shoguns and were strictly controlled through alternate attendance in the capital city of Edo (modern Tokyo) and other regulations. Samurai gradually were transformed into scholar-bureaucrats under the chivalric code of *bushido* ("way of the warrior") and the bureaucratic principles of Neo-Confucianism. Urban merchants or townspeople (*chonin*) became wealthy as the samurai class declined. Feudalism ended when authority was returned to the emperor with the Meiji Restoration of 1868 and the Meiji government (1868–1912) abolished the special privileges of the samurai class. See also ALTERNATE ATTENDANCE; ARCHERY; ARMOR; ASHIKAGA SHOGUNATE; BAKUFU; BOSHIN CIVIL WAR; BUSHIDO; CASTLES; CLASS STRUCTURE; CONFUCIANISM; DAIMYO; EDO ERA; HEIAN ERA; HORSE; HORSE-RIDER THEORY; KAMAKURA SHOGUNATE; KOFUN ERA; LANDED ESTATE SYSTEM;

FIFTH-GENERATION ADVANCED COMPUTER SYSTEMS

An advanced computer system planned by the Electronics Policy Division of the Japanese Ministry of International Trade and Industry (Tsusho Sangho Sho or Tsusansho), MITI, to promote advanced computer research in Japan. An international conference was held in Tokyo in October 1981 to initiate the Fifth Generation project. In 1982 the Institute for New Generation Computer Technology (ICOT) was founded to coordinate a 10-year research and development program for knowledge information processing systems (KIPS), in order to make Japan competitive in the world computer market, especially against the dominant American corporation IBM. Their goal is for the Fifth Generation computers to supercede the first four "generations": electronic-vacuum tube computers, transistorized computers, integrated circuit computers and very large-scale integrated computers (VLSI). Computers in these four stages have all operated with the same serial data-processing system; the Fifth-Generation computer project is intended to have an entirely new type of system for programming and organizing memory, called parallel processing, which greatly reduces processing time. Fifth-Generation systems are important in so-called artificial intelligence (AI) research, which will process knowledge by means of intelligent human reasoning rather than mathematical calculation. Pilot projects that use AI in this way are known as "expert systems." See also COMPUTER INDUSTRY; MINISTRY OF INTERNATIONAL TRADE AND INDUSTRY.

FIGURE PAINTING (jimbutsuga)

One of the three general categories of Japanese and East Asian painting, along with landscape painting (sansuiga) and bird-and-flower painting (kachoga).

The earliest types of figure painting in Japan were depictions of the many gods of the Buddhist religion introduced from India through China in the 6th century A.D. Statues and paintings (butsuga) of gods such as Amida and Kannon are focal points of Buddhist temples. Buddhist stories were also illustrated by narrative paintings (monogatari-e) on horizontal-rolling scrolls (emakimono). From the Heian Era (794–1185) onward, a native Japanese style of painting known as Yamato-e developed and was commonly used for secular scroll and album illustrations of vernacular literature, including novels such as The Tale of Genji (Genji Monogatari), poetry, folktales, and historical or military tales. Daily activities were also painted on screens and scrolls, known as genre paintings.

The Zen sect of Buddhism, introduced into Japan from China in the 12th century A.D., had a strong tradition of figure painting. Although Zen emphasizes self-enlightenment and has no pictures of transcendent gods, Daruma (Bodhidharma), traditionally held to be the founder of Zen (Ch'an in Chinese) in China is a popular subject in Zen ink painting. Monks, hermits and sages are also portrayed in paintings known as Zen doshakuga. Zen masters often gave colored portraits of themselves, known as chinso, to disciples who completed their training.

Secular portraits were made of emperors and military figures seated on raised platforms or riding horses in full battle armor. The 13th-century painting of the military ruler Minamoto no Yoritomo has been designated a Japanese National Treasure. Portraits of prominent women were sometimes painted, such as Oichi no Kata, sister of the 16th-century national unifier Oda Nobunaga, and wives of daimyo (feudal lords). The Tosa school of painting carried on the ancient Yamato-e style and influenced the Edo Era (1600–1868) style of painting and woodblock prints known as ukiyo-e ("pictures of the floating world"). Such works have become popular collector's items around the world. They often portray figures in the licensed pleasure quarters of Japanese cities, including Kabuki actors, courtesans and geisha.

Westerners appeared for the first time in Japan in the 16th century, and their activities were painted on screens, scrolls and albums in a style known as namban ("southern barbarian") art. Western-style painting (yoga), including portraiture, was introduced into Japan during the Meiji Era (1868–1912) and has been employed alongside Japanese-style painting (Nihonga). See also BIRD-AND-FLOWER PAINTING; BUDDHISM; CHINA AND JAPAN; DARUMA; FLOATING WORLD; INK PAINTING; LANDSCAPE PAINTING; NAMBAN; SCREENS; SCROLLS; SCULPTURE; TOSA SCHOOL OF PAINTING; WOODBLOCK PRINTS; ZEN SECT OF BUDDHISM.

FILIAL PIETY (ko)

A central principle of Confucianism, filial piety requires that children respect and obey their parents and take care of them in their old age. The Treatise on Filial Piety is one of the most important books in the canon of Confucian writings. In Confucian thought, the family is the basic unit of society and political organization, and the Japanese Neo-Confucian scholar Nakae Toju (1608–1648) argued that filial piety distinguishes human beings from animals and constitutes the highest moral virtue. The Japanese traditionally revered the emperor as the father of the nation, and considered themselves to be his children.

The samurai class, which controlled Japan from the 12th through the mid-19th centuries, followed a code known as bushido, that demanded absolute loyalty to one's master. This principle often came into conflict with the notion of filial piety. Popular Bunraku (puppet) and Kabuki dramas in the Edo Era frequently portrayed this conflict, as well as the conflict that people experienced between duty (giri) to their family and their own personal feelings (ninjo). Suicide was often the only way to resolve these conflicts.

Traditionally, the oldest son in a Japanese family has been obligated to live with his parents, even after marriage. This placed a hard burden on the son's wife, who was often badly treated by her mother-in-law. When the parents retired or died, the son and his wife succeeded them as heads of the household. Even today, the Japanese maintain close relations between older and younger generations. Young unmarried people in Japan usually live at home with their parents rather than get their own apartments.

Japanese hesitate to place their elderly parents in nursing homes, and while today they often do not live in the same home with them, they tend to live close enough to care for them. Japanese mothers maintain especially close relationships with their children throughout their lives. See also BUNRAKU; BUSHIDO; CONFUCIANISM; DEPENDENCY; DUTY AND FEELINGS; EMPEROR; FAMILY; KABUKI; MOTHER; RETIREMENT.

FILM (*eiga*) Japan has a rich tradition of filmmaking. Western movies were first shown in Japan in the late 1890s, and by 1899 the Japanese were shooting their own films. The first movie studio in Japan was built in Tokyo in 1912 by Nikkatsu Corporation, Japan's oldest movie company. Makino Shozo (1878–1929), who began to direct films in 1907, is considered the father of Japanese cinema. The earliest movies drew upon traditional Kabuki theater and a modern form of theater known as *shimpa*. Silent movies were narrated by a performer (*benshi* or *katsuben*) who sat next to the screen and was accompanied by musical instruments. Talking pictures were produced in Japan starting in the 1930s. The two basic types of stories in Japanese films have been contemporary domestic dramas (*gendaigeki*) centered on families and the emotional conflicts of their members, and historical costume dramas (*jidaigeki*), often with sword-fighting samurai. In 1920 the entertainment conglomerate Shochiku Co., Ltd., opened a movie studio. The other top studios have been Daiei Co., Ltd., Toho Co., Ltd., and Toei Co., Ltd. A large faction left Toho in 1948 to form Shin (New) Toho Co., Ltd.

Japanese movies in the late teens and 1920s were made by people from the left-wing new theater movement known as *shingeki* and show an interest in lower-class characters. The Japanese military government forced the movie industry to serve its purposes during World War II, and movies made then emphasize self-sacrifice of Japanese citizens. Movies made after the war often explored social concerns such as crime and gangsters or troubled human relationships. The 1950s are considered the "golden age" of Japanese cinema.

The greatest Japanese filmmakers include Kurosawa Akira, Mizoguchi Kenji, Ozu Yasujiro and Ichikawa Kon. Hayakawa Sesshu and Mifune Toshiro have been the Japanese film actors best known abroad. Mifune made numerous films with Kurosawa, including *Rashomon* (1950), which won first prize at the Venice Film Festival for that year. Kyo Machiko and Tanaka Kinuyo are the best-known film actresses. Many Japanese actresses got their start in the Takarazuka Girls Opera Company. Japanese films display great technical skill and visual beauty. They have slower pacing than most Western movies, and their dialogue is often spare, leading the audience to discern nonverbal cues as well as spoken dialogue.

In the 1960s, "new wave" directors such as Nagisa Oshima made radical films with political and sexual content. The popularity of television caused half of the movie theaters in Japan to close in that decade. In 1971 Daiei went bankrupt; Nikkatsu stopped producing feature films and turned to soft-core pornography; and the other studios underwent major reorganization. Independent filmmakers became increasingly active, and documentaries became a popular form. Toho turned to production of television programs and live shows. Daiei later reorganized and resumed limited movie production. Japanese movies have revived somewhat in the 1980s. Some directors have been critical of Japan, such as the humorous Itami Juzo, whose satirical movies *Tampopo* and *A Taxing Woman* became international hits. The Tora-san movie series, about a meek man who never wins the women he loves, is the longest-running film series in the world, with two episodes released annually. Feature animated cartoons are also very popular in Japan. Many Japanese movies are shown in foreign countries and are available on videotape. Some Japanese filmmakers have collaborated on international productions, such as *Merry Christmas, Mr. Lawrence*, starring British actors Tom Conti and David Bowie and Japanese popular musician Sakamoto Ryuichi. Kurosawa's latest films were financed by Francis Ford Coppola and other American filmmakers. See also ICHIKAWA KON; KABUKI; KUROSAWA AKIRA; KYO MACHIKO; MIZOGUCHI KENJI; OSHIMA NAGISA; OZU YASUJIRO; RASHOMON; SAKAMOTO RYUICHI; STORYTELLING; TAKARAZUKA OPERA COMPANY; TANAKA KINUYO; THEATER, MODERN; TORA-SAN.

FINANCIAL AND BUSINESS CIRCLES (*zaikai*) A term used by the Japanese media and the general public for leading groups that represent the business community in Japan. Four major Japanese business associations are connected in popular literature with the *zaikai*: the prominent Federation of Economic Organizations (Keidanren), which represents big business; the Japan Chamber of Commerce and Industry (Nihon Shoko Kaigisho), which represents small business interests; the Japan Committee for Economic Development (Keizai Doyu Kai), whose members are individual businessmen concerned with management practices; and the Japan Federation of Employers' Associations (Nikkeiren), which represents employers in negotiations with labor unions. The Keidanren is the major contributor to the dominant Liberal Democratic Party (LDP; Jiyu Minshuto) and thus has great political influence. The chairman of the Keidanren is often referred to in the Japanese media as the "prime minister of the business community." The powerful Japanese bureaucracy has closely guided Japan's economic development since the Meiji Era (1868–1912), giving rise to the slogan, "Japan, Incorporated," which implies that business and government act as one large corporation. See also CORPORATIONS; FEDERATION OF ECONOMIC ORGANIZATIONS; JAPAN CHAMBER OF COMMERCE AND INDUSTRY; "JAPAN INC."; LABOR UNIONS; LIBERAL DEMOCRATIC PARTY.

FIRE FIGHTING Most cities and large towns in Japan maintain their own fire departments. Containing fires has always been a major problem in Japanese cities because traditional homes are built of wood and earthquakes are frequent. Starting in A.D. 1629, the Tokugawa Shogunate developed a government system of fire fighters (*hikeshi*) to protect its castle in Edo (modern Tokyo) and homes, shrines and temples in the samurai district surrounding the castle. Two branches of this system came into operation: *daimyo*

Firemen in Tokyo wearing traditional heavy quilted jackets decorated with the crest of their brigade. Japanese cities have often been destroyed by fire because buildings were traditionally made of wood.

hikeshi, maintained by *daimyo* (feudal lords) to protect Edo Castle, the Tokugawa family shrine, and *daimyo* mansions in Edo and in the capitals of their home provinces; and *jobikeshi,* companies of fire fighters made up of samurai bannermen *(hatamoto).* In 1718 each neighborhood in the commoner districts of Edo also organized fire companies, known as *machi hikeshi,* which were administered by the city commissioners and were often assisted by volunteers. Designated members carried company standards *(matoi)* on long poles. Competition between fire brigades was keen, and volunteers were rowdy, which often hampered the putting out of fires. Every *daimyo* and commoner fire brigade had its own colorful firemen's uniform. *Daimyo* firemen wore brightly colored wool or leather jackets *(kaji-baori)* lined with silk damask and decorated with white embroidered crests *(mon),* undervests *(muneate)* dyed in the same color as the coat, and a helmet. Commoners wore heavy quilted cotton jackets *(hanten)* and leather or quilted cotton hoods *(zukin).* The jackets were decorated with the crests of the neighborhood groups *(kumi)* to which they belonged. Japanese firemen's jackets are popular collector's items today.

The Meiji government (1868–1912) disbanded the *daimyo* and samurai brigades, and reorganized the volunteer *machi hikeshi* into fire-fighting companies known as *shobogumi* *(keibodan* in 1939, *shobodan* from 1947). These companies fell under the jurisdiction of police forces until the 1948 Law of Fire Defense Organization made them independent.

Today, the national Fire Defense Agency is supervised by the Ministry of Home Affairs; each prefecture has a fire defense school to train professional and volunteer firemen. Firemen not only fight fires, but plan for fire disasters, warn citizens when conditions indicate the potential for fires, and investigate the cause of fires. They also operate a comprehensive program of fire prevention and public education, as well as ambulance and rescue services. A traditional fire-brigade festival *(dezomeshiki)* is held near the Imperial Palace in Tokyo during the New Year Festival, in which firemen perform acrobatic stunts on ladders and display modern fire-fighting equipment and techniques. See also CRESTS; DAIMYO; EDO ERA; NEW YEAR FESTIVAL; SAMURAI.

FIREARMS, INTRODUCTION OF *(teppo denrai)* European guns became widely used in Japan after they were introduced in 1543 by Portuguese sailors shipwrecked on Tanegashima Island, off the southern Japanese island of Kyushu. These firearms transformed the art of warfare in Japan. Explosive weapons were known to the Japanese, especially during the Mongol invasions of the 13th century, but swords and other samurai weapons remained the basic instruments of battle before the mid-16th century. The *daimyo* (feudal lord) of Tanegashima ordered craftsmen to copy the European guns, and many other *daimyo* soon followed suit. Japanese blacksmiths began making large numbers of firearms, mainly muskets that were even better than those manufactured in Europe. In 1549 the warlord Oda Nobunaga (1534–1582) added a 500-gun firearm brigade to his army in Owari Province (modern Aichi Prefecture) and took control of the most important musket factories, located in Omi Province and the city of Sakai. Takeda Shingen, *daimyo* of Kai Province (modern Yamanashi Prefecture) also trained some of his soldiers to fight with guns. Oda Nobunaga's firearm brigade played decisive roles in the Battle of Anegawa in 1570 and the Battle of Nagoshina in 1575. His military successor, Toyotomi Hideyoshi (1536–1598), also used firearms when he fought the Shimazu clan on Kyushu Island in 1586 and the Hojo clan in the Odawara Campaign of 1590. Firearms had become the most important offensive weapon in Japan by the end of the 16th century and changed the way battles were waged, as direct combat between men with spears and swords was replaced by long-range musket fire from foot soldiers. Since the soldiers who learned to fire muskets were usually from the peasant class, their new skill enabled them to improve their social status, although they did not displace the samurai class. The use of firearms also contributed to new methods of fortifying castles, including thick stone walls, metal doors and wide moats. However, the use of firearms was banned by the Tokugawa Shogunate (1603–1867), and samurai swords were reinstated as the primary weapons. See also ARMOR; CASTLES; ODA NOBUNAGA; SAMURAI; SWORD; TOKUGAWA SHOGUNATE; TOYOTOMI HIDEYOSHI.

FIREFLY (*hotaru*)   There are 10 luminous species of firefly among the 25–30 species found in Japan. The Japanese have always enjoyed firefly viewing (*hotarugari*) on summer evenings. Firefly viewing began as a pastime of the aristocratic class during the Heian Era (794–1185) but became a popular amusement during the Edo Era (1600–1868), when people dressed in *yukata* (informal cotton robes) and went to the banks of rivers such as the Sumida River in Edo (now Tokyo), or in special boats on the Uji River outside Kyoto and Lake Biwa, northeast of Kyoto, to watch the fireflies. The Japanese believed that the lights of fireflies represented the souls of the dead. Many poems in the eighth-century collection *Manyoshu* use fireflies as a metaphor for passionate love. The celebrated novel *The Tale of Genji (Genji Monogatari)*, written by Murakaki Shikibu (c. A.D. 1000), includes a scene where a prince first sees his beloved in the light created by fireflies. Sei Shonagon, famous for writing *The Pillow Book (Makura no soshi)* in the late 10th century A.D., also praised the sight of fireflies on a dark summer evening. See also BIWA, LAKE; GENJI, THE TALE OF; SEI SHONAGON; SUMIDA RIVER; UJI; YUKATA.

FIREWORKS (*hanabi*)   Introduced to Japan by the Portuguese at the end of the 16th century, fireworks were soon manufactured commercially by the Japanese and sold in famous shops in Edo (now Tokyo) such as Tamaya and Kagaya. In 1614 the shogun Tokugawa Ieyasu held the first recorded fireworks display (*hanabi taikai*) in Japan. The first summer fireworks festival was held on the banks of the Sumida River in 1733 and continues to be a popular entertainment in Tokyo today. This festival at the end of July marks the opening of the river's fishing season for sweet trout. Another popular festival is held in Omagari on the fourth Saturday in August. River carnivals (*kawabiraki*) climaxed by fireworks displays take place around the country during the summer.

There are two types of Japanese fireworks. *Uchiage* are shot high into the air from cannons and explode outward to look like cherry blossoms, chrysanthemums, plum blossoms and other flowers. They may also release flags or parachutes. This type of projectile fireworks, invented in China, traditionally has been made by placing gunpowder inside a paper ball, inserting the ball into a cylinder and igniting it to send it up. *Shikake* are "set pieces" that are tied onto wooden frames. When ignited, they show the outline in fire of various objects, calligraphy and scenes. Chemicals are added to produce colors, smoke and other special effects. Japanese fireworks are famous around the world for their spectacular beauty. See also SUMIDA RIVER.

FISH AND FISHING INDUSTRY   Fish is a basic part of the Japanese diet. About half the animal protein consumed in Japan is comprised of fish and other seafood. Because Japan is a small island nation, no place there is more than 100 miles from the sea, and thus an abundance of fresh- and salt-water fish is available. Buddhist proscriptions against eating many kinds of meat have also influenced the Japanese to consume fish.

Some of the most popular fish in Japan are the sea bream (*tai*), blowfish (*fugu*; poisonous if prepared improperly), tuna (*maguro*), and sweetfish (*ayu*), which are still caught in a few regions by the traditional method of using cormorant birds. The Japanese eat a large proportion of their fish sliced raw as sashimi or sushi (over small portions of rice). They also grill, smoke, pickle and dry fish. Dried flakes of bonito (*katsuo*) are used to make the basic stock (*dashi*) for Japanese soups.

The waters off the northeast (Pacific Ocean) coast of Japan contain rich fishing grounds, especially where the warm Black Current (Kuroshio) flowing up from the south meets the cold Parent Current (Oyashio) from the north. Japan has a large deepsea fishing fleet, including large factory ships that process fish at sea. By 1976, the fleet totaled more than 370,000 gross tons, including trawlers and factory ships. However, Japanese deepsea fishing has decreased since many countries enacted 200-mile exclusive zones around their coasts. Japan has long disputed with Russia the fishing grounds around the northern Kuril Islands. Japan's coastal fishing industry is also diminishing due to overfishing and pollution. Nevertheless, Japan remains one of the world's largest fishing nations, catching around 10 million tons a year. It is also one of the last whaling nations, for which it is strongly criticized. Fish are also cultivated on many farms in the Inland Sea. Much of the commercially caught fish is auctioned at the Tsukiji Tokyo Central Wholesale Market.

Sport fishing is a popular leisure activity in Japan. See also BLOWFISH; BONITO; CLIMATE OF JAPAN; COOKING; CORMORANTS, FISHING WITH; FISH PASTE AND FISH CAKES; GEOGRAPHY OF JAPAN; INLAND SEA; KURIL ISLANDS; PACIRIC OCEAN; SASHIMI; SEA BREAM; SEAFOOD; SUSHI; TOKYO CENTRAL WHOLESALE MARKET; TUNA; WHALING.

FISH PASTE AND FISH CAKES *(kamaboko)* Fish paste is a puree of ground fish that is molded into firm loaves or cylinders that can be sliced and served. Kamaboko (derived from a 14th-century word for "swamp plant" or "cattail," a reference to the cake's shape) is made from white fish such as cod or shark, squid and eel. The fish is mixed with salt and a binder such as potato starch, ground into a fine paste and filtered through a sieve, shaped into a desired form, and then steamed. It becomes firm as it cools. A fish cake is usually about 8 inches long, 1–2 inches wide and weighs 5–8 ounces. Cylindrical fish cakes, called *chikuwa* ("bamboo wheels"), are made by molding fish paste around a steel rod (formerly, a piece of bamboo), steaming it and then browning the outer layer by grilling it over charcoal. The form now called *kamaboko* has a semicircular shape and was formerly molded and steamed on boards of fragrant cedar wood *(ita)*. *Kamaboko* is white with the surface dyed red to look festive, and is often cut into slices or different shapes. It can be served at room temperature or heated in boiling water. The slices can be eaten by dipping them cold into a sauce made of soy sauce and *wasabi* (horseradish paste), grilling them brushed with soy sauce, deep frying them or simmering them in a liquid. *Kamaboko* slices are a common ingredient in soups and noodle dishes. They are also found in *oden,* a stew of vegetables, eggs, fish cake and other ingredients cooked for many hours in a broth of kelp (seaweed) and bonito and sold at food stalls. *Naruto* is a fish cake that has a red swirl design when sliced. *Hampen* is a soft white fish cake made by mixing the fish paste with yam *(yama-imo)* before steaming, which gives it a fluffy texture. These two types of fish cake are also served by slicing them and adding them to soups and stews. *Datemaki* is fish paste mixed with sugar and eggs and then grilled. Its sweet taste makes it a popular tradtional new year delicacy *(osechi-ryori).* See also COOKING; FISH AND FISHING INDUSTRY; FOOD STALLS; NOODLES; SEAWEED; SOUP; SOY SAUCE; WASABI.

FISH PRINTING *(gyotaku)* A technique for making decorative prints of fish and other natural objects, such as shells and flowers. *Gyotaku* means literally "fish rubbing." To print a fish, a thin coat of black carbon-based ink *(sumi;* also used for calligraphy or *shodo,* the "art of writing"), is brushed onto a recently caught and cleaned fish from head to tail. The fish is then brushed from tail to head to spread the ink under the edges of the scales and spines. A piece of white handmade plant-fiber paper *(washi),* which is absorbent and tolerates moisture, is then placed on top of the inked fish and pressed firmly. The entire fish is rubbed with the fingers or a *baren* (bamboo fiber disc, traditionally used to make *hanga* or woodblock prints) to transfer the ink to the paper. The paper is gently lifted from the fish, revealing the print. The eyes are painted in with a small brush. This process can be repeated to create up to 10 good prints from one fish. See also CALLIGRAPHY; PAPER, HANDMADE; WOODBLOCK PRINTS.

FITTINGS FOR SWORDS See SWORD; SWORD GUARD.

552nd FIELD ARTILLERY BATTALION See 442ND REGIMENTAL COMBAT TEAM.

FLAGS AND BANNERS *(hata; nobori)* The current Japanese national flag *(hinomaru)* is a white rectangle with a red circle in the center symbolizing the rising sun and is thus called *nisshoki,* the "rising sun flag." Before World War II, the sun had red rays to the edge of the flag; Nippon or Nihon, the Japanese term for Japan, means "source of the rising sun." Flags with the rising-sun design may have been used in Japan as early as the 13th century A.D., and they were used by various warriors in the 16th century. Toyotomi Hideyoshi (1536–1598), one of the three unifiers of Japan, used a rising-sun flag when he invaded Korea in 1592 and 1597. This flag was also used by the powerful Shimazu clan who ruled Satsuma Province on southern Kyushu Island and who persuaded the Tokugawa Shogunate (1603–1867) to fly rising-sun flags on Japanese ships. The Meiji government (1868–1912), which was controlled largely by leaders from Satsuma, made the rising-sun flag the official Japanese flag on January 27, 1870.

In the Heian Era (794–1185), the imperial court flew flags known as *ban* to represent their authority. When military families became increasingly powerful in the late Heian Era, each one had its own flag. The two most powerful families were the Taira, who used a red flag, and the Minamoto, who used a white flag. When the Minamoto defeated the Taira in 1185, ruling power in Japan was transferred from the imperial court to military governments *(bakufu)* for seven centuries. Warfare was common between *daimyo* (feudal lords) who controlled the Japanese provinces, and colorful banners known as *nobori* were flown in battles to identify various groups of samurai fighting under different *daimyo.* These banners were long rectangles attached vertically with loops to bamboo poles. They were dyed in different colors and marked with names, crests *(mon)* or other emblems.

During the Edo Era (1603–1868), Japanese families began hanging *koi-nobori,* kites in the shape of carp *(koi)* derived from military banners, at the Boys' Day Festival on May 5th, now known as Childrens' Day. The carp is a fish that represents courage and strength, traits the Japanese want their sons to have.

Another type of banner used in Japan is the *hata,* a long rectangle of cloth that is hung from a pole so that it flies freely. *Hata* were also decorated with written characters or symbols. The Tokugawa Shogunate retained about 5,000 samurai known as *hatamoto,* or bannermen, who were descendants of samurai who had helped Tokugawa Ieyasu (1543–1616) establish the shogunate. *Hata* inscribed with religious sayings may also be carried in processions. See also BAKUFU; CREST; DAIMYO; MEIJI RESTORATION OF 1868; SAMURAI; SHIMAZU CLAN; TOKUGAWA SHOGUNATE.

FLOATING WORLD *(ukiyo)* A 17th- and 18th-century concept of the pleasure of life and its impermanence. *Ukiyo* was originally a Buddhist term indicating the sad and impermanent nature of human life. During the Heian Era (794–1185) the term meant "sorrowful world." During the

Genroku Era (1688–1704), a period of lively cultural activity within the Edo Era (1600–1868), *ukiyo* assumed a new meaning based on the homonym of *uki,* which means either "sorrowful" or "floating." Thus the Buddhist view that life is sad was transformed to the notion that since life is transient, one might as well enjoy its pleasure while one can.

Genroku culture was the art of the pleasure quarters licensed by the Tokugawa Shogunate (1603–1868) for sex and entertainment, such as the Yoshiwara in Edo (modern Tokyo). The teahouses, bathhouses and theaters of these quarters were frequented by the wealthy urban merchant class, who were low on the social scale but controlled the Japanese economy. Money, sex and style were the chief interests of the floating world, as described by the popular novelist Ihara Saikaku (1642–1693). Amusement was provided by courtesans and prostitutes, geisha, and Kabuki and Banraku (puppet theater) performers. Numerous artists of the Edo Era portrayed the pleasures of the floating world in paintings and woodblock prints known as *ukiyo-e,* "pictures of the floating world." The most popular subjects of these pictures are Kabuki actors and women of the pleasure quarters. See also BATH; BUNRAKU; EDO ERA; GEISHA; GENROKU ERA; KABUKI; PROSTITUTION; SAIKAKU; WOODBLOCK PRINTS; YOSHIWARA.

FLOWER ARRANGING *(ikebana)* Ikebana, the art of combining flowers and other plant materials in appropriate containers according to prescribed rules, comes from *ikeru,* "to keep alive," and *hana,* "flower." It is also called *kado,* "the way of flowers." Seasonal flower arrangements are displayed in traditional Japanese homes in a special alcove called a *tokonoma.* Flower arranging originated with flower offerings *(kuge)* in Buddhism, which was introduced into Japan from China in the 6th century A.D. In the 15th century, *ikebana* became a highly developed art form with different schools teaching their own styles of arrangement, which fall into several broad categories. The *rikka* ("standing flowers") style was created by 15th-century masters of the Ikenobo school. It derived from the earlier Buddhist arrangements, also known as standing flowers *(tatebana)* in which the stem of the central flower stood one and one-half times the height of the metal container, and two more flowers were placed symmetrically on either side. The *rikka* style had complex rules of design. Seven branches (later nine) were required to represent natural landscapes, including a mountain, waterfall and valley. The *shoka* ("living flowers"), or *seika,* style, which evolved in the 17th century, aimed for a simpler design following the natural lines of the flowers, using only three curving branches to form an asymmetrical triangle. The primary branch (the *shin*) is from one and one-half to three and one-half times the height or width of the container; the middle branch (the *soe*) is two-thirds the height of the *shin;* and the third branch (the *tai*) is one-third the height of the *shin.* Flowers and leaves are held in place by clamps *(hanakubari)* inside the container, such as a forked twig *(matagi)* or a spiked metal holder *(kenzan).* The *shoka* style is taught by most of the

A flower arrangement *(ikebana)* in the *shoka,* or "living flowers," style. It is displayed next to a hanging scroll in a decorative alcove known as a *tokonoma.*

contemporary several thousand Japanese flower-arranging schools.

Today, the three largest *ikebana* schools are the Ikenobo, Ohara and Sogetsu, which have millions of students, and branches in foreign countries. Japanese women still study flower arranging as one of the three traditional arts they ought to know in order to be good wives, along with cooking and the tea ceremony. There is also a special way of arranging flowers for the tea ceremony which is called *chabana* (*cha* means tea). Such arrangements are to be natural and spontaneous, and often have only one flower in a simple vase. They derive from the *nageire* ("to throw" or "to fling into") style created by Sen no Rikyu (1522–1591). See also BUDDHISM; FLOWERS; SEN NO RIKYU; TEA CEREMONY; TOKONOMA.

FLOWER FESTIVAL (Hana Matsuri) The celebration on April 8 of the birthday of the Buddha (Enlightened One), the founder of the Buddhist religion. Siddhartha Gautama (Buddha) was born in India in the 6th century B.C. The religion he taught spread across Asia to China and Korea, and eventually to Japan in the 6th century A.D. Tradition maintains that when The Buddha was born, eight dragons appeared and sprinkled him with fragrant perfume. The main ceremony of the Japanese Flower Festival is *Kambu-tsue,* the bathing of statues of the baby Buddha with *amacha,* a sweet tea prepared with hydrangea leaves. At many large Buddhist temples, the priests use long-handled dippers to pour the tea on the statues of the Buddha. After this service, the crowds of worshippers in the temple compound take their turn bathing the Buddha, and mothers rub the tea onto children to ensure good health. In Tokyo, a procession of Buddhist priests carrying a statue of the baby Buddha and accompanied by many children dressed in kimono formerly went from the Asakusa Kannon Temple through the districts of Ueno and Ginza to Hibiya Park adjoining the Imperial Palace. During the ceremony held there, the priests scattered pink, white and yellow papers cut in the shape of lotus flower petals and leaves. The lotus, representing purity, is the sacred flower of Buddhism and is found in many temple decorations. See also BUDDHISM; CHILDREN IN JAPAN; LOTUS.

FLOWERS (hana) The Japanese closely identify with the changing seasons and keenly observe the annual "floral calendar" of blooming plants and trees. They do not prefer flowers that have bright colors and strong scents, but those that embody the emotional associations of the seasons. Traditional Japanese gardens have only a few flowers, which harmonize with the natural beauty of moss, pine and maple trees, bamboo, stones, sand and water. Some favorite flowers of the Japanese, in the order in which they bloom, include the plum, peach, cherry, iris, hollyhock, morning glory, peony, wisteria, autumn flowers and grasses, chrysanthemum and camellia. The most beloved flower in Japan is the delicate pink cherry blossom, which falls from the trees after blooming briefly. The peach is associated with the Doll Festival, also known as Girls' Day. Flower-viewing parties (hanami), especially for cherry blossoms, have been held in spring since ancient times. The pure white lotus flower is a symbol of enlightenment in the Buddhist religion. A major theme in Japanese painting and literature, especially waka and haiku poetry, is the beauty of nature, as summarized by the phrase "flowers, birds, wind, and moon" (kacho fugetsu). Flowers have been one of the most common decorative motifs on textiles, lacquer ware and other ornamental objects since the Heian Era (794–1185). Flower arranging (ikebana) is a highly developed Japanese art. Traditional homes have decorative alcoves known as tokonoma where flower arrangements and scrolls are displayed. Umbrellas and hats decorated with flowers are included in many Japanese festivals, because flowers entice the kami (sacred spirits) to enter sacred areas. Pretty young women hired to serve tea in offices are known as hana. See also DOLL FESTIVAL; FESTIVALS; FLOWER ARRANGING; FLOWER FESTIVAL; GARDENS; HAIKU; HOLLYHOCK FESTIVAL; LACQUER WARE; PAINTING; TEXTILES; TOKONOMA; TREES; WAKA; NAMES OF INDIVIDUAL FLOWERS.

FLUTES (fue) A variety of flutes are used in gagaku, classical orchestral court music. A flute known as nokan is played along with hand drums (tsuzumi) to accompany actors and singers in classical Noh drama. The shinobue is a flute played with large drums and bells at popular festivals (matsuri-bayashi, festival music). Japanese flutes, made of wood or bamboo, have a piercing, mysterious sound. Related musical instruments include the shakuhachi, a large vertical end-blown bamboo flute, and the sho, a mouth organ with 17 vertical narrow bamboo pipes. See also DRUMS; FESTIVALS; GAGAKU; NOH DRAMA; SHAKUHACHI; SHO.

FOLK CRAFTS See BAMBOO; BASKETS; BOXES; DOLLS; HAMADA SHOJI; HEMP; KASURI; KITES; LACQUER WARE; LEACH, BERNARD; LIVING NATIONAL TREASURES; MASHIKO; METALWORK; MINGEI; PAPER, HANDMADE; POTTERY; TEXTILES; TOYS; WOODWORKING; YUZEN DYEING.

FOLK SONGS (min'yo) Japanese folk songs are classified by their musical structure, function or the region of the country where they are sung. Some min'yo are religious songs performed for kagura (Shinto religious dances) or Buddhist dances, such as the Bon odori. Others are sung for specific tasks, such as rice-planting, cutting grass, making sake or sailing a boat. Certain min'yo may be sung at weddings or other social gatherings. There are also children's folk songs, such as counting songs and lullabies. Folk songs are not always easy to classify by region because many of them have become known all over Japan. Regions that still have distinct folk songs include Niigata and Akita prefectures in northern Japan, and the southern Ryukyu Islands (Okinawa Prefecture). The lyrics of ancient folk songs have been recorded as poems in a number of anthologies, such as the eighth-century Manyoshu. Japanese folk songs usually have either two or four beats to a measure. Fast songs often have cross-rhythms and syncopation. They often include repeated refrains and expressions from local dialects.

Folk songs are usually accompanied by musical instruments. The most common are the shamisen, a banjo-like stringed instrument; the taiko (drum); and the shinobue (a high-pitched flute). An ensemble of these instruments is called hayashi. The shakuhachi (vertical bamboo flute) is sometimes used to accompany slow folk songs.

The Japan Broadcasting Corporation (NHK) has made extensive collections of traditional Japanese songs, and has published transcriptions and issued field recordings of many songs from their collections. A national min'yo competition is held each year for performers from every region of Japan. Japanese scholars have also collected folk songs, often by interviewing elderly people in rural villages. See also BON FESTIVAL; DRUMS; FLUTES; JAPAN BROADCASTING CORPORATION; KAGURA; MANYOSHU; RICE PLANTING AND HARVESTING FESTIVALS; SHAKUHACHI; SHAMISEN; SINGING.

FOLKTALES See BAMBOO CUTTER, THE TALE OF THE; HEARN, LAFCADIO; KINTARO; MOMOTARO; MONOGATARI; STORYTELLING; YANAGITA KUNIO.

FOOD See BENTO; COOKING; GARNISHES FOR FOOD; FOOD MODELS, PLASTIC; FOOD STALLS; FISH AND FISHING INDUSTRY; NOODLES; PICKLES; RICE; SEAFOOD; SEASONING FOR FOOD; SEAWEED; NAMES OF INDIVIDUAL DISHES AND INGREDIENTS.

FOOD MODELS, PLASTIC *(mihon)* Replicas of meals or items on a menu, which are displayed in a restaurant window to attract customers and show them which items are available. Prices are usually indicated as well. Food models are known by the generic term for model or sample, *mihon.* Their shapes, colors and details are extremely realistic, from sushi and sukiyaki to spaghetti and meatballs, ice cream, and cups of coffee. Some people consider them a form of modern folk art *(mingei).* The models are especially helpful to foreign tourists who cannot read Japanese menus. Food models may have originated when many Americans lived in Japan during the postwar Allied Occupation (1945–1952). They were formerly made of colored wax, which tended to melt, but are now made of plastic. Restaurant supply houses in large cities, such as those on Kappabashi Street in the Asakusa district of Tokyo, sell models of standard dishes. Tourists like to buy them as amusing souvenirs. See also ASAKUSA; RESTAURANTS.

FOOD STALLS *(yatai)* Portable stands on wheels that have cooking facilities to produce a variety of different types of food and drink. Some food stalls are pulled around the streets of a city by the owners on foot. Others are pulled by bicycle or have small motors to move them. Many food stalls are set up on the grounds of shrines and temples during festivals. Every night stalls cluster around railroad stations to offer quick, inexpensive dishes for commuters on their way home. The stalls tend to specialize in one type of food. One of the most popular late-night snacks is *ramen,* a bowl of Chinese-style noodles in a hot broth. *Ramen* stalls are commonly open very late, to feed people after the bars close. They usually have a few stools or boxes or a bench in front of the stall for customers to sit on. *Soba* is another type of noodle, made of buckwheat, sold by the stalls. *Oden* is a combination of vegetables, tofu (bean curd), fish cake, hard-boiled eggs, and other ingredients, boiled for hours in a broth made with *kombu* (kelp, a kind of seaweed). The diner picks a number of items and eats them with mustard or *miso* (soybean paste). *Okonomiyaki* is a round pancake with a filling of vegetables, cooked egg, seafood or meat, and eaten with the hands. A smaller version, *takoyaki,* consists of round wheat dumplings filled with boiled octopus *(tako).* One of the most popular fast foods is *yakitori,* small grilled pieces of chicken. In autumn and winter, sweet potato *(satsuma-imo)* vendors bake the potatoes in their carts by burying them in hot stones and cry out, "*Ishiyaki-imo*" to advertise their wares. See also COOKING; NAMES OF INDIVIDUAL FOODS.

FOOTWEAR, TRADITIONAL Special sandal-like shoes are worn with kimono, the traditional Japanese garment for both men and women. These sandals are of two general types, *zori* and *geta.* Each *zori* is held on the foot by one thong that fits between the big toe and the other toes. Divided socks known as *tabi* (like mittens for the feet) are worn with *zori. Tabi* are usually white. *Jika tabi,* worn by gardeners and other laborers, are dark-colored and have thick soles. Women's *zori* usually have padded soles that rise up slightly from front to back; they may have toe

protectors. They may be made of leather or artificial materials, and can be decorated with colors and small designs. Men wear flat *zori* made of woven straw. There is also a leather-soled flat sandal similar to *zori* known as *setta.*

Geta are flat wooden sandals, usually made of paulownia wood, which have two cross-pieces underneath to raise the sole off the ground. Seta are worn with bare feet on casual occasions with an informal cotton robe called *yukata.* Similar sandals with even higher supports and with toe protectors are worn on rainy days and are called *takageta, ashida* or *tsumagake.* In former times, straw sandals known as *waraji* were commonly worn. See also KIMONO; YUKATA.

FOREIGNERS IN JAPAN *(gaijin)* The term *gaijin* (short for *gaikokujin*), "outsider," is applied to all foreigners in Japan, including some ethnic minorities who are permanent residents in Japan, such as Koreans. Legally, the term *gaikokujin* (foreigner or alien) applies to all persons who do not have Japanese citizenship, which is available only to those having a Japanese father. The principal minority groups in Japan include Koreans, Chinese and Ainu (indigenous inhabitants of northern Honshu Island), and *burakumin* or "hamlet people," who are similar to ethnic Japanese but are socially segregated by occupation. Until 1990, all foreigners residing in Japan, even second- and third-generation Koreans born in Japan, were required to obtain certificates of alien registration and to be fingerprinted; the latter was controversial. Persons who hold dual citizenship for Japan and another country are regarded as aliens. Apart from native minorities, resident foreigners in Japan today tend to be teachers from North America and Europe; students from Asia, North America, and Europe; businessmen and diplomats from all over the world; and unskilled workers, mostly from Taiwan, the Philippines and other Asian countries, including women who work in bars and massage parlors.

Portuguese traders and Roman Catholic Jesuit missionaries were the first Europeans to appear in Japan, in the mid-16th century. They were called *namban* ("southern barbarians") because they sailed to Japan from islands to the south. The Tokugawa Shogunate, viewing Christians as a threat to its authority, banned all foreigners from the country and instituted a policy of national seclusion that lasted from 1639 until Japan was forcibly opened to Western trade in the mid-19th century. For two centuries, only a few Dutch Protestants and Chinese were allowed to trade with Japan, the southern city of Nagasaki; the Dutch were confined to Dejima Island. "Dutch studies" *(rangaku)* became the channel by which Japanese learned about the outside world. The movement that overthrew the Tokugawa Shogunate and brought about the Meiji Restoration of 1868 had as its slogan Revere the Emperor, Expel the Barbarians *(Sonno joi).* However, the Meiji government (1868–1912) actually modernized Japan by employing many foreign experts *(oyatoi gaikokujin,* "hired foreigners") to advise the government and teach Western culture and technology.

Japan had in fact adapted widely from foreign cultures throughout its history. The Buddhist religion, a system of writing, government organization and silk weaving are some of the fundamental aspects of Japanese culture imported from China starting in the 6th century A.D. Groups of immigrants came to Japan from China and Korea before the middle of the Heian Era (794–1185), such as the Aya, Hata and Soga clans. After that time, however, only small numbers of other Asians came to Japan, such as Buddhist priests and diplomatic missions. Some Koreans were also brought to Japan following two invasions of that country by the Japanese warlord Toyotomi Hideyoshi (1537–1598). But unlike other Asian nations, Japan had never been conquered or colonized by an outside power before it surrendered to the Allies in World War II. The Allied Occupation (1945–52) brought many foreigners, mainly American soldiers, to Japan. Thousands of American soldiers are still stationed on bases in the country. As inhabitants of a relatively isolated small island nation, the Japanese have remained a fairly homogeneous ethnic group. Although they have eagerly incorporated aspects of foreign cultures throughout their history, they have resisted mingling with foreign peoples. Recently, Japanese have been having wider contacts with foreigners by going abroad in large numbers, both as tourists and as businessmen representing Japanese companies. See also CHINA AND JAPAN; DEJIMA; DUTCH IN JAPAN; KOREA AND JAPAN; MINORITIES IN JAPAN; MEIJI RESTORATION OF 1868; NAMBAN; OCCUPATION OF JAPAN; PORTUGUESE IN JAPAN; REVERE THE EMPEROR, EXPEL THE BARBARIANS; SECLUSION, NATIONAL.

FOREIGN EXCHANGE See BANKING SYSTEM.

FOREIGN SERVICE See MINISTRY OF FOREIGN AFFAIRS.

FOREIGN TRADE See BANKING SYSTEM; DEJIMA; EXPORTS AND IMPORTS; FUKUOKA; INVESTMENTS OVERSEAS, JAPANESE; JAPAN EXTERNAL TRADE ORGANIZATION; JOINT-VENTURE CORPORATION; KAGOSHIMA; MINISTRY OF INTERNATIONAL TRADE AND INDUSTRY; NAGASAKI; RYUKYU ISLANDS; SAKAI; SATSUMA PROVINCE; SECLUSION, NATIONAL; VERMILION SEAL SHIP TRADE; TRADING COMPANY, GENERAL.

FORESTRY Forestry has been an important industry in Japan since ancient times. Trees remain abundant today, with forests covering 61 million acres, or nearly 70% of the Japanese islands, although the mountainous terrain has made access to forests very difficult. Wood has always been important to Japanese culture. Homes and other buildings such as Shinto shrines and Buddhist temples have traditionally been constructed of wood, mainly cedar or cypress. Numerous household objects are made of wood, such as boxes, trays, chests and chopsticks. Charcoal, made from wood, has been a common fuel for cooking and heating. The cities of Kyoto, Osaka and Tokyo became major centers of wood consumption, especially since frequent fires necessitated major rebuilding efforts. Lumber was transported from forests to urban markets along principal rivers.

The Tokugawa Shogunate (1603–1867) and *daimyo* (feudal lords) actively planted and cultivated forests, and the

sale of wood was a major source of revenue for them. The Meiji government (1868–1912) divided Japanese forest land into government-owned and privately owned regions. Today, about a third of Japanese forest land is owned by the national government. National forests, located in remote mountain ranges, cover about 17.3 million acres and play an important role in land conservation. Local governments administer about 2 million acres of public forest, leasing much of the land to local residents. Private forests, accounting for about 17 million acres, are owned by individuals, companies, cooperatives, and religious shrines and temples. Most individual owners are farmers, who generally own plots of less than 25 acres, which they harvest in addition to farming.

In 1984 there were about 150,000 forestry workers in Japan. Forestry is most active on the large northern island of Hokkaido. About one-third of the lumber used in Japan comes from domestic forests, and the rest, mainly specialty woods, is imported from Southeast Asia, the United States, Canada and the Soviet Union. In 1980 wood was Japan's second largest import item, after petroleum. That year Japan consumed more than 3.53 billion cubic feet of wood. The Japanese pulp and paper industry also uses large quantities of wood. In 1983 the production of pulp was 8.9 million tons, and production of paper reached a record high of 10.9 million tons.

Traditional wooden buildings are being replaced with concrete structures in Japanese cities, causing a decreasing demand for lumber. Large cedar and cypress forests were planted in mountainous areas of Japan after World War II, but the lower demand for this wood is a major problem for the forestry industry. See also AGRICULTURE; ARCHITECTURE; BOXES; CHEST; CHOPSTICKS; CYPRESS; EXPORTS AND IMPORTS; FARMHOUSE; GEOGRAPHY OF JAPAN; HIBACHI; HOMES AND HOUSING; NATIONAL PARKS; PAULOWNIA; PINE TREE; SHRINES, SHINTO; TEMPLES, BUDDHIST; TRAYS; TREES; WOODWORKING.

FORTUNE TELLING *(uranai-shi)* There are numerous methods of fortune telling in Japan, many of which were introduced from China in ancient times. One of the most popular is palm reading *(teso-uranai)*. Palm readers set up folding tables in the evening in busy districts of Japanese cities. Candle lanterns on the tables enable the palm readers to study the palms of their clients, especially young women eager to know whether the future will bring them love and a happy marriage. Fortune tellers also practice physiognomy *(ninso-uranai)*, fortune telling by facial features and other bodily characteristics. Various divination techniques are also used. Thin sticks *(zeichiku)*, usually in bundles of 50, are allowed to fall into a pattern, which is interpreted to make predictions about the client. Blocks *(sangi)* with long and short markings representing different basic elements of the universe are also scattered, with the fortune teller reading the patterns made by the markings; they are based on the Chinese classic text *I Ching*, which divides the universe into a system of yin (negative) and yang (positive) aspects. A person's future is also believed to be influenced by the year in which he or she is born, according to the traditional 12-year cycle of the animal zodiac. The 12 animals in order are the rat, ox, tiger, rabbit, dragon, snake, horse, sheep, monkey, dog, rooster and boar. Since ancient times in Japan, deities of the Shinto and Buddhist religions have been thought to control human destinies, and many shrines and temples offer chances for finding out the views of the gods. One of the most popular is *omikuji*, fortunes written on papers that are drawn at random or even dispensed by vending machines; unfavorable fortunes are tied on tree branches within the sacred grounds to prevent them from coming true. Many kinds of amulets and talismans can also be purchased to help bring good fortune. The Japanese especially want to learn their fortunes at the New Year. Many traditional festivals represent the ancient Japanese attempt to divine their fate. For example, in former times when a farming community wanted to know whether it would have a successful harvest, methods of prediction included the performance of tug-of-war competitions, races or sumo wrestling matches before the deities. See also AMULETS; FESTIVALS; NEW YEAR FESTIVAL; SUMO; TALISMANS; ZODIAC; NAMES OF INDIVIDUAL ANIMALS.

FORTY-SEVEN RONIN INCIDENT   Also known as the Ako Incident; a famous vendetta in which 47 *ronin,* or masterless samurai, avenged the death of their *daimyo* (feudal lord). These 47 ronin are known as *Shijushichishi.* In 1701 Asano Naganori (1665–1701), the lord of Ako in Harima Province (part of modern Hyogo Prefecture), was appointed by the Tokugawa Shogunate in the capital city of Edo to receive envoys who were delivering New Year's greetings from the emperor in Kyoto. Kira Yoshinaka the shogun's chief of protocol, treated Asano so badly that Asano was provoked to attack Kira with his sword in Edo Castle. The Shogunate required Asano to commit suicide, and confiscated his feudal estate in Harima. The 47 samurai who served Asano made a vow to avenge his death, but their leader, Oishi Yoshio, convinced them not to attack Kira right away but to see if the shogun would give the Ako estate to Asano's younger brother. The shogun refused, so after waiting two years, the *ronin* killed Kira in his mansion and carried his head to the grave of their master Asano at Sengakuji, a Buddhist temple 5 miles away. Although the *ronin*'s revenge was demanded by a longstanding samurai code *(bushido),* their act violated the legal code by which the Tokugawa shoguns ruled a unified and peaceful Japan. Therefore the *ronin* were ordered to commit suicide, and were buried with their master at *Sengakuji.* The Japanese public regarded them as heroes for their loyalty and bravery, and many plays were written about the incident, including one by Japan's preeminent playwright, Chikamatsu Monzaemon (1653–1724). The most famous play is *The Treasury of Loyal Retainers* (*Kanadehon chushingura;* 1748, translated as *Chushingura* in 1971), by Takedo Izumo et al. More than 100 modern novels and movies have also used the theme of the 47 *ronin* incident. See also BUSHIDO; CHIKAMATSU MONZAEMON; DAIMYO; SAMURAI; TOKUGAWA SHOGUNATE.

FOUR *(shi)*   The number four is avoided in Japan because it is pronounced the same as the word for death. Floor numbers of tall buildings skip the number four, just as Western buildings often have no 13th floor. Tea and sake sets usually have five cups. The desirable number of guests at a traditional tea ceremony is three or five. The Japanese prefer odd numbers in general, a reflection of their aesthetic preference for asymmetry, as embodied in the concepts of *sabi* and *wabi.* However, the four seasons of the year, with distinctive climate changes, flowers and plants are widely appreciated in Japanese culture. See also SABI AND WABI; SAKE; TEAPOTS; TEA CEREMONY.

442ND REGIMENTAL COMBAT TEAM   A U.S. Army combat unit in World War II, composed entirely of *nisei* (second generation) Japanese Americans, which became the most highly decorated unit in American military history. The unit included the 442nd Infantry Regiment, the 522nd Field Artillery Battalion and the 232nd Engineer Combat Company and fought against Nazi troops in France and Italy. *Nisei* men petitioned the U.S. government to form the unit so that they could demonstrate their loyalty to the United States. Japanese-Americans had been forced into relocation camps, suspected of being enemies and saboteurs, after Japan attacked the American fleet at Pearl Harbor, Hawaii on December 7, 1941. President Franklin D. Roosevelt ordered the War Department to organize the 442nd Regimental Combat Team on January 22, 1943. Ten thousand *nisei* men volunteered, and 2,686 were initially chosen. More than 10,000 served with the unit altogether during the course of the war. The unit began basic training at Camp Shelby, Mississippi, on February 1, 1943, and left for combat in Italy on May 1, 1944. Its motto was Go for Broke. In Europe the unit fought in the Rome–Arno River campaign, the Vosges Mountain campaign, the Battle of Bruyeres, and the final assault against German forces in Italy in 1945. Soldiers of the 442nd were awarded 18,143 medals for valor. *Nisei* also served honorably as combat interpreters with American units fighting Japanese forces in the Pacific theater of the war; more than 6,000 were trained at the Military Intelligence Service Language School in Minnesota. Nearly 30,000 Japanese Americans served in the U.S. armed forces during World War II, thus helping Japanese Americans gain acceptance in the United States after the war. The 100th/442nd/MIS World War II Foundation is erecting a memorial to the Japanese-American veterans of World War II. See also IMMIGRANTS, JAPANESE; NISEI; WORLD WAR II.

FOUR-POWER TREATY   See ANGLO-JAPANESE ALLIANCE.

FOX *(kitsune)*   This small carnivorous animal appears in many Japanese folktales. The fox is thought to have supernatural powers and to be able to bewitch human beings and transform itself into human form. Many stories, often dramatized in Noh and Kabuki, tell of a fox changing into a woman to marry a man. The Japanese traditionally believed that a person suffering from insanity or depression was possessed by the spirit of a fox.

The great Buddhist priest Kukai (774–835; also known as Kobo Daishi) was believed to have driven all the foxes from his home island of Shikoku after a fox attempted to deceive him. On Shikoku, badgers, cats or dogs take the place of evil foxes in folk stories.

The fox is also the messenger of Inari Dai Myojin, the god of rice, and shrines to Inari have fox statues in them. The favorite food of the fox is thought to be *aburage*, thin sheets of deep-fried *tofu* (bean curd). A dish of noodles and broth with *aburage* is called "fox noodles" (*kitsune udon*). See also BADGER; CAT; DOG; INARI; KUKAI; SHIKOKU ISLAND; TOFU.

FRIENDS OF CONSTITUTIONAL GOVERNMENT PARTY (Rikken Seiyukai or Seiyukai)   Also known as the

Political Friends Society; a leading political party in Japan between 1900 and 1940 and a predecessor of the Liberal Democratic Party (LDP; Jiyu Minshuto), which has dominated Japanese politics since 1955. The Seiyukai, as the Friends of Constitutional Government Party is commonly known, was founded in 1900 by Ito Hirobumi (1841–1909), the first prime minister of Japan (1885–1888). Ito joined his followers with the group begun by another political leader, Itagaki Taisuke (1837–1919). In 1874 Itagaki had established the "Freedom and Peoples' Rights Movement," which became the first Japanese political party and dominated early imperial legislatures under the name of the Liberal Party (Jiyuto, "Freedom Party"). After its founding in 1900, the Seiyukai contolled the Imperial Diet (Parliament) for nearly two decades. In 1918 the Seiyukai held a plurality in the House of Commons (lower house of the Diet), and the party's leader, Hara Takashi (also known as Hara Kei or Hara Satoshi; 1856–1921), was selected as prime minister of Japan. He was the first Japanese prime minister to be chosen because of political party leadership rather than from the aristocratic members of the House of Peers (upper house of the Diet). Hara kept the Seiyukai in power until he was assassinated in 1921. In 1924 the People's Government Party, or Minseito (or Rikken Minseito), took power. Between 1924 and 1932, ruling cabinets were formed from either the Seiyukai or the Minseito. Whichever party held the most seats in the Diet formed the cabinet and selected the prime minister. The power of these parties weakened after 1932, when the army began directly controlling the government in Japan, although they continued to be influential in the House of Commons. In April 1937 the two parties combined forces and won a victory that forced Prime Minister Hayashi Senjuro (1876–1943), a former army general, to resign after four months in office. However, the military regained control within a month when Japan went to war with China (Sino-Japanese War of 1937–1945). The Seiyukai was revived after World War II as the Liberal Party (Jiyuto). In 1955 it combined with the Japan Democratic Party (Nihon Minshuto) to form the Liberal Democratic Party. See also DIET; ELECTIONS; ITAGAKI TAISUKE; ITO HIROBUMI; LIBERAL DEMOCRATIC PARTY; PEOPLE'S GOVERNMENT PARTY; POLITICAL PARTIES; PRIME MINISTER; SINO-JAPANESE WAR OF 1937–1945.

FRUIT   See CITRUS FRUIT; PEACH TREE; PERSIMMON; PLUM TREE.

FUDE   See BRUSHES; CALLIGRAPHY; INK PAINTING.

FUDO MYOO   A ferocious divine figure who uses the power of his anger to conquer evil. Fudo, whose name means "immovable," is the most popular of the category of *myoo*, "kings of light or wisdom," the third level of deities in the Buddhist religion, after Buddhas (*nyorai*) and bodhisattvas (*bosatsu*). The *myoo* were originally deities worshiped in the Hindu religion in India, but were absorbed into the iconography of esoteric Buddhism, which was introduced into Japan through China in the 9th century A.D.

Fudo worship is centered at Shinshoji Temple in Chiba Prefecture north of Tokyo. Statues of Fudo Myoo are found in many temples in Japan, such as Mudoji-dani, connected with Enryakuji on Mount Hiei. Fudo is also worshiped in the Otowa no taki ("Sound of Feathers") waterfall at scenic Kiyomizudera Temple in the eastern part of the old capital city of Kyoto. See also BUDDHISM; ENRYAKUJI; KIYOMIZUDERA; TEMPLES, BUDDHIST.

FUGU   See BLOWFISH.

FUJI HEAVY INDUSTRIES, LTD.   See AUTOMOBILE INDUSTRY.

FUJI, MOUNT (Fujisan)   The highest and most graceful mountain in Japan, and a world-famous symbol of the country. Mount Fuji, or Fujisan (Fuji, possibly from the Ainu word *fuchi*, for "fire," plus *san* meaning "mountain") is located 60 miles southwest of Tokyo on central Honshu Island. Fuji, a perfectly shaped volcanic cone that rises to 12,385 feet, has always been revered in Japan, especially by members of a religious sect known as Fujiko, and male religious pilgrims have climbed it since ancient times. Women were not allowed on sacred mountains until the modern era. A Shinto shrine to Konohana Sakuya Hime, a divine princess who is the spirit of the cherry blossom, is maintained on the summit by the main Sengen Shrine (Fujisan Hongu Sengu Jinja) in the town of Fujinomiya just south of Fuji. Mount Fuji is open to the public for climbing from July 1st to August 26th, and every year around 400,000 people climb the five trails, marked off at 10 levels or stations. Most people take a bus to Station 5 halfway up the mountain and make a day's roundtrip hike to the top; from the Kawaguchiko Fifth Station the ascent takes five to nine hours and the descent three hours. Campers may stay overnight in huts on the volcanic hillside and experience the sunrise from the top of Fuji. There are also three difficult trails for advanced climbers. Women, who are associated with pollution in the Shinto religion, were not permitted to climb Mount Fuji until 1868.

Still classified by geologists as an active volcano, Fuji has erupted 18 times in recorded history. The most recent eruption, in 1707, dropped half a foot of ash on the city of Edo (modern Tokyo). The crater on Fuji's summit is 1,640 feet in diameter and 820 feet deep. Above the timberline, ranging from 7,900–9,200 feet, the naked slope is usually covered with snow. The slope is steep at the top but wide at the base, where the diameter averages 30 miles. Mount Fuji is actually composed of three active volcanoes: Komitake and Ko Fuji have been covered by lava from Shin Fuji.

Mount Fuji, the highest and most graceful mountain in Japan, and a world-famous symbol of the country. Fuji is a volcanic cone 12,385 feet high that has always been revered by the Japanese. Half a million people climb Mount Fuji every summer.

Mount Fuji belongs to the Fuji Volcanic Zone, a chain of volcanoes extending from the Mariana Islands in the Pacific Ocean up through the Izu Peninsula to Niigata Prefecture on Honshu Island. Fuji sits on a large fissure in the earth's crust that divides Honshu into northeast and southwest sections.

Mount Fuji is frequently covered with clouds, but on a clear day it can be seen 100 miles away. It has been immortalized in poetry and portrayed in numerous paintings and prints. The famous artist Hokusai (1760–1849) made series of woodblock prints titled Thirty-Six Views of Mount Fuji and One Hundred Views of Mount Fuji. North of Fuji lies the Fuji Five Lakes district, a popular vacation spot. From east to west, the lakes are Motosu, Shoji, Saiko, Kawaguchi and Yamanaka. Mount Fuji is the central attraction in Fuji-Hakone-Izu National Park. See also FUJI-HAKONE-IZU NATIONAL PARK; HOKUSAI; MOUNTAINS; SHINTO; VOLCANO.

FUJI-HAKONE-IZU NATIONAL PARK The most heavily visited national park in Japan, located 60 miles southwest of the capital city of Tokyo. The park includes several separate areas that are treated as one administrative unit: Mount Fuji; the Fuji Five Lakes area; Hakone; the tip of Izu Peninsula; and the Seven Isles of Izu. Fuji-Hakone National Park was formed in 1934, and the Seven Isles of Izu, which on a clear day are visible from the summit of Mount Fuji, were added to it in 1964. Hakone is a popular hot-springs resort area that lies within the 25-mile-wide crater of an extinct volcano at the base of Mount Fuji. In

addition to the numerous spas, some attractions in the Hakone region are boat rides on Lake Ashinoko, natural caves and ponds that emit sulphur fumes, a Natural Science Museum in the town of Owakudani, and many festivals throughout the year. The mountains bloom with pink cherry blossoms in April, azaleas in May and June and red maple leaves in autumn. The old Tokaido Road between Kyoto, Osaka and Edo (modern Tokyo) ran through Hakone, and the old Barrier Guardhouse, which served as a government checkpoint on the road, has been reconstructed and several miles of the old, narrow, winding road have been preserved. The Izu Peninsula has a beautiful coastline that juts into the Pacific Ocean on the east coast of Honshu Island, south of Fuji. See also FUJI, MOUNT; HOT SPRING; IZU PENINSULA; NATIONAL PARKS; TOKAIDO ROAD.

FUJI PHOTO FILM CO., LTD. See CAMERAS AND PHOTOGRAPHY.

FUJITSU, LTD. See COMPUTER INDUSTRY.

FUJIWARA CLAN A powerful group existing in Japan since earliest times that dominated the Heian Era (794–1185) imperial court from A.D. 858 and remained influential in the court into the 19th century. For this reason, the late Heian Era is also known as the Fujiwara Period (858–1158).

The Fujiwara, originally named Nakatomi, were an immigrant group from the Asian mainland. Japanese prince Naka no Oe (later Emperor Tenji) awarded the name Fujiwara ("Wisteria Field") to Nakatomi Kamatari (614–669), who, working in a wisteria garden, hatched the plan that led to the downfall of the rival Soga clan. The Fujiwara helped the imperial court institute the Taika Reform of 645, which adopted the Chinese bureaucratic system of government, claimed all land in Japan for the emperor and recompensed local land-owning nobles by assigning them ranks in the court and positions as provincial governors. Fujiwara no Kamatari's son Fuhito (659–720) promulgated the first legal code in Japan, the Taiho Code of A.D. 702. His four sons in turn founded the four main branches of the Fujiwara clan. The Fujiwara became prominent by acquiring land from small provincial landowners in return for their protection, and by securing for their daughters the positions of empress or imperial concubine. Reigning emperors thus had Fujiwara fathers-in-law, who exercised a great deal of control over court affairs.

In A.D. 858 Fujiwara no Yoshifusa (804–872) took the position of regent (sessho) for the underage emperor, becoming the first imperial regent not to be born into the imperial family. His nephew and successor, Fujiwara no Mototsune (836–891), became regent and then kampaku, regent for an emperor who had come of age, speaking for and issuing commands on behalf of the emperor. Rule by powerful regents became typical in Japan.

Fujiwara no Michinaga (966–1028) became the most important figure in the court from 995 to 1027 and brought Fujiwara power to its height. However, his successor as regent, Fujiwara no Yorimichi (990–1074), saw his power circumvented by Emperor Go-Sanjo, whose mother did not belong to the Fujiwara clan. Go-Sanjo created a type of rule known as "cloister government" *(insei),* whereby the emperor directed the affairs of state from behind the scenes while a young heir sat on the throne and performed public ceremonial duties. Fujiwara power also declined because the women of the family died young or gave birth only to girls, who could not become emperors. Moreover, in the late Heian Era the samurai class was taking control of the provinces, with rival samurai factions claiming that they had the right to rule in the name of the emperor. The Taira clan in eastern Japan rebelled against the imperial throne and were finally defeated by the Minamoto clan, whose leader, Minamoto no Yoritomo (1147–1199), founded the Kamakura Shogunate (1192–1333), the first military regime *(bakufu)* in Japan. Yoritomo did not claim the position of regent, which was held by the Fujiwara, but allowed the Fujiwara regents and the emperors to continue their affairs in Kyoto while he made his headquarters in the eastern town of Kamakura and functioned as the de facto ruler with the title of *shogun* (generalissimo). The Hojo clan came to function as regents for the shogunate, and they always selected as shogun a member of the Fujiwara clan or the imperial family. This dual system of imperial and military rulers lasted for nearly seven centuries in Japan, until the Meiji restoration of the emperor in 1868. See also BAKUFU; EMPEROR; FUJIWARA NO MICHINAGA; FUJIWARA NO TEIKA; HEIAN ERA; KAMAKURA SHOGUNATE; NAKATOMI CLAN; SHOGUN; SOGA CLAN; TAIHO CODE; TAIKA REFORM; TAIRA-MINAMOTO WAR; WISTERIA.

FUJIWARA NO MICHINAGA (966–1028) A member of the influential Fujiwara clan, who brought the power of the Fujiwara during the Heian Era (794–1185) to its zenith. Michinaga's father, Fujiwara no Kaneie (929–990), held the highest court positions of grand minister of state *(dajo daijin)* and regent for his grandson, Emperor Ichijo. The Fujiwara had built up their power by marrying their daughters to emperors. Michinaga received his first court post in A.D. 980 and became head of the Fujiwara clan in 995, upon the death of his father and brothers. He was appointed to the powerful position of minister of the right *(udaijin)* and awarded the prestigious honorary title of examiner of imperial documents *(nairan).* Michinaga gained full control of the imperial court by exercising power through Fujiwara family relations. Four emperors were Michinaga's sons-in-law, two emperors were his nephews and three were his grandsons. Michinaga also expanded his power base with the miliary class, which was gaining control of the Japanese provinces, particularly the Seiwa Genji branch of the Minamoto clan. Minamoto descendants would end the power of the Heian court two centuries later and initiate military rule in Japan with the Kamakura Shogunate (1192–1333).

Michinaga became regent *(sessho)* for his grandson, Emperor Go-Ichijo (r. 1016–1036) in 1016, but the next year he became grand minister of state and passed the regency to his son Fujiwara no Yorimichi (990–1074). He also made his other sons imperial ministers and advisors. In 1019 Michinaga retired from public life and became a monk of the Pure Land (Jodo) sect of Buddhism, which had been

introduced from China in the ninth century, and built the magnificent Hojoji monastery as his retirement residence. However, he continued to exercise power in the court through Yorimichi. Michinaga wrote a diary, *Mido Kampaku Ki,* which provides much information about politics and daily life at the Heian court. Skilled in poetry and music, Michinaga may have been a model for Prince Genji, the main character in *The Tale of Genji (Genji Monogatari,* c. A.D. 1000). Michinaga had been a lover of Murasaki Shikibu, *Genji's* author. See also DIARY; EMPEROR; FUJIWARA CLAN; GENJI, THE TALE OF; HEIAN ERA; KAMAKURA SHOGUNATE; MINAMOTO CLAN; MURASAKI SHIKIBU; PURE LAND SECT OF BUDDHISM.

FUJIWARA NO TEIKA (1162–1241) Also known as Fujiwara no Sadaie; the most important poet of his time, and a scholar and critic who developed the aesthetic principles of Japanese literary taste in the medieval era (12th–16th centuries). Teika's father was Fujiwara no Shunzei (also known as Fujiwara no Toshinari; 1114–1204), the chief classical Japanese poet of the imperial court. Teika succeeded him as court poet. Emperor Go-Toba (1180–1239; r. 1183–89) chose Teika to help compile the eighth imperial anthology of classical poetry, the *New Collection of Ancient and Modern Times (Shin Kokinshu;* c. 1205), and Emperor Go-Horikawa (1212–34; r. 1221–32) honored Teika by making him sole compiler of the ninth imperial anthology, the *New Imperial Collection (Shin chokusenshu;* 1235). Collections edited and published by Teika established the canons of classical Japanese poetry. He also edited classical diaries, Buddhist scriptures and collections of stories from the Heian Era (794–1185). One collection, *Single Poems by 100 Poets (Hyakunin Isshu),* remains the best-known poetry anthology in Japan and is used in a card game *(utagaruta)* Japanese play during New Year celebrations. Teika wrote some 4,600 poems including the anthology *Foolish Verses of the Court Chamberlain (Shui guso;* 1216). Among his important works of literary criticism is *Guide to the Composition of Poetry.* Teika advised Japanese poets to continue using the language, forms and themes of earlier classical poets, and literate Japanese were expected to acquire an extensive knowledge of earlier poetry. Teika's central aesthetic concept was the Heian ideal of courtly refinement and elegance *(miyabi),* which evolved into the medieval concept of *yugen,* that which is mysterious and can only be expressed by subtle intimations. See also CARD GAMES; DIARIES; NEW YEAR FESTIVAL; POETRY; YUGEN.

FUJIWARAKYO See NARA.

FUKUDA TAKEO (1905–) A leading Japanese politician belonging to the conservative faction of the Liberal Democratic Party (LDP) who was prime minister from 1976 to 1978. Fukuda, who was born in Gumma Prefecture, graduated from Tokyo University and became a career bureaucrat in the Japanese Ministry of Finance. He was named chief of the Budget Bureau in 1947, but a government scandal forced him to resign in 1948. In 1952 he became a member of the House of Representatives (Lower House) of the Japanese Diet (Parliament). Fukuda served as Minister of Agriculture, then Minister of Finance and finally as Minister of Foreign Affairs, after which he became deputy Prime Minister and Director General of the Economic Planning Agency. He has a reputation as a financial expert. In 1976 Fukuda was selected as president of the LDP and since the party was in the majority, he became prime minister of Japan. Two years later he was replaced by a different faction leader, Ohira Masayoshi. Fukuda has retained his seat in the Diet and is a senior statesman and influential member of the LDP. See also DIET; LIBERAL DEMOCRATIC PARTY; MINISTRY OF FINANCE; OHIRA MASAYOSHI; PRIME MINISTER.

FUKUOKA   The largest city on Kyushu Island (the southernmost of the four main islands of Japan); the capital of Fukuoka Prefecture; and a major center for industry, culture and education. The city covers 99 square miles and has a population of over 1 million. Situated on Hakata Bay, and at one time called Hakata City, Fukuoka was the center of northern Kyushu as far back as the seventh century. The port of Hakata served as the merchant shipping link between Japan and China, and Chinese influence stimulated cultural development very early in the Fukuoka region. This area may have been the site of an ancient Japanese kingdom called Yamatai that is mentioned in the Chinese *Wei Chronicle* (*Wei Zhi* or *Wei Chih*). Archaeological sites dating from the Yayoi Era (c. 300 B.C.–c. A.D. 300) have yielded an enormous number of prehistoric artifacts. Numerous tomb mounds *(kofun)* have also been excavated. The ancient center of government for all of Kyushu, Dazaifu, was located 9 miles to the south of Fukuoka.

Fukuoka and the port of Hakata, divided by the Nakagawa River, remained separate until 1889, when they were joined to form the city of Fukuoka. Hakata, a commercial center inhabited by merchants, became very prosperous from trade with China, particularly during the 15th and 16th centuries, when China was ruled by the Ming dynasty (1368–1644). The only premodern attempt by a foreign power to invade Japan occurred at Hakata in the 13th century. The Mongols, who ruled China at that time under Kublai Khan, launched their first invasion in 1274 and a second one in 1281, but both were floundered off Hakata in typhoons. This encouraged the Japanese to believe that their land is protected by "divine wind" *(kamikaze)* of the gods *(kami)*. Some ruins of the Japanese fortifications built to defend against the Mongols can still be seen. The feudal lord of this region constructed a castle in western Hakata in 1601. The name Fukuoka was given to this castle and the surrounding area. Today a public park, Ohori-Koen, is on the site of Fukuoka Castle, and the history of Fukuoka is displayed in the collections of the Fukuoka City Art Museum. Of the city's many famous shrines and temples, two have special importance. Shofukuji is considered the oldest Zen Buddhist temple in Japan. The Zen priest Eisai, who spent four years in China and brought Zen Buddhism and seeds of tea plants back to Japan, founded this temple in A.D. 1195. Sumiyoshi-jinja is one of the oldest Shinto shrines on Kyushu. Dedicated to the god of seamen, its buildings are approximately 400 years old. The nearby town of Dazaifu also has an important Shinto shrine, Temmangen, that was originally founded in A.D. 950. Its main building was erected in 1590. Since Temmangen is dedicated to the god of scholarship, secondary school students come here to pray for help in passing the rigorous university entrance examinations. The shrine's grounds are famous for beautiful plum and camphor trees and iris flowers.

Fukuoka Prefecture is a major tourist destination because of its historical remains and its beautiful coastline, which is part of the Seto Inland Sea National Park. Commercial fishing is still an important industry. The prefecture includes the major industrial center of Kita Kyushu (North Kyushu). In the 19th century, the area's large coal deposits were mined for the development of heavy industries. See also CHINA AND JAPAN; EISAI; FOREIGN TRADE; KAMIKAZE; KITA KYUSHU; KYUSHU ISLAND; INLAND SEA; MONGOL INVASIONS OF JAPAN; TOMB MOUND.

FUKUROKUJU   See JUROJIN; SEVEN GODS OF GOOD FORTUNE.

FUKUSA   A small square of expensive silk used for covering an important gift when presenting it to the recipient. In Japan, textiles play a significant role in gift-giving, which is an important element of Japanese culture. Gifts are often wrapped in squares of cloth known as *furoshiki*, but for a distinguished gift, a *fukusa* has traditionally been laid over the gift to symbolize high regard or when paying tribute to a superior. If the *fukusa* is a family heirloom, the recipient ceremoniously returns it to the giver. A *fukusa* may be beautifully decorated with embroidery. The most elaborate embroidered *fukusa* were created during the centralized feudalism of the Tokugawa Shogunate (1603–1867), when *daimyo* (feudal lords) were required to present many gifts to the shogun in Edo (modern Tokyo). Since Japan was then at peace after a century of warfare, the country became prosperous, and the creation of textiles and other arts flourished. *Fukusa* were exchanged between members of the aristocratic class or given by wealthy persons to powerful superiors. A *fukusa* is also used by the host in a Japanese tea ceremony to ritually wipe the tea container and the tea scoop. Men frequently use purple *fukusa* and women red ones, but *fukusa* are now being designed in a variety of colors and decorated with seasonal and other motifs. See also DAIMYO; FUROSHIKI; GIFTS; SILK; TEA CEREMONY; TEXTILES; TOKUGAWA SHOGUNATE.

FUKUZAWA YUKICHI (1835–1901)   A leading educator in the early Meiji Era (1868–1912) who stressed the need for a complete restructuring of Japanese society through the adoption of Western science and civilization. Fukuzawa was born to a poor samurai family on Kyushu, the southernmost of the four main islands of Japan. In 1854 he went to the cosmopolitan city of Nagasaki, which for 200 years had been the only Japanese city allowed by the Tokugawa Shogunate (1603–1867) to trade with Western nations, on the nearby island of Dejima where Dutch traders were confined, and to Osaka to study Dutch, the language of the only Westerners permitted to trade with Japan. He went to Edo (now Tokyo) in 1858 to start a new school for the Dutch language, but when he made contacts with the new foreign trading community in nearby Yokohama, he discovered that they spoke English. He immediately began to learn English, and was a member of Japan's first mission to the United States in 1860. In 1862 he was part of Japan's first mission to Europe. He described the knowledge of Western civilization that he gained on this trip in a three-volume book, *Conditions in the West*, published from 1866 to 1870, which was a best-seller in Japan. His mission was to educate his fellow Japanese about what he felt were the most important aspects of Western civilization: science and a spirit of independence, which he popularized in the slogan, "independence and self-reliance" *(dokuritsu jison)*. His writings were collected in 30 volumes. Fukuzawa founded a school in Tokyo, Keio Gijuku, which became Keio University, and a newspaper, *Jiji Shimpo*. His tireless efforts to educate the Japanese people by "enlightening" *(keimo)* them through Western knowledge brought him nationwide fame. He published his autobiography in 1898, which was translated into English (revised edition, 1966) as *The Autobiography of Yukichi Fukuzawa*. See also DEJIMA; DUTCH IN JAPAN; MEIJI RESTORATION OF 1868; NAGASAKI; UNIVERSITIES; YOKOHAMA.

FUNERALS Japanese funerals have traditionally been held at home, although many families now use professional undertakers. When near death, a person is given water to drink by close relatives. If the family is holding the funeral, they wash the dead body with hot water *(yukan)* and dress it in either a white robe *(kyokatabira)* or the dead person's favorite outfit. The body is placed in a plain wooden coffin and laid out in front of the *tokonoma*, an alcove in the most formal room of a traditional home. A white cloth is placed over the face, and the hands are clasped.

Most funerals in Japan are conducted under the Buddhist rite because the Shinto religion regards the dead as impure. For a Buddhist funeral, a low table is placed near the head of the deceased to hold offerings of incense, flowers and candles. Offerings of rice and water are also used for Shinto funerals. A knife to drive evil spirits away is placed on the deceased's chest for a Buddhist funeral and beside the head for a Shinto one. A sword that is a family heirloom may also be displayed. The family pastes a paper inscribed with the characters *mo-chu* (in mourning) on the entrance gate to the home, and the doors of the home altar *(kamidana)* are closed. Relatives and friends are notified of the death, and they promptly call on the family to express their sympathy. A priest is called to make arrangements for the ceremonies.

Most funerals last two days. During the evening and night of the first day, called *tsuya* ("wake" or "vigil"), a Buddhist priest chants scriptures. Guests may be invited into a separate room for refreshments after they have offered incense to the deceased so they can reminisce about him or her. The ceremony on the second day is called *kokubetsushiki*, "leave-taking," and is held at home or in a temple or funeral parlor. Along with the coffin, an altar is set up with a tablet *(ihai)* inscribed with the name of the

deceased, a photograph *(iei)*, incense burners, flowers and Buddhist ritual objects. A priest recites scriptures and then mourners offer incense to the deceased in a ritual known as *shoko*. Each family member and friend bows to the bereaved family and looks at the memorial tablet and the picture while placing his or her hands together in prayer. A mourner takes powdered incense from the container on the table with the right hand, raises it while bowing slightly and places the incense in the incense burner. He or she does this two more times, places his or her hands together in prayer, and bows again to the bereaved family. Men wear black suits and black ties to a funeral, and women wear black kimono or black dresses. Persons attending a funeral place condolence money *(koden)* for the bereaved family inside a special envelope *(kodenbukuro)* and leave it on a table when they sign the register book at the funeral. The amount varies depending on one's relationship to the family. The envelope is tied with black and white string and is inscribed with the characters for *goreizen*, "before the spirit of the departed."

Japanese law requires that all bodies be cremated. Afterward, pieces of bone are placed in a jar *(kotsutsubo)*, which the family takes home and places on an altar with the memorial tablet, picture and an incense burner. Upon returning from a funeral, a person is sprinkled with salt for purification before entering the home. On the seventh day after the funeral and on every seventh day until the 49th, family and friends stand around the altar while a priest chants scriptures. They also offer incense and eat a meal together. The jar is buried in a cemetery during this period. On the 49th day, the family of the bereaved send letters of thanks to all the people who attended the funeral service, and give them reciprocal gifts of half the value of their *koden*. Memorial services are held on the first, third, seventh, 13th, 17th, and 33rd anniversaries *(hoyo)* of a person's death. Families visit graves on the spring and autumn equinox *(higan)* and during the Bon Festival in midsummer to offer food, flowers and incense to the deceased. See also BON FESTIVAL; BUDDHISM; CALENDAR; FAMILY; HIGAN; INCENSE.

FURNITURE, TRADITIONAL Traditional Japanese homes have very little furniture. People sit on *tatami*, or straw floor mats, and sleep on *futon*, mattress and quilt sets that are laid on the floor at night and stored during the day in closets built into the walls. Low wooden tables are used for eating and writing. A special table with a heating device, called a *kotatsu*, derived from the charcoal brazier known as a *hibachi*, is used in cold weather. Clothing and other necessities are stored in wooden chests, called *tansu*, and small boxes. Shoes are not worn inside but are stored in special chests in the entrance halls of homes. Rooms can be divided with folding screens *(byobu)* or sliding screens *(shoji)*. Art objects are displayed in a *tokonoma*, an alcove recessed into the wall. Wealthy families have traditionally kept their valuable objects in a fireproof storehouse *(kura)* separate from the main home. See also BOXES; CHEST; FUTON; HIBACHI; HOMES AND HOUSING; SCREENS; STOREHOUSE; TATAMI; TOKONOMA.

FURO See BATH.

FUROSHIKI A decorative square cloth used for wrapping and carrying objects. The use of *furoshiki* dates back to the early Edo Era (1600–1868), when Japanese wrapped items in them to take to the public bathhouses. They also spread the *furoshiki* on the floor to stand on while undressing. The word *furoshiki* literally means "bath spread." *Furoshiki* range in size from 2 to 8 feet square. The most common way of wrapping an object in a *furoshiki* is to place it in the center of the cloth, with the corners of the *furoshiki* laid out. The front and back corners are lapped over each other and then the right and left corners are tied in a square knot. *Furoshiki* are traditionally made of cotton or silk, although today they are frequently made of polyester and other synthetic fabrics. They can be plain or decorated with colorful designs. Gifts may also be beautifully wrapped in fine silk *furoshiki*. See also BATH; GIFTS; SILK; WRAPPING.

FURUTA ORIBE (1544–1615) A warrior who became a renowned master of the Japanese tea ceremony. Oribe was born in Mino Province (modern Gifu Prefecture) and served the warlords Oda Nobunaga (1534–1582) and Toyotomi Hideyoshi (1536–1598), who helped unify Japan in the late 16th century. His name was originally Furuta Shigenari, but Toyotomi rewarded him with a large estate near Kyoto and an official title, Oribe no Kami. A student of Toyotomi's personal tea ceremony master, Sen no Rikyu (1522–1591), Oribe succeeded Rikyu as the greatest tea master in Japan. Among Oribe's own students were the second Tokugawa shogun, Tokugawa Hidetada, several of his *daimyo* (feudal lords) and the artist Hon'ami Koetsu (1558–1637). Oribe's taste for boldly decorated tea utensils differed from the quiet, restrained taste of Rikyu. The style of pottery known as Oribe ware (*oribe-yaki*) was named for him. Oribe also showed a preference for tea utensils in the styles of Bizen ware (*bizen-yaki*) and Karatsu ware (*karatsu-yaki*). He designed the *oribedoro*, a type of stone lantern for tea ceremony gardens, and Christian motifs on some of these lanterns support the claim that Oribe was a convert to Christianity, which had recently been introduced into Japan. Oribe later served Tokugawa Ieyasu (1543–1616), who founded the Tokugawa Shogunate (1603–1867), and fought for him during the Battle of Sekigahara (1600). However, during Ieyasu's siege of Osaka Castle in 1615, Oribe secretly changed his allegiance and betrayed the ultimately victorious Ieyasu to the pro-Toyotomi forces headquartered there. Ieyasu then ordered Oribe to commit suicide. See also BIZEN WARE; CHRISTIANITY IN JAPAN; HON'AMI KOETSU; KARATSU WARE; LANTERNS; ODA NOBUNAGA; ORIBE WARE; POTTERY; SEKIGAHARA, BATTLE OF; SEN NO RIKYU; TEA CEREMONY; TOKUGAWA IEYASU; TOYOTOMI HIDEYOSHI.

FUSUMA See HOMES AND HOUSING; RIMPA SCHOOL OF PAINTING; SCREENS.

FUTAMIGAURA An area along the eastern coast of Honshu Island, facing Ise Bay, which is the site of the famous Wedded Rocks (Meotoiwa). These two partially submerged rocks are compared by the Japanese to the husband and wife creator gods Izanagi and Izanami. Large straw ropes, used in the Shinto religion to mark sacred spaces and to symbolize marriage, connect the two rocks. On top of the larger, "husband" rock is a *torii* gate, which is also used to denote a sacred place. Futamigaura is about 3 miles long and belongs to Ise-Shima National Park. See also ISE-SHIMA NATIONAL PARK; IZANAGI AND IZANAMI; ROCKS; SHINTO; STRAW WARE; TORII.

FUTON A set of bedding unrolled at night for sleeping on the floor. The same room of a home can be used for sleeping, eating and the activities of daily life, all of which take place on the *tatami* or straw mats that cover the floor. In the morning the *futon* are put away in built-in closets (*oshiire*) with sliding doors. A *futon* set consists of an under-*futon* or mattress (*shikibuton*) and a quilt (*kakebuton*) that covers the sleeper. The quilt can be encased in a sheet-like cover called *shikifu* to keep it clean. Both the under-*futon* and quilt are fabric cases stuffed with cotton, or occasionally down. Ordinary *futon* are covered with printed cotton, while expensive *futon* have silk cases that are hand-dyed with beautiful colors and patterns.

The Japanese began using cotton quilting for their bedding in the middle of the 16th century. Before that time, people of the noble and samurai classes slept on thick matting made of woven rushes, and covered themselves with *fusuma*, kimono-shaped covers made of cotton stuffed with silk floss. Common people slept on thin straw mats or even loose straw and used thick covers made from hemp cloth that was heavily quilted or stuffed with fibers of hemp or other plants. Today the Japanese add sheets and regular blankets to their *futon* and use pillows (*makura*) made of buckwheat chaff. They also like to place a light towel-like blanket (*taoruketto*) on top of the mattress which helps absorb moisture. Because *futon* absorb body moisture, they must be aired in the sun as often as possible. Each morning housewives hang *futon* outside on long poles or balcony rails before storing them for the day; the sun kills bacteria in *futon*. In a ryokan, or traditional Japanese inn, maids lay out *futon* for guests in the evening and put them away in the morning. See also HOMES AND HOUSING; PILLOWS; RYOKAN; TATAMI.

G

GAGAKU "Elegant music"; traditional music performed for the Japanese imperial court. The word *gagaku* comes from the Chinese word *yayue (ya-yueh)* for music played for rituals in ancient times. The music, played by an orchestra of various instruments from Tang (T'ang) dynasty China (618–906), including bronze bells, flutes and drums, accompanies a form of dance, known as *bugaku*, also performed for the court. *Bugaku* and *gagaku* are very slow, solemn and majestic. Both were introduced into Japan from China in the seventh and eighth centuries A.D. and constitute the oldest continuously performed arts in the world. They are performed by the Imperial Court Orchestra in Tokyo. *Gagaku* music played a central role in court life of the Heian Era (794–1185) and was performed by aristocrats as well as professional musicians, who were organized into guilds. Descendants of the eighth century guild musicians perform *gagaku* music today as members of the Imperial Palace Music Department. *Gagaku* declined during the centuries when Japan was ruled by military governments, from the Kamakura Shogunate (1192–1333) until the Meiji Restoration of 1868. However, the Meiji government revived official *gagaku* and *bugaku* performances.

There are three broad categories of *gagaku* music: *togaku*, Chinese-style music from the Tang dynasty, plus some pieces from other Asian countries; *komagaku*, a style of music from ancient Korea; and native Japanese music for rituals performed for the divine spirits of Shinto. Shinto court music and dance are often termed *mikagura* (court *kagura*), to distinguish them from folk Shinto music, known as *kagura*.

Different instruments are used, depending on the type of *gagaku* being played. The *hichiriki*, a double-reed pipe that resembles an oboe, is played for all three types. *Togaku* ensembles also use a *sho*, a mouth organ having 17 small bamboo pipes that plays many notes at one time. *Togaku* and *komagaku* use various percussion instruments, such as a large hanging drum (*taiko*), a small bronze gong (*shoko*) and a small hourglass-shaped drum (*tsuzumi*), in addition to two stringed instruments, the *biwa* and the *koto*. Shinto ritual music is performed mainly by singers, who rhythmically strike a pair of wooden clappers, known as *shakubyoshi*. All types of *gagaku* music are very complex, with many different scales and modes, and extremely slow compared to other types of music. See also BIWA; BUGAKU; CHINA AND JAPAN; DRUMS; FLUTES; KOTO; SHINTO; SHO.

GAIJIN See FOREIGNERS IN JAPAN.

GAMBLING (*tobaku, bakuchi*) In Japan today, the only legal forms of gambling are government-operated lotteries (*takarakuji*) and horse, bicycle, motorcycle and speedboat racing. However, the tradition of gambling games in Japan dates back to the sixth century A.D. when a board game known as *sugoroku*, involving dice, was introduced from China. From the eighth century on, many other gambling games using dice became popular as well, although the government sometimes tried to prohibit them. Card games (*karuta*) were introduced by the Dutch and Portuguese in the 16th century, over the prohibition of the Japanese government. In the late 18th century a game played with flower-decorated cards (*hanakaruta*, now called *hanafuda*) became very popular, and since World War II has replaced dice games as the main form of gambling in Japan.

Eighteenth-century professional gamblers took their name, *yakuza*, from a card game played at that time. The *yakuza* operated gambling dens and became highly organized gangsters who still control gambling and other illegal activities in Japan. Private gambling establishments, rarely prosecuted by the government, offer *hanafuda*, dice games (*saikoro*) and mah-jongg. *Pachinko*, a game similar to pinball, also has connections to illegal gambling. Horse racing had existed since ancient times in the form of religious pageants to entertain the gods and predict the fortunes of the year ahead and was introduced as a sport in 1880 by Europeans living in the port city of Yokohama. When the Japanese government allowed betting on horse races in the early 20th century, racetracks were built throughout the country. Dog racing was also legalized, and after World War II, betting on bicycle, motorcycle and speedboat races became more popular. So-called "public gambling" now takes place at more than 150 government-sponsored racetracks of all kinds in Japan, mostly in large cities. Public lotteries became popular in the 18th century, and today, local or municipal governments operate public lotteries as a way of supplementing their revenue. Some Japanese also bet on illegal bullfights and dogfights. See also CARD GAMES; HORSE; PACHINKO; YAKUZA.

GAMES (*asobi*) Aristocrats in the Heian Era (794–1185) court enjoyed a type of kickball, played in a circle. They also enjoyed poetry-writing competitions in which they would alternate sections in writing a poem. A game that became popular during the Edo Era (1600–1868) is *kendama*, in which the player tries to catch a small ball in a wooden cup. Today children also like to toss small beanbags (*otedama*) in time to a popular children's song.

Many kinds of traditional toys have been enjoyed in Japan, including kites (*tako*), spinning tops (*koma*) and dolls of various types. *Origami*, the art of folding small pieces of paper into birds, animals and other shapes, is learned by all Japanese. One of the first games that Japanese children learn is a hand game called scissors-paper-stone (*jan-ken-*

pon). Robot toys and computer video games have become widespread in Japan. Card games *(karuta)* have been played in Japan since they were introduced by the Portuguese in the 16th century. Some popular Japanese card games· are *hanafuda* and *uta karuta,* the matching of flowers *(hana)* or classical poems *(uta)* portrayed on the cards. A similar traditional game known as *kai awase* matches pictures of literary episodes painted on the insides of clamshells. *Go* and *shogi* are popular board games similar to chess and checkers. One of the most popular modern games is *pachinko,* a vertical machine similar to Western pinball machines. Legal forms of gambling include horse, bicycle, motorcycle and speedboat races. At the New Year Festival, girls play *hanetsuki,* a game similar to badminton, in which they hit a shuttlecock with a decorated paddle or battledore *(hagoita).* Popular sports are golf, baseball, skiing and tennis. Martial arts such as judo, karate, archery *(kyudo)* and *kendo* (swordfighting), which were traditionally practiced by samurai, have become popular competitive sports in Japan and abroad. See also CARD GAMES; CHILDREN IN JAPAN; COMPUTER INDUSTRY; DOLLS; FESTIVALS; GAMBLING; GO; KITES; MARTIAL ARTS; NEW YEAR FESTIVAL; ORIGAMI; PACHINKO; ROBOTS AND ROBOTICS; SCISSORS-PAPER-STONE; SHELLS; SHOGI; TOYS, TRADITIONAL.

GANGSTERS See POLICE SYSTEM; TATTOO; YAKUZA.

GARDENS *(niwa)* Gardens in Japan differ from Western gardens that have expansive lawns and colorful flowers planted in symmetrical beds. Japanese gardens, while carefully maintained and cultivated, are designed as microcosms, displaying nature on a small scale. Major features of Japanese gardens include moss, bamboo groves, pine and maple trees, rocks, streams and ponds, and sand. Some flowering trees are used, such as cherry, peach and plum, as are flowering shrubs, especially azaleas, camellias, wisteria and rhododendron. There are also varieties of evergreen shrubs, and ferns planted near water. Groupings of rocks are a basic element of Japanese gardens. Rocks and streams represent mountains and rivers. Ponds, narrow streams and waterfalls are featured in many gardens and provide coolness in the hot summer. Aristocrats in the Heian Era (794–1185) enjoyed oval boating ponds in the center of their gardens. Buddhist temple compounds included gardens representing the tranquil beauty of paradise. Three basic types of gardens developed in Japan, the "hill style" garden *(tsukiyama),* dry-landscape or rock garden *(kare sansui)* and tea garden *(chaniwa).*

The hill-style garden, also known as the pond style, contains hills, ponds and streams. A bridge is built to an island in a pond, and stepping stones are placed in a stream. There are small hills landscaped with pine, maple and cherry trees. Iris are often planted near a pond. Water flows through a *kakei,* or bamboo pipe, and can pour into a *shishiodoshi,* a piece of bamboo that moves up and down as it fills and empties, striking a rock and making a hollow sound when it falls. A variation of the hill style is the socalled "stroll" *(shuyu)* style garden, which has been built around many traditional Japanese mansions and temples.

A garden of white raked sand and rocks at Myoshinji, a Zen Buddhist temple in Kyoto. This style of garden is unique to Japan.

The garden path leads from one vantage point to another, where changing scenes can be viewed. Also classified as a stroll garden is the "many pleasure" *(kaiyu)* style, which contains several gardens constructed around a central pond. During the Edo Era (1600–1868), *daimyo* (feudal lords) built *kaiyu* gardens that synthesized hill and teahouse garden styles and brought in elements from other Japanese arts. These gardens, which provide natural scenes of mountains, rivers and valleys, employ a design concept known as "borrowed views" *(shakkei)* or "capturing alive" *(ikedori).* Such gardens incorporate views of features that lie beyond them in their design. For example, many gardens in Kyoto use pine trees, thick hedges, gateposts and so forth to frame a view of distant mountains.

Dry-landscape style gardens *(karesansui)* are also known as the "dry mountain stream style" gardens and as rock gardens; they are composed solely of white sand or fine gravel and a few rocks, and sometimes enclosed by a few trees and shrubs. The sand is carefully raked, and the rocks are placed in asymmetrical groupings. This style of garden is unique to Japan and is associated with Zen Buddhism. It is related to the sparse aesthetic of Zen Buddhist calligraphy and monochromatic black ink painting *(sumi-e),* especially the portrayal of rocky mountain peaks and dry riverbeds. The dry-landscape garden is an abstract expression of the universe within a limited space. The most famous garden of this type is located at Ryoanji, a Zen Buddhist temple in Kyoto.

The teahouse style *(chaniwa, roji)* is a simple garden built around a teahouse *(chashitsu)* to enhance the peaceful, spiritual quality of the tea ceremony *(chado* or *chanoyu).* A *chaniwa* has a natural appearance but is a carefully arranged composition of plants, path and teahouse. It is encountered on the way to a teahouse, not observed from the house, and so the design of the pathway is important. Steppingstones *(tobi-ishi)* are specially chosen to be placed asymmetrically on the path. This type of garden is also called *roji,* "dew ground" or "dewy path." A waiting arbor *(machiai)* with a bench is placed in the garden where guests gather before entering the tearoom together. A tea garden is divided by a small gate (*chumon*) into an outer garden (*soto roji*) around the waiting room and an inner garden (*uchi roji*) around the teahouse. The inner garden contains a stone water basin (*tsukubai*) where guests can rinse their hands and mouths to purify themselves for the tea ceremony. Vegetation in a tea garden includes evergreen trees and shrubs, ferns, and moss covering the ground. Rocks, bamboo lattice-work fences and stone lanterns are also used. Katsura Detached Palace and Kinkakuji, both on the outskirts of Kyoto, have famous tea gardens. See also BAMBOO; BONSAI; CALLIGRAPHY; INK PAINTING; KATSURA DETACHED PALACE; KINKAKUJI; LANTERNS; MOSS; MOUNTAINS; ROCKS; RYOANJI; SHOIN STYLE OF ARCHITECTURE; TEA CEREMONY; TEAHOUSE; ZEN SECT OF BUDDHISM; NAMES OF INDIVIDUAL TREES AND PLANTS.

GARNISHES FOR FOOD (*mukimono*) Small decorative shapes cut from vegetables and fruits to enhance the appearance of food. *Mukimono* is the name given to this art. *Kaishiki* is the technique by which very sharp knives, vegetable peelers and special cutting tools are used to make a variety of forms, such as flowers, animals and fans. Carrots, cucumbers, radishes, lotus root and tomatoes are the most frequently used vegetables for garnishes. *Mukimono* derives from the ancient practice of serving food on leaves that were folded or cut to embellish the presentation. The art of creating food garnishes became highly developed in the 1720s in the capital city of Edo (modern Tokyo).

Japanese cuisine considers the appearance of food as much as its taste. Some food is simply garnished by small piles of finely shredded daikon (Japanese radish) or finely grated or pickled ginger. Such garnishes, called *tsuma* when they accompany sashimi (slices of raw fish), are thought to aid digestion as well. Other foods can be garnished with seasonings such as toasted sesame seeds, grated rind of a citrus fruit (*yuzu*) or tiny shoots of edible plants, including parsley, trefoil (*mitsuba*) and chrysanthemum leaves. See also CITRUS FRUIT; CHRYSANTHEMUM; COOKING; DAIKON; GINGER; KNIVES; SASHIMI; SEASONING FOR FOOD.

GEISHA Also known as *geigi* or *geiko*; women skilled in classical dancing, singing, playing a banjo-like stringed instrument called the *shamisen* and witty conversation who entertain wealthy clients at banquets. *Geisha* means "art person." They are very knowledgeable about etiquette and the wearing of elaborate kimono. Geisha as an occupational category originated in the 18th century in the "floating world" (*ukiyo*) of government-licensed pleasure quarters of large Japanese cities, such as the Yoshiwara in Edo (modern Tokyo), where geisha were hired to entertain at parties for courtesans (*oiran* or *tayu*) and their clients. By the 19th century, geisha were considered trendsetters, and influenced fashions with their elegant style, described as *iki* (chic). They also inspired the literary, musical and graphic arts, and were depicted by many artists of woodblock prints (*ukiyo-e*). With the modernization of Japan and changing values, today there are fewer than 1,000 geisha of high degree in Japan, concentrated in the cities of Kyoto and Tokyo, and fewer than 20,000 geisha of all types. There

Maiko ("dancing girls") performing in traditional kimono, makeup and hairstyles. Girls who want to become entertainers known as *geisha* learn dancing, singing and other arts while serving an apprenticeship as *maiko*.

are five geisha districts (*hanamachi*, "flower towns") in Kyoto, notably Gion and Pontocho, and 20 districts in Tokyo, notably Shimbashi and Akasaka, the favorite district of powerful leaders of political factions.

The geisha world is poetically known as *karyukai*, the "flower and willow world." Geisha still wear beautiful, expensive kimono and elegant hairstyles and stylized white makeup known as *shiroi*. Now that Japanese women wear Western styles, geisha have changed from being fashion innovators to being the conservators of traditional Japanese styles. Their function has also been largely assumed by bar hostesses, who pour drinks and provide companionship for men, but who wear expensive Western dresses and do not engage in the difficult study of the traditional arts.

Geisha are not prostitutes, but they usually have intimate relations with their patrons (*danna*). They also have a number of favorite customers (*gohiki*) who hire them for parties and also help pay their formidable expenses for kimono and ongoing lessons in classical dancing, *shamisen* playing and several styles of singing. Many geisha also study flower arranging, the tea ceremony and calligraphy. A girl who is apprenticing to become a geisha is called a *maiko* ("little dancer"). She wears a special long-sleeved kimono and a particular hairstyle. In former times, poor girls were often indentured to geisha houses by their parents and were required to work hard as maids before training to be geisha. Now women make their own choice to become geisha, and they are legally required to stay in school through age 15. Many become geisha in their 20s without a period of apprenticeship.

Each geisha *hanamachi* (district) has its own *kenban* (registry office), which handles the assignments for geisha to entertain at parties in private restaurants (*ryotei; chaya*, "teahouse," in Kyoto; also known as *kashi zashiki*, "rental banquet rooms"). The geisha union (*geigi kumiai*) regulates the times of attendance and the fees paid for geisha. Every geisha is affiliated with a geisha house (*okiya* or *geigiya*), which is licensed by the *kemban*, and some of them live on the premises. Geisha houses are managed by older women, usually former geisha, who are called "mother" (*okasan*). Customers hire geisha through the restaurants where they hold their parties. The restaurant managers tell the *kemban* how many geisha they require, and the *kemban* contacts the *okiya*. A geisha may be called to more than one party in an evening. Geisha receive generous tips in addition to standard hourly wages.

Some geisha districts sponsor annual public stage performances of singing and dancing, such as the autumn Kamo River Dances (Kamogawa *odori*) in Pontocho. There are small numbers of regional *chiho* geisha in other Japanese cities. In addition, there are so-called *onsen* geisha, who entertain at hot spring resorts (*onsen*) and who engage in prostitution as well as entertain customers. Liza Crihfield Dalby (b. 1949), the only foreign woman to have studied the geisha, wrote *Geisha* (1983), a book on their history and activities. See also AKASAKA; COURTESAN; DALBY, LIZA CRIHFIELD; DANCE, TRADITIONAL; FLOATING WORLD; GION; HAIRSTYLES; HOT SPRING; KIMONO; KYOTO; MAKEUP; PONTOCHO; SHAMISEN; TEA CEREMONY; TOKYO; WOODBLOCK PRINTS; YOSHIWARA.

GENJI CLAN   See MINAMOTO CLAN; TAIRA-MINAMOTO WAR.

GENJI, THE TALE OF (*Genji Monogatari*)   The greatest work of classical Japanese fiction. *The Tale of Genji* was written in the early 11th century by Murasaki Shikibu (fl. c. A.D. 1000), a woman in the imperial court also known as Lady Murasaki. A complex work, it describes in 54 chapters the life and love affairs of Genji, the Shining Prince, and Kaoru, his supposed son who is actually his friend's grandson. Dwelling on the refinements of daily life in the court during the Heian Era (784–1185), the novel is tinged with the Heian concept of *mono no aware*, a feeling of gentle sadness about the ephemeral nature of things influenced by Buddhism. *Genji* is a psychological novel that explores the deep yet delicate passions that motivate human actions.

Prince Genji is born in the first chapter. His father is the reigning emperor and his mother is the emperor's favorite wife. She dies when Genji is very young. Although the boy is the emperor's favorite son, for various reasons he cannot inherit the throne. Like other imperial sons who are denied the right to rule, he is given the name Genji (also known as Minamoto). Genji is attracted to women who resemble his dead mother; his greatest love is a girl named Murasaki (Purple). The episodes of the novel describe Genji's exile for several years, his return to the court, and his marriages and affairs with various court ladies. As the novel progresses, many sad events unfold, including the death of Murasaki.

Genji enjoyed immediate popularity at the Heian court.

The earliest surviving texts, however, date from the medieval era. Critical commentaries of the work have been written throughout Japanese history, and every Japanese student reads passages from *The Tale of Genji*. Episodes have been adapted for Noh and Kabuki plays and modern movies and television shows, and have been depicted by many painters. The first and most famous illustrations were the 12th-century Genji Scrolls (*Genji Monogatari Emaki*), also known as the Takayoshi Scrolls. *The Tale of Genji* has been translated into English several times, most precisely by Edward Seidensticker (1976). Many critics believe that Arthur Waley (1935, reprint 1960), despite taking liberties with the text, produced the most beautiful translation. See also HEIAN ERA; KABUKI; MONO NO AWARE; MURASAKI SHIKIBU; NOH DRAMA; NOVELS; PAINTING; SCROLLS; WALEY, ARTHUR.

GENRO   Elder statesmen; a group of government leaders of the Meiji Era (1868–1912). (It is not to be confused with the Genroin, a legislative body known as the Chamber of Elders, which played a role in the Japanese government from 1875 to 1890.) Members of the *genro* headed government ministries and eventually selected the prime ministers of Japan in the name of the emperor. Some also took turns holding the position of prime minister. The term *genro* was first used in 1892 to refer to key figures in government from the Meiji Restoration of 1868 who had become older and more influential. The *genro* were honored as "elder statesmen" (*genkun*) by the emperor for service to the country and chosen to advise him on political matters. While two members, Ito Hirobumi and Okubo Toshimichi, seemed to dominate, the group exercised its power collectively. Ito Hirobumi and Kuroda Kiyotaka were the first to be awarded the title *genro*, in 1889. Five more *genro* were added in the next decade, Inoue Kaoru, Matsukata Masayoshi, Oyama Iwao, Saigo Tsugumichi and Yamagata Aritomo. This original group of seven *genro* was in fact the same group of imperial councillors (*sangi*) that had been established in 1869 to advise the emperor. They therefore remained in office even though this title was officially discontinued in 1885.

The *genro* were mostly from samurai families of the regions of Satsuma (now Kagoshima Prefecture) and Choshu (now Yamaguchi Prefecture), whose forces had played the major role in bringing about the downfall of the Tokugawa Shogunate (1603–1867) and the restoration of imperial authority.

In 1912 two more *genro* were named, Katsura Taro and Saionji Kimmochi. Saionji, an aristocrat, was the last surviving *genro* and continued to select prime ministers until 1937. The broader powers of the *genro*, however, lasted only until the start of the Taisho Era (1912–1926). Other factions had begun to exercise greater power by then, including the Diet (Parliament) and its constituent political parties, government ministries, the military and large corporations. There had also been much resentment against the concentration of power in representatives of the Satsuma-Choshu faction. Yet in the years they exercised authority, the *genro* made a great contribution to the stable development of the modern Japanese state. See also CHOSHU

PROVINCE; CONSTITUTION, MEIJI; DIET; EMPEROR; MATSUKATA MA-
SAYOSHI; MEIJI RESTORATION OF 1868; POLITICAL PARTIES; PRIME
MINISTER; SAIONJI KIMMOCHI; SAMURAI; SATSUMA PROVINCE; TAISHO
ERA; TOKUGAWA SHOGUNATE; YAMAGATA ARITOMO.

GENROKU ERA (1688–1704) A period during the Tokugawa Shogunate (1603–1867) marked by active cultural
development, especially among the *chonin* (townspeople
and merchants) of urban Edo (modern Tokyo). This culture
is characterized by the term *ukiyo*, "floating world." This
term had originally meant "sorrow" (*uki*), referring to the
temporal and sad nature of the world, conveyed in literature of the Heian Era (794–1185) and Buddhist writings,
but the middle class in the Genroku Era applied its homonym, *uki*, meaning "floating," to the sensual and aesthetic
pleasures of their new culture. The word referred above
all to the arts and entertainment that developed in the
Yoshiwara, the district of Edo that was licensed by the
government for entertainment and prostitution. Licensed
pleasure quarters also thrived in Kyoto and Osaka.

When the Tokugawa clan unified Japan after centuries
of military struggle, they transformed the samurai into
government bureaucrats, using the Chinese ethic of Confucianism as a means of social control. By the end of the
peaceful 17th century, the Japanese economy had become
very prosperous, and members of the urban middle class,
showing their independence from the samurai class, spent
their disposable income on luxuries and amusements. This
"floating world" of enjoyment was depicted in the vibrant
woodblock prints known as *ukiyo-e*. These prints often
showed famous Kabuki (traditional theater) actors and
courtesans. Kabuki and Bunraku (puppet theater) appealed
to the growing middle class, in contrast to the austere Noh
drama associated with the samurai class. Many Kabuki and
Bunraku plays were written by Chikamatsu Monzaemon
(1653–1724). New woodblock printing techniques introduced from Korea aided the mass-market publishing of
popular fiction, such as that of Ihara Saikaku (1642–1693).
The poet Matsuo Basho (1644–1694) helped make the *haiku*
form of poetry popular as well. The colorful Rimpa school
of painting was founded by Korin (Ogata Korin; 1658–
1716). Thus, many cultural items that have come to be
considered typically Japanese developed during the Genroku Era. See also BASHO; BUNRAKU; CHIKAMATSU MONZAEMON;
CONFUCIANISM; EDO; FLOATING WORLD; HAIKU; KABUKI; KORIN; NOH
DRAMA; NOVELS; PROSTITUTION; RIMPA SCHOOL OF PAINTING; SAI-
KAKU; SAMURAI; TOKUGAWA SHOGUNATE; WOODBLOCK PRINTS;
YOSHIWARA.

GEOGRAPHIC REGIONS Japan is divided into eight
major regions by the Japanese government for document-
ing statistical data. The eight regions follow natural geo-
graphical divisions. Three of these are the northernmost
island of Hokkaido; the southern main island of Kyushu
and related islands, such as the Ryukyu Islands (Okinawa
Prefecture); and Shikoku, the smallest of the four main
islands of Japan. Honshu, the largest island of Japan, is
divided into five geographic regions. Tohoku is the mountainous rural northeastern region, which includes Sendai

City. Kanto, on east central Honshu, is Japan's most ur-
banized region and includes Tokyo, the national capital.
Chubu is the mountainous central region of Honshu, in-
cluding the Japan Alps. Kinki lies to the west and includes
Japan's second largest industrialized area, centering on the
cities of Osaka and Kobe, and the historical capitals of
Kyoto and Nara. Chugoku on west Honshu is an agricul-
tural and fishing region. See also GEOGRAPHY OF JAPAN; HOK-
KAIDO ISLAND; HONSHU ISLAND; KANSAI AND KANTO; KINKI; KYUSHU
ISLAND; SHIKOKU ISLAND; NAMES OF INDIVIDUAL CITIES.

GEOGRAPHY OF JAPAN Japan is a chain of volcanic
mountainous islands separated from mainland Asia to the
west by the Sea of Japan. The Korean peninsula, about 150
miles from Japan, is the closest point on the mainland. The
Pacific Ocean lies to the east of the main Japanese islands.
Honshu is the largest and central island of Japan. Next
largest are Hokkaido to the north, Kyushu to the south
and Shikoku to the southeast. These four main islands,
lying along a northeast-southwest axis, are separated only
by narrow straits. Japan also includes more than 3,000
small adjacent islands and islets; more than 200 smaller
island groups, including the historically important southernmost Ryukyu Island chain (Okinawa Prefecture); and
several islands about 800 miles out in the Pacific. Japan has
a territorial dispute with the Soviet Union about two islands
of the Kuril group and several other islands near Hokkaido.
The Japanese archipelago lies between the latitudes of 45°
and 25°, roughly comparable to the east coast of North
America. Japan is long and narrow, and no place is more
than 100 miles from the sea.

The Japanese islands are actually tops of mountain ridges
that have been lifted up out of the water by violent activity
beneath the earth's crust. Japan has many volcanoes and
hot springs, and experiences over 1,500 earthquakes every
year. Only about 25% of the total land area is level enough
for agriculture or dense habitation. One large basin, the
Kanto Plain on eastern Honshu, is where the capital city
of Tokyo is located. A long chain of mountains down the
center of the archipelago divides Japan into the "front,"
facing the Pacific Ocean, and the "back," facing the Sea of
Japan. Three mountain chains join to form the Japan Alps
on northern Honshu. Mount Fuji, a dormant volcano 12,385
feet high, is the highest point in Japan. Because rivers in
Japan are generally not navigable, water transportation has
always been conducted in coastal waters, particularly those
of the Inland Sea. The Sea of Japan coast and the Pacific
coast north of Tokyo have few natural harbors. See also
AGRICULTURE; CLIMATE OF JAPAN; EARTHQUAKES; FUJI, MOUNT; HOT
SPRING; JAPAN ALPS; KANSAI AND KANTO; KOREA AND JAPAN; KURIL
ISLANDS; MOUNTAINS; PACIFIC OCEAN; RYUKYU ISLANDS; SEA OF
JAPAN; SHIPPING AND SHIPBUILDING; VOLCANO.

GERMANY AND JAPAN See IMPERIAL JAPANESE ARMY AND
NAVY; PACIFIC OCEAN; RUSSO-JAPANESE WAR; SINO-JAPANESE WAR OF
1894–1895; SINO-JAPANESE WAR OF 1937–1945; TRIPARTITE PACT;
WORLD WAR I; WORLD WAR II.

GETA See FOOTWEAR.

GHOSTS See DEMONS AND GHOSTS.

GIFTS (*kurimono; miyage*)   Gift-giving is one of the basic ways by which the Japanese strengthen social relationships. There are two major gift-giving seasons in Japan, *chugen* and *seibo*. *Chugen* is associated with the Bon Festival in midsummer, when families make offerings to the souls of their deceased members, who return to visit during Bon. Traditionally, families handed out these offerings to relatives and other important people as a way of symbolically connecting them with the sacred souls of the dead. *Seibo* means "year end," the gift-giving season in December to thank people for special favors during the past year. Gifts at *chugen* and *seibo* are given to persons of higher social position to express gratitude for their assistance, such as teachers (*sensei*, especially of traditional arts such as tea ceremony or flower arranging), doctors, employers, business clients and go-betweens (*nakodo*) who helped arrange one's marriage. Gifts at *chugen* and *seibo* especially represent the thanks of one family to another or one business to another. The two gift-giving seasons have been highly commercialized by Japanese department stores and by the business practice of giving large bonuses to employees at these times. During *chugen* and *seibo*, department stores offer special gift packs for sale. Popular gifts include consumable items such as fruit, wine, whiskey, canned goods and cooking oil, as well as soap. The stores will also wrap and deliver the gifts, although traditional etiquette requires that the gifts be delivered in person.

Japanese also give gifts for coming of age (*seijin*), weddings, funerals, the birth of a child, or an illness or other disaster. They also like to take gifts known as *temiyage*, which are often sweets or other edible items, when making social calls. This custom is called *hangaeshi*. Farewell gifts (*sembetsu*) are given by relatives and friends to a person who is going away for an extended time. People who go on trips are expected to bring souvenirs (*miyage*) back for family and friends. These are often regional food specialties or folk crafts; the recipient of a *miyage* or other gift is expected to give a gift in return. Children are given pocket money (*otoshidama*) at the New Year by relatives and family friends. The money is handed out in special envelopes (*otoshidamabukuro*) bought from stationery stores. It is very important that gifts be wrapped in special ways according to the nature of the gifts themselves and the status of the persons receiving the gifts; the way a gift is wrapped usually indicates what is inside. The Japanese believe it is impolite to open a gift in front of the person who has given it. See also BON FESTIVAL; DEPARTMENT STORES; ETIQUETTE; FUNERALS; GO-BETWEEN; NEW YEAR FESTIVAL; SENSEI; SWEETS; WEDDINGS; WRAPPING.

GINGER (*shoga*)   A root crop that is used for its sharp, refreshing flavor, especially when pickled. There are two main types of pickled ginger. *Hajikama shoga* ("blushing ginger"), is pickled in rice vinegar and sugar and has a delicate pink color with a taste that is both sweet and sour. It is eaten with foods that have been cooked by grilling. *Beni shoga* (red ginger) is pickled in salt and vinegar and has a tart, salty flavor. Traditionally, this kind of pickle was made with a red-colored brine left from the pickling of plums with the red leaves of the *shiso* (beefsteak) plant. Thinly shaved slices of pickled ginger are eaten with sushi and other Japanese foods. Many dipping sauces made with a base of soy sauce have fresh ginger grated into them. See also PICKLES; SOY SAUCE; SUSHI.

GINKAKUJI (Temple of the Silver Pavilion)   A temple of the Rinzai sect of Zen Buddhism located at the foot of Mount Hiei on the eastern side of the city of Kyoto. In A.D. 1483 Ashikaga Yoshimasa, the eighth shogun during the Ashikaga Shogunate (1338–1573), took up residence at this site, which was formerly that of a monastery of the Tendai sect of Buddhism. Yoshimasa took the tonsure in 1485 as a monk of the Shokokuji, a Zen Buddhist temple. He decreed that when he died, his residence should be turned into a temple named Joshoji, from his religious name, Jishoin. This occurred in 1490. The temple became known as the Silver Pavilion because Ashikaga Yoshimasa had intended to cover one of the temple's 12 buildings, the Kannon (Goddess of Mercy) Hall, with silver leaf. In this he was influenced by the Kinkakuji, or Temple of the Gold Pavilion, which his grandfather Ashikaga Yoshimitsu had erected in 1397. The silver was never applied, but the name remains. A fire in the Tembun Era (1532–1555) destroyed all of the temple's buildings except two, the Ginkakuji and the Togudo. After centuries of disrepair, the temple was restored in the Meiji Era (1868–1912). Ginkakuji and Togudo are the only original buildings of the Ashikagas that remain today in Japan. (Kinkakuji was burned down in 1950 and later rebuilt.) The Ginkakuji has two stories. The lower one served as Yoshimasa's meditation room, and the upper story houses a statue of the goddess Kannon. The Togudo, which was Yoshimasa's private residence, houses statues of Amida Buddha and Yoshimasa on its altars, as well as the memorial tablets of the Ashikaga shoguns. There is also a famous tearoom (*chashitsu*), which is thought to be the oldest room in Japan designed for the tea ceremony. A garden separates the two buildings. See also AMIDA; ASHIKAGA SHOGUNATE; ASHIKAGA YOSHIMASA; HIEI, MOUNT; KANNON; KINKAKUJI; RINZAI SECT OF ZEN BUDDHISM; TEAHOUSE.

GINKGO TREE (*icho*)   A tree with fan-shaped leaves native to East Asia and introduced to the West. The ginkgo has fruit with a strong, unpleasant odor, but the fruit has small, round nutlike kernels, called *ginnan*, which can be cooked and eaten. The tree can grow up to 100 feet tall and have a diameter of 7 feet. It flowers in the spring, and in the autumn its leaves turn yellow. Because ginkgo trees resist fire, pollution and cold weather, they are often planted along roads and as screens and firebreaks. The ginkgo leaf is the symbol of the Urasenke school of the tea ceremony because a ginkgo tree diverted a fire from the Sen family home in the 16th century. Another ginkgo tree was famous for saving a home in the fire caused by the Great Kanto Earthquake of 1923, which destroyed the city of Tokyo; the ginkgo is now the official tree of Tokyo. Ginkgos are traditionally believed to help mothers maintain a good supply of milk to nurse their babies. A famous ginkgo tree, which still stands in the Tsurugaoka Hachiman Shrine compound in Kamakura, was the site of the assassination of Minamoto no Sanetomo, who was the second son of Minamoto Yoritomo, founder of the Kamakura Shogunate, which governed Japan 1192–1333. See also EARTHQUAKE; KAMAKURA; KAMAKURA SHOGUNATE; TREES; URASENKE SCHOOL OF THE TEA CEREMONY.

GINZA The main shopping, commercial and entertainment district of Tokyo, bordering the southeast edge of the Imperial Palace. Many of Japan's largest department stores are located here, along with smaller shops, boutiques, galleries, restaurants and bars. The name *Ginza* means "place where silver is minted" and refers to the government mint established in this area by the Tokugawa Shogunate (1603–1867) on land reclaimed from the sea after 1612. During the 18th century the mint's administrators grew quite powerful by illegal practices that caused the shogunate to close the mint. It was reopened in the 19th century but finally abolished by the imperial government that took power with the Meiji Restoration of 1868. The Ginza then became the first modernized district of Tokyo, with Western-style buildings, expensive imported goods for sale and wide, tree-lined streets. Together with the districts of Shimbashi and Nihonbashi, the Ginza remains the most popular district in Tokyo for shopping, eating and drinking. A large number of hotels are also located here. The current Imperial Hotel was built in 1970 on the site of the original Imperial Hotel, which opened in 1890. A later Imperial Hotel was designed and built on this site in the early 20th century by American architect Frank Lloyd Wright. This hotel became famous for surviving the destruction caused by the Great Kanto Earthquake of 1923, and it continued to be one of the world's grand hotels until pressures of real estate development led to its destruction and replacement in 1970 with a high-rise hotel. The Kabuki Theater (*Kabuki-za*) sits at the intersection of two main streets in the Ginza, Harumi-Dori and Showa-Dori. This home for the colorful traditional Japanese theater was destroyed during World War II but rebuilt soon after the war by contributions from people all over Japan. Hibiya Park adjoins the grounds of the Imperial Palace. The park was opened as part of a program to modernize and beautify Tokyo in the early 1900s. Protest demonstrations often group here and march to the prime minister's residence. Tokyo Station, surrounded by office buildings, is the starting point for the Bullet Train (Shinkansen) to Kyoto and other cities west of Tokyo. See also BULLET TRAIN; DEPARTMENT STORES; IMPERIAL HOTEL; IMPERIAL PALACE (TOKYO); KABUKI; MEIJI RESTORATION OF 1868; TOKUGAWA SHOGUNATE; TOKYO.

GION A district located on the east bank of the Kamo River in the former capital city of Kyoto. Gion, first licensed as an entertainment district by the government in the early 1700s, houses the most famous of the six communities of geisha in Kyoto. Twice a year the geisha of Gion hold a public dance performance called *Miyako odori* in the Gion Geisha Theater.

Also in the district is Yasaka Shrine (popularly known as Gion Shrine) of the Shinto religion. This very large shrine, dedicated to Gozu Tenno, a god of good health, holds an annual festival, Gion Matsuri, which is also known as Gion *goryoe* (service for souls of the dead), during the entire month of July. The festival was begun in A.D. 869 to drive away an epidemic in Kyoto; in the original ceremony 66 long spears *(hoko)*, one for each province of Japan, were mounted on a portable shrine and carried to a sacred pond in the Imperial Park (Shinsen-en). Today this event is represented by a parade on July 17th with enormous floats decorated with tall poles and carrying groups of musicians playing a type of music known as Gion-*bayashi*. Smaller floats are also carried on men's shoulders. Many other summer festivals throughout Japan are modeled on the Gion festival, such as the Sanno Festival in Tokyo and the Gion Yamagasa in Hakata. See also FESTIVALS; GEISHA; KAMO RIVER; KYOTO; PONTOCHO.

GIRLS' FESTIVAL See DOLL FESTIVAL.

GLOVER, THOMAS, and GLOVER MANSION AND GARDEN See NAGASAKI.

GO (or IGO) A game of strategy played on a square board marked with a grid of 19 horizontal and 19 vertical lines that have 361 intersections. Two players, using black and white polished round stones (markers), take turns placing their stones on the intersections in order to capture as much territory as possible. The player whose stones occupy the highest number of intersections wins the game. *Go* seems like a relatively simple game, with only a few basic rules, yet it requires great skill. Many players go so far as to consider it an art and a way of life. A handicapping system called *teawari* gives the higher ranked player the white stones and lets black play the first stone. Black has 181 stones to play, and white has 180. Black is also permitted to put a number of stones on specific points before the game starts. Once a stone is placed on the board it cannot be removed, unless it is captured by being surrounded by the opponent's stones. Then it is removed from the board. One point is awarded for each captured stone and for each intersection that is surrounded by stones. When there are no more possible ways that either player can gain more territory or capture stones, or when all the stones have been played, the game is over. Whichever player controls the most squares is the winner.

The game of *go* has been traced back to ancient China, and may have originated in India more than 4,000 years ago, as did the game of *shogi*, which is similar to chess. *Go* was brought from China (where it was called *weiqi* or *wei-ch'i*) to Korea (where it was known as *patuk*) and eventually to Japan in the fifth or sixth century A.D. The Imperial Treasure House (Shosoin) in the ancient capital city of Nara houses the oldest *go* board in Japan. The game was played by the nobility during the Heian Era (794–1185), and is featured in an episode of the renowned 11th-century novel

The Tale of Genji. Go was later supported by the Tokugawa Shogunate (1603–1867), which subsidized four schools of *go* and held annual competitions. The greatest player of this era, called the "saint of *go*," was Dosaku, Hon'imbo IV (1645–1702). The Meiji Restoration of 1868 ended subsidies for professional *go* players, who then formed a private group that led to the formation of the Japan Go Association (Nihon Kiin) in 1924. At present there are about 400 professional *go* players in Japan. They are ranked into nine grades, the ninth, or highest, being kudan. There are also many amateur players, who are ranked by nine degrees and seven grades. There are *go* associations in the United States and Europe, under the International Go Federation, which was founded in Tokyo in 1982. A *go* match between an elderly master and a young player who defeats him is the plot in Kawabata Yasunari's famous modern novel, *The Master of Go* (*Meijin*; 1942–1954, translated into English in 1972). A movie about a match between a Chinese and a Japanese *go* master, set in the 1920s, was released in English as *The Go Masters* (*Mikan no Taikyoku* in Japanese). See also GAMES; KAWABATA YASUNARI; SHOGI.

GO-BETWEEN (*nakodo*)   A man or woman who helps arrange a marriage. Usually a husband and wife act together as mediators to introduce the couple, assist in negotiating the arrangements between their two families, run the wedding and reception, and counsel the married couple if problems arise in their relationship. A go-between is often a good family friend or relative who knows the characters of the two people. Although about half of the marriages in Japan today are self-arranged "love marriages" (*ren-ai kekkon*), many couples still prefer a marriage in which they are "matched" (*miai-kekkon*). Even couples who marry for love have an honorary go-between at their wedding. The go-between arranges a meeting, known as a *miai*, between a man and a woman who have similar social status, education and hobbies. Their personalities and occupations are also considered. The go-between usually initiates the relationship by sending a letter from the man to the woman. Their two families often hire detective agencies to check the potential spouse's background, examine household registers (*koseki*), which are official lists of family members, and question people who know the man or woman.

Marriage has traditionally been a union between two families more than an individual choice in Japan. Families belonging to higher social classes, particularly nobles, samurai and wealthy landowners, wanted to ensure proper connections through marriage. Go-betweens became important to Japanese of all social classes during the past century, especially since many people migrated from their villages to large cities. If the families find each other acceptable, they will agree to a *miai*, in which the go-between, the two young people and their parents or other family members will meet at a restaurant or theatrical performance. Either party can refuse the marriage if they do not like the person they meet at the miai. Many families, in fact, have *miai* with several different people. If they do like each other, they may date for a while before announcing

their formal engagement (*yuino*). The go-between takes charge of the official engagement ceremony and the wedding. At the wedding reception, the go-between and his spouse sit on either side of the bride and groom, and the go-between makes the main speech. After the honeymoon, the married couple pays a thank-you visit to the go-between and keeps in touch with gifts and New Year visits or cards. The Japanese also use go-betweens in other social situations where they want to avoid a direct confrontation with another person. See also FAMILY; HOUSEHOLD REGISTER; WEDDINGS.

GO-DAIGO, EMPEROR (1288–1339)   The 96th reigning emperor (*tenno*) of Japan (r. 1318–1339), who attempted to overthrow the military government of the Kamakura Shogunate (1192–1333) and restore to power the imperial line in Kyoto. The Hojo clan, whose members were regents of the Kamakura Shogunate, pressured him to rebel. Go-Daigo was exiled to the remote Oki Islands in the Sea of Japan when the Kamakura Shogunate discovered that he was plotting to overthrow it. In 1333 Go-Daigo escaped and gathered support from members of the court and the samurai class in western Japan. Ashikaga Takauji, commander of an army sent from the shogun's headquarters in the eastern city of Kamakura to defeat Go-Daigo, switched allegiance to the emperor and helped to bring down the Kamakura Shogunate. Go-Daigo's rule in Kyoto is known as the Kemmu Restoration (Kemmu no Chuko; 1333–1336). However, Takauji turned against Go-Daigo and in 1336 forced him to flee south to the mountains in Yoshino, where Go-Daigo established a court that became known as the Southern Court. Ashikaga placed the puppet emperor Komyo (1322–1380; r. 1336–1348) on the throne in Kyoto, which became known as the Northern Court. This divided court lasted for nearly 60 years and is known as the Nambokucho Era (1336–1392). In 1339 Emperor Go-Daigo abdicated the throne to his son Emperor Go-Murakami (1328–1368; r. 1339–1368) and died the next day. In 1392 the third Ashikaga shogun persuaded the southern emperor, grandson of Go-Daigo, to come back to Kyoto. But neither he nor the southern line of the imperial family ever held power. After Go-Daigo, the emperors did not actively rule Japan until the Meiji Restoration of 1868. See also ASHIKAGA SHOGUNATE; ASHIKAGA TAKAUJI; BAKUFU; EMPEROR; EXILE; KAMAKURA; KAMAKURA SHOGUNATE; MEIJI RESTORATION OF 1868; NAMBOKUCHO ERA; SHOGUN.

GODS   See AMIDA; AMATERASU O MIKAMI; BENTEN; BISHAMON; BODHISATTVA; BUDDHISM; DAIKOKU; DAINICHI; EBISU; FESTIVALS; FUDO MYOO; HACHIMAN; HOTEI; IZANAGI AND IZANAMI; JIZO; JUROJIN; KAMI; KANNON; MIROKU; MOUNTAINS; NINIGI NO MIKOTO; OKAME; ROCKS; SCULPTURE; SEVEN GODS OF GOOD FORTUNE; SHINTO; SUSANOO NO MIKOTO; TREES.

GODZILLA   A monstrous dinosaur-like beast that appeared in Japanese movies since 1954. Godzilla was supposedly created under the sea by the effects of radiation from the atomic bombs that had been dropped on Japan in 1945. He was originally evil and destructive, reflecting

Japanese fears about the bombs. However, in the 1960s he was transformed into a good creature who defended Japan against threatening evil creatures like the Smog Monster and Megalon. Many Godzilla movies have been shown in the United States and other countries. A plastic Godzilla on wheels was one of the first monster *(monsutaa)* toys to become extremely popular in Japan. Monsters and robots figure strongly in Japanese culture, not only as toys but in comic books and television shows for children. They act out a clearly defined conflict between good and evil, heroes and villains. The 17th Godzilla movie was released in 1989. See also ATOMIC BOMB; COMIC BOOKS; DEMONS AND GHOSTS; FILMS; ROBOTS; TOYS.

GOFU See AMULETS.

GOLDEN PAVILION See KINKAKUJI.

GOLDEN WEEK A period in the spring when three Japanese national holidays fall close together. The birthday of former Emperor Hirohito (Showa; 1901–1989; r. 1926–1989) was celebrated on April 29; Constitution Day falls on May 3, and the Children's Day Festival is held on May 5. Hirohito's birthday was designated in 1990 as a new national holiday, "Greenery Day," to encourage the planting and cultivation of natural vistas. Many Japanese use Golden Week as their spring vacation period from work and take trips or visit their families in the towns where they grew up. See also CHILDREN'S DAY FESTIVAL; CONSTITUTION OF 1947; HIROHITO, EMPEROR; HOLIDAYS, NATIONAL.

GOLF The Western game of golf, which has become very popular in Japan, was introduced there by Arthur H. Groom, an English merchant, who opened a golf course at Kobe in 1901 and founded the Kobe Golf Club in 1903. Since World War II, golf has become associated with big business in Japan, because corporations use country clubs to entertain clients, and many Japanese businessmen are required to learn the game. Japan is second only to the United States in the number of country clubs, with about two thousand in use and close to a thousand more being planned. The northern island of Hokkaido is the nation's golf capital, with more than 130 country clubs. Metropolitan Tokyo and surrounding prefectures have banned new projects because the region is saturated with courses. Few Japanese country clubs are public; memberships are necessary, very expensive, and bought and sold as investments by corporations. Today there are about 12 million golfers in Japan, second only to the United States. There are also more than a thousand professional Japanese golfers. Netted driving ranges, often placed on rooftops, are popular in cities.

GOVERNMENT See CABINET, PRIME MINISTER'S; CONSTITUTION OF 1947; DIET; ELECTIONS; JAPAN SOCIALIST PARTY; LIBERAL DEMOCRATIC PARTY; NEIGHBORHOOD ASSOCIATION; POLICE SYSTEM; PREFECTURE; PRIME MINISTER; SUPREME COURT; TAX SYSTEM; WARD.

GRAVES See BON FESTIVAL; FUNERALS; HIGAN.

GREAT BRITAIN AND JAPAN See ADAMS, WILLIAM; ANGLO-JAPANESE ALLIANCE; WASHINGTON CONFERENCE AND NAVAL TREATY OF 1922; WORLD WAR I; WORLD WAR II.

GREAT BUDDHA See ASUKA; BUDDHISM; DAIBUTSU; KAMAKURA; NARA; SCULPTURE; TODAIJI.

GREATER EAST ASIA COPROSPERITY SPHERE (Dai Toa Kyoeiken) A slogan used in the late 1930s and early 1940s for Japan's political, military and economic expansion in East Asia. Japanese Prime Minister Konoe Fumimaro proclaimed Japan's New Order in East Asia *(Toa Shinchitsujo)* on November 3, 1938. Japan was at war with China (Sino–Japanese War of 1937–1945), and Konoe asked China to cooperate with Japan against imperialistic Western nations, which had exploited China since the British Opium War (1839–1842), and also against communism. Unlike China and other Asian countries, Japan had resisted Western exploitation and had become a modern, industrialized country. Yet Japan itself was similarly expanding imperialistically and had already seized Korea, Taiwan and Manchuria. The nationalist Chinese leader Chiang Kai-shek rejected Japan's demands, but his rival, Wan Jingwei (Wang Ching-wei), collaborated with the Japanese in 1940 to create the so-called Reorganized National Government of the Republic of China. Japan increased its expansion in Asia upon signing the Tripartite Pact in September, 1940 with Germany and Italy, which were at war with other Western nations. Japan attacked Pearl Harbor on December 7, 1941, and the U.S. declaration of war brought Japan into World War II. The Greater East Asia Coprosperity Sphere, which included Japan, China, and Manchuria, was then extended militarily to include French Indochina, the Dutch East Indies, the Pacific Islands and Southeast Asia. Some Japanese even wanted to add India, Australia and New Zealand to the sphere. The government of Prime Minister Tojo Hideki created the Greater East Asia Ministry (Dai Toa Sho) in 1943. Leaders of five nations in the Coprosperity sphere, who believed that the Japanese were liberating their countries from Western imperialism, attended the Greater East Asia Conference (Dai Toa Kaigi) in Tokyo the same year. See also KONOE FUMIMARO; KOREA AND JAPAN; TOJO HIDEKI; SINO-JAPANESE WAR OF 1937–1945; WORLD WAR II.

GREENERY DAY See GOLDEN WEEK; HOLIDAYS, NATIONAL; HIROHITO, EMPEROR.

GUADALCANAL, BATTLE OF See WORLD WAR II.

GUAM, BATTLE OF See WORLD WAR II.

GUILDS See APPRENTICE SYSTEM; TOWNSPEOPLE.

GUNS See FIREARMS, INTRODUCTION OF.

H

HACHIKO See DOG; SHIBUYA.

HACHIMAKI See HEADWEAR.

HACHIMAN The god of warriors, the protector of the Japanese nation and one of the Seven Gods of Good Fortune. Hachiman is a spirit of Shinto, the indigenous Japanese religion. During the Heian Era (794–1185), he came to be revered as the deified spirit of the legendary Emperor Ojin. By the sixth or eighth century, Hachiman was being worshipped at a shrine called Usa Jingu, which survives as the oldest and most important shrine dedicated to him. A branch of this shrine, called Iwashimizu Hachiman Shrine, was built in Kyoto in A.D. 859 by the Buddhist monk Gyokyo. Hachiman had become identified with Buddhism after an oracle decreed in A.D. 749 that he would protect the Great Buddha statue then being constructed in the city of Nara. From that time on, Hachiman was regarded as a protector of Buddhism, the religion brought from China to Japan, and was awarded the Buddhist title Daibosatsu (Great Bodhisattva, or enlightened being). Because of his military associations, Hachiman was chosen by the powerful Minamoto clan as their patron deity. Minamoto no Yoritomo, the founder of the Kamakura shogunate, which ruled Japan (1192–1333), built the Tsurugaoka Hachiman Shrine in 1211 in Kamakura. This is where Minamoto established the headquarters for his military government, and the shrine is the most important Hachiman shrine in eastern Japan. Today there are about 25,000 shrines dedicated to Hachiman throughout the country. See also BUDDHISM; DAIBUTSU; KAMAKURA SHOGUNATE; MINAMOTO CLAN; MINAMOTO NO YORITOMO; NARA; SEVEN GODS OF GOOD FORTUNE; SHINTO; SHRINES, SHINTO.

HAGI WARE *(hagi-yaki)* A type of pottery made in the towns of Hagi and Fukawa on the southwest coast of Honshu Island. Hagi ware is made with rough clay, and decorated with thick reddish or cream glazes that crackle and deepen with use. Hagi tea bowls *(chawan)* are highly valued for the tea ceremony *(chanoyu)*. The first Hagi potters were Koreans who were brought to Japan during the Japanese invasions of Korea under Toyotomi Hideyoshi in 1592 and 1597. The rough and asymmetrical simplicity of Korean rice bowls was appreciated by Toyotomi's tea ceremony master, Sen no Rikyu, and other tea connoisseurs, and feudal lords brought skilled Korean potters to establish seven pottery centers in Japan's western provinces. The Miwa and Saka families ran the Hagi kilns. An early wood-fired kiln on a rising slope *(noborigami)* with 14 chambers has been excavated in the Hagi area. At first, Hagi potters made heavy tableware and storage containers with local clay that was rich in iron. Such Old Hagi Ware was made until 1770, when Hagi masters began using white, sandy clay discovered nearby to make lighter tea bowls. The soft, warm feel of Hagi bowls, valued second in rank only to Raku ware, is compared by the Japanese to warm human flesh. Pockmarks and scars made on glazes while bowls are fired in the kiln are considered beautiful. The most highly prized Hagi tea bowls, known as *Ido chawan*, have high "feet," or bases, and show marks left by the potters who turned them on the potter's wheel. More than a hundred potters still produce Hagi ware, and the potter Miwa Kyusetsu was named a Living National Treasure by the Japanese government. Three museums in Hagi display collections of tea bowls and other traditional objects: the Hagi-yaki Togei Kaikan, the Ishii Teabowl Art Museum and the Kumaya Art Museum. See also KILN; KOREA AND JAPAN; LIVING NATIONAL TREASURES; POTTERY; RAKU WARE; SEN NO RIKYU; TEA CEREMONY; TOYOTOMI HIDEYOSHI.

HAGOITA See ASAKUSA; GAMES; NEW YEAR FESTIVAL; TOYS, TRADITIONAL.

HAIKU An important form of traditional Japanese poetry that comprises three lines with 17 syllables in a 5-7-5 pattern. The Japanese language lends itself to short poetry because it has few vowel sounds and consists of short open syllables, each made up of a consonant and vowel. So many words sound alike that it is almost impossible to write long poems in Japanese. *Haiku* is related to two other poetic terms, *hokku* and *haikai*. *Hokku* ("starting verse") was the first link in a long chain of short verses known as *haikai no rengai*, or *haikai*. All three terms refer to the 5-7-5 syllabic pattern that became known as the independent Japanese poetic form *haiku* in the late 19th century, mainly through the efforts of the poet Masaoka Shiki (1867–1902). But even in the 16th century, *haikai* had become a separate poetic genre in contrast to *renga*, a serious classical form of poetry with complex rules of composition. *Haikai* verse was lighter, more humorous and used colloquial expressions *(haigon)*, which had previously been thought unworthy of poetry. The greatest *haikai* poet was Basho (1644–1694), who developed the form into something greater than just witty amusement, to express deep and sudden insights about nature and human life. His style set the standard for later *haiku* poets, and about 1,000 of his *haiku*, to use the modern term, survive. *Haiku* became a very popular poetic form, not only in Japan but in foreign countries as well, ever since Basho's poems were first translated into English and French in the early 20th century. At present, several *haiku* magazines are published in English. See also BASHO; POETRY; RENGA.

HAIR ORNAMENTS   See COMBS AND HAIR ORNAMENTS.

HAIRSTYLES, TRADITIONAL (*kamigata*)   Japanese hairstyles evolved over different historical eras and often reflected the age and social rank of the wearer. In the earliest historical era, the fourth to sixth centuries A.D., men wore their hair parted in the middle and looped over the ears (*mizura* style). Women pulled their hair up into a flat loop fastened on top of the head (*shimadamage* style). Chinese hairstyles became fashionable among the Japanese aristocracy when Chinese culture was being introduced in the seventh and eighth centuries. Noblemen pulled their hair up into a large topknot at the back of the head (*kanka no ikkei* or *chommaga* style). Noblewomen wore their hair in a single or double large topknot (*kokei* style) decorated with a flower-shaped ornament (*saishi*). Common people usually wore their hair straight. The samurai class, which controlled Japan from the 12th to mid-19th centuries called for simpler hairstyles. Samurai men still pulled their hair into a topknot; however, they shaved the front of their heads to decrease the heat of their battle helmets, and undid their topknots to let their remaining hair fall straight inside when they put on helmets. This hairstyle for men, with shaved forehead and topknot (known as *sakayaki, osakayaki, hondamage,* or *chasemmage* in different historical eras), lasted into the 19th century. During the Tokugawa Shogunate (1603–1867), the samurai hairstyle was also worn by merchants and other lower classes, although the styles of their topknots differed from those of samurai. Women wore their hair straight and very long during the ninth–14th centuries. By the 16th century, women of the merchant class were piling their hair on top of their heads in the *karawamage* style, which imitated men's topknots. Elaborate hairstyles became fashionable for women in the Tokugawa era. The hair was coated with a substance such as camellia oil, and divided into five sections: front hair smoothed back over the head in a high mound, right and left sections, a large bun in the lower back, and a rounded section in the back known as the *tabo*. The most popular hairstyles of the late Tokugawa Era were known as *katsuyamamage* and *shimadamage*. Decorative combs and other ornaments were worn in the hair. Variations of styles were strictly prescribed, especially for geisha and courtesans of the urban districts licensed for prostitution by the Tokugawa Shogunate, such as the Yoshiwara in Edo (modern Tokyo). The Meiji government encouraged Japanese men to cut off their topknots in 1871 and adopt Western hairstyles. Japanese women also gradually changed to Western styles in the 20th century. Geisha, brides and other women still wear traditional hairstyles, especially the *shimadamage* style for formal events and the New Year Festival. These styles expose the neck and beautifully complement kimono (traditional Japanese clothing) which have high collars. An elaborate rolled hairstyle known as *momoware* ("split peach"), traditionally worn by young Japanese girls, is now worn only by *maiko* (apprentice geisha) in Kyoto. See also CAMELLIA; COMBS AND HAIR ORNAMENTS; COURTESAN; GEISHA; KIMONO; SAMURAI; WEDDINGS; YOSHIWARA.

HAKAMA   A traditional formal garment for men, the *hakama* is a pleated, divided skirt worn over a man's kimono. It is made of subtly striped gray silk, or another subdued color. A *hakama* has no buttons or other fasteners to hold it on, but rather has two long ties that are wrapped around the waist and knotted in a special tight bow in front. Men's clothing for ceremonial occasions is known as *montsuki hakama*. The *montsuki* is a jacket (*haori*) with a man's family crest (*mon*) printed on the shoulders, which is worn with *hakama* and kimono. The most formal jacket worn with *hakama* is the *habutae haori*, which is black and has five crests, two on the front shoulders, two on the back shoulders, and one at the neck. A Japanese bridegroom wears the *montsuki hakama* at a traditional Shinto wedding ceremony. See also CREST; KIMONO; SILK; WEDDINGS.

HAKATA   See FUKUOKA.

HAKE   See BRUSHES.

HAKODATE   A city with a population of about 350,000, on southwest Hokkaido, the northernmost of the four main Japanese islands. Hakodate is the gateway to Hokkaido, due to its location on the tip of Oshima Peninsula on the Tsugaru Strait, which separates Hokkaido from the main island of Honshu. The 33.5-mile-long Seikan Railroad Tunnel (Aomori-Hakodate Tunnel), the longest underwater tunnel in the world, was completed in 1985 to connect Hokkaido and Honshu islands. Ferries also sail between Hakodate on Hokkaido and Aomori City on Honshu Island. The city has been an active fishing port since the 1700s. Russian expansion north of Japan led the Tokugawa Shogunate (1603–1867) to open the Office of the Commissioner of Hakodate (Hakodate bugyo) in the early 19th century. Fort Goryokaku, in Hakodate, was the site of the final battle in the overthrow of the Tokugawa Shogunate and the Meiji Restoration of imperial authority in 1868. The Kanagawa Treaty of 1854 made Hakodate one of the first Japanese ports open to foreign trade after 250 years of isolation, along with Kobe, Nagasaki and Yokohama. Hakodate remained the largest city on Hokkaido until a fire destroyed most of the city in 1934. It was devastated again, by bombing during World War II. In 1952 the city began to revive when fishing intensified in the northern waters of Japan. Today the major industries in Hakodate include seafood processing and shipbuilding, and rice and vegetables are grown on the Hakodate Plain. Mount Hakodate, a 1,100 foot-high extinct volcano, is a popular tourist attraction. See also FERRIES; FISH AND FISHING INDUSTRY; HOKKAIDO ISLAND; MEIJI RESTORATION OF 1868; RAILROADS; SEAFOOD; SHIPPING AND SHIPBUILDING; TOKUGAWA SHOGUNATE; VOLCANO.

HAKONE, LAKES   See FUJI-HAKONE-IZU NATIONAL PARK.

HAKUIN EKAKU (1686–1769)   A master of the Rinzai sect of Zen Buddhism and a painter and calligrapher. Born in the village of Hara in what is now Shizuoka Prefecture, Hakuin joined Shoinji, the local Zen temple, at the age of

14. At 19 he undertook a pilgrimage to find a religious answer to his deep despair. At 23, Hakuin had an experience of enlightenment (satori) when a temple bell rang while he was meditating. He continued traveling to study with Zen masters at different temples, and achieved ultimate enlightenment under a strict teacher named Shoju Rojin.

Hakuin returned to Shoinji in his native village when he was 31, where he became a great Zen teacher with many followers. He required his pupils to strive diligently in their quest for enlightenment, and gave them a strict regimen of meditation and daily work in the temple compound. Hakuin also systematized a method of Zen instruction that uses koans, paradoxical questions that cannot be solved by ordinary logic but which point directly to ultimate reality. He translated many koans created by earlier Zen masters in China, and added one of his own that has become famous: "What is the sound of one hand clapping?" Hakuin's religious methods are still practiced in Japanese temples of the Rinzai sect of Buddhism. At the same time, Hakuin was sympathetic to ordinary people, such as farmers, and respected the various forms of Buddhism they practiced. Hakuin's ink paintings and calligraphy, which he began doing in his sixties, express his profound religious insight through simple but powerful brush strokes. He is best known for his paintings of Daruma (Bodhidharma), the legendary teacher who brought Zen Buddhism to China from India. Hakuin also wrote extensively about Zen, and one of his books has been translated into English as *The Embossed Tea Kettle (Orategama)*. See also CALLIGRAPHY; DARUMA; INK PAINTING; KOAN; MEDITATION; PILGRIMAGE; RINZAI SECT OF ZEN BUDDHISM; SATORI.

HAMADA SHOJI (1894–1978) The most important modern Japanese potter and a founder of the folk-crafts (mingei) movement. Hamada was born in Kawasaki and educated at Tokyo Industrial College (now Tokyo Institute of Technology), where he studied the science and technology of making pottery. His teacher was Itaya Hazan, who was from the famous pottery-making village of Mashiko, where Hamada later settled. After he graduated, Hamada took a job at the Kyoto Ceramic Testing Institute with his friend and fellow potter Kawai Kanjiro. For several years they experimented there with glazes and other pottery techniques, and studied with the famous potter Tomimoto Kenkichi. Hamada became friends with the great English potter Bernard Leach (1887–1979), who spent many years in Japan and was a friend of Yanagi Soetsu (1889–1961), the founder of the Japanese folk-craft movement. Hamada went to England with Leach in 1919 to help him establish a pottery-making center with a traditional wood-firing kiln in the town of St. Ives. He returned to Japan after five years, but maintained a lifelong relationship with Leach. Hamada traveled widely over the years throughout Europe, the United States, China and Korea, lecturing, teaching pottery and learning about the crafts of other countries. In 1936, Hamada, Kawai and Yanagi founded the Japan Folk-craft Museum (Nippon Mingei Bijutsu-kan). They also published *Kogei*, a magazine about crafts.

Hamada developed his own pottery center in Mashiko, where his collection of crafts is now open to the public. A prolific potter, Hamada was an expert in many traditional Japanese styles, ranging from the asymmetrical, subdued tea bowls used in the tea ceremony to colorful pieces in the style of Okinawa (the southernmost islands of Japan), where he often spent the winter. The Japanese government honored Hamada by naming him a Living National Treasure in 1955 and awarding him the Order of Culture in 1968. Bernard Leach compiled a tribute to him in 1975, titled *Hamada, Potter*, which includes Hamada's own remembrances and descriptions of his pottery. See also DECORATIONS, CIVILIAN; KILN; LEACH, BERNARD; LIVING NATIONAL TREASURES; MASHIKO; MINGEI; OKINAWA ISLAND; POTTERY; TEA BOWL; YANAGI SOETSU.

HANAE MORI See MORI HANAE.

HANEDA AIRPORT See AIRLINES AND AIRPORTS.

HANIWA "Clay ring"; hand-formed, unglazed clay cylinders and hollow sculptures that were placed on earthen tomb mounds (kofun) of Japanese nobles during the fourth to seventh centuries A.D. *Haniwa* were arranged upright on cylindrical bases in rows around the tomb mound to protect a tomb and define it as a sacred space. Precursors of *haniwa* were the hourglass-shaped stands of the preceeding Yayoi Era (c. 300 B.C.–c. A.D. 300), that held large jars containing ritual offerings for burial ceremonies. The stands evolved into cylindrical shapes that replaced the jars. The eighth-century A.D. chronicle *Nihon Shoki* claims that *haniwa* took the place of human sacrifices, although there is no physical evidence of sacrificial victims in Japan. The pieces included human figures, animals, houses and household objects, boats, and ceremonial objects. The most common shape was the clay cylinder or ring, which averaged 16–20 inches in diameter and 3.3 feet high. Some cylinders have holes representing eyes and mouths. Mounted warriors in armor suggest the military nature of Japan's rulers at the time, some of whom may have been northeastern Asian nomads who invaded Japan through Korea in the late third or fourth century A.D. Other human figures include entertainers, dancers, musicians and mourners, who would belong to the ceremonial procession accompanying the deceased to the tomb. *Haniwa* originated in the Kinki region around Osaka and Nara on western Honshu Island, where the rule of Japan by an imperial court was centralized. However, the majority of *haniwa* have been excavated in the Kanto region around Tokyo on eastern Honshu. Haniwa were not made after the Buddhist religion was introduced from China in the sixth century A.D. and the Japanese took up the Buddhist custom of cremating rather than burying their dead. See also FUNERALS; KOFUN ERA; NIHON SHOKI; TOMB MOUNDS; YAYOI ERA.

HAORI A loose "half-coat" or jacket that is worn over a kimono by both men and women. A *haori* is shaped the same way as a kimono, with long, straight panels of cloth and hanging sleeves. Whereas the sides of a kimono overlap and are held tight by an *obi* (sash), a *haori* remains open in the front and is held on by two small braids of silk thread that are tied into a knot. *Haori* and kimono are both stored flat by folding them in a specified way along their seams. The custom of wearing *haori* was originated in the 1800s by geisha of the Fukagawa district of Tokyo and taken up by other geisha. *Haori* were considered chic *(iki)*, but geisha stopped wearing them by the 1930s because by then they had become popular among ordinary Japanese women. Women's *haori* usually have designs that differ from but complement the kimono over which they are worn. The simple shape of the *haori* can be decorated by an infinite variety of colors and designs, which often fit the season of the year. Men wear *haori* in dark, solid colors. For formal occasions, such as a wedding, men wear *mont-suki*, a black *haori* with five family crests *(mon)* on the front and back shoulders and at the neck. The *montsuki* is worn with a *hakama*, a formal divided skirt worn over a kimono. Women do not wear *haori* for formal occasions. See also CORD, BRAIDED; CREST; GEISHA; HAKAMA; KIMONO.

HAPPI COAT   A jacket traditionally worn by firemen and certain types of servants during the Edo Era (1600–1868). It became a common garment for workmen, such as carpenters and fishmongers. Today happi coats are worn by workmen and by people taking part in festivals. They are made of straight panels of cloth that fit the body loosely. Often there is a decoration on the back, such as a calligraphic character. Happi coats are also made in bright colors as popular souvenirs for foreign tourists to Japan. See also CALLIGRAPHY; FESTIVALS; FIRE FIGHTING.

HARAJUKU   A district of Tokyo that has become a trendy place for Japanese young people to spend their leisure time. They flock to the international shops and cafes on the main avenue, Omotesando Street, where famous designers such as Mori Hanae have their boutiques. On Sunday afternoons the street becomes a promenade and performance place for young people known as the "Bamboo Shoot Tribe," who, wearing clothing of the 1950s, dance to American rock and roll music. Omotesando Street leads to Yoyogi Park, the site of the 1964 Olympic Village. Yoyogi Sports Facility is still used for public events. Originally this area served as the parade ground for the Imperial Japanese Army, but during the Allied Occupation of Japan after World War II, Americans turned the area into a virtual American city named Washington Heights. Just north of Yoyogi Park is the most revered Shinto shrine in Tokyo, Meiji Shrine, built to honor the great Emperor Meiji, who died in 1912. See also BAMBOO SHOOT TRIBE; IMPERIAL JAPANESE ARMY AND NAVY; IRIS; MORI HANAE; OCCUPATION OF JAPAN; OLYMPIC GAMES; MEIJI SHRINE; TOKYO; TORII.

HARA-KIRI   See BUSHIDO; MISHIMA YUKIO; SUICIDE; SWORD.

HARIBAKO   See BOXES.

HARRIS, TOWNSEND (1804–1878)   The first U.S. consul general in Japan, he was responsible for getting Japan to sign its first commercial treaty with the United States, in 1858. This treaty was officially named the United States-Japan Treaty of Amity and Commerce (Nichibei Shuko Tsusho Joyaku), but was commonly known as the Harris Treaty.

Harris was a politically active merchant in New York who decided to investigate the commercial potential of Asia. Between 1849 and 1855, he traveled to the major trading cities in China and Southeast Asia. He persuaded the U.S. government to appoint him as first consul general in Shimoda, a Japanese port on the Izu Peninsula that had been opened to Western trade by the Kanagawa Treaty of 1854. Harris arrived in Shimoda in August, 1856, along with a Dutch interpreter named Henry Heusken. Japanese officials in Shimoda gave a local woman named Tojin Okichi to Harris, and their brief relationship was later turned into a famous legend and was one source for the opera, *Madama Butterfly*. Harris undertook extensive negotiations with the Tokugawa Shogunate (1603–1867), and in 1857 he received permission to meet with the shogun in the capital city of Edo (modern Tokyo) and begin negotiating a commercial treaty. He relied on the threat of the European powers, at that time fighting a war with China, to persuade the shogunate to agree to the American demands.

The Harris Treaty was signed at Kanagawa on July 29, 1858, and ratified by the U.S. Senate. Major points agreed to in the 14 articles of the treaty included the opening of the Japanese ports of Hyogo (modern Kobe), Kanagawa (later changed to Yokohama), Nagasaki and Niigata to American trade and residents; the opening of Edo for trade in 1862 and Osaka in 1863; full diplomatic relations between Japan and the United States; and the right of Japan to buy American ships and arms, and to hire American soldiers, scientists and technicians as advisors. Great Britain, France, the Netherlands and Russia soon concluded similar treaties with Japan, known as the Ansei Commercial Treaties. Its concessions to the United States contributed to Japanese opposition to the Tokugawa Shogunate, which was overthrown in 1867. The Harris Treaty remained in force until a new commercial treaty between Japan and the U.S. went into effect in 1899. Harris remained in Japan until 1862, and then went into retirement in the United States. See also ANSEI COMMERCIAL TREATIES; BUTTERFLY; EDO; IZU PENINSULA; TOKUGAWA SHOGUNATE; YOKOHAMA.

HARRIS TREATY   See HARRIS, TOWNSEND.

HARUNOBU (1725?–1770)   A well-known woodblock print *(hanga)* artist, and the first to produce full-color woodcuts known as *nishiki-e* ("brocade pictures"). Nothing is known of Harunobu's early years, except that his full name was Suzuki Harunobu. His earliest prints were made in Edo (modern Tokyo) in the early 1760s; most are of Kabuki (traditional theater) actors. He was commissioned to make pictorial calendars *(egoyomi)* in 1765 and 1766 for private collectors, many of them Harunobu's friends and patrons, who were members of the samurai class that ruled Japan under the Tokugawa Shogunate (1603–1867). Harunobu utilized the full-color technique, with black outlines and as many as 10 pigments, to make the prints for these calendars. Woodblock prints were formerly made with only two or three colors, and the calendars helped stimulate the production of full-color woodblock prints by other artists. In the years that Harunobu worked until his untimely death in 1770, he created nearly 20 black-and-white illustrated books, hundreds of individual color prints, and some paintings. Many of his pictures show women of the licensed pleasure quarters or middle-class women going about their domestic activities. Other subjects included illustrations of poems, references from mythology and literature, and erotic prints, known as *shunga*. Harunobu's print sets include the *Thirty-Six Poetic Geniuses (Sanjurok-kasen)*, the *Seven Gods of Good Fortune (Shichifukujin)*, flowers of the four seasons, and the festivals of the 12 months. Harunobu's works have been acquired by collectors around the world. It is often hard to prove which prints are his originals because imitations, reprints, and reproductions were made after his death as late as the Meiji Era (1868–1912). See also EDO ERA; KABUKI; SHUNGA; WOODBLOCK PRINTS.

HARVEST RITUALS See AGRICULTURE; FESTIVALS; RICE PLANTING AND HARVESTING FESTIVALS; SHINTO.

HASEDERA TEMPLE See JIZO; KAMAKURA; KANNON.

HASEGAWA SCHOOL OF PAINTING See KANO SCHOOL OF PAINTING.

HASHI See CHOPSTICKS.

HATA CLAN A powerful and wealthy family in ancient Japan that held high diplomatic positions, supervised government storehouses and was involved in the silk and metalworking industries and economic development. The family name *Hata*, although written with the Chinese character for the Qin (Ch'in) dynasty (221 B.C.–207 B.C.), was given the same pronunciation in Japanese as the word for looms (*hata*) used to weave textiles.

The Hata clan likely descended from a man of Chinese origin named Yuzuki no Kimi, who came to Japan from Paekche, a kingdom in Korea, around A.D. 400. A large group of people emigrated with him, and their descendants were called *hatahito*. (The term *kikajin* is also applied to the Hata and several other clans who came from Korea, such as the Aya, and their descendants; *kika* means to change one's country of allegiance.) The main branches of the Hata clan settled in the Kyoto region on west-central Honshu Island, and Hata no Kawakatsu became close to Prince Shotoku (574–622), who is considered the "Father of Japanese Culture." In A.D. 784 Emperor Kammu moved the capital city from Nara (then known as Heijokyo) to Nagaokakyo, the power base of the Hata clan. But several unfortunate incidents persuaded the imperial court to move, in A.D. 794, to Heiankyo, now known as Kyoto.

Members of the Hata clan founded several Shinto shrines in the Kyoto area. The Fushimi Inari Shrine was built by Hata no Kimi Irogu in A.D. 711 to enshrine the Hata clan deity *(ujigami)*, Ta no Kami, the god of the fields. Inari, who is associated with rice cultivation and is the most widely worshipped deity in Japan, developed from this deity. See also AYA CLAN; INARI; KOREA AND JAPAN; NARA; SHOTOKU, PRINCE; SHRINES, SHINTO; SILK.

HAYAKAWA SESSHU (1886–1973) A Japanese movie actor who made 40 movies in Hollywood under the name Sessue Hayakawa. He was born in Chiba Prefecture, just north of Tokyo and in 1906 went to the United States to attend the University of Chicago. As an amateur actor he later met the American director Thomas Ince, who gave Hayakawa his first movie role in 1914 in *Typhoon*. Hayakawa received critical praise for his acting in two movies, *Yoshiwara* (1936, directed by Max Ophuls) and *Bridge over the River Kwai* (1957, directed by David Lean), in which he played an iron-willed Japanese army officer. Hayakawa also acted in many Japanese movies after he returned home in 1949, although he was not as successful in his native country as he was in the United States. See also FILM.

HAYASHI RAZAN (1583–1657) A Neo-Confucian scholar who served as adviser to Tokugawa Ieyasu (1542–1616), founder of the Tokugawa Shogunate (1603–1867), and three of his successors. Razan helped spread the principles of the Chu Hsi (Tei Shu in Japanese) school of Neo-Confucianism, which the Tokugawa Shogunate used as its ideology for ordering Japanese society and transforming the samurai from warriors into peaceful civil servants based on the Chinese model of the scholar-bureaucrat.

Razan was born in the old capital city of Kyoto and studied Rinzai Zen Buddhism at Kenninji. He then studied the classics of Confucianism and won the acceptance of Tokugawa Ieyasu, who made him an official Confucian adviser in 1607 and gave him the name Doshun. Hayashi drew up many laws that governed Japan under the Tokugawa Shogunate, including the Laws Governing the Military Households and the Imperial Court.

Whereas Buddhism was the predominant philosophy during the medieval era (12th–16th centuries), Confucian learning supplanted it during the Tokugawa Shogunate, virtually becoming an orthodox creed in Japan with the performance of Confucian rituals and reverence for Chinese sages. Razan strongly opposed Buddhism, largely because it tended to be too individualistic, and Christianity. His arguments with Buddhist thinkers led him to explore Shinto, the indigenous Japanese religion, and associate its *kami* (sacred spirits) with principles of Confucian thought. Chu Hsi's philosophy emphasized morality, the fulfillment of duties required by one's station in life, loyalty in human relationships and respect for one's superiors. This philosophy was combined with the feudal Japanese notion of loyalty by samurai to their lords, to create the ethical code of *bushido*.

Razan edited and published numerous Confucian works, and wrote 150 scholarly books altogether. His home in the capital city of Edo (modern Tokyo) became a major center of Confucian studies known as the Shohei-ko. Hayashi's son Shunsai (also known as Gaho; 1618–1680) and grandson Hoko (1644–1732) inherited the position of official Confucian adviser to the shogunate. The official title Head of the State University (Daigaku-no-kami) was awarded to Hayashi Hoko by the fifth Tokugawa Shogun, Tsunayoshi (1646–1709), and became hereditary in the Hayashi family. The 12th and last holder of that title was Hayashi Gakusai (1833–1906). See also BUDDHISM; BUSHIDO; CLASS STRUCTURE; CONFUCIANISM; SAMURAI; SHINTO; TOKUGAWA IEYASU; TOKUGAWA SHOGUNATE.

HEALTH-SPORTS DAY   See HOLIDAYS, NATIONAL.

HEARN, LAFCADIO (1850–1904)   A European-born writer of Irish-Greek ancestry who spent three decades in the United States before moving to Japan in 1889, where he wrote 11 books that introduced Japanese culture to readers in the West. Hearn led a poor and troubled life in the United States, but his flamboyant writing won him jobs on various newspapers around the country. He also lived for a time on the French island of Martinique.

Hearn arrived in Japan in 1890, the 23rd year of the Meiji Era (1868–1912), when Japan was becoming Westernized and undergoing a complete political, cultural and economic transformation. Hearn had been commissioned by Harper and Brothers Publishing Company to write books and articles in Japan. However, he quarreled with them, and instead took a position teaching English at a Japanese school in Matsue, on the west coast of Honshu Island. Hearn lived for 15 months in Matsue, where he married a Japanese woman, Koizumi Setsuko, and took the Japanese name Koizumi Yakumo. The Hearn Residence and Memorial Hall (Koizumi Yakumo Kyuko) in Matsue exhibits his manuscripts and personal belongings. Hearn supported his wife's whole family, and her parents legally adopted him as a son in 1896 so he could become a Japanese citizen. He and his wife had four children. The oldest, a son named Kazuo, later wrote a book, translated into English as *Father and I.*

Hearn moved his family to Kumamoto on Kyushu Island, where he took a college teaching position and published his first book on Japan, *Glimpses of an Unfamiliar Japan* (1894). He then took a job in Kobe writing for an English-language newspaper, the *Kobe Chronicle*, and after that taught English literature at Tokyo University until 1903. During those years, Hearn published many books on Japan, including *Kokoro* (1896), *Gleanings in Buddha-Fields* (1897), *Exotics and Retrospectives* (1898), *In Ghostly Japan* (1899), *Shadowings* (1900), *A Japanese Miscellany* (1901) and *Kotto* (1902). Hearn was in love with "old Japan" and disliked the new developments that were rapidly modernizing the country. Accordingly, he chose to write about the exotic and strange. Many of his books are collections of folktales. Hearn could not read or write Japanese very well, so his wife and students collected old stories and legends for him, which he adapted into English with great literary skill. When Hearn died in 1904, he was given a Japanese Buddhist funeral, and his family moved the household altar into his former study. After his death, Hearn's university students published their notes of his lectures in a total of nine volumes. His best-known book, *Japan: An Attempt at Interpretation*, was published just after his death. In 1905 an anthology of his writing was published under the title *The Romance of the Milky Way and Other Studies and Stories.* See also KOBE; KUMAMOTO; MATSUE; MEIJI RESTORATION OF 1868; TOKYO UNIVERSITY.

HEARTH (*irori*)   A square opening, cut in the floor of a traditional farmhouse or a room for the tea ceremony, where a charcoal fire is burned to heat water for tea in a large iron kettle (*kama*). The *irori* is a major feature of farmhouses in central and northern Japan where the winter is long and snowy. It serves as the focus of rural family life and represents warmth and sustenance. A kettle is always hung over the *irori*, except when a cooking pot is hung in its place to prepare a one-dish meal. In farmhouses, the kettle is suspended over the *irori* on an iron pot hook (*jizai kagi*, "free moving hook"), which itself is hung on a large carved wooden hanger (*jizai gake*), suspended from the rafters. The pot hook can also be in the chain (*kusari*) style, and thus attached directly to the rafters. The hook can be adjusted to raise or lower the height of the kettle over the fire. The *irori* has a wooden frame about 18 inches square inside which the folor walls are coated with plaster. An attractive plain or lacquered wood board is inserted around the inside of the *irori*. In the tea ceremony (*chanoyu*, "boiling water for tea"), a large kettle is heated on a metal tripod in an *irori* from November through April; a smaller kettle is heated on a *furo*, a portable clay or iron brazier, from May through October. See also FARMHOUSE; KETTLE; SNOW COUNTRY; TEA CEREMONY.

HEIAN ERA (794–1185)   The aristocratic age of Japanese history, characterized by the flowering of classical culture. The name *Heian* derives from Heiankyo, Capital of Peace and Tranquility (now known as Kyoto). Emperor Kammu relocated the imperial court to the newly constructed capital in A.D. 794. The four centuries of the Heian Era are divided into the Early Heian Period (794–857) and the Late Heian, or Fujiwara, Period (858–1158), when the Fujiwara clan dominated the imperial court. During the Heian era, a centralized bureaucratic government was adapted along the lines of the Chinese model, land cultivation was extended and military expeditions were sent to conquer the Ainu (indigenous tribes) in northern Japan. Court nobles and Buddhist temples acquired large plots of land in the provinces known as *shoen* (landed estates or manors).

The Chinese system of writing with ideographs had earlier been adopted, but during the Heian Era a phonetic syllabic system of Japanese writing, known as *kana*, was developed, stimulating the creation of poetry and prose works, mainly diaries and novels, by members of the court, especially women. The most important Heian work of literature is *The Tale of Genji (Genji Monogatari)* by Murasaki Shikibu. Perhaps the world's earliest novel, it provides a glimpse of the highly refined court life at the time, which valued calligraphy, the other arts, and sensitivity to human emotions and the fleeting beauty of nature, as expressed in the esthetic concept known as *mono no aware*. A narrative style of secular painting developed, known as *yamato-e*, which combined calligraphy, painting and poetry and which favored natural subjects such as landscapes, the seasons of the year and famous places of Japan.

The Buddhist religion had been introduced from China in the sixth century A.D., and during the Heian Era important new Buddhist sects were founded by Japanese monks who had studied in China, notably the Tendai, Shingon, and Pure Land *(Jodo)* sects. Pure Land, which preached salvation through faith in the deity Amida Buddha, became extremely popular, and Shinto, the indigenous Japanese religion, became synthesized with Buddhism.

Politically, the Fujiwara clan dominated the imperial court from 858 to 1158, serving as regents for the Yamato emperors and gaining enormous tax-free estates, which gradually eroded the court's tax base and led to its decline. By the end of the 11th century, the samurai class was gaining power in the provinces, as powerful local leaders organized their own armies to protect and increase their holdings. This happened especially in the Kanto region of eastern Japan. Two great rival warrior clans, the Taira (Heike) and Minamoto (Genji), fought a major war 1180–1185, which brought the Heian Era to a close. The victorious Minamoto no Yoritomo established the Kamakura Shogunate (1192–1333), a military government *(bakufu)* that initiated seven centuries of feudalism in Japan. Although he did not depose the emperor, Minamoto exercised de facto governing power. Kyoto remained the imperial capital until the Meiji Restoration of 1868. Heian Shrine was built in Kyoto in 1895 to commemorate the 1,100th anniversary of the city. It holds the Festival of the Ages (Jidai matsuri) every October 22, with a procession of 2,000 people dressed in costumes representing the various historical eras from the Meiji Restoration back to the Heian Era. See also BUDDHISM; CALLIGRAPHY; CHINA AND JAPAN; DIARIES; EMPEROR; FESTIVAL OF THE AGES; FUJIWARA CLAN; GENJI, THE TALE OF; HEIAN SHRINE; HEIANKYO; IMPERIAL PALACE (KYOTO); KAMAKURA SHOGUNATE; KANA; KYOTO; LANDED-ESTATE SYSTEM; MINAMOTO CLAN; MINAMOTO NO YORITOMO; MONO NO AWARE; MURASAKI SHIKIBU; NARA; PAINTING; POETRY; PURE LAND SECT OF BUDDHISM; SAMURAI; SCROLLS; SHINGON SECT OF BUDDHISM; TAIRA CLAN; TAIRA-MINAMOTO WAR; TENDAI SECT OF BUDDHISM; WRITING SYSTEM, JAPANESE; YAMATO.

HEIAN SHRINE (Heian Jingu) A Shinto shrine located in the former capital city of Kyoto, erected in 1895 to celebrate the 1,100th anniversary of the city's founding. Heian Shrine is dedicated to the spirits of two emperors particularly important to Kyoto. The first is Emperor Kammu (r. 781–806), during whose reign Kyoto was made capital of Japan. At that time it was called Heiankyo, Capital of Peace and Tranquility. The second is Emperor Komei (r. 1846–1867), the last emperor to reign in Kyoto before the capital was transferred to present-day Tokyo, which as Edo had been the seat of the Tokugawa military regime (1603–1867). Set in beautiful gardens, Heian Shrine is very large and replicates an even larger shrine that had been constructed in A.D. 794. The main gate and oratory also replicate portions of the original imperial palace in Kyoto.

Heian Shrine holds annual festivals on January 30th to honor Emperor Komei and April 3rd to honor Emperor Kammu. It also sponsors the Festival of the Ages (Jidai matsuri), a magnificent procession on October 22nd with thousands of people dressed in authentic historical costumes, dating from the Meiji Era (1868–1912) back to the eighth century A.D. See also EMPEROR; FESTIVAL OF THE AGES; HEIANKYO; KYOTO; SHINTO; SHRINES.

HEIANKYO "Capital of Peace and Tranquility"; the original name of the city of Kyoto, the imperial capital of Japan from A.D. 794 until the Meiji Restoration of 1868. Previously the imperial court had been located in the city of Nara 28 miles to the south. Emperor Kammu (r. 781–806), aided by members of the dominant Fujiwara and Hata clans, attempted to move the capital in 784 to a site known as Nagaokakyo, to halt meddling in government matters by priests of Buddhist sects that had become powerful in Nara. Nagaokakyo soon came to be regarded as an unfavorable location because of natural disasters and political disagreement regarding the site, so Kammu decided to build the capital instead in Uda village (Ukyo Ward in modern Kyoto) between the Kamo and Katsura rivers.

The location for the new capital of Heiankyo was advantageous for the imperial court's expansion into northern and eastern regions of Japan. Heiankyo, like Nara, was laid out in a symmetrical grid pattern modeled on the Tang (T'ang) Chinese capital of Chang'an (Ch'ang-an, modern Xian). The imperial palace and government offices were situated in the northern part of the city, which measured 2.8 miles west to east and 3.2 miles north to south. A 276-foot-wide avenue called Suzaku Oji divided Heiankyo into eastern and western districts, called Sakyo and Ukyo. The course of the Kamo river (Kamogawa) was moved to flow east of the city, and north-south canals were dug to enhance transportation by water. The name Kyoto, which means "capital" or "site of the imperial palace," had been used as an alternate name for Nara and Heijokyo, former imperial capitals. By the end of the 11th century, the name Kyoto had replaced the former name Heiankyo for the city. The historical period from the city's founding in 794 until 1185 is known as the Heian Era. See also BUDDHISM; FUJIWARA CLAN; HATA CLAN; HEIAN ERA; IMPERIAL PALACE (KYOTO); KAMO RIVER; KYOTO; NARA; NARA ERA.

HEIJI WAR OF 1159–1160 See MINAMOTO NO YORITOMO; TAIRA CLAN; TAIRA-MINAMOTO WAR.

HEIKE CLAN See HEIKE, THE TALE OF THE; TAIRA CLAN; TAIRA-MINAMOTO WAR

HEIKE, THE TALE OF THE (Heike monogatari) A famous prose work, similar to a historical novel, which tells the story of the conflict between two great clans, the Taira, also known as Heike, and the Minamoto, or Genji. For 20 years in the late 12th century A.D., the Taira family held power after defeating their Minamoto rivals and also removing the powerful Fujiwara family, who had controlled the imperial court. In 1180 the Minamoto took up arms against the Taira, causing a five-year war, which ended with the terrible defeat of the Taira at the Battle of Dannoura in A.D. 1185.

The first section of *The Tale of the Heike* describes the life and death of the hateful figure Taira no Kiyomori. The second part centers on the general Minamoto no Yoshinaka, who dies, and the third on the heroic Minamoto no Yoshitsune, who is wrongly accused of treachery by his brother Minamoto no Yoritomo. Belonging to the genre of "war tales" *(gunki monogatari), The Tale of the Heike* concentrates on warriors and the battles they fight. The episodes were spread through Japan by wandering blind Buddhist priests who played the *biwa,* similar to a lute, and were thus called *biwa hoshi.* Their songs about the Heike were collected into a 200-piece repertoire for the *biwa* known as *heikyoku.* The Buddhist doctrine that everything is a temporary illusion, and that salvation is gained only through faith in Amida Buddha, colors the episodes of *The Tale of the Heike.* They were first written down in the early 13th century by a member of the aristocracy. However, the art of chanting the episodes created a number of variations in the text. Many Japanese writers have drawn upon stories in *The Tale of the Heike* for their own works. It has also been translated into English. See also AMIDA; DANNOURA, BATTLE OF; BIWA; MINAMOTO CLAN; MINAMOTO NO YORITOMO; MONOGATARI; TAIRA CLAN; TAIRA-MINAMOTO WAR.

HEISEI ERA (1989–) The official name for the reign, which began January 9, 1989, of the current emperor of Japan, Akihito (born December 23, 1933). The two written characters in the name Heisei mean "Achieving [or Accomplishing] Peace," or "Peace and Concord." This name is appropriate for the reign of Akihito, who was born before World War II and experienced the devastation of Japan during the war, the country's renunciation of warfare, and its economic, political and cultural rebirth. The name Heisei also calls to mind the Heian Era (794–1185), the "golden age" of Japanese classical culture in the new imperial capital of Heiankyo (later known as Kyoto). The Heisei Era began when the Showa (Enlightened Peace) Era (1926–1989) ended upon the death of Akihito's father, Emperor Hirohito (1901–1989), now known as Emperor Showa for the name of his reign. Upon Emperor Akihito's death, he will be known as Emperor Heisei. His birthday is now a Japanese national holiday. See also AKIHITO, EMPEROR; EMPEROR; HEIAN ERA; HIROHITO, EMPEROR; HOLIDAYS, NATIONAL; IMPERIAL HOUSEHOLD; SHOWA ERA.

HELMET, WARRIOR'S See ARMOR.

HEMP *(asa)* A type of plant belonging to the mulberry *(kozo)* family that is used to make textiles for clothing. Mulberry fibers are also used for handmade paper *(washi,* erroneously translated as "rice" paper). The Japanese term *asa* includes not only hemp but other plants, except cotton, whose fibers are used for textiles. Some examples are ramie, which belongs to the nettle family; *basho,* a type of plantain often translated as "banana"; and fibers from the inner bark of other trees and shrubs, including wisteria *(fuji)* and types of mulberry known as *kaji, kozo* and *shina.*

In Japan, techniques for stripping, softening and twisting fibers from wild hemp, mulberry and nettle to make clothing date back to the Jomon Era (c. 10,000–c. 300 B.C.). Ramie, known in Japan as *choma* or *karamushi* (China grass), was introduced into Japan from China during the Yayoi Era (c. 300 B.C.–c. A.D. 300), and the Japanese began to cultivate it for its long, strong fibers. Techniques for spinning, dyeing and weaving plant fibers were introduced from China and Korea during the Nara Era (710–794). Hemp has been widely used for clothing throughout Japanese history. Its proper name is *taima,* but it is often called *hon'asa,* "original" or "basic" *asa.* Clothing made of *asa* or plant fibers is strong and durable but rather stiff. It keeps the wearer cool in summer but does not provide warmth in the winter. However, most Japanese wore *asa* clothing until cotton was introduced into Japan at the end of the Muromachi Era (1333–1568). Only small numbers of the upper classes could afford to wear silk throughout Japanese history. *Asa* was frequently decorated with patterns created by dipping the textiles in vats of blue dye made from indigo plants *(ai).* Today only a few artisans continue the tradition of making textiles from plant fibers. A woman named Ayano Chiba who grows and weaves hemp was honored by the Japanese government by being designated a Living National Treasure in 1955. See also CHINA AND JAPAN; CLOTHING; INDIGO; LIVING NATIONAL TREASURES; MULBERRY BUSH; PAPER, HANDMADE; TEXTILES.

HERALDRY See ARMOR; CREST; FLAGS AND BANNERS; SWORD GUARD.

HERBAL MEDICINE See MEDICINE, TRADITIONAL.

HIBACHI A square or round ceramic or wood brazier that has traditionally been used to burn charcoal as a source of indoor heat. The *hibachi* is half-filled with ash, on which pieces of burning charcoal are arranged. Used mainly for heating a room rather than for cooking, the Japanese *hibachi* is different from the device used in North America to grill food which is also called a *hibachi.* There are several shapes of Japanese *hibachi.* The round type, made of a hollowed-out log, or wood, metal or ceramic, is called *maruhibachi.* A simple wooden box shape is called *hakohibachi.* A *Nagahibachi* is a *hibachi* with small drawers to hold such items as pipes and tobacco. Several utensils are used with a *hibachi.* The metal chopsticks used to handle the hot charcoal are called *hibashi.* A metal scraper used to level the ash left by the burned charcoal is called *hainarashi.* Sometimes a teakettle is placed in the *hibachi* on a metal tripod known as *gotoku. Hibachi* were used in Japan as far back as the Nara Era (710–794), and several made of copper and nickel have been preserved at the Shosoin, a storehouse dating from that time. However, only members of the upper class used *hibachi* before the middle of the Edo Era (1600–1868), when they were adopted by people of all classes. The use of *hibachi* dwindled when the safer methods of gas, electric, and central heating became available in Japan, although *hibachi* still have a place as decorations in traditional restaurants and inns *(ryokan).* Another traditional heating device, the *kotatsu*, is still used in Japan. See also HOMES AND HOUSING; KETTLE; KOTATSU; RESTAURANTS; RYOKAN.

HIBAKUSHA See ATOMIC BOMB; MINORITIES IN JAPAN.

HIBIYA PARK See GINZA; IMPERIAL PALACE (TOKYO).

HIDEYOSHI TOYOTOMI See TOYOTOMI HIDEYOSHI.

HIE SHRINE (Hie Taisha; Hiyoshi Taisha) A Shinto shrine in Otsu City, Shiga Prefecture, which is closely linked with Enryakuji, the main Tendai Buddhist temple on Mount Hiei in northeast Kyoto. Nearly 4,000 branches of Hie Shrine have been established throughout Japan.

Hie Shrine is divided into two sections, the East Shrine and the West Shrine. The West Shrine, built by Emperor Tenji (r. 661–672) when he made Otsu his capital in A.D. 668, housed Onamuchi no Mikoto, the deity of Omiwa Shrine, who protected the imperial family and the Yamato court. Tradition claims that the East Shrine, dedicated to the deity Oyamakui no Kami, was founded in 91 B.C. Saicho (767–822), a great religious leader who founded the Tendai Sect of Buddhism in Japan, worshipped Oyamakui no Kami, whom he claimed to have found on top of Mount Hiei, where he founded the Tendai temple Enryakuji. He renamed the deity Sanno (Mountain King).

Hie Shrine was given the Buddhist name Sanno Gongen and became the guardian of Enryakuji. Saicho thus initiated the process by which Buddhism, introduced into Japan from China in the sixth century A.D., accepted deities of Shinto, the indigenous Japanese religion, and identified them with Buddhist deities.

During the medieval era (12th–16th centuries), powerful bands of warrior-monks from Mount Hiei periodically threatened the court at Kyoto, when they felt their privileges imperiled. They enforced their demands by carrying a sacred palanquin *(mikoshi)* from Hie Shrine into the city. The palanquin was considered so sacred that people were afraid to touch it. The East and West Shrine buildings of Hie Shrine were destroyed in 1571 by the warlord Oda Nobunaga (1534–1582) when he took control of Kyoto. They were rebuilt by the warlord Toyotomi Hideyoshi (1536–1598) and have been designated National Treasures by the Japanese government. Hie Shrine holds its annual festival on April 12–15. The Tokugawa shoguns (1603–1867) revered the deity housed at Hie Shrine in Edo (modern Tokyo) as the guardian of the city, and Hie Shrine's Sanno Festival, held annually June 10–16, is one of the two largest shrine festivals in Tokyo. See also ENRYAKUJI; HIEI, MOUNT; KYOTO; PALANQUIN, SACRED; ODA NOBUNAGA; SAICHO; SHINTO; SHRINES, SHINTO; TENDAI SECT OF BUDDHISM; TOYOTOMI HIDEYOSHI.

HIEI, MOUNT (Hiezan) A mountain in the northeast sector of the old capital city of Kyoto on which is located Enryakuji, headquarters of the Tendai sect of Buddhism founded by the Japanese monk Saicho (767–822). Saicho left Nara, the capital of Japan at the time, to found a small Buddhist temple on Mount Hiei where he could live a quiet religious life. After studying at the Chinese headquarters of the Tiantai (T'ien-t'ai; Tendai in Japanese) sect Saicho formally established the Japanese Tendai sect on Mount Hiei. Saicho's temple, which became known as Enryakuji, developed into an enormous complex where many important Japanese religious leaders studied. Mount Hiei grew in prominence when Emperor Kammu moved the capital from Nara to Kyoto in A.D. 794. Enryakuji was believed to guard the capital city from evil spirits, who were thought to attack from the northeast. The names Enryakuji and Mount Hiei are often used interchangeably to refer to Tendai headquarters in Japan. See also BUDDHISM; ENRYAKUJI; KYOTO; SAICHO; TENDAI SECT OF BUDDHISM.

HIGAN Literally, "the other shore"; two seven-day Buddhist memorial services held around the spring and autumn equinoxes, which fall on March 21st or 22nd and September 23rd or 24th and are national holidays in Japan. The spring equinox is also known as *Shumbun no hi*, and the autumn equinox as *Shubun no hi*. The memorial services, formally known as *higan'e*, were first held in A.D. 806 and are practiced by all Buddhist sects in Japan but not in other Buddhist countries. Their aim is to help souls to move from "this shore" *(shigan)*, the world of pain and suffering, to the "other shore" of enlightenment, the Western Paradise of the Pure Land. *Higan* is held around the time of the equinoxes because on those two days the sun rises due east and sets due west. They also mark the change of seasons, ending the cold of winter and the heat of summer. At *higan*, Japanese families tend the graves of their ancestors, and offer them special dumplings and other foods they enjoyed in life. Services are held at Buddhist temples, and religious scriptures are read to assist lost souls. See also BUDDHISM; CALENDAR; FUNERALS; HOLIDAYS, NATIONAL; PURE LAND SECT OF BUDDHISM; SCRIPTURES, RELIGIOUS.

HIGH-TECHNOLOGY See COMPUTER INDUSTRY; ELECTRONICS INDUSTRY; FIFTH-GENERATION ADVANCED COMPUTER SYSTEMS; RESEARCH AND DEVELOPMENT; ROBOTS AND ROBOTICS; SEMICONDUCTOR INDUSTRY; TELECOMMUNICATIONS SYSTEM; TSUKUBA ACADEMIC NEW TOWN.

HIMEJI CASTLE (Himeji-jo) The finest surviving castle in Japan and the second largest after Osaka Castle. Located in the town of Himeji, west of the city of Kobe, on Honshu Island, Himeji Castle is known as Shirasagi, or White Egret (or Heron), because it is tall, pure white and graceful. The castle's main structure sits on a hill about 150 feet high at the center of three rings of compounds, to which the castle owes its beauty and its effectiveness as a stronghold. It was originally constructed in the 14th century by the Akamatsu clan and then acquired by the Kodera clan. The warlord Toyotomi Hideyoshi, who unified Japan after the country underwent several centuries of military struggle, took possession of Himeji Castle in 1580. Terumasa Ikeda acquired the castle in 1609 as a reward for his service in the Battle of Sekigahara (1600). Terumasa, the son-in-law of Tokugawa Ieyasu, founder of the Tokugawa Shogunate (1603–1867), fortified Himeji Castle as a strong defense

Himeji Castle, considered the finest castle in Japan, has been restored to its early 17th-century beauty. It is also called White Heron Castle (Shirasagi) because it is tall, white and graceful.

against western lords who threatened the Tokugawa government. Himeji Castle was closed from 1956 until 1964 so that it could be restored to its 16th-century beauty. See also CASTLES; OSAKA; SEKIGAHARA, BATTLE OF; TOKUGAWA IEYASU; TOKUGAWA SHOGUNATE; TOYOTOMI HIDEYOSHI.

HIMIKO (fl. c. third century A.D.) A queen who reportedly ruled a regional political alliance named Yamatai in northern Kyushu Island or the Yamato (Nara) region of Japan. Himiko (or Pimiko) is mentioned in a Chinese document, *History of the Kingdom of Wei,* or *Wei Chronicle (Wei zhi or Wei Chih),* written around A.D. 297, which refers to Japan as the "Land of Wa." This document records that battles took place among political factions of the Wa people A.D. 170–180 and that Himiko, a young woman, emerged the winner and was declared the queen of the Land of Wa. References to *kido,* the "Way of the Demons," indicate that she may have been a shaman, or one thought to have religious powers. Along with a thousand female slaves, Himiko remained in seclusion with a military guard. Only one man was permitted to enter her private quarters, to serve her food and deliver messages. Stories suggest that Himiko's brother acted for her in public affairs of state. Himiko sent a mission with tribute to establish relations with the government of China in A.D. 239. The Wei emperor Ming accepted Himiko's tribute and granted her the title "Ruler of Wa friendly to Wei" (*qinwei Wo wang* or *ch'in-wei Wo wang;* in Japanese, *shingi wao*). This title was made official by a gold seal with a purple cord that was sent to Himiko from China, along with other gifts, including textiles and bronze mirrors. A Chinese mission accompanied Himiko's mission back to the Land of Wa (or Yamatai), and this was followed by a second Chinese mission. In A.D. 245 the Wei court of China supported Yamatai, led by

the warrior Nanshomai, in a battle against another region of Japan known as Kona (or Kunu). It is not recorded which side won the battle, but it is recorded that Himiko died. More than a hundred female and male slaves were killed and buried with her, and a large mound of earth was reportedly piled above her grave. See also CHINA AND JAPAN; MIRROR; SHAMANS AND SHAMANISM; TEXTILES; YAMATO.

HINOKI See CYPRESS TREE.

HIRADO See ADAMS, WILLIAM; ARITA WARE; DEJIMA; NAGASAKI; SAGA PREFECTURE; XAVIER, ST. FRANCIS.

HIRAGANA A syllabic system for writing native Japanese words, grammatical elements such as verb inflections and adjectival endings, and words loaned from the Chinese language that cannot be written with the 1,945 Chinese characters, or *kanji,* officially approved by the Japanese Ministry of Education. *Hira* means "commonly used," "rounded" and "easy." *Hiragana* characters are cursive and thus are easy to write compared with *kanji. Hiragana* is one of the syllabic writing systems, known collectively as *kana,* which the Japanese developed in the ninth century A.D. Japanese writing eventually became an extremely complex mixture of *kanji* and *kana.* Modern Japanese uses two syllabic systems, *hiragana* and *katakana,* both of which have 48 characters representing the basic syllables of the Japanese language. Both also developed out of *manyogana,* an early set of *kana* which was used to write the *Manyoshu,* a classic eighth-century Japanese poetry anthology.

Hiragana derived from a cursive form of *manyogana,* known as *sogana.* At first usually Japanese women wrote with *hiragana,* and men wrote in *kanji.* Thus early *hiragana* was also known as *onnade,* "women's hand." This system of writing became widespread in the Heian Era (794–1185), and by the ninth century, *onnade* or *hiragana* was used by both men and women to write poetry. The system gained official recognition when poems were written in *hiragana* for the anthology *Kokinshu (Kokin wakashu;* c. A.D. 905) sponsored by the imperial court. The use of *hiragana* became more complicated over the centuries. In 1900 it was simplified so that, as in its original use, one *hiragana* character corresponds to one syllable of spoken Japanese. Variants of *hiragana* used prior to 1900 are termed *hentai-gana.* See also CALLIGRAPHY; CHINA AND JAPAN; KANA; KANJI; KOKINSHU; LANGUAGE, JAPANESE; MANYOSHU; POETRY; WRITING SYSTEM, JAPANESE.

HIRANUMA KIICHIRO (1867–1952) A powerful right-wing political leader in the 1920s and 1930s who served as prime minister of Japan in 1939. Born in what is now Okayama prefecture, Hiranuma studied English law at Tokyo University. During his student years in the 1880s, the Japanese were reacting against the rapid Westernization of the early Meiji Era (1868–1912) and finding renewed pride in their own national traditions. Hiranuma believed in *kokutai,* the concept of a unique Japanese political essence based on a sacred moral relationship between the emperor and his subjects. As an official in the Ministry of Justice,

Hiranuma successfully prosecuted 25 members of the Japanese Diet (Parliament) for bribery in 1909 and forced a cabinet minister to resign in 1915 for suspected bribery. Throughout his life Hiranuma opposed the influence of political parties and foreign ideas on the Japanese government. He served as minister of justice 1923–1924 and was then appointed to the Privy Council, of which he was vice president for 10 years. In 1924 he also founded an organization known as Kokuhonsha to promote his political ideology, which opposed democracy, liberalism and socialism; the group was dissolved in 1936 because of opposition from government leaders such as Saionji Kimmochi. Saionji then allowed Hiranuma to be appointed president of the Privy Council that same year. In 1939 Hiranuma became prime minister, but was forced to resign eight months later because of his desire for a military alliance between Japan and Nazi Germany. After serving in the cabinet of Prime Minister Konoe Fumimaro, Hiranuma served as an unofficial senior advisor (jushin) to the emperor during World War II, and helped remove General Tojo Hideki from power. During the Allied Occupation of Japan, the war crimes trials sentenced Hiranuma to life imprisonment. He died in prison several years later. See also DIET; EMPEROR; KOKUTAI; KONOE FUMIMARO; PRIME MINISTER; SAIONJI KIMMOCHI; TOJO HIDEKI; WAR CRIMES TRIALS; WORLD WAR II.

HIRATSUKA RAICHO   See BLUESTOCKING SOCIETY.

HIRO, CROWN PRINCE   See AKIHITO, EMPEROR; CROWN PRINCE; IMPERIAL HOUSEHOLD.

HIROHITO, EMPEROR (1901–1989)   Now known as Emperor Showa; the 124th reigning emperor (tenno) of Japan, according to the traditional count, who reigned for 62 years, from 1926 to 1989, the longest reign of any emperor in Japanese history. Since his death in January 1989, Hirohito has been known by his reign name, Showa, "Enlightened Peace" or "Enlightenment and Harmony." His eldest son, Akihito (b. 1933), is the current emperor of Japan.

Hirohito's father, Emperor Taisho (1879–1926), ascended the throne in 1912 when Emperor Meiji died. However, he became too ill to perform his official duties, and in 1921 Hirohito was named regent for his father. That same year Hirohito traveled to England, the first Japanese crown prince to visit a foreign country. In January 1924 Hirohito married Princess Nagako (1903–   ), the eldest daughter of Prince Kuni no Miya Kunihiko. They had two sons and four daughters. Upon the death of Emperor Taisho on December 25, 1926, Hirohito became emperor of Japan. His main advisor in the 1920s and 1930s was the genro (elder statesman) Saionji Kimmochi (1849–1940). Hirohito served as a symbol for the Japanese people but was discouraged from directly exercising political power. However, he did take a strong public stand against the military officers who attempted a coup d'etat in the February 26th Incident of 1936.

Hirohito's long reign was marked by many tumultuous events that wrought enormous changes on Japan. The military became increasingly powerful and carried out a policy of aggressive Japanese expansion in East Asia, culminating in the Pacific Theater of World War II. The war devastated the country, and after atomic bombs were dropped on Hiroshima and Nagasaki in August 1945, Hirohito surrendered unconditionally to the Allied Powers and renounced the traditional claim to his divinity. During the postwar Occupation of Japan, which was headed by U.S. General Douglas MacArthur (1880–1964), a new Japanese constitution was promulgated and many political, economic and social reforms were enacted to make the country more democratic. MacArthur decided not to prosecute Emperor Hirohito as a war criminal, the merit of which is still being debated.

Following the Occupation, Japan rapidly grew into a global economic power. Hirohito became the first reigning Japanese emperor to travel abroad when he visited Europe in 1972 and the United States in 1975.

Hirohito died on January 7, 1989. His funeral, held at the Shinjuku Gyoen Imperial Garden, was attended by 10,000 Japanese and foreign dignitaries and was televised around the world. In 1990 his birthday, April 29, was designated a new national holiday, "Greenery Day," to encourage the cultivation and planting of natural vistas. Since Hirohito's death, many Japanese have questioned the role that he played in the war and the place of the imperial throne in the modern industrialized democracy that Japan has become. The Japanese constitution denies any political power to the emperor and regards him as merely a symbol of the Japanese state. See also AKIHITO, EMPEROR; CONSTITUTION OF 1947; CROWN PRINCE; EMPEROR; GENRO; MACARTHUR, U.S. GENERAL DOUGLAS; OCCUPATION OF JAPAN; SAIONJI KIMMOCHI; TAISHO ERA; TENNO; WAR CRIMES TRIALS.

HIROSHIGE (1797–1858)   Full name: Ando Hiroshige; a famous woodblock print (hanga) artist, book illustrator and painter. Hiroshige was born to a fireman's family in the city of Edo (modern Tokyo). Tokutaro, as he was called, lost his parents when he was 12. Desiring to be an artist, he was finally accepted as a student by Utagawa Toyohiro, who gave him the artist's name Hiroshige. He began his career by making book illustrations, but to support his wife and son, he also worked as a fireman until 1832. Starting in 1818, Hiroshige produced single-sheet woodblock prints depicting Kabuki theater actors and beautiful women of the licensed pleasure quarters, conventional subjects for print artists. Hiroshige next changed his style from the heavily outlined figures common in woodblock prints to bird-and-flower prints that incorporated subtler effects used by painters. In 1830 a publisher commissioned him to design a set of prints showing 10 views of Edo. The prints made Hiroshige so famous that for two decades he produced thousands of landscape prints, more than 1,000 of which were views of Edo. A trip to the old capital city of Kyoto inspired Hiroshige to design his most famous set of prints: *Fifty-three Stations of the Tokaido Road (Tokaido gojusantsugi)*. Altogether, Hiroshige designed 20 sets of views of the Tokaido Road. The trip also led Hiroshige to produce other sets of prints showing famous sites in Kyoto and Osaka, and the famous *Eight Views of Omi*. Some of his greatest prints were made in the late 1830s to complete a set of views of the Kiso Kaido, another route between Edo and Kyoto. Hiroshige returned to book illustration in the 1840s. In the 1860s he produced more print sets of landscapes, including *Views of Over Sixty Famous Places (Rokujuyoshu meisho zue)*, *One Hundred Views of Edo (Meisho Edo hyakkei)*, and *Thirty-six Views of Mount Fuji (Fuji sanjurokkei)*. When Hiroshige died in a cholera epidemic, he had created numerous book illustrations, paintings and more than 10,000 print designs. Succeeding artists carried on his work as Hiroshige II, III and IV. When Japanese art became popular in France in the 1860s, the prints of Hiroshige were most admired, and influenced many Western artists. Toulouse-Lautrec and Van Gogh, among others, copied Hiroshige's treatment of perspective. See also EDO; FUJI, MOUNT; KYOTO; OSAKA; TOKAIDO ROAD; WOODBLOCK PRINTS.

HIROSHIMA A city on western Honshu Island facing Hiroshima Bay on the Seto Inland Sea, with a population of nearly 1 million. It is the capital of Hiroshima Prefecture. Hiroshima is best known as the target of the first atomic bomb, dropped on August 6, 1945, during World War II. The city was completely devastated and about half of the 400,000 people in the city were killed immediately. Many others continue to suffer from cancer, disfigurement, and other effects of radiation. The bombing is commemorated every year on August 6 in the Peace Memorial Park. Within the park the Peace Memorial Museum houses exhibits on the effects of the bomb on the city and its residents and in the Peace Memorial Hall documentary films about the bomb are screened. A stone chest in the Memorial Cenotaph bears the names of the bomb's victims, and a Peace Flame burns in the hope that atomic weapons will be abolished. The skeleton of Hiroshima's Industrial Promotion Hall, known as the Atomic Bomb Dome, has been left standing as a testament to the bomb's destruction. The children who died are symbolized by a statue of a girl with a crane rising above her that symbolizes long life and happiness. The statue was inspired by a girl who believed she could be cured of her radiation sickness by folding 1,000 folded-paper *(origami)* cranes but died after folding the 964th crane. Japanese schoolchildren leave strings of paper cranes in the Peace Memorial as a tribute to her. Another famous site in Hiroshima is Shukkei-en, a miniature landscape garden laid out in 1620 for the Asano clan. Hijima Park is well known for its beautiful cherry blossoms.

Hiroshima Bay became a commercial center under the Taira clan during the latter part of the Heian era (794–1185) and since then has been a center for shipping on the Inland Sea. Hiroshima grew from a fishing village into a castle town during the Edo Era (1600–1868). The castle was originally built by the Asano clan in 1593; rebuilt in 1958, the castle houses a museum in its five-story structure. By the 20th century, Hiroshima was the seventh largest city in Japan and an important military and industrial center. There was an important naval base in Hiroshima Bay, one reason it was a target during World War II. Today, Hiro-

shima has been totally rebuilt. Its main industrial products are ships, automobiles and machinery. Boats depart from Hiroshima for cruises on the Seto Inland Sea and excursions to Miyajima (Shrine Island), a Shinto shrine that is regarded as one of the three most famous landscapes in Japan (Nihon Sankei). See also ATOMIC BOMB; CASTLES; CRANE; INLAND SEA; MIYAJIMA.

HISAMATSU SHIN'ICHI (1898–1976) A major modern philosopher of the Zen sect of Buddhism. Hisamatsu was born in Gifu Prefecture and educated at Kyoto University, where he studied with Nishida Kitaro, Japan's greatest modern philosopher. Hisamatsu was professor of religion and Buddhism at Kyoto University from 1926 to 1946, after which he taught at several Buddhist universities. He studied the Rinzai form of Zen Buddhism with master Ikegami Shozan at Myoshinji in Kyoto. In 1957 Harvard University appointed Hisamatsu a visiting lecturer on Zen Buddhist culture. The following year he lectured on Zen culture and met with Western philosophers and artists in Europe, the Middle East and India. In Japan, Dr. Hisamatsu helped found the FAS Society for the practice and study of Zen. The initials FAS stand for the society's motto, Awakening to the Formless self, taking the standpoint of All mankind, creating Superhistorical history. He also helped found the Shinchakai, a society for the spiritual practice of the Japanese tea ceremony. Hisamatsu's many writings have been published in a collected edition in Japan. Several of his works have been translated into English, most notably *Zen and the Fine Arts (Zen to Bijutsu*, 1957; translated 1971). See also NISHIDA KITARO; RINZAI SECT OF ZEN BUDDHISM; TEA CEREMONY; ZEN SECT OF BUDDHISM.

HISTORICAL ERAS *(jidai)* Periods into which Japanese history is classified according to the type of government and the social class that held power. Every October the Festival of the Ages (Jidai Matsuri), with thousands of people dressed in authentic costumes, is held in the old capital city of Kyoto to commemorate the periods of Japanese history from ancient times to the late 19th century. The major eras of Japanese history are:

Jomon Era (c. 10,000 B.C.–c. 300 B.C.)
    Prehistoric period; hunter-gatherer way of life; Shinto religious beliefs
Yayoi Era (c. 300 B.C.–c. A.D. 300)
    Introduction of wet rice cultivation and civilization from Asian mainland; distinctive poetry; transition from nomadic to agricultural way of life
Kofun (Tomb Mound) Era (also known as Yamato Era; c. 300–710)
    Appearance of mainland Asian horse-riding warrior group that became ruling elite and developed imperial system and Yamato court; Prince Shotoku (Shotoku Taishi; 574–622), "Father of Japanese Culture"; Buddhism, culture, and systems of writing and government introduced from China
Nara Era (710–794)
    Imperial capital moved to Heijokyo (modern Nara)

Heian Era (794–1185)
Imperial capital moved to Heiankyo (modern Kyoto); landed estate *(shoen)* system important; powerful Buddhist groups emerge; golden age of classical Japanese literature and culture

Bushi or Samurai Era (military rule, 1185–1868)
Emergence of feudal warriors and elite military class as central control periodically breaks down and is reimposed

Kamakura Shogunate (1192–1333)
First feudal military government *(bakufu);* domination by samurai class after Taira-Minamoto War (1180–1185)

Kemmu Restoration (1333–1336)
Direct imperial rule by Emperor Go-Daigo (1288–1339; r. 1218–1339)

Nambokucho Era (1336–1392)
Imperial line divided between Southern and Northern courts

Ashikaga Shogunate (1338–1573)
Second military government; also known as the Muromachi Era (1333–1568); growth of regional lords with powerful armies; conflicts between *daimyo* (feudal lords); introduction of Zen Buddhism, flowering of related arts such as ink painting, Noh drama, tea ceremony

Sengoku (Warring States) Era (1467–1568)
Century of warfare among *daimyo;* Europeans enter Japan

Azuchi-Momoyama Era (1568–1600)
Unification of Japan into centralized feudalism by three powerful warriors, Oda Nobunaga (1534–1582), Toyotomi Hideyoshi (1536–1598) and Tokugawa Ieyasu (1543–1616); decisive Battle of Sekigahara (1600)

Tokugawa Shogunate (1603–1867)
Third military government; centralized feudal bureaucracy, conversion of samurai from warriors to government bureaucrats; also known as Edo Era (1600–1868); rapid economic growth, flourishing of cities and popular culture, such as Kabuki and Bunraku theaters and woodblock prints; seclusion of Japan from West; national seclusion (1639–1854)

Meiji Era (1868–1912)
Breakdown in central military authority leads to restoration of imperial power; named for reign of Emperor Meiji; modern government and economic system copied from West established; wars with China and Russia

Taisho Era (1912–1926)
Reign of Emperor Taisho; continued political and economic modernization

Showa Era (1926–1989)
Reign of Emperor Hirohito (1901–1989); rise of militarism, World War II, Japan's defeat and occupation; democratization of political, economic and social institutions; rapid postwar growth, Japan becomes global economic power

Heisei Era (1989–present)
Reign of Emperor Akihito (1901–   )

See also FESTIVAL OF THE AGES; NAMES OF INDIVIDUAL HISTORICAL ERAS, FIGURES, ETC.

HITACHI, LTD. See COMPUTER INDUSTRY; ELECTRONICS INDUSTRY.

HITACHI, PRINCE See AKIHITO, EMPEROR; IMPERIAL HOUSEHOLD.

HIZEN PROVINCE See SAGA PREFECTURE.

HOGEN WAR OF 1156 See TAIRA CLAN.

HOJO CLAN A powerful samurai group that controlled the Kamakura Shogunate (1192–1333), the military government *(bakufu)* that initiated the feudal era in Japan. Minamoto no Yoritomo (1147–1199), founder of the Kamakura regime, was exiled as a young man to Izu Province (part of modern Shizuoka Prefecture), where he came to know Hojo Tokimasa (1138–1215). Tokimasa's ancestors belonged to the Taira clan, enemies of the Minamoto clan, but his grandfather had adopted the name Hojo from a place in Izu where he was governor. Hojo Masako (1157–1225), daughter of Tokimasa, married Minamoto no Yoritomo in 1177. Yoritomo led the Minamoto in their defeat of the Taira in 1185, and established his shogunate in Kamakura in eastern Japan, executing his brother and other close relatives to eliminate his rivals. When Yoritomo died suddenly in 1199, the Hojo family moved into a position of power. In 1203 Tokimasa, with Masako's assistance, created for himself the position of regent *(shikken)* for Yoritomo's ineffectual sons. Two years later, Masako had her father exiled and her brother, Hojo Yoshitoki (1163–1224), installed as regent. He ruled until 1224, when his grandson Hojo Yasutoki (1183–1242) became regent, until 1242. These three generations of Hojo regents consolidated the power of the Kamakura Shogunate, with Masako actually in control. Because she took vows as a Buddhist nun, she became known as the "nun shogun" *(ama shogun)*. Yasutoki put down an imperial rebellion against the shogunate and promulgated a legal code for the military class, the *Goseibai Shikimoku*, which helped establish the feudal system in Japan. Seven more members of the Hojo family exercised power as regents until 1333. As they chose each successive shogun, they always insured that he was a member of the imperial family or the Fujiwara clan, who were regents in the Heian court (794–1185), which held power before the Kamakura Shogunate.

Hojo Tokimune (1251–1284) organized Japan's defense against two attempted invasions by the Mongols in 1274 and 1281. However, when the samurai that had played the largest role in repelling the Mongols did not receive any recompense from the Hojo-controlled shogunate, they joined Emperor Go-Daigo (1288–1339; r. 1318–1339) in his attempt to restore imperial rule, known as the Kemmu Restoration. Hojo Takatoki (1303–1333; ruled 1316–1326) sent his general Ashikaga Takauji (1305–1358) against Emperor Go-Daigo, but Takauji switched his allegiance to the emperor and overthrew the Kamakura Shogunate in 1334. After their defeat Hojo Takatoki, the last Hojo regent, and 700 family members and followers, committed suicide. Takauji then turned against the emperor and founded the Ashikaga

Shogunate (1338–1573), the second military government of Japan. See also ASHIKAGA TAKAUJI; BAKUFU; FEUDALISM IN JAPAN; GO-DAIGO, EMPEROR; KAMAKURA SHOGUNATE; MINAMOTO NO YORITOMO; MONGOL INVASIONS OF JAPAN; SAMURAI; SHOGUN.

HOKKAIDO ISLAND The northernmost of the four main islands of Japan, Hokkaido is second in size to Honshu Island, to which it is connected by the 33-mile-long Seikan Tunnel, the world's longest tunnel, which runs under the Tsugaru Strait. The Pacific Ocean borders Hokkaido to the east and south, the Sea of Japan to the west and the Sea of Okhotsk to the northeast. Hokkaido has a total area of 32,236 square miles and a population of over 5.5 million, which gives it 21% of Japan's total landmass yet only 5% of its population. The climate is much colder and drier than the rest of Japan and Hokkaido is very mountainous except for the Ishikari Plain, a flat stretch of land in the southwest. The capital city is Sapporo, which holds a popular Snow Festival every February and which hosted the Winter Olympic Games in 1972. The other major city is Hakodate, a major commercial fishing port.

The name *Hokkaido*, meaning "Northern Sea Circuit," was given to the island in 1869. At that time Japan was divided into districts called prefectures *(ken)*. Hokkaido, though administratively equivalent to a prefecture, is called a circuit *(do)*. It did not officially belong to Japan until the Meiji government (1868–1912) established a colonial office *(kaitakushi)* to promote Japanese settlement and development on the island, which had economic potential because of its natural resources and strategic location close to Japan's menacing neighbor Russia. Hokkaido was populated by the Ainu, indigenous tribes of nomadic hunters thought to belong to the Caucasian race and having a unique language and culture, which survivors find difficult to keep alive today. In 1881 the Japanese government decided to sell the assets of the Hokkaido Colonization Office to private concerns, and Kuroda Kiyotaka, the office's director, sold them to a friend at a very low cost, sparking a political crisis that canceled the sale. More recently, the government created the Hokkaido Development Agency (Hokkaido Kaihatsu Cho) in 1950 to upgrade housing, transportation, communication and industrial development on the island. Hokkaido has spectacular natural beauty with many national parks and forests, ski resorts, and hot springs, such as Noboribetsu Spa (Noboribetsu Onsen). See also AINU; FISH AND FISHING INDUSTRY; HAKODATE; HOT SPRING; NATIONAL PARKS; OLYMPIC GAMES, PACIFIC OCEAN; SAPPORO; SEA OF JAPAN; SNOW FESTIVAL.

HOKUSAI (1760–1849) One of the greatest Japanese illustrators, *ukiyo-e* ("pictures of the floating world") woodblock print designers and painters. Hokusai was born in the city of Edo (now Tokyo) and was adopted into a family that made mirrors for the Tokugawa Shogunate (1603–1867). Displaying artistic talent at a young age, Hokusai began working with the famous *ukiyo-e*–style painter Katsukawa Shunsho, who specialized in portraits of well-known actors. Hokusai also made theatrical prints until around 1785, when he began working in other styles and

The *Great Wave*, a woodblock print by Hokusai (1760–1849), from his series, *Thirty-six Views of Mount Fuji* (c. 1831). This print has become a world-famous symbol of Japan.

studying painting and book illustration with various artists. He also used a number of different names to sign his works; Hokusai, the name by which he is best known, means "north studio," referring to the north star, which was important in the Nichiren sect of Buddhism, the religion that Hokusai followed. From 1798–1806, Hokusai made a series of prints of scenes from the popular drama about the forty-seven ronin incident *(Chushingura)*. He portrayed daily life along the Sumida River in a long rolled scroll of the *makimono* style. Two separate sets of prints on the *Fifty-three Stations of the Tokaido Road* done in the early 1800s became famous. Hokusai gained notoriety when he painted large pictures at temple festivals, such as a portrait of Daruma, legendary founder of the Zen Sect of the Buddhist religion.

When Utamaro (1753–1806) died, Hokusai became the preeminent *ukiyo-e* artist in Japan. He began to innovate in designing prints of landscapes and bird-and-flower motifs, and created his finest works between 1820 and 1832. Prior to these years, he concentrated on book illustration, and also published two books of sketches to instruct other artists. In the 1820s, Hokusai produced many print series on natural themes. The most popular set, *Thirty-six Views of Mount Fuji (Fugaku sanjurokkei)*, contains a print known as the *Great Wave*, which is now a world-famous symbol of Japan. Little is known about Hokusai's two wives, but he had five children altogether, several of whom also became artists. Hokusai was exiled from Edo in 1834–1836, during which time he published *One Hundred Views of Mount Fuji*. He returned to find a terrible famine in Edo, which forced him to turn out an enormous number of paintings and drawings in order to survive. In 1839 he lost everything in a fire, and so produced less in the last few years of his life. Hokusai's works became well known in Europe and influenced many Western artists particularly the post-impressionists, with their elegant simplicity. See also DARUMA; EDO ERA; FLOATING WORLD; NICHIREN SECT OF BUDDHISM; PAINTING; TOKAIDO ROAD; UTAMARO; WAVES; WOODBLOCK PRINTS.

HOLIDAYS, NATIONAL *(kyujitsu)* There are 12 annual public holidays celebrated throughout Japan. When a national holiday falls on a Sunday, the holiday is celebrated on the following Monday. Government offices, banks and public schools are closed on national holidays, but department stores and smaller shops remain open. January 1 is the first national holiday, New Year's Day (Ganjitsu). The New Year Festival is one of the two main holiday seasons in Japan, along with the Bon Festival in the summer. Because of the family and religious nature of New Year and Bon, many Japanese travel back to their hometowns to celebrate. Everyone takes at least three days off from work for the New Year. Government offices close from December 27 through January 3. Most schools close from December 25 until January 7, and from July 25 to August 31. January 15 is Adults' Day (Seijin-no-hi), a festival to celebrate the adulthood of all Japanese who have turned 20 within the past year. February 15 is National Foundation Day (Kenkoku Kinen-no-hi), commemorating the ascent to the throne of the legendary first emperor of Japan, Jimmu Tenno. This holiday was abolished after World War II but reinstated in 1967. March 20 or 21 is Vernal Equinox Day (Shumbun-no-hi). Autumnal Equinox Day (Shubun-no-hi) is celebrated on September 23 or 24. The weeks around these days are called *higan* and are important in the Buddhist calendar; special religious services are held and Japanese visit the graves of their ancestors. April 29, the birthday of the late Emperor Showa (1901–1989; formerly known as Hirohito) was a national holiday during the 62 years of his reign. In 1990 it was designated "Greenery Day," a national holiday to encourage the planting and cultivation of natural vistas. May 3 is Constitution Day (Kempo Kinenbi), which commemorates Japan's current constitution, established on this date in 1947. May 5 is the Children's Day Festival (Kodomo-no-hi). The week within which these three holidays fall is called Golden Week, and many people take the whole week off. Tenno Tanjobi, the national holiday celebrating the birthday of the reigning emperor of Japan, is observed beginning in 1989 on December 23, the birthday of reigning Emperor Akihito (1933–). September 15 is Respect for the Aged Day (Keiro-no-hi). The week starting on this day is called "Senior Citizens' Welfare Week." October 10 is Health-Sports Day (Taiiku-no-hi). It promotes the health and physical development of the people and commemorates the Olympic Games held in Tokyo in 1964. Many schools and companies hold sports meets on this day. November 3 is Culture Day (Bunka-no-hi), a holiday established in 1948 to appreciate peace and freedom and to promote culture. The emperor holds a garden party to award Cultural Orders of Merit *(Bunka Kunsho)* to people who have made major contributions to the promotion of Japanese culture. November 23 is Labor Thanksgiving Day (Kinro-Kansha-no-hi). When Japan was an agricultural society, this was the harvest thanksgiving festival (Niiname-sai). It is now celebrated in recognition of all people who work. See also ADULTS' DAY; AKIHITO, EMPEROR; BUDDHISM; CHILDREN'S DAY; CONSTITUTION OF 1947; DECORATIONS, CIVILIAN; EMPEROR; FESTIVALS; GOLDEN WEEK; JIMMU TENNO; OLYMPIC GAMES; SPORTS.

HOLLYHOCK FESTIVAL (Aoi Matsuri) A festival held on May 15 by Kamigamo and Shimogamo shrines in Kyoto that features a procession of hundreds of people wearing costumes of the ancient imperial Japanese court. The procession reenacts the pilgrimages that emperors made during the Heian Era (794–1185) to worship the gods at Kamigamo (Upper Kamo River) and Shimogamo (Lower Kamo River) Shinto shrines. It is called the Hollyhock Festival because the shrine buildings and objects used on this occasion are all decorated with hollyhock leaves to protect the city from earthquakes and thunderstorms, in obedience to an ancient oracle. Many of the costumes are also made of textiles that have hollyhock motifs. At the center of the festival procession is an imperial cart drawn by an ox and decorated with hollyhock leaves. It is followed by an imperial messenger riding a fine horse and is attended by Shinto priests, pages, military retainers, government officials, servants and musicians. The Goddess Saioh, the principal deity of this festival, is represented by a portable shrine, or palanquin *(mikoshi)*, carried on the shoulders of court officials. The procession begins at the old Kyoto Imperial Palace and goes first to Shimogamo Shrine, where a formal ceremony is performed to receive the imperial messenger. Musicians perform ancient court music while a dance called Azuma-asobi is performed. The procession then moves along the Kamo River to Kamigamo Shrine, where the ceremonies, music, and dance are repeated. A Shinto religious service is performed to conclude the festival. See also EMPEROR; FESTIVALS; FLOWERS; IMPERIAL PALACE (KYOTO); KAMO RIVER; KYOTO; PALANQUIN; SHINTO.

HOMES AND HOUSING The Japanese live in extremely crowded conditions because most of the country's land is too mountainous to be inhabited, and three-quarters of the population now reside in urban areas. Land is very expensive, especially in cities. Many Japanese cannot afford to buy their own homes but live in cramped apartments in high-rise buildings *(danchi)*, which have been described as rabbit hutches. Families of workers for large corporations often live together in housing provided by their company at low rents or even rent free. The average apartment or single home averages four to five small rooms, with 29 *tatami* (straw mats) per residence, for a total of 86 square meters (1,283 sq. ft.).

Japanese homes are traditionally made of wood, with post-and-beam construction and sloping tiled roofs. Modern dwellings are built of concrete because they are less prone to fires and wood is becoming scarce, but even they contain many features of a traditional Japanese residence. Traditional homes, modeled after the Buddhist *shoin* style, are usually built to face south, but also have an opening on the northern side, so air can pass through the house to provide cooling in summer and warmth in winter. Wooden homes are raised up from the ground on pillars that rest on small foundation stones, which help absorb the shock of frequent earthquakes and protect from dampness in the humid climate. A wooden verandah surrounds the house. The tiled roof has wide eaves to protect the home from the frequent rain. Walls are made of mud and finished on the surface with fine sand or plaster. Wood ceilings, posts and beams are left their natural color.

The main entryway is known as a *genkan*. Shoes are removed and left there to protect *tatami*. Slippers are worn on wooden floors in corridors but not on *tatami*. *Shoji* and *fusuma*, sliding screens made of wood frames covered with handmade paper *(washi)*, serve as opaque windows and room dividers. There are also sliding wooden doors called *sugito* or sliding glass doors. The traditional guest reception room or parlor, known as the *zashiki* or *kyakuma*, has a *tokonoma*, an alcove where hanging scrolls and flower arrangements are displayed. The space in front of the *tokonoma* is the place of honor. This style of architecture derives from the *shoin* style, used for studies in Buddhist temples and *samurai* homes, in which the main room contains a *tokonoma* and built-in desk and shelves *(chigaidana)*. *Shoji* can be opened to provide a view of the garden. There is a close relationship between the home and garden. The Japanese traditionally kneel on the floor or sit on flat pillows called *zabuton*. Homes traditionally have very little furniture, usually only a low table and wooden chests called *tansu*. The same room is used for sitting, eating and sleeping. Bedding, consisting of mattresses and quilts known as *futon*, is taken out from a built-in closet and spread on the floor at night. In the morning it is aired and then stored away. The bath, the place of purification, is kept separate from the toilet, considered the most unclean part of a house. A traditional farmhouse *(minkan)* has a hearth *(irori)* in the center where an iron kettle of water is boiled over a charcoal fire to provide heat. Most homes do not have central heating. Japanese keep warm in winter by sitting with their legs under a *kotatsu*, an electric (formerly charcoal) heater under a table covered with a large quilt. Modern Japanese homes have Western-style kitchens, and usually at least one room containing Western furniture. Young Japanese often sit on chairs and sleep on beds. See also ALTARS IN HOMES; APARTMENT HOUSE; BATH; FAMILY; FARMHOUSE; FURNITURE; FUTON; GARDENS; HEARTH; HIBACHI; KETTLE; PILLOWS; ROOF TILES; SCREENS; SHOIN STYLE OF ARCHITECTURE; SHOJI; TATAMI; TOILET; TOKONOMA; WOODWORKING.

HON'AMI KOETSU (1558–1637)   Known as Koetsu; a renowned calligrapher and creator of lacquer ware, painting and pottery. Koetsu was born to a family that appraised swords for great warlords and the imperial court. In 1615 he moved to Takagamine, northwest of the old capital city of Kyoto, perhaps forced into exile there by Shogun Tokugawa Ieyasu (1543–1616), and developed a community of craftsmen from Kyoto. Koetsu studied the tea ceremony *(chanoyu* or *chado)* with the famous tea master Furuta Oribe (1544–1615), and learned pottery from the Raku family, whose style of tea bowls *(chawan)* was created specifically for the tea ceremony. One of Koetsu's Raku tea bowls is a famous Japanese National Treasure. He studied the techniques of lacquer ware as well, and a number of beautiful boxes for calligraphy equipment and other lacquered objects are attributed to him. However, Koetsu is most celebrated for his calligraphy. His graceful style, derived from the aesthetic calligraphy of the Heian Era (794–1185), led

him to be called one of the "three great brushes" of his time. Many scrolls, letters, copies of religious scriptures and *shikishi* (paper mounted on pieces of cardboard) have survived. Koetsu worked closely with the artist Sotatsu (?–1643?), founder of the decorative style of painting and design known as the Rimpa school. Sotatsu frequently decorated the papers on which Koetsu wrote calligraphy. See also CALLIGRAPHY; LACQUER WARE; POTTERY; RAKU WARE; RIMPA SCHOOL; SOTATSU; TEA CEREMONY.

HONDA MOTOR CO., LTD.   See AUTOMOBILE INDUSTRY; MOTORCYCLE INDUSTRY.

HONEN (1133–1212)   A Buddhist priest who founded the Pure Land sect of Buddhism. Honen, whose real name was Genku, was born to a samurai family in a region of Japan that is now part of Okayama Prefecture. At the age of eight, after his father died, Honen began studying Buddhism at Enryakuji on Mount Hiei, the headquarters of the Tendai sect of Buddhism. He was ordained as a monk when he was 15. However, he became disillusioned with the elite nature of Tendai teachings and practices, and found religious salvation in the practice of the *nembutsu*, which was the recitation of the name of the god Amida Buddha, who was believed to have taken a vow that he would save any person who called on his name with complete faith.

Honen went to the city of Kyoto in A.D. 1175 to spread his faith in the *nembutsu*, and wrote a book entitled *Senchaku hongan nembutsushu* explaining his beliefs. Honen explained that it is not necessary to practice the strict discipline and meditation methods that are taught by other sects of Buddhism. One just has to recite Amida's name without any doubt of his compassion, and one will be saved. Although the *nembutsu* has been practiced in Japan for many centuries, and all of the Buddhist sects, including Tendai, had statues of Amida in their temples, Honen took the decisive step of proclaiming the *nembutsu* the only religious practice that ought to be followed. He gained many converts among the common people, and the Tendai monks on Mount Hiei grew so angry with his success and his criticisms of their political activities that they burned all the copies of Honen's book they could find, along with the woodblocks from which they were printed. They persecuted his movement, and four of his disciples were executed in 1206. The following year, at the age of 74, Honen was exiled to a remote region on Shikoku Island. The Pure Land sect increased in popularity, however, and in 1211 Honen was allowed to return to Kyoto, where he died a few months later. See also AMIDA; BUDDHISM; ENRYAKUJI; EXILE; HIEI, MOUNT; NEMBUTSU; PURE LAND SECT OF BUDDHISM; SHIKOKU ISLAND; TENDAI SECT OF BUDDHISM.

HONNE AND TATEMAE   See ETIQUETTE.

HONORIFIC LANGUAGE   See LANGUAGE, JAPANESE; O-, -SAN.

HONSHU ISLAND   The main island of Japan, with an area of 89,126 square miles and a population of about 100 million, counting a number of tiny offshore islands, Honshu is the most densely populated island in the country, especially in the plains of Kansai (site of Osaka, Kyoto and Kobe) and Kanto (site of Tokyo and Yokohama). These areas also contain the highest concentration of industry, business, educational facilities and cultural activities. Major cities on Honshu include Sendai, Nagoya and Hiroshima. As much of Honshu is covered by mountain ridges, most of the cities lie close to the Pacific Ocean or Inland Sea on the east coast. Central Honshu Island is also the area where most of the important events and cultural developments in Japanese history took place. Northern Honshu was inhabited mostly by nomadic tribes known as Ainu until the late 19th century. The mountain ridges in this region are the cause of heavy snowfall and long winters, giving it the nickname Snow Country. Most of the island's climate is temperate and humid with high average precipitation. Western Honshu, along the Sea of Japan, has also been less heavily developed, and agriculture and fishing remain the major economic activities there. Shikoku Island borders Honshu to the south, and Kyushu Island, the place of origin of earliest Japanese culture, lies one mile to the southwest. Honshu is connected to Hokkaido by the Seikan Tunnel, to Shiko by the Seto-Ohashi Bridge, and to Kyushu by tunnels and a bridge. Most foreign visitors enter Japan through the international airports at Tokyo and Osaka, and most Japanese exporting and importing also takes place in the Kansai and Kanto regions of Honshu Island. See also AINU; AIRLINES AND AIRPORTS; CHIBA PREFECTURE; HIROSHIMA; EXPORTS AND IMPORTS; HOKKAIDO ISLAND; INLAND SEA; ISLANDS; KANSAI AND KANTO; KOBE; KYOTO; KYUSHU ISLAND; MOUNTAINS; NAGOYA; OSAKA; PACIFIC OCEAN; SEA OF JAPAN; SENDAI; SHIKOKU ISLAND; SNOW COUNTRY; TOKYO; YOKOHAMA.

HORSE (uma) Two breeds derived from Mongolian horses were introduced into Japan from the Asian mainland in the mid-Jomon Era (c. 10,000 B.C.–c. 300 B.C.). Small horses with a shoulder height of about 43–47 inches known as tokara uma were used in the Ryukyu Islands of southern Japan. Medium-size horses with a shoulder height of 51–59 inches, known as misaki uma and kiso uma, were used in the main Japanese islands for pulling heavy loads and carrying warriors. Bronze and iron bits, stirrups and ornaments have been excavated from tomb mounds (kofun) in which the ruling elite were buried during the Kofun Era (c. 300–710). The so-called horse-rider theory (kiba minzoku setsu) held by most modern scholars argues that a nomadic mounted warrior people invaded Japan from Manchuria and Korea in the second century A.D. and became the imperial rulers of the country.

During the Heian Era (794–1185), Chinese-style saddles, known as karakura, were adopted by the Japanese and became quite ornate. Other trappings, known as yamato-gura, were works of art crafted from metal, leather and wood, decorated with lacquer, mother-of-pearl inlay and gold. The samurai, who ruled Japan for 700 years from the 12th century, were trained in horsemanship (bajutsu) as one of their principal skills, along with archery (kyudo) and fighting with spears and swords (yari and kendo). Over time at least 20 different schools of horsemanship developed in

Japan. A form of archery, known as kasagake, in which warriors on horseback shoot at targets, flourished during the Kamakura Shogunate (1192–1333). Yabusame, a type of ceremonial mounted archery performed by warriors at Shinto shrines to request peace and a good harvest from the kami (sacred spirits), originated during the Heian Era. It is still performed at annual festivals at Tsurugaoka Hachiman Shrine in Kamakura and at Meiji Shrine in Tokyo. In ancient times, horses were believed to be sacred to the kami of Shinto, and horse races were held to divine the will of the kami and to predict fortunes for the coming year. Horses are still kept at shrines and paraded through shrine districts during religious festivals. Since the medieval era (12th–16th centuries), ceremonial horse races known as kurabe uma have been performed at Kamo Shrines in the old capital city of Kyoto. The Soma Wild Horse Chase (Soma Nomaoi) by horse riders dressed as medieval samurai is a famous event held every July in Haramachi (Fukushima Prefecture). Ema, or wooden plaques painted with a white horse, are still used as talismans by worshippers at Shinto shrines to make a vow or a request of the kami. Daimyo (feudal lords) enjoyed breeding horses and especially valued those bred in Nambu Province (modern Iwate Prefecture).

In the 20th century, larger breeds were developed by the Japanese government for military use. Since World War II, horses have been bred on Hokkaido Island and in the Tohoku district of northern Honshu for racing, which was introduced from the West in 1861 and is one of the few legal gambling activities in Japan.

The horse is one of the 12 animals in the traditional 12-year zodiac calendar. People born in the Year of the Horse are believed to be quick, independent, clever, good with money and lovers of entertainment. Women born in the Year of the Horse, associated with the element of fire, sometimes have trouble getting married because they are thought to cause harm to their husbands. The Fire Horse Year, which last fell in 1966, comes every 60 years. See also ARCHERY; DAIMYO; GAMBLING; HEIAN ERA; HORSE-RIDER THEORY; KAMAKURA SHOGUNATE; KOFUN ERA; LACQUER WARE; SAMURAI; SHINTO; SHRINES, SHINTO; TALISMANS; TOMB MOUND; ZODIAC.

HORSERADISH, JAPANESE See WASABI.

HORSE-RIDER THEORY (kiba minzoku setsu) A widely held theory that the first unified state in ancient Japan was established by a warrior group who rode horses and invaded Japan from the Asian mainland through Korea. The standard version of the horse-rider theory was developed by Professor Egami Namio (b. 1906) of Tokyo University, who explained the theory at a symposium in 1948 on the origins of the Japanese people and culture, and in his book The Horse-Rider State (Kiba minzoku kokka, 1967). Previous Japanese scholars had recognized cultural influences and immigrants from China, Korea, Northeast and Southeast Asia, and Pacific islands, but they maintained that these were additions to a unique Japanese culture that had developed within the country itself. The symposium in 1948 was inspired by Oka Masao, another Japanese historian, who proposed a theory that three different cultural strata in prehistoric Japan had been introduced from southern China and Southeast Asia, and a fourth through Korea from Manchuria. This fourth type of culture, it was suggested, was brought into Japan by an invading group that had descended from nomadic herders who spoke an Altaic language, was organized militarily into five tribes and had a hereditary patriarchal (okoteki) pattern of leadership. Oka termed this group the "imperial race" (tenno zoku) and associated it with the tomb mound culture of the Kofun Era (c. 300–710) in Japan. Egami argued that the horse-riding warriors invaded Japan in the Late Kofun Era and that they founded the imperial line of the Yamato clan as recorded in the Kojiki, an eighth-century official Japanese chronicle. Some Japanese scholars have been skeptical of Egami's theory about Altaic invaders. However, the horse-rider theory raises important issues for future historical and archaeological research in Japan. See also EMPEROR; HORSE; KOFUN ERA; KOJIKI; KOREA AND JAPAN; TENNO; TOMB MOUND; YAMATO.

HORYUJI   The oldest surviving Buddhist temple and monastic complex in Japan. Located in the Nara region of western Honshu Island, Horyuji owns a magnificent collection of Buddhist art objects and other treasures, including many pieces from the Asuka Era (late sixth century–710). Horyuji was originally founded by Empress Suiko (554–628) and her regent, Prince Shotoku (574–622), between A.D. 601 and 607, and was rebuilt in the early eighth century after being destroyed by fire. The main hall (Kondo), pagoda, roofed gallery and gate survive from that time, as do some paintings, statues and other treasures kept in the hall. The beautiful main hall may be the oldest wooden building in the world. Horyuji and its artistic treasures are associated with Prince Shotoku, a great patron of Buddhist religion and culture, which had been introduced into Japan from China in the sixth century A.D. Shotoku was venerated as a saint in Japan by the time of the Kamakura Era (1192–1333). The 1,350th anniversary of Shotoku's death was commemorated in 1941 by the construction of the Daihozoden, a museum at Horyuji to exhibit Horyuji's art treasures. The bulk of Horyuji's art collection, known as "Treasures Donated by Horyuji" (Horyuji Kenno Homotsu), were moved in the late 19th century to the Tokyo National Museum in Ueno Park, Tokyo, where they are housed in a gallery called the Horyuji Treasure House (Horyuji Homotsukan). Among the treasures are written documents, lacquer ware, metal objects, paintings, sculptures, textiles, bows and arrows, musical instruments, and masks for gigaku, an ancient court dance often performed as part of Buddhist ceremonies. Many of these objects are older than (and just as fine as) the treasures preserved in the Shosoin (Imperial Treasure House), built in the eighth century A.D. in Nara, then capital of Japan. See also ASUKA; BUDDHISM; NARA; PAGODA; SHOTOKU, PRINCE; SHOSOIN; SUIKO, EMPRESS; TEMPLES, BUDDHIST; UENO.

HOSOKAWA CLAN   A family of daimyo (feudal lords) and deputies to the Ashikaga Shogunate (1338–1573), who remained prominent during the Tokugawa Shogunate (1603–1867). The Hosokawa were in fact a branch of the Ashikaga clan who were named for their estate in Hosokawa, Mikawa province (part of modern Aichi Prefecture). Hosokawa Akiuji (Yoriharu; 1299–1352) aided Ashikaga Takauji (1305–1358) in founding the Ashikaga Shogunate, and the Hosokawa were soon appointed military governors (shugo) of seven provinces on Shikoku and Honshu islands. In A.D. 1367 Hosokawa Yoriyuki (1329–1392) was given the title of shogunal deputy (kanrei), and served as advisor to Shogun Ashikaga Yoshimitsu (1358–1408). The Hosokawa attained their greatest power under Hosokawa Katsumoto (1430–1477) and Hosokawa Masamoto (1466–1507). As kanrei, they controlled the affairs of state through a line of puppet shoguns they had appointed. The Hosokawa lost much of their wealth and power during the Onin War (1467–1477), although they still controlled the declining Ashikaga Shogunate. The clan's fortunes rose again under Hosokawa Yusai (Fujitaka; 1534–1610), a poet-scholar and daimyo who served the national unifiers Oda Nobunaga (1534–1582) and Toyotomi Hideyoshi (1536–1598). Yusai's son Hosokawa Tadaoki (Sansai; 1563–1646) served Nobunaga and Hideyoshi and fought on the side of Tokugawa Ieyasu (1542–1616) at the Battle of Sekigahara in 1600. After Ieyasu had won the battle and completed the unification of Japan, he rewarded Hosokawa Tadaoki with a wealthy domain, which included Buzen Province and part of Bungo Province (parts of modern Fukuoka and Oita prefectures). Tadaoki was married to Hosokawa (Tama) Gracia (1563–1600), a Christian convert who is regarded as the ideal brave and virtuous samurai wife. Their son Hosokawa Tadatoshi (1586–1641) was transferred to a larger domain at Kumamoto in Higo (modern Kumamoto Prefecture). He was a poet, painter and one of the main disciples of the renowned tea ceremony master Sen on Rikyu (1522–1591). The Hosokawa were foremost among daimyo who mastered the art of bun, or cultural pursuits such as poetry, painting and tea, along with the art of bu, or military pursuits. See also ASHIKAGA SHOGUNATE; ASHIKAGA TAKAUJI; DAIMYO; HOSOKAWA (TAMA) GRACIA; ODA NOBUNAGA; ONIN WAR; SEKIGAHARA, BATTLE OF; SEN NO RIKYU; SHOGUN; TOKUGAWA IEYASU; TOKUGAWA SHOGUNATE; TOYOTOMI HIDEYOSHI.

HOSOKAWA (TAMA) GRACIA (1563–1600)   Japanese name, Hosokawa Tama; the wife of the daimyo (feudal lord) Hosokawa Tadaoki (1563–1646), and a Christian convert who is regarded as a model of the brave and virtuous samurai wife. Hosokawa Tama, or Gracia, was the daughter of Akechi Mitsuhide (1526–1582), a military general who served the national unifier Oda Nobunaga (1534–1582) but led a coup against him that resulted in Nobunaga's death. Akechi was killed two weeks later, and most of his family, including Tama's sisters and their husbands, were killed or committed suicide. Tama and her husband escaped, and the national unifier Tokugawa Ieyasu (1542–1616) had her installed in the newly built Hosokawa clan mansion near Osaka Castle, as a virtual hostage, to guarantee the loyalty of her husband. During this period she began learning about the Christian religion, introduced to the Japanese by Portuguese Roman Catholic missionaries in the mid-1600s, from two Japanese converts: Kiyohara Maria, daughter of a noble in the imperial court in Kyoto, and Takayama Justo

Ukon, a *daimyo* convert to Christianity and close friend of Tama's husband, Hosokawa Tadaoki. In 1587, Tama was baptized in her residence by Maria, who was instructed in her actions by two Jesuit priests, and she took the baptismal name Gracia. Tadaoki was infuriated but could not persuade her to renounce her Christian faith. In 1600 Tadaoki went north on a military campaign and his enemy Ishida Mitsunari sent troops to move Gracia into Osaka Castle. She refused to leave the Hosokawa residence without her husband's permission, and ordered her chamberlain to kill her to defend her husband's honor and prove his loyalty to Ieyasu. Gracia's dramatic death caused such commotion in Osaka that the other hostages captured by Ishida escaped the city and declared their allegiance to Ieyasu. Two months later, Ieyasu was able to defeat his remaining enemies in the decisive Battle of Sekigahara, after which he rewarded Gracia's husband, Tadaoki, by doubling the size of his domain. Gracia was commemorated by a large Christian memorial service. James Clavell used Hosokawa Gracia as the model for the character Lady Mariko in his best-selling novel *Shogun* (1975). See also CHRISTIANITY IN JAPAN; DAIMYO; HOSOKAWA CLAN; ODA NOBUNAGA; PORTUGUESE IN JAPAN; SEKIGAHARA, BATTLE OF; SHOGUN; TOKUGAWA IEYASU.

HOSSO SECT OF BUDDHISM (Hossoshu) Predominant sect of the Buddhist religion during the Nara Era (710–794). The Hosso, or Dharma Character sect, is also known as the Yuishiki sect. *Yuishiki* means "only consciousness," referring to the sect's teaching that everything is created by the mind. The Hosso sect was introduced into Japan from China by the Japanese monk Dosho around A.D. 650. This was very soon after the Chinese monk and pilgrim Hsuang-Tsang (Xuang-Zang) translated the sect's scripture, which had been written in Sanskrit by the Indian philosopher Vasubandhu, into Chinese in A.D. 648. This scripture is known in Japanese as the *Joyuishiki-ron*.

The Hosso sect was centered in the temples of Genkoji, Kofukuji and Horyuji, but also influenced rich and powerful temples such as Todaiji. Horyuji was the headquarters of the Hosso sect until it split from the sect in 1950. Kofukuji and Yakushiji remain the central Hosso temples, and there are 35 other Hosso temples in Japan. Hosso continued to be an important Buddhist sect during the medieval era of Japanese history (13th–16th centuries), but the sect has few members at present. See also BUDDHISM; CHINA AND JAPAN; HORYUJI; NARA ERA; TODAIJI.

HOSTESSES IN BARS See ALCOHOLIC BEVERAGES; EMPLOYMENT; EXPENSE ACCOUNT; INCOME; WATER TRADE.

HOT SPRING (*onsen*) Japan has natural hot springs in abundance, particularly on the southern island of Kyushu. Hundreds of hot springs have developed into popular resort towns. Two of the most famous are Atami, outside Tokyo, and Beppu, on Kyushu. Hot springs are very popular in Japan, especially those which have high mineral contents. Different minerals are thought to cure specific ailments. Many hot springs are channeled into pools in roofed public bathhouses (*sento*). There are also beautiful

open-air bathing pools (*rotemburo*), often with natural features such as rocks and waterfalls. In some places, one can bathe in hot sand or mud. After bathing in hot springs, the crowds of visitors enjoy eating, drinking and strolling around the town while wearing *yukata*, informal cotton robes supplied by each hotel.

Legends associate the origins of hot spring bathing in Japan with the religious act of purification, as well as the healing of illness by supernatural power. Hence hot springs were called *kami no yu*, or "hot water of the gods." Many were reputedly discovered by Buddhist monks, especially Gyoki (668–749) and Kukai (774–835).

Today the Japanese government publishes a guidebook to the country's hot springs, which range from large resorts to small bubbling pools in remote areas. Scientific research institutes also study balneotherapy, or the medical benefits of hot springs in treating bodily injuries and diseases, such as rheumatism and neuralgia. The Ministry of Health and Welfare has designated dozens of hot springs where medical treatments can be received. See also ATAMI; BATH; BEPPU; BUDDHISM; KUKAI; PURIFICATION; SHINTO.

HOTEI The god of contentment and happiness, and one of the Seven Gods of Good Fortune. Hotei is depicted as a fat man with a round naked belly. He holds a large bag of treasures and a fan (*ogi*). Although Hotei is said to be the only human being among the Seven Gods of Good Fortune, he is also considered an incarnation of the Buddhist god Maitreya (Miroku in Japanese), the Buddha of the future. Maitreya is known in China as Pu-tai (Pu-tei), the derivation of the name Hotei. See also FANS; MIROKU; SEVEN GODS OF GOOD FORTUNE.

HOUSE OF COUNCILLORS See DIET; ELECTIONS.

HOUSE OF REPRESENTATIVES See DIET; ELECTIONS.

HOUSEHOLD APPLIANCES See ELECTRONICS INDUSTRY.

HOUSEHOLD REGISTER (*koseki*) The legal record of information about members of a Japanese household. This register, or *koseki*, is kept in the municipal office of the city or town where the household resides, and is bound into a *kosekibo*, a book containing household registers. A copy is held by the regional bureau of the Japanese Ministry of Justice. At birth, every Japanese child is registered in the *koseki* of his or her parents. Required information includes name, date of birth, name of mother and father, and date of death. Additions and changes to a *koseki* must be legally made within a required time period. The first name listed in the *koseki* is the *hittosha*, the person whose family name is used by both husband and wife (in Japan, husbands sometimes take their wives' surnames). When a couple marries, they begin compiling a new *koseki*, and lines are drawn through their names in the *koseki* in which they were first listed. In some cases, a person's listing may be returned to a former *koseki*, for example, when returning to a former surname after being divorced or widowed. A child born to an unmarried woman is recorded in her family's *koseki*. Being listed in a *koseki* proves that a person is a Japanese citizen. The child of a Japanese man and a foreign wife can be listed in his *koseki* and regarded as a citizen, and so can the wife. Since 1984 the child of a Japanese woman and a foreign husband can become Japanese citizens. Information in a *koseki* is used for many purposes, such as entering school, getting a job, applying for a passport or getting married. *Koseki* were compiled in ancient Japan, but fell out of use until the Tokugawa Shogunate (1603–1867) restored them. The government of the Meiji Restoration of 1868 continued this practice by means of the Household Register Law (Koseki Ho) of 1871 and the Civil Code of 1898. The information in *koseki* is used to discriminate against minorities such as *burakumin*. See also BURAKUMIN; FAMILY; MEIJI RESTORATION OF 1868; MINORITIES IN JAPAN; TOKUGAWA SHOGUNATE.

HOUSEWIFE See CHILDREN IN JAPAN; DEPENDENCY; FAMILY; MOTHER; WOMEN'S ASSOCIATIONS.

HUMOR COMIC BOOKS; HAIKU; KYOGEN; LANGUAGE, JAPANESE; OKAME; SAIKAKU; SHUNGA; SIGNBOARDS; STORYTELLING.

HYOTTOKO See OKAME.

I

ICHIKAWA FUSAE (1893–1981)   A feminist politician who led the Japanese women's suffrage movement and was elected to five terms in the House of Councillors (upper house) of the Diet (Parliament). Ichikawa was born into a farm family in Aichi Prefecture and was educated to be a teacher in the city of Nagoya. She was also the first woman reporter for the newspaper *Nagoya shimbun*. In 1918 she went to Tokyo and became affiliated with Hiratsuka Raicho (1886–1971), a feminist who founded the Bluestocking Society (Seitosha). In 1920, Ichikawa, Hiratsuka and Oku Mumeo founded the New Woman's Association (Shin Fujin Kyokai), which won the right for Japanese women to attend political meetings. Ichikawa then spent two and a half years in the United States, where she learned much from American groups advocating women's rights. In Japan in 1924 she helped found the Women's Suffrage League (Fusen Kakutoku Domei). She also worked with liberal politicians in the Diet to get laws passed giving political rights to Japanese women. Although the militarization of Japan during World War II halted liberal movements, Ichikawa worked to help women deal with domestic problems caused by the war. After the war, Ichikawa founded the Japan League of Women Voters (Nihon Fujin Yukensha Domei) in 1945. Japanese women were given the right to vote by the new Japanese constitution enacted in 1947 during the postwar Occupation of Japan. In 1953, Ichikawa ran successfully as an independent for a seat in the House of Councillors. Over the next three decades she won five of the six elections she entered, including landslides in 1975 and 1980, even though she was not helped by a political party or business interests. She also worked for a women's political group, the Women's Suffrage Hall (Fusen Kaikan). See also CONSTITUTION OF 1947; DIET; FEMINIST MOVEMENTS; OCCUPATION OF JAPAN; WOMEN IN JAPAN.

ICHIKAWA KON (1915–)   Film director. Ichikawa was born in Ise in Mie Prefecture. He left school to be a cartoonist and designer, and after World War II he turned to filmmaking. His wife, Wada Natto, cowrote many of his fine early movies, such as *Pusan* (*Mr. Pu*; 1953) and *Okuman Choja* (*A Billionaire*; 1954). They also collaborated on his most highly regarded film, *The Harp of Burma* (*Biruma no tategoto*; 1956), about a Japanese soldier who stays in Burma after the war to seek personal peace by becoming a Buddhist monk. Ichikawa also filmed adaptations of Japanese literature. He based *Enjo* (*The Conflagration*; 1958) on the novel *Kinkakuji* (1956) by Mishima Yukio (1925–1970), which itself was based on the true story of a monk who burned down a famous golden Buddhist temple in Kyoto in 1950. *Kagi* (*The Key*, shown abroad as *Odd Obsession*; 1959) was based on a novel of the same title by Tanizaki Jun'ichiro

(1886–1965), and *Hakai* (*The Broken Commandment*, shown abroad as *The Outcast*; 1961) was based on a novel by Shimazaki Toson. The renowned Japanese actress Kyo Machiko (1924–) starred in *Kagi*, a story of sexual conflict between a husband and wife. Between 1976 and 1978, Ichikawa filmed melodramas based on mystery novels by Yokomizo Seishi. In addition to filming numerous fictional stories, Ichikawa also made two excellent documentaries: *Tokyo Orimpikku* (*Tokyo Olympiad*; 1965) depicts athletes and spectators at the 1964 Tokyo Olympic Games, and *Seishun* (*Youth*; 1968) is about high school baseball, a very popular sport in Japan. Ichikawa's style of filmmaking is characterized by masterful editing, excellent acting, beautifully composed and photographed scenes and a concern for the human qualities of the characters. See also FILM; KYO MACHIKO; MISHIMA YUKIO; TANIZAKI JUN'ICHIRO.

IDEOGRAPHS, CHINESE   See KANJI; LANGUAGE, JAPANESE; WRITING SYSTEM, JAPANESE.

IEMOTO   "Household or family root"; a term used for the grand master or head of a school of traditional Japanese art, such as dance, flower arrangement, Kabuki theater, Noh drama, or the tea ceremony. *Iemoto* usually refers to the founder of a school and his direct male descendants. For example, in the Urasenke tea ceremony school, the current *iemoto*, Sen Soshitsu, in the 15th generation descendant from the school's founder, Sen no Rikyu (1522–1591). His son will succeed him as the 16th Urasenke *iemoto*. A school of traditional Japanese art is like an extended family where every member looks to the *iemoto* as the father figure who has final authority. In many cases the *iemoto* is so involved in the lives of his closest followers that he even acts as the go-between for their weddings. He also inherits his school's valuable objects of art and maintains its traditional practices, which his followers must learn without deviation if they are to remain in the school. As they progress in their studies, students are awarded certificates of accomplishment by the *iemoto*; the highest followers are accredited as master teachers (*natori*) and are permitted to have their own students. As in other areas of Japanese life, all relationships within the school are hierarchical, with junior members subordinate to and dependent upon members who are higher in rank. This is true even for the large schools of flower arrangement and tea ceremony that have millions of members in branch chapters in Japan and around the world. See also FLOWER ARRANGING; GO-BETWEEN; KABUKI; NOH DRAMA; SEN NO RIKYU; TEA CEREMONY; URASENKE SCHOOL OF THE TEA CEREMONY.

IEYASU   See TOKUGAWA IEYASU.

IEYASU SHRINE   See NIKKO; TOSHOGU SHRINE.

II NAOSUKE   See ANSEI COMMERCIAL TREATIES.

IKAT   See KASURI.

IKEBANA   See FLOWER ARRANGING.

IKEDA CLAN   See BIZEN WARE.

IKEDA TERUMASA   See AZUCHI-MOMOYAMA ERA; HIMEJI CASTLE.

IKKYU SOJUN (1394–1481)   A Zen Buddhist monk known for his poetry and calligraphy and for his eccentric ways. Ikkyu was probably the son of emperor Go-Komatsu (1377–1433; r. 1382–1412) and a lower ranking noblewoman. When he was five, Ikkyu was sent to Ankokuji in Kyoto, where he was educated in the Buddhist scriptures and Chinese classical literature. In 1410 he began studying and practicing meditation with Ken'o Soi, and after Ken'o died in 1415, Ikkyu went to the town of Katata on Lake Biwa, where he studied Zen Buddhism under a strict teacher named Kaso Sodon (or Keso Shudon; 1352–1428). Ikkyu attained enlightenment (*satori*) in 1420 when he heard the cry of a crow while meditating at night in a boat on Lake Biwa. He moved to the port town of Sakai, where he scandalized the residents by going to wineshops and brothels. His actions gained him a reputation as a "mad" Zen monk. For example, to demonstrate the Buddhist teaching of the impermanence of all things, he once waved a human skull at people celebrating the New Year. At the same time, he made connections with the rich merchants of Sakai.

Ikkyu spent a period wandering, and gathered a number of artists, poets and playwrights as disciples. The best known of these was the painter Bokusai (or Motsurin Shoto; d. 1496), who wrote a biography of Ikkyu and made a portrait of him that has become famous. Ikkyu himself was a renowned writer and calligrapher, producing poetry in both the classical Chinese and the Japanese style. His main work is a collection of more than one thousand Chinese poems called *The Crazy-Cloud Anthology (Kyounshu)*. Eight works of prose, mostly sermons for lay audiences, are also ascribed to Ikkyu. During his life, Ikkyu attacked what he felt was the "inauthentic" teaching of Zen Buddhism in the temples of Gozan and Daitokuji in Kyoto, yet in 1474 he was appointed the 47th abbot of Daitokuji. The temple had been destroyed in the Onin War of 1467–1477, and Ikkyu oversaw the rebuilding of the temple, with financial assistance from the merchants of Sakai. He also helped solve political differences within its community. As abbot of Daitokuji, he taught the ritual for making tea that was practiced in Zen monasteries. Shuko Murata (1422–1502), one of Ikkyu's disciples, adapted many Japanese customs into the ritual and thereby originated the Japanese tea ceremony. In his later years, Ikkyu gained notoriety when he had a love affair with a blind woman singer named Mori. After spending several years in retreat at Shuon'an, his hermitage in the village of Takigi between Kyoto and Sakai, Ikkyu died in 1481 at the age of 87. See also DAITOKUJI; POETRY; SAKAI; SATORI; ZEN SECT OF BUDDHISM.

IMARI   A city on the southern Japanese island of Kyushu through which a type of colorful enameled porcelain known as Arita ware (*arita-yaki*) was shipped to Western nations, starting in the 17th century A.D. Arita ware thus became known in Europe and America by the name Imari. See also ARITA WARE; PORCELAIN.

IMMIGRANTS, JAPANESE   The Tokugawa Shogunate (1603–1867), which forbade Japanese from leaving the country from the early 17th century, lifted its ban on emigration in 1866. Japanese immigrants came to Hawaii in 1868 to work on sugar plantations. A small group came to California in 1869. Starting in 1885, Japanese laborers, farmers and samurai emigrated to the West Coast of the United States to meet the demand for cheap labor in California, after the U.S. Congress passed a federal law excluding Chinese in 1882. Many came from the southern Ryukyu Islands, which were formally acquired by Japan as Okinawa Prefecture in 1872. First-generation Japanese immigrants (born in Japan) are called *issei*, their children are known as *nisei* (second generation) and their grandchildren as *sansei* (third generation).

By 1890 there were about 2,000 Japanese in the United States, and 72,000 two decades later. Many more were brought under the American flag when the United States annexed Hawaii in 1898. Hamada Hikozo (1837–1897) was the first Japanese to become an American citizen. Japanese women frequently came to America as "picture brides," selected by Japanese men in the United States from their photographs. Japanese immigrants suffered greatly from prejudice, as Chinese immigrants had before them. In the so-called Gentleman's Agreement of 1907–1908, the Japanese government agreed not to issue passports to Japanese laborers who wanted to come to the United States; and it stopped issuing passports to picture brides in 1920. Anti-Japanese feeling became so strong, especially on the West Coast, that in 1924, Congress exluded new Japanese from the United States. Japan, by now a world power, regarded this law as an insult.

The United States went to war with Japan after it attacked the U.S. naval fleet at Pearl Harbor, Hawaii, on December 7, 1941. Because of a fear of disloyalty, more than 100,000 Japanese-American citizens and Japanese resident aliens on the West Coast were deprived of their property and forcibly interned in ten relocation camps, the best known of which is Manzanar Relocation Center near Lone Pine, California, which held more than 10,000 inmates. *Nisei* men proved their loyalty to the U.S. by persuading the government to form the 442nd Regimental Combat Team, an all Japanese-American military unit which bravely fought the Nazis in Europe and became the most decorated combat unit in American military history. Japanese-Americans later sought redress for their incarceration during the war, and in 1988 President Ronald Reagan signed into law a national act of contrition for the incarceration, which provided recompense of $20,000 for each surviving internee.

During the Occupation of Japan following the war, some Japanese women married American soldiers who were stationed there and came to the United States as war brides. Japanese were permitted to immigrate to the United States once more with the passage of the McCarran-Walter Act of 1952, and 40,000 Japanese emigrated to America between 1952 and 1960. Since the U.S. Immigration Act of 1965 revised the terms by which foreign immigrants could enter the United States, 10–20,000 Japanese have emigrated there each year. Today there are about 700,000 Japanese-Americans, with about 250,000 living in Hawaii. The Japanese-American National Museum was founded in Los Angeles in 1989. They have achieved a high standard of living and education, and have become integrated into the American population. In addition, tens of thousands of Japanese businessmen and their families and Japanese students have temporarily moved to the United States.

There are also significant populations of Japanese immigrants in South America, primarily Brazil, and Canada. Japanese began emigrating to Canada in the late 1870s, and there were about 7,600 in British Columbia in 1908. Riots against Chinese and Japanese in Vancouver in 1907 caused the Canadian government to limit Japanese immigrants to 150 a year. The 20,000 Japanese-Canadians and Japanese nationals living in Canada in 1941 were also interned in relocation camps or remote towns during World War II, for which they later sought redress. Japanese-Canadians won full citizenship rights after the war. There are about 40,000 Japanese-Canadians today, the majority living in Ontario Province. Japanese began emigrating to Brazil as coffee plantation workers in 1908. There are 1.2 million persons of Japanese descent living in Brazil, of whom about 20% were born in Japan. Seventy-five percent of the total reside in the state of Sao Paolo. Peru has Latin America's second largest Japanese immigrant community. A *nisei* named Alberto Fujimori became president of Peru in 1990. See also 442ND REGIMENTAL COMBAT TEAM; ISSEI; JAPANESE-AMERICAN CITIZENS' LEAGUE; NISEI; PICTURE BRIDE; RYUKYU ISLANDS; SANSEI.

IMPERIAL HOTEL (Teikoku Hoteru)   A hotel designed by the American architect Frank Lloyd Wright (1869–1959) and constructed facing Hibiya Park and the Imperial Palace in Tokyo. Wright had first visited Japan in 1905. On a return trip in 1913, he received a commission from representatives of the emperor to build a deluxe new hotel to replace the old German-built Imperial Hotel. Wright's new Imperial Hotel became a famous landmark for visitors to Tokyo. Completed in 1922, it required six years of construction, which was supervised by Paul Meuller, an engineer who constructed many of Wright's most important buildings. Wright's architectural assistant on the project was Antonin Raymond, who worked in Japan from 1919 to 1937 and returned in 1948 and who designed numerous buildings in Japan and trained many modern Japanese architects. Wright floated the hotel's structure on thousands of short concrete pillars to allow it to withstand the earthquakes that frequently occur in Japan. Its basic material was reinforced concrete, but Wright used wood for the

roof trusses, and a Japanese stone known as *oyaishi*. When a massive earthquake struck Tokyo in 1923 and leveled much of the city, the Imperial Hotel remained standing. Wright's ferro-concrete design for the Imperial Hotel still influences modern Japanese architecture. However, the hotel was demolished in 1976, and a new, much larger Imperial Hotel was erected on the same site. The lobby of Wright's original structure was moved to the open-air Meiji Mura Museum just north of Nagoya City.

Wright designed other buildings in Japan, including the Odawara Hotel (1917), a movie theater in the Ginza district of Tokyo (1918), the Yamamura House (1924) and a school known as Jiyu Gakuen (1927), which his Japanese pupil Endo Arata helped design. In addition, Wright collected Japanese woodblock prints, about which he became an authority. See also EARTHQUAKE; IMPERIAL PALACE (TOKYO).

IMPERIAL HOUSEHOLD (koshitsu)   The term for the extended imperial family. This could include the reigning emperor (tenno), the empress (kogo), the grand empress dowager (tai kotaigo; grandmother of the emperor), the empress dowager (kotaigo; mother of the emperor), imperial princes (shinno; sons of the emperor or of his eldest son) and their wives (shinnohi), imperial princesses (naishinno; daughters of the emperor or of his oldest son), princes (o; grandsons of the emperor) and their wives (ohi), and princesses (joo; granddaughters of the emperor). The eldest son of the emperor, who is first in the line of succession, is called the crown prince (kotaishi). There is no surname for members of the imperial household. Princes and princesses use the titles of their fathers and their personal names.

Although a number of women held imperial power in ancient Japan, from the Nara Era A.D. (710–794) until the present only males have been allowed to sit on the imperial throne. After the crown prince, the next men in line to succeed to the throne are the oldest son of the crown prince, followed by his other sons and his grandsons. Then come the second oldest son of the emperor and his sons and grandsons, followed by other sons and grandsons of the emperor, brothers of the emperor and their sons and grandsons, and uncles of the emperor and their sons and grandsons. Except for the crown prince and his oldest son, who may not refuse the throne, it is possible for other sons, daughters, grandsons and granddaughters of the emperor to give up their status as members of the imperial family. For example, daughters of former Emperor Showa (earlier known as Hirohito) and of his brother Prince Mikasa became commoners through marriage and took the surnames of their husbands. Issues concerning the Imperial Household, such as renunciation of imperial status, are decided upon by an advisory body called the Imperial Household Council (Koshitsu Kaigi), which includes two members of the imperial family, the speakers and vice-speakers of the House of Representatives (lower house) and House of Councillors (upper house) of the Japanese Diet (Parliament), the prime minister, the chief justice and another justice of the Supreme court, and the head of the Imperial Household Agency (Kunaicho), which administers the affairs of the imperial family. The Imperial Household Law (Koshitsu Tempan), passed by the Diet in 1947 to replace the former Imperial Household Law that was passed along with the Meiji Constitution in 1889, governs important decisions regarding the Imperial Household. These include succession to the throne, titles assigned to family members, the appointment of a regent when the emperor is too young or otherwise unable to fulfill his duties, and the creation of the Imperial Household Council. See also CONSTITUTION OF 1947, JAPANESE; CROWN PRINCE; DIET; EMPEROR; IMPERIAL HOUSEHOLD AGENCY.

IMPERIAL HOUSEHOLD AGENCY (Kunaicho) An agency of the Japanese government that administers the affairs of the emperor and his family, known collectively as the Imperial Household (koshitsu). The Imperial Household agency, which belongs to the cabinet of prime minister, was created in 1947 to carry out the duties of the former Imperial Household Ministry (Kunaisho). The prime minister appoints the grand steward (Kunaicho chokan) who heads the Imperial Household Agency. Divisions of the agency include the Secretariat of the Grand Steward, the Board of Chamberlains, the Board of Ceremonies, the Office of the Crown Prince's Household, the Archives and Mausolea Department, and the Maintenance and Works Department. The agency keeps records for the imperial family, and maintains imperial tombs and property owned by the state but used by the imperial family. It also keeps two seals or stamps that are used to legitimize imperial documents: the imperial seal (gyoji) and the seal of state (kokuji). See also CABINET, PRIME MINISTER'S; CROWN PRINCE; EMPEROR; IMPERIAL HOUSEHOLD; PRIME MINISTER; SEALS AND SIGNATURES.

IMPERIAL JAPANESE ARMY AND NAVY (Dai Nippon Teikoku Rikugun and Kaigun) The official names of the army and navy established in 1868 following the Meiji Restoration. They were created from the military forces of Satsuma, Choshu, and other southwestern domains that overthrew the Tokugawa Shogunate (1603–1867) in the Boshin Civil War (1867–1868) and brought about the Meiji Restoration of 1868. The founders of the new armed forces were largely of upper and lower samurai (warrior) background. The army command was from Choshu and the navy command from the trading province of Satsuma. They adapted military training methods and principles of organization from Western nations, particularly Prussia (Germany), including the conscription of soldiers from non-samurai classes. In later years the Imperial Japanese Army fought in a number of military actions in Asia, the major ones being the Sino-Japanese War of 1894–1895, the Russo-Japanese War (1904–1905), the Sino-Japanese War of 1937–1945 and the Pacific phase of World War II (1941–1945). The Meiji Constitution (1889) placed the Imperial Japanese Army and Navy under the direct command of the emperor. The army later took actions that it claimed were carried out on behalf of the emperor's wishes. Through such actions as the Manchurian Incident in 1931 and the February 26th Incident in 1936, the military took greater control

of the nation's politics. It also pursed a policy of aggressive Japanese expansion into other Asian countries. Nearly 1 million Japanese soldiers were fighting in China and Manchuria by 1939. Military leaders had Japan sign the Anti-Comintern Pact (1936) and the Tripartite Pact (1940) with Germany and Italy. Army General Tojo Hideki served as prime minister from 1941 to 1945. Japanese troops moved into Southeast Asian countries to gain oil and other resources badly needed by Japan. Japan attempted to immobilize American intervention by attacking the U.S. Pacific Fleet at Pearl Harbor on December 7, 1941, but the U.S. declared war on Japan. At the height of the Pacific phase of World War II, the Imperial Japanese Army was organized into 172 infantry divisions, four armored divisions and 13 air units. Its 6,400,000 soldiers had a reputation as fierce and devoted fighters. The Imperial Japanese Navy won major victories in the Sino-Japanese War of 1894–1895, the Russo-Japanese War (1904–1905), and World War I. Japan proved itself a major world power when, under Admiral Togo Heihachiro's command, the Japanese navy destroyed Russia's Baltic fleet at the Battle of Tsushima in 1905. Admiral Yamamoto Isoroku planned the attack on Pearl Harbor and served as commander of the Japanese navy during World War II. He was killed when American forces shot down his plane, and the Japanese navy was destroyed by the end of the war. The Imperial Japanese Army and Navy were disbanded in 1945 following Japan's surrender to the Allied powers. The new Japanese constitution enacted in 1947 during the postwar Occupation states that Japan renounces war and the threat or use of force, and forbids Japan from maintaining land, sea and air forces. However, Japan has established voluntary Self-Defense Forces (Jietai), which provide defensive security and disaster relief. See also CHOSHU PROVINCE; CONSTITUTION, MEIJI; CONSTITUTION OF 1947; FEBRUARY 26TH INCIDENT; MANCHURIAN INCIDENT; MEIJI RESTORATION OF 1868; PEARL HARBOR, JAPANESE ATTACK ON; RUSSO-JAPANESE WAR (1904–1905); SAMURAI; SATSUMA PROVINCE; SELF-DEFENSE FORCES; SINO JAPANESE WAR OF 1894–1895; SINO-JAPANESE WAR OF 1937–1945; TOGO HEIHACHIRO; WORLD WAR II; YAMAMOTO ISOROKU.

IMPERIAL PALACE (KYOTO) (Kyoto Gosho) The residence of the reigning emperor of Japan and his family while Kyoto was the imperial capital from 794–1868. The old Imperial Palace, known as Kyoto Gosho, still stands in Kyoto and is open to the public by application to the Kyoto office of the Imperial Household Agency. The original Gosho was constructed by Emperor Kammu (737–806; r. 781–806), who built the city of Heiankyo (later known as Kyoto) and moved the capital there in A.D. 794. The imperial court centered in the Gosho ruled over a brilliant period of cultural flowering known as the Heian Era (794–1185). The original Gosho burned down in 1788, and a reconstruction was also destroyed by fire. The current Kyoto Gosho, constructed in 1855, survives because Kyoto was spared from bombing by the Allied powers during World War II.

The palace is surrounded by acres of carefully raked white gravel and enclosed by a tile-roofed earthwork wall.

The south gate, Kenrei-mon, is used exclusively by the emperor. Members of the Imperial Family and royal peers entered through the near west gate, called Gishu-mon (Nobles' Gate). There are two other gates in the west wall, the Seisho-mon, through which visitors enter today, and the Junko-mon. The north gate, the Sakuhei-mon, was used by Imperial consorts and their ladies-in-waiting. There is also the Kimon, a gate on the unlucky northeast corner. The main palace enclosure covers more than 27 acres, with an outer garden of nearly 220 acres. There are 18 structures joined by covered corridors and separated by gardens with streams and bridges, rocks, and artificial hills. The main buildings are the Shishinden (Ceremonial Hall), where emperors were enthroned and state functions were held; and the Seiryoden (Pure Cool Hall), originally the living quarters of the imperial family. The imperial throne and other furnishings and decorations, such as painted sliding screens, are exhibited.

The remains of Sento Imperial Palace (Sento Gosho), originally a residence for ex-emperors, stand outside the walls of the palace in the southeast section of the Imperial Park. Its beautiful garden was built in the early 17th century by the famous landscape designer Kobori Enshu. Omiya Palace (Omiya Gosho), northwest of Sento Palace, was built in the 17th century by Emperor Go-Mizunoo for his wife, Empress Tofukumon-in. His mother and every empress-dowager after her until 1868 resided in Omiya Palace. Today it is used by members of the imperial family and official state visitors when they are in Kyoto. Many annual festivals are held at the Kyoto Imperial Palace, including the Hollyhock Festival (Aoi Matsuri) in May and the Festival of the Eras (Jidai Matsuri) in October. See also EMPEROR; FESTIVAL OF THE AGES; GARDENS; HEIAN ERA; HEIANKYO; HOLLYHOCK FESTIVAL; IMPERIAL HOUSEHOLD; IMPERIAL HOUSEHOLD AGENCY; IMPERIAL PALACE (TOKYO); KYOTO; MEIJI RESTORATION OF 1868.

IMPERIAL PALACE (TOKYO) The current residence of the reigning emperor of Japan and his family. The imperial palace is located in the business center of Tokyo (formerly known as Edo), on the former site of Edo Castle (also known as Chiyoda Castle), the residence of the Tokugawa shoguns (1603–1867). After the Meiji Restoration of 1868, when the emperor moved from Kyoto to Tokyo, construction was begun on the imperial palace; it was completed in 1888. Most of the buildings were destroyed by air raids during World War II, although the surrounding moats and stone bridges were not harmed. Reconstruction of the palace was completed in 1968. Nijubashi Bridge is the main bridge into the private palace grounds, which are opened to the public twice a year, at the New Year and on the emperor's birthday. Special permission to take a tour of the palace at other times may be arranged with the Imperial Household Agency. The Outer Garden and East Garden (Higashi Gyoen) are open to the public, and the stone foundation of the central structure of Edo Castle remains in the East Garden. To the north of the palace lies Kitanomaru Park (Kitanomaru Koen), formerly the private grounds of the Imperial Guard and now the home of several mu-

seums. Adjacent to the imperial palace are Hibiya Park, with a concert hall, and Tokyo's main government, financial and shopping districts. See also CASTLES; EDO ERA; EMPEROR; IMPERIAL HOUSEHOLD; IMPERIAL HOUSEHOLD AGENCY; IMPERIAL PALACE (KYOTO); MEIJI RESTORATION OF 1868; TOKUGAWA SHOGUNATE; TOKYO.

IMPERIAL REGALIA (*sanshu no jingi [shimpo, shingu]*) Also known as the three sacred treasures; sacred objects that symbolize the authority and legitimacy of the emperor of Japan. The imperial regalia consist of curved jewels (*magatama*), a sacred mirror (*kagami*), and a sacred sword (*tsurugi*). Legends recorded in the eighth century A.D. in the Japanese chronicles *Kojiki* and *Nihon Shoki* claim that the gods of heaven gave these treasures to Sun Goddess Amaterasu o Mikami, the central deity of Shinto. Amaterasu withdrew into a cave after her brother Susano no Mikoto made her angry, and the deities used the sacred mirror to help lure her out of the cave. When she emerged, they gave her the curved jewels, and her brother gave her the sacred sword, which he had taken from the tail of a serpent named Yamata no Orochi that he had killed in Izumo, to indicate his submission. Amaterasu gave the sacred mirror, jewels and sword to her grandson Ninigi no Mikoto when she sent him down to earth to found the dynasty that became the Japanese imperial family. The sacred treasures were tokens that he and his descendants should rule the islands of Japan forever.

Amaterasu told her grandson that when he looked in the mirror, it would be as though he were looking at her. Ninigi no Mikoto's grandson was the legendary first Japanese emperor, Jimmu Tenno, who supposedly founded the imperial line in 660 B.C. An important Shinto document, *The Records of the Legitimate Succession of the Divine Sovereigns* by Kitabatake Chikafusa (1293–1354), claims that the mirror represents the sun, the jewel the moon, and the sword the stars. The mirror reflects the true qualities of all things and is thus the source of honesty. The jewel is gentle and submissive and is the source of compassion. The sword is strong and resolute and is the source of wisdom.

According to legend, the imperial regalia were handed down to each succeeding emperor and were kept in the Imperial Palace. During the reign of the legendary 10th Emperor Sujin (supposedly 97–30 B.C.), the sacred mirror and sword were replaced by replicas after an oracle decreed that the original mirror and sword should be removed from the palace to prevent them being polluted by contact with human beings. Legends claim that in 4 B.C. the mirror and sword were enshrined at Ise, which has become the central shine of Shinto. Later, a priestess of Ise Shrine lent the sword to the legendary prince Yamatotakeru when he was attempting to conquer eastern Japan for the imperial family based in western Japan. The sword saved his life and was renamed Kusanagi no Tsurugi, The Sword That Cut the [Burning] Grass. Atsuta Shrine in Nagoya City claims to house this sword. The replica of the sword that was supposedly made in Emperor Sujin's time disappeared in the Battle of Dannoura in 1185, when the boy Emperor Antoku was drowned, and a sword from Ise Shrine took its place.

Today the supposedly original curved jewels and the replicas of the mirror and sword are housed in the Imperial Palace in Tokyo. The replica mirror is enshrined in the *Kashikodokoro*, Place of Awe, one of the three Shinto shrines in the palace. The jewels and sword are kept in a room called the *Kenji no Ma*, or Room of the Sword and Seal. When a new emperor takes the throne, the sword and jewels are presented to him in a ceremony known as the Kenji Togyo no Gi. This ritual was televised in 1989 when Akihito (1933–) became emperor after the death of his father, Emperor Showa (1901–1989; formerly known as Hirohito). See also AKIHITO, EMPEROR; AMATERASU O MIKAMI; ATSUTA SHRINE; DANNOURA, BATTLE OF; EMPEROR; IMPERIAL PALACE; ISE SHRINE; JIMMU TENNO; KOJIKI; MIRROR; NIHON SHOKI; NINIGI NO MIKOTO; SHINTO; SUSANOO NO MIKOTO; SWORD.

IMPERIAL TREASURE HOUSE See SHOSOIN.

IMPORTANT CULTURAL PROPERTIES See NATIONAL TREASURES.

IMPORTS See EXPORTS AND IMPORTS.

INARI Popularly known as Inari Daimyojin; the Shinto *kami* (sacred spirit) associated with cereals and rice cultivation. Inari is the most widely worshipped *kami* in Shinto, the indigenous Japanese religion. Rice is the most important and sacred food in the Japanese diet. The name Inari may be an abbreviation of *ine-nari*, which means "ripening of rice." Worship of Inari originated in ancient Japan with the Hata clan, which enshrined its clan deity (*ujigami*), the *kami* of rice fields, at the Fushimi Inari Shrine. Legend states that this occurred in A.D. 711 on the first Day of the Horse in the second month, according to the traditional lunar and zodiac calendars. The festival of Inari is still held on this day throughout Japan. When the Japanese capital was moved to Kyoto in A.D. 794, the Hata Clan grew powerful and the Fushimi Inari Shrine became a popular religious site. The great religious leader Kukai (774–835), who founded the Shingon sect of Buddhism, made Inari even more important by identifying this Shinto *kami* with the Buddhist deity Dakiniten (Dakini). During the medieval era (13th–16th centuries), Inari also came to be worshipped as the deity of blacksmiths and commerce, and was popular with members of the samurai class. The fox, believed to have sacred powers and to control the financial success of families, came to be identified as the messenger of Inari. Fried *tofu* (soybean curd), believed to be the favorite food of the fox, is a traditional offering at Inari shrines. During the Edo Era (1600–1868), many Japanese placed Inari shrines in their households to worship the "Inari of success" (*shusse* Inari). Today there are about 40,000 Inari shrines in Japan. The most important are the Fushimi Inari Shrine in Kyoto, the Takekoma Inari Shrine in Miyagi Prefecture, the Kasami Inari Shrine in Ibaraki Prefecture, the Toyokawa Inari, which is actually the Buddhist Temple Myogonji in Aichi Prefecture, and the Yutoku Inari Shrine in Saga Prefecture. There are also numerous small Inari shrines around the country, as well as household shrines to Inari as a guardian deity (*yashikigami*). See also ALTARS IN HOMES; FOX; HATA CLAN; KAMI; KUKAI; RICE; SHINTO; SHRINES, SHINTO; TOFU; ZODIAC.

INCENSE (*ko*) Small pieces of wood, or pellets of ground wood mixed with other materials, that are scented with fragrance. Incense is burned in small decorative metal containers. The use of incense goes back to ancient times, when it was used as an offering in Buddhism, the religion introduced into Japan from China in the sixth century A.D. The practice of burning incense in front of statues of Buddhist deities is still followed, both in temples and in homes. This type of incense for Buddhist rituals, known as *senko*, is on long sticks that can be stood upright in large containers. During the Heian Era (794–1185), incense was also used to give rooms and clothing a pleasing scent. Literature of the time, such as the novel *The Tale of Genji* (*Genji Monogatari*), provides descriptions of court women scenting their multilayered robes with incense, and of incense-smelling competitions that were an aristocratic pastime. Typically, 10 participants smelled four different types of incense, 10 times each, passing the incense burner among them. The goal was to guess the name and place of origin of each type of incense. By the 15th century A.D., Japanese of other classes were also enjoying the incense ceremony, or *kodo* ("Way of Incense"). Rules for the ceremony were formalized by various scholars, such as San-jonishi Sanetaka and Shino Munenobu. *Kodo* was widely practiced during the Genroku Era (1688–1704), along with flower arranging and the tea ceremony. Today the ceremony is still taught by the Sanjonishi and Shino schools, but interest in *kodo* has declined. However, incense still plays an important role in the tea ceremony. The host places incense on the charcoal fire that heats the tea kettle. Guests enjoy the soothing and gentle fragrance and admire the *kogo*, or container in which the incense has been brought into the room. See also ALTARS IN HOMES; BUDDHISM; GENJI, THE TALE OF; HEIAN ERA; TEA CEREMONY; TEMPLES, BUDDHIST.

INCOME The Japanese national income grew very rapidly in the 1950s and 1960s, and by 1968 Japan had achieved the third highest gross domestic product (GDP) in the world after the United States and the Soviet Union. The share of GNP from family-run small businesses is around 17%, much higher than in other industrialized countries. The average wages of Japanese workers in the manufacturing sector are nearly the same as those in Western industrialized nations. The highest wages are earned by regular employees in finance, public service, publishing, iron and steel, and petroleum, and the lowest in the clothing and textiles, furnitures, and leather products industries. Farmers have comparatively low income. Administrative and technical workers earn around 20% more than production workers. Women workers earn a little more than half the income of men. A 1988 British report comparing executive salaries in the seven leading industrial nations ranked Japan first in nominal income, but last in terms of real buying power. The cost of land and homes are so high in Japanese cities that many people are no longer able to buy their own homes. Automobiles, food, and other consumer goods are also very expensive in Japan, largely because of the complex distribution system and control of imports by large corporations.

Full-time workers receive promotions and pay raises based on seniority. Companies give regular employees large bonuses twice a year, at midsummer and the end of the year, which are the two main gift-giving seasons in Japan. Other benefits include social security and health insurance, retirement and pension funds, and assistance in paying for education and home mortgages. Labor unions generally cooperate with companies in negotiating pay increases and benefits. Business executives receive generous expense accounts from their companies for entertaining clients after work. Most women who work for companies or in retail sales are considered part-time employees and receive only 70% of the wages of full-time women workers, with no benefits or job security. The Japanese have a very high rate of savings and investment. See also CORPORATIONS; EMPLOYMENT; EXPENSE ACCOUNTS; GIFTS; LABOR UNIONS; SALARYMAN; SENIORITY SYSTEM; TAX SYSTEM; WATER TRADE.

INDEBTEDNESS (on) A moral, psychological, and social term for the debt a person incurs when receiving a favor or large gift. The word *on* originally referred to the benevolence or favor of one's parent, feudal lord or ruler. However, the modern usage of the word indicates the vast debt of gratitude and obligation that the receiver owes the giver. While indebtedness is an indigenous Japanese concept, it may have been influenced by two sources. The Chinese character for *on* means "blessing" or "favor." The Buddhist religion, introduced into Japan from China in the sixth century A.D., conceives of *on* as the debt a person has to mankind and to the compassion of the Buddha, founder of the religion. During the feudal era, *on* referred to the debt of samurai to their lords. The samurai code obligated them to serve their lord, even to die for him in battle, as repayment for land or money and protection they received from him. *On* also refers to the debt one owes one's parents and ancestors for the gift of life itself. Children must take care of their parents when they get old, have children to carry on the family and do nothing to shame the family's name. This obligation is defined as filial piety (ko), a major concept of the Chinese philosophy of Confucianism, which was also introduced into Japan. A person is indebted as well to superiors, such as teachers and employers, and to people who have bestowed exceptional favors, such as saving one's life. The concept of indebtedness is related to that of duty, or *giri*, which indicates the need to repay favor or *on*. In one sense, the debt can never be erased, yet one is required to repay it to one's utmost ability. This binds the individual in a continuous give-and-take network of social relationships in which one is expected to subordinate personal feelings to duty, and to remain loyal to the person to whom one is indebted. See also BUDDHISM; CONFUCIANISM; DUTY AND FEELINGS; FAMILY; FILIAL PIETY; LOYALTY; SAMURAI.

INDIGO (ai) A plant used to make blue dye for textiles. The variety of indigo commonly used in Japan is native to Indochina and is known as *tadeai* in Japanese. When crushed leaves of the indigo plant are placed in water, oxygen and fermentation cause a substance in the plant called indikan to bind with textile fibers and turn them blue. Each time a textile is dipped in the indigo solution, it turns a darker blue. The technique of dyeing with indigo, known as "raw-leaf dyeing" (namahazome), was used in Japan as far back as the seventh century A.D. A piece of indigo-dyed fabric from c. A.D. 620 is owned by Horyuji in Nara. Japanese records from the eighth and 10th centuries A.D. describe the cultivation of indigo plants and methods for producing indigo-blue dyes. Only members of the aristocracy wore indigo-dyed textiles through the Nara Era (710–794). By the end of that era, a "vat-dye" technique (tatezome) had been invented, which enabled larger amounts of textiles to be dyed so commoners could wear them as well. This technique produces *sukumo*, a dye made by drying indigo leaves, sprinkling them with water, letting them ferment, and pounding them to a paste (aidama). Fermentation is controlled by mixing the paste in large vats with lime, a starch such as wheat bran paste, liquid from wood-ash and water. During this week-long process, the mixture is also heated to about 100° F. Numerous textiles can be dyed many different shades of blue with this technique. After being dipped in the mixture, they are hung up to dry. Blue and white designs are created by using stencils and wax or paste to cover areas that will resist the blue dye. Today synthetic chemical dyes are often used in place of or along with *sukumo*, although some artisans continue to follow the traditional methods. Cotton is the textile most frequently dyed with indigo, and is used mainly for informal robes known as *yukata*. Hemp (asa) was commonly used to make *yukata* in the past. See also HEMP; STENCIL; TEXTILES; YUKATA.

INDUSTRIAL ZONES (kogyo chitai) Industrial zones were originally created by the Meiji government (1868–1912) when Japan was being modernized and industrialized. They are located around major ports and mouths of large rivers along the coast, to facilitate the import of raw materials and the export of finished goods. The Keihin Industrial Zone in the Kanto region surrounding Tokyo and Yokohama, and including the prefectures of Chiba, Kanagawa, Saitama and Tokyo, is the most important. (Chiba Prefecture is sometimes referred to as the Kaiyo Industrial Zone.) Second is the Hanshin Industrial Zone around the cities of Osaka and Kobe. Third is the Chukyo Industrial Zone around Nagoya City and including Aichi, Gifu and Mie Prefectures. These three zones are all on Honshu, the main Japanese island. Fourth is the Kita (Northern) Kyushu Industrial Zone, including Fukuoka Prefecture, on Kyushu Island to the south. These four zones on or near the Pacific Ocean account for around half of Japanese manufacturing. The coastal area connecting them is known as the Pacific Ocean Belt Industrial Zone. There are several other important zones. Setouchi Industrial Zone around the Inland Sea includes part of southwest Honshu and northern Shikoku Island. Tokai lies between Nagoya and Tokyo. Hokuriku includes Niigata, Toyama, Fukui and Ishikawa Prefectures on northwestern Honshu. See also EXPORTS AND IMPORTS; GEOGRAPHY OF JAPAN; MEIJI RESTORATION OF 1868; PACIFIC OCEAN; SHIPPING AND SHIPBUILDING; NAMES OF INDIVIDUAL CITIES, ISLANDS AND PREFECTURES.

INDUSTRY See AUTOMOBILE INDUSTRY; BIOTECHNOLOGY INDUSTRY; CAMERAS AND PHOTOGRAPHY; CORPORATIONS; COMPUTER INDUSTRY; ELECTRONICS INDUSTRY; EXPORTS AND IMPORTS; FORESTRY INDUSTRY; INDUSTRIAL ZONES; MINISTRY OF INTERNATIONAL TRADE AND INDUSTRY; SEMICONDUCTOR INDUSTRY; SHIPPING AND SHIPBUILDING; STEEL INDUSTRY.

INK PAINTING *(suibokuga; sumi-e)* A style of monochrome painting that uses blocks of black ink *(sumi)*, diluted with water and applied with brushes onto handmade paper *(washi)* or silk. Ink paintings are usually mounted on vertical hanging scrolls *(kakemono)*. Japanese painters adopted this style from China in the 14th century. Ink painting was originally associated with the Zen Buddhist religion, which had been introduced from China in the 12th century. Known as *suibokuga* ("water-ink pictures"; *shuimohua* in Chinese) or *suim-e* ("ink pictures"), ink painting is closely related to calligraphy *(shodo,* "the way of writing"), which is also done with black ink and brushes.

The ink block has a charcoal or soot base and is compressed into hard sticks. Liquid ink is made by rubbing an ink stick on an inkstone and adding drops of water to produce the desired darkness and consistency. Many different shades of ink can be created, which are often termed the "colors of ink." An ink painting cannot be painted over or corrected. The artist contemplates the intended painting, then executes it rapidly with sure strokes of the brush. An ink brush is absorbent, flexible and often pointed, and slight changes in pressure by the artist alter the thickness or thinness of a stroke. The angle at which a brush is held also creates a strong, hard line or a soft, weak one. In both ink painting and calligraphy, the brush strokes are considered to reveal the personality of the artist.

Common subjects in Japanese ink painting are landscapes, including mountains, trees, grasses and rocks, and Buddhist subjects, such as hermits and Daruma (Bodhidharma), the founder of Zen Buddhism. Poetic inscriptions are often written in the corner by the painters or their associates. Literature and ink painting are thus intimately related.

The Muromachi Era (1333–1568) is often termed the period of ink painting in Japanese art history. The shogunate patronized Zen Buddhism and related arts, such as Noh Drama and ink painting. *Suibokuga* became the official court style under priest-painter Shubun (active 1430s to early 1460s), who was head of the first Bureau of Painting *(E-dokoro)* under the Ashikaga Shogunate (1338–1573). During the Azuchi-Momoyama Era (1568–1600), artists of the Kano school combined the techniques of monochrome ink painting with colorful Japanese-style painting *(Yamato-e)*. This decorative style was frequently executed as screen paintings for castles built by powerful *daimyo* (feudal lords). During the Edo Era (1600–1868), the Japanese interest in Confucianism revived ink painting as the art form of schol-ars and other literati, who painted nature scenes in a style known as *Bunjin-ga* (literati painting) or as *Nanga* ("southern painting"). Because of the association of Zen and ink painting, some of the finest ink painters have been Zen priests or laymen, such as Josetsu (early 15th century), Sesshu Toyo (1420–1506), Hakuin Ekaku (1686–1769) and Sengai Gibon (1750–1837). Three generations of secular painters connected with the Ashikaga Shogunate, Noami (1397–1471), Geiami and Soami (c. 1455–1525), are also famous masters of this art form. See also ASHIKAGA SHOGUNATE; CALLIGRAPHY; DAIMYO; HAKUIN EKAKU; JOSETSU; KANO SCHOOL OF PAINTING; MUROMACHI ERA; NOAMI; PAINTING; SCREENS; SCROLLS; SENGAI GIBON; SESSHU TOYO; SOAMI; ZEN SECT OF BUDDHISM.

INLAND SEA (Seto Naikai) Also known as the Seto Inland Sea; a body of water that separates the main Japanese island of Honshu from Shikoku Island. The Seto-Ohashi Bridge was recently completed connecting the two. It is actually six bridges connecting islands in the sea. Kyushu Island lies just west of the Inland Sea.

The Inland Sea covers 3,667 square miles and has an average depth of 144 feet. The picturesque beauty of the sea is renowned, due to its mountainous coastline and more than 1,000 small, pine-covered islands. The largest islands in the sea are Awajishima, separated from Shikoku Island by the violent whirlpools of the Naruto Strait, and Shodoshima, famous for its scenic Kankakei gorge. The entire Inland Sea, along with coastal areas on Honshu and Shikoku, make up a national park (Seto Naikai Kokuritsu Koen), which extends for 248 miles and draws many tourists. From the beginning of Japanese history, the Inland Sea has been the major route for the transportation of goods and the spread of culture between northern Kyushu and the old capitals of Nara and Kyoto on central Honshu. In recent decades, the regions bordering the sea have become highly industrialized, in an area known as the Inland Sea Industrial Region (Setouchi Kogyo Chitai). Major products manufactured here include automobiles, petrochemicals and steel. Shipbuilding is also an important industry, but the once-active fishing industry has declined because of polluted waters. See also HONSHU ISLAND; KYUSHU ISLAND; NARUTO STRAIT; NATIONAL PARKS; SHIKOKU ISLAND.

INLAY WORK See LACQUER WARE; METAL WARE; WOODWORKING.

INNS See RYOKAN.

INRO "Seal basket"; a decorative carrier for a name seal. An *inro* is a miniature lacquer-ware container with several compartments that fit together. It can be hung from the *obi* (sash) of a kimono by means of a silk cord and a miniature carving known as a *netsuke*. The cord runs through two vertical channels along the two sides of an *inro* and ends in a decorative knot underneath. The top ends of the cord go through a sliding bead *(ojime)* and are fastened to the *netsuke*, which is pulled up in back of the *obi* and suspended over it. The bead can be moved up or down the cord to open the *inro's* compartments or fit them back together.

An *inro*, a small container with several compartments, which is hung from the *obi* (sash) of a kimono on a braided silk cord with a *netsuke* or toggle. This 19th-century *inro* is made of wood decorated with lacquer.

The original function of an *inro* was to carry the seals *(inkan)* and red ink paste with which the Japanese stamped their names on documents. However, medicines and tobacco were the items most commonly carried in *inro*. *Inro* were first used in Japan in the 17th century, and Japanese men wore them as a major fashion accessory during the middle and late Edo Era (1600–1868). *Inro* lacquer work was magnificent even on a small scale. Craftsmen had to painstakingly build up the body of an *inro*, applying numerous layers of lacquer to a wood base and smoothing and fitting the pieces. Artists then applied *maki-e*, intricate lacquer decorations that often included gold. Each *inro* had a unique design that made it a work of art. Flowers, birds, animals and other natural motifs were popular. When the Japanese began wearing Western clothing with pockets during the Meiji Era (1868–1912), *inro* fell out of fashion, but they were still made for the many foreign collectors who became fascinated with the beautiful little containers. See also KIMONO; LACQUER WARE; NETSUKE; OBI; SEALS AND SIGNATURES.

INSECTS See BUTTERFLY; CRICKET; FIREFLY.

INTANGIBLE CULTURAL ASSETS See LIVING NATIONAL TREASURES; NATIONAL TREASURES.

INTEGRATED CIRCUITS See COMPUTER INDUSTRY; FIFTH-GENERATION ADVANCED COMPUTER SYSTEMS; SEMICONDUCTOR INDUSTRY.

INTERNATIONAL MILITARY TRIBUNAL FOR THE FAR EAST See SUPREME COMMANDER FOR THE ALLIED POWERS; WAR CRIMES TRIALS.

INTERNATIONAL TRADE See EXPORTS AND IMPORTS; INVESTMENTS OVERSEAS, JAPANESE; JAPAN EXTERNAL TRADE ORGANI-ZATION; JOINT-VENTURE CORPORATION; MINISTRY OF INTERNATIONAL TRADE AND INDUSTRY; TRADING COMPANY, GENERAL.

INVESTMENTS OVERSEAS, JAPANESE Japanese companies have invested in foreign manufacturing either by establishing new, wholly owned facilities or by taking a minority or joint venture position in established operations. The largest Japanese investments have been made in East and Southeast Asian countries and more recently the United States. Investments are also important in Great Britain and Latin America. Around 26% of foreign investment funds go to the United States, 14% to Indonesia, 7% to Brazil, 5% to Australia and 4% to Great Britain. Close to 60% of Japanese foreign manufacturing investments are in manufacturing subsidiaries in Asia. Japanese investments in the United States and Europe have been mainly in commerce and finance, primarily to support the marketing of its export goods. Japanese companies are now increasing their investment in manufacturing in the United States, partly to avoid protectionist legislation against Japanese imports and partly to offset the rising value of the yen in the 1980s. Japan is now one of the world's largest exporters of capital, with net capital outflows of more than $50 billion annually. In March 1989, Japanese companies had invested $136.9 billion abroad. Japan is also the second largest shareholder in and provider of funds to the World Bank. Most of Japan's largest foreign investors are general trading companies such as Mitsubishi, Mitsui, and Marubeni.

When the yen was very strong from 1984 through March 1989, Japan invested $72 billion in the United States, $32 billion in Latin America and the Caribbean, $32 billion in Asia, and $30 billion in Europe. Japan is the second largest investor, after the United States, in Latin America, especially Chile, Mexico and Brazil. Japanese overseas investment is estimated to approach $160 billion in 1990, with more than half of that amount going to Asia and North America. The Institute for International Economics in Washington, D.C., estimates that by the year 2000, direct Japanese investment in the United States will total $300 billion. At present, Japan has around $53 billion invested in the United States, ranking it second to Great Britain ($97 billion). One reason the Japanese invest heavily in the United States is that it is the world's largest market for consumer goods, many of which are manufactured and exported by Japanese companies. Major investments include acquisitions and mergers of companies, joint ventures between Japanese and foreign companies, real estate and manufacturing plants. One example is the purchase of the Firestone Tire and Rubber Company by the Bridgestone Corporation of Japan. Bridgestone intended to invest $1.5 billion in Firestone, including research and plant modernization. Sony Corporation acquired CBS Records and Columbia Pictures; Matushita acquired Motorola's Quasar television division; Toyota established a joint venture with General Motors; and Nissan established an automobile manufacturing plant in Tennessee.

American companies have called for protectionist legislation against Japanese investors because they feel that they have been prevented from directly competing in many

Japanese markets. Officials in Washington are also concerned that Japanese investment in American companies, especially in strategic industries such as aerospace and semiconductors, is a threat to American national security. However, many state and local governments welcome Japanese investment because it brings jobs and economic prosperity to their regions. Japanese government agencies and corporations have become active lobbyists with the U.S. government, spending around $150 million a year on information gathering, legal counsel, and political campaigns to ensure Japanese access to American markets and scientific and technical research. See also CORPORATIONS; EXPORTS AND IMPORTS; JOINT-VENTURE CORPORATION, RESEARCH AND DEVELOPMENT; TRADING COMPANY, GENERAL.

IO ISLANDS (VOLCANO ISLANDS) See BONIN ISLANDS; IWO JIMA.

IOJIMA ISLAND AND BATTLE See BONIN ISLANDS; IWO JIMA; WORLD WAR II.

IRIOMOTE ISLAND See CAT; RYUKYU ISLANDS.

IRIS Several varieties of iris are native to Japan, and are called in Japanese *ayame, kakitsubata, shaga* and *hanashobu*. They grow both wild and under cultivation. A flower called *shobu*, commonly identified as an iris but actually the sweet flag, has been associated with the Boys' Day Festival (Tango no Sekku; now called the Children's Day Festival (Kodomo no hi), which is held on May 5th (traditionally, the fifth day of the fifth month in the lunar calendar). Because the leaves of the *shobu* look like swords, they were thought to make boys strong warriors. On Boys' Day, Japanese traditionally drank sake (rice wine) with *shobu* petals in it and floated *shobu* leaves in bath water. Before going into battle, samurai drank sake with chopped *shobu* leaves, because the word *shobu* has the same pronunciation as the Japanese word for victory. Japanese wore garlands of *shobu* on their heads on this day during the Nara Era (710–794) because they believed that the flower could repel evil spirits. During the Heian Era (794–1185), they practiced the Chinese custom of hanging irises from the eaves of roofs as protection from evil spirits. The *kakitsubata* variety of iris, which grew in Korea, China and Siberia, was the first variety of iris that was known in Japan. The Japanese used its juice as a clothing dye. Cultivation of irises became highly developed in the Edo Era (1600–1868), especially in a garden in Edo (present-day Tokyo), which is now called Horikiri. Other iris gardens in Tokyo are located in Meiji Shrine, Yasukini Shrine, Jindai Botanical Garden and Tokyo Shobu Garden (Shobu-en). See also BATH; CHILDREN'S DAY FESTIVAL; GARDENS; MEIJI SHRINE; SAKE; SAMURAI; SWORD; YASUKUNI SHRINE.

IRORI See FARMHOUSE; HEARTH; KETTLE.

ISE, TALES OF (*Ise Monogatari*) A collection of more than 100 stories that was compiled in the 10th century A.D. *Tales of Ise* is the oldest surviving text of the genre *uta monogatari*, or stories written in a combination of prose and poetry.

Members of the court in the late Heian Era (794–1185) had to know the *Tales of Ise,* along with the *Kokinshu,* an anthology of poems commissioned by the imperial government c. A.D. 905, in order to be considered well bred. Different versions of the *Tales of Ise* contain from 125 to 140 episodes. The book's title comes from episode number 69 in a 10th-century version that tells of the ninth-century poet Ariwara no Narihira visiting Ise, the most sacred shrine of Shinto. The *Tales of Ise* influenced many later literary works in Japan, including *The Tale of Genji* by Murasaki Shikibu. Commentaries were written about *Tales of Ise* beginning in the 12th century, and it was one of the most read and imitated classical literary works in the Edo Era (1600–1868), when beautifully illustrated editions of the book were printed. See also GENJI, THE TALE OF; HEIAN ERA; KOKINSHU; MONOGATARI; POETRY.

ISE-SHIMA NATIONAL PARK (Ise-Shima Kokuritsu Koen) A heavily visited national park on Shima Peninsula jutting into the Pacific Ocean on eastern central Honshu Island. The park covers 214.4 square miles and includes the mountainous interior of the peninsula and a beautiful coastline. Tour buses travel along the Ise-Shima Skyline Highway. The most important sites within the park are Ise Shrine; the "wedded rocks" (*meotoiwa*), two rocks in Ise Bay at Futamigaura that are bound by a straw rope that represents fidelity in marriage; and the cultured pearl farms at Toba, where traditional women pearl divers (*ama*) provide a popular attraction. The Marine Land Aquarium is located in the town of Kashikojima. Ago Bay on the southern coast of Shima Peninsula is the most scenic area of the park and is also a center for pearl cultivation and fishing. See also FUTAMIGAURA; ISE SHRINE; NATIONAL PARKS; PEARL.

ISE SHRINE (Ise Jingu) The most important shrine of Shinto, the indigenous Japanese religion. Ise Shrine, located on the Shima Peninsula jutting into the Pacific Ocean on east central Honshu Island, enshrines Sun Goddess Amaterasu o Mikami, ancestral *kami* (divine spirit) of the Japanese imperial line.

Members of the Japanese imperial family still go to Ise Shrine to report important family events. The prime minister of Japan also visits Ise upon being elected, and returns every New Year to pray for the nation's prosperity. Ise Shrine also houses the sacred mirror (*kagami*), one of the three imperial regalia symbolizing imperial power.

The *Nihon Shoki*, an official chronicle compiled in A.D. 720, records the founding of Ise Shrine. During the reign of Emperor Suinin, probably around A.D. 260, the mirror revered as the embodiment of Amaterasu was transported to Ise, whose site was chosen by the emperor's daughter, Princess Yamatohime. From her time until the reign of Emperor Go-Daigo (r. 1318–1339), every priestess of Ise Shrine was an imperial princess. Ise Shrine was closed to the Japanese public until after the Onin War in 1467. On its reopening, it quickly became a popular pilgrimage site, and today millions of Japanese visit Ise on New Year's Day.

The main building of the Inner Shrine (Ko Taijingu or

Naiku) is made of unpainted cypress wood (hinoki), joined without nails in the natural, unadorned style typical of Shinto shrines. The simple crossbeams and thatched roofs resemble storehouses and granaries in ancient Japan. The building is torn down and rebuilt every 21 (formerly every 20) years. This rite, known as shikinen sengu, was last performed in 1973. The old wood is cut into small pieces and given to the thousands of pilgrims who attend the ceremony. Among the other rituals held at the shrine, the most important is Kannamesai, the dedication of the harvest of new rice every October.

The Outer Shrine (Toyouke [or Toyuke] Daijingu or Geku), erected in the fifth century A.D., is dedicated to Toyouke (Toyuke) Daijin, kami of food, clothing and housing. A white stallion belonging to the emperor accompanies the offerings of food that are made every morning at the shrine. The chronicle Kojiki (A.D. 712), records how this shrine was moved from the imperial palace to Ise. It too is made from cypress and is torn down and rebuilt periodically.

The buildings of Ise Shrine, approached through large wooden torii gates, are surrounded by a tranquil forest of camphor and cryptomeria trees. Chickens are kept in the shrine precincts because a crowing rooster supposedly helped lure Amaterasu out of the cave where she was hiding in anger from her wicked brother Susanoo no Mikoto. In the vicinity of Ise there are 14 affiliated shrines. See also AMATERASU O MIKAMI; ARCHITECTURE; CYPRESS WOOD; EMPEROR; IMPERIAL REGALIA; KOJIKI; MIRROR; NIHON SHOKI; PILGRIMAGE, SHINTO; SHRINES, SHINTO; TORII; WOODWORKING.

ISHIGAKI ISLAND   See RYUKYU ISLANDS.

ISHII MITSUJIRO (1889–1981)   A senior politician who helped form and later became an elder statesman of the Liberal Democratic Party (LDP), Japan's major political party. He graduated from the Tokyo Higher School of Commerce (now Hitotsubashi University) and pursued a career in journalism, which led to his position as managing director of the newspaper Asahi Shimbun Sha. In 1946 he was elected to the House of Representatives, the Lower House of the Japanese parliament (known as the Diet). In 1953 he was appointed Minister of Transportation, after which he held several other cabinet posts, the most important of which was head of the Ministry of International Trade and Industry (MITI). By 1960 Ishii was a prominent leader of the Liberal Democratic Party and waged an unsuccessful campaign to become party president. In 1967 he was elected Speaker of the House of Representatives. See also DIET; LIBERAL DEMOCRATIC PARTY; MINISTRY OF INTERNATIONAL TRADE AND INDUSTRY.

ISHIKAWA JUN (1899–)   A modern Japanese novelist, translator and literary critic. Ishikawa was born in Tokyo and educated in French literature at the Tokyo School of Foreign Languages. He and his classmate Yamanouchi Yoshio (1894–1973) first translated the novels of French writer Andre Gide into Japanese in the 1920s. In 1935 Ishikawa published a number of first-person fictional re-

flections of a struggling writer living in Tokyo. The next year he published his first novel, The Bodhisattva (Fugen), which won the prestigious Akutagawa Prize for Japanese literature. In 1939 he published his novel A Plain Sketch (Hakubyo). Ishikawa attempted to leave Japan during World War II but the authorities refused to grant him permission to do so. The Japanese military banned his work "I Hear the War God Singing" ("Marusu no uta"; 1938). During the war he published a literary critique and a biography of two Japanese authors, as well as an essay, "All about Literature" ("Bungaku undo"; 1942), advancing his theory of writing and living. Ishikawa found relief from the war by immersing himself in Japanese literature written during a period of the Edo Era (1600–1868) called the Temmei Era (1781–1789). He believed this literature, especially a form of comic verse known as kyoka, was the first truly modern writing in Japan. Ishikawa gained notoriety in the postwar era as a member of the "libertine" (buraiha) or "new burlesque" (shingesaku) literary movement, so-named for their nonconformist life-style, which mirrored the riotous living in the novels (gesaku, burlesque parodies) of the lively Edo Era. He published a number of short stories between 1946 and 1948 that brought him fame, including "Legenda Aurea" ("Ogon densetsu"; 1946) and "Christ amidst the Ruins" ("Yakeato no Iesu," 1946). From 1950 on, Ishikawa turned to writing surreal and experimental novels, the best known of which are Hawks (Taka; 1953), Lays of the White-Haired (Hakutogin; 1957), Wild Spirits (Aratama; 1963) and The Millenium (Shifukusennen; 1965). Ishikawa's novel Asters (Shion Monogatari; 1956, translated 1961) was awarded the Prize of the Minister of Education for the finest work of Japanese literature in 1957. He also continued to write short stories and essays on many aspects of literature and on art in general. Ishikawa revived a literary form known as kijinden, or sketches of interesting people in Japanese history, under the title, Eccentrics and Gallants around the Country (Shokoku kijinden; 1955–1957). The wide body of writing produced by Ishikawa combined a 20th-century modernist outlook with literary traditions from the Temmei Era. Ishikawa's interest in French literature and universal themes have led him to be classified as one of Japan's three "internationalist" writers, along with Abe Kobo (1924–) and Oe Kenzaburo (1935–). See also ABE KOBO; AKUTAGAWA RYUNOSUKE; EDO ERA; NOVELS; OE KENZABURO.

ISLANDS   See AMAMI ISLANDS; FERRIES; BONIN ISLANDS; DEJIMA; GEOGRAPHY OF JAPAN; HOKKAIDO ISLAND; HONSHU ISLAND; IWO JIMA; KURIL ISLANDS; KYUSHU ISLAND; RYUKYU ISLANDS; SHIKOKU ISLAND; TSUSHIMA ISLAND.

ISOLATION OF JAPAN   See DEJIMA; DUTCH IN JAPAN; PERRY, MATTHEW CALBRAITH; PORTUGUESE IN JAPAN; SECLUSION, NATIONAL; TOKUGAWA SHOGUNATE.

ISSEI   The first generation of Japanese immigrants to other countries, primarily the United States, Canada, and Brazil. Issei were born in Japan but went abroad to work and save money with hopes that they could return to a comfortable life in Japan. In 1868, a group of 1418 Japanese men were recruited by an American to work on sugar plantations in Hawaii. Their harsh treatment there led the Japanese government to forbid immigration to Hawaii until 1885. In 1869 about two dozen Japanese men went to California to farm, but were not successful. Only in 1885–1886, when the Japanese government made migration much easier for its citizens, did large numbers of workers leave Japan. Most of them were single young men who had grown up on farms. They worked as contractual laborers on sugar plantations, farms or railroads, or for lumber and mining industries. Japanese workers often took the place of Chinese immigrants, who had been excluded from the United States in 1882. A "picture bride" system developed, whereby the men could be married by proxy and have their wives sent from Japan. The children of these *issei* parents were born in the new countries and are known as *nisei,* or "second generation." The grandchildren of *issei* are known as *sansei,* or "third generation." Many *issei* parents sent their children back to Japan to live with their relatives and to be educated or find better economic opportunities. However, few *issei* returned to live in Japan. They worked very hard to support their children, and suffered a great deal from racial prejudice. About 270,000 Japanese came to the United States from 1868 until they were excluded by the U.S. Immigration Act of 1924. Nearly half of them came in the short period 1901–1908. A much small number emigrated to the western Canadian province of British Columbia. During World War II, *issei* and *nisei* on the West Coast of the United States and Canada were forced into internment camps, for which they have successfully sought redress. Japanese still emigrate to Brazil, where they are active mainly in agriculture. *The Issei: The World of the First Generation Japanese Immigrants, 1885–1924,* by Yuji I. Chioka, was published in 1989. See also IMMIGRANTS, JAPANESE; NISEI; PICTURE BRIDE; SANSEI.

ISSEI MIYAKE   See FASHION DESIGNERS, CONTEMPORARY.

ISUZU MOTOR CO., LTD.   See AUTOMOBILE INDUSTRY.

ITAGAKI TAISUKE (1837–1919)   The founder of the Liberal Party, the first major political party in Japan. Itagaki was born to a samurai family in the Tosa region of Shikoku Island and was sent to the capital city of Edo (now Tokyo) to be educated. After a period of conflict with Tosa officials, Itagaki was appointed to handle financial and military concerns in the Edo residence of the *daimyo* (lord) of Tosa. He joined Saigo Takamori (1827–1877), a leader from the southern region of Satsuma, and others in overthrowing the Tokugawa government (1603–1867) and returning the emperor to a central position with the Meiji Restoration of 1868. Itagaki served in the new Meiji government but resigned in 1873 to protest the rejection by other Meiji leaders of Saigo Takamori's plan to invade Korea. Itagaki and his companions from Tosa (by then called Kochi Prefecture) organized the Public Party of Patriots (Aikoku Koto) in Tokyo, which in 1874 issued the Tosa Memorial criticizing the Meiji government and calling for a Japanese national assembly. Itagaki then founded two more political organizations, the Self-Help Society (Risshisha) and the Society of Patriots (Aikokusha), which advocated *minken,* or popular rights. This was a new concept in Japan, stimulated by the interest in Western political institutions.

Itagaki rejoined the Meiji government in 1875 but soon resigned again because the newly created *Genroin,* a group of respected elder statesmen, had no real legislative power. In 1877 Itagaki called for a Japanese constitution, and he continued to work for a national assembly that would represent the Japanese people. In October 1881 he helped found the Liberal Party (Jiyuto; literally, the "Freedom Party"), the first real political party in Japan. The following year he went to Europe to study constitutional systems of government, and the Liberal Party disintegrated while he was away, finally closing in 1884. Itagaki's campaign for popular rights enabled the party to be reborn as the Rikken Jiyuto in 1890, when the first session of Japan's Diet (Parliament) was held. Prime Minister Ito Hirobumi (1841–1909) appointed Itagaki as home minister of his second cabinet. Itagaki also negotiated with Okuma Shigenobu, head of the Shimpoto (Progressives), Japan's second major political party, to unite the two parties. They did so in 1898 under the name Constitutional Party (Kenseito), but the coalition lasted only four months. After a brief attempt to continue his political party, Itagaki left politics altogether to write books. However, the two political movements led by Itagaki and Okuma have lasted in various way to the present day in Japan. Since World War II, the Liberal Democratic Party (LDP) has been the dominant force in Japanese politics. See also GENRO; ITO HIROBUMI; LIBERAL DEMOCRATIC PARTY; MEIJI RESTORATION OF 1868; POLITICAL PARTIES; OKUMA SHIGENOBU; SAIGO TAKAMORI; TOKUGAWA SHOGUNATE.

ITAMI AIRPORT   See AIRLINES AND AIRPORTS.

ITAMI JUZO   See TAX SYSTEM.

ITO HIROBUMI (1841–1909)   A Meiji statesman who became the first prime minister of Japan. Ito worked to overthrow the Tokugawa Shogunate (1603–1867) and bring about the Meiji Restoration of 1868, helped draft the first Japanese constitution, and served as prime minister four times (1885–1888, 1892–1896, 1898, 1900–1901). He also founded the political party Seiyukai (Friends of Constitutional Government Party) in 1900, which was revived after World War II as the Liberal Party.

Ito was born in Choshu Province (modern Yamaguchi Prefecture) on the southwestern tip of Honshu Island, a stronghold of opposition to the Tokugawa Shogunate. He was educated in a school that advocated the restoration of imperial power, and studied Western military methods in Nagasaki. In 1862 he went to Edo (modern Tokyo), the Tokugawa capital, with Kido Takayoshi (1833–1877), who became another important Meiji leader. They joined the proimperial, anti-Western movement, which was known by its slogan: Revere the Emperor, Expel the Barbarians *(Sonno joi).* Choshu made Ito a member of the samurai class in 1863 and sent him abroad (despite the Tokugawa policy of national seclusion) with other young samurai to learn about the West. His experiences convinced Ito that Japan should open itself to Western nations. He conducted negotiations after Choshu and Western powers attacked each other in the Straits of Shimonoseki, and worked for an alliance between Choshu and Satsuma Province (modern Kagoshima Prefecture), which also produced anti-shogunal forces. Leaders from Satsuma and Choshu guided the overthrow of the Tokugawa Shogunate and the founding of a modern system of government under the Meiji Restoration of 1868. Ito became a junior councillor *(san'yo)* for foreign affairs and then held numerous other positions in the Meiji government. In 1870 he studied Western systems of currency in the United States, then joined the Iwakura Mission of 1871, sent by the Meiji government to examine political and educational systems in the United States and Europe. Ito remained in the Meiji government when many other leaders resigned during political crises over a proposed Japanese military invasion of Korea in 1873 and a Japanese military expedition to Taiwan in 1874. He helped suppress the Satsuma Rebellion of disgruntled samurai against the Meiji government, led by Saigo Takamori (1827–1877), in 1877. Saigo committed suicide, Kido died soon after, and another Meiji leader, Okubo Toshimichi (1830–1878), was assassinated in 1878. Ito and Okuma Shigenobu (1838–1922) remained as the two most powerful leaders, but Okuma was removed from government in 1881 because he pressed for a rapid change to representative government in Japan. Ito became the first prime minister in 1885, while also serving as imperial household minister and chairman of the Constitutional Commission. He negotiated the Treaty of Shimonoseki after the Sino-Japanese War of 1894–1895. Ito had been put in charge of a government bureau to draft a constitution and was sent to Europe in 1882 to study European constitutional systems of government; he was impressed by the Prussian model. He decided that the emperor should remain at the center of Japan's new constitutional system because the imperial throne symbolized the unique "body politic" or "national essence" *(kokutai)* of Japan. The constitution established a two-house Diet (Parliament), but kept the ministers of state, army and navy responsible to the emperor rather than to the Diet. The Meiji Constitution was promulgated by the emperor on February 11, 1889. The two-house Diet was established in 1890, with Ito chairing the House of Peers (upper house). He became prime minister a third time in 1898 but dissolved the Diet due to opposition to his tax policies from the political parties in the lower house. Those parties merged into one party, the Kenseito (Constitutional Party), led by Okuma and Itagaki Taisuke (1837–1919), who formed a new cabinet when Ito resigned as prime minister. In 1900 Ito founded a pro-government political party, the Friends of Constitutional Government Party (Rikken Seiyukai), and formed a fourth cabinet as prime minister. Ito left politics in 1901 and traveled to Russia to strengthen trade relations between Japan and that nation. In 1903 Ito for the third time became head of the Privy Council (Sumitsuin), the highest-ranking advisory body to the emperor and Meiji government. After the Russo-Japanese War (1904–1905) gave Japan control over Korea's foreign relations, Ito became the first Japanese resident-general in Korea. In 1907 he forced the Korean emperor to abdicate so that Japan could claim a full protectorate over Korea. In 1909 An Chung-gun, a Korean nationalist, assassinated Ito in Manchuria. See also CHOSHU; CONSTITUTION, MEIJI (1889); DIET; FRIENDS OF CONSTITUTIONAL GOVERNMENT PARTY: ITAGAKI TAISUKE; IWAKURA MISSION; KIDO TAKAYOSHI; KOKUTAI; KOREA AND JAPAN; MEIJI RESTORATION OF 1868; OKUBO TOSHIMICHI; OKUMA SHIGENOBU; POLITICAL PARTIES; PRIME MINISTER; REVERE THE EMPEROR, EXPEL THE BARBARIANS; RUSSO-JAPANESE WAR; SAIGO TAKAMORI; SATSUMA PROVINCE; SATSUMA REBELLION OF 1877; SEIYUKAI; SHIMONOSEKI; SINO-JAPANESE WAR OF 1894–1895; TOKUGAWA SHOGUNATE.

ITOH, C., & CO., LTD. (Itochu Shoji) The third-largest general trading company *(sogo shosha)* in Japan. The company was begun in 1858 when Ito (or Itoh in different phonetics) Chubei sold cloth in the Japan provinces. In 1885 Ito started trading with other Asian countries, and developed the company into a trading firm that imported raw cotton and exported cotton yarn. The company's success made it Japan's third-largest general trading company during World War II. After the war, it was reorganized as C. Itoh & Co., Ltd., and diversified from textiles into many other industries, including chemicals, machinery, metals, processed food and petrochemicals. C. Itoh has been active in the field of energy resources, such as developing oil fields in Indonesia and importing oil from Middle East countries. After the oil crisis of 1973 in Japan, Ataka & Co., the 10-largest trading company, declared bankruptcy and merged with C. Itoh. In 1976 C. Itoh acquired the Ataka Corporation, a producer of chemicals, iron and steel. C. Itoh has close to 100 overseas branches and offices, and about half as many foreign affiliates. Head offices are in Tokyo and Osaka. See also CORPORATIONS; EXPORTS AND IMPORTS; TRADING COMPANY, GENERAL.

ITSUKUSHIMA SHRINE See MIYAJIMA.

IWAKURA MISSION (Iwakura Kengai Shisetsu) A delegation sent to the United States and Europe to study Western government and culture by the Meiji government for 18 months (1871–1873) shortly after the establishment of the Meiji regime in 1868. The purpose of the mission was to gather information about Western society and government, visit leaders of 15 Western countries with which Japan had signed diplomatic and economic treaties (Ansei Commercial Treaties), and learn what Japan could do to press for revisions of those treaties, which the Japanese recognized as unfavorable to them. The mission was named for its chief ambassador, Iwakura Tomomi (1825–1883), a powerful senior minister in the Japanese government. Others who served as vice-ambassadors of the mission were Ito Hirobumi, Kido Takayoshi, Okubo Toshimichi and Yamaguchi Naoyoshi, all new Meiji leaders. Heads of government bureaucracies, interpreters, secretaries and attendants brought the number of members to approximately 50 (some members were replaced by other appointees during the mission). Fifty-four Japanese students also accompanied the mission, including five girls, from 6 to 15 years old, who were the first Japanese females to study outside Japan. Tsuda Umeko, the youngest girl, stayed in the United States for 11 years and later founded Tsuda College for Women in Tokyo. The Iwakura Mission spent seven months in the United States, four months in Great Britain and seven months on the European continent. On the return voyage they stopped at leading ports in South Asia and China. Members of the mission were always ceremoniously received by royalty and heads of state. The delegates realized that they would not be able to immediately revise the Ansei Commercial Treaties. However, the information they acquired led to the development of a Japanese constitution in 1889. They also brought back a knowledge of modern manufacturing and trading practices that would enhance the Japanese economy. The delegates, however, recognized that Japan did not have to borrow Western culture on a wide scale but could retain its uniqueness. Iwakura's private secretary, Kume Kunitake, compiled a five-volume account of the journey, *A True Account of the Tour in America and Europe of the Special Embassy (Tokumei zenken taishi: Beio kairan jikki)*. See also ANSEI COMMERCIAL TREATIES; CONSTITUTION, MEIJI (1889); ITO HIROBUMI; KIDO TAKAYOSHI; MEIJI RESTORATION OF 1868; OKUBO TOSHIMICHI.

IWO JIMA (Io Jima) An island of the Volcano Island (Io Island) group in the Pacific Ocean nearly a thousand miles south of Tokyo. This island group, and the Bonin Islands to the northeast, were claimed as Japanese territory in the late 1800s. The largely uninhabited Volcano and Bonin Islands became strategically important for Japan during World War II. American military forces wanted to take Iwo Jima to establish an air base from which escort planes could accompany B-29 planes bombing the main islands of Japan. The Americans could also use Iwo Jima to block Japanese sea-lanes and defend American bomber bases in the Mariana Islands to the south. The Japanese general on Iwo Jima, Kuribayashi Tadamichi, had his army of 23,000 soldiers dig bunkers into the volcanic soil and fortify its caves with machine guns and mortars. Thirty-thousand American marines landed on Iwo Jima on February 9, 1945. During the terrible fighting, the Americans pushed the Japanese back to Mount Suribachi, where a famous photograph was taken of five Marines and a Navy corpsman raising the American flag on February 23rd. A statue of this flag raising on Iwo Jima was erected in Arlington National Cemetery in Washington, D.C. The Battle of Iwo Jima, which lasted for nearly one month, was one of the bloodiest of World War II. Close to 7,000 Americans were killed and another 18,000 wounded. Only about 1,000 Japanese survived the battle. Two monuments have been placed on Mount Suribachi, a black marble stone for the Japanese and a statue of the flag raising for the Americans. Iwo Jima was administered by the United States during the Occupation of Japan after the war but was returned to Japanese rule in 1968. Now it is uninhabited except for Japanese and American scientific research teams. See also BONIN ISLANDS; PACIFIC OCEAN; WORLD WAR II.

IZANAGI AND IZANAMI Brother and sister deities who were the male and female creators of Japan and the *kami* (divine spirits) of Shinto, the indigenous Japanese religion. Their full names are Izanagi no Mikoto and Izanami no Mikoto. Myths recorded in the eighth-century A.D. historical chronicles *Kojiki* and *Nihon Shoki* relate that Izanagi and Izanami stood on the Floating Bridge of Heaven and dipped the Heavenly Jeweled Spear down into the ocean. Drops of brine that fell from the spear formed the island of Onokorojima, where they descended and married. Izanami gave birth to the islands of Japan and numerous *kami*, who are associated with aspects of nature such as the sea, mountains, rivers, trees and agriculture. She was burned and died while giving birth to the fire deity, Kagutsuchi no Kami. Izanagi killed him and went to the Land of Darkness *(Yomi no kuni)* to find Izanami. Despite her pleas not to, he looked at her and saw how terribly her body had decayed. Izanagi had to perform a ceremony of purification *(misogi)* by bathing in the sea. This act created many more gods, including the Sun Goddess Amaterasu O Mikami, the Moon God Tsukumi no Mikoto, and Amaterasu's brother Susanoo no Mikoto. See also AMATERASU NO MIKAMI; KAMI; KOJIKI; NIHON SHOKI; PURIFICATION; SHINTO; SUSANOO NO MIKOTO.

IZU PENINSULA A popular resort area on the Pacific Ocean southwest of Tokyo, with a dramatic coastline, fine beaches and hot springs. The Japanese imperial family maintains a resort on Izu Peninsula, which is part of the Fuji-Hakone-Izu National Park. The main town on the peninsula is the crowded hot-spring resort of Atami, whose name means "hot sea." One of the best public beaches is Yumigahama on the southeast tip of the peninsula. Near this beach is the town of Shimoda, where U.S. Commodore Matthew Perry anchored his ships in 1854. At Rosenji Temple in Shimoda, Perry and Tokugawa Shogunate (1603–1867) representatives signed a Treaty of Friendship to open Japan to the Western world. Shimoda is also where Townsend Harris, the first American consul in Japan, resided when he came to Japan in 1856 before moving permanently to Yokohama. Hofukuji Temple houses the tomb and personal belongings of Okichi, the Japanese mistress chosen for Harris who tragically drowned herself after he left Shimoda. The less-developed west side of Izu Peninsula offers beautiful scenery. See also ATAMI; FUJI-HAKONE-IZU NATIONAL PARK; HARRIS, TOWNSEND; HOT SPRING; PACIFIC OCEAN; PERRY, MATTHEW CALBRAITH; TOKUGAWA SHOGUNATE; YOKOHAMA.

IZUMI SHIKIBU (fl. c. 1000) The most talented poet of the mid-Heian Era (794–1185). Her poems number over 1,500 and are in the *waka* style (in which each poem has 31 syllables). Most of these poems are preserved in two collections, known as the *Seishu (Main Collection)* and the *Zokushu (Continued Collection)*. The *Shuishu*, the third anthology of *waka* sponsored by the imperial Government and published during Izumi's lifetime, contained one poem by her. The fourth such anthology, published after her death, contained 67 of her poems, more than any other poet. She wrote poems in every style that was used at that time, from simple verses about nature to complex philosophical works. Izumi was known to have been romantically involved with a number of men, and many of her poems have love as their theme. Her greatest love was Prince Atsumichi (981–1007), and she wrote more than 100 poems to mourn his early death. A literary diary has been preserved that recounts the love story of Izumi and Prince Atsumichi, the *Diary of Izumi Shikibu (Izumi Shikibu Nikki)*. Scholars are divided as to whether she herself actually wrote this story, although most believe that she did. Izumi also wrote on Buddhist themes such as enlightenment and the renunciation of passion. See also DIARIES; HEIAN ERA; POETRY; WAKA.

IZUMO SHRINE (Izumo Taisha; Izumo no Oyashiro) A Shinto shrine at Taisha in Shimane Prefecture on southwest Honshu Island. The Japanese believe that the *kami* (divine spirits) of Shinto leave their own shrines for a month in October or November (depending on the lunar calendar) and travel to Izumo Shrine. In Izumo, this month is traditionally called *kamiarizuki* ("the month of the present gods"), whereas in the rest of Japan it is called *kannazuki* ("the month without gods"). A festival is held October 11–17 according to the old lunar calendar to welcome the gods to Izumo. Celebrants carry lighted torches from the beaches to lead the *kami* to the shrine, where they dwell in small box-shaped buildings that have been erected for their visit. The chief *kami* residing at Izumo Shrine is Okuninushi no Mikoto. Mythology recorded in the eighth century A.D. chronicles *Kojiki* and *Nihon Shoki* relate that Okuninushi gave his land to Ninigi no Mikoto when Ninigi was sent by his grandmother, the Sun Goddess Amaterasu o Mikami, from heaven to rule Japan. Okuninushi's actions so pleased her that she had a large shrine erected to him at Izumo. Japanese folk religion also associates Okuninushi with the Buddhist god Daikoku, one of the Seven Gods of Good Fortune. Stories about Okuninushi's father courting and marrying his mother at Izumo make the shrine a special place for weddings, and many Japanese travel to be married there. About 3 million people visit Izumo Shrine every year. See also AMATERASU O MIKAMI; DAIKOKU; KAMI; KOJIKI; NIHON SHOKI; NINIGI NO MIKOTO; SHRINES, SHINTO; SEVEN GODS OF GOOD FORTUNE.

J

JACL See JAPANESE-AMERICAN CITIZENS LEAGUE.

JAL See JAPAN AIR LINES CO., LTD.

JAPAN AIR LINES CO., LTD. (Nihon Koku) The primary Japanese international airline company, with a reputation for world-class service, safety and reliability. Japan Air Lines, known as JAL, is one of the world's largest international airline companies. Its famous logo is a crest *(mon)* of a red crane in a circle. JAL began as a joint-stock company in 1951, with corporate headquarters in Tokyo. It was reorganized in 1953 when the Japanese government acquired 50% of the company's shares and granted it exclusive rights to fly international routes into and out of Japan. The first JAL trans-Pacific flight took place in 1954. In 1967 JAL became the third international airline to fly around the world, and in 1970 it was the first non-Soviet airline permitted to fly regularly over Siberia. By 1982 the company was flying 82 airplanes abroad and within Japan, and its domestic routes handled more than 100 flights every day. JAL has an automated freight-handling operation, named JALTOS, based at New Tokyo International Airport at Narita. The airline also operates a chain of hotels around the world under the name JAL Hotel System International, and offers package tours under the names of JALPACK and ZERO. By 1987 JAL controlled 39% of the Pacific market, and had 50 Boeing 747 airplanes, the largest fleet of any company. The Japanese government sold its controlling shares of JAL in 1987 to end the special privileges that had enabled the company to become a monopoly, so as to make it more competitive. JAL has been restructured into three separate divisions: international passenger service, domestic passenger service, and cargo and mail service. See also AIRLINES AND AIRPORTS; CREST.

JAPAN ALPS Three picturesque mountain ranges across the spine of the main island of Honshu. They were first called the Japan Alps in 1896 by Walter Weston, a British missionary and mountaineer, who compared them to the European Alps. Northernmost is the Hida Range, comprising Central Mountains (Chubu Sangaku) National Park, in Nagano Prefecture. In the middle are the Central Alps, or Kiso Range. The third is the Southern Alps, or Akaishi Range. Kitadake (North Peak) on Mount Shirane in the Southern Alps is the second highest peak in Japan, after Mount Fuji. Next highest are Mount Hotakadake and Mount Yarigatake in the Hida Range. Weston called Yarigatake the "Matterhorn of Japan." All of these peaks are higher than 10,000 feet at above sea level.

Before modern times, mountains in Japan were believed to be the sacred dwelling places of divine spirits. A few mountains were climbed and consecrated by early Buddhist leaders, such as Kukai, opening them to religious pilgrims. Weston popularized mountain climbing, and now many Japanese vacation in the Japan Alps. A festival honoring Weston is held in Kamikochi Village in the northern Hida Range every year on the first Sunday in June, when the mountain-climbing season begins. The Northern Alps, which meet the Sea of Japan on the west coast of Honshu, receive heavy snowfall in winter, and snow lies on peaks and in valleys all year round. Nights are cold even in summer, and storms are always a threat to climbers. Some peaks of this range are in fact active volcanoes. Mount Yakedake (Burnt Mountain) erupted in 1962. Tateyama, a group of three mountains in the Hida Range, is one of the three holy mountains in Japan, along with Fuji-san and Hakusan in central Honshu. The Southern Alps comprise Minami Alps National Park and are close to Mount Fuji in central Honshu. The peaks of this range are not as rugged as those of the Northern Alps, and rather than being volcanoes, are composed of granite, sandstone or slate. As they are less accessible to mountain climbers and tourists, their natural beauty has remained unspoiled. See CLIMATE OF JAPAN; FUJI, MOUNT; HONSHU ISLAND; KUKAI; MOUNTAINS; NATIONAL PARKS; SEA OF JAPAN; SNOW; SNOW COUNTRY.

JAPAN-AMERICAN SOCIETIES Also known as Japan Societies; organizations throughout the U.S. that have an interest in relations between Japan and the United States. The first Japan Societies were founded in Boston (1905), San Francisco (1905), New York (1907), Los Angeles (1909), and Portland, Oregon (1907). They were social and business organizations whose leaders were mostly missionaries and socially prominent businessmen with connections in Japan. Commercial interests led to the founding of societies in Seattle (1923), the center of U.S. trade with Japan at the time, and Chicago (1930). Members of the Seattle Japan Society actively protested the 1924 U.S. law excluding all Japanese from emigrating to the U.S. Japan Societies ceased to function during World War II but reorganized themselves following the postwar Allied Occupation of Japan (1945–1952). Membership in the societies is open to the general public. The New York Japan Society is the wealthiest and most prominent of the societies, and sponsors a wide variety of lectures, Japanese film and theatrical programs, art exhibits, language classes, and political and economic programs. David Rockefeller donated a building opened officially in September 1971 and an extensive Japanese art collection to the New York Japan Society.

During the 1970s, as Japan became a world economic power rivaling the U.S., a growing number of Americans became interested in Japan. Scholarship on Japan and Asia in general also developed into a major academic field. The Japan-America Societies established programs to educate the American public about Japanese arts and culture, government and economics. In 1975, the U.S. Congress established the Japan-U.S. Friendship Commission, which promotes education and cultural exchange programs and which contributes administrative and financial support to the Japan-America Societies. In 1979, the Associated Japan-America Societies of the United States, a nonprofit national advisory organization, was established. Japan-America Societies have been founded in many other cities and states, including Atlanta, Los Angeles, Washington, D.C., and Fort Lee, N.J. and Tampa. There are also six U.S.-government-sponsored American Centers in Japan. In 1981 the Japanese government contributed $2 million to the endowment of the Japan-U.S. Friendship Commission, to which it gave another $3 million in 1986. The Japanese Ministry of Foreign Affairs established the Japan Foundation in 1972 to promote international cultural exchange, particularly in the humanities and social sciences. There are also Japan Societies in other countries, including Germany, Italy and France. See also JAPAN FOUNDATION.

JAPAN ATOMIC ENERGY RESEARCH INSTITUTE See SCIENCE AND TECHNOLOGY AGENCY.

JAPAN BROADCASTING CORPORATION (Nippon Hoso Kyokai) The Japanese national public broadcasting system. The government-owned Japan Broadcasting Corporation system, known as NHK, is supported by a service charge on television sets. There are two national channels. One broadcasts foreign-language courses and other educational programs, and the other offers news and popular entertainment similar to that on Japan's private networks—comedies, dramas, traditional and Western music and dance, and quiz shows. The NHK system also includes three radio networks, two FM and one AM. NHK has a reputation for the high quality of its programming. It broadcasts in more than 21 languages to an international audience in 18 world broadcast zones. Around 16,000 people are employed by NHK in Japanese and foreign cities.

Broadcasting began in Japan when the Tokyo Broadcasting Station was incorporated in 1925. The next year this station merged with two stations in the cities of Osaka and Nagoya to become Nippon Hoso Kyokai. During the American Occupation of Japan following World War II, NHK was controlled by the Supreme Commander of Allied Powers (SCAP). The Broadcast Law of 1950 reorganized NHK as a public corporation that would broadcast to all of Japan. The law also allowed for commercial broadcasting networks, which began operations in 1951. NHK is headed by an operation committee whose 12 members are appointed by the Japanese prime minister and approved by the Diet (Parliament). The Diet also controls the administration and budget of NHK. Operation committee members select the chairman of the board, who manages the network's operation. The NHK Center, located in the Shibuya district of Tokyo, is open to the public for daily tours. See also BROADCASTING SYSTEM; DIET; HARAJUKU; OCCUPATION OF JAPAN.

JAPAN CHAMBER OF COMMERCE AND INDUSTRY (Nihon Shoko Kaigisho) The national organization for chambers of commerce located in nearly 500 Japanese cities. Japanese chambers of commerce and industry first appeared in 1878 in the largest cities, such as Tokyo and Osaka. In 1922 the Japan Chamber of Commerce and Industry, or Nissho, as it is known, was formed to coordinate smaller businesses in Japan and to speak for their commercial interests both within Japan and abroad. Various international economic organizations maintain offices with Nissho, including the Federation of Asian Chambers of Commerce and Industry and the Pacific Economic Committee. See CORPORATIONS; EXPORTS AND IMPORTS; FOREIGN TRADE.

JAPAN COMMITTEE FOR ECONOMIC DEVELOPMENT See FEDERATION OF JAPANESE ECONOMIC ORGANIZATIONS.

JAPAN COMMUNIST PARTY (Nihon Kyosanto) A major opposition political party. The Japan Communist Party, or JCP, was founded in 1922 as a branch of Comintern, the international communist movement controlled by the Soviet Union. The goal of the JCP was to make Japan a worker's nation without an emperor. The Japanese government suppressed the JCP in the 1920s and 1930s until the party ceased functioning in 1935. The JCP became a legal political party for the first time in 1945, right after World War II. In 1949 the party won nearly 3 million popular votes and 35 seats in the House of Representatives (lower house of the Diet, or Japanese parliament). In 1948 student members of the JCP founded the Zengakuren (Zen Nihon Gakusei Jichikai Sorengo; All-Japan Federation of Student Self-Governing Associations), the largest student organization in Japan. The Zengakuren was controlled by the Communist Party until the mid-1950s, but since then has split into several factions.

The JCP lost popularity in the 1950s due to anticommunist sentiment during the Korean War and terrorist acts by some of its members. In the 1952 election the party lost all its seats in the House of Representatives. Years later the party regained some popularity, by emphasizing its independence from China and the Soviet Union and by developing a new image of responsibility and moderation. It broke with the Soviet Union in 1963 and with the Chinese Communists in 1965. The JCP won 39 seats in the House of Representatives, its highest number ever, in 1979, after which it reestablished formal ties with the Communist Party in the Soviet Union. It is still estranged from the Communist Party in China but has relations with communist parties in Western Europe. The JCP had 400,000 members in 1981, in addition to student members in a movement on university campuses known as Minsei (Nihon Minshu Seinen Domei; Democratic Youth League of Japan). The JCP has a large income, much of which comes from the sale of its publications. *Akahata (Red Flag)* had 3.5 million subscribers in 1981. In the 1980s, the Communist Party has advocated a neutral Japanese foreign policy, the cutting of military ties with the United States, and welfare and "quality of life" social issues in Japan. It also attacks what it calls the "monopoly capitalism" of the dominant

Liberal Democratic Party (Jiyu Minshuto). The JCP lost 11 of its 27 House of Representatives seats in the February 1990 elections. See also DIET; ELECTIONS; LIBERAL DEMOCRATIC PARTY; POLITICAL PARTIES; ZENGAKUREN.

JAPAN ECONOMIC JOURNAL See NEWSPAPERS.

JAPAN EXTERNAL TRADE ORGANIZATION (Nihon Boeki Shinkokai) Formerly called Japan Export Trade Research Association; a governmental association that promotes Japanese foreign trade. The Japan External Trade Organization (JETRO) was established in 1958 by the Ministry of International Trade and Industry (MITI) to promote exports by providing export information to Japanese companies. By the 1970s, Japanese exporters had become so successful that the balance of trade turned from a deficit to a surplus. JETRO slowly shifted from solely promoting exports to encouraging imports into Japan, furthering relations with Japan's trading partners, disseminating trade data, conducting marketing research and planning, and serving as a liaison between small businesses in Japan and other countries. To carry out these activities, JETRO opened offices in major foreign trading centers. By late 1981 JETRO had offices in more than 60 countries. In Japan, JETRO has sponsored trade exhibitions for foreign products and helped found the World Trade Mart in Tokyo, where foreign products are displayed for potential Japanese purchasers. See also EXPORTS AND IMPORTS; MINISTRY OF INTERNATIONAL TRADE AND INDUSTRY (MITI).

JAPAN FEDERATION OF EMPLOYERS' ASSOCIATIONS See FEDERATION OF ECONOMIC ORGANIZATIONS.

JAPAN FOLKCRAFT MUSEUM See HAMADA SHOJI; MINGEI; YANAGI SOETSU.

JAPAN FOUNDATION (Kokusai Koryu Kikin) A public corporation under the Japanese Ministry of Foreign Affairs that promotes international cultural exchange, with an emphasis on the humanities and social sciences. The Japan Foundation, founded in 1972, was developed from the Japan Cultural Society (Kokusai Bunka Shinkokai,) which was established in 1934. Today the Japan Foundation has 10 offices in foreign countries and a staff of nearly 150. Its headquarters are in Tokyo, with a branch office in Kyoto. The Japan Foundation invites foreign scholars, educators, artists, journalists and researchers to work in Japan and helps interested Japanese to study in other countries. So far the foundation's programs have invited nearly 4,000 people to Japan and sent more than 2,500 Japanese abroad. More than 4,000 high school teachers and other professionals have also visited Japan in group programs sponsored by the Japan Foundation. The foundation has promoted the study of Japanese culture and society by awarding more than 850 grants, sending hundreds of Japanese abroad as visiting scholars, and donating nearly a quarter of a million books to foreign institutions that study Japan. Moreover, the foundation has sent more than 1,000 Japanese language teachers abroad and brought hundreds of foreign teachers and students to take intensive courses in

Japan. In 1990 the Japan Foundation opened a Japanese language school in Saitama, near Tokyo. The foundation sends traditional and contemporary Japanese art exhibitions, performers and films to other countries, and sponsors foreign exhibitions, performances and films in Japan, especially from developing countries. It also maintains the Japan Foundation Library, a collection of 15,000 foreign-language books and journals about Japan. The library publishes collection guides and bibliographies on specific topics. The Japan Foundation receives tax-free contributions from private organizations and individuals who wish to support international cultural exchange programs. See also MINISTRY OF FOREIGN AFFAIRS.

JAPAN HOUSING CORPORATION See APARTMENT HOUSE.

"JAPAN INC." A phrase applied by foreigners to explain the unusually close working relationship between government and business in Japan, which makes it seem that the two form one powerful unit, "Japan Inc." The success of the Japanese economy has been due in large part to subsidies and privileges given to Japanese companies, starting in the Meiji Era (1868–1912). Large financial and industrial combines known as *zaibatsu* became very powerful in the 20th century. The Allied Occupation of Japan after World War II dissolved the *zaibatsu* and established an Anti-Monopoly Law and a Fair Trade Commission to encourage free enterprise. However, the Japanese government continued to place strong controls on Japanese business. It has done so mainly through the Ministry of International Trade and Industry (MITI), which has closely directed Japan's industrial growth. See also CORPORATIONS; MINISTRY OF INTERNATIONAL TRADE AND INDUSTRY; OCCUPATION OF JAPAN; ZAIBATSU.

JAPAN INDUSTRIAL COUNCIL See FEDERATION OF ECONOMIC ORGANIZATIONS.

JAPAN INFORMATION CENTER FOR SCIENCE AND TECHNOLOGY See SCIENCE AND TECHNOLOGY AGENCY.

JAPAN LINE, LTD. See SHIPPING AND SHIPBUILDING.

JAPAN NATIONAL TOURIST ORGANIZATION See JAPAN TRAVEL BUREAU.

JAPAN RAILWAYS (Nihon Tetsudo) Also known as JR; the company that operates the major passenger and freight railroad lines in Japan, as well as bus and ferry systems. The Japanese government founded JR as a public corporation named Japanese National Railways (JNR) in 1949. The government already owned the majority of Japanese railway lines, which had been destroyed during World War II, and wanted to reorganize the railroad system. However, by the 1980s JNR was sustaining large financial losses, so the Japanese government converted it into a private corporation in 1987, known as Japan Railways. Billions of passengers every year still ride more than 28,000 daily trains operated by JR on 13,200 miles of tracks which run throughout the main islands. JR is the largest enterprise in

Japan with assets of $48.5 billion in 1980. The company is headed by a president appointed by the prime minister's cabinet, a vice president, a chief engineer and directors and auditors, and has around half a million employees. JR is world famous for its efficient service and advanced railway technology, especially the high-speed Bullet Train (Shinkansen), which began operating in 1964. See also BULLET TRAIN; RAILROADS.

JAPAN SEA See SEA OF JAPAN.

JAPAN SOCIALIST PARTY (Nihon Shakaito) Also known as the Socialist Party of Japan; the second largest political party in postwar Japan and the largest opposition party. The Japan Socialist Party (JSP) was founded in 1906 but had to disband a year later because radical members antagonized the Japanese government. The party was founded once more after World War II by members of socialist groups that were active prior to the war. In 1947, during the postwar political turmoil, the JSP won a plurality of seats in the House of Representatives (lower house of the Diet, or Japanese parliament) which enabled it to form a coalition government. However, fighting between left-wing and right-wing factions within the JSP brought down its government in 1948, and the party was soundly defeated by conservative groups in the 1949 elections.

The party has always been divided by these two internal factions. In 1955 the factions agreed to come back together. However, the issues of foreign policy, the nationalization of major industries, the rearmament of Japan, and foreign alliances split the JSP during the 1950s. The JSP opposed Prime Minister Kishi Nobusuke's policies regarding the revision of the Mutual Security Treaty between Japan and the United States in 1960. Asanuma Inejiro (1898–1960), the chairman of the JSP, was assassinated by a right-wing fanatic during an election speech in 1960. In 1961 the moderate conservative wing of the JSP split off to form the Democratic Socialist Party (Minshato). The larger progressive faction remained as the JSP. In the 1960s and 1970s these two socialist parties together held about a third of the seats in the Diet's House of Representatives. Factional infighting within the JSP continued during this time. With economic growth, support for the party declined in Japanese cities, although it remained constant in rural areas. The JSP is largely supported by Sohyo, the General Council of Trade Unions of Japan, a federation of white-collar workers, teachers and other government employees. However, some unions belonging to Sohyo have supported the Japan Communist Party (Nihon Kyosanto). The Japan Socialist Party advocates the improvement of general social welfare, the holding down of consumer prices, and the abolition of high school and college entrance examinations. It has opposed the proposed revision of the Japanese constitution and wants to abolish the country's Self-Defense Forces (Jietei; abbreviated SDF). The current head of the JSP is Doi Takako (1928–), the first woman to head a political party in Japan. The JSP handed the LDP its first defeat in elections held July 23, 1989 for the House of Councillors (upper house of the Diet). The JSP won 46

seats, 25% of the House, which gave it a total of 86 seats and leadership in coalition with other opposition parties. The House of Councillors selected Doi as prime minister, but the House of Representatives chose Kaifu Toshiki, and its decision prevailed because the constitution gives priority to the lower house. In the February 18, 1990 elections for the House of Representatives, JSP jumped from 83 to 141 seats, but other oppisition parties lost ground, so they could not unite to elect Doi as prime minister. However, the JSP continues to play a leading role in Japanese politics. See also ASANUMA INEJIRO; DEMOCRATIC SOCIALIST PARTY; DIET; DOI TAKAKO; ELECTIONS; JAPAN COMMUNIST PARTY, LIBERAL DEMOCRATIC PARTY; POLITICAL PARTIES; PRIME MINISTER; RECRUIT SCANDAL; SECURITY TREATY BETWEEN JAPAN AND THE UNITED STATES.

JAPAN TIMES, THE See NEWSPAPERS.

JAPAN TRAVEL BUREAU, INC. (Nihon Kotsu Kosha) The largest travel agency in Japan, commonly known as the JTB. A semi-governmental agency with corporate headquarters in Tokyo, the JTB was founded in 1912 as the Japan Tourist Bureau to interest foreigners in visiting Japan. Its name was changed to the Japan Travel Bureau when it was incorporated as a nonprofit foundation in 1945. In 1963 the bureau's business department was reorganized as an independent private corporation, Japan Travel Bureau, Inc. The JTB makes reservations for hotel rooms and transportation, sells tickets for Japan Railways and other transport companies, offers tour packages, and publishes travel information and maps. It has 300 branch offices in Japan and more than a dozen overseas offices. Travel within Japan and abroad is becoming very popular with the Japanese, especially since the government has recently promoted the five-day work week to encourage leisure activities. In 1989, around 2 million Japanese traveled abroad. Popular destinations were Hawaii, California and Europe. Many Japanese newlyweds spend their honeymoons in Hawaii. Travel information is also provided to foreigners by the Japan National Tourist Organization (JNTO), another official agency with offices around the world. In Japan, JNTO maintains three Tourist Information Centers (TIC) in Tokyo, Kyoto and at New Tokyo International Airport in Narita. See also AIRLINES AND AIRPORTS; JAPAN RAILWAYS.

JAPAN-U.S. FRIENDSHIP COMMISSION See JAPAN-AMERICAN SOCIETIES.

JAPANESE-AMERICAN CITIZENS LEAGUE Abbreviated as JACL; an organization founded in 1930 to promote the political and civil rights of Japanese-Americans. Membership in JACL was originally limited to American citizens of Japanese descent, who at that time belonged to the second generation of Japanese-Americans, known as *nisei*. This policy excluded the first generation, known as *issei*, who had been born in Japan and immigrated to the United States and other countries. The JACL supported the U.S. military effort against Japan during World War II, and even acquiesced in the U.S. government's incarceration of West

Coast Japanese-Americans during the war, for which many members of JACL in the ten relocation camps were severely criticized by their fellow inmates. The JACL lobbied for the admittance of *nisei* into the American armed forces and the return to their homes of *nisei* who were proven loyal to the United States. After the war, the JACL continued its lobbying efforts, calling for a Japanese-American Claims Act; for a change in the naturalization laws that would apply the same conditions for naturalization to Asian as to European and African immigrants; and the end of long-standing discriminatory policies against Asians by the U.S. immigration system. Even though Japanese-Americans have been more readily accepted in American society during the past few decades, especially the *sansei* or third generation, the JACL has remained an influential organization. By 1980, the organization had more than 30,000 members. The JACL Legislative Education Committee worked for the passage of the Civil Liberties Act of 1988, which provides financial redress to Japanese-Americans who were incarcerated during World War II. A similar bill was passed in Canada for financial redress to Japanese-Canadians interned during the war. See also IMMIGRANTS, JAPANESE; ISSEI; NISEI; SANSEI; WORLD WAR II.

JAPANESE-AMERICANS See 442ND REGIMENTAL COMBAT TEAM; IMMIGRANTS, JAPANESE; ISSEI; JAPANESE-AMERICAN CITIZENS LEAGUE; NISEI; PICTURE BRIDE; SANSEI.

JAPANESE CONFEDERATION OF LABOR See DEMOCRATIC SOCIALIST PARTY; LABOR UNIONS.

JAPANESE METEOROLOGICAL AGENCY See TYPHOON; VOLCANO.

JAPANESE NATIONALITY LAW See MINORITIES IN JAPAN.

JAPANESE RED ARMY See RED ARMY FACTION.

JAPONISME See EXPOSITIONS, INTERNATIONAL; WOOODBLOCK PRINTS.

JAZZ See AKIYOSHI TOSHIKO.

JETRO See JAPAN EXTERNAL TRADE ORGANIZATION.

JEWELS, SACRED See AMATERASU O MIKAMI; EMPEROR; IMPERIAL REGALIA; NINIGI NO MIKOTO; TOMB MOUND; YAYOI ERA.

-JI See TEMPLES, BUDDHIST.

JICST (JAPAN INFORMATION CENTER FOR SCIENCE AND TECHNOLOGY) See SCIENCE AND TECHNOLOGY AGENCY.

JIJI PRESS See NEWSPAPERS.

JIMMU TENNO (Emperor Jimmu) The legendary first reigning emperor (*tenno*) of Japan as recorded in the ancient chronicles *Kojiki* (A.D. 712) and *Nihon Shoki* (A.D. 720). These texts date his reign as 660–585 B.C. However, these dates are far too early for Emperor Jimmu to be a historical figure. That he is a legend is seen in the story that he was the grandson of Ninigi no Mikoto, who was in turn the grandson of the Sun Goddess Amaterasu o Mikami. She gave her grandson Ninigi the three imperial regalia (the sacred sword, mirror, and jewel) that symbolize his power to rule Japan, and ordered him to descend from the sky to earth to establish his reign. The Japanese have believed that this mandate validates the rule of the imperial family from its legendary origin with Jimmu Tenno in 660 B.C. to the present.

The name Jimmu is a posthumous title that was given to this figure in the eighth century A.D. The ancient chronicles call him by several names, including Kamu Yamato Iware Hiko no Mikoto. They state that Jimmu was raised in Hyuga on Kyushu, the southernmost of the four main islands of Japan, and that he led an expedition in 667 B.C. to conquer the Yamato region of the main island of Honshu to the northeast. The story of this expedition, which supposedly took several years, does reflect the eastward expansion of an armed force of invaders from southwest Japan into the Yamato region. They were said to have taken a long route using the Seto Inland Sea, moved into the areas of present-day Okayama and Osaka, and defeated local warriors. The invaders finally came to the area currently known as Nara and enthroned Jimmu Tenno at a palace called Kashihara, according to the legend. Many issues and dates remain unsettled about the different versions of this legend, but it can be said that the ancestors of Japan's imperial family did migrate from Kyushu Island to the region of Yamato, where the emperors ruled, constructing capitals in the Asuka region, then Nara and finally Heiankyo, later known as Kyoto. See also AMATERASU O MIKAMI; ASUKA; EMPEROR; HEIANKYO; IMPERIAL REGALIA; INLAND SEA; KOJIKI; KYOTO; KYUSHU ISLAND; NARA; NIHON SHOKI; NINIGI NO MIKOTO; YAMATO.

JINGU, EMPRESS Also known as Empress Jingo; a legendary nonreigning empress (*kogo*). Modern scholars argue that Jingu is actually a composite of several women who ruled as shamans, or powerful religious mediators with divine spirits. The *Nihon Shoki*, a historical document written in A.D. 720, records that Jingu ruled as regent between the reigns of two legendary emperors, Chuai and Ojin, in the late fourth and early fifth centuries. Jingu was supposedly a consort of Chuai, and the daughter of Princess Katsuragai no Takanuka and Okinaga no Sukune. According to tradition, Chuai died fighting the Kumaso people of Kyushu Island. Jingu completed the conquest and then sailed to Korea to bring military assistance to the Korean state of Silla. It is a historical fact that Japanese military campaigns were waged against Korea in the late fourth century. When she returned to Japan, the story goes, Jingu gave birth to a son but did not allow him to take the throne. After her death her son became Emperor Ojin. See also EMPEROR; KOREA AND JAPAN; KYUSHU ISLAND; NIHON SHOKI; SHAMANS AND SHAMANISM; TENNO.

-JINJA See SHRINES, SHINTO.

JITO, EMPRESS (645–703) The 41st Japanese reigning sovereign (*tenno*), following the traditional method of counting. She reigned A.D. 686–697. Jito was the daughter of Emperor Tenji and the wife of Emperor Temmu. She assumed control when Temmu died in 686, and after the crown prince also died, Jito became the official reigning empress in 690. She followed the Buddhist religion, which had been introduced into Japan from China in the sixth century A.D. Jito also wrote poems in the *waka* style, and these were included in the *Manyoshu*, an important eighth-century poetry collection. She is best known for enacting the first set of laws in Japan, known as the Asuka Kiyomihara Code. Jito abdicated the throne to her grandson Prince Karu (who later became Emperor Mommu) in 697. She was the first imperial ruler to take the official title "retired sovereign" (*dajo tenno*). See also BUDDHISM; CHINA AND JAPAN; EMPEROR; MANYOSHU; TEMPLES, BUDDHIST; WAKA.

JIZO A popular Buddhist god who is the patron deity of children who have died and who also protects travelers. Jizo derives from an Indian god whose Sanskrit name is Ksitigarbha, "womb of the earth." He is depicted as a Buddhist monk holding a jewel and a staff. As a bodhisattva, or enlightened being, he has taken a vow to help all suffering beings. Faith in Jizo was introduced into Japan by Chinese Buddhist missionaries during the Heian Era (794–1185) and soon became associated with indigenous Japanese spirits. Stone statues of Jizo can be found in many temple compounds and along roadsides. Many of the statues have red bibs, like those worn by children, which have been placed on them by grateful worshippers. The grounds of Hasedera Temple in Kamakura contain more than 50,000 statues of Jizo. See also BUDDHISM; BODHISATTVA; CHILDREN IN JAPAN; KAMAKURA; SCULPTURE.

JOCHO (?–1057) The preeminent Japanese sculptor during the middle Heian Era (794–1185), and the originator of the workshop system (*bussho*) for the production of sculpture. During the Heian Era, all sculptures was associated with the Buddhist religion, which had been introduced from China in the sixth century A.D. Jocho, a Buddhist priest in the imperial capital of Kyoto, was one of the first artists in Japanese history to be honored by the imperial court, when imperial regent Fujiwara no Michinaga awarded him the rank of *hokkyo* ("bridge of the law"), in A.D. 1022 for his work at Hojoji Temple. In 1048 Jocho was raised to the higher rank of *hogen* ("eye of the law") for his sculpture and restoration work at Kofukuji Temple. These titles, usually awarded to highest-ranking Buddhist priests, set a precedent benefiting artists in later eras as well. Jocho's workshop system was made by possible by a new sculpture method known as the assembled or joined woodblock technique (*yosegi-zukuri*). Heian sculptors worked in wood and developed a method to carve portions of a sculpture from several smaller wood blocks and then join them together. Teams of craftsmen who specialized in different parts could work simultaneously, a kind of early mass production. The only sculpture by Jocho that has survived is a beautiful gilt-wood statue of Amida Buddha seated in meditation in the Phoenix Hall (Hoodo) of the Byodoin Temple (A.D. 1053) in Uji, near Kyoto. The elegance and graceful lines of Jocho's work, as seen in this statue, influenced Japanese Buddhist sculpture through the 12th century. See also AMIDA; BUDDHISM; FUJIWARA NO MICHINAGA; SCULPTURE; UJI.

JODO SHIN SECT OF BUDDHISM See PURE LAND SECT OF BUDDHISM.

JOINERY See HOMES AND HOUSING; JOCHO; SCULPTURE; WOODWORKING.

JOINT STAFF COUNCIL See SELF-DEFENSE FORCES.

JOINT-VENTURE CORPORATION (*goben kaisha*) A company that is jointly owned by Japanese and foreign partners. There have been many joint ventures in Japan because of Japanese laws that limited foreign investment in the country from the 1950s through the early 1970s. Because foreign companies were not able to establish wholly owned branches in Japan, especially in industries deemed crucial for economic development by the Ministry of International Trade and Industry (MITI), many foreign companies established relationships with Japanese companies in industries related to their own. Japanese companies entered into joint ventures as a way to access foreign technology and funds, for which their employees provided business expertise and channels for distributing products. This arrangement enabled the Japanese to successfully manufacture and market such products as computers, electronics and automobiles. More recently, as the Japanese economy has prospered, Japanese companies have gone abroad to benefit from foreign natural resources, cheap labor, and to get around foreign laws restricting imports, sometimes forming joint ventures. By the late 1970s, Japanese multinational corporations had operations throughout the world, in the areas of manufacturing, development of natural resources such as oil, and marketing and other service activities. Japanese joint ventures abroad have frequently been organized by Japanese general trading companies (*sogo shosha*) and specialty trading companies (*semmon shosha*), who locate business partners in host countries for Japanese manufacturers, thus forming three-way joint ventures. In some cases, Japanese companies that compete at home will combine their expertise to build a manufacturing plant in a foreign company for their mutual benefit. In other cases, individual Japanese companies will establish their own foreign subsidiaries for manufacturing and distributing their products. Japanese companies prefer to maintain majority ownership and control of their foreign subsidiaries. See also CORPORATIONS; TRADING COMPANY, GENERAL.

JOMON ERA (c. 10,000 B.C.–c. 300 B.C.) The first of the three prehistoric periods of Japanese history after the Paleolithic and Mesolithic eras. The hunting and gathering Jomon Era preceded the development of settled villages and agriculture, particularly wet-rice cultivation, in the

Yayoi Era (c. 300 b.–c. a.d. 300). The name Jomon, meaning "rope pattern" or "cord-marked," refers to pottery excavated at many sites dating from that era. Jomon pots had flat bottoms and were made by coiling clay and making decorative marks with cords of twisted plant fibers, sticks or shells. Clay figures (dogu) of animals and human beings, especially pregnant women, were also made. Hunting, fishing and gathering of shellfish, nuts and plants were the main methods of sustenance in the Jomon Era. People lived in small settlements with square covered pits in the ground for homes and storage places. They used tools made of stone or bone, and they stored and prepared food in pottery containers and wicker baskets. They may have worn simple robes made of bark from mulberry trees. Certain features of later Japanese culture appeared during the Jomon Era, such as the language, shamanism and characteristic beliefs about religion and nature. Various kinds of Jomon artifacts have been discovered throughout all of the Japanese islands. However, only those dating from the Late Jomon Era (c. 2500 b.c.–c. 1000 b.c. or c. 2000 b.c.–c. 1000 b.c.) show the same decorative styles regardless of where in Japan they were made. By the Final Jomon Era (c. 1000 b.c.–c. 300 b.c.), southern Japan was becoming a highly organized and ritualistic society. Rice was just beginning to be cultivated on Kyushu Island, where it probably had been introduced from southern China. See also kyushu; mulberry bush; pottery; rice; shamanism; shinto; yayoi era.

JORURI   See bunraku; chikamatsu monzaemon.

JOSETSU (early 15th century)   A Buddhist priest of Shokokuji Temple in Kyoto who worked in a style of painting known as suibokuga, "water-ink" painting, also known as sumi-e, "painting with ink." Josetsu was influenced by Chinese ink painting of the Song (Sung; 960–1279) and Yuan (1260–1368) dynasties. Two paintings by Josetsu are known to survive. Catching a Catfish with a Gourd (Hyonenzu) depicts a Zen Buddhist koan, or religious riddle, that compares the attainment of Buddhist enlightenment to a man trying to catch a catfish with a gourd. A range of distant mountains is gently painted behind the man. This was one of the first ink landscape paintings in Japan, commissioned by the Shogun Ashikaga Yoshimochi (1386–1428). The painting was pasted on one side of a screen, and 31 poems by Zen monks about the koan were pasted on the other. Wang Xizhi [Wang Hsi-chih] Writing on Fans (O Gishi shosen zu) was actually painted on a fan, and later mounted as a hanging scroll. Two Buddhist monks also wrote inscriptions on the painting. Another famous painting attributed to Josetsu is The Three Sages, which depicts the three Asian religious philosophers Buddha, Lao-Tzu and Confucius in an amusing manner. See also ink painting; screens; scrolls; zen sect of buddhism.

JR   See japan railways.

JUBAKO   See boxes.

JUDO   "The Way of Softness [or Flexibility]"; a martial art emphasizing throwing and grappling techniques. Judo originated in jujutsu, an ancient Chinese way of self-defense without using weapons. This method was introduced in Japan from China almost 2,000 years ago, and its techniques of holding and throwing were practiced by sumo wrestlers and samurai. During the Tokugawa Shogunate (1603–1867), jujutsu was used for self-defense and for nonviolent arrests by authorities. During this time, many schools arose to teach variations of basic jujutsu. Kano Jigoro (1860–1938) combined and modernized various jujutsu techniques to develop the popular sport of judo. He named his technique kodokan-judo, and established the Kodokan Dojo (training hall) in Tokyo in 1882. The philosophy of jujutsu and judo is that a strong opponent can be brought down by being thrown off balance. The seemingly weaker person does this by keeping a basic posture that is soft and flexible, enabling him to deflect the opponent's strength back on himself. It is necessary to maintain a calm and alert state of mind, as well as self-control, and to become aware of the opponent's weak points. Students of judo practice kata, or systematized forms of movement, such as kicking, hitting, and chopping. They also practice randori, or freestyle methods of throwing and holding opponents. Learning how to fall when grappling with an opponent is the fundamental technique of judo. Students are grouped in 10 ranks, symbolized by the belts they wear on their white practice clothes (judogi). Beginners wear a white belt; adults in the first to third class (kyu) wear a brown belt and young people wear a purple belt; students in the fourth and fifth class wear a white belt. Above the classes are ranked grades (dan); first to fifth dan wear black; sixth to eighth dan wear red and white; and higher levels of dan wear scarlet. In 1911 the Japanese Ministry of Education added judo to the physical education programs of middle schools, and in 1939 it required judo training for all male students above the fifth grade. Prohibited from schools during the Allied Occupation of Japan after World War II, judo was revived in 1949 with the founding of the All-Japan Judo Federation (Zen Nihon Judo Remmei). The International Judo Federation was founded in 1952, with members in 17 countries; today over 100 countries belong. Judo was made a medal event in the Olympic Games held in 1964 in Tokyo. Aikido is a new martial art similar to judo. See also aikido; martial arts.

JUJUTSU   See aikido; judo.

JUKU   A private tutoring school that many Japanese students attend in addition to their regular schools, especially in large cities. Juku began during the Edo Era (1600–1868) as small schools founded by individual teachers who gave lessons in martial arts or other specific subjects. When the Japanese government established a nationwide elementary school system during the Meiji Era (1868–1912), juku became private tutorial schools that often taught individual subjects, such as English, in distinction to regular public or private schools, which offered a complete range of subjects. Juku proliferated in the 1970s as a result of increasing pressure on students to excel academically as the means for economic success. *Juku* give students extra training in subjects such as English, Japanese or mathematics so they can pass the rigorous examinations for entrance into universities, high schools and even junior high schools. *Juku* stress rote learning and standardized answers to test questions. A student has to take a separate examination for each university to which he or she applies. There are also "cram schools" (*yobiko*), which prepare students to pass the "examination hell" of university entrance examinations. Japanese mothers push their children so hard to succeed in school that they have been disparagingly nicknamed "education mamas" (*kyoiku mama*). See also CHILDREN IN JAPAN; EDUCATION SYSTEM; MOTHER; UNIVERSITIES.

JUROJIN The God of Long Life and Wealth and one of the Seven Gods of Good Fortune. He is actually a combination of two divine figures, Jurojin and Fukurokuju, who are depicted as dwelling together in the body of an old man with an elongated head. He holds a long cane with a scroll (*makimono*) tied to it and a leaf-shaped fan known as an *ogi* and is often accompanied by a deer. See also CRANE; DEER; FAN; SCROLLS; SEVEN GODS OF GOOD FORTUNE.

"JUST IN TIME" INVENTORY PRODUCTION SYSTEM (JIT) A system of manufacturing in which materials and parts are produced and delivered by suppliers just as they are needed. This is known as the JIT system, and also as the *kanban* system, because all parts carry a *kanban* (small card), which describes the part's origin, destination, description and quantity required. The JIT system enables factories to maintain continuous production while keeping low inventories, hence decreasing costs. Toyota Motor Corporation developed the JIT system in the 1930s, and implemented it on a large scale in the 1950s and 1960s. Hence it is also known as the Toyota Production System. This system is one reason Japanese companies are extremely competitive in the world market, and many western companies, such as General Motors, have been adapting the JIT system and are requesting parts suppliers to relocate next to manufacturing plants. See also AUTOMOBILE INDUSTRY; CORPORATIONS; EXPORTS AND IMPORTS; QUALITY CONTROL CIRCLE.

K

KABUKI The most popular form of traditional Japanese theater. Kabuki is characterized by stylized dialogue and movements, vivid costumes and makeup, lively and often violent action, dancing, and emotional tension in the stories. Singers and an orchestra of drums *(taiko, tsuzumi)*, flutes *(fue)*, wooden clappers *(hyoshigi,* or *ki* for short), and *shamisen,* a stringed instrument similar to a banjo, accompany a Kabuki performance and also create sound effects. Kabuki developed from a risque form of dance first performed in 1603 by a woman named Okuni, who was associated with Izumo Shrine in Kyoto, and her female troupe. The name Kabuki comes from the lively Kabuki *odori* ("stylish and provocative or shocking dance"), which Okuni created from popular folk and street dances of the time, known as *furyu odori* ("fashionable dances"). During the Edo Era (1603–1868), Kabuki grew into a colorful theatrical art form that uses elaborate costumes and makeup, intricate sets and special effects, and dramatic postures and dialogue. Ever since the Tokugawa Shogunate (1603–1867) banned women from performing in Kabuki, accusing them of being prostitutes, men actors have played all the roles. Actors who specialize in female roles and their elaborate costumes and makeup are known as *onnagata.* Kabuki appealed to the urban merchant class, which became wealthy during the Edo Era and patronized the licensed pleasure quarters in Edo (modern Tokyo) and Osaka, known as the "floating world" *(ukiyo).* Woodblock prints, or "pictures of the floating world" *(ukiyo-e),* portrayed top Kabuki actors, who were idolized as the pop stars of their time.

Kabuki actors wear thick makeup that is designed to express their characters. Some actors also have boldly colored lines painted on their faces to show anger, bravery and so forth. Actors move in stylized patterns known as *kata.* Stage hands known as *kuroko,* dressed in black so as to be less visible, appear on stage to move props or adjust an actor's costume. The Kabuki stage has a runway, known as the "flower way" *(hanamichi),* from the back of the auditorium through the audience to stage right. Some actors make dramatic entrances and exits on the *hanamichi,* and even perform important scenes on it. The Kabuki stage has many contraptions to thrill the audience, such as a trap door *(seri)* in the floor through which a character disappears or emerges, and a revolving stage *(mawari-butai)* for quick changes of scenery. Costumes and wigs can also be changed rapidly to reveal a character's true identity.

Most Kabuki plays still performed today were written by Chikamatsu Monzaemon (1653–1724) and Mokuami Kawatake. Kabuki and Bunraku (puppet theater), which developed at the same time, share much the same repertoire.

The plays fall into two types: historical dramas *(jidaimono),* which are acted mainly in the *aragoto* or "rough stuff" style, and contemporary (i.e., Edo Era) "talk of the town" social dramas *(sewamono)* based on real events. Dramatic tension is created in both types of plays by the conflict between duty to society and human feelings *(giri* and *ninjo).* The most famous historical drama in the Kabuki and Bunraku repertoires is Chikamatsu's *The Tale of the Forty-Seven Ronin (Chushingura),* about *ronin* (masterless samurai) who avenge the murder of their lord. Popular contemporary dramas often portray love suicides.

Every Kabuki actor belongs to a hierarchically ordered acting family whose name he takes and with whom he spends many years training as an apprentice. An actor's promotion to a higher rank is celebrated by a *shumei,* or name-assuming ceremony. The head of each family is a leading Kabuki actor who has assumed the theatrical name of a predecessor. Some well-known young Kabuki actors today are Ichikawa Ennosuke II (b. 1939), Matsumoto Koshiro (b. 1942), Nakamura Kankuro V (b. 1955) and Bando Tamasaburo (b. 1950), who is internationally famous for playing women. The main Kabuki theater is the Kabuki-za in Tokyo, and Kabuki is performed at other theaters in Tokyo and Osaka as well. Performances usually last around five hours, with several intermissions during which audience members eat in the theater's restaurants or enjoy *bento* (boxed lunches). Tickets can be bought for one or two scenes as well as for the entire day's performance. See also BUNRAKU; CHIKAMATSU MONZAEMON; DANCE; DRUMS; DUTY AND FEELINGS; EDO ERA; FLOATING WORLD; FLUTES; SHAMISEN; WOODBLOCK PRINTS; YOSHIWARA.

KADOMATSU See BAMBOO; NEW YEAR FESTIVAL.

KAGOSHIMA A city at the southern tip of Kyushu, the southernmost of the four main islands of Japan. Kagoshima has a population of more than a half million and is the capital of Kagoshima Prefecture. The first encounter between Japan and the Western world took place in Kagoshima. The Portuguese Jesuit missionary St. Francis Xavier landed here in 1549 and converted more than 600 Japanese to Christianity during his 10 months in the city. Trade with China was also active even before the 16th century under the regulation of the Shimazu Clan, which ruled Kagoshima for 29 generations (695 years) prior to the Meiji Restoration of 1868. Much of this trade came through the Ryukyu Islands (now Okinawa Prefecture) to the south, which the Shimazu controlled for several centuries before they were formally acquired by Japan in 1879. The Shimazus built Tsurumaru Castle in Kagoshima in 1602 and later provided much of the impetus for the modernization of Japan by building the country's first Western-style factory in Kagoshima in the 1850s; this structure is now the Shokoshuseikan Museum exhibiting historical objects of the Shimazu Clan. Iso Garden (Iso Koen), laid out by the Shimazus in the 1600s, is a popular tourist attraction today. The Kagoshima Prefectural Museum of Culture, on the site where Tsurumaru Castle once stood, displays the history of Kagoshima going as far back as the Jomon Era (c.10,000–300 B.C.). One hundred and two castle towns ringed the border of the Shimazu region during the Edo Era (1600–1868). Chiran, one of those towns south of Kagoshima, has six gardens and numerous homes of samurai that are open to the public.

In 1865, despite the isolation of Japan enforced by the Tokugawa Shogunate (1603–1867), the Shimazus sent 17 men to Great Britain to learn Western languages and technology. These men became leaders in the Meiji Restoration. Two of them, Saigo Takamori and Okubo Toshimichi, were born in Kagoshima Prefecture. Saigo became the leader of former samurai who felt mistreated by the new Meiji government after they had fought for its establishment. The last battle of the Satsuma Rebellion (1877), an uprising against the Meiji government, took place on Shiroyama Hill in Kagoshima. Saigo committed suicide in a cave on the hill. A statue in Ueno Park in Tokyo commemorates him.

The city of Kagoshima was destroyed during World War II but has been completely rebuilt. Major industries include food processing, wood crafts and the weaving of *oshima tsumugi*, a type of silk dyed with mineral-rich mud. Satsuma pottery is also made here. Railroad lines and national highways terminate in Kagoshima, and boats leave the port for southern islands, including Okinawa. Across Kinko Bay, the active volcano Mount Sakurajima pours out steam and sometimes deposits ash on Kagoshima. Its last big eruption, in 1914, sent forth enough lava to connect the volcano with Osumi Peninsula across the channel of the bay. Mount Sakurajima and the city of Kagoshima are part of the Kirishima-Yaku National Park. Kagoshima Prefecture has a mild subtropical climate and a primarily agricultural economy. Major products are rice, sweet potatoes, vegetables, citrus fruit, tea, sugar cane and tobacco. Since World War II there has been a marked decline in population in the prefecture. See also AGRICULTURE; CHRISTIANITY IN JAPAN; FERRIES; KYUSHU ISLAND; MEIJI RESTORATION OF 1868; OKINAWA ISLAND; PORTUGUESE IN JAPAN; RAILROADS; RYUKYU ISLANDS; SAIGO TAKAMORI; SATSUMA PROCINCE; SATSUMA REBELLION; SATSUMA WARE; SECLUSION, NATIONAL; SHIMAZU CLAN; TOKUGAWA SHOGUNATE; VOLCANO; XAVIER, ST. FRANCIS.

KAGURA A ritual performance of sacred dances, often by dancers wearing masks, during festivals at Shinto shrines. *Kagura*, a category of Japanese folk performing arts (*minzoku geino*), is performed to the music of flutes, drums, gongs and singing. In a *kagura* ritual, *kami* (sacred spirits) are invoked, and then songs and dances are performed in their presence to bring long life or renewal to the community. There are two basic types of *kagura*: mikagura, performed at the imperial court and in related shrines, and sato or

minkan kagura (village or provincial *kagura*), performed outside the court. In ancient times, *mikagura* were performed on numerous occasions during the year. Musicians belonging to the imperial household still perform *mikagura*. Today the most important performances are for the ceremonies to enthrone a new emperor (*Daijoe* or *Daijosai*), held in the first November after the emperor comes to the throne; and the *Naishidokoro mikagura*, a special court performance held in December. Subcategories of *sato kagura* include *miko kagura*, dances of Shinto priestesses (*miko*); Ise or *yudate kagura*, the offering of boiling water (*yudate*) to *kami*; Izumo *kagura*, dances in which sacred objects are held by performers; and *shishi kagura*, lion (*shishi*) dances. There are many variations within each of these types in different regions of Japan.

Miko kagura, the earliest form of *kagura*, originated as a dance to induce the possession by a *kami* of a shaman through whom the *kami* would give an oracle. This was performed at the main Shinto shrines of Ise, Izumo and Kasuga, and became practiced at many smaller shrines as a means of offering prayers to *kami* on behalf of worshippers. It is still performed before shrines by young priestesses, who wear white kimono and red *hakama* (divided skirts), with long hair tied in the back with a red ribbon. This dance includes circular movements and repetition of movements in each of the four directions. *Kagura* offering boiling water to invoke kami is no longer performed at Ise Shrine but is held in many other shrines. It often includes a performer who wears a mask to represent a *kami* and who blesses or speaks with an unmasked person representing the community that has invoked the *kami*. Performers of Izumo *kagura* dance without masks while holding objects sacred to the *kami* being invoked, or wear masks to dance dramas based on myths. The most important element of *shishi* (lion) *kagura* is the large lion-head mask, in which the *kami* is present. Dancers do not wear the mask but carry it about the performance area. Traditionally, troupes would take lion masks to farmhouses to perform rituals for benefits such as fire prevention. See also DANCE, TRADITIONAL; DRUMS; FESTIVALS; FLUTES; ISE SHRINE; LION AND LION DANCE; MASKS; PRIESTS AND PRIESTESSES, SHINTO; SHAMANS AND SHAMANISM; SHINTO; SHRINES, SHINTO; WATER.

KAGUYAHIME See BAMBOO CUTTER, THE TALE OF THE.

KAI AWASE See CARD GAMES; SHELLS.

KAIFU TOSHIKI (1931–) A politician in the dominant Liberal Democratic Party (LDP; Jiyu Mishuto) who was selected as prime minister of Japan in August 1989. Kaifu replaced Uno Sosuke, who was chosen to replace Prime Minister Takeshita Noboru (p.m. 1987–1989) when Takeshita was forced to resign on April 25, 1989 after being implicated in the Recruit Scandal, the worst political scandal in postwar Japan. After a few weeks in office, Uno himself became implicated in a sex scandal, and resigned immediately after the LDP suffered a crushing defeat in the July 23, 1989, national elections for the House of Councillors (upper house of the Japanese Diet, or parliament).

The LDP chose Kaifu as its new president and consequently prime minister, because he belonged to the Komoto faction, the only one not tainted by the Recruit Scandal. The second youngest man to become prime minister, Kaifu is a skilled debater and attractive vote getter.

During World War II, Kaifu was drafted at age 14 to work in a factory in Nagoya City, near his birthplace. Two years later, he qualified to become a junior airman, but the war ended in 1945 before he became a flier. After the war he attended Waseda University. When Kaifu was arrested in 1951 for a speech criticizing U.S. Occupation authorities' security regulations against free speech during the Korean War, a local politician named Kono Kinsho secured his release from jail. Kaifu worked for Kono while completing his education at Waseda. In 1960, at age 29, Kaifu was elected to the Diet for the first of his 10 terms. Kaifu served as Prime Minister Miki Takeo's deputy chief cabinet secretary (1974–1976), and twice served as minister of education. However, Kaifu has never held an LDP executive post, nor any party or government position having to do with foreign affairs. Despite his lack of experience, Kaifu led the LDP to a victory in the February 18, 1990 elections for members of the House of Representatives, and so he was reelected LDP president and, in turn, prime minister on February 27, soon after the Diet was convened for a 120-day extraordinary session. Kaifu was also nominated prime minister by the House of Councillors because the opposition parties, which had nominated Doi Takako of the Japan Socialist Party as prime minister after the July, 1989 elections, could not agree on a candidate. See also DIET; DOI TAKAKO; ELECTIONS; FACTIONS, POLITICAL; JAPAN SOCIALIST PARTY; LIBERAL DEMOCRATIC PARTY; MIKI TAKEO; POLITICAL PARTIES; PRIME MINISTER; TAKESHITA NOBORU; UNO SOSUKE.

KAIHO SCHOOL OF PAINTING See KANO SCHOOL OF PAINTING.

KAISEKI A special light meal served at a sake party in a restaurant or during a tea ceremony (chanoyu), where it is known as chakaiseki. This type of cooking, termed kaiseki ryori, originated with the tea ceremony in the late 15th-early 16th century. The name kaiseki, "stones in the pocket," comes from the practice of Zen Buddhist monks who placed small heated stones on their stomachs to keep from getting hungry while meditating and fasting. Kaiseki is a light meal that is not meant to be filling but to provide an aesthetic and social experience. In a complete tea ceremony, the host starts a charcoal fire in the tearoom to boil water for tea and then serves chakaiseki. The meal usually consists of two kinds of soup (miso and clear), three dishes of fish and vegetables, rice, pickles and sake. Sashimi (raw fish), sunomono (sliced vegetables and fish with a vinegar dressing) and aemono (fish and vegetables with sesame seeds, bean paste or vinegar) are types of cold dishes that may be served, collectively known as mukozuke. Next come cooked foods and broiled fish or seafood. There are also appetizers called hassun, which are specialties from "land and sea." The meal concludes with tsukemono (pickles). Guests and host also exchange cups of sake in a ritual

known as sakazukigoto. When the meal is finished, the fire has burned hot enough to make tea. The host serves sweets (kashi) and ritually prepares the tea in front of the guests. Kaiseki food is very fresh and seasonal, simply yet carefully prepared, and served on beautiful lacquer or pottery dishes. Kaiseki meals served at parties in restaurants date back to the early 19th century, when poets would meet to write renga and haikai (haiku) linked verses. The food was similar to that for tea ceremonies, but was served without the elaborate tea rituals. Today anyone can enjoy a kaiseki meal at a first-class Japanese restaurant known as a ryotei. See also COOKING; FISH AND FISHING INDUSTRY; LACQUER WARE; PICKLES; POETRY; POTTERY; RICE; SOUP; SWEETS; TEA CEREMOHY.

KAISHA See CORPORATIONS.

KAKIEMON WARE (Kakiemon-de) A type of glazed enameled porcelain ware produced from around A.D. 1643 in the town of Arita, Hizen Province (modern Nagasaki and Saga Prefectures), on the southern Japanese island of Kyushu. Kakiemon ware is named for Sakaida Kizaemon, at whose kiln it was first made. The lord of his domain gave him the name Kakiemon in 1644 to reward him for a porcelain decorative object he had made in the shape of two persimmons (kaki). Kakiemon objects have an underglaze of blue and white, in designs patterned after Chinese motifs, or an overglaze decoration of enamels in bright colors. A glossy, milk-white body is a distinctive feature of Kakiemon ware. Colorful decorations are predominantly red, orange and blue. By the late 1600s, distinctive Japanese motifs of birds and flowers were used to decorate Kakiemonware. These were often derived from paintings of the Tosa and Kano Schools. The majority of Kakiemon objects are decorative items such as dishes and bowls, vases, teapots, containers and candlesticks. They were exported to Europe in great quantities, especially after the fall of the Chinese Ming dynasty (1368–1644) prevented Chinese objects from reaching foreign markets. Kakiemon designs were copied by porcelelain factories in China and Europe, including Meissen in Germany, Chelsea in England and Chantilly in France. Kakiemon ware is still produced in Japan by family descendants. See also ARITA WARE; EXPORTS AND IMPORTS; KANO SCHOOL OF PAINTING; PORCELAIN; TOSA SCHOOL OF PAINTING.

KAMA See KETTLE.

KAMABOKO See FISH PASTE AND FISH CAKES.

KAMAKURA A city of 175,000 people on Sagami Bay, 28 miles southwest of Tokyo, best known for a great statue of Amida Buddha (Daibutsu). The Daibutsu is the second largest bronze statue in Japan, after the one at Nara. Cast in 1252, it is 37.7 feet high and weighs 93 tons. The statue now sits in the open because the wooden temple that originally housed it was destroyed by a tidal wave in 1495. Also known for its 65 Buddhist temples and 19 Shinto shrines, Kamakura was for about 150 years the capital of Japan. When the warlord Minamoto no Yoritomo (1146–

1149) seized control of the country, he located his military government at Kamakura in 1192, because it was far away from Kyoto, the capital of the imperial court, which had ruled Japan until Minamoto's time. After Minamoto's sons were assassinated, the Hojo clan, the family of Minamoto's widow, ran the military government until emperor Go-Daigo sent troops from Kyoto and destroyed the Kamakura Shogunate in 1333.

The Tsurugaoka Shrine was erected by Minamoto no Yoritomo and dedicated to Hachiman, the Shinto god of war and patron deity of the Minamoto clan. The City Museum of Kamakura and the Kanagawa Prefecture Art Museum are also within the shrine precincts. Five Zen Buddhist temples located in Kamakura, collectively known as Kamakura Gozan, include Kenchoji, Engakuji, Jochiji, Jufukuji and Jomyoji temples. Kenchoji is known for its cedar trees and a wooden ceremonial gate. Engakuji, founded in 1282, is a fine example of architecture of the Kamakura Era. Another Buddhist temple, Tokeji, founded in 1285, provided refuge for women to escape from cruel husbands and their families. Hasadera Temple houses an 11-headed statue of Kannon, the Buddhist Goddess of Mercy, more than 30 feet tall. Carved from one piece of camphor wood in the eighth century, this is the largest wooden statue in Japan. The grounds of Hasadera also contain more than 50,000 stone statues of Jizo, the god who protects children. Two more famous temples in Kamakura are Miyohonji, of the Nichiren sect of Buddhism, and Komyoji, of the Pure Land Sect of Buddhism. See also BAKUFU; DAIBUTSU; GINKGO TREE; HACHIMAN; HONSHU ISLAND; KAMAKURA SHOGUNATE; KANNON; KYOTO; MINAMOTO NO YORITOMO; SCULPTURE; SHRINES, SHINTO; SHOGUN; TEMPLES, BUDDHIST; WAVES; ZEN SECT OF BUDDHISM.

KAMAKURA SHOGUNATE (1192–1333)   The first of three military governments (*bakufu*, or shogunates) that ruled Japan for nearly seven centuries. The Kamakura Shogunate was founded by Minamoto no Yoritomo (1147–1199), who was awarded the title of *seii tai shogun* ("barbarian-subduing generalissimo"; abbreviated as *shogun*) by the emperor in 1192. In 1180 Yoritomo led a rebellion against the Taira clan, which controlled the government of the Heian imperial court in Kyoto. Many warriors joined Yoritomo's cause in a lord-vassal relationship, taking a pledge of loyalty to him as "houseman" (*gokenin*). That same year, he established his *bakufu* in Kamakura on east central Honshu Island, away from the imperial capital of Kyoto on western Honshu. In 1185, which is often given as the founding date of the Kamakura Shogunate, the Minamoto clan decisively defeated the Taira clan at the Battle of Dannoura. Yoritomo then established a system of appointed governors (*shugo*) and stewards (*jito*) to control the country. The Kamakura shoguns rewarded their vassals by giving them rights over certain lands and appointing them stewards, which altered the landed-estate (*shoen*) system of the Heian aristocracy. During the Kamakura Era, the samurai class gradually solidified as the ruling class in Japan. However, the shogunate permitted the imperial court in Kyoto to retain a symbolic function.

After Yoritomo died in 1199, members of the Hojo clan

gained control of the Kamakura Shogunate, starting with Hojo Masako, Yoritomo's wife and the mother of his two successors. The Hojo clan were known as *shikken*, or shogunal regents. They took members of court families from Kyoto to Kamakura and gave them the title of shogun. The lords of some provinces became wealthy and powerful enough to challenge the authority of the Kamakura Shogunate, and the shogunate was further undermined after the Mongols attempted to invade Japan in 1274 and 1281. The Mongols were repelled, but the Hojo regents had no resources to reward their vassals who had fought off the invaders. The Kamakura Shogunate ended in 1333 when Emperor Go-Daigo attempted to restore imperial rule in Kyoto, aided by Ashikaga Takauji, a turncoat Kamakura general. Takauji then betrayed the emperor and founded the second military government in Japan, known as the Ashikaga Shogunate (1338–1574). See also ASHIKAGA SHOGUNATE; ASHIKAGA TAKAUJI; BAKUFU; DANNOURA, BATTLE OF; FEUDALISM; GO-DAIGO, EMPEROR; HEIAN ERA; HOJO CLAN; KAMAKURA; LANDED-ESTATE SYSTEM; MINAMOTO NO YORITOMO; MONGOL INVASIONS OF JAPAN; SAMURAI; TAIRA-MINAMOTO WAR.

KAMBAN   See SIGNBOARDS.

KAMBUN MASTER   See MORONOBU.

KAMI   The term for the sacred spirits of Shinto ("The way of the *kami*"), the indigenous Japanese religion. *Kami* literally means "upper" or "above." Shinto is the Chinese pronunciation of the two Chinese characters, or *kanji*, used to write the name of this religion. The characters are traditionally given the Japanese pronunciation *kami no michi*, for "the path of the *kami*."

Although *kami* is usually translated as "divinity," "deity," or "god," a *kami* is not a transcendent, all-powerful god in the Western sense. Numerous legends about *kami* are recorded in the eighth century A.D. chronicles *Kojiki* and *Nihon Shiko*. The Japanese revere as *kami* anything in nature that inspires awe or possesses some kind of superior power, including mountains, trees, rocks, streams, animals and plants. Human beings may also be revered as *kami*, particularly the emperors, military heroes and ancestors. The phrase *yaoyorozu no kami*, "vast myriads of *kami*," indicates the countless number of *kami* in Japan. Many are benevolent, but there are also harmful *kami* who cause misfortune if they are not appeased or exorcised. These are frequently the "vengeful spirits" (*goryo*) of people who were forced to commit suicide or die in exile. *Kami* that represent the powers of fertility and reproduction are especially important. Izanagi and Izanami, the *kami* couple who created other *kami* and the islands of Japan, are referred to as "the *kami* of the mysterious generative spirit" (*musubi no kami*).

The Sun Goddess Amaterasu o Mikami, who was born from Izanagi, is the central *kami* of the Shinto pantheon. Ancient legends tell how she sent her grandson Ninigi no Mikoto down from the "High Celestial Plain" (*Takamagahara*) to rule Japan, and how his grandson Jimmu Tenno supposedly became the first emperor in 606 B.C. Japanese traditionally believe that the imperial family descended from him in an unbroken line and that every emperor is thus sacred. *Kami* worshipped in Shinto shrines generally have human qualities. These include Amaterasu as the divine ancestor of the imperial family, *kami* who play a role in ancient myths about the origin of Japan, ancestors of major clans, *kami* of rice and agriculture, and important historical figures. In ancient Japan, each clan (*uji*) had its own titulary deity or *ujikami*, for whom the head of the clan performed religious rituals. Innumerable other *kami* may be propitiated with religious rituals, such as those performed when construction is begun on a new building. Since *kami* are spirits, Shinto has not had a tradition of religious paintings and sculptures of deities, which was richly developed in Buddhism. In Shinto there is neither a sharp distinction between the many sacred spirits and humans, nor one transcendent god. Human beings, sacred spirits and nature are harmoniously interrelated. A person becomes an ancestral *kami* (*sosenshin*) when a prescribed number of memorial services are held after his or her death. Japanese homes contain a small altar to *kami* known as a *kamidana*, or "*kami* shelf," where family members offer prayers and food.

Leaders of the Shingon Sect of Buddhism associated Buddhist deities with Shinto *kami*. In time the Buddhist theory of *honji-suijaku*, "original substance manifests traces," became widespread. In this view, Japanese *kami* are the "manifest traces" (*suijaku*) of the "original substance" (*honji*) of particular Buddhas and bodhisattvas. Shinto shrines were incorporated into Buddhist temples of the Shingon and Tendai Sects.

At Shinto shrines, worshippers pass through a sacred gate known as a *torii* and purify themselves with water before they approach the *kami*. Shrines hold festivals (*matsuri*) to honor and entertain the *kami* that they enshrine. During festivals, *kami* are paraded through the shrine districts in sacred palanquins known as *mikoshi*. Children are taken to shrines and presented to the *kami* a month after they are born and at the Seven-Five-Three Festival. Weddings are frequently held before the *kami* in Shinto shrines. See also ALTARS IN HOMES; AMATERASU O MIKAMI; BUDDHISM; FESTIVALS; IZANAGI AND IZANAMI; JIMMU TENNO; KOJIKI; NIHON SHOKI; NINIGI NO MIKOTO; PALANQUIN, SACRED; PURIFICATION; SEVEN-FIVE-THREE FESTIVAL; SHINGON SECT OF BUDDHISM; SHINTO; SHRINES, SHINTO; TORII; WEDDINGS.

KAMIKAZE "Wind of the gods" or "divine wind"; the name for typhoons (*taifu*, violent storms) that destroyed much of the armed fleet of the Mongols who attempted to invade Japan in 1274 and 1281. The Japanese believed that the storms that saved their country from foreign invasion were sent by the *kami* (gods) of Ise Shrine, the major shrine of Shinto.

In World War II, the name *kamikaze* was given to Japanese pilots who made suicide attacks on enemy ships. The units of these specially trained pilots were called the Kamikaze Special Attack Forces (Kamikaze Tokubetsu Kogekitai, or Tokkotai). The idea of suicide pilots was suggested by Vice Admiral Onishi Takijiro of the First Air Fleet, and *kamikaze*

attacks were first made in October 1944, on the Allied fleet off Leyte in the Philippine Islands. Five pilots of Zero fighter planes, each loaded with a 250-kilogram bomb, dived into American ships. More than 2,000 *kamikaze* attacks were made in the next 10 months, until Japan surrendered in August 1945, and altogether the *kamikaze* sunk 34 Americans ships and damaged 288 more. They were widely used in the Battle of Okinawa, which began in April 1945. At the close of the war, Japanese forces were attempting to use other types of suicide attack, such as manned torpedoes, explosive-laden motorboats, small submarines and frogmen.

Today, reckless automobile drivers in Japan are jokingly called *kamikaze*. See also KAMI; ISE SHRINE; MONGOL INVASIONS OF JAPAN; OKINAWA, BATTLE OF; SHINTO; WORLD WAR II; ZERO FIGHTER PLANE.

KAMMON STRAIT See SHIMONOSEKI.

KAMMU, EMPEROR See EMPEROR; FESTIVAL OF THE AGES; HEIAN SHRINE; HEIANKYO; KYOTO; NARA; SAICHO; TAIRA CLAN; TENDAI SECT OF BUDDHISM.

KAMO NO CHOMEI (1156?–1216) A poet and critic who symbolizes the literary recluse worn down by the futility of life who leaves the world to lead a life of quiet refinement in a mountain hut. Chomei lived during the turbulent time when the courtly refinement of the Heian Era (794–1185) was yielding to the military rule of the Kamakura Shogunate. As a young man, Kama no Chomei published poems in several anthologies commissioned by the imperial court, and his abilities brought him into the highest literary circles in Japan. Chomei published a collection of his poetry, the *Kamo no Chomei shu*, and presented his *Second Hundred-Poem Sequence of the Shoji Era* (*Shoji ninen nido hyakushu*) to the retired Emperor Go-Toba (1180–1239). His literary treatise, *Nameless Notes* (*Mumyosho*; written after 1211), promoted the aesthetic concept of *yugen*, whereby the infinite is exprssed in subtle and elegant allusions. Chomei also wrote a poetic diary of the travels he made, *Accounts of Ise* (*Iseki*; c. 1186). In 1204 he became a Buddhist monk after he was prevented from inheriting a post due him at the Kamo Shrines in the capital city of Kyoto. In 1209 he built a small hut on Mount Hino (Hinoyama) near the town of Uji, south of Kyoto. In this retreat his wrote *The Ten-Foot Square Hut* or *An Account of My Hut* (*Hojoki*, 1212), in which he reflected on the impermanence of all things, as taught by the Buddhist religion. He also wrote about the great rivalry between the Taira (Heike) and Minamoto clans in the late 12th century that led to the defeat of the Tairas and the founding of the Kamakura Shogunate (1185–1333) by the Minamotos. Chomei's final work, *Collection of Religious Awakenings* (*Hosshinshu*; c. 1214), was an anthology of Buddhist stories with moral lessons. See also BUDDHISM; DIARIES; HEIAN ERA; KAMAKURA SHOGUNATE; MINAMOTO CLAN; POETRY; TAIRA CLAN; YUGEN.

KAMO RIVER (Kamogawa) A river that flows through the city of Kyoto, the former capital of Japan. The Kamo begins in the Tamba Mountains north of the city and flows south for 22 miles until it meets the Katsura River (Katsuragawa) in southwestern Kyoto. The districts of Gion on the east bank of the Kamo and Pontocho on the west bank are famous for their communities of geisha, women trained in traditional Japanese arts who entertain at banquets for affluent male patrons. Their teahouses provide romantic views of the river. Every spring and autumn the geisha of the Pontocho district hold public performances of the Kamo River Dance (Kamogawa *odori*).

The river's course was diverted to flow east of the imperial palace that was constructed when Kyoto became the capital of Japan in A.D. 794. Wide stone banks have been laid out along the Kamo River, and parks have been situated on dry places in the riverbed where popular entertainers used to perform. Since the river cannot be navigated easily, the Takase barge canal was built along its west side for the transportation of goods.

In earlier days, the Kamo River was used for rinsing long pieces of silk that had been beautifully dyed with the *yuzen* technique for which Kyoto textiles have been famous. Many paintings and poems depict the cloth, from which kimono are made, in the clear water of the Kamo. River birds named plovers (*chidori*) are another traditional symbol of the river. See also GEISHA; GION; HEIAN ERA; IMPERIAL PALACE (KYOTO); KIMONO; KYOTO; PLOVER; PONTOCHO; TEXTILES; YUZEN DYEING.

KAMPAI A drinking toast that means "bottoms up" or "to your health." The Japanese wait until everyone in the group has a drink, then they all say *"kampai!"* while raising their sake (rice wine) cups or glasses. Custom prescribes that drinkers fill each other's cups. See also ALCOHOLIC BEVERAGES; SAKE.

KANA Written symbols representing the 48 syllables in the Japanese language. *Kana*, developed to write the Japanese language phonetically, originally meant writing that is "not regular," to distinguish it from *mana* ("regular" writing), which uses Chinese characters (*kanji*). The Chinese system of writing was adapted by the Japanese when Chinese culture was introduced into Japan in the sixth century A.D. years ago. The Japanese language can be written solely using *kana*, but the writing system actually combines *kana* and *kanji*. At present two styles of *kana* are used. *Hiragana* is a cursive form, that is, written with flowing strokes that were derived from Chinese characters. *Hiragana* is used for native Japanese words, grammatical aspects such as verb inflections and adjectival endings, and words derived from Chinese that are not written using Chinese characters. *Katakana* is a square form of writing that is commonly used to write foreign words. *Hiragana* and *katakana* developed from an ancient system of *kana* known as *manyogana*, which was used to write poems in the *Manyoshu*, an important eighth-century poetry anthology. This system used abbreviated Chinese characters to denote the syllables of the Japanese language. A Chinese-speaker would not understand the meanings of these characters as written in Japanese. See also HIRAGANA; KANJI; KATAKANA; LANGUAGE, JAPANESE; MANYOSHU; WRITING SYSTEM, JAPANESE.

KANAGAWA TREATY OF 1854 See ABE MASAHIRO; HAKODATE; PERRY, MATTHEW CALBRAITH; SECLUSION, NATIONAL.

KANAMI KIYOTSUGU See KASUGA SHRINE; NOH DRAMA; ZEAMI.

KANAZAWA A city bordering the Sea of Japan on Honshu Island that is the capital of Ishikawa Prefecture, the gateway to the scenic Noto Peninsula and a center for traditional Japanese crafts and manufacturing. Some historic wooden buildings still stand because Kanazawa, like the historic city of Kyoto, was spared from being bombed during World War II. The Nagachi samurai district preserves a street of lovely wooden homes still privately owned. Kanazawa is well-known for Kenrokuen Garden, one of the three finest landscape gardens in Japan (along with Kairakuen Garden in Mito and Korakuen Garden in Okayama), which offers charming views of miniature landscapes composed of streams and ponds, rocks, hills, trees and shrubs. The garden was originally begun by the fifth lord of the Maeda clan in the 1670s, during the Tokugawa Shogunate (1603–1867), and added to by each generation until the 12th lord of Maeda completed it in the early 1800s. Korakuen was opened to the public in 1875. Adjoining the garden are Seisonkaku Villa, built by the 13th lord of Maeda in 1863, and the Ishikawa Prefectural Museum for Traditional Products and Crafts. Kanazawa is famous for a decorative style of pottery called Kutani Ware (*Kutani-yaki*). Another important craft is a technique for dyeing silk with colorful designs called *yuzen*. Lacquer ware, wood products, folk toys, baskets and handmade paper are also well-known Kanazawa products.

Kanazawa became an independent region five centuries ago, unique in Japan, when rebellious Buddhist priests and peasants overthrew their feudal lord. It remained autonomous until the warlord Oda Nobunaga subdued the region and awarded it to his retainer Maeda Toshiie. The Maeda clan controlled Kanazawa for centuries and because of the wealth in the area were second in power in Japan only to the Tokugawa clan, who unified and ruled Japan from 1603 until the Meiji Restoration of 1868. Kanazawa prospered with Maeda patronage of the arts and local skill in agriculture, particularly in the cultivation of rice. See also BASKETS; FEUDALISM; GARDENS; HONSHU ISLAND; KAMAKURA SHOGUNATE; KUTANI WARE; KYOTO; LACQUER WARE; MAEDA CLAN; MEIJI RESTORATION OF 1868; ODA NOBUNAGA; PAPER; SAMURAI; SEA OF JAPAN; TOYS, TRADITIONAL; WOODWORKING; YUZEN DYEING.

KANDA The bookstore and university district of Tokyo. The streets of Kanda and the neighboring districts of Jimbocho and Ochanomizu, with major train stations, are lined with hundreds of new and secondhand bookstores. Many specialize in English and other foreign-language books. One shop, Ohya Shobo, claims to have the world's largest collection of old Japanese illustrated books, maps and woodblock prints. Kanda is also known for two Shinto Shrines: Kanda Myojin and Yushima Seido. Kanda Myojin was originally founded in A.D. 730, although its present buildings were erected in 1934 after the Great Kanto Earthquake. Behind the red main building, smaller shrines house the portable palanquins (mikoshi) that are used to carry the gods of the shrine through the streets during the famous Kanda Festival in May. Steps next to the shrine lead steeply up a hill with ginkgo trees on top, which in earlier days were used as navigation by fishing boats. Yushima Seido Shrine, founded in the 14th century and rebuilt in 1935, is dedicated to the Chinese sage Confucius. A large library for the study of Confucian ethics marks the site of a school that was a forerunner of modern Tokyo University. Many scholars and statesmen were educated at this shrine during the Tokugawa Shogunate (1603–1867). Students often pray at the shrine and write their prayers for acceptance into a university on wooden plaques. The shrine also hosts a famous plum blossom festival in late February and early March. See also BOOKS AND BOOKSTORES; CONFUCIANISM; FESTIVALS; GINKGO TREES; PALANQUIN, SACRED; SHRINES, SHINTO; TALISMANS; TOKUGAWA SHOGUNATE; TOKYO UNIVERSITY; UNIVERSITIES; WOODBLOCK PRINTS.

KANEKO KENTARO (1853–1942) An official in the Meiji government. Kaneko was born in 1853 in the Fukuoka region on Kyushu, the southernmost of the main Japanese Islands. In 1871 he traveled to the United States and enrolled at Harvard, where he studied political science, law and economics. Upon graduating, in 1878, he returned to Japan and became a lecturer at Tokyo Imperial University. In 1880 he became a secretary in the Senate (Genroin) of the Meiji government. Kaneko was appointed to the Office for the Investigation of Institutions (Seido Torishirabe Kyoku) in 1884, when he assisted Ito Hirobumi and other government leaders in drafting Japan's first constitution (Constitution of 1889). The next year, when Ito became the first prime minister of Japan, Kaneko became his secretary. Kaneko continued to move up in the government, with appointments to the House of Peers (Upper House of the prewar Diet, or Parliament) in 1890 and several cabinet positions in the following decade. The government sent Kaneko to Washington, D.C. to promote its position with President Theodore Roosevelt during the Russo-Japanese War of 1904–1905. He was also given an honorary degree by Harvard University. Kaneko returned to Japan in 1906 and served in the Privy Council until he died in 1942. He also wrote books on the Meij Constitution and chaired an official committee to compile historical documents about the Meiji Restoration and the constitution. See also CONSTITUTION, MEIJI (1889); DIET; ITO HIROBUMI; MEIJI RESTORATION OF 1868; PRIME MINISTER; RUSSO-JAPANESE WAR.

KANJI Characters, or ideographs, from Chinese script that are used for writing Japanese words. They are combined with two Japanese syllabic systems, or kana, known as hiragana and katakana. The Japanese adopted many elements of Chinese civilization during the Nara Era (710–794), including the Chinese system of ideographic writing, which was transmitted primarily through translations of Buddhist scriptures. However, because Chinese and Japanese have different linguistic roots with different grammatical systems, the monosyllabic Chinese characters were inadequate for writing Japanese, which is polysyllabic and has many grammatical forms different from Chinese. Although the Japanese language can be written entirely with its own phonetic scripts (kana), kanji continued to be used, either alone or in combination, to write the meanings and sounds of some words. However, a Chinese-speaking person would have difficulty reading the meanings of kanji in Japanese. The Japanese give Chinese characters their own sometimes multiple pronunciations; they may read the same Chinese character in three or more different ways. Large Japanese dictionaries list between 40,000 and 50,000 kanji, but most of these characters are not commonly used. In 1946 the Japanese Ministry of Education issued a list of 1,850 basic kanji to be used by the government and in the schools. This list was revised to 1,945 kanji in 1981. Academic texts require the use of more kanji, but 2,000 kanji are usually sufficient for popular literature, and no more than 5,000 kanji are ever used in printed matter. See also CHINA AND JAPAN; HIRAGANA; KANA; KATAKANA; LANGUAGE, JAPANESE; SCRIPTURES, RELIGIOUS; WRITING SYSTEM, JAPANESE.

KANNON Also known in Japan as Kanzeon or Kanjizai; the Buddhist Goddess of Mercy, one of the most popular deities in Japan. Kannon, whose name means "the one who hears their cries," is revered as the bodhisattva (enlightened being) who embodies infinite compassion. Kannon derived from a male deity named Avalokitesvara in India, but when Buddhism was introduced into China, the deity, there called Guanyin or Kuan-yin, came to be depicted as a female. She was especially popular as the protector of women in pregnancy and childbirth. The worship of Guanyin, or Kannon, was introduced into Japan with Buddhism in the sixth century A.D. Stories about the miraculous power of Kannon were recorded in a major Buddhist sutra (religious scripture), the Lotus Sutra (Hokke Kyo), which has been the basic document of the Tendai and Pure Land (Shin) sects of Buddhism in Japan. The Pure Land sect, which became a popular Japanese religious movement during the medieval era (12th–16th centuries A.D.), teaches that Kannon is the main attendant of the Buddhist deity Amida, who rules over the Pure Land, where people who have faith in him will go after they die. Kannon is believed to carry them on a white lotus flower to the Pure Land of Amida. Statues of Kannon were erected at 33 beautiful spots in Japan, and people of all social classes enjoyed making pilgrimages to these shrines. A seventh-century A.D. wooden sculpture of Kannon at Horyuji in Nara, and the 1,000 statues of the Thousand-Armed Kannon in Sanjusangendo, a 12th–century temple in Kyoto, have been designated as National Treasures by the Japanese government. Japanese Christians on the southern island of Kyushu secretly worshiped Maria Kannon, a goddess who combined attributes of the Virgin Mary and Kannon, when Christianity was banned in Japan by the Tokugawa government. See also AMIDA; BUDDHISM; CHRISTIANITY IN JAPAN; HORYUJI; LOTUS; LOTUS SUTRA; NATIONAL TREASURES; PILGRIMAGE; PURE LAND SECT OF BUDDHISM; TENDAI SECT OF BUDDHISM.

KANO SCHOOL OF PAINTING The most important Japanese school of painting in the Chinese style, known as kanga, founded by Kano Masanobu (1434–1530), which dominated Japanese painting for several centuries. Kano paintings were originally pure ink paintings (sumi-e) with strong linear designs, done mostly on rolling handscrolls (emakimono) and vertical scrolls (kakemono). Artists of the Kano school were patronized by the shogunates (military governments, or bakufu) from the late Muromachi Era (also known as the Ashikaga Shogunate; 1333–1568) through the Azuchi-Momoyama (1568–1600) and Edo (1600–1868) eras.

Kano Masanobu (1434–1530), who settled in Kyoto, then the capital city, learned the Chinese Southern Song (Sung; 1127–1279) and Yuan (1279–1368) styles of monochromatic ink painting (suibokuga or sumi-e) from a painter-priest named Shubun (d. c. 1460) at the workshop of the Zen Buddhist temple Shokokuji, which, patronized by the Ashuikaga shoguns, was the center for ink painting, known as suibokuga. A set of Chinese landscape, bird-and-flower, and figure wall paintings created by Masanobu for a sub-temple of Myoshinji Zen temple are considered the first Kano-style ink paintings. In the 1480s Masanobu became the acknowledged master of this painting style and was named official artist (goyo eshi) to the Ashikaga Shogunate in the kanga, or Chinese monochromatic ink painting, style. He thus began the first line of professional artists other than Zen priests to paint in this style. Masanobu's son Kano Motonobu (1476–1559) introduced colors and decorative styles typical of Yamato-e or "Japanese-style painting," which had developed during the aristocratic Heian Era (794–1185), into the more somber Kano style. He also developed a network of support for the Kano School among members of the Muromachi upper class and created a studio system to train Kano artists. Motonobu painted on sliding doors and screens as well as scrolls. A beautiful example of his work is Birds and Flowers of the Four Seasons, painted on four sliding doors in Daisenin temple in Kyoto. Kano Eitoku (1543–1590; real name Kano Kuminobu), Motonobu's grandson, became the greatest Kano painter during the Azuchi-Momoyama Era (1568–1600) and was commissioned by the great warlords Oda Nobunaga (1543–1582) and Toyotomi Hideyoshi (1536–1598) and others to decorate their castles. Eitoku executed paintings on large spaces, such as the sliding doors (fusuma) and folding screens (byobu) that decorated the castles, and originated the use of gold leaf as a background on which to paint natural scenes in vivid colors. His opulent style combined strong compositional forms and finely painted details. For example, a strong, diagonal pine tree trunk might fill half the painting, and be accompanied by delicate flowers. In addition to his work for Azuchi Castle, Eitoku created paintings for other notable buildings, including Osaka Castle, Sento Palace, the Imperial Palace and Jurakudai, the residence built by Hideyoshi. None of these works survived the military turbulence of his era; however, some of his screens and other paintings still exist in Japanese collections. Eitoku also painted many genre subjects, or scenes of daily life and annual festivals in Kyoto, the capital city at the time. His son Kano Mitsunobu (1561 or 1565–1608) worked with him on many of his commissions. When Eitoku died while working on the Imperial Palace, Mitsunobu completed the painting and took over as head of the

Kano family. Eitoku's son-in-law Kano Sanraku (1559–1635) continued the Kano tradition in Kyoto, and his grandson Kano Tan'yu (1602–1674) brought it to the new capital city of Edo (modern Tokyo), where several branches of the Kano style developed. During the Azuchi-Momoyama and Edo eras, paintings of the Kano began to resemble those of the Tosa school. Two rival schools to the Kano school also arose, the Hasegawa school and the Kaiho school. The highly decorative Rimpa school of painting evolved out of the Kano school. The Kano school lasted longer as a vital tradition than any other major school of painting in Japan, due largely to its studio system of training professional artists and its patronage by military rulers and the imperial court. Its influence lingered into the 20th century. Hashimoto Gaho (1835–1908), the last Kano artist, helped found and taught at the school that is now known as the Tokyo University of Fine Arts and Music. See also ASHIKAGA SHOGUNATE; AZUCHI-MOMOYAMA ERA; BAKUFU; CASTLES; EDO ERA; FLOATING WORLD; INK PAINTING; MUROMACHI ERA; PAINTING; RIMPA SCHOOL OF PAINTING; SCREENS; SCROLLS; TOSA SCHOOL OF PAINTING; ZEN SECT OF BUDDHISM.

KANSAI AND KANTO The two most heavily populated and industrialized regions of Japan. Kansai, meaning "west of the pass [or barrier]," refers to the region around the cities of Osaka, Kobe and Kyoto. Kanto, "east of the pass (or barrier)," refers to the region around the city of Tokyo. The division between Kansai and Kanto was established in the 10th century when a dividing line was designated by an official government station (Sekisho) in what is now Shiga Prefecture. During the Kamakura Era (1192–1333), Kansai and Kanto were separated by three barrier stations located at Suzuka (Mie Prefecture), Fuwa (Gifu Prefecture) and Arachi (Fukui Prefecture). Later the dividing barrier was moved further east to Hakone (Kanagawa Prefecture). The terms Kansai and Kanto are used in both a historical sense and culturally to refer to customs and manners, for example, regional dialects in Kansai (Kansai namari or Kansai ben). In this usage the word Kansai is similar to kamigata, another term used to refer to the Kyoto-Osaka area in general. Kansai can also be used more broadly to include Shikoku Island and the Chugoku region of western Honshu Island. In Kansai, Osaka is Japan's second most important city for commerce and industry after Tokyo, and Kobe serves as its port. Kyoto is important as a cultural center and was capital of Japan until the 17th century.

Kanto as a broad regional category comprises the east central area of Honshu Island and includes the current prefectures of Tokyo, Chiba, Saitama, Kanagawa, Gumma, Ibaraki and Tochigi, as well as the Pacific Islands of Izu and Ogasawara. The Kanto Plain is the largest plain in mountainous Japan and has the densest population. With Tokyo as the capital and largest city, Kanto is now the political, economic, industrial and cultural center of the country. Kanto was an undeveloped frontier area prior to the 13th century. When the Tokugawa Shogunate (1603–1867) moved the capital from Kyoto to the new city of Edo (later called Tokyo), Kanto underwent rapid development. The cities of Tokyo, Yokohama and Kawasaki together form the center of heavy manufacturing known as the Keihin Industrial Zone. Traditional industries also continue to operate, such as textile weaving, sake brewing and silkworm cultivation, and agriculture is still practiced. Kanto has five national parks, including Fuji-Hakone-Izu and Nikko. See also AGRICULTURE; CHIBA PREFECTURE; HONSHU ISLAND; INDUSTRIAL ZONES; NATIONAL PARKS; SHIKOKU ISLAND; TOKUGAWA SHOGUNATE; NAMES OF INDIVIDUAL CITIES AND PARKS.

KANZA TROUPE   See NOH DRAMA; ZEAMI.

KAPPA   A small yellow-green mythical creature, ugly but appealing, which is thought to live in rivers, ponds or lakes. A *kappa* has a long snout and is shaped like a monkey, but instead of fur it has fish scales or a tortoise shell. The main feature of a *kappa* is a hollow, saucer-like indentation on top of its head that must always be filled with water. A *kappa* loses its power immediately if the water is spilled out. A *kappa* is believed to be a vampire that feeds on the blood of humans, horses and cattle. Drowning victims were traditionally thought to be caught and pulled under by *kappa*. Oddly, the *kappa* is also very polite. If a *kappa* can be tricked into bowing to its intended victim, it will lose the water on its head and thus lose its strength. It can also be tamed by offering it a cucumber. The *kappa* also keeps promises it makes, and some folktales tell of weakened *kappa* that give humans useful knowledge or vow not to attack humans anymore. The famous Japanese author Akugatawa Ryunosuke (1892–1927) wrote a novel titled *Kappa*. See also AKUGATAWA RYUNOSUKE; DEMONS AND GHOSTS.

KAPPABASHI STREET   See ASAKUSA; FOOD MODELS, PLASTIC.

KARAOKE   An entertainment popular in private homes and bars, in which amateurs sing to recorded music. *Kara* means "empty," and *oke* is short for "orchestra." Some bars also show videos while the singers are performing. *Karaoke* songs are often popular Japanese ballads (*enka*) with sentimental words and plaintive melodies. Western songs are also popular, such as "Yesterday" and "My Way," the favorite song of businessmen. Songbooks provide the words for the singers. The talented and untalented alike all are required to take their turn. See also EXPENSE ACCOUNTS; FOLK SONGS; SALARYMAN; SINGING.

KARATE   Literally, "empty hand"; a martial art that uses hand, arm and leg movements in self-defense. Karate was introduced into Japan from Okinawa (Ryukyu Islands) to the south. Okinawans had learned Chinese techniques of unarmed combat from masters of kung fu (*quanfa* or *ch'uanfa* in Chinese, meaning "rules of the fist"; *kempo* in Japanese) during the five centuries when Ryukyu was a tributary kingdom of China. Weapons were forbidden there by rulers of the Ryukyu kingdom, and then by the Shimazu clan of Satsuma Province on the southern Japanese island of Kyushu who took control of Ryukyu in 1609. Okinawans combined Chinese fighting techniques, called "Tang [T'ang Dynasty] hand" (*tode* in Japanese), with native Okinawan

techniques, known as *te*, or "hand." After Okinawa became a prefecture of Japan in 1872, karate became an organized sport. In 1922 Okinawan karate master Funakoshi Gichin was invited by the Japanese Ministry of Education to demonstrate karate in Tokyo. Karate clubs were soon established in Japanese universities following Funakoshi's Shotokan School of Karate. Two other schools and many variations on the techniques evolved. However, all karate schools train their members in basic formal exercises (*kata*) and sparring (*kumite*) with a partner. The three basic karate techniques are thrusts, strikes and kicks. Students train in a wooden-floored hall known as a *dojo*. During the 1950s, karate became a popular sport in Japan. Today there are a student federation with about 7,000 student members and a general federation of karate organizations in Japan, as well as karate associations in many foreign countries. Tournaments are held throughout the world. See also CHINA AND JAPAN; DOJO; MARTIAL ARTS; RYUKYU ISLANDS.

KARATSU WARE   (Karatsu-yaki)   Pottery produced for 300 years at many kilns south of Karatsu City in Hizen Province (modern Saga Prefecture) on Kyushu Island. Shapes, designs and methods for making Karatsu ware were derived from pottery made in Yi dynasty Korea during the early 16th century. Being very close to the Korean peninsula, Kyushu was the place through which Korean and Chinese culture was introduced into Japan since ancient times. By the 17th century, Korean wood-burning kilns with many chambers built on a slope, known as *nobori-gama*, were used for the first time in Japan, to fire Karatsu ware. Korean emigrant potters also introduced the foot-driven pottery wheel. Karatsu ware was made of coarse, hard clay containing iron and coated with a hard feldspath glaze that crackled. Simple designs such as flowers, grasses or abstract patterns were often painted under the glaze. The many variations of Karatsu ware have been classified into three categories: plain Karatsu (*muji karatsu*) with a single glaze; Korean Karatsu (*Chosen karatsu*) combining opaque white and dark brown or black iron glazes; and "picture Karatsu" (*ekaratsu*) having iron oxide designs painted under a semitransparent glaze.

Karatsu kilns produced functional objects for daily use, such as rice bowls, dishes and storage jars, which were shipped all over Japan. Their designs were simple and unpretentious yet had a refinement that appealed to masters of the Japanese tea ceremony. Karatsu tea bowls (*chawan*), vases and water containers became especially prized. During the two invasions of Korea through Kyushu conducted by the warlord Toyotomi Hideyoshi (1536–1598), a great patron of the tea ceremony, many Korean potters were brought back to Kyushu, and production of Karatsu ware increased tremendously. The discovery of kaolin clay in Kyushu in the 17th century caused many of the kilns to convert to making porcelain, but a few Karatsu kilns have remained in operation up to the present time. The Karatsu potter Nakazato Taroemon XII (b. 1895) has been named a living National Treasure by the Japanese government. See also KOREA AND JAPAN; KYUSHU; LIVING NATIONAL TREASURES; POTTERY; TEA CEREMONY; TOYOTOMI HIDEYOSHI.

KASUGA SHRINE (Kasuga Taisha) A Shinto shrine in the ancient capital city of Nara. Kasuga Shrine was founded in A.D. 709 by Fujiwara no Fuhito, and dedicated to the divine spirits (kami) of three other shrines that were associated with the powerful Fujiwara clan. Kasuga was also a national shrine intended to protect the new Japanese capital of Nara that would be constructed starting in A.D. 710. About A.D. 768, the shrine was moved into Nara. The shrine building, according to Shinto tradition, used to be reconstructed every 20 years, until the Edo Era (1600–1868), 57 times altogether. Kasuga Shrine has 3,000 bronze and stone lanterns, which are lit twice a year: on February 3rd or 4th to celebrate the coming of spring, and on August 15th to welcome souls of the dead who return for the Bon Festival. Kasuga also holds an annual festival (Kasuga Matsuri) on March 13th, which was first held by the imperial family in A.D. 850. Many sacred deer roam the grounds of the shrine and are believed to be messengers of the divine spirits.

Kasuga Shrine has been important throughout Japanese history. In the 11th and 12th centuries, warrior-monks of Kofukuji Buddhist temple, connected with Kasuga Shrine, often made demands on the Japanese government by carrying into the capital city of Kyoto the shrine's sacred symbol, which no one dared to touch. Kanami, the founder of the Kanze school of the Noh drama and father of the great actor and playwright Zeami (1363–1443), was a Shinto priest connected to Kasuga Shrine. See also BON FESTIVAL; DEER; FUJIWARA CLAN; NARA; NOH DRAMA; SHINTO; SHRINES, SHINTO; ZEAMI.

KASURI A type of cloth, known outside Japan by the Indonesian name ikat, which has been tie-dyed and woven by a complicated process that produces a "splash pattern." There are several steps in tie-dyeing, also known as a thread-resist technique. First, the thread to be used in weaving a piece of cloth is tied into bundles. Then the bundles of thread are tightly bound with white threads so that when they are dyed, the sections of thread bundles that are bound will resist being colored by the dyes, while the unbound sections do take on the colors. After dyeing, the bundles are untied and woven together, and a geometric pattern emerges. Kasuri is generally made from plant fibers such as hemp (asa), ramie or cotton, and has white patterns on an indigo background. Basic kasuri patterns are geometric cross and parallel cross designs, although more complex pictorial motifs can be woven, such as pine trees, bamboo and cranes. These are known as e-gasuri ("picture kasuri"). Some dye inevitably bleeds into the bound threads. This creates a fading and merging of dyed and undyed sections, which makes the edges of the woven designs a bit hazy and gives kasuri a unique quality appreciated by the Japanese.

Kasuri clothing was worn by many Japanese farmers and urban merchants from the mid-18th to the early 20th centuries. The kasuri technique originated in India, then was brought to Southeast Asia. In the 14th century it reached the southern Ryukyu Islands (modern Okinawa Prefecture), from where it was introduced into Japan proper. In

1609 the Shimazu clan, which governed the Satsuma domain (modern Kagoshima Prefecture) on southern Kyushu Island, took control of Ryukyu, and a large portion of the annual tribute paid by Ryukyu to Satsuma was in the form of kasuri. Weavers throughout Japan soon learned the kasuri technique, and traditional kasuri is still woven in a few regions. Today, a kimono made from kasuri woven in Okinawa will sell for thousands of dollars. The Japanese have utilized various other tie-dyeing techniques since ancient times. One technique still popular is known as shibori-zome, in which small portions of a piece of cloth are bound with thread before dyeing, to create a pattern made up of large or small dots. See also HEMP; INDIGO; KIMONO; RYUKYU ISLANDS; TEXTILES.

KATAKANA A syllabic system of writing foreign words incorporated into the Japanese language, such as terms derived from non-Chinese sources, foreign names, technical terms and telegrams, as well as various Japanese words that are given emphasis. Kana is the general term for syllabic systems that the Japanese derived from Chinese characters (kanji) in the ninth century A.D. Japanese writing became an extremely complex mixture of kanji and kana. Modern Japanese uses two syllabic systems, katakana and hiragana. The latter is used to write native Japanese words and Chinese words that cannot be written with kanji. It is a cursive form, that is, its characters are round and flowing in style. Katakana is a non-cursive form. Both kana systems have 48 characters, which represent the basic syllables of the Japanese language. Katakana and hiragana both developed out of manyogana, an early set of kana that was used to write the Manyoshu, a classic eighth-century Japanese poetry anthology. Katakana was originally used to help Japanese readers remember how to pronounce Buddhist scriptures written in Chinese. By the ninth century, Japanese were writing with a system known as kanamajiri bun, meaning a combination of Chinese characters and katakana. By the mid-10th century, katakana was being used to write classical poetry of the type known as waka. Japanese folktales and other prose literature were being written in a combination of katakana and kanji by the 12th century. The katakana system of writing was routinized in the Muromachi Era (1333–1568), and was standardized in its modern form in 1900. See also CALLIGRAPHY; CHINA AND JAPAN; HIRAGANA; KANA; KANJI; LANGUAGE, JAPANESE; MANYOSHU; POETRY; SCRIPTURES, RELIGIOUS; WAKA; WRITING SYSTEM, JAPANESE.

KATAZOME See STENCILS; TEXTILES; YUZEN DYEING.

KATO TAKAAKI (1860–1926) Also known as Kato Komei; a statesman and politician who, as foreign minister, was responsible for Japan's decision to enter World War I in 1914.

Kato was born Hattori Sokichi in Owari Province (part of modern Aichi Prefecture) and raised by his grandparents in Nagoya City. He was educated in English law at Tokyo University, and admired the English parliamentary system. The Mitsubishi Corporation sent Kato to England for two years to study the shipping business, after which he worked in the Mitsubishi head office in Tokyo and married the daughter of the company's founder.

Kato decided to enter government service, and in 1888 became the private secretary for then Foreign Minister Okuma Shigenobu (1838–1922). He was appointed Japanese minister to Great Britain in 1894, where he laid the foundations for the Anglo-Japanese Alliance of 1902. Prime Minister Ito Hirobumi (1841–1909) appointed Kato foreign minister in 1900, and two years later Kato was elected to the Diet (Parliament) representing Kochi Prefecture. In 1908 Kato again became minister to Britain, where he worked for the revision of the Anglo-Japanese Alliance which took effect in 1911. Kato also served brief terms as Japanese foreign minister in 1906 and 1913, and in 1914 was again appointed to this position in the cabinet of Prime Minister Okuma Shigenobu. Kato angered the *genro* (elder statesmen), who had great influence in the Japanese government, when he brought Japan into World War I in 1914 and presented the Twenty-One Demands to increase Japanese control over China in 1915, and opposition to his actions forced Kato to resign.

In 1916 he became president of a newly organized political party, the Kenseikai (Constitutional Association). Although this party won the majority of seats in the Diet, which meant that Kato ought to have been appointed prime minister by the *genro*, they appointed General Terauchi Masatake instead. The Kenseikai lost power until 1924, when it joined with two other parties and became the majority party in the Diet. At that time, the Kenseikai took the new name of Minseito, or People's Government Party, and Kato became premier of Japan. The new three-party cabinet passed the Universal Manhood Suffrage Law of 1925, which gave the vote to all Japanese males over age 25. The Peace Preservation Law of 1925 was also passed, which enabled the government to suppress communism and other radical movements. Political differences forced the cabinet to resign, but Kato remained in office, and in August 1925 a new Kenseikai cabinet was formed under his leadership. Kato died in office on January 28, 1926. He had wielded great political influence during the period of the so-called Taisho Democracy (1913–1932), a time of liberalization begun in the Taisho Era (1912–1926). See also ANGLO-JAPANESE ALLIANCE; CABINET, PRIME MINISTER'S; DIET; GENRO; ITO HIROBUMI; MITSUBISHI CORPORATION; OKUMA SHIGENOBU; POLITICAL PARTIES; TAISHO ERA; TWENTY-ONE DEMANDS ON CHINA; WORLD WAR I.

KATSU KAISHU (1823–1899)   The chief negotiator for the Tokugawa Shogunate (1603–1867) when power was transferred to the Meiji government in 1868, and an important naval figure. Also known as Katsu Rintaro and Katsu Awa, Katsu Kaishu was born in the city of Edo (now Tokyo) to a samurai family. Trained in swordsmanship and Western military science and technology, he also learned the Dutch language. Katsu opened his own school in 1850.

When U.S. Commodore Matthew Perry opened Japan to Western nations in 1854, Katsu advised the Tokugawa government of the need for an official Japanese school for Western military studies. After receiving naval instruction from the Dutch headquartered in the southern Japanese city of Nagasaki, Katsu was appointed captain of Japan's first modern warship, the Dutch-built *Kanrin Maru*, which was sent to the United States in 1860 with a Japanese mission to ratify the Harris Treaty between the United States and Japan. When he returned to Japan, Katsu was appointed commissioner of warships (*gunkan bugyo*) and made an unsuccessful attempt to train sailors for a national navy.

In 1866 he negotiated a peace settlement between the shogun Tokugawa Yoshinobu and the extreme anti-shogun feudal domain of Choshu (now Yamaguchi Prefecture), but the shogun refused to honor the settlement. Choshu joined with the powerful Satsuma Province (now Kagoshima Prefecture) in bringing down the Tokugawa Shogunate in 1867, which led to the Meiji Restoration of 1868. On Katsu's advice, the shogun surrendered. Katsu worked out a compromise with Saigo Takamori, the leader of the pro-imperial factions, which allowed the Tokugawas to retain some power while surrendering Edo Castle, thus preventing outright civil war. When some forces loyal to the Tokugawa Shogunate took arms against the imperial forces, they were quickly defeated, and the Tokugawas were sent into exile in Suruga (now part of Shizuoka Prefecture). Katsu went into exile with them, but in 1872 the new Meiji government appointed him minister of the navy. After he left this position in 1875, he edited a collection of historical documents from the Tokugawa Shogunate. See also CHOSHU PROVINCE; DUTCH IN JAPAN; IMPERIAL JAPANESE ARMY AND NAVY; MEIJI RESTORATION OF 1868; NAGASAKI; PERRY, MATTHEW CALBRAITH; SAIGO TAKAMORI; SATSUMA PROVINCE; TOKUGAWA SHOGUNATE.

KATSURA DETACHED PALACE (Katsura Rikyu)   Also known as Katsura Imperial Villa; a 17th-century country retreat built on the Katsura River (Katsuragawa) west of the old capital city of Kyoto. The site had long been used by Kyoto aristocrats, but most of the buildings in place today were erected by two members of the Hachijo no Miya family. Prince Toshihito (1579–1629) built the original part of the main house, known as the Old Shoin (Ko Shoin). His son, Prince Toshitada (1619–1672), built the other three sections of the main house, known as the Middle Shoin (Chu Shoin), Music Room (Gakki no Ma), and New Shoin (Shin Shoin). The New Shoin contains a dais, or raised platform, built to accommodate visits from the retired emperor Go-Mizunoo, who built Shugakuin Detached Palace in Kyoto. The rooms of the house, averaging 12 feet by 30 feet each, lie in a diagonal line and are connected by a veranda along their south side.

Katsura Detached Palace is a celebrated example of traditional Japanese architecture. The deceptively simple design, executed with the finest woodworking skills, gives it a natural refinement. The main house is in harmony with equally famous gardens, which include ponds, islands, bridges and manmade hills. Many elements of the gardens resemble actual places in 16th-century Japan. The entire Katsura complex, covering about 17 acres, also contains small pavilions, teahouses and a Buddhist chapel.

A garden in Katsura Detached Palace in Kyoto, one of the most beautiful traditional residences in Japan. Rocks, moss, maple trees and ponds are commonly found in Japanese gardens.

Katsura was designed by the renowned gardener Kobori Enshu under the patronage of the great warlord Toyotomi Hideyoshi (1537–1598). Kobori stipulated that Hideyoshi should spare no expense, give him no time limit and never visit Katsura until it was completed. Hideyoshi died without ever seeing it. The Imperial Household Agency administers Katsura Detached Palace and admits a limited number of visitors who have obtained permission in advance. Many 20th-century Western architects have been influenced by the natural materials and simple yet elegant design of the palace. See also GARDENS; IMPERIAL HOUSEHOLD AGENCY; SHOIN STYLE OF ARCHITECTURE; SHUGAKUIN DETACHED PALACE; TOYOTOMI HIDEYOSHI; WOODWORKING.

KAWABATA YASUNARI (1899–1972) A modern Japanese novelist who was awarded the Nobel Prize in Literature in 1968. Born in Osaka, Kawabata lost his parents, sister and grandparents when he was young, which contributed to the melancholy nature of his writing. He attended high school in Tokyo and in 1924 received a degree in Japanese literature from Tokyo University, where he also studied English literature. His first published story was "Izu no odoriko" (tr. "The Izu Dancer," 1955).

Kawabata was influenced by *renga* (linked verse), a traditional Japanese form of poetry that makes use of associated images. He also subscribed to the aesthetic principle of "elegant sadness" *(mono no aware)* found in the monumental 11th-century Japanese novel *The Tale of Genji*. The works of Kawabata are subtle and suggestive rather than direct, and have connected episodes that do not lead to definite conclusions. The natural world plays a central role in his novels, at times overshadowing the human characters. *Snow Country (Yukiguni*; 1935–1948, translated 1956), one of Kawabata's greatest novels, dwells on the mountains and snow in the wintry region of northwest Honshu Island. Against that backdrop, the main character has a brief affair with a local geisha. Another of his greatest novels is *The Master of Go (Meijin*; 1942–1954, translated 1972), about a master of the game of *go* who loses to a young contender. This story was later made into a critically praised movie. *Thousand Cranes (Sembazuru*; 1951, translated 1959) is about the love of a man for several women, one of whom teaches the tea ceremony. *The Sound of the Mountain (Yama no oto*; 1949–1954, translated 1970) describes the frustrations of a man who is attracted to his daughter-in-law and sister-in-law. Other translated works by Kawabata include *House of Sleeping Beauties (Nemureru bijo*; 1960–1961, tr. with "Birds and Beasts" and "One Arm," 1969); *Beauty and Sadness (Utsukushisa to kanishimi to*; 1961–1963, tr. 1975); and *The Lake (Mizuumi*; 1954, tr. 1974); and *Palm-of-the Hand Stories* (translated 1988). Kawabata wrote literary criticism as well as fiction, and he discovered the young Japanese writer Mishima Yukio, who became a famous novelist in his own right. Kawabata's own life ended as sadly as many of his novels; he was discovered in a room filled with gas, apparently a suicide, although this has not been proven. See also GENJI, THE TALE OF; GO; MISHIMA YUKIO; MONO NO AWARE; NOVELS; SNOW COUNTRY; TEA CEREMONY.

KAWAKUBO REI See FASHION DESIGNERS, CONTEMPORARY.

KAWASAKI An industrial city on the Tamagawa River along the southwest border of Tokyo that is the center of the Keihin Industrial Zone. Oil, coal, iron ore and food are imported through the large port of Kawasaki. Kawasaki was a town during the Edo Era (1600–1868), but in 1907 it began to become industrialized with the building of factories along the Tamagawa River and on land reclaimed from Tokyo Bay. The city was rebuilt after being destroyed during World War II, and petrochemicals, electrical machinery and appliances, automobiles, and steel have become some of its major products. Kawasaki Heavy Industries, Ltd. (Kawasaki Jukogyo), is one of the largest manufacturing companies in Japan, producing ships, airplanes, motorcycles, engines, steel and industrial machinery. The company, an offspring of the Kawasaki Tsukiji Shipyard, founded by Kawasaki Shogo in 1878, exports heavily and has established many overseas subsidiaries and sales offices. Kawasaki Kisen Kaisha, Ltd., operating abroad as the K Line, is the largest Japanese ocean shipping line. Kawasaki Daishi (previously known as Heigenji), a temple of the Shingon (Pure Word) sect of Buddhism, 9draws the most visitors of any temple or shrine in Japan during the New Year Festival. The shrine dates to A.D. 1127, when a statue of Kukai (Kobo Daishi, the founder of the Shingon Buddhist sect in Japan) was pulled from the sea by the warrior Hirama Kanenori. The temple was destroyed in 1945 and completely rebuilt after the war. See also INDUSTRIAL ZONES; KUKAI; NEW YEAR FESTIVAL; SHINGON SECT OF BUDDHISM; TOKYO; NAMES OF INDIVIDUAL INDUSTRIES.

KAWASAKI HEAVY INDUSTRIES, LTD. See MOTORCYCLE INDUSTRY.

KAWASAKI KISEN KAISHA, LTD. See SHIPPING AND SHIPBUILDING.

KDD See NIPPON TELEGRAPH AND TELEPHONE CORPORATION; TELECOMMUNICATIONS SYSTEM.

KEGON SECT OF BUDDHISM A flourishing sect in the early centuries of Buddhist history in Japan, and one of the six sects of Nara Buddhism (Nara Era: 710–794). The Kegon sect was introduced by the Chinese monk Daoxun (Tao-hsuan; Japanese: Dosen, 702–760) and also by the Korean monk known in Japan as Shinjo (d. 742). *Kegon*, from the Chinese term *Huayan (Huayen)*, means "Flower Wreath." The basic *sutra* (religious scripture) of the sect is the *Kegonkyo (Flower Wreath Sutra)*, Japanese for the Sanskrit name *Avatamsakasutra*; this *sutra* is believed to have been the teaching delivered by the Buddha immediately after he attained enlightenment. Its principle doctrine is the harmony of the cosmos ruled by Lochana Buddha, who sits on a lotus flower throne, and through whom all beings are related. Emperor Shomu (701–756; r. 724–794), who patronized the Kegon sect, was responsible for the erection of the enormous temple in Nara named Todaiji and the casting of its 53-foot high Daibutsu (Great Buddha; a bronze sculpture of Lochana Buddha). The Kegon sect is still centered at Todaiji and has 47 other temples. It went into a decline after the Nara Era, but its doctrine of the interrelation and interdependence of all things influenced later Buddhist teachings, such as those of Kukai (774–835), founder of the Shingon sect, and the popular practice of a ritual chant known as *nembutsu*. See also BUDDHISM; DAIBUTSU; KUKAI; NARA; NARA ERA; NEMBUTSU; SHINGON SECT OF BUDDHISM; TODAIJI.

KEGON WATERFALL (Kegon no Taki) The most famous and heavily visited waterfall in Japan, Kegon Waterfall is located on the Daiyagawa River, which flows out of Lake Chuzenji. The lake and 318-foot-high waterfall are part of Nikko National Park, which is located 87 miles north of Tokyo. A Buddhist temple and a hot spring resort are also situated on Lake Chuzenji. Tourists can take an elevator to an observation point at the bottom of the river gorge for a thrilling view of the waterfall. This was a favorite site for love suicides. See also HOT SPRING; NIKKO NATIONAL PARK; SUICIDE.

KEIDANREN See FEDERATION OF JAPANESE ECONOMIC ORGANIZATIONS.

KEIHANSHIN INDUSTRIAL BELT See BIWA, LAKE; INDUSTRIAL ZONES.

KEIHIN INDUSTRIAL ZONE See INDUSTRIAL ZONES; KAWASAKI; YOKOHAMA.

KEIRETSU See CORPORATIONS.

KELP See SEAWEED.

KEMMU RESTORATION See ASHIKAGA TAKAUJI; GO-DAIGO, EMPEROR; MUROMACHI ERA; NAMBOKUCHO ERA.

KENDO "The Way of the Sword"; a martial art based on samurai sword fighting or fencing. In *kendo*, a split-bamboo sword known as a *shinai* is used in place of a dangerous metal sword. The *shinai*, made of four strips of bamboo bound together with a leather grip and cap, is about 38 inches long and weighs 3 pounds. A *kendo* student wears protective armor, consisting of a *keikogi* (tunic) and *hakama* (divided skirt); a *tare*, or heavy cotton padding to protect the hips; a *do*, or breastplate; *kote*, or heavy gloves with forearm protectors; and a *men*, or helmet, to protect the face and head. Even with the armor, a blow from the bamboo sword can be painful.

Sword fighting was introduced into Japan from China between the sixth and ninth centuries A.D. The use of longer blades in Japan made it necessary to hold the sword with two hands. Fencing techniques developed during the military rule of the Kamakura Shogunate (1192–1333) and the Muromachi Era (1333–1568). During the peaceful era of the Tokugawa Shogunate (1603–1867), *kenjutsu* acquired a moral and spiritual element as a method for training the mind as well as the body. Bamboo swords and protective armor were also developed during this time.

Sword fighting was known as *kenjutsu* or *gekken* until the word *kendo* came into use during the Showa Era (1926–1989) to emphasize the spiritual discipline of fencing. *Kendo* was made a compulsory sport in Japanese schools in 1911, but it and other martial arts were banned in Japan by the Allied Occupation authorities after World War II. After the Occupation, in 1952 the All Japan Kendo Federation (Zen Nihon Kendo Rimmei) was established to oversee the awarding of grades. *Kendo* students train by studying movements (*waza*) for attack and defense, in particular stance, footwork, and sword cuts, thrusts and parries, and make special shouts during these movements. Students progress through six beginner classes (*kyu*), and then 10 grades (*dan*). Members of higher grades can also qualify for teaching degrees. Each prefecture in Japan has its own *kendo* federation (*kendo remmei*); the International Kendo Federation was founded in 1970. Tournaments are held throughout Japan and in many foreign countries. See also BAMBOO; MARTIAL ARTS; SAMURAI; SWORD.

KENZAN (1663–1743) A renowned potter and painter who was the successor to his teacher, the acclaimed Japanese potter Nonomura Ninsei (fl. mid-17th century A.D.). Kenzan was also a talented calligrapher, painter, poet and lacquer artist.

Born to the family of a wealthy textile merchant in the old capital city of Kyoto, Kenzan's real name was Ogata Shinsei. His brother, Ogata Korin (1658–1716), became a famous painter. They were descended from a celebrated Japanese artist, calligrapher, potter, and lacquer and metal designer named Hon'ami Koetsu (1558–1637).

Kenzan's pottery featured strong, simple designs with colored enamel overglazes, especially in gray-blue, green, tan, white, dark brown and black. His favorite motifs were snow-covered pine trees or villages, and bamboo, but he also employed red, blue, green and yellow enamels to create floral designs, often in the style of his ancestor Koetsu. Some of Kenzan's most famous works of pottery were square plates decorated with landscapes or poetry.

Kenzan built a pottery kiln in 1609 at Narutaki, northwest of Kyoto, and named it *Inuiyama* (Northwest Mountain). The written characters for *Inuiyama* can also be read as *kenzan*, and so he took the name Kenzan as his art name. Succeeding generations of potters still use the name today. Despite his artistic genius, Kenzan was unable to keep his kiln in operation and was forced to close it in 1712. In 1731 he moved to the capital city of Edo (modern Tokyo), where he was supported during his remaining years by a wealthy patron. See also CALLIGRAPHY; HON'AMI KOETSU; KILN; KORIN; NONOMURA NINSEI; POTTERY; PAINTING.

KENZO TAKADA See FASHION DESIGNERS, CONTEMPORARY.

KETTLE (*kama*) A large cast iron pot used for boiling water for tea over a charcoal fire. A kettle is cast by pouring molten iron into a clay and sand or wax mold. Patterns can be inscribed on the mold to decorate the kettle. Iron kettles have been used since ancient times in Japan. With the development of the tea ceremony in the late Muromachi Era (1333–1568), kettles became appreciated as works of folk art (*mingei*) as well as functional objects. Two regions became famous for producing kettles, Ashiya (in modern Fukuoka Prefecture) and Temmyo (or Temmei, in Tochigi Prefecture). Ashiya kettles have a smooth surface, a refined form and graceful decoration. The Temmyo type has a coarse surface and a simple, rustic look. According to Sen no Rikyu (1522–1591), who established the rituals of the tea ceremony, the kettle is the most important tea utensil. *Chanoyu*, a term for the tea ceremony, means "boiling water for tea." Large kettles are heated on metal tripods in *irori* (an open hearth cut in the floor) from November through April, and smaller kettles are heated on *furo* (portable clay or iron braziers) from May through October. Most tea kettles are round, but they are found in various shapes and styles. For example, "hailstone" kettles have a bumpy surface, and "cloud dragon" kettles have a narrow cylindrical shape. A kettle has two small "ears" on its sides through which circular handles can be slid to pick it up. It also has a smooth metal lid with a knob on top. The kettle is one of the many folk art elements incorporated by tea masters into the tea ceremony. See also TEA; TEA CEREMONY.

KI See AIKIDO; MEDICINE, TRADITIONAL; SHIATSU.

KICHIJO(TEN) A female deity of Buddhism; the Japanese name for the Indian goddess of beauty and fertility whose Sanskrit name is Srimahadevi. A sumptuous eighth-century painting of Kichijo at Yakushiji, a Buddhist temple in Nara Prefecture, is designated a Japanese National Treasure. Even more famous is a wooden statue of Kichijo dating from A.D. 1212 in Joruriji (also known as Kutaiji), a Shingon Buddhist temple in Kamo Cho in Kyoto Prefecture; the statue is carved with ornate robes and jewelry in the style of the imperial court of the late Heian Era (794–1185), and is richly colored and decorated with *kirikane*, thin strips of gold leaf that are applied to resemble textile designs. Kichijo is sometimes associated with the Seven Gods of Good Fortune (Schijifukujin). See also BUDDHISM; HEIAN ERA; NATIONAL TREASURES; SCULPTURE; SEVEN GODS OF GOOD FORTUNE; SHINGON SECT OF BUDDHISM; TEMPLES, BUDDHIST.

KIDO KOICHI (1889–1977) A politician who persuaded the Japanese government to accept the conditions of the Potsdam Declaration for the surrender of Japan that ended World War II. The grandson of Kido Takayoshi (1833–1877), an important leader of the Meiji Restoration of 1868, Kido Koichi held a number of government positions, including minister of education (1937) and home minister (1939). In 1940 he was made lord keeper of the privy seal (*naidaijin*, an administrative post established by the Meiji government in 1885). As such he was not supposed to engage in political decisions. However, Kido took action that year to recommend that Konoe Fumimaro be made prime minister, and in 1941, just before World War II, he supported General Tojo Hideki as successor to Konoe. During the war crimes trials after the surrender of Japan, Kido was judged a class-A war criminal and sentenced to life imprisonment but was released in 1955 because of poor health. The diary he kept from January 1930 to December 1945, published in 1966 as *Kido nikki* (*The Diary of Kido*), is one of the most important Japanese sources of historical information for the latter period of World War II. See also KIDO TAKAYOSHI; KONOE FUMIMARO; SURRENDER OF JAPAN; TOJO HIDEKI; WAR CRIMES TRIALS; WORLD WAR II.

KIDO TAKAYOSHI (1833–1877) Also known as Kido Koin; a statesman who was one of the three main leaders of the Meiji Restoration of 1868, along with Saigo Takamori (1827–1877) and Okubo Toshimichi (1830–1878). Kido was born to a samurai family in the town of Hagi in Choshu Province (modern Yamaguchi Prefecture) on the southwestern tip of Honshu Island. He was adopted by a family of higher social standing named Katsura and educated at a private academy that emphasized loyalty to the emperor.

In 1852 Kido moved to Edo (modern Tokyo), seat of the

Tokugawa Shogunate, where he was trained in the use of the sword and made political connections with pro-imperial leaders from various regions of Japan. Kido served in the Choshu military forces defending the Japanese coast 1853–1854 against the naval squadron of U.S. Commodore Matthew C. Perry. An official in the Choshu bureaucracy, Kido also had ties with the lower-level Choshu samurai who supported the emperor. In 1862 the shogunate transferred Kido from Edo to Kyoto, the imperial capital, where he served as chief representative of the Choshu domain.

A coup in 1863 in Kyoto by leaders of the Satsuma and Aizu domains drove the Choshu faction out of the city. The following year, Choshu forces failed in an attempt to capture the Imperial Palace in Kyoto, and Kido went into hiding. He went to Choshu in 1865 when a radical army of samurai and farmers, known as the *shotai*, led by Takasugi Shinsaku, took control of the domain. Under Kido and Takasugi, the *shotai* defeated forces sent against them by the Tokugawa Shogunate.

In 1866, with the support of Sakamoto Ryoma (1836–1867), an important pro-imperialist leader from Tosa Province (modern Kochi Prefecture) on Shikoku Island, Kido negotiated a secret alliance between Satsuma and Choshu, which overthrew the shogunate and restored imperial power in 1868. Kido was the chief Choshu representative in the new Meiji government. The most important of the various positions he held was councillor *(sangi)* in 1870–1874 and 1875–1876. The Meiji government centralized authority and modernized Japan. Kido replaced the feudal system of domains ruled by *daimyo* (feudal lords) with a system of official government prefectures *(ken)*. He was a member of the Iwakura Mission (1871–1873), which visited Western countries to study their political and educational systems. He recommended that Japan develop a constitutional government modeled on that of Germany, and presided over meetings of prefectural governors that were early attempts at representative government. Kido opposed the pro-military faction in the Japanese government that wanted to invade Korea and Taiwan, which he felt would hamper efforts to improve the social conditions of the Japanese people. By 1873, Kido had lost his position as the preeminent Meiji leader to Okubo Toshimichi. He opposed the Satsuma Rebellion of 1877, led by Saigo Takamori, which was suppressed by the Meiji government. Kido died that year of poor health. See also CHOSHU PROVINCE; CONSTITUTION, MEIJI (1889); IWAKURA MISSION OF 1872; MEIJI RESTORATION OF 1868; OKUBO TOSHIMICHI; PREFECTURE; SAIGO TAKAMORI; SATSUMA PROVINCE; SATSUMA REBELLION; TOKUGAWA SHOGUNATE.

KIKKOMAN CORPORATION

The largest and most famous producer of soy sauce in Japan. The company was founded as the Noda Shoyu Company by the Mogi family and other investors. In 1957 it established a subsidiary in San Francisco named Kikkoman International. Soy sauce sold so well abroad that in 1972 the company built a soy sauce manufacturing plant in Walworth, Wisconsin, under the name Kikkoman Foods, Inc. There is a European sales subsidiary of Kikkoman called Trading Europe, GmbH. Kikkoman sells light and dark soy sauces, other sauces such as teriyaki sauce, wine and processed foods; it sells a number of famous American brand name foods to the Japanese market. It also operates restaurant chains in Japan and abroad. See also SOY SAUCE; TERIYAKI.

KIKU See CHRYSANTHEMUM.

KILN An enclosure for firing pottery and porcelain wares until the clay is hardened. Japanese kilns were traditionally fired with wood. During the Jomon Era (c. 10,000–c. 300 B.C.) and Yayoi Era (c. 300 B.C.–c. A.D. 300), pottery was fired in simple pits dug in the ground. Because this method could not produce very high temperatures, the pottery was soft and easily broken. Techniques for firing pottery in chambers above the ground were introduced into Japan from the Asian mainland starting in the fourth century. During the medieval period (12th–16th centuries), the most commonly used kiln was a single-chamber through-draft type known as a cellar kiln *(ana-gama)*, built with a chimney in the rear to enable heat to flow to the back of the kiln. Such klins could reach temperatures of around 2,200 to 2,400 degrees F, which produced very hard pottery. The *ana-gama* was used to produce Sue ware, which evolved into Bizen ware and Tamba ware. Longer *ana-gama* kilns with several chambers were also developed.

The climbing kiln, or *nobori-gama*, was introduced by Korean potters who were brought to Japan in the early 17th century. A climbing kiln is built on the slope of a hill and may have as many as 20 chambers. Each chamber is placed on a flat step dug above the preceding chamber. The chambers are connected by openings at ground level in the wall of each next higher chamber. Pottery to be fired is stacked on shelves in each chamber, and a wood fire is built in a small chamber at the base of the kiln. A chimney behind the highest chamber draws the heat up through the successive chambers, each of which has a flame vent, a spy hole and a stoking hole for adding wood. Temperatures of around 2,400 to 2,600 degrees F are reached, allowing for high-fired porcelain as well as pottery. The pottery or porcelain is generally fired for 35–40 hours in the climbing kiln. Then it must be left to cool for 4–7 days before being removed.

Raku ware is made with a low-fire kiln consisting of a 3-foot-high cylinder of bricks or curved tiles plastered on the outside with fireclay mud. The firebox consists of a brick tunnel extending 2–3 feet at ground level from an opening in the cylinder wall. Because black Raku must be fired at a higher temperature, only one piece at a time is fired in a very small kiln.

In the late 19th century the down-draft kiln was introduced from Europe. It has one chamber on a flat surface, with either an outside pit for a wood fire or burners built in the side walls for a gas fire. Recently the electric kiln has become widely used in Japan, especially by potters in Kyoto who produce overglaze enamel porcelain ware. Although *nobori-gama* with three to five chambers are still used, climbing kilns or single-chamber down-draft kilns fired by oil or gas are most commonly used in Japan today. See also PORCELAIN; POTTERY; NAMES OF INDIVIDUAL WARES.

KIMIGAYO See NATIONAL ANTHEM.

KIMONO Literally, "a thing worn" (*mono*, "thing"; *kiru* "to wear"); a robe that is the traditional garment of Japanese men and women. A kimono is cut from straight narrow panels of fabric that are sewn together in straight lines. It is wrapped around the body and tied with a sash called an *obi*. The left side of a kimono is always crossed over the right side, except on the deceased. Kimono may be made of silk, cotton, hemp, linen, wool and even synthetic fabrics such as polyester. Yukata, informal kimono-like robes made of cotton, are worn for bathing and at hot spring resorts and summer festivals.

Women wear several layers of undergarments beneath a kimono that are tied with narrow sashes. A *nagajuban* is the kimono-like layer worn just under the kimono. A kimono is also tied with sashes and then wrapped with an *obi*, which is secured by a small pillow and sashes and a braided cord called an *obi-jime*. There are numerous ways of tying girls' and women's *obi* into decorative shapes on the backs of kimono. White split-toed socks called *tabi* and thong sandals called *zori* are worn with kimono. Short jackets called *haori* are sometimes worn over kimono. Women traditionally wore their hair up in elaborate styles to display the nape of the neck. Upper-class women also wore long trailing robes over their kimono known as *uchikake*.

The standard style of kimono is more precisely known as *kosode*, literally "small sleeves," with sleeve ends sewn up except for the small opening at the wrist. This style came into use by women of the dominant samurai class during the Kamakura Era (1192–1333). Formerly the outer garment for lower classes and the undergarment for upper classes, the *kosode* replaced the *hirosode* ("wide sleeves"; sleeve ends left entirely open) style worn by court nobles during the Heian Era (794–1185). The *kosode* style, which became commonly worn in Japan by the 16th century, has remained much the same for eight centuries. *Katabira* are unlined *kosode* made of hemp or ramie that are crisp and cool for summer.

By the 19th century, the kimono became less flowing and more tubular in shape. Today, young unmarried women wear kimono with long hanging sleeves, known as *furisode* ("swinging sleeves"). Married women wear kimono with shorter sleeves, properly called *kosode*. Women wear certain colors and patterns of kimono based on their age and the season of the year. The simple style of the kimono functions like a blank canvas that can be decorated with a great variety of design motifs, patterns, and colors. The Japanese have taken textile weaving and dyeing to a high level of skill and beauty. Some examples are brocade weaving, *kasuri* (tie-dye weaving, known abroad as *ikat*) and *yuzen* dyeing of patterns using paste-resist techniques. Designs from nature are commonly used, such as plants and flowers, as well as abstract or geometric patterns such as plaids, stripes and small dots. A design may be large or small, and may decorate the entire kimono, or just the bottom edge, shoulders or sleeves. Kimono in solid colors that harmonize with the seasons may also be worn. The most formal kimono for married women is the black *tomesode*, which has five family crests (*mon*) on the neck and shoulders and a hand-painted decoration on the lower section. Younger women wear brighter colors, especially pink, red and orange, while older women wear more restrained colors such as lavender. Men's kimono are usually black,

Women of the licensed pleasure quarters in 18th-century Edo (modern Tokyo) wearing kimono. This woodblock print is by Torii Kiyonaga (1752–1815).

gray or dark brown, and their *obi* are narrower and tied in simple flat knots in the back. For formal occasions, men wear over their kimono a divided skirt called a *hakama* and a black *haori* that has crests on the neck and shoulders. This outfit is called a *montsuki hakama*.

Most Japanese wear Western clothing and only put on kimono for auspicious occasions such as a wedding or the New Year Festival. Girls also wear kimono for the Adults' Day Festival when they turn 20 years old. Traditional women entertainers known as geisha still wear kimono all the time. Kimono are also worn for Japanese tea ceremonies. Heirloom kimono are often handed down in families from mother to daughter. After wearing, a kimono should be hung to air it out. It should then be carefully folded flat along the seams and stored in a wrapper made of white handmade paper *(washi)*. There are special wooden chests *(tansu)* with shallow, wide drawers for storing paper-wrapped kimono. A good silk kimono is usually taken apart for washing and then sewn back together by hand. See also ADULTS' DAY; BROCADE; CHEST; CLOTHING; CORD, BRAIDED; CREST; FOOTWEAR; GEISHA; HAIRSTYLES, TRADITIONAL; HAKAMA; HAORI; KABUKI; KASURI; OBI; PAPER, HANDMADE; SILK; TEA CEREMONY; TEXTILES; WEDDINGS; YUKATA; YUZEN DYEING.

KING See EMPEROR.

KINKAKUJI (Temple of the Golden Pavilion) A temple of the Rinzai sect of Zen Buddhism, Kinkakuji is located at the foot of Mount Kinugasa and Mount Saimonjiyama on the western side of Kyoto. Ashikaga Yoshimitsu (1358–1408, the third shogun during the Muromachi Era (1338–1568), acquired an estate on this site and erected a complex of buildings known as Kitayama Palace (Kitayama-dono) there. Yoshimitsu intended this to be a retreat, but he actually ruled Japan from here while his young son Yoshimochi held the title of shogun. According to his wishes, the palace was converted to a temple after Yoshimitsu died in 1408, and was named Rokuonji for the religious name given to him posthumously. The Kinkaku, or Golden Pavilion, is a three-story building within the complex that is covered with gold leaf and houses Buddhist altars and statues of Amida Buddha, Kannon and other religious figures. This building and Fudo Hall (Fudodo) were the only original buildings to survive a fire that destroyed the temple complex in the 16th century, but the Golden Pavilion was destroyed in 1950 when a young Buddhist monk set it on fire. This event was the basis of Mishima Yukio's novel *The Temple of the Golden Pavilion (Kinkakuji;* 1956). In 1955 a reproduction of the original Kinkaku, including the gold leaf (regilded 1988), was completed. Another restoration was completed in 1990. Kinkakuji contains many Buddhist art treasures and a beautiful landscape garden with a large pond. See also AMIDA BUDDHA; ASHIKAGA YOSHIMITSU; GARDENS; GINKAKUJI; KANNON; KYOTO; MISHIMA YUKIO; MUROMACHI ERA; RINZAI SECT OF ZEN BUDDHISM; SHOGUN; TEMPLES, BUDDHIST.

KINKI NIPPON RAILWAY CO., LTD. See KINKI REGION; RAILROADS.

KINKI REGION (Kinki chiho) A region on west-central Honshu Island that includes Hyogo, Kyoto, Mie, Nara, Osaka, Shiga and Wakayama prefectures. It is bounded by the Sea of Japan to the west, the Inland Sea to the southwest and the Pacific Ocean to the southeast. Japanese culture and government have been centered in the Kinki region for almost 2,000 years. Nara and Kyoto served as the former capitals of Japan and the seat of the imperial family until the emperor moved to Tokyo after the Meiji Restoration of 1868. Kyoto remains the preeminent center for traditional Japanese culture and is heavily visited by tourists. The Kinki region also contains Lake Biwa, Japan's largest lake; the major Shinto shrine at Ise; Amanohashidate, a beautiful sandbar that is one of the three "famous sites of Japan" *(Nihon sankei);* and the industrial and commercial cities of Osaka and Kobe, which constitute the heart of the Keihanshin industrial region, the second largest in Japan after Tokyo-Yokohama. In 1963 the Japanese government enacted the Kinki Region Development Law to help the Kinki region become equal in economic and cultural importance to the Tokyo Metropolitan Area. The region is served by the Kinki Nippon Railway Co., Ltd. (Kinki Nippon Tetsudo; known as Kintetsu), the largest private railroad company in Japan. The Kyoto-Osaka-Kobe region is also commonly known as Kansai ("West of the Pass"). See also AMANOHASHIDATE; BIWA, LAKE; INLAND SEA; ISE SHRINE; KANSAI AND KANTO; KOBE; KYOTO; NARA; OSAKA; PACIFIC OCEAN; RAILROADS; SEA OF JAPAN.

KINOKUNIYA SHOTEN See BOOKS AND BOOKSTORES.

KINSHIP See CLAN; FAMILY.

KINTARO "Golden Boy"; the hero of several versions of a folktale about a boy who grew up in the forest. Kintaro is a hero to Japanese boys. As the highest ideal for them to emulate, he represents the virtues of strength, loyalty and a good nature.

One version of the legend is that as a baby, Kintaro was stolen by bears, who taught him sumo-style wrestling and raised him with the animals of the forest. Kintaro had enormous strength, like the Greek mythological figure Hercules. Another version is that Kintaro grew up in an remote forest area with his widowed mother and was a devoted and dutiful son who always helped her, especially by chopping wood; he is therefore depicted holding a hatchet (the weapon also associated with the god of thunder).

Kintaro and his animal companions had many adventures and, possessing enormous strength, Kintaro eventually became King of the Forest. One day he saved a little girl from wolves, and discovered that she was his sister. Some stories also tell how he grew up to be a great sumurai, brought his mother to court and gave her a fine house to live in. Stories about Kintaro may have been based on a historical person named Sakata no Kintoki, a follower of a warrior named Minamoto no Yorimitsu, who was mentioned in an 11th-century anthology of stories called *Konjaku Monogatari*. See also CHILDREN IN JAPAN; MINAMOTO CLAN; SAMURAI; SUMO.

KIRI See PAULOWNIA.

KIRIN BREWERIES, LTD. See ALCOHOLIC BEVERAGES.

KISHI NOBUSUKE See SECURITY TREATY BETWEEN JAPAN AND THE UNITED STATES.

KITA KYUSHU "North Kyushu"; a highly industrialized city in northern Kyushu, the southernmost of the main islands of Japan. Kita Kyushu was formed in 1963 when the five cities of Kokura, Moji, Tobata, Wakamatsu and Yawata were merged. The population is now over 1 million. In earlier days this was a rural region with villages where farming and fishing were the main economic activities. Mining of the extensive deposits of the Chikuho Coalfield on northwestern Kyushu during the Meiji Era (1868–1912) provided the means for industrial development. The ports of Moji and Wakamatsu began shipping coal, and the government opened the Yawata Iron and Steel Works (now the private Nippon Steel Corporation) in Yawata in 1901. Steel and iron have continued to be thriving industries, along with chemicals, ceramics, machinery, electrical appliances and food processing. Many factories have been built on reclaimed land along the 20-mile coast between Kammon Strait and Dokai Bay. Kita Kyushu, with a large port and a major airport, is the gateway to Kyushu. An underwater tunnel and a bridge now connect this city with Honshu, Japan's main island. See also BRIDGES; HONSHU ISLAND; INDUSTRIAL ZONES; KYUSHU ISLAND; STEEL INDUSTRY.

KITAGAWA UTAMARO See UTAMARO.

KITANO SHRINE (Kitano Temmangu; also known as Kitano Jinja and Kitano Tenjin) A Shinto shrine in the city of Kyoto dedicated to the spirit of Sugawara no Michizane (845–903), a famous scholar and official in the imperial court. Sugawara was exiled for opposing the powerful Fujiwara clan, and when he died in disgrace, it was believed that his vengeful spirit was the cause of several disasters in Kyoto. To appease his spirit, the court awarded him the posthumous title "God of Thunder" (Karai Tenjin), and had Kitano Shrine built to commemorate the 44th anniversary of his death. He became the patron saint of scholarship and calligraphy, and many Tenjin shrines in Japan were dedicated to him.

Kitano Shrine owns a famous scroll painting (emakimono) known as Kitano Tenjin engi, which portrays the events of Sugawara's life and the construction of his shrine. Kitano Shrine was the site of a tea ceremony held by the great warlord Toyotomi Hideyoshi (1537–1598) in November 1587. He invited everyone in Japan to take part, and the massive Kitano tea party lasted several days. The shrine holds a public market on the 25th day of every month that is popular with antiques collectors. See also CALLIGRAPHY; FUJIWARA CLAN; KYOTO; SUGAWARA NO MICHIZANE; SHINTO; TEA CEREMONY; TOYOTOMI HIDEYOSHI.

KITE (tako; ika; ikanobori) Traditional Japanese kites are often made with bamboo frames and are decorated with brightly painted designs such as legendary warriors, calligraphy, birds and insects, or abstract patterns.

Kites were introduced into Japan, probably from China by priests of the Buddhist religion, before the 10th century A.D. The oldest Japanese term for kite, ika, short for ika-nobori, refers to the characters for "paper hawk" (kami tobi). In ancient Japan, kites were used for military and religious purposes. They were flown to ask the divine spirits (kami) of Shinto, the indigenous Japanese religion, for good harvests, good health and strong children; to thank them or celebrate festivals; and to purify an area and keep evil away. Military uses for kites included sending messages and signals, and perhaps even helping warriors to soar over obstacles. A famous Kabuki play tells the story of Kinsuke, who sailed on a large kite to steal golden scales from the fish statue on top of Nagoya Castle.

During the Edo Era (1600–1868), members of the wealthy merchant class in the city of Edo (now Tokyo) began flying kites for enjoyment. They had the kites decorated with colorful paintings similar to famous prints in the ukiyo-e style. Kites became works of art and popular souvenirs, and the custom of kite flying soon spread throughout Japan. The modern Japanese word for kite, tako, originated in the dialect of 18th-century Edo. Tako means octopus, and ika, another word for kite (derived from different characters from the ika previously mentioned), means squid (ika nobori is a squid banner).

Today there are many different forms of Japanese kites, some of which are folk art produced in various regions of the country. Japanese kites are divided into five groups according to their shapes; rectangular, polygonal, kimono or windbag, round or intricate. Kites are flown for the New Year, Doll and Children's Day Festivals. Battles between

A giant paper kite decorated with calligraphy. The team of men is preparing for the kite battle held every May in Hamamatsu.

teams of fighting kites are held in some places in Japan. Many tourists watch the kite battles held at Hamamatsu (Shizuoka Prefecture) and Shirone (Niigata Prefecture). The Japan Kite Association operates a Kite Museum in Tokyo. Kites were given to parents when their first son was born and were decorated with pictures to protect babies, such as the legendary strong boy Kintaro. Kites shaped like the carp (koi nobori) are still flown on Children's Day (formerly Boys' Day) to symbolize strength and courage. See also CARP; CHILDREN'S DAY FESTIVAL; DOLL FESTIVAL; EDO ERA; FESTIVALS; KABUKI; KAMI; KINTARO; NEW YEAR FESTIVAL; SHINTO; WOODBLOCK PRINTS.

KIYOMIZUDERA "Temple of Clear Water"; a temple of the Hosso sect of Buddhism built on a hillside in the eastern area of the city of Kyoto. One end of the temple's Main Hall (Hon-do) projects over a cliff, supported by wooden scaffolding and columns 456 feet high. The veranda provides a beautiful view of Kyoto.

Kiyomizudera (also known as Seisuiji) was supposedly founded in A.D. 798 by a monk named Enchin, who was supported by Kanoue no Tamuramaro (758–811), a leader of military campaigns to conquer eastern Japan for the rulers based in Kyoto. Enchin and Tamuramaro built a temple next to a waterfall to house a statue of Kannon (Buddhist Goddess of Mercy) with 11 faces (Juichisen Kannon), which can still be seen in the Main Hall. Kiyomizudera received imperial patronage and was named a national temple in A.D. 810 and became number 16 of 33 temples devoted to Kannon (Saikoku San-ju-san Sho) on a pilgrimage route in western Japan. Although the temple remained independent during the frequent religious wars that broke out in Kyoto, its buildings were destroyed many times by fighting, fires and earthquakes. Most of the buildings that exist today were completed in 1633 under the patronage of Tokugawa Iemitsu (shogun 1623–1651), the third ruler of the Tokugawa Shogunate (1603–1867).

At present, Kiyomizudera contains seven halls, a three-story pagoda, and a few smaller buildings. The Amida Hall (Amida-do) is the site where Honen (1133–1212), founder of the Jodo sect of Buddhism, publically initiated the practice of reciting a prayer known as the nembutsu in A.D. 1188. Visitors use dippers to drink water from the sacred waterfall, named "Sound of Feathers Waterfall" (Otowa-no-taki), which is dedicated to the god Fudo Myoo and believed to be purifying. See also FUDO MYOO; HOSSO SECT OF BUDDHISM; KANNON; KYOTO; KYOTO WARE; NEMBUTSU; PAGODA; TEMPLES, BUDDHIST; TOKUGAWA IEMITSU.

KNEELING BOWING; PILLOWS; TATAMI.

KNIVES (hocho) Traditional Japanese knives are very sharp and of high quality. They are made from steel, using techniques similar to those for making swords. The finest quality knives are known as hon-yaki ("true-forged"), for the process by which the metal is coated with a special mud while being heated at very high temperatures to protect it from overheating and breaking. These knives cost hundreds of dollars and are used by professional chefs. Ordinary kitchen blades, known as (hon-gasumi or kasumi,

"haze" or "mist"), have a thin layer of hard steel inside a thick layer of soft iron. The finished blade has just a thin line of hard steel exposed to form the cutting edge. Japanese knives last a lifetime if properly cared for. They must be honed on a whetstone to sharpen them before use, and wiped immediately after use to prevent rusting. Most Japanese knives are sharpened on the right side only.

More than a hundred different types of knives are used in Japan for cutting food and other purposes. In many cases, one type of knife is used only to cut one type of food, particularly fish, one of the most important foods in the Japanese diet. For example, an unagi saki is used to cut eel, and a katsuo bushi to slice bonito fish. A knife for cutting tuna, a large fish, is as long as a sword.

Twenty different types of knives are commonly used for cooking in Japan. They fall into three general categories, each with a number of sizes and weights with blades of different lengths. Short but pointed kitchen cleavers or carvers (deba-bocho) are used for making basic cuts of fish, chicken and meat. Vegetable knives (nakiri-bocho or usuba-bocho) resemble flat cleavers but are very light-weight. They are used for paring, slicing, chopping, mincing and cutting decorative garnishes from vegetables. Nakiri-bocho are vegetable knives used in home kitchens. The term usuba refers to a variety of vegetable knives used by professional chefs. Fish slicers (sashimi-bocho) are long, thin-bladed knives used to slice fish fillets into thin pieces.

Carpenters, furniture makers, and other craftsmen also use a variety of knives and other tools, such as chisels and planes. They prefer to have their tools made to order by local blacksmiths rather than to buy mass-produced ones. Blacksmiths also make special types of scissors for flower arranging and gardening. See also COOKING; FLOWER ARRANGING; SASHIMI; SUSHI; SWORD; WOODWORKING.

KOAN "Public case"; a religious question that cannot be solved by ordinary logic but that points directly to the ultimate nature of reality. Koan are a method used in the Rinzai sect of Zen Buddhism, along with meditation and other techniques, to attain satori (enlightenment). The Soto sect of Zen Buddhism also employs koan but places greater emphasis on meditation.

The word koan comes from the Chinese word kung-an or gongan, which refers to records in courts of law which provide the opinions of wise men that serve as precedents in deciding legal cases. Collections of koan were compiled in China which contain teachings of earlier Zen masters instructive for Zen students. Two classic collections of koan translated into Japanese have been published in English as the Blue Cliff Record (Hekiganroku; 1125), and the Gateless Gate (Mumonkan; 1228). The Japanese Zen master Hakuin Ekaku (1686–1769) systematized the method of koan study that is still practiced in Japanese Rinzai temples. He also added a koan of his own that has become famous: "What is the sound of one hand clapping?" See also EISAI; HAKUIN EKAKU; MEDITATION; RINZAI SECT OF ZEN BUDDHISM; SATORI; SOTO SECT OF ZEN BUDDHISM; ZEN SECT OF BUDDHISM.

KOBAKO See BOXES; INCENSE.

KOBAN See POLICE SYSTEM.

KOBE A city built on a hillside overlooking Osaka Bay that rivals Yokohama as one of Japan's two busiest ports and serves as the port for the busy commercial city of Osaka. The city has a population of over 1.3 million and is the capital and largest city in Hyogo Prefecture. Kobe has been an important port as far back as the Nara Era (710–794). Trade between Japan and China brought Kobe great prosperity, especially during the 15th and 16th centuries. Kobe has long been a cosmopolitan city. When Japan was opened to trade with Western nations in the mid 1800s, the Ansei Commercial Treaties signed in 1858 designated Hyogo (now merged with Kobe) as an open port, officially opened on January 1, 1868. Western traders who moved into Kobe were at first confined to an island separated by canals from the rest of the city. They had their own municipal council, laws, police and tax system, and built Victorian-style homes, some of which still exist. Exhibits in the Kobe Maritime Museum show the history of the port. The Kobe City Museum shows the Western influences on furniture, printing and shipbuilding, and also screens and scrolls that depict the Japanese view of Westerners. The Hakutsuru Fine Art Museum was one of Japan's first private museums. (Hakutsuru is a brand of sake whose name means "white crane.") The old pre–World War II building houses Japanese art and a collection of antique Chinese pottery and bronze objects amassed by the brewing family. Mount Rokko to the north provides a good view of the city; the top can be reached by cable car. Ships, iron and steel, railroad cars, textiles, and sake are some of Kobe's principal products. Kobe beef is also famous for its high quality. See also ANSEI COMMERCIAL TREATIES; FOREIGN TRADE; HONSHU ISLAND; OSAKA; SAKE; SHIPPING AND SHIPBUILDING; STEEL INDUSTRY; TEXTILES; YOKOHAMA.

KOBE DAISHI See KUKAI.

KODANSHA, LTD. One of the largest publishing companies in Japan. At present Kodansha publishes several dozen magazines for the Japanese mass market, as well as a wide range of books (1,565 books in 1980). In 1963 Kodansha established Kodansha International, Ltd., which has become the preeminent publisher of Japanese books in English. In 1983 the company published the monumental eight-volume *Kodansha Encyclopedia of Japan.*

Kodansha was founded in 1911 to publish a magazine for the Greater Japan Oratorical Society (Dai Nippon Yuben Kai), which had been established in 1909 by Noma Seiji (1878–1938), a clerk at Tokyo University Law School. Noma went on to publish many popular magazines in the 1920s under the company name Dai Nippon Yuben Kai Kodansha, and prior to World War II 70% of all magazines circulated in Japan were published by this company. During the Allied Occupation of Japan after the war, Kodansha was strongly criticized for having supported the war effort, and all the company's officers were forced to resign. See also BOOKS AND BOOKSTORES; MAGAZINES; OCCUPATION OF JAPAN.

KODO See DRUMS.

KOETSU See HON'AMI KOETSU.

KOFUN ERA (c. 300–710) A period in ancient Japanese history named for *kofun,* large tombs constructed of mounded earth for the burial of aristocrats. This practice may have derived from burial mounds of the Yayoi Era (c. 300 B.C.– c. A.D. 300). Many ritual and decorative objects were buried in tomb mounds, some of which have been excavated. The mounds were often decorated with pottery figures known as *haniwa.* The Kofun Era is usually divided into three phases based on different types of mounds: Early (fourth century A.D.), Middle (fifth century) and Late (sixth–seventh centuries). This last coincides with the Asuka Era (late 6th century–710) when the Yamato clan established the Japanese imperial court, when urban areas were developing and when the Buddhist religion with its complex culture were introduced from China. The Kofun Era was followed by the Nara Era (710–794), when a bureaucratic imperial government was established in the new capital city of Nara. See also HANIWA; NARA; NARA ERA; TOMB MOUND; YAMATO; YAYOI ERA.

KOI AND KOINOBORI See CARP; CHILDREN'S DAY FESTIVAL; KITE.

KOISO KUNIAKI See OKINAWA, BATTLE OF; SUZUKI KANTARO; WORLD WAR II.

KOIZUMO YAKUMO See HEARN, LAFCADIO.

KOJIKI *Record of Ancient Things;* a collection of early Japanese mythology, religious rituals, songs and history compiled in A.D. 712. The *Kojiki* and the *Nihon Shoki* (or *Nihongi;* compiled A.D. 720) are the earliest extant Japanese documents. They contain similar materials and were commissioned by the ruling family of the Yamato region of western Honshu Island to legitimize their power and increase their prestige.

The *Kojiki* and *Nihon Shoki* both present genealogies that trace the descent of the imperial family from the Sun Goddess, Amaterasu o Mikami. According to legend, the Sun Goddess was born to Izanagi and Izanami, the god and goddess who created the islands of Japan, the ocean, rivers, mountains and trees. Amaterasu sent her grandson Ninigi no Mikoto down from heaven to rule Japan, giving him three sacred treasures, a jewel, a sword and a mirror, to symbolize the eternal reign of his dynasty, and these three objects, known as the imperial regalia, still symbolize the power of the Japanese emperors. According to the creation story, Ninigi went to Kyushu, the southernmost of the four main islands of Japan. His own grandson, Jimmu Tenno, supposedly became the first Japanese emperor in 660 B.C. Although this date is many centuries too early to be the historical founding of the rule of the imperial family, their ancestors probably did in fact come from western Kyushu Island and gradually migrate to the Yamato region on Honshu Island. The Japanese imperial family, whose origins are recorded in the *Kojiki* and the *Nihon Shoki*, is claimed to be the longest unbroken dynasty in the world.

The *Kojiki* records the generations descended from Jimmu Tenno down through the seventh century A.D. The imperial court moved to the newly built city of Nara in A.D. 710. The Soga clan, the most powerful faction at court, supported the importation of Chinese culture, which was introduced into Japan in the sixty century A.D., primarily by priests of the Buddhist religion. The Chinese emphasis on recording historical events to serve as a guide to the present likely influenced the way that events were selected and recorded in the *Kojiki*. While the *Nihon Shoki* was written in the Chinese language, the *Kojiki* was written in a complex style that uses Chinese ideographs both in the customary way and also to imitate phonetically the way the Japanese language sounded in the eighth century A.D. This way of writing was so difficult to understand that whereas the *Nihon Shoki* remained an important text over the centuries, the *Kojiki* was virtually neglected for a thousand years, until the Japanese scholar Motoori Norinaga (1730–1801) made his life's work the deciphering of the *Kojiki*. See also AMATERASU O MIKAMI; BUDDHISM; CHINA AND JAPAN; EMPEROR; JIMMU TENNO; NARA; NIHON SHOKI; SHINTO; SOGA CLAN; WRITING SYSTEM, JAPANESE; YAMATO.

KOKEDERA See MOSS; SAIHOJI.

KOKINSHU *Collection from Ancient and Modern Times*; the first Japanese poetry anthology officially commissioned by the imperial court. Altogether there were 21 such official anthologies. The *Kokinshu* was commissioned during the reign of Emperor Daigo (r. 897–930) and completed c. A.D. 905. Its proper name is *Kokin wakashu, Collection of Japanese Poems from Ancient and Modern Times*. The anthology includes more than 1,100 poems in the *tanka* form, a "short poem" having 31 syllables in a five-line pattern of 5-7-5-7-7. One of the *Kokinshu*'s four compilers, the great poet Ki no Tsurayuki, also wrote a preface to the collection c. A.D. 922, which was the first major Japanese work of literary criticism. The *Kokinshu* set the aesthetic standards for all later classical Japanese poetry and Japanese culture in general. The most valued aesthetic quality in ancient Japan was *miyabi*, or refined sensibility, which was highly developed by the aristocracy of the Heian Era (794–1185). Another principle, *yugen*, or sad awareness of the temporary nature of things, is mentioned in the preface to the *Kokinshu*. Closeness to nature another Japanese trait, is evident in the many poems about the seasons. Love poetry also has an important place in the *Kokinshu*. The lyrics for the unofficial Japanese national anthem, "Kimigayo" ("His Majesty's Reign"), taken from a poem in the *Kokinshu*, were set to music in the late 19th century. See also HEIAN ERA; NATIONAL ANTHEM; POETRY; TANKA; YUGEN.

KOKORO A term used in the Buddhist religion to mean both the human heart and mind, or emotion and intellect, in the broad sense. It is sometimes translated as "soul." *Kokoro* is the Japanese pronunciation of the Chinese Bud-

dhist term *hsin*. The term *kokoronashi* or *mushin* ("no mind"; to be empty of or to lack heart or depth of feeling) is used in Buddhism to describe a person who has realized *satori*, that is, who has become enlightened and is thus free of ordinary attachments and desires. *Kokoronashi* is also applied as an aesthetic term to literary expressions lacking elegance and refinement, such as comic linked verse. During the Heian Era (794–1185), *kokoronashi* referred to a person who lacked discretion, good taste or artistic and emotional sensitivity. Natsume Soseki (1867–1916) wrote a novel titled *Kokoro* (1914; translated 1957) about the suicide of General Nogi Maresuke and his wife on the day of the funeral of Emperor Meiji (r. 1867–1912) as an act of loyalty to the emperor. A *kokorozuke* (or *shugi*; "in celebration") is a tip, usually money but occasionally a gift, to thank a person of lower status for services rendered, such as a maid in a *ryokan* (Japanese inn) or a chauffeur. The money is handed to the recipient in a specially decorated envelope. See also BUDDHISM; GIFTS.

KOKU A unit of measure, most commonly applied to a certain volume of rice, which was used to determine tax payments, stipends for samurai, agricultural productivity and the wealth of *daimyo* (feudal lords). One *koku* of rice is the equivalent of 5.12 bushels (about 0.18 cubic meters), which was the amount considered sufficient to feed one person for one year. The Japanese historically measured wealth in terms of rice, the basic crop, an important medium of exchange, and the form in which taxes were collected.

Starting with the Taika Reform of 645–649, when the *koku* as a unit of measure was adapted from China, the imperial court acquired its revenues by taxing a percentage of the rice crop grown by the Japanese people. The size of a *koku* was standardized by Toyotomi Hideyoshi (1537–1598), one of the three warlords who unified Japan. See also DAIMYO; EDO ERA; FEUDALISM; MAEDA CLAN; RICE; SHINTO; TAIKA REFORM OF 645–649; TOKUGAWA SHOGUNATE; TOYOTOMI HIDEYOSHI.

KOKUSAI DENSHIN DENWA CO., LTD. See NIPPON TELEGRAPH AND TELEPHONE CORPORATION; TELECOMMUNICATIONS SYSTEM.

KOKUTAI Literally, "body politic," usually translated as "national essence" or "national polity"; a pre-World War II concept used to define the uniqueness of the Japanese state.

The ancient term *kokutai* was developed by the 17th-century scholar Yamaga Soko to argue that Japanese government and ethics were not adapted from China but arose in Japan in conjunction with Shinto, the indigenous Japanese religion. But the modern sense of *kokutai* also drew upon Confucian ethics, which advocate unquestioning obedience to one's superiors. Ito Hirobumi (1841–1909) and other leaders of the Meiji Restoration of 1868 used *kokutai* to convey the idea that Japan is a family-state centered on the emperor, who is the figurative father of his subjects.

As Japan entered the modern era, the emperor was used

as a symbol of *kokutai* to heighten nationalist feelings. Reverence for and loyalty to the emperor rallied the Japanese against the threat they felt from "Western barbarians" in the 19th century, and enabled Japan to incorporate Western science and culture without destroying its traditional identity and political structure.

During the 1930s, the Japanese military suppressed ideas that countered the nationalistic ideology of *kokutai*. The Ministry of Education issued a tract in 1937 titled *The Fundamental Principles of Our National Polity (Kokutai no Hongi)* to educate the Japanese on their duty to loyally serve the state. They were not to criticize the military, it explained, because it represented the emperor, and they must be willing even to die for him in support of Japan's sacred mission. After World War II, authorities of the Occupation banned this tract and denounced the nationalistic ideology of *kokutai*. Japan's new constitution, enacted in 1947, declared the emperor to be a human symbol of the state, rather than a sacred being, and Japan to be a republic that guarantees personal freedoms to its citizens. See also AMATERASU O MIKAMI; CONFUCIANISM; CONSTITUTION OF 1947; EMPEROR; ITO HIROBUMI; MEIJI RESTORATION OF 1868; OCCUPATION OF JAPAN; SHINTO; WORLD WAR II.

KOMAINU   See DOG;, LION.

KOMBU   See SEAWEED.

KOMEI, EMPEROR   See MEIJI, EMPEROR.

KOMEITO   See CLEAN GOVERNMENT PARTY; SOKA GAKKAI.

KOMYO, EMPEROR   See ASHIKAGA SHOGUNATE.

KONBU   See SEAWEED.

KONGOBUJI   A Buddhist temple on Mount Koya (Koyasan), located on south-central Honshu island, that is the administrative headquarters of the Mount Koya Shingon sect (Koyasan Shingonshu) of Buddhism. The Shingon complex on Mount Koya was founded in A.D. 816 by the Japanese monk Kukai (774–835; known posthumously as Kobo Daishi). Today Kongobuji is the name of a specific temple, but formerly the entire complex of temples and monasteries was known by that name. By the 12th century, Kongobuji had become a flourishing center for Buddhist studies. Fires and rivalry between lay workers and religious clergy destroyed the buildings several times, but they were always reconstructed. Internal dissension was ended in 1869 when Seiganji, the temple belonging to the *gakuryo* religious faction, was named Kongobuji and made the head temple of the sect.

Kukai died at Mount Koya in A.D. 835. He is buried in a mausoleum in the center of the temple complex, known as the Oku no In. According to believers, he is in deep meditation to bring about the salvation of all beings. Two hundred-fifty thousand others are buried in surrounding plots, including Buddhist leaders and *daimyo* (feudal lords) from the Edo Era (1600–1868). Mortuary tablets of deceased Japanese emperors are kept in the *jibutsudo*, a room in the main building of Kongobuji. The Kongobuji temple complex includes more than 100 other buildings, including the Fudodo, which was built in A.D. 1198 and has been designated a Japanese National Treasure. The Koyasan Treasure House (Koyasan Reihokan) contains calligraphy, paintings, sculpture, Buddhist ritual objects and religious scriptures from the Heian (794–1185) and Kamakura (1192–1333) eras, including documents written by Kukai, Minamoto no Yoritomo (1147–1199), the great warrior who founded the Kamakura Shogunate, and his brother, Minamoto no Yoshitsune (1159–1189). Today more than 3,600 temples throughout Japan are affiliated with the Mount Koya Shingon Sect. See also BUDDHISM; KOYA, MOUNT; KUKAI; NATIONAL TREASURES; SHINGON SECT OF BUDDHISM; TEMPLES, BUDDHIST.

KONICA   See CAMERAS AND PHOTOGRAPHY.

KONISHIROKU PHOTO INDUSTRY CO., LTD (SAKURA FILM)   See CAMERAS AND PHOTOGRAPHY.

KONOE FUMIMARO (1891–1945)   A politician who served as prime minister of Japan 1937–1939 and 1940–1941. Konoe promoted the concept of a Greater East Asia Coprosperity Sphere (Dai Toa Kyoeiken), in which Asia would be united politically and economically under Japanese military domination and liberated from Western influence.

Konoe was born in Tokyo to an aristocratic family and inherited the title of prince. He was educated at Kyoto University and in 1916 was appointed to the House of Peers (upper house) of the Imperial Diet (the Japanese parliament between 1889 and 1947). In the 1920s he encouraged Japanese support of nationalists in China who opposed Western imperialism in Asia. He also supported Japanese military incursions against China in the 1930s and the Japanese puppet state in Manchuria (Manchukuo). Konoe became vice president of the House of Peers in 1931 and served as its president from 1933 to 1937. He chose not to accept his first appointment as prime minister, which was made just after the February 26th Incident of 1936. He did become prime minister in June of 1937. War with China broke out that year, but Japan's failure to force China to acquiesce to Japanese demands caused Konoe to resign as prime minister in 1939. He served two more terms as prime minister, from July 22, 1940 to July 18, 1941, and July 18, 1941 to October 18, 1941. Konoe led Japan during the height of the militarization that would bring it into World War II, and he allied Japan with the European Axis powers through the Tripartite Pact in 1940. Konoe realized that Japan's military expansion could not succeed against American opposition and resigned as prime minister two months before Japan bombed Pearl Harbor on December 7, 1941. In 1945 he helped remove General Tojo Hideki, who had succeeded him as prime minister. When Konoe was accused of being a war criminal after the war, he committed suicide on December 16, 1945. See also GREATER EAST ASIA COPROSPERITY SPHERE; MANCHURIAN INCIDENT; OCCUPATION OF JAPAN; PEARL HARBOR, JAPANESE ATTACK ON; PRIME MINISTER; SINO-

JAPANESE WAR OF 1937–1945; TOJO HIDEKI; TRIPARTITE PACT; WAR CRIMES TRIALS; WORLD WAR II.

KOREA AND JAPAN

The peninsula of Korea is the closest point on the Asian mainland to the Japanese islands, only 150 miles away, and was historically Japan's main link with the continent. Many early settlers crossed the Tsushima Strait from Korea to the southern island of Kyushu. After China established a colony in Korea in 108 B.C., Chinese culture and Asian religions were introduced into Japan through Korea. Contents of tomb mounds in Japan indicate that during the Kofun Era (A.D. 300–710), nomadic mounted warriors arrived from Korea and northeast Asia, bringing crafts such as metallurgy and silk weaving, and became the ruling elite in Japan. The Japanese attacked the Korean kingdom of Silla 25 times from the first through fifth centuries, establishing a foothold on the southern tip of Korea from A.D. 369 to 562. After Japanese troops moved against the Korean kingdom of Koguryo in A.D. 391, the king of Paekche thanked them by sending Korean scholars of the Chinese classics to the Yamato court in western Japan. In A.D. 522 King Song of Paekche sent a mission to Yamato requesting military aid and bringing presents, including Buddhist sculptures and scriptures written on scrolls. Chinese culture and the Buddhist religion were adopted by the Yamato court, creating the first flowering of culture in Japan. Immigrant groups from Korea such as the Aya and Hata clans settled in the Yamato area and brought skills such as silk cultivation. Japan continued to have diplomatic and trading relations with Korea.

Mongols from northern Asia, led by Kublai Kahn, attempted to invade Japan through Korea in 1274 and 1281 but failed both times, with much of their fleet destroyed by typhoons, called "divine wind" (*kamikaze*) by the Japanese. The Japanese national unifier Toyotomi Hideyoshi invaded Korea in 1592, capturing Pusan and Seoul and marching to the Manchurian border. Ming China claimed suzerainty over Korea and sent an army to halt the Japanese advance. Hideyoshi launched a second invasion in 1597, but Chinese troops pushed the Japanese back to the southern coast of Korea. After Hideyoshi died suddenly in 1598, the Japanese troops made their final evacuation.

In 1868 the Meiji government (1868–1912) sent a diplomatic mission to Korea to negotiate trade agreements, but Korea rejected its proposals. Saigo Takamori planned to send a Japanese military force to Korea in 1873, but other members of the government vetoed this plan. They did send a naval force to Korea, however, to persuade the country to sign the Treaty of Kangwha of 1876, opening two ports to Japanese trade in addition to the one at Pusan. Japan intervened in political crises in Korea in 1882 and 1884 but was challenged by a large Chinese military presence. After China claimed sovereignty over Korea in 1894, Japan fought and easily won the Sino-Japanese War of 1894–1895, after which Japan took control of Korea. Russia, Germany and France protested this action, sparking the Russo-Japanese War (1904–1905), in which the Japanese again easily defeated a much larger neighbor. The Japanese

army took control of Korea despite Korea's declaration of neutrality. In 1905 the United States and Great Britain recognized Japanese rights in Korea, and Japan signed an agreement with Korea making the country a protectorate of Japan. Ito Hirobumi, who had been first prime minister of Japan, became the first Japanese resident-general in Korea, bringing with him Japanese officials, troops and a suppressive military police force. In 1909 Ito was assassinated by a Korean. Japan forced Korean emperor Kojon to abdicate in 1907, and forced Korea to sign a treaty of annexation to Japan in 1910. Renamed Chosen, Korea remained remained a colony of Japan until August 15, 1945, when Japan surrendered to the Allied Powers, ending World War II.

Japanese policies in Korea remain a deep source of resentment between the two countries. After Japan invaded China in 1937 and the war in the Pacific broke out in 1941, the entire Korean economy was structured to support Japanese military efforts, and the Korean people were required to declare their loyalty to the Japanese empire and take Japanese family names. They were drafted into the Japanese army starting in 1942, and thousands were sent to work in Japanese factories, mines and military bases. After Japan's defeat, the Republic of Korea was created in 1948 and more than a million Koreans in Japan were repatriated to Korea. During the Allied Occupation of Japan (1945–52), Japan was a staging area for American troops fighting the Korean War, which broke out in 1950, led by U.S. General Douglas MacArthur. The war ended in a stalemate in 1953, with Korea divided in half along the 38th parallel. The Republic of Korea (South Korea) has seen successful economic development, and is now beginning to rival Japan, its former colonial master, in important industries such as automobiles, consumer electronics, shipbuilding and steel. Today Japan and South Korea have close diplomatic and trade ties. Koreans remain one of the largest minority groups in Japan, numbering about 700,000. In May 1990 Emperor Akihito expressed "deepest regret" to South Korean President Roh Tae Woo for the suffering Japan had caused Korea, and Prime Minister Kaifu Toshiki expressed Japan's "sincere remorse and honest apologies." See also AYA CLAN; BUDDHISM; CHINA AND JAPAN; HATA CLAN; HORSE-RIDER THEORY; ITO HIROBUMI; KAMIKAZE; KOFUN ERA; KYUSHU ISLAND; MACARTHUR, DOUGLAS; MEIJI RESTORATION OF 1868; MINORITIES IN JAPAN; MONGOL INVASIONS OF JAPAN; OCCUPATION OF JAPAN; RUSSO-JAPANESE WAR; SAIGO TAKAMORI; SINO-JAPANESE WAR OF 1894–95; TOMB MOUND; TOYOTOMI HIDEYOSHI; TSUSHIMA ISLAND; WORLD WAR II; YAMATO.

KOREANS IN JAPAN

See KOREA AND JAPAN; MINORITIES IN JAPAN.

KORIN

(1658–1716) Also known as Ogata Korin; a painter and designer who worked in the style of the Rimpa school of painting. Born Ogata Koretomi, he studied with Yamamoto Soken (d. 1706), an ink painter of the Kano school, but he is best known for carrying on the work of Sotatsu (?–1643?; also known as Tarawaya Sotatsu), founder of the Rimpa school, which is also known as the Sotatsu-Korin school. Korin was the older brother of the famous painter and potter Kenzan (1663–1743; also known as Ogata Kenzan), to whose pottery bowls and plates he applied painting and calligraphy. The two artists were distantly related to another great Japanese artist, Hon'ami Koetsu (1558–1637).

The Ogata family were merchants who sold textiles in the old capital city of Kyoto, where Korin first became an influential designer of *kosode* ("small sleeve"), a type of kimono that was a basic women's garment in the Edo Era (1600–1868). In 1704 Korin moved to Edo (modern Tokyo), where he spent seven years painting works commissioned by wealthy *daimyo* (feudal lords) and merchants, but he returned to Kyoto in 1711 in pursuit of artistic freedom. During this final period of his life he created his greatest work, screens entitled *Red and White Plum Trees (Kohakubai zu)*, which now belong to the MOA Museum of Art in Atami. Korin's masterful decorative style is also seen in his famous screen paintings, *Iris Screens (Kakitsubatazu)*, in which the blue iris flowers and green leaves stand out against a vivid gold background. The screens are now in the collection of the Nezu Art Museum in Tokyo. See also HON'AMI KOETSU; IRIS; KENZAN; KANO SCHOOL OF PAINTING; KIMONO; PAINTING; PLUM TREE; RIMPA SCHOOL OF PAINTING; SCREENS; SOTATSU.

KOSE SCHOOL OF PAINTING (Koseha)   The first school of painters in ancient Japan, it began in the ninth century A.D. and continued until the 15th century. The Kose style was originated by a painter in the imperial court in Kyoto named Kose no Kanaoka (fl. ninth century A.D.), in reaction to the Chinese painting styles (*kara-e*) and subjects that had dominated Japanese art in the seventh and eighth centuries. Kose no Kanaoka, in fact, was commissioned in A.D. 880 to paint portraits of Confucian sages on the walls of the Japanese Imperial University (Daigakuryo), and in A.D. 888 to paint similar portraits for the Imperial Palace. But he also painted Japanese subjects, such as the changing seasons of the year, and thus helped initiate an indigenous style of painting, known as *Yamato-e*. During the late Heian Era (794–1185), members of the Kose school held the position of professional artists (*eshi*) at the Imperial Court Painting Bureau (Kyutei Edokoro). Kose no Kanaoka's great-grandson Hirotaka, whose paintings were commissioned for the Imperial Palace and by the powerful Fujiwara clan, ensured that the Kose school remained dominant in the imperial court during the 11th and 12th centuries. The Kose school declined in influence during the Kamakura Shogunate (1192–1333), when a branch the school moved to the old capital city of Nara to work in the painting workshops of Kofukuji Buddhist temple. By the start of the Muromachi Era (1333–1568), the Kose had been supplanted by the *Yamato* style of painting. See also CHINA AND JAPAN; FUJIWARA CLAN; HEIAN ERA; IMPERIAL PALACE (KYOTO); NARA; PAINTING; YAMATO STYLE OF PAINTING.

KOSODE   See CLOTHING; KIMONO.

KOTATSU   A traditional device for heating a room that is still commonly used in Japan. Formerly a *kotatsu* was a large clay pot containing ash and burning charcoal. The pot was placed on the floor or in an opening cut into the floor, and was covered with an open wooden frame and a quilt. Family members sat with their legs under the quilt to keep warm. Until the 19th century the *kotatsu* was the major method for heating homes. The modern type of *kotatsu* uses electricity and is much safer. It consists of an open wooden frame with an electric heating bulb underneath. The frame is covered with a large cloth, over which is placed a removable table top and a quilt to cover the legs of family members. See also HOMES AND HOUSING.

KOTO   A rectangular musical instrument similar to a zither or harp that is played by plucking its 13 strings. The *koto* is about 6 feet long and is made of paulownia wood (*kiri*). Its strings are made of silk and the *koto* is tuned by adjusting moveable bridges between the strings. The *koto* is placed flat on the floor, and the musician kneels on the floor behind it, plucking the strings with picks that are attached to the thumb and first two fingers of the right hand. Pressing the strings with the left hand changes the pitch. The range of a *koto* is two and a half octaves. A musician may also sing while playing. First brought to Japan during the Nara Era (710–794), the *koto* was one of an ensemble of musical instruments in a standard Chinese court orchestra (called *Gagaku* in Japanese). The *koto*, which was called *zheng* in Chinese, remained an aristocratic instrument in Japan to the present time. The use of the *koto* as a solo instrument was developed by new musical schools beginning in the late 15th century. The *koto* was also taken up, along with a three-string banjo-like instrument called a *shamisen*, by a class of blind musicians known as *kengyo*. Two classical styles of *koto* playing became standardized,

Women dressed in kimono playing zither-like classical instruments called *koto*. They are kneeling on thick straw mats called *tatami* in front of sliding screens called *shoji*.

with a large repertoire as a solo instrument and in an ensemble. The *Ikuta* style of *koto* music in Kyoto combines playing of the *koto* and *shamisen,* while the *Yamada* style in Tokyo has the *koto* play the melody. Some 20th-century composers have created *koto* with 12, 17, 20 and even 80 strings. The earliest Japanese *koto* actually had five or six strings.

The *Shichigenkin,* an instrument similar to the *koto* and also known as a *kin* (from the Chinese *gin* or *ch'in*) has seven strings with no moveable bridges, is about four feet long and less than a foot wide, and is plucked like a zither. The Chinese associated this instrument with poets and scholars. The *kin* was also brought to Japan during the Nara Era, but later declined in use. A Chinese monk who emigrated to Japan in 1677 made the instrument popular with the literati during the Edo Era (1600–1868). See also GAGAKU; PAULOWNIA; SHAMISEN.

KOUTA See GEISHA; SHAMISEN; SINGING.

KOYA, MOUNT (Koyasan; sometimes abbreviated Ya-san)
The headquarters of the Shingon sect of Buddhism founded by the Japanese monk Kukai (774–835). Mount Koya, one of the most sacred places in Japan, lies about 24 miles east of Wakayama City on the Kii Peninsula in the Pacific Ocean on south central Honshu Island.

The Shingon complex of more than 100 temples and monasteries on Mount Koya is often referred to by the general name Koyasan. The complex as a whole was also called Kongobuji, but in 1869 that name was assigned to one large temple on Koyasan.

In A.D. 816 Emperor Saga gave Kukai permission to found a religious community on Mount Koya, far from the capital city of Kyoto on western Honshu. At that time Koyasan was already revered as sacred and had religious ascetics living on it. Most of the Shingon buildings on Koyasan were constructed during the time of its second abbot, Shinnen (804–891). Many were destroyed by fire in 994 but were restored under the abbot Myosan (1021–1106). Koyasan's reputation grew in the 12th century, due partly to patronage by retired Japanese emperors. Members of the Pure Land (Jodo) Sect of Buddhism also flocked to study Buddhism at Koyasan. Further, members of the noble and samurai classes sought refuge at Koyasan after the Taira-Minamoto War (1180–1185), which displaced the aristocratic domination of the Heian Era (794–1185) and ushered in seven centuries of military rule in Japan.

The Pure Land Buddhists who settled at Koyasan became known as *hijiri* (later, *Koya hijiri*). *Koya hijiri* who took to wandering the country influenced many Japanese to make pilgrimages to Koyasan to deposit hair or ashes of deceased relatives. They also raised money for Koyasan, and taught the religious beliefs of Pure Land Buddhism and reverence for Kobo Daishi, the honorary title given to Kukai after his death. Kukai had died on Mount Koya in 835.

During the 14th and 15th centuries, lay workers at Koyasan, who became known as the *gyonin-gata,* took control of the wealthy complex from the religious leaders (*gakuryo* or *shuto*). The warlord Oda Nobunaga (1534–1582), in his drive to unify Japan, attacked Koyasan and killed many residents. The Tokugawa Shogunate (1603–1867) exiled leaders of the *gyonin-gata,* destroyed their temples and forced the *hijiri* to merge their Pure Land religion into the Shingon sect of Buddhism. In 1868 Seiganji, the temple of the religious or *gakuryo* faction, was given the name Kongobuji and made the head temple of Koyasan. In 1872 women were finally given permission to enter Koyasan. See also BUDDHISM; KONGOBUJI; KUKAI; ODA NOBUNAGA; PILGRIMAGE; PURE LAND SECT OF BUDDHISM; SHINGON SECT OF BUDDHISM; TAIRA-MINAMOTO WAR; TOKUGAWA SHOGUNATE.

KOZO See MULBERRY BUSH; PAPER, HANDMADE.

KUKAI (774–835)
A Buddhist priest who founded the Shingon (True Word) Sect of Buddhism in Japan and became one of the preeminent figures in Japanese history. Kukai, known posthumously as Kobo Daishi, "Great Teacher," was born on Shikoku Island to an aristocratic family and was educated in the Confucian and Taoist teachings that had been introduced into Japan from China. But he renounced these philosophies and gave up a potential career in the government bureaucracy to study the Buddhist religion, which had also been introduced from China. In A.D. 804 he went to China and studied esoteric Buddhism with the great master Hui-kuo (Keika in Japanese; 746–805), returning to Japan two years later.

In A.D. 816 Kukai received imperial permission to build a monastery on Mount Koya, east of the capital city of Kyoto, where he could teach Shingon Buddhism. He taught that everything that exists is a manifestation of the universal being Dainichi (Japanese for the Indian deity Vairochana), and that believers could realize the oneness of existence by practicing rituals that involved the recitation of spells (*shingon,* or "true words," from *mantrayana* in Sanskrit), meditation postures and various hand gestures (*mudras*). Shingon deities were associated with the *kami,* or spirits, of Shinto, the indigenous Japanese religion. For example, the name of the god Dainichi was written with characters that mean "Great Sun," identifying this god with the Sun Goddess, Amaterasu o Mikami, the highest Shinto deity.

Court nobles in the Heian Era (794–1185) found the complex symbols and practices of Kukai's esoteric Buddhism very appealing. In A.D. 823 Kukai received from Emperor Saga (r. 809–823) a temple at Kyoto named Toji, which became Shingon headquarters. He taught Shingon to his rival Saicho (767–822), founder of the Tendai sect headquartered on Mount Hiei, the other great Buddhist sect of the Heian Era. Kukai established a route for religious pilgrimage among 88 temples on his home island of Shikoku, which is still followed today. He wrote many books on Shingon Buddhism and compiled the oldest surviving Japanese dictionary. His beautiful calligraphy earned him the reputation of being one of the three "great brushes" of his time. Kukai is believed to be the originator of *kana,* a syllabic script that is one of several basic elements of the Japanese writing system. See also AMATERASU O MIKAMI; BUDDHISM; CALLIGRAPHY; DAINICHI; HEIAN ERA; HIEI, MOUNT; KOYA, MOUNT; PILGRIMAGE; SAICHO; SHIKOKU ISLAND; SHINGON SECT OF

BUDDHISM; SHINTO; TENDAI SECT OF BUDDHISM; WRITING SYSTEM, JAPANESE.

KUMAMOTO   A city in the center of Kyushu Island that has one of Japan's largest and most important castles. Kumamoto Castle was built from 1601 to 1608 by the great warrior Kato Kiyomasa on land given to him by Shogun Tokugawa Ieyasu, in gratitude for his support during the Battle of Sekigahara (1600), which established the rule of the Tokugawa Shogunate (1603–1867). Built on top of a hill, the massive castle has three main buildings, 49 towers, 18 gatehouses and curved walls with defensive overhangings. The castle was acquired by the Hosokawa clan in 1632 and remained a stronghold for the Tokugawa government until the Meiji Restoration of 1868. Much of the castle was destroyed by fire during the Satsuma Rebellion of 1877, when samurai troops under Saigo Takamura unsuccessfully attacked the imperial troops stationed at the castle. Kumamoto remained an imperial garrison (chindai) until the end of World War II. In 1960 the castle was reconstructed of ferro-concrete on a smaller scale. Today it houses a museum of objects from the Kato and Hosokawa clans, as well as samurai armor and weapons.

Kumamoto City has a population of about half a million and serves as the capital of Kumamoto Prefecture. Its role as a provincial center dates back to the seventh century. This area, called Higo Province after the Taika Reform of 645, was strongly influenced by the culture of mainland China. It later figured in the Shimabara Uprising of 1637, which led to the torture and murder of Japanese Christian converts by the Tokugawa Shogunate.

Kumamoto has been famous for products in damascene, a decorative technique for inlaying gold and silver on iron, which was used to decorate samurai armor. Along with the castle, there are two other scenic sites in the city. Suizenji Garden was laid out in 1632 by the Hosokawa family and has a 400-year-old teahouse. Tatsuta Park contains the grave of Hosokowa Gracia, a renowned convert to Christianity.

The Kumamoto region has been remote from Japan's economic and industrial centers, so agriculture continues to be its main occupation. However, the city is trying to increase industrial development and is planning to open a technological research center in 1995. Kumamoto Prefecture is a major high-tech producing area, generating about 50% of Kyushu's total output of semiconductors. The Japanese government has developed Kumamoto Technopolis, which includes research and development centers in a planned area similar to Tsukuba Academic New Town. Kumamoto Prefecture has two National Parks, which include the scenic coastline of the Amakusa Islands and Mount Aso (Asosan), a large active volcano. See also CASTLES; HOSOKAWA CLAN; HOSOKAWA GRACIA; KYUSHU ISLAND; NATIONAL PARKS; SAIGO TAKAMURI; SAMURAI; SATSUMA REBELLION; SHIMABARA UPRISING; SHOGUN; TOKUGAWA SHOGUNATE.

KUMON METHOD   A method for teaching arithmetic and mathematics to children through a system of self-learning. The Kumon method was developed by a Japanese educator in 1958 with the aim of giving children confidence and creativity. Children work through Kumon course materials at their own pace, but they must complete a worksheet perfectly within a time limit in order to advance to the next lesson. Around 1.4 million students in Japan now learn math in Kumon classes, which are given privately after school hours. Juku or "cram schools" for all subjects are heavily attended in Japan. Kumon teachers are usually mothers and housewives who are devoted and enthusiastic about educating children. Since the first Kumon center in the U.S. was established in Los Angeles in 1983, the Kumon method has been spreading throughout the country. A school district in Sumiton, Alabama, was the first in the U.S. to use the Kumon method in its classes, with good results. The Kumon Institute has established special programs for U.S. school districts, such as Kumon Mathematix Inc. in Houston, Texas. See also EDUCATION; JUKU.

KURIL ISLANDS (Chishima Retto)   Also known as the Kurile Islands; a chain of more than 30 islands between the northernmost main Japanese island of Hokkaido and the Kamchatka Peninsula of northeastern Siberia in the Soviet Union. Possession of four of the Kuril Islands is disputed by the two countries. Japan claimed the southern part of the Kuril Islands chain in 1855. In 1875, an agreement with tsarist Russia gave Japan the northern section of the Kurils, except for Sakhalin Island, known in Japanese as Karafuto. After Japan's defeat in World War II, the Soviet Union was awarded the Kuril Islands (including Japanese-occupied Sakhalin), along with Habomai and Shikotan, two small islands off Hokkaido. In the late 1960s, the Japanese government began to press for the return of these offshore islands and the two southernmost Kuril islands of Kunashiri and Etorofu. The Soviets have refused to admit these Japanese claims, and maintain armed forces on the islands. The Kuril Islands, which are valuable not only for their strategic location, but for their natural resources, especially rich mineral deposits, remain a sore point in Japanese-Soviet relations. Japan and the Soviet Union have reopened negotiations on this issue.

Soviet Deputy Foreign Minister Vladimir Petrovsky proposed early in 1990 that the two countries undertake joint ecological studies in the Kuril Islands and Sakhalin. This proposal was initially put forward by Soviet Foreign Minister Eduard Shevardnadze in an interview published in Izvestia on April 12. Petrovsky proposed that the two countries set up a joint research mission, with a station on Sakhalin Island, to study the ecosystem of the Kuril archipelago and undertake joint conservation efforts and environmental monitoring. Japan has traditionally tied the establishment of full economic ties with the Soviet Union to a resolution of the territorial dispute and the conclusion of a peace treaty. Japan desires unconditional return of the islands to Japanese sovereignty. Actually, no international agreement has ever recognized the incorporation into the Soviet Union of Sakhalin Island and the Kurils. See also HOKKAIDO ISLAND; WORLD WAR II.

KUROSAWA AKIRA (1910–)   A leading Japanese movie director whose films have garnered him international acclaim. He has also written more than 20 scripts that have been filmed by other directors.

Kurosawa was born in Tokyo, the youngest of seven children. His father was an educator from the old samurai class. After middle school, Kurosawa studied painting at the Doshusha School of Western Painting and worked as an artist. In 1936 he took a job as an assistant film director at P.C.L. Studios, where he worked under director Yamamoto Kajiro.

Kurosawa is a perfectionist with strong convictions about what he wants to portray on film. His first film was *Sugata Sanshiro* (1943; shown abroad as *Sanshiro Sugata*), about a judo master. Kurosawa's first popular movie was *Drunken Angel* (*Yoidore tenshi*; 1948), about a sick gangster, played by Mifune Toshiro (1920–   ), who acted in many of Kurosawa's later movies and gained fame for his samurai roles. *Rashomon* (1950), based on two stories by Akutagawa Ryunosuke (1892–1927), was the first Kurosawa movie to win international recognition. Starring Mifune and the actress Kyo Machiko (1924–   ), it presents conflicting accounts of a rape. *Rashomon* was adapted as *The Outrage* by the American director Martin Ritt (1964). Kurosawa's film *Ikiru* (*To Live*; 1952), about a man who is dying of cancer, continued the theme of illusion versus reality. *The Seven Samurai* (*Shichinin no samurai*; 1954), regarded as one of Kurosawa's greatest movies, was his first *jidai-geki*, or historical drama. The story of villagers who hire samurai to help defend themselves against bandits was adapted by the American director John Sturges as *The Magnificent Seven* (1961).

Kurosawa has made dozens of films and has worked with the major Japanese film studios Toho, Daiei and Shochiku, although their executives have not always agreed with his artistic goals. In 1960 Kurosawa made the first film with his own unit, Kurosawa Productions, titled *The Bad Sleep Well, (Warui yatsu hodo Yoko nemuru)* about bureaucratic corruption. Well-known movies starring Mifune as a lone samurai are *Yojimbo* (1961) and *Tsubaki Sanjuro* (1962; shown abroad as *Sanjuro*). The Italian director Sergio Leone adapted the story of *Yojimbo* in his 1964 movie shown in English as *For a Few Dollars More*. Kurosawa filmed adaptations of numerous Western literary works, such as *The Idiot* (*Hakuchi*; 1951), based on the novel by Fedor Dostoevsky; *The Throne of Blood* (*Kumonosojo*; 1957), based on Shakespeare's *Macbeth*; and *The Lower Depths* (*Sonzoko*; 1957), based on a play by Maxim Gorky. After *Dodesukaden* (1970), about a disturbed boy who acts as if he is a train, Kurosawa did not make a movie for 10 years because he had trouble getting financial backers. His next film, *Kagemusha* (*The Warrior's Double*; 1980), is about a commoner who is forced to impersonate a great feudal lord who has died while a civil war is raging. *Ran* (1985), a historical military epic based on Shakespeare's *King Lear*, received international acclaim. Kurosawa's latest film, *Dreams*, a series of dream tales, opened the 1990 Cannes Film Festival. A detailed study of Kurosawa's earlier work, *The Films of Akira Kurosawa*, was published by Donald Richie in 1965. His memoirs were translated by Audie E. Bock in 1982 as *Something Like an Autobiography*. In 1990 Kurosawa was presented a special Academy Award for lifetime achieve-

ment. See also AKUTAGAWA RYUNOSUKE; FILM; KYO MACHIKO; MIFUNE TOSHIRO; RASHOMON; SAMURAI.

KUROSHIO (Black Current)   See CLIMATE OF JAPAN; GEOGRAPHY OF JAPAN; PACIFIC OCEAN; SEA OF JAPAN.

KUSUNOKI MASAHIGE (?–1336)   A warrior who became regarded by the Japanese as a great legendary hero for his loyalty to the emperor. Prior to World War II, young people in Japan were taught to dedicate their lives to the emperor just as Kusunoki did. A bronze statue of Kusunoki stands in front of the Imperial Palace in Tokyo. Kusunoki fought to the death for Emperor Go-Daigo (1288–1339) in the overthrow of the Kamakura Shogunate (1192–1333), Japan's first military government, or *bakufu*. The story of Kusunoki Masahige comes from the *Taiheiki*, a chronicle of legends about the civil warfare from the time Go-Daigo became emperor in 1318 until he was overthrown in 1337. Kusunoki's army defeated Kamakura forces at Chihaya in Kawachi Province. Other Kamakura forces led by Ashikaga Takauji (1305–1358) marched west from the military headquarters in Kamakura on eastern Honshu Island to the imperial capital of Kyoto, but Takauji switched allegiance and joined Go-Daigo's rebellion, and the combined forces brought about the downfall of the Kamakura Shogunate in 1333. Kusunoki was rewarded by being made a provincial governor. However, Ashikaga Takauji revolted against the new government of the emperor in 1335, and Kusunoki's advice to withdraw from Kyoto and ambush Takauji's forces when they occupied the city was rejected by court nobles. In 1336 Kunusoki decided to confront Takauji at Minatogawa (near modern Kobe City), but he lost the battle and committed suicide. See also ASHIKAGA TAKAUJI; BAKUFU; GO-DAIGO, EMPEROR; KAMAKURA SHOGUNATE; SAMURAI; SHOGUN.

KUTANI WARE (*kutani-yaki*)   A type of richly decorated porcelain ware. Powerful *daimyo* (feudal lords) of the Maeda clan established the Kutani kilns in Kaga Province (modern Ishikawa Prefecture), where they were in operation from 1655 to 1704 and from 1807 to the present day. Kutani ware is bold and lively in its forms, and has a creamy white background decorated with blue-and-white motifs or colorful overglaze enamels. Such enamels, ground into powders and painted onto the objects, are low-fire glazes that melt and fuse to the surface of a higher-fired glaze. "Blue" Kutani ware (*ao-kutani*) has blue overglaze enamel on a white surface. Red, green, purple and gold are also common on Kutani ware. Design motifs, such as flowers and trees, were inspired by the Kano and Tosa schools of Japanese painting, Ming and Qing (Ch'ing) dynasty Chinese porcelains, and colorful textiles.

Goto Saijiro (d. 1704) ran the old Kutani kiln (1655–1704), which produced bowls, plates, containers with lids and sake bottles used by the Maeda both as tableware and for the tea ceremony. Kutani and Arita were the leading centers of porcelain production in Japan from the mid-17th into the 18th century. During the 19th century, a number of kilns in Kaga (Ishikawa Prefecture) began producing porcelain in the style of Old Kutani ware, especially red and gold objects for export to the West, where they were much admired. The finest decorative Kutani ware was made by Eiraku Wazen XII (1823–1896) at the Eiraku kiln, which had been established in the 1860s. See also ARITA WARE; KANO SCHOOL OF PAINTING; MAEDA CLAN; PORCELAIN; TEA CEREMONY; TOSA SCHOOL OF PAINTING.

KYO MACHIKO (1924–) An internationally famous movie actress who starred in many acclaimed Japanese movies, including *Rashomon* (1950) by Kurosawa Akira (1910–), *Ugetsu* (Ugetsu Monogatari; 1953) by Mizoguchi Kenji (1898–1956); *Gate of Hell* (Jigokumon; 1953) by Kinugasa Teinosuke, which won the Grand Prize at the 1954 Cannes Film Festival; and *Odd Obsession* (Kagi, or The Key; 1959) by Ichikawa Kon (1915–). Kyo Machiko was born Yano Motoko in Osaka. In 1936 she became a member of the Osaka Shochiku Girl's Opera. In 1949 she signed with Daiei Motion Picture Co. and played her first feature role in *He Who Laughs Last* (Saigo no warau otoko; 1949). Her fine performance as the raped bride in *Rashomon* made her famous. She also appeared in the American movie set during the Occupation of Japan, *Teahouse of the August Moon* (1956) by Donald Mann. In 1976 she talked about working with Mizoguchi in the documentary *Kenji Mizoguchi: The Life of a Film Director*. See also FILM; ICHIKAWA KON; KUROSAWA AKIRA; MIZOGUCHI KENJI; RASHOMON.

KYODO NEWS SERVICE See NEWSPAPERS.

KYOGEN "Crazy words"; comic drama or farce, performed as an interlude between serious plays in a performance of Noh drama. Kyogen and Noh developed in the 14th century from an earlier theatrical tradition introduced into Japan from China in the eighth century. Known as *sarugaku* ("monkey music") or *sangaku* ("scattered [or miscellaneous] entertainment"), this form included popular entertainment such as acrobatics, juggling, magic and humorous parodies. *Sarugaku* performances came to be associated with Shinto shrines and Buddhist temples, especially in the Kyoto-Nara region of west-central Honshu Island, where the imperial court was centered.

The broad use of the term Noh includes Kyogen, and some comic roles within Noh plays are also termed Kyogen. However, Noh and Kyogen became separate forms, particularly under the famous Noh actor and playwright Zeami (1363–1443), who was patronized by the founder of the Ashikaga Shogunate (1338–1573). Kyogen retained its earthy and spontaneous aspects. Whereas masks are used by principal characters in Noh, independent Kyogen plays are usually performed without masks, although humorous masks may be used on occasion. Kyogen costumes are simple, in contrast to sumptuous brocaded Noh robes. The musicians and chorus that accompany Noh plays leave the stage during a Kyogen performance, during which two Kyogen players interact using dialogue in an ancient form of the Japanese language. They may also sing a type of "small song" known as *kouta*. Kyogen is fast-paced, witty and amusing. Many Kyogen plays actually parody Noh plays. Another category of Kyogen consists of an encounter

between a *daimyo* (feudal lord) and his servant who tricks him. Some other stock characters in Kyogen include the country bumpkin, bridegroom, son-in-law, devils, Buddhist priests and blind men.

Three separate schools of Kyogen were established in the late 16th and early 17th centuries, the Okura, Sagi and Izumi schools. The first two were patronized by the ruling family of the Tokugawa Shogunate (1603–1867), based in Edo (modern Tokyo), which the Izumi school was supported by a branch of the Tokugawa and the Maeda clan, and also performed for the imperial court in the old capital of Kyoto. The schools lost their patrons with the Meiji Restoration of 1868. However, groups within the Izumi and Okura schools kept the Kyogen tradition alive, and these two schools have continued to the present time. Since World War II, there has been a new interest in Kyogen as a theatrical art. A repertoire of around 260 independent plays is drawn upon by the two schools. See also ASHIKAGA SHOGUNATE; NOH DRAMA; TOKUGAWA SHOGUNATE; ZEAMI.

KYOIKU MAMA See CHILDREN IN JAPAN; EDUCATION SYSTEM; MOTHER.

KYOTO A major city on the Kamo River in southwest Honshu Island that was the imperial capital of Japan from 794 to 1868, and is today the capital of Kyoto Prefecture. The numerous historical and religious sites in Kyoto make it the cultural and spiritual center of Japan, and the Allies spared the city from bombing during World War II for this reason. More than 30 million tourists a year visit Kyoto. Some of its attractions are Nijo Castle, the Kyoto Imperial Palace, Katsura and Shugakuin Detached Palaces, the geisha districts of Gion and Pontocho, and the sand and rock garden at Ryoanji. Other famous Buddhist temples in Kyoto are Daitokuji, Ginkakuji (Temple of the Silver Pavilion), Kinkakuji (Temple of the Gold Pavilion), Kiyomizudera and Saihoji, known for its moss garden. Major Shinto shrines include Heian, Kamo and Kitano. There are many popular annual festivals, such as the Hollyhock Festival, Gion Festival and Festival of the Ages. Kyoto is also renowned for traditional Japanese crafts, especially pottery, lacquer ware, woodblock prints, fans, Yuzen silk dyeing and Nishijin silk weaving. Major schools of the tea ceremony, flower arranging, classical dance and Noh drama have their headquarters in Kyoto. Kyoto also has numerous museums and a botanical and zoological garden. The city is situated in a basin surrounded by mountains, the most famous being Mount Hiei, which rises above the city to the east.

Members of the Hata clan, an immigrant group from Korea skilled in silkworm cultivation and silk weaving, had settled the Kyoto basin in the sixth century A.D. Emperor Kammu (737–806) built the city of Heiankyo ("Capital of Peace and Tranquility") there in A.D. 794 as the new home for the imperial court, which had been located in Nara to the south. Heiankyo, like Nara, was laid out in a grid pattern modeled on Chang'an (Ch'ang-an; modern Xian), the capital of Tang (T'ang) dynasty (618–907) China. The name Heiankyo was later changed to Kyoto, "Western Capital." Classical Japanese culture flourished in aristocratic Kyoto during the Heian Era (794–1185). The military government (bakufu) known as the Kamakura Shogunate (1192–1333) moved the locus of ruling power to east Honshu, but the Ashikaga Shogunate (1338–1573) chose Kyoto as its headquarters. A brilliant culture flowered under Ashikaga patronage until warfare among provincial daimyo (feudal lords) led to the Onin War (1467–1477), which devastated much of the city. After a century of civil war, Kyoto was taken over in 1568 by Oda Nobunaga (1534–1582), the first of three national unifiers. Toyotomi Hideyoshi (1537–1598), the second unifier, initiated a building program in Kyoto that included the richly decorated Jurakudai mansion and Fushimi Castle (neither of which survive). During the Azuchi-Momoyama Era (1568–1600), Kyoto experienced a third period of remarkable cultural flowering. Tokugawa Ieyasu (1534–1616) built the city of Edo (modern Tokyo) on eastern Honshu as the headquarters of the Tokugawa Shogunate (1603–1867). Yet while political power was centered in Edo, Kyoto remained an important artistic and religious center. However, after the Meiji Restoration of 1868, the capital of Japan was moved to Tokyo, where Emperor Meiji took up residence.

Kyoto made up for this loss by undergoing rapid modernization. Today the city covers 235.7 square miles and has a population of around 1.5 million. Kyoto Prefecture (Kyoto Fu) covers 1,781 square miles and has a population of around 2.5 million. It lies within the so-called Kinki and Kansai regions. Facing the Sea of Japan and divided by the Tamba Mountains, Kyoto Prefecture includes Lake Biwa, the largest lake in Japan. The southern half, including Kyoto City, is an extension of the Hanshin Industrial Zone. Major industries include machinery, metal, synthetic fiber and fishing. Rice and vegetables are cultivated, and tea is grown in the area of Uji City near Kyoto. See also BIWA, LAKE; HEIANKYO; KANSAI AND KANTO; KINKI; NARA; UJI; NAMES OF INDIVIDUAL CRAFTS, DISTRICTS, FESTIVALS, HISTORICAL ERAS AND FIGURES, SHRINES AND TEMPLES.

KYOTO WARE (kyo-yaki) The general term for porcelain and pottery produced in and around the old capital city of Kyoto. Decorative enameled Kyoto pottery (faience) is also known as Kiyomizu ware (kiyomizu-yaki), after the porcelain kilns that were established at the base of Kiyomizu Temple in eastern Kyoto in the mid-17th century. The street called Higashiyama Dori, leading to the temple, is still lined with shops selling ceramics ranging from inexpensive souvenirs to valuable works of art. Another type of Kyoto ware is Awa ware, a crackled buff-colored faience decorated with colored enamels and gold. Raku ware (raku-yaki) was also developed in Kyoto for tea ceremony bowls, but its rough, asymmetrical style differs from decorative Kyoto wares. As Kyoto was the imperial capital for more than a thousand years, its potters were patronized by the court and the aristocratic class, and Kyoto ware is famous for its delicate refinement. During the Edo Era (1600–1868) there were more potters in Kyoto than in any other area of Japan.

Many early Edo potters came to Kyoto from kilns at Seto and Shigaraki. Nonomura Ninsei (fl. mid-17th century), one of the preeminent figures in Japanese pottery, influenced potters in Kyoto, especially Kiyomizu. Formerly a potter at Tamba, where he was known as Seiemon Nonomura, Ninsei began applying the technique of overglaze enamel to earthenware in Kyoto around A.D. 1650. He set up a kiln near the palace of his patron, Prince Ninnaji, who awarded him the title nin, which he combined with the first character of his given name to create his art name, Ninsei. His work was carried on by Kenzan Ogata (1663–1743), another major Japanese potter who also worked in enameled earthenware. Kiyomizu techniques were adapted by the Tateno kiln at Kagoshima in southern Japan, which developed an overglaze enameled earthenware known as white Satsuma ware. See also KENZAN; KILN; KIYOMIZUDERA TEMPLE; KYOTO; NONOMURA NINSEI; PORCELAIN; POTTERY; NAMES OF INDIVIDUAL WARES.

KYUDO See ARCHERY.

KYUSHU ISLAND The southernmost and third largest of the four main islands of Japan. Kyushu, along with its surrounding islands, covers 16,623 square miles and has a population of more than 14 million. The administrative region of Kyushu includes the Amami and Ryukyu Islands, comprising Okinawa Prefecture, that stretch for a thousand miles to the south. Kyushu is separated from the largest island of Honshu by the mile-wide Kammon Strait, which is crossed by railroad and automobile tunnels. The climate of Kyushu is generally warm and humid, with heavy rainfall and subtropical vegetation. Because northern Kyushu is close to the Korean peninsula, the island was the first to receive many migrants and cultural innovations from the Asian mainland. The Yamato clan, which established the Japanese imperial line on central Honshu nearly 2,000 years ago, are believed to have emigrated from Kyushu. Japanese rulers attempted to invade Korea many times from northern Kyushu, and in the 13th century, Mongols threatened to invade Japan through this area but were repelled.

Mountain ridges divide Kyushu into northern and southern regions. Mount Aso has the largest crater basin in the world, containing five volcanic cones. The island has numerous hot springs, some of which are resort towns, such as Beppu and Unzen Spa. Kyushu also has six national parks and 10 quasi-national parks administered by prefectures. The city of Kagoshima on Kyushu's southern tip is faced by an active volcano, Sakurajima. On the island's western side are Kumamoto, an old castle town, and Nagasaki, the only city in Japan that was permitted to trade with foreigners after Japan was closed to outsiders in A.D. 1639. Portuguese Jesuits converted many Japanese to Christianity in this area, but Christianity was outlawed and believers were persecuted by the warlord Toyotomi Hideyoshi and the Tokugawa Shogunate (1603–1867). Kita Kyushu (North Kyushu), the largest city, is highly industrialized. Neighboring Fukuoka is a center for administration, commerce and culture. Saga Prefecture is famous for pottery, especially Karatsu ware, and porcelain that was exported from the town of Arita. See also ARITA WARE; BEPPU; CHRISTIANITY IN JAPAN; FUKUOKA; HOT SPRING; KAGOSHIMA; KARATSU WARE; KITA KYUSHU; KOREA AND JAPAN; KUMAMOTO; MONGOL INVASIONS OF JAPAN; NAGASAKI; NATIONAL PARKS; OKINAWA ISLAND; PORCELAIN; PORTUGUESE IN JAPAN; POTTERY; RYUKYU ISLANDS; SAGA PREFECTURE; TOKUGAWA SHOGUNATE; TOYOTOMI HIDEYOSHI; VOLCANO; YAMATO CLAN.

L

LABOR THANKSGIVING DAY See HOLIDAYS, NATIONAL.

LABOR UNIONS The first labor unions in Japan were organized among blue-collar workers such as printers and metalworkers in the 1890s. During World War II, the Japanese military government disbanded all labor unions, but the new Japanese constitution promulgated in 1947 during the Allied Occupation of Japan guaranteed the fundamental rights of workers to organize labor unions, engage in collective bargaining and strike to give weight to their demands, although this right may be suspended in times of national emergency. By 1949 more than half of all Japanese workers were organized into unions. Today there are about 74,000 corporate and federal labor unions in Japan, with around 12.3 million members, about one-third of the entire Japanese work force.

Most unions are organized within individual companies rather than by trade. They are known as "enterprise unions," meaning that a union's members are regular employees of one particular enterprise, or company. White- as well as blue-collar workers, and lower-level managers, automatically become members of company unions when they are hired. Managers at the level of section head *(kacho)* and above do not belong to a union, nor do temporary and subcontract workers. Union dues are deducted from a worker's salary and comprise around 1–2% of his or her annual pay. Union officers are elected from within the union ranks. While a union bargains hard for good wages and working conditions, it identifies its economic interests with those of the company that permanently employs its members; and so keeps its demands reasonable. Strikes are usually symbolic displays of union solidarity rather than battles that cripple a company.

Branch operations of large enterprises each have their own unions, which belong to an enterprise-wide federation of branch unions. Single-enterprise unions and federations of branch unions in one industry or a number of related industries are further organized into industry-wide federations. Such federations in turn combine to form national labor federations. In the early 1980s there were four Japanese national labor federations, each having its own political position: Sohyo, Domei, Churitsu Roren and Shinsambetsu. Sohyo (General Council of Trade Unions of Japan) is the largest, and most of its members work in the public sector. It is closely aligned with the Japan Socialist Party (JSP; Nihon Shakaito). Sohyo organizes the so-called Spring Labor Offensive (Shunto), during which brief strikes are held during negotiations between unions and enterprises. Domei (Japanese Confederation of Labor) is the second-largest union and is more moderate. Its members are blue-collar workers in private industry. Domei is associated with the Democratic Socialist Party (DSP; Minshato). Internationally, Domei is affiliated with the International Confederation of Free Trade Unions (ICFTU). Some industry-wide federations are also affiliated with the ICFTU, while others are affiliated with appropriate industrial divisions of the World Federation of Trade Unions (WFTU). Churitsu Roren (Federation of Independent Unions) is much smaller and cooperates with Sohyo in collective bargaining strategy. Shinsambetsu (National Federation of Industrial Labor Organizations) maintains a politically neutral position. About 24% of single-enterprise unions are independent, and belong to neither industry nor national federations.

The only industry-wide unions are for government employees, teachers, telecommunications workers and seamen. More than half of all Japanese teachers belong to Nikkyoso (Japan Teacher Union), one of Japan's most radical unions and the largest such labor organization in the world. The International Metalworkers' Federation-Japan Council (IMF-JC) has also been active in Japan since the mid-1960s.

Collective bargaining is usually conducted directly between the union and the enterprise, with little involvement by the industry and national federations. The Spring Labor Offensive demonstrates the unified power of labor movement in one pattern-setting industry, and the agreement it achieves regarding workers' wages and benefits is usually followed by major industries in Japan. Small businesses, which do not have formal labor pacts, generally work out piecemeal agreements with their workers. All public employees in Japan are prohibited from striking by law, and some classes of public employees are also restricted from collective bargaining or organizing labor unions. The Labor Relations Adjustment Law protects labor unions from unfair employer practices and established a labor relations commissions to adjudicate disputes. The Japanese government has the legal right to end labor disputes temporarily if such action is necessary. See also CORPORATIONS; CONSTITUTION OF 1947; EDUCATION SYSTEM; INCOME; SPRING LABOR OFFENSIVE.

LACQUER WARE *(shikki)* Also known as Japan ware; utensils and art objects coated in an elaborate and time-consuming way with sap from the Japanese lacquer tree *(urushi no ki)*. Lacquer gives these objects a beautiful appearance and protects them from moisture and damaging elements.

The lacquer tree *(urushi)* is related to poison ivy, so lacquer is very toxic and must be collected and handled with great care. Both cultivated and wild trees are tapped. A horizontal cut is made in the bark of a 3 to 10-year-old lacquer tree and a bucket is suspended to catch the drops

A set of lacquer ware food dishes. Rice and soup are served in round lidded bowls. Foods such as sushi or sweets may be served in square lidded boxes.

of sap. This is the raw lacquer, which is is brown and gummy and has a strong smell. Each tree produces 6–7 ounces of lacquer. The best quality is collected in August and September.

Raw lacquer is refined by a process known as *nayashi,* which removes the water and thickens and homogenizes the lacquer. In this process, lacquer is heated and stirred under direct sunlight. Colors are added to the lacquer, usually black or red. Lacquer is usually applied in 20–90 thin coats to a thin core of wood (*kiji*) or other material, such as paper, leather, porcelain, a basket, or metal, which is shaped into a tray, box or some other object. The core object to be coated is smoothed, painted with priming (*shitaji*) made from a fine powder and then covered with layers of cloth impregnated with a mixture of liquid lacquer and clay, over which the layers of lacquer are brushed on. The brush must be held steady and the workshop kept dust-free. Lacquer dries slowly at a temperature of 25–30 degrees C (77–86 degrees F) and humidity of 75–85%. Humidity hastens the hardening of lacquer, whereas dry air and cold temperatures slow it. After each coat of lacquer dries, the object is polished with charcoal or stone. A final coat of highly refined clear lacquer is applied, after which the object is given its final polishing with deerhorn powder and seed oil.

The best known technique for decorating lacquer ware is *maki-e,* in which gold and silver powders and particles are sprinkled on damp lacquer to make designs. Designs may be worked in relief (*taka maki-e*), "flat" (*hira maki-e*) or by coating *maki-e* with lacquer and burnishing it to bring out the design (*togi-dashi*). The *maki-e* technique is unique to Japan and was already being used by the eighth century A.D. Another decorative technique is *raden,* inlays made from pieces of mother-of-pearl (*aogai*) or abalone (*awabi*) or other shells. Inlays are also made of semiprecious stones and other materials. *Guri* (or *guri-bori*) is lacquer that is applied in layers of contrasting colors, usually red and black, then carved with grooves to make spiral designs. *Heidatsu* is a decoration of sheet gold or silver shapes applied to the surface, covered with lacquer, then burnished to expose the decoration. Designs are also created by special techniques for carving and modeling, texturing the surface and special polishes.

Lacquer ware can last for thousands of years. The oldest pieces found in Japan date from the Jomon Era (c. 10,000 B.C.–c. 300 B.C.), and the oldest Japanese lacquer paintings are found on a seventh-century shrine in the Horyuji temple complex. Many ancient pieces have been preserved in the Shosoin, an eighth-century storehouse in Nara. The height of lacquer ware production in Japan came in the 16th–18th centuries under the patronage of *daimyo* (feudal lords) and wealthy urban merchants. Two renowned lacquer artists of the period were Hon'ami Koetsu (1558–1637) and Korin (1658–1716).

Most lacquer ware, while decorative, is intended for daily use. Common lacquered objects include trays, writing boxes, tables, cabinets, altars, cosmetic boxes, mirror stands, wooden pillows, serving trays, soup bowls, multilayered food boxes, fine chopsticks, tea containers, small multi-layered containers (*inro*) suspended from *obi* (sashes) with *netsuke* (toggles), and even suits of armor.

Some famous types of Japanese lacquer ware include *wajima-nuri* from Ishikawa Prefecture, *aizu-nuri* from Aizu-Wakamatsu in Fukushima Prefecture, and *tsugaru-nuri* from Hirosaki in Aomori Prefecture. Colorful lacquer ware produced in the Ryukyu Islands (modern Okinawa Prefecture) of southern Japan is also highly admired. Contemporary lacquer artist Genroku Matsuda has been designated a Living National Treasure. See also BOXES; DAIMYO; EDO ERA; HON'AMI KOETSU; HORYUJI; KORIN; LIVING NATIONAL TREASURES; NETSUKE; RYUKYU ISLANDS; SHELLS; SHOSOIN; TRAYS.

LAKES See BIWA, LAKE; FUJI-HAKONE-IZU NATIONAL PARK; GARDENS.

LAND RECLAMATION (*tochi zosei*) The conversion of wasteland into fields for agriculture or of shallow water along coasts into land for industrial use or habitation. Japan underwent a major program of land reclamation starting in the 17th century, when a large portion of the capital city of Edo (modern Tokyo) was created by reclaiming land from Edo Bay (Tokyo Bay). During the Meiji Era (1868–1912), land reclamation projects were undertaken to create large industrial zones. New rice paddies were also created by building embankments to drain lakes, ponds and marshes. A third round of massive land reclamation took place after World War II, when dredging along coastal areas provided new land for suburban housing and for industry. The Tokyo-Yokohama-Chiba region has developed largely on reclaimed land, and recent studies have warned of massive destruction there from a major earthquake, which is always a threat in Japan. Other cities have also developed by land reclamation. For example, the port city of Kobe spent 15 years reclaiming land from the sea to create Kobe Port Island for both residential and industrial use. Another island is now being reclaimed. The city of Osaka is constructing a new airport on reclaimed land in Osaka Bay. See also CHIBA PREFECTURE; EARTHQUAKES; EDO ERA; INDUSTRIAL ZONES; KOBE; LANDED ESTATE SYSTEM; OSAKA; RICE; TOKYO; YOKOHAMA.

LANDED ESTATE SYSTEM (*shoen*) An ancient system of private land ownership in which *shoen*, large estates in the provinces, were granted to members of the ruling class or Buddhist temples in the capital city of Kyoto. *Shoen* originated in the eighth century and developed into important centers of economic production in medieval Japan (12th–16th centuries). A landed estate was worked by peasants and craftsmen who lived on the land and produced agricultural and other products for its absentee owner. A resident manager oversaw the daily operations of the estate.

The *shoen*, which replaced the earlier *ritsuryo* system of public ownership of land, often arose from government-supported projects to reclaim land for rice cultivation. A person who was responsible for reclaiming a plot of land became its owner and appointed agents to live on the *shoen* and administer its cultivation and the collection of taxes, which included specified percentages of the grain, roof tiles, pottery and other materials produced on the estate. Proprietorship became hereditary and owners of *shoen*, especially Buddhist temples, eventually came to be exempt from taxes to the imperial government in Kyoto, which eroded the Heian Era (794–1185) government's financial resources and eventually led to its loss of authority. Proprietors of *shoen* began grouping scattered plots together to create conglomerates of land holdings. By the end of the 11th century, managers who were responsible for dues and labor services on plots of land had gained rights of tenure to that land. These persons were known as *myoshu*, holders of "designated fields" (*myoden*). Provincial sumurai lords became known as *daimyo; dai* means "great," and *myo* (name or title) is derived from *myoden*. The Kamakura Shogunate (1192–1333), reflecting this new balance of power, created the offices of military governor (*shugo*) and military estate steward (*jito*), which transferred authority over landholdings from central proprietors in the capital to the *daimyo*. Local *jito* began acquiring full rights to *shoen*. During the Ashikaga Shogunate, *shugo* (or *shugo daimyo*) replaced former provincial governors, and became both the civil and military authorities in the Japanese provinces. During the civil warfare of the Sengoku (Warring States) Era (1467–1568), the *shugo daimyo* and the shogunate became so weakened by the conflicts that other local military leaders, known as *sengoku daimyo*, took control of the land and the people who worked it. The *shoen* system had disappeared by the 16th century, except for large estates held by great Buddhist temples that had large bands of warrior-monks (*sohei*). These powerful temples were defeated by the national unifier Oda Nobunaga (1534–1582), bringing the landed-estate era to a close and establishing the *han* (domain) system that characterized the centralized feudalism of the Tokugawa Shogunate (1603–1867). See also ASHIKAGA SHOGUNATE; BUDDHISM; DAIMYO; HEIAN ERA; KAMAKURA SHOGUNATE; ODA NOBUNAGA; RICE; RITSURYO SYSTEM; SAMURAI; SHOGUN.

LANDSCAPE PAINTING (*sansuiga*) One of the three general styles of Japanese and East Asian painting, along with bird-and-flower painting (*kachoga*) and figure painting (*jimbutsuga*). Paintings are traditionally executed on horizontal rolling scrolls (*emakimono*) or vertical hanging scrolls (*kakemono*).

Landscape painting was developed in China by the fifth century and introduced into Japan with Buddhist religion and culture starting in the sixth century. Trees, mountains, rocks and rivers have been common subjects in landscape painting, which can be an expression of philosophical concepts as well as of natural forms. *Yamato-e*, the colorful painting style of Heian Era (794–1185) Japan, used landscapes to illustrate Buddhist stories about the gods and paradise, or to depict the four seasons (*shiki-keibutsuga*) and famous places mentioned in poetry and prose narratives (*meisho-keibutsuga*). In the 15th century, Japanese priest-painters of the Zen Buddhist religion adapted the monochromatic style of black ink painting (*sumi-e* or *suibokuga*), which had developed in China during the Song (Sung; 960–1279) and Yuan (1280–1368) dynasties. This style does not seek to realistically depict nature, but uses sparse black lines on white backgrounds to portray landscapes with philosophical themes, such as sturdy pine trees on remote, rugged mountains.

The Japanese and Chinese languages are traditionally written with brushes and black ink, and so there is a close association between the art of writing, or calligraphy (*shodo*), and painting in Japan and China. The Japanese artists Shubun (?–c. 1460) and Sesshu Toyo (1420–1506) became known for their idealized landscapes that utilized Chinese motifs. Artists of the Kano school of painting adapted this style to create decorative landscapes on large screens, especially for use in castles during the Azuchi-Momoyama Era (1568–1600). During the Edo Era (1600–1868), ink landscapes (*suibokuga* or *sansuiga*) and literati (*bunjinga*), or "southern," landscapes (*nanga sansuiga*) were popular. Literati landscape painting, adapted in the 18th century from the style used by Chinese scholar-painters, employs ink washes to create a soft, misty atmosphere. In the late Edo Era, a realistic style of painting landscapes (*fukeiga*) also developed in Japan. See also BIRD-AND-FLOWER PAINTING; BRUSHES; BUDDHISM; CALLIGRAPHY; CHINA AND JAPAN; FIGURE PAINTING; INK PAINTING; KANO SCHOOL OF PAINTING; SCREENS; SCROLLS; SESSHU TOYO; ZEN SECT OF BUDDHISM.

LANGUAGE, JAPANESE Japanese is acknowledged to be perhaps the most complex and difficult language in the world. Japanese has very different spoken and written forms, is very idiomatic and has a grammatic structure that makes it extremely difficult for English speakers to learn. It is related to the Hungarian-Magyar and Finnish (Altaic) languages, and all three may have originated in a common source in Central Asia. Japanese words consist of short syllables. In many cases, words with the same pronunciation may have several different meanings, which are discerned by the context in which they are spoken or the characters with which they are written.

Vowels are pronounced in Japanese much like those in Romance languages, especially Italian. *A* is pronounced *ah*; *e* as in *pen*; *i* as in *inn* when in the middle of a word, like *e* in *see* when at the end of a word; *o* is pronounced *oh*; *u oo.* Some vowels have a double, or long, pronunciation; two words may be similar except for the double vowel sound, such as *okashi* (sweets) and *okashii* (strange). Consonants are always followed by a vowel and are pronounced the same as in English. *G* has a hard sound when it begins a word. There are also some double consonants: *kk, pp, tt, tch,* and *ss.* The Japanese language has no sound for "th" or "l"; the latter is usually pronounced as an "r" sound. The "v" sound usually comes out more like a "b," as in "balbe" for "valve."

Syllables are given fairly even stress in pronunciation. Intonation is dropped slightly when asking a question. The word order of a Japanese sentence is subject-object-verb, much as in German. A modifier precedes the word it modifies. There is no differentiation between singular and plural, but plurals are understood in the context of a sentence or indicated by special counting words. Verbs have present and past tenses; the future is indicated by the use of adverbs. The Japanese language uses numerous connecting words. For example, subject nouns are followed by the participle *ga* or *wa,* and object nouns are followed by *e* to indicate direction or *o* to indicate action. A question is indicated by the syllable *ka* at the end of a sentence.

Japanese is written with a complex combination of Chinese characters, or *kanji;* and two native syllabic systems *(kana),* *hiragana* and *katakana,* which correspond precisely to the syllables of the Japanese language. Roman letters, or *romaji,* can also be used to write or print Japanese. Many Chinese characters have at least two and even five or more alternate pronunciations in Japanese, depending on whether they are used for a borrowed Chinese word or a native Japanese word. Chinese characters are classified according to their Chinese, *on,* or Japanese, *kun,* readings.

The Japanese language also has many levels of politeness depending on the sex of the speaker and the person being spoken to, and the relationship between them. Different words and grammatical forms are used to make the language more or less formal when speaking to a social superior or inferior, respectively. Honorific language, known as *keigo,* is extremely important. Traditionally, Japanese women use honorifics more frequently, and traditional women's speech is very different from that of men. There are four levels of honorific speech: (1) *sonkeigo,* honorific or formal expressions used when one is talking to a superior; (2) *kenjogo,* words one uses to humble oneself before a superior; (3) *keibetsugo,* casual words used with close friends or to speak to an inferior; (4) *teineigo,* derived from *sonkeigo* and used by modern Japanese to speak to people in general situations. The Japanese language has many different words for *I* and *you,* which are used depending on the relationship and gender of the people talking. The honorific prefix *o-* is often added to words as a sign of respect; for example, sweets *(kashi)* are called *okashi.* People do not call each other by their given names, but by their family names with the suffix "-san"; for example, Suzuki-san, which is the equivalent of Mr., Mrs. or Miss Suzuki. Family members and close friends may use the more intimate suffix-chan with the personal name; for example, Midori-chan.

Japanese children spend many years learning their language by copying *kana* and *kanji* characters. They begin writing *kanji* in the first year of grade school. They know 881 kanji after six years of elementary school, and close to 2,000 *kanji* by the time they complete high school. The Japanese have always valued calligraphy *(shodo,* the "Way of Writing") as the highest form of art. Japanese students also study English for six years in junior and senior high school. Numerous English and other Western words have been adapted into the Japanese, such as *depato* for department store and *golufu* for golf. See also CHINA AND JAPAN; HIRAGANA; KANA; KANJI; KATAKANA; O-; -SAN; WRITING SYSTEM, JAPANESE.

LANTERNS *(toro)* Japanese lanterns can be made of stone, paper, or iron. *Ishidoro,* stone lanterns, made of granite or syenite, have many different shapes and are frequently about 6 feet high. Smaller stone lanterns are also used to decorate gardens or illuminate footpaths. A stone lantern has an empty chamber with windows set on top of the base. It is lit by placing a candle inside the chamber and covering the windows with opaque paper. There are three general types of stone lanterns: the tall, thin type that has a hexagonal chamber and roof; short, wide ones, often having four legs, with a mushroom-shaped top; and small pagodas that have several chambers stacked vertically. Stone lanterns were brought to Japan from China in the sixth century. The oldest stone lantern in Japan was supposedly placed in a Buddhist temple for Prince Shotoku in A.D. 594. Lanterns became a regular feature of Japanese Buddhist temples and Shinto shrines. Kasuga Shrine in Nara is famous for the 2,000 stone lanterns that line its walkway. The lanterns are lighted twice a year, in February and mid-August. Tokoji in the city of Hagi has 500 moss-covered stone lanterns lining its path. Eventually stone lanterns also came to be used as garden decorations. During the Azuchi-Momoyama Era (1568–1600), masters of the tea ceremony placed them in gardens outside teahouses. Tea masters valued lanterns that had a weathered look and moss growing on them. Such lanterns are still preferred by the Japanese in their gardens.

Lanterns made of bronze or iron have also been widely used. Bronze hanging lanterns are known as *tsuri-doro.* One thousand bronze lanterns hang in the precincts of Kasuga Shrine in Nara. Todaiji, also in Nara, has a 13-foot-high octagonal bronze lantern that dates back to the Nara Era (710–794). Small iron lanterns that stand on the floor, called *andon,* are used in homes. They too have many different shapes and sizes. There is a pan at the base to catch dripping oil or candle wax, although many of these lanterns are now fitted for electricity. *Bombori* are hexagonal-shaped lanterns that are attached to poles by which they can be carried.

Paper lanterns, or *chochin,* are made by stretching paper over a collapsible round frame of bamboo strips. Family crests, symbols, or calligraphy often decorate these lanterns, which can be illuminated with candles or electric bulbs. *Chochin* are used outdoors and can be carried with poles or hung on buildings, especially homes, restaurants, and temples and shrines during festivals. At the lantern festival held in the city of Akita on August 5–7, men balance 30-foot-high bamboo poles with nine cross-poles on which 46 paper lanterns are hung. Some other festivals that use many lanterns to decorate floats and sacred palanquins (mikoshi) to carry the gods take place in September at Kishima Shrine in Shirawaki-shi and October in Nihonmatsu-shi. Aka-chochin, red paper lanterns, hang in front of bars and restaurants serving inexpensive quick snacks, such as yakitori (grilled chicken). See also BAMBOO; BUDDHISM; CALLIGRAPHY; CREST; FESTIVALS; GARDENS; KASUGA SHRINE; METALWORK; PAPER, HANDMADE; RESTAURANTS; TODAIJI.

LAWS AND LAWYERS   See LEGAL SYSTEM; SUPREME COURT.

LDP   See LIBERAL DEMOCRATIC PARTY.

LEACH, BERNARD HOWELL (1887–1979)   An Englishman who studied pottery in Japan and became the best-known Western potter, as well as a teacher, philosopher and writer who introduced Japanese styles of pottery to the Western world. Leach was born in Hong Kong but was educated in England. After studying at the Slade School of Art and the London School of Art, Leach went to Japan in 1909, where he introduced the artistic technique of etching. After two years in Japan, Leach began to learn pottery with a sixth-generation master of the Kenzan school, which was founded in the early 18th century by Kenzan Ogata, a brother of the famous artist Kenzan Korin. Leach and his friend Kenkichi Tomimoto received certificates that qualified them to represent the seventh generation of Kenzan pottery. Leach also developed a close friendship with Hamada Shoji (1894–1978), who was to become the most famous contemporary Japanese potter.

Leach and Hamada went to England in 1920 and started the Leach Pottery in St. Ives, Cornwall, where they built the first traditional Asian-style sloping wood-fired kiln in the West. Professional potters and student apprentices have come from the world over to study pottery at the St. Ives studio, which has been managed since 1956 by Leach's third wife, Janet Darnell, who had studied pottery with Hamada in Japan. Leach also built a small pottery studio at Dartington, England, in 1929.

Altogether Leach spent over 18 years in Japan during more than a dozen visits there. He joined with Hamada and Yanagi Soetsu (1889–1961) in founding the Japanese craft movement to promote folk crafts (mingei) and adapted Yanagi's book on the aesthetics of folk craft, which he published in English as The Unknown Craftsman (1972). He also wrote Hamada, Potter (1975) in tribute to his friend and colleague. Leach had written two earlier books to present his own aesthetic views and describe how he became a potter: A Potter's Book (1940) and A Potter's Portfolio (1950).

His principal output was stoneware with glazes perfected in Asia such as celadon and Chinese-style temmoku. He took inspiration from the Raku style of pottery and objects made for tea ceremony, which have a rough and imperfect beauty greatly valued by the Japanese.

Leach won many awards for his pottery, including the Binns Medal of the American Ceramic Society, the Gold Medal in Milan and an honorary doctorate from the University of the South-West (Exeter, England). In 1953 the first traveling exhibition of his pottery was held in the United States, with exhibits in New York City and Washington, D.C. Leach, accompanied by Hamada, made a 10,000 mile tour of the country, then continued on to Japan, where Leach stayed until 1955. He published his diary of that trip, first in Japan, and then in England as A Potter in Japan, 1952–55 (1960). Leach made another 10,000-mile tour of the United States to exhibit and lecture with his wife Janet. He was knighted by Queen Elizabeth II in appreciation of his great influence on the British craft movement. In 1961, a major retrospective of Leach's work was held in the gallery of the Arts Council in London. In 1966 Leach received the Order of the Sacred Treasure, Second Class, from the Japanese government. Other books by Leach include Kenzan and His Tradition (1966), A Potter's Work (1967) and Beyond East and West (1978). See also APPRENTICE SYSTEM; DECORATIONS, CIVILIAN; HAMADA SHOJI; KILN; MINGEI; POTTERY; RAKU WARE; TEA BOWL; TEA CEREMONY; YANAGI SOETSU.

LEAGUE OF NATIONS AND JAPAN   Japan was a charter member of the League of Nations, an organization that developed out of the meetings held in 1919 in Paris for the Treaty of Versailles after World War I. Japan had entered the war as an ally of Great Britain, and had equal rank with Britain, France and the United States at the Paris meetings. The Treaty permitted Japan to keep the territories it had taken from Germany in the war, including Shandong (Shantung) Province in China and several Pacific islands. The League of Nations was founded on January 10, 1920, with the goal of keeping world peace, arbitrating disputes between nations and persuading them to corporate. The League's basic organization consisted of the Secretariat, the League Council and the League Assembly, a general meeting of all members. Various other committees were also drawn up. The Permanent Court of International Justice and the International Labor Organization (ILO) were formed later as affiliates. Japan had a permanent seat on the League Council with other major Allied and Associated Powers, attended all council and committee meetings and had a seat on the assembly's executive board. The Japanese scholar-diplomat Nitobe Inazo became under-secretary-general of the League of Nations, as well as director-general. In 1926 Sugimura Yotara replaced Nitobe as under-secretary-general, and also became director of political affairs. Several other Japanese diplomats took part in council and assembly meetings.

In 1928 China appealed to the League of Nations about Japanese military activities in Shandong (Shantung) Province, but Japan prevented the League from taking action other than sending technological aid. After the Manchurian Incident in 1931, when Japanese troops seized the region of Manchuria bordering China, Korea and the Soviet Union, and set up a puppet state known as Manchukuo, the League of Nations sent the so-called Lytton Commission to Manchuria, whose report convinced the assembly to condemn Japan as the aggressor in Manchuria. Matsuoka

Yosuke led the Japanese delegation in walking out of the meeting. On March 27, 1933, Japan gave notice that it was withdrawing from the League. In 1937, the start of the Sino-Japanese War of 1937–1945, the League again charged Japan with aggression in China. Japan did not accept the League's invitation to discuss the matter, and the League Council called for sanctions against Japan, but could not enforce them. Germany and Italy also withdrew from the League, and World War II broke out in 1939, thus ending the League, which was repaced after the war by the United Nations. See also MANCHURIAN INCIDENT, SINO-JAPANESE WAR OF 1937–1945; UNITED NATIONS AND JAPAN; WORLD WAR I; WORLD WAR II.

LEGAL SYSTEM   Japan's legal system is based on the Six Codes (Roppo) of civil law: the Constitution, the Civil Code, the Code of Civil Procedure, the Commercial Code, the Penal Code, and the Code of Criminal Procedure. The Constitution, the primary document governing law and politics; it establishes popular sovereignty, human rights, and a two-chamber Diet (Parliament) counterbalanced by a judiciary. The *Six Codes Book* (*Roppo Zensho*) is available in major bookstores in Japan and is more widely understood by Japanese than equivalent legal codes in other countries are understood by their citizens. The modern Japanese legal system was adopted from civil law systems of European countries by the Meiji government (1868–1912), and the principle of individual rights and Western court procedures were instituted. The Commercial Code was modeled on the French Napoleonic Code, and the Code of Civil Procedure was based on the Prussian system. During the postwar Occupation of Japan (1945–1952), a new constitutional law was established modeled on the Constitution of the United States. The Constitution of 1947 and the Civil Code (1948) gave the Japanese many basic individual rights, including equality of the sexes and equal treatment under the law.

The constitution established the judicial branch of government, independent from the legislative and executive branches. The highest court is the Supreme Court, which administers the court system throughout the country, including eight high courts, 50 district courts in 50 different cities, 50 family courts on a level with district courts and 570 summary courts in cities and towns. High courts function as courts of appeal in criminal and civil cases and have jurisdiction over election disputes. District courts have jurisdiction in criminal and civil cases except petty offenses and certain cases assigned to other courts. Family courts have jurisdiction in matters of inheritance, divorce and juvenile delinquents and their rehabilitation. Summary courts have jurisdiction over minor offenses and small civil claims. Procurators present cases for the government in the various courts, and they also direct penal and probation officials who administer disciplinary programs to convicted criminals. Lawbreakers are prosecuted by attorneys under the Supreme Public Procurators Office, which is administered by the Ministry of Justice and operates under rules of the Supreme Court. Trial by jury was instituted in Japan by the 1923 Jury Law, but was suspended in 1943 and has not

been reinstated. The Japanese prefer mediation to litigation, and rely less on lawyers and law courts than citizens of most other countries. Lawyers and courts are used more to help differing parties reach a compromise than to issue a judgment in the case. Business is conducted with an emphasis on human relationships rather than binding contracts and legal documentation.

Japanese lawyers-to-be study law as undergraduates, and since there are no graduate law schools as known in the West, Japanese go directly into corporations or government to handle legal issues. A law training school, however, is used to prepare judges. In the United States there are around 150 lawyers per 100,000 people, 33 in West Germany and eight in Japan. 60% of all Japanese practicing attorneys are located in the cities of Tokyo and Osaka. Most Japanese lawyers have their own practice or belong to law firms that have two to four attorneys. Many graduates of university law faculties do not become lawyers, judges or prsecutors, but work as government officials or in corporate legal departments. The government elite has generally been trained in the Law Faculty of Tokyo University. See also CONSTITUTION OF 1947; MEIJI RESTORATION OF 1868; OCCUPATION OF JAPAN; POLICE SYSTEM; SUPREME COURT; TOKYO UNIVERSITY.

LEYTE GULF, BATTLE OF   See WORLD WAR II; YAMATO.

LIBERAL DEMOCRATIC PARTY   (LDP; Jiyu Minshuto)   The largest and most powerful political party in postwar Japan. The moderately conservative LDP, as it is known, initially drew its power from agricultural interests but today has diversified its support. Since its founding in 1955, the LDP has held the majority of seats in the Japanese Diet (Parliament). The only exception was in 1976, following the Lockheed Scandal, which brought down Prime Minister Tanaka Kakuei (prime minister 1972–1974) and his cabinet. The LDP was also seriously harmed in 1989 by the worst postwar political scandal, known as the Recruit Scandal, which brought down the government of Prime Minister Takeshita Noboru and contributed to the party's loss of a majority in the House of Councillors (upper house of the Diet) in the July 1989 elections, after which Takeshita's replacement, Prime Minister Uno Sosuke resigned and was replaced by Kaifu Toshiki, the current prime minister.

The LDP was formed in November 1955 when the two major conservative political parties, the Liberal Party and the Japan Democratic Party, merged in response to the uniting of socialist political factions as the Japan Socialist Party (JSP; Nihon Shakaito), which remains a major opposition party in the Diet. These two parties were the heirs of the Rikken Seiyukai and Rikken Minseito parties that had dominated party politics (however weak) in Japan prior to World War II. Both had their roots in the first Japanese political parties, formed by the Meiji government leaders Itagaki Taisuke (1837–1919) and Okuma Shigenobu (1838–1922) in the 1880s.

The LDP has been supported by businessmen, white-collar workers, government workers and farmers. The Federation of Economic Organizations (Keidanren), which represents big business in Japan, provides significant funding to the LDP, and the LDP-dominated Japanese government advocates policies supporting big business. Powerful LDP politicians have developed close relations with wealthy corporate executives. The LDP has overseen Japan's rapid economic growth and the development of the country's export economy and maintained a policy of close cooperation with the United States for mutual defense. However, the party does not have a well-defined political philosophy and has not always been consistent in its policies. It has favored free enterprise, free trade, academic freedom and better conditions for workers, but it has also supported national social welfare programs, including medical insurance and old-age pensions, protection of rice and other staple crops from competitive imports and government control of the education system. Right-wing members of the LDP have supported revision of the Japanese constitution, which was enacted in 1947 during the post-war Allied Occupation of Japan, although party leaders prefer to keep this issue in the background. Different factions within the party hold different positions on various issues, and faction leaders must work out compromises, which sometimes result in contradictory national policies. The Japanese public generally views the LDP as conservative, riddled with factions and in debt to business interests. They are critical of the party's recent bribery and sex scandals, and the 3% national consumption tax, the first ever in Japan, passed by the LDP-dominated Diet in 1989. However, in elections held February 18, 1990 for the House of Representatives (lower house of the Diet), the LDP won 275 of the house's 512 seats. This was a decline from the 295 seats it held before the elections, but 18 seats more than a simple majority, so the party remained in power. Kaifu was reelected president of the LDP and, in turn, prime minister on February 27, 1990. See also CABINET, PRIME MINISTER'S; CONSTITUTION OF 1947; DIET; ELECTIONS; FACTIONS, POLITICAL; FEDERATION OF ECONOMIC ORGANIZATIONS; ITAGAKI TAISUKE; JAPAN SOCIALIST PARTY; KAIFU TOSHIKI; OKUMA SHIGENOBU; PRIME MINISTER; RECRUIT SCANDAL; TAKESHITA NOBORU; TAX SYSTEM; UNO SOSUKE.

LIFETIME EMPLOYMENT SYSTEM (*shushin koyo*) The practice followed by many Japanese companies of retaining full-time employees for their entire working life. This applies especially to college-educated male managers and highly skilled blue-collar workers. Even when a company is in serious financial difficulty and has to reduce its staff, it will attempt to find alternative work for permanent employees or transfer them to subsidiaries rather than lay them off. In return, employees are expected to remain loyal and work for the company until retirement age, which is usually 55 or 60, although a company may ask an employee to retire "voluntarily" when he is no longer needed. Employees are hired when they graduate from high school or college, after careful screening. Conversely, young people also are very careful about which companies they apply to for permanent employment. Employees hired in the same class are formed into groups that stay together throughout their careers. They traditionally have received promotions

and pay raises based on how many years they have worked for the company (seniority system, *nenko joretsu-sei),* but this system is on the decline as job mobility is on the rise. Older workers are also handicapped because they do not know how to use new technology. See also CORPORATIONS; EMPLOYMENT; RETIREMENT; SENIORITY SYSTEM.

LION (*shishi*) This is not an actual lion, but a lion-like mythical creature that is depicted by statues at Japanese shrines, temples and tombs to ward off evil spirits. The creature was introduced into Japan and other East Asian countries from China, and is frequently seen in the southernmost islands of Okinawa Prefecture (Ryukyu Islands), which have close cultural ties with China. Lion statues are often found in pairs, one snarling with an open mouth and the other growling with a closed mouth. The *shishi-mai,* frequently translated into English as "lion dance," is performed in many regions of Japan. The dancers wear costumes and headdresses representing mythical lions or deer. Several dancers may form one lion under a large costume with a lion's head. This type of *shishi-mai* belongs to the category of *kagura,* or sacred dance, which is a form of exorcism. It derives from a Chinese dance introduced into Japan as *gigaku* ("masked dance") during the Heian Era (794–1185) and became popular throughout Japan in the medieval era (13th–16th centuries). Another type of *shishi-mai* is performed by dancers who each wear an individual costume and headdress. Its origin lies in the *shishi odori,* or "deer dance," that has been traditionally performed in eastern Japan, and in the *Nembutsu odori,* a religious dance for the deity Amida performed by members of the Pure Land sect of Buddhism. Many *shishi-mai* have been incorporated into the repertoire of Japanese classical dance, accompanied by a stringed instrument called the *shamisen.* See also CHINA AND JAPAN; DANCE, TRADITIONAL; PURE LAND SECT OF BUDDHISM; RYUKYU ISLANDS; SHAMISEN.

LIQUOR See ALCOHOLIC BEVERAGES.

LITERATURE See CALLIGRAPHY; DIARIES; GENJI, THE TALE OF; HAIKU; HEIKE, THE TALE OF; ISE, TALES OF; MANYOSHU; NOVELS; POETRY; RENGA; TANKA; WAKA.

LIVING NATIONAL TREASURES (Ningen Kokuho) People who have been honored by the Japanese government for their exceptional skills in traditional Japanese arts and crafts. "Living National Treasures" is a popular term for these men and women, who are actually designated Bearers of Important Intangible Cultural Properties (Juyo Mukei Bunkazai Hojisha). There can be no more than 70 at one time.

During the Meiji Era (1868–1912) the Japanese government recognized the importance of preserving major art objects, and in 1929 the Preservation of National Treasures Law (Kokuho Hozon Ho) was finally passed. Following World War II, the Law for the Protection of Cultural Assets (Bunkazai Hogo Ho) was passed in 1950 and amended in 1954 and 1970 to recognize intangible artistic assets (*mukei bunkazai*) as well as objects of art. In 1955 the government established the Ningen Kokuho Award for those Living [or Human] National Treasures who have mastered the technical skills to create beautiful things that have been used in Japanese daily life, such as dolls, handmade paper, lacquer ware, pottery, swords, textiles and wooden objects. Kabuki (traditional theater), Noh drama, puppet theater (Bunraku) and traditional dance and music are also among the more than 60 categories that have been designated as worthy of the award. In some cases whole groups are given this award, such as dancers in Okinawa (the southernmost islands of Japan) and lacquer makers in Wajima. Recipients of the award, which includes an annual stipend, must have not only the highest technical abilities but also a commitment to teaching their craft or performing art to apprentices who may become future masters. They are expected to exhibit or perform around the country and to leave records of their personal knowledge so that others can learn from their achievements. The best known Living National Treasure has been the potter Hamada Shoji, whose work has been exhibited widely outside Japan. Ningen Kokuho awards are given out every year through a program in the Agency for Cultural Affairs of the Japanese Ministry of Education. Regional and local governments in Japan may also honor people as Bearers of Intangible Cultural Assets, but only those who have received the national award of Ningen Kokuho are called Living National Treasures. See also APPRENTICE SYSTEM; BASKETS; BOXES; BUNRAKU; DANCE, TRADITIONAL; DOLLS; HAMADA SHOJI; HEMP; INDIGO; KABUKI; KASURI; LACQUER WARE; METALWORK; NOH DRAMA; PAPER, HANDMADE; POTTERY; STENCILS; SWORD; TEXTILES; WOODBLOCK PRINTS; WOODWORKING.

LOBSTER See SEAFOOD.

LOCKHEED SCANDAL See FUKUDA KAKUEI; MARUBENI CORPORATION; MIKI TAKEO; OHIRA MASAYOSHI; TANAKA KAKUEI.

LOINCLOTH (*fundoshi* or *shitaobi*) A long strip of white cloth, usually cotton, traditionally worn by men as a kind of underwear or as a work outfit. Peasants wore loincloths for agricultural work in the fields, as did palanquin bearers and other laborers. The loincloth is tied around the waist, wrapped between the legs and tucked into or tied to the material in back, leaving the buttocks uncovered. Loincloths were worn in Japan since ancient times, and were made of linen until cotton was introduced during the Edo Era (1600–1868). Upper-class men wore silk loincloths. Japanese men began wearing Western-style underwear during the Meiji Era (1868–1912), but a loincloth remained part of the military uniform worn by soldiers of the Imperial Japanese Army through World War II. Men still wear loincloths for traditional festivals when they engage in activities such as carrying torches or sacred palanquins (*mikoshi*) bearing *kami* (sacred spirits) in street processions. They are sometimes also worn by men who perform with large drums known as *kodo*. Sumo wrestlers wear a special dark loincloth made of heavy silk, known as a *mawashi* or *shimekomi*. See also DRUMS; FESTIVALS; PALANQUIN; SUMO.

LONDON NAVAL CONFERENCES (1930 and 1935–36) Conferences held in London that revised the Washington Naval Treaty (1922) limiting naval armament. Japanese delegates to the London Naval Conference of 1930 were former Prime Minister Wakatsuki Reijiro, Ambassador Matsudaira Tsuneo and Navy Minister Admiral Takarabe Takeshi. The cabinet of Prime Minister Hamaguchi Osachi instructed the representatives to demand that the Japanese navy be allowed a ratio of seven ships to every 10 American and every 10 British ships, but American and British delegates refused to accept this proposal. A compromise worked out at the conference came fairly close to Japanese demands, but angered hard-line leaders in Japan. The Japanese delegates were also unsuccessful in trying to have the Philippine Islands, an American colony, declared a neutral territory. Although Japan reluctantly ratified the conference's treaty, Japanese politicians and naval administrators who opposed the unequal treaty gained more domestic influence as a result. Pressure from the Navy Minister, Admiral Osumi Mineo (1876–1941), finally caused the cabinet of Prime Minister Okada Keisuke to announce in 1934 that it would abrogate the entire Washington Naval Treaty of 1922. Great Britain called a meeting with Japan, the United States, France and Italy in London in December 1935 to save the treaty. The Japanese delegates, Ambassador Nagai Matsuzo and Admiral Nagano Osami, demanded that Japan be allowed the same number of ships as the American and British navies and that all naval fleets be expanded. The other nations rejected these demands, and Japan left the conference. Even though an agreement was made between remaining nations at the conference to continue naval arms limitations, the conference in fact was a failure, and Japanese military efforts increased, leading to fighting in the Pacific Theater in World War II. See also IMPERIAL JAPANESE ARMY AND NAVY; WASHINGTON CONFERENCE AND NAVAL TREATY; WORLD WAR II.

LOTTERIES See GAMBLING.

LOTUS (*hasu*) A flowering plant that grows in water such as ponds and rice paddy fields. Lotus flowers grow on long, straight stalks and lie on the surface of the water. The fragrant flowers are about 8 inches in diameter and can be white, pink or red. They stay in bloom for four days, opening their long petals in the morning and closing them in the afternoon.

The lotus may have originated in India, and was brought to Japan from China. It is mentioned in the *Kojiki*, an official chronicle recorded in A.D. 712. The lotus flower is an important symbol in the Buddhist religion and is commonly depicted on statues and other Buddhist objects. As the lotus rises out of the mud, so an enlightened human being rises above the impurity of the ordinary world. The lotus is also a symbol of the Pure Land where believers in the salvation provided by Amida Buddha are thought to go after death. Hence may temple compounds have had ponds with lotus flowers.

The seeds of the lotus, contained in the oval-shaped fruit, have been used as cures by Asian medical traditions, along with lotus flowers, leaves and roots. The creamy whit lotus "root" (renkon), actually a rhizome, is also used in Japanese and Chinese cooking. When the root, which is about 5–8 inches long and 2½ inches wide, is cut into slices, a lacy pattern emerges due to hollow areas that run lengthwise through the root. The crunchy texture and mild flavor of lotus root slices are popular in vinegared dishes, simmered dishes, and as a vegetable in *tempura*. See also AMIDA; BUDDHISM; COOKING; FLOWERS; KOJIKI; LOTUS SUTRA; MEDICINE, TRADITIONAL; PURE LAND SECT OF BUDDHISM.

LOTUS SUTRA (*Hokke Kyo*) The most important *sutra* (scripture) of the branch of the Buddhist religion known as Mahayana Buddhism, or the Greater Vehicle. After Buddhism originated in India in the sixth century B.C. it divided into two main branches, Theravada (or Hinayana), the Lesser Vehicle, and Mahayana. The latter was brought through Central Asia to China and Korea, and was introduced into Japan in the sixth century A.D. The *Lotus Sutra*, or the *Sutra of the Lotus of the Wonderful Law*, was translated from Indian Sanskrit into Chinese in the third century A.D. It supposedly contains the last sermon given by Siddhartha Gautama, the founder of Buddhism, just before his death and entry into Nirvana. The *Lotus Sutra* teaches that all human beings have the potential for Buddhist enlightenment, and this universal outlook is the main principle of Mahayana Buddhism. A passage in the *Lotus Sutra* proclaims that all people who call upon the name of Kannon, the Goddess of Mercy (known as Avalokiteshvara in Sanskrit), will be saved. The lotus, a flower that grows in water, is the Buddhist symbol for ultimate perfection. Just as the beautiful lotus flower rises up from the mud, so do purity and truth rise above evil, and all people have the lotus of the Buddha nature within them.

In Japan, the *Lotus Sutra* became the basic scripture of the influential Tendai sect of Buddhism, which was introduced from China by the Japanese monk Saicho (767–822) and centered at the Enryakuji on Mount Hiei northeast of the capital city of Kyoto. The *Lotus Sutra* was also used by other religious teachers, notably Nichiren (1222–1282), who had trained at Mount Hiei but left the Tendai sect to preach his own interpretation of this scripture. Nichiren taught that people could attain salvation from suffering and death only by having absolute faith in the *Lotus Sutra*. They did not have to read the scripture, but simply recite the phrase "Praise to the Wonderful Law of the Lotus Sutra." Nichiren even felt that such faith would save the entire Japanese nation. His name is a combination of two terms: *nichi*, "the sun," symbolizing the light of truth and also the Land of the Rising Sun, as Japan has been named; and *ren*, "lotus." Nichiren's teachings based on the *Lotus Sutra* gained a large following among the Japanese people and are currently experiencing a revival. See also BUDDHISM; ENRYAKUJI; HIEI, MOUNT; KANNON; LOTUS; NICHIREN; PURE LAND SECT OF BUDDHISM; SAICHO; SCRIPTURES, RELIGIOUS; SUN; TENDAI SECT OF BUDDHISM.

LOVE HOTEL (*tsurekomi hoteru* or *rabu hoteru*) A hotel where couples, married or unmarried, can rent rooms for a short time for sexual purposes without social stigma. The room rate is calculated by the hour or by the night, although most couples stay only a few hours. Rooms in love hotels are often decorated with exotic or fantastic themes. A love hotel is identified by a brightly colored heart-shaped neon sign on its roof. The hotel is also surrounded by a wall and has a separate entrance and exit. Japanese go to love hotels because they offer privacy that is often lacking in Japanese homes, where rooms are small, walls are thin and several generations may live together. There are around 35,000 love hotels throughout Japan, usually close to railroad stations. See also HOMES AND HOUSING.

LOYALTY (*chu, chusei, shugi*) A major ethical concept in Japanese culture, which has been influenced both by Confucianism and feudal social structure. Confucianism, introduced from China in the fifth–sixth centuries A.D., teaches that society maintains its order through hierarchical relationships, starting with the parent-child relationship in the family. Confucianism regards loyalty to one's parents, and by extension to one's family, as essential. According to Confucianism, people ought to be loyal and obedient to those of higher social rank, especially parents. In turn, parents and other superiors nurture and assist those underneath them. Loyalty to one's parents is termed filial piety (*ko; koko; oya koko*). The parent-child relationship has served as the model for all relationships in Japan. This remains true today, even in the business world and among gangsters (*yakuza*). Loyalty and duty (or obligation; *giri*) are interrelated principles.

During the feudal era in Japan, which began in the 12th century, loyalty to one's lord (*daimyo*) took precedence over loyalty to one's family as the central ethical requirement. In the feudal lord-vassal relationship, vassals owed their lords absolute obedience. In return, lords gave their vassals patronage and favors (*on*) such as land grants or property rights. The lords in turn were vassals of the shogun, or military ruler. The Tokugawa Shogunate (1603–1867) combined feudal ethics with Confucianism to reinforce loyalty as a universal ethical virtue in Japanese society. Loyalty is central for the ethical code known as *Bushido*, the "Way of the Warrior," which became formalized during the Tokugawa era.

The Meiji government (1868–1912), which modernized Japan, also promoted loyalty and filial piety as central principles. Moreover, it transformed the concept of loyalty to feudal lords into the notion of loyalty to the emperor as the embodiment of the Japanese state (*kokutai*, "body politic" or "national essence"), in the religion of so-called State Shinto.

After Japan was defeated in World War II, the emperor renounced the traditional Japanese belief that he was divine, and loyalty to the emperor is no longer official Japanese policy. However, the concept of loyalty has survived as a dominant social force. Modern companies are like families in that they receive complete loyalty from their employees, who in turn receive job security and personal benefits. Hence Japanese employees seldom leave one company for another. Most Japanese also still feel strong bonds of loyalty to their parents and to their teachers. See also BUSHIDO; CONFUCIANISM; DAIMYO; DUTY AND FEELINGS; EMPLOYMENT; FAMILY; FEUDALISM; FILIAL PIETY; KOKUTAI; MEIJI RESTORATION OF 1868; SAMURAI; SHOGUN; STATE SHINTO; TOKUGAWA SHOGUNATE.

LUNCH BOX   See BENTO.

LUZON, BATTLE OF   See WORLD WAR II.

MA A traditional Japanese aesthetic concept that indicates a pause or an interval in time, or empty space. *Ma* has to do with rhythm, timing and balance. This concept originated with Japanese music, which uses rests, or brief periods of silence, juxtaposed to sound. Singers, musicians and dancers are free to add or lengthen pauses in the music or body movements to heighten the dramatic intensity of a performance. This is especially true in classical Noh drama, where the main actor stops for a short time in the middle of a movement. Zeami (1363–1443), who developed the philosophical concepts of Noh, wrote that an actor reveals his heart in such an interval where there is no sound and no motion. Kabuki theater also employs intervals; an example is when an actor pauses and looks silently at the audience as a way of expressing deep emotion. *Ma* as timing is also important in popular theatrical forms such as storytelling *(rakugo)* and comic dialogues *(manzai)*. A Japanese proverb states that a performer's life depends on *ma*.

Ma as empty space is utilized by Japanese painters who leave portions of their pictures blank. This is especially true in calligraphy *(shodo)* and ink painting *(sumi-e* or *suibokuga)* influenced by Zen Buddhism. This emptiness, which makes the painted or decorated area even more noticeable, is similarly employed in Japanese gardens. The rock garden at Ryoanji in Kyoto, for example, is famous for the spacing of a few rocks in a large field of white raked sand.

The emptiness of *ma* is a positive force and filled with energy. Related to *ma* is the concept of *yugen*, which indicates that which is deeply mysterious and is expressed indirectly. In the Zen-influenced martial arts *(budo)*, such as sword fighting, the interval *(ma-ai)* or spatial distance between two opponents in combat is crucial. *Ma* also plays a role in Japanese literature. For example, 17-syllable *haiku* poetry is written in three lines of 5-7-5 syllables, with three intervals or beats. Empty space is also important in Japanese architecture. A traditional room is plain and has mostly empty space; there is little furniture. Rather than filling a room with paintings and other decorations, a *tokonoma*, or alcove, is placed in one wall where a scroll and a flower arrangement can be appreciated. Even in Japanese social relationships, there is the sense of *nakama*, or being "inside" *(naka)* a close circle of friends or associates, who are able to communicate without words *(haragei*, "belly language") because of their silently shared feelings. See also "BELLY LANGUAGE"; DANCE, TRADITIONAL; GARDENS; HAIKU; HOMES AND HOUSING; INK PAINTINGS; KABUKI; MARTIAL ARTS; NOH DRAMA; RYOANJI; STORYTELLING; TOKONOMA; YUGEN; ZEAMI; ZEN BUDDHISM.

MACARTHUR, DOUGLAS (1880–1964) The commander of the U.S. Army in the Pacific Theater during World War II and Supreme Commander for the Allied Powers (SCAP) during the Allied Occupation of Japan following the war, until U.S. President Harry S Truman dismissed him in April 1951. MacArthur, the son of a U.S. army general who served in the Philippines, was born in Arkansas and educated at West Point Military Academy. He served in the Philippines and East Asia, in Europe during World War I, and at West Point after the war, and was Army chief of staff 1930–1935. He then returned to the Philippines and reorganized the Philippine army. In July 1941 President Franklin D. Roosevelt appointed him commander of the U.S. forces in the Far East, shortly before the Japanese attacked Pearl Harbor and the Philippines on December 7, 1941. MacArthur was forced to abandon the Philippines and flee to Australia, making his famous proclamation, "I shall return." He successfully led the Pacific island-hopping military campaign by which the Allied Powers defeated the Japanese in 1945. MacArthur was then appointed Supreme Commander for the Allied Powers and accepted the Japanese unconditional surrender on the U.S. battleship *Missouri* on September 2, 1945. MacArthur's policies were more moderate and less punitive of the Japanese than other Allied Powers desired. He resisted Allied demands to try Emperor Hirohito (1901–1989) as a war criminal because he felt that the Japanese needed the emperor as a symbol of national and social unity. But Hirohito acquiesced to Allied demands to renounce the traditional belief in the emperor's divinity.

MacArthur was hard-working and conscientious but aloof and impersonal. The Japanese respected him for these traits and regarded him almost as a shogun, but many Americans felt he was egocentric and arrogant. MacArthur oversaw the demilitarization of Japan and the reorganization of the Japanese government along the lines of American democracy. Major changes included land reforms, partial dissolution of giant financial combines known as *zaibatsu*, women's rights and a system of compulsory education. MacArthur also had a new constitution drawn up, which was promulgated in 1947 by the new Japanese government under Prime Minister Shidehara Kijuro (1872–1951) and still remains in effect. One article of this new constitution forbids Japan from rearming itself.

In 1948–1950 Manchuria and mainland China were taken over by the Chinese Communists and South Korea was invaded by North Korea. From Japan, MacArthur staged an amphibious landing of American troops at Inch'on, behind North Korean lines, on September 15, 1950. But the Chinese Communists surprised him by entering the war to defend North Korea. In order to replace American troops in Japan, MacArthur ordered the Japanese to build up a national police reserve, which in 1954 took the name Land, Sea, and Air Self-Defense Forces and was placed under a Defense Agency. President Truman's administration wished to refrain from American military involvement with China, but MacArthur wanted to retaliate against China and carry the war into Manchuria. On April 11, 1951, Truman dismissed MacArthur as SCAP and replaced him by General Matthew Ridgeway. This action shocked the Japanese. The American people welcomed MacArthur back home as a hero. In an address to the U.S. Congress, MacArthur quoted the lines from a famous military song, "Old soldiers never die; they just fade away." He retired with the rank of five-star general. See also CONSTITUTION OF 1947; EDUCATION; HIROHITO, EMPEROR; OCCUPATION OF JAPAN; SELF-DEFENSE FORCES; SHOGUN; SUPREME COMMANDER FOR THE ALLIED POWERS; WORLD WAR II; ZAIBATSU.

MADAME BUTTERFLY See BUTTERFLY; HARRIS, TOWNSEND; NAGASAKI.

MADE IN JAPAN (Nihonsei) By the end of World War II, with the Japanese economy and industry shattered and the country without natural resources, the Japanese were able to produce only cheap goods made of poor materials. "Made in Japan" became an epithet used by foreigners to denigrate the country's exports. However, government and commercial leaders carefully guided the rebuilding of Japanese industry, and in a few decades the export-based Japanese economy had become the rival of the other developed countries. Today the phrase "Made in Japan" refers to products with high quality and reliability, and Western countries are struggling to make products that are as good. Morita Akio (1921–), president of Sony Corporation, published a best-selling autobiography, *Made in Japan* (1987). See also MINISTRY OF INTERNATIONAL TRADE AND INDUSTRY; MORITA AKIO; QUALITY CONTROL CIRCLE.

MAEDA CLAN A family whose leaders became very powerful *daimyo* (feudal lords) during the Edo Era (1600–1868) through alliances with the great warlords who unified Japan, Oda Nobunaga (1534–1582) and Toyotomi Hideyoshi (1536–1598). Maeda Toshiie (1538?–1599) served Nobunaga until his death in 1582, and then joined with Hideyoshi. For his military service, these warlords awarded him lands in Noto Province and Kaga Province (both part of modern Ishikawa Prefecture) and Etchu Province (modern Toyama Prefecture), and Toshiie settled at Oyama Castle in Kanazawa City. Under the Maeda, Kanazawa became the largest and wealthiest domain of the Edo Era, with an annual income of more than 1 million *koku* (a measurement of rice equal to approximately five bushels). The Maeda were known in Japan as lords of the "million *koku* of Kaga" (*Kaga hyakuman-goku*) and were classified as *tozama daimyo*, or "outside lords," by the Tokugawa Shogunate, because they had been powerful before the shogunate began its rule and were thus permitted to retain a great deal of autonomy. They developed Kanazawa into a lovely castle town, known as the "little Kyoto" of Japan, which is a popular tourist attraction today. Maeda Tsunanori (1643–1724) made reforms in the Kanazawa domain that changed samurai (warriors) into salaried bureaucratic administrators, placed a fixed amount (*jomen*) system of taxes on agricultural villages and gave local peasant officials more responsibility over their villages. Tsunanori was also a scholar of Confucianism and promoted the preservation and editing of old books, thus forming the core collection of the present Sonkeikau Library, which contains more than 100,000 works in both Japanese and Chinese. The Maeda invited many scholars to take up residence in Kaazawa, and also patronized the Noh drama and other performing arts and crafts. See also CASTLES; DAIMYO; EDO ERA; KANAZAWA; KOKU; MAEDA TOSHIIE; ODA NOBUNAGA; TOKUGAWA IEYASU; TOYOTOMI HIDEYOSHI.

MAEDA TOSHIIE (1538?–1599) The founder of the Maeda clan, which became the most powerful *daimyo* (feudal lord) family of the Edo Era (1600–1868). Toshiie served the great warlord Oda Nobunaga (1534–1582) from 1551 until he was assassinated in 1582. Toshiie fought in Nobunaga's major military campaigns, including the Battle of Nagoshino (1575), where he commanded musketeers (*teppo ashigaru*) trained to fight with firearms recently introduced into Japan from the West. Nobunaga made Toshiie a *daimyo* in 1581 when he awarded him Noto Province (part of modern Ishikawa prefecture). After Nobunaga's death, Toshiie sided with Toyotomi Hideyoshi, (1536–1598), the enemy of Toshiie's long-term ally Shibata Katsuie, in the Battle of Shizugatake (1583). Following his victory, Hideyoshi awarded Toshiie two districts of Kaga Province (part of modern Ishikawa Prefecture). Toshiie settled in Kanazawa, which under the Maeda Clan became the largest domain during the Edo Era. He served in the military campaigns that brought all of Japan under Hideyoshi's control, and in 1595 Toshiie became a member of Hideyoshi's council of "Five Great Elders," (*Gotairo*), which headed his military government. Hideyoshi adopted two of Toshiie's daughters and took a third as his concubine. When Hideyoshi died in 1598, Toshiie became the main protector of his son and heir, Toyotomi Hideyori (1593–1615). However, when Toshiie died the following year, other warlords struggled for control of the country. Tokugawa Ieyasu defeated his rivals at the Battle of Sekigahara (1600) and became military ruler of all Japan. See also AZUCHI-MOMOYAMA ERA; CASTLES; DAIMYO; FIREARMS, INTRODUCTION OF; KANAZAWA; KOKU; MAEDA CLAN; ODA NOBUNAGA; SEKIGAHARA, BATTLE OF; TOKUGAWA IEYASU; TOKUGAWA SHOGUNATE; TOYOTOMI HIDEYOSHI.

MAEKAWA REPORTS A series of reports submitted to Japanese Prime Minister Nakasone Yasuhiro (prime minister 1982–1987) in 1986 recommending ways for Japan to decrease its enormous trade surplus, which caused international political and economic problems for Japan, by increasing imports. The report was prepared by the Advisory Group on Economic Structural Adjustment for International Harmony, a private group chaired by Maekawa Haruo (b. 1911), a former official with the Bank of Japan. The trade surplus, which rose rapidly in the 1980s, was the result of Japan's great success at exporting its high-quality products around the world. The value of the yen (Japanese currency) also increased dramatically against other currencies. Among their proposals, the Maekawa Reports recommended government policies that would stimulate domestic consumption and imports, improve access of foreign companies to the Japanese market, liberalize financial markets, stabilize international financial exchange rates and encourage economic cooperation with other countries. A government Task Force on Economic Structural Adjustment, headed by Nakasone, was subsequently formed to implement these recommendations. See also CORPORATIONS; EXPORTS AND IMPORTS; INVESTMENTS OVERSEAS, JAPANESE; NAKASONE YASUHIRO; STOCK MARKET; YEN.

MAGATAMA   See AMATERASU O MIKAMI; EMPEROR; IMPERIAL REGALIA; NINIGI NO MIKOTO; TOMB MOUND; YAYOI ERA.

MAGAZINES (*zasshi, shukanshi*) Magazines were first published in Japan in the late 19th century. The earliest magazines were mostly political forums or literary magazines (*bungei zasshi*) in which the work of many new writers was published. The 20th century saw a boom in magazines on the arts, entertainment and interests of women and children. General interest magazines (*sogo zasshi*) are published monthly. Weekly magazines (*shukanshi*) were first published in 1922 by the Asahi and Mainichi Newspaper companies. The Japanese love to read and have a literacy rate of close to 100%. Specialized magazines are published for every segment of the reading public. More than 2,000 monthly magazines and about 100 weekly magazines are published in Japan. Comic books (*manga*) are very popular with Japanese children. There are also adult comic books enjoyed by college students and businessmen. Weekly photo magazines containing celebrity gossip sell about 3 million copies a week. Highly illustrated sports magazines also sell extremely well. Women's magazines have a big format and and are printed on good quality glossy paper, with color photographs, an assortment of articles and advertising filling 20–60% of the pages. *The Housewife's Friend (Shufu no Tomo)*, which has been published since 1917, set the standard for women's magazines, with a circulation of about half a million copies. Young women's fashion magazines contain pictures of the latest fashions, articles on new trends in cooking, travel and recreation, personal advice columns, and popular fiction. Foreign magazines of all types are readily available, and many Japanese magazines are sold abroad. See also ADVERTISING; BOOKS AND BOOKSTORES; COMIC BOOKS; NEWSPAPERS.

MAHAYANA BUDDHISM   See BUDDHISM; MONASTICISM, BUDDHIST.

MAIKO   See APPRENTICE SYSTEM; GEISHA.

MAINICHI SHIMBUN   See NEWSPAPERS.

MAKEUP   Makeup has always played an important role in Japanese society. From ancient times, aristocratic women have worn heavy makeup emphasizing a very white face and small red lips. White face powder, lipstick, rouge and other cosmetics were introduced into Japan from China and Korea by the sixth century A.D. Until the 19th century, Japanese women blackened their teeth after they were married. They also shaved their eyebrows and drew new ones with a paste (*mayuzumi*) that included lampblack. They applied red rouge (*beni*) to their lips and, infrequently, to their cheeks. Contemporary Japanese women spend the equivalent of millions of dollars every year on cosmetics. The largest Japanese cosmetic company is the world-famous Shiseido Co., Ltd., which was founded in Tokyo in 1872. With many overseas branches and manufacturing plants, the company has a high reputation for research and development of cosmetics and skin products. Japanese women have traditionally used rice bran, juice from gourds and cucumbers, and nightingale excrement to cleanse their skin and maintain beautiful complexions.

Women entertainers known as geisha ("art persons") still wear a traditional style of heavy makeup for formal banquets and dance performances. They cover their faces and necks with a thick paint-like white makeup known as *o-shiroi*, "honorable white," that is a powder mixed with water and applied with a brush. Until the late 19th century, this makeup (also worn by Kabuki actors and courtesans) contained lead and was highly toxic; now it is made of safe ingredients. Geisha also use red makeup to outline their eyes. They cover their lips with white makeup and then paint in smaller, bright red lips. Their own hair is covered with an elaborate wig decorated with ornaments. Geisha are trained to cover their mouths when they laugh, partly because the stark white makeup makes their teeth seem yellow in contrast. Japanese women who perform classical dances wear a similar type of makeup. Actors in the Kabuki traditional theater wear stylized makeup, which is quite exaggerated for historical dramas (*jidai-mono*) and more realistic for plays about daily urban life (*sewa-mono*) set in the Edo Era (1600–1868). Heavy makeup is worn by actors who specialize in female roles, known as *onnagata*, when playing courtesans, court ladies and young women, and by actors playing young men in urban dramas and noble military heroes in historical dramas. Very bold and colorful mask-like makeup, known as *kumadori*, is worn by leading actors in historical dramas. There are around 100 *kumadori* face styles that define particular characters. The color red symbolizes passion, goodness or supernatural powers. Blue symbolizes fear, jealousy and other evil negative qualities, or even demons. These makeup styles resemble those in the Chinese theater known as Peking Opera. See also BRUSHES; COMBS AND HAIR ORNAMENTS; COURTESAN; DANCE, TRADITIONAL; EDO ERA; GEISHA; HAIRSTYLES, TRADITIONAL; KABUKI; MIRROR; SHISEIDO CO., LTD.; TOOTH BLACKENING; WHITE.

MAKI-E TECHNIQUE.   See BOXES; INRO; LACQUER WARE.

MANAGEMENT   See CORPORATIONS; EMPLOYMENT; EXPENSE ACCOUNTS; JOINT-VENTURE CORPORATION; SALARYMAN; TRADING COMPANY, GENERAL.

MANCHUKUO   See LEAGUE OF NATIONS AND JAPAN; MANCHURIAN INCIDENT; SINO-JAPANESE WAR OF 1937–1945.

MANCHURIAN INCIDENT (1931) (Manshu Jihen) The invasion of Manchuria, a region bordering China, Korea and the Soviet Union, by the Japanese Guandong (Kwantung) Army in Manchuria. Japan had maintained a military presence in Manchuria since the Russo-Japanese War (1904–1905), during which 100,000 Japanese had been killed in Manchuria. When Japan defeated Russia it acquired the Liadong (Liaotung) Peninsula (known as the Guandong [Kwantung] Leased Territory), which China had leased to Russia, along with mining rights, other commercial interests and control of the South Manchurian Railway. Japan treated Manchuria as a colony and moved about a million Japanese subjects into the region. Chinese resistance, and an alliance between the warlord of Manchuria and Chinese Nationalists led by Chiang Kai-shek, convinced the officers of the Japanese Guandong Army that they had to take control of Manchuria. On September 18–19, 1931, the Japanese attacked the main Chinese military garrison in Mukden (now Shenyang). In Tokyo, the prime minister's cabinet protested this plan to the army minister, who in turn sent a letter to the commander of the Guandong Army, but it did not arrive in time. The cabinet was unable to prevent the army from occupying all of southern Manchuria and the capitals of all three Manchurian provinces by the end of 1931. By January 1933 Japanese troops controlled all of Manchuria. Japan appointed Pu Yi, the last Chinese emperor, head of the newly created puppet state known as Manchukuo. The League of Nations condemned the Japanese occupation of Manchuria, and Japan withdrew from the League in 1933, thus isolating itself from other world powers. Japan's actions in Manchuria created a massive Soviet military buildup along the border. It also created intense animosity between China and Japan, which resulted in the Sino-Japanese War of 1937–1945. See also LEAGUE OF NATIONS AND JAPAN; RUSSO-JAPANESE WAR; SINO-JAPANESE WAR OF 1937–1945.

MANDALA See BUDDHISM; DAINICHI; SHINGON SECT OF BUDDHISM.

MANDARIN ORANGE See CITRUS FRUIT.

MANGA see COMIC BOOKS.

MANUFACTURING See AUTOMOBILE INDUSTRY; CAMERAS AND PHOTOGRAPHY; COMPUTER INDUSTRY; CORPORATIONS; ELECTRONICS INDUSTRY; EXPORTS AND IMPORTS; INDUSTRIAL ZONES; "JUST IN TIME" INVENTORY PRODUCTION SYSTEM; LABOR UNIONS; MOTORCYCLE INDUSTRY; QUALITY CONTROL CIRCLE; RESEARCH AND DEVELOPMENT; ROBOTS AND ROBOTICS; SEMICONDUCTOR INDUSTRY; SHIPPING AND SHIPBUILDING; STEEL INDUSTRY.

MANYOSHU *Collection of Ten Thousand* [or *Myriad*] *Leaves;* an anthology compiled in the eighth century A.D. that is the earliest and best surviving collection of Japanese poetry known as *waka.* A standard version of the *Manyoshu* comprises 20 books with 4,520 poems, most of which were written in the century prior to A.D. 760. During this time, especially in the Nara Era (710–794), Chinese culture was being rapidly embraced by the Japanese, and poets of the

Manyoshu used Chinese characters to write the Japanese language phonetically, in a technique known as *manyogana,* from the words *manyo* and *kana* (a script) meaning "borrowed names." The result was a complex writing style difficult to understand today.

Some of the poems in the *Manyoshu* are ascribed to peasants or derive from ancient folks songs, but most were composed by members of the Japanese aristocracy. The poems are written in several forms. Four thousand two hundred are *tanka* ("short poems") having five lines of 5, 7, 5, 7 and 7 syllables, 260 are *choka* ("long poems") and 60 are *sedoka* ("head-repeated poems"—having a recurring pattern of 5-7-7-5-7-7 syllables). The Japanese have always preferred the direct and spontaneous expressions of short poems. Unlike later Chinese-influenced poetry in Japan, which was often more refined and limited in theme, poems in the *Manyoshu* deal with a wide range of human emotions. These include grief for a loved one who has died and sorrow over human suffering as well as joyful declarations of love and praise for natural beauty like that of Mount Fuji.

There are many variations on the text of the *Manyoshu,* the earliest dating from the late Kamakura Era (1192–1333), and all include footnotes, letters and other explanatory materials, all written in Chinese. The texts have been studied by scholars throughout Japanese history, particularly in the Edo Era (1600–1868), when many critical commentaries on the work were written. There are many English translations of poems from the *Manyoshu.* See also CHINA AND JAPAN; NARA ERA; POETRY; TANKA; WAKA; WRITING SYSTEM, JAPANESE.

MANZAI See STORYTELLING.

MANZANAR RELOCATION CENTER See IMMIGRANTS, JAPANESE; JAPANESE-AMERICAN CITIZENS LEAGUE.

MAPLE TREE (*kaede; momiji,* red maple leaves) More than 20 species of maple tree are native to Japan. Non-native maples, such as those from North America, are also grown in Japan. Maples from China are used in *bonsai,* the cultivation of miniature trees. Japanese maple trees are especially beautiful in autumn when their leaves turn bright red. Maple leaves in autumn, known as *momiji,* have always been celebrated in Japanese art and literature, and are a common decorative motif. The Japanese enjoy viewing autumn leaves, a custom known as *momijigari,* especially in the mountains around the old capital cities of Kyoto and Nara. This custom dates back to the Heian Era (794–1185), when aristocrats held parties in their gardens to view cherry blossoms (*sakura no hana*) in spring and maple trees in autumn while writing poetry and playing music, and also made trips into the mountains during these seasons. See also AUTUMN; BONSAI; CHERRY BLOSSOMS; KYOTO; MOUNTAINS; NARA; POETRY.

MAPPO See NICHIREN; PURE LAND SECT OF BUDDHISM.

MARRIAGE See FAMILY; FATHER; GO-BETWEEN; HOUSEHOLD REGISTER; MOTHER; WEDDINGS.

MARTIAL ARTS *(bujutsu; bugei; budo)* Traditional methods of fighting both with and without weapons. There are more than 20 different martial arts developed in Japan. The best known are archery *(kyudo); kendo*, sword-fighting techniques using split bamboo sticks; and judo, karate and *aikido*, methods of weaponless fighting in which opponents are thrown or restrained. A central concept of Japanese martial arts is the technique of pulling one's opponent off balance, known as *kuzushi*, while defending against an opponent's attack.

The martial arts were developed from the late 12th century by members of the samurai class. During the Edo Era (1600–1868), Japan was no longer at war, but the code of *bushido* ("Way of the Warrior") required samurai to learn seven martial arts for self-defense but more importantly for spiritual discipline: military strategy, Western firearms, archery, swordfighting, judo, horseback riding and use of the spear. Sumo, a unique Japanese form of wrestling, and *ninjutsu* (the "art of stealth"), practiced by spies and assassins known as *ninja*, have also been traditionally associated with the martial arts.

Following the Meiji Restoration of 1868, the emphasis of the martial arts changed. Studied by members of all social classes and no longer practiced for warfare, the martial arts became known as *budo* ("Martial Way") to emphasize their nature as spiritual disciplines. In the 20th century, martial arts developed into competitive sports in which students acquire physical skills and test them in competitions.

Knowledge of a martial art is transmitted directly from master to student. Students of a martial art traditionally train in a hall known as a *dojo* under the strict guidance of a *sensei* (teacher) who has mastered the art. Each martial art is taught by many different schools *(ryuha)*, each having its own philosophy and teaching style. During training, students usually wear special white pants and jackets, with colored belts to indicate the rank they have attained. Students learn *kata* (form), which involves correct posture and movements, by diligently practicing established forms or patterns of movement. See also AIKIDO; ARCHERY; BUSHIDO; DOJO; JUDO; KARATE; KENDO; NAGINATA; NINJA; SAMURAI; SENSEI; SUMO; SWORD.

MARUBENI CORPORATION One of the largest Japanese trading companies *(sogo shosha)* and a member of the Fuyo Group. Marubeni was founded in 1858 and reorganized in 1949. Its head offices are in Tokyo, with 50 domestic branches, 128 overseas branches and subsidiaries, 231 affiliates in Japan and 150 in foreign countries. The company is involved in many industries, such as chemicals, energy, machinery and textiles. Marubeni has also diversified into the fields of insurance underwriting, financing of construction projects and property leasing. In 1981, Marubeni was number four in sales among all Japanese trading companies, with sales of Y10.1 trillion, of which the domestic market accounts for more than a third. Marubeni was the trading corporation that was the Japanese partner of Lockheed Corporation, the American airplane manufacturer that bribed Japanese government officials in the 1970s, resulting in a major political scandal and the resignation and indictment of Prime Minister Tanaka Kakuei in 1976. See also CORPORATIONS; EXPORTS AND IMPORTS; TANAKA KAKUEI; TRADING COMPANY, GENERAL.

MARUOKA CASTLE See CASTLES.

MARUZEN See BOOKS AND BOOKSTORES.

Martial arts masters giving an exhibition fight with a chained sickle weapon *(kusarigama)*. Students kneel respectfully on the floor of the *dojo* (training hall).

MASHIKO A town in Tochigi Prefecture north of Tokyo that is famous for its 150-year-old folk craft pottery industry. The heavy earthen stoneware produced in Mashiko for tableware and kitchenware, such as dishes, teapots and grinding mortars (suribachi), is known as Mashiko ware (mashiko-yaki). Professional potters moved to the Mashiko area toward the end of the Edo Era (1600–1868) to supply the new capital city of Edo (now Tokyo). The feudal lord (daimyo) of the Mashiko area patronized its pottery industry.

In 1924 the Japanese potter Hamada Shoji (1894–1978) decided to live and work in Mashiko. His pottery later became world famous, and the Japanese government designated him a Living National Treasure (Ningen Kokuho). Today tourists flock to Mashiko to see Hamada's home, workshop, traditional wood-fired kiln and a museum exhibiting folk-art objects he collected during his many trips to Europe, North America and Asia. Hamada's son and former students continue to make pottery in the Hamada style. Many foreign potters have also settled in Mashiko, and many villagers remain active in producing Mashiko ware, which has exerted an important influence on the Western potters. See also HAMADA SHOJI; KILN; LIVING NATIONAL TREASURES; MINGEI; POTTERY.

MASKS (men) Face or head coverings representing deities, animals or demons, and worn with elaborate costumes in Japanese dance, religious ceremonies, and festivals. The concept of "face" or "appearance" (kao) is important in Japan, and many types of masks have been important in Japanese culture. They are usually made of painted or lacquered wood or clay, although some have been made of cloth or paper. The earliest masks that have been preserved were used during the Nara Era (710–794) for gigaku, a ceremonial dance form introduced from the Asian mainland and performed outdoors in front of temples. Fourteen different types of masks were used in a gigaku program, all of which had oversized, almost grotesque facial features. Another imported ceremonial dance form known as bugaku also used masks. Dating from the aristocratic Heian Era (794–1185), many bugaku masks are more stylized, and were carved by sculptors of Buddhist statues. Some of the figures they represent are birds and drunken foreigners. Noh drama, a highly stylized theatrical form that originated in the 14th century and is still performed, uses more than 200 types of masks. Noh masks often portray human beings, but as representative types of characters, for example an old man, young woman, demons and ghosts. Noh masks are still carved in the same way as they were many centuries ago. The carver of a Noh mask uses cypress wood (hinoki) and colors it with chalk powder, black ink (sumi) and mineral pigments. Kyogen, a type of comic drama performed along with Noh, uses humorous masks with exaggerated features. Masks are also used in dance dramas known as sato kagura, which act out myths of Shinto, the indigenous Japanese religion. Masks worn in popular religious festivals often resemble demons or animals, and serve to exorcise evil spirits or to petition the kami (sacred spirits) for a good harvest. The lion dance (shishiodori) is widely performed throughout Japan, as are dances performed with crane or deer masks. Rituals performed for spring festivals when rice seedlings are transplanted include dancers wearing masks of women or old men, symbolizing fertility and longevity. Humorous masks of Okame, a plump young woman, and Hyottoko, a man with a twisted face, are commonly worn for comic dances at agricultural festivals. See also BUGAKU; CRANE; CYPRESS; DANCE; DEER; DEMONS AND GHOSTS; "FACE"; FESTIVALS; LION; NOH DRAMA; OKAME; RICE PLANTING AND HARVESTING FESTIVALS.

MASSAGE See MEDICINE, TRADITIONAL; SHIATSU.

MATCHA See TEA; TEA CEREMONY.

MATS See FURNITURE, TRADITIONAL; HOMES AND HOUSING; STRAW WARE; TATAMI.

MATSU See PINE TREE.

MATSUE A city on lake Shinji near the west coast of Honshu Island, and the capital of Shimane Prefecture. The population of Matsue is about 140,000. Many Japanese tourists visit the city, which has the traditional charms of Kyoto on a smaller scale. Lafcadio Hearn, a European who wrote many books about Japan and became a Japanese citizen, taking the name Koizumi Yakumo and marrying a Japanese woman in 1891, lived in Matsue for 15 months in 1890–1892. Hearn's manuscripts and personal belongings are exhibited in the Hearn Memorial Hall (Koizumi Yakumo Kinenkan). The Matsue Cultural Museum (Matsue Kyodokan), built in 1903, shows objects and photographs of daily life from the Meiji Era (1868–1912). Traditional Japanese architecture can be seen in the teahouse Meimei-an, built in 1779, and a house known as Buke Yashiki, built in 1703 for the Shiomi samurai clan. Matsue Castle is one of the most beautiful examples of castle architecture in Japan, and one of the few remaining original castles. It was built in 1611 by Yoshiharu Horii, who had been rewarded for his part in the Battle of Sekigahara, and was partly reconstructed in 1642. The five-story structure exhibits samurai battle armor and weapons. Gesshoji, the family temple of the Matsudaira clan, was begun by Matsudaira Naomasa, grandson of Shogun Tokugawa Ieyasu, who united Japan under the Tokugawa Shogunate (1603–1867). Izumo-Taisha Shrine outside Matsue is the oldest shrine site in Japan, although its present buildings were erected in 1744 and 1874. This shrine is the most heavily visited of any place in the Matsue area. See also ARMOR; CASTLE; HEARN, LAFCADIO; KYOTO; SAMURAI; SEKIGAHARA, BATTLE OF; TEAHOUSE; TOKUGAWA IEYASU.

MATSUKATA MASAYOSHI (1835–1924) A statesman who served as minister of finance, prime minister and genro (elder statesman) in the Meiji government (1868–1912). Matsukata's policies as finance minister prepared the framework for Japan's later economic growth as a modern nation.

He was born in Kagoshima in Satsuma Province (modern

Kagoshima Prefecture), the domain of the powerful Shimazu clan which took a leading role in the overthrow of the Tokugawa Shogunate (1603–1867) and the Meiji Restoration of 1868. Matsukata was educated as a samurai and entered the service of the Shimazu lords. In 1866 he went to Nagasaki to learn Western science and naval affairs from the officers of British warships stationed there. He also served as the liaison between the Shimazu bureaucracy in Satsuma and the Satsuma leaders Okubo Toshimichi (1830–1878) and Saigo Takamori (1827–1877), who were in the imperial capital of Kyoto plotting to overthrow the Tokugawa Shogunate and restore imperial authority. Matsukata purchased naval ships and ammunition for their forces. He was in Nagasaki at the time of the Meiji Restoration and helped maintain order when shogunate forces fled. The Meiji government appointed Matsukata a provincial governor, then brought him to Tokyo to play a central role in the Ministry of Finance, where he drafted laws for and implemented the Land Tax Reform, which enabled the government to have a stable tax system on which it could prepare annual budgets. As the official Japanese representative to the Paris International Exhibition in 1878, Matsukata was able to study the governments of Western industrialized countries, on which the Meiji government was attempting to model itself. In 1881 he became minister of finance and successfully reduced inflation, which inspired the confidence of the Japanese people and encouraged economic development. Matsukata served as finance minister in seven of the 10 cabinets between 1881 and 1901. He composed the articles on finance in the Meiji Constitution of 1889, enacted the Finance Law, which established the government's financial administration and enacted policies that led to Japan's adoption of the gold standard in 1897. Since leaders from Satsuma and Choshu provinces alternated as prime minister, Matsukata held that position in 1891–1892 and 1896–1898. A number of political crises troubled his first term, but his second term was more successful. In 1898 Matsukata was named a *genro,* and although he retired from active service in 1901, he continued to advise the government. He was honored with the title of prince and the post of lord keeper of the privy seal (*naidaijin*). He also served as president of the International Red Cross of Japan from 1903 to 1912. See also CABINET, PRIME MINISTER'S; CONSTITUTION, MEIJI (1889); GENRO; MEIJI RESTORATION OF 1868; NAGASAKI; OKUBO TOSHIMICHI; PRIME MINISTER; SAIGO TAKAMORI; SATSUMA PROVINCE; SHIMAZU CLAN.

MATSUMOTO CASTLE See CASTLES.

MATSUO BASHO See BASHO; HAIKU.

MATSUSHIMA "Pine Tree Islands;" a group of more than 260 small islands in Matsushima Bay near Sendai on the northeast coast of Honshu Island. The beauty of these islands covered with gnarled pine trees has ranked Matsushima as one of Japan's three most famous sites (*Nihon sankei*), along with Miyajima and Amanohashidate. Seventeenth-century haiku poet Basho wrote poems praising the scenery of Matsushima. Zuiganji, a temple thought to date back to A.D. 828 and belonging to the Zen sect of Buddhism, has been designated a National Treasure. Its main building was constructed in the early 1600s by command of the powerful feudal lord Date Masumune, and caves and grottoes filled with Buddhist Sculptures and memorial tablets were used by Zen priests for meditation. The temple's treasure hall, Seiryuden, displays objects belonging to the temple and the Date family. Godaido, a wooden temple scenically located on an island connected by a bridge to the mainland, is administered by Zuiganji. Also associated with the Date family are Entsuin Temple and gardens, and Kanrantei, a wooden water-viewing pavilion. Oshima Island was used as a retreat by Buddhist priests, although its religious statues and carvings have fallen into disrepair. See also AMANOHASHIDATE; BASHO; HAIKU; MIYAJIMA; NATIONAL TREASURES; PINE TREE; SCULPTURE; SENDAI; ZEN SECT OF BUDDHISM.

MATSUSHITA ELECTRIC INDUSTRIAL CO., LTD. (PANASONIC) See ELECTRONICS INDUSTRY.

MATSUYAMA CITY AND CASTLE See SHIKOKU ISLAND.

MAZDA See AUTOMOBILE INDUSTRY.

MEDICINE, TRADITIONAL The three types of traditional medical treatments in Japan are herbal (*kampoyaku* or Chinese) medicine, acupuncture and moxabustion. In addition, various ancient religious and folk treatments are still practiced to exorcise evil spirits believed to cause disease. Some religious festivals originated as ways of asking the deities to prevent epidemics. Children are taken to shrines of Shinto, the indigenous Japanese religion, shortly after birth and for the Seven-Five-Three Festival to ensure good health. Some foods are also thought to have medicinal value in Japan. For example, many Japanese eat a pickled plum (*umeboshi*) at breakfast every day to keep healthy. Ginseng, garlic and daikon radish are other popular foods believed to have medicinal properties.

Chinese medicine, or *kampo,* was introduced into Japan in the sixth and seventh centuries A.D. This system prescribes teas boiled or steeped with dried leaves, roots or bark of various plants, depending on the illness or condition being treated. Some *kampo* medicines are also made from animal or mineral sources. Herbal medicines are sold in special stores and in herbal sections of drugstores in Japan. The doctor examines the patient's face, tongue, fingernails, pulse and even dreams, before making a diagnosis. *Kampo* emphasizes the treatment of the person as a whole, rather than concentrating on isolated symptoms. Its underlying theory is that diseases are caused by the blocked flow within the patient of *ki* (qi or ch'i in Chinese), the vital energy, or life force, that fills the universe.

This belief is shared by the external treatments of acupuncture and moxabustion, which assume that *ki* flows in channels, or meridians, throughout the body. If *ki* is blocked, certain points on the body can be stimulated to promote its flow. Charts of the body illustrate the meridians and the points where they are likely to become blocked and require opening up. Acupuncture *(hari kyu)* does this by inserting needles into the blocked points. In a related treatment known as *shiatsu,* or acupressure massage, fingers are pressed on these points. Moxabustion attempts to unblock the points by burning little wads of dried *mogusa* leaves on the patient's skin.

Surgery, drugs and other elements of Western medicine were introduced into Japan by the Portuguese, Spanish and Dutch in the 16th–19th centuries. Western medicine is known in Japan as *rampo* ("Dutch practice"). After the Meiji Restoration of 1868, the Japanese government took German medicine as the model for medical treatment in Japan. Today Japan has a modern health-care system, with Western-style hospitals, surgery and drug treatments. However, traditional medical practices are still widely accepted, and are now being studied by many Western doctors and scientists. See also DAIKON; PLUM; SHIATSU.

MEDIEVAL ERA See ASHIKAGA SHOGUNATE; AZUCHI-MOMOYAMA ERA; FEUDALISM; KAMAKURA SHOGUNATE; MUROMACHI ERA; ONIN WAR; SAMURAI; SENGOKU ERA; SHOGUN.

MEDITATION *(zazen)* A technique used in the Buddhist religion, introduced into Japan from China in the sixth century A.D., to attain *satori,* enlightenment or the awakening of the "True Self." *Zazen,* the Japanese term for meditation, derives from the Indian word *dhyana* (*Chan* or *Ch'an* in Chinese). Buddhism was founded in India in the sixth century B.C. by Siddhartha Gautama, who became known as the Buddha, or Enlightened One. This religion adopted from yoga the practice of sitting in the so-called lotus position. The back is kept straight, the legs are crossed and the hands, one resting on the other, are kept in the lap. This position enables the disciple to calm the body and mind, shut out distractions and concentrate on transcending the limits of the ordinary self to attain *satori.* In Japan, meditation is primarily associated with the Meditation, or Zen, sect of Buddhism, which was introduced by Eisai in the 12th century A.D., but it is practiced by other sects as well. See also BUDDHISM; EISAI; SATORI; ZEN SECT OF BUDDHISM.

MEIJI, EMPEROR (1852–1912) The 122nd reigning emperor *(tenno)* in the traditional count; he reigned 1867–1912. The Meiji emperor's given name was Mitsuhito, but after his death he became known by the name of his reign, Meiji, "Enlightened Peace." He became emperor at age 14 upon the death of his father, Emperor Komei (1831–1867; r. 1846–1867), although an imperial regent *(sessho)* exercised power on his behalf until he came of age. Emperor Meiji married Ichijo Haruko (1850–1914; later known as Shoken Kotaigo, Empress Dowager Shoken). He took the throne at the same time as a movement led by samurai from southern Japan overthrew the military government of the Tokugawa Shogunate (1603–1867) and restored authority to the emperor, in the Meiji Restoration of 1868. The new Meiji government (1868–1912) moved the capital from Kyoto to Tokyo (formerly Edo) and embarked on a program to modernize Japan along Western models. A constitution

was promulgated in 1889 that declared that "the Emperor is sacred and inviolable" and that he combines "in himself the rights of sovereignty." Emperor Meiji took seriously his role as supreme commander of the military and worked closely with Japanese officers during the Sino-Japanese War of 1894–1895 and the Russo-Japanese War of 1904–1905. He maintained an interest in traditional Japanese cultural and historical sites, and did not allow the government to discard traditional rites and ceremonies performed by the emperor. The death of Emperor Meiji symbolized the conclusion of the process by which Japan was transformed into a modern nation. In 1913 Meiji Shrine (Meiji Jingu) was built in Tokyo to honor the spirits of Emperor Meiji and Empress Shoken. Emperor Meiji's son Yoshihito succeeded him and is known as Emperor Taisho (1879–1926; r. 1912–1926). His grandson Hirohito (1901–1989 r. 1926–1989), now known as Emperor Showa, enjoyed the longest reign of any emperor in Japanese history. See also BOSHIN CIVIL WAR; CONSTITUTION, MEIJI (1889); EMPEROR; MEIJI RESTORATION OF 1868; MEIJI SHRINE; RUSSO-JAPANESE WAR, SINO-JAPANESE WAR OF 1894–1895; TAISHO ERA.

MEIJI RESTORATION OF 1868 The restoration of political authority to the emperor; the beginning of the modern era of Japan. After 1868 Japan abolished feudalism and adopted Western institutions to become a modern, industrialized state. The Meiji government was dominated by former samurai from Satsuma and Choshu provinces in southwest Japan, who had led the overthrow of the Tokugawa Shogunate (1603–1867). They included Saigo Takamori, Itagaki Taisuke, Ito Hirobumi, Katsu Kaishu, Matsukata Masayoshi, Okubo Toshimichi, Okuma Shigenobu and Saionji Kimmochi. The imperial court moved from Kyoto to Tokyo ("Eastern Capital"), the new name for Edo, the Tokugawa capital. The system of provinces *(han)* led by *daimyo* (feudal lords) was replaced by a prefectural system *(ken),* and *daimyo* received court titles and retired to Tokyo. The southern Ryukyu Islands, which had been controlled by Satsuma Province since 1609, were designated Okinawa Prefecture. The Japanese government sent a large mission abroad in 1872 led by Iwakura Tomomi to study Western government, technology and culture. Japan sent exhibits to many international expositions in Europe and the United States. A modern, largely Prussian-style educational system was established in Japan, and a modern army and navy based on Western models were formed under the leadership of Yamagata Aritomo. In 1873 a universal conscription law was enacted that deprived samurai of their feudal privileges, and in 1876 samurai were forbidden from wearing two swords, the symbol of their elite position. Samurai anger over these policies, and over the government's rejection of Saigo Takamori's proposal to invade Korea, fomented the unsuccessful Satsuma Rebellion of 1877, led by Saigo. During the Meiji Era, Finance Minister Matsukata Masayoshi established the Bank of Japan, placed Japan on the gold standard, and undertook other measures to stimulate economic growth. Large financial and manufacturing combines known as *zaibatsu* came to dominate the economy in later years. A constitution was promulgated in 1889 that established an Imperial Diet (Parliament) and the office of prime minister, whose first occupant was Ito Hirobumi. Japan's first two political parties were formed, and retired government leaders continued to exercise great influence as *genro* (elder statesmen). In 1902 Japan signed the Anglo-Japanese Alliance for mutual security with Great Britain. Japan went to war over Korea and Manchuria on the Asian mainland and defeated China in the Sino-Japanese War of 1894–1895 and Russia in the Russo-Japanese War (1904–1905), which established Japan as the dominant power in East Asia and which established Korea and Taiwan as colonies of Japan. The Meiji Era ended in 1912 with the death of Emperor Meiji and accession to the throne of his son, the Emperor Taisho, during whose reign (Taisho Era, 1912–1926) Meiji policies were continued. See also ANGLO-JAPANESE ALLIANCE; BANK OF JAPAN; BOSHIN CIVIL WAR; CHOSHU PROVINCE; CONSTITUTION, MEIJI (1889); DAIMYO; DIET; EMPEROR; EXPOSITIONS, INTERNATIONAL; GENRO; IMPERIAL JAPANESE ARMY AND NAVY; IWAKURA MISSION; KOREA AND JAPAN; MEIJI, EMPEROR; POLITICAL PARTIES; PREFECTURE; PRIME MINISTER; RUSSO-JAPANESE WAR; RYUKYU ISLANDS; SAMURAI; SATSUMA PROVINCE; SATSUMA REBELLION; SINO-JAPANESE WAR OF 1894–1895; TAISHO ERA; TAIWAN AND JAPAN; TOKUGAWA SHOGUNATE; ZAIBATSU; NAMES OF INDIVIDUAL LEADERS.

MEIJI SHRINE (Meiji Jingu) A Shinto shrine in the Harajuku section of Tokyo dedicated to the spirit of Emperor Meiji (1852–1912; r. 1867–1912) and his wife, Empress Shoken (1850–1914). Emperor Meiji, who ascended the throne just before imperial power was restored after the military government of the Tokugawa Shogunate (1603–1867) was overthrown, did much to modernize Japan.

In 1913 it was resolved that a shrine should be built to honor Emperor Meiji. The shrine was completed in 1920 with labor volunteered by more than 100,000 Japanese people. It was destroyed in World War II but rebuilt in the 1950s. The wooden *torii* (gate) leading to the shrine, at over 30 feet, is one of the tallest in Japan. The shrine has a beautiful inner garden that is especially famous for its irises. Meiji Shrine is a major Japanese pilgrimage center. Crowds of people visit from all over Japan, especially at the New Year Festival. November 3rd, the birthday of Emperor Meiji, is the date of the shrine's annual festival. This is also Culture Day, a national holiday in Japan. See also HARAJUKU; HOLIDAYS, NATIONAL; IRIS; MEIJI RESTORATION OF 1868; PILGRIMAGE; SHINTO; SHRINES, SHINTO; TOKYO; TORII.

MEISHI (name cards) Calling cards that are printed with a person's name, place of employment, title, address, and telephone number. *Meishi* are business cards but are used extensively in Japan even on social occasions. Since Japan is a very status-conscious society where relationships are formal, *meishi* are always exchanged between people who are meeting for the first time, so that they can determine their relative status. *Meishi* are necessary for everyone doing business in Japan, even foreigners, who can have *meishi* printed up quickly there. One side of the *meishi* can be printed in English and the other side printed in *katakana*, the Japanese script used for writing words of foreign origin.

A woman's *meishi* is usually smaller and has rounded edges, in contrast to the square edges of the man's larger card. The idea of name cards may have been introduced to Japan from England. They were first used in Japan during the last years of the Tokugawa Shogunate (1603–1867) by government officials who had to deal with foreigners when Japan was forcibly opened to Western countries in the 1850s. Beginning with the Meiji Restoration of 1868, name cards came into common use by the Japanese people. The exchange of *meishi* follows strict rules of etiquette to ensure that the cards are handled with respect. People bow when they exchange them. It is impolite to write on a card received from another person. However, one can write messages on *meishi* that one hands to someone else, even a note of introduction to be given to a third person. Many people carry their *meishi* in special cloth-covered holders that fit easily into a pocket. See also BOWING; EMPLOYMENT; ETIQUETTE; WRITING SYSTEM, JAPANESE.

MEMORIAL SERVICE See BON FESTIVAL; FUNERALS; HIGAN.

MEMORIAL TABLETS See ALTARS IN HOMES; FUNERALS; HIGAN.

METALWORK Five metals, known collectively as *gokin*, were traditionally worked in Japan: gold, silver, copper, tin and iron. They were used for Buddhist sculpture and ritual objects, swords and armor, bells, mirrors, jewelry, furnishings, food and beverage containers, tools, and other objects for household and personal use. Metal crafts began during the Yayoi Era (c. 300 B.C.–c. A.D. 300), when new cultural influences, including bronze and ironwork, were introduced to Japan from the Asian mainland. The introduction of the Buddhist religion from India through China in the sixth century A.D. was accompanied by a wide variety of crafts. Temples housed bronze statues of Buddhist deities, incense burners, openwork banners (large metal banners with pierced designs), large bells and other ritual objects, and pagodas were topped with bronze spires. Silver was not widely used, and gold was used mainly to gild Buddhist statues and vessels. Most objects were made by casting molten metal, but other techniques were employed, such as forging, embossing, engraving and hammering. Coins and official bronze seals were cast. Different alloys were employed. The Japanese invented a gold and copper alloy known as *shakudo* for inlay work. *Hakudo,* "white bronze," is copper alloy with a high tin content. *Shakudo* is a copper alloy. *Sawari* is a brasslike alloy of copper, tin, and lead or silver. *Chujaku* is natural brass. The rise of the samurai class, which became the ruling elite during the Kamakura Shogunate (1192–1333) brought the art of sword making to its greatest height. The development of the tea ceremony during the Muromachi (1333–1568) and Azuchi-Momoyama (1568–1600) eras made the production of iron tea kettles (*kama*) an important art. The introduction of Western firearms and other objects led to their production in Japan. During the Edo Era (1600–1868), there was a great demand for various small metal objects, such as water droppers, brush stands and portable cases for calligraphy; miniature figures known as *netsuke;* smoking pipes; women's hair ornaments; metal fittings for wooden chests of drawers; and so forth. Cloisonne, decorative metal objects colored with enamels, also became popular during this period. The Meiji government (1868–1912) prohibited the wearing of samurai swords in 1876, but provided the means for sword makers and other traditional metal artists to continue their work. The major Japanese metal crafts are still produced today, such as swords, kettles, gongs, mirrors, and inlay work. Some metalworkers have been designated as Living National Treasures by the Japanese government. See also BELLS; BUDDHISM; CALLIGRAPHY; CHEST; CLOISONNE; COMBS AND HAIR ORNAMENTS; KETTLE; LIVING NATIONAL TREASURES; MIRROR; NETSUKE; SCULPTURE; SWORD; SWORD GUARD.

MIAI See GO-BETWEEN; WEDDINGS.

MICHIKO, EMPRESS See AKIHITO, EMPEROR; CROWN PRINCE; IMPERIAL HOUSEHOLD.

MICROCHIPS See COMPUTER INDUSTRY; FIFTH-GENERATION ADVANCED COMPUTER SYSTEMS; SEMICONDUCTOR INDUSTRY.

MIDWAY ISLAND, BATTLE OF See WORLD WAR II; YAMAMOTO ISOROKU; YAMATO.

MIFUNE TOSHIRO (1920–) An internationally famous Japanese movie actor and producer. Mifune was born to a Japanese family in China and returned to Japan after World War II. In 1947 he began his acting career with Toho Co., Ltd., a major Japanese movie company. His first film was *The New Age of Fools* (*Shin baka jidai; 1947*), directed by Taniguchi Senkichi. Upon seeing him in his second movie (*Ginrei no hate; To the End of the Silver-capped Mountains*), the director Kurosawa Akira cast Mifune as a gangster in his film *Drunken Angel* (*Yoidore tenshi; 1948*). This was the start of a long-lasting collaboration between the two men, and Mifune acted in 16 of Kurosawa's 26 movies. Their last picture together was *Red Beard* (*Akahige; 1965*). The role of the bandit Tajomaru in *Rashomon* (1950), a movie Kurosawa adapted from a story by Akutagawa Ryunosuke, brought Mifune international acclaim. He is also known for his roles in such movies as *Yojimbo* (1961)and *Tsubaki Sanjuro* (1962). Some believe that he did his finest acting as the thief in *The Lower Depths* (*Donzoko; 1957*). Mifune has also worked in television and foreign films. He directed a film, *Legacy of the Five Hundred Thousand* (*Gojuman no isan; 1963*). Mifune also appeared in *The Life of Oharu* (1952) by Mizoguchi Kenji and *Rebellion* (1967) by Kobayashi Masaki. Western films in which he has appeared include John Frankenheimer's *Grand Prix* (1966), John Boorman's *Hell in the Pacific* (1967), and Jack Smight's *Battle of Midway* (1976). Many critics felt that Mifune's later roles did not match the fine performances that he gave under Kurosawa's direction. However, he has been acclaimed for his performance in Kumai Kei's *The Death of a Tea Master* (*Honkakubo ibun: Sen no Rikyu; 1989*), about the ritual suicide of Sen no Rikyu (1522–1591), which won a Silver Lion Award at the 1989 Venice International Film Festival. See also AKUGATAWA RYUNOSUKE; FILMS; KUROSAWA AKIRA; MIZOGUCHI KENJI; RASHOMON; SEN NO RIKYU.

MIKI TAKEO (1907–1988) Prime minister of Japan from 1974 to 1976. Born in Tokushima Prefecture, Miki was educated at Meiji University in Tokyo and the University of California at Berkeley. In 1937 he was elected to the House of Representatives, the Lower House of the Japanese Diet (Parliament). After belonging to a number of conservative political parties, in 1955 Miki joined the Liberal Democratic party (Jiyu Minshuto; known as the LDP), Japan's dominant party and therefore the one from which the prime ministers are chosen. He was director-general of the Economic Planning Agency (1958), minister of international trade and industry (1965–1966), and minister of foreign affairs (1966–1967). Miki became prime minister when Tanaka Kakuei (prime minister 1972–1974) resigned because of the major scandal over bribes by the Lockheed Corporation, an American aircraft company trying to enter the Japanese market. Miki was selected to replace Tanaka because although he was only the leader of a small faction in the LDP, he had a reputation for honesty that would help the party's image. Also, the LDP wanted to avoid a conflict between the leaders of its two major factions, Fukuda Takeo (who became prime minister 1976–1978) and Ohira Masayoshi (prime minister 1978–1980). The Japanese public supported Miki's investigation of the Lockheed scandal, as a result of which Tanaka and the other defendants were indicted and forced to resign from the LDP. However, in December 1976 they were reelected to the Diet as "independents," and Miki was replaced by Fukuda as prime minister. While in office, Miki also had to deal with the Japanese economic recession caused by the 1973 oil crisis in the Middle East. See also DIET; FUKUDA TAKEO; LIBERAL DEMOCRATIC PARTY; OHIRA MASAYOSHI; OIL CRISIS OF 1973; POLITICAL PARTIES; PRIME MINISTER; SATO EISAKU; TANAKA KAKUEI.

MIKIMOTO PEARL See PEARL.

MILITARY See ARMOR; ASHIKAGA SHOGUNATE; BAKUFU; BUSHIDO; CASTLES; DAIMYO; FEUDALISM; IMPERIAL JAPANESE ARMY AND NAVY; KAMAKURA SHOGUNATE; KAMIKAZE; MARTIAL ARTS; RUSSO-JAPANESE WAR; SAMURAI; SELF-DEFENSE FORCES; SHOGUN; SINO-JAPANESE WAR OF 1894–1895; SINO-JAPANESE WAR OF 1937–1945; SWORD; TOKUGAWA SHOGUNATE; WORLD WAR I; WORLD WAR II; YASUKUNI SHRINE.

MINAMATA DISEASE A disease caused by high levels of mercury dumped without treatment by the Chisso Corporation into Minamata Bay, Kumamoto Prefecture, on the southern Japanese island of Kyushu. The victims were fishermen and their families, who consumed large amounts of fish with mercury deposits. They began showing symptoms of mercury poisoning in 1953, including loss of sight and hearing, mental and speech disorders, tremors, paralysis, and mental retardation and severe birth defects in their children. By 1981 the number of confirmed cases reached 1,293, of whom 305 had died. Chisso lost a court battle and was required to pay U.S. $200 million in compensation to the 15,000 victims who had filed claims by June 7, 1985. Fishing was banned in Minamata Bay in 1973, and no new cases of the disease appeared thereafter.

Minamata Disease and the insensitivity of the polluting companies were major factors in the rise of the Japanese environmental movement and spurred the Japanese to improve the quality of the air and water in urban and industrialized regions. Japanese now use the term Minamata Disease to refer to a whole category of physical problems caused by air, water and soil pollution. Incidents of chemical poisoning in Niigata, Toyama and Yokkaichi in the 1960s also ended in court-ordered compensation to victims from the companies responsible for the pollution. See also ENVIRONMENTAL ISSUES; FISH AND FISHING INDUSTRY; KYUSHU ISLAND.

MINAMOTO CLAN One of the four great ancient clans, along with the Fujiwara, Tachibana and Taira, that controlled the Japanese imperial court during the Heian Era (794–1185). Members of the Minamoto family played an important role in the Japanese government up to the Meiji Restoration of 1868. The clan originated in A.D. 814, when Emperor Saga (r. 809–823) gave the family name Minamoto to 33 of his 50 children, in order to decrease the number of people who would vie to inherit the throne and to balance the power of the Fujiwara clan. Because the Chinese characters for the name Minamoto can also be pronounced *gen* in Japanese, the Minamoto have also been known as the Genji (*ji* means clan or family). Prince Genji, the main character of the great 11th-century novel *The Tale of Genji,* belonged to the Minamoto family. Ten different lines of the Genji or Minamoto family descended from emperors who ruled after Emperor Saga. Members held civil posts in the government in the capital city of Kyoto. The Murakami Genji line became powerful in the court during the 11th century A.D. At the same time, the Seiwa Genji line produced a number of military leaders who directed battles against the rival Taira clan (also known as the Heike) in support of the Fujiwara. But in the 12th century, the Seiwa Genji (or Minamoto) warriors suffered many losses, and Taira no Kiyomori seized power. However, he spared the lives of young Minamoto warriors, and in 1180 Minamoto no Yoritomo (1147–1199) led a successful war against the Taira clan. Yoritomo concluded the Taira-Minamoto War (Gempei no Soran) in 1185 by completely destroying the Taira. He also conquered eastern Japan and established a military government in Kamakura, known as the Kamakura Shogunate (1192–1333), thus beginning nearly 700 years of military rule in Japan. Although the line of Seiwa Genji ended in 1219, other family lines continued to control Japan during the medieval era. These included the Ashikaga family, which founded the Ashikaga Shogunate (1338–1573; also known as the Muromachi Era); and Tokugawa Ieyasu (1543–1616), who founded the Tokugawa Shogunate (1603–1867). See also CLAN; FEUDALISM; FUJIWARA CLAN; GENJI, THE TALE OF; HEIKE, THE TALE OF THE; TAIRA CLAN; TAIRA-MINAMOTO WAR.

MINAMOTO NO YORITOMO (1147–1199) A warrior who founded the Kamakura Shogunate (1192–1333), thus initiating nearly seven centuries of military rule in Japan.

Yoritomo's life had been spared by Taira no Kiyomori after his father, Minamoto no Yoshitomo, led the Minamoto (or Genji) clan in an unsuccessful rebellion against the rival Taira (or Heike) clan (Heiji War of 1159–1160). Yoritomo was exiled, but gained the support of his captor, Hojo Tokimasa whose daughter, Hojo Masako, married Yoritomo. In the 1170s the Minamoto rebelled against the powerful Taira no Kiyomori. Yoritomo raised a large army and established his military headquarters (*bakufu*) at Kamakura in eastern Japan. He strengthened his base of power there between 1180 and 1183, and then began battling Taira forces. Yoritomo's brother, Minamoto no Yoshitsune (1159–1189), defeated the Taira on Shikoku Island in 1185 and forced them south to Kyushu Island. His fleet defeated the Taira fleet in the Battle of Dannoura in the Strait of Shimonoseki (now known as Kammon Strait) between Kyushu and Honshu Islands, in which the seven-year-old Emperor Antoku was drowned. After the war, Yoritomo became jealous of his brother Yoshitsune, who led an unsuccessful revolt against him and fled north to seek protection from members of the Fujiwara clan. He was forced to commit suicide, and Yoritomo conquered the northern territory.

Rather than abolishing the imperial court at Kyoto, the victorious Yoritomo sought to have the court legitimize his power. In 1192 he was given the title of shogun, which acknowledged that he was in fact the supreme military commander of Japan. Although Yoritomo's sons became shogun after him, they could not hold on to political power, and the Hojo family took control of the Kamakura Shogunate when Hojo Tokimasa had himself declared regent in 1203.

A famous portrait of Minamoto no Yoritomo by Fujiwara no Takanobu has been designated a Japanese National Treasure. See also BAKUFU; DANNOURA, BATTLE OF; HEIKE, THE TALES OF THE; HOJO CLAN; KAMAKURA SHOGUNATE; MINAMOTO CLAN; MINAMOTO NO YOSHITSUNE; SHIMONOSEKI; SHOGUN; TAIRA CLAN; TAIRA-MINAMOTO WAR.

MINAMOTO NO YOSHITSUNE (1159–1189) Renowned for his bravery and handsome looks, Yoshitsune was the most prominent tragic warrior in Japanese history. He and his loyal retainer, a warrior-monk named Benkei, became the heroes of many Japanese plays and historical dramas.

Yoshitsune was the youngest brother of Minamoto no Yoritomo (1147–1199), who established military rule in Japan with the Kamakura Shogunate (1192–1333), based in eastern Japan. The brothers were exiled by Taira no Kiyomori after their father led an unsuccessful rebellion against him. Yoshitsune escaped the Buddhist temple where he was held and sought protection with a member of the Fujiwara clan, into which his mother had married after his father was killed. When Yoritomo raised an army against the Taira (or Heike) clan, Yoshitsune served as his general and defeated the Taira forces in many battles. In 1185 he led a fleet of more than 800 boats that finally destroyed the Taira at the Battle of Dannoura in the Strait of Shimonoseki (now known as Kammon Strait). However, Yoritomo became jealous of his brother Yoshitsune, especially his close relationship with the imperial court in Kyoto. Yoshitsune led a failed rebellion against his brother in the Kamakura area and was forced to flee to the Fujiwara for protection once again. However, in 1189 he was betrayed to Yoritomo, and rather than surrender, he killed his wife and daughter and committed suicide. The story of Yoshitsune's life and death gave rise to the Japanese phrase for an underdog, *hogan-biiki; hogan* was Yoshitsune's title as chief of imperial police, and *biiki* means partiality toward this ill-fated man. See also BENKEI; DANNOURA, BATTLE OF; FUJIWARA CLAN; MINAMOTO NO YORITOMO; SHIMONOSEKI; SUICIDE; TAIRA-MINAMOTO WAR.

MINGEI Folk crafts or handmade objects used in daily life. *Mingei*, a combination of *min* (the people or folk) and *gei* (skill or art), is thus "the people's art." A movement for the appreciation of folk crafts in Japan was initiated in the early 20th century by Yanagi Soetsu (1889–1961), who coined the term *mingei* to distinguish folk crafts from *bijutsu*, or fine art, which is solely aesthetic in purpose and is associated with the ruling aristocracy. He also differentiated *mingei*, which is handmade, from *kogei*, or folk art, which is primarily functional and may be mass-produced by machines. Besides its practical function *(yo)*, *mingei* is further characterized by a religious aspect *(kokoro)* that is simple and unassuming yet has a beauty of its own. Yanagi used the term *minshu*, "the people," for ordinary Japanese who have selflessly created useful objects by hand. Yanagi founded the Japan Folk Art Society with a Japanese and an English potter, Hamada Shoji (1894–1978) and Bernard Leach (1887–1979). He also established the Folk Art Museum (Mingei Kan) in Tokyo. His goal was to preserve traditional Japanese *mingei* and to encourage and support contemporary Japanese folk artists. Japanese *mingei* are noted for beautiful shapes, colors and use of local materials. They include pottery, textiles, lacquer ware, bamboo objects, metalwork, wooden objects such as chests, handmade paper, dolls and toys, and even signboards for shops. Some types of painting, sculpture, and calligraphy are also classified as *mingei*. Such crafts have been highly regarded by the Japanese throughout their history.

Craft techniques developed greatly during the Muromachi Era (1333–1568), and were especially stimulated by the tea ceremony, which reached its height of popularity during the Azuchi-Momoyama Era (1568–1600). The aesthetic principles of *sabi* and *wabi*, or beauty that is simple and unpretentious, led Japanese tea masters to incorporate into the tea ceremony numerous objects used by ordinary people in daily life. Patronage by *daimyo* (feudal lords) during the Edo Era (1600–1868) supported flourishing pottery and textile weaving industries. Folk crafts declined in the 20th century as machine production and synthetic materials became widespread. However, after World War II many Japanese had a renewed interest in folk crafts, and many *mingei* museums were founded around the country. Although *mingei* have been created in villages and rural areas throughout Japan, some regions specialize in certain types of items. For example, the finest textiles have been made in Okinawa (Ryukyu Islands), the finest stencil-dyed and embroidered kimono in Tohoku, fine woven textiles and pottery in Tamba, and the finest bamboo ware in Kyushu and western Shikoku Island. The Japanese government designates the greatest traditional potters, textile dyers and weavers, lacquer makers, metalworkers and other artisans as Living National Treasures (Ningen Kokuho). The Japan Traditional Craft Center was established in Tokyo by the Diet (Parliament) in 1979 to encourage the formation of craft guilds and to sell their products. Traditional crafts are those that date to before the Meiji Era (1868–1912), made by hand of traditional materials, and used in daily life. One hundred seventy-one craft guilds have registered with the center. See also HAMADA SHOJI; LEACH, BERNARD; LIVING NATIONAL TREASURES; SABI AND WABI; TEA CEREMONY; YANAGI SOETSU; NAMES OF INDIVIDUAL CRAFTS.

MINISTRY OF EDUCATION, SCIENCE AND CULTURE (Mombusho) The ministry that sets education standards for and administers the national public school system, and promotes cultural activities. The minister of education, science and culture is appointed by the prime minister. The ministry exercises a great deal of control over textbooks, curricula and teacher training, and has direct jurisdiction over the Japanese national universities, national junior and technical colleges, museums, and education research institutes. It works closely with local boards of education in the 47 Japanese prefectures and the major cities. The Japan Teachers Union (Nikkyoso) often clashes with the education ministry over its policies, which many teachers believe are too conservative. The Central Council on Education advises the ministry on problems in the education system and recommends reforms. The ministry provides scholarships for foreign students to study in Japan, and oversees exchange programs for Japanese and foreign students. The Agency for Cultural Affairs was set up in 1968 as a special body of the ministry. It includes the Cultural Affairs Division, which disseminates information about the arts in Japan and abroad, and the Cultural Properties Protection Division, which protects the cultural heritage of Japan. This division administers more than 1,000 historic sites and designates important art objects as National Treasures or as Important Cultural Properties. See also CABINET, PRIME MINISTER'S; EDUCATION SYSTEM; NATIONAL TREASURES; UNIVERSITIES.

MINISTRY OF FINANCE (Okurasho) The most prestigious and powerful agency in the Japanese government. The Ministry of Finance (MOF) is responsible for Japan's tax and financial affairs, including banking and investment regulations. Its bureaus include those of the budget, tax, customs and tariff, financial, securities (stocks and bonds), banking and international finance. The MOF also administers local finance bureaus, customhouses and the auxiliary mint and printing bureaus, as well as the semi-autonomous National Tax Administration Agency.

Since the MOF is responsible for the national budget, it

provides the funds for all ministries and agencies in the Japanese government. The Budget Bureau of the MOF prepares budgets for each fiscal year (which begins April 1) based on requests from other ministries and affiliated agencies, and submits them to the Diet for approval. The Constitution of 1947 gives the Diet (Parliament) the power to amend the budget. Although it rarely exercises this power, Diet members belonging to the dominant Liberal Democratic Party have great influence on the preparation of the budget. The Japanese budget has grown rapidly in the postwar era, reflecting rapid GNP growth, but expenditures have been kept stable.

The Tax Bureau estimates tax revenues and adjusts the tax schedules. It also oversees the liquor industry, which is very large in Japan. Government revenues come primarily from individual, corporate and sales taxes, and contributions to social security. In 1989 the Japanese government initiated its first national consumption tax, set at 3% on all purchases.

The MOF issues government bonds and controls government borrowing of money. It administers the Fiscal Investment and Loan Program, funded mainly from postal savings, which provides loans to public and private enterprises.

The Ministry of Finance was established by the Meiji government (1868–1912) in 1869. Finance Minister Matsukata Masayoshi (in office 1881–1900) stabilized the Japanese economy by putting the yen on the gold standard and establishing the Bank of Japan in 1882. The Bank of Japan still conducts the government's monetary policy. Since World War II, the government has controlled Japan's remarkable economic recovery by expanding or restricting the nation's money supply, to stimulate or restrain economic growth and to control inflation. The policy was generally expansionist until the oil crisis of 1973, when the realization of Japan's dependence on foreign resources caused the government to restrain the growth of the money supply. The Ministry of Finance works closely with the Ministry of Foreign Affairs on issues of customs, foreign trade, international finance and tariffs. Japan is a member of international organizations concerned with trade and economic development, such as the International Monetary Fund (IMF), the General Agreement on Tariffs and Trade (GATT) and the Organisation for Economic Cooperation and Development (OECD). It has also played the leading role in the Asian Development Bank. See also ALCOHOLIC BEVERAGES; BANKING SYSTEM; CABINET, PRIME MINISTER'S; DIET; EXPORTS AND IMPORTS; LIBERAL DEMOCRATIC PARTY; MATSUKATA MASAYOSHI; MINISTRY OF FOREIGN AFFAIRS; OIL CRISIS OF 1973; TAX SYSTEM; YEN.

MINISTRY OF FOREIGN AFFAIRS (Gaimusho) A ministry of the Japanese government responsible for Japan's foreign policy and diplomatic relations. The Ministry of Foreign Affairs, one of the most important government ministries, has regional bureaus for Asia, North America, Latin America, Europe, the Middle East and Africa, economic affairs and cooperation, treaties, the United Nations, and public information and cultural affairs. There are also

departments for consular and emigration affairs, and research and planning. The ministry's Foreign Service Personnel Committee administers Japan's elite career foreign service corps, whose officers are chosen by competitive examination and trained by the ministry's Foreign Service Training Institute. Many have also received law degrees from Tokyo University, the leading university in Japan. Japanese ambassadors are almost exclusively appointed from within the career diplomatic ranks. The Ministry of Foreign Affairs maintains more than 150 embassies, more than 60 consulates and consulates-general, and several permanent missions or delegations overseas.

The Ministry of Foreign Affairs was established in 1869 by the Meiji government (1868–1912), which developed formal relations with Western countries after more than two centuries of national seclusion from the outside world.

Japanese foreign relations and economic issues are closely related. The Ministry of International Trade and Industry (MITI), which is responsible for Japanese exports and imports, coordinates its trade policy with the Ministry of Foreign Affairs. For example, the ministries persuaded the Japanese automobile industry to go along with voluntary export restraints in 1981 to help maintain good relations with the United States and Canada. The Ministry of Foreign Affairs also works closely with the Ministry of Finance on issues of customs, foreign aid, international finance and tariffs; with the Ministry of Agriculture, Forestry and Fisheries regarding foreign agricultural imports and fishing rights; and with many other government agencies, such as the Japan External Trade Organization (JETRO), the Export-Import Bank and the Overseas Technical Cooperation Agency. See also CABINET, PRIME MINISTER'S; JAPAN EXTERNAL TRADE ORGANIZATION; MINISTRY OF INTERNATIONAL TRADE AND INDUSTRY.

MINISTRY OF INTERNATIONAL TRADE AND INDUSTRY (MITI; Tsusho Sangyo or Tsusansho) An important government ministry that develops and implement policies for Japanese trade and industry. Various agencies of the Japanese government have controlled private industry since the Meiji Restoration of 1868. MITI was founded in 1949 by combining the older Trade Agency and the Ministry of Commerce and Industry. American officials of the Occupation of Japan following World War II acknowledged that a centralized ministry was essential to help rebuild Japanese industry and foreign trade. Until the mid-1960s, MITI controlled all Japanese exports and imports and directed Japan's rapid industrial growth. As the architect of Japanese industrial policy, it set goals for crucial heavy industries: coal, electric power, steel and shipbuilding. MITI also stimulated productive competition between rival companies, the formation of industrial cartels and the acquisition of weak, small companies by strong, large ones. MITI's informal "administrative guidance" of Japanese companies also adjusted marketing strategies and helped slow business investments when the economy was growing too quickly, to prevent inflation and imbalance of payments. The shift was made from heavy industries such as steel and shipbuilding to such industries as automobiles, electronics and computers. MITI controlled Japanese foreign exchange, erected trade barriers against other countries and ensured that Japanese companies acquired the best foreign technology that was essential for their own needs. In the 1960s, other countries began to complain about these policies and the close association between Japanese government and business, which foreigners dubbed "Japan, Inc."

Some of the more important agencies within MITI are the Japan External Trade Organization (JETRO), the Agency of Natural Resources and Energy, the Patent Office, and the Agency of Industrial Science and Technology, which oversees government research institutes. Research in the 1980s has been aimed at developing technologies for alternate energy, information processing, biotechnology and new industrial materials. MITI receives advice from business leaders through 20 civilian advisory commissions (shingikai), such as the Industrial Structure Council. Industry-caused problems in Japan, especially pollution and overcrowding, are currently being addressed by MITI. See also CABINET, PRIME MINISTER'S; EXPORTS AND IMPORTS; FOREIGN TRADE; JAPAN EXTERNAL TRADE ORGANIZATION; JAPAN, INC.; OCCUPATION OF JAPAN; RESEARCH AND DEVELOPMENT.

MINISTRY OF POSTS AND TELECOMMUNICATIONS
See POSTAL SERVICE; TELECOMMUNICATIONS SYSTEM.

MINKA See FARMHOUSE.

MINO WARE (mino-yaki) Pottery made in Mino Province (modern Gifu Prefecture) on central Honshu Island. Mino ware developed from ancient Sue ware, ash-glazed wares made during the Heian Era (794–1185), Yamachawan ware during the medieval era and glazed pottery of the Chinese Song (Sung) dynasty (960–1279) imported into Japan during the 14th and 15th centuries. Mino ware was associated with an important type of Japanese pottery known as Seto ware (seto-yaki), produced in Seto City in the neighboring province of Owari (modern Aichi Prefecture).

The warlord Oda Nobunaga (1534–1582) took control of Mino Province in 1567. Oda and other warlords during the Azuchi-Momoyama Era (1568–1600), especially Toyotomi Hideyoshi (1536–1598), took a great interest in the tea ceremony. This stimulated the production of several styles of Mino ware for tea utensils, such as tea bowls (chawan), vases, water containers and dishes for kaiseki, the special tea ceremony meal.

The most important Mino styles were Shino ware, Oribe ware and temmoku, a brown glaze introduced from China. Their production was enhanced by the introduction of the nobori-gama, a wood-fired climbing kiln with many chambers, from the Karatsu pottery center on Kyushu Island. See also AZUCHI-MOMOYAMA ERA; KAISEKI; KARATSU WARE; KILN; ODA NOBUNAGA; ORIBE WARE; POTTERY; SETO WARE; SHINO WARE; TEA CEREMONY; TEMMOKU; TOYOTOMI HIDEYOSHI.

MINOLTA CAMERA CO., LTD. See CAMERAS AND PHOTOGRAPHY.

MINORITIES IN JAPAN Minority groups in Japan include the Ainu, burakumin ("hamlet people" or "people of special hamlets"), Chinese, Koreans and Okinawans. The Ainu, of Caucasian stock, were nomadic hunters and fishers who inhabited much of northern Honshu Island until Japanese settlement pushed them to the northernmost island of Hokkaido, where a small group resides today. There are about 50,000 Chinese in Japan. Most of them live in several large Japanese cities, especially Yokohama and Nagasaki, and operate restaurants and small businesses.

About 680,000 Koreans live in Japan, mainly in Osaka. Japan annexed Korea in 1910, and between 1939 and 1945, about 1 million Koreans were brought to Japan as forced laborers or military draftees. Most Koreans in Japan today are their second- or third-generation descendants. Even though they were born in Japan and speak Japanese, first-and-second-generation Korean residents are required to register as aliens every three years with the Japanese government. The Alien Registration Law requires the fingerprinting of all residents in Japan who are not ethnic Japanese. Citizenship is determined by household register (koseki), which until recently was permitted to list only children of Japanese fathers. Few Koreans can even qualify to become naturalized citizens under the Japanese Nationality Law (Kokuseki Ho) and thus are denied the advantages of citizenship, including equal housing, education, jobs and most social welfare benefits. Several recent court cases in Japan have challenged discrimination against Koreans. In a bilateral accord reached in Seoul, South Korea, in April 1990, Japan will exempt third-generation Korean residents of Japan from the controversial fingerprinting requirements and work out an alternative system to identify them. Third-generation Korean residents will get Japanese reentry permits valid for up to five years, and an alternative will also be found to replace the existing law that Korean residents carry alien registration cards.

Okinawans inhabit the chain of islands, known as the Ryukyus, which lie south of Kyushu, the southernmost main island of Japan. Since the Ryukyu kingdom was a tributary state of China for five centuries, Okinawan culture has many Chinese elements, although Okinawans speak a dialect of Japanese. The Japanese government made the Ryukyus a prefecture of Japan, called Okinawa Prefecture, in 1879. However, Okinawans continue to have lower education and income levels and higher unemployment than the ethnic Japanese. Many of them have emigrated to the United States and Latin America over the past century.

The largest minority group in Japan is the burakumin ("hamlet people" or "people of special hamlets"), who number about 2 million. Their ancestors worked mainly at tasks such as taking care of the dead, butchering animals and working with leather, all of which are considered polluting occupations by the Buddhist and Shinto religions. The burakumin do not differ physically or culturally from other Japanese but are forced to live in segregated communities. In 1871 the Meiji government decreed that burakumin should be accepted as "new common people" (shin *heimin*), but the household register system labels them as outcastes. *Burakumin* are still not integrated into the Japanese educational system and are unable to get good jobs.

Another group which suffers discrimination in Japan is the *hibakusha*, victims of the atomic bombs dropped on Hiroshima and Nagasaki in 1945 at the end of World War II. Contrary to medical evidence, their offspring are feared to be susceptible to rare diseases, and they have trouble finding marriage partners. Persons of mixed ancestry are also shunned as "polluted" by the Japanese. See also AINU; ATOMIC BOMB; BURAKUMIN; HOKKAIDO ISLAND; HOUSEHOLD REGISTER; IMMIGRANTS, JAPANESE; KOREA AND JAPAN; OKINAWA ISLAND; RYUKYU ISLANDS.

MINSEITO   See PEOPLE'S GOVERNMENT PARTY.

MINSHUKU   See RYOKAN.

MINTS TO PRODUCE COINS   See GINZA; YEN.

MIRIN   A sweet rice wine with a golden color and somewhat syrupy consistency that is used for cooking. *Mirin* is used in place of sugar to improve the flavor of fish and meat, and to add a gloss to sauces. It is often mixed with soy sauce for basting such grilled dishes as teriyaki and yakitori. The sweet taste of *mirin* balances the saltiness of soy sauce and the tartness of vinegar, with which it is also mixed. *Mirin* is made by fermenting a mixture of glutinous rice, rice malt and sake. After one month of fermentation, a clear liquid called *shochu* is distilled from the mixture, mixed with cooked sweet rice and more rice malt, and fermented for three more months. Then a clear liquid is pressed out, which in turn is aged for six months to two years. Mirin has an alcoholic content of about 13%, but the alcohol usually evaporates during cooking. It is not used for drinking. See also COOKING; SAKE; SEASONING FOR FOOD; SOY SAUCE; TERIYAKI; YAKITORI.

MIROKU   A deity also known as Miroku Bosatsu, who is the "Buddha of the Future" in the Buddhist religion, which was introduced into Japan from China in the sixth century A.D. Miroku, one of the earliest Buddhist deities worshiped in Japan, belongs to the complex pantheon of the Mahayana (Greater Vehicle) branch of Buddhism (in contrast to Hinayana, or Theravada, Buddhism, the Lesser Vehicle), which originated in India. Miroku's name in Sanskrit is Maitreya, the "Benevolent One." Miroku is among the top five of 13 Mahayana Buddhist deities that the Japanese classified as specially worthy of worship. It is believed that Miroku will be born 5,000 years after Shaka (Shakyamuni), the "historical Buddha," attained *satori* (enlightenment) in India in the sixth century B.C. Miroku will come down to earth from the Tosotsu (Tusita) heaven and bring all beings to enlightenment. Buddhist scriptures promise that people who worship Miroku will be reborn after death in Miroku's Tosotsu heaven. In 12th-century Japan the worship of Amida Buddha as taught by the Pure Land Sect of Buddhism became more popular than Miroku

worship. Yet Miroku still has a place in Japanese Buddhism and in so-called "new religions" that have emerged in modern Japan, such as O-omoto. Miroku, a benevolent deity, is often portrayed at village festivals by a man wearing traditional robes and a large mask of a white, smiling face with long ears. The deity Hotei, one of the Seven Gods of Good Fortune, is considered an incarnation of Miroku. See also AMIDA; BUDDHISM; FESTIVALS; HOTEI; MASKS; NEW RELIGIONS; O-OMOTO; PURE LAND SECT OF BUDDHISM.

MIRROR *(kagami)*   Traditionally, a piece of bronze or other metal, generally round in shape, which is highly polished so that it reflects images. Many bronze mirrors made in China were placed in tomb mounds *(kofun)* in Japan during the Kofun Era (c. 300–710). Japanese artisans soon began to produce mirrors decorated with native designs. The Shoshoin, an eighth-century imperial repository, contains 58 Chinese and Japanese mirrors made in various shapes and sizes from bronze, iron, cupronickel and silver, and decorated on the back with motifs of birds, flowers, animals and landscapes.

The mirror is associated with the Sun Goddess Amaterasu o Mikami, divine ancestor of the imperial family. Legends relate that when Amaterasu sent her grandson Ninigi no Mikoto to rule over the Japanese islands, she gave him three sacred treasures, a mirror, sword and curved jewel *(magatama)*. These treasures, known as the imperial regalia, still symbolize the authority of the Japanese emperor. According to the legend, the mirror was used to lure Amaterasu out of a cave where she had withdrawn after her brother treated her rudely. Legendary emperor Sujin supposedly installed the sacred mirror of Amaterasu at Ise, the central shrine of Shinto, the indigenous Japanese religion. This mirror is believed to embody the *kami* (sacred spirit) of Amaterasu herself. A replica of the sacred mirror is housed in a shrine in the Imperial Palace. The *Kojiki,* and official eighth-century chronicle, also relates that the creator god Izanagi (father of Amaterasu) gave his children a polished silver disc and told them to kneel before it each morning and evening, subduing their passions and evil thoughts so that the disc would reflect only a pure spirit.

Two proverbs express the significance of mirrors in Japanese culture: "When the mirror is dim the soul is unclean," and "Just as the sword is the spirit of a samurai, the mirror is the spirit of a woman." A bride was traditionally given a mirror that symbolized her honor and virtue as a married woman. In the second half of the 16th century, a type of round mirror with a handle, known as an *e-kagami,* was developed in Japan. The handle and back of the mirror were highly decorated with metalwork or ornate lacquer techniques. Lacquer cosmetic and mirror sets were part of dowries for wealthy brides in the Edo Era (1600–1868). See also AMATERASU O MIKAMI; IMPERIAL REGALIA; KOJIKI; LACQUER WARE; MAKEUP; SHOSOIN; TOMB MOUND.

MISHIMA YUKIO (1925–1970)   An important modern Japanese writer who is also remembered for his dramatic suicide. Mishima's real name was Hiraoka Kimitake. He was born in Tokyo and educated at the elite Peer's School (Gakushuin), where he published his first poems in the school's literary magazine. His teachers published his first story, "The Forest in Full Flower" ("Hanazakari no mori," 1941), in their own highly regarded literary magazine in 1944 and gave him the pen name Mishima Yukio. During the turbulent time at the end of World War II, Mishima continued writing stories while a law student at Tokyo University. His work was praised by the great Japanese writer Kawabata Yasunari (1899–1972), who shared an interest in the traditions of Japanese culture. Mishima gained fame as a writer with his novel *Confessions of a Mask (Kamen no kokuhaku;* 1949, translated 1958), about a boy who painfully realizes he cannot live a normal life in Japanese society. Mishima's books often dwell on male beauty and homosexual desires. Some of his major novels include *Thirst for Love (Ai no Kawaki;* 1950 translated 1969) *The Sound of Waves (Shiosai;* 1954, translated 1956), based on the Greek myth of Daphnis and Chloe; *The Temple of the Golden Pavilion (Kinkakuji;* 1956, translated 1959), about the actual burning down of Kinkakuji by a deranged monk; and *The Sea of Fertility (Hojo no umi)*, about death and reincarnation, published serially from 1965 until his death.

As an artist, Mishima was obsessed with the expression of truth and beauty in his work. Yet he also had a nationalistic bent. In 1967 he trained with the Japanese Self-Defense Forces (Jietai), and the following year he formed his own private army of 100 men, the Shield Society (Tate no Kai), sworn to defend the Japanese emperor. Mishima became frustrated that his attempts to revive traditions relinquished by Japan after World War II, such as emperor worship, did not succeed. He made a final protest by storming the Japanese military barracks and publicly committing suicide *(seppuku)* in the traditional Japanese manner, by slitting his belly open and then having one of his soldiers cut off his head with a sword.

Mishima's novels have been translated into English and other languages. A movie was made about his life and art by the American director Paul Schrader in 1985. See also KAWABATA YASUNARI; KINKAKUJI; NOVELS; SUICIDE.

MISO (soybean paste) A thick paste made from fermented soybeans; a basic ingredient of Japanese cooking. There are many different types of *miso*, which are all made by the same basic method. Soybeans are boiled, crushed and mixed with wheat, barley, or rice. *Koji,* a grain inoculated with *Aspergillus* mold, which causes the fermentation process, is added to the soybean mixture, which is then left to ferment for a period of several months up to three years. The three basic types of *miso* are light, red, and dark. Light *miso* is sold as "sweet" (kyo-miso), white (shiro-miso) or yellow (inaka-miso). It has the lowest salt content and a high *koji* content, so it ferments naturally in a few weeks. Dark *miso* and red *miso* have more salt and soybeans and less *koji*. They take one to three years to ferment. Red *miso* (aka-miso), which is very good for making *miso* soup, is made from soybeans, rice and barley. Dark *miso* is fermented with a mold made solely of soybeans and is very thick and dark brown. It is usually mixed with red *miso* to make soup. Light *miso* is very high in lactic acid bacteria, whereas dark *miso* is high in protein and fatty acids, and is saltier. *Miso* is so rich that only a small amount is needed to flavor other foods. In general, darker types of *miso* taste better in winter dishes that require long simmering, such as vegetable stews and soups. The Japanese like to vary their *miso* soup from light to dark as the seasons change. Many Japanese people consume *miso* every day, particularly as a bowl of hot *miso* soup at breakfast, because it is considered healthful. *Miso* provides essential amino acids, minerals and vitamin B-12, and it has enzymes and bacteria that aid the digestion and assimilation of other foods. *Miso* soup, rice and pickles are considered a complete meal when eaten together. Japanese cooking often combines *miso* with other basic ingredients such as sake, *mirin* (sweet rice wine for cooking) and vinegar to flavor a wide variety of foods. See also COOKING; PICKLES; RICE; SAKE; SEASONING FOR FOOD; SOUP; SOYBEANS.

MITI See MINISTRY OF INTERNATIONAL TRADE AND INDUSTRY.

MITSUBISHI The largest corporate group in Japan. Mitsubishi was founded in the 1870s by Iwasaki Yataro, who acquired the trading and shipping company operated by the Japanese domain of Tosa (modern Kochi Prefecture) when the Meiji government (1868–1912) abolished the feudal domains and their business activities. In 1873 Iwasaki made the company a private enterprise and named it the Mitsubishi Commercial Company (Mitsubishi Shokai). The name Mitsubishi, meaning "three diamond shapes," comes from the crest *(mon)* used by Iwasaki as his trademark. The company soon owned most of the Japanese commercial steamships and was renamed the Mitsubishi Steamship Company (Mitsubishi Kisen Kaisha) in 1875. In 1887, it acquired the shipyards in Nagasaki, which are still an important part of the company. Iwasaki astutely diversified into many other areas, such as mining and metallurgy, banking, real estate and warehousing. He organized the company as a limited partnership named Mitsubishi, Ltd. (Mitsubishi Goshi Kaisha) in 1893 and made its subsidiaries independent joint-stock corporations. Mitsubishi became a great Japan *zaibatsu* (business conglomerate) and expanded enormously before and during World War II. It was broken up between 1946 and 1950, when the Allied Occupation of Japan dissolved the *zaibatsu*. However, during the 1950s, the subsidiaries of Mitsubishi came together again as a *keiretsu* (enterprise grouping). Today there are close to 100 companies within the Mitsubishi group, active in chemicals, electrical machinery and household appliances, electronic equipment, mining and metallurgy, and other industries.

Mitsubishi Heavy Industries, Ltd. (Mitsubishi Jukogyo) is the largest manufacturer of heavy machinery in Japan. Revenues for Mitsubishi Heavy Industries totaled $12.4 billion for fiscal year (FY) 1989, and $6.6 for the first half of FY 1990. Earnings totaled $405 million for FY 1989 and $204 million for the first half of FY 1990. Breakdown of sales by product category for the first half of FY 1990: power systems 32.4%, machinery, 24.7%, ships and steel

13.3%, aircraft and special vehicles 15.4%, and general machinery 14.5%. Mitsubishi Heavy Industries makes Japan's largest heavy rockets. A consortium of companies is attempting to sell launch services using Japan's next-generation rocket, the H-II, which will be introduced in 1993. Mitsubishi Heavy remains the Japanese government's major arms contractor. Mitsubishi Bank (Mitsubishi Ginko), dating back to 1880, is the fourth largest city bank (a city-based bank with a widespread network of branches) in Japan. Mitsubishi Motors Corporation (Mitsubishi Jidosha Kogyo) manufactures automobiles, trucks and buses that are exported all over the world. Mitsubishi Corporation (Mitsubishi Shoji) is the largest Japanese trading company (sogo shosha), with more than 60 domestic and 130 overseas offices and subsidiaries. Mitsubishi headquarters are in Tokyo. In 1989 Mitsubishi Real Estate bought a controlling interest in Rockefeller Center in New York City. See also BANKING SYSTEM; CORPORATIONS; EXPORTS AND IMPORTS; TRADING COMPANY, GENERAL; ZAIBATSU.

MITSUI The second-largest corporate group in Japan. Mitsui Takatoshi founded the House of Mitsui in 1673 as a chain of dry goods stores in Kyoto and Edo (modern Tokyo), and soon after branched into moneylending and currency exchanging. In 1691 the company became an official transmitter of tax monies for the Tokugawa Shogunate (1603–1867). Mitsui also established connections with the Meiji government that took power in 1868. It became the largest zaibatsu (business conglomerates) in Japan, with banking, mining and trading as the main activities of its subsidiaries. The Mitsui family, which had grown into many branches and associated families, controlled Mitsui until 1892, when the conglomerate was reorganized as a limited partnership. During the 1890s, Mitsui diversified into heavy industries. A holding company (Mitsui Gomei Kaishi) was formed as an unlimited partnership in 1909 to oversee the numerous subsidiaries. In turn, they were reorganized as independent joint-stock corporations. Mitsui expanded greatly during World War II, but was broken up between 1946 and 1950 when the Allied Occupation of Japan dissolved the zaibatsu. However, the separate Mitsui companies came together again in the 1950s as a keiretsu (enterprise grouping). The Mitsui group now compromises nearly 100 companies, in such areas as construction, mining, shipbuilding and shipping, petrochemicals, and real estate. Mitsui Bank, Ltd. (Mitsui Ginko) was founded in 1876 as the first private bank in Japan. It remains one of the largest Japanese city banks (city-based bank with numerous branches). Mitsui & Co., Ltd. (Mitsui Bussan), also founded in 1876, is the second-largest Japanese trading company (sogo-shosha). It has the most overseas investments and more than 150 foreign offices, branches and incorporated companies. Mitsui corporate headquarters are in Tokyo. See also BANKING SYSTEM; CORPORATIONS; EXPORTS AND IMPORTS; TRADING COMPANY, GENERAL.

MITSUKOSHI, LTD. See DEPARTMENT STORES.

MIYAJIMA "Shrine Island;" an island in the Seto Inland Sea off Hiroshima that is considered one of the "Three Famous Sites" in Japan (Nihon sankei) along with Matsushima and Amanohashidate. Miyajima has been a sacred place throughout Japanese history. The entire island is considered a shrine, but it is also the setting for a Shinto shrine named Itsukushima. This shrine's enormous red torii (gate) rising out of the water is the largest in Japan and one of the country's most famous landmarks. Over 53 feet tall and made of camphor wood, the torii has guarded Itsukushima Shrine since 1875. The shrine itself dates back to A.D. 592 and honors several female deities who were thought to have appeared at this site and commanded local inhabitants to build the shrine. During the medieval era (12th to 16th centuries), when the Buddhist and Shinto religions intermingled, the Buddhist goddess Benten became associated with Itsukushima Shrine. Several other deities worshiped here are believed to protect sailors and fishermen. The bright red shrine is built directly over the water so it appears to be floating when the tide is high. There are actually several buildings, including a main hall and a pagoda, which are connected by walkways. A 770 foot covered dock winds around the main shrine building and is the oldest stage for Noh drama in Japan. Bugaku, a type of ancient Japanese court dance, is often performed on this stage for visitors to the shrine. Many religious ceremonies also take place there throughout the year, and the shrine's annual festival is celebrated on June 17th. There are two museums, the Miyajima Museum of Historic Treasures, and the Miyajima Municipal History and Folklore Museum. Itsukushima Shrine houses a rich variety of national treasures, such as decorative scrolls of the Lotus Sutra, a Buddhist scripture. Miyajima's natural beauty is beloved by the Japanese people, in particular the dense woods, the cherry blossoms in spring, and the red maple leaves in autumn. Tame deer wander freely and monkeys swing through the trees in a hilltop park. Women were not permitted on the island until after World War II. See also AMANOHASHIDATE; BENTEN; BUDDHISM; BUGAKU; CHERRY BLOSSOM; DEER; HIROSHIMA; INLAND SEA; LOTUS SUTRA; MAPLE TREE; MONKEY; NATIONAL TREASURES; NOH DRAMA; SHINTO; SHRINES, SHINTO; TEMPLES, BUDDHIST; TORII.

MIYAKE ISSEI See FASHION DESIGNERS, CONTEMPORARY.

MIYAKO ISLAND GROUP See RYUKYU ISLANDS.

MIZOGUCHI KENJI (1898–1956) An internationally famous Japanese film director. Mizoguchi was first a painter and then began directing movies in 1922. His earliest movies were concerned with the problems of poor people and conflict between social classes. Mizoguchi became particularly interested in the sacrifices Japanese women were required to make for their families or to help their men succeed in life. This theme was first explored in his 1929 film Nihombashi, about a woman who becomes a wealthy man's mistress in order to pay for her brother's college education. Two movies he directed in 1936, now considered among the greatest Japanese films, continued this theme: *Osaka Elegy (Naniwa erejii)* and *Sisters of the Gion (Gion no shimai)*. The former is about a woman who is rejected by the family whom she has had to support by becoming the mistress of a banker. The latter is about the plight of two sisters who are geisha in the Gion district of Kyoto. During World War II, Japanese military pressure for nationalistic movies led Mizoguchi to film a famous story about *ronin* (masterless samurai), *The Loyal Forty-Seven Ronin of the Genroku Era (Genroku chushingura; 1941–42)*. After the war, Mizoguchi made more movies about suffering women, such as *Women of the Night (Yoru no onnatachi; 1948)*, *A Story from Chikamatsu or Crucified Lovers (Chikamatsu monogatari; 1954)*, and *Street of Shame (Akasen shitai; 1956)*. *Ugetsu (Ugetsu Monogatari [1953], Ghost Story)*, about a woman who died in the military conflicts that wracked Japan in the 16th century, became well known abroad. *The Life of Oharu (Saikaku ichidai onna; 1952)* won Mizoguchi the prize for best director at the Venice Film Festival. It tells the story of an aristocratic woman whose strong love for a man brings her down to the lowest social class and forces her to become a prostitute. Mizoguchi directed more than 80 movies during his career. A documentary about Mizoguchi was made in 1976 entitled *Kenji Mizoguchi: The Life of a Film Director*. See also FILM; FORTY-SEVEN RONIN INCIDENT; GEISHA; GION.

MOA MUSEUM OF ART   See ATAMI.

MOCHI   Small, dense cakes of pounded glutinous rice *(mochi-gomi)*. Sweet glutinous rice is soaked, steamed and pounded with a large mortar and pestle, then left to dry until it solidifies. *Mochi* is often pounded the traditional way by placing the cooked rice in a wooden tub or log with a hollowed out section *(usu)* and pounding it with a large wooden mallet *(kine)*. One person pounds the rice with the mallet while another turns it until it has an even consistency. The pounded rice is made into small, round cakes or rolled out and cut into 2-inch squares. Then it is stored in a cool place or refrigerated until it is used. Machine-made *mochi* is commonly sold in packages in Japan today, and *mochi*-making machines are available as home appliances. *Mochi* is cooked by broiling, baking or grilling the cakes over a charcoal fire. They puff up and their surface becomes crisp, while the inside turns soft and sticky. They can be eaten with soy sauce and grated *daikon* (Japanese radish), or filled with sweetened bean paste. *Shiruko* is a sweet, hot dish of grilled *mochi* and cooked and sweetened red beans *(azuki)*. *Mochi* should be chewed slowly and carefully because it is hard to swallow and can stick in the throat.

Mochi is generally associated with ceremonial events such as the New Year Festival (Shogatsu). The concentrated rice symbolizes wealth and long life. Big round cakes of white *mochi* (*kagami* or "mirror" *mochi*) are displayed as decorations. These cakes are also used as offerings for a number of religious ceremonies throughout the year. The most important New Year's food is *o-zoni*, a soup made with different ingredients, depending on the region of Japan, but always containing *mochi*. Many celebrities, such as

sumo wrestlers, actors and politicians, are invited to pound *mochi* as part of the public celebration of the New Year. Japanese folk literature identifies a rabbit in the moon pounding *mochi* with a big mallet. Seeing the rabbit in the moon brings the viewer a year of good luck. *Mochi* was used very early in Japanese history and was brought to Japan from southern China through Korea. It is also eaten in some Southeast Asian countries. See also BEANS; DAIKON; MOON; NEW YEAR FESTIVAL; RABBIT; RICE; SOY SAUCE.

MOMIJI   See MAPLE TREE; SEASONS OF THE YEAR.

MOMOTARO   "Peach Boy." The hero of a popular folktale about a boy who was born from a peach found by an old woman. There are many versions of the story. In all of them, the old woman takes the peach home and a little boy is born from it. She and her husband call him Momotaro, or "Peach Boy," and raise him as their own son. He grows up rapidly, leaves home to overcome the monsters on Ogre Island and brings home the treasures there for his parents. This version of the folktale became popular in the Edo Era (1600–1868). Momotaro falls into the category of stories about children born in an unusual way who perform great deeds, known as "Tales of a Tiny Child" *(Chiisako Monogatari)*. See also DEMONS AND GHOSTS; MONOGATARI; PEACH.

MOMOYAMA ERA   See AZUCHI-MOMOYAMA ERA.

MON   See CREST.

MONASTICISM, BUDDHIST *(soryo)*   The Buddhist religion, which began in India and was introduced into Japan from China through Korea in the sixth century A.D., has a complex hierarchy of monks, priests and nuns. *Sogya* (*samgha* in Sanskrit) is the Japanese term for communities known as monasteries where such people reside and follow the Buddhist law or *vinaya*. A *sogya* is a community with more than four monks or nuns. *So* is the Japanese term for monks, who are also called *soryo*. Women can join Buddhist orders as nuns, known as *ama*. Priests are called *shinpu*. Hermitages, often in remote areas, are called *in* or *an*. Buddhist monks and nuns traditionally take vows of celibacy and poverty and shave off their hair, a practice called *tokudo*, although this changed in most Japanese Buddhist sects. Their primary activities include meditation, studying Buddhist scriptures and performing religious rituals.

The ordination *(jukai)* of Buddhist monks was officially instituted in Japan at Todaiji in A.D. 754 by the Chinese Buddhist monk Ganjin (Jianzhen or Chien-chen in Chinese). In Japan the *sogya* was closely associated with the ruling powers, who patronized and closely regulated the Buddhist religion. The powerful Soga clan were early patrons of Buddhism, especially Empress Suiko (554–628) and her regent, Prince Shotoku (574–622). Monastic communities grew rapidly during the Nara Era (710–794). Monks, priests and nuns were placed under the administrative and penal code known as the *ritsuryo* system. The government established the office of *sogo*, chief administrator of Buddhist monks, and created a ranking system for monks. From

Buddhist monks wearing traditional robes and shaved heads. The Buddhist religion, introduced to Japan from India through China and Korea in the sixth century A.D., has had a widespread influence on Japanese culture.

highest to lowest, monks were known as *sojo, sozu* or *risshi*. Priests of the Hosso, Kegon and other sects of Buddhism in Nara became so powerful that the imperial court built new cities where it could move to escape Buddhist political influence. In A.D. 794 the court moved to Heiankyo (later known as Kyoto), where it remained until the modern era.

Buddhist monasteries became great centers of learning and culture, in particular Enryakuji on Mount Hiei outside Kyoto and Kongobuji on Mount Koya. Many of Japan's great Buddhist leaders studied at Enryakuji. Buddhist temples acquired large provincial estates (*shoen* or landed estates), which developed into active centers of commerce, moneylending and artistic activities, and sponsored entertainers and merchant guilds. Enryakuji and other large Buddhist complexes also developed armies of warrior-monks that sometimes fought each other. In the 12th and 13th centuries, itinerant monks took Buddhism to the common people and the Pure Land, True Pure Land and Nichiren sects flourished, blurring the distinction between monks and lay people. Buddhist monks and priests were required to be celibate until Shinran (1173–1263), who advocated the marriage of priests. Eventually all Buddhist sects in Japan allowed their priests to marry, which sets Japanese Buddhism apart from Theravada Buddhism as practiced in Southeast Asia and Sri Lanka, which stresses celibate monasticism.

The Zen Sect of Buddhism, introduced into Japan in the 13th century, reemphasized monasticism under Chinese Zen monastic rules (*shingi*), as well as the technique of meditation (*zazen*) to achieve *satori* (enlightenment). The center of a Zen monastery is the communal meditation hall (*sodo*). In the 16th century, the national unifers Oda Nobunaga and Toyotomi Hideyoshi destroyed many powerful Buddhist monasteries and confiscated their lands. However, the Tokugawa Shogunate (1603–1867) used Buddhist

monasteries and temples as centers of administrative control, by requiring all Japanese to register at their local temples. The shogunate closely regulated monks and nuns, and encouraged them to study rather than preach or engage in social welfare.

Buddhist priests controlled many shrines of Shinto, the indigenous Japanese religion. The Meiji government (1868–1912) attempted to purify Shinto of Buddhist influences, and removed Buddhist statues and priests from Shinto shrines. Monks and priests were criticized for being corrupt, and Buddhism suffered a decline. However, Buddhist sects attempted to reform themselves, and since World War II they have been experiencing a revival. The Meiji government abolished the official awarding of the titles of *sogo* and *soi* in 1872, although Buddhist sects continued to award these titles. The secretary-general (*kansho*) is the highest rank among Buddhist priests. However, some sects have experienced conflicting claims between their elected *kancho* or chief secretary of religious matters (*shumu*) and the hereditary chief abbot.

In Japan, major activities of Buddhist priests have become the performance of funerals and memorial services for the dead, and the maintenance of temple graveyards. Buddhism is sometimes called in Japan a "religion of the dead." Many priests have also studied Western philosophy and become scholars of religion, and have introduced Buddhism to Western countries. See also BUDDHISM; ENRYAKUJI; FUNERALS; HIEI, MOUNT; HOSSO SECT OF BUDDHISM; KIYOMIZUDERA TEMPLE; KOYA, MOUNT; KONGOBUJI; LANDED ESTATE SYSTEM; MEDITATION; MEIJI RESTORATION OF 1868; NARA ERA; NICHIREN; ODA NOBUNAGA; PRIESTS, SHINTO; PURE LAND SECT OF BUDDHISM; RITSURYO SYSTEM; SCRIPTURES, RELIGIOUS; SHAMANS AND SHAMANISM; SHINGON SECT OF BUDDHISM; SHINRAN; SHOTOKU, PRINCE; SOGA CLAN; SUIKO, EMPRESS; TEMPLES, BUDDHIST; TENDAI SECT OF BUDDHISM; TODAIJI; TOKUGAWA SHOGUNATE; TOYOTOMI HIDEYOSHI; ZEN SECT OF BUDDHISM.

MONEY See BANKING SYSTEM; INVESTMENTS OVERSEAS, JAPANESE; MINISTRY OF FINANCE; TAX SYSTEM; YEN.

MONGOL INVASIONS OF JAPAN (A.D. 1274 and 1281) Two armed naval expeditions were sent to invade Japan by the Mongol emperor of China Khubilai Khan (1215–1294). These attempted invasions are known in Japanese as the Bun'ei War (Bun'ei no Eki; 1274) and the Koan War (Koan no Eki; 1281). Khubilai had completed his grandfather Chinghis Khan's conquest of the Asian mainland when he united China under the Yuan dynasty (1270–1368). He wanted to make Japan, like other Asian countries, a tributary state of China, but Japan had refused this type of relationship ever since Chinese culture was adopted under Prince Shotoku (574–622). In 1268 Khubilai Khan sent envoys from Korea, with a letter to the Japanese emperor in Kyoto, in which he threatened to invade if Japan did not submit to his demands. At the time, Japan was actually being governed by the military regime of the Kamakura Shogunate (1192–1333) centered in Kamakura on Honshu's east coast, and the shogunate mobilized its vassals (*gokenin*) to resist the Mongols. In November 1274 an armada of close to 900 ships with 40,000 troops sailed from the southern tip of Korea toward the southern Japanese island of Kyushu, about 150 miles away. Mongol troops landed at Hakata on northwest Kyushu, attacked Japanese troops, and then returned to their ships. That night a violent typhoon (taifu) destroyed much of the Mongol fleet, and the remaining ships retreated to Korea.

In 1275 and 1279, Khubilai Khan sent more envoys with threatening demands to Japan. Both times the Japanese responded by beheading the envoys and strengthening their military defenses along the coast. In June 1281 two Mongol fleets with 4,400 armed ships and 140,000 troops sailed toward Japan from Korea and southern China. Japan was saved from invasion once more by a typhoon, on August 16, which destroyed almost the whole Mongol fleet in Hakata Bay and killed more than half the troops. Again the survivors were forced to retreat. The Japanese, believing these storms were sent by the gods to protect their country, called them kamikaze, or "divine wind." They also believed that the kamikaze made their country invincible against outside attacks. The attempted Mongol invasions were the last threat to Japan by foreign powers until the mid-19th century, and the last time foreign invaders set foot on Japanese soil until the Battle of Okinawa in 1945 near the end of World War II. The Kamakura Shogunate used the need for defenses against the Mongols to extend its power in western Japan, but resentment against its power there contributed to its downfall in 1333. See also CHINA AND JAPAN; KAMIKAZE; KAMAKURA SHOGUNATE; KOREA AND JAPAN; KYUSHU ISLAND; SHOTOKU, PRINCE; TYPHOON.

MONKEY (saru) The Japanese macaque plays a large role in Japanese literature and folklore. Monkeys are common wild animals in wooded areas of Japan, living in large troops with hierarchical social systems. About 2 feet long with a 3-inch tail and weighing about 26 pounds, the monkeys have yellow-brown fur and red faces and buttocks. The Japanese regard the monkey as a clever but foolish trickster. Monkeys steal crops and even go into the farmhouses. Many Japanese legends portray monkeys with human characteristics. Monkeys were kept in stables because they were believed to protect horses from disease. Myths about a monkey god named Sarutahiko led to the practice at some Shinto shrines of treating monkeys as messengers of sacred spirits. The three monkeys (san en) that "hear no evil, see no evil, speak no evil", and cover their ears, eyes and mouth respectively with their paws are considered messengers of Koshin, the God of Roads; stone statues of the three monkeys are often found along roadsides in Japan. The most famous portrayal depiction of the three monkeys is a wooden carving over a gate at Toshogu Shrine, the mausoleum of Tokugawa Ieyasu (1543–1616), founder of the Tokugawa Shogunate (1603–1867), at Nikko. A type of ancient Chinese entertainment introduced into Japan and known as sarugaku, or "monkey music," was the origin of the classical theatrical form called Noh drama. A popular type of Japanese street entertainment was sarumawashi, or shows by trained dancing monkeys. Numerous Zen Buddhist ink paintings (sumi-e) depict mon-

keys, such as a monkey trying to grasp the moon reflected in a lake. The monkey is one of the 12 animals in the 12-year zodiac cycle; people born in the Year of the Monkey are thought to be clever, practical and inventive. Japanese research on monkeys is world famous, and the Japan Monkey Center is a major primate research facility. See also NOH DRAMA; TOSHOGU SHRINE; ZEN SECT OF BUDDHISM; ZODIAC.

MONKS, BUDDHIST See MONASTICISM, BUDDHIST.

MONO NO AWARE A literary and aesthetic concept that is usually translated as "sensitivity to or deep feeling for things." The term aware, describing an emotional response to the momentary beauty that can be seen in nature or in human relationships, first appeared in the Manyoshu, an eighth-century collection of poetry. During the Heian Era (794–1185) the term acquired a connotation of sadness or melancholy, indicating a sensibility to the "sadness of things" because of their impermanence, a central teaching of the Buddhist religion introduced into Japan from China in the sixth century A.D. Murasaki Shikibu used the concept aware more than a thousand times in her famous 11th-century novel The Tale of Genji (Genji Monogatari). She described the fleeting beauty, for example, of a leaf blown by the wind. An 18th-century literary critic, Motoori Norinaga (1730–1801), made a study of the concept of aware as used in The Tale of Genji. He was the first critic to emphasize that mono no aware was the most important aesthetic concept in all literature of the Heian Era, expressed in such images as an unshed tear or a fallen flower. Norinaga concluded that mono no aware is a deep feeling for the reality of life that is awakened in any sensitive human being. However, after the Heian Era the concept of aware was used less frequently, and it came to have the current more negative connotation of "pathos" or wretched sorrow. See also BUDDHISM; GENJI, THE TALE OF; HEIAN ERA; MURASAKI SHIKIBU; POETRY.

MONOGATARI Literally, "talk of things," or tales; in the strict sense, the term for works of prose narrative written in Japan from the ninth through 15th centuries. Narrative literature is termed monogatari bungaku, and is distinguished from poetry (waka bungaku), diary literature (nikki bungaku) and essays or random writings (zuihitsu bungaku). The monogatari form of literature was developed by women in the imperial court of the Heian Era (794–1185) who amused themselves with stories, which were recorded in vernacular language with the newly developed Japanese syllabic writing system known as kana. Court romances are termed uta or tsukuri monogatari. The best known is the 11th-century novel The Tale of Genji (Genji Monogatari) by Murasaki Shikibu. Such works contain many poems even though they are considered prose works. Other well-known monogatari include Tales of Ise (Ise Monogatari), a collection of tales from the early 10th century, and The Tale of the Bamboo Cutter (Taketori Monogatari), a 10th-century narrative that draws on earlier fairy tales. Other basic types of monogatari are historical tales (rekisha monogatari), which arose in the late 11th century, and military tales *(gunki monogatari)*, which developed following the civil warfare of the late 12th century. *The Tale of the Heike (Heike Monogatari;* early 13th to late 14th century), tells the story of the war between the Taira (or Heike) and Minamoto (or Genji) clans, which led to the founding of Japan's first military government, the Kamakura Shogunate (1192–1333). A type of short, often humorous popular tale also developed out of Buddhist miracle stories and is known as tale literature *(setsuwa bungaku).* See also BAMBOO CUTTER, THE TALE OF THE; GENJI, THE TALE OF; HEIKE, THE TALE OF; ISE, TALES OF; KANA; MURASAKI SHIKIBU; POETRY; TAIRA-MINAMOTO WAR; WRITING SYSTEM, JAPANESE.

MONSTERS   See DEMONS AND GHOSTS; GODZILLA; KAPPA.

MOON *(tsuki)*   The moon is beloved by the Japanese for its many romantic associations. Moonlight is one of the most common themes in Japanese poetry, especially the forms of poetry called *haiku* and *waka.* Moonlight's subtle quality especially appeals to the Japanese, who traditionally celebrated a "Little New Year" (Koshogatsu) during the full moon on the 15th day of the first month in the lunar calendar. The Bon Festival, a Buddhist festival celebrating the visit of ancestors to their families, is held during the full moon on the 15th day of the seventh lunar month. A Moon-Viewing Festival is held on the 15th night of the eighth lunar month (Jugoya), which is regarded as the harvest moon. Moon viewing, along with cherry blossom viewing in the spring and snow viewing in the winter, is a popular time for romantic expressions of love.

The word *tsukimi* is used in Japanese poetry to represent the full moon at harvest time. When the Japanese look at the full moon, they see a rabbit in the moon pounding *mochi* (glutinous rice cakes) with a mortar and pestle. Ancient Japanese creation myths tell of the Moon God who was born from the creator god Izanagi. The Moon God is the brother of the Sun Goddess Amaterasu no Mikami, who is traditionally believed by the Japanese to be their divine ancestor. See also AMATERASU O MIKAMI; BON FESTIVAL; CALENDAR; CHERRY BLOSSOM; HAIKU; IZANAGI AND IZANAMI; MOCHI; MOON-VIEWING FESTIVAL; POETRY; RABBIT; SNOW; WAKA.

MOON-VIEWING FESTIVAL (Tsukimi)   The celebration of the clearest and most beautiful full moon of the year, held in mid-autumn on the 15th day of the eighth month in the traditional Japanese lunar calendar (around September 22 in the Western calendar now used in Japan). Although it is generally thought that this festival was brought to Japan from China during the Muromachi Era (1333–1568), there is a record of a moon-viewing festival being observed in A.D. 851 during the reign of Emperor Montoku. This festival became quite popular during the Edo Era (1600–1868), when citizens of Edo (modern Tokyo) enjoyed a festival in honor of the moon held on the banks of the Sumida River. A three-day moon-viewing festival has also traditionally been held at Hyakka-en (Hundred Flowers Garden) in Tokyo, which, designed by a group of artists and writers in the 18th century, has many literary associations. The moon has always been one of the three most

popular subjects of Japanese poetry, along with flowers and snow. The autumn harvest moon has many romantic associations for the Japanese people, and families traditionally sat outside on the verandas of their homes to enjoy the moon and eat a meal of special foods, including seasonal fruits and vegetables, rice balls, sweet potatoes, taro, chestnuts and sake. Following a very old custom, they also ate the Seven Herbs of Autumn, the foremost of which is *susuki,* or Japanese pampas grass. See also AUTUMN FLOWERS AND GRASSES; CALENDAR; FLOWERS; MOON; POETRY; RICE; SAKE; SNOW; SUMIDA RIVER; SWEET POTATO.

MORI HANAE (1926–)   Known outside Japan as Hanae Mori; the first Japanese fashion designer to open branch stores in foreign cities and to become internationally famous. Mori was born near Kyoto and studied literature at Tokyo Christian Women's College. Also trained as an artist and textile designer, she married a prominent Japanese textile manufacturer right after she graduated. She designed textile prints that he produced commercially. In the 1950s Mori began designing Western-style clothing, and opened her first shop on the Ginza in Tokyo in 1955. She also designed costumes for more than 500 Japanese movies, as well as skiwear for the 1972 Sapporo (Japan) Winter Olympic Games. In 1964 the International Silk Association sponsored the first showing of her fashion collection in America. Mori opened a shop in New York City in 1973. That year she was given the American Nieman Marcus Award for her designs. She brought her first couture (custom-made high fashion) collection to Paris in 1977 and the next year opened her own building in Tokyo, which houses boutiques, a couture studio, and the business offices for her company. Mori maintains a similar building in Paris, where she plays a prominent role in the world of high fashion. Her ready-to-wear clothes are sold all over the world, and she has branched out into the design of accessories, fabrics, sportswear, lingerie, sheets and towels, which draw upon Japanese design motifs. Mori specializes in cocktail and evening dresses that utilize materials and shapes of kimono. See also FASHION DESIGNERS, CONTEMPORARY; KIMONO; SILK; TEXTILES.

MORITA AKIO (1921–)   Founder, with Ibuka Masaru (1908–), of Sony Corporation, a premiere Japanese electronics company.

Morita was born in Aichi Prefecture and educated at Osaka University. In 1946, he and Ibuka began their company, originally named Tokyo Tsushin Kogyo Kabushiki Kaisha (Tokyo Telecommunications Engineering Corporation), on the second floor of a former Tokyo department store that had been burned out during the war. In 1953, when Morita traveled abroad to represent the company and learned that foreigners could not pronounce the company's name, the partners changed it to Sony. Morita handled the company's financial affairs and became president of Sony in 1971, and chairman and chief executive officer in 1976. He always promoted an international perspective and successfully marketed Sony products all over the world. He built Sony manufacturing plants in California, Great Britain and other foreign locations, and opened business offices in many countries. He also organized the Sony Trading Corporation, which exports Sony products. One of the company's greatest successes has been the Sony Walkman portable radio and cassette player, which Morita invented. Due to Morita's efforts, Sony became the first Japanese company to be listed on the New York Stock Exchange. In 1988 Sony acquired Columbia Pictures CBS Records. Morita published a book about his experiences and philosophy as a businessman, *Made in Japan* (1987), which became a best-seller in Japan and abroad. Morita also collaborated with Japanese politician Ishihara Shintaro on a controversial best-seller in Japan, *The Japan That Can Say No*, in 1989. Morita did not authorize an English edition, because it strongly criticized American corporate management and trade policies, but bootleg translations were widely circulated; the book's rights were then sold to foreign publishers in 1990. See also ELECTRONICS INDUSTRY; MADE IN JAPAN; SONY CORPORATION.

MORNING GLORY (*asagao*) A plant with funnel-shaped flowers and large leaves that grows by twining around fences, poles, hedges and other supports. Blooming in the summer, morning glory flowers open early in the morning and close before noon. They can be blue, purple, white, red or variegated. The morning glory was brought to Japan from the Asian mainland as a medicinal plant over 1,000 years ago. The seeds are still used as a diuretic and laxative.

During the Heian Era (794–1185) aristocrats cultivated morning glories in their gardens for the fleeting beauty of their flowers. During the Edo Era (1600–1868), many varieties of morning glory were cultivated, and large flowers were especially prized. They are still commonly grown in Japanese gardens, and competitive exhibitions of morning glory plants are held throughout Japan in early summer. A morning glory fair (*asagaoichi*), with many stalls selling potted plants, is held in early July every year at Kishibojin Temple in Tokyo, and at other temples around the country.

A famous *haiku* poem about a morning glory was composed by Chiyo of Kaga (1703–1775). One morning she found a morning glory vine twined around the bucket of her household well, and rather than disturb the plant with its beautiful flower, she went to borrow water from a neighbor. The morning glory is also the subject of a story about the national unifier Toyotomi Hideyoshi (1536–1598) and his tea ceremony master, Sen no Rikyu (1522–1591). Hideyoshi, who loved extravagance, heard of the beautiful morning glories blooming in Rikyu's teahouse garden and went early in the morning to see them, but Rikyu had cut down all the flowers, and when Hideyoshi entered the tea ceremony room, he saw only a single morning glory flower displayed in a vase. See also FAIR DAY; FLOWERS; GARDENS; TEAHOUSE STYLE; HAIKU; SEN NO RIKYU; TOYOTOMI HIDEYOSHI.

MORONOBU (?–1694) Full name Hishikawa Moronobu; an important woodblock print artist and painter in the Edo style known as *ukiyo-e* (pictures of the ''floating world'' or the pleasure quarters). Moronobu was born north of Edo (modern Tokyo) and was taught by his father to make brocade, that is, silk textiles woven with raised designs. In the mid-1660s he moved to Edo and studied the techniques and style of *ukiyo-e* art, which portrayed Kabuki actors, courtesans and related entertainers in the licensed pleasure quarters of Japanese cities. He was likely a student of the great *ukiyo-e* artist known as the Kambun Master, and he studied the artistic styles of the Kano and Tosa schools of painting. In the 1670s, he succeeded the Kambun Master as the foremost *ukiyo-e* artist in Edo.

Moronobu produced many paintings and at least 150 print albums and illustrated books, including novels, poetry anthologies, plays, books of *shunga* (erotic art) and design books for kimono. By combining elements of illustration and genre paintings (depictions of daily activities), Moronobu created the definitive *ukiyo-e* style that influenced Japanese artists for 200 years. See also EDO; FLOATING WORLD; KABUKI; KANO SCHOOL OF PAINTING; KIMONO; SHUNGA; TOSA SCHOOL OF PAINTING; WOODBLOCK PRINTS; YOSHIWARA.

MORSE, EDWARD SYLVESTER (1838–1925) An American who acquired an excellent collection of Japanese objects while he lived and worked in Japan between 1877 and 1879 and who introduced Japanese art and culture to America. Morse was born in Portland, Maine, trained as a zoologist at Harvard university, and taught at Bowdoin College in Maine. He traveled to Japan in 1877 to study a species of shellfish known as brachiopods, only two decades after Japan had been opened to the West by U.S. Commodore Matthew Perry after more than two centuries of isolation. While there Morse became fascinated by the Japanese people and culture, and constantly made notes and drawings of all that he observed. Accepting a teaching position in the zoology department at newly founded Tokyo University, Morse helped organize the department and introduced Darwin's theory of evolution and Western methods of scientific research. He also helped found the Japanese Imperial Museum, and discovered the ancient Omori Shell Mounds (Omori *kaizuka*) which contained pottery, tools and skeletons from the Jomon Era (c. 10,000–c. 300 B.C.). On a return trip to Japan 1882–1883, Morse gathered a fine collection of Japanese ceramics, which now belong to the Boston Museum of Fine Arts. Morse served as director of the Peabody Museum of Salem, Massachusetts, from 1880 to 1916, and director emeritus there until he died in 1925.

Morse interested many Americans in Japanese art and culture, including Ernest Fenollosa, an expert on Asian art, who spent many years in Japan and acquired a fine collection of Japanese art objects for the Boston Museum of Fine Arts. The Peabody Museum of Salem commemorated the 100th anniversary of Morse's first trip to Japan with a special exhibition of Morse's acquisitions, accompanied by a catalog with his drawings and observations, *Japan Day by Day* (1977). The Japanese government awarded Morse the Order of the Rising Sun (Kyokujitsusho) in 1898 and the Order of the Sacred Treasure (Zuihosho) in 1922. See also DECORATIONS, CIVILIAN; FENOLLOSA, ERNEST; PERRY, MATTHEW CALBRAITH; SECLUSION, NATIONAL; SHELL MOUNDS; TOKYO UNIVERSITY.

MOSS *(koke* or *kokerui)* About 2,000 species of moss grow in the humid Japanese climate. Subarctic species grow on Hokkaido Island and northern Honshu Island; tropical species grow in southwest Japan; and species growing in the central forest areas of Japan resembling those in the Himalaya and the North American Appalachian mountain ranges.

The Japanese cultivate moss, which is one of the basic elements of Japanese gardens, along with bamboo, rocks, water and sand. Moss is planted in gardens surrounding traditional teahouses. In the moss garden *(kokeniwa)*, rocks and hardwood trees are surrounded by carpets of various species of moss. Many Buddhist temples in the old capital city of Kyoto have lovely moss gardens, notably Saihoji Temple, which is nicknamed Kokedera, or "Moss Temple." Moss is also the featured element in a type of miniature landscape garden placed in a shallow wooden box, known as moss tray gardening *(koke bonkei)*. Moss embodies *sabi*, a central aesthetic concept in Japanese culture, which means taking pleasure in the unpretentious, antique, and worn. See also BONSAI; GARDENS; ROCKS; TEAHOUSE; SABI AND WABI; SAIHOJI.

MOTHER *(haha* or *okaasan)* The most important social role for Japanese women. *Okaasan,* the term used for their mothers by upper-class children in the late Edo Era (1600–1868), became used by all social classes in the early 20th century. Since World War II, young Japanese children have also called their mothers "mama," but generally switch to *okaasan* as they grow older. *Okaachan* is a more intimate term also used for mother. When speaking of their mothers to other people, the Japanese use an alternate pronunciation of the written character for mother, *haha*. The character for mother comprises that for woman *(onna)* with two dots added to represent breasts.

The primary relationship in a Japanese family is that between mother and child, rather than between husband and wife as in most Western families. The relationship between mothers and sons is especially close. Traditionally, the eldest son has lived with the mother and father even after marriage, with wives becoming members of their husbands' families and mothers-in-law *(shutome* or *shuto)* training the new wives in family customs. Tyranny of mothers-in-law over their sons' wives was common, although less so today. A wife moved up in the family hierarchy by becoming a mother, especially of a son, and eventually took her place as matriarch of the household. This was symbolized by the mother-in-law handing over the family's wooden rice paddle *(shamoji)* to her successor. The word mother-in-law is written by adding the character for "old" next to that for "female." Pregnant wives have traditionally returned home to be with their own mothers when they give birth for the first time; the grandmothers go to their daughter's homes to help care for subsequent newborns. The term for grandmother, *obaasan,* joins the characters for "woman" and "wave," referring to her wrinkles. A less common term for one's own grandmother is *sobo*, "ancestor mother."

Japanese mothers maintain a great deal of physical contact with their children and carry them in a sling both inside and outside the home until they are about two years old. This practice, known as *onbu*, contributes to the dependency *(amae)* that is a primary emotional tie in Japanese society. Japanese children also sleep in the same room with their mothers until they are about 10 years old. Until recently, few Japanese women worked outside the home after they had children, and most Japanese still believe that women should care for their own children and not rely on babysitters or day-care centers. Women who do not have children are regarded with pity. Many wedding traditions indicate the importance of having children, such as the inclusion of *konbu* (a type of seaweed) in engagement gifts exchanged between the couple's families, because it sounds similar to *ko o umu*, "bearing a child." An informal term used by sons about their own mothers is *ofukuro*, "the old lady" or "the great sack," indicating the family money bag or purse, which the mother controls.

Fathers usually turn over all responsibility for their children's education to the mothers. Examinations to get into good schools are difficult, and mothers push their children very hard to succeed. This has earned some mothers the disparaging nickname "education mama" *(kyoiku mama)*. When schools for Japanese females were opened in the late 19th century, their philosophy for educating women was to create "good wives and wise mothers" *(ryosai kenbo)*. Even today, women high school graduates usually attend two-year colleges to learn secretarial skills, and work only a few years until they marry. Japanese women usually marry between ages 23 and 25, and have children within a few years. Recently, more mothers have begun working again after their children start school. See also CHILDREN IN JAPAN; DEPENDENCY; EDUCATION SYSTEM; FAMILY; FATHER; WEDDINGS.

MOTHER-OF-PEARL See LACQUER WARE; SHELL.

MOTORCYCLE INDUSTRY In the early 1950s there were more than 50 manufacturers of two-wheeled motor vehicles in Japan. Honda Motor Co., Ltd. (Honda Giken Kogyo) soon dominated the industry and became the world's leading producer of motorcycles. Honda remains the largest motorcycle manufacturer, followed by Yamaha Motor Co., Ltd. (Yamaha Hatsudoki) and Suzuki Motor Co., Ltd. (Suzuki Jidosha Kogyo). Kawasaki Heavy Industries, Ltd. (Kawasaki Jukogyo) is another well-known motorcycle manufacturer.

Honda was founded in 1946 by Honda Soichiro, and began producing a small motorcycle in 1949. Soon thereafter it began producing motorcycles with large engines to sell in the international market. Honda diversified into automobiles and industrial engines in the 1960s, and developed a low-pollution Compound Vortex Controlled Combustion (CVCC) engine, which was one of the first to meet U.S. environmental standards enacted in 1975. When Yamaha threatened to overtake Honda in the motorcycle market in the 1970s, Honda countered the attack and dealt

Yamaha a severe blow by introducing a large variety of new motorcycle models. Honda's corporate headquarters are in Tokyo, but the company has always had an international perspective. In 1959 it opened an American subsidiary, Honda Motor Co., Inc. It now has dozens of foreign production plants, with many joint ventures and technology exchange agreements. About one-third of its total sales come from motorcycles.

Yamaha Motor Co., Ltd. produces motorcycles, motorboats, sailboats, golf carts, snow mobiles and several types of engines. The company was established in 1955 when it separated from Nippon Gakki Co., Ltd. Motorcycles total about 70% of Yamaha's annual sales, and about 70% of its total annual production of motorcycles is exported. Yamaha has several overseas branch offices, as well as joint ventures and technology exchange agreements in many countries. Corporate headquarters are in Iwata, Shizuoka Prefecture.

Suzuki Motor Co., Ltd. manufactures minicars and outboard motors as well as motorcycles. Now affiliated with Isuzu Motors, Ltd. and General Motors Corporation, the company was founded by Suzuki Michio in 1920 to manufacture textiles, but during the 1950s it changed to the manufacture of motor vehicles. Suzuki has its corporate headquarters in Hamamatsu, Shizuoka Prefecture, and motorcycle assembly plants in several South and Southeast Asian countries.

Japan's success in motorcycles has forced American companies out of the market. Today only Harley Davidson is active in America, producing larger models. See also AUTOMOBILE INDUSTRY; CORPORATIONS; EXPORTS AND IMPORTS.

MOUNTAINS (yama) Mountainous terrain covers 85% of the islands of Japan. Two hundred and twenty-five Japanese mountains are volcanoes, and 60 of them can become active. Mount Aso on southern Kyushu Island is the world's largest active volcano. Sakurajima is another active volcano on Kyushu, near Kagoshima City. The northern region of Honshu, the main Japanese island, has large mountain ranges known as the Japan Alps, which have been designated national parks. Since ancient times, the Japanese have revered mountains as dwelling places of kami, sacred spirits of Shinto, the native Japanese religion. A mountain where a kami dwells is known as a "spirit mountain" (reizan) or "divine body mountain" (shintai-zan). Mountain worship is known as sangaku shinko ("mountain beliefs"). Shinto shrines and Buddhist temples have been built on many Japanese mountains. Fuji is the highest and most famous mountain in Japan. It has been devoted to the worship of Kono Hana Sakuyahime no Mikogo, consort of Ninigi no Mikoto. Ninigi is the grandson of the central Shinto deity, the Sun Goddess Amaterasu o Mikami, and the grandfather of Jimmu Tenno, the legendary first Japanese emperor. A small shrine stands on the edge of Fuji's crater, and large shrines are located around its base. Every summer, thousands of Japanese make a pilgrimage to climb Mount Fuji. Mount Nantai near Nikko is another famous sacred mountain. Its main shrine, Futarasan Shrine, is in Nikko near Toshogu Shrine; the Inner Shrine is at the peak

and an intermediate shrine is located near Lake Chuzenji. The mountain is ascended by thousands of worshipers during its festival every August. Enryakuji, one of the most important Buddhist temples in Japan, was built on Mount Hiei in northeast Kyoto. Other sacred mountains include Mount Koya, Mount Omine and Mount Takesan. A special type of mountain religion combining Shinto and Buddhist practices developed, known as Shugen-do, which emphasizes pilgrimages to sacred mountains and ascetic retreats on the mountains. Its priests are male shamans who are called yamabushi, mountain ascetics. Women were forbidden on sacred mountains in Japan until the late 19th century. Western-style mountain climbing was introduced into Japan at that time and has become very popular. Japanese gardens often contain miniature mountains or include views of neighboring mountains. See also ASO, MOUNT; BUDDHISM; FUJI, MOUNT; GARDENS; GEOGRAPHY OF JAPAN; HIEI, MOUNT; JAPAN ALPS; KAGOSHIMA; KAMI; KOYA, MOUNT; NATIONAL PARKS; PILGRIMAGE; SHAMANS AND SHAMANISM; SHINTO; SHRINES, SHINTO; TEMPLES, BUDDHIST; VOLCANO.

MOUSE See RAT AND MOUSE.

MOVIES See FILMS.

MULBERRY BUSH (kozo) Also known as the paper mulberry; used to produce handmade paper (washi) sometimes erroneously called rice paper, clothing and stencils (katagami) for dyeing textiles. The leaves of one type of mulberry known as kuwa are used to feed silkworms. Paper made from the paper mulberry tree is durable and water resistant, and is used for making woodblock prints (ukiyo-e). It is also pasted on shoji (sliding opaque window screens) and sliding panels (fusuma) in traditional homes.

Until cotton was cultivated in Japan in the 15th century, commoners wore clothing made of mulberry fiber, or kozo, which is made by a time-consuming process that entails stripping the tough bark and beating it to bring out the long thin fibers. Most of the kozo used for fiber production in Japan today is grown in Kochi Prefecture on Shikoku Island, and in Tochigi Prefecture.

Some small communities of papermakers still grow and strip their own kozo trees. Kozo bark is harvested in November and December after the leaves fall from the trees. The sticks are steamed to soften them and make it easier to strip the black and green outer layers of bark from the inner white fiber. After they are stripped, the fibers are loosened by being gently beaten with wooden mallets. The fibers are then hung on bamboo racks to dry. Finally, the kozo fibers are cooked and washed to make paper or textiles. See also CLOTHING; PAPER, HANDMADE; SCREENS; SHOJI; TEXTILES.

MUNAKATA SHIKO (1903–1975) A woodblock print artist whose work has been exhibited widely in North America and Europe as well as Japan. Munakata was born to a large, poor family. Though he received only an elementary school education, he learned to draw and studied Western art on his own. He moved to Tokyo in 1924 to become an oil painter. In 1982 he began studying the art of woodblock prints with the famous printmaker Hiratsuka Un'ichi. By the 1930s Munakata was himself an established printmaker, and his works were shown in many Japanese exhibitions. In this decade he became friendly with members of the *mingei* (folk craft) movement, such as the potter Hamada Shoji and the collector and critic Yanagi Soetsu, who founded the Japan Folkcraft Museum (Nihon Mingeikan). During World War II Munakata's home and woodblocks were destroyed in a bombing raid. However, he was never deterred from creating prints, paintings, scrolls and illustrated books at a rapid pace. He drew his inspiration from many sources, including traditional Japanese screen paintings and ink paintings, *mingei,* and Western artists, such as Toulouse-Lautrec, Matisse, Van Gogh, and German expressionists. The ceremonies and beliefs of the Shinto and Buddhist religions were very meaningful for him. Munakata's work has a dynamic and intense quality. He created strong designs, many in bold black lines on white paper. Among his greatest works are the series, *Ten Disciples of the Buddha* (*Shaka ju dai deshi;* 1939) and 12 prints of the Buddhist deity Kannon (*Avalokitesvara;* 1949). Munakata's prints are found in art collections around the world. The numerous Japanese and international awards he received include the Grand Prix, Venice Biennale (1956) and the Japanese Order of Culture (1970). See also BUDDHISM; HAMADA SHOJI; MINGEI; SCREENS; SCROLLS; SHINTO; WOODBLOCK PRINTS; YANAGI SOETSU.

MURASAKI SHIKIBU (c. A.D. 1000) The most highly regarded fiction writer in Japanese history and the author of *The Tale of Genji* (*Genji Monogatari),* considered the earliest novel in the world and Japan's most important work of classical fiction. Lady Murasaki, as she was known, is also credited with *The Diary of Murasaki Shikibu* (*Murasaki Shikibu nikki)* and a collection of 123 poems entitled *Murasaki Shikibu shu.* She was probably born in the A.D. 970s; her parents were related to the influential Fujiwara clan. Her father, a well-known writer, held several government positions in the capital city of Kyoto and was then named governor, first of Echizen Province and then of Echigo Province to the north of Kyoto. Lady Murasaki learned the Chinese language, very unusual for a woman of her time, by attending her brother Nobunori's Chinese lessons. She was married to Fujiwara no Nobutaka, a soldier in the imperial guard, between 994 and 998, and had at least one daughter before he died in A.D. 1001. By A.D. 1008 she was a lady-in-waiting to her relative Empress Akiko (Fujiwara no Shoshi).

Copies of *The Tale of Genji* were circulated among members of the court. The book narrates events in the life of the "Shining Prince," Genji, especially his love affairs, and provides information about court life during the Heian Era (794–1185). The name Murasaki, which means "purple," is the name of Genji's greatest love. It became applied to Lady Murasaki, whose real name was To no Shikibu, in the late Heian Era. Nothing is known of Lady Murasaki's later life, except for an entry in a court member's diary A.D. 1013 that notes that she was still serving Empress Akiko. A grave in Kyoto is claimed to be that of Lady Murasaki. She is often compared with another Heian writer, Sei Shonagon, but Murasaki's exceptional novel about Genji gives her a unique place, not only in Japanese, but in world literature. There are several English translations of *The Tale of Genji,* most notably those by Arthur Waley and Edward Seidensticker. See also DIARIES; GENJI, THE TALE OF; HEIAN ERA; KYOTO; NOVELS; SEI SHONAGON; WALEY, ARTHUR.

MUROMACHI ERA (1333–1568) A period in Japanese history that coincided with the military government, or *bakufu,* of the Ashikaga Shogunate (1338–1573; also known as the Muromachi Shogunate). The name Muromachi is taken from a district in the old capital city of Kyoto where the palace and administrative headquarters of the Ashikaga shoguns were located. Scholars assign different dates to the Muromachi Era but generally consider it to have begun with the defeat of the military government of the Kamakura Shogunate (1192–1333) by a rebellion under Emperor Go-Daigo (1288–1339) and Ashikaga Takauji (1305–1358). This is termed the Kemmu Restoration. Three years later, Takauji took control of Kyoto and founded the Ashikaga Shogunate (1338–1573). The first half of the Muromachi Era is also known as the era of Southern and Northern Courts (Nambokucho), when in 1336 Go-Daigo and his family fled south of Kyoto and established an imperial court that challenged the northern court in Kyoto controlled by the Ashikaga Shogunate. This was the last time until the Meiji Restoration of 1868 that the imperial court took an active part in governing Japan. However, Ashikaga Yoshimitsu (1358–1408) ended the southern imperial line in 1392.

The Ashikaga shoguns supported the Zen Buddhist religion that was introduced from China in the 13th century and that had an enormous impact on Japanese culture. They also patronized art forms that flourished during this time, such as Noh drama, flower arrangement *(ikebana),* the tea ceremony *(chanoyu),* linked-verse poetry known as *renga,* and ink painting *(sumi-e).* The Muromachi Era was a time of great cultural activity, expansion of military power, social unrest and regional warfare between local *daimyo* (feudal warlords) and their samurai armies. The Onin War (1467–1477) between the son and brother of the eighth Ashikaga shogun, Yoshimasa, destroyed Kyoto and virtually ended the power of the Ashikaga *Bakufu.* It was followed by a century of warfare in Japan, known as the Warring States (Sengoku) Era. The Muromachi Era came to a close when the great warlord Oda Nobunaga (1534–1582) entered Kyoto in 1568 and initiated the process of unifying Japan. See also ASHAKIGA SHOGUNATE; ASHIKAGA TAKAUJI; ASHIKAGA YOSHIMASA; ASHIKAGA YOSHIMITSU; BAKUFU; DAIMYO; EMPEROR; FEUDALISM; FLOWER ARRANGING; GO-DAIGO, EMPEROR; INK PAINTING; KYOGEN; NAMBOKUCHO ERA; NOH DRAMA; ODA NOBUNAGA; ONIN WAR; RENGA; SAMURAI; SENGOKU ERA; SHOGUN; TEA CEREMONY; ZEN SECT OF BUDDHISM.

MUSASHI, PLAIN OF A large, flat area of land to the north, south and east of Tokyo. One of the few large, open areas in mostly mountainous Japan, this region includes metropolitan Tokyo and Saitama and eastern Kanagawa prefectures. It was organized as Musashi Province (Musashi no Kuni; also known as Bushu) in A.D. 646 during the Taika Reform of 645–649 and was administered by the Yamato Court on western Honshu Island. In the Heian Era (794–1185), the province was divided up into large private estates (shoen) owned by families of court nobles who had been sent to govern Musashi. Starting in the 10th century A.D., local clans formed their own warrior bands (bushidan), which became known as the Seven Bands of Musashi (Musashi Shichito) Their lord-vassal relationship marked the origin of a feudal system that would dominate Japan from the late 12th through the 16th centuries. The clans who controlled the Seven Bands of Musashi eventually became vassals of the powerful Minamoto clan. The Minamoto defeated the Taira (or Heike) clan and founded the Kamakura Shogunate (1192–1333), initiating seven centuries of military rule in Japan. Musashi Province was later administered by the Uesugi and Hojo clans until the warlord Toyotomi Hideyoshi (1536–1598) took control of the region in 1590. The shogun Tokugawa Ieyasu (1543–1616), founder of the Tokugawa Shogunate (1603–1867), moved the capital of Japan from Kyoto on western Honshu to the new city of Edo (modern Tokyo) in Musashi Province. Musashi became the political, cultural and economic center of Japan. See also CLAN; EDO ERA; FEUDALISM; MINAMOTO CLAN; TAIKA REFORM; TOKUGAWA SHOGUNATE; YAMATO.

MUSEUMS IN JAPAN (hakubutsukan) Japan has more than 2,000 museums, many of which have been built since World War II. These include national, prefectural, municipal and private museums, as well as collections held by Shinto shrines and Buddhist temples.

Since the early days of their history, the Japanese have carefully preserved as many objects of beauty or historical significance as they could, despite disasters such as earthquakes, typhoons, fires and civil wars. The Japanese did not display all their objects, but carefully wrapped them in silk, placed them in special boxes, and stored them in storehouses. This collecting impetus began in the sixth century A.D. with the introduction of Chinese civilization and the Buddhist religion and related arts.

The Shosoin (Imperial Treasure House), built in the eighth century in the old capital city of Nara, houses a priceless collection of art and other objects, such as musical instruments, textiles and written documents. Other notable treasure houses include those at Kofukuji, Horyuji, and Toshodaiji temples in Nara, and at Enryakuji on Mount Koya. Many shrine and temple collections are located in the former capital city of Kyoto and its environs.

Many great daimyo (feudal lord) families also developed large collections, some of which are now displayed in private museums. These include the Tokugawa Art Museum in Nagoya; the Eisei Bunko Foundation in Tokyo, which exhibits the Hosokawa family collection; and the Seisonkaku in Kanazawa, which exhibits the collection of Maeda Nariyasu (1811–1884) in the Maeda family villa.

Many private collections were developed following the Meiji Restoration of 1868, particularly by families who founded zaibatsu (trading companies) and by contemporary business leaders. Some examples include the Goto Art Museum, Nezu Art Museum, Suntory Art Gallery and Idemitsu Art Gallery, all in Tokyo; the Fukuoka Art Museum in Fukuoka, the Fujita Art Museum in Osaka, and the Yamato Bunkakan near Nara.

The first museum opened to the public in Japan was the Tokyo National Museum, opened in 1871 and moved to its present site in Ueno Park in 1882. There are also National Museums in Kyoto, opened to the public in 1897, and Nara, established in 1895, and a National Treasure House in Kamakura. National Museums are operated by the Agency for Cultural Affairs, a division of the Ministry of Education. Nearly every prefecture and city in Japan has one or more museums.

There are a great many Japanese museums specializing in modern or Western art; particular items such as ceramics, calligraphy, swords, arms and armor, or paper; or the works of individual artists. Archaeological museums have been built on or near major excavation sites. Japanese museums publish catalogues of their holdings and special exhibits, and some also publish regular art journals. In order to preserve objects in their collections, museums exhibit only a limited number at any one time. The finest pieces are usually put on display in the autumn. Large department stores also present seasonal exhibits in their own art galleries. See also DAIMYO; DEPARTMENT STORES; FOLK CRAFTS; FUKUOKA; HORYUJI; HOSOKAWA CLAN; KAMAKURA; KOYA, MOUNT; KYOTO; MAEDA CLAN; NARA; OSAKA; SHOSOIN; SHRINES, SHINTO; STOREHOUSE; TEMPLES, BUDDHIST; TOKYO; UENO; NAMES OF INDIVIDUAL ARTS AND CRAFTS.

MUSHROOMS (take) Mushrooms are commonly used in Japanese cooking. The best known mushroom is shiitake, which is dark brown with a thin stem and a cap that looks like an umbrella. This mushroom is easy to cultivate on farms on cut logs of the shii (golden oak) and other oak varieties. These mushrooms are in season in the spring and fall. Shiitake can also be bought dried in small packages containing 8–10 caps. They must be soaked 30 minutes or more to soften them before use in cooking. Two ways of cooking shiitake are salting and grilling them over charcoal or simmering them in broth. The enokidake mushroom grows in clusters of thin white stems with button caps. Enoki is the name for the Chinese nettle tree or hackberry, on which this variety of mushroom is easily cultivated. With a mild flavor and a crisp texture, enokidake are served in soups, one-pot dishes and salads. Matsutake, or "pine mushroom," is the most treasured of all Japanese mushrooms, as the flavorful fungus grows only in the wild under red pine trees and is available for just a few weeks in October. It has a thick stem and is eaten before the cap opens up. Lightly cooked before serving, the matsutake is often the featured ingredient of a dish. The shimeji, "oyster" or "abalone mushroom," has a thick stem and a flat gray cap and grows in clusters. The kikurage ("wood jellyfish"), is well known in dried form as a black "cloud ear" or "wood ear" mushroom. Sold in packages, it is generally used in

Chinese-style, stir-fry dishes. *Kikurage* must be soaked in water, which softens and expands them. They are then cut into small pieces for cooking. See also COOKING; PINE TREE.

MUSIC AND MUSICAL INSTRUMENTS   See BIWA; BUGAKU; BUNRAKU; DANCE, TRADITIONAL; DRUMS; FESTIVALS; FOLK SONGS; FLUTES; GAGAKU; GEISHA; KABUKI; KARAOKE; KOTO; NOH DRAMA; SHAKUHACHI; SHAMISEN; SHO; SINGING.

MUTUAL SECURITY TREATY   See SECURITY TREATY BETWEEN JAPAN AND THE UNITED STATES; YOSHIDA SHIGERU.

MYOSHINJI TEMPLE   See BELLS.

MYTHOLOGY   See AMATERASU O MIKAMI; DEMONS AND GHOSTS; EMPEROR; IMPERIAL REGALIA; IZANAGI AND IZANAMI; JIMMU TENNO; KAMI; KOJIKI; MONOGATARI; NIHON SHOKI; NINIGI NO MIKOTO; RIKKOKUSHI; SHINTO; SUSANOO NO MIKOTO; YANAGI SOETSU.

N

NABEMONO See SOUP.

NABESHIMA WARE (*nabeshima-yaki*)   A type of porcelain ware made between 1628 and 1871 in the region of Arita, Hizen Province (modern Saga Prefecture), on the southern island of Kyushu. This porcelain was named for the Nabeshima clan, who ruled the Saga domain in Hizen and who strictly controlled the kilns and secret techniques for the production of Nabeshima ware. The kiln at Iwayagawachi produced underglaze blue and white ware, and the kiln at Nangawara made blue and white and also multicolored objects.

Clan officials protected the secret techniques by moving the Nabeshima kiln and its 31 official potters to the valley of Okawachi, north of Arita, in 1695. After the pieces were fired, they were sent to Arita, where they were decorated with colored enamels in the "red-painting," or enameling, workshop run by the famous artist Imaizumi Imaemon. Red, yellow and bluish green were the predominant colors used for the vivid Nabeshima designs, which were composed mainly of flowers and other vegetation. The majority of pieces were food dishes made exclusively for use by the Nabeshima clan or for gifts to the Tokugawa Shogunate (1603–1867). Vases, storage and water containers, and incense burners were occasionally produced. Nabeshima ware made in the late 17th and early 18th centuries was the highest quality porcelain produced in Japan during the Edo Era (1600–1868). See also ARITA WARE; KILN; PORCELAIN.

NAGAKO, EMPRESS   See AKIHITO, EMPEROR; HIROHITO, EMPEROR; IMPERIAL HOUSEHOLD.

NAGAOKAKYO   See KYOTO.

NAGASAKI   With a population of half a million people, Nagasaki is located on Kyushu, the southernmost of the four main islands of Japan, and is the capital of Nagasaki Prefecture. A beautiful city built on hills rising from the harbor, Nagasaki has been a major port since it was opened to Portuguese Jesuit missionaries and traders in 1571 by the feudal lord Omura Sumitada. Chinese traders were also active in the city. In 1587 the warlord Toyotomi Hideyoshi banned Christianity and executed more than 600 Japanese Christians on Nishizaka Hill in the city. A monument and museum occupy the site today.

After the Tokugawa Shogunate (1603–1867) closed Japan to the outside world in 1639, Nagasaki was for two centuries the only city in Japan where foreign trade was permitted, and only Chinese and Dutch were allowed to trade with the Japanese. This took place on Dejima, a small man-made island in Nagasaki Bay that housed a limited number of Dutch traders. A self-governing merchant's organization, known as Nagasaki Kaisho ("Nagasaki Meeting Place"), had the legal right to control all foreign transactions in the city until 1867.

The opening of Japan and the signing of the Ansei Commercial Treaties with foreign nations in 1858 ended Nagasaki's monopoly of foreign trade, although it remained an important port. Foreigners took up residence in Nagasaki during the Meiji Era (1868–1912) after Japan was opened to the world again. Some remaining Meiji Western-style houses can be seen in Glover Garden. The best-known is the Glover Mansion, built in 1863 by Thomas Glover, an Englishman married to a Japanese woman. The home has been romantically associated with the fictional opera character Madame Butterfly. The first modern Japanese shipbuilding facility, the Nagasaki Shipyards (now a division of Mitsubishi Heavy Industries, Ltd.), was opened here in 1861. These were the largest privately owned shipyards in Japan. Because of its shipyards, port and industries, Nagasaki was targeted for the second atomic bomb, dropped by the Allied Powers on August 9, 1945.

The city was completely rebuilt after the war. Shipbuilding continues to be a major industry, and other economic activities include commercial fishing, cultured pearl cultivation, the manufacture of objects made of tortoise shell and coral, and processing of fish paste (*kamaboko*) and dried mullet roe (*karasumi*). A famous product of Nagasaki is *kasutera*, a sponge cake that was introduced by the Portuguese.

The Nagasaki Traditional Performing Arts Museum, in Glover Garden, exhibits the Chinese-style dragons and floats used in the Okunchi Festival in October. This festival is celebrated at Suwa Shrine, a Shinto shrine built by the government to promote the native Japanese religion when it was trying to eradicate Christianity. The first mansion built by the U.S. for its consul in Japan is now a museum named the 16th Mansion (Jurokuban-kan Mansion). Other attractions include the Oura Catholic Church, the Nagasaki City Museum of History and Folklore, a shrine to Confucius and the Historical Museum of China. There are also two Buddhist temples, Sofukuji and Kofukuji. The history of Nagasaki is shown in the Nagasaki Municipal Museum. While the old Dutch island of Dejima has been incorporated into the city through reclamation of land in Nagasaki Bay, exhibits on the history of Dutch trade can be seen in the Nagasaki Municipal Dejima Museum, along with a model of the island during the Edo Era (1600–1868).

The atomic bomb explosion is commemorated in Peace Park, where a demonstration is held every year on the anniversary of the bombing. A black stone pillar in the park indicates the epicenter of the explosion. The Nagasaki

International Cultural Hall has exhibits on the destruction of the city.

Nagasaki Prefecture, on the northwest coast of Kyushu Island, comprises the four peninsulas of Kita Matsuura, Nagasaki, Nishi Sonogi and Shimabara, and several groups of small off-shore islands. This area was a primary point of contact between Japan and China even in ancient times. The Jesuit missionary St. Francis Xavier landed at Hirado in 1550. He was followed by missionaries and traders from many European countries. When the Tokugawa Shogunate persecuted Christians, they rebelled in the Shimabara Uprising of 1637.

The prefecture has a mild climate. Major economic activities are commercial fishing, cultivation of pearls, edible seaweed and sweet potatoes, and shipbuilding. Coal was actively mined during the Meiji Era. There are four national parks: Genkai, Iki-Tsushima, Saikai and Unzen-Amakusa. See also ANSEI COMMERCIAL TREATIES; ATOMIC BOMB; CHRISTIANITY IN JAPAN; DEJIMA; DUTCH IN JAPAN; FISH AND FISHING INDUSTRY; FOREIGN TRADE; KYUSHU ISLAND; NATIONAL PARKS; PEARL; PORTUGUESE IN JAPAN; SEAWEED; SECLUSION, NATIONAL; SHIMABARA UPRISING; SHIPPING AND SHIPBUILDING; TOKUGAWA SHOGUNATE; TOYOTOMI HIDEYOSHI; XAVIER, ST. FRANCIS.

NAGAUTA See SHAMISEN; SINGING.

NAGINATA "Halberd"; a spear-like weapon and martial art. The halberd or *naginata* is a wooden pole 4–8 feet long with a sharp curved blade on the end that ranges from 1–3 feet in length. It is the Japanese version of the Chinese *kwanto,* or bronze halberd, that was introduced in ancient times. Starting in the Heian Era (794–1185), the *naginata* was used to train warrior-monks in Buddhist temples. From the 11th through the 15th centuries, foot soldiers used the *naginata* to wound horses and fend off the samurai who rode them. A *naginata* was swung around in a circle with the aid of centrifugal force, and cut down everything around it. The *naginata* played a prominent role in the Taira-Minamoto War (1180–1185). However, it became less important, as did the samurai sword, when firearms were introduced into Japan from the West in 1542. During the Tokugawa Shogunate (1603–1867), the *naginata* became strongly associated with women of the samurai class, although men continued to use this weapon. From the Meiji Era (1868–1912) to the present, *naginata* has been taught as a martial art; four to five years are required to learn the two dozen different combat techniques. Around half a million people in Japan and other countries study *naginata* techniques under the auspices of the All-Japan Naginata Federation. In tournaments, competitors wear the same protective equipment as do students of *kendo* (sword fencing). *Naginata* and *kendo* teach many of the same movements and *kata* (forms) for wielding the weapons. See also KENDO; MARTIAL ARTS; SWORD.

NAGOSHINA, BATTLE OF See FIREARMS, INTRODUCTION OF; ODA NOBUNAGA.

NAGOYA The fourth largest city in Japan, with a population of more than 2 million, and the capital of Aichi Prefecture. Situated in central Honshu Island on the Nobi Plain near Ise Bay, Nagoya is the economic, political and cultural center of the region between the major cities of Tokyo-Yokohama and Osaka. It is also the center of the Chukyo Industrial Zone. Industrial products include steel, chemicals, machinery, textiles and porcelain, which are exported through Nagoya's large port. Most of the commerce in Nagoya has to do with wholesaling. Noritake Co. manufactures its world-renowned porcelain in Nagoya. The city is also known as the center for cloisonne (shippo), a technique for decorating objects with colored enamels. Exhibits and demonstrations can be seen at the Shippo-Cho Industrial Hall (Shippo Sangyo Kaikan).

The main tourist attraction is Nagoya castle. The castle was rebuilt in 1959 after the five-story donjon was destroyed in World War II. A castle was built on this site by the Imagawa clan, who used it as their military base. It was then taken over by the warlord Oda Nobunaga but subsequently abandoned. The shogun Tokugawa Ieyasu, who unified Japan under the Tokugawa Shogunate (1603–1867), built a larger castle here between 1609 and 1614. His ninth son, Yoshinao, lived in the castle, and it was controlled by his descendants until the end of the Tokugawa Era. The castle now houses many historical art treasures such as paintings on screens and sliding doors. Two valuable bronze dolphins covered with gold scales were reconstructed and sit atop the castle roof. They are believed to protect the castle from fire. Nimoru garden is next to the castle. Also in Nagoya, the Tokugawa Art Museum exhibits many belongings and art objects of the Tokugawa clan, including famous scrolls that depict scenes from *The Tale of Genji.* The scrolls are shown only every five years.

Nagoya city developed around the base of the castle. However, this area was settled early in Japanese history, as evidenced by ancient tomb mounds (kofun), one of which is supposedly that of the legendary Prince Yamatotakeru, who was associated with Atsuta Shrine (Atsuta Jingu), which was originally founded in the third century and later brought prosperity to Nagoya during the 13th–16th centuries. Atsuta Shrine houses the sacred sword that is one of the three imperial regalia, Japan's most treasured objects which traditionally validate the rule of the emperor. The sword is called *Kusanagi-no-Tsurugi,* or "Grass-Mowing Sword." Many Japanese come to the shrine on pilgrimage even though the sword is not displayed. The shrine holds the Ohoho Festival every year in May. See also ATUSATA SHRINE; CASTLE; CLOISONNE; IMPERIAL REGALIA; INDUSTRIAL ZONES; ODA NOBUNAGA, TOKUGAWA IEYASU; TOMB MOUND.

NAHA A city of 300,000 people on the southern island of Okinawa; the capital of Okinawa Prefecture (formerly called the Ryukyu Islands). Okinawa Prefecture was occupied by the American military from the end of World War II until the United States returned it to Japan in 1972. Okinawa is the largest island of the Ryukyu Island chain, which has a distinct culture closer to that of Japan but influenced by China and Southeast Asia. For many centuries the kingdom of Ryukyu, with Naha as its port, conducted extensive trade with Japan, China and Southeast

Asia. Shuri, now a district of Naha, was the capital of the Ryukyu dynasty from 1429 to 1879, when Okinawa was made a prefecture of Japan. Naha was destroyed in 1945 during the Battle of Okinawa, the final battle of World War II, but a portion of Shuri Castle remains on a hill and is now part of Ryukyu University. The castle's reconstruction was completed in 1990. Shurei no Mon, the Gate of Courtesy, which was the second gate to the castle built by King Sho-Sei (1527–1555), was restored in 1958. The gate is an example of traditional Okinawan architecture, and is the symbol of Naha and the hospitality of the Okinawan people. Near the gate are remains of the castle wall, Ryutan Pond and several old shrines and temples, some of which were rebuilt after the war. Five stone gates also remain from the Buddhist Sogen Temple, which have been restored and designated a National Treasure. Naminoue-gu (Above-the-Waves Shrine), adjoined by Gokoku-ji Buddhist temple, is the site where emissaries from China and other notables were feted when they departed from Naha. The shrine is a popular gathering spot.

Several lively festivals are held in Naha throughout the year, notably Jiriuma on January 20, a parade of women dressed in colorful kimono of the pleasure quarter; Hari, dragon-boat races on May 3–4; and Naha Otsunahiki on October 10, a tug-of-war between thousands of people pulling two enormous ropes, one male and one female. The main street, Kokusai-Dori (International Street), has a large market along its eastern side on Heiwa-Dori (Heiwa Street). Behind the market lies the Tsuboya district, with many traditional workshops that produce colorful Okinawan-style pottery. Other local crafts include *bingata,* colorfully dyed textiles; lacquer ware; and a liquor called *awamori.* The Okinawa Prefectural Museum exhibits folkcrafts of the Ryukyu Islands. Numerous performances are given by traditional dance troupes. Naha has an international airport and a ferry terminal, and is the link between the main islands of Japan and the smaller Ryukyu Islands. See also LACQUER WARE; OKINAWA, BATTLE OF; OKINAWA ISLAND; OCCUPATION OF JAPAN; POTTERY; RYUKYU ISLANDS; SHRINES, SHINTO; TEMPLES, BUDDHIST; TEXTILES; WORLD WAR II.

NAKADAKE VOLCANO   See ASO, MOUNT.

NAKAJIMA AIRCRAFT CO.   See ZERO FIGHTER PLANE.

NAKAMISE STREET   See ASAKUSA.

NAKASHIMA, GEORGE (1905–)   An American woodworker of Japanese descent who is world renowned for his furniture and architectural designs based on traditional Japanese styles. Nakashima was born in 1905 in Spokane, Washington, to Japanese parents who both came from wealthy samurai families. George's mother spent six years as an attendant to an official in the imperial Japanese court before going to the United States to marry George's father, who was well-known to her own family. In 1925 George Nakashima traveled to Japan and met his relatives. After receiving architectural degrees from the University of Washington and the Massachusetts Institute of Technol-

ogy, he studied for a year in France. Then he traveled through Asia to Japan, where he worked for an architectural firm in Tokyo. Visiting shrines and temples all over Japan taught him much about the natural beauty of Japanese wooden buildings. Nakashima then went to the Sri Aurobindo Ashram, a religious community in India, to oversee the construction of a dormitory for the community's disciples. He was so impressed with the spiritual life there that he became a member for two years.

Returning to Japan just before World War II, Nakashima met his future wife, also Japanese-American, Marion Okajima, and the two went back to America. They and their newborn daughter were forced into a detention camp for Japanese-Americans in Idaho during World War II. Despite the hardships, he was able to learn traditional Japanese woodworking techniques from a carpenter also in the camp. During the war, the Nakashimas were able to leave the camp and move to New Hope, Pennsylvania, where he and several assistants set up a workshop to make wood furniture. They performed every step in furniture production themselves, starting with milling the raw lumber. Nakashima's furniture and architectural designs became famous for bringing out the inherent beauty of the various kinds of wood he worked with, using their natural forms and grains. One of his most famous commissions was for Pocantico Hills, the country home of then governor of New York Nelson A. Rockefeller. Nakashima has exhibited widely in the United States and Japan, winning many awards for craftsmanship. He has recorded his philosophy as a Japanese woodworker in the book, *The Soul of a Tree: A Woodworker's Reflection* (Kodansha, 1981). See also FURNITURE, TRADITIONAL; IMMIGRANTS, JAPANESE; TREES; WOODWORKING.

NAKASONE YASUHIRO (1918–)   Prime minister of Japan from 1982 to 1987. Nakasone was born in Gumma Prefecture. He joined the Liberal Democratic Party (Jiyu Minshuto; known as the LDP), Japan's predominant postwar political party. In 1947 he won a seat in the House of Representatives, the lower house of the Japanese Diet (Parliament), and won every election after that. (He still holds a seat in the Diet, but he was replaced as head of the fourth-ranked faction in the Liberal Democratic Party by Watanabe Michio, former chairman of the LDP Policy Research Council.) He was also appointed to a number of ministerial positions, including minister of transport in the cabinet of Sato Eisaku (1901–1975), who was prime minister from 1964 to 1972, and director-general of the Defense Agency. Nakasone was elected president of the LDP in 1982 and became the prime minister of Japan when Prime Minister Suzuki Zenko (1911–) resigned in November 1982. During his administration, Nakasone had to deal with major issues regarding international relations, economics, defense and Japan's trade surplus with the United States and other nations. Nakasone traveled to the United States in May 1983 to take part in the ninth summit meeting of the world's most industrialized nations. American President Ronald Reagan also visited Japan to meet with Nakasone in November 1983. That same year, the LDP suffered large losses in the general elections, but Nakasone managed to be reelected president of the LDP in 1984, and the LDP won a large victory in the 1986 elections. Nakasone never controlled a powerful faction in the LDP. Many Japanese accused him of being a "weathervane" who followed popular trends. He also stirred up controversy when he made an official visit to Yasukuni Shrine, a Shinto shrine dedicated to Japanese war heroes where military leaders convicted by the post-World War II war crimes trials were buried. Although Nakasone was required to retire from office when his second term as party president expired in October 1986, the LDP permitted a one-year extension of his term until October 1987. In May 1989 Nakasone was called by the Diet to testify under oath about his role in the Recruit Scandal. He had received thousands of shares of stock from the Recruit Company, but prosecutors could not directly link Nakasone to political and economic favors given to the company, and criminal charges were not brought against him. See also DIET; LIBERAL DEMOCRATIC PARTY; PRIME MINISTER; RECRUIT SCANDAL; SUZUKI ZENKO; YASUKUNI SHRINE.

NAKATOMI CLAN   One of the two most powerful families that governed the ancient Yamato imperial court. The Nakatomi clan was responsible for maintaining the shrines dedicated to the indigenous Japanese religion, which came to be known as Shinto ("Way of the Gods"), in distinction to the Buddhist religion, which was introduced from China in the sixth century A.D. Twice a year the hereditary priests of the Nakatomi clan performed the ritual of the Great Purification (*Oharai*) in which the *kami* (sacred spirits) were asked to purify the Japanese people. The Nakatomi opposed the new religion of Buddhism, which was supported by the rival Soga clan and the imperial regent Prince Shotoku (574–622). The two clans contended for nearly a century until the leader of the Nakatomi clan, Nakatomi Kamako (Kamatari; 614–669), helped Prince Naka no Oe overthrow Soga Emishi and his son Soga Iruka, who had amassed too much power in the imperial court. Kamatari assisted Prince Naka no Oe in reforming the Japanese system of government based on the Chinese mode of centralized bureaucratic administration. This change, known as the Taika Reform of 645–649 (*Taika no Kaishin*; "Great Reform"), increased the impact of Chinese and Buddhist influences on Japanese government and culture. The prince awarded Kamatari a new family name, Fujiwara ("Wisteria Field"). Fujiwara no Kamatari thus founded the Fujiwara clan, which dominated the imperial court from the ninth through 12th centuries and remained influential into the 19th century. See also CHINA AND JAPAN; BUDDHISM; FUJIWARA CLAN; PURIFICATION; SHINTO; SHOTOKU, PRINCE; SOGA CLAN; TAIKA REFORM; YAMATO COURT.

NAMBAN   Literally, "Southern Barbarian"; the term applied to Westerners, primarily Portuguese and Spaniards, who came to Japan in the 16th and 17th centuries from the Portuguese island of Macau near Hong Kong and the Spanish-dominated Philippine Islands, all of which lie south of Japan. The expression was used originally by the Chinese, who regarded all foreigners as barbarians, to refer to the people of Indochina and other countries south of China.

The Japanese originally applied the term to the people of Thailand, Indonesia, and the Philippines. Westerners from Britain and the Netherlands, who entered Japan in the early 17th century, were termed *komojin*, "red-haired men," from their fair appearance. *Namban* influences were important in Japan for a century, dating from A.D. 1543, when shipwrecked Portuguese traders appeared near Tanegashima island south of Kyushu Island and introduced Western firearms into Japan, revolutionizing the nature of Japanese warfare. The Roman Catholic Jesuit missionary St. Francis Xavier (1506–1562) landed at Kagoshima on the southern tip of Kyushu in A.D. 1549 and introduced Christianity into Japan. Some Japanese converted to the new religion, but *daimyo* (feudal lords) were mainly interested in the material culture and lucrative trading opportunities brought by the *nambanjin* ("southern barbarian people"). *Namban* trade took place through the ports of Hirado and especially Nagasaki on Kyushu. The Portuguese traded Chinese raw silk and silk cloth, Western wool, velvet and tapestries, armor, tobacco, playing cards, and other luxury items. The Japanese paid for these items primarily with silver and copper, which was refined for export in Osaka City by a technique called *nambanbuki*, "Southern Barbarian refining," which the Japanese learned from the Portuguese. Many Japanese terms that are still used for various textiles, foods and so forth were adapted from the Portuguese language, such as *tempura*. *Namban* art was produced by the Japanese to depict European ships and traders on folding screens (*byobu*), mostly by painters of the Kano school. In the narrow sense, *namban* art refers to paintings that were done in the Western style by Japanese artists. Jesuits also brought Christian paintings to decorate their churches, although most were destroyed in the anti-Christian persecutions during the late 16th and early 17th centuries. A Jesuit church built in Kyoto in 1576 was known as the Nambanji, or Southern Barbarian Temple. *Namban* design motifs such as crosses were also used on tea bowls, sword guards and lacquer boxes. The Tokugawa Shogunate decided that *namban* missionaries and traders threatened its authority in Japan, and by 1638 it had expelled all Spaniards and Portuguese and banned Christianity in Japan. For more than two centuries after that, only Dutch traders (who were not Roman Catholics) were permitted to trade with Japan, and they were confined to the tiny island of Dejima in Nagasaki. See also CHRISTIANITY IN JAPAN; DEJIMA; DUTCH IN JAPAN; FIREARMS, INTRODUCTION OF; KANO SCHOOL OF PAINTING; KYUSHU ISLAND; NAGASAKI; PORTUGUESE IN JAPAN; SCREENS; TOKUGAWA SHOGUNATE; XAVIER, ST. FRANCIS.

NAMBOKUCHO ERA   (1336–1392) "Southern and Northern Courts; a period in Japanese history, also known as the Northern and Southern Courts Era, when there were two rival imperial courts. This division began in the 13th century when competition for the imperial throne arose between descendants of Emperor Go-Fukakusa (r. 1246–1260), known as the Jimyoin, or senior line, and descendants of his younger brother, Emperor Kame-yama (r. 1260–1274), known as the Daikakuji, or junior line. The Kamakura Shogunate (1192–1333) temporarily resolved the dispute by forcing the lines to alternate in placing emperors on the throne. However, Emperor Go-Daigo (r. 1318–1339), a member of the junior line, decided not only to make his own line the sole successors, but also attempted to overthrow the Kamakura Shogunate and restore imperial power in the capital city of Kyoto. In 1333 the successful Go-Daigo instituted the so-called Kemmu Restoration (Kemmu no Chuko; 1333–1336) of imperial rule with the help of several military factions. However, the warrior Ashikaga Takauji (1305–1358), who had supported Go-Daigo, turned against him in 1336, forcing Go-Daigo to abdicate, and placed a member of the rival senior line on the throne as Emperor Komyo (r. 1336–1348). Go-Daigo fled to the mountains of Yoshino (in modern Nara Prefecture), where he established a southern court rivaling the northern court that remained the Ashikaga Shogunate's puppet in Kyoto. After nearly 60 years of schism and civil war, the third Ashikaga shogun, Yoshimitsu (1358–1408), convinced the southern emperor Go-Kameyama (Go-Daigo's grandson; r. 1383–1392) to return to Kyoto. Under the Shogun's compromise, the northern emperor Go-Komatsu (r. 1382–1412) would reign as sole emperor, with succeeding emperors chosen alternately from the southern and northern lines. However, this promise was never kept, and the southern imperial line disappeared. During the Nambokucho Era, the court aristocracy in Kyoto lost its traditional rights of land ownership under the landed-estate (shoen) system, and the military rulers controlling the Japanese provinces increased their power.

The rival claims of the southern and northern courts became an issue in later eras of Japanese history. Pro-imperial scholars in the Edo Era (1601–1868) and militarists in the 1930s denounced Ashikaga Takauji as a traitor. Even after World War II, a merchant in Nagoya City named Kumazawa Hiromichi (1889–1966) unsuccessfully pressed his claim with Occupation authorities that he should be recognized as emperor because he was a descendant of the southern court. The fact that Japanese emperors from the Nambokucho Era to the present have been descendants of the northern rather than the southern line diminishes their traditional claim to divinity based on their unbroken decent from the Sun Goddess Amaterasu o Mikami. See also AMATERASU O MIKAMI; ASHIKAGA SHOGUNATE; ASHIKAGA TAKAUJI; ASHIKAGA YOSHIMITSU; EMPEROR; GO-DAIGO, EMPEROR; KAMAKURA SHOGUNATE; KYOTO; LANDED-ESTATE SYSTEM.

NAME CARD   See MEISHI.

NAMES, JAPANESE   Japanese names are written with the family name first, followed by the given name. In formal relationships, a person is addressed by his or her family name with the honorary suffix -san (standing for Master, Mister, Ms., or Mrs.) to show respect; for example, Suzuki-san. Family members and close friends may use the more intimate suffix -chan with the personal name; for example, Midori-chan. Children are given names that are carefully chosen to have auspicious meanings and positive connotations. Names may also be chosen because they are written with a specific number of brush strokes in the Chinese

characters used for their names. Brothers are often given names that indicate their birth order (first son, second son, etc.). Many girls are given names that are written with characters for flowers or beauty. Girls' names often end in -ko, meaning "child" or "little one." For example, the name Hanako means "flower child." Husbands and wives respectfully address each other not with their given names but with other terms such as "father" and "mother." Until the law was changed in 1976, a divorced woman was required to give up her husband's family name and return to using her own maiden name, even though her children continued to bear the husband's name. The same was true for mukoyoshi, men "adopted" into their wives' families and bearing their wives' family names, a common practice in Japan. Japanese law still requires both spouses to use the same family name.

In ancient Japan, only nobles and members of military families had family names, while commoners were known only by their personal names or terms that indicated the places they inhabited or their ways of making a living. In 1870 the Meiji government permitted all Japanese to take a family name. Some of the most common family names in modern Japan are Sato, Suzuki, Tanaka, Yamamoto, Watanabe and Kobayashi.

A reigning emperor is never referred to by his personal name, but by the phrase tenno heika, or reigning emperor. After his death, he is known by the name of his reign. For example, Emperor Hirohito (1901–1989), as he was called earlier, is now referred to as Emperor Showa ("Enlightenment and Harmony"). Sons and daughters born to an emperor are given names ending in -hito and -hime to indicate their royal descent. Japanese can have several names or titles during their lives.

Before the 20th century, upper-class men were first given birth names, and then coming-of-age names when they were teenagers. Literary or artistic names have been commonly used, and it can be confusing to trace the career of an artist such as Hokusai (1760–1849), who used 30 artistic names during his lifetime. A person who masters a traditional art such as the tea ceremony can be given an "art name" in a special ceremony. Such a name may be passed on to succeeding generations, such as the name of the Kabuki actor Kokugoro VI. A person who dies is given a kaimyo, or posthumous Buddhist name for the spirit of the dead, which is engraved on the tombstone. See also FAMILY; HOUSEHOLD REGISTER; MEISHI; -SAN.

NANJING (NANKING)   See CHINA AND JAPAN; SINO-JAPANESE WAR OF 1937–1945; WORLD WAR II.

NANSEI ISLANDS   See RYUKYU ISLANDS.

NANZENJI   An important temple in the old capital city of Kyoto belonging to the Rinzai branch of the Zen sect of Buddhism. The original building was the residence of the retired Emperor Kameyama, who converted it into a Zen temple. Nanzenji prospered because of its connections to the imperial court. In 1334 Emperor Go-Daigo designated Nanzenji number one among the Gozan ("Five Temples"), the most important Buddhist temples in Japan. It was awarded even higher status above the Gozan in 1386 by the Shogun Ashikaga Yoshimitsu (1358–1408). Warrior-monks from the rival temple Enryakuji destroyed much of Nanzenji in 1393. After it was rebuilt by Shogun Ashikaga Yoshimochi (1386–1428), fires again destroyed Nanzenji in 1447 and 1467. In the late 16th and 17th centuries, the temple enjoyed the patronage of the imperial court, the great warlord Toyotomi Hideyoshi and the Tokugawa shoguns, and most of the buildings surviving at Nanzenji today date from that time. The temple compound formerly contained around 100 *tatchu*, or sub-temples, of which about a dozen remain. The sub-temple Nanzen'in serves as the mausoleum of Emperor Kameyama (1249–1305) and has one of the most important gardens in Kyoto. The large and small living quarters for the abbot of Nanzenji (*daihojo* and *shohojo*) are National Treasures. Nanzenji owns a large collection of important art works, such as ink paintings (*sumi-e*) and painted screens and murals. See also ENRYAKUJI; NATIONAL TREASURES; PAINTING; RINZAI SECT OF ZEN BUDDHISM; TEMPLES, BUDDHIST; ZEN SECT OF BUDDHISM.

NARA   A city on western Honshu Island that was the capital of Japan from A.D. 710 to 794, known as the Nara Era. In ancient Japan, the imperial court moved to a different location on the succession of a new emperor. Nara was constructed in the Nara Basin, or Yamato Basin, when the imperial court moved from Fujiwarakyo, the capital from 694 to 710. Nara was carefully laid out on a grid after the city of Chang'an (Ch'ang'an; modern Xian or Sian), the capital of China during the Tang (T'ang) dynasty (618–906). The introduction of Chinese civilization into Japan, beginning in the sixth century A.D., led to the first great flowering of Japanese culture during the Nara Era.

Heijokyo (the original name for Nara) extended 3 miles from north to south and 2.7 miles from east to west, with streets laid out in a checkerboard pattern. The Heijo Imperial Palace was located in the north-central part of the city, and from there a wide boulevard extended to the main entrance gate in the south. Kasuga, a Shinto shrine, and Kofukuji and Todaiji, Buddhist temples, were constructed in the eastern part of Nara. The Shosoin (Imperial Treasure House) was also built on the grounds of Todaiji. Buddhism was promoted by the Japanese imperial court in Nara as a way of unifying the country under its rule.

In A.D. 784 the capital was transferred to Nagaokakyo; in 794 it moved to Heiankyo, and Nara declined, although its temples remained powerful during the Heian Era (794–1185). The city was attacked by the Taira clan in A.D. 1180 but recovered during the Kamakura Era (1192–1333). Today more than a million tourists visit Nara each year to see the origins of Japanese civilization at Kasuga Shrine, Kofukuji, Todaiji, the Nara National Museum and other sites. The seventh-century A.D. Horyuji lies 12 miles to the southwest. Nara Park, the largest municipal park in Japan, has many tame sacred deer. On January 15th the Grass Burning (Yama Yaki) Festival on Wakakusayama Hill is held, in which surrounding hillsides are burned for an hour to purify the Buddhist temples of Nara. Other religious festivals are held throughout the year. Modern Nara is the capital of Nara Prefecture and has a population of 300,000. Local crafts include production of brushes and Chinese ink (*sumi*) for calligraphy, dolls, lacquer ware and fans. See also BUDDHISM; CHINA AND JAPAN; DEER; EMPEROR; HEIAN ERA; HORYUJI; KASUGA SHRINE; KOFUKUJI; NARA ERA; SHOSOIN; TODAIJI; YAMATO CLAN.

NARA ERA (710–794)   The period of Japanese history when the capital was located at the city of Nara. The imperial court modeled Nara on the Chinese Tang (T'ang) dynasty capital of Chang'an (Ch'ang'an; modern Sian or Xian). Chinese culture had been introduced into Japan in the sixth century A.D., largely through the Buddhist religion, and stimulated the original flowering of Japanese culture during the Nara Era. The court officially supported six Buddhist sects as a way of heightening its power and prestige. Chinese Buddhist art and architecture, the Chinese writing system, and the Chinese system of centralized bureaucratic government were adopted by the Japanese. Japan was divided into provinces, districts, hamlets and villages, governed by officials appointed by the emperor. All Japanese people were regarded as the emperor's subjects and expected to obey his representatives. Many Japanese missions were sent to China, and in turn many foreigners visited Japan. Todaiji (Great Eastern Temple), the world's largest wooden structure, was built to emulate the large Buddhist temples in China, and the world's largest bronze Buddhist statue, or Daibutsu, was placed inside. The Shosoin (Imperial Treasure House) was constructed on the temple's grounds to house a vast collection of art and craft items acquired from all over the world. The golden age of Buddhist art in Japan, particularly sculpture, is known as the Tempyo Era (729–794). In imitation of the Chinese interest in written historical records, the *Kojiki* and *Nihon Shoki* were compiled to provide the legendary origins of the Japanese imperial family. The great poetry anthology *Manyoshu* was also compiled during this era. The court was moved from Nara to Heiankyo (Kyoto) in A.D. 794, to sever the government from its strong Buddhist connections and because Heian provided better access to the rest of the country, among other reasons. See also BUDDHISM; CHINA AND JAPAN; DAIBUTSU; HEIANKYO; KOJIKI; MANYOSHU; NARA; NIHON SHOKI; SCULPTURE; TEMPYO ERA.

NARITA AIRPORT   See AIRLINES AND AIRPORTS; CHIBA PREFECTURE; JAPAN AIR LINES.

NARUHITO, CROWN PRINCE   See AKIHITO; CROWN PRINCE; EMPEROR.

NARUTO STRAIT (Naruto Kaikyo)   A narrow strait of water between Awaji Island (Awajishima) and Naruto City on northeastern Shikoku Island. The Naruto Strait connects the eastern Inland Sea (Seto Naikai) and the Kii Channel, which in turn links Osaka Bay with the Pacific Ocean. Naruto means "roaring gate," referring to its treacherous whirlpools caused by tidal currents; at high tide the water rushes at a speed of 12 miles an hour or more. The whirlpools, named Awa-no-Naruto, are famous in Japanese literature. Today they can be seen up close from sightseeing boats. A section of the Seto Ohashi Bridge, which was opened in 1988 to connect Honshu and Shikoku Islands, is built over the Naruto Strait. See also INLAND SEA; SHIKOKU ISLAND.

NATIONAL AEROSPACE LABORATORY See SCIENCE AND TECHNOLOGY AGENCY.

NATIONAL ANTHEM ("Kimigayo"; "His Majesty's Reign") A song praising the emperor that the Japanese consider their national anthem, even though it has never been officially designated as such. The words of "Kimigayo" come from an anonymous poem of the *waka* type included in the *Kokinshu,* a 10th-century A.D. poetry collection, and express the wish that the reign of the emperor will be happy and last for thousands of years. Over the centuries this poem was frequently performed by singers of traditional Japanese music. A 19th-century composer named Hayashi Hiromori wrote music for "Kimigayo" that was chosen by the Imperial Household Ministry to be performed for the birthday of Emperor Meiji on November 3, 1880. The song continued to be used on ceremonial occasions, and in 1893 the Ministry of Education ruled that it should be sung in all Japanese schools on national holidays. "Kimigayo" also came to be sung before sports competitions. The Japanese Diet (Parliament) has never passed a law designating the national anthem and the rising sun flag *(hinomaru)* as the official symbols of the nation. Since World War II, many Japanese have associated the national anthem and the flag with proimperial Japanese militarism that culminated in the disastrous war. The Ministry of Education designated the anthem and flag as national symbols in 1977, but the directive it issued in 1990 that schools should fly the flag and sing "Kimigayo" at entrance and graduation ceremonies has aroused widespread opposition by teachers and parents. See also EMPEROR; FLAGS AND BANNERS; KOKINSHU; MEIJI RESTORATION OF 1868; MINISTRY OF EDUCATION; WAKA.

NATIONAL DEFENSE ACADEMY See SELF-DEFENSE FORCES.

NATIONAL DEFENSE COUNCIL See CABINET, PRIME MINISTER'S; SELF-DEFENSE FORCES.

NATIONAL DIET LIBRARY See DIET.

NATIONAL MUSEUM OF WESTERN ART See MUSEUMS IN JAPAN; UENO.

NATIONAL PARKS (*kokuritsu koen*) The Environment Agency of the Office of the Prime Minister administers the 27 Japanese national parks. There are also 51 quasi-national parks (*kokutei koen*) and many prefectural parks, both types administered by the governments of prefectures. In 1873 the Japanese government established public parks (*koen*) to protect areas popular for their cherry blossoms (*sakura*) in the spring and red maple leaves (*momiji*) in the autumn;

Ueno Park in Tokyo is one example. By 1911, people were requesting the government to protect the Shinto shrines and cedar forests at Nikko. This led to the establishment of the National Parks Association of Japan in 1929. The National Parks Law was passed two years later. Between 1934 and 1936, 12 Japanese national parks were created, the first two being the Inland Sea (Seto Naikai) and the Unzen (now Unzen-Amakusa). Today the most heavily visited national parks are Fuji-Hakone-Izu, which is close to Tokyo and receives about 100 million visitors a year, and Ise-Shima, east of Kyoto on the Pacific coast, which encompasses the main shrine of Shinto. The national parks together cover about 7,600 square miles, 5½% of Japan's total land area. See also CHERRY BLOSSOM; FUJI-HAKONE-IZU NATIONAL PARK; INLAND SEA; ISE-SHIMA NATIONAL PARK; MAPLE TREE; SHINTO; SHRINES, SHINTO; UENO.

NATIONAL POLITY See KOKUTAI.

NATIONAL SCIENCE MUSEUM See MUSEUMS IN JAPAN; UENO.

NATIONAL SPACE DEVELOPMENT AGENCY See SCIENCE AND TECHNOLOGY AGENCY.

NATIONAL TREASURES (Kokuho) Historical objects or works of art that have been designated by the Japanese government as having the highest cultural and historical importance. This system of preserving valued objects was created by the Preservation of Ancient Shrines and Temples Law (Koshaji Hozon Ho) in 1897 and the Preservation of National Treasures Law (Kokuho Hozon Ho) in 1929. The need to preserve traditional Japanese culture became apparent when Japan was rapidly modernizing and adopting Western culture in the late 19th century. The preservation movement was spurred by Ernest F. Fenollosa, an American teacher in Japan, and his associate Okakura (Kakuzo) Tenshin. The Meiji government passed a law in 1871 to protect old Buddhist temples and Shinto shrines, and in 1897 it passed the Preservation Law. Many rare works of art were destroyed during World War II. In 1950 the Law for Protection of Cultural Assets (Bunkazai Hogo Ho) was passed, to preserve remaining objects. The law was revised in 1954 and 1975. It replaced the previous categories used to designate National Treasures, and added the term "Important Cultural Properties" (Juyo Bunkazai), some of which are given the greater designation of National Treasures. In addition to honoring physical objects, such as paintings, decorative objects and buildings, the new law created the category of "Intangible Cultural Assets" (Mukei Bunkazai). People who are highly skilled in traditional performing arts or crafts, such as weaving or pottery, are designated "Bearers of Important Cultural Assets." They are popularly known as "Living National Treasures" (Ningen Kokuho). The annual selection of Important Cultural Properties and National Treasures is made by the Committee for the Protection of Cultural Assets from suggestions made by the Agency for Cultural Affairs of the Japanese Ministry of Education. By 1978, more than 10,000 buildings and art objects had been designated Important Cultural Properties, with 1,000 of these designated National Treasures. The largest number of such objects are sculpture and calligraphy. By 1981 the Cultural Properties Protection Division was also preserving and administering more than 1,000 historic sites in Japan. See also FENOLLOSA, ERNEST F.; LIVING NATIONAL TREASURES; MUSEUMS IN JAPAN; OKAKURA KAKUZO.

NATIONALISM See EMPEROR; KOKUTAI; STATE SHINTO; YASUKUNI SHRINE.

NATSUME See BOXES; TEA CEREMONY.

NATSUME SOSEKI (1867–1916) Japanese novelist and literary scholar. Born Natsume Kinnosuke in Tokyo, Soseki studied classical Chinese and majored in English literature at Tokyo University. After going to England to study in 1900, Soseki took a position teaching literary criticism at Tokyo University. During the early years of his career, he wrote *haiku* and other forms of poetry, as well as literary sketches and a book on literary theory. After the critical success of his first published novel, *I Am a Cat (Wagahai wa neko de aru;* 1905, translated 1961), he concentrated on fiction.

Soseki wrote his novels and short stories during the Meiji Era (1868–1912), when Japan was rapidly transforming itself from a feudal society into a modern one, and he expressed the anxiety and loneliness many Japanese suffered while trying to cope with social change. Some other novels by Soseki that have been translated into English are *Botchan* ("Little Master"; 1906, translated as *Botchan* in 1972), *The Three-Cornered World (Kusamakura,* "Grass Pillow"; 1906, translated 1965), *Red Poppy (Gubinjinso;* 1907, translated 1918), *Sanshiro* (1908, translated as *Sanshiro* in 1977), *And Then (Sorekara;* 1909, translated 1978), *Mon* ("The Gate"; 1910, translated as *Mon* in 1972), *Kokoro* ("The Heart"; 1914, translated as *Kokoro* in 1957), *Grass on the Wayside (Michikusa;* 1915, translated 1969), *The Wayfarer (Kojin;* 1913, translated 1967) and *Light and Darkness* (1916, translated 1971). A number of like-minded writers formed a group around Soseki that later Japanese dubbed "the Soseki mountain range." Soseki died shortly before he completed *Light and Darkness (Meian;* 1916, translated 1971), about a new type of relationship between a husband and wife, which some critics regard as his greatest work. See also HAIKU; LITERATURE; MEIJI ERA; NOVELS.

NATTO See SOYBEANS.

NATURE See AGRICULTURE; CLIMATE OF JAPAN; EARTHQUAKES; FLOWERS; FORESTRY INDUSTRY; GARDENS; GEOGRAPHY OF JAPAN; KAMI; RAIN; RICE PLANTING AND HARVESTING FESTIVALS; ROCKS; SEASONS OF THE YEAR; SHINTO; SNOW; TREES; TYPHOONS; VOLCANO; WAVES.

NAVY See IMPERIAL JAPANESE ARMY AND NAVY; SELF-DEFENSE FORCES.

NCR JAPAN, LTD. See COMPUTER INDUSTRY; ELECTRONICS INDUSTRY.

NEC (NIPPON ELECTRIC CO., LTD.) See COMPUTER INDUSTRY.

NEIGHBORHOOD ASSOCIATION (*chokai*) A formal organization (*kai*) in a neighborhood (*cho*) of a Japanese city or town that provides a common identity for local residents and handles issues that directly concern them. It provides services such as waste recycling, installation of street lights and fund raising to buy a new sacred palanquin (*mikoshi*) for festivals held by the neighborhood's Shinto shrine. A neighborhood association works closely with the local shopkeeper's association (*shotenkai*) and other local groups, such as the old people's club. These local organizations enable Japanese citizens to maintain some local autonomy in the face of a highly centralized government. Neighborhood associations do not always give in to the government and will actively oppose any policies that negatively affect the neighborhood. Japanese have a high level of participation in their neighborhood associations, which are operated by male residents but have women's auxiliaries. See also PALANQUIN, SACRED; WARD.

NEMBUTSU A Buddhist invocation or prayer; an abbreviation of *Namu Amida Butsu,* meaning "Homage to [or I take refuge in] Amida Buddha." Amida (originally an Indian god whose Sanskrit name is Amitabha, "Lord of Boundless Light") is the god who presides over the Western Paradise or Pure Land, into which one who recites *nembutsu* hopes to be reborn. Amida supposedly vowed that everyone who calls on his name shall be saved.

The practice of reciting *nembutsu* became widespread in China after the Buddhist religion was introduced there from India in the first century A.D. In the ninth century A.D., when Chinese devotion to Amida was at its height, a Japanese missionary of the Tendai sect of Buddhism named Ennin (794–864) introduced Amida worship and *nembutsu* into Japan. Ennin had gone to China to study Buddhism in A.D. 838 and returned to Japan in A.D. 847. Other monks of the Tendai sect who popularized the practice of calling upon Amida for salvation were Kuya (903–972); Ryonin (1072–1132); and Genshin (942–1017), who wrote an important book on *nembutsu, Essentials of Salvation* (or *Essentials of Pure Land Rebirth, Ojoyoshu*). Whereas Genshin taught that this method of salvation is available to all people, including women and lay persons as well as men and monks, Ryonin went further and taught that if one person practices *nembutsu,* he or she accumulates enough religious merit to save all other beings. These teachings contributed to the popularization of Buddhism in Japan.

The monk Genku (1133–1212), a follower of Genshin's teachings who became known by the Buddhist name Honen Shonin, founded the Pure Land sect of Buddhism in 1175. According to Honen, any person from any social class can be reborn into the Pure Land, simply by repeating the name of Amida without having any doubt of the god's compassion. Thus faith in Amida, not good works or great learning, was considered the way to salvation. Honen's follower Shinran (1173–1263) went so far as to state that one sincere repetition of *nembutsu* is enough to guarantee one's salvation. Shinran founded the True Pure Land sect of Buddhism (Jodo Shinsu), an offshoot of the Pure Land sect. See also AMIDA; BUDDHISM; HONEN; PURE LAND SECT OF BUDDHISM; SHINRAN; TENDAI SECT OF BUDDHISM.

NEOLITHIC AGE See JOMON ERA.

NETSUKE A miniature decorative carved figure used to attach an *inro* ("seal basket"; small lacquered box) and other personal items to the *obi* (sash) of a kimono. The word *netsuke* is written with two Chinese characters meaning "root" and "to attack." A silk cord attaches the *inro* to a small sliding bead *(ojime)*, which is moved up or down to open or close the *inro* and the *netsuke*. The *netsuke* is drawn up behind the *obi* and suspended over it to hold the *inro* in place. Since kimono have no pockets, *netsuke* and *inro* were an ingenious solution to the problem of how to carry things. They were usually worn by men, as women had large sleeves in which they could carry objects. Tobacco pouches, pipe cases, money purses and small writing sets *(yatate)* were also suspended from *netsuke*. Such hanging objects were known as *sagemono*.

Netsuke and *inro* were widely used during the Edo Era (1600–1868). Their designs were influenced by the popular taste of the urban merchant class, known as *chonin* or townspeople, who grew wealthy during this time. Carved stone and ivory toggles imported from China in the 18th

An ivory *netsuke* of a man and a dog. A *netsuke* is a miniature sculpture that is used to fasten a small container known as an *inro* to the *obi* (sash) of a kimono.

century also stimulated the creation of *netsuke* in Japan. Subjects and designs seem to be infinite in number. Animals were the most popular motif, especially the 12 animals of the zodiac cycle. Other popular motifs included flowers, masks, mythical creatures, deities and human beings. A set of *netsuke* and *inro* would be designed with the same theme, since they would be used together. However, most sets have been separated over the years. *Netsuke* were occasionally made of lacquered wood, as were *inro*, but the majority were carved from hard materials such as wood, ivory, tortoise shell, porcelain, hornbill, cloisonne, animal horns and tusks, and even nuts and double gourds. After production of *netsuke* and *inro* peaked in the 19th century, it dwindled when Japanese men began wearing Western-style clothing with pockets. At the same time, *netsuke* and *inro* became valuable collector's items with Westerners because of their beautiful designs and craftsmanship. Netsuke have been made up to the present time, but as a self-conscious art form rather than as functional objects. See also EDO ERA; INRO; KIMONO; LACQUER WARE; OBI; ZODIAC.

NEW RELIGIONS *(shinko shukyo)* A general term applied to religious movements that arose in 19th- and early 20th-century Japan. These religions have not regarded themselves as new, however, but as lay movements that have developed out of old Japanese religious traditions. They have adapted elements from Japanese folk traditions, such as shamanism and ceremonies connected with rice cultivation, Shinto, the indigenous Japanese religion, Buddhism, the religion introduced into Japan from China in the sixth century A.D., Confucianism and Taoism, also introduced from China, and Christianity, introduced from the West in the 16th century A.D. The new religions have all been founded by a living man or woman with charismatic qualities that made him or her seem divine to followers. These religions have claimed that believers could find answers to all of their problems through faith and worship. Faith healing is a common aspect of new religions. Many of them, especially Soka Gakkai ("Value-Creating Society") also emphasize faith in a Buddhist scripture known as the *Lotus Sutra* and the chanting of its title: *Namu myoho renge kyo*, as taught by the Japanese Buddhist leader Nichiren (1222–1282). The new religions' emphasis on personal faith contrasts with that of the established Japanese religions *(kisei shukyo)*, to which members belonged because of family tradition or neighborhood connections. The new religions appealed to poor farmers, urban laborers and other people of the lower classes who had suffered during the rapid modernization and social changes in Japan during the Meiji Era (1868–1912). The religions also became a powerful social force following Japan's defeat in World War II. In 1951, many new religions cooperated to form the Union of New Religious Organizations of Japan (Shin Nihon Shukyo Dantai Rengokai). The most important of the new religions include Oomoto, Tenrikyo, and Soka Gakkai, which has an affiliated political party, the Clean Government Party (Komeito). See also BUDDHISM; CLEAN GOVERNMENT PARTY; LOTUS SUTRA; MEIJI ERA; NICHIREN; OOMOTO; TENRIKYO; SHAMANS AND SHAMANISM; SHINTO; SOKA GAKKAI.

NEW TOKYO INTERNATIONAL AIRPORT (Narita) See AIRLINES AND AIRPORTS; CHIBA PREFECTURE; JAPAN AIR LINES.

NEW YEAR FESTIVAL (Shogatsu) The largest and most important annual holiday in Japan. Since it has a religious dimension, it is comparable to Christmas in America. New Year's Day (ganjitsu or gantan) is celebrated on January 1st. Most business and schools close on January 2nd and 3rd as well, so people can travel to their hometowns and spend three days celebrating with their families. In earlier times the holiday lasted even longer.

Many traditional customs are associated with the New Year as a time of purification and renewal. Hatsumode is the first visit to a Shinto shrine or Buddhist temple in the New Year. Many Japanese arrive at temples just before midnight to hear the bells ring 108 times (joya no kane) to dispel evil spirits of the old year and welcome in the new year. They pray for health and happiness in the year ahead, and buy good-luck amulets, lucky fortunes written on slips of paper, and sacred arrows. Many women wear beautiful kimono on this occasion. In Tokyo, Meiji Shrine is the most popular shrine for hatsumode. Hundreds of thousands of Japanese also visit Ise, the most important Shinto shrine, during the first week of the New Year.

The Japanese thoroughly clean their homes in late December to welcome the toshigami, the deity of the New Year. Entrances to some homes are still decorated with kadomatsu, or decorations of pine, plum and bamboo branches that symbolize longevity and prosperity. Straw ropes known as shimenawa, hung with white paper strips or shide, mark the temporary dwelling of the toshigami and keep evil spirits out.

Family members celebrate together on the first day of the New Year. They drink sweet spiced sake known as toso, and enjoy special New Year's food (osechi-ryori), that is prepared ahead of time, including fish cakes (kamaboko), shrimp, vegetables and a soup known as zoni, which contains mochi (pounded glutinous rice cakes). Special altars known as toshidana ("year shelf") are placed in tokonoma (alcoves) of Japanese homes, on which are displayed New Year's foods to honor the toshigami, including large, round rice cakes known as kagami (mirror) mochi, citrus fruit called daidai and bottles of sake; shida, or fern leaves, are also displayed as offerings to the toshigami. Such New Year's items are bought at special year-end fairs (toshi no ichi): Girls dressed in kimono play hanetsuki, a traditional game similar to badminton, in which they hit a shuttlecock back and forth with paddles known as hago-ita. Bought at special fairs held before the New Year Festival, hago-ita are decorated with paintings, mainly of famous Kabuki actors. Boys fly kites (tako) decorated with pictures of samurai or comic book characters. Other popular games at the New Year are spinning tops (koma) and card games (karuta) in which poems or pictures of flowers are matched. Children are given otoshidama, gifts of money in special red envelopes, by their parents and relatives. The Japanese send New Year's postcards (nengajo) to friends, relatives, business associates and old school friends. Cards posted between

A girl dressed in traditional kimono and hairstyle for the New Year Festival, the most important holiday in Japan.

the middle and end of December are held by the post office until New Year's morning, when they are delivered all at once by students hired as temporary mailmen. The Japanese government makes a large annual profit from the sale of nenga hagaki, New Year's cards printed with lottery numbers. Winning numbers are announced on January 16th. On January 2nd, the first calligraphy of the New Year (kakizome), is usually performed, and the Japanese write poems or New Year's sayings or resolutions with brushes and black ink on paper scrolls. Many schools hold kakizome contests. On this day, friends and business associates visit each other, drink sweet spiced wine, express gratitude for favors done during the previous year and create good will for the new year. The inner grounds of the Imperial Palace in Tokyo are opened to the public on January 2nd, only one of two days each year, the second being the emperor's birthday. The Japanese believe that dreams during the night of January 2nd–3rd, called hatsuyume ("first dream"), are likely to come true. Some Japanese place pictures of the legendary "treasure ship" (takarabune) of the Seven Gods of Good Fortune under their pillows to ensure auspicious dreams.

Many other activities traditionally begin again on the 2nd, 4th, or 11th, such as sewing, fishing and using a hoe to till the fields. On January 6th, firemen throughout Japan hold parades and perform acrobatic stunts on high bamboo ladders to show their agility and skill. This traditional event, known as Dezomeshiki, has taken place since the Edo Era (1600–1868). New Year decorations are taken down and burned on January 7th or 11th, depending on the region of the country. January 16th is a traditional holiday known as *yabuiri*, when apprentices, daughters-in-law and servants visited their parents.

All the above activities celebrated Oshogatsu, "Big New Year," according to the Gregorian calendar, which Japan adopted in 1873. There is also a "Small New Year," Koshogatsu, celebrated according to the traditional lunar calendar. It begins with the first full moon, which falls around January 15th, and is mainly observed in rural areas to ensure a good harvest in the new year. According to the ancient lunar calendar, New Year's Day falls on a day in early February and is the traditional beginning of spring, or Risshun. This day is preceeded by the Bean-Throwing Festival, or Setsubun, which is still celebrated in Japan with the tossing of soybeans to drive away evil spirits and welcome good fortune. See also AMULETS; BAMBOO; BEAN-THROWING FESTIVAL; BELLS; CALENDAR; CALLIGRAPHY; CARD GAMES; FIRE FIGHTING; FISH PASTE AND FISH CAKES; ISE SHRINE; KIMONO; KITES; MEIJI SHRINE; MOCHI; PINE TREE; PLUM TREE; PURIFICATION; SAKE; SEVEN GODS OF GOOD FORTUNE; SHINTO; SHRINE, SHINTO; STRAW WARE; TEMPLES, BUDDHIST; TOKONOMA.

NEWSPAPERS (*shimbun*) There are more than 120 daily newspapers in Japan, with a combined circulation of more than 65 million. Newspapers have morning editions, evening editions or both. They are sold at newsstands and bookstores and by home or office subscription. The average Japanese household subscribes to one or two daily newspapers. Rival companies actively compete for subscribers, and salesmen often visit homes with premiums such as hand towels to try to persuade readers to change their newspapers. The five national Japanese-language dailies are the more progressive *Asahi Shimbun* and *Mainichi Shimbun*; the more conservative *Yomiuri Shimbun* and *Sankei Shimbun*; and the economic paper *Nihon Keizai*. These five account for half of total newspaper circulation. Every prefecture also has from one to six local dailies. There are local and regional papers as well, such as the *Hokkaido Shimbun*, and 11 sports papers. Many other newspapers are published on a daily, weekly or monthly basis on special-interest topics, such as economics, trade, political parties, labor unions, manufacturing, books, and concerns of women, children or students. There are also English-language newspapers with a total daily circulation of more than 125,000. The largest is *The Japan Times*, which is published only in English. The large Japanese companies also put out English-language editions: the *Asahi Evening News*, the *Mainichi Daily News*, the *Daily Yomiuri* and the weekly *Japan Economic Journal*. Two major news agencies created after World War II, Kyodo News Service and Jiji Press, maintain extensive news-gathering operations around the world. Many smaller news agencies distribute news on specialized topics, and the Radio Press (RP) translates news from

foreign short-wave broadcasts. See also BROADCASTING SYSTEM; BOOKS AND BOOKSTORES; MAGAZINES.

NHK See JAPAN BROADCASTING CORPORATION.

NICHIREN (1222–1282) One of the most important figures in Japanese history and religion; a Buddhist monk who founded the Nichiren sect of Buddhism, also known as the Hokke or Lotus sect.

Nichiren was born in a fishing village in Awa Province (part of modern Chiba Prefecture). He entered a nearby Buddhist temple when he was 12 and was ordained as a monk when he was 16. Nichiren studied at the headquarters of the Tendai sect of Buddhism on Mount Hiei. The basic scripture of Tendai was the *Lotus Sutra,* and Nichiren came to believe that faith in this scripture was the only way to achieve salvation. He also subscribed to the theory of *mappo*, "the latter days of the Buddhist law," to explain the widespread suffering in Japan, caused by military dictatorship and a series of national disasters. According to *mappo*, the suffering was the result of the spread of false teachings by the Buddhist sects in Japan, which Nichiren denounced as heretical. He directed his strongest criticism toward the Pure Land Sect of Buddhism, which taught salvation by faith in Amida Buddha. Nichiren proclaimed that ultimate truth could be found only in the *Lotus Sutra*. People could not save themselves but needed to be rescued through faith in true Buddhist teachings. It was not necessary even to read the *Lotus Sutra*. Believers simply had to recite a formula (similar to the *nembutsu* chant of the Pure Land Sect), "Praise to the Wonderful Law of the *Lotus Sutra*" (*Namu myoho renge kyo*). Nichiren often beat a drum to accompany his chanting.

Nichiren's public denunciation of the Zen and Pure Land sects of Buddhism in 1253 led to his expulsion from Awa Province. He moved south to Kamakura, the headquarters of the military government, (*bakufu*) with whom he was frequently at odds over their support for heretical Buddhist sects. Nichiren was convinced that the age of *mappo* would end shortly and a new Buddhist era would begin, with Japan at the center. The characters in Nichiren's name stand for sun (*nichi*), and lotus (*ren*); the latter represents the *Lotus Sutra*, and the former represents the "Light of Truth" and the "Land of the Rising Sun," Japan. His *Treatise on the Establishment of the Legitimate Teaching for the Security of the Country (Rissho ankoku ron;* 1260) expressed his political as well as religious concerns and his strong sense of Japanese nationalism.

The *bakufu* exiled Nichiren from Kamakura in 1257 until 1263. When the Mongols were threatening to invade Japan, Nichiren's criticism of the government caused him to be tried for treason in 1271. He barely escaped execution and was exiled again, to Sado Island in the Sea of Japan, off Japan's west coast. While there he wrote several more religious texts.

In 1274, Nichiren was allowed to return to Kamakura, where he claimed that Japan could escape disaster only if the country converted to his religious teaching. When this did not happen, Nichiren retired from Kamakura to live in a hermitage in the mountains. Events in Japan, including two attempted invasions by the Mongols, proved his predictions about imminent disaster to be correct.

The *Lotus Sutra* remained for Nichiren the only true expression of religious truth. He was a scholar and moral leader as well as an outspoken religious fanatic. He gained many followers among the lower ranks of the samurai class. Nichiren Buddhism, the only major Japanese Buddhist sect founded in Japan rather than being introduced from China, prospered despite oppression and has been enjoying a revival since World War II. See also AMIDA BUDDHA; BAKUFU; BUDDHISM; EXILE; HIEI, MOUNT; HOJO CLAN; KAMAKURA; LOTUS SUTRA; NICHIREN SECT OF BUDDHISM; PURE LAND SECT OF BUDDHISM; SAMURAI; ZEN SECT OF BUDDHISM.

NICHIREN SECT OF BUDDHISM

Also known as the Hokke or Lotus Sect; founded by the great religious leader Nichiren (1222–1282). Nichiren taught that individual salvation, and the salvation of Japan, could be attained only through faith in one Buddhist scripture, the *Lotus Sutra.* Believers must chant the phrase, "Praise to the Wonderful Law of the *Lotus Sutra (Namu myoho renge kyo;* abbreviated as *Hokkekyo).* After Nichiren's death, three sect leaders carried on his preaching: Nichiji (1250–?), who preached to the Ainu people on the northern island of Hokkaido, and perhaps in Siberia; Nisshin (1407–1488), who went to the southern island of Kyushu and then to the capital city of Kyoto on western Honshu Island; and Nichiro (1565–1630), who was exiled after he denounced the warlords Toyotomi Hideyoshi (1536–1598) and Tokugawa Ieyasu (1543–1616) for not following Nichiren. The lack of a central leader after Nichiren's death caused many divisions within the Nichiren sect, yet it was successful in attracting converts. In 1469, when about half the population of the capital city of Kyoto practiced Nichiren Buddhism, the sect made itself an independent power in Kyoto and neighboring provinces. In 1536, armies of monks from Mount Hiei, headquarters of the rival Tendai sect of Buddhism, destroyed Nichiren temples in Kyoto. These were rebuilt, but the warlord Oda Nobunaga (1534–1582) further persecuted the sect. The major branches of the Nichiren sect in Japan decided to cooperate with the government, and religious activities were redirected from zealous preaching to scholarship and education. Members of the merchant class, which prospered during the Tokugawa Shogunate (1603–1867), were attracted to the Nichiren sect by its pilgrimages and promises of success in worldly affairs. In the 20th century, Nichiren's political ideas were used by many members of the sect to support Japanese militarism in the 1930s and 1940s. However, after World War II they turned to antinuclear pacifism. The Soka Gakkai, or "Value-Creating Society," a modern religious organization with an affiliated political party known as the Clean Government Party (Komeito), is connected with the Nichiren sect. See also BUDDHISM; CLEAN GOVERNMENT PARTY; NICHIREN; ODA NOBUNAGA; SOKA GAKKAI; TOKUGAWA SHOGUNATE; TOYOTOMI HIDEYOSHI.

NICHIREN SHOSHU
See NICHIREN SECT OF BUDDHISM.

NIGHTINGALE
See BUSH WARBLER.

NIHON KEIZAI SHIMBUN
See NEWSPAPERS.

NIHON SANKEI
See AMANOHASHIDATE; MATSUSHIMA; MIYAJIMA.

NIHON SHOKI
Chronicles of Japan; a collection of early Japanese mythology, religious rituals, songs and history compiled in A.D. 720. The *Nihon Shoki* and the *Kojiki (Record of Ancient Things;* compiled A.D. 712) are the earliest extant Japanese documents. They contain similar materials and were commissioned by the ruling family of the Yamato region of western Honshu Island to legitimize their power and increase their prestige. The *Nihon Shoki* and *Kojiki* both present genealogies that trace the descent of the imperial family from the Sun Goddess Amaterasu O Mikami. In the legend, the Sun Goddess was born to Izanagi and Izanami, the god and goddess who created the islands of Japan, the ocean, rivers, mountains and trees. These aspects of nature have always been regarded as sacred manifestations by the indigenous Japanese religion, Shinto. Amaterasu sent her grandson Ninigi no Mikoto down from heaven to rule Japan, giving him three sacred treasures, a jewel, a sword, and a mirror, to symbolize the eternal reign of his dynasty. These three objects, known as the imperial regalia, still symbolize the power of the Japanese emperor. According to the creation story, Ninigi went to Kyushu, the southernmost of the four main islands of Japan. His grandson, Jimmu Tenno, supposedly became the first Japanese emperor in B.C. 660. Although this date is many centuries too early to account for the historical founding of the imperial family, the story does reflect the fact that their ancestors probably did come from western Kyushu Island and gradually migrated to the Yamato region on Honshu Island. The *Nihon Shoki* records the generations descended from Jimmu Tenno down through the seventh century A.D. The *Chronicles* also describe the founding of the shrine to Amaterasu at Ise, which is the most sacred of all Shinto shrines and houses the sacred mirror.

Because the Japanese had no script, they borrowed Chinese ideographs to write their own language. Hence the *Nihon Shoki* was written in Chinese. The Nara court valued the classical learning of China, and Chinese emphasis on recording historical events to serve as a guide to the present likely influenced the way that events were selected and recorded in the *Nihon Shoki.* The *Chronicles* was the first of six national histories that were officially compiled to record events up to A.D. 887. It has remained an important document throughout Japanese history. See also AMATERASU O MIKAMI; BUDDHISM; EMPEROR; IMPERIAL REGALIA; ISE SHRINE; IZANAGI AND IZANAMI; JIMMU TENNO; KOJIKI; NARA; NARA ERA; NINIGI NO MIKOTO; SHINTO; SOGA CLAN; WRITING SYSTEM, JAPANESE; YAMATO.

NIHONBASHI
See ADAMS, WILLIAM; BRIDGES; GINZA.

NIJO CASTLE (Nijo-jo) A castle built in the early 17th century in Kyoto by the shogun Tokugawa Ieyasu (1543–1616). Ieyasu began the castle just after he unified Japan under the Tokugawa Shogunate (1603–1867) and moved the capital from Kyoto to the new city of Edo (now Tokyo). The castle was intended to be a reminder of his power. Later Tokugawa shoguns added to the castle and stationed armies there to remind the inhabitants of the region, including the imperial court, that the shoguns were the de facto rulers of the country. However, this display of power was no longer felt to be necessary after the mid-17th century; Tokugawa Iemitsu was the last shogun to come to Nijo Castle, in 1634, until the end of the shogunate more than two centuries later. Although Ieyasu built the castle in the style of a fortress, it is smaller than many other castles in Japan, and its halls are designed for ceremonial occasions rather than battles. The interior is richly decorated with paintings, wood carvings, metalwork and even cloisonne covers for nails in the walls and ceilings. The rooms were laid out in concentric rings; only high-ranking people could enter the interior halls closer to the shogun's personal apartment, while those of lower rank were forced to stay in the outer halls. The Tokugawa were fearful of threats to their power, so hidden rooms for bodyguards were also built into the castle. The castle's most distinctive feature, to protect against a surprise attack, is the "nightingale floors" that "sing," or squeak, when anyone walks on them. The inner buildings of Nijo Castle were destroyed over the years by fires. The outer buildings that remain along with the moats and stone walls, are well preserved. Behind the castle is a large garden, which was laid out with ponds, bridges and plants, but no trees, so the shogun would not have to see falling leaves and be reminded of his mortality. See also CASTLES; KYOTO; SHOGUN; TOKUGAWA IEYASU; TOKUGAWA SHOGUNATE.

NIJUBASHI BRIDGE See IMPERIAL PALACE (TOKYO).

NIKKO NATIONAL PARK (Nikko Kokuritsu Koen) One of the most heavily visited national parks in Japan, located 87 miles northwest of Tokyo. The park's center is the town of Nikko, which dates to A.D. 782, when a Buddhist temple was founded there by the priest Shodo (735–817). Upon the death of the great shogun Tokugawa Ieyasu (1543–1616), founder of the Tokugawa Shogunate (1603–1867), the opulent Toshogu Shrine was built in Nikko as his mausoleum. The town was already famous as a center for religious devotees, who still make a pilgrimage every August to the sacred cone-shaped mountain known as Nataisan. Toshogu Shrine also attracts many secular tourists, especially for the massive samurai processions during the shrine's Grand Festivals. There are many other shrines and temples in Nikko. Chuzenji temple houses an 8th century statue of Kannon, Buddhist Goddess of Mercy, that was carved from a living tree.

Nikko National Park covers 543 square miles and contains numerous volcanic mountains and lakes. At the base of Nantaisan lies Lake Chuzenji, with Kegon Waterfall, the highest in Japan, on its eastern side. To the northwest is Shiranesan, a mountain 6,560 feet high. Chuzenji, Shiobara, and Nasu are popular hot spring resorts. Along the old roads around the mountains of Nikko can be seen many impressive trees, such as evergreens, large cryptomerias, and maples, whose foliage turns a beautiful red in autumn. See also HOT SPRING; KEGON WATERFALL; MAPLE TREE; MOUNTAINS; NATIONAL PARKS; PILGRIMAGE; SHRINES, SHINTO; TEMPLES, BUDDHIST; TOSHOGU SHRINE.

NIKKO SECURITIES CO., LTD. See SECURITIES COMPANIES.

NIKON See CAMERAS AND PHOTOGRAPHY.

NINIGI NO MIKOTO A major figure in Japanese legend and mythology who was sent to rule over the islands of Japan by his grandparents, Takamimusubi no Kami, the God of Creation, and Amaterasu o Mikami; the Sun Goddess and central deity of Shinto. Ninigi no Mikoto's father was Amaterasu's son, Ame no Oshihomimi no Mikoto, and his mother was Takuhata Chijihime, who was also a daughter of Takamimusubi. Amaterasu decreed that Ninigi no Mikoto should rule the land of Japan, fertile with rice, and that his dynasty would rule forever. She gave him three tokens of his divine mission and power, a mirror, a sword, and curved jewels, which became the imperial regalia that have legitimized the rule of the imperial family in Japan to this day. Ninigi no Mikoto supposedly descended from heaven to earth on a mountain called Takamagahara on the southern island of Kyushu, accompanied by ancestors of the five major clans in ancient Japan. He married a divine spirit named Konohana no Sakuyahime, who represents a flower in bloom. According to Japanese mythology, Ninigi's grandson became the first reigning emperor in Japan, Jimmu Tenno, in 660 B.C. Ninigi no Mikoto is worshiped at various shrines in Japan, notably the Kirishima Shrine in Kagoshima Prefecture. His wife is believed to be the divine spirit of Mount Fuji, the most sacred mountain in Japan and the symbol of the country. See also AMATERASU O MIKAMI; EMPEROR; FUJI, MOUNT; IMPERIAL REGALIA; JIMMU TENNO; KYUSHU ISLAND; MIRROR; SWORD.

NINJA Spies and assassins trained in *ninjutsu*, the "way of invisibility," a method of stealth and subterfuge. *Ninja* acted as secret agents who gained information about enemies for their masters. Legends place the origin of *ninja* in ancient Japanese history, but *ninja* were active primarily during feudal times, particularly the Sengoku Era (1467–1568). Because the power of *ninja* lay in secrecy as well as physical strength, teachers of *ninjutsu* wrote very little about their art. Two schools of *ninjutsu* developed, known as the Koga and Iga schools for the home areas of their practitioners. *Ninja* learned a multitude of techniques, foremost of which was disguising themselves by dressing in black, moving quickly and quietly in the dark, and confusing or diverting guards. They underwent intensive physical training and learned specific techniques for using their fists and bodily postures to fight opponents. *Ninja* also used a variety of small but effective weapons, such as *shiruken*, pointed shapes thrown at enemies; *tennenbishi,* tiny pointed objects thrown on the ground to injure the feet of people chasing them; and *shinobi kumade,* a rope with pieces of bamboo and a hook used to climb walls. Women who practiced *ninjutsu* were called *kunoichi.* They could get inside enemy camps by disguising themselves as entertainers or servants. *Ninja* are fascinating legendary figures who are often shown in historical television shows and movies in Japan. See also FEUDALISM; MARTIAL ARTS.

NINJUTSU See NINJA.

NINSEI See NONOMURA NINSEI.

NIPPON (OR NIHON) The Japanese word for Japan, made up of the Chinese ideographs for "the root (origin) of the sun" or "the place where the sun rises." Hence Japan is known as the "Land of the Rising Sun." The term derives from two Chinese ideographs that the Japanese Prince Shotoku (574–622) used for his country's name in an official letter to China. The Chinese characters are pronounced in Japanese as Nippon or Nihon.

The name *Japan* that is used in Western languages may derive from Jihpenkuo, the name for Japan that was used in northern China and romanized by the Portuguese in Asia either as *Zipangu* or *Jipangu.* However, an alternate theory argues that the name comes from the Dutch word *Yatpun,* which was used in southern China to refer to the country of Japan. See also CHINA AND JAPAN; DUTCH IN JAPAN; PORTUGUESE IN JAPAN; SHOTOKU, PRINCE.

NIPPON ELECTRIC CO., LTD. (NEC) See COMPUTER INDUSTRY.

NIPPON TELEGRAPH AND TELEPHONE CORPORATION (Nihon Denshin Denwa Kosha; abbreviated as Denden Kosha) Also known as NTT; the formerly public corporation, privatzed, by the government in 1985, that controls electronic telecommunications in Japan. (Japanese telecommunications with foreign countries are now handled by a separate corporation, Kokusai Denshin Denwa Co., Ltd., also known as KDD. It is the largest corporation in Japan, with 280,000 employees and more capital than any other company in the world, $80.3 billion in assets. The government has been considering breaking up NTT, as AT&T was broken up in the United States, but the company is attempting to prevent this. NTT is developing a fiber-optic telecommunications system that by 2015 will run into every home and every office in Japan. Known as the "integrated services digital network" (ISDN), it will require an investment by NTT of more than $200 billion.

NTT was founded in 1952 as one of three main public service and monopoly corporations, along with Japanese National Railways (now privatized as Japan Railways) and Japan Tobacco and Salt. By 1989, half of NTT's stock was sold to Japanese investors; foreigners were not allowed to buy shares in the company. NTT is headed by a five-person committee whose members are corporate executives and communications experts. Within Japan, NTT monop-

olizes communications and the sale of communications technology. It has been a major source of funds for technology research and development in Japan. NTT's demand for electronic equipment and machinery stimulated the production of powerful computer microchips that have dominated world markets. Telephone service continues to provide nearly 90% of NTT's income. NTT also began a data communication service in 1968; one of its first experiments was to link home and office computers into a large computer network in two districts of Tokyo. By the 1980s, the corporation was developing various non-telephone services to link computer data systems. In 1989 it spent $1.7 billion, or 4.3% of revenues, on research and development. See also COMPUTER INDUSTRY; ELECTRONICS INDUSTRY; RESEARCH AND DEVELOPMENT; TELECOMMUNICATIONS SYSTEM.

NIPPON YUSEN (NYK) See SHIPPING AND SHIPBUILDING.

NISEI The second generation of Japanese immigrants to other countries, particularly the United States. *Nisei* are the children of first-generation Japanese immigrants, known as *issei,* who left Japan and settled abroad in the late 19th and early 20th centuries. The children of *nisei* are known as *sansei* (third generation). A large number of *nisei* were well-educated yet had to take low-paying jobs because of racial discrimination against them. Many *nisei* went to Japan, either to be educated or to seek better opportunities. The Japanese American Citizens League (JACL), an organization founded in 1930 to promote the political and civil rights of Japanese Americans, was limited to *nisei* members only.

As a group, *nisei* suffered through the Depression and the incarceration of Pacific Coast Japanese-Americans by the U.S. government during World War II. Yet *nisei* loyally supported the U.S. military effort against Japan and formed two *nisei* fighting units, the 442nd Regimental Combat Team and the 100th Battalion, which were the most decorated military units in the war. Nearly 30,000 Japanese-Americans, mostly *nisei,* served in the two units, and over 6,000 more served as translators and interpreters in the Pacific war zone. Many *nisei* were in Japan during the war, and an unknown number were killed by the atomic bombs dropped on Hiroshima and Nogosaki in 1945. After World War II, more than 500 war survivors, known as *nisei hibakusha,* returned to the United States. At present there are thousands of *nisei* living in Japan. Because they know both Japanese and American languages and cultures, they often work in the areas of foreign trade and Japanese-American relations. See also IMMIGRANTS, JAPANESE; ISSEI; JAPANESE-AMERICAN CITIZENS LEAGUE; SANSEI; WORLD WAR II.

NISHIDA KITARO (1870–1945) The first and most important modern Japanese philosopher, and the founder of the Kyoto school of philosophy that has shaped the thinking of all subsequent Japanese philosophers. His writings over a 40-year period have been collected in 19 volumes. Many of his books and essays have been translated into English over the past three decades, and his ideas have influenced a number of Western scholars. Nishida became very knowledgeable about Western philosophy, which he combined with the concepts of Zen Buddhism. Nishida was born in 1870 near the city of Kanazawa. As a student he established a close friendship with the well-known Zen Buddhist philosopher Suzuki Daisetz Teitaro, who introduced Zen to the West. Nishida was also interested in mathematics, and studied with the Japanese mathematician Hojo Tokiyoshi, but chose philosophy as his life work. Although his earlier education was erratic, Nishida was a brilliant student at Tokyo University, from which he graduated in 1894. He became a teacher and married his cousin, Tokuda Kotomi, who bore him eight children. In 1896 he took up Zen meditation while teaching in Kanazawa. The next year he began a diary to record his religious crisis, which was intensified by his break from his father and temporary separation from his wife.

Nishida's first published work was *Zen no Kenkyu* (1911), in which he presented his concept that "pure experience" is the fundamental aspect of human life. Nishida taught at Kyoto University from 1910 until he retired in 1928. His philosophical work during this time developed the concepts of "absolute free will" and *basho*, the "place" of "absolute Nothingness" where the "true self" is seen. This latter concept comes from the Buddhist definition of the ultimate reality of life as "absolute Nothingness." Nishida first presented these views in the book *From the Acting to the Seeing (Hataraku mono kara miru mono e*; 1927). He continued his philosophical speculation and wrote many books even after his retirement. Rising militarism in Japan during the 1930s, which culminated in the Pacific Theater of World War II, deeply upset Nishida, but he struggled to continue his philosophical work even during the war. He died in June 1945, shortly before the surrender of Japan to the Allied Powers. Nishida's earliest work was translated into English as *An Inquiry into the Good* in 1990 by Masao Abe and Christopher Ives. See also SUZUKI DAISETZ TEITARO; ZEN SECT OF BUDDHISM.

NISHIJIN A district in northwest Kyoto that is the center of the traditional Japanese silk-weaving industry. Nishijin became an important textile center when weavers who had fled Kyoto during the Onin War of 1467–1477 returned and established workshops in this district. The warlord Toyotomi Hideyoshi, who took control of Japan in 1582, protected the Kyoto weaving center. During the 17th century, Chinese refugees settled in Nishijin and taught Japanese weavers how to make the gold thread that Nishijin weavers incorporated into their silk. The thread was made by pasting pieces of gold leaf on paper and twisting them around thin silk strips. *Nishijin-ori*, the heavy brocade fabrics made with gold thread, are known as *karaori*, or Chinese weaving. Tightly woven in complex patterns, these fabrics are still used in Japan for costumes in the traditional theatrical form, Noh and for formal *obi*, the stiff sash wound around kimono. In 1874 Nishijin weavers began to use the French jacquard loom, which uses punched cards to feed threads into the pattern being woven and reduces the amount of human labor required. Lately the Nishijin district has been experiencing a decline because few Japanese wear kimono

except for very special occasions. See also BROCADE; KIMONO; KYOTO; NOH DRAMA; OBI; SILK; TEXTILES; TOYOTOMI HIDEYOSHI.

NISSAN MOTOR CO., LTD. (Nissan Jidosha) The second largest automobile manufacturer in Japan after Toyota Motor Corporation. Nissan's vehicles were formerly marketed under the name Datsun. The company also manufactures automobile parts, trucks, textile machinery, large boat engines and aerospace components. Nissan was founded by Aikawa Yoshisuke in 1933 and began mass production of small cars at its plant in Yokohama in 1934. By 1938 it was producing more than 8,000 cars a year. After World War II, Nissan invested in new assembly plants, equipment and technology, and widened its sales network in Japan and overseas. The company's assembly lines were highly automated by the mid-1950s. Nissan began selling automobiles in the United States in 1960. In 1966 it increased its product lines by absorbing the Prince Motor Co., Ltd., and also absorbed Minsei Diesel and took control of Fuji Heavy Industries' domestic production. Nissan has thousands of dealers in about 150 foreign countries, and many overseas assembly plants. At least half its total annual sales come from foreign markets. Nissan corporate headquarters are in Tokyo. See also AUTOMOBILE INDUSTRY; TOYOTA MOTOR CORPORATION.

NOAMI (1397–1471) Also known as Shinno; a famous painter and connoisseur who served the shogun Ashikaga Yoshimasa (1436–1490), the eighth shogun of the Ashikaga Shogunate (1338–1573). The shoguns who ruled Japan during this era were great patrons of the arts. They also favored the Zen Buddhist religion, which was introduced from China in the 12th century A.D. and had a vast influence on Japanese art and culture. Noami was curator of the shogun's collection of art treasures and wrote a manual about it. He also helped compile information about painters whose works were owned by the shogun, and he mounted and exhibited the paintings Yoshimasa had acquired from China. Noami's taste set the critical standards for art appreciation in his time. He was also a master of the incense and tea ceremonies, linked-verse poetry known as *renga*, and landscape gardening. Noami painted in many styles, including ink painting (*sumi-e*), landscapes, bird-and-flower subjects, and human and divine figures. One of Noami's paintings, *White-robed Kannon (Byakue Kannon*; 1468), has survived. Kannon is the Buddhist Goddess of Mercy. Noami's son Geiami (Shingei; 1431–1485) and his grandson Soami (Shinso; c. 1455–1525) became painters and curators for the Ashikaga shogun as well. See also ASHIKAGA SHOGUNATE; GARDENS; INCENSE; INK PAINTING; KANNON; RENGA; SOAMI; TEA CEREMONY; ZEN BUDDHISM.

NOBUNAGA ODA See ODA NOBUNAGA.

NOGUCHI, ISAMU (1904–1988) A world-renowned Japanese-American sculptor and designer. Isamu Noguchi was born in Los Angeles to a Japanese father, Noguchi Yonejiro, and an American mother, Leonie Gilmour. The family went to Japan in 1906, where the father, a poet, taught English at Keio University. Noguchi was raised in Japan until 1918, when his mother sent him back to the United States for his education. He studied at private high schools and attended Columbia University, but gave up his plans to be a doctor in favor of studying sculpture. In 1927 he went to Paris on a Guggenheim Fellowship and worked for two years with the sculptor Constantin Brancusi. Noguchi returned to New York, but spent much time in the 1930s traveling through Europe, Russia, China, Japan and Mexico. When Japanese-Americans on the West Coast were forcibly interned in relocation camps during World War II, Noguchi voluntarily lived in a camp in Arizona for seven months. Following the war, he returned to Japan many times and studied traditional Japanese arts such as pottery and garden design. A Japanese influence can be seen in many of Noguchi's sculptures, as well as his gardens and architectural projects. These include gardens for Keio University in Tokyo and the UNESCO building in Paris, the Billy Rose Sculpture Garden for the Israeli Museum in Jerusalem, a marble garden at Yale University and a sculpture garden at the Museum of Fine Arts in Houston. Noguchi collaborated on ballet set designs with Martha Graham, and also designed furniture and lighting equipment. His sculptures, made of marble, wood, metal, stone, cement or terra-cotta, have been exhibited throughout the world. The Isamu Noguchi Garden Museum in Long Island City, New York, includes 12 galleries and an outdoor sculpture garden. In 1986 Noguchi received the Kyoto Prize from the Inomori Foundation in Japan. In 1987 he was awarded the National Medal of Arts by President Ronald Reagan. In 1988 he received the Third Order of the Sacred Treasure from the Japanese government and the first Award for Distinction in Sculpture from the Sculpture Center. A documentary about Noguchi's life and work was made in 1980–1981. See also GARDENS; IMMIGRANTS, JAPANESE; POTTERY; SCULPTURE.

NOH DRAMA A highly stylized form of traditional theater that incorporates music, singing and dance. In a performance, serious Noh plays are alternated with comic vignettes known as Kyogen. These two forms are classified together as Nogaku. Noh performances consist of a main protagonist (shite) and a supporting actor (waki). The actors chant and move in a slow, restrained manner. At first the shite appears to be an ordinary person. The waki calls the shite to the stage and asks questions that lead the shite to express his real nature, such as a defeated warrior or a woman who has lost her son or her lover. The climax of the drama is the dance by the shite, during which the waki takes an unobtrusive position in a corner of the stage. Occasionally the shite is accompanied by a servant (tomo), friend (tsure) or child (kokata). A stage assistant (koken) dressed in black adjusts the shite's costume, hands him props and costume parts, and takes them when they are no longer needed. Every Noh actor trains throughout his lifetime as either a shite or waki. While characters played by waki are always human males, such as imperial ministers, priests, warriors or villagers, a shite plays a wide range of characters, including women, warriors, ghosts, old men,

deities and even animals. The shite usually wears a mask to express his character, such as an old man (okina), young woman (ko-omote), court noble (chujo), male demon (kobeshimi), female demon (hannya), and so forth. When playing a middle aged man in a "bare face play" (hitamen-mono) or "present play" (gendai-mono), he does not wear a mask but keeps his face masklike and devoid of expression. All Noh actors, musicians and singers keep their faces expressionless during every performance. The actors wear elaborate costumes made of a silk brocade kimono, over-jacket, hakama (divided skirt), and the shite wears a wig and headband to hold the wig in place. The shite and waki also carry large folding fans (chukei) that can be opened or closed to represent a large variety of objects and activities.

Noh is performed on a special stage that developed from outdoor platforms in shrines for sacred Kagura dance performances. There are no sets, and only a few simple props are used to symbolize objects, such as a boat, house or torii (shrine gate). A modern indoor Noh theater (Nogakudo) has a roofed platform about 20 feet square made from cypress wood (hinoki) that projects into the audience. The stage is open but has a pillar at each corner. A stylized pine tree (matsu) is painted on the back wall (kagami-ita, "mirror board" or "resounding board") of the stage. The floor boards are highly polished to facilitate the sliding movements of the actors' feet. Large earthenware jars buried under the boards magnify the sound when the dancing actors stamp their feet. White gravel (shirasu) is spread on the floor between the stage and the audience. A roofed walkway or "bridge" (hashigakari) leads from the actors' waiting or "mirror" room (kagami-no-ma) to the main stage. Three live pine trees are placed in front of the bridge and two behind it. A large curtain (age-maku) with five stripes that divides the bridge from the waiting room is lifted when the actors enter or leave the stage. The musicians (hayashi) sit in a row at the back of the stage. Instruments include the large stick drum (taiko), medium-sized hand drum (otsuzumi), small hand drum (kotsuzumi) and flute (fue). Six to 10 singers forming a chorus (jiutai) sit along the right of the stage and chant a recitative known as utai or yokyoku.

The emphasis of a Noh play is not plot development but the gradual intensification of a single emotion to its most concentrated point. There are five categories of plays: deity or celebratory plays (Waki Noh): ghost plays (Shura Mono) in which the shite is the ghost of a warrior of the Taira or Minamoto clans; woman or wig plays (Katsura Mono), in which the shite is a beautiful woman; miscellaneous subjects (Zatsu Noh), especially deranged or mad woman plays (Kyojo Mono); and demon plays (Kichiku Mono). As Noh is music-drama that is chanted and danced, its lyrics are called "song music" (yokyoku).

The majority of plays in the Noh repertoire were written by two actors who formalized the art of Noh, Kanze Kan'ami (1333–1384) and his son Zeami (1363–1443). Noh developed out of many sources, including a lively Chinese burlesque performance known as sarugaku ("monkey music"), rural temple and shrine performances (dengaku, "field music") derived from ancient rice planting and harvesting

The main character in a traditional Noh drama wearing a mask and gorgeous silk brocade robes. Drummers at the back of the stage, and singers and flute players to the right, accompany the performer.

rituals, a popular song form known as *kouta,* an ancient masked dance drama known as *Gigaku,* ancient court dance known as *bugaku,* Shinto religious ritual dances *(kagura),* and Buddhist religious liturgy *(shomyo).* Kan'ami adapted a lively narrative women's song-and-dance style *(kusemai)* as the heart of Noh. Zeami, patronized by Shogun Ashikaga Yoshimitsu (1358–1408), developed an aesthetic philosophy based on the concept of *yugen* (mysterious profundity). Noh became associated with the samurai and aristocratic classes in Japan, whereas the traditional Kabuki theater was associated with the urban merchant class. Five schools or troupes of Noh that existed by the time of the Tokugawa Shogunate (1603–1867) still perform Noh today: Kanze, which has the highest rank; and Komparu, Hosho, Kongo, and Kita. See also ASHIKAGA YOSHIMITSU; BUGAKU; DANCE, TRADITIONAL; DRUMS; FAN, FLUTES; HAKAMA; KIMONO; MASKS; PINE TREE; RICE PLANTING AND HARVESTING FESTIVALS; SILK; ZEAMI; YUGEN.

NOMURA KICHISABURO (1877–1964)
A Japanese naval officer and diplomat active in negotiations between Japan and the United States prior to World War II. Nomura graduated from the Japanese Naval Academy in 1898. He held many naval posts and was made naval attache at the Japanese embassy in Washington, D.C. during World War I. Nomura was made an admiral in 1933. After serving as director of the Peers' School in 1937, he was appointed foreign minister in 1939. In that capacity he held discussions with Joseph Grew, then the American ambassador to Japan, regarding the strained relations between the United States and Japan. Nomura was sent by the Japanese government to America as ambassador extraordinary and plenipotentiary in 1941, by which time, relations between Japan and the United States were at the breaking point. Nomura negotiated with American Secretary of State Cordell Hull, but their meetings did not prevent war between the two countries, which began with the Japanese attack on Pearl Harbor on December 7, 1941. After the war, Nomura wrote a book about his experiences during these negotiations called *Envoy to the United States* (*Beikoku no tsukaishite;* published in 1946). He was also elected to two terms in the House of Concillors, the upper house of the Japanese Diet (Parliament). See also DIET; IMPERIAL JAPANESE ARMY AND NAVY; PEARL HARBOR, JAPANESE ATTACK ON; WORLD WAR II.

NOMURA SECURITIES CO., LTD., AND NOMURA RESEARCH INSTITUTE
See SECURITIES COMPANIES.

NONOMURA NINSEI (fl. mid-17th century A.D.)   A highly regarded potter who utilized the technique of overglaze colored enamels. Born in the village of Nonomura in Tamba Province (part of modern Kyoto Prefecture), he was originally called Nonomura Seiemon or Seibei. Tamba was a center for the production of large pottery jars to store tea. Ninsei, as he was known professionally, studied pottery in Seto (modern Aichi Prefecture) on the southern Japanese island of Kyushu, whose Seto ware (*seto-yaki*) was famous for tea caddies (*chaire*) used in the Japanese tea ceremony. Ninsei was educated by the important tea master Kanamori Sowa (1584–1656) about the preference of tea masters for enameled ware with simple designs and pottery with dark brown monochrome glazes. Yet Ninsei became renowned for decorating his pieces in brightly colored enamels, even using gold and silver. He worked in varying styles, from rough Shigaraki ware (*shigaraki-yaki*) vases and tea jars to austere Seto ware tea caddies to decorated incense burners, tea bowls (*chawan*), water containers, and serving dishes for the special tea ceremony meal, *kaiseki*. Ninsei settled near the old capital city of Kyoto and established a pottery kiln at Ninnaji, a Buddhist temple. He took his professional name, Ninsei, from the first character in the name Ninnaji and the first character of his own name. Ninsei was the first Japanese to apply his own seal to the works he created. His work was widely imitated by other potters in Japan, and many pieces attributed to Ninsei could not have been made by him. Ninsei's genuine successor was his former student Ogata Kenzan (1663–1743). Pottery in the style of Ninsei is still produced in the area of Kyoto adjacent to Kiyomizudera Temple. See also KAISEKI; KENZAN; KIYOMIZU-DERA; POTTERY; SETO WARE; TEA CEREMONY.

NOODLES (*menrui*)   Noodle dishes (*menrui*) were introduced into Japan from China and are not a part of formal Japanese cooking, yet they are one of the most popular foods in Japan and are often eaten fast as a complete meal. Large cities have many restaurants and food stalls serving noodles, and even small-town restaurants serve noodles as the main dish. There are many different types of noodles in Japan. The two most popular are *udon*, made from wheat flour, and *soba*, made from a mixture of buckwheat flour (*soba-ko*) and wheat flour. *Udon*, associated with Osaka and southern Japan, is thick and light-colored. *Soba*, associated with Tokyo and northern Japan, because buckwheat requires cooler and drier growing conditions, is long, thin and light brownish gray. It has strong connotations of the old city of Edo (now Tokyo) and the working classes.

Both *soba* and *udon* can be served with a sauce into which the noodles are dipped before eating, or in a large bowl of hot broth. *Wasabi* (a paste of Japanese horseradish) and chopped green onions are mixed into the dipping sauce to give it a sharper flavor. Different geographic areas have different kinds of broth and sauce for noodles. In the Kansai region around Osaka and Kyoto, noodles are eaten with a combination of soy sauce and a stock made from bonito fish and kelp (an edible seaweed). In the Kanto region of Tokyo and Yokohama, a mixture of bonito stock and darker soy sauce is preferred. Other ingredients are added to noodle dishes, such as green onions, chicken, shrimp *tempura*, and slices of fish paste cake (*kamaboko*). A popular dish called "fox noodles" (*kitsune-udon*) includes deep-fried *tofu* (soybean curd), which is thought to be a favorite food of the fox.

There are other types of wheat noodles, such as *kishimen*, which are wide and flat, and *somen*, which are like very thin spaghetti. *Hiyamugi* are thin noodles that are always served cold in the summer with a dipping sauce. *Soba* can also be eaten cold, as *mori-soba*, served on a bamboo rack in a lacquer box. *Cha-soba* is buckwheat noodles with green tea (*cha*) added to the dough. *Ramen* is the Japanese name for Chinese-style noodles, which have egg added to the dough and are served in a pork or chicken broth seasoned with soy sauce or *miso* (fermented soybean paste). Grilled pork, spinach, slices of fish paste cake and other ingredients are usually added to the soup. Dried instant *ramen* noodle soups sold in individual packages have become very popular. *Ramen* noodles can also be served on a plate with various accompaniments. Some noodles are made of ingredients other than wheat, such as *konnyaku*, the starch of a tuber called "devil's plant," which is used in a stew called *sukiyaki*; and potatoes, which are used to make a cellophane-like vermicelli known as "spring rain" (*harusame*).

When Japanese move into a new home, they give *soba* to their neighbors because *soba* also means "next to" or "near." *Hikkoshi soba* announces that "we have moved near you," and the shape of the noodles symbolizes the wish that relations with the neighbors will last a long time but remain "narrow," or proper. On New Year's Eve, the Japanese eat *soba* while listening to the temple bells ring in the New Year. This dish is called *toshikoshi*, or "year passing," and the long noodles represent the desire for a long life.

Storytellers of the *rakugo* tradition amuse audiences by imitating people eating noodles. In Japan, noodles are eaten by lifting them with a pair of chopsticks and sucking them into the mouth while making a loud slurping noise to show enjoyment. See also CHOPSTICKS; COOKING; FOOD STALLS; FOX; KANSAI AND KANTO; MISO; NEW YEAR FESTIVAL; RESTAURANTS; SOY SAUCE; STORYTELLING; WASABI.

NOREN   A split cloth hung like a door at the entrance of a Japanese restaurant, shop or bathhouse. It serves as a sign decorated with the symbol or crest (*mon*) of the shop as well as information about its services. A popular color combination is indigo with white calligraphy. *Noren* are also popular souvenirs, often hung as decorations in private homes. Old *noren* have great value and are handed down as family heirlooms. These may include large silk *noren* with family crests and beautifully dyed symbols such as cranes and tortoises, symbolic of good fortune and used at wedding celebrations. See also BATH; CALLIGRAPHY; CRANE; CREST; FAMILY; INDIGO; RESTAURANTS; SILK; TORTOISE; WEDDINGS.

NORI   See SEAWEED; SUSHI.

NORITAKE CO.   See NAGOYA.

NORTHERN AND SOUTHERN COURTS ERA See NAMBOKUCHO ERA.

NOVELS (*shosetsu*) Japan is rich in literary forms, and the novel has a long history there. Novels were composed as far back as the Heian Era (794–1185) when a syllabic system of writing known as *kana* was developed. *Kana* was used primarily by women, in contrast to the system of *kanji*, or Chinese characters, that was used by men. *The Tale of Genji* (*Genji Monogatari*) by Murasaki Shikibu (fl. c. A.D. 1000) is generally considered to be not only the first Japanese novel, but the first novel in world literature. It describes the life and loves of Prince Genji and daily life in the Heian imperial court. Ancient Japanese novels such as *The Tale of Genji* are concerned with psychological and emotional nuances, aesthetic subtleties such as color combinations of the multilayerd robes worn by court ladies, and the fleeting beauties of nature. They contain a great deal of poetry, regarded by the Japanese as the highest literary form, as do the diaries that comprise an important related form of literature in Japan. The concerns of early modern Japanese novels in the Edo Era (1600–1868) are somewhat different, as seen in the works of Saikaku Ihra (1642–1693), whose erotic fiction describes the exploits of men and women in urban licensed pleasure quarters (*ukiyo*, "floating world"). Modern Japanese novelists and short story writers are influenced by the realism of writers such as Saikaku, the aesthetic and emotional subtleties of ancient court novels, and Western existentialist literature. During the late Meiji Era (1868–1912), a type of modern fiction known as the I-novel (*watakushi shosetsu* or *shishosetsu*) developed, in which the author's experiences and feelings take precedence over structured form and plot. Some of the best-known modern Japanese novelists include Natsume Soseki (1867–1916), Tanizaki Junichiro (1886–1965), Akutagawa Ryunosuke (1892–1927), Nobel Prize winner Kawabata Yasunari (1899–1972), Endo Shusaku (1923–), the controversial Mishima Yukio (1925–1970), Abe Kobo (1924–) and Oe Kenzaburo (1935–). See also DIARIES; FLOATING WORLD; GENJI, THE TALE OF; KANA; KANJI; POETRY; WRITING SYSTEM; JAPANESE; NAMES OF INDIVIDUAL WRITERS.

NUNS, BUDDHIST See MONASTICISM, BUDDHIST.

NYK See SHIPPING AND SHIPBUILDING.

O

O- An honorific prefix added to certain nouns and used in verb phrases in the Japanese language to show respect. The addition of o- to words such as that for a palanquin to carry the statue of a god in a procession (o-mikoshi) is a feature of Japanese honorific language (keigo). Other examples are o-cha for tea, o-mizu for water and o-bento for a portable box that holds a quick meal. Different levels of speech reflect the many different levels of formality in social relationships. Japanese men and women have different levels and styles of language, and women's speech is more deferential and uses o- more frequently than does that of men. In most cases, o- is added to words that were originally Japanese, in contrast to the many words that came into Japanese from the Chinese language. Chinese loanwords were given the respectful prefix go- or gyo-, which has become associated with the emperor. An example is gyo-en, "imperial gardens." Respect or deference is shown to persons by adding the suffix -san to their names, as in Yamada-san. See also LANGUAGE, JAPANESE; NAMES, JAPANESE; -SAN; WRITING SYSTEM, JAPANESE.

OBI A long cloth sash that is wrapped around traditional robes known as kimono and yukata. An obi is both decorative and functional because it holds the kimono on the wearer's body—no pins, buttons or other fasteners are used. Until the 16th century, obi were simply thin cords. During the Edo Era (1600–1868), the kosode, an early form of the modern kimono made from long straight panels of fabric, became the main article of clothing. Obi worn over kosode by women became wider and more elaborate and were influenced by styles worn by actors in the Kabuki theater who played women's roles (onnagata). Married women and high-ranking courtesans tied their obi in front, and single women and girls tied them in back. Today all obi are tied in the back. By the middle of the Edo Era, obi became standardized to the 10–13 foot length that is still worn today. Obi were soft and pliant until around 1800, when stiff, heavy textiles became popular. Obi are made from a great variety of fabrics. Formal obi are made of heavy silk, such as brocade (nishiki) or figured brocade (tsuzure-ori), and can cost as much as kimono. The Nishijin district of Kyoto is famous for woven brocade obi. Synthetic fabrics such as polyester are also used today.

Obi are classified according to their fabrics, designs and colors, the seasons and occasions for which they are worn, whether they are worn by single or married women, and so forth. The most elegant obi is the maru obi, made of patterned brocade and double the width of an ordinary obi, and worn folded in half lengthwise. Today this is worn mainly by brides over wedding kimono. The fukuro (lined) obi is worn on formal occasions. A folded obi known as a Nagoya obi can be worn for formal or informal occasions. Unlined woven obi known as hitoe ("one layer") obi are worn in the summer, especially with casual kimono or the informal yukata. Half-width (han haba) obi with stiff linings are worn year-round for casual occasions. There are even "instant" obi (tsuke obi) made of two parts, a ready-tied bow and a sash on which it is attached.

Before a woman puts on an obi, she folds her kimono over at the waist and ties it with undersashes to create a panel of material over which the obi is wrapped. The obi is held in place with a braided cord (obi-jime) that is tied in a knot in front. A stiff lightweight panel (obiita) is placed behind the front of the obi to keep it smooth. A light silk sash (obi-age) is wrapped around the top with its ends tucked into the front of the obi. It covers the small pillow (obimakura) in back, which supports the shape of the bow.

There are several hundred ways of tying an obi. The most common style today is the taiko ("drum"), which creates a large rounded surface that displays a woven or hand-painted design. Chidori (plover bird) has two small "wings" coming out of the top of the taiko style. Fukura-suzume ("pouting sparrow") is a dramatic large bow worn by girls and young single women. Some other styles are cho-no-mai ("dancing butterfly") and tateya ("standing arrow"). Maiko, young women apprenticing to become geisha, wear a special elaborate drooping style of obi known as darai obi over colorful kimono with long sleeves.

Men today wear two styles of obi, a stiff kaku obi or a soft heko obi, both of which are about 3½ inches wide. The kaku obi is tied in a small "shellfish" bow in back. The soft obi is tied in a loose bow and worn over a yukata. See also BROCADE; CORD, BRAIDED; GEISHA; KABUKI; KIMONO; NISHIJIN; SILK; TEXTILES; WEDDINGS.

OCCUPATION OF JAPAN (1945–1952) The Occupation technically began when Japan formally surrendered to the Allies on August 14, 1945, and ended on April 28, 1952, when the peace treaty signed in San Francisco by Japan and 48 other nations went into effect. The Japanese people were in a desperate condition by the time Japan surrendered and largely cooperated with the occupying forces. The head of the Allied occupation was the Supreme Commander for the Allied Powers (SCAP), U.S. General Douglas A. MacArthur (1880–1964). The term SCAP was also applied to the building housing occupation headquarters in Tokyo. In October 1945 the SCAP office issued a directive on civil liberties in Japan, which strictly limited the power of the Ministry of Home Affairs and the centralized police system, released political prisoners, removed restrictions on fundamental individual rights and enabled political parties to revive themselves. More than 200,000 officials judged to have been involved in starting the war were purged. A new cabinet approved by SCAP was formed by Shidehara Kijuro (1872–1951), who served as prime minister 1945–1946. By early 1946, SCAP had completed demobilization of the Imperial Japanese Army, Navy, and Air Force, and had begun implementing extensive political, economic and educational reforms. SCAP worked through the Japanese bureaucracy rather than trying to replace it altogether.

A new Japanese constitution to replace the Meiji Constitution of 1889 was promulgated in November 1946 and took effect on May 3, 1947. The Japanese Constitution of 1947, still in effect without changes, was prepared by SCAP but retained the British parliamentary system on which the previous Japanese government had been modeled. The constitution made the popularly elected two-chamber Diet (Parliament) the highest organ of government; retained the emperor as the symbol of the Japanese state and the unity of its people but transferred political power from the emperor to the people; placed executive power in a cabinet formed by the majority political party in the Diet, and made the cabinet responsible to the Diet; made the courts independent of other branches of government and gave the Supreme Court the power of constitutional review; and strengthened regional and local self-government. It emphasized civil liberties, gave women full equality with men and permitted labor unions to organize. Article IX of the constitution renounced Japan's right to make war, maintain armed forces or use the threat of force in international disputes.

The first major economic reform undertaken by SCAP was land reform. Absentee landowners were required to sell excess land to the government, which sold it at moderate prices to the peasants who worked the land. The prewar business and financial combines known as *zaibatsu*, considered responsible for financing the war, were dissolved to decentralize the economy. The police system was reorganized to decrease central government control. The education system, considered the key to the democratization of Japan, was reorganized on the U.S. model. The International Military Tribunal for the Far East, established in Tokyo in 1948, handled the punishment of Japanese war criminals, but MacArthur decided not to prosecute Emperor Hirohito (now known as Emperor Showa; 1901–1989) as a war criminal. From 1948 on, SCAP paid greater attention to economic recovery, to ensure Japan's stability and the success of reforms already made, and to relieve the United States of the heavy expense of maintaining the Japanese economy. These aims were supported by the conservative new prime minister Yoshida Shigeru (1878–1967; prime minister 1946–1954). Agitation by labor unions was curtailed, the breakup of the *zaibatsu* was slowed down and intense efforts were made to halt inflation and revive exports.

The eruption of the Korean War in June 1950 strengthened these policies. Japan served as the main staging area for U.S. troops entering Korea, and the American need for goods and services greatly stimulated the Japanese economy. The deployment of American troops to Korea also

caused MacArthur to allow Japan to create a paramilitary force to maintain internal security, the National Police Reserve, now the Self-Defense Forces (SDF), which was unpopular with many Japanese because it ran counter to the spirit of the constitution. In 1951 MacArthur was removed as SCAP by U.S. President Harry S Truman over policy disagreements. The Occupation of Japan was the third time in Japanese history that Japan was transformed by reforms adopted from foreign sources, along with the Taika Reform of 645–649 and the Meiji Restoration of 1868. On the whole, the Allied Occupation was a success. Run principally by the United States, it created a close relationship between Japan and the United States, which, despite problems such as trade policy, remains strong today. See also CABINET, PRIME MINISTER'S; CONSTITUTION OF 1947; DIET; EDUCATION SYSTEM; HIROHITO, EMPEROR; IMPERIAL JAPANESE ARMY AND NAVY; MACARTHUR, DOUGLAS; PEACE TREATY OF 1952; POLICE SYSTEM; PRIME MINISTER; SELF-DEFENSE FORCES; SHIDEHARA KIJURO; SUPREME COMMANDER FOR THE ALLIED POWERS; SURRENDER OF JAPAN; WAR CRIMES TRIALS; WORLD WAR II; YOSHIDA SHIGERU; ZAIBATSU.

ODA NOBUNAGA (1534–1582) A military warlord who helped unify Japan after a century of warfare known as the Sengoku Era (1467–1568). Nobunaga was born into a military family in Owari Province (part of modern Aichi Prefecture). His father, Nobuhide, was the *daimyo* (lord) of Nagoya Castle. Nobunaga expanded his father's power base by defeating enemies in his own family as well as in neighboring regions. His first major victory was the Battle of Okehazama (modern Toyoake in Aichi Prefecture) in 1560, when he defeated the superior army of Imagawa Yoshimoto. In 1562 a vassal of Imagawa named Matsudaira Motoyasu, who later became Tokugawa Ieyasu, founder of the Tokugawa Shogunate (1603–1867), joined Nobunaga's side. Their alliance proved decisive for the course of Japanese history. An ambitious and ruthless warrior whose personal signature seal was inscribed with the motto, "to bring the whole country under one sword" (*tenka-fubu*), Nobunaga became a major *daimyo* in 1567 when he conquered the rich province of Mino. He was very receptive to two aspects of Western civilization recently introduced by the Portuguese: the Christian religion and firearms. He waged a lifelong campaign against the Buddhist institutions that had wielded great power during Japan's medieval era (12th–16th centuries) and against the Buddhist priests, who were his principal opponents. Nobunaga established a firearms brigade in his army and conquered the two important musket foundries in Sakai City and Omi Province, which gave him superior firepower over his enemies. Nobunaga was also the first Japanese military leader to use ironclad ships, when he blockaded the port of Osaka.

In 1568 Nobunaga made a large step toward unifying Japan when he led his armies into the old capital of Kyoto, which had suffered greatly during the warfare of the Sengoku Era. Rebellious lords had burned the palace of Shogun Ashikaga Yoshiteru, who was forced to commit suicide, and the imperial court had asked Nobunaga to come to the aid of the city. Nobunaga installed Ashikaga Yoshiaki as the new shogun but in fact exercised military rule himself. He destroyed Enryakuji, the influential Tendai Buddhist temple compound on Mount Hiei, and slaughtered its 20,000 monks, who had opposed his campaign to control the central Japanese provinces. From 1570 on, Nobunaga was forced to fight a coalition of enemy *daimyo,* after he invaded Echizen (part of modern Fukui Prefecture), as well as his most powerful enemy, Honganji, headquarters of the Jodo Shin (True Pure Land) sect of Buddhism. Shogun Ashikaga Yoshiaki joined the fight against Nobunaga in 1573. Nobunaga responded by burning the environs of Kyoto and then driving him into exile, which in effect ended the military rule of the Ashikaga Shogunate. In 1576 Nobunaga began constructing his heavily fortified castle at Azuchi. He won his second great victory in 1580 with the surrender of Honganji.

In 1574, Nobunaga accepted the title of court noble *(kuge),* and in 1577 he was given the third highest of all imperial court positions, minister of the right *(udaijin).* Nobunaga was also a patron of the arts and retained the services of the great tea ceremony master Sen no Rikyu (1522–1591). Nobunaga might have accepted the emperor's offer to name him shogun, but he died in a surprise attack during a tea ceremony by one of his generals, Akechi Mitsuhide; defeated, Nobunaga committed suicide. At the time, he controlled more than half the provinces of Japan, mainly in the region of Kyoto. His general, Toyotomi Hideyoshi (1537–1598), avenged his death and carried on his efforts to control the rest of Japan. The three generals, Nobunaga, Hideyoshi and Ieyasu, are known as the "Three Heroes" of Japan's unification. See also ASHIKAGA SHOGUNATE; AZUCHI-MOMOYAMA ERA; DAIMYO; EMPEROR; ENRYAKUJI; FIREARMS, INTRODUCTION OF; HIEI, MOUNT; KYOTO; PORTUGUESE IN JAPAN; PURE LAND SECT OF BUDDHISM; SEN NO RIKYU; SENGOKU ERA; SHOGUN; TEA CEREMONY; TOKUGAWA IEYASU; TOKUGAWA SHOGUNATE; TOYOTOMI HIDEYOSHI.

ODORI   See BON FESTIVAL; DANCE, TRADITIONAL.

OE KENZABURO (1935–) A leading contemporary Japanese novelist, short story writer, and essayist. Oe is described as an existentialist writer because his work has been affected by World War II and the atomic bomb, the postwar Occupation of Japan, some personal tragedies and the philosophy of modern Western thinkers.

Oe was born to a large family on Shikoku Island. He studied French literature at Tokyo University and wrote his graduation thesis on the novels of Jean-Paul Sartre. In 1957 Oe published his first important short story, "Lavish Are the Dead" ("Shisha no ogori"; translated 1965). The next year his short story "The Catch" ("Shiiku"; translated 1959), won the prestigious Akutagawa Prize. Oe's first novel, *Memushiri kouchi,* also published in 1958, earned him a reputation as one of Japan's best young writers. His writing became more consciously political and leftist around 1959, when the Japanese were debating the renewal of the Security Treaty between Japan and the United States. Oe published two collections of essays in 1962, about the Conference of Afro-Asian Writers he attended in Tokyo and about his trips to Europe and the Soviet Union. In the 1960s his novels and short stories were also influenced by the pain he experienced over the birth of his son, who had a congenital defect, and his visit to Hiroshima, where the first atomic bomb was dropped. Oe's novel *A Personal Matter (Kojinteki na taiken;* 1964, translated 1968) won the Shincho Literary Prize. A later novel, *The Silent Cry (Man'en gannen no futtoboru;* 1967, translated 1974), won the Tanizaki Junichiro Prize. Oe's journeys to North America and to Okinawa, which was governed by the United States at the time, stimulated his thinking about the course Japan had taken over the last century. He published two editions of collected essays in 1965 and 1968. A collection of his stories was translated into English in 1972 as *Teach Us to Outgrow Our Madness (Warera no kyoki o ikinobiru michi o oshieyo;* 1969). Oe has continued to publish novels and collections of essays. See also AKUTAGAWA RYUNOSUKE; ATOMIC BOMB; HIROSHIMA; NOVELS; OKINAWA ISLAND, SECURITY TREATY BETWEEN JAPAN AND THE UNITED STATES; TANIZAKI JUNICHIRO.

OFFICE LADY (OL) The popular term for Japanese women who do secretarial work in offices. Around one-third of working women in Japan are OLs (pronounced *o-eru).* The term *OL* was chosen in 1963 from entries to a competition held by *Josei Jishin,* a Japanese women's magazine. Many Japanese women hold jobs that are classifed as part-time in Japan, legally defined as up to 35 hours a week, but they usually put in enough overtime to make their jobs equal to full-time employment in the West. However, as "part-time" workers, the women receive lower wages and fewer benefits than men and women who hold full-time jobs. An "office flower" *(shokuba no hana)* is a decorative variety of OL. Office flowers are young women hired to look pretty, answer the telephone and do photocopying. These tasks are usually referred to as "serving tea" *(ochakumi),* another basic task of office flowers. Office flowers often marry men they meet at work. Women have been expected to stop working when they get married, although this is changing. The Japanese regard marriage as "eternal employment" *(eikyu shushoku)* for women. OLs are depicted in television soap operas as single women who have well-paying or exciting jobs but who are always unhappy because they really want to be married. See also CORPORATIONS; EMPLOYMENT.

OGATA KORIN   See KORIN.

OH SADUHARU   See BASEBALL.

OHIRA MASAYOSHI (1910–1980) Prime minister of Japan 1978–1980. Ohira was born in Kagawa Prefecture and educated at Tokyo Shoka Daigaku (now Hitotsubashi University). He became a bureaucrat in the Ministry of Finance, and in 1952 he won a seat in the House of Representatives, the lower house of the Japanese Diet. Ohira belonged to the Liberal Democratic Party (LDP; Jiyu Minshuto), Japan's dominant political party and therefore the one from which prime ministers are chosen. He held appointments as foreign minister and minister of finance in the cabinets of prime ministers Tanaka Kakuei and Miki Takeo. In 1976 he became secretary-general of the LDP, and in 1978 he was chosen president of the party and prime minister. Ohira hosted the economic summit meeting of leaders of the most developed countries held in Tokyo in 1979. In 1980 he suffered a political crisis when his cabinet received a vote of no-confidence. In response Ohira decided to dissolve the House of Representatives of the Diet. He died just 10 days before the LDP won a large victory in the next election. Ohira was also a scholar, a Christian and one of the last great Japanese postwar political faction leaders. See also DIET; LIBERAL DEMOCRATIC PARTY; MIKI TAKEO; MINISTRY OF FINANCE; POLITICAL PARTIES; PRIME MINISTER; TANAKA KAKUEI.

OIL CRISIS OF 1973 (sekiyu kiki)   Also known as the "oil shock" (sekiyu shokku); the threat to the Japanese economy resulting from the Arab oil embargo of October 1973. The Organization of Petroleum Exporting Countries (OPEC) placed an embargo on oil exports when the fourth Arab-Israeli war broke out on October 6, 1973. This caused a shock to the Japanese economy, because Japan was importing 99% of its crude oil, mostly from the Middle East and North Africa. Japan is a small island nation with few resources, and at the time of the oil crisis it was the world's largest importer of oil, needed to fuel the heavy industries that manufactured three quarters of Japan's exports. The worldwide recession along with the sudden rise in oil prices 1973–1976 affected Japan more than any other country. Its growth rate fell from around 11% to −2%, which was Japan's first postwar decline in industrial production, combined with severe inflation. However, although the Japanese experienced high inflation and loss of income in real terms, they did not fall into political or social instability, as might have happened in other countries. The oil supply stabilized, but subsequent hiking of prices by OPEC led to the quadrupling of oil costs and a consequent increase in the prices of many other raw materials Japan imports. The Japanese have been concerned with foreign dependency and economic strangulation ever since the oil shock. Many of the country's most energy-intensive industries reduced their dependence on oil during late 1970s and enhanced their productivity. At the same time, technological advances in microcircuits enabled Japan to shift to less energy-intensive industries through the expansion of the consumer electronics and computer industries. The prime minister's cabinet also developed more conciliatory policies toward Arab nations and increased its programs to assist their development, thus straining Japan's relationship with Israel. When international oil prices suddenly increased once more in 1979, the Japanese economy was strong enough to avoid the double-digit inflation suffered by other industrial nations and that Japan itself had suffered during the first oil crisis. By 1981 oil prices had dropped slightly, import demand had weakened and rapid growth in exports had yielded a trade surplus once more. Although the Japanese economy remains dependent on the prices of imported petroleum and other raw materials, its export sector can respond rapidly to match increases in imports. See also EXPORTS AND IMPORTS.

OKAKURA KAKUZO (1862–1913)   Also known as Okakura Tenshin; a Japanese writer and art conservator who helped spread knowledge about Japanese art in the Western world.

Okakura was born in Yokohama and learned English at the Tokyo School of Foreign Languages. At Tokyo University he studied with Ernest F. Fenollosa, an American scholar of traditional Japanese art and culture. Okakura became Fenollosa's interpreter and helped him found the Painting Appreciation Society (Kangakai), which received a commission from the Japanese government to catalog and display Japanese art treasures. In 1886 Okakura accompanied Fenollosa to Europe and the United States and studied Western art history and museum techniques. In 1889 Okakura helped found the first art academy in Japan, now known as Tokyo University of Fine Arts and Music, and served as its director until 1898. At the same time, he was also curator of the Imperial Household Museum (now Tokyo National Museum), helped publish Japan's first art magazine National Flower (Kokka) and organized exhibits of work by young artists. A conflict with the Ministry of Education led him to resign and to help found the private Japan Fine Arts Academy (Nihon Bijutsuin). Okakura traveled widely to study the art treasures of China and India. In 1904 he began making frequent trips to the United States and Europe to lecture and exhibit Asian art objects. He visited Fenollosa, who was curator of Oriental Art at the Boston Museum of Fine Arts, and met the influential patron Isabella S. Gardner. Okakura became advisor to the Boston Museum in 1905, and in 1911 he was named its curator of Chinese and Japanese art. He built a world-famous Asian collection for the museum, returning to Asia every year to acquire objects, as well as to visit his wife and children in Japan. Okakura wrote many articles and books about Asian art, including The Book of Tea (1906), in which he discusses the origin and unique history of tea in Asian culture, particularly the Japanese tea ceremony. See also FENOLLOSA, ERNEST F.; MUSEUMS IN JAPAN; TEA; TEA CEREMONY; TOKYO UNIVERSITY.

OKAME   Also known as Otafuku; a comic mask of a young, jolly, fat-cheeked woman who symbolizes prosperity and well-being. Okame masks are often worn in kagura, folk dance performances at Shinto festivals. They are also used for signboards (kamban) that advertise shops. The male equivalent is the Hyottoko mask, a comic face of a man with bulging lips that bend to the side of his face. His pursed lips may indicate that he is trying to blow on a fire, or that he often tells lies. A pair of comic dancers wearing Okame and Hyottoko masks often perform during traditional agricultural festivals in Japan. The masks may have derived from masks used in a traditional comic theater known as Kyogen. See also DANCE, TRADITIONAL; FESTIVALS; KYOGEN; SHINTO; SIGNBOARDS.

OKHOTSK, SEA OF   See CLIMATE OF JAPAN; GEOGRAPHY OF JAPAN; HOKKAIDO ISLAND; KURIL ISLANDS; SEA OF JAPAN.

OKI ELECTRIC INDUSTRY CO., LTD.   See COMPUTER INDUSTRY.

OKICHI   See BUTTERFLY; HARRIS, TOWNSEND; IZU PENINSULA.

OKINAWA, BATTLE OF (1945)   The final battle between Japan and the Allied Powers in World War II. Allied forces defeated the Japanese on the Pacific island of Saipan in July 1944, turning the tide against Japan and bringing U.S. bombers within range of Tokyo. Heavy American bombing of the Japanese islands forced the resignation of Prime Minister Tojo Hideki and also his successor, General Koiso Kuniaki. The Allies prepared for a major invasion of Okinawa Island in the Ryukyu Islands of southern Japan. Tens of thousands of Okinawan civilians were evacuated to other islands, and 100,000 Japanese troops were brought in to defend Okinawa. The first Allied air strike, on October 10, 1944, destroyed the city of Naha, but Japanese commanders decided to make a stand against the forthcoming Allied invasion, which began on April 1, 1945. The U.S. 10th Army established a beachhead, and five American army divisions, supported by naval barrage and aerial bombardment, invaded the island. Japanese troops were able to hide in the many natural caves on the island, and *kamikaze* pilots attacked American warships. The bloody battle lasted for 82 days, until the American flag was finally raised on June 22, 1945. On Mabuni Hill, tens of thousands of soldiers died in the final fighting, and General Ushijima committed suicide when Japanese defeat was imminent. Two hundred fifty thousand Japanese soldiers and civilians died altogether, as opposed to 12,500 Americans killed and 37,000 wounded. Many civilians committed suicide out of fear of the invaders. Okinawa's cities were in ruins and its economy devastated. Although Japan lost the Battle of Okinawa, it gave no sign that it intended to surrender, and the Allies feared they would have to engage in even bloodier fighting by invading the main islands of Japan. In August 1945, the U.S. dropped two atomic bombs on the cities of Hiroshima and Nagasaki, and Japan finally surrendered on August 14, 1945. Following the war, the U.S. occupied Okinawa Prefecture and established large military bases on Okinawa Island, which is strategically located near China and Korea. Not until 1972 did the United States return Okinawa to Japan; it still maintains bases there. Today the Okinawa Old Battlefield Quasi-National Park commemorates the battle with several monuments to the war dead. See also ATOMIC BOMB; KAMIKAZE; NAHA; OCCUPATION OF JAPAN; OKINAWA ISLAND; RYUKYU ISLANDS; SUICIDE; SURRENDER OF JAPAN; TOJO HIDEKI; WORLD WAR II.

OKINAWA ISLAND   The largest of the southernmost islands of Japan, and the most important part of the Ryukyu Islands, which lie in a chain 800 miles long between Kyushu Island and the Republic of Taiwan. Today these islands are commonly referred to as Okinawa and comprise the Prefecture of Okinawa. The Chinese character for Okinawa means "floating rope," but the name comes from a local dialect. Okinawa Prefecture has a population of more than 1 million and a total land area of around 866 square miles, of which Okinawa Island covers 53%. Okinawa's capital and largest city is Naha, with a population of about 300,000. Naha has been completely rebuilt since its destruction by Allied bombing and the Battle of Okinawa, April 1–June 22, 1945, the final battle, and one of the bloodiest, between the Allied Powers and Japan during World War II. The worst fighting took place on the southern end of the island, especially Mabuni Hill, where the Okinawa Old Battlefield Quasi-National Park commemorates those who died there. The U.S. administered Okinawa after the war until it finally agreed to return it to Japan in 1972. That year the Japanese government established the Okinawa Development Agency in the prime minister's office to administer the economic development of the prefecture. There are still American bases on Okinawa Island, where about 35,000 U.S. military personnel are stationed. Okinawa City (formerly Koza) has grown up around the bases. On the northern end of Okinawa Island are Nago City and a memorial park, which was built for Ocean Expo 1965. The island has a subtropical climate and many tourist beaches. A large cave named Gyokusendo in the south is another popular attraction. There are many castle sites dating as far back as the 12th century.

Okinawa was organized into three kingdoms in the 14th century and unified in 1372. In 1406 the founder of the Sho dynasty, which ruled Ryukyu until 1879, established his capital at Shuri in Naha. Shuri Castle has recently been rebuilt. Ryukyu, a great island trading kingdom, had a tributary relationship with China for five centuries. In 1609 it was taken over by the Shimazu clan of Satsuma Province (modern Kagoshima Prefecture) on southern Kyushu; this was kept hidden from China so as not to impair Ryukyu's trade with China, which made Satsuma wealthy. U.S. Commodore Matthew Perry paid two visits to Okinawa in 1853 and 1854 when he attempted to open Japan to Western trade. In 1879 Japan incorporated the Ryukyu Islands as Okinawa Prefecture. Although Okinawa is part of Japan, it has a unique and rich heritage reflecting its contacts with many Asian cultures. See also NAHA; OCCUPATION OF JAPAN; OKINAWA, BATTLE OF; PERRY, MATTHEW CALBRAITH; RYUKYU ISLANDS; SATSUMA PROVINCE; SHIMAZU CLAN; WORLD WAR II.

OKUBO TOSHIMICHI (1830–1878)   A leader of the proimperial movement that brought about the Meiji Restoration of 1868, and one of the main proponents of modernization in Japan. Okubo was born to a samurai family in Kagoshima on the southernmost Japanese island of Kyushu. As a boy he received a military education but also studied Chinese Confucian learning and Zen Buddhism. He became an official in the government of the Satsuma region (now Kagoshima Prefecture), where there was much opposition to the Tokugawa Shogunate (1603–1867), stemming especially from its failure to protect Japan from foreign influences. Okubo assumed the leadership of a Satsuma group that pressed the shogunate for reforms in 1862. He joined with Saigo Takamori, also from Satsuma, and Kido Takayoshi of the Choshu domain in 1866 to form the secret Satsuma-Choshu Alliance, which forged the links that eventually led to the Meiji Restoration. Upon the death of Emperor Komei, members of the Satsuma-Choshu alliance seized the Imperial Palace in Kyoto on January 3, 1868, and announced that power had been restored to Komei's son, who took the name Emperor Meiji. Okubo, Saigo and Kido directed the reforms of the Japanese government that created the modern Japanese state.

Okubo was a member of the Iwakura Mission that visited the United States and Europe (1871–1873). Back in Japan he became head of the Home Ministry (Naimusho) and exercised power equal to that of a prime minister. Okubo advocated the modernization of Japanese industry, agriculture and communications, and the development of a Japanese constitutional government that would retain limited powers for the monarchy. He opposed the plans of Saigo, Kido and Itagaki Taisuke, another powerful leader, to invade Korea in 1877, arguing that this would harm the Japanese economy, government and foreign relations. All three men resigned in protest of Okubo's policy. In 1877, Okubo put down the Satsuma Rebellion, led by his old friend Saigo Takamori, which was an attempt by anti-reform samurai to seize control of the government of Japan. After eight months of fighting, the military under Okubo's command defeated the rebellion. Samurai in his home area of Satsuma regarded Okubo as a traitor, and he was assassinated on May 14, 1878. See also ITAGAKI TAISUKE; IWAKURA MISSION; KIDO TAKAYOSHI; MEIJI RESTORATION OF 1868; SAIGO TAKAMURA; SATSUMA PROVINCE; SATSUMA REBELLION; TOKUGAWA SHOGUNATE.

OKUMA SHIGENOBU (1838–1922) A prominent politician during the Meiji (1868–1912) and Taisho (1912–1926) eras who was prime minister twice as well as a cabinet minister, leader of a political party and the founder of Waseda University.

Okuma was born near the city of Nagasaki in the region of Hizen (now Saga Prefecture). Hizen belonged to a coalition of rebellious *han* (feudal domains), known as the Satsuma-Choshu Alliance, in the southwest region of Honshu Island, which produced the leaders of the Meiji Restoration of 1868. Okuma received the traditional schooling for sons of samurai families, then went to Nagasaki, the only Japanese city where trade with Western countries was allowed by the Tokugawa Shogunate (1603–1867), and learned Western business and accounting methods as well as the Dutch and English language.

Okuma supported the movement to restore the emperor as ruler of Japan, which culminated in the overthrow of the Tokugawa government and the Meiji Restoration of 1868. The Meiji government appointed Okuma to handle commercial and diplomatic relations with foreign countries in Nagasaki. He did so well that he was appointed to several government posts in the capital city of Tokyo. By 1873 he was active in the ministries of foreign affairs and finance, and soon became minister of finance. He did much

to modernize Japan by developing systems for currency and telecommunications, founding the national mint and a ministry of industry. He borrowed money from Great Britain to build the first Japanese railroad. He also prepared the first national budget while most of the leaders of the new Meiji government were in Europe and the United States on the Iwakura Mission. Other measures that Okuma helped put into effect while they were away included a military draft and plans to invade Korea. This latter plan angered the members of the Iwakura Mission, although Okuma did find support from another prominent government leader, Okubo Toshimichi.

Okuma was removed from the Meiji government in 1881 when he requested that the emperor establish a parliamentary type of government based on a constitution and political parties, and advocated that the prime minister be chosen from the major political party. He also exposed a scandal in the government office responsible for colonization of the northern island of Hokkaido. In 1882, Okuma and other men who had quit the ministry of finance in sympathy with him founded a political party, the Constitutional Reform Party (Rikken Kaishinto), which was Japan's second major party, after the Liberal Party (Jiyuto), founded by Itagaki Taisuke in 1881. At this time Okuma also founded a university named Tokyo Semmon Gakko, which later became Waseda University. He was back in government in 1888 as foreign minister. In this position he negotiated with Western nations to revise the unequal treaties. His concessions to the foreign powers angered the public, and an attempted assassination helped force him out of politics. Yet he became foreign minister again in 1896, and the next year he was also named minister of agriculture and commerce. Two years later he helped form another political party, the Constitution Party (Kenseito); then in 1900 Okuma became head of a splinter party. In 1907 he left this position to serve as the president of Waseda University.

Okuma was selected by the leaders of the Meiji government as prime minister in 1914. He was the first prime minister in Japan to campaign for public support of his programs, and he even held press conferences for journalists to question his policies. His cabinet is best known for presenting the Twenty-one Demands on China in 1915. Okuma finally retired from politics when he and his cabinet resigned in 1916 due to an election scandal over bribery of Diet members by Home Minister Oura Kanetake and controversy over the Twenty-one Demands on China. See also ANSEI COMMERCIAL TREATIES; DUTCH IN JAPAN; HOKKAIDO ISLAND; ITAGAKI TAISUKE; MEIJI RESTORATION OF 1868; OKUBO TOSHIMICHI, POLITICAL PARTIES; PRIME MINISTER; SATSUMA PROVINCE; TWENTY-ONE DEMANDS ON CHINA; UNIVERSITIES.

OKUNCHI FESTIVAL See NAGASAKI.

OKUNI (fl. 1600 A.D.) Also known as Izumo no Okuni; a female entertainer who is popularly credited with founding the Kabuki theater. Okuni was apparently a priestess *(miko)* at Izumo, a major Shinto shrine, but became head of an exciting troupe of women entertainers, whose performances in Kyoto in 1603 at Kitano Shrine and on the dry riverbed (kawara) of the Kamo River (Kamogawa) made them nationally famous and spawned many imitators. People who lived along dry riverbeds were known as *kawaramono* and were social outcasts because their occupations, such as collecting night soil, digging graves and working with leather, were considered "unclean." Various singers, dancers, acrobats and other popular entertainers belonged to the *kawaramono,* and since they were free to perform on dry riverbeds without government interference or taxation, these areas developed into popular entertainment centers. Okuni's style of performance, which mingled singing, dancing, music and short plays, became known as Okuni Kabuki. The term *Kabuki* derives from a verb that means to act in an eccentric and suggestive yet stylish way. Okuni drew upon many sources for her theater, including popular songs, fashion and dances, such as a type of Buddhist folk dancing and chanting known as Nembutsu Odori. She performed in men's clothing in such roles as a samurai and a drunken man seeking pleasure. Okuni Kabuki appealed to the newly wealthy members of the urban merchant class (chonin, "townspeople") during the Edo Era (1600–1868). Performances by Okuni's troupe were boldly erotic, and the women engaged in prostitution as well as entertainment. In 1629 the Tokugawa Shogunate (1603–1867) banned Okuni's performances to prevent the corruption of public morals. Since that time, only males have acted in the Kabuki theater. *Onnagata* are Kabuki actors who specialize in playing women's roles. See also DANCE, TRADITIONAL; EDO ERA; IZUMO SHRINE; KABUKI; KAMO RIVER; KITANO SHRINE; NEMBUTSU; PRIESTS AND PRIESTESSES, SHINTO; TOKUGAWA SHOGUNATE; TOWNSPEOPLE.

OKUNINUSHI NO MIKOTO   See DAIKOKU; EBISU; IZUMO SHRINE.

OLYMPIC GAMES   The 18th Modern Olympic Games were held in Tokyo October 1–24, 1964, the first time ever in Asia. More than 5,500 athletes from 94 countries competed. Japan had actually been scheduled to host the 12th Olympic Games in 1940, but they were cancelled due to the outbreak of war between Japan and China. In 1964 the Japanese were proud to show off their country, which was developing rapidly after having been devastated in World War II. The high-speed Bullet Train (Shinkansen) was put in operation in time for the Olympics, and Tokyo underwent a massive building effort that cost about $3 billion. The Olympic Village was built in Yoyogi Park just east of Meiji Shrine in the Harajuku district of central Tokyo. Two modern gymnasia were built to house a swimming pool and basketball courts. Today the green spaces of Yoyogi Park and the Yoyogi National Gymnasia are open to the public.

In February 1972 the Winter Olympic Games were held in Sapporo, capital of the northernmost Japanese island of Hokkaido. These were the first winter games to take place in an Asian country. One thousand six hundred forty-one athletes from 35 countries participated. A Japanese ski jumper, Kasaya Yukio, won the first gold medal Japan ever

received in a Winter Olympics. See also BULLET TRAIN; HARAJUKU; MEIJI SHRINE; SAPPORO; TOKYO.

OLYMPUS OPTICAL CO., LTD.   See CAMERAS AND PHOTOGRAPHY.

OMAMORI   See AMULETS.

OMOTESANDO STREET   See HARAJUKU.

ONI   See DEMONS AND GHOSTS.

ONIGIRI   See BENTO; RICE.

ONIN WAR   A war fought from 1467 until 1477 in the old capital city of Kyoto and its surrounding region on western Honshu Island. This war initiated a century of military struggle in Japan known as the Sengoku or Warring States Era (1467–1568).

The Onin War erupted as a dispute between the brother and son of the shogun Ashikaga Yoshimasa (1436–1490) over who would succeed him. More broadly, the Onin War was a conflict among so-called *shugo daimyo,* military officials who governed the provinces of central and western Japan. The *shugo daimyo* had been given autonomous powers by the Ashikaga Shogunate (1338–1573) but remained dependent on the shogunate and each other in a delicate balance of power. The *shugo daimyo* needed the authority of the shogun to help them control the local military leaders (kokujin) in the territories they governed. The relationship between the shogunate and the *shugo daimyo* began breaking down after Ashikaga Yoshimitsu (1358–1408) died, and further declined after the assassination of Ashikaga Yoshinori (1394–1441). Whenever a *shugo daimyo* died without naming his successor, the lack of a strong shogun to support one candidate over other contenders resulted in fighting between factions in that *daimyo*'s territory. By the mid-1400s, succession disputes were tearing apart the Ogasawara, Togashi, Hatakeyama and Shiba *shugo daimyo* houses.

In 1464 Ashikaga Yoshimasa decided to give up his official responsibilities. Since his wife, Hino Tomiko, had not borne a son to be his heir, he asked his brother Yoshimi (1439–1491) to leave the Buddhist priesthood and become his successor. But the next year, Tomiko gave birth to a son, Yoshihisa (1465–1489), and demanded that he be named successor. The Onin War was triggered when two *shugo daimyo* houses took opposing sides in this dispute. The Hosokawa clan, under the leadership of Hokosawa Katsumoto, supported Yoshimi, and the Yamana clan, led by Yamana Sozen, supported Tomiko's son Yoshihisa. The location of their army camps in Kyoto led to the name Eastern Army for the Hosokawa faction and Western Army for the Yamana faction. During the decade of brutal fighting, factions within other *shugo daimyo* houses, such as the Hatakeyama and Shiba clans, used the Onin War to fight their own struggles for succession. Yoshihisa became shogun in 1473, but the war dragged on for four more years. Kyoto was destroyed, the Ashikaga Shogunate had lost its governing authority, and the great *shugo daimyo* houses declined while Japan endured a century of civil war. See also ASHIKAGA SHOGUNATE; ASHIKAGA YOSHIMASA; ASHIKAGA YOSHIMITSU; DAIMYO; HOSOKAWA CLAN; KYOTO; SENGOKU ERA; SHOGUN.

ONNAGATA   See KABUKI; MAKEUP.

ONO YOKO (1933–   )   Known outside of Japan as Yoko Ono; an avant-garde artist, musician, and filmmaker who became world famous as the wife of John Lennon (1940–1980), of the British rock band the Beatles.

Ono was born into a wealthy family in Tokyo. In 1952 she went to New York City with her banker father, later attending nearby Sarah Lawrence College. Her first two husbands were Ichiyanagi Toshi (1933–   ), a Japanese composer, and Anthony Cox, an American artist. After their divorce, Cox kidnapped their daughter, Kyoko (b. 1963). Ono married John Lennon in 1969. Many people blamed her for breaking up the Beatles as well as Lennon's first marriage, but the four musicians had already started working on separate projects. Ono was also controversial for her experimental and conceptual art. Her first show was at the AG Gallery in New York in 1961. Lennon and Ono collaborated on various artistic projects, made experimental films and recorded several albums under the name Plastic Ono Band. They also gained notoriety for their antiwar activities and unconventional life-style. The couple separated briefly but reconciled and lived a quiet life in New York. Lennon helped care for their son Sean (b. 1975) while Ono managed their considerable financial holdings. In 1980 the couple released another album, *Double Fantasy*. After Lennon was murdered that year, Ono recorded an album in his memory, *Age of Glass* (1981). She then resumed her artistic activities. In 1989 the Whitney Museum of American Art in New York held an exhibition of her art.

OOMOTO   One of the major so-called "new religions" that appeared in Japan in the 19th century. Oomoto was founded in 1892 by Deguchi Nao (1837–1918), who was born in the Kyoto region and who married a carpenter with whom she had eight children. He died in 1887, and in 1892 she began seeing visions, experiencing trances and claiming that the god Ushitora no Konjin spoke through her. Nao wrote down the messages, and these scriptures, called *ofudesaki*, became the heart of Oomoto. Nao preached that the end of the world was imminent and a messiah would come to establish a peaceful "Kingdom of Heaven." Human beings must cooperate with this god, who is present in the human heart, for the "Reconstruction of the World." Many people claimed to be cured of illness by Nao. A man named Ueda Kisaburo (1871–1948; later known as Deguchi Onisaburo) promoted Nao's teachings and helped organize the Oomoto religion. He married Nao's daughter Sumi (1883–1952) and became the movement's leader.

The religion of Oomoto combines beliefs and rituals from Shinto, the native Japanese religion; Japanese folk traditions, in particular shamanism; and Buddhism, the religion introduced into Japan from China in the sixth century A.D. However, Oomoto claims to be an international religion and teaches world peace and brotherhood. The religion had around 2 million members in the 1920s and 1930s, when it was persecuted by the Japanese government for its denounciation of war and militarism. Onisaburo and other Oomoto leaders were imprisoned in 1935, but was released after World War II. After Onisaburo died in 1952, Oomoto was unable to regain its former membership, although it has continued to be active, centered in the towns of Kameoka and Ayabe in Kyoto Prefecture. In 1976 the Oomoto School of Traditional Arts was founded to teach traditional arts, such as the tea ceremony, flower arranging, pottery, calligraphy and Noh drama, to foreign students. There were 160,000 members of Oomoto in 1977. See also BUDDHISM; NEW RELIGIONS; SHINTO; SHAMANS AND SHAMANISM.

OPENING OF JAPAN   See ANSEI COMMERCIAL TREATIES; HARRIS, TOWNSEND; PERRY, MATTHEW CALBRAITH; SECLUSION, NATIONAL; "REVERE THE EMPEROR, EXPEL THE BARBARIANS"; TOKUGAWA SHOGUNATE.

ORIBE   See FURUTA ORIBE.

ORIBE WARE (*oribe-yaki*)   A type of pottery named for the tea ceremony master Furuta Oribe (1544–1615). Oribe ware is associated with another type of pottery known as Shino ware. Shino and Oribe were two styles of Mino ware (*mino-yaki*), pottery made in the province of Mino (modern Gifu Prefecture) on central Honshu Island. Tea ceremony masters during the Azuchi-Momoyama Era (1568–1600), when tea was patronized by great warlords, valued Shino and Oribe tea utensils such as water containers and tea bowls (*chawan*). Oribe ware is made from clay that turns salmon pink when fired in the kiln, and is covered with white, tan, green and light brown feldspath glazes. Pieces known as *e* ("picture") Oribe are decorated with bold, spontaneous designs in dark reddish brown iron-oxide glaze. A distinctive copper-green glaze (*ao* or "green," Oribe) was used for the first time in Japan on Oribe ware. Production of Oribe reached its height in the late 16th and early 17th centuries when the *noborigama*, a wood-fired "climbing" kiln with many chambers on a rising slope, was introduced from the region on Kyushu Island where Karatsu ware was made. Typical Oribe pieces are tea bowls, vases, incense burners, and dishes, bowls and cups for serving the special tea ceremony cuisine called *kaiseki*. See also FURUTA ORIBE; KAISEKI; KARATSU WARE; KILN; MINO WARE; SHINO WARE; TEA CEREMONY.

ORIGAMI ("folding paper")   The art of folding paper into different shapes or objects, such as birds and animals, dolls, boats and so forth. The term *origami* also refers to the objects that are created by this technique. Although this art form is now practiced primarily for enjoyment, *origami* is rooted in ancient Japanese religious rituals. Paper has always been highly valued in Japan. When a Buddhist priest brought the skill of making paper to Japan from China in A.D. 538, the Japanese began using paper for ceremonial occasions and folded pieces of strong, fibrous handmade paper (*washi*) into various shapes according to

strictly prescribed rules. The earliest religious use of *origami* was at the main Shinto shrine at Ise, where gods were represented by figures cut from special paper *(jingu yoshi)*. Paper still plays an important function in Shinto purification ceremonies. Pieces of white paper are specially cut and folded to make an implement called a *gohei* or *shide* that a priest shakes during the ceremony. Paper figures of human beings are also used in some purification ceremonies.

Bottles of sake placed on Shinto altars were covered with folded white paper and tied with a complex knot of silver and gold cords *(mizuhiki)*. This custom is still practiced today, as is the ornamentation of sake bottles at weddings with male and female *origami* butterflies. Gifts in Japan have always been wrapped according to formal rules of etiquette depending on the social rank of the recipient and the type of occasion. Wrapped gifts are decorated with a folded paper shape called *noshi*. This follows the custom of *noshi-awabi*, which originated in the 12th century, whereby a thin strip of dried abalone, a symbol of good fortune, was placed in a piece of folded paper on a gift.

The crane *(tsuru)*, a bird that the Japanese regard as an omen of "a thousand years" of long life and good fortune, is the oldest and most popular *origami* shape. The auspicious nature of this symbol is heightened by a complex *origami* of connected figures representing a Thousand Cranes (Sembazuru). Folding and stringing together a thousand cranes and offering them to the gods is thought to make a wish come true. Sembazuru may also be given as expressions of sympathy to someone who is in the hospital or who has lost a relative or friend. Schoolchildren leave many Sembazuru at the Peace Park in Hiroshima to honor those killed by the atomic bomb in World War II. The *origami* crane shape is also depicted as a decorative motif on textiles, particularly ones used for theatrical costumes.

Although *origami* has undergone changes through the centuries, it still follows specified roles for folding paper, emphasizing straight lines and sharp angles. Most *origami* shapes begin with a square piece of paper, often with different colors on the two sides. It is folded as required by following four types of preparatory folds. These folds are (1) the diagonal (opposite corners meet), (2) double diagonal, (3) book fold (vertically through the center), and (4) double book fold. The addition of more geometric folds, and the layering and manipulation of the paper and its angles, will build up a desired shape. *Origami* is a good practical technique for educating children about spatial and angular relationships using artistic creativity. Different kinds of paper can be used to add interest to the flat, angular shapes. *Origami* paper is usually brightly colored on one side, and it is available in different degrees of thickness and stiffness. The shape may also be other than square, such as a rectangle, triangle, circle, pentagon, or hexagon. The technique of folding a shape with layers of different-colored paper is called *kasaneori*. Folding one piece of paper that is printed with a colorful design is known as *kawari-e origami*. These techniques are used to make costumed paper dolls *(oshi-e origami)*. Functional objects like a paper wallet

that is carried in the fold of a kimono, and small boxes can also be made. See also ATOMIC BOMB; CRANE; GIFTS; MULBERRY BUSH; PAPER, HANDMADE; PURIFICATION; SHINTO; WRAPPING.

OSAKA The third-largest city in Japan, after Tokyo and Yokohama, the hub of the Hanshin Industrial Zone, and an important center for finance and wholesaling. Major industrial products include chemicals, machinery, steel and textiles, many of which are exported through the ports of Osaka and Kobe on Osaka Bay. Osaka also has an international airport and is constructing a new one, the Kansai International Airport, on a site in Osaka Bay. Situated in southwest central Japan, the Osaka region was inhabited as far back as the Yayoi Era (c. 300 B.C.–c. A.D. 300), and has a distinct cultural and historical tradition. Osaka always served as a port, for trade with China in the seventh and eighth centuries A.D. and to serve the ancient Japanese capitals of Nara and Kyoto, north of Osaka. Toyotomi Hideyoshi, the warlord who unified Japan, built Osaka Castle (Osaka-jo) in 1583 on a strategic hilltop in the city's northern district and used it as his headquarters. After he died, armies of the Tokugawa Shogunate (1603–1867) took Osaka Castle in 1615. The castle was also damaged in the fighting that led to the Meiji Restoration of 1868. The main gate and several towers have survived, but the tower keep was rebuilt using ferroconcrete in 1931. Merchants poured

Osaka Castle, originally built in the late 16th century by Toyotomi Hideyoshi (1536–1598), one of three warlords who helped unify Japan. The castle was destroyed twice and rebuilt in 1931 using ferroconcrete.

into the city during the Edo Era (1600–1868) and made Osaka Japan's largest center for the distribution of goods, particularly rice that was collected as tax payments.

Osaka was destroyed during World War II but has since been rebuilt. It covers 80 square miles and has a population of more than 3 million. The city is also capital of Osaka Prefecture in the central part of the main Japanese island of Honshu. The region around Osaka, Kobe and Kyoto is called both Kinki and Kansai. Tourist attractions include Shitenno Temple, Sumiyoshi Shrine, Osaka Municipal Museum and Osaka Municipal Museum of Fine Arts. The National Museum of Ethnology is located on the site of the world's fair Expo '70, which was held in Osaka. In 1990 Osaka hosted Expo '90, the International Garden and Greenery Exposition. Remains from the ancient capital of Naniwakyo can also be seen. Osaka is known for its multitude of excellent restaurants and for a traditional form of puppet theater known as Bunraku. See also BUNRAKU; CASTLES; EXPO '70; EXPORTS AND IMPORTS; INDUSTRIAL ZONES; KANSAI AND KANTO; KOBE; KYOTO; TOYOTOMI HIDEYOSHI.

OSAKA INTERNATIONAL AIRPORT See AIRLINES AND AIRPORTS.

OSHIMA NAGISA (1932–) An internationally renowned film director. Oshima was born in Kyoto and studied law at Kyoto University, but was unable to get a job because he had been a student activist. In 1954, the Shochiku Motion Picture Company gave him a position as an assistant director. He also wrote screenplays and film criticism. In 1959 he began directing his own movies. Influenced by the French "new wave" (nouvelle vague) film movement, in the 1960s Oshima became the leader of a group of radical Japanese movie directors known as Shochiku New Wave (Nuberu Bagu). Many of Oshima's movies are about two themes that he admits have particularly interested him: sex and crime. An early movie, Cruel Story of Youth or Naked Youth: A Story of Cruelty (Seishun zankoku monogatari; 1960) takes place during violent Japanese demonstrations against the renewal of the U.S.-Japan Security Treaty in 1960. In the film, a juvenile delinquent who represents the nihilism of young people in Japan commits sexual violence against his girlfriend. Oshima left Shochiku Motion Picture Company in 1960 and in 1965 formed his own production company, Sozosha. Oshima's interest in Western movies led him to work on many international coproductions. He gained worldwide notoriety with his French-produced film about sexual obsession, In the Realm of the Senses (Ai no korida; 1976). The sequel, Empire of Passion (Ai no borei; 1978), won him the Best Director award at the Cannes International Film Festival. For many years, however, Oshima encountered legal obstacles to having his work shown in Japan. Two of his recent coproductions include Merry Christmas, Mr. Lawrence (1983), which features English actors Tom Conti and David Bowie, and Max Mon Amour (1987). In 1973 Oshima also became the host of a popular morning television program in Tokyo, on which he advises women on marriage and social problems. See also FILM.

OTAFUKU See OKAME.

OYASHIO (PARENT CURRENT) See CLIMATE OF JAPAN; GEOGRAPHY OF JAPAN; PACIFIC OCEAN.

OYSTER See PEARL; SEAFOOD; SHELL.

OZAWA SEIJI (1935–) A world-renowned Japanese classical orchestra conductor. Ozawa was born in Shenyang, China, and was educated in Japan at the Toho Gakuen School of Music, where he studied conducting with Saito Hideo (1902–1974). In 1959 Ozawa was awarded first prize in the International Competition of Orchestra Conductors, held at Besancon, France. After serving as assistant conductor of the New York Philharmonic and music director of the Toronto Symphony Orchestra, in 1970 Ozawa was named conductor and music director of the San Francisco Symphony Orchestra, a position he held until 1976. In 1972 he also became conductor of the New Japan Philharmonic Orchestra in Tokyo, and was given the Japan Arts Academy Prize. In 1973 Ozawa took his current position as music director of the Boston Symphony Orchestra.

OZU YASUJIRO (1903–1963) Japanese film director. Ozu was born in Tokyo but raised by his mother in his father's hometown of Matsuzaka, near Nagoya City, while his father remained in Tokyo. In 1923 Ozu became an assistant cameraman with an important Japanese movie company named Shochiku Co., Ltd. He was promoted to director by 1927. At first he filmed short comedies, but in the 1930s he began making serious movies, most of them dealing with problems related to the breakdown of modern Japanese families. Ozu's first major movie, I Was Born, But . . . (Umarete wa mita keredo; 1932), about a boy growing up, was the first cinematic work of social realism in Japan. Perhaps reflecting his own upbringing, children in Ozu's films are often raised by one parent. Conflict between children and parents who nonetheless share a deep affection is another important theme. Ozu drew directly from his own life experiences in There Was a Father (Chichi ariki; 1942), about a father and son, who are close despite their long separation imposed by their careers. Ozu made his most famous movie soon after World War II. Tokyo Story (Tokyo Monogatari; 1953) poignantly portrays the neglect of an aging couple by their children, who move from their small town to selfishly pursue their own interests in hectic postwar Tokyo. A number of the relatives lack any emotional concern for other family members, another common theme in Ozu's films. Ozu produced and directed 53 movies during his career. In concentrating on family dramas, he provided viewers an intimacy with his characters by using low camera shots, slow pacing and everyday dialogue. He is considered the most "Japanese" of Japan's great movie directors. See also FAMILY; FILM.

P

PACHINKO A pinball game played on vertical machines. *Pachinko* was introduced to Japan from America as a children's game in 1920. Since World War II it has become one of the most popular recreational activities in Japan, with 70% of the men and 30% of the women spending $70 billion a year on the game. By law, players must be over 18 years old. *Pachinko* parlors are recognized by their bright gaudy lights, loud music, and the constant noise of the machines. A player purchases small steel balls, chooses a machine, pours the balls into a feed chute and rapidly snaps a knob or presses an automatic feed lever to shoot the balls into the pinball grid. If a ball slips into a winning hole or catcher, known as a "tulip" because of its shape, the "petals" open up and several more balls may land in it before the petals suddenly close. Every ball that is caught this way releases about a dozen additional balls into play. Winning is a combination of luck and skill. The machine gives the winner a batch of steel balls that can be traded in at a counter for various prizes, including chocolates, cookies, canned food, cigarettes and magazines. Although gambling is strictly controlled in Japan and it is illegal to trade the balls in for cash, there are places near pachinko parlors where this can be done. Most people play for fun and relaxation. See also GAMBLING; GAMES.

PACIFIC OCEAN The largest body of water in the world, which lies off the east and southeast coasts of Japan. The Pacific Ocean has served as a buffer between the islands of Japan and the non-Asian world until modern times. Most cultural influences traveled east across the Asian continent and entered Japan from China and Korea, which lie directly west of Japan, through Kyushu Island. Many immigrants to Japan also followed this route.

Rich fishing grounds lie in the Pacific Ocean, especially off the Sanriku Coast of northeastern Honshu, where the warm Kuroshio (Black Current, also known as the Japan Current) flowing up from the south meets the cold Oyashio (Okhotsk Current or Kuril Current) flowing down from the north. The current also accounts for the fact that Honshu, the principal island of the Japanese archipelago, enjoys a milder climate on the eastern side than on the western.

The Pacific Plate, comprising the bed of the Pacific Ocean, moves west at a speed of several centimeters each year. The point along the east coast of Japan where the Pacific Geologic Plate pushes below the Eurasia Plate to its west is called the Japan Trench. Movement of this plate creates severe earthquakes and volcanic eruptions in Japan. See also CHINA AND JAPAN; CLIMATE OF JAPAN; EARTHQUAKES; FISH AND FISHING INDUSTRY; GEOGRAPHY OF JAPAN; HONSHU ISLAND; HOKKAIDO ISLAND; KOREA AND JAPAN; SECLUSION, NATIONAL; VOLCANO.

PACIFIC WAR See WORLD WAR II.

PACKAGING See WRAPPING.

PADDIES See AGRICULTURE; RICE; RICE PLANTING AND HARVESTING FESTIVALS.

PAGODA (*to*) "Tower"; a tall structure, usually made of wood and having five stories, which is an important feature of Japanese Buddhist temple or monastery architecture. The Buddhist religion, introduced into Japan from China in the sixth century A.D., originated in India in the sixth century B.C. Pagodas developed from ancient Indian *stupas*, low, round structures that enshrined religious scriptures (*sutras*) and sacred body parts or relics of the Buddha. In

A five-story pagoda of Kofukuji in the ancient capital city of Nara. A pagoda, commonly erected in a Buddhist temple compound, houses scriptures and sacred relics.

China the *stupa* evolved into the tall, wooden pagoda, retaining its function as a holy storage place. Pagodas were constructed in Japan beginning in A.D. 585. The oldest surviving Japanese pagoda, dating back to A.D. 711, can be seen at Horyuji in the ancient capital of Nara. Since the Japanese prefer odd numbers, nearly all surviving pagodas have three or five stories. A typical five-storied pagoda (*goju-no-to*) has a square, circular or multisided base and five stories, representing sky, wind, fire, water and earth, and is topped by an ornamented spire (*sorin*). A central pillar (*shimbashira*) in the center of the pagoda holds relics of the Buddha and points to heaven. The location of the pagoda within a temple compound varies according to the different sects of Buddhism. Towers similar to pagodas can be found at temples of the Shingon and Tendai sects of Buddhism. These towers, called *tahoto*, have a square base and a circular upper story, with a spire at the top. See also BUDDHISM; HORYUJI; NARA; TEMPLES, BUDDHIST; SCRIPTURES, RELIGIOUS.

PAINTING See BIRD-AND-FLOWER PAINTING; BRUSHES; CALLIGRAPHY; CASTLES; FIGURE PAINTING; INK PAINTING; KANO SCHOOL OF PAINTING; LANDSCAPE PAINTING; RIMPA SCHOOL OF PAINTING; SCREENS; SCROLLS; TOSA SCHOOL OF PAINTING; WOODBLOCK PRINTS; YAMATO.

PALACE See IMPERIAL PALACE (KYOTO); IMPERIAL PALACE (TOKYO); KATSURA DETACHED PALACE; SHUGAKUIN DETACHED PALACE.

PALANQUIN (*kago*) A bamboo or wooden box large enough for one or two people to be carried in. The palanquin was a traditional method of transporting members of the upper class in Japan, beginning in the Muromachi Era (1333–1568). Palanquins were originally made of bamboo, with a floor, roof and enclosed front and back. The sides were open or had screens that could be rolled up or down. A long pole through the roof was carried on the shoulders of two men. Palanquins were widely used during the Edo Era (1600–1868) and were made in various shapes and materials for people of different social classes. Commoners rode in bamboo palanquins known as *machikago* or *tsujikago*. Japanese of the highest rank, including aristocrats, *daimyo* (feudal lords) and chief priests, rode in beautifully lacquered enclosed wooden palanquins known as *norimono*. See also EDO ERA; MUROMACHI ERA; PALANQUIN, SACRED.

PALANQUIN, SACRED (*mikoshi*) A portable shrine, also known as a *shin'yo*, used for carrying the spirits of Shinto deities (*kami*) in processions during festivals. The *mikoshi*, usually referred to with the honorary prefix o- as o-*mikoshi*, is a miniature version of the shrine in which the deity resides. It is decorated with black lacquer and gilded metal, and a phoenix (*hoo*; a mythical bird) often sits on its roof. A *mikoshi* can be small enough for children to carry, or so large that hundreds of men are needed. Large *mikoshi* rest on two long poles that the men bear on their shoulders. The bearers wear short jackets and headbands (*hachimaki*) dyed with the symbol of the local shrine association to which they belong. The deity's spirit is believed to descend into the *mikoshi* when it is taken out and paraded through

the shrine's district. A sacred mirror (*shinkyo*) is often carried inside the *mikoshi* to represent the divine spirit. The bearers run and shake the *mikoshi* vigorously to signify the spirit inside. Along the procession route, the *mikoshi* may be set down in places where religious rituals were originally performed (*otabisho*), and residents offer food and sake to the deity in gratitude for divine protection during the coming year. In some festivals, *mikoshi* are carried into a river or the sea to ask the shrine deity for bountiful fishing. The first recorded use of *mikoshi* in Japan dates from the eighth century A.D. Prior to that time, divine spirits were symbolically carried in a mirror and another sacred object, such as a branch of the *sakaki* tree. In the 10th century *mikoshi* were carried in the then capital city of Kyoto to help prevent epidemics. See also FESTIVALS; KAMI; SHINTO; SHRINES, SHINTO.

PALM READING See FORTUNE TELLING.

PANASONIC (MATSUSHITA ELECTRIC INDUSTRIAL CO., LTD.) See ELECTRONICS INDUSTRY.

PANDAS See ZOOLOGICAL GARDENS.

PAPER BOOKS See BOOKBINDING, TRADITIONAL; BOOKS AND BOOKSTORES; COMIC BOOKS.

PAPER, HANDMADE (*washi*) Paper made by hand from fibers of the mulberry bush (*kozo*) or other plants. Japanese handmade paper is not made from rice plants, although it is often referred to as "rice paper" by foreigners. Paper was introduced to Japan around the seventh century A.D. Koreans were the master papermakers, and legends tell of a Korean monk named Doncho who came to the court of Empress Suiko in 610 and taught Japanese the techniques for making Chinese paper, ink and writing brushes. During the Nara Era (710–794), the imperial court encouraged papermaking by promoting the copying of thousands of Buddhist scriptures. Papermaking was important in the aristocratic culture of the Heian Era (794–1185) because literature became the main cultural activity, especially with the development of native syllabic systems of writing (*kana*). Writing became an art form for its own sake, known as calligraphy (*shodo*), and papers with a variety of decorative colors and textures were used.

Techniques for making Japanese-style *washi* were developing during this time. Whereas Chinese paper mixes cloth and plant fibers, *washi* is made from plant bark, usually mulberry, and not mixed with cloth. It has a rough surface and irregular edges, and is very strong. Making *washi* is a time-consuming and laborious process. First the plant branches are steamed, and the bark is peeled away and soaked in cold water. The tough outer bark is then scraped away with sharp knives. The inner layer of soft white fibers is heated in an alkaline solution and rinsed in cold water. Impurities are picked out of the fibers, which are then beaten with mallets or heavy sticks or mechanized beaters until completely broken down and separated. Next, the fibers are mixed with water, and a vegetable mucilage called *neri* is added to the pulp to maintain the proper consistency. The papermaker dips a wooden frame *(keta)* lined with a fine bamboo screen *(su)* into the pulp, lifts it up and gently shakes it to pour off excess pulp. Water is drained from the screen, and the layer of pulp is lifted from the frame, turned over and placed face down onto a pile of newly made sheets of *washi*. The wet stack of paper is pressed until partially dried. Each damp sheet is then separated and brushed onto a wooden drying board. When dry, the sheets are trimmed, colored with dye if desired and packaged for sale. Abe Eishiro, a modern *washi* maker, has been designated a "Living National Treasure" by the Japanese government.

Because it is strong and resistant to water, *washi* is used for the arts of calligraphy, ink painting, woodblock prints and *origami* (paper folding). It is pasted on wooden frames to make sliding screens and doors known as *shoji* and *fusuma*, as well as lanterns. Stencils are cut from *washi* for making woodblock prints and for printing designs on silk textiles. Kimono, other traditional articles of clothing and objects, and gifts of money are all stored or wrapped in white *washi* according to specified methods of folding and wrapping. Strips of white *washi* are hung on straw ropes for Shinto religious ceremonies and used in purification rites. *Chiyogami* are brightly colored hand-printed patterned papers decorated with techniques that use stencils, similar to woodblock prints. These papers are used to make boxes, dolls and other decorative items. See also CALLIGRAPHY; DOLLS; GIFTS; INK PAINTING; KIMONO; LANTERNS; LIVING NATIONAL TREASURES; MULBERRY BUSH; ORIGAMI; PURIFICATION; SCREENS; SHINTO; STENCILS; WHITE; WOODBLOCK PRINTS; WRAPPING.

PARENT-CHILD RELATIONSHIP See APPRENTICE SYSTEM; DEPENDENCY; FAMILY; FATHER; IEMOTO; MOTHER, SAMURAI; YAKUZA.

PARENT CURRENT (OYASHIO) See CLIMATE OF JAPAN; GEOGRAPHY OF JAPAN; PACIFIC OCEAN.

PARKS See FUGI-HAKONE-IZU NATIONAL PARK; GARDENS; HARAJUKU; HIROSHIMA; IMPERIAL PALACE (TOKYO); MEIJI SHRINE; NATIONAL PARKS; NIKKO NATIONAL PARK; RIKUGIEN GARDEN; UENO.

PARLIAMENT See DIET.

PAULOWNIA *(kiri)* A hardwood tree that does not grow wild in Japan but is widely cultivated for its fine wood. The paulownia, which grows 30 feet high, may have been introduced into Japan from China or Korea more than a thousand years ago. Its leaves grow in large ovals with pointed tips. In early summer, tubular purple flowers bloom on the top branches, followed by oval fruits, which are not eaten but used for decorations. The paulownia flower is used in many designs for family crests *(mon)*. Paulownia wood is soft and light, resists warping, and has a fine grain. It is highly prized for making *tansu*, large wooden storage chests used in homes and shops. Many other objects for daily use are also made of paulownia, such as boxes, *hibachi* (charcoal braziers) and informal raised wooden

sandals called *geta*. Since paulownia grows quickly, parents traditionally planted a paulownia tree on the birth of a daughter. When she grew up, the tree was cut down to make a chest for her wedding trousseau. See BOXES; CHEST; CRESTS; FOOTWEAR; FURNITURE; HIBACHI; WOODWORKING.

PEACE MEMORIAL PARK See ATOMIC BOMB; HIROSHIMA.

PEACE TREATY OF 1952 Formally known as the Treaty of Peace with Japan, but also known as the San Francisco Peace Treaty; a treaty that ended the Allied Occupation of Japan following World War II and restored full independence to Japan. The peace treaty was signed by Japan, the United States, and 47 other countries at San Francisco on September 8, 1951, and went into effect on April 28, 1952. On the same day in San Francisco, Japan and the United States also signed a security treaty that allowed the American government to maintain military bases and troops in Japan, and specified that U.S. forces would deal with external aggression against Japan, while Japanese Self-Defense Forces would deal with internal problems and natural disasters. The U.S.-Japan Security Treaty took effect in February, 1952. As early as 1947, the United States, which had administered the Occupation of Japan, attempted to negotiate a treaty of peace, but met continued opposition from the Soviet Union. In 1950 the U.S. initiated negotiations without Soviet participation, which, with several other countries, including India and Burma, refused to sign the peace treaty. (India signed a separate peace treaty with Japan in 1952, and Burma did so in 1954). The treaty restored Japanese sovereignty over the four main islands of Honshu, Kyushu, Hokkaido and Shikoku, and small adjacent islands but removed Japanese sovereignty over all territories seized by Japan since 1895, including Korea, Taiwan, the Kuril Islands and southern Sakhalin Island. The Soviet Union had occupied the Kurils and southern Sakhalin since 1945; however, their status was left unresolved since the Soviets did not sign the treaty, and Japan still disputes the Soviet claim to these islands. The United States was given trusteeship of the Ryukyu Island chain, including Okinawa Island, to the south of the main Japanese islands. In the treaty, Japan also agreed not to pardon war criminals that had been convicted by the International Military Tribunal for the Far East unless permission was granted by the majority of the 11 nations that took part in the trials. Japan also agreed that the United States would administer the payment of war reparations to countries that made claims to Japan. The treaty declared that Japan had the right of self-defense and that it could authorize the stationing of foreign troops in Japan. In 1952 Japan also signed a peace treaty with the Chinese Nationalist regime which had relocated to the island of Taiwan from mainland China in 1949, although this treaty did not deny Japan the right to negotiate with the People's Republic of China on the mainland. Japan began informal trade relations with the P.R.C. in 1953. See also KURIL ISLANDS; OCCUPATION OF JAPAN; OKINAWA ISLAND; RYUKYU ISLANDS; SECURITY TREATY BETWEEN THE U.S. AND JAPAN; SELF-DEFENSE FORCES; U.S. AND JAPAN; WAR CRIMES TRIALS; WORLD WAR II.

PEACH FESTIVAL   See DOLL FESTIVAL; PEACH TREE.

PEACH TREE (*momo no ki*)   Peach trees were brought to Japan from China in the 1870s. There is too much rainfall in Japan for Western peach trees to be cultivated successfully, although Japanese and Western peaches have been crossed to make a hybrid for commercial canning. In Japan the peach is mainly eaten fresh. Peach flowers are associated with the Doll Festival (Hina Matsuri) held for girls every year on March 3rd, because they bloom at this time; the festival is also known as the Peach Festival (Momo-no-Sekku). Delicate pink peach flowers symbolize the grace and gentleness that are traditional ideals for young women in Japan. A vase of flowering peach branches is often placed next to the set of dolls dressed in imperial court costumes that is displayed during the festival. Momotaro (Peach Boy) is a popular folktale about a boy born from a peach who is raised by an elderly couple, slays demons on Ogre Island, and brings home treasures. See also DOLL FESTIVAL; MOMOTARO.

PEARL (*shinju*)   A pearl is made of a substance termed nacre that is secreted by a shellfish if an irritating object gets inside the shell. Natural pearls have always been valued as decorative gems, and classified according to their quality, shape and color, which can range in tone from white to pink, gold, green, blue and even black. Japanese women pearl divers (*ama*) have long been active in the Pacific Ocean off Toba on the Shima Peninsula in Mie Prefecture. In the 1890s a Japanese man named Mikimoto Kokichi (1858–1954) developed a method to artificially stimulate oysters to produce pearls by inserting small mother-of-pearl beads into the oysters and keeping them in seawater until the "seeds" were coated with many layers of nacre. These so-called "cultured pearls" were soon harvested on a large scale in the Pacific Ocean off the Shima Peninsula. In 1899 Mikimoto began selling his pearls in a store in Tokyo, and two years later he opened branch stores in cities in the United States and other countries.

Pearls have become a world-renowned product of Japan,

Women diving for pearls in the Pacific Ocean off Toba on the Shima Peninsula, Mie Prefecture. Pearls have been cultivated for a century in Japan.

and three-quarters of all Japanese cultivated pearls are still produced in the same area where Mikimoto began his experiments. Small pearls are formed in six months, while larger pearls require two or three years. Harvested in November, the total annual number of Japanese pearls amounts to nearly 100,000 pounds about half of which are exported to the United States and Europe. Pink freshwater pearls are also cultivated in Lake Biwa and Kasumigaura and are exported to India and Southeast Asia, where they are used to make jewelry and are also ground for cosmetic and medicinal use. See also BIWA, LAKE; EXPORTS AND IMPORTS; PACIFIC OCEAN.

PEARL HARBOR, JAPANESE ATTACK ON (December 7, 1941)   The surprise attack by Japanese fighter planes on the U.S. Pacific Fleet in Pearl Harbor, Hawaii was planned by Admiral Yamamoto Isoroku and was timed to coincide with Japan's delivery of a declaration of war to the U.S. government in Washington. At Pearl Harbor the Japanese sank four American battleships and two other ships, damaged four battleships and 12 other ships, and killed or wounded 3,700 men. Three American aircraft carriers were at sea and thus escaped the attack. Japanese losses included 29 planes and five small submarines, with 64 men killed. The United States had intelligence information that the Japanese were planning an attack, but thought it would take place in the Philippine Islands. Six hours after the Japanese attacked Pearl Harbor, they attacked and destroyed most of the American planes based in the Philippines. Within a few days, Japan also attacked Guam, Wake, Midway and Hong Kong islands, thereby destroying or immobilizing 90% of U.S. air and sea forces in the Pacific Ocean.

When Pearl Harbor was attacked, Japanese diplomats were in Washington, D.C., negotiating with the U.S. government. Tensions were high between the two countries because of U.S. opposition to Japan's aggression in China, Japan's alliance with Italy and Germany, and American economic sanctions against Japan, including the banning of oil shipments that Japan desperately needed. Destroying the U.S. naval fleet freed Japan to expand southward and capture the oil-rich Dutch East Indies (Indonesia). Japan calculated that the United States would be too preoccupied with the war in Europe to mobilize in the Pacific. However, the attack on Pearl Harbor incensed the American people and united them into a concerted effort against both Japanese and European fascism. The attack is commemorated at its site by the Arizona Memorial Museum. See also SINO-JAPANESE WAR OF 1937–1945; WORLD WAR II.

PENTAX   See CAMERAS AND PHOTOGRAPHY.

PEONY (*botan, shakuyaku*)   A flowering plant introduced to Japan from China during the Nara Era (710–794) as a medicinal plant. In China the peony, a symbol of wealth and honor, was known as the "king of flowers." Starting in the Edo Era (1600–1868), many beautiful varieties of peony have been cultivated in Japan, especially on Daikonjima, an island in Shimane Prefecture. Two species of peony belonging to the buttercup family are still widely cultivated in Japan as ornamental plants, the tree peony (*botan*) and a herbaceous peony (*shakuyaku*). The tree peony grows to a height of 3–10 feet and produces single or double round flowers about 6 inches in diameter. They may be pink, white, purple or particolor. Single flowers have seven to nine petals, while doubles have many more. After the flowers bloom in early summer, they produce large seeds. The herbaceous peony grows about 2 feet high and produces large flowers with around 10 petals, each 2 inches long. The flowers may be red, white or particolor.

Peonies have been exported to the West from Japan since the Edo Era. Peony flowers have been a popular design motif in Japan since the Nara Era, and are often combined with lotus, honeysuckle and other flowers in complex patterns known as scrolling vine motifs (*karakusa*). Another popular pattern is peonies and butterflies. The Japanese do not usually include peonies in flower arrangements because the flowers drop off the stems suddenly, like human heads cut off by samurai swords. See also BUTTERFLY; FLOWER ARRANGING; FLOWERS; LOTUS.

PEOPLE, JAPANESE The Japanese are one of the most racially homogeneous population in the world. The basic ethnic Japanese stock developed during the Jomon Era (c. 10,000 B.C.–c. 300 B.C.). Before the ninth century A.D., some Korean and Chinese immigrant groups, as well as members of various indigenous tribes in the Japanese islands, were absorbed into the Japanese stock. For well over a thousand years the population of Japan has consisted of ethnic Japanese, who speak the Japanese language. The Japanese are of Mongolian stock, with a fold in the eyelid, yellow skin pigmentation, flat faces with high cheekbones, black hair, relatively hairless bodies and short limbs. One strain of the Japanese people may have originated in Central Asia. A second strain may have originated in southern China, giving the Japanese a more delicate bone structure and smaller size than the Mongolian types who settled in northern China. Some scholars argue that there is also a Malaysian or Polynesian strain in the Japanese people, as evidenced by ancient Japanese architecture, although this is a controversial point.

Japan has become one of the most densely populated of the world's major industrialized nations. Three-fourths of the population live in urban areas, especially in the Kansai and Kanto regions around Osaka and Tokyo. The population more than tripled between 1872 and 1985, from 34.8 million to 121 million. However, birth and death rates have been declining in recent years. The population as a whole is aging, and it is estimated that by the year 2020, the population will total around 128 million, with about 28 million aged 65 or over. The Japanese have the highest longevity rate in the world, with an average life expectancy in 1985 of 74.84 years for men and 80.46 years for women.

Around 1 million Japanese emigrated to other countries during the past century, but 70% of those left before World War II, and settled mostly in Hawaii, the mainland United States, and South America.

Several minority groups in Japan suffer social and eco-

nomic discrimination, including the Ainu, an indigenous proto-Caucasian group in northern Japan; the *burakumin* ("hamlet people"), who are racially Japanese but who are occupational outcastes; and Koreans and Chinese born in Japan but not given full citizenship. The people of the Ryukyu Islands (Okinawa Prefecture), which became a prefecture of Japan in 1879, are related to the Japanese people but speak different dialects, have some different cultural traits and have darker, hairier bodies than the mainland Japanese. See also AINU; BURAKUMIN; CHINA AND JAPAN; HORSE-RIDER THEORY; JOMON ERA; KANSAI AND KANTO; KOREA AND JAPAN; MINORITIES IN JAPAN; RYUKYU ISLANDS.

PEOPLE'S GOVERNMENT PARTY (Minseito) The name given in 1927 to a political party earlier known as the Progressive Party or Constitutional Government Party (Kenseito), and revived after World War II as the Democratic Party (also known as the Progressives). This party, the second in Japan, was founded in 1882 by Okuma Shigenobu (1838–1922). For three decades after its founding, the People's Government Party trailed the first Japanese political party, founded in 1874 by Itagaki Taisuke (1837–1919) and known first as the Liberal Party (Jiyuto, "Freedom Party"), then as the Friends of Constitutional Government Party (Seiyukai), and after World War II as the Liberal Party. In 1915 Okuma's party won a plurality, and in 1924 it produced its first prime minister, Kato Takaaki (1860–1926). These two political parties alternated in controlling the Diet (Parliament) and office of prime minister into the 1930s. Both parties were moderate and represented big business, wealthy agrarian interests, landlords and the upper middle class. The Manchurian Incident of 1931, in which Japanese troops seized Manchuria, brought down the Minseito cabinet in December 1931. Assassinations of political and business leaders and the rising influence of the Japanese military in the prewar years ended the power of the political parties to influence the government. The People's Government Party was revived as the Japan Democratic Party (Nihon Minshuto) after the war, and in 1955 it joined with the Liberal Party (Jiyuto) to form the Liberal Democratic Party (Jiyu Minshuto), which has dominated Japanese politics to the present time. See also DIET; ELECTIONS; FRIENDS OF CONSTITUTIONAL GOVERNMENT PARTY; ITAGAKI TAISUKE; KATO TAKAAKI; LIBERAL DEMOCRATIC PARTY; POLITICAL FRIENDS SOCIETY; MANCHURIAN INCIDENT; OKUMA SHIGENOBU; POLITICAL PARTIES.

PERRY, MATTHEW CALBRAITH (1794–1858) A U.S. naval officer who was instrumental in opening Japan to Western nations after it had been closed by the Tokugawa Shogunate (1603–1867) in 1639. During his long naval career, Perry served in many regions of the world and was awarded the honorary title of Commodore in 1841. In 1852, President Fillmore's administration authorized him to head a naval expedition to establish diplomatic and commercial relations between the United States and Japan. Perry's squadron first landed at Naha on Okinawa Island in southernmost Japan, then sailed to Edo Bay (modern Tokyo Bay), arriving on July 8, 1853, and anchored at Uraga off the Izu Peninsula. Perry came ashore with 300 armed marines and met with the *daimyo* (feudal lord) of Uraga. He presented a letter from President Fillmore addressed to the emperor, asking for normalization of trade relations between Japan and the United States and permission for American ships to anchor in Japanese ports so they could resupply with coal, water and food. Perry said he would return in one year to receive an answer to the U.S. demands.

After sailing to Hong Kong and Macao, Perry returned to Japan in February 1854 to receive the government's reply. His fleet, termed the "black ships" by the Japanese, now included three steam frigates and 6 other vessels. This time he demanded that negotiations be held at Kanagawa (part of modern Yokohama), located close to the capital city of Edo (modern Tokyo). When Perry arrived, Japan had already been suffering attempts by other nations to open it to trade. Russia was pushing down from Siberia in the north, and European powers, which controlled India and much of Southeast Asia, were forcing unequal treaties on China. Clearly, Japan's geographic isolation would no longer provide security from foreign nations. Perry's ships, armed with modern cannon, could have destroyed Edo, or cut off food supplies by blocking the entrance to Edo Bay.

The Tokugawa Shogunate was unable to make a forceful stand against Perry's black ships. It took the unprecedented step of consulting with the imperial court and with leading *daimyo* (feudal lords), who opposed giving in to American demands. The shogunate decided to acquiesce, however, and signed the Kanagawa Treaty with the United States on March 31, 1854. the first modern treaty that Japan signed. The treaty stipulated that two Japanese ports, Shimoda on the Izu Peninsula and Hakodate on the northern island of Hokkaido, would be opened to American ships. The treaty did not establish trade relations between the two countries, but it did allow for the United States to station a consular official at Shimoda. Townsend Harris took this position in 1856.

This reversal of the established shogunal policy to exclude foreigners created agitation against the Tokugawa Shogunate throughout Japan and contributed to the shogunate's downfall in 1867 and the Meiji Restoration of 1868. "Expel the Barbarians" became a slogan of opposition to the Tokugawa Shogunate. After signing the Kanagawa Treaty, Perry continued to explore the coast of Japan and the Ryukyu Islands (modern Okinawa prefecture) to the south, then returned home to much acclaim. See also EDO; HAKODATE; HARRIS, TOWNSEND; IZU PENINSULA; OKINAWA ISLAND; RYUKYU ISLANDS; SECLUSION, NATIONAL; TOKUGAWA SHOGUNATE.

PERSIMMON *(kaki)* An Asian fruit often eaten as a dessert, the persimmon is grown throughout Japan except for the northernmost island of Hokkaido. Many Japanese grow persimmon trees in their home gardens, harvesting the fruit from September through November. There are many types of persimmon belonging to two basic varieties, astringent *(amagaki)* and non-astringent *(shibugaki)*. The astringent variety has a bitter taste due to a high tannin content. These persimmons can be eaten only after being

treated with alcohol and carbon dioxide, or when they have been dried. Sugars in the fruit create a white powder on dried persimmons. Strings of persimmons were traditionally hung from the eaves of farmhouse roofs in the autumn to dry in the sun. Non-astringent persimmons, the most widespread of which are called *fuyu*, have a sweet taste. They have an orange color and a round shape, similar to a tomato, and are eaten when firm. See also FARMHOUSE.

PHARMACEUTICAL INDUSTRY See BIOTECHNOLOGY INDUSTRY.

PHILIPPINE SEA, BATTLE OF THE See WORLD WAR II, YAMATO.

PHILOSOPHY See BUDDHISM; CONFUCIANISM; HAYASHI RAZAN; HISAMATSU SHIN'ICHI; NISHIDA KITARO; SHINTO; SUZUKI DAISETZ TEITARO.

PHOENIX *(ho)* A mythical bird that represents the South and summer and is believed to appear only once in a thousand years to mark an auspicious event, such as the rule of a virtuous emperor. The phoenix has features of the peacock and the pheasant, such as bright colors and a long tail. In Japan as in China, the bird became a symbol of the empress as the *kirimon* or phoenix crest. The empress doll displayed by families at the Doll Festival (also known as Girls' Day; March 3) has phoenix designs on her kimono sleeves and crown. The phoenix motif has been used to decorate many types of objects in Japan, such as scroll mountings, screens, and ladies' accessories. The Phoenix Pavilion (known as the Hoodo) of the Byodoin, an 11th-century temple at Uji, is constructed in the shape of a stylized phoenix and has two phoenixes decorating the roof. This building, a fine example of late Heian Era (794–1185) aristocratic architecture, has been designated by the government as a National Treasure. See also DOLL FESTIVAL; NATIONAL TREASURES; UJI.

PHOTOGRAPHY See ADVERTISING; BROADCASTING SYSTEM; CAMERAS AND PHOTOGRAPHY; FILMS; MAGAZINES; MOVIES.

PICKLES *(tsukemono)* Rice and pickles are eaten together and are even thought to constitute a complete meal. Their nutrients complement each other, and the sharp flavor of the pickles enhances the plainer taste of the rice. Thousands of types of pickles are made in Japan by over 100 methods. Each region of Japan has its own special type of pickles, which are often packaged and sold as gifts for travelers to bring home as souvenirs. A number of basic types of pickles are commonly eaten, especially in the cities. These include pickled daikon (Japanese radish), Chinese cabbage, eggplant, turnip, cucumber, ginger, scallion, and plum. Japanese consider pickled eggplant *(nasu-zuke)* to be the best of all pickles. Picked ginger *(shoga-zuke)* is always served with sushi (rice topped with raw fish, vegetables, and other ingredients) and has a very sharp flavor. Pickled *daikon (takuan-zuke)* is another favorite.

Pickles can be made at home and represent "Mom's

cooking" (ofukuro no aji) to the Japanese, although most people now buy pickles in stores. The basic method for preparing pickles is very simple. A vegetable such as daikon or cabbage is put into a wooden barrel and covered with salt. When the barrel is full, a lid is placed on top, weighted down by a large stone. The weight and salt work together to force the juices out of the vegetables, and the salt preserves and seasons them. Some other methods pickle vegetables in a mash made of rice bran, in miso (soybean paste), or in a by-product of sake. Pickles have an important place at Japanese weddings and the introductory meetings (miai) between prospective brides and grooms, at which fish and meat pickled in sake or miso are served.

The only fruit that is pickled in Japan is umeboshi, which is usually called a plum (ume) but is actually a species of apricot. Records from the 10th century illustrate that pickled plums were used then as a disinfectant and for medicinal purposes. They are so salty and sour that they also stimulate the eating of large quantities of rice. For this reason the Japanese often eat them at breakfast. Pickled plums are said to also aid digestion and the intestinal tract. They are added to a rice gruel to help cure illness. Yellow plums are harvested just before they ripen in June. Traditional methods pickle them for a month, dry them in the summer sun, and put them back into the pickling liquid along with shiso leaves, which color them a dark red. The pickled plums are ready to eat when the weather turns cold. See also DAIKON; GINGER; MISO; PLUM; RICE; SAKE; SUSHI; WEDDING.

PICKS, WOODEN (tsuma-yoji, kashi-yoji) Small pointed pieces of wood used as toothpicks (tsuma-yoji) or as cake picks (kashi-yoji) for cutting and eating moist Japanese-style sweets (kashi), especially in the tea ceremony. The finest picks are made from kuromoji, a small tree of the camphor species. They are cut by hand and have a dark strip of bark on one side. Cheaper picks are cut by machine from inexpensive wood such as white birch and do not have bark strips. There are special carrying cases for toothpicks and cake picks. Small wood or ceramic toothpick holders are kept on the tables of many Japanese restaurants and homes. Etiquette requires that one cover one's mouth with the left hand while using a toothpick. Picks are sold in gift packages by department stores and specialty shops at the New Year season. Kiri-bako-iri are toothpicks wrapped with red tipped papers, inscribed with fortune poems. See also NEW YEAR FESTIVAL; SWEETS; TEA CEREMONY.

PICTURE BRIDE A Japanese woman who married a Japanese man who had immigrated to another country without meeting him. The man and woman exchanged photographs through the mail. If they agreed to marry, their marriage was legalized in Japan without the man being present. The bride then left the country to live with her husband.

Japanese women who became picture brides were often from the lower social classes and wanted to make a better life or escape unhappy situations. Marriages arranged by go-betweens (nakodo) had been common for a long time in Japan. According to Japanese law, no ceremony was required for a marriage to be legal. The families only had to present to their local registrar a document stamped with the personal seals of the bride and groom. The bride was then officially entered in the groom's household register (koseki).

Many Japanese immigrants went to the United States as laborers after the Chinese were excluded in 1890. More than 125,000 Japanese immigrated to the United States between 1901 and 1908. In 1908 a "Gentlemen's Agreement" between Japan and the United States halted Japanese immigration, but immigrants already in America were able to acquire passports for their parents, wives and children. The picture bride system became a convenient way for them to establish families. U.S. immigration officials acknowledged the legality of picture bride marriages, although they often required the couple to have an American marriage ceremony after the bride arrived. Continued opposition to Japanese immigration forced Japan to stop giving passports to picture brides to the United States in 1920–1921. Many still came to the U.S. territory of Hawaii until the U.S. Immigration Act of 1924 excluded Japanese immigrants from Hawaii as well. See also GO-BETWEEN; HOUSEHOLD REGISTER; IMMIGRANTS, JAPANESE; ISSEI.

PILGRIMAGE (junrei) The term junrei is commonly used for a journey to a distant religious site. Pilgrimage has always been an important religious and social activity in Japan. The custom began during the Nara Era (710–794) and was frequently practiced during the Heian Era (794–1185), when aristocrats and monks of the Buddhist religion, which had been introduced into Japan during the sixth century A.D., traveled to mountains in the countryside that were revered as sacred. Regular pilgrimage circuits of temples were already mapped out on western Honshu Island and Shikoku Island by the late Heian Era. In the medieval era, pilgrimage was principally a way of demonstrating one's religious devotion, but it became more of a social event for all classes of society during the Edo Era (1600–1868), when the country was at peace, merchants prospered, and transportation became easier. Some of the most heavily visited pilgrimage sites were the "88 Buddhist Temples of Shikoku Island," the Shinto Shrine at Ise and Mount Fuji, but numerous other pilgrimage centers also developed. The famous haiku poet Matsuo Basho (1644–1694) wrote many of his poems while making pilgrimages.

Modern travel as a leisure activity in Japan often follows earlier pilgrimage routes. Japanese travelers enjoy visiting famous Buddhist temples and Shinto shrines on their vacations. Temple and shrine festivals also attract large crowds of visitors all through the year and especially at the New Year Festival. See also BASHO; BUDDHISM; FUJI, MOUNT; ISE SHRINE; MOUNTAINS; NEW YEAR FESTIVAL; SHIKOKU ISLAND; SHINTO.

PILLOW BOOK, THE See SEI SHONAGON.

PILLOWS (makura, zabuton) Cushions are used in Japan to sit on or to rest the head on while sleeping. Hard pillows for sleeping are known as makura. Today they are made of cloth and often stuffed with buckwheat chaff. Traditionally, raised pillows made from hard materials such as wood or pottery were used under the neck to keep elaborate hairstyles neat. A book by the famous Japanese woman writer Sei Shonagon (fl. late 10th century) is known as the *Pillow Book (Makura no soshi)*, perhaps because she stored the manuscript in her wooden sleeping pillow, or perhaps because she discusses intimate relationships. The term "pillowing" has been used in Japan to refer to sexual relations, and just before their weddings young women were often shown "pillow books" *(makura-e)* containing detailed pictures of sexual activity.

Traditional Japanese homes have very little furniture. People kneel or sit on *tatami* (thick straw floor mats), on top of which may be placed thin square stuffed cushions known as *zabuton. Zaisu*, seats on the floor without legs, may also be used for sitting at low tables or writing desks *(tsukue).* See also FURNITURE, TRADITIONAL; HAIRSTYLES, TRADITIONAL; HOMES AND HOUSING; SEI SHONAGON; TATAMI.

PINE TREE *(matsu)* Because pine trees remain green in winter and stand strong against wind and rain, they have always been revered in Japan. There are several native varieties. Most common is the red pine *(akamatsu),* which grows 130 feet high and has a trunk as large as 6 feet in diameter. Red pine wood is often used to build houses and boats, and the rare edible mushroom known as *matsutake* ("pine mushroom") grows only near roots of red pine trees. The black pine *(kuromatsu)* is as tall as the red pine but has a narrower trunk. It is used for landscaping, prevention of soil erosion and construction wood. Black pines are also used in *bonsai,* the art of cultivating miniature trees, as are smaller varieties of Japanese pine, such as *goyomatsu* and *kita goyomatsu.*

Pine branches are combined with bamboo for the New Year's decoration known as *kadomatsu.* Bamboo, pine, and plum blossoms are often combined in a popular decorative motif known as the "three friends of winter." Stages for classical Noh drama have a painting of a pine tree for a backdrop, and live pine trees are planted in front of the actor's walkway to the stage. Noh is closely related to the religion of Zen Buddhism, which admires the sturdiness of an ancient pine tree that has withstood the buffeting of weather over time. Pine trees have been a frequent subject of Japanese painting and ink painting *(sumi-e).* Ashes of burned pine are used to make paints and black ink *(sumi)* for calligraphy and ink painting. A scenic place known as Matsushima (Pine Tree Islands) on the northeast coast of Honshu Island is regarded as one of the "Three Famous Sites" (Nihon Sankei) of Japan. See also BAMBOO; BONSAI; INK PAINTING; MATSUSHIMA; MUSHROOMS; NEW YEAR FESTIVAL; NOH DRAMA; PAINTING; THREE FRIENDS OF WINTER; ZEN SECT OF BUDDHISM.

PIONEER ELECTRONIC CORPORATION See ELECTRONICS INDUSTRY.

PLANTS See BONSAI; FLOWER ARRANGING; FLOWER FESTIVAL; FLOWERS; GARDENS; MOSS.

PLOVER *(chidori)* Small birds found along rivers and the seashore and in marshes and rice paddies. Plovers have long legs, round bodies, short beaks and large eyes. There are 12 species of this shorebird in Japan, which are generally gray, black, brown or white. Plovers feed in flocks and have a melancholy cry. They have been featured in Japanese poetry and decorative motifs since ancient times. A pattern known as "plovers and waves" *(chidorigata)* is frequently found on kimono (traditional clothing) and sliding doors *(fusuma).* The traditional geisha community of Pontocho in the city of Kyoto uses the plover for its crest. "Plovers on the Beach" is a well-known dance in Okinawa (Ryukyu Islands). See also CREST; KAMO RIVER; KIMONO; PONTOCHO; SCREENS.

PLUM TREE *(ume)* A tree brought to Japan from China around the eighth century A.D. that grows about 20 feet high and bears a yellow fruit that resembles an apricot rather than a Western plum. Plum flowers, which have five petals and a lovely fragrance, are important in Japanese culture as the first flowers to bloom in the New Year, based on the traditional lunar calendar. Both red and white plum blossoms have been cultivated in Japan. The plum blossom has been used as a decorative motif for textiles and lacquer ware, and in family crests *(mon).* The plum is combined with the pine tree *(matsu)* and bamboo *(take),* which also remain fresh in winter, in a popular decorative motif known as the "three friends of winter." This motif, also popular in China, is used on festive and auspicious occasions. The plum tree was mentioned in many poems of a type known as *waka* written by members of the ancient Japanese court. Since the plum fruit ripens during the rainy season *(tsuyu)* in early summer, the rain at this time is often called "plum rain" *(bai-u).* The Japanese make plum wine and plum vinegar, and use dried strips of plum to make sweets known as *noshiume.* Plums are also thought to have medicinal value, and every morning many Japanese eat pickled plums *(umeboshi)* with rice to aid their digestion. Bark of the plum tree is used to dye textiles. Plum wood is used for interior features of homes, such as the *tokobashira,* a wooden post next to the *tokonoma,* an alcove where art objects are displayed. See also CALENDAR; CREST; NEW YEAR FESTIVAL; PICKLES; RAIN; SWEETS; THREE FRIENDS OF WINTER; TOKONOMA; WAKA.

POETRY Ever since the Japanese adopted the Chinese writing system along with many other aspects of Chinese culture beginning in the sixth century A.D., they have admired poetry as the highest form of literature. The Japanese language is traditionally written with brush and ink on scrolls that are viewed by unrolling or hanging, and calligraphy (shodo, the "Way of Writing"), closely associated with poetry, is regarded as the highest form of the visual arts. *Waka,* "Japanese poems or songs," is the term for classical forms of Japanese poetry written in the vernacular using *kana* (syllabic scripts), as distinguished from Chinese-style poetry *(kanshi,* "Chinese verse") written in *kanji* (ideographs) by early Japanese poets. Specifically, the term *waka* is applied to Japanese poetry written in the classical form known as *tanka* ("short poem"), which became dominant by the ninth century A.D. A *tanka* consists of five lines with 31 syllables in a 5-7-5-7-7 pattern and is written in *kana*. Because the Japanese language comprises a limited number of syllables, many words sound alike, and the language lends itself to short poems with a limited number of syllables. In the 14th century the *tanka* form was adapted into the *renga* ("linked verse") form, which has two parts alternately composed by two or more people: three lines of 5-7-5 syllables and two lines of 7-7 syllables. By the 17th century the *haiku* (also known as *hokku* or *haikai* form, with three lines of 5-7-5 syllables, which is expressive and spontaneous in contrast to the rigid *tanka* form, became popular. In the broad sense, the term *waka* includes all of these poetic forms. The term *waka* is now associated with poets who wrote in the classical 31-syllable *tanka* form prior to the 20th century, while the term *tanka* refers to 20th-century poets who attempt to use the *tanka* form in a more creative manner.

The earliest and perhaps greatest anthology of Japanese poetry is the *Manyoshu*, comprising 20 books with a total of 4,154 *waka*. Most of these are *tanka* ("short poems"); there are also 260 *choka* ("long poems") and 60 *sedoka* ("head-repeated poems"). Anthologies of poetry were compiled by imperial order during the Heian Era. The first was the *Kokinshu* (*Kokin wakashu*; A.D. 905), which contains 1,111 poems arranged by topics, such as the four seasons and love. Sugawara no Michizane (845–903), an official in the imperial court, is regarded as the greatest master of Chinese-style poetry in early Japan, and was also a master of the Japanese poetic style. The most highly regarded poet of the mid-Heian Era was Izumi Shikibu (fl. c. 1000), a court lady who mastered every poetic style of the time. More than 1,500 of her *waka* have survived. Diary (*nikki*) literature, a major Heian literary form dominated by women authors such as Murasaki Shikibu (fl. c. 1000) and Sei Shonagon (fl. late 10th century), contains a large proportion of poetry. Fujiwara no Teika (1162–1241) is the literary figure most responsible for establishing Japanese taste in poetry. He is believed to have compiled *Hundred Poets, a Poem Each (Hyakunin Isshu)*, the best-known anthology of Japanese verse. Most Japanese still memorize the poems in this anthology, and learn them by playing a popular poem-matching card game known as *utagaruta*. Teika also preserved the classical tradition of poetry by compiling the influential anthology known as the *New Collection* and by his literary criticism in *Guide to the Composition of Poetry*.

During the transition from the imperial Heian Era to samurai rule under the Kamakura Shogunate (1192–1333), the court poet and literary critic Kamo no Chomei (1156?–1216) became the symbol of the literary recluse who lives a quiet life in the mountains and uses poetry as a means of religious awakening. From the 12th through 16th centuries, the *renga* form of poetry became popular. A *renga* is based on the five-line *waka* or *tanka* form but is composed by two or more people in succession: one gives the first three lines of 5-7-5 syllables, the next supplies the two successive lines of 7-7 syllables, then three 5-7-5 lines are created, and so on. Public *renga* competitions were fre-

Thirty-Six Immortal Poets, a painting on a two-fold screen attributed to Tatebayashi Kagei (fl. mid-18th century). The Japanese have always regarded poetry as one of the most important arts.

quently held. Whereas the *tanka* form was associated with the imperial court, members of all social classes enjoyed composing *renga*. During this era, monochromatic ink painting (*suibokuga* or *sumi-e),* associated with Zen Buddhism, became the dominant artistic style, and artists often wrote poems alongside their depictions of mountains and other natural scenes. In the 16th century, the first three lines of the *renga* form of poetry were developed into the lighthearted *haiku* form, which comprises only 17 syllables in a 5-7-5 pattern. The best known *haiku* poet is Matsuo Basho (1644–1694). *Haiku* remains very popular in Japan and is practiced by poets around the world. Another beloved Japanese poet is the Soto Zen monk Ryokan (1758–1831); more than 400 of his poems in Chinese and 1,400 of his poems in Japanese have been preserved. Many Japanese enjoy composing poetry today, and a poetry competition is held every New Year in which thousands of people submit a *waka* on the theme announced by the emperor. Numerous collections of Japanese poetry have been translated into English. See also BASHO; CALLIGRAPHY; DIARIES; FUJIWARA NO TEIKA; HAIKU; HEIAN ERA; INK PAINTING; IZUMI SHIKIBU; KAMO NO CHOMEI; KOKINSHU; MANYOSHU; RENGA; RYOKAN [POET]; SCROLLS; SUGAWARA NO MICHIZANE; TANKA; WAKA; WRITING SYSTEM, JAPANESE.

POLICE SYSTEM *(keisatsu)* The current police system was established by the Police Law of 1954, and combines the centralized police system that operated before World War II and the decentralized local police units created during the postwar Occupation. The police system is administered by the National Public Safety Commission, which reports to the prime minister and controls the National Police Agency (Keisatsucho), located in Tokyo. Each prefecture maintains a police force administered by the National Police Agency. Tokyo also has its own police force, known as the Metropolitan Police Department (Keishicho). The National Public Safety Commission also administers the National Police Academy, bureaus of criminal investigation, traffic, security and communications, police bureaus in the eight general administrative regions of Japan, and the Imperial Guard Headquarters. Cities, towns and villages are divided into districts, each of which is serviced by numerous small police stations (hashutsujo, commonly known as koban) in the cities or by residences for policemen and their families (chuzaisho) in rural areas. They are staffed 24 hours a day by patrol police (gaikin keisatsu; also known as Omawarisan, or "Mr. Honorable Walking Around") who patrol the neighborhood on foot, bicycle or motorbike, mediate family quarrels and other disputes, help people with directions, and recover lost property. Other police specialize in criminal investigation (keiji), traffic control (kotsu), crime prevention (bohan), security (koan) or administration (keimu). The emergency police number is 110, commonly known as hyakutoban. There are around 200,000 policemen in Japan. Policemen are highly respected and receive cooperation from most citizens, which is one reason why the crime rate in Japan is less than one-fifth that of the United States. Japan also has strict laws forbidding the possession of firearms or dangerous weapons without a license. Drug use is also forbidden. Policemen conduct surveys of homes in their areas twice a year to check the names, ages, occupations, business addresses and automobile license numbers of residents. They also find out who is old or home alone and might require emergency assistance, as well the hours kept by local businesses and their employees. Such information often proves helpful in criminal investigations. Neighborhood associations (chonaikai) work actively with the police, as do other citizen's groups, and at times even known gangsters (yakuza). Special police riot units were formed in each prefectural department and the Metropolitan Police after riots occurred at the Imperial Palace in 1952. They handle violent demonstrations, aid in natural disasters such as earthquakes and control crowds during festivals. Policemen are hired and promoted through 10 ranks on the basis of examinations, and must pass strict background checks to show no radical activities, mental illness or criminal record. Police schools require one-year courses for high school graduates and six-month courses for college graduates and women. Police also must take continuing education courses in various fields related to their work. See also LEGAL SYSTEM; NEIGHBORHOOD ASSOCIATION; PREFECTURE; WARD; YAKUZA.

POLITICAL PARTIES See CLEAN GOVERNMENT PARTY; DEMOCRATIC SOCIALIST PARTY; DIET; ELECTIONS; FACTIONS; FRIENDS OF CONSTITUTION GOVERNMENT PARTY; JAPAN COMMUNIST PARTY; JAPAN SOCIALIST PARTY; LIBERAL DEMOCRATIC PARTY; PEOPLE'S GOVERNMENT PARTY; POLITICAL FRIENDS SOCIETY; PRIME MINISTER.

POLITICAL SYSTEM See CONSTITUTION OF 1947; DIET; ELECTIONS; PREFECTURE; PRIME MINISTER; WARD.

POLLUTION See ENVIRONMENTAL ISSUES; MINAMATA DISEASE.

PONTOCHO A section of the former capital city of Kyoto known as an entertainment district, with many restaurants, bars and traditional theaters. Pontocho is best known for having one of the six communities of geisha in Kyoto (another such famous district is Gion), which today is directed by the Pontocho Geisha Association. Geisha are women skilled in traditional Japanese dance and music who entertain at parties held in teahouses for wealthy businessmen and government leaders. They give public performances called Kamogawari Odori ("Kamo river dances") in spring and autumn at the Kaburenjo theater. Pontocho is located on the west side of the Kamo River (Kamagawa), which is lined with graceful willow trees, a symbol of the slim and delicate geisha. The crest (mon) of the Pontocho geisha is the plover (chidori), a water bird commonly seen along the river. In the summer, colorful red paper lanterns are hung on verandas of teahouses built out over the river. Before Pontocho became an entertainment district during the Edo Era (1600–1868), charcoal makers lived there, and boatmen poled barges of charcoal to the city of Osaka through the Takase Canal built along the west side the Kamo River. The name Pontocho may come from ponte, Portuguese for "bridge." Another name for the district, Sentocho, can mean "the street of boatmen." See also CREST; GEISHA; GION; KAMO RIVER; KYOTO; PLOVER.

PORCELAIN Dishes, tea cups, vases and other objects that have a thin but hard white clay base and are decorated with colored glazes. A glaze is a thin, hard coating of silicate and other substances that is applied on the surface of clay objects before they are fired in a kiln. The alkaline glaze used for porcelain must be fired at a high temperature, which makes the finished product hard and translucent.

The Japanese potter Gordoya Shonzui studied porcelain techniques in China for five years, from A.D. 1510, and brought back a limited supply of porcelain clays and blue cobalt glaze to decorate his wares. In the early 17th century, Japanese potters learned techniques for porcelain making from Li Sanping (Li San-p'ing; Ri Sampei in Japanese), a Korean potter who discovered fine porcelain stone at Izumiyama in the Arita region (modern Saga Prefecture) on the southern island of Kyushu. Porcelain was also found on Amakusa Island in 1712 and is still used today for most porcelain ware in Japan; the stone is crushed and mixed with water to make porcelain clay. Arita became the center for Japanese styles of decorative porcelain, known as Arita ware, Kakiemon ware, Nabeshima ware, and Imari ware, for the port city through which porcelain was exported in large quantities to the West. The Kakiemon technique of decorating porcelain with colorful enamel overglazes was adopted by potters at the Kutani kiln (in modern Ishiwaka Prefecture). Porcelain techniques were also brought to the old capital city of Kyoto and are still used there. Commercial factories were also set up in Kyoto, Arita and other cities to manufacture porcelain ware on a large scale for domestic use and for export. See also ARITA WARE; KAKIEMON WARE; KILN; KUTANI WARE; KYOTO WARE; NABESHIMA CLAN; POTTERY; SAGA PREFECTURE.

PORTUGUESE IN JAPAN

The Portuguese were the first Westerners to appear in Japan. Portuguese traders were shipwrecked in 1543 by a typhoon off Tanegashima, a small island near the southern island of Kyushu. Their muskets, the first firearms ever seen in Japan, were recognized by the lord of Tanegashima as new and powerful weapons. Firearms were soon manufactured by the Japanese and changed the nature of warfare during the civil war that was then wracking the country.

In 1549 the Portuguese Jesuit missionary St. Francis Xavier (1506–1552) landed at Kagoshima on Kyushu and began preaching the Christian religion. He converted many Japanese on Kyushu, but failed in his attempt to meet with the Japanese emperor or the shogun, and left for India in 1551. Other Portuguese Jesuits came to Japan and introduced Western science and culture along with the religion. Japanese *daimyo* (feudal lords) were interested in the material goods brought by Portuguese traders accompanying the missionaries, such as clocks, wine, wool and velvet, and tobacco. The Portuguese introduced playing cards, known in Japanese as *karuta* after the Portuguese word *carta*, and *tempura*, a type of batter-coated fried food.

Portuguese trading ships began to make regular calls at the port of Hirado from around 1550. In 1570 Nagasaki was opened to foreign trade and became the center of trade between Japan and Portugal, which controlled Asian colonies in Goa (India) and Macao (China). Each year a Portuguese ship from Goa stopped at Macao to sell goods from India and pick up raw silk and silk textiles from China to sell in Japan. Japan's main export was copper, which was processed in Osaka, along with fans, screens, swords and textiles. The Portuguese were called *namban*, "Southern Barbarians," because their ships came to Japan from the south.

Otomo Yoshishige, a Kyushu *daimyo*, converted to Christianity in 1578, by which time more than 100,000 Japanese had become Christian converts. The Jesuits developed close relationships with Japanese priests of the Zen Buddhist religion, who were involved with the import of Chinese goods through the port of Sakai near Kyoto. Oda Nobunaga (1534–1582), one of the three warlords who unified Japan, was receptive to Christianity, but Toyotomi Hideyoshi (1536–1598), the second unifier, opposed it. Tokugawa Ieyasu (1543–1616), the third unifier, who founded the Tokugawa Sogunate (1603–1867), regarded Portuguese traders and missionaries as subversives who threatened his rule. The Spanish, who sailed up from the Philippine Islands and began trading with Japan in 1596, were also suspect. In 1606 the shogunate issued anti-Christian edicts that began the active persecution of Christians. In 1624 all Spaniards were banned from Japan. Following the rebellion of Japanese Christians known as the Shimabara Uprising of 1637–1638, all Portuguese were expelled from Japan,

and the shogunate instituted a policy of national seclusion that lasted more than two centuries. See also CHRISTIANITY IN JAPAN; CARD GAMES; DAIMYO; FIREARMS, INTRODUCTION OF; NAMBAN; ODA NOBUNAGA; SECLUSION, NATIONAL; SHIMABARA UPRISING; TEMPURA; TOKUGAWA IEYASU; TOKUGAWA SHOGUNATE; TOYOTOMI HIDEYOSHI; ZEN SECT OF BUDDHISM.

POSTAL SERVICE

The official mail delivery system of the Japanese government, administered by the Ministry of Posts and Telecommunications. This system efficiently handles the world's second largest volume of mail, after that of the United States, over three-quarters of which is business mail. Japan has about 23,000 post office branches throughout the country. In addition to mail, they handle the payment of government bills such as tax, electricity, telephone and national health, the transfer of money by telephone or telegram, and savings accounts and pension funds. In 1968 the Japanese postal service developed the first postal code address system, along with machinery that automatically reads and sorts postal code numbers to speed mail delivery. Japanese postal code numbers have three or five digits. Mechanization became necessary as the Japanese population concentrated in a number of large cities and the economy grew at a rapid rate. Several central facilities in Tokyo use containerized transport equipment to move letters and packages to other post office branches.

As far back as A.D. 646, a system for delivering mail was put in use in what is now the Kyoto-Osaka area of Japan, modeled on the Chinese system of relays of messengers on horses between post-station towns. Other Japanese provinces instituted their own post-horse systems to aid communications between the provinces and the capital of Nara (then called Heijokyo). After a period of decline, the post-horse system was rejuvenated by the military rulers of the Kamakura Shogunate (1192–1333), with the addition of couriers on foot. The unification of Japan under the Tokugawa Shogunate (1603–1867) brought a renewed communications system using post-horse and foot messengers, which was used to exercise military and government control over provincial lords. A postal service for private individuals was inaugurated in 1615 with a courier system for families of the samurai class in the cities of Osaka, Kyoto and Edo (modern Tokyo). The merchant families of these cities began their own courier system in 1633.

The government under the Meiji Restoration of 1868 established a postal system between Tokyo and Osaka on April 20, 1871. This postal service was developed and modeled on European systems by Maejima Hisoka, called the Father of the Post in Japan. Within two years the postal service was operating throughout the country, setting rates for mail delivery and issuing postage stamps. Japan joined the Universal Postal Union in 1872. The symbol for Japanese post zones is $\overline{T}$; this symbol also identifies a post office. Mailboxes are red and have a rectangular shape. Mail is collected two or three times a day in the cities. The postal service offers limited issues of commemorative stamps or series on a regular schedule. The 23rd day of each month is known as "letter day" (*fumi no hi*). All New Year's greeting cards that are posted by a certain date in mid-December are held by the postal service and then delivered together on New Year morning by students who are hired for this job. The Japanese also like to send greeting cards in summer. The cards are called *shochumimai,* which means that the senders are inquiring after the health of their friends and relatives in the hot season. Although the government postal service is very efficient in Japan, there are also many private delivery services which handle large packages. See also BANKING SYSTEM; MEIJI RESTORATION OF JAPAN; NEW YEAR FESTIVAL; TELECOMMUNICATIONS SYSTEM.

POTSDAM DECLARATION See ATOMIC BOMB; HIROHITO, EMPEROR; SURRENDER OF JAPAN; WORLD WAR II.

POTTERY Plates, bowls, vases, storage jars, figures and other objects made with clay and fired to hardness in a kiln. Pottery has attained an exceptional degree of refinement in Japan and has utilized a wide variety of materials and techniques. The clay used for making pottery is coarser than that used for fine porcelain, which is also important in Japan. The earliest Japanese pottery was cord-marked earthenware made in the Jomon Era (c. 10,000 B.C.–c. 300 B.C.). Clay figures known as *haniwa* were placed around tomb mounds (*kofun*) during the Kofun Era (c. 300–710). Over the centuries, new pottery-making techniques were introduced from China and Korea, including the potter's wheel, technology for coloring objects with glazes, and chambered kilns built on the slopes of hills (*ana-gama*). Sue ware was the main type of Japanese pottery during the Nara (710–794) and Heian (794–1185) eras. It was followed by the so-called "six old kilns of Japan," which date back

A craftsman bringing a large pottery storage jar out of the kiln where it was fired.

at least to the early Kamakura Era (1192–1333): Seto, Tokoname, Shigaraki, Tamba, Bizen and Echizen. Pottery making was further stimulated by the tea ceremony, which was introduced from China as a Zen Buddhist ritual in the 12th century. Small glossy brown tea bowls (*chawan*) known as *temmoku* were adapted by the Japanese. The tea ceremony developed as a complex art over several centuries and was formalized by Sen no Rikyu (1522–1591), who created the Raku style of tea bowl. Numerous kilns, especially in the Kyoto region and on Kyushu Island, began producing great quantities of tea bowls, cold water jars, vases, tea storage jars and serving dishes for the tea ceremony. *Daimyo* (feudal lords) patronized local pottery kilns, some of the most important being Hagi, Karatsu, Kutani, and Oribe, Raku, Seto and Shino, as well as the six old kilns. Many of these older Japanese kilns are still producing pottery today, and some master potters have been designated Living National Treasures by the Japanese government. The *mingei* (folk art) movement of the 1920s, led by Hamada Shoji (1894–1978) and his English colleague Bernard Leach (1887–1979), revived interest in rough, traditional pottery made in Japanese villages, such as Mashiko. See also HAMADA SHOJI; HANIWA; JOMON ERA; KILN; LEACH, BERNARD; LIVING NATIONAL TREASURES; MINGEI; MASHIKO; PORCELAIN; SAGA PREFECTURE; SEN NO RIKYU; TEA BOWL; TEA CEREMONY; NAMES OF INDIVIDUAL WARES.

PRAWN See SEAFOOD; TEMPURA.

PREFECTURE (*ken*) An administrative district below the national government in Japan; similar to a state in the United States, a county in England or a province in other countries. There are 47 such districts: one metropolitan region (*to;* city of Tokyo); two urban prefectures (*fu;* cities of Kyoto and Osaka); one district (*do;* Hokkaido Island); and 43 rural prefectures (*ken*). Prefectures are in turn administratively divided into cities (*shi*), towns (*cho*) or villages (*mura*). Large cities are further subdivided into wards (*ku*). Each prefecture or district has a governor and a one-chamber legislative assembly. The governor and legislators face elections every four years and maintain departments of general affairs, finance, health, labor and welfare. Some also have departments of agriculture, commerce, fisheries, forestry and industry. The 47 Japanese prefectures are also grouped into eight major regions for statistical purposes in government documents. The islands of Hokkaido, Kyushu and Shikoku each form one region, and the main island of Honshu is divided into five regions.

This centralized prefectural system (*ken*) was established by the Meiji government (1868–1912) in 1871, when it abolished the former system of feudal domains (*han*) that had been governed by hereditary local lords known as *daimyo. Haihan chiken,* meaning "abolish *han* and establish *ken,*" was the name given to this act of political centralization. The *daimyo* were given generous compensations for the surrender of their lands and the dissolution of their standing armies. See also DAIMYO; ELECTIONS; FEUDALISM; GEOGRAPHIC REGIONS; GOVERNMENT; MEIJI RESTORATION OF 1868.

PREHISTORIC ERA See KOFUN ERA; JOMON ERA; YAYOI ERA.

PRESIDENT See PRIME MINISTER.

PRIESTS AND PRIESTESSES, SHINTO Persons authorized to perform the sacred rituals of Shinto, the native Japanese religion. In Shinto, priests and priestesses serve as mediators between human beings and gods. In ancient Japan, religious rituals were performed by shamans, frequently women, who functioned as mediums through whom the gods spoke. Later, important rituals were performed by local clan chieftains *(kuni no miyatsuko)*. The Nakatomi clan became responsible for religious ceremonies in the imperial court. Shinto is not centralized, so various titles have been used for priests in different regions and historical eras in Japan. *Kannushi* and *shinkan* are general terms often used for Shinto priests. *Kannushi* became institutionalized at some larger Shinto shrines during the Heian Era (794–1185), and the office of *kannushi* became hereditary.

Before the Edo Era (1600–1868), small village shrines did not have professional priests. Laymen who were heads of powerful local households took turns presiding over village festivals. Large shrines came to have several ranks of priests who performed administrative as well as ritual functions. These include head priests *(guji)*, assistant chief priests *(gon-guji)*, senior priests *(negi)*, and junior priests *(gon-negi)*. The Shinto priesthood was hereditary until 1871, when the Meiji government (1868–1912) decreed that Shinto priests were civil servants who were to perform rituals for the nationalistic religion known as State Shinto. The present constitution of Japan, enacted in 1947 following World War II, makes religious organizations independent of the government. Priests are now appointed by the nationwide Association of Shinto Shrines (Jinja Honcho), following seminary training or the passing of a licensing examination. At Ise, the central Shinto shrine, there is also a high priestess *(saishu)*. This is an ancient postion that has traditionally been held by an imperial princess. At many shrines there are also young unmarried women known as *miko,* who perform ceremonial dances before the *kami* at shrine festivals and various minor shrine duties. These women wear white kimono, red *hakama* (divided skirts), and *tabi* (white split-toed socks), and have long hair tied in the back with a red ribbon. Priests wear a costume similar to that of Heian Era court officials. It consists of a white kimono, *hakama*, large-sleeved outer robe *(kariginu)* that comes to the knees, a special cap *(kammuri)*, *tabi*, and thonged sandals or large black lacquered shoes *(asa-gutsu)*. The *hakama* and outer robe may be white or another color. They carry a long piece of wood *(shaku)* as a symbol of their priestly office.

The indigenous religion of the southern Ryukyu Islands (Okinawa Prefecture), which became a prefecture of Japan in 1879, is conducted by priestesses known as *noro* or *nuru*. Depending on the local community, these priestesses are either hereditary or selected. The Buddhist religion, which was introduced into Japan from China and India in the sixth century A.D., has a complex monastic organization composed of priests, monks and nuns. See also BUDDHISM; CLAN; FESTIVALS; HAKAMA; ISE SHRINE; KAGURA; KIMONO; MONASTICISM, BUDDHIST; NAKATOMI CLAN; PURIFICATION; RYUKYU ISLANDS; SHAMANS AND SHAMANISM; SHINTO; SHRINE; SHINTO; STATE SHINTO.

PRIESTS, BUDDHIST See MONASTICISM, BUDDHIST.

Prime Ministers (from 1945)*

July 1944–April 1945	Kumaki Koiso
April 1945–August 1945	Kantaro Suzuki
August 1945–October 1945	Navuhiko Higashikuni
October 1945–May 1946:	Kijuro Shidehara
May 1946–May 1947:	Shigeru Yoshida (Liberal Party)
May 1947–February 1948:	Tetsu Katayama (Japan Socialist Party)
February–October 1948:	Hitoshi Ashida (Democratic Party)
October 1948 –December 1954:	Shigeru Yoshida (Liberal Party)
December 1954 –December 1956:	Ichiro Hatoyama (Democratic Party, Liberal Democratic Party)
December 1956 –February 1957:	Tanzan Ishibashi (Liberal Democratic Party)
February 1957–July 1960:	Nobusuke Kishi (Liberal Democratic Party)
July 1960–November 1964:	Hayato Ikeda (Liberal Democratic Party)
November 1964–July 1972:	Eisaku Sato (Liberal Democratic Party)
July 1972–December 1974:	Kakuei Tanaka (Liberal Democratic Party)
December 1974 –December 1976:	Takeo Miki (Liberal Democratic Party)
December 1976 –December 1978:	Takeo Fukuda (Liberal Democratic Party)
December 1978 –June 1980:	Masayoshi Ohira (Liberal Democratic Party)
June–July 1980:	Masayoshi Ito (acting) (Liberal Democratic Party)
July 1980–November 1982:	Zenko Suzuki (Liberal Democratic Party)
November 1982 –November 1987:	Yasuhiro Nakasone (Liberal Democratic Party)
November 1987 –June 1989:	Noboru Takeshita (Liberal Democratic Party)
June–August 1989:	Sosuke Uno (Liberal Democratic Party)
August 1989–	Toshiki Kaifu (Liberal Democratic Party)

*Names of prime ministers give surnames after given names, in Western fashion.

PRIME MINISTER (*naikaku sori daijin*) The leader of the ruling political party and hence the chief executive officer in the Japanese government. The prime minister and his cabinet form the executive organ of the Japanese Diet (Parliament). The Japanese constitution instituted in 1947 during the postwar Occupation stipulates that the House of Councillors (upper house) and House of Representatives (lower house) of the Diet elect the prime minister from among their members. If the houses disagree, the individual elected by the House of Representatives becomes prime minister. In theory, the Japanese emperor appoints the prime minister chosen by the Diet; in practice, the prime minister is chosen by the majority political party. Since 1955, the president of the Liberal Democratic Party (LDP; Jiyu Minshuto) has become prime minister of Japan, through a process of negotiation among factions within the LDP.

The prime minister in turn chooses the ministers for his cabinet, most of whom are also members of the Diet and who usually hold office for a shorter period than the prime minister. Career bureaucrats staff government operations up to the level of the cabinet ministries. There is also an Office of the Prime Minister (Sorifu), comparable to the White House Executive Office in the U.S. government. Among its functions are the administration of government personnel affairs and coordination of various executive agencies.

The system of prime minister and cabinet was adapted by the Meiji government in 1885. At first there were nine ministries, headed by the Prime Minister, which were independent from the Diet. Before World War II the prime minister had the power to appoint many government officials, but he shared power with a body of elder statesmen known as the *genro*, as well as with the emperor's councillors and officers of the imperial household. The *genro* chose the prime minister from leaders of the major political parties. Military leaders and cabinet ministers were independent and reported directly to the emperor. The system was revised after the war to resemble the British system, whereby all executive authority is assigned to the prime minister and his cabinet. The prime minister was given power over the military; the *genro* and other imperial advisory bodies were abolished; and executive authority was removed from the emperor. The prime minister's cabinet was made responsible to the Diet, and the upper and lower houses and committees of the Diet can require the prime minister and cabinet ministers to attend their sessions to answer questions about their policies. The Diet, through a no-confidence vote, can also force the prime minister and cabinet to resign or to call a new election, which may or may not return them to power. See also CABINET, PRIME MINISTER'S; CONSTITUTION OF 1947; DIET; GENRO; LIBERAL DEMOCRATIC PARTY; MEIJI RESTORATION OF 1868; OCCUPATION OF JAPAN; POLITICAL PARTIES.

PRINTS See WOODBLOCK PRINTS.

PROSTITUTION It has long been the practice in Japan that men have sex with their wives for procreation and with other women for pleasure. The Tokugawa Shogunate (1603–1867) licensed certain districts of Edo (modern Tokyo) and other large cities as pleasure quarters for brothels and other adult entertainment, such as Kabuki and Bunraku (puppet) theaters. The best-known district was the Yoshiwara in Edo. The pleasure districts became known collectively as the "floating world" (*ukiyo-e*).

Prostitutes (*yujo*) in these districts were officially registered with the government. The highest class of prostitutes were known as courtesans (*tayu*). Women entertainers known as geisha also originated in the pleasure quarters. They are not prostitutes, but sing, dance and entertain men at private banquets.

Even before the Edo Era (1600–1868), a poor family often sold a daughter into prostitution. The family was paid a sum of money, and the girl was usually indentured for a 10- or 20-year contract. She had a hard life and had only a slight hope of being bought out of her contract by an admirer. After the Meiji Restoration of 1868, organized prostitution continued in red-light districts. As many as 100,000 Japanese girls were sold into prostitution in China, Southeast Asia and other countries before the government banned this practice in 1920. Japanese prostitutes in foreign countries were known as *karayuki-san*, literally "one who went to China"; many of them died abroad before their 30th birthday.

In the early 20th century, Japanese brothels were highly organized. By 1930, there were more than 50,000 prostitutes in 511 licensed quarters. During World War II, the Japanese military sent more than 100,000 "comfort women" (*ianfu*) to serve as prostitutes for Japanese soldiers in war zones. Around 80% of these were Korean girls; Korea had become a Japanese colony in 1910, and Koreans are still a large minority group in Japan. Japanese women received the vote in 1945, and due largely to pressure from women's associations, the Japanese Diet (Parliament) outlawed prostitution in 1956. On April 1, 1957, prostitution became officially banned for the first time in Japan. However, prostitution has not disappeared, but is practiced by "soap ladies" working in so-called "soaplands," bathhouses and massage parlors in the same districts that were formerly legal red-light districts. Hostesses in bars and nightclubs now entertain men in the "water trade" (*mizu shobai*) that has replaced the old "floating world," and some hostesses engage in prostitution. Today, many women from Thailand, Taiwan, the Philippines and other countries go to Japan to become prostitutes. They are known as *Japayuki-san*, "one who goes to Japan," or "Miss Japan-Bound." Prostitution is controlled by gangsters called *yakuza*. See also COURTESAN; EDO ERA; FLOATING WORLD; GEISHA; KOREA AND JAPAN; WATER TRADE; YAKUZA; YOSHIWARA.

PUBLISHING See BOOKS AND BOOKSTORES; KODANSHA, LTD.; MAGAZINES; NEWSPAPERS.

PUPPET THEATER See BUNRAKU.

PURE LAND SECT OF BUDDHISM (Jodoshu) A sect of Buddhism, the religion introduced into Japan from China in the sixth century A.D., that was established in Japan by

Honen (1133–1212); the most popular sect of Buddhism in Japan today. The Pure Land sect emphasizes worship of Amida, the Japanese name for the deity called Amitabha in Sanskrit. Amida is the Buddha of Boundless (or Unlimited) Light who presides over the Western Paradise, or the Pure Land (Jodo). Worshippers believe that Amida made an "Original Vow," in which he asserted with utmost compassion for all sinful people that any one who calls upon him with faith and sincerity will be reborn in the Pure Land after death.

Amida worship existed for centuries in India and China before it was practiced in Japan by the Tendai and Shingon sects of Buddhism, which were favored by the aristocratic class in the Heian Era (794–1185). Statues of Amida and his attendants, Seishi and Kannon (Goddess of Mercy), were placed in all Japanese Buddhist temples. In the late Heian Era, some monks began to preach Amida worship to commoners and to emphasize the religious practices of singing, dancing and reciting a chant known as the *nembutsu*. The monk Kuya (903–972) traveled throughout Japan teaching Amida worship at this time. The chant *Namu Amida Butsu*, abbreviated as the *nembutsu*, means "I take refuge in Amida Buddha." The *nembutsu* was also advocated by the monks Genshin (942–1017) and Ryonin (1072–1132), and *nembutsu* dancing (*nembutsu odori*) was further popularized in the Kamakura Era by the monk Ippen (1239–1289). This dance evolved into an entertaining folk dance that is still performed in Japan at the annual summer Bon Festival, which welcomes visiting ancestral spirits. Genshin, who wrote a popular religious book called the *Essentials of Salvation (Ojo Yoshu)*, taught that salvation was possible for all people, laymen and monks, women and men alike. This insistence on universal salvation through faith in Amida was a new development that laid the foundation of Pure Land Buddhism. Neither meditation nor ritual, two important aspects of other Buddhist sects, are necessary in the Pure Land sect, but only total reliance on the compassion of the Amida Buddha. The Japanese term for salvation by faith is *tariki*, the "strength of another," as opposed to *jiriki*, "one's own strength."

Honen established Amida worship as the separate Pure Land Buddhist sect. Pure Land Buddhism became a mass movement in Japan at the same time as the Taira and Minamoto clans fought a bitter civil war that ended the imperial rule of the Heian Era in 1185 and initiated seven centuries of military government, starting with the Kamakura Shogunate (1192–1333). According to the Buddhist theory of *mappo* (The End of The Law), the world was in such chaotic decline that people were unable to gain salvation by their own efforts. Thus the Pure Land sect offered people of all social classes the hope of universal salvation through simple devotion to Amida. Rather than being required to give up the ordinary world and become a celibate monk or priest, anyone, even women, could lead a religious life, the sect taught.

Honen's disciple Shinran (1173–1263) traveled throughout Japan to spread Amida worship, especially to members of the peasant class, teaching that a believer need recite the *nembutsu* only once with absolute faith and sincerity in

order to be saved. Shinran described the Pure Land as a state of grace that the believer can experience in this life. His teaching gave rise to the most important branch of Pure Land Buddhism, known as the True Pure Land Sect (Jodo Shinsu; abbreviated as Shinsu); after his death, his followers established their headquarters in Honganji, Temple of the Original Vow, where they placed his ashes. Pure Land Buddhism was opposed by the great religious teacher Nichiren (1222–1282), who taught his own concept of universal salvation by faith alone and established another Buddhist sect that takes its name from him. Ippen (1239–1289) used the methods of singing and dancing to further popularize Pure Land Buddhism. Rennyo (1415–1499), eighth abbot of Honganji, led the Shinsu sect to attract many followers among the common people and become very influential in Japan.

In the 16th century, the city of Osaka began growing around Honganji, which had become a military stronghold; the temple fought off attack by the great warlord Oda Nobunaga (1534–1582) in a 10-year siege. For their fanatic devotion, followers of True Pure Land were called *Ikko*, or "Single-Minded." Shinran was the first Buddhist leader in Japan to renounce celibacy. His descendants have inherited the leadership of the True Pure Land branch of Pure Land Buddhism. Starting in the late 16th century, this branch divided into many factions. When the Meiji government (1868–1912) attempted to suppress Buddhism in favor of Shinto, the indigenous Japanese religion, the True Pure Land sect led Buddhist opposition to this policy. Pure Land Buddhism remained very popular in Japan and grew rapidly in the 20th century.

Among the numerous *amidado*, or halls built for worship of Amida, the most famous is the Hoodo in Byodoin, a Buddhist temple in Uji City. See also AMIDA; BON FESTIVAL; BUDDHISM; DANCE, TRADITIONAL; HONEN; KAMAKURA SHOGUNATE; KANNON; NEMBUTSU; NICHIREN; ODA NOBUNAGA; OSAKA; SCULPTURE; SHINRAN; TEMPLES, BUDDHIST; UJI.

PURE WORD SECT OF BUDDHISM   See SHINGON SECT OF BUDDHISM.

PURIFICATION *(harai or harae)* One of the basic elements of worship in Shinto, the indigenous Japanese religion, along with offerings *(shinsen)*, prayer *(norito)* and a symbolic feast *(naorai)*. The word for purification derives from the verb *harau*, "to cleanse." Purification drives away evil spirits *(magatsuhi)* that interfere with relations between humans and *kami* (sacred spirits). Japanese traditionally believe that the thing most offensive to the *kami* is pollution or uncleanness *(tsumi)*. A person is required to wash his or her body and put on clean clothing in preparation for religious observances.

Sources of uncleanness, connected primarily with blood and death, include menstruation, childbirth, sexual intercourse, wounds, disease and death. Many traditional taboos were enforced to protect people in these circumstances. The word for wound or injury, *kega*, is related to that for death, misfortune, defilement or impurity *(kegare)*. Ancient chronicles record that the creator god Izanagi no Mikoto went to the land of the dead to see his wife, Izanami no Mikoto, and upon returning had to cleanse himself of defilement from contact with the dead. Shinto is concerned with ceremonial impurity or pollution rather than moral guilt or sin. Impurity is removed by washing it away, or ritual ablution (misogi). Bathing is a central activity in Japanese culture, with religious and social as well as practical aspects. In front of every Shinto shrine (jinja), there is an ablution pavilion (temizuya) with a stone basin of water (temizu, "hand water") and a bamboo ladle. Worshippers ceremonially remove pollution and purify themselves by rinsing their hands and mouths before entering the central part of a shrine. In ancient times such purification was performed at a stream, spring or the seashore. The sacred purity of a Shinto shrine is demarcated by an entrance gate known as a torii. Sprinkling salt or salt water is another means of purification in Shinto. Shinto priests perform symbolic ritual purification by reciting a prayer and waving a wand known as a haraigushi in front of worshippers or objects to be purified. The wand, which is made of bamboo or sakaki wood, with many long streamers of white paper and a few strands of flax, is kept on a stand on the altar.

A small branch of the evergreen tree known as sakaki is sometimes waved in place of this wand. An ancient ritual may also be performed to purify the entire country or world, known as Oharai, "Great Purification." A shrine is purified for a religious festival (matsuri) by having all its buildings and ritual objects cleaned and the grounds swept. Shimenawa, rice straw ropes hung with white paper folded in zig-zags and flax pendants, are placed around sacred areas. Sakaki branches and pieces of bamboo are also hung in the precincts as symbols of purification. Priests purify themselves before festivals with a period of abstinence called saikai, or "restraint and rules." This includes frequent bathing (kessai), putting on clean robes, eating specified food and abstaining (imi) from acts forbidden during this time. In some festivals, men wearing loincloths carry a sacred palanquin (mikoshi) into a river or the sea, an act of purification known as hama-ori ("going to the beach"). Ascetics perform the austere practice of mizugori, or washing away impurity by standing under a waterfall or pouring buckets of cold water over themselves. See also BAMBOO; BATH; FESTIVALS; PALANQUIN, SACRED; PAPER, HANDMADE; PRIESTS AND PRIESTESSES, SHINTO; SAKAKI TREE; SHINTO; SHRINE, SHINTO; WATER; WHITE.

QUALITY CONTROL CIRCLE Also known in Japan as Total Quality Control (TQC); groups of workers that are organized on assembly lines to analyze and correct existing problems in each step of the manufacturing process, so that a company's products will meet high standards of reliability. Japanese companies have very high rates of worker participation in groups that suggest ways to improve quality and productivity.

Methods for quality control *(hinshitsu kanri)* are now associated with Japanese companies, but they were introduced to Japanese corporations by American business experts after World War II. In 1948 a quality-control seminar was held at the recommendation of American representatives of the Western Electric Co., who were in Japan helping to reconstruct the Japanese telecommunications system. Quality-control methods taught at the seminar by American lecturers were widely adapted by Japanese corporations. In 1949 the Industrial Standards Law was passed in Japan, which specified standards of quality that products had to meet before they could receive authorization to display the JIS (Japan Industrial Standard) mark. In 1950 W. Edward Deming, an American authority on statistical methods for quality control, was invited to lecture in Japan by the Japan Union of Scientists and Engineers (JUSE). The next year JUSE established the Deming Prize, and it is still awarded annually to the Japanese company that has made the most effective use of quality-control methods. Deming presented an alternative to the way companies usually handle the problem of defective products, which is to have workers inspect the products after they are manufactured and reject the ones that do not meet specified standards of quality. Deming taught it is more productive and less costly to analyze each phase in the manufacturing system, in order to identify problems in product design, utilization of equipment, materials and steps followed by workers. The best way for a company to do this is to get its employees involved in quality circles, which

work together to make such an analysis. Japanese companies form quality control circles in all departments, including manufacturing, design, marketing and services for products already sold. The final result is a marked decrease in the number of finished products that are rejected for poor quality. Ideally, the goal is to have "zero defects." Many American companies are now beginning to follow Deming's principles and organize quality control circles. See also COMPANIES; EXPORT AND IMPORT.

QUILTING *(sashiko)* A method of stitching layers of fabric together to mend or reinforce garments, decorate them or make them warmer. In Japan a quilted garment is made by stitching two or more layers of indigo-dyed hemp or cotton fabric. *Sashiko* uses running stitches that spread in all directions to create dots over the garment, known as *tsuzurezashi*. A variation known as *kogin* employs white and dark blue stitches that run parallel between the edges of the fabric. Straight and curved stitches are often combined in quilting to make traditional designs on the garment, such as tortoise shells, plum blossoms, bamboo joints, leaves or waves. This technique has been used mainly for work clothes, especially those worn by farmers and fishermen in the cold, snowy regions of northern Japan. The Ainu, an indigenous group on northern Hokkaido Island, create quilted garments with elaborate curvilinear designs. Heavy jackets worn by firemen were also traditionally made by the *sashiko* technique. Practitioners of martial arts such as judo and karate wear clothing that is reinforced with *sashiko* stitching. A style of weaving textiles to imitate quilting is also referred to as *sashiko*. Quilted clothing began to disappear in the 20th century but was revived with the *mingei* (folk crafts) movement, initiated by Yanagi Soetsu (1889–1961), which celebrates the beauty of handmade objects for everyday use. The *sashiko* technique has become popular abroad. See also AINU; CLOTHING; HEMP; INDIGO; MINGEI; TEXTILES; YANAGI SOETSU.

R

RABBIT *(usagi)* The most common among the many varieties of rabbit in Japan are the *nousagi,* which turn white in snowy areas in the winter, found on the main islands of Honshu, Kyushu and Shikoku, and the *yukisage* ("snow hare"), found in mountainous areas on the northernmost island of Hokkaido. These rabbits (or hares) average slightly less than 2 feet in length and are a nuisance to farmers. The rabbit, a popular character in Japanese folktales and mythology, is often portrayed as a shrewd trickster. The oldest Japanese story about a rabbit is the "White Hare of Inaba," which appears in the *Kojiki,* an official chronicle recorded in A.D. 712. The hare wanted to visit the Inaba region, but when it tried to trick the crocodiles that prevented it from getting there, a crocodile pulled the hare's fur off. Prince Okuninushi helped the hare grow its fur back, and in turn, the hare helped the prince marry the princess of Inaba, and the couple made the hare their companion. The rabbit is one of the animal symbols in the 12-year zodiac calendar cycle. People who are born in the year of the rabbit, are thought to be gentle, affectionate, lucky and trustworthy. The Japanese also believe that when the moon is full, a rabbit can be seen in the moon pounding glutinous rice into cakes known as *mochi.* See also KOJIKI; MOCHI; MOON; ZODIAC.

RACCOON DOG See BADGER.

RADIO See BROADCASTING SYSTEM; ELECTRONICS INDUSTRY; JAPAN BROADCASTING CORPORATION; MORITA AKIO; SONY CORPORATION.

RADISH, JAPANESE See DAIKON.

RAILROADS *(tetsudo)* The heart of the system is Japan Railways (Nihon Tetsudo, abbreviated as Kokutetsu; also known as JR), which operates over 13,000 miles of tracks. More than 7 billion passengers a year ride on nearly 30,000 JR trains. JR was formerly run by the Japanese government, but was privatized in 1987 to halt its huge financial losses. The number of railroad passengers in Japan has declined as automobiles and airplanes have become popular; coastal shipping of goods has also reduced the need for freight cars. In addition to JR, there are 14 smaller Japanese railroad lines, with 3,500 miles of track, which mainly serve commuters and visitors to resort areas. The largest of these is the Kinki Nippon Railway Co., Ltd. (Kinki Nippon Tetsudo; abbreviated as Kintetsu), operating between Osaka, Kyoto, Nagoya, Ise and Nara. Some lines are world famous for their speed and efficiency, in particular the JR Bullet Train (Shinkansen) operated out of Tokyo Station. More than 200 Bullet Trains run each day in the most heavily traveled corridor between the cities of Tokyo and Osaka. The Bullet Train route extends all the way from Honshu Island in northern Japan to Kyushu Island in the south. There are also two types of regular long-distance trains: limited express trains *(tokkyu),* and express trains *(kyuko),* which make more stops. Slower, local trains *(futsu)* stop at all stations. Japanese railroads connect with bus and subway systems in large cities and with an extensive regional system of buses and ferries. A montly timetable *(Speedo Jikokuhyo)* is published for nationwide long-distance and private trains, express buses, ferries and airlines.

The first railroad line was opened in Japan in 1872, making the 17.4-mile run between Tokyo and the nearby port of Yokohama. Because the Japanese government brought in British technicians and equipment to construct its railroad system, trains and cars still keep to the left in Japan. During the late 1800s, trunk lines were built southwest of Tokyo to the cities of Osaka, Kobe, Kyoto and Shimonoseki, north to Sendai and Aomori, and west to the Sea of Japan. Lines were also constructed on Hokkaido and Kyushu Islands. The railroad lines in place in Japan by the early 20th century are the same ones used today. Most were destroyed by bombing during World War II but were soon rebuilt and upgraded. See also BULLET TRAIN; JAPAN RAILWAYS; SUBWAYS.

RAIN *(ame)* A major feature of the Japanese climate, averaging 64 inches annually. The southern islands of Okinawa Prefecture receive as much as 84 inches of rain a year. Japan experiences a rainy season *(tsuyu)* from mid-June to mid-July, which is also called *bai-u* ("plum rain") because plums ripen at this time. Heavy rains may also fall from the end of August through mid-September, when violent storms called typhoons *(taifu)* stike the Japanese islands, especially in the south. There is also a rainy season in September following the typhoons, known as *shurin.*

Since it rains so much, the Japanese have many poetic names for different kinds of rain. Some examples are *yudachi* (an evening shower in summer), *konukame* (misty rain), and *shigure* (icy rain in winter). The high rainfall favors the wet-paddy cultivation of rice, the central food in the Japanese diet. In the past, many religious rituals were performed to make the gods send rain for the rice crops. A category of dance known as "rain dances" *(amagoi odori)* is still performed as a folk art.

Traditional Japanese rainwear *(amagu)* included straw raincoats *(mino),* consisting of capes *(katamino)* and various long or short body coverings, and woven straw rain hats *(kasa).* Aristocrats in the Heian Era (794–1185) wore oiled silk coverings *(amaginu).* Rain capes *(kappa)* were adapted from the Portuguese in the 16th century. Upper classes wore wool capes and lower classes wore capes of handmade paper *(washi)* waterproofed by being soaked in paulownia-seed oil. Umbrellas *(kasa)* came to be used for rain starting in the Edo Era (1600–1868), as did cotton capes. Special sandals, known as *ashida,* had platforms raised above the ground to help keep the feet dry. The Japanese began wearing Western rainwear during the Meiji Era (1868–1912). Waterproof cloth raincoats in the shape of kimono are still worn with traditional clothing. See also CLIMATE OF JAPAN; DANCE, TRADITIONAL; FOOTWEAR; KIMONO; PLUM; RICE; STRAW WARE; TYPHOON; UMBRELLA.

RAKU WARE *(raku-yaki)* A type of pottery created in the late 1600s specifically for bowls used in the Japanese tea ceremony. The renowned tea master Sen no Rikyu (1522–1591) worked with the potter Chojiro (1516–1592) to create bowls that were wide enough for a bamboo whisk to whip the powdered tea and hot water into a frothy beverage. Hence the bottom of a Raku bowl is called a "tea pool" *(chadamari).* They also chose a clay that was porous and fired at a low temperature so the tea bowl would gently warm the drinker's hands and not transmit heat too quickly. Rikyu designed Raku bowls to have a rough, asymmetrical shape formed by hand rather than on a pottery wheel. This shape embodies the concept of *wabi,* or "poverty that surpasses riches."

Raku ware is made by quickly firing the clay object in a kiln at 1,472–1,832 degrees F. A lead oxide glaze is then poured over the object, which is fired again. There are two types of Raku ware, black and red, since Rikyu felt that these colors look best with the bright green tea used in the tea ceremony. The glaze for black Raku had dust of rocks from the Kamo River mixed into it; red Raku is painted with a yellow slip, a mixture of clay and water and then glazed. In addition to tea bowls, vases, incense and tea containers, and water jars were also made at the Raku kilns.

The name Raku was taken from a gold seal presented to Chojiro's son Jokei by the great warlord Toyotomi Hideyoshi (1536–1598), whom Rikyu served as tea master. The seal was inscribed with the character *raku,* meaning "pleasure (or enjoyment)," part of the name of Hideyoshi's palace, Jurakudai.

Radu ware is still produced near Kyoto by descendants of Chojiro. Many artisans around the world make pottery with *raku* techniques, but traditionally in Japan, only pottery made at the Raku kilns has been given the name Raku. See also CHOJIRO; POTTERY; SABI AND WABI; SEN NO RIKYU; TEA BOWL; TEA CEREMONY; TOYOTOMI HIDEYOSHI.

RAMEN See NOODLES.

RASHOMON A film made in 1950 by Kurosawa Akira (1910–) about the murder of a nobleman and the rape of his wife by a bandit in the late Heian Era (794–1185). Kurosawa based the story of *Rashomon* on two stories by the modern Japanese writer Akutagawa Ryunosuke (1892–1927). In the movie, several different characters involved with the incident give their own versions of what happened. As none of them agree, the viewer comes to realize that it is impossible to determine what the reality is. *Rashomon* won first prize at the Venice Film Festival in 1951, and has been acclaimed throughout the world. The well-known Japanese actor Mifune Toshiro played the role of the bandit, and Kyo Machiko the murdered nobleman's wife. See also AKUTAGAWA RYUNOSUKE; HEIAN ERA; KUROSAWA AKIRA; KYO MACHIKO; MIFUNE TOSHIRO.

RAT AND MOUSE *(nezumi)* The term *nezumi* is used for all types of small gray rodents in Japan. *Nezumi* are generally divided into those that inhabit people's homes *(ienezumi)* and those found in farms and natural habitats *(nonezumi).* Rats and mice are pests because they eat rice and other stored foods. Yet since rats are only found where there is an abundance of grain, the rat also symbolizes prosperity and is often depicted in Japanese folk art. A rat is usually shown nibbling a bale of rice next to Daikoku, the God of Wealth and one of the Seven Gods of Good Fortune. The rat is also the first of the animals that characterize the 12-year zodiac cycle. People born in the Year of the Rat are thought to be ambitious, hard-working and thrifty. See also DAIKOKU; ZODIAC.

RECRUIT SCANDAL The most extensive political scandal in postwar Japan, which broke in 1988 and brought down the government of Prime Minister Takeshita Noboru and seriously damaged the prestige of the dominant Liberal Democratic Party (LDP). The scandal was uncovered by *Asahi Shimbun* reporters and named for the Recruit Company, an information-services, employment and real estate conglomerate. Recruit sought to gain favors and influence by making available large amounts of cash and 2 million shares of stock to leading Japanese politicians and their associates, including former Prime Minister Nakasone Yasuhiro (p.m. 1982–1987). Those who broke the law were accused of accepting inexpensive unlisted shares of stock in Recruit Cosmos, the real estate branch of the company, and later selling it at high profits when the stock was traded publicly. Nippon Telegraph and Telephone (NTT), a former public corporation that was recently privatized, was also accused of aiding Recruit in two telecommunications and computer ventures, and some of its executives were arrested for bribery. Hiromasa Ezoe, chairman of Recruit, was jailed on February 13, 1989. Takeshita took responsibility and resigned in April 1989, after 17 months in office. Aoka Ihei, Takeshita's former private secretary and chief political fund-raiser, who had handled all of Takeshita's financial dealings, committed suicide. The majority LDP had a hard time finding a replacement for Takeshita since most senior party leaders were tainted by the scandal, and they faced an unpopular election in July 1989. Uno Sosuke was finally chosen, but he quickly became embroiled in a scandal surrounding his relationship with a geisha, which further damaged the LDP. The Japanese public became furious about the scandals and about the 3% national consumption tax, the nation's first, which the LDP had pushed through the Diet in the spring of 1989. When elections were held in July for half of the seats in the House Councillors (upper house of the Japanese Diet, or parliament), voters handed the LDP its first significant defeat in 34 years, by electing a large number of socialists and putting a majority in opposition party hands. Uno resigned shortly after and was replaced by Kaifu Toshiki.

In 1976 the LDP had suffered another major bribery scandal, the Lockheed Scandal, in which the American Airplaine manufacturer bribed Prime Minister Tanaka Kakuei (p.m. 1972–1974) and other officials. Tanaka also resigned. See also DIET; ELECTIONS; KAIFU TOSHIKI; LIBERAL DEMOCRATIC PARTY; NAKASONE YASUHIRO; NIPPON TELEGRAPH AND TELEPHONE CORPORATION; PRIME MINISTER; TANAKA KAKUEI; TAKESHITA NOBORU; UNO SOSUKE.

RED ARMY FACTION (Sekigunha) A Marxist terrorist group that grew out of the radical student movement on Japanese university campuses in the 1960s, partly in protest against the U.S. war in Vietnam. After the radical movement was not able to rally mass support on Okinawa Day, April 28, 1969, for a protest calling for removal of the U.S. military from Okinawa Island, dissident communists decided to organize the more violent Red Army splinter group on September 4, 1969. Members of the faction committed bombings and robberies in Japan until they were defeated by Japanese police and their own internal fighting in February 1971. The international wing of the Red Army Faction, known as the Japanese Red Army (Nihon Sekigun), became closely connected with a network of international terrorists, primarily in the Middle East. Its members hijacked passenger airplanes and committed violent acts around the world. In their most notorious attack, they murdered 26 people at Lod Airport in Israel on May 30, 1972, in support of the Popular Front for the Liberation of Palestine (PFLP). In 1974 they attacked a Shell oil refinery in Singapore and seized the French embassy in the Netherlands. When they hijacked a Japan Airlines airplane over India in 1977, Japan yielded to their demands for the equivalent of U.S. $6 million in ransom and the release of six Red Army members from prison. For this concession the Japanese government was heavily criticized at home and abroad, and in response it formed a special police unit to keep track of Red Army Faction activities and tightened security measures at Japanese airports. Although the Red Army Faction continued to issue threats in the early 1980s, its activities decreased considerably. Members were reported to be training in North Korea and Lebanon and available for hire by other terrorist groups. See also POLICE SYSTEM; UNIVERSITIES.

REDRESS BILL See JAPANESE-AMERICAN CITIZENS LEAGUE.

REI KAWAKUBO See FASHION DESIGNERS, CONTEMPORARY.

REISCHAUER, EDWIN OLDFATHER (1910–1990) An American scholar of Japanese history and U.S. ambassador to Japan (1961–1966). Reischauer was born in Tokyo to missionary parents and raised in Japan. After graduating from the American School in Japan in 1927, he went to the United States and graduated from Oberlin College in 1931. Reischauer did graduate work at Harvard University in early Japanese and Chinese history and also spent five years studying in Tokyo, Kyoto, Beijing and Paris. He wrote his doctoral dissertation at Harvard on Ennin, the Japanese Buddhist monk. After he joined the Harvard faculty, Reischauer became one of the first American scholars to offer courses on East Asia, and was director of the Harvard-Yenching Institute from 1956 to 1961. During World War II, Reischauer served in the Department of War and of State, and the U.S. Army. Named ambassador to Japan in 1961, one year after many Japanese demonstrated against the revised United States-Japan Security Treaty, Reischauer attempted to improve relations between the two countries. He recognized that Japan could no longer be treated as it had been during its occupation by the United States but must be made an equal partner. After his first wife died, Reischauer married Matsukata Haru in 1956. This marriage, and his fluency in the Japanese language, made Reischauer very popular with the Japanese people. In 1966 he returned to the faculty of Harvard University, from which he retired in 1981. He has written many books on Japan, including the best-seller *The Japanese Today* (Cambridge: Harvard University Press, 1988). Haru Matsukata Reischauer, granddaughter of Prime Minister Matsukata Masayoshi, wrote a book about her family, *Samurai and Silk: A Japanese and American Heritage* (Cambridge: Belknap Press of Harvard University Press, 1986). See also MATSUKATA MASAYOSHI; OCCUPATION OF JAPAN; SECURITY TREATY BETWEEN JAPAN AND THE UNITED STATES; WORLD WAR II.

RELIGION See ALTARS IN HOMES; BUDDHISM; CHRISTIANITY IN JAPAN; EMPEROR; FESTIVALS; HOSSO SECT OF BUDDHISM; KAMI; MONASTICISM, BUDDHIST; NEW RELIGIONS; OOMOTO; PAGODA; PRIESTS AND PRIESTESSES, SHINTO; PURE LAND SECT OF BUDDHISM; PURIFICATION; RICE PLANTING AND HARVESTING FESTIVALS; SCRIPTURES RELIGIOUS; SHAMANS AND SHAMANISM; SHINGON SECT OF BUDDHISM; SHINTO; SHRINE, SHINTO; SOKA GAKKAI; TEMPLES, BUDDHIST; TENDAI SECT OF BUDDHISM; TENRIKYO; ZEN SECT OF BUDDHISM.

RELIGION OF DIVINE WISDOM See TENRIKYO.

RENGA "Linked verse"; a form of poetry in which two or more people compose alternating parts of the poem. These parts are known as the upper unit (*kami no ku*), which has three lines of 5-7-5 syllables, and the lower unit (*shimo no ku*) in two lines of 7-7 syllables. A sequence of 100 five-line stanzas (*hyakuin*) comprises the normal length of a *renga* poem. There are also 1,000-stanza (*senku*) *renga* sequences. As many as six or more poets may take turns creating the units of a poem in the *renga* form. The custom of creating linked verses was practiced as a party entertainment by court nobles during the Heian Era (794–1185). It became an accepted Japanese art form in the 14th century, when poets abandoned the stifling rules of the *tanka* form of classical Japanese poetry in favor of the freer expression offered by *renga*. Members of the peasant, merchant and samurai classes also enjoyed creating *renga* at social gatherings. Nijo Yoshimoto (1320–1388) compiled the first *renga* anthology authorized by the imperial court. The greatest *renga* master was the Zen Buddhist priest Sogi (1421–1502), whose famous *renga*-composing session with two other poets, Shohaku and Socho, resulted in the 100-verse poem, "A Hundred Stanzas by the Three Poets of Minase" (A.D. 1488). *Renga* spawned a related form of poetry known as *haikai* ("comic" or "free"), *hokku*, or *haiku*, as it is known today. *Haiku* allows for more freedom and spontaneity than *renga*, as well as humor. It consists of the first *renga* unit of three lines having 5-7-5 syllables. The best known *haiku* poet was Matsuo Basho (1644–1694). See also BASHO; HAIKU; HEIAN ERA; POETRY; TANKA.

RESEARCH AND DEVELOPMENT (R&D) R&D has been important in Japan since the Meiji Era (1868–1912), when the Ministry of Engineering was established in 1870 to build railroads, telegraph systems, and modern factories. The government had established 13 research institutes by 1900. After World War II, in order to catch up with global scientific developments, the government established the Science and Technology Agency to plan program development and coordinate government administration of research in science and technology. In 1961 Japan enacted a law providing for the formation of cooperative ventures known as technology research associations, which aimed at catching up with the West by acquiring foreign technology for Japanese industries. The long-term policy was to move Japan from dependence on foreign technology to independent and innovative technological research, and to use cooperative ventures to stimulate R&D by private companies. Around 80 technology research associations have been established in Japan, most administered by the Ministry of International Trade and Industry (MITI). The associations do not usually perform research themselves but facilitate information exchange and mutual coordination of research, which is conducted by companies belonging to the associations. The government provides financial support, and tax and regulatory policies favorable to R&D. MITI has a Venture Enterprise Center (VEC) that guarantees up to 80% of private bank loans to entrepreneurs who propose viable projects.

Japanese companies perform most R&D on their own, especially leading companies that do not wish to jeopardize their competitive edge by sharing information. Major companies often spend more than 5% of their profits for R&D projects, increasing their R&D expenditures by around 20% annually. A preliminary report by the Management and Coordination Agency stated that in fiscal year 1988 total Japanese research spending rose 8% to just over $75.9 billion, equal to 2.85% of that year's gross national product. Private companies increased their R&D spending by 11.2% to $51.6 billion. Research spending by universities totaled $14.4 billion and research laboratories $10 billion, slight increases over the previous year. Some companies, such as Nippon Telegraph and Telephone (NTT), develop a group of private companies as suppliers who cooperate in the development of appropriate technology. In 1974 the Japanese Supreme Court extended the R&D tax deducation to new jointly funded research concerns, even if their research was not related to the business of the investors that started them, and by the mid-1980s hundreds of R&D limited partnerships were established. The best-known cooperative research project has been the Very Large Scale Integration (VLSI) computer project of the late 1970s and early 1980s to compete with the American company IBM by developing semiconductor (microchip) technology. The Fifth-Generation Advanced Research Systems is a ten-year R&D project, begun in 1982, guided by MITI. Two areas currently emphasized in Japanese R&D are biotechnology and new materials, both of which will help Japan free itself from the need to import raw materials and energy. Japan's low level of defense expenditures has allowed R&D to concentrate on nonmilitary projects.

Some early private R&D institutes were the Toyoto Central Research and Development Laboratories, Inc. (1960) for automobiles and the Sony Corporation Research Center (1961) for consumer electronics. National institutes have also been established at Japanese national universities, such as the Institute for Nuclear Studies at Tokyo University, and other institutes serve the universities but are not attached to particular ones. The Japanese government has built a special "science city" in Tsukuba outside Tokyo as a national research center where many research institutes have been brought together. Known as Tsukuba Academic New Town, the city was completed in 1978 and is administered by the Science and Technology Agency. See also AUTOMOBILE INDUSTRY; COMPUTER INDUSTRY; ELECTRONICS INDUSTRY; FIFTH-GENERATION ADVANCED COMPUTER SYSTEMS; MINISTRY OF INTERNATIONAL TRADE AND INDUSTRY; SCIENCE AND TECHNOLOGY AGENCY; SEMICONDUCTOR INDUSTRY; TSUKUBA ACADEMIC NEW TOWN.

RESPECT FOR THE AGED DAY See HOLIDAYS, NATIONAL; RETIREMENT.

RESTAURANTS Restaurants in Japan frequently specialize in one type of food, and usually do not serve both Japanese and Western dishes. The suffix "-ya" means restaurant; for example, a place that serves sushi is called a *sushi-ya*. Some other popular restaurants serve eel (*unagi-ya*), soba noodles (*soba-ya*), pork cutlets (*tonkatsu-ya*) or grilled pieces of chicken (*yakitori-ya*). Such restaurants are generally small, and customers often sit at counters where they can watch the food being prepared. A short panelled curtain known as a *noren* is hung over the entrance to a restaurant. Large red paper lanterns (*aka-chochin*) are hung outside *yakitori-ya* and some other types of eating and drinking establishments. Many restaurants have window displays of realistic plastic models to show what type of food they offer. Outdoor food stalls (*yatai*) are popular places to eat quick snacks, especially in the evening. *Ryotei* are elegant restaurants that serve numerous courses of traditional Japanese haute cuisine, known as *kaiseki*. A *ryotei* is set off from the street and does not have a sign indicating its entrance. Guests are served in private rooms, where they sit on *tatami* (straw floor mats) and look out on a garden. Some Buddhist temples operate restaurants that serve a special vegetarian cuisine called *shojin ryori*. Japanese people rarely entertain guests at home but prefer to meet with friends or business clients in restaurants. A *miai,* or arranged meeting between potential marriage partners and their families, is often held in a restaurant. Many restaurants will deliver. Portable food boxes (*bento* or *o-bento*) containing rice, *sushi* and other popular bite-sized foods are widely available in train stations, department stores and specialty shops. See also BENTO; COOKING; FOOD MODELS, PLASTIC; FOOD STALLS; KAISEKI; LANTERNS; NOREN; TATAMI; WEDDINGS; NAMES OF INDIVIDUAL DISHES.

RETIREMENT (*inkyo; teinen*) Traditionally, the custom by which the head of a Japanese household handed over his duties and withdrew from public life when his oldest son was married (often by age 20) and was ready to continue the family line. The retiree and his spouse would usually move to a separate house or separate quarters within the main house. In folk tradition, the household head's wife, called *shufu,* also retired symbolically by "handing over the rice ladle" (*shamoji*) to her successor. By extension, the term for this kind of retirement, *inkyo* ("seclusion"), is generally applied today to any retiree or old person.

During the Edo Era (1600–1868), samurai, who became bureaucrats during this period, compulsorily retired from their duties at age 60. *Inkyo* was followed more frequently in samurai families; the stipend paid by the samurai's lord ended at retirement and was transferred to the head of the family's next generation. Farmers, merchants and craftsmen were not forced out of active life so directly, and their retirement was often a gradual process. At age 60, villagers were no longer required to work a full day on collective tasks, but they usually continued to perform various chores.

The 60th year has traditionally been considered the start of old age in Japan because that is when a person completes a full zodiac cycle (*kanreki*). Japanese still have large private celebrations when they turn 60, but employees of large companies and government bureaus are usually required to retire at age 55, to allow for the promotion of junior employees. This compulsory retirement is called *teinen,* or "fixed year." A law was passed in 1986 to set 60 as the legal retirement age, and payments of employee pension benefits begin at age 60. Benefits of the National Pension (Kokumin Nenkin) program, which takes care of workers not covered by their employer pensions, begin at age 65. Pensions do not usually cover all of a retired person's expenses, which may include supporting children and perhaps even parents. Men who have dedicated their lives to their jobs also often find it difficult to retire. Thus many people seek another job after official retirement.

Older people have always been highly respected in Japan. They were honored by special ceremonies in the Edo Era, and in 1963 the Japanese government established Respect for the Aged Day (Keiro no Hi) on September 15th as a national holiday. Japanese laws require children to take responsibility for the welfare of their aged parents. The low birth rate and high longevity rates in Japan are producing an ever-growing older population that will require increased welfare services in the years to come. By 2020, 20% of the population will be over age 65. See also BIRTHDAY; EMPLOYMENT; FAMILY; FILIAL PIETY; SENIORITY SYSTEM; ZODIAC.

REVERE THE EMPEROR, EXPEL THE BARBARIANS (*Sonno joi*) A 19th-century revolutionary slogan advocating the restoration of imperial rule in Japan and the expulsion of foreigners, who were making demands on Japan. This was a slogan of the political movement that eventually overthrew the Tokugawa Shogunate (1603–1867) and brought about the Meiji Restoration of 1868. The Tokugawa Shogunate secluded Japan from all foreign influences in 1639, but in the 19th century, Russian, British and American traders opening Asia attempted to gain access to Japan. In 1854 U.S. Commodore Matthew C. Perry, under the threat of force, compelled the shogunate to reverse its policy of national seclusion by signing a treaty opening up two Japanese ports, Shimoda and Hakodate, to foreign trade. Soon after, the shogunate made similar one-sided agreements with other Western powers, concluding the Ansei Commercial Treaties, which resulted in widespread regional agitation against the seemingly weak and ineffectual shogun. The strongest intellectual position was taken by scholars of the Mito school of Japanese historical studies, who promoted the concept that the emperors, descendants of the Sun Goddess Amaterasu o Mikami, were the ordained rulers of Japan. *Sonno,* or reverence for and loyalty to the emperor, was declared necessary to unite the Japanese people, so they could drive out the barbarians (*joi*). These concepts became the core of the emerging nationalistic ideology that was later referred to as *kokutai,* the Japanese "national essence or polity" or the "body politic." The Mito school took its name from Mito Province (part of modern Ibaraki Prefecture), home of Aizawa Seishisai (1782–1863), the first scholar to elaborate the doctrine of *sonno joi.* Aizawa's political treatise, *New Proposals* (*Shinron;* 1825), argued that the will of the Japanese people should be directed toward a single national purpose. He argued that this could be done by establishing a political order based on the authority of the emperor, and by increasing nationalism through confrontations with foreign enemies. The *sonno joi* slogan was later taken up by other leaders, primarily from the rebellious southern provinces of Satsuma and Choshu, who wanted to overthrow the shogunate. Ironically, leaders of the new Meiji government sent missions abroad to learn as much as possible about Western government and technology, which they adopted to modernize Japan. See also AMATERASU O MIKAMI; ANSEI COMMERCIAL TREATIES; EMPEROR; FOREIGNERS IN JAPAN; KOKUTAI; MEIJI RESTORATION OF 1868; PERRY, MATTHEW CALBRAITH; SECLUSION, NATIONAL; TOKUGAWA SHOGUNATE.

RICE (*kome*) A cereal grass whose grain is the staple food crop of Japan. The cultivation of rice in wet paddy fields was introduced into Japan from the Asian mainland during the Yayoi Era (c. 300 B.C.–c. A.D. 300). Japan's abundant rainfall made it ideal for rice culture. At first, rice seeds were planted directly in paddy fields, but in the fifth–sixth centuries, farmers started growing rice seedlings in nursery

Rice being cultivated in wet paddy fields. Rice is the most important and sacred food in the Japanese diet.

beds and then transplanting them into the paddies. The transplanting of rice seedlings in May or June is a major traditional festival season in Japan, as is the autumn rice harvest. Religious rituals were traditionally performed for each critical stage in the rice growing cycle, to ask the sacred spirits of the rice plant *(inadama)* for a bountiful harvest. Inari, the *kami* (sacred spirit) associated with rice, is widely worshipped in Japan. The Japanese emperor, who functions as the head priest in Shinto, the indigenous Japanese religion, traditionally performs rice transplanting and harvesting rituals to ensure a good crop for the nation.

Because rice cultivation is labor-intensive and depends on controlled irrigation of the fields, it requires intense periods of cooperation by all members of the community. This work method became the foundation of the Japanese social structure based on the extended family or household *(ie)*.

In Japan, three main types of rice are consumed: *hakumai,* or white rice that is highly polished and has had the bran and rice germ removed; *haigamai,* which has the rice germ left in; and *genmai,* unpolished brown rice, which can be mixed with green tea *(cha)* to make a beverage called *genmaicha.* Short-grain sticky white boiled rice is always served in a traditional Japanese meal, usually at the end with soup, pickles and green tea. The three dishes of rice, pickles and tea are even considered sufficient to comprise a basic meal by themselves. The terms for cooked rice,

meshi, gohan and *raisu,* can also indicate the meal itself. White rice is served plain in its own bowl. The rice grains are tender but cling together and are thus easily eaten with chopsticks. Rice is also used to make sushi, small portions of vinegared rice with raw fish or other toppings. Rice balls *(onigiri)* are a basic ingredient in portable food boxes known as *bento.*

The alcoholic beverage sake is brewed from white rice and is drunk before a meal with appetizers but is usually not served during the meal when rice is being eaten. Sake drinking plays an important role in Japanese religious life because the beverage is considered sacred to the *kami.* Rice vinegar and *mirin* (sweetened rice wine) are used in cooking.

Noodles may also be made of rice. Rice crackers *(sembei)* are a popular snack food. Fermented rice is used to make pickles and *miso* (fermented soybean paste), basic foods in the Japanese diet. *Mochi,* cakes made from pounded glutinous rice, and *sekihan,* rice cooked with red beans, are popular foods at Japanese religious festivals. When a person dies, a bowl of white rice is placed at the head of the body, with one chopstick stuck upright in it. For this reason, the Japanese never leave chopsticks in their bowls of rice during meals.

Rice consumption has been declining in Japan in recent decades with the increased consumption of bread and cakes. However, since the 1930s, the Japanese government has subsidized rice farmers to keep the country self-sufficient in rice production. It buys rice from farmers' cooperatives at high prices set by the government, and sells the rice to retailers, who then sell the rice to consumers at slightly lower government-established prices. This practice, initiated by the Rice Control Law of 1933 to control fluctuations in supply and demand, has created a large rice surplus, which is stockpiled. Yet, bowing to pressure from rice growers, the Japanese government resists demands by the United States to allow foreign rice, which would be cheaper for consumers, to be sold in Japan.

Since ancient times, rice has been a measure of wealth, based on a unit of volume known as the *koku* (about 5 bushels). Tax payments were assessed in *koku,* and samurai were paid stipends in *koku.* Rice straw, the dried stalks of rice plants from which the grain has been harvested, has been used to make many household items, including *tatami* (thick floor mats), ropes, rainwear and various wrappings and containers. Although handmade paper is often called rice paper in English, it is not made from rice but from other plants, such as the mulberry bush *(kozo).* See also AGRICULTURE; ALCOHOLIC BEVERAGES; BENTO; CHOPSTICKS; COOKING; CRACKERS; RICE; KOKU; MIRIN; MOCHI; NOODLES; PICKLES; RICE PLANTING AND HARVESTING FESTIVALS; SAKE; STRAW WARE; SUSHI; TATAMI; TEA.

RICE PLANTING AND HARVESTING FESTIVALS   Rice is the staple food of the Japanese diet. Since the introduction of wet-rice cultivation during the Yayoi Era (c. 300 B.C.–c. A.D. 300), Shinto, the indigenous Japanese religion, has been concerned with the phases of rice cultivation.

Japanese folk religion holds that the *kami* (sacred spirit) of rice lives in the fields while the rice is growing.

Taue, the festival for transplanting rice seedlings into large wet fields, or paddies, is held in June. During the festival, young women in a long row bend over to place the seedlings in the paddies, while young men in a row behind the women accompany them with vigorous drumming and singing. Other musicians play flutes and gongs. A leader *(sanbaisan)* sings each line, which is echoed by the group. Participants wear brightly colored kimono and straw hats. In the evening the entire village enjoys a feast with more singing and dancing to celebrate the successful planting of the rice. The emperor of Japan, acting as a priest for the nation as a whole, symbolically plants a few rice seedlings in a sacred paddy in the imperial palace to ensure a good harvest. Rice planting has sentimental associations for Japanese even though only 5% of the population is rural and engaged in farming. Farming villages also hold summer festivals to ward off natural disasters such as storms and droughts that threaten the crops.

The most important festivals are held at harvest time in the autumn, when harvested rice from the new crop is offered to the *kami*. Harvest festivals include processions from Shinto shrines of people in colorful costumes carrying banners, playing drums and other musical instruments, and singing. Purification rituals are performed and prayers of thanksgiving are offered by Shinto priests and a group of laymen chosen from the community. The entire village then enjoys a feast. The enthronement ceremony for a new Japanese emperor is modeled on the annual harvest thanksgiving ceremony. See also DRUMS; EMPEROR; FESTIVALS; KAMI; RICE; SHINTO; YAYOI ERA.

RICE WINE See SAKE.

RICKSHAW *(jinrikisha)* Literally, "man power *(jinriki)* vehicle *(sha)"*; a small two-wheeled carriage pulled by a man to transport people. The rickshaw was supposedly invented by three Japanese men in 1869, shortly after foreign horse-drawn carriages were introduced into Japan. In 1870 the Japanese government gave permission for production of rickshaws on a large scale. Within a few years, up to 50,000 rickshaws were in use in Tokyo. The rickshaw became popular because it was quicker and more easily handled than the palanquin *(kago)*, the traditional Japanese means of transporting people, a box-like enclosure on poles carried by two or more men. The rickshaw was originally a carriage for two people on iron wheels with two poles in the front which were grasped by the man pulling it. Around 1887 the size of the carriage was decreased to hold one person. Iron wheels were later replaced by solid rubber wheels, and then by penumatic tires, resembling modern bicycle tires. Japanese rickshaws were exported to other Asian and Southeast Asian cities such as Hong Kong and Shanghai. In Japan, after the turn of the century, bicycles and automobiles gradually replaced rickshaws, and they were rarely used after much of Tokyo was destroyed in the Great Earthquake of 1923. For a short time after World War II the *rintaku*, a carriage similar to a rickshaw but pulled by a man on a bicycle, was used in Japan. These conveyances are still used in some Southeast Asian cities. In Japan today, geisha occasionally ride to their parties in rickshaws. See also PALANQUIN.

RICOH CO., LTD. See CAMERAS AND PHOTOGRAPHY; ELECTRONICS INDUSTRY.

RIKKEN SEIYUKAI See FRIENDS OF CONSTITUTIONAL GOVERNMENT PARTY.

RIKKOKUSHI "Six National Histories"; the general name for six official histories *(seishi)* compiled by order of the imperial court during the Nara Era (710–794) and early Heian Era (794–1185). The term *Rikkokushi* was first applied to the six histories as a group in the introduction to a book on Japanese foreign relations written in A.D. 1470, the *Zenrinkoku Hoki*. The chronicles record the history and mythology of Japan, from the perspective of the Yamato court on west central Honshu Island, up to A.D. 887. Information in the six histories was taken from court records compiled by the Ministry of Central Imperial Affairs (Nakatsukasasho) and biographies of court officials written for the Ministry of Ceremonial (Shikibusho), and each was compiled by a committee of court officials and scholars overseen by the Office for the Compilation of the National History (Senkokushi-dokoro). The histories were written after Chinese culture was introduced into Japan, and were modeled on Chinese "annals" *(pen-chi; benji* in Japanese) or histories of imperial dynasties.

The first of the six official chronicles was completed in A.D. 720. Named the *Nihon Shoki* (abbreviated as *Nihongi; Chronicle of Japan*), it is the only one of the six that preserves ancient legendary material as well as straightforward history. The second chronicle is the *Shoku nihongi* (or *Shokki; Chronicle of Japan*), compiled in several versions covering the reigns of nine Japanese emperors from 697–791; it is the most reliable source for the history of the Nara Era. The other four chronicles include *Nihon koki (Later Chronicle of Japan, Continued)*, covering the years 792–833; *Shoku Nihon koki (Later Chronicle of Japan, Continued)*, covering the reign of Emperor Nimmyo 833–850; *Nihon Montoku Tenno jitsuroku* (or *Montoku jitsuroku; Veritable Record of Emperor Montoku of Japan*), covering 850–858; and *Nihon sandai jitsuroku* (or *Sandai jitsuroku; Veritable Record of Three Generations [of Emperors] of Japan*), providing a wealth of historical details for the years 858–887. Later official histories were compiled but have not survived. Summaries of material in the *Rikkokushi* were compiled by the scholar Sugawara no Michizane in the *Ruiju Kokushi (Classified National History;* A.D. 892), and by unknown authors in the *Nihon Kiryaku (Outline Record of Japan;* date unknown). See also EMPEROR; NIHON SHOKI; YAMATO.

RIKUGIEN GARDEN A large 18th-century landscape garden that many consider the most beautiful garden in Tokyo. Rikugien Garden, a favorite of Shogun Tokugawa Tsunayoshi (1646–1709; ruled 1680–1709), is typical of the so-called "stroll" style of garden *(kaiyu shiki teien)*, which has different views that can be enjoyed as one moves through the garden. Rikugien Garden covers 25 acres and includes a pond with an island, a hill with a grove of large old trees, and a teahouse. It was given to the city in 1938 and converted to a public park. See also GARDENS; TEAHOUSE.

RIKYU   See SEN NO RIKYU.

RIMPA SCHOOL OF PAINTING   A school of decorative painting that originated in the early 17th century with the artist Sotatsu (?–1643?), and was also influenced by Sotatsu's friend and collaborator, Hon'ami Koetsu (1558–1637). This school takes its name from Korin (1658–1716), who revived its style in the 17th century, along with his brother, a potter named Kenzan (1663–1743): *Rimpa* combines the second syllable of Korin's name (*rin*) and the Japanese term for school (*ha*, pronounced *pa*).

The Rimpa style developed by Sotatsu was bold and simple in design and composition yet lavish in its use of brilliant colors to paint fine details. Many of the paintings were done on sliding wall panels (*fusuma*) and large folding screens (*byobu*) used to decorate Japanese castles. Sotatsu drew inspiration from an old Japanese style of painting known as *Yamato-e*, which depicted nature during the four seasons, the yearly cycle of human activities, beautiful sites in Japan and episodes from classical literature, such as *The Tale of Genji* (*Genji Monogatari*; 11th century A.D.). *Yamato-e* was regarded as the true artistic expression of native Japanese taste.

Sotatsu had a workshop in the old capital city of Kyoto from 1600 to his death around 1643, where he received the patronage of the imperial court centered there. Thus the Rimpa style came to be associated with the Japanese aristocracy. Korin and Kenzan brought the Rimpa style to the new capital city of Edo (modern Tokyo). This style was revived once more in the 17th century by Sakai Hoitsu (1761–1828), whose family had financed Korin and owned many of his works. Rimpa paintings became popular with European and American collectors in the late 19th century. See also KENZAN; KORIN; PAINTING; SCREENS; SOTATSU.

RINZAI SECT OF ZEN BUDDHISM   One of the two main sects of the Zen Buddhist religion. Zen emphasizes meditation (*zazen*) as a means of attaining *satori* or *kensho* (enlightenment or the awakening of a person's true self or Buddha nature). Personal experience rather than the study of written documents is central to Zen. Rinzai Zen teaches that enlightenment comes suddenly, or "all at once," in contrast to the process of "gradual enlightenment" taught by Soto, the other main Zen sect. Besides meditation, other Rinzai techniques for bringing about sudden enlightenment are the study of *koan* (religious questions or riddles), meetings with enlightened masters (*sanzen*), questions and answers between masters and disciples (*mondo*), and radical methods such as shouts (*katsu*) and being hit on the shoulders during meditation with a bamboo stick (*bo*).

The Rinzai Sect originated in China, where it is known as the Linji (Lin-chi) sect of Chan (Ch'an; Zen in Japanese) Buddhism, named for Linji Yixuan (Lin-chi I-hsuan; Rinzai Gigen in Japanese; d. A.D. 867). Rinzai Zen was established in Japan during the 12th and 13th centuries by several Buddhist monks, notably Eisai (1141–1215), who studied Linji Buddhism in China for four years. Eisai taught Rinzai Zen in the capital city of Kyoto, but in the face of opposition by monks of the powerful Tendai and other Buddhist sects, he moved east to Kamakura, headquarters of the new warrior government known as the Kamakura Shogunate (1192–1333). The shogunate supported Eisai and enabled him to found Kenninji Zen monastery in Kyoto. Rinzai Zen spread during the medieval era (12th-16th centuries) under patronage of the Kamakura Shogunate and Ashikaga Shogunate (1338–1573) and leading warlords in the Japanese provinces. Several hundred Rinzai monasteries were built and organized under the Gozan, or five leading monasteries, in Kyoto and Kamakura. However, two prominent monasteries, Daitokuji and Myoshinji, were founded outside the Gozan network. Their abbots, such as the iconoclast Ikkyu Sojun (1394–1481), criticized the material concerns and bureaucracy of the Gozan monasteries and emphasized a more severe life of meditation. In the 18th century, Japanese Rinzai Zen was stimulated by the monk Hakuin Ekaku (1686–1769), who belonged to Myoshinji. Hakuin taught Zen to people of all social classes, produced many of the greatest Zen ink paintings and reorgainzed the *koan* system.

Today there are 14 branches of Rinzai Zen in Japan, all of which derive from Hakuin. Rinzai is practiced in more than 6,000 temples and convents, and many lay people practice Rinzai meditation in schools and businesses. The Rinzai Sect was introduced to the West by Suzuki Daisetz Teitaro (1870–1966), Hisamatsu Shin'ichi (1889–1980), and other Rinzai masters. See also DAITOKUJI; EISAI; HAKUIN EKAKU; HISAMATSU SHIN'ICHI; IKKYU; INK PAINTING; KOAN; MEDITATION; SATORI; SUZUKI DAISETZ TEITARO; SOTO SECT OF ZEN BUDDHISM; ZEN SECT OF BUDDHISM.

RISSHUN   See BEAN-THROWING FESTIVAL; CALENDAR; NEW YEAR FESTIVAL.

RITSURYO SYSTEM   A system of government, based on complex legal codes (*ritsuryo*), established by the Yamato imperial court in the late seventh and eighth centuries. These codes were adopted from the more complex Chinese imperial system of administrative and legal centralization. *Ritsu* refers to a body of injunctions and prohibitions that specify punishments for particular crimes, comprising a penal code. *Ryo* refers to a code that has to do primarily with the financing and administration of the government bureaucracy. An important example was the Taiho Code (Taiho Ritsuryo) promulgated in A.D. 701–702.

The *ritsuryo* codes were concerned with matters of property and inheritance, but their main function was to enhance the authority of the court bureaucracy over all levels of society. The system called for the compilation of population registers, which administrative officials used to determine and collect taxes from each household, which were paid both in labor and in goods. Reforms enacted under Prince Shotoku (Shotoku Taishi; 574–622) strengthened the *ritsuryo* system, through which a small number of court officials were able to govern moderately well a population of around 5 million. The Grand Council of State (Dajokan) was the highest body in the bureaucracy and issued all ruling edicts in the name of the emperor. There were many other bureaucratic levels, and court nobles vied with each other for the highest positions in the bureaucracy. Under the *ritsuryo* system, local hereditary clan chiefs and regional governments lost their autonomy and were required to give their allegiance to the imperial court and its central bureaucracy. The *ritsuryo* system reached its height in the eighth century and remained in effect until A.D. 967, when the power of the imperial bureaucracy became overshadowed by the so-called regency government controlled by the powerful Fujiwara clan. See also CHINA AND JAPAN; CLAN; EMPEROR; FUJIWARA CLAN; SHOTOKU, PRINCE; TAIHO CODE; YAMATO.

RIVERS See BRIDGES; KAMO RIVER; SUMIDA RIVER; TOKYO.

ROBE See CLOTHING; KIMONO; YUKATA.

ROBOTS AND ROBOTICS Computer-driven machines used in manufacturing that can perform functions previously done by human beings. Industrial robots (*sangyoyo robotto*) have been introduced into many Japanese factories, such as those producing automobiles and electronic machinery. In 1980 Japanese companies were using 75,000 robots on production lines, three quarters of all the world's robots, and some factories were completely automated. Industrial robots have increased productivity in Japan by reducing the number of blue-collar workers needed and by eliminating defects in products. Japanese workers have generally not been threatened by automation, though, because the lifetime employment system in large companies gives full-time workers job security and expanding job opportunities. Moreover, the workers receive bonuses calculated on their company's profits, and therefore are receptive to new technology that gives the company a competitive advantage. Robots are routinely used in Japanese factories to handle materials, assemble parts and perform such functions as painting cars, often relieving workers of repetitive and dangerous jobs. Although the United States initially developed robot technology, Japan became the world leader in applying that technology by emphasizing the manufacture of small, low-cost robots that can be programmed to work on short production runs. The Japanese government has provided financial incentives to help companies automate their plants, and money for research into industrial applications of robots. In 1968 Kawasaki Heavy Industries, Ltd. was the first company in Japan to license robot technology from the United States. By the late 1970s, around 200 Japanese companies were involved in robot production, and 85 universities and research institutes were advancing robot technology. During the 1980s, Japan has increased its production of robots by at least 40–50% each year and has become an exporter of industrial robots. Research is now being completed on so-called third-generation robots. First-generation robots worked by rote, repeating the same motions over and over; second-generation

robots have some sensing abilities but are stationary; third-generation robots are being developed to have humanlike sensors and free-moving hands and arms. The Japanese Ministry of International Trade and Industry (MITI) has funded an eight-year program for an intelligent third-generation robot, in conjunction with the so-called fifth-generation (artificial intelligence) computer project. This Advanced Robot Technology Project will be completed in 1991. More than 20 companies have joined university researchers and robotic scientists in Tsukuba Science City to develop robot hands, senses of vision and touch, locomotion, and remote operation. One use for remote control is "hazard" robots, which can be sent into dangerous places where humans cannot go, such as radioactive interiors of nuclear reactors, the ocean floor, and even burning buildings, to rescue people. Robot toys were developed in Japan and are popular around the world. See also AUTOMOBILES; COMPUTER INDUSTRY; CORPORATIONS; ELECTRONICS INDUSTRY; EMPLOYMENT; FIFTH-GENERATION ADVANCED COMPUTER SYSTEMS; LABOR UNIONS; MINISTRY OF INTERNATIONAL TRADE AND INDUSTRY; TSUKUBA ACADEMIC NEW TOWN.

ROCKS Since ancient times, rocks and other natural objects have been venerated as dwelling places of *kami* (sacred spirits) in Shinto, the indigenous religion of Japan. A number of Shinto shrines honor rocks, such as Suwa Shrine in Nagano Prefecture. Two large rocks in the sea at Futamigaura represent Izanagi and Izanami, the mythical creators of the Japanese islands. Tied together by a large rope made of rice straw, they are popularly known as the "Wedded Rocks." Stone water basins are placed at Shinto shrines and in tea ceremony gardens (*chaniwa*) for worshippers or guests to purify themselves by rinsing their hands and mouths. Rocks and stones are an important feature in all Japanese gardens, even those squeezed into tiny courtyards. Flat stepping stones are placed asymmetrically to form a path through a tea garden. The austere "dry landscape" (*karesansui*) style of garden, influenced by the Zen Buddhist religion, consists of white sand and a few large rocks. Rocks are also used to represent mountains in miniature tray plantings known as *bonsai*. Individual rocks displayed as art objects are known as *suiseki* ("viewing stones"). See also BONSAI; FUTAMIGAURA; GARDENS; IZANAGI AND IZANAMI; PURIFICATION; SHINTO; SHRINES, SHINTO.

RONIN See FORTY-SEVEN RONIN INCIDENT; SAMURAI.

ROOF TILES (*kawara*) Tiles made of terracotta or fired clay are frequently used to cover the roofs of traditional Japanese homes and other buildings. Clay tiles are good roofing material because they are strong, fireproof and water-resistant. The technique of covering roofs with overlapping parallel rows of upwardly curving "pan" tiles (*hiragawara*) was introduced into Japan from China in the sixth century A.D. The tiles were placed into a clay bed on a roof. Semicylindrical tiles (*marugawara*) were aligned between rows of pan tiles to keep water from coming through the roof. The end tiles, which project over the walls, were decorated with lotus flowers or linear designs. This style of roofing, known as *hongawara-buki* ("normal" or "orthodox" style), was used on Buddhist temples and other important buildings. In the 17th century, a new technique of overlapping tiles by hooking them together, known as *sangawara-buki,* was developed. These tiles were easier to place on roofs and thus more practical for homes. The Tokugawa Shogunate (1603–1867) required the replacement of straw-thatch (*warabuki*) and reed-thatch (*kayabuki*) roof coverings with clay tiles to resist the spread of fires, a constant threat in Japanese cities. Various tile decorations were also placed on roofs, such as dolphins (*shachigawara*), gargoyles (*onigawara*) and family crests (*mon*). Many different shapes of roof tiles have been used in Japan, and some are associated with particular regions of the country. Roof tiles are still commonly used on traditional homes and are often made of concrete or synthetic materials such as plastic. Today they are also available in bright colors. See also CREST; HOMES AND HOUSING; POTTERY; TEMPLES, BUDDHIST.

ROOSTER See CHICKEN AND ROOSTER.

ROPPONGI See AKASAKA.

RUSSIA AND JAPAN See ANGLO-JAPANESE ALLIANCE; HOKKAIDO ISLAND; KOREA AND JAPAN; KURIL ISLANDS; MANCHURIAN INCIDENT; RUSSO-JAPANESE WAR; SINO-JAPANESE WAR OF 1894–1895; SINO-JAPANESE WAR OF 1937–1945; TSUSHIMA ISLAND; UNITED NATIONS AND JAPAN; WORLD WAR I; WORLD WAR II.

RUSSO-JAPANESE WAR (1904–1905) A war between Japan and Russia for control of Korea and Manchuria. Japan had disputes with Russia over trade and territory starting in the late 18th century, and claimed the southern Kuril Islands in 1855. In 1875 Japan signed an agreement with Russia that gave Japan the northern Kuril Islands and conceded Sakhalin (Karafuto in Japanese) Island to Russia. After Japan defeated China in the Sino-Japanese War of 1894–1895 it won control of Korea, but was forced to return the Liaodong (Liaotung) Peninsula to China due to a tripartite intervention by Russia, France and Germany. Japan did gain control of Formosa (Taiwan) and the strategically important base of Port Arthur (modern Lushun). Yet Russia, supported by France and Germany, soon forced the Japanese out of Port Arthur and seized the Liaodong Peninsula. In 1900 Russia also sent troops into Manchuria during the Boxer Rebellion in China and then broke its promise to withdraw them. In 1902 Japan and Great Britain signed the Anglo-Japanese Alliance to offset a pact between France and Russia and to protect British interests in the North Pacific.

By the end of 1903, anti-Russian feeling was running very strong in Japan. Negotiations between the two countries regarding Korea and Manchuria were unsuccessful, and Japan ended diplomatic relations with Russia on February 6, 1904. On February 8th, the Japanese navy attacked the Russian fleet at Port Arthur. Japan declared war against Russia two days later. The first Japanese army landed in Korea and marched north across the Yalu River into Manchuria. The second Japanese army landed on the Liaodong

Peninsula. The third army attacked Port Arthur and took it from Russia in January 1905. Japanese troops won the battles of Liaoyong, Shahe (Shaho) and Mukden (modern Shenyang), but suffered terrible casualties without completely routing the Russian forces. However, the Japanese navy destroyed the Russian Baltic Fleet at the Battle of Tsushima in May 1905. Japan asked U.S. President Theodore Roosevelt to mediate, and the war was concluded by the Treaty of Portsmouth on September 5, 1905. Under the pact, Japan acquired control of Korea, the South Manchuria Railway and southern Sakhalin Island, and acquired Russian leases in Port Arthur and Dalian. China also gave Japan further rights in Manchuria. Japan did not gain all that it wanted from the war, but it did have its first foothold in China and gained control of Korea, which it annexed in 1910. The outcome of the Russo-Japanese War thus made Japan an imperialistic power equal to Western nations. See also ANGLO-JAPANESE ALLIANCE; IMPERIAL JAPANESE ARMY AND NAVY; KOREA AND JAPAN; SINO-JAPANESE WAR OF 1894–1895.

RYOANJI A temple in Kyoto belonging to the Rinzai branch of Zen Buddhism on whose ground is found the best-known Zen garden, composed of rocks and sand. Ryoanji was the former estate of Hosokawa Katsumoto (1430–1473), a general who died in the Onin War of 1467–1477 and who instructed that it be turned into a Zen temple. Abbot Giten of the neighboring Rinzai temple Myoshinji became the first abbot of Ryoanji. Both temples were burned in the Onin War and rebuilt in the 15th century. Ryoanji was supported by the warlord who unified Japan, Toyotomi Hideyoshi (1536–1598), and Shogun Tokugawa Ieyasu (1543–1616), founder of the Tokugawa Shogunate (1603–1867). Since Ryoanji burned again in 1797, only the abbot's quarters, priests' quarters, a pond, tombs of the Hosokawa family and the rock garden remain. Added to Ryoanji around A.D. 1500, the garden measures about 100 feet by 50 feet and is surrounded on three sides by a low wall, with a veranda on the fourth side from which people can view the garden. The garden's design, attributed to the artist Soami (c.1455–1525), is in the *karesansui* or "dry landscape" style. It contains no trees or plants, but only white sand that is raked every day, showing grooves created by the rake, and 15 rocks in several irregular groupings. Many attempts have been made to interpret the "meaning" of the rocks and sand, by describing them as tigers fording a river, mountains and clouds, islands in a sea and so forth. The "emptiness" of the garden is precisely its meaning from the Zen Buddhist perspective. See also GARDENS; HOSOKAWA CLAN; RINZAI SECT OF ZEN BUDDHISM; ROCKS; SOAMI; ZEN SECT OF BUDDHISM.

RYOKAN A Japanese-style inn with traditional architecture and service. The old wooden structures used as *ryokan* are frequently the former homes of wealthy merchant or samurai warrior families. They tend to be small, with only one or two stories and no more than about two dozen rooms. Guests enter through a gate and a small but carefully landscaped garden. A woman dressed in kimono bows to greet them, helps them take off their shoes and

Ryokan Hiiraguya, a traditional inn in Kyoto. Most *ryokan* are old wooden structures that were formerly the homes of wealthy merchant or samurai families.

put on slippers, and leads them down a long wooden corridor to their room. Here the guests remove their slippers and enter the room, which has *tatami* (straw mats) covering the floor and is furnished with a low table and cushions (*zabuton*) to sit on. A scroll and a flower arrangement are displayed in an alcove called a *tokonoma*. While the guests relax and look out on the garden the maid brings them green tea and sweets, as well as the guest register for them to sign. The guests then take a Japanese-style bath and put on casual robes called *yukata* that the inn provides during their stay. After this the maid serves them dinner in their room. Dinner and breakfast are included in the cost of the room. Dinner is specially prepared by a chef, who presents the dishes in artistic arrangements. The maid then clears away the dinner dishes and lays out the *futon* (Japanese-style bedding) on the *tatami* for the guests to sleep on. In the morning she stores the *futon* in a built-in closet and serves a Japanese breakfast of fish, seaweed, pickles and *miso* soup. When the guests leave, she accompanies them to the door and bows and waves goodbye.

Minshuku are private homes with extra rooms that offer Japanese-style accommodations at a lower cost than *ryokan* but without the constant service of a maid. Guests put out their own *futon* at night and put them away in the morning. Everyone eats dinner and breakfast together at the family table. Similar arrangements are offered at *shukubo*, Japanese-style lodgings with vegetarian meals in Buddhist temples. See also BATH; COOKING; FURNITURE, TRADITIONAL; FUTON; HOMES AND HOUSING; TATAMI; TOKONOMA; YUKATA.

RYOKAN (1758–1831) A monk of the Soto branch of the Zen sect of Buddhism, which was introduced from China into Japan by the Japanese monk Dogen (1200–1253). Ryokan is beloved in Japan for his poetry and calligraphy and for his personality, reflected in the name he took: *ryo* means "good" and *kan* means "generosity" or a "big heart." Ryokan was born in what is now Niigata Prefecture, a remote area in the Snow Country of northwestern Honshu Island. As the oldest son, he was expected to take over the position of village headman from his father, but Ryokan gave up the office because he was too kind-hearted to deal with village conflicts. Undergoing a deep spiritual crisis about the meaning of life, in 1777 Ryokan began studying Zen Buddhism at Koshoji, a local Soto Zen temple. He then spent more than a decade training with a Zen priest named Kokusen (d. 1791), and another decade making a pilgrimage to study with masters at various Zen temples in western Japan.

Ryokan settled in a small hut in the mountains and lived a simple life of absolute poverty. Yet he was close to the farmers in the nearby village, dancing at their festivals and playing with their children. He lived a Zen life instead of teaching about Zen. Ryokan also wrote more than 400 poems in Chinese, and well over 1,000 poems in various Japanese styles, such as the *tanka* form, *waka* form and *haiku*, and folk songs; many have been translated into English. His poems express in a simple, direct way the deep human feelings that underlie daily life. Ryokan also wrote love poems to Teishin (d. 1872), a Buddhist nun he met when he was 69 and she was 29. They spent happy hours together writing poems and discussing religion and literature. Four years after Ryokan died in 1831, Teishin published a collection of his poetry called *Dew on the Lotus* (*Hachisu no tsuyu*; 1835). Today many tourists visit Ryokan's hermitage on Mount Kugami and an art museum and Ryokan memorial hall near Izumozaki village where he was born. See also DŌGEN; HAIKU; MANYOSHU; RINZAI SECT OF ZEN BUDDHISM; SNOW COUNTRY; SOTO SECT OF ZEN BUDDHISM; TANKA; WAKA; ZEN SECT OF BUDDHISM.

RYORI See COOKING.

RYUKYU ISLANDS A chain of more than 70 islands that extend for 800 miles between Kyushu Island and the Republic of Taiwan. The islands have a population of more than 1 million and cover around 866 square miles, of which Okinawa Island comprises 53%. The next largest islands are Iriomote, which is covered by forests and is known for the Iriomote Wild Cat, and Ishigaki. The islands fall into three groups, the Okinawa Island group, the Miyako Island group, and the Yaeyama group. They have a subtropical climate with frequent rainfall and are surrounded by coral reefs. Violent typhoons often strike the islands in late summer and autumn. The Ryukyu Islands are also known as the Nansei Islands (Nansei Shoto, Southern Islands) in Japanese. Today they are generally referred to as Okinawa because they form one administrative unit, Okinawa Prefecture, with the capital city of Naha on Okinawa Island. Ryukyu is the Japanese pronunciation of Liuqiu (Liu-ch'iu), the name given to these islands by Ming dynasty (1368–1644) China, to which Ryukyu paid tribute in exchange for trading privileges. Ryukyu was settled in prehistoric times and the people are related to the Jomon Era (c. 10,000 B.C.–c. 300 B.C.) Japanese, Chinese and Polynesians. The many dialects spoken on the islands are related to the Japanese language but are unintelligible to speakers of standard Japanese or other dialects. Ryukyu was organized into

three kingdoms in the 15th century. In 1372 Satto, king of Chuzan (Central Okinawa), established a tributary relationship with China. In 1406 the first Sho dynasty was founded in Chuzan, and the capital was moved to Shuri, around which the city of Naha grew. The second Sho dynasty, founded in 1470, lasted until Okinawa became a prefecture of Japan in 1879. For centuries Ryukyu was a great trading kingdom and the hub of trade between China, Korea, Southeast Asia and Japan. Goods exchanged included Japanese swords and copper, Chinese raw silk, silk textiles, pottery and Southeast Asian spices. In 1609 the Shimazu Clan of Satsuma Province (modern Kagoshima) on southern Kyushu took control of Ryukyu, but allowed Ryukyu to continue paying tribute to China so as not to disrupt lucrative trade.

Many cultural items were introduced into Japan from Ryukyu, including *kasuri* (a tie-dye weaving technique), sweet potatoes and a banjo-like instrument called the *shamisen*. Ryukyu is especially known for colorful lacquer ware, pottery and textiles. *Bashofu* is a cloth woven from banana plant fiber used to make kimono). *Bingata* is beautiful cloth dyed by a paste-resist technique adopted in Japan as *yuzen* dyeing of textiles; designs are created by covering certain areas with rice paste to resist colored dyes in which the cloth is dipped, and then removing the paste. Ryukyu's rich cultural heritage reflects many influences from various Asian cultures. It has a strong tradition of classical court and folk music and dances. The indigenous religion is similar to Shinto but is conducted by priestesses (*nuru* or *noro*). *Kami* (sacred spirits) are worshiped in natural things such as trees and rocks, and in the spirits of ancestors. Religious rituals and festivals are concerned with the agricultural cycle and a good harvest.

In 1816 European ships began putting into port in Ryukyu, and U.S. Commodore Perry visited Okinawa twice in 1853 and 1854 when he attempted to open Japan to Western trade. After the islands became Okinawa Prefecture in 1879, the people became so impoverished that many of them emigrated to Hawaii, South America and the Philippine Islands. Okinawa Island was devastated during the final battle between Japan and the Allied Powers in World War II. The U.S. administered the islands until 1972, when it finally agreed to return them to Japan. That year the Japanese government established the Okinawa Development Agency, and the islands have since been making an economic recovery. They are now being promoted as a tourist resort area. The main products are crafts, sweet potatoes, sugar cane and a potent distilled liquor called *awamori*. See also IMMIGRANTS, JAPANESE; KASURI; LACQUER WARE; NAHA; OCCUPATION OF JAPAN; OKINAWA ISLAND; OKINAWA, BATTLE OF; PERRY, MATTHEW CALBRAITH; SATSUMA PROVINCE; SHAMISEN; SHIMAZU CLAN; SHINTO; SWEET POTATO; TYPHOON; WORLD WAR II, YUZEN DYEING.

S

SABI AND WABI Two important related aesthetic concepts. The word *sabi* was used in ancient Japan to mean "desolate" or "lonely" and later acquired the further meanings "to grow old" and "to grow rusty." By the 13th century, *sabi* was used to describe the pleasure found in something that is old, faded, unpretentious, lonely. It was connected with another aesthetic term, *yugen*, which indicates beauty that is mysterious and subtle and cannot be expressed with words. The great Noh dramatist Zeami (1363–1443) helped develop these concepts, and similar uses of *sabi* can be found in *The Tale of the Heike* (13th century) and in *Essays in Idleness,* a work on aesthetics by Yoshida Kenko (1283–1350). Zeami and poets of the *renga* form also connected *sabi* with "chill beauty" (*hie*), expressed in such images as withered grass on a moor. The great tea ceremony masters Murata Shuko (d. 1502), Takenoo Joo (1502–1555) and Sen no Rikyu (1522–1591) valued tea utensils that were *sabi*, that is, imperfect, used, coarse. The character for *sabi* can also be pronounced *jaku*, a Buddhist term for peace and tranquility (*shanti* in Sanskrit).

Wabi, meaning "poverty," describes a life that is lived with an enjoyment of poverty surpassing riches. The adjective *wabishi* meant "lonely" or "without comfort" in ancient Japan, but during the medieval era (12th–16th centuries) it became a positive concept describing a life of non-attachment to material concerns such as wealth or power. A life of *wabi* is one of tranquillity that finds the highest beauty in simplicity and austerity. The Zen Buddhist notion of non-attachment further contributed to the meanings of *sabi* and *wabi*. These concepts are also expressed in the simple *haiku* poems of Basho (1644–1694) and his followers. See also BASHO; HAIKU; NOH DRAMA; TEA CEREMONY; SEN NO RIKYU; YUGEN; ZEAMI; ZEN BUDDHISM.

SACRED TREASURES See AMATERASU O MIKAMI; EMPEROR; IMPERIAL REGALIA; JIMMU TENNO; NINIGI NO MIKOTO; MIRROR; SWORD; TENNO.

SADO ISLAND See DRUMS; EXILE.

SAGA PREFECTURE A region on northwest Kyushu, the southernmost of the four main Japanese islands, that is a famous center for the production of pottery and porcelain. The most important kiln sites are Arita, Imari and Karatsu.

Saga was formerly known as Hizen Province. During the Edo Era (1600–1868), it was controlled by the Nabeshima clan, who patronized the pottery kilns. Saga lies only about 150 miles from the Korean Peninsula and was a staging area for Toyotomi Hideyoshi's invasions of Korea in the late 16th century. Many Korean potters were brought to Saga after the invasions and taught new techniques to Japanese potters. Just off Saga is Hirado Island, associated with the English navigator William Adams (1564–1620), who stayed in Japan.

Religious pilgrims come to Saga to purify themselves by bathing in Tamasudare (Bead Curtain) Waterfall. There are many hot spring resorts (*onsen*) in Saga, and legend claims that Empress Jingu (first century A.D.) bathed in Takeo hot spring. Saga has a beautiful coastline and contains one of the largest coastal pine forests in Japan. Sasebo, the headquarters of Japan's Maritime Self-Defense Force, is also located in Saga Prefecture. Saga Prefecture covers 933 square miles and has a population of nearly 1 million. The capital is Saga City. See also ADAMS, WILLIAM; ARITA WARE; HOT SPRING; IMARI WARE; JINGU, EMPRESS; KARATSU WARE; KYUSHU ISLAND; NABESHIMA CLAN; PINE TREE; PORCELAIN; POTTERY; SELF-DEFENSE FORCES; TSUSHIMA ISLAND.

SAICHO (767–822) Also known by his posthumous name, Dengyo Daishi; a Japanese monk who founded the Tendai sect of Buddhism in Japan. Saicho was born to a clan named Mitsukube, which had immigrated from China, in Omi Province (modern Shiga Prefecture). He was named Hirono, but took the name Saicho when he became a Buddhist monk in Nara, then the capital of Japan. Saicho left Nara to found a small temple on Mount Hiei northeast of Kyoto where he could live a quiet religious life, but disciples sought him out there. In A.D. 804 Saicho joined a diplomatic mission to China so that he could study at the important center of the Buddhist religion on Mount Tiantai (T'ien-t'ai; Tendai in Japanese). After nine months, Saicho became accredited as a master of Tiantai Buddhism. He returned to Japan and established the Japanese Tendai sect at his temple on Mount Hiei. This temple became known as Enryakuji.

Tendai teachings are based on the *Lotus Sutra*, an important scripture of the Mahayana (Great, or One, Vehicie) branch of Buddhism, which teaches that all human beings, not only monks, can attain enlightenment. Saicho taught this universal principle in opposition to Hosso and other esoteric sects of Buddhism based in Nara, which taught that only select individuals could become Buddhas. Emperor Kammu, who moved the capital from Nara to Kyoto in A.D. 794, supported Saicho's Tendai sect. Enryakuji, fortuitously located on Mount Hiei, was believed to guard Kyoto from evil spirits.

Saicho studied the teachings of Shingon (True Word or Esoteric) Buddhism with Kukai (774–835; later known by his posthumous name Kobo Daishi, Great Teacher Kobo). Kukai had also studied on Mount Hiei and had joined the same mission to China in A.D. 804. Saicho and Kukai became the two greatest religious leaders of ancient Japan, but their close relationship ended in 816 when Kukai asserted the superiority of the Shingon sect of Buddhism and one of Saicho's main disciples left to join Kukai.

Saicho's greatest contribution was not as a religious philosopher but as a practical administrator. He petitioned the imperial court for independence for the Tendai sect, which was granted a week after his death in A.D. 822. He also initiated a new system for ordaining monks, who formerly could be officially ordained only by Nara sects. He simplified the rules that monks were required to follow, although he asserted that monks must study for 12 years on Mount Hiei, and then serve the imperial court as religious teachers or leaders of public works projects. Through Saicho's efforts Enryakuji on Mount Hiei became a national center for the study of Buddhism in Japan. See also BUDDHISM; CHINA AND JAPAN; ENRYAKUJI; HIEI, MOUNT; HOSSO SECT OF BUDDHISM; KUKAI; KYOTO; LOTUS SUTRA; NARA; SHINGON SECT OF BUDDHISM; TENDAI SECT OF BUDDHISM.

SAIGO TAKAMORI (1827–1877) A samurai who commanded the army from Satsuma Province that was instrumental in the overthrow of the Tokugawa Shogunate (1603–1867) and the return to power of the emperor under the Meiji Restoration of 1868. Saigo Takamori later led the Satsuma Rebellion (1877) protesting the new policies of the Meiji government.

Saigo was born to a large family in Satsuma Province (modern Kagoshima Prefecture) on Kyushu, the southernmost of the four main Japanese islands. After holding provincial posts there, in 1854 he went to the capital city of Edo (modern Tokyo) in the service of Shimazu Nariakira, *daimyo* (feudal lord) of Satsuma. During the Ansei purge (1858) conducted by Ii Naosuke against those who threatened the powers of the Tokugawa Shogunate, Saigo escaped to Kagoshima but was then exiled to Amami (Oshima) Island for three years. Shimazu Hisamitsu, the new *daimyo* of Satsuma, exiled Saigo once again because Saigo opposed Shimazu's plan to lead a rebellion against the shogunate in Kyoto. Saigo was recalled in 1864, however, because he was the only man who could lead the restless Satsuma samurai. In 1866 Saigo negotiated an agreement with Choshu Province, whose forces were led by Kido Takayoshi (1833–1877), that gave birth to the Satsuma-Choshu Alliance against the shogunate. The shogun resigned in 1867 but decided to wage a military campaign against Saigo's forces. After defeating the former shogun's troops at Toba and Fushimi, Saigo led his pro-imperial army to Edo in a campaign known as the Boshin Civil War. With a minimum of fighting, the transfer of power to Emperor Meiji was negotiated with Katsu Kaishu (1823–1899), the representative of the Tokugawa Shogunate.

Under the Meiji Restoration of 1868, Saigo served as commander of the imperial guards and commanding general of the army. He also assisted Okubo Toshimichi (1830–1878), Kido Takayoshi, Yamagata Aritomo (1838–1922) and Iwakura Tomomi (1825–1883) in establishing the new Meiji government. The latter three left the government in Saigo's hands when they went to Europe and North America on the Iwakura Mission of 1871, during which time a crisis

arose over Korea. When members of the Iwakura Mission finally returned to Japan in 1873, they opposed Saigo's plan to invade Korea after it had turned down Japanese demands for commercial and diplomatic relations. Saigo felt that Japan needed Korea in order to resist Russian expansion in Asia, and, also resisting the rapid Westernization of Japan being effected by the Meiji government and its poor treatment of the samurai, he withdrew from the government. He returned to Kagoshima (Satsuma) with many disgruntled samurai who left their army and police posts to accompany him. In 1877, when dissident samurai attacked Meiji government troops in Kagoshima, Saigo felt loyalty gave him no choice but to lead the rebellion. His army was defeated by government troops in Kumamoto. The survivors fought back to Kagoshima, made their final charge, and at Kagoshima Saigo committed suicide. He was posthumously pardoned by the emperor.

Saigo's allegiance to the samurai spirit and his heroic martyrdom inspired patriotic Japanese soldiers who fought on many Asian battlegrounds from the late 19th century through World War II. A Memorial to the Satsuma Loyal Retainers has been erected in Kagoshima, along with a museum on the life of Saigo Takamori. See also BOSHIN CIVIL WAR; CHOSHU PROVINCE; DAIMYO; EXILE; IWAKURA MISSION; KAGOSHIMA; KIDO TAKAYOSHI; KOREA AND JAPAN; KUMAMOTO; KYUSHU ISLAND; MEIJI RESTORATION OF 1868; OKUBO TOSHIMICHI; SAMURAI; SATSUMA PROVINCE; SATSUMA REBELLION; SHIMAZU CLAN; SHOGUN; SUICIDE; TOKUGAWA SHOGUNATE; YAMAGATA ARITOMO.

SAIHOJI A Buddhist temple popularly known as Kokedera, Moss Temple, because of its famous moss garden. Saihoji is located in the former capital city of Kyoto and belongs to the Rinzai branch of the Zen sect of Buddhism. Tradition claims that Saihoji was founded in the mid-eighth century A.D. by a monk named Gyogi. Two major Japanese religious figures, Kukai (774–835), who founded the Shingon sect of Buddhism, and Honen (1133–1212), founder of the Pure Land Sect of Buddhism, may have spent time at this temple. Saihoji became associated with Rinzai Zen in 1139 when the renowned Zen master Muso Soseki (1275–1351) moved there. A beautiful teahouse for the Japanese tea ceremony was built in the compound of Saihoji in the late 16th century. See also MOSS; TEA CEREMONY; TEAHOUSE; RINZAI SECT OF ZEN BUDDHISM; TEMPLES, BUDDHIST; ZEN SECT OF BUDDHISM.

SAIKAKU (1642–1693) Also known as Ihara Saikaku or Ibara Saikaku; a poet and novelist who created a genre of popular fiction in Japan known as "books of the floating world" (*ukiyo-zoshi*). The "floating world" (*ukiyo*) refers to the life of artistic entertainment and physical enjoyment in the licensed pleasure quarters of large Japanese cities during the Edo Era (1600–1868). Saikaku produced a great number of stories, novels and amusing sketches of contemporary life and customs, which are mostly set in the pleasure quarters of Osaka.

Saikaku was born into a merchant family in Osaka. His name may originally have been Hirayama Togo. He later took the literary name of Ihara Kakuei, and then used

Saikaku. When his wife died in 1675, even though he was only in his thirties, Saikaku retired from the family business. He became a writer and teacher of *haikai*, a short form of poetry known today as *haiku*, and made a reputation by participating in marathon competitions of *haikai* improvisation. In 1684 he composed 23,500 *haikai* verses in one 24-hour session. Meanwhile, Saikaku published his first novel in 1682, *The Life of an Amorous Man* (*Koshoku ichidai otoko*; translated 1964), a work of erotic fiction based on popular guidebooks to the women in Osaka's pleasure quarters at the time. The book consists of short episodes describing the sexual adventures of an "amorous man" named Yonosuke. Although Saikaku did not give up poetry, he began turning out prose works at a rapid pace, many of which continued the sexual themes of his first novel. He also wrote books about townsmen (*chonin*), the urban merchant class that became wealthy during the Edo Era and frequented the pleasure quarters, and members of the samurai class. Saikaku was a product of and contributed to the explosion of popular culture in Japan during the Genroku Era (1688–1704). His stories, telling lively tales with a style that combines humor and pathos, constitute the first great realist fiction in Japan and are now admired as classic Japanese literary works. Some others of Saikaku's books that have been translated into English are *Five Women Who Loved Love* (*Koshoku gonin onna*; 1686, translated 1956); *The Life of an Amorous Woman* (*Koshoku ichidai onna*; 1686, translated 1963); and *The Japanese Family Storehouse* (*Nippon eitaigura*; 1688, translated 1959). See also EDO ERA; FLOATING WORLD; GENROKU ERA; HAIKU; NOVELS; OSAKA; PROSTITUTION; SAMURAI; STOREHOUSE; YOSHIWARA.

SAIONJI KIMMOCHI (1849–1940) Prime minister of Japan from 1906–1908 and from 1911–1912. He was born into the Tokudaiji family and adopted into the Saionji family, both of which are branches of the Fujiwara clan, the most prominent family connected with the imperial court throughout Japanese history. Saionji was a representative on the pro-imperial side during the Boshin Civil War of 1868, which overthrew the Tokugawa Shogunate (1603–1867) and brought about the Meiji Restoration of 1868. He studied law in France from 1871 to 1880 and visited several other European countries. When he returned to Japan he founded Meiji Law School (Meiji Horitsu Gakko), which later became Meiji University. In 1882 he joined a group led by Ito Hirobumi that traveled to Europe to study constitutions of various governments. Saionji was then appointed Japanese minister to Austria and Germany. Back in Japan he took a number of government positions, including vice-president of the House of Peers and minister of education. In 1903 he succeeded Ito Hirobumi as president of a new political party called the Friends of Constitutional Government Party (Rikken Seiyukai). Between 1901 and 1913, Saionji alternated terms as prime minister of Japan with another statesman, Katsura Taro. The two men were honored by being appointed *genro*, "elder statesmen" who exercised political authority during the Meiji Era (1868–1912) and Taisho Era (1912–1926). Saionji was the only member of the nobility to receive this honor, and he became the last surviving *genro*.

Saionji resigned as president of the Seiyukai political party when he lost the party's support during the Taisho Political Crisis of 1912 when the third cabinet of Prime Minister Katsura Taro was overthrown by an opposition movement. He then represented Japan at the Paris Peace Conference that produced the Treaty of Versailles after World War I. During the 1920s and 1930s, he acted as an advisor to the emperor, although he often was unable to promote the emperor's desire for peace in the face of increasing aggression against other countries by the Japanese military. As the last of the *genro*, Saionji continued to exercise some influence in the choice of prime ministers, the last time in 1937, when he supported General Hayashi Senjuro. See also BOSHIN CIVIL WAR; FRIENDS OF CONSTITUTIONAL GOVERNMENT PARTY; FUJIWARA CLAN; GENRO; ITO HIROBUMI; MEIJI RESTORATION OF 1868; POLITICAL PARTIES; PRIME MINISTER; TAISHO ERA; TOKUGAWA SHOGUNATE.

SAIPAN, BATTLE OF See WORLD WAR II.

SAKAI A port city on the eastern end of the Inland Sea (Seto Naikai) near modern Osaka that was an important commercial center from the mid-14th through the mid-17th centuries. The Ashikaga Shogunate (1338–1573) and the Hosokawa clan used Sakai as a trading center when the Onin War (1467–1477) prevented them from using the port of Hyogo (modern Kobe). Sakai merchants invested in ships sponsored by the Hosokawa that sailed on four missions to Ming dynasty China (1368–1644). The merchants became wealthy and powerful through trade with China, Korea, the Ryukyu Islands to the south and European countries. Sakai also grew into a center for brewing, printing, ironwork and the production of firearms, silk damask and bleached cotton. Cultural activities such as *renga* poetry and the tea ceremony flourished. The great tea master Sen no Rikyu (1522–1591) came from a family of wealthy Sakai merchants. The city was governed by a council of merchants and had considerable autonomy, which led one Jesuit missionary in Japan to compare it to the great European trading city of Venice. Sakai merchants constructed towers and a moat around the city to defend it during the civil warfare that raged in Japan during the Sengoku (Warring States) Era (1467–1568). The national unifier Oda Nobunaga (1534–1582) took control of Sakai in 1569. The Tokugawa Shogunate (1603–1867) claimed the city as a shogunal domain (*tenryo*) but gave monopoly privileges for raw silk trading with China to Sakai's raw-silk-importing guild. However, Sakai declined as a center of trade after the shogunate instituted national seclusion in 1639 and designated Nagasaki and Osaka as Japan's major trading centers. Sakai is now a modern port and a center for chemical, textile and other industries, with a population of more than 800,000. See also ASHIKAGA SHOGUNATE; HOSOKAWA CLAN; NAGASAKI; ODA NOBUNAGA; ONIN WAR; OSAKA; RYUKYU ISLANDS; SECLUSION, NATIONAL; SEN NO RIKYU; SENGOKU ERA; SILK; TOKUGAWA SHOGUNATE.

SAKAKI TREE A tree that is sacred to Shinto, the indigenous Japanese religion. The *sakaki*, which has broad leaves and is related to the camellia, remains green and blooms even in the winter. The *sakaki* tree grows about 33 feet high and has 3-inch-long oval leaves. Five-petaled white flowers bloom on the tree in early summer. The *sakaki* grows wild in mountainous areas in the warmer regions of Honshu, Kyushu and Shikoku islands in Japan, and also in northeastern China, Korea and northern Taiwan. Because of the ancient Shinto belief that *kami* (sacred spirits) dwell in evergreen trees, the *sakaki* is used to indicate a sacred space and to decorate Shinto shrines. Its branches are also used as offerings to *kami* in Shinto rituals. A priest may wave a *sakaki* branch to purify worshippers or objects. Sprigs of *sakaki* are placed in vases on *kamidana*, small Shinto altars in homes.

Ancient legends about the central Shinto deity, the Sun Goddess Amaterasu o Mikami, tell that when she withdrew into a cave in anger over her brother's actions the other gods lured her out with various objects including 80 combs made from *sakaki* wood; a mirror and jewels were also hung on the branches of a *sakaki* tree, which caused her to peer out of the cave and bring light to the world again. See also ALTARS IN HOMES; AMATERASU O MIKAMI; PURIFICATION; SHINTO; SHRINES, SHINTO.

SAKAMOTO RYUICHI (1952–) A world-famous Japanese musician, composer and actor. Sakamoto has played two movie roles, Captain Yonoi in the acclaimed film *Merry Christmas, Mr. Lawrence* (1983), by controversial Japanese director Oshima Nagisa, for which he also composed the soundtrack, and a secret service man in *The Last Emperor* (1987), by Italian director Bernardo Bertolucci. On the latter film he collaborated with American musician David Byrne and Chinese musician Su Cong to compose the music, for which they won a Golden Globe Award and an Academy Award in the United States.

Sakamoto began studying piano at the age of three and was composing music by age 10. While studying musical composition at Tokyo's prestigious University of Arts, he also attended experimental music performances by Western artists. After graduating, he began working in pop music, and formed the Yellow Magic Orchestra (YMO) with Hosono Haruomi and Takahashi Yukihiro. Their experiments with new technology began a musical revolution in Japan. In 1978 Sakamoto recorded his first solo album, *The Thousand Knives of Ryuichi Sakamoto*. After recording several albums, YMO made its farewell tour in 1983, and its final concerts at Tokyo's Budokan were recorded for a live album, *After Service*, and a video, *Propaganda*, both released in 1984. Sakamoto also worked with Yano Akiko, a Japanese popular singer and songwriter whom he married in 1983. He released his fourth solo album in 1984, a comprehensive recording entitled *Ongakuzukan* (*Illustrated Musical Encyclopedia*). New York choreographer Molissa Fenley commissioned Sakamoto to compose a piece for her dancers entitled "Esperanto"; an album of this music was released in 1985. In 1986, Sakamoto recorded another album

and went on tour with American musicians, producing a live recording and a video. Sakamoto recently acquired a new partner, Bill Laswell, an American bassist and record producer. They created an album, *Neo Geo*, by sending tapes between Tokyo and New York for digital recording and computer mixing. Sakamoto's next solo album, *Beauty*, has recently been released. See also OSHIMA NAGISA.

SAKE An alcoholic beverage made from rice; the best-known indigenous Japanese drink. The correct term for sake is *nihonshu*, "Japanese wine or spirits," and sake is also the generic term for all alcoholic beverages in Japan. Although sake is usually translated as "rice wine," it is actually made by a brewing method similar to the one for making beer. To make sake, rice is steamed so that its starches will turn into sugar; then an aspergillus mold (*koji kabi*) is added to the mixture to stimulate the process of fermentation. This takes about 45–60 days, after which the liquid is refined into a clear beverage with a 15–17% alcohol content. No aging or distilling is involved. The dregs (*sake-kasu*) are used for cooking and making pickles (*tsukemono*). Nearly 3,000 companies in Japan, especially in the western and northern regions, make many different grades of sake. Sake producers are regulated by the Japan Sake Brewers Association. Sake is naturally sweet (*amakuchi*), but some types are treated to make them dryer (*karakuchi*). The traditional way of serving sake is to warm it to release its flavor and aroma. About 6 ounces of sake are poured into a small pottery or porcelain container (*tokkuri*), which is set in a pot of boiling water for several minutes. At the table, sake is poured from the *tokuri* into tiny cups (*choko* or *sakazuki*). Japanese etiquette requires that each person pour sake for another. When everyone has their drinks, they raise their cups and shout "*kampai!*" ("to your health" or "bottoms up!"). Because sake is made from rice, it is usually not served with rice dishes. The best accompaniment to sake is small pieces of food known as *otsumami* (snacks) or *sake no sakana* (fish), such as dried fish, fish roe, raw fish (sashimi) and pickles.

Because it is made from rice, the Japanese believe that sake is the drink of the gods (*kami*) of Shinto, the indigenous Japanese religion. The gods supposedly brewed sake from the first rice harvested every year, and it has always been one of the major offerings in ceremonies at Shinto shrines and altars in homes. At a Shinto wedding ceremony, the bridal couple performs the "three times three" ceremony of exchanging lacquer cups and drinking sake. Sake is also heavily drunk at the numerous annual festivals held throughout Japan, which are associated with the agricultural cycle.

In the Heian Era (794–1185), only priests and aristocrats were permitted to drink sake, which at that time was a thick milky or yellow beverage (still sold as *doburoku* or *nigori-zake*, unrefined sake). Other Japanese began enjoying sake during the 12th century. Brewing techniques were refined during the rise of the urban merchant class in the Edo Era (1600–1868). Today sake is exported to many foreign countries. The Japanese also drink a type of powerful alcoholic beverage known as *shochu*, which is distilled from grain, sweet potatoes or other ingredients. See also AGRICULTURE; ALCOHOLIC BEVERAGES; ALTARS IN HOMES; FESTIVALS; KAMI; KAMPAI; RICE; SHINTO; WEDDINGS.

SAKHALIN ISLAND   See KURIL ISLANDS; RUSSO-JAPANESE WAR.

SAKURA   See CHERRY BLOSSOM.

SAKURA FILM   See CAMERAS AND PHOTOGRAPHY.

SAKURAJIMA, MOUNT   See KAGOSHIMA; MOUNTAINS; VOLCANO.

SAKYAMUNI   See BUDDHISM.

SALARYMAN (*sarariman*)   White-collar workers who are salaried employees of large companies and government agencies. *Sarariman* is a Japanese-English term coined after World War I to differentiate between blue-collar workers who performed manual labor and white-collar administrators and managers in large companies. The term applies only to men, as very few women hold managerial positions in Japanese companies. The stereotypical salaryman is a short-haired, clean-shaven man wearing a white shirt, tie and dark suit with a company lapel pin on the jacket; he carries a briefcase on his long commute between his home in the suburbs and his office in the city. There are about 38 million salarymen in Japan, 70% of whom are university graduates. They are expected to be loyal to their companies, which usually offer these men lifetime employment, and to participate in social activities sponsored by the companies. Salarymen are very concerned with upward mobility (*shoshin*) within their company, which is based partly on the relative prestige of the universities they attended. Fearful of doing anything to jeopardize their lifetime job security, they tend to be conservative and conform to company policies. See also CORPORATIONS; EMPLOYMENT; LIFETIME EMPLOYMENT SYSTEM; OFFICE LADY; UNIVERSITIES.

SALT (*shio*)   Salt is a traditional means of purification in Shinto, the indigenous Japanese religion. This may be because salt is taken from the sea, where ancient cleansing rituals were performed. As a nation of small islands, the sea is very important to Japan. Salt is scattered in front of religious processions and is used in various religious ceremonies. After a funeral, Japanese scatter salt at the entrance of a house to protect returning mourners from contamination after contact with the dead. A small mound of salt is placed at the entrance of a restaurant to keep evil away. This custom, called *mori-jio*, is also seen in farmhouses at the New Year Festival, when salt is placed alongside the hearth or the well. *Sumo* wrestlers scatter salt during rituals held before a match. Starting in the Nara Era (710–794), salt was produced in Japan in salt fields, known as *enden*, at sea shores. Seawater was partially evaporated in the sun and then boiled to produce salt. Japanese cuisine is quite salty, including soy sauce, the basic flavoring ingredient. *Shio-yaki* is a method for grilling fish and other foods with salt. See also COOKING; FUNERALS; NEW YEAR FESTIVAL; PURIFICATION; SHINTO; SUMO.

SAMURAI   Literally, "one who serves"; also known as *bushi*, "military gentry"; a member of the warrior class that arose in Japan during the late Heian Era (794–1185) and developed into the feudal warrior class that ruled Japan from the late 12th century until the Meiji Restoration of 1868. The samurai originated as military retainers of the provincial manors or estates (*shoen*) owned by court nobles and Buddhist temples located in the capital city of Kyoto. Warriors became organized into bands or military units, known as *bushidan*, made up of members of local rival clan chieftains, which were especially powerful in the Kanto region of east central Honshu Island. At first the *bushidan* were formed only when they were needed to fight specific battles, after which they returned to being managers of farmlands. By the 11th century, however, larger and more centralized warrior bands were becoming established in which samurai pledged their loyalty as vassals to their lords. This was the basis of the feudal system, which placed samurai in a fictive child-parent relationship with their lords as "housemen" (*kenin*) or "children of the house" (*ienoko*). Peasants were required to stay on the land and pay rent to samurai, who held rights to the land in the form of fiefs (*chigyo*).

The largest warrior families were led by descendants of

Men dressed in medieval samurai battle armor for the Soma Wild Horse Chase held every July in Haramachi, Fukushima Prefecture.

A 17th-century samurai wearing battle armor and two swords. Samurai governments ruled Japan from the late 12th through the mid-19th century.

the imperial family. Emperors had numerous children by many concubines, and most did not keep their royal status but were given new family names, mainly Taira and Minamoto, and appointments in the provinces. The rival Taira and Minamoto clans fought a civil war (Taira-Minamoto War; 1180–1185) in which the Minamoto clan soundly defeated the Taira. After the war, Minamoto no Yoritomo (1147–1199) founded the Kamakura Shogunate (1192–1133), the first of three military "tent" governments (bakufu) that ruled Japan for nearly seven centuries, not replacing the imperial court in Kyoto but wielding the actual ruling power.

During the samurai-dominated feudal era of Japan (12th–16th centuries), local, regional and national lords, known as daimyo, fought each other to increase their power and their land holdings. The second and third bakufu were the Ashikaga Shogunate (1338–1573) and the Tokugawa Shogunate (1603–1867). A century of feudal warfare, known as the Sengoku (Warring States) Era (1467–1568), also divided Japan between the Onin War (1467–1477) and the unification of Japan during the Tokugawa Shogunate (1603–1867).

Samurai originally fought on horseback with large swords. The Japanese regarded a samurai's sword, so critical to survival, as his "soul" or "spirit." Samurai were trained in sword fighting, archery and other martial arts, which are still practiced as competitive sports by many Japanese

today. The samurai virtues, which became embodied in a code known as bushido (the Way of the Warrior), are obedience and loyalty to one's lord, bravery and self-discipline. Samurai who lost or left their masters were known as ronin, "floating (or drifting) men" and could be retained by other lords to fight in their armies.

The Tokugawa Shogunate, which brought centuries of peace to a unified Japan, sharply differentiated the samurai from the peasant and artisan classes, and transformed the samurai from warriors into civil bureaucrats. Cities grew up around castles built by daimyo, and samurai values were spread to all levels of Japanese society. However, there were different social levels of samurai, according to their wealth and rank. Lower levels of samurai served as foot soldiers, guards or clerks.

Samurai from rebellious southern provinces led the overthrow of the Shogunate and the Meiji Restoration of 1868. The privileged position of the samurai class was officially ended in the 1870s, when the Meiji government ended stipends to samurai and forbade them from wearing their swords, yet it was former samurai who were leaders in the Meiji government that guided Japan from feudalism into the modern era.

The Japanese are fascinated by samurai, just as Americans idealize the western cowboy. Dramas about samurai have been a mainstay of popular culture in Japan, from Kabuki and Bunraku (puppet theater), which developed in the Edo Era, to present-day movies and television shows. The story of the Forty-Seven Ronin who avenged their master's murder is frequently performed under the title Chushingura, and has been made into a movie. A world-famous samurai movie set in the Edo Era is The Seven Samurai, written and directed by Kurosawa Akira (b. 1910). See also ARMOR; ASHIKAGA SHOGUNATE; BAKUFU; BUNRAKU; BUSHIDO; CASTLE; DAIMYO; FORTY-SEVEN RONIN INCIDENT; KABUKI; KAMAKURA SHOGUNATE; KANSAI AND KANTO; KUROSAWA AKIRA; MARTIAL ARTS; MINAMOTO CLAN; MINAMOTO NO YORITOMO; SHOGUN; SWORD; TAIRA CLAN; TAIRA-MINAMOTO WAR; TOKUGAWA SHOGUNATE.

-SAN A suffix added to the name of a person to show respect. This practice reflects the formal and hierarchical nature of social relationships in Japan. For example, someone whose family name is Yamada is called Yamada-san. -San stands for Mr., Mrs., Ms. or Miss. Variations of this suffix are -sama, which is more formal and is now used mainly for addressing letters, and -chan, a term of affection used for children. In Japan, even Mickey Mouse is extended the courtesy, as "Miki-chan." The suffix -sama also occurs in fixed phrases or terms. For example, the Star Festival is called Tanabata-sama because of the gods in attendance at the festival. See also ETIQUETTE; LANGUAGE, JAPANESE; NAMES, JAPANESE.

SAN FRANCISCO PEACE TREATY See PEACE TREATY OF 1952.

SANDALS See FOOTWEAR.

SANJA FESTIVAL See ASAKUSA.

SANJUSANGENDO See ARCHERY.

SANKAIJUKU TROUPE See BUTOH.

SANSEI The name given to the third generation of Japanese immigrants in other countries, primarily the United States. The first generation is known as *issei,* and the second as *nisei. Sansei* have become more integrated into American and other societies than their parents were able to be, and many *sansei* are now marrying spouses not of Japanese descent. Unlike their parents, few *sansei* are familiar with the Japanese language and culture. See also IMMIGRANTS, JAPANESE; ISSEI; NISEI.

SANSOM, SIR GEORGE BAILEY (1883–1965) A British diplomat who also wrote influential works on the history and language of Japan. Sansom became a member of the British consular service when he was only 19. Assigned to the Far East in 1904, beginning as an interpreter in Nagasaki, he served in Japan for nearly 40 years. In the 1920s Sansom also became known as the foremost Western scholar of Japanese history and culture. His first book, published in 1928, was *An Historical Grammar of Japanese.* Three years later he published *Japan: A Short Cultural History,* a classic English-language text on Japan that is still widely used in university courses. In 1935 Sansom was knighted. Following World War II, during the Allied Occupation of Japan, he came to Washington, D.C. to serve on the Far Eastern Commission. In 1947 Columbia University in New York made him the first director of its East Asian Institute, where he led the much-needed development of Western scholarship about Japan. While at Columbia he published *The Western World and Japan.* Sansom accepted an appointment to Stanford University in 1954, which enabled him to write his most important scholarly study, *The History of Japan,* which was published in three volumes from 1958 to 1963. He died two years later at the age of 82. See also HISTORICAL ERAS; OCCUPATION OF JAPAN.

SAN'YO ELECTRIC CO., LTD. See ELECTRONICS INDUSTRY.

SAPPORO The capital of Hokkaido, Japan's northernmost island. A relatively new city, Sapporo has a population of 1½ million, making it the largest Japanese city north of Tokyo. In 1869 the Meiji government established a colonial office *(kaitakushi)* on Hokkaido, which at that time was a wilderness inhabited only by tribes of indigenous nomadic people called Ainu. The chosen site for the new administrative center, Sapporo took its name from an Ainu place-name meaning "big, dry river." The Meiji government sent 76 foreign experts (46 Americans among them) to advise the Japanese on Hokkaido on how to develop the rich natural resources there. They designed the new city, located on the Toyohiragawa River plain, with a uniform grid or checkerboard pattern. Sapporo Agricultural College was founded in 1875. A Western-style building erected for the college in 1878 has a clock tower that is still Sapporo's most famous landmark. Dr. William S. Clark, an American who taught there for one year and is remembered for his famous advice to the students, "Boys, be ambitious," is commemorated with a statue. The college is now a national university, Hokkaido University, and maintains a natural history museum within the city's Botanical Garden (Shokubutsu-en). Other museums in Sapporo include the Historical Museum of Hokkaido (Kaitaku Kinenkan), showing the development of Hokkaido, and the Historical Village of Hokkaido (Kaitaku-no-Mura), an outdoor museum containing homes, a school and a shrine. Exhibits on Ainu culture are displayed at the Batchelor Memorial Museum, named for John Batchelor, an English minister who collected Ainu artifacts during the Meiji Era. There is also a museum in the factory of Sapporo Breweries, Ltd., the second largest brewing company in Japan, after Kirin Brewery Co., Ltd. The Sapporo company dates back to 1876 and produces beer and soft drinks. Sapporo beer is exported to many countries. After World War II, the city of Sapporo became more industrialized. Mining, food processing and construction are some major economic activities. Sapporo gained world attention when it hosted the 11th Winter Olympic Games in February 1972. The Teine Olympia Ski Grounds, site of many Olympic events, is now open to the public. Many tourists come to the city every February for the Snow Festival, which features large snow and ice sculptures along the city's central boulevard, which lines Odori Park. See also ALCOHOLIC BEVERAGES; AINU; HOKKAIDO ISLAND; MEIJI RESTORATION OF 1868; OLYMPIC GAMES; SNOW FESTIVAL.

SAPPORO BREWERIES, LTD. See ALCOHOLIC BEVERAGES; SAPPORO.

SARASHINA DIARY (*Sarashina nikki*) A book of memoirs written in prose and poetry shortly after A.D. 1059 by a Heian Era (794–1185) court lady. Her personal name is unknown, and she is referred to as Sugawara no Takasue no Musume (Daughter of Sugawara no Takasue; b. A.D. 1008). She was a descendant of Sugawara no Michizane (845–903), an important scholar, poet and court official, and the niece of a court lady who wrote *The Gossamer Years* (*Kagero nikki;* A.D. 974, translated 1964), the earliest surviving diary by a Japanese woman.

The *Sarashina Diary* is unusual for a Heian diary in that much of it was written long after the fact and in that it covered most of the author's life, beginning when she was 12 and continuing until she was in her 50s. She was raised in Kazusa Province (modern Chiba Prefecture, bordering Tokyo), where her father was vice-governor. In 1020 her family traveled across Japan to the capital of Kyoto. In the diary she describes Mount Fuji and other wonders of nature that she saw and people that she encountered on the three-month journey. Afterward she remained in Kyoto but went on many pilgrimages. After serving for a short period as lady-in-waiting to an imperial princess, she married Tachibana no Toshimichi, governor of Shinano Province (modern Nagano Prefecture), and had three children. After several people close to her died, including her husband, she apparently became a Buddhist nun. The diary dwells on the sad events in her life, and on her passion for romantic tales (monogatari). She also records that she was given a copy of The Tale of Genji (Genji Monogatari), the first Japanese novel, by its author and her aunt, Murasaki Shikibu (fl. c. A.D. 1000).

The Sarashina Diary was translated into English by Ivan Morris under the title As I Crossed a Bridge of Dreams (1963). Two other works are attributed to the diary's author: Nights of Fitful Waking (Yoru no Nezame) and Tale of the Hamamatsu Middle Counselor (Hamamatsu Chunagon Monogatari). See also DIARIES; GENJI, THE TALE OF; HEIAN ERA; MONOGATARI; MURASAKI SHIKIBU; PILGRIMAGE; SUGAWARA NO MICHIZANE.

SASA See BAMBOO; BUSH WARBLER.

SASHIKO See QUILTING.

SASHIMI Slices of fresh raw saltwater fish and other seafood. Sashimi is the most important dish in a Japanese meal. In formal meals sashimi is served at the beginning, or right after the appetizers and soup, when it can be properly appreciated. Even when all the dishes are served together in a home-style meal, sashimi is eaten first. Freshness is essential, requiring fish that is not only freshly caught but also in season. Some varieties of popular fish such as tuna, bream and mackerel are available throughout the year, but others are best eaten in designated seasons. For example, in the spring, Japanese enjoy bonito, karei flounder and sea bream (tai), which they regard as "king of saltwater fish." Summer is the season for perch and anago eel. Mackerel, clams, oysters and hirame flounder are some autumn specialties, and winter brings yellowtail tuna (maguro), sawara mackerel and a small fish called "whitebait" (shirauo). Varieties of freshwater fish are generally not used for sashimi because they may contain parasites. Other seafood used for sashimi includes abalone, scallops, clams and shrimp. When slices of raw fish or seafood are served on small portions of vinegared rice, they are known as sushi.

Slices of sashimi are ¼ to ½ inch thick. There are special techniques for cutting the fresh fish into fillets, and also for the final step of slicing the fillets into small pieces for serving, which requires a special long, thin knife called a sashimi-bocho. Two slicing techniques are most commonly used. One is the "flat cut" (hira-zukuri), by which the knife is drawn through the fillet toward the person cutting, working from the right side of the fillet. Another is the "slant cut" (sogi-zukuri, also called usu-zukuri), used to cut firm, white-fleshed fish into paper-thin slices. Working from the left side of the fillet, the knife is held almost horizontal, with the sharp edge slicing toward the left. These slices are arranged on a serving dish in the shape of a flower, such as a chrysanthemum, or a bird. The most notorious fish served as sashimi is the blowfish (fugu), which can be fatally poisonous if improperly prepared and which is served only by restaurants with specially trained and licensed chefs.

The presentation of sashimi is valued as highly as is the freshness of the fish. Served on flat dishes or plates, perhaps five or six slices will be laid against a bed of shredded daikon (white Japanese radish) and artistically garnished with leaves, such as those of the shiso (beefsteak plant). A dipping sauce is provided to add flavor. Soy sauce is always used as the base, and sake is added to dipping sauces in restaurants. Wasabi (a paste of Japanese horseradish) or grated ginger (shoga) is mixed into the sauce to give it a sharper taste. Ponzu is another popular sauce, in which lemon, vinegar and other ingredients are mixed with the soy sauce. See also BLOWFISH; BONITO; DAIKON; EEL; FISH AND FISHING INDUSTRY; GINGER; SAKE; SEAFOOD; SOY SAUCE; TUNA; WASABI.

SATO EISAKU (1901–1975) Prime minister of Japan from November 1964 to July 1972, the longest term of any prime minister in Japanese history. Born in Yamaguchi Prefecture, Sato was educated at Tokyo University. After graduating in 1924, he entered government service and held various administrative jobs, starting in the Ministry of Railways (now the Ministry of Transport). In 1948 Prime Minister Yoshida Shigeru appointed Sato to several consecutive posts, including director of the Prime Minister's Cabinet secretariat, minister of posts and telecommunications and minister of construction. A member of the Liberal Democratic Party (Jiyu Minshuto; known as the LDP), Japan's predominant political party, Sato was elected to the House of Representatives (lower house of the Japanese Diet, or parliament) in 1949, and Yoshida named Sato secretary-general of the LDP in 1953. Sato's political career was interrupted in 1954 by his indictment for taking bribes from an association of shipbuilders, but he was freed in a general amnesty issued by the Japanese government when Japan entered the United Nations in 1956. Two years later Sato became finance minister in the cabinet of Prime Minister Kishi Nobusuke. He then became minister of international trade and industry in the cabinet of Ikeda Hayato, and was in charge of the Tokyo Olympic Games in 1964. That year Sato lost a bid to replace Ikeda as president of the LDP, but Ikeda then developed terminal cancer and chose Sato as his successor.

Under the leadership of Prime Minister Sato, Japan became the third largest economic power in the world, Japanese relations with Korea and Southeast Asia were strengthened, the United States–Japan Security Treaty of 1960 was extended in 1970 and the islands of Okinawa Prefecture (Ryukyu Islands) were returned to Japan by the United States in 1972. Sato's opponents criticized him for being too lenient in allowing the U.S. to use its bases in Okinawa for potential crises in other Asian countries. Sato worked to maintain a cooperative relationship with the United States, although certain issues created dissension, such as Japanese textile exports to America, revaluation of the yen and President Nixon's trip to the People's Republic of China. In 1974 Sato was awarded the Nobel Peace Prize, largely because of his advocacy of the "three nonnuclear principles" (hikaku sangensoku) for Japan, which were the basis of a non-official policy of nonmanufacturing, nonpossession and nonintroduction of nuclear weapons into

Japan. See also CABINET, PRIME MINISTER'S; DIET; LIBERAL DEMOCRATIC PARTY; OKINAWA ISLAND; OLYMPIC GAMES; PRIME MINISTER; SECURITY TREATY BETWEEN JAPAN AND THE UNITED STATES; YEN; YOSHIDA SHIGERU.

SATORI Enlightenment, or the awakening of the True Self, which is the ultimate goal of religion according to the Zen sect of Buddhism. Enlightenment has been the central point of Buddhist teachings from the religion's founding in India in the sixth century B.C. *Satori* is the Japanese word for the Chinese term *wu*, which literally means "awakening" or "apprehending." Zen, which was introduced into Japan from China (where it was known as *Chan*) by the Japanese monk Eisai (1141–1215), uses many techniques, such as meditation and *koans* (religious riddles or questions), to help a religious seeker break through the limits of his or her ordinary self, or ego, to attain *satori*. Zen teaches that the "death" or transcendence of the ego is at the same time the awakening of the True Self. Zen masters have paradoxically described the True Self as the "original face" a person has prior to the birth of one's parents. The Zen concept of enlightenment as self-awakening differs from some other sects of Buddhism that offer salvation through faith in a deity, such as Pure Land Buddhism, which worships Amida Buddha. Meditation is also practiced by other Buddhist sects, however. See also BUDDHISM; KOAN; MEDITATION; ZEN SECT OF BUDDHISM.

SATSUMA PROVINCE A region on the southern tip of Kyushu, the southernmost of the four main Japanese islands, which forms the western half of modern Kagoshima Prefecture. The former Province of Osumi comprises the eastern half.

Satsuma Province was established in A.D. 646, one of 11 provinces in the region known as the Western Sea Circuit (Saikaido) on Kyushu. The dominant Fujiwara clan owned many estates (*shoen*) in Satsuma starting in the mid-Heian Era (794–1185), as did many temples and shrines in the capital city of Kyoto. The Shimazu clan, which functioned as steward (*gesu* or *geshi*) on estates in Satsuma owned by the Konoe Family, served as military governors (*shugo* or *shugo daimyo*) of Satsuma from the 12th through the 16th centuries, expanding their power until they controlled most of Kyushu Island in the Sengoku (Warring States) Era (1467–1568). Under Shimazu control, Satsuma was the site where many foreign influences entered Japan, including the sweet potato (known as *satsuma-imo*), Western firearms and the Christian religion, which was introduced by the Jesuit missionary St. Francis Xavier (1506–1552). The warlord Toyotomi Hideyoshi (1536–1598) subdued the Shimazu clan in 1587. However, in 1609 the Shimazu annexed to Satsuma Province the great trading empire of the Ryukyu Islands (modern Okinawa Prefecture) to the south. In 1866, Satsuma Province and Choshu Province (modern Yamaguchi Prefecture on Kyushu Island) formed the secret Satsuma-Choshu Alliance (Satcho Domei) to overthrow the Tokugawa Shogunate (1603–1867), in which the Satsuma samurai leaders Saigo Takamori (1827–1877) and Okubo Toshomichi (1830–1878) played an important role. When the Tokugawa Shogunate was overthrown in the Boshin Civil War and power was returned to the emperor with the Meiji Restoration of 1868, Satsuma and Choshu leaders held the most important positions in the new government. In 1877 Saigo Takamuri led disgruntled samurai in the so-called Satsuma Rebellion against the Meiji government. Satsuma is also world famous for a type of decorated pottery known as Satsuma ware. See also BOSHIN CIVIL WAR; CHOSHU PROVINCE; CHRISTIANITY IN JAPAN; DAIMYO; FIREARMS, INTRODUCTION OF; FUJIWARA CLAN; KAGOSHIMA; KYUSHU ISLAND; LANDED ESTATE SYSTEM; MEIJI RESTORATION OF 1868; OKUBU TOSHIMICHI; RYUKYU ISLANDS; SAIGO TAKAMORI; SAMURAI; SATSUMA REBELLION; SATSUMA WARE; SENGOKU ERA; SHIMAZU CLAN; SWEET POTATO; TOKUGAWA SHOGUNATE; TOYOTOMI HIDEYOSHI; XAVIER, ST. FRANCIS.

SATSUMA REBELLION (1877; Seinan Senso or Seinan no Eki) Also known as the Southwest Campaign; the largest and last armed uprising by members of the samurai class against the policies enacted by the new Meiji government (1868–1912). The Satsuma Rebellion was led by Saigo Takamori (1827–1877), a samurai from Satsuma Province (part of modern Kagoshima Prefecture) on southern Kyushu Island who had commanded the army that overthrew the Tokugawa Shogunate (1603–1867) and returned power to the emperor in the Meiji Restoration of 1868. The *daimyo* (feudal lords) whom the samurai served had been persuaded to hand over their domains to the Meiji government, which designated the domains as government prefectures in 1871. In exchange, the *daimyo* were made governors of the provinces they once ruled, given government bonds in compensation for wealth they had lost and made peers of the realm in 1885. The samurai did not fare as well. A number of them, mostly from Choshu Province, became army officers or entered the police force or government bureaucracy. However, thousands of samurai had no means of supporting themselves in the new order and became impoverished. The government first promised them pensions, but then replaced the pensions with token sums of money. Samurai were also offended by new rules that forbade them from carrying their two traditional swords, considered the soul of the samurai, and that required them to give up their top-knot for Western-style haircuts. They were further angered by the new conscription system developed by Yamagata Aritomo (1838–1922), which brought members of the peasant class into the army.

Saigo Takamori became dissatisfied with the rapid changes being effected by the Meiji government, especially by the government's refusal to invade neighboring Korea after it refused Japanese demands for commercial and diplomatic relations in 1873. Saigo left the capital city of Tokyo for Kagoshima (Satsuma), and many samurai left their positions in the army and police force to go with him. In 1877 the Meiji government suspected a rebellion and sent troops to remove ammunition stored at an army depot and navy yard in Kagoshima. Young samurai attacked the government troops. Saigo had not anticipated such action, but once it occurred, he felt he had no choice but to lead the rebel force to the capital city of Tokyo. At Kumamoto City on southwestern Kyushu they were opposed by government forces led by General Tani Kanjo. After 50 days of fighting and the destruction of Kumamoto Castle (1607), the rebel army was rebuffed and fought its way back through southern Kyushu to Kagoshima. The remaining 400 soldiers made their final charge, and Saigo committed suicide.

Saigo's traditional samurai forces were defeated by the new Japanese conscript army of 40,000 soldiers, who had the advantage of modern training and weapons. Following the Satsuma Rebellion, dissidents established the first political parties in Japan, the Liberal Party in 1881 and the Progressive Party in 1882, as a peaceful means of opposing government policies. See also CHOSHU PROVINCE; DAIMYO; IMPERIAL JAPANESE ARMY AND NAVY; KAGOSHIMA; KUMAMOTO; KYUSHU; MEIJI RESTORATION OF 1868; POLITICAL PARTIES; SAIGO TAKAMORI; SAMURAI; SATSUMA PROVINCE; SUICIDE; SWORD; TOKUGAWA SHOGUNATE; YAMAGATA ARITOMO.

SATSUMA WARE (*satsuma-yaki*) A type of pottery produced at kilns in Satsuma Province (modern Kagoshima Prefecture) on southern Kyushu Island. Satsuma ware originated around 1600 when Korean potters, who had been brought to Japan during the two Japanese invasions of Korea under the warlord Toyotomi Hideyoshi (1537–1598), were settled in the region by its ruler, Lord Shimazu Yoshihiro, who himself was a potter and a student of the great tea ceremony master Sen no Rikyu (1522–1591). One group of Satsuma potters made tea ceremony utensils known as old Chosa or old Satsuma ware. The tea bowls (*chawan*), tea caddies (*chaire*) and other pieces were simple in design and coated with a dull black or warm reddish brown glaze. Another group made functional objects, known as Kushikino ware, for daily use. Satsuma potters often studied at Seto, Bizen and other important Japanese pottery centers. The discovery of white clay at Kirishima Mountain in 1614 initiated the manufacture of white Satsuma ware. In the mid-17th century, decorations made of brightly colored enamels were introduced from Kyoto. Porcelain makers from the Arita region also taught their techniques to Satsuma potters. Enamelled Satsuma pottery was exported to Europe in large quantities during the 19th century. These pieces, many of which were actually made at factories in Tokyo and Kyoto, had crackled white glazes and colorful red, green and gold enamelled decorations, known as "brocade" designs. See also ARITA WARE; BIZEN WARE; KOREA AND JAPAN; KYUSHU ISLAND; POTTERY; SATSUMA PROVINCE; SEN NO RIKYU; TEA CEREMONY; TOYOTOMI HIDEYOSHI.

SAUCES See COOKING; SOY SAUCE; SEASONING FOR FOOD.

SAYONARA The Japanese expression meaning "goodbye." This word is familiar to Americans as the name of a novel set in Japan by American author James Michener. *Sayonara*, published in 1954, tells the story of a sad love affair between an American Air Corps major named Gruver and a beautiful Japanese woman named Hana-ogi. It was made into a film in 1957 by the American director Joshua Logan starring Marlon Brando and Japanese actress Mi-yoshi Umeki, who won an Academy Award for best supporting actress; co-star Red Buttons won the Academy Award for best supporting actor.

SCAP See MACARTHUR, GENERAL DOUGLAS; OCCUPATION OF JAPAN; SUPREME COMMANDER FOR THE ALLIED POWERS.

SCHOOLS See EDUCATION SYSTEM; SENSEI; TOKYO UNIVERSITY; UNIVERSITIES.

SCIENCE AND TECHNOLOGY AGENCY (Kagaku Gijutsu Cho) An agency in the Office of the Prime Minister that promotes scientific and technological research in Japan. The Science and Technology Agency also coordinates research and development programs in science and technology that are sponsored by various government ministries. The director-general of the agency is appointed by the prime minister and is a member of his cabinet. The Japanese government established the Science and Technology Agency in 1956 to lessen Japan's dependence on foreign technology and to help Japan catch up with global scientific developments, from which it had been cut off during World War II. The Japan Atomic Energy Research Institute, the National Space Development Agency, the National Aerospace Laboratory and the Japan Information Center for Science and Technology are administered by the Science and Technology Agency. The agency also supervises Tsukuba Academic New Town, a government-planned national educational and scientific research center north of Tokyo. See also CABINET, PRIME MINISTER'S; RESEARCH AND DEVELOPMENT; TSUKUBA ACADEMIC NEW TOWN.

SCIENCE CITY See TSUKUBA ACADEMIC NEW TOWN.

SCISSORS-PAPER-STONE (*jan-ken-pon*) A hand game that is often played by Japanese adults as well as children to determine who will go first or is "it," similar to the way Westerners toss a coin to decide who has priority. Two players shout "*jan ken pon!*" and on the cry of "*pon!*" rapidly form their hands into one of three shapes: the index and middle fingers in the shape of scissors; an open hand with palm up, for paper; or a clenched fist, for a stone. A hand with a scissors shape beats paper, because scissors can cut paper. Paper beats stone because it can wrap a stone. Stone beats scissors because scissors cannot cut stone. This is one of the first games that Japanese children learn. It is also known as "stone-paper-scissors" (*gu-choki-pa*). This is a popular game at parties with geisha (women entertainers), where the person who becomes "it" has to drink a cup of sake. Various types of "fist" games, such as guessing the number of fingers a person is holding up behind his back, have long been played in Japan, especially among the common people at drinking parties. See also CHILDREN; GAMES; GEISHA.

SCREENS (*byobu; fusuma*) There are two basic kinds of Japanese screens, folding screens (*byobu*, "barrier against the wind") and sliding screens (*fusuma*, "blocking" or separating"). Folding screens, introduced from China in the seventh century A.D., have been used in Japanese homes, castles, shrines, temples and restaurants to protect against drafts, to divide rooms and to create privacy. A folding screen consists of a large standing wooden frame in two or more sections, covered with thick paper, silk or other textiles. An upside-down folding screen is a traditional sign of mourning in Japan. Sliding screens, also used to divide a room, consist of light wooden frames covered with thick, opaque paper on each side. They slide on tracks placed along the edge of *tatami* (straw floor mats) to form a wall. One opens and closes a sliding screen by kneeling and gripping a small lined recess placed low on the screen. Sliding screens are light and can be easily taken out of their tracks to enlarge a room. The paper on the screens can be replaced when it becomes worn. Thinner and lighter sliding screens known as *shoji* are also used in traditional Japanese homes to let in diffused light. They are made of lattice frameworks with translucent paper pasted on one side. Sliding screens are usually cream-colored, although they can be decorated with paintings, known as *shohekiga*. This term, also pronounced *shobyoga*, is sometimes used to refer to all types of screen paintings. Folding screens are frequently decorated with paintings, termed *byobu-e*. Screen painting was a developed art form in Japan by the Nara Era (A.D. 710–794). The most popular themes of Japanese screen paintings have been landscapes, the four seasons, birds and flowers, and daily activities (genre paintings). Monochromatic ink paintings (*sumi-e*) were created on screens during the 14th–16th centuries, especially with the influence of Zen Buddhism. Decorative screen painting reached its height during the Azuchi-Momoyama Era (1568–1600), when warlords decorated their castles with gorgeous screens painted by artists of the Kano and Tosa schools. Artists of the Rimpa school added to this tradition through the 18th century. See also CASTLES; HOMES AND HOUSING; INK PAINTING; KANO SCHOOL OF PAINTING; RIMPA SCHOOL OF PAINTING; TATAMI; TOSA SCHOOL OF PAINTING.

SCRIPTURES, RELIGIOUS Japan had no written language before Chinese culture was introduced with the Buddhist religion in the sixth century A.D. Shinto, the indigenous Japanese religion, does not have one definitive set of religious scriptures. Myths about Japanese creator and ancestral deities are recorded in two eighth-century chronicles, the *Kojiki* and the *Nihon Shoki*, compiled by the imperial court. Some poems with religious themes are also included in the important eighth-century poetry anthology *Manyoshu*. However, ancient Shinto was not centralized, and religious beliefs and practices have been associated with numerous local *kami* (sacred spirits) throughout the Japanese islands. Shinto is not concerned with such things as guilt, morality, or study and chanting of scriptures, but rather with ritual purification, dispelling of evil spirits and enshrinement of *kami* at festivals (*matsuri*) to gain their blessings and ensure good harvests.

The Buddhist religion is divided into many different sects and has no one definitive text but a multitude of written scriptures (*sutras*). After its founding in India in the sixth

century B.C., Buddhism split into two main branches. Theravada Buddhism, with a monastic emphasis, spread throughout Southeast Asia, whereas Mahayana, with an emphasis on universal salvation, spread through Central Asia, China and Korea to Japan. When the Japanese were first learning the Chinese writing system, they needed trained Buddhist priests to explain the Chinese translations of Buddhist scriptures, which were originally written in Sanskrit in India, the home of the Buddha. The Japanese imperial court made Buddhism a state religion to enhance its power and prestige, and the court encouraged the copying of Buddhist *sutras*. Prince Shotoku (Shotoku Taishi, the "Father of Japanese Culture"; 574–622) patronized Buddhism and even wrote commentaries on three *sutras*. Various Buddhist sects have emphasized particular scriptures. The copying and reciting of Buddhist *sutras* has been a means by which believers can accumulate religious power and merit. The most important popular Buddhist scripture has been the *Lotus Sutra* (*Hokkekyo*), central to the Tendai sect, the Nichiren sect, and to new sects such as the Soka Gakkai. Writings by Nichiren (1222–1282), Saicho (767–822), Honen (1133–1212) and many other Buddhist teachers are widely studied. The Zen sect has repudiated a reliance on written scriptures, although it developed compilations of written sayings of Zen masters and *koan*, or religious riddles, as teaching devices. From the ninth through 19th centuries, the Japanese buried *sutras* in small earthen mounds (*sutra* mounds, *kyozuka*) to preserve them, bring repose to dead souls, ensure rebirth in paradise or gain material benefits. Buddhist temple compounds include pagodas (*to*), structures that house Buddhist *sutras* and relics. Priests chant *sutras* while beating rhythmically on a wooden fish drum (*mokugyo*) in daily religious services and at other important occasions, such as funerals. Lay followers may also chant *sutras* in front of Buddhist household altars (*butsudan*). See also ALTARS IN HOMES; BUDDHISM; CALLIGRAPHY; FUNERALS; KAMI; KOAN; KOJIKI; LOTUS SUTRA; MANYOSHU; MONASTICISM, BUDDHIST; NIHON SHOKI; PAGODA; SHINTO; WRITING SYSTEM, JAPANESE; NAMES OF INDIVIDUAL SECTS AND TEACHERS.

SCROLLS (*emakimono, kakemono*) Rolls of paper or cloth decorated with calligraphy or paintings. There are two types of scrolls, vertical and horizontal. Scrolls that unroll vertically and are hung, usually in a *tokonoma* (alcove in a traditional Japanese room to display art objects), are known as *kakemono*. Long scrolls that unroll horizontally are known as *emakimono*, or *emaki* for short. These scrolls were the original "books" of East Asia. *Emaki* are made from paper or silk rectangles that are pasted together horizontally and rolled around a cylinder (*jiku*). Most *emaki* are 30–40 feet long, although they can be as long as 80 feet; they may be narrow or as wide as 20 inches. Sets of *emaki* may contain several dozen scrolls. An *emaki* is viewed from right to left, which is the same direction in which the Japanese language is written. An *emaki* must be laid flat on a small table and viewed by no more than a few people at a time. The right hand rolls up a 12-inch section of the scroll after it is seen, and the left hand unrolls the new section to be looked at.

Emaki were introduced into Japan from China with the Buddhist religion in the sixth century A.D. Many ancient *emaki* were copies of *sutras* (Buddhist scriptures). During the Nara Era (710–794), the Japanese court encouraged the copying of thousands of *sutras*. During the Heian Era (794–1185), scrolls became secularized, and Japanese-style paintings and illustrations were created on *emaki*, depicting landscapes, daily activities at the court, legends and popular stories. Poetry was also written on *emaki* in beautiful calligraphy, and literary tales were illustrated. A famous 12th-century handscroll known as the *Genji Monogatari Emaki* illustrated the famous novel, *The Tale of Genji (Genji Monogatari)* by Murasaki Shikibu (fl. c. A.D. 1000). Only fragments of this scroll survive, but they are regarded as the finest example of illustrated stories in the *emakimono* style. Paintings of classical literary works are quite colorful and use techniques such as "blown-away roofs" *(fukinuki yatai)* to show people inside buildings. Another famous 12th-century *emaki* set, *Scrolls of Frolicking Animals and Humans (Choju giga)*, contains monochrome ink paintings *(sumi-e)* that humorously portray animals acting like human beings. A variety of *emaki* types were painted during the military warfare of the Kamakura Era (1192–1333), including battle tales, daily activities, and religious themes, such as the Buddhist hell *(Hell Scroll, Jigoku zoshi)*.

Emakimono declined and *kakemono* took precedence when monochrome ink painting became popular, especially through Zen Buddhism, which was introduced into Japan in the 12th century. However, *emaki* paintings continued to be done by artists of the Tosa school, and one of the last great *emaki* artists was Tosa Mitsunobu (1434–1525). *Kakemono* had also been introduced from China with Buddhism in the sixth-century A.D. and were originally paintings of the Buddha hung in temples. As *kakemono* came to be decorated with calligraphy and ink painting, landscapes and bird-and-flower motifs became common themes. A piece of paper or silk containing calligraphy or an ink painting is carefully mounted on a paper scroll. Geometric proportions for placement of a painting on the scroll and patterns of gold brocade or silk applied along the edges are strictly specified. Several styles of mounting are used, from simple to elaborate. In the Japanese tea ceremony, a *kakemono* is hung in the tearoom as the focal point during the first part of the ceremony, then is replaced by a flower arrangement. The scroll is calligraphy by a Zen priest or a tea master and is chosen to harmonize with the season of the year or with the particular occasion for the ceremony. See also BUDDHISM; CALLIGRAPHY; GENJI, THE TALE OF; HEIAN ERA; INK PAINTING; NARA ERA; PAPER, HANDMADE; SILK; TEA CEREMONY; TOSA SCHOOL OF PAINTING; ZEN SECT OF BUDDHISM.

SCULPTURE *(horimono, chokoku)* Horimono is the Japanese term for carved and engraved objects. Before the modern era, Japanese sculpture was primarily religious (particularly Buddhist) or decorative, such as small figures known as *netsuke*. *Chokoku* refers to sculpture as an independent form of plastic arts, introduced in Japan from the West during the Meiji Era (1868–1912). Clay human-like figures known

as *dogu* were made in Japan during the Jomon Era (c. 10,000 B.C.–c. 300 B.C.). *Haniwa*, cylindrical and figural clay objects, were placed on burial mounds *(kofun)* during the Kofun Era (c. 300–710).

When the Buddhist religion was introduced into Japan in the sixth century, skilled immigrants from China and Korea brought with them the techniques for many art forms, including sculpture, which was associated with Buddhist temples built by the Yamato court in western Japan. Statues of Kannon, Miroku and other gods in the Buddhist pantheon were made of bronze, clay, lacquer and wood; stone was not commonly used for Japanese sculpture. Gilt-bronze Buddhist images, known as *kondo butsu*, were often made by the lost-wax technique. A clay core was formed, and a layer of wax was applied over the clay core and modeled into the final figure. An outer mold was then placed over the wax layer and heated so that the wax would melt out through channels in the mold. Into the space between the two molds the sculptor poured melted bronze to cast the figure. After the sculpture cooled, it was smoothed and polished, and an engraver sometimes applied designs. The statue was then plated with gold. Large clay sculptures were made by forming the clay around a wooden core, drying and painting it. Dry lacquer sculptures are known as *kanshitsuzo*. Hollow dry-lacquer statues were made by covering a clay core with layers of linen cloth soaked with lacquer *(urushi)* and modeling the linen into the desired image. When the lacquer dried, the clay center was removed and a wooden frame was placed inside to reinforce the sculpture and prevent it from warping. The surface was then painted. Woodcore dry-lacquer stat-

The sculpture of a Benevolent King (Nio), a Buddhist protector deity, at Horyuji in the ancient capital city of Nara.

ues built on wooden armatures led to the development of wooden sculpture.

Eighth-century Japanese sculpture was dominated by Chinese styles of Tang (618–906) dynasty and many images enshrined in the old capital city of Nara. The Nara Era (710–794) was the golden age of Japanese Buddhist art. During this period, the imperial court built the massive Todaiji at Nara, and other temples around the country, thus creating a demand for many Buddhist statues. The largest was the Daibutsu (Great Buddha) at Todaiji, over 53 feet high.

In the ninth century, wood sculptures became the preferred form. Wood was abundant in Japan, and trees were revered in Shinto, the native Japanese religion, which coexisted with Buddhism. At first, wooden sculptures were constructed from single blocks of wood (ichiboku-zukuri; ichiboku meaning "one trunk") that were hollowed out to prevent the formation of cracks. Joined or assembled woodblock construction next developed, known as yosegi-zukuri. In this technique, a log was split and its core was removed. Then two pieces of wood were joined together to form an image, and each section was carved to almost the same thickness. The head and torso of a statue were assembled from pieces of separately carved and hollowed-out wood from different trees. The statue was then coated with cloth and sabi urushi (thick raw lacquer mixed with crushed stone), then with black lacquer. Finally, it was painted with colored pigments. Cut gold leaf was used for hair and other features.

During the Heian Era (794–1185), when the capital was moved to Heiankyo (later known as Kyoto), sculptors were patronized by the aristocracy, especially the powerful Fujiwara clan. Life-size wooden sculpture from late Heian and later eras typically employed the assembled woodblock technique, which was refined by the 11th-century Buddhist sculptor Jocho, who also developed the private workshop system (bussho) for sculpture production.

In Japanese art, each deity is depicted with particular iconographic traits, such as hair styles, draped robes, halos, hand gestures and objects. For example, Kannon, Goddess of Mercy, carries a lotus flower and water container. Buddhist deities usually stand or sit with their legs crossed in the meditation pose, and are often placed on lotus pedestals. The smallest sculptures are about 1 foot high, but most range from 3 to 8 feet. Daibutsu are more than 50 feet high. Small statues are housed in zushin, miniature shrines with doors. Hollowed-out statues often carry inscriptions telling how, when and why they were made. Some also contain relics, miniature sculptures, documents and other objects inside that help scholars to determine their age.

During the Taira-Minamoto War (1180–1185), the largest Nara temples, Todaiji and Kofukuji, were burned and much of their contents were lost. The Kamakura Shogunate (1192–1333) sponsored their restoration, and sculptures were recreated by the Nara sculptor Kokei, his son Unkei and his disciple Kaikei.

New sects of Buddhism became widespread in Japan during the Kamakura Era, including Zen, Nichiren and Pure Land, which increased demand for statues. Some sculptures of Shinto kami (sacred spirits) were produced similar to Buddhist images beginning in the ninth century. Medieval artists combined Shinto with Buddhism. For example, a sculpture depicts the Shinto war god Hachiman as a human-looking Buddhist priest. Shugo bijutsu is the term for images produced through the combination of Buddhist and Shinto figures.

Buddhist sculpture waned from the 15th century onward, and polychromed wood sculptures of important ruling figures were produced in seated position, such as Minamoto no Yoritomo, founder of the Kamakura Shogunate. Buddhist priests were also carved in seated positions, such as chinso, images of Zen Buddhist priests, either sculpted or painted. Buddhism declined in the late Muromachi (1333–1568) and Azuchi-Momoyama (1568–1600) eras, and traditional workshops for Buddhist sculptures were closed, spelling the end of monumental sculptures that had been created for Buddhist temples and some Shinto shrines for a thousand years. In consequence, the skills of wood carvers were applied to other smaller forms, such as masks for bugaku (ancient ritual dances) and Noh drama. Traditional religious sculpture had disappeared by the Meiji Era (1868–1912), since Buddhist temples had lost state support. Miniature carving, such as netsuke, made primarily from wood or ivory, developed into an art in its own right.

Western forms of sculpture such as those by Auguste Rodin, were adopted in Japan in the late 19th century. In the postwar era, Japanese sculptors have utilized modern and avant-garde forms and new materials, such as steel, plastic and aluminum. The new Open-Air Museum, opened at Hakone in 1969 to exhibit Japanese and Western outdoor sculpture, has had a wide influence on sculpture exhibits in other cities. Modern Japanese sculptors work in kinetic and tensile forms, and create environmental sculptures using lights. Architects often include sculpture as an integral part of their buildings. The Japanese-American sculptor Isamu Noguchi (1904–1988) became world famous. See also BUDDHISM; BUGAKU; DAIBUTSU; GODS; HANIWA; JOCHO; MASKS; METALWORK; NARA; NETSUKE; NOGUCHI, ISAMU; NOH DRAMA; SHINTO; TODAIJI; WOODWORKING

SDF See SELF-DEFENSE FORCES.

SEA BREAM (tai) A saltwater fish that has a delicate but firm white flesh and a light, sweet taste. Sea bream is often served raw in thin slices as sashimi. The Japanese consider the sea bream the finest of all fish and regard it as a symbol of good luck. The god Ebisu, one of the Seven Gods of Good Fortune and the patron deity of fishermen, is depicted carrying a sea bream under his left arm. The pink-skinned sea bream, named sakuradai for the color of cherry blossoms (sakura), is salted and grilled whole over charcoal to serve at wedding banquets and other festive events. The head is also used in a salty soup called ushio-jiru. See also CHERRY BLOSSOM; COOKING; EBISU; FISH AND FISHING INDUSTRY; SOUP; WEDDINGS.

SEA OF JAPAN (Nihonkai) The body of water between the west coast of Japan and the eastern coasts of China and Korea. The Sea of Japan is the smallest of three seas around Japan, the other two being the East China Sea to the south and the Okhotsk Sea to the north. The Straits of Kammon, Mamiya, Soya, Tsugaru and Tsushima connect the Sea of Japan with the other two seas. The average depth of the Sea of Japan is 4,428 feet, and its deepest point is 12,175 feet; it covers an area of 389,000 square miles. A current that flows north toward the main islands of Japan divides into the Black Current (Kurashio) on the eastern, or Pacific Ocean, side and the smaller Tsushima Current on the western, or Sea of Japan, side. During the winter, high pressure systems over Siberia send cold air over the Sea of Japan. The cold air picks up moisture, runs into ridges of mountains on the central-west coast of the main Japanese island of Honshu, and drops heavy snowfall. This region is known as the Snow Country, or the Japan Alps. There are many good fishing grounds in the Sea of Japan for salmon, mackerel, cod, herring, cuttlefish, walleye pollack and king crab. The sea is also being studied as an important ecological region. See also CLIMATE OF JAPAN; FISH AND FISHING INDUSTRY; GEOGRAPHY OF JAPAN; HONSHU ISLAND; JAPAN ALPS; PACIFIC OCEAN; SNOW COUNTRY; WATER.

SEA OF OKHOTSK See CLIMATE OF JAPAN; GEOGRAPHY OF JAPAN; HOKKAIDO ISLAND; KURIL ISLANDS; SEA OF JAPAN.

SEA URCHIN See SEAFOOD.

SEAFOOD Seafood is one of the main sources of protein in the Japanese diet. In addition to a great variety of fish, the Japanese eat many kinds of shellfish and other seafood. Many species of crab (kane) live in the seas surrounding Japan. Crabs are usually boiled and served with vinegar dressings. Because crabs regularly shed their shells and grow new ones, and can also grow claws to replace ones that have been torn off, they symbolized the power of life and regeneration to the ancient Japanese. Old legends tell of ghosts that inhabit some types of crab that have a pattern similar to a human face on their shells.

Sea urchins (uni) are a type of shellfish that have always been a delicacy in Japan. Sea urchin roe (nama uni) is eaten raw with a soy sauce dip, and served as a garnish.

Shrimps, prawns and lobsters are classed together as ebi in Japan. They are found in both fresh and salt water. Because shrimps, prawns and lobsters also shed their shells and grow new ones, they too symbolize regeneration to the Japanese. In earlier times, red cooked lobsters were used for New Year decorations, along with rice cakes, citrus fruit, ferns and seaweed. Shrimp was eaten at coming-of-age or adulthood ceremonies. Today, shrimp is commonly eaten fried in *tempura* batter, and boiled and served on top of rice as sushi.

More than 100 species of squid and cuttlefish (ika) are found off the coast of Japan. They are eaten raw or in dried form (surume). Dried squid was used for religious offerings to *kami* (divine spirits), and is still given as a present on auspicious occasions in Japan.

There are about 6,000 species of marine shellfish and 90 species of freshwater shellfish in Japan. Clams (hamaguri), harvested from shallow coastal waters, can be eaten raw, steamed or fried. Symbolizing union, their double shells make clams an auspicious comestible at wedding banquets. Abalone (awabi), large edible marine snails, have a similar significance. Oysters are not only eaten, but used for cultivating pearls. The iridescent inner lining of shells known as mother-of-pearl is also used to make decorative inlays on lacquer ware. Archaeologists have learned much about early Japanese culture by excavating ancient shell mounds, of which there are about 2,000 in Japan. See also ABALONE; FISH AND FISHING INDUSTRY; PEARL; SASHIMI; SEAWEED; SHELL; SOY SAUCE; SUSHI; TEMPURA.

SEALS AND SIGNATURES (hanko, imban, in, inkan, insho, rakkan) Engraved stamps that Japanese people use to fix their names or signatures on important documents. Whereas a personal signature is legally required on such documents in the West, in Japan the impression made by a seal known as a *hanko, inkan* or *insho* is required. An *inkan* is usually a small cylinder made of wood, ivory, precious stone or another material with the person's family name carved on one end. The *inkan* is pressed on a pad of red ink known as a *shuniku* and then pressed onto the piece of paper. There are two kinds of *inkan*, a *mitome-in* for ordinary use such as stamping documents at work, and a *jitsuin* ("true seal") for more important documents, such as the contract to buy a car or a house. *Jitsuin* must be legally registered at a local registry office, which keeps an impression of it on file.

Seals were originally used in Japan from the eighth to the 10th century by the imperial government, following Chinese custom. Individuals began to use personal seals from the 12th century, especially monks of the Zen sect of Buddhism and military warlords. But these seals were affixed to books and works of art, and were not used for government documents. Painters and calligraphers also took up the practice of applying seals, or *rakkan*, to their creations. Following the Chinese custom, artists had their seals uniquely carved with their given or artistic name in an ancient Chinese script known as *tensho*. Other information may be included in the seals, which sometimes helps to identify the date and artist of the work on which it appears. Most Japanese artists still use *rakkan* today.

After the Onin War of 1467–1477, autonomous feudal lords known as *daimyo* used personal seals on official documents within their domains, and the warlords who unified Japan continued this custom as a way of asserting their authority. During the rule of the third Tokugawa shogun, Iemitsu (ruled 1623–1651), when there was a rapid increase in economic activities, the entire Japanese population found personal seals very useful for official records and contracts. In 1694, as a way of halting counterfeiting, the Tokugawa government required registration of *jitsuin* for the first time. See also CALLIGRAPHY; DAIMYO; NAMES, JAPANESE; TOKUGAWA SHOGUNATE; ZEN SECT OF BUDDHISM.

SEAMI See ZEAMI.

SEASONING FOR FOOD *(yakumi)* A number of basic ingredients give Japanese cooking its distinctive flavor. Soy sauce *(shoyu*, a brown liquid made from fermented soybeans) and *mirin* (sweetened rice wine) are used in cooked dishes and in dipping sauces. These sauces often have grated ginger or daikon (large white Japanese radish) added to them to enhance flavor and aid digestion. *Wasabi* (Japanese horseradish) is a green paste also used in dipping sauces and some types of sushi. *Miso*, a brown paste made from fermented soybeans, is another frequently used ingredient, especially in soups. A variety of seaweed known as *nori* can be toasted, crumbled and sprinkled on food. Dried flakes of the bonito fish are also used as a topping on some dishes. Rice vinegar *(komezu)*, which is milder than Western vinegars, is used in sauces and cooked foods. A mixture of seven dried and ground spices called "seven-taste pepper" *(shichimi togarashi)* is sprinkled on noodle dishes, soups and other dishes. This mixture consists of powdered red pepper, brown pepper, poppy seeds, hemp seeds, dried orange peel, rakeseeds and *nori*. It is available in packages and is also sold by spice vendors at shrine festivals and local fairs. Sesame seeds *(goma)*, both black and white, are used in sauces and dressings and are briefly toasted before use. A deeper flavor is released by grinding them with a pestle in a special ridged bowl called a *suribachi*. See also BONITO; COOKING; DAIKON; GINGER; MIRIN; SEAWEED; SOY SAUCE; WASABI.

SEASONS OF THE YEAR See AUTUMN FLOWERS AND GRASSES; CALENDAR; CLIMATE OF JAPAN; FESTIVALS; FLOWERS; GARDENS; RAIN; RICE PLANTING AND HARVESTING FESTIVALS; SEVEN HERBS OF SPRING; SNOW; SNOW COUNTRY; SNOW FESTIVAL; THREE FRIENDS OF WINTER; TYPHOON.

SEAWEED The two basic types of edible algae are *konbu*, or dried kelp, and *nori*, dried sheets or squares that are often called "laver" in English. *Konbu* (also known as *kombu* or *kobu*) is harvested between July and September in the cold waters off the northernmost island of Hokkaido. Deep brown in color, *konbu* leaves grown 2½–12 inches wide and several feet long, sometimes reaching a length of 30 feet or more. They are dried in the sun, cut, folded and packaged for market. Two basic kinds of *konbu* are consumed in Japan. *Nikonbu* is the type of kelp that is eaten in sushi and other dishes. *Dashi-konbu* is kelp that is simmered in water to make a stock known as *dashi* that is the basic ingredient of Japanese soups. *Konbu* can also be roasted and ground into a powder for seasoning food. Decorations for the New Year always include *konbu* because it is associated with the word *yoroko-bu*, which means "rejoice."

Nori is seaweed that is pressed and dried into thin, square sheets, known as *Asakusa nori*. The sheets are sold in cellophane bags in a standard size of 7 x 8 inches and are used to wrap rice balls *(onigiri)* and a type of rolled sushi called *nori-maki*. *Nori* tastes best when it is toasted briefly over a flame to make it crisp. The Japanese eat small pieces of toasted *nori (yakinori)* by dipping them in soy sauce and placing them on hot rice. They also enjoy several other types of seaweed. *Wakame* are dried strips that swell up when soaked in water. They are eaten in soups or salads. *Ao nori* is crumbled green seaweed that is sprinkled over food as a seasoning. Dried bits of black seaweed called *hijiki* are soaked in water and eaten in salads. See also COOKING; HOKKAIDO ISLAND; NEW YEAR FESTIVAL; SEASONING FOR FOOD; SOUP; SUSHI; TUNA; WASABI.

SECLUSION, NATIONAL (1639–1854; Sakoku) A policy of the Tokugawa Shogunate (1603–1867) to isolate Japan from foreign influences and to remove challenges to its own control over the country. Westerners, especially Spanish and Portuguese missionaries and traders, had come into Japan through Kyushu, where they established strong relations with the *daimyo* (feudal lords) and made many Christian converts. Between 1633 and 1639, the senior councillors *(roju)* of the shogunate in Edo (modern Tokyo) sent five orders to the shogunate's two councillors *(bugyo)* in Nagasaki on the southern island of Kyushu that banned the Christian religion in Japan, expelled Roman Catholic missionaries and traders, and prohibited Japanese from traveling to foreign countries. The third shogun, Tokugawa Iemitsu (1604–1651) enforced the seclusion policy and tortured and executed Christians to eradicate the religion from Japan. Controlled foreign trade was permitted only with the Dutch (who were Protestant), Chinese and Koreans, but Dutch traders were confined to an artificial island known as Dejima constructed in Nagasaki Harbor; Chinese were permitted only in Nagasaki; and only Japanese traders and government officials from the provinces of Satsuma (modern Kagoshima Prefecture) and Tsushima were allowed to travel to Korea and the Ryukyu Islands (modern Okinawa Prefecture).

By the 19th century, the policy of national seclusion was being challenged by military threats from the United States, Great Britain, Portugal and Russia; all wanted to trade with Japan. Western studies *(Yogaku)* and Dutch studies *(Rangaku)* had already become widespread in Japan, and in 1811 the shogunate founded a center to translate Western books. The Japanese began questioning the policy of seclusion, which the nationalistic Mito school of scholars supported. Many Japanese became attracted to the new National Learning *(Kokugaku)* movement, which drew upon ancient Japanese texts and the Shinto religion and which led to the conservative Japanese reaction against foreign threats, including the slogan Revere the Emperor, Expel the Barbarians *(Sonno joi)*. Commodore Matthew Perry of the United States used naval power to force the shogunate to sign the Kanagawa Treaty of 1854 between the United States and Japan. In 1858 the shogunate signed the Ansei Commercial Treaties with other Western powers, which opened Japanese ports to them and thus ended the period of national seclusion. See also ANSEI COMMERCIAL TREATIES; CHRISTIANITY IN JAPAN; DUTCH IN JAPAN; KYUSHU ISLAND; NAGASAKI; PERRY, MATTHEW CALBRAITH; RYUKYU ISLANDS; SATSUMA PROVINCE; TOKUGAWA IEMITSU; TOKUGAWA SHOGUNATE.

SECURITIES COMPANIES Companies that broker, underwrite and trade corporate and public stocks and bonds. There are more than 200 securities companies in Japan, about half of which are members of the Tokyo Stock Exchange (TSE), with the rest belonging to regional exchanges. The market is dominated by the "big four," Nomura Securities Co., the largest brokerage house in the world, Nikko Securities Co., Ltd., Daiwa Securities Co., Ltd. and Yamaichi Securities Co., Ltd., which account for nearly half of total turnover on the TSE.

Nomura Securities Co., Ltd., the largest, founded in 1925, has more than 100 branches in Japan and more than two dozen overseas branches and subsidiaries. It also operates the leading Japanese think tank, the Nomura Research Institute. Nikko Securities Co., Ltd., the second largest, established in 1944, maintains overseas offices and subsidiaries in New York and many other cities and operates Nikko Research Center. Daiwa Securities Co., Ltd., founded as a bond dealer in 1902, has nearly 100 domestic branches and more than a dozen overseas subsidiaries. The fourth major securities company, Yamaichi Securities Co., Ltd., established in 1897, suffered a major setback in 1965 but recovered with the aid of special funds from the Bank of Japan. Since 1980, all of these Japanese securities companies have become very aggressive in the American stock market, which they perceive as having a large growth potential. In the 1980s American stocks have become very attractive to Japanese investors because of the dollar's weakness against the Japanese yen. See also BANK OF JAPAN; CORPORATIONS; INVESTMENTS OVERSEAS, JAPANESE; STOCK MARKET; YEN.

SECURITY TREATY BETWEEN JAPAN AND THE UNITED STATES (1952; revised 1960, renewed 1970 [Nichibei Anzen Hosho Joyaku; abbreviated Ampo Joyaku]) A treaty of mutual security signed by Japan and the United States at the same time as the Peace Treaty of 1952 concluding the Allied Occupation of Japan following World War II. The security treaty, which was largely motivated by the outbreak of the Korean War in 1950, permitted the United States to maintain military bases and facilities and to station troops in Japan, and guaranteed that the United States would defend Japan in case of attack. The constitution of Japan enacted in 1947 forbids Japan from maintaining military forces, although Japan later established Self-Defense Forces (SDF; Jietai) for its internal security.

In 1960 a revised Treaty of Mutual Cooperation and Security (Nichibei Sogo Kyoryoku Oyobi Anzen Hosho Joyaku), also known as the Mutual Security Treaty (MST), was signed between Japan and the United States. When the House of Representatives (lower house) of the Japanese Diet (Parliament) ratified this treaty in 1960, massive protest demonstrations broke out in Japan, with rioting by members of the radical student federation Zengakuren and of labor unions. Prime Minister Kishi Nobusuke (b. 1896; p.m. 1957–1960) was forced to resign, but the treaty was passed by default when the House of Councillors (upper house of the Diet) did not vote on the issue within the required period of 30 days. In this revised security treaty, Japan and the United States agreed to assist each other in case of armed attack on territories administered by Japan. The treaty also contained provisions for international and

economic cooperation. The treaty would last for 10 years, after which it could be revoked by either side after one year's notice. When the security treaty came up for renewal, the issue of reversion of Okinawa Prefecture (Ryukyu Islands) to Japan became a focal point of Japanese political campaigns. The United States had retained administration of the southern Ryukyu Islands after the Occupation and established large military bases on Okinawa Island. Opposition Japanese politicians demanded that Okinawa Prefecture be returned to Japan and that the security treaty not be renewed. There was also much opposition in Japan to U.S. involvement in the Vietnam War. Japanese Prime Minister Sato Eisaku (1901–1975; p.m. 1964–1972) calmed much of the opposition by visiting Washington, D.C. in 1969 and signing a joint communique with President Richard M. Nixon, in which the United States agreed to return Okinawa to Japan in 1972. Japan and the United States also reaffirmed the importance of the security treaty in maintaining peace in East Asia. In 1970 the Japanese government automatically renewed the security treaty. Later that year the United States announced that it would reduce the number of troops it had stationed in Japan. In 1981 Japan announced that it would continue to rely on the arrangements of the treaty to guarantee its national security. See also DIET; LABOR UNIONS; OCCUPATION OF JAPAN; RYUKYU ISLANDS; SATO EISAKU; ZENGAKUREN.

SEI SHONAGON (c. A.D. 1000) A writer during the Heian Era (794–1185) famous for *The Pillow Book (Makura no soshi)*, which was the first of the Japanese literary genre known as *zuihitsu* ("running brush" or "to follow the brush"), which consisted of a miscellaneous collection of brief episodes, aphorisms and personal impressions without a structured plot. Like Lady Murasaki (Murasaki Shikibu; fl. A.D. 1000), her famous contemporary who wrote *The Tale of Genji (Genji Monogatari)* and who mentioned her in her diary, Sei Shonagon lived at the imperial court in the capital city of Kyoto. While she served as a lady-in-waiting to Empress Sadako, she kept an ongoing record of her witty observations about court life. The book's title may come from the fact that she always kept it by her side, perhaps even in her wooden pillow. Much of *The Pillow Book* has to do with love affairs, a common theme in Heian literature. The book is filled with lists of things she liked or disliked, of birds and other natural phenomena, and of names and other things that she found interesting. She also composed imaginary scenes, such as a lover writing to his mistress. Her opening description of the four seasons of the year and the moods associated with them has been much imitated in Japanese literature. Sei Shonagon idolized Empress Sadako and other members of the royal family whom she served but often made fun of people beneath her and of herself as well, with keen observations about styles of dress and behavior.

Little is known about Sei Shonagon's early or later years. Her father was a famous scholar and poet named Motosuke (908–990), and she was educated in the Chinese classics, unusual for a Japanese woman of that time. A brilliant and original author, she also wrote a number of poems that were collected under the title *Sei Shonagon shu*. See also DIARIES; GENJI, THE TALE OF; HEIAN ERA; KYOTO; MURASAKI SHIKIBU; PILLOWS.

SEIKAN TUNNEL   See HOKKAIDO ISLAND.

SEISHI   See AMIDA; KANNON.

SEISMOLOGY   See EARTHQUAKES.

SEIWA GENJI CLAN   See ASHIKAGA TAKAUJI; MINAMOTO CLAN.

SEKIGAHARA, BATTLE OF (A.D. 1600)   A battle at Sekigahara in Mino Province (modern Gifu Prefecture) in which Tokugawa Ieyasu (1543–1616), founder of the Tokugawa Shogunate (1603–1867), defeated his major opponents. Ieyasu was the third of ''Three Heroes'' who unified Japan in the late 16th century. The first, Oda Nobunaga (1534–1582), had been assassinated at the height of his power, after which Nobunaga's general, Toyotomi Hideyoshi (1537–1598), continued the campaign to unify the Japanese provinces. After Hideyoshi's death, Ieyasu was the most powerful warlord in Japan, and strove to complete the unification of the country. His power base was Japan's eastern provinces. Ieyasu's most dangerous enemy was Ishida Mitsunari, who persuaded other *daimyo* (feudal lords) of the western provinces, including the powerful Mori, Shimazu and Ukita clans, to join forces with him and march against Ieyasu. Their armies, totaling 100,000 men, met on October 21, 1600 at Sekigahara, a strategic pass between the plain surrounding Nagoya City and the plain east of Lake Biwa. Mitsunari's side gained an early advantage, but the tide was turned when regiments led by Kobayakawa, one of Mitsunari's commanders, and four other *daimyo* changed allegiance. Ieyasu won a decisive victory, then captured Mitsunari's castle at Sawayama and marched to the city of Osaka to overtake the remaining supporters of Hideyoshi's son Toyotomi Hideyori (1593–1615). The Battle of Sekigahara was the last major conflict after more than a century of civil warfare in Japan. After Ieyasu's victory at Sekigahara, he reduced the feudal domains of his remaining opponents to prevent them from joining together against him and awarded many of the confiscated lands to his loyal retainers. See also DAIMYO; ODA NOBUNAGA; TOKUGAWA IEYASU; TOKUGAWA SHOGUNATE; TOYOTOMI HIDEYOSHI.

SEKIHAN   See BEANS; BIRTHDAYS; BOXES.

SEIYUKAI   See FRIENDS OF CONSTITUTIONAL GOVERNMENT PARTY.

SELF-DEFENSE FORCES (Jieitai; abbreviated SDF)   The air, ground and naval armed services of Japan. Article IX of the Japanese constitution, enacted in 1947 during the Allied Occupation following World War II, states, ''The Japanese people forever renounce war as a sovereign right of the nation or the threat or use of force as a means of settling international disputes.'' Thus the Self-Defense Forces are forbidden to possess any offensive or nuclear weapons or to be deployed outside Japan.

After the war, Occupation policies aimed to disarm and demilitarize Japan. However, when the outbreak of the Korean War in 1950 forced the United States to shift to Korea American troops stationed in Japan, U.S. General Douglas MacArthur (1880–1964), the Supreme Commander for Allied Powers (SCAP) in occupied Japan, authorized the creation of a 75,000-man Japanese National Police Reserve with more powers than a regular police force. In 1952 the Reserve became the National Safety Forces and, along with the Maritime Guard, was placed under the jurisdiction of the new Safety Agency. In 1954, after the end of the Occupation, the conservative faction in the Japanese Diet (Parliament) passed the Self-Defense Forces Law, which transformed the Safety Agency into the Defense Agency (Boeicho) and reorganized the armed forces into the current Self-Defense Forces. These include the Air Self-Defense Force (Koku Jieitai), Ground Self-Defense Force (Rikujo Jieitai), and Maritime Self-Defense Force (Kaijo Jieitai). The stated goal of the Self-Defense Forces is to preserve the peace and independence of Japan, to defend against aggression that threatens its security, to preserve public order when necessary, and to maintain emergency preparedness for disaster relief. Opposition political parties have criticized the SDF, arguing that they violate the constitution and open the door for a revival of militarism, but the Japanese public now generally accepts the SDF as necessary for defense of the country. However, because of political opposition to the SDF, the Defense Agency, while belonging to the Prime Minister's Cabinet, has not been elevated to ministry status. The director-general of the Defense Agency reports to the prime minister and administers the SDF. He is assisted by the Joint Staff Council, members of SDF command staffs and civilian personnel in the Defense Agency. Each of the three defense forces has a chief of staff.

There is no conscription, and the SDF find it hard to recruit good personnel between the ages of 18 and 25. Women were first admitted in 1974 and now constitute 2% of the total forces, but are excluded from combat. In 1970 a volunteer reserve corps of SDF members who had resigned from active duty was created. The National Defense Academy trains many SDF officers, and some officers are trained for higher-level commands at the National Defense College. Women will be admitted to the National Defense Academy in 1992. Civilian and military SDF personnel altogether total around 300,000.

The Ground Self-Defense Force has 13 divisions, in five regional armies stationed throughout the country. The Maritime Self-Defense Force has its headquarters at Yokosuka (Kanagawa Prefecture) near Tokyo and is most active in antisubmarine warfare. The Air Self-Defense Force has three regional forces in the main Japanese islands plus a Southwestern Composite Air Division on the southern island of Okinawa. The Air Defense Command in Tokyo directs the missiles posted in all of the Japanese air zones.

The U.S. military maintains several major bases in Japan and still has a major commitment to defending Japan. The Japanese government has placed a ceiling on the defense budget so that it totals no more than 1% of Japan's annual estimated gross national product (GNP), and many American politicians now argue that, considering the strength of the Japanese economy, the country should take more responsibility for its own military defense. However, Asians who suffered Japanese invasions during World War II continue to fear a remilitarized Japan. See also CABINET, PRIME MINISTER'S; CONSTITUTION OF 1947; DIET; MACARTHUR, DOUGLAS; OCCUPATION OF JAPAN; SECURITY TREATY BETWEEN JAPAN AND THE UNITED STATES.

SEMBEI See CRACKERS, RICE.

SEMICONDUCTOR INDUSTRY The production of integrated silicon circuits, also known as memory chips or microchips, which are the basic elements of computers and other electronic products. Semiconductors are a major industry in Japan. Invented in America but developed quickly in Japan, the semiconductor industry was given its first boost by the success of the Sony Corporation in developing transistor radios in 1954. The Japanese government and industry worked together to acquire semiconductor technology from abroad, and to coordinate research and development of more advanced semiconductors. Japan's success in this industry has been related to its ability to take the lead in the electronics market. Until 1977 Japan imported semiconductors, mainly from the United States, which was the leader in semiconductor technology. In 1979 American companies experienced a severe shortage of semiconductors, and began to buy a large supply from Japanese producers. By 1980, Japan was exporting more semiconductors than it imported, and by 1981 it had caught up to the United States in many aspects of semiconductor technology. By 1982 Japan had captured about 70% of the world's market for 64K-RAM semiconductors. In 1984, the total capital investment of the Japanese semiconductor industry surpassed that of the U.S. industry for the first time, and this gap is expected to increase. Today Japan dominates the manufacturing equipment and chip production industry.

The Japanese semiconductor industry was aided in its early years by the VLSI (very large-scale integrated circuit) project (1976–1979), which the Ministry of International Trade and Industry (MITI) structured so that strong vertically integrated companies, comparable to the American IBM, could be built up in Japan to produce semiconductors, computer hardware and software. Today, the Japanese semiconductor industry still maintains a policy of fast growth and increased competitiveness in the world market. Japanese companies concentrate on gaining a large market share by offering quality products at low cost to buyers. Many Japanese electronics firms have located semiconductor plants on the southern island of Kyushu to take advantage of plentiful labor, clean air, good water supply and convenient airports. Kyushu has became known as "Silicon Island." Most advanced research is still performed in the Tokyo area, however. See also COMPUTER INDUSTRY; ELECTRONICS INDUSTRY; KYUSHU ISLAND; MINISTRY FOR INTERNATIONAL TRADE AND INDUSTRY; RESEARCH AND DEVELOPMENT; SONY CORPORATION.

SEN NO RIKYU (1522–1591) A tea master who established many of the rules, utensils and aesthetic principles that became central to the Japanese tea ceremony (chado, the "Way of Tea," or chanoyu, "hot water for tea"). Rikyu was born into the wealthy and influential merchant class in the town of Sakai (near modern Osaka), the main port at that time in the lucrative foreign trade with China. He studied the tea ceremony with several famous masters and Zen Buddhism at Daitokuji in the capital city of Kyoto. The warlord Oda Nobunaga (1534–1582) chose Rikyu to serve as one of the masters for his tea ceremonies from 1570 to 1573, after which Toyotomi Hideyoshi (1537–1598), the warlord who unified Japan, made Rikyu his own tea master. Although Rikyu presided at the grand outdoor party Hideyoshi held at Kitano Shrine in 1587 for the general population, and other tea gatherings at which Hideyoshi used sumptuous utensils, his personal aesthetic was at variance with the ostentation preferred by Hideyoshi. Rikyu followed his teacher Takeno Joo (1502–1555), himself a student of the tea school founded by Murata Shuko (1422–1502), in conducting tea ceremonies according to the principle of wabi. Wabi cha, or "poverty tea," calls for simplicity, naturalness, the use of simple utensils taken from daily life and an austere spiritual nature. Rikyu worked with the potter Chojiro (1516–1592) to create black, rough, asymmetrical bowls, known as Raku ware, to serve the bright green ceremonial tea. He also designed an intimate style of tea ceremony in a rustic teahouse (chashitsu) the size of two tatami (straw floor mats). Many stories have been preserved about the creative interaction between Rikyu and Hideyoshi, but for a number of possible reasons, in 1591 Hideyoshi became angry with Rikyu and forced him to commit ritual suicide (seppuku). The Death of a Tea Master (Honkakubo ibun: Sen no Rikyu; 1989), a film directed by Kumai Kei and starring Mifune Toshiro, won a Silver Lion Award at the 1989 Venice International Film Festival. Rikyu's descendants formed the main schools of the tea ceremony, the largest of which, Urasenke, now has branch schools around the world as well as throughout Japan. See also CHOJIRO; MIFUNE TOSHIRO; ODA NOBUNAGA; POTTERY; RAKU WARE; SABI AND WABI; SUICIDE; TATAMI; TEA CEREMONY; TEAHOUSE; TOYOTOMI HIDEYOSHI; URASENKE SCHOOL OF THE TEA CEREMONY.

SEN SOSHITSU See IEMOTO; URASENKE SCHOOL OF THE TEA CEREMONY.

SENCHA See TEA; TEAPOTS.

SENDAI The economic and political center of the northeast region of Honshu Island and the capital of Miyagi Prefecture. Located on the Hirosegawa River a little more than 200 miles north of Tokyo, Sendai has a population of nearly 1 million. It became Greater Sendai City in March 1988 when it merged with the adjacent towns of Miyagi, Akyu and Izumi City. The Japanese city closest to the United States, Sendai is the main distribution center for northeastern Japan.

This area was the administrative center of northern Japan as far back as the eighth century A.D. The city of Sendai was founded in 1602 by the warlord Date Masamune, who built a large castle and laid out the city streets. His mausoleum is a popular tourist attraction. Tourists also visit the Osaki Hachiman Shrine and attend the parade to celebrate the Star Festival (Tanabata-sama) on August 7th each year. Sendai was destroyed during World War II but has been rebuilt. Its nickname is the "City of Trees." There are 12 colleges and universities, including the national Tohoku University (founded in 1907), which is on the site of Sendai Castle on top of Aobayama Hill. Major industries produce steel, rubber, silk, wood and food products. The surrounding agricultural area produces rice and vegetables. Sendai is also becoming a center for high technology, and is developing the "Tohoku Intelligent Cosmos" project that will have research and development facilities. See also CASTLES; HONSHU ISLAND; RESEARCH AND DEVELOPMENT; STAR FESTIVAL; TREES; UNIVERSITIES.

SENGAI GIBON (1750–1837) A monk of the Zen sect of Buddhism and a famous painter and calligrapher. Sengai was born to a farm family in what is now Gifu Prefecture. He became a novice monk at the age of 11, and at 19 went on the first of two *angya*, or pilgrimages, to study with masters at different Zen temples. Sengai was eventually ordained the 123rd abbot of Shofukuji, the first Japanese Zen temple, founded in 1195 by Eisai (1141–1215) in Hakata on the southern island of Kyushu. After Sengai retired from this position in 1811 at age 61, he spent the last 26 years of his life creating ink paintings and calligraphy. Although not a professional artist, his work has been greatly admired for its spontaneity and sense of humor. He often combined poems with visual depictions, which covered a wide range of religious themes, such as Kannon (Goddess of Mercy) and Daruma (the legendary founder of Zen Buddhism), to animals, flowers and human figures. During the past three decades, Sengai's works have been exhibited many times outside Japan. His paintings have been reproduced in annual calendars by Idemitsu Sazo, founder of the Idemitsu Kosan Company, who owns the largest collection of Sengai's works and displays them in the Idemitsu Art Gallery in Tokyo. See also CALLIGRAPHY; DARUMA; EISAI; INK PAINTING; KANNON; PILGRIMAGE; POETRY; ZEN SECT OF BUDDHISM.

SENGAKUJI TEMPLE   See FORTY-SEVEN RONIN INCIDENT.

SENGOKU ERA (1467–1568) "Warring States" Era or Era of the "Country at War"; a period in Japanese history characterized by political unrest and widespread military conflict between *daimyo* (lords) of various provinces. The Sengoku Era falls within the period when Japan was ruled by the Ashikaga Shogunate (1338–1573; also known as the Muromachi Era). The balance of power between the Ashikaga shoguns, based in Kyoto on western Honshu Island, and provincial *daimyo* broke down in the 15th century, and the Onin War (1467–1477), which devastated Kyoto, is usually considered the beginning of the Sengoku Era. It ended when the warlord Oda Nobunaga (1534–1582), one of the great military leaders who helped to unify Japan,

took control of Kyoto in 1568. The Sengoku Era is often characterized by the term *gekokujo,* "the overturning of those on top by those below." Local military leaders, known as *shugodai* and *kokujin,* wrested control of the provinces away from the powerful *shugo daimyo* families who had been governing the Japanese provinces. These new leaders, called *Sengoku daimyo,* actually stimulated economic development, particularly through projects to reclaim land, control floods and increase rice production; the cultivation of cotton, which aided the Japanese textile industry; the mining of gold, silver, copper and iron, which helped the growth of metallurgy; and trade between provinces, which encouraged overland and boat transportation, and the growth of commercial cities. Commercial and political centers developed around the castles built by rival *daimyo.* Culture was also spread throughout the country by Zen Buddhist monks and poets (*rengashi*), whom the *daimyo* invited to their domains. *Renga* and *haiku* poetry, Japanese and Chinese classical literature, ink painting (*sumi-e*), the tea ceremony, Noh drama and book publishing all flourished. The Christian religion and Western culture and firearms were also introduced into Japan during the Sengoku Era. The former was initiated by St. Francis Xavier (1506–1552), a Roman Catholic missionary who came to Japan in 1549. The Sengoku Era was followed by the Azuchi-Momoyama Era (1568–1600), when Japanese culture reached what some regard as its zenith and the country was unified under the rule of the Tokugawa shoguns. See also ASHIKAGA SHOGUNATE; AZUCHI-MOMOYAMA ERA; CASTLES; CHRISTIANITY IN JAPAN; DAIMYO; FIREARMS, INTRODUCTION OF; INK PAINTING; MUROMACHI ERA; NOH DRAMA; ODA NOBUNAGA; ONIN WAR; RENGA; TEA CEREMONY; TOKUGAWA IEYASU; TOKUGAWA SHOGUNATE; TOYOTOMI HIDEYOSHI; XAVIER, ST. FRANCIS; ZEN SECT OF BUDDHISM.

SENIORITY EMPLOYMENT SYSTEM (*nenko joretsu*) A system of employment in Japanese companies whereby employees are promoted and given pay raises based on the number of years they have worked for the company. Other determining factors are the university the employee attended and the employee's sex and type of work. The seniority system began during World War I in Japan and has become widely practiced, particularly by large corporations. It evolved out of the need to maintain a stable work force, since employees know their jobs are secure and that their salaries will increase as they grow older. Building employee loyalty is another goal of the seniority system. Japanese white-collar workers are hired in groups when they graduate from school. Since workers at the same level receive virtually the same salaries, they are less inclined to compete and more willing to cooperate with each other. However, on the negative side, exceptional younger employees may be frustrated by not being able to advance more quickly than their coworkers. Japanese employees usually retire in their late fifties, and their pensions are also based on seniority. The seniority system is starting to create problems for Japanese companies as the majority of the population increasingly falls into an older age bracket, leaving less room for younger employees to advance. Some companies are beginning to experiment with merit systems that take an employee's abilities into account. See also CORPORATIONS; EMPLOYMENT; LIFETIME EMPLOYMENT SYSTEM; LOYALTY; RETIREMENT.

SENSEI A term of respect that students generally use to address a schoolteacher, or an instructor of martial arts or traditional arts such as dance and the tea ceremony. An older person who is not a teacher may also be addressed with respect as *sensei*, "master." See also DANCE, TRADITIONAL; EDUCATION SYSTEM; TEA CEREMONY.

SENSOJI TEMPLE See ASAKUSA; FAIR DAY.

SENTO See BATH.

SEPPUKU See BUSHIDO; MISHIMA YUKIO; SUICIDE; SWORD.

SESSHU TOYO (1420–1506) An important painter in the *suibokuga*, or "water-ink," style, also known as *sumi-e*, "ink pictures." Sesshu was born in Bitchu Prefecture (part of modern Okayama Prefecture), and as a young man became a Buddhist monk at Shokokuji in Kyoto, where Josetsu, the first major ink painter in Japan, had also been a monk in the early 15th century. Josetsu's style of ink painting influenced the monk Shubun, with whom Sesshu studied painting. In 1464 Sesshu joined the Unkokuan art studio in Yamaguchi (in modern Yamaguchi Prefecture), far from the culture of Zen Buddhist temples in the capital city of Kyoto. In 1467 he went to China for two years with a trade mission sent by the Ouchi clan, which controlled Yamaguchi. There Sesshu was able to view many Chinese ink paintings and famous landscapes in the Chinese countryside. He also spent time at a Chinese Buddhist monastery and created a wall painting in the Board of Rites building in Beijing. Sesshu painted most of his famous works after his trip to China, and art historians have pointed out the influence of Chinese ink painters from the Song (Sung; 960–1279), Yuan (1260–1368) and Ming (1368–1644) dynasties on Sesshu's work. By 1476 he opened his own studio in Bungo Province (part of modern Oita Prefecture).

Some of Sesshu's best-known landscape ink paintings include two hanging scrolls, *Autumn and Winter Landscapes;* a horizontal scroll, *Landscapes of the Four Seasons;* and *Haboku Landscape.* He painted many sets of screens, often using bird-and-flower motifs. Two of his famous portraits are *Portrait of Masuda Kanetaka* and *Huike (Hui-k'o) Severing His Arm.* The latter portrays one of the central stories of Zen Buddhism, in which Huike cuts off his own arm to convince the Zen teacher Daruma of his desperate need to be enlightened. Sesshu trained many other Japanese ink painters, and his strong, dynamic style continued to influence later generations of artists. See also CHINA AND JAPAN; INK PAINTING; JOSETSU; SCREENS; SCROLLS; ZEN SECT OF BUDDHISM.

SESSUE HAYAKAWA See HAYAKAWA SESSHU.

SETO INLAND SEA See INLAND SEA.

SETO-OHASHI BRIDGE See BRIDGES; HONSHU ISLAND; INLAND SEA; SHIKOKU ISLAND.

SETO WARE (*seto-yaki*) A type of pottery made in the city of Seto in Owari Province (modern Aichi Prefecture) on central Honshu Island from the 12th century to the late 15th century. Seto, regarded as the oldest of all Japanese pottery kilns, dating back at least to the Heian Era (794–1185) and classified as one of the "six old kilns" of Japan, produced the only glazed pottery in Japan until the late 13th century A.D. In the ninth century A.D., kilns in the Owari area began using the green celadon glaze that was introduced from China, and by the 12th century, Seto was the center of celadon production in Japan. For the next 400 years, Seto remained the dominant Japanese pottery center, with the production of Seto ware reaching its apogee in the 14th century. Seto celadon glazes tended to be not green but yellow (*ki-zeto*) or amber (*ame*) in color. Pieces were often decorated with stamped or incised designs of flowers. A dark brown Chinese glaze known in Japan as *temmoku* was also produced by Seto potters. *Temmoku* utensils were important in the tea ceremony, which had been brought back from Chinese temples by Japanese Zen Buddhist monks. Tea masters admired 15th-century Seto *temmoku* tea bowls (*chawan*) and tea caddies (*chaire*), which had a glossy, deep brown glaze. In the 16th century, Seto ware was surpassed by Mino ware (*mino-yaki*) in neighboring Mino Province (modern Gifu Prefecture). However, Seto ware has continued to be produced in small quantities up to the present. See also MINO WARE; POTTERY; TEA BOWL; TEA CEREMONY.

SETSUBUN See BEAN-THROWING FESTIVAL.

SEVEN-FIVE-THREE FESTIVAL (Shichi-Go-San) A festival for children that takes place on November 15th. Parents take girls aged three and seven and boys aged five to Shinto shrines to give thanks for their health and to pray for continued good health and happiness. The children attend a ceremony during which Shinto priests offer them sacred sake. Traditionally, girls began wearing their hair up at three, and girls of seven changed from a girl's kimono to an adult-style kimono secured with an *obi* or sash. Boys of five put on the *hakama*, or formal pleated divided skirt that men wear over their kimono. Today boys often wear their best suits to the festival, but girls still wear silk kimono and decorative hair ornaments. Large crowds throng the shrine compounds to see the children, and their proud parents take many photographs. In Tokyo the most popular shrines to visit for this festival are Hie Shrine in the Akasaka district and Myojin Shrine in the Kanda district. People buy "thousand-year candy" (*chitose-ame*), red and white candy sticks in decorated paper bags, to give the children a thousand years of happiness. See also AKASAKA; CHILDREN IN JAPAN; FESTIVALS; HAKAMA; KANDA; KIMONO; SAKE; SHINTO; SHRINES, SHINTO.

SEVEN GODS OF GOOD FORTUNE (Shichifukujin) A group of associated gods worshipped by many Japanese people, particularly those of the merchant class in the 16th and 17th centuries. The number seven has religious symbolism in Buddhism, as evidenced by the Buddhist notion of the Seven Misfortunes and Seven Blessings. The Seven Gods (actually, six gods and one goddess) of Good Fortune were taken from several different religions, including Buddhism, Shinto (the native Japanese religion), Chinese Taoism and Indian Brahmanism. Three of the Gods, Ebisu, Daikoku(ten) and Bishamon(ten), are gods of good fortune. Ebisu is the god of fishermen and carries a large fish. Daikoku, the god of wealth, holds a bag of treasures and a mallet that, when shaken, grants wishes. Bishamon, the god of warriors, is dressed in armor. The god of long life and wealth is actually a combination of two figures, Jurojin and Fukurokuju, who dwell together in the body of an old man with an elongated head who holds a long cane with a scroll tied to it and a leaf-shaped fan. Hotei, the god of happiness, has a contented smile and a round exposed belly and holds a large sack and a leaf-shaped fan. Hotei is regarded as a Zen Buddhist priest who was a reincarnation of the Buddhist god Maitreya; his name comes from the Chinese name Budai or Putai. Benten (or Benzaiten) derives from an Indian goddess called Sarasvati in the Sanskrit language. The goddess of music, wisdom and water, she plays the *biwa*, a Japanese mandolin. The Seven Gods of Good Fortune play a special role at the New Year Festival, when the shrines and temples associated with them are visited by many Japanese. These gods are believed to enter port on a ship filled with treasures (*Takarabune*) on New Year's Eve. Decorations portraying the gods on their treasure ship are displayed to bring good fortune. Many Japanese place these pictures by their pillows so that their first dream in the New Year will be filled with fortune. See also BUDDHISM; NEW YEAR FESTIVAL; SHINTO; SHRINES, SHINTO; TEMPLES, BUDDHIST; NAMES OF INDIVIDUAL GODS.

SEVEN HERBS OF SPRING (*nanakusa*) Seven edible herbs that are traditionally eaten in a rice gruel (*nanakusagayu*) on January 7th, as part of the New Year Festival, to ensure good health. They include Japanese dropwort (*seri*), shepherd's purse (*nazuna*), cudweed (*gogyo*), *Stellaria media* (a type of chickweed; *hakobe*), *Lapsana apogonoides* (*hotokenoza*), turnip (*suzuna* or *kabu*) and daikon. The seven herbs of spring parallel the autumn flowers and grasses (*akigusa*), which are not consumed but displayed in flower arrangements in August and September. See also AUTUMN FLOWERS AND GRASSES; DAIKON; NEW YEAR FESTIVAL.

SEVENTEEN-ARTICLE CONSTITUTION (Jushichijo no Kempo) A set of ethical principles for Japanese government officials issued in A.D. 604 by Prince Shotoku (574–622), regent for Empress Suiko (554–628; r. 593–628). Although usually translated as "constitution," *kempo* does not mean a constitution in the modern sense. Shotoku's constitution is a collection of general principles derived from Chinese Confucian ideology and the teachings of the Buddhist religion, which had both been introduced into Japan during the sixth century A.D. Shotoku was a convert to Buddhism and used the religion to increase the power

and prestige of the imperial court and to improve social harmony. The articles claim that imperial rule is the highest authority because it has divine origins, and government officials ought to be its loyal servants. The Seventeen-Article Constitution was part of Shotoku's extensive reorganization of the Japanese government based on Chinese models. See also BUDDHISM; CHINA AND JAPAN; CONFUCIANISM; EMPEROR; SHOTOKU, PRINCE; SUIKO, EMPRESS.

SEX See COURTESAN; FLOATING WORLD; LOVE HOTEL; OKUNI; PROSTITUTION; SAIKAKU; SHUNGA; TANIZAKI JUN'ICHIRO; WATER TRADE; WOODBLOCK PRINTS; YOSHIWARA.

SHABU-SHABU See SUKIYAKI.

SHADES, BAMBOO (*sudare*) Rolling shades, made from small strips of bamboo or thin reeds, that are hung for decorative purposes or to divide rooms. They are handmade by artisans who have mastered the difficult craft of matching slightly uneven strips of bamboo so that a finished shade will hang perfectly straight. The strips are bound together with long strings, which can be pulled to roll up, or loosened to roll down, the hanging shade. Special shades for teahouses are made from thin reeds. Shades known as *misu*, hung along corridors of Shinto shrines and Buddhist temples, have silk brocade bindings on their four edges and two elaborate silk tassels suspended from thick braided silk cords. See also BAMBOO; SHRINES; SHINTO; TEAHOUSE; TEMPLES, BUDDHIST.

SHAKUHACHI A musical instrument made of bamboo that is similar to a flute but played like a recorder. The name *shakuhachi* comes from the traditional Japanese units of measure for its length, that is, 1 *shaku* and 8 (*hachi*) *sun*, equivalent to 21.46 inches. The player blows into a hole in the top of the bamboo and sounds the notes by covering or opening the finger holes, which usually number from five to eight. The *shakuhachi* produces a low, breathy tone capable of many variations despite the simple appearance of the instrument. It also has a lonely, melancholy sound that calls to mind the *shakuhachi* playing of wandering Zen Buddhist monks (*komuso*, "priests of nothing"), who wore baskets over their heads to symbolize their non-attachment to the world, during the Edo Era (1600–1868). One of several imperial court instruments introduced into Japan from China in the seventh century A.D., a six-hole *shakuhachi* was played in the Japanese imperial court orchestra (*gagaku*) through the ninth century. Only in the 16th century did a five-hole *shakuhachi* become associated with mendicants belonging to the Fuke sect of Zen Buddhism, who played the instrument as a way of practicing meditation. When the Meiji government (1868–1912) abolished their sect in 1871, the *shakuhachi* became a more common secular instrument taught by a number of different schools. Even during the Tokugawa Era (1603–1867), the *shakuhachi* was played in a trio called *sankyoku*, along with two stringed instruments known as *koto* and *shamisen*, by women of the growing merchant class.

The repertoire of music for the *shakuhachi* now includes

"original pieces" *(honkyoku)* that derive from Fuke religious solos, "outside pieces" *(gaikyoku)* played in 19th-century *sankyoku* ensembles, and "contemporary pieces" *(gendaimono)* combining Western and traditional Japanese styles. The *shakuhachi* still retains its Zen associations, and thus the solo *honkyoku* style is the most prominent, emphasizing breathing techniques practiced in Zen Buddhist meditation and producing sounds that vary subtly in pitch and intensity. According to Zen Buddhism, the long phrases played by the *shakuhachi* seem to come from and return to the Nothingness that is the ultimate Zen principle. See also FLUTES; GAGAKU; KOTO; SHAMISEN; ZEN SECT OF BUDDHISM.

SHAMANS AND SHAMANISM *(miko; gyoja* or *yamabushi)*

Shamanism is the belief that certain persons, known as shamans, have supernatural powers of healing, exorcising evil spirits and going into a trance to divine the will of the sacred spirits. Shamanism originated in central Asia, and the Japanese shamanistic tradition has its roots in this and Korean practices. A shaman, who can be male but is usually female in Japan, is "called" into the religious life by a supernatural figure who appears in visions and becomes the shaman's guardian spirit. This spirit *(kami)* enters and takes possession of the body of the shaman, making it possible for him or her to communicate with the dead and other spirits. A shaman undergoes training and ascetic practices, such as fasting and isolation, to heighten the ability to communicate with *kami.*

Shamans played an important function in ancient Japan, and shamanism has survived in Japanese folk religious traditions. Ancient Chinese documents mention female "queens" with shamanistic traits who ruled areas of ancient Japan, such as Empress Himiko (third century A.D.). The two types of shamans still practicing in Japan are known as the *miko* and the *gyoja* or *yamabushi.*

A *miko,* or "medium," is usually a woman who goes into a trance so that the *kami* speaks through her mouth. In ancient Japan, a *miko* acted as the medium for a spirit during a religious ritual. The term *miko* is also applied to young girls who hold the office of priestesses at Shinto shrines, although they do not claim shamanistic powers. In rural areas of Japan, women continue to function as mediums for *kami.* The indigenous religion of the southern Ryukyu Islands (modern Okinawa Prefecture) is still conducted by women priestesses, known as *nuru* or *noro.*

The type of shaman known as *gyoja* or *yamabushi* is usually a man who is a drifting mountain dweller of a syncretistic Shinto-Buddhist sect known as Shugendo and who has undergone Buddhist and other ascetic practices that are thought to give him the powers of healing, exorcism and calling *kami* into his body. Ascetic training includes bathing in cold water, fasting, taking retreats on holy mountains, reciting sacred scriptures and walking on fire. *Yamabushi* literally means "one who lives in the mountains." A *yamabushi* wears a distinctive outfit with baggy trousers, tunic and black cap, and carries a staff, Buddhist rosary and conch-shell trumpet.

Japanese still go to ascetic shamans for healing and exorcism of evil spirits. Founders of many modern so-called New Religions in Japan have functioned as shamans. See also BUDDHISM; HIMIKO, EMPRESS; KAMI; MOUNTAINS; NEW RELIGIONS; PRIESTS AND PRIESTESSES, SHINTO; RYUKYU ISLANDS; SHINTO.

SHAME *(haji)* This social and psychological characteristic of the Japanese people has been described by American anthropologist Ruth Benedict (1887–1948) in her classic study *The Chrysanthemum and the Sword* (1946; translated into Japanese as *Kiku to katana,* 1949). Benedict characterized Japanese society as being concerned more with shame, and less with guilt, which is a central concept of Western culture. For Benedict, a guilt culture is guided by absolute moral standards and instills a personal conscience that makes a person feel guilty for committing sinful acts. In a shame culture, people are more concerned about how they are judged by other people. Although Benedict's theory has been criticized for making an artificial distinction between shame and guilt, it can be said that for the Japanese, keeping up social appearances and presenting a good "face" *(kao)* in public are very important. Individual feelings *(ninjo)* must be subordinated to duty *(giri)* to family and society. The Japanese are conscious of their position in the social hierarchy, and usually avoid doing things in public that would bring shame to themselves, their families and their other social groups. The obverse is expressed in a well-known saying, When on a trip, shame can be thrown away *(Tabi no haji wa kakisute);* that is, one can do what one wants in the absence of the social group that judges one's actions. Benedict's insights were reinforced by Japanese psychiatrist Doi Takei's best-seller *The Anatomy of Dependence* (*Amae no kozo;* 1971, translated 1973), which elaborated on the psycho-linguistic characteristics of Japanese culture. See also DEPENDENCY; DUTY AND FEELINGS; FACE; FAMILY; FILIAL PIETY.

SHAMISEN A musical instrument similar to a banjo that has a round body, long neck and three fretless strings that are plucked. The wooden frame is made of mulberry, red sandalwood or quince, and ranges from about 3½ to 4½ feet in length. The front and back of the body are covered with the skin of cats or dogs. Those made of dog skin are cheaper and are used for practice. High humidity during the rainy season in June may cause the cat or dog skin to split, and the *shamisen* will have to be covered with new skin. The strings are silk or nylon, and the three pegs at the end of the neck that hold the strings tight are made of ivory, plastic or wood. The small plectrum *(bachi)* that is used to pluck the strings is made from ivory, tortoiseshell or plastic. The *shamisen* probably originated in China, where it is called *sanxian* or *san-hsien,* and was brought to Japan through Korea and the Ryukyu Islands in the middle of the 16th century. In the Ryukyus (modern Okinawa Prefecture) it is known as *sanshin* or *jamisen,* and the body is covered with snakeskin. In Japan the *shamisen* (called *samisen* in the Kansai region of Kyoto and Osaka) quickly became associated with the pleasure quarters and the performing arts patronized by urban merchants. Its lively twang contrasts with the refined sound of the *koto,* the stringed instrument preferred by the samurai and nobility.

At times the Japanese government even tried to ban the *shamisen*, but the instrument never lost its popularity. Orchestras for Kabuki (traditional theater) and puppet theater (Bunraku) use *shamisen* to accompany the singers who chant the stories being portrayed on stage.

The *shamisen* is the instrument played by geisha. At one time, all geisha studied the instrument, although today they specialize in *shamisen* or classical Japanese dance. There is a geisha saying, If you have three strings, you can eat (*Sanbon ga areba, taberaru*). At a geisha party the *shamisen* player must be skilled enough to follow the male guests at banquets who wish to sing short songs known as *kouta*. While there is some written notation of *shamisen* music, geisha learn to play by ear and memorize the music. The three schools of *shamisen* music heard most often today are the ballad style (*tokiwazu*), the lyric style (*kiyomoto*) and long songs (*nagauta*). The *nagauta* style is the one learned by most amateur students of the *shamisen*. See also BUNRAKU; GEISHA; KABUKI; KOTO; RYUKYU ISLANDS; SINGING.

SHARP CORPORATION   See ELECTRONICS INDUSTRY.

SHELLS (*kai*)   Evidence that prehistoric people in Japan gathered shellfish is found in approximately 2,000 piles of shells, known as shell mounds (*kaizuka*), that date from the Jomon Era (c. 10,000 B.C.–c. 300 B.C.). Some shell mounds also exist from the Yayoi Era (c. 300 B.C.–c. A.D. 300) and Kofun Era (c. 300–710). Shell mounds also contain other archaeological materials, such as plant and animal remains, pottery and human burials, that provide much valuable information about the food, customs and environment of ancient Japanese. Most of the shell mounds are located near the beaches and warm water along Japan's east coast, particularly in the Kanto area around Tokyo. Excavation of the shell mounds was begun by an American teacher in Japan named Edward Sylvester Morse (1838–1925), who began research work on the Omori Shell Mounds in 1877.

Shells were used during the medieval era (12th–16th centuries) in Japan for religious offerings, known as *kaigarakyo*. The Japanese would write characters from a Buddhist *sutra* (religious scripture) on shells taken from a beach and bury them in so-called sutra mounds (*kyozuka*).

A game played with shells, known as *kai-awase*, is associated with aristocrats of the Heian Era (794–1185). The purpose of the game is to match clamshell halves that are painted or decorated with lines from poems of a type known as *waka*. The clams were stored in beautiful lacquer containers, or "shell pots" (*kai oke*), that were included in trousseaus of wealthy brides during the Edo Era (1600–1868). *Kai-awase* was the source for several card games that became popular in Japan during the Edo Era and are still played today.

Small iridescent pieces of the inner sides of shells, known as mother-of-pearl, have been used in Japan since the eighth century A.D. to make beautiful decorative inlays. *Raden* is the technique of making decorative inlays, especially on lacquer ware, with mother-of-pearl from a type of shell known as *yakogai*. *Aogai* is the technique of making inlays with blue-green fragments of abalone (*awabi*) shell.

Cultivation of pearls inside oyster shells is a large Japanese industry. See also CARD GAMES; EDO ERA; HEIAN ERA; KOFUN ERA; JOMON ERA; LACQUER WARE; MORSE, EDWARD SYLVESTER; PEARL; SCRIPTURES, RELIGIOUS; SEAFOOD; YAYOI ERA; WAKA.

SHELLFISH   See ABALONE; SEAFOOD; SHELLS; SUSHI.

SHIATSU   "Finger pressure"; a therapeutic technique in which the practitioner presses on key points of the body with fingers, elbows, knees, palms of the hand, or feet. The pressure points (*tsubo*) are thought to lie in meridians (*keiraku*) that run through the body. Traditional Japanese and Chinese medicine maintains that disease occurs when the life force (*ki*, or *chi* in Chinese) is blocked from flowing naturally through the meridians. Pressure on blocked points is thought to help stimulate the body's internal organs, relax the muscles and reduce stress. *Shiatsu* is said to be particularly helpful for headaches, rheumatism, high blood pressure and other conditions caused by stress and fatigue. A practitioner is expected to detect the internal condition of the body by analyzing problems along the spinal column, similar to chiropractic. *Shiatsu* is often called massage, but it differs from the active and rhythmic manipulation of the body performed by a massage therapist. This type of massage is known in Japan as *amma* ("press stroke") and has been influenced by traditional Chinese medicine. During the Edo Era (1600–1868), massage was performed by a guild of blind masseurs who were protected by their local lords. See also MEDICINE, TRADITIONAL.

SHIBORI   Small damp towels made from thick white fabric such as cotton terrycloth that restaurants give customers to wipe their hands and faces before eating. *Shibori* are also traditionally used in place of napkins. The term *shibori* is usually preceded by the honorary suffix *o-*, as *o-shibori*. Hot in the winter and cold in the summer, *shibori* are very refreshing. Japan Air Lines flight attendants hand out *shibori* to passengers on international flights, and this practice has been picked up by many other airlines. See also JAPAN AIR LINES; O-; PURIFICATION; RESTAURANTS.

SHIBORI-ZOME   See KASURI.

SHIBUI   "Astringent," like the acidic taste of a persimmon before it is ripe; an aesthetic term developed in the Muromachi Era (1333–1568) in Japan to connote beauty that is subtle and restrained yet profound. *Shibui* indicates that which is subdued rather than brightly colored. Objects can be *shibui*, such as a piece of pottery, yet the adjective can also be used to describe a color or pattern, a work of architecture, a singer's voice, an actor's performance and even a person's artistic taste or way of behaving in a refined, dignified manner. Modern Japanese still value the aesthetic principle of *shibui* and appreciate things that are old, seemingly worn and have a patina. The concept of *shibui* is related to similar aesthetic terms, *sabi* and *wabi*, all of which were influenced by the philosophy and cultural activities of the Zen sect of Buddhism. See also MUROMACHI ERA; PERSIMMON; SABI AND WABI; ZEN SECT OF BUDDHISM.

SHIBUYA A popular shopping and entertainment district of Tokyo centered around one of the city's busiest railroad stations, handling over a million passengers each day. Shibuya Castle formerly stood here, and the Shibuya River supplied power for a milling industry that was in operation until the 1920s. The symbol of Shibuya is the bronze statue of a dog named Hachiko that stands in front of the station and is a popular meeting place. In 1923, Hachiko began accompanying his master to the station and home again each workday. Even though his master died away from home in 1925, Hachiko waited 10 years at the station for him to return. When Hachiko himself died in 1935, the Japanese people raised a statue to commemorate his loyalty. Hachiko was stuffed and placed in the National Science Museum in Ueno Park. See also TOKYO; UENO.

SHICHIGENKIN See KOTO.

SHIDEHARA KIJURO (1872–1951) Prime minister of Japan October 1945–April 1946. Shidehara was born to a wealthy family in Osaka and received a law degree from Tokyo University in 1895, after which he served from 1896 to 1919 in the Japanese foreign service in Korea, the United States and Europe, and in the home office in Tokyo. In 1903 he married Iwasaki Masako, whose father was head of the powerful Mitsubishi company. Shidehara was named ambassador to the United States in 1919 and was a delegate to the Washington Conference held in 1921–1922, which dealt with the issue of limiting naval powers in the Pacific Ocean. He also used the conference to lessen tension between Japan and China, mainly by negotiating the return of Shandong (Shantung) Province (which Japan had taken) to China. During the 1920s, his policy of Japanese conciliation toward China and cooperation with other nations was known as "Shidehara Diplomacy." Unlike many Japanese leaders, Shidehara opposed military intervention in the Chinese revolution at that time, although he did favor the promotion of Japanese economic interests there. After he was appointed minister of foreign affairs, he prevented the Japanese military from intervening in several political and military crises that erupted in China, which brought him public criticism for supposed weakness.

Shidehara served as interim premier of Japan November 1930–March 1931 after Prime Minister Hamaguchi Osachi was wounded in an assassination attempt, but he had little success in influencing the Diet. The last crisis Shidehara faced as foreign minister was the Manchurian Incident in September 1931, when he was unable to stop the Japanese Guandong (Kwantung) Army from occupying Manchuria. From 1931 to 1945, Shidehara held a seat in the House of Peers (Upper House of the Diet) but refrained from active participation in politics. During the Occupation of the country after the war, Shidehara was chosen to be the second postwar prime minister of Japan. He took credit for Article IX in the 1947 constitution that prohibited Japan from maintaining military forces, and for recommending that the emperor of Japan, in order to continue the imperial system, renounce the traditional Japanese belief that he is divine. Shidehara's Japan Progressive Party (Nihon Shim-poto) lost the first general election after the war, held in April 1946, but he later served two sessions in the House of Representatives (lower house of the Diet) and was made Speaker of the House in 1949. See also CHINA AND JAPAN; CONSTITUTION OF 1947; DIET; EMPEROR; MANCHURIAN INCIDENT; MITSUBISHI; OCCUPATION OF JAPAN; PRIME MINISTER; WASHINGTON CONFERENCE AND NAVAL TREATY; WORLD WAR II.

SHIFUKU See BROCADE; TEA CEREMONY.

SHIGARAKI WARE (*shigaraki-yaki*) A type of pottery produced in the Shigaraki Valley in Shiga Prefecture on west-central Honshu Island. Roof tiles were made here for the Shigaraki Imperial Palace (Shigaraki no Miya) built A.D. 742–745 for Emperor Shomu (r. A.D. 724–749). Pottery bowls, jars and other items used by farm households were first produced at Shigaraki during the Kamakura Shogunate (1192–1333). Shigaraki ware has a rough, ancient look. Its granular surface is created when white feldspar or quartz granules in the clay melt and protrude when fired in a kiln. The objects are reddish brown with a natural ash glaze. Originally they were fired in small underground or tunnel kilns (*anagama*). The Korean-style *noborigama*, or "climbing" kilns built on a hillside, were first used at Shigaraki in the 16th century. Shigaraki ware resembles Bizen ware, and it is possible that some Bizen potters moved to Shigaraki. Many of the best-known Shigaraki pieces are large storage jars with rounded bodies and small mouths. These have been especially valued by tea ceremony masters for storing tea. The tea masters Takeno Jo-o and Sen no Rikyu (1522–1591) patronized the Shigaraki kilns for tea jars, tea bowls and vases. In 1632 the Tokugawa Shogunate (1603–1867) selected Shigaraki ware as the official storage jars for tea grown for the shogunate in Uji. During the 19th century, Shigaraki potters began mass-producing many types of objects for domestic use. Today, individual potters continue to make storage jars, water jars and tea bowls in the old manner. Shigaraki is among the "Six Old Kilns" in Japan. See also BIZEN WARE; KILN; POTTERY; ROOF TILES; SEN NO RIKYU; TEA BOWL; TEA CEREMONY; UJI.

SHIITAKE MUSHROOMS See MUSHROOMS.

SHIKOKU ISLAND The smallest of the four main islands of Japan. Shikoku lies off the southeast coast of Honshu, the main island, from which it is separated by the Seto Inland Sea. The Bungo Channel separates Shikoku from Kyushu, the southernmost main island of Japan. Shikoku includes the prefectures of Kagawa, Tokushima, Ehime and Kochi, as well as many nearby small islands. Matsuyama and Takamatsu are the two largest cities. Much of Shikoku is covered with steep mountains that have hampered development and have blocked communications between towns. A lack of natural resources has also limited the development of heavy industries on Shikoku. This situation may be improved by the Seto-Ohashi Bridge, opened in 1988 after 10 years of construction, linking Shikoku and Honshu. It is actually six bridges that connect a number of small islands in the Seto Inland Sea to the main island of Honshu. The primary economic activities on Shikoku have been commercial fishing, livestock raising, and the growing of rice, citrus fruit and vegetables. Shikoku has a subtropical climate with mild winters and hot summers, although the southern coast bordering the Pacific Ocean has heavy summer rainfall and typhoons. The northern side of the island bordering the Seto Inland Sea was developed early in Japanese history because the Inland Sea was a major transportation and shipping route. There are two national parks, Inland Sea and Ashizuri-Uwakai, on Shikoku.

Matsuyama city on the northwest coast has a population of half a million. Although most of the city was destroyed during World War II, one of Japan's best-preserved medieval castles, Matsuyama Castle, still stands here. The Dogo Onsen in Matsuyama, which dates back at least 3,000 years, claims to be the oldest hot spring in Japan. Thousands of people a day bathe in the Dogo Onsen Honkan, a three-story wooden bathhouse built in 1894 that still has tatami floor mats and sliding screens (shoji). Connected to it is a bathhouse erected for the imperial family in 1899, which is open to the public for tours. Dolls are made in Matsuyama with an oval shape designed after the legendary empress Jingu, who supposedly came to Dogo Spa when she was pregnant. Other crafts for which the city is known are *iyo kasuri*, indigo-dyed cotton that is used to make workclothes, and Tobe ware (tobe-yaki), thick white porcelain with blue designs.

Shikoku is famous for its 88 Buddhist temples, which are popular as pilgrimage sites. They honor Kukai (Kobo Daishi) who was born on Shikoku in A.D. 774 and founded the Shingon (True Word) sect of Buddhism. Making a pilgrimage to all 88 temples is believed to release one from the cycle of death and rebirth. Eight of the temples are in Matsuyama. The most popular one is Ishiteji, which was built in 1318 in the combined Chinese and Japanese architectural styles of the Kamakura Era (1192–1333).

Takamatsu, the second largest city on Shikoku, was the capital of the Matsudaira clan (1642–1868). The family's summer retreat is now a public park named Ritsurin. The "borrowed landscape" style of garden within the park incorporates the view of nearby Mount Shiun. There are six ponds, 13 scenic hills, rocks, pine trees and cherry trees in Ritsurin Park, and a teahouse named Kiku-getsu-tei. Yashimaji Temple in Takamatsu is number 84 on the pilgrimage route of 88 temples. It was the site of a battle in the 12th century between the Taira and Minamoto clans.

The town of Kotohira has one of the oldest Kabuki theaters in Japan, the Kyu Kompira Oshibai, the only complete Edo Era (1603–1868) Kabuki playhouse that survives. It was built in 1835 in traditional style with *tatami* and *shoji* screens. The revolving stage is turned by eight men in the basement. Plays are staged here once a year in April. Kotohiragu Shrine, a popular pilgrimage site also known as Kompira-san, was originally founded in the 11th century, but the present main shrine buildings were erected in the 19th century. One of Japan's largest and oldest Shinto shrines, it houses models and photographs of boats that fishermen have left to ask for the protection of the

gods. Kabuki performances are also held at this shrine. See also CASTLE; GEOGRAPHY OF JAPAN; HONSHU ISLAND; HOT SPRING; INLAND SEA; KABUKI; KUKAI; KYUSHU ISLAND; PILGRIMAGE; SHINGON SECT OF BUDDHISM; TAIRA-MINAMOTO WAR; TAKAMATSU; TYPHOON.

SHIMABARA UPRISING (1637–1638) An uprising of 37,000 peasants, *ronin* (masterless samurai) and others suffering from famine, high taxes and desperate economic and political conditions in the Shimabara domain (part of modern Nagasaki Prefecture) of the *daimyo* (feudal lord) Matsukura Katsuie (d. 1638) on southern Kyushu Island. The uprising quickly spread to the nearby Amakusa Islands (part of modern Kumamoto Prefecture) in the domain of the *daimyo* of Karatsu, Terazawa Katataka (1609–1647). Many of the rebels were converts to the Christian religion, which had been introduced by Portuguese Roman Catholic missionaries in the 16th century and become widely practiced on Kyushu. The Tokugawa Shogunate (1603–1867) regarded the foreign religion as a threat to its authority, and in 1614 Shogun Tokugawa Ieyasu (1543–1616) issued an edict banning Christianity in Japan and began persecuting Christians. The persecution came to a climax when the rebels made a stand in Hara Castle on the Shimabara Peninsula. Their leader was a samurai named Amakusa Shiro (also known as Masuda Shiro Tokisada and by the Christian name Jeronimo; 1622?–1638), whose *daimyo*, Konishi Yukinaga, had been killed by Ieyasu. Many samurai who had served Konishi joined with the rebellious peasants when their uprising broke out on December 11, 1637. Shogun Tokugawa Iemitsu (Ieyasu's son) sent 100,000 troops to defeat the rebels, and Dutch naval ships assisted by bombarding the castle. After three months, the castle fell, on April 12, 1638, and all 37,000 rebels were horribly slaughtered, including women and children. The Shimabara Uprising caused the Tokugawa Shogunate to banish all Portuguese and Spanish from Japan, and the Protestant Dutch, who had aided the shogunate, became the only Westerners permitted to engage in trade with Japan. In 1639 the shogunate proclaimed the seclusion of Japan to isolate the country from Western political and religious influences. Although some Japanese continued to hold Roman Catholic masses in secret, the Christian religion was effectively stamped out in Japan until modern times. See also CHRISTIANITY IN JAPAN; DAIMYO; DUTCH IN JAPAN; KYUSHU ISLAND; NAGASAKI; PORTUGUESE IN JAPAN; SAMURAI; SECLUSION, NATIONAL; TOKUGAWA IEMITSU; TOKUGAWA IEYASU; TOKUGAWA SHOGUNATE.

SHIMAZU CLAN A powerful family based in Satsuma Province (the western half of modern Kagoshima Prefecture) on Kyushu, the southernmost of the four main Japanese islands. The Shimazu clan functioned as stewards (*gesu* or *geshi*) on landed estates in Satsuma owned by the Konoe family, who resided in the capital city of Kyoto. From the 12th through the 16th centuries, the Shimazus served as military governors (*shugo* or *shugo daimyo*) of Satsuma. Shimazu Tadahisa (1179–1227), a vassal of Minamoto no Yoritomo (1147–1199), who founded the Kamakura Shogunate (1192–1333), was appointed *shugo* of Satsuma and Omi provinces. By the time of Shimazu Yoshihisa (1533–1611), the Shimazu had expanded their power until they controlled most of Kyushu Island. Many foreign influences entered Japan through Satsuma under the Shimazu, including the Christian religion and Western firearms. The warlord Toyotomi Hideyoshi (1536–1598), one of the three great unifiers of Japan, defeated Shimazu Yoshihisa in 1587 and confiscated all of Kyushu controlled by the Shimazu except for Satsuma and Omi Provinces. The family suffered another setback in 1600 when Yoshihisa's brother Shimazu Yoshihiro (1535–1619) fought unsuccessfully against Tokugawa Ieyasu (1543–1616), founder of the Tokugawa Shogunate (1603–1867) at the Battle of Sekigahara. The Shimazu regained some of their lost power when Yoshihiro's son Shimazu Iehisa (1578–1638) took control of the Ryukyu Islands (modern Okinawa Prefecture), a wealthy trading kingdom to the south of Kyushu. This greatly enhanced Shimazu wealth and power and gave them the sugar monopoly in Japan. The Tokugawa permitted the Shimazu, who were classified as *tozama*, or "outside vassals," to serve as *daimyo* of Satsuma. The Shimazu also adopted Western industrial and military techniques to strengthen Satsuma Province. They played an important role in the Meiji Restoration of 1868. The Shimazu flag, which has a red sun in the middle of a white field, became the national flag of Japan. See also CHRISTIANITY IN JAPAN; DAIMYO; FIREARMS, INTRODUCTION OF; FLAGS AND BANNERS; KAGOSHIMA; KAMAKURA SHOGUNATE; KYUSHU ISLAND; LANDED ESTATE SYSTEM; MEIJI RESTORATION OF 1868; RYUKYU ISLANDS; SATSUMA PROVINCE; SEKIGAHARA, BATTLE OF; TOKUGAWA IEYASU; TOKUGAWA SHOGUNATE; TOYOTOMI HIDEYOSHI.

SHIMBASHI   See BRIDGES; GINZA.

SHIMODA   See HARRIS, TOWNSEND; IZU PENINSULA; PERRY, MATTHEW CALBRAITH.

SHIMONOSEKI   A city on the southwest tip of the main island of Honshu with a population of nearly 300,000. Shimonoseki is connected to the industrial area of Kita Kyushu on Kyushu Island by the longest suspension bridge in Japan. Kammon Bridge crosses Kammon Strait, a mile-wide body of water separating the two islands, also formerly known as the Strait of Shimonoseki. Two undersea railroad tunnels and a highway tunnel also connect the islands. Ferries sail between Shimonoseki and the port of Pusan in South Korea. Ships sailing the Inland Sea would pass through Kammon Strait to get to the major trading city of Nagasaki on the western side of Kyushu. Shimonoseki is an industrial city and one of Japan's largest centers for commercial fishing. Two major sea battles took place in the waters off Shimonoseki. The Minamoto clan defeated the Taira (or Heike) clan in the Battle of Dannoura in 1185, thus beginning nearly seven centuries of military rule in Japan known as *bakufu*. The destruction of the Taira Clan is memorialized in an important work of classical literature, *The Tale of the Heike (Heike Monogatari)*. In September 1864 Shimonoseki was bombarded by a naval expedition of American, British, French and Dutch ships,

retaliating for attacks by forces of Choshu Province (modern Yamaguchi Prefecture on Honshu Island) against Western ships passing through the Strait of Shimonoseki, which bordered Choshu. Choshu forces wanted to expel all foreigners, whom the Tokugawa Shogunate (1603–1867) had granted trading concessions by the Ansei Commercial Treatics of 1858. The bombardment of Shimonoseki underscored the weakness of the Tokugawa and led to the Meiji Restoration of 1868. Choshu leaders were important in the Meiji Restoration and served as the army elite until 1945. Shimonoseki also had a role in the conclusion of the Sino-Japanese War of 1894–1895, at the end of which China acceded to Japanese demands and signed the Treaty of Shimonoseki there on April 17, 1895. See also ANSEI COMMERCIAL TREATIES; DANNOURA, BATTLE OF; FISH AND FISHING INDUSTRY; HEIKE, THE TALE OF THE; KITA KYUSHU; MEIJI RESTORATION OF 1868; MINAMOTO CLAN; SHIPPING AND SHIPBUILDING; SINO-JAPANESE WAR OF 1894–1895; TAIRA CLAN; TOKUGAWA SHOGUNATE.

SHIMPA   See THEATER, MODERN.

SHIN BUDDHISM   See PURE LAND SECT OF BUDDHISM.

SHINGEKI   See THEATER, MODERN.

SHINGON SECT OF BUDDHISM   "True Word" sect of Buddhism, also known as the Shingon-darani sect, Daini-chi sect, Mandara sect, Yuga sect and Mikkyo (Esoteric Buddhism); an important sect of the Buddhist religion in Japan. The Shingon sect was founded in the ninth century A.D. by the Japanese monk Kukai (774–835; known posthumously as Kobo Daishi, or Great Teacher Kobo). Esoteric Buddhism, also known as Tantrism, originated around A.D. 600 in India, and spread through Tibet and Central Asia to China. It emphasized the secret transmission of its teachings, along with the ritual use of incantations and spells. In A.D. 804 Kukai traveled to China and became adept in Esoteric Buddhism. When he returned to Japan, he founded a Shingon Buddhist monastery named Kongobuji on Mount Koya near modern Osaka. Kukai taught that everything that exists is a manifestation of Dainichi, the Japanese name for the deity Vairocana, the cosmic or universal Buddha. A believer can realize oneness with Dainichi through the body, speech and mind.

A major Shingon practice is the recitation of spells or "true words" (*shingon* in Japanese; *mantras* in Sanskrit). The most famous *mantra* of Esoteric Buddhism is a phrase in the Tibetan language, *Om mani padme hum*, meaning "The jewel is in the lotus." While chanting, the believer makes prescribed gestures or poses with the hands, known as *mudras*. Visual representations of reality or diagrams of the cosmos, known as *mandalas*, are also employed in Shingon rituals. *Mandalas* portray Dainichi in the center, surrounded by other Buddhist deities in hierarchical order. A *mandala* can be a temporary drawing on the ground, or a carving or painting on a wall or a hanging scroll. Sacred objects such as the lotus flower and the *vajra*, or symbolic thunderbolt, are also handled during Shingon rituals. Its secret rituals, hierarchical teachings and symbolic art made

Shingon Buddhism the most popular religion among the Japanese aristocracy during the Heian Era (794–1185). There was much rivalry between Shingon and Tendai, the other major sect of Buddhism in Heian Japan. Kukai wrote Dainichi's name with the same Chinese characters (kanji) as "great sun," which led Japanese to identify him with the Sun Goddess, Amaterasu o Mikami, the supreme deity of Shinto, the indigenous Japanese religion. In medieval Japan, other Shinto deities became identified with Buddhist deities, in a system developed by Shingon known as Shugendo. Kukai systematized Shingon beliefs in his numerous writings, many of which have been translated into English. These beliefs have not changed in Japan since Kukai's time. However, Kukai's disciples divided the sect into two major branches, Old (kogi) and New (shingi) Shingon, which have been further subdivided into 47 subsects. Today there are more than 12,000 Shingon temples in Japan and 12 million members of the sect. See also BUDDHISM; CHINA AND JAPAN; KONGOBUJI; KOYA, MOUNT; KUKAI; LOTUS; TENDAI SECT OF BUDDHISM.

SHINJUKU A district of Tokyo that has the largest railroad station and transfer point in Japan. More than 2 million commuters and shoppers a day pass through Shinjuku Station, using nine railroad and subway lines and numerous bus routes. The station has a large complex of shops and restaurants both above and underground. The area west of the station is filled with high-rise office buildings and luxury hotels. The eastern side is a busy shopping area during the day and a lively entertainment district at night. Shinjuku was a country village surrounded by rice paddies when the station was originally built in the 1880s. The district soon provided nightlife and lodgings for travelers. While most of Tokyo was destroyed by the Great Kanto Earthquake of 1923, Shinjuku was spared and grew rapidly. The current station building was opened in May 1964. Shinjuku Imperial Gardens (Shinjuku Gyoen Kokuritsu Koen) is a 144.5-acre park containing Japanese and European-style gardens and a tropical greenhouse. The grounds, once belonging to a family of feudal lords named Naito, were turned over to the imperial household of Emperor Meiji in 1872, and modeled on the style of European parks in 1906. After World War II the grounds were opened to the public. Shinjuku Imperial Gardens are famous for cherry blossoms in the spring and chrysanthemums in autumn. The Japanese prime minister hosts a cherry blossom-viewing party here every April for Japanese and foreign dignitaries. South of the gardens is the beautiful National Noh Theater (Kokuritsu Nohgaku-do). See also CHERRY BLOSSOM; CHRYSANTHEMUM; EARTHQUAKES; PRIME MINISTER.

SHINKANSEN See BULLET TRAIN; RAILROADS.

SHINO WARE (shino-yaki) A type of pottery made from clay with a low iron content that turns a pale cream color when fired. Shino ware is covered with a thick white glaze of feldspar. There are several types of Shino ware. Red Shino is made by applying glaze thinly; the glaze becomes semitransparent when fired and the thinnest areas are stained red (hi-iro, "fire color" or koge, "scorch"). E Shino ("picture" Shino), is painted with simple iron oxide decorations such as grasses or birds before the glaze is applied. Nezumi Shino ("gray" Shino) is covered with a dark brown iron-oxide slip in which decorations are incised, after which it is covered with thick feldspar glazes. Rough, asymmetrical Shino tea bowls (chawan) and other utensils for the tea ceremony have been highly valued by tea masters. Shino ware belongs to the style of pottery known as Mino ware (mino-yaki) produced in Mino Province (modern Gifu Prefecture) on central Honshu Island. Mino ware was associated with Seto ware, made in the major pottery center of Seto in the neighboring province of Owari (modern Aichi Prefecture). During the Azuchi-Momoyama Era (1568–1600), the great warlords and tea patrons Oda Nobunaga (1534–1582) and Toyotomi Hideyoshi (1536–1598) stimulated production of certain Mino styles for tea utensils, especially Shino ware, Oribe ware and wares with a type of brown glaze introduced from China known as temmoku. Production of Shino ware was revived in the 20th century by the potter Arakawa Toyozo. He found the old Mino kiln sites in 1930 and was named a Living National Treasure by the Japanese government in 1955. See also AZUCHI-MOMOYAMA ERA; ODA NOBUNAGA; ORIBE WARE; POTTERY; SETO WARE; TEA CEREMONY; TEMMOKU; TOYOTOMI HIDEYOSHI.

SHINOBAZU PON See BENTEN; BLOWFISH; UENO.

SHINRAN (1173–1263) Founder of the True Pure Land (Jodo Shin) Sect of Pure Land (Jodo) Buddhism. The Pure Land sect, which became a mass movement in 12th-century Japan, is dedicated to the Buddhist deity Amida. He is believed to have made an "Original Vow" to save all suffering beings, and anyone who calls on his name is thought to enjoy rebirth in Amida's heavenly Pure Land. Believers recite the nembutsu, an invocation that is short for Namu Amida Butsu, "I put my faith in Amida Buddha."

Shinran became a Tendai Buddhist monk at Enryakuji on Mount Hiei, outside the capital city of Kyoto, in 1181 when he was eight years old. In 1201 he became a follower of Honen (1133–1212), who established Pure Land Buddhism as a separate sect. Honen was exiled due to opposition to his teaching, and Shinran was also exiled from 1207–1212. Shinran, perhaps obeying Honen's command, was the first Buddhist priest in Japan to break the vow of celibacy and take a wife, setting a precedent for all Japanese Buddhist sects. Shinran identified with ordinary people and wanted to offer them salvation through faith in Amida. He went so far as to claim that it was not necessary to keep repeating the nembutsu, as Honen taught, because nothing a person does is able to bring him salvation. Shinran taught that if one truly has faith in the compassionate saving grace of Amida, a single sincere invocation of Amida's name would be enough to bring salvation. After Shinran's death, his followers formally organized the True Pure Land Sect, which has become one of the wealthiest and most widespread sects in Japan. See also AMIDA; BUDDHISM; HONEN; PURE LAND SECT OF BUDDHISM.

SHINTO The indigenous religion of Japan with deep traditional ties to Japanese values and history. The term *Shinto*, the "Way of the Gods" *(kami)*, was applied to collective religious beliefs and rituals in Japan in the sixth century A.D., to differentiate them from the organized religion of Buddhism (called *Butsudo*, the "Way of the Buddha," in Japanese), which was introduced through China from India at that time.

Shinto is centered on the belief that *kami* (meaning "upper" or "above," rather than "transcendent") are all-pervasive and inhabit mountains, trees, rocks and streams, as well as living beings. There are numerous *kami*, which are associated with the local communities that worship them. Shinto shrines are built on sites where *kami* are believed to be manifest and house sacred objects that embody *kami*. Shrine buildings are constructed from plain wood with thatched roofs, in a simple style that harmonizes with their natural surroundings. They are often surrounded by groves of trees.

Shinto has no religious scriptures and no concept of sin or ethics, but is concerned with pollution or defilement, which can be removed by acts of purification *(harai* or *harae)*. Bathing in water *(misogi)* or the symbolic sprinkling of water by a priest waving a wand of white paper strips *(gohei)* is the primary means of Shinto purification.

Shinto creation legends were recorded in the official eighth-century chronicles *Kojiki* and *Nihon Shoki* to legitimize the authority of imperial rule by the Yamato court. The Japanese islands were supposedly created by brother and sister *kami*, Izanagi and Izanami. The emperor is traditionally believed to be the descendant of Izanagi's daughter, the Sun Goddess Amaterasu o Mikami, who gave her grandson Ninigi no Mikoto three sacred treasures, a mirror, sword and curved jewels *(magatama)*, when she sent him to rule the islands. These treasures are known as the imperial regalia. Ise, the central Shinto shrine, houses the mirror of Amaterasu. During the eighth century, the Yamato imperial court organized Shinto shrines and the performance of national religious ceremonies to extend its authority. Since that time the emperor has functioned as a mediator between the Japanese people and the *kami* world.

Shinto is especially concerned with the cultivation of rice, and rice planting and harvest ceremonies have always been major festival times in Japan. Many other festivals *(matsuri)* are held at shrines each year, the most important being the New Year Festival.

Shinto is a positive force in Japanese spirituality, usually associated with auspicious occasions. Children are taken to shrines to be blessed shortly after birth and at the ages of three, five and seven for the Seven-Five-Three Festival held on November 15th. Marriages are frequently held at Shinto shrines. Japanese visit shrines at other important times in their lives when they wish to gain the power of the *kami*, and they purchase amulets and talismans at shrines to help attain their wishes. During festival processions, sacred objects embodying *kami* are carried in palanquins known as *mikoshi*. Families traditionally have Shinto altars *(kamidana,* "god shelf") in their homes.

Shinto and Buddhism, both major religious forces in Japanese history, became intertwined in various ways. A theory developed, known as *honji suijaku*, which regarded Shinto *kami* as specific manifestations of universal Buddhist deities. Buddhist temples incorporated features of Shinto shrine architecture, and shrines and temples were even constructed in the same compounds.

Following the Meiji Restoration of 1868, the Japanese government established State Shinto as a means of using the Shinto faith to instil nationalistic fervor. State Shinto, an ideology based on belief in the divinity of the emperor and the notion of *Kokutai*, or Japanese "national essence," was abolished following World War II, when the emperor also renounced his divine status. However, Sect or Shrine Shinto still plays an important role in Japanese life. See also ALTARS IN HOMES; AMATERASU O MIKAMI; AMULETS; BATH; BUDDHISM; EMPEROR; FESTIVALS; IMPERIAL REGALIA; ISE SHRINE; KAMI; KOJIKI; NEW YEAR FESTIVAL; NIHON SHOKI; PALANQUIN, SACRED; PRIESTS AND PRIESTESSES, SHINTO; PURIFICATION; RICE PLANTING AND HARVESTING; FESTIVALS; SHRINES, SHINTO; STATE SHINTO; TALISMANS; WATER.

SHIPPING AND SHIPBUILDING Because Japan is an archipelago of several thousand mountainous islands, the shipping industry has been important since ancient times. The ancient Japanese learned shipbuilding techniques from the Korean kingdom of Silla. Later shipbuilding was influenced by Japan's 20 diplomatic missions to China between A.D. 600 and A.D. 894, and 17 more from about 1401 to 1547. Western shipbuilding techniques were introduced into Japan in the 16th century by the Portuguese, Spanish and Dutch, and by William Adams (1564–1620), an English navigator who settled in Japan.

Japanese merchants had carried on an active foreign trade with China, as early as the Heian Era (794–1185), and with Southeast Asia and Western nations in the 15th and 16th centuries, until the early 17th century, when the Tokugawa Shogunate (1603–1867) closed Japan to foreign trade, except for limited trade with the Dutch and Chinese at the southern port of Nagasaki. During this period, the Japanese were forbidden to build ocean-going ships, although large coastal cargo ships were used to transport rice and other goods throughout the country. A well-traveled route extended from ports on the Sea of Japan (western) coast around Honshu Island via the Seto Inland Sea to the ports of Osaka and Edo (modern Tokyo-Yokohama).

Modern steamships were first brought to Japan in 1853–1854 by U.S. Commodore Matthew C. Perry, who forcibly opened the country to foreign trade. At this time, the shogunate built several shipyards and removed the restriction on ocean-going vessels. A modern shipbuilding industry developed after the Meiji Restoration of 1868, when the government pursued a policy of industrialization and modernization, and organized a modern navy. The government designated shipbuilding a priority industry and invested in several shipyards, which it later sold to private companies. Western experts on steel and shipbuilding were brought to Japan, and schools for shipbuilding engineering were established. In fact, the shipping and shipbuilding industries received about three-quarters of all Japanese government subsidies between 1897 and 1903. The Japanese merchant fleet tripled in size between 1896 and 1913. The Imperial Japanese Navy also expanded greatly in the 20th century and proved Japan to be a world naval power by destroying the Russian Baltic fleet in the Russo-Japanese War (1904–1905).

During World War I, Japan became the world's third-greatest ship producer and exported ships to England, the United States and France. The industry became depressed in the 1920s, but rising militarism in the 1930s spurred Japan to become the world's second-ranking ship producer by 1937.

The Imperial Japanese Navy and merchant marine fleet were destroyed during World War II, and after the war, the Japanese government established a policy of planned shipbuilding (keikaku zosen). The Ministry of International Trade and Industry (MITI) encouraged industrial growth by favoring shipbuilding and other heavy industries, and in the 1950s Japan became the world's largest shipbuilding nation. New welding and assembly technologies were utilized and shipyards were automated to increase production. Because of its reliance on imported oil and raw materials and competition from Taiwan and South Korea, Japanese shipbuilding declined somewhat after the Oil Crisis of 1973. However, Japan is still a major shipbuilding nation. In the early 1980s, vessels totalled around 3.5% of Japan's exports, and nearly two-thirds of the ships it produced were exported. The largest Japanese shipbuilders have been Mitsubishi Heavy Industries, Ltd.; Mitsui Engineering & Shipbuilding Co., Ltd.; Kawasaki Heavy Industries, Ltd.; Ishikawajima-Harima Heavy Industries Co., Ltd.; and Hitachi Zosen Corporation.

Shipping is a major industry because the Japanese economy relies heavily on exports and imports. Japan Line, Ltd. merged in 1988 with Yamashita-Shinnihon Steamship Co., Ltd., to form Nippon Liner System, Ltd. In 1989 they formed Navix Line, Ltd., Japan's fourth-largest shipping line. Kawasaki Kisen Kaisha, Ltd., known abroad as the K Line, is the leading Japanese ocean freight carrier. Nippon Yusen K.K., known as NYK, and Mitsui OSK Lines, Ltd. are the two largest lines. Kawasaki Kisen Kaisha, Ltd. is another important shipping line. In FY 1989 the four largest shipping companies earned profits of about $223.3 million, after suffering losses in FY 1986 and 1987 and earning a profit of $130 million in 1988. The largest Japanese seaports are Yokohama-Tokyo and Kobe-Osaka. Fishing is also an important Japanese industry, and ferries are a common means of transportation among the Japanese islands. See also ADAMS, WILL; EXPORTS AND IMPORTS; FERRIES; FISH AND FISHING INDUSTRY; IMPERIAL JAPANESE ARMY AND NAVY; KOBE; MITSUBISHI; MITSUI; YOKOHAMA.

SHISEIDO CO., LTD. The leading Japanese manufacturer of cosmetics and soap. Shiseido was founded in Tokyo in 1872 as a Western-style pharmacy. Five years later it began selling cosmetics. The company is famous for its high level of research and development for skin care and cosmetic products. Corporate laboratories are located in Yokohama, and headquarters are in Tokyo. Shiseido's beautifully packaged products are sold in more than 20 countries under such names as Murasaki, Zen, Inoui, Moisture, and Mist. A new Shiseido "face" is created each year by Serge Lutens, a French makeup designer. The American subsidiary, established in 1965 as Shiseido Cosmetics (America) Ltd. has seen sales of its products recently grow by more than 30% annually. In 1968 Shiseido established a second overseas subsidiary in Italy. The company also has manufacturing plants in several countries. Shiseido's domestic marketing system has a total of 25,000 chain stores throughout Japan under 98 sales companies. See also MAKEUP.

SHISHI See LION.

SHITAMACHI Literally, "downtown"; the term for the traditional commercial district of an older Japanese city, especially Edo (modern Tokyo). Shitamachi specifically refers to the districts "below" a castle where merchants (shonin) and craftsmen (shokunin) resided. They ran small businesses or shops from their homes. The merchant and artisan classes were kept separate from the samurai, who controlled Japan for 700 years from the Kamakura Shogunate (1192–1333) until the Meiji Restoration of 1868. Urban merchants and craftsmen, collectively known as chonin, or townspeople, developed their own popular culture and social customs. Some of these are still preserved in a few close-knit old neighborhoods that fall in the category of shitamachi, such as Asakusa and Ueno in Tokyo. Shitamachi culture flourished during the Edo Era (1600–1868), especially in the government-licensed pleasure quarters, such as Yoshiwara and Asakusa in Tokyo, Shimabara and Gion in Kyoto, and Dotombori and Shimmachi in Osaka. Many types of art and entertainment now considered traditionally Japanese arose there, including Bunraku (puppet theater), Kabuki (traditional theater), rakugo (storytelling), ukiyo-e (woodblock prints), and geisha, who play a stringed instrument called the shamisen. Residents of shitamachi have always been lively, outgoing, fashionable (iki, "chic") and knowledgeable about the arts. The unique qualities of shitamachi have been lessened in the 20th century by education and by government policies that have made the Japanese more homogeneous. Much of Tokyo's shitamachi was destroyed by the Great Kanto Earthquake of 1923 and by bombing during World War II and subsequently rebuilt. Yet many members of the middle class still hold to the old values and close social relationships identified with shitamachi that are described in the book Low City, High City: Tokyo from Edo to the Earthquake 1867–1923 (1983) by Edward Seidensticker. The Shitamachi Museum in Ueno Park exhibits items related to Tokyo's old "downtown." See also ASAKUSA; BUNRAKU; CASTLES; CITIES; EDO ERA; GEISHA; GION; KABUKI; KYOTO; OSAKA; SAMURAI; SHAMISEN; STORYTELLING; TOKYO; UENO; WOODBLOCK PRINTS; YOSHIWARA.

SHO A wind instrument played in traditional orchestras that perform ancient ritualistic Japanese court music, or gagaku. This type of orchestra was introduced into Japan from China during the Nara Era (710–794). The *sho* is related to traditional mouth organs played in various Asian countries. In China it is called the *sheng*. The Japanese *sho* has a small lacquered wood base in the shape of a cup. Seventeen thin bamboo tubes or pipes of different lengths rise from the base and are bound together in a cluster. The musician blows air into a mouthpiece on the side of the base. The air vibrates small pieces of metal inside the pipes, and single notes and chords are played by closing finger-holes on various pipes. The continuous sound produced by the *sho* is simple yet mysterious. It is sometimes played for rituals connected with shrines of Shinto, the native Japanese religion. See also GAGAKU; SHINTO.

SHOCHIKU CO., LTD. See MOVIES; TAKARAZUKA OPERA COMPANY.

SHOCHU CONSPIRACY See GO-DAIGO, EMPEROR; KAMAKURA SHOGUNATE.

SHODO See CALLIGRAPHY.

SHOES See FOOTWEAR.

SHOFUKUJI TEMPLE See EISAI; FUKUOKA; ZEN SECT OF BUDDHISM.

SHOGI A board game similar to chess. Two players use 20 pieces each on a square wooden board that is marked into a grid of 81 squares. The pieces are also made of wood and have an elongated five-sided shape. Chinese calligraphic characters are written on the pieces to identify them. The main piece is the king (*osho*). However, since an emperor once forbade the use of two kings on the same board, the less skilled player uses a "jewel" (*gyokusho*) in place of a king (the character for jewel is written the same as that for king but with one additional brush stroke). The king and the jewel are both moved one square in any direction, the same as a king in chess. Other pieces include a rook (*hisha*), a bishop (*kakugyo*), two gold generals (*kinsho*), two silver generals (*ginsho*), two knights (*keima*), two lancers (*kyosha*) and nine pawns (*fuhyo*) on each side. Each of these pieces is moved around the board according to rules and can capture the opponent's pieces. A player can also put captured pieces into play on his own side. If a piece is moved into the opponents' territory (the first three rows of squares on the opponent's side), that piece can be "promoted," that is, moved like a piece of higher rank. A promoted piece is called a *narigoma*. Rooks can be moved any distance forward or sideways. Bishops can be moved any distance diagonally. Gold generals are moved one square in any direction except diagonally backward, and silver generals move one square in any direction except backward or sideways. Knights move forward to either of the two squares to the left or right of the two squares in front of them. Lancers move to any square forward but cannot go backward. Pawns move forward one square at a time. As in chess, the goal of *shogi* is to checkmate the king or jewel of the opponent.

Shogi derives from an ancient Indian game brought to Japan through China, where it was called *xiang qi* or *hsiang-ch'i*; *shogi* is the Japanese pronunciation of this word. Japanese diplomats who went to China during the Nara Era (710–794) may have brought a form of the game back with them. A number of versions were played by members of the nobility in the Heian Era (794–1185). *Shogi* was given its current form during the Muromachi Era (1333–1568). The Tokugawa Shogunate (1603–1867) took an interest in the game and formed an office for *shogi* (and another board game called *go*), assigned to the commissioner of shrines and temples. It was first headed by a monk named Hon'imbo Sansa and then by Ohashi Sokei (1555–1623), who was the first player to be designated "master" (*meijin*). His son Soko (1613–1660) drew up the standardized rules that are still followed by *shogi* players. The system for ranking players was also developed, and the highest rank of *meijin* was made hereditary. *Shogi* lost its official organization during the Meiji Era (1868–1912). New associations were formed in 1924 and 1936, and in 1947 the Japan Shogi Federation (Nihon Shogi Remmei) was founded. This federation supports more than 100 professional players, administers their ranking system, trains and licenses new professionals, and publishes the magazines *Shogi World* (*Shogi sekai*) and *Shogi Magazine* (*Shogi Magajin*). There are nine levels (*dan*), below which are several classes (*kyu*). The federation holds tournaments, which are sponsored by Japanese newspapers; some are even shown on television. Amateurs are also licensed by the federation up to the sixth level and participate in amateur competitions, many of which are held by schools and places of employment. About 20,000 members belong to the 568 chapters of the Japan Shogi Federation in Japan and abroad. See also GAMES; GO; NEWSPAPERS; WRITING, JAPANESE.

SHOGUN An abbreviation of the title *seii tai shogun*, or "barbarian-subduing generalissimo." The title of shogun was formally conferred by the Japanese imperial court upon military commanders or dictators. It was first used by the Nara court (Nara Era, 710–794) for government officials ordered to lead armies against nomadic tribes living in northeast Honshu Island. After the tribes were subdued in the eighth century, the title of shogun was not used until the Taira-Minamoto War (1180–1185) between the rival Taira (or Heike) and Minamoto (or Genji) clans. When Minamoto no Yoshinaka routed Taira forces from the imperial capital of Kyoto he gave himself the title *seii tai shogun*. Yoshinaka was killed, but his cousin Minamoto no Yoritomo (1147–1199) finally defeated the Taira, established a military government in Kamakura on east central Honshu Island, and had the emperor confer on him the title shogun in 1192. The government he founded is known as the Kamakura Shogunate after the town of Kamakura, where it was centered.

Shogunate is the usual English translation of the Japanese term *bakufu*, literally "tent government." It is applied to three military governments that controlled Japan from the late 12th through late 19th centuries: the Kamakura Shogunate (1192–1333), the Ashikaga Shogunate (also known as the Muromachi Shogunate; 1338–1573), and the Tokugawa Shogunate (1603–1867). Shoguns who ruled each of these governments claimed to be distant descendants of the original Minamoto clan and the office of shogun became hereditary. In each case, the shogun did not attempt to do away with the imperial court, but used the court to legitimize his power. Moreover, the shoguns never functioned as absolute military dictators who ruled all of Japan. Many regions were controlled by independent *daimyo*, or "great lords," with whom the shoguns were forced to share power. The term shogun became well known in the Western world in the early 1980s due to James Clavell's popular novel about 16th-century Japan, *Shogun* (1975), which was made into as television mini-series. See also ASHIKAGA SHOGUNATE; BAKUFU; DAIMYO; KAMAKURA SHOGUNATE, MINAMOTO CLAN, MINAMOTO NO YORITOMO; TOKUGAWA SHOGUNATE.

SHOGUN (Novel by James Clavell)   See ADAMS, WILLIAM; HOSOKAWA GRACIA; SHOGUN.

SHOIN STYLE OF ARCHITECTURE (*shoin-zukuri*)   A traditional style of residential architecture whose elements have been incorporated into contemporary traditional-style Japanese houses. The *shoin* style is characterized by open space, clean lines and rectangular shapes, and harmony between interior privacy and openness to nature. It evolved out of the *shinden-zukuri* style of architecture used in aristocratic mansions and residences of high-ranking Buddhist priests and samurai from the Heian Era (794–1185) through the 15th century.

The *shoin* style originally referred to the studies (*shoin*) of Buddhist priests. This type of room has a projection on its south side to give more light to the study. It contains a *tokonoma* (decorative alcove), staggered shelves (*chigaidana*), built-in desk (*shoin*) and decorative doors (*chodaigamae*). These four elements were arranged in a standardized design, and were often placed on a raised floor area known as a *jodan*. They were originally functional but later became quite decorative. The floors came to be completely covered with *tatami* (thick straw mats).

The *shoin* style was used in samurai mansions, guest halls of Buddhist temples and private quarters of Zen Buddhist abbots in the Azuchi-Momoyama (1568–1600) and Edo (1600–1868) eras. By the Edo Era, walls consisted of *shoji*, sliding wooden frames paneled with handmade paper that allowed more light to filter into the room, which were opened for viewing a well-trimmed landscape garden outside. In bad weather *shoji* were protected by sliding wooden rain doors (*amado*).

Shoin eventually became quite elegant and decorated with gold and multicolored paintings, carved wooden transoms, and other ornamental details, as can be seen at Nijo Castle in Kyoto. Here *shoin* are large, impressive reception areas. They have finished walls covered with paintings, hexagonal rails on the ceiling, and horizontal timbers (*nageshi*) that connect grooved square columns. *Sukiya-zukuri*, a simpler and less formal variation of the *shoin* style, came into use for rustic teahouses (*chashitsu*) during the Azuchi-Momoyama Era. Members of the urban merchant and artisan classes adapted this style during the Edo Era. It uses *shoin* elements such as the *tokonoma*, *tatami* and *shoji*, but is built on a smaller scale with natural materials and plain earthen walls. This style can be seen at Katsura Detached Palace in Kyoto. See GARDENS; KATSURA DETACHED PALACE; NIJO CASTLE; SHOJI; TATAMI; TEAHOUSE; TOKONOMA; WOODWORKING.

SHOJI   A sliding wooden frame partition with an open wood framework that has white handmade paper (*washi*) pasted on one side to make it translucent. The paper allows some light to filter through the screen but provides privacy. The *shoji*, usually used in front of windows or verandas, fits into a carved wooden track in the floor. The formal way to open or close a *shoji* is to kneel on the floor, place both hands on the frame below its center, and slide it quietly open or shut. A sliding wooden frame covered on both sides with thick, opaque paper, known as a *fusuma*, is used to divide rooms internally. See also HOMES AND HOUSING; PAPER, HANDMADE; SCREENS.

SHOJIN RYORI   See BUDDHISM; COOKING; TOFU.

SHOPPING   See ADVERTISING; AKIHABARA; DEPARTMENT STORES; DISTRIBUTION SYSTEM; GIFTS; GINZA; NOREN; SHINJUKU; SIGNBOARDS; WOMEN'S ASSOCIATIONS; WRAPPING.

SHOSOIN   The imperial storehouse at Todaiji (Great Eastern Temple) in Nara, the ancient capital of Japan, which contains about 10,000 art objects and other treasures from the Nara Era (710–794). Most of the objects were used to dedicate the enormous Daibutsu (bronze statue of the Buddha) installed at Todaiji in A.D. 752, or were given by the Empress Komyo in A.D. 756. The Shosoin is a large rectangular building in three sections that sits on 40 columns, each 8 feet above the ground. Completed in A.D. 761, it is made of logs of cypress wood (*hinoki*), which are criss-crossed to ventilate the interior and control humidity. As an imperial repository, the Shosoin and its treasures are managed by the Imperial Household Agency. In earlier times, the building was rarely opened, but at present a selection of its treasures, which have been remarkably well preserved, is displayed every October in the Nara National Museum. The Shosoin houses a wealth of objects imported from many Asian and European countries, as well as creations by Japanese artists. The collection includes textiles and clothing, books and other documents, glass and ceramic utensils and decorative items, paintings, swords, mirrors, screens, musical instruments, games, sculptures, lacquer ware, medicines, religious objects and masks used in *gigaku*, a classical dance form introduced into Japan and frequently performed at Buddhist temples during the Nara Era. See also BUDDHISM; DAIBUTSU; CYPRESS; IMPERIAL HOUSEHOLD AGENCY; NARA; NARA ERA; STOREHOUSE; TODAIJI.

SHOTOKU, PRINCE (Shotoku Taishi; 574–622)   A leader who served as regent during the reign of his aunt, Empress Suiko (554–628; r. 593–628) and became the architect of major government reforms in Japan based on concepts of centralized government introduced with Buddhism from China. Shotoku was made regent by the Soga clan, which became the most powerful faction in the Yamato court on western Honshu Island during the sixth century. As regent, Shotoku wielded political power on behalf of the imperial court. To weaken the powerful clans, he reorganized the government, initiating a system of ranking court members according to 12 cap ranks or levels of status. In A.D. 604 he issued the Seventeen-Article Constitution (Jushichijo no Kempo), literally a "splendid law," which was not a constitution in the modern sense but a statement of ethical principles by which the Yamato area was to be governed, based on Confucian ideology and Buddhist teachings. A follower of the Buddhist religion. Shotoku issued an imperial edict in A.D. 594 promoting Buddhism and erected many Buddhist temples in Japan. He established formal relations between Japan and China by sending a mission to China in A.D. 600. In A.D. 607 he sent a second mission, which carried a letter to the Chinese emperor referring to Japan as the "Land of the Rising Sun" (Nippon or Nihon) for the first time in history. China had always referred to Japan by the perjorative term Wa (Dwarf), but Shotoku's use of Nippon claimed equal status for Japan with China. In A.D. 602 Shotoku sent his brother Prince Kume (d. A.D. 603) on an unsuccessful military campaign to conquer the Korean kingdom of Silla. In A.D. 620 Shotoku also helped compile two official historical chronologies, Tennoku and Kokki, which were later destroyed. The term tenno, "Heavenly Sovereign," referred to the supposedly divine nature of the Japanese emperor.

Legends about the birth of Shotoku, whose given name was Prince Umayado, were recorded in the official chronology, Nihon Shoki (A.D. 720). As Prince Shotoku, he became a revered figure in Japanese history. Shotoku Taishi, the title applied to him, means "Crown Prince Virtuous Sage." See also BUDDHISM; CHINA AND JAPAN; EMPEROR; NIHON SHOKI; NIPPON; SEVENTEEN-ARTICLE CONSTITUTION; SOGA CLAN; SUIKO, EMPRESS; TEMPLES BUDDHIST; TENNO; YAMATO.

SHOWA ERA (1926–1989) The name of the 62-year reign of Emperor Hirohito (1901–1989), the 124th emperor of Japan in the traditional count, who reigned longer than any other emperor in Japanese history. Since his death on January 7, 1989, Hirohito has been known as Emperor Showa. The two written characters in the name Showa mean "Enlightened Peace." When Emperor Showa's father, Emperor Taisho (Emperor Yoshihito; 1879–1926, r. 1912–1926), became too ill to perform his imperial duties, Crown Prince Hirohito was appointed regent (sessho) for him in 1921. On Taisho's death in 1926, Hirohito became emperor in his own right.

During the Showa Era, Japan underwent many dramatic changes. An experiment in democracy following World War I gave way to Japanese militarism, which exploited the symbol of the emperor as divine to promote aggressive expansion in the Pacific region, culminating in the Sino-Japanese War of 1937–1945 and the Pacific Theater of World War II. At the end of the war, Emperor Hirohito accepted unconditional surrender and renounced the traditional be-

lief in his divinity. Devastated by the war, Japan was occupied by the Allied Power until 1952. The Occupation brought Japan a new constitution and many political, economic and social reforms. During thee postwar period, Japan rapidly grew into a global economic power, and Hirohito became a symbol of the newly democratic and prosperous country. However, his death caused the Japanese to engage in national debate about the events of the Showa Era and the role the emperor played in shaping them. Hirohito was succeeded as emperor by his eldest son, Akihito (b. 1933), whose reign name is Heisei, meaning "Achieving Peace" or "Peace and Concord." See also AKIHITO, EMPEROR; CONSTITUTION OF 1947; EMPEROR; HEISEI ERA; HIROHITO, EMPEROR; OCCUPATION OF JAPAN; TAISHO ERA; SURRENDER OF JAPAN; WORLD WAR II.

SHRIMP See SEAFOOD; TEMPURA.

SHRINES, SHINTO (jinja) Sacred sites where rituals are performed and prayers are offered to the kami (sacred spirits) of Shinto, the native Japanese religion. A Shinto shrine, the dwelling place for one or more kami, is an enclosed rectangular area entered through a large gateway known as a torii. The entrance is often guarded by a pair of stone animals sacred to the kami, such as dog-lions (komainu), deer, monkeys or foxes, to keep away evil spirits. Shimenawa, ropes of rice straw on which are hung bunches of straw and white zigzag-shaped pieces of paper, are suspended from torii at festival times to keep out impurity. Most shrines are located in places where kami manifest themselves in natural objects, such as a tree, a rock or a mountain, although they may also enshrine a defied ancestor (ujigami). Rural shrines are often concealed in dense groves of trees. A dirt or stone path ("the approach," sando) leads from the torii to the sanctuary. Worshippers symbolically purify themselves by rinsing their mouths and finger tips at a stone basin in an ablution pavilion (temizuya).

Most shrines came to have one sanctuary, which has

Izumo, a major shrine of Shinto, the indigenous Japanese religion. The shrine is built of wood in the most ancient style, dating back more than 1,500 years.

two parts: an inner compartment (honden), which houses the sacred symbol of the kami, called the "divine body" (shintai) or "august-spirit-substitute" (mitamashiro), such as a mirror or sword, and a worship hall (haiden) in front, where Shinto priests make offerings of food and other sacred objects. Shrines devoted to several kami may have a separate honden for the sacred symbol of each. Worshippers are not permitted to enter the honden or the haiden, and priests may enter them only on special occasions. Two swinging doors at the front of the honden protect the sacred symbol. They are always closed and locked except during special rituals, and a curtain of split bamboo or some other material is hung in front of the honden. Shrines may have auxiliary buildings, such as a place to prepare food offerings, a shrine office, a stage for sacred dances and a pavilion for offerings of talismans. Large shrines also have a ceremonial hall, a stable for sacred horses, a storehouse for the sacred palanquin (mikoshi) used to carry the kami in festival processions, a storehouse for shrine treasures and a residence hall for priests.

There are various ancient styles of shrine architecture, but all are very simple and natural. The sanctuary is constructed of plain cypress wood (hinoki) on poles above the ground, and has a roof thatched with cypress or miscanthus bark. The rafters of the roof cross at both ends of the ridge and continue upward for several feet. There is a large offering box where worshippers deposit money in front of the sanctuary. Some shrines have a bell above the box to which a rope is attached to summon the kami.

There are around 80,000 Shinto shrines in Japan, ranging from very small rural shrines to large compounds. The Grand Shrine of Ise is the most important Shinto shrine in Japan. Meiji Shrine and Yasukuni Shrine were constructed in Tokyo as centers for government-sponsored State Shinto. Many Japanese families have a small Shinto altar, known as a kamidana ("god shelf"), in their homes. See also ALTARS IN HOMES; CYPRESS; FESTIVALS; ISE SHRINE; KAMI; MEIJI SHRINE; PRIESTS AND PRIESTESSES, SHINTO; PURIFICATION; SHINTO; STATE SHINTO.

SHUBUN   See LANDSCAPE PAINTING.

SHUGAKUIN DETACHED PALACE   Also known as Shugakuin Imperial Villa; a retreat for the imperial family built in the 17th century in the former capital of Kyoto on western Honshu Island. Shugakuin Detached Palace was built as the retirement villa of Emperor Go-Mizunoo (1596–1680; r. 1611–1629) with the support of the Tokugawa Shogunate (1603–1867). Years after Go-Mizunoo abdicated the throne in 1629, he finally chose Shugakuin village in the foothills of Mount Hiei northeast of Kyoto as the site for his villa. He designed several pavilions, which were completed by 1659, along with upper and lower gardens on the hillside. A middle garden was added after Go-Mizunoo's death in 1680 when his daughter Akenomiya erected a convent on the grounds, known as the Rinkyuji. Over the next two centuries, Shugakuin Detached Palace

went through several cycles of neglect and restoration by various emperors, and in 1883 Emperor Meiji (1852–1912; r. 1868–1912) restored it to its current condition. In contrast to the renowned architecture of Katsura Detached Palace, also in Kyoto, Shugakuin is admired for its large, park-like gardens with ponds and waterfalls. The gardens are designed in the style known as "borrowed scenery" (shakkei) to incorporate views of hills in the distance, as well as the city of Kyoto. The Imperial Household Agency administers Shugakuin Detached Palace and admits a limited number of visitors, who must obtain permission in advance. See EMPEROR; GARDENS; IMPERIAL HOUSEHOLD AGENCY; KATSURA DETACHED PALACE, KYOTO; TOKUGAWA SHOGUNATE.

SHUNGA   "Spring pictures"; a general term for erotic paintings, prints and book illustrations. Today the preferred term for such pictures is higa, "secret pictures." The Japanese have always regarded sex as natural and enjoyable, and pictures of sexual activity have been preserved from as far back as the eighth century A.D. Shunga as an art form, however, came into being with the advent of scrolls called emakimono that are viewed horizontally. The earliest documented shunga scroll was The Phallic Contest (Yobutsu kurabe), supposedly by an abbot named Toba Sojo (1053–1140), which portrays a test of male sexual powers by ladies of the imperial court. The oldest surviving shunga scroll is The Catamites' Scroll (Chigo no soshi), dated A.D. 1321 and preserved in the Samboin temple of Daigoji, a Buddhist temple compound. It depicts homosexual activity by Buddhist monks. Shunga were a popular art form during the Edo Era (1600–1868), due to the widespread use of woodblock printing in the old capital of Kyoto and the new city of Edo (modern Tokyo). Shunga was associated with ukiyo-e, the woodblock prints that portray the "Floating World" (ukiyo) of the government-licensed pleasure quarters, such as the Yoshiwara in Edo. Printed shunga are considered to date from 1660, when the first surviving, dated shunga collection was published in Edo. An artist known as the Kambun Master was the first ukiyo-e artist who produced shunga in Edo. His student, Moronobu (d. 1694), created more than two dozen sets of shunga book illustrations during his career. Many other ukiyo-e artists worked in the shunga form. The pictures are fresh and almost innocent and even have a humorous quality.

In 1722 the Tokugawa Shogunate (1603–1867) forbade the artistic portrayal of sex, but this actually created an increased demand for nude pictures. One of the greatest ukiyo-e artists, Suzuki Harunobu (c. 1725–1770), produced a dozen collections of shunga prints. The acknowledged master of shunga was Utamaro (1753–1806); his first album of shunga prints, Pillow of Song (Uta makura; 1788), is regarded as his greatest erotic work. Hokusai (1760–1849) was another famous ukiyo-e artist who worked in the shunga form. The high point of shunga art came at the end of the 18th century. Later print artists continued to produce shunga but never created work as masterful as their predecessors. Some hand-painted shunga have also been preserved from the Edo Era. Shunga decreased during the Meiji Era (1868–

1912), and since then, due partly to government censorship, this form has had only a minor place in Japanese art. See also ERO ERA; HARUNOBU; HOKUSAI; MORONOBU; SCROLLS; TOKUGAWA SHOGUNATE; UTAMARO; WOODBLOCK PRINTS; YOSHIWARA.

SHURI See NAHA; OKINAWA ISLAND; RYUKYU ISLANDS.

SIDDHARTHA GAUTAMA See BUDDHISM.

SIGNATURES See SEALS AND SIGNATURES.

SIGNBOARDS *(kamban)* Large signs that have traditionally been hung outside Japanese shops and restaurants to advertise goods, food or services for sale. The use of signboards developed during the rise of an urban merchant culture during the Edo Era (1600–1868), when Japanese cities became crowded with rows of small shops. Owners advertised by hanging *noren* (short panelled curtains) in the doorways, displaying highly visible signboards, and hanging brightly colored lanterns at night. Starting in 1682, the Tokugawa Shogunate (1603–1867) frequently attempted to regulate the size and form of signboards. Billboards for Kabuki theatrical performances had to be written with a particular style of characters known as *kantei,* which is still used for Kabuki advertisements. Shop signs were creatively decorated with strong patterns and written characters. Puns, in which the Japanese delight, were often used. Signboards had to be seen from both directions on the street. They were often simple wooden rectangles, but they could also be realistic three-dimensional shapes. For example, a *geta* (raised sandal) maker would hang out a large wooden *geta,* or an umbrella maker an oversize umbrella. Signboards were carved by craftsmen with fine skill and great originality. Today old signboards are collected as folk art *(mingei).* Japanese merchants still like to decorate their shops or restaurants with eye-catching signs, such as a large red crab over the entrance to a seafood restaurant. See also CALLIGRAPHY; EDO ERA; LANTERNS; MINGEI; NOREN; RESTAURANTS; WOODWORKING.

SILK *(kinu)* A fabric woven from very fine yet strong threads made from the cocoons of larvae of silkworm moths *(kaiko).* Japanese silkworms have a breeding cycle of six months or one year and reproduce in large numbers. The silkworm larvae are fed mulberry leaves. The larvae then form white, yellow or pale green cocoons, which are spun into threads to make either raw silk or glossed silk.

Raw silk is made by leaving sericin, a natural, sticky substance found on the cocoon fibers, in the strands when they are twisted together to form the silk thread. The threads are woven into cloth, and then boiled in soap and water to remove the sericin. The most common type of raw silk in Japan is *chirimen,* a crinkly silk crepe. Glossed silk is woven from threads that have been dyed and boiled to remove the sericin before weaving. Woven patterns in stripes, plaids and *kasuri* (a tie-dye weaving technique) are popular, as is *Nishijin-ori,* a type of silk brocade traditionally woven in the Nishijin district of Kyoto and used for *obi* (sashes for kimono).

Techniques for breeding silkworms and spinning silk thread, known as sericulture, as well as techniques for spinning and weaving skill, were introduced to Japan from China and Korea by the mid-third century A.D. Mulberry bushes were also cultivated about this time for feeding the silkworms. Japanese already knew how to weave hemp *(asa),* mulberry *(kozo)* and other plant fibers into cloth. There are many ancient Japanese legends about sericulture and weaving. A Korean emperor supposedly sent gifts of woven silk to Japan c. A.D. 200. That emperor's son, Prince Yuzu, supposedly emigrated to Japan with several thousand refugees who were members of the Aya clan. They settled in the Yamato basin near what was later the city of Kyoto, and their village, Uzumasa, became the first center of Japanese silk production. Organized into government workshops, they produced two types of silk, *aya* (figured twill) and *nishiki* (silk woven in a multicolored design, sometimes called brocade). Silk was worn only by court aristocrats; the common people continued to wear cloth made from plant fibers. Commoners often used silk to pay taxes or tribute to the court.

From its introduction, sericulture became an important Japanese industry. It declined during the warfare of the feudal era (12th–16th centuries), but revived in the 16th century. Chinese-style silk-weaving techniques were introduced then, such as *kara-ori* (an ornate brocade), *kinran* and *ginran* (gold and silver brocade), *donsu* (damask), and *shusuu* (satin). The Tokugawa Shogunate (1603–1867) and the *daimyo* (provincial lords), patronized the silk industry. Member of the growing urban merchant class also became wealthy enough to wear silk. During the seclusion of Japan from 1639 to the mid-19th century, the native Japanese silk industry was stimulated by rising demand and by restrictions on silk imports. After Japan was opened to the West, silk was exported to foreign countries beginning in 1859 through the treaty port of Yokohama. The Meiji government (1868–1912) encouraged the export of raw silk and made Japan the leading silk producer and exporter in the early 20th century. World War II disrupted the Japanese silk industry, but it has since revived. Now, however, Japan imports silk from China to meet its domestic needs. See also AYA CLAN; CLOTHING; HEMP; KASURI; KIMONO; MULBERRY BUSH; NISHIJIN; OBI; TEXTILES; YUZEN DYEING.

SILVER PAVILION See GINKAKUJI.

SINGING There are many types of singing in Japan, some of which date back to ancient times. *Kagura uta* are songs performed for ceremonial dances *(kagura)* of Shinto, the indigenous Japanese religion. They comprise a body of ancient court songs in the court orchestra style that is known as *gagaku,* and are accompanied by *gagaku* instruments. The standard modern repertory for *kagura uta* contains about 88 numbers. Numerous chants are sung in the Buddhist religion, introduced to Japan in the sixth century A.D. In addition, each region of Japan has its own folk

An artist hand-painting silk fabric with floral motifs, a common element of Japanese design.

songs *(minyo)*, which are frequently sung at festivals, such as the rice planting festival. The Japan Broadcasting Corporation sponsors a *minyo* competition each year.

Several types of singing developed in the urban popular culture of the Edo Era (1600–1868). *Nagauta*, "long songs," became the most important type of music to accompany dances in the Kabuki theater by the end of the 18th century. These songs are accompanied by a banjo-like instrument called the *shamisen*, drums and flutes. *Nagauta* for concert performances developed in the 19th century. The total repertory of dance and concert songs includes more than 100 numbers. *Kouta*, "short songs," are a type of popular song accompanied by the *shamisen*. Also known as Edo *kouta*, they are performed mainly by geisha. The songs are sung in a high pitch and are too fast for dancing.

Jiuta, "local songs," originated in the 17th century in the Kyoto-Osaka regions. They are quiet and elegant and are accompanied by the *shamisen*, the zither-like *koto*, and a vertical bamboo flute called a *shakuhachi*. Another style of restrained, elegant singing developed for the traditional Noh drama, which originated in the 14th century. *Ryukoka* are popular urban songs, which date back to ancient times. During the Edo Era, *yose*, or musical recitation, became popular. *Joruri* is a style of singing narration that became associated with the Bunraku puppet theater. Songs composed when Japan was modernizing during the Meiji Era (1868–1912) were influenced by Western music. Many popular songs were recorded during the 1920s and 1930s. They often had sad themes such as loneliness and the parting of lovers. Since World War II, Japanese popular music has followed Western popular styles. Many television shows feature singing contests. *Karaoke*, "empty orchestra," in which individuals take turns singing to pre-recorded music, is very popular, especially in bars. See also BUDDHISM;

BUNRAKU; DRUMS; EDO ERA; FESTIVALS; FLUTES; FOLK SONGS; GAGAKU; GEISHA; JAPAN BROADCASTING CORPORATION; KABUKI; KAGURA; KARAOKE; NOH DRAMA; SHAKUHACHI; SHAMISEN; SHINTO.

SINO-JAPANESE WAR OF 1894–1895

A war between Japan and China for control of Korea. The newly organized Japanese Imperial Army, led by Yamagata Aritomo (1838–1922), believed that the security of Japan depended on Japanese control over Korea, and the Meiji government (1868–1912) wanted to protect the rights of Japanese business and fishing rights in Korea. China sent troops into Korea when an anti-Japanese riot broke out in Seoul in 1882. In 1884 the Japanese supported a coup d'etat in Korea, and the Korean queen Min asked Chinese troops to come to her aid. Japanese military leaders planned to go to war with China that year, but they needed another 10 years to develop an adequate army and navy and to overcome domestic opposition to the war. Meanwhile, military expansion in Asia by France, Great Britain and Russia in the 1880s convinced the Japanese that they could take similar actions in Korea. In 1893 the Korean ruling dynasty, threatened by the Tonghak Rebellion, asked China to send more troops into the country. Japan responded by sending in troops as well, and then declaring war on China on August 1, 1894. China had a large, modern navy, but its army lacked training and leadership. Japan easily defeated Chinese land and naval forces, to the amazement of Western nations, in the battles of P'yongyang, Yalu river and Weihaiwei. China and Japan signed the Treaty of Shimonoseki on April 17, 1895. The terms, which exacted financial reparations from China, made Japan the dominant nation in Asia and gave it the status of an international imperialist power. Japan also gained control of Korea, the strategically important base of Port Arthur (modern Lushun), and Formosa (modern Taiwan). Japan acquired the Liaodong (Liaotung) Peninsula on the southern tip of Manchuria, but was soon forced to return it to China due to a tripartite intervention by Russia, France and Germany. These three powers then forced the Japanese out of Port Arthur, and Russia took control of Port Arthur and the Liaodong Peninsula. Hostility between Japan and Russia over control of Korea and Manchuria increased, until Japan declared war against Russia in 1904 (Russo-Japanese War of 1904–1905). See also CHINA AND JAPAN; KOREA AND JAPAN; MEIJI RESTORATION OF 1868; RUSSO-JAPANESE WAR; YAMAGATA ARITOMO.

SINO-JAPANESE WAR OF 1937–1945 (Nitchu Senso)

A term used in Japan to identify that aspect of World War II in which Japanese troops fought on the Chinese mainland against two groups of Chinese forces, the Nationalist army led by Chiang Kai-shek and the Communist army led by by Mao Zedong (Mao Tse-tung). The second half of this war coincided with the war fought between Japan and the Allied Powers in the Pacific, referred to as the Greater East Asia War by some Japanese. In the West, the term World War II is commonly used to include all theaters of Japanese military operations between 1937 and 1945.

The Sino-Japanese War of 1937–1945 represents the cul-mination of Japanese aggression in China, which began with Japan's 1931 invasion of Manchuria and the setting up of a puppet state there known as Manchukuo. Japanese forces expanded into China, causing the Nationalist and Communist forces to suspend their civil war and unite in a war of resistance against Japan. The war technically began when Japanese and Chinese troops exchanged shots at Luguoqiao (Lukouchiao; known as Marco Polo Bridge in English). Chinese cities quickly fell to the Japanese, and the capture of Nanjing (Nanking), during which tens of thousands of Chinese civilians were tortured, raped and murdered, has become notorious as the "Rape of Nanjing." Chinese troops retreated into the interior to use guerrilla tactics against the Japanese forces.

After the United States declared war on Japan following the attack on Pearl Harbor, on December 7, 1941, America and Britain supported China, but Chinese troops provided only weak resistance against the Japanese. Many defected to the collaborationist provisional government, headed by Wang Kemin (Wang K'o-min). By the end of 1944, Japan had taken control of eight Chinese provinces. However, by this time Japan was succumbing to Allied victories in the Pacific islands and to bombing raids on the Japanese home islands.

The war between Japan and China finally ended when Japan surrendered to the Allies on August 15, 1945. Japan signed a peace treaty with the Republic of China (Taiwan) on April 29, 1952, at the end of the postwar Allied Occupation of Japan. But Japan was not able to negotiate a formal end to the war with the People's Republic of China until 1978, when the two countries ratified the China-Japan Peace and Friendship Treaty.

The Sino-Japanese War of 1937–1945 caused the deaths of at least 1,300,000 Chinese and 571,000 Japanese soldiers, as well as countless Chinese civilians, and the destruction of enormous amounts of Chinese farmland and other property. It also weakened the Nationalists and helped lead to their overthrow by the Communists under Mao Zedong in 1949. See also CHINA AND JAPAN; MANCHURIAN INCIDENT; OCCUPATION OF JAPAN; PEARL HARBOR, JAPANESE ATTACK ON; SURRENDER OF JAPAN; WORLD WAR II.

SIX OLD KILNS

See BIZEN WARE; POTTERY; SETO WARE; SHIGARAKI WARE; TAMBA WARE; TOKONAME WARE.

SNAKE (hebi)

The many species of snake found throughout Japan are generally not poisonous, except for the species mamushi, on all of the islands, and habu, on the southern island groups of Amami and Okinawa (Ryukyu Islands). The snake has traditionally been regarded as a god of the rice paddies where it can be found in the spring, and of the mountains, where it migrates in the autumn to hibernate. The ancient Japanese also believed that snakes were immortal because they shed their skins and grew new ones, like an eternal cycle of death and rebirth. Because snakes eat rats, they were also considered guardians of homes, and the species aodaisho was sometimes allowed to live in country homes for that reason. Snakes also came to have negative associations, such as the belief that they could sexually attack women. They also symbolize human passion. *Dojoji*, a famous play in the repertoires of Kabuki theater and Noh drama, tells the story of Kiyohime, a woman who fell in love with a young celibate priest. When he resisted her advances, her intense passion turned her into a hissing snake. The priest hid under a large bell, but the snake wrapped itself around the bell and melted it, killing the priest. The snake is used as a decorative motif for such objects as *netsuke* and sword guards; a snake design on the latter symbolizes the swordsman's ability to strike his opponent swiftly. The snake is one of the 12 animals in the traditional Japanese 12-year zodiac cycle. People born in the year of the snake are thought to be wise, lucky with money, passionate and good-looking, especially the women. See also AMAMI ISLANDS; KABUKI; NETSUKE; NOH DRAMA; RYUKYU ISLANDS; SWORD GUARD; ZODIAC.

SNOW (*yuki*) Although regions south of Tokyo receive little snowfall, a great deal of snow falls on the Japan Sea, or northwestern, side of Honshu Island and on Hokkaido Island to the north. Northwestern Honshu is referred to as snow country (*yukiguni*). Every February Sapporo, like other towns in northern Japan, holds a large snow festival, which is a popular tourist attraction. The custom of *yukimi*, or observing snow-covered landscapes while enjoying food and sake, was practiced by Japanese aristocrats in the Heian Era (794–1185) and taken up by the general population in the Edo Era (1600–1868). Snow viewing is a common subject in Japanese literature and art. See also CLIMATE OF JAPAN; HOKKAIDO ISLAND; SAKE; SAPPORO; SNOW COUNTRY; SNOW FESTIVALS.

SNOW COUNTRY (*yukiguni*) A popular name for the mountainous northern region of Honshu, the main Japanese island, which receives heavy snowfall in winter. Winter winds from Siberia and Mongolia pick up water as they cross the Sea of Japan, run into the mountains, and drop snow on Honshu's northwest coast. Snow country, a popular ski resort area, is dominated by three mountain ranges known collectively as the Japan Alps. *Snow Country* (*Yukiguni*; 1935–1948, translated 1956) is also the title of a novel by Japanese author and Nobel Prize winner Kawabata Yasunari (1899–1972). The book describes an affair between a man from Tokyo and a geisha in a mountain town in the snow country. See also CLIMATE OF JAPAN; GEOGRAPHY OF JAPAN; JAPAN ALPS; KAWABATA YASUNARI; SNOW.

SNOW FESTIVALS (*yuki matsuri*) Winter festivals held in northern areas of Japan that have heavy snowfalls. The largest and best-known snow festival is held every February in Sapporo, capital of the northernmost island of Hokkaido. Two million tourists attend this festival each year. The Sapporo Snow Festival features a competition of about 150 statues, buildings and other imaginative forms carved from snow, much of which has to be brought by trucks from mountains outside the city. Elaborate ice carvings are also displayed. Different from this is a religious snow festival held January 14–15 at Izu Shinto Shrine in Anan,

A huge sculpture made of ice for the Snow Festival held in February in Sapporo, capital of the northern island of Hokkaido. Sapporo was the site of the 1972 Winter Olympic Games.

Nagano Prefecture, at which an offering of snow is made to the gods because snow is believed to bring a good harvest in the coming year. Many places in northern Japan hold *kamakura* festivals for children during the winter. A *kamakura* is a cave made by building a mound of snow about 7 feet in diameter and hollowing out the middle. A small altar (*kamidana*) dedicated to the God of Water (*Suijin-sama*) is placed inside the cave. Children sit around a hibachi inside the caves and cook and eat *mochi* (small cakes made of glutinous rice) and drink a sweetened rice wine called *amazake*. Such a festival is held February 15–17 in Yokote-shi in Akita Prefecture. Candy figures of lucky cranes, tortoises and dogs are sold during the festival. The practice of snow viewing (*yukimi*) while enjoying food and sake dates back to ancient time in Japan, as recorded in chronicles from the Nara Era (710–794). During the Heian Era (794–1185), members of the imperial court and the aristocracy enjoyed such occasions, often making journeys to view snow. Snow viewing has also been a popular theme in Japanese literature. In the Edo Era (1600–1868), the general population also began to enjoy this custom. See also CRANE; DOG; FESTIVALS; HIBACHI; HOKKAIDO; MOCHI; SAKE; SAPPORO; SHINTO; SNOW; SNOW COUNTRY; TORTOISE.

SOAMI (c. 1455–1525) Also known as Shinso; a painter and connoisseur who served as curator of the art collection owned by Ashikaga Yoshimasa (1436–1490), the eighth shogun of the Ashikaga Shogunate (1338–1573). This position had also been held by Soami's father, Noami (1397–1491), and his father, Geiami (1431–1485). The "three Amis" set the critical standards for art appreciation in Japan at that time. Curatorial duties included the mounting, preservation, labeling and exhibiting of paintings in the Ashikaga collection. The Ashikaga Shoguns were great patrons of the arts and of Zen Buddhism, which was introduced into Japan from China in the 12th century A.D. and had a pervasive influence on Japanese arts and culture. Soami wrote the *Kundaikan-sochoki*, (1511) a private catalog of the treasures in the Ashikaga art collection, which is a valuable source for determining the authenticity of paintings brought to Japan from China during that era. In 1485 Soami facilitated the choice of paintings for the artist Kano Masanobu to use as inspiration for his paintings at Ginkakuji (Temple of the Silver Pavilion), a retreat built by Yoshimasa. Soami may also have written *Okazari ki* (1524), a book describing the proper ceremonial display of art objects. He painted in several styles, including Chinese ink-painting *(sumi-e)* landscapes, and figure and bird-and-flower subjects. His paintings of the "Eight views" have been preserved in the Daisenin, a temple in the Daitokuji compound in the old capital city of Kyoto. See also ASHIKAGA SHOGUNATE; DAITOKUJI; GINKAKUJI; INK PAINTING; NOAMI; ZEN SECT OF BUDDHISM.

SOBA See NOODLES.

SOCIAL CLASSES See CLASS STRUCTURE; MINORITIES IN JAPAN.

SOCIALIST PARTY OF JAPAN See DOI TAKAKO; JAPAN SOCIALIST PARTY.

SOGA CLAN A powerful family associated with the ancient Yamato imperial court, which wielded political power in the sixth and seventh centuries A.D. The Soga clan also had connections with the influential Aya clan, which had immigrated from Korea. The Soga were largely responsible for the adoption in Japan of many aspects of Chinese civilization, including the Buddhist religion and the Chinese model of government. The pro-Buddhist Soga were opposed by the Nakatomi clan, who maintained the shrines of the indigenous Japanese religion later known as Shinto, and by the Mononobe clan, the leading military family and protectors of the imperial court. Beginning with Soga no Iname (d. 570), four generations of Soga held the position of chief minister *(oomi)* in the court. In A.D. 587 Soga no Umako (d. 570), son of Iname, defeated the Mononobe and Nakatomi at the Battle of Shigisen. He placed his nephew on the imperial throne as Emperor Sushun, and then replaced him with his niece and Iname's granddaughter, who reigned as Empress Suiko (r. 593–628). The court centralized its rule during her reign, with the guidance of her nephew and regent Prince Shotoku (Shotoku Taishi; 574–622), who is regarded as the father of Japanese culture. Soga power increased under Umako's son Emishi (d. 645) and grandson Soga no Iruka (d. 645), but resentment against the Soga came to a head with a coup d'etat in A.D. 645 in which Emishi and Iruka were killed. However, Umako's grandson Soga no Akae served as chief minister of the court during the Taika Reform of 645–649, which further strengthened the government's power. See also AYA CLAN; BUDDHISM; CHINA AND JAPAN; CLAN; NAKATOMI CLAN; SHOTOKU, PRINCE; SUIKO, EMPRESS; TAIKA REFORM; YAMATO COURT.

SOKA GAKKAI "Value-Creating Society"; the largest of the so-called new religions in Japan. Soka Gakkai, the lay organization of Nichiren Shoshu, a branch of the Nichiren sect of Buddhism, claims 16 million members but probably has about 6 million. It was founded in Tokyo in 1930 by a schoolteacher named Makiguchi Tsunesaburo, and most of its original members were also teachers. The purpose of Soka Gakkai was to reform Japanese society through reforming the educational system in accordance with the teachings of the Japanese Buddhist religious leader Nichiren (1222–1282). Makiguchi and Toda Josei, the general director of Soka Gakkai, were imprisoned during World War II for opposing the war and not revering the state religion of Shinto. Makiguchi died in jail, but Toda reorganized Soka Gakkai after the war and became its president in 1951. His successor, Ikeda Daisaku, oversaw the group's rapid expansion in the 1960s and 1970s. Later presidents have continued his policies. Soka Gakkai teaches that the Buddha nature resides in each person and that the same principle that transforms a person from within will bring about peace and happiness for the whole world. Members must have absolute faith in the teachings of Nichiren Shoshu. They chant the *daimoku*, a phrase that proclaims "Devotion to the *Lotus Sutra*" (Namu Myoho Renge Kyo), which is the basic religious scripture of Nichiren Buddhism. Members recite passages from the *Lotus Sutra* in front of their household altars, in which they have placed the *Gohonzon*, a copy of a scroll inscribed by Nichiren. They are also required to promulgate the religion's teachings. Intolerant of other religions, even other Buddhist sects, Soka Gakkai has grown rapidly since the 1970s through its appeal to young, less-educated urban Japanese workers of the lower classes and other people not in the mainstream of Japanese society. It has about 6 million members in Japan and half a million members overseas. The organization holds frequent meetings, mass rallies and festivals. It established its own educational system and founded Soka University in Tokyo in 1971. It also publishes many books, journals and a daily newspaper called *Seikyo shimbun*. Soka Gakkai entered the political sphere when it founded the Clean Government Party *(Komeito)* in 1964. The Komeito is now a major independent opposition political party in Japan. See also ALTARS IN HOMES; CLEAN GOVERNMENT PARTY; LOTUS SUTRA; NEW RELIGIONS; NICHIREN; NICHIREN SECT OF BUDDHISM.

SOLOMON ISLANDS See YAMAMOTO ISOROKU; WORLD WAR II.

SOMA WILD HORSE CHASE See HORSE.

SONY CORPORATION One of the largest audio and video electronics manufacturing companies in Japan. Net consolidated profits for the six months ending September 1989 rose 6.8% over the same period in 1988, to $351 million; consolidated sales in the the six months ending September 1989 rose 23.8% to $8.78 billion. Sony Corporation was founded in Tokyo in 1946 by two Japanese entrepreneurs, Morita Akio and Ibuka Masaku, as Tokyo Tsushin Kogyo (Tokyo Telecommunications Engineering Corporation). In 1950 the company made the first tape recorders in Japan. In 1952 it bought the rights from Western Electric to manufacture transistor radios in Japan. When the company began to market its products abroad in the 1950s, foreigners found the name too difficult to pronounce, so in 1958 the company's name was changed to Sony Corporation. The Japanese Ministry of International Trade and Industry (MITI) prevented foreign electronics companies from opening branches in Japan unless they had Japanese partners. In 1965 Sony made the first partnership of this kind, with the American company Texas Instruments, and acquired essential patented electronics technology such as integrated circuits. Sony and other Japanese companies began using these circuits in a wide range of products and thus closed the technological gap between Japan and the United States by the mid-1970s. Ibuka became president of the company in 1970 and served as its chairman 1971–1976. Morita became president of Sony in 1971 and chairman and chief executive officer in 1976. His marketing genius and innovative ideas made Sony an international success. Morita invented the popular portable radio and cassette player known as the Sony Walkman. The company also developed many other important new products, such as the first Japanese tape recorder and transistor radio, the Trinitron color television, the Betamax videocassette system, the compact disc and the world's first transistor 8-inch television. Sony's main products are televisions, videocassette recorders, tape recorders and radios. Recent products are the 8 millimeter video format and the laser videodisc. The Sony trademark is registered in more than 175 countries and territories, and the company operates manufacturing plants and distribution subsidiaries in many foreign countries. Under Morita's leadership, in 1961 Sony issued American Depositary Receipts to become the first Japanese company to be listed on the New York Stock Exchange. Sony stock is now listed on 18 major stock exchanges in 10 countries. In 1988 Sony acquired the American company CBS Records and in 1989 it acquired Columbia Pictures. Between 1986 and 1989, Sony also bought more than 100 companies in Europe. See also ELECTRONICS INDUSTRY; MINISTRY OF INTERNATIONAL TRADE AND INDUSTRY; MORITA AKIO.

SOROBAN see ABACUS.

SOTATSU (?–1643?) Also known as Tawaraya Sotatsu; an artist who founded a decorative style known as the Rimpa school of painting. Little is known about Sotatsu's life. He was born into the upper merchant class, perhaps to a family of fan makers, and his family name may have been Kitagawa or Nonomura. Sotatsu worked closely with another great artist, Hon'ami Koetsu (1588–1637), who may have been related to him by marriage and who was especially skilled in calligraphy. Sotatsu painted animals and flowers on many handscrolls on which Koetsu wrote *tanka*, or classical poems, taken from 10th- and 13th-century poetry anthologies and other ancient sources. In addition to decorating scrolls (*emakimono*) and fans (*sensu*), Sotatsu is best known for his large paintings on folding screens (*byobu*). He drew inspiration from the native Japanese style of painting, known as *Yamato-e*, which represented classical themes from the Nara Era (710–794) and Heian Era (794–1185). These themes had been important for the Tosa school of painting, which had dwindled by Sotatsu's time. Sotatsu's screen paintings depicting *bugaku*, an ancient dance form, and the 11th-century classical novel *The Tale of Genji* (*Genji Monogatari*) are greatly admired. Sotatsu executed his works with bold designs and strong brushstrokes yet delicately painted fine details. He used bright colors, often including gold and silver. However, he also mastered the form of black-and-white ink paintings (*sumi-e*), for painting bird-and-flower motifs and subjects important for the Zen sect of Buddhism. Sotatsu ran a busy workshop in the old capital of Kyoto from 1600 until his death around 1643. He received the patronage of the imperial court and important feudal lords. The Rimpa style that he originated was revived in the 17th century by the painter Korin (1658–1716). See also FANS; HON'AMI KOETSU; INK PAINTINGS; KORIN; PAINTING; SCREENS; SCROLLS.

SOTO SECT OF ZEN BUDDHISM One of the two main sects of the Zen Buddhist religion. Zen emphasizes meditation (*zazen*) as a means of attaining *satori* or *kensho* (enlightenment or the awakening of a person's true self or Buddha nature). Personal experience rather than the study of written documents is central to Zen. Soto Zen teaches that enlightenment comes in a gradual process, in contrast to the "sudden enlightenment" that is taught by Rinzai, the other main Zen sect, which was the dominant Zen sect in China and which was established in Japan in A.D. 1191 by Eisai (1141–1215). The Soto sect also originated in China, where it is known as the Caodong (Ts'ao-tung) sect, and was founded in Japan by Dogen (1200–1253) in A.D. 1227 when he returned from studying Zen in China. During the the 13th and 14th centuries, many Japanese Zen monks went to China to study with Zen masters, and many Chinese masters traveled to Japan. While most of them belonged to the Rinzai sect, Dogen became dissatisfied with Rinzai and chose to study with a Soto master, Tiantong Rujin (T'ien-t'ung Ju-Ching; Tendo Nyojo in Japanese; 1163–1228). He was a strict teacher who emphasized the practice of sitting in quiet meditation (*mokusho* Zen or "silent illumination Zen"), as distinct from the so-called "active Zen," which prescribed the study of *koan* (religious riddles or questions) along with meditation. Dogen founded a small temple outside the capital of Kyoto, but in 1243 he left Kyoto to escape opposition from Rinzai, Tendai and other Buddhist sects. Traveling north to the remote mountains of Echizen Province (part of modern Fukui Prefecture), Dogen established Eiheiji for the training of Soto Zen monks. The temple was named for the Eihei Era (A.D. 58–A.D.75) when Buddhism was introduced into China from India, its place of origin, a momentous event in the development of the Buddhist religion.

After Dogen died in 1253, a dispute among his disciples created a division in the Soto sect. One faction that favored Dogen's practice of strict meditation remained at Eiheiji but went into decline, while another faction moved to Daijoji in Kaga Province (modern Ishikawa Prefecture). This faction, led by the priest Gikai (1219–1309), became successful and dominated the Soto sect in Japan. Keizan Jokin, Gikai's successor, spread Soto Zen throughout the country and was revered as Dogen's equal. He and his disciples brought various folk and esoteric religious traditions into Soto Zen and lessened the emphasis on austerity and meditation. Soto monks built many public works, such as bridges and irrigation projects, and worked to help the common people during the warfare of the feudal era (12th–16th centuries). Soto and Rinzai Zen were supported by *daimyo* (feudal lords), but during the Tokugawa Shogunate (1603–1867), the military government placed strict controls on Buddhist sects. However, Soto priests became active in studying and publishing Dogen's books, and a Soto school known as the Sendanrin in Edo (modern Tokyo) evolved into modern Komazawa University. Many of Dogen's works have now been translated into English. Today there are more than 14,000 Soto temples and close to 7 million practitioners of Soto Zen in Japan. See also BUDDHISM; DOGEN; EISAI; MEDITATION; KOAN; RINZAI SECT OF ZEN BUDDHISM; SATORI; TEMPLES, BUDDHIST; ZEN SECT OF BUDDHISM.

SOUP *(shirumono)*   Soup is one of the basic dishes in a Japanese meal. There are two types of soup in Japanese cuisine. The more formal soup, known as *suimono* ("something to drink"), is a clear soup made from *dashi*, a stock of water cooked with flakes of the bonito fish and an edible seaweed called *konbu*. *Suimono* is seasoned with salt and soy sauce, and may have herbs, spices and seasonal garnishes added. Two popular garnishes are *kinome*, the leaf of the prickly ash *(sansho)*, in spring and summer, and a decoratively cut slice of *yuzu*, a citrus fruit, rind in autumn and winter. Other small pieces of food may be added to *suimono*, including chicken, fish, shellfish, eggs, vegetables such as bamboo shoots or mushrooms, and *tofu* (soybean curd). The other type of soup, called *miso shiru*, has a thick stock made with *miso*, or fermented soybean paste. *Miso* soup is less formal and calls to mind home-style cooking. There are many types of *miso* that are used in different combinations according to the season. In general, red *miso* is saltier and white *miso* is sweeter. As *miso* is a good source of protein and digestive enzymes, it is the central dish in a traditional Japanese breakfast, accompanied by rice, fish, pickles and tea. *Miso* soup is also served at lunch and dinner, and may have added ingredients, such as *tofu*, vegetables and edible seaweed. For the New Year Festival, the Japanese eat a soup called *ozoni*, which has many varieties and ingredients depending on the region of the country. *Mochi*, a small cake made of pounded glutinous rice, is always added to *ozoni*. Japanese soup is served very hot in a lacquered bowl with a lid. The diner savors the aroma when the lid is removed, picks up the bowl with the left hand, and drinks the soup, using chopsticks in the right hand to eat the small ingredients.

Nabemono ("things in a pot") are soup-like stews cooked in a large pot or pan at the table, mainly in cold weather. Pieces of beef, chicken, or fish, vegetables, *tofu* and a noodle made of devil's-tongue starch *(shirataki)* are added to the broth. This dish originated with the large soup pots that were hung over the open hearth *(irori)* in farmhouses in the snow country of Japan, and soon became popular in the cities as well. *Sukiyaki* is a well-known dish of the *nabemono* type. See also BONITO; COOKING; FARMHOUSE; GARNISHES FOR FOOD; MISO; MOCHI; NEW YEAR FESTIVAL; SEASONING FOR FOOD; SUKIYAKI; TOFU.

SOUTHEAST ASIA AND JAPAN   See EXPORTS AND IMPORTS; DUTCH IN JAPAN; NAMBAN; PEARL HARBOR, JAPANESE ATTACK ON; PORTUGUESE IN JAPAN; RYUKYU ISLANDS; SATSUMA PROVINCE; SHIMAZU CLAN; VERMILION SEAL SHIP TRADE; WORLD WAR II.

SOUTHERN AND NORTHERN COURTS ERA   See NAMBOKUCHO ERA.

SOUVENIR GIFTS   See GIFTS.

SOVIET UNION AND JAPAN   See ANGLO-JAPANESE ALLIANCE; HOKKAIDO ISLAND; KOREA AND JAPAN; KURIL ISLANDS; MANCHURIAN INCIDENT; RUSSO-JAPANESE WAR; SINO-JAPANESE WAR OF 1894–1896, SINO-JAPANESE WAR OF 1937–1945; TSUSHIMA ISLAND; UNITED NATIONS AND JAPAN; WORLD WAR I; WORLD WAR II.

SOY SAUCE *(shoyu)*   A salty, strong-tasting dark liquid made from the slow brewing of fermented soybeans, wheat and brine. Soy sauce is the ingredient most commonly used to season Japanese food. Only small quantities are needed to enhance the flavors of food. There are several different kinds of soy sauce. The regular variety is called *koikuchi shoyu*, referring to its dark color. This is widely used for basting sauces, marinades and simmered dishes. Light soy sauce *(usukuchi shoyu)* is saltier than regular soy sauce and preferred by professional chefs, especially in the Kansai area around the cities of Osaka and Kyoto. White soy sauce *(shiro shoyu)*, made primarily from wheat and brine and light in color, is used in the Nagoya region. A mild soy sauce with half the salt content is now being made as well. *Tamari* is thicker and darker than soy sauce and has a richer flavor. It is actually the dark liquid that forms on top of soybeans when they are fermenting to make *miso* (soybean paste). This is generally used as a dipping sauce, especially with sashimi (raw fish), and in basting sauces.

Soy sauce acts as a preservative for foods and aids the digestion of grains and acidic foods. The Japanese learned some techniques for brewing soy sauce from the Chinese in the eighth and ninth centuries, but Japanese soy sauce is distinctive, with a thinner consistency and a lighter, less salty taste. In Japan, soy sauce was originally made by farm families for consumption at home until the 16th century, when it began to be widely used and commercially manufactured. It is made by mixing roasted soybeans and toasted cracked wheat, then inoculating them with an *Aspergillus* fermenting mold. In three days a mold grows, called *koji*, which is mixed with brine to make a mash. The mash is put into fermentation vats to brew for one or two years. Then the liquid soy sauce is pressed from the mixture, refined, and pasteurized. This method is called natural brewing. Most commercially brewed soy sauce in Japan is fermented from three to six months and is often bottled with added ingredients. Soy sauce can even be made in three or four days by cooking the mixture at high temperatures and adding hydrolyzed vegetable protein, hydrochloric acid, caramel, and corn syrup. This type of soy sauce is quite thick and black.

Soy sauce was known in Europe as early as the 17th century. Dutch traders on Dejima Island outside Nagasaki sent barrels of soy sauce back to Europe. It eventually came to be used by chefs for King Louis XIV of France. Today the Kikkoman Corporation is the most famous brand and the largest producer of soy sauce in Japan. See also COOKING; DEJIMA ISLAND; KIKKOMAN CORPORATION; MISO; SASHIMI; SOYBEANS; TERIYAKI.

SOYBEANS (*daizu*) A variety of bean with a high protein content that is roasted and fermented to make a number of basic Japanese foods, including tofu, *miso* and soy sauce. Tofu is a white cheese-like substance that is often eaten in place of meat. *Miso* is a paste that is used for flavoring and to provide important enzymes, primarily in soups. Soy sauce is a basic flavoring ingredient in Japanese cooking. *Natto*, another food made from fermented soybeans, has a slippery texture and a strong scent similar to cheese. These foods are all made from soybeans that have been dried. The Japanese also like to eat fresh soybeans. From May through September, soybean plants are sold in food markets. The beans grow in clusters of pods about 2½ inches long on the stems of bushy plants about 20 inches tall. *Edamame*, fresh green soybeans that are salted and boiled in water in the pods, and eaten right after cooking, are a popular snack. Mature, dried soybeans are sold in packages and are known as *daizu*, "great beans." They can be softened by soaking and boiling in water, then simmered in a seasoned broth and served as a vegetable. Soybeans were cultivated in ancient China and introduced into Japan in the early Yayoi Era (c. 300 B.C.–A.D. c. 300), where they have remained one of the major food crops. The Japanese also import soy beans from the United States. See also COOKING; MISO; SOUP; SOY SAUCE; TOFU.

SPANISH IN JAPAN See CHRISTIANITY IN JAPAN; NAMBAN; PORTUGUESE IN JAPAN; SHIMABARA UPRISING OF 1637–1638; TOKUGAWA SHOGUNATE.

SPORTS See AIKIDO; BASEBALL; DOJO; JUDO; KARATE; KENDO; MARTIAL ARTS; NAGINATA; SUMO.

SPRING See BEAN-THROWING FESTIVAL; CHERRY BLOSSOM; CLIMATE OF JAPAN; DOLL FESTIVAL; FLOWER FESTIVAL; RAIN; RICE PLANTING AND HARVESTING FESTIVALS.

SPRING WAGE OFFENSIVES (*shunto*) Also known as "scheduled struggles"; a technique used by labor unions every spring since 1955 to secure nationwide pay raises and benefits adjustments based on economic growth. The annual spring wage offensive has been organized by Sohyo (General Council of Trade Unions of Japan), one of the two largest labor federations in Japan and the principal supporter of the Japan Socialist Party (JSP). Many of Sohyo's member unions are composed of government employees, such as teachers, and employees of public corporations, such as the National Railway Workers Union (although Japan National Railways was recently privatized). By the 1970s, most organized labor in Japan participated in the spring work stoppages and demonstrations. A central committee plans the offensive but plays no direct role in direct bargaining between unions and management. Months of planning and publicity precede the spring wage offensive, and the committee announces the level wage and benefit increases they are seeking, as well as the probable schedule of work stoppages. The offensive is often a highly ritualized annual show of force and solidarity, with dancing and banners, rather than a crippling strike. Wage settlements are sometimes actually made in the industry before its labor offensive takes place. Railway workers also use the work slow-down tactic of "work-to-rule" which means adhering to prescribed rules for times to start and stop trains, which disrupts the flow of rush hour trains. Labor and management have closer working relations in Japanese companies than in those of most other industrialized countries. Management usually keeps the union members informed of the company's financial condition, and unions do not make wage demands that would undermine the corporations' financial health. The Central Labor Relations Commission helps the two sides reach an agreement. See also CORPORATIONS; EMPLOYMENT; INCOME; JAPAN RAILWAYS; LABOR UNIONS.

SQUID See SEAFOOD.

STAR FESTIVAL (Tanabata-sama or Tanabatsume) A festival held on the seventh day of the seventh month in old Japanese lunar calendar and now celebrated on July 7th (August 7th in some regions). The Star Festival derives from an old Chinese legend about a weaver princess, called Shokujo by the Japanese, and a cowherd named Kengyu; they personify the stars Vega and Altair. According to the legend, the beautiful princess was the daughter of the King of the Sky. She was a very skillful weaver and sat at her loom day and night weaving magnificent garments for her father. One day the cowherd visited her, and they fell in love at first sight. The princess began to neglect her weaving, and her jealous father forbade the two lovers to meet, except for once a year on the seventh day of the seventh month. For the rest of the year they had to live on opposite banks of the Milky Way, known as the "River of the Sky."

When the long-awaited night finally arrived for the two lovers to meet, they found the river so wide that neither could cross it. The disappointed princess began to weep, and a flock of magpies flew to her and made a bridge with their outspread wings for her to cross over the river and meet her lover. The festival based on this story was brought from China to Japan during the reign of Emperor Koken (752–756). Imperial families in the Heian Era (794–1185) made offerings to the two stars Vega and Altair and wrote poems for the occasion. The Star Festival is one of five festivals of a Chinese origin still celebrated in Japan. People believe that if it rains on this day, the River of the Sky will overflow and the lovers will not be able to meet. During the festival, young women pray for skill in weaving, sewing, calligraphy and other handcrafts, and special decorations are displayed to express these wishes. *Tanzaku*, strips of colored paper on which people have written *tanka* or *haiku* poems, are hung on bamboo poles or branches. Sendai, Hiratsuka, and several other cities have large parades a month later, on August 7th, to celebrate the Star Festival with many elaborate floats and paper lanterns and decorations. See also CALENDAR; CALLIGRAPHY; FESTIVALS; HAIKU; SENDAI; TANKA.

STATE See PREFECTURE.

STATE SHINTO (Kokka Shinto) The Japanese national Shinto-related ideology created by the government after the Meiji Restoration of 1868. The ideology known as State Shinto was based on the reinterpretation of certain practices and beliefs of Shinto, the indigenous Japanese religion, especially the divinity of the emperor and *kokutai*, the concept of a "body politic" or "national essence" for Japan. State Shinto became a nationalistic cult, centered on the divinity of the emperor and manipulated by the government to unify the Japanese people to incite them to fulfill his divine mission to the country and expand militarily in Asia.

In State Shinto the religion was combined with ethical principles of Confucianism, especially those of loyalty and filial piety. Conversely, the Meiji government separated Shinto from Buddhism, with which it had become entwined over the centuries, in order to return to the distinctive ancient Japanese concept of *saisei itchi*, "unity of religious ritual and government administration." Buddhism, like Christianity, was seen as an alien faith at the time, owing to its Indian and Chinese origins.

In 1869 a government Office of Shinto Worship (Jingikan) was created, which had an Office of Propaganda (Senkyoshi) to promulgate reverence for Shinto and the emperor and obedience to the imperial will. In 1871 State Shinto was formally created through decrees establishing Shinto shrines as government institutions supported by the state, stipulating that Shinto priests be appointed by the government, and requiring all Japanese citizens to become registered members of their local shrine. The Grand Shrine of Ise, sacred to the Sun Goddess Amaterasu o Mikami, believed to be the ancestor of the imperial family, was declared the highest ranking shrine. The government also created new national shrines, including two major shrines in Tokyo: Meiji Shrine, dedicated to Japan's first modern emperor, and Yasukuni Shrine, where the souls of soldiers and sailors who had died in battle defending the imperial throne since 1853 were given repose. The Japanese Constitution of 1889 officially declared the emperor to be "sacred and inviolable." The Imperial Rescript on Education of 1890 called for loyalty to the Japanese state, associated with reverence for the imperial ancestors who founded the state. Students were required to revere pictures of the emperor and empress hung in their schools. State Shinto was a major factor contributing to the rise of Japanese nationalism prior to World War II. In 1911, the Ministry of Education required schools to take pupils to shrines during festivals, especially at Yasukuni Shrine. In 1932 the Ministry declared that shrines were not religious but government institutions, and that shrine visits were required to inculcate patriotism and loyalty to the emperor and the nation.

After Japan's defeat in World War II, State Shinto was abolished by General Douglas MacArthur, Supreme Commander for the Allied Powers during the Occupation of Japan. The Japanese government was ordered to end its financial support of Shinto shrines and its control of their affairs. Emperor Hirohito (now known as Emperor Showa; 1901–1989) renounced his divinity and became simply a symbol of the state. The Japanese Constitution of 1947 guarantees religious freedom and forbids the government from taking part in any religious activity. However, Yasukuni Shrine has been paid official visits by several Japanese prime ministers, and conservative members of the Diet (Parliament) have attempted to make Yasukuni Shrine an official national holy place. Controversy also surrounded the funeral of Emperor Hirohito in 1989, when Shinto rituals performed by priests were combined with government ceremonies. Some Japanese complained that this violated the constitutional separation of government and religion. See also AMATERASU O MIKAMI; EMPEROR; HIROHITO, EMPEROR; ISE SHRINE; KOKUTAI; MEIJI RESTORATION OF 1868; MEIJI SHRINE; OCCUPATION OF JAPAN; YASUKUNI SHRINE.

STATUES See DAIBUTSU; HANIWA; JOCHO; JOMON ERA; NOGUCHI ISAMU; SCULPTURE.

STEEL INDUSTRY Steel, now a declining industry in Japan, had been Japan's major export since the mid-1950s. The Meiji government (1868–1912) built Japan's first modern steel plant in 1898, the Yawata Iron and Steel Works. Several private steel companies were established soon thereafter. In 1934 the government established Nippon Steel Corporation, formerly the state-run Yawata Iron and Steel Works, as a national company. Technology for producing iron and steel have been developed in Japan since ancient times, although modern steel-manufacturing technology was imported from the West. Traditional Japanese iron and steel swords are the finest ever produced anywhere in the world.

After World War II, Japanese steel companies had to completely rebuild, and the first advanced steel plant was completed in 1957. Steel and shipbuilding companies worked closely together to develop durable alloys. The Japanese shipbuilding industry rapidly became the largest in the world. The steel industry was closely guided by the Ministry of International Trade and Industry (MITI), which recognized that a strong steel industry could help build up other basic industries, including shipbuilding. The Japan Development Bank provided capital for steel companies, and the government extended tax breaks and funds for research and development, to stimulate the growth of the steel industry. Steel companies rigorously strove to reduce costs in order to maintain high growth rates. Postwar production of steel jumped from 5 million tons in 1950 to nearly 150 million tons in 1980. In 1980 Japanese iron and steel production surpassed that of the United States for the first time, and Japan became the world's largest exporter of steel. The Japanese steel industry became the most efficient in the world by the mid-1970s, producing the largest tonnage and the highest quality of steel in the world, at prices 25–30% lower than American steel. In response the United States has enacted measures to protect its own steel industry.

Japan's steel industry has been declining recently because the world demand for steel has decreased, and other steel producers such as South Korea, Taiwan and Brazil are becoming competitive with Japan. Japanese companies have also had to invest heavily in pollution control equipment following the industry's switch from oil to coal after the oil crisis of 1973. Steel firms now invest in foreign steel companies or are diversifying into high-tech industries. See also EXPORTS AND IMPORTS; MINISTRY OF INTERNATIONAL TRADE AND DEVELOPMENT; OIL CRISIS OF 1973; SHIPPING AND SHIPBUILDING.

STENCILS (*katagami*)   Pieces of thick paper made from the bark of the mulberry bush (*kozo*) that have a pattern cut into them for use in dyeing textiles for kimono (Japanese robes). Two or three sheets of handmade paper are glued together with persimmon juice (*kakishibu*) and hung to dry in a smokehouse. The stencil paper then has a detailed picture or geometric pattern cut into it with a knife and an awl. Many traditional patterns consist of tiny holes that are punched out to make an overall *komon* ("small dot") pattern. Stripes and tortoiseshell are some other popular designs. Geometric designs were commonly used in the city of Edo (modern Tokyo), while *yuzen* dyeing of flowers and other natural motifs has been popular in Kyoto. A stencil will not warp, and it can be used and washed many times. The method for dyeing textiles with stencils, known as *katazome*, involves placing stencils on the fabric and rubbing glutinous paste through the open sections of the stencils. The paste resists the absorption of colored dyes that are then applied. The stencil-covered fabric is then rinsed to remove the rice paste. These steps may be repeated many times for the application of different colors. Each time, rice paste is rubbed over all portions, whether already dyed or not, which are not to be dyed in the next color. From the Edo Era (1603–1868) to the present, stencils have been made by artisans in Shiroko and Jike villages (together known today as Suzuka city) in Mie Prefecture.

The Japanese government has designated several stencil cutters as Living National Treasures. Stencils have become popular collectible works of art in their own right. See also LIVING NATIONAL TREASURES; PAPER, HANDMADE; TEXTILES;

STOCK MARKET (*shoken torihikijo*)   Exchanges began in Japan in the late 1870s for the trading of government bonds issued to members of the former samurai class. The Japanese stock market grew rapidly with the development of manufacturing during and after World War I. During World War II, Japanese stock trading came to a halt, but the stock markets were opened again in 1949 under the Allied Occupation of Japan, and a Securities Exchange Law based on the U.S. model was passed.

Tokyo is today one of the three main stock markets of the world, along with New York and London. The largest exchange in Japan is the Tokyo Stock Exchange (TSE), which handles around $\frac{3}{4}$ of all transactions and in March, 1990 was valued at $3 trillion, comparable to the New York Stock Exchange. Next largest is the Osaka Stock Exchange. There are also exchanges in Fukuoka, Hiroshima, Kyoto, Nagoya, Niigata and Sapporo, which list many stocks on the TSE "first section" (of major corporations) along with those of regional companies not listed in Tokyo. There are also "second sections" in Tokyo, Osaka and Nagoya where securities of smaller capital companies or less active stocks are traded. In addition, there is an over-the-counter market where various unlisted securities are traded. At the end of 1987, the Tokyo Stock Exchange had 93 member firms and listed 1,532 domestic and 88 foreign companies. The total market value was US$ 2.7 trillion in stocks and $1 trillion in bonds.

Because Japanese women traditionally control the family finances, stockbrokers often work as door-to-door salesmen, and brokerage houses have branches in most major shopping areas to attract investors. Around 20 million Japanese own stocks and bonds, but the majority of shares in Japanese companies are owned by banks, rather than by individual shareholders. In 1980 there were 256 brokerage companies in Japan, employing nearly 90,000 people. The four largest are Nomura, Nikko, Yamaichi and Daiwa, which have opened branches in foreign countries. Nomura is the world's leading brokerage house. A large portion of foreign investment in Japan is in the TSE.

The standard source of information for the Japanese stock market is *Kaisha Shikiho*, published in English twice a year as *The Japan Company Handbook*. The main Japanese daily financial newspaper, *Nihon Keizai Shimbun*, publishes a weekly international English edition, *The Japan Economic Journal*.

In 1990 Japan's financial markets suffered their worst volatility in decades, with the Nikkei 225, a stock index of blue-chip companies in Japan, falling 25% from a high of nearly 39,000 on December 29, 1989 to 28,000 at the beginning of April 1990. Reasons for the fall included the yen's decline by more than 10% against the American dollar; a steep rise in the cost of borrowing money, with Japan's official discount rate rising from 2.5% to 5.25% by March 30, 1990; increasing oil prices worldwide; and Japanese fears of rising inflation and trade tensions with the United States. See also BANKING SYSTEM; CORPORATIONS; SECURITIES COMPANIES; YEN.

STOREHOUSE *(kura)* A building originally used by farmers to store rice and other grains. In ancient Japan, a farm storehouse, or granary, held the first rice that was harvested each year. This rice was offered to the deity of grain and then used as seed rice the following year to grow the next rice crop. The work *kura* also means "seat," which indicates that a granary was the sacred home of the grain deity. A storehouse was built of wood in a simple rectangular shape with a pitched roof and a platform floor raised off the ground. The emperor, who embodied the grain deity, also lived in a palace that was made of wood with a raised floor.

Shrine buildings to house the *kami* (sacred spirits) of Shinto, the native Japanese religion, were modeled on the simple architectural style of a storehouse. During the Nara Era (710–794), wealthy aristocrats and Buddhist temples constructed storehouses to safekeep their valuable art objects, written documents and religious scriptures. The Shosoin was built at Todaiji in Nara to house the temple's numerous treasures, most of which were gifts from Empress Komyo or were ritual objects used in the dedication of the Daibutsu (Great Buddha statue) in A.D. 752.

During the Heian Era (794–1185), farmhouses came to have sections enclosed with thick walls of clay plaster, known as *nema* (bedrooms) or *nando* (storerooms). Used for storing household objects, they developed into *dozo*, freestanding rectangular buildings with small windows and thick plaster walls to protect stored items in case of fire. Storehouses of this type were also used in cities, such as Edo (modern Tokyo), where fires were a constant problem.

Wealthy families had their own storehouses. In cities and villages alike, collective storehouses stored rice and other goods for the whole community. The vast wealth kept in Japanese storehouses also helped finance Japan's transformation into a modern, industrialized country during the Meiji Era. See also DAIBUTSU; EMPEROR; HEIAN ERA; NARA; PALACE; RICE; SHINTO; SHOSOIN; SHRINES, SHINTO; TEMPLES, BUDDHIST; TODAIJI.

STORES See DEPARTMENT STORES; DISTRIBUTION SYSTEM; GIFTS.

STORYTELLING *(rakugo)* Comic storytelling by a professional storyteller *(rakugoka)* who uses his voice, facial expressions and pantomime to tell deliver a monologue is popular in Japan. The storyteller wears a dark kimono and sits alone on a pillow *(zabuton)* in the center of the stage with no scenery. He acts out the episodes of a long story using only a hand towel and a fan for props, eating imaginary noodles, pouring sake into an imaginary cup, and so forth. The audience already knows the story very well but takes pleasure in the original way a particular storyteller portrays the characters in it. He also makes up his own introduction to the story, incorporating references to current events and his own experiences. The word *rakugo* is written with two Chinese characters that indicate the pun delivered by the storyteller as the punch line ("the drop") at the end of the story. *Raku* (also pronounced *ochi*) means "drop" and *go* means "word." *Rakugo* became the accepted Japanese term for comic storytelling in the late 19th century, although this type of storytelling dates back to the 17th century when entertainers called *otogishu* traveled with the armies of the warlords. In the 17th century, storytellers called *hanashika* ("talkers") became popular in the cities of Edo (modern Tokyo), Kyoto and Osaka. They also traveled through the countryside to perform at outdoor shows and restaurants and were hired for private parties. In 1791 the first *rakugo* theater was founded in Edo. Since that time, *rakugo* has gone through several periods of popularity and decline. Today performances are held at many *rakugo* halls in Tokyo, and there are *rakugo* clubs in universities where members study and perform storytelling. *Rakugo* is often broadcast on radio and television. In 1983 *rakugo* master Katsura Shijaku began performing in English as well as Japanese, and has performed in many countries.

Another type of popular traditional storytelling is *manzai*, a comic dialogue with expressive hand gestures engaged in by two comedians, a "wit" *(tayu)* and a "straight man" *(saizo)*. *Manzai* dates back over a thousand years in Japan. Such performers also traveled, and their clever dialogues were thought to spread blessings for the coming year. In the late 19th century, *manzai* was being performed in theaters, and even today this art has a major place in Japanese television shows. See also BROADCASTING SYSTEM; EDO ERA; KIMONO; NOODLES; PILLOWS; SAKE.

STRAW WARE Items woven from dried stalks of rice and other grain plants, such as barley. The Japanese make both religious and functional objects from the straw of rice, which is the most important and sacred food in the Japanese diet. In shrines of Shinto, the indigenous Japanese religion, sacred rice straw ropes *(shimenawa)* are hung to define sacred spaces, to hang offerings to *kami* (sacred spirits), or to enclose sacred trees. These ropes are also hung at festivals and around entrances to homes at the New Year Festival. Strips of white paper *(gohei)* are hung on the straw ropes for purification. At the midsummer Bon Festival to welcome visiting ancestral spirits, little straw boats known as "boats of the blessed ghosts" *(shoryobune)* are sailed away on streams and rivers. Newly woven mats of rice straw are also placed in front of Buddhist altars in homes *(butsudan)*. The floors of traditional homes are covered with thick rice straw mats called *tatami*; thin straw mats known as *mushiro* are also used. Farmhouses are covered with thatched roofs *(kayabuki)* made of straw or pampas grass. Straw ropes are also used to tie stalks of bamboo to make latticework fences and gates.

Straw is a strong material with a simple, natural look that appeals to the Japanese. Straw objects are considered *mingei* or folk crafts. Innumerable household objects are woven from straw, especially baskets and boxes of all sizes for carrying and storing food, clothing and other items. Japanese traditionally wore raincoats *(mino)*, rain hats *(amigasa)*, sandals *(zori, waraji)*, boots *(waragutsu)* and gloves woven of straw. Many traditional folk toys are woven of straw, particularly horses, and they originally played a role in agricultural rituals. See also AGRICULTURE; BASKETS; BON FESTIVAL; BOXES; MINGEI; NEW YEAR FESTIVAL; PURIFICATION; RICE; SANDALS; SHINTO; SHRINES, SHINTO; TATAMI; TOYS, TRADITIONAL.

STUDENTS   See APPRENTICE SYSTEM; CHILDREN IN JAPAN; DOJO; EDUCATION SYSTEM; UNIVERSITIES; ZENGAKUREN.

SUBARU   See AUTOMOBILE INDUSTRY.

SUBWAYS (*chikatetsu*)   The first subway in Japan was the Ginza Line in Tokyo, which was opened in 1927 by the Tokyo Underground Railway Company and ran for 1.4 miles between the districts of Asakusa and Ueno. Ten lines now operate in the Tokyo system, covering a distance of 150 miles, and the system is constantly being expanded. The Tokyo subways have not kept pace with the increase in ridership, and the busiest stations use white-gloved guards to help pack riders into the cars. The city of Osaka opened a subway system in 1933. By the 1980s, subways were also operating in the cities of Osaka, Nagoya, Kobe, Sapporo (built for the 1972 Winter Olympic Games held there), Yokohama, Kyoto, Fukuoka and Sendai. Every Japanese subway system bases the cost of fares on the distance traveled. Japanese subways are built to connect with major railroad lines, usually at large stations, which are major

Employees of the Tokyo subway system packing riders into overcrowded subway cars during rush hour.

commercial areas in Japan that contain restaurants, department stores and smaller shops. See also FUKUOKA; KOBE; KYOTO; NAGOYA; OSAKA; RAILROADS; SAPPORO; SENDAI; TOKYO; YOKOHAMA.

SUE WARE   See BIZEN WARE; POTTERY.

SUGAWARA NO MICHIZANE (845–903)   A scholar, poet and court official in the Heian Era (794–1185) who became venerated after his death as the patron saint of scholarship in Japan. Michizane was born into a family of important scholars and poets. His father and grandfather played a major role in the Japanese adoption of Chinese culture during the ninth century. They were editors of Chinese-language poetry anthologies, taught Chinese Confucianism at the court university (Daigakuryo), and were members of the last two in a series of early Japanese official missions to China. Michizane was educated in the Chinese classics, taught Chinese literature and became a civil servant in the court bureaucracy. He also wrote the finest Chinese-language poetry in early Japan, as well as Japanese-language poetry. Moreover, Michizane contributed to the court-sponsored histories of Japan, known as *Rikkokushi*, which provide useful information for modern historians. In A.D. 886 Michizane began a four-year term as governor of Sanuki Province (modern Kagawa Prefecture) on Shikoku Island. When he returned to the capital city of Kyoto, Emperor Uda (867–931; r. 887–897) appointed him to high court positions in order to help offset the great power exercised by the Fujiwara clan. In 894 Michizane persuaded the Japanese court to stop sending official missions to China because of political instability there. He thus influenced the development of Japanese culture by halting the adoption of Chinese culture. In 899 Michizane was appointed minister of the right (*udaijin*), the second highest court office. By then Emperor Uda had abdicated the throne to his son, Daigo, who was allied with the Fujiwara clan. In 901 Fujiwara leaders falsely accused Michizane of a plot against the emperor and had him banished to the southern Japanese island of Kyushu, where he died in 903. Subsequent calamities at the imperial court were thought to be caused by Michizane's angry ghost, and to oppose the spirit the court pardoned Michizane posthumously and awarded his descendants hereditary positions as court scholars. Kitano Shrine in Kyoto and Dazaifu Shrine in Dazaifu were dedicated to Michizane, revered as the sacred spirit Karai Tenjin. Shrines dedicated to him throughout Japan still sell amulets to students taking school entrance examinations. See also AMULETS; CHINA AND JAPAN; CONFUCIANISM; FUJIWARA CLAN; HEIAN ERA; IMPERIAL COURT; KITANO SHRINE; POETRY; RIKKOKUSHI; SHRINES, SHINTO.

SUGINOI PALACE HOTEL AND BATHS   See BEPPU.

SUIBOKUGA   See INK PAINTING.

SUICIDE   Suicide was often required of samurai during the feudal era (12th–16th centuries) in Japan. Samurai were expected to be loyal to their *daimyo* (feudal lords), disciplined, brave in battle and ready to face death at any time. When defeated, samurai took their own lives to save their honor. The warrior Minamoto no Yoshitsune (1159–1189) became a famous hero when he committed suicide rather than be captured by the enemy troops of his own brother, Minamoto no Yoritomo (1147–1199). The method of committing suicide by cutting open one's abdomen became ritualized and is properly known as *seppuku*, although also known by the vulgar term *harakiri*, or "belly slitting." *Seppuku* is no longer an accepted practice in Japan but remains a popular theme in Kabuki and Bunraku (puppet) theater, movies and television dramas. The best-known tale about *seppuku* is *Chushingura*, the true story of the Forty-Seven Ronin (masterless samurai) who avenged their lord's death by taking his enemy's head, and then committed suicide to make amends for breaking the peace mandated by the Tokugawa Shogunate (1603–1867). A famous act of *seppuku* as an expression of loyalty occurred when Emperor Meiji died in 1912 and General Nogi, a hero of the Russo-Japanese War (1904–1905), and his wife followed the emperor into death.

In Japan, suicide has also been a traditional way of shaming another person. Committing suicide on an enemy's doorstep caused him to "lose face" for having driven someone to such a desperate act. When Japan was on the verge of defeat at the end of World War II, young men known as *kamikaze* pilots were trained for the suicidal missions of dive-bombing enemy ships. More recently, the novelist Mishima Yukio (1925–1970) committed *seppuku* as a dramatic political statement.

In Japan, suicide has also been a way of wiping out shame and of escaping from a hopeless situation. Many plays in the Bunraku and Kabuki repertoire tell of love suicides committed to resolve the conflict between duty (*giri*) to one's family and society and one's personal feelings (*ninjo*). The most famous play on this theme is *The Love Suicides at Sonezaki (Sonezaki Shinju)* by the great playwright Chikamatsu Monzaemon (1653–1724). Although the conflict between duty and feelings is not as strong in modern Japanese society, suicide can still be a way of resolving a difficult situation. Students can be driven to suicide by the intense pressure to pass entrance examinations for the best high schools and universities, known as the so-called "examination hell" (*juken jigoku*). Older people, especially widows, may also resort to suicide because of feeling of loneliness and uselessness. See also BUNRAKU; CHIKAMATSU MONZAEMON; DIAMYO; DUTY AND FEELINGS; EDUCATION SYSTEM; FORTY-SEVEN RONIN; KAMIKAZE; LOYALTY; MINAMOTO NO YOSHITSUNE; MISHIMA YUKIO; SAMURAI; SWORD.

SUIKO, EMPRESS (554–628) Reigning empress (*tenno*) from 593 to 628, she is 33rd in the traditional Japanese count of rulers. She was the daughter of Emperor Kimmei (509–571, ruled 531 or 539–571) and a member of the Soga clan. Suiko was married to her half-brother, Emperor Bidatsu, who reigned 572–585, by whom she had seven sons. After Bidatsu's death the Soga clan, led by the Great Minister Soga no Umako, defeated the rival Mononobe clan in 587. Soga placed the next emperor, Sushun, on the throne in 588, then had him assassinated, and put his niece Suiko on the throne, making her the first reigning empress in Japan since the legendary matriarchal rulers of the prehistoric era. Umako broke with precedent in order to ensure that a child born to a Soga mother would be on the throne, which helped maintain a balance of power with the rivals of the Soga clan, the Mononobe and Nakatomi clans. Soga also named a nephew of Suiko, Prince Umayado, rather than one of her own sons, as heir apparent and regent, because Soga valued Umayado's strong support for the importation of the Buddhist religion from China, which provided Japan with new knowledge and culture; Umayado became famous in Japanese history as Crown Prince Shotoku (Shotoku Taishi; 574–622). Many significant developments took place during Suiko's reign. Diplomatic relations were begun with the Sui dynasty of China; a system of court ranks (*kan'i junikai*, the "twelve cap ranks") was established; national histories, known as *Tennoki* and *Kokki*, were compiled; a seventeen-article constitution was issued; and the religious teachings and arts of Buddhism were encouraged, as exemplified by the building of temples, including Horyuji. See also BUDDHISM; CHINA AND JAPAN; EMPEROR; HORYUJI; NAKATOMI CLAN; SEVENTEEN-ARTICLE CONSTITUTION; SHOTOKU, PRINCE; SOGA CLAN; TENNO.

SUKIYAKI A meal cooked in a large pan over heat at the table. The ingredients can be thin sliced beef, tofu (bean curd), especially *yakidofu* (broiled bean curd), seasonal vegetables such as mushrooms, onion, celery, cabbage and scallions, and stringy, translucent noodles made of devil's-tongue starch (*shirataki*). Oil is heated in the pan; the beef is lightly fried; and the rest of the ingredients are added. A sauce called *warashita*, made of soy sauce, mirin (sweet rice wine for cooking) and sugar, is poured over the ingredients while they are cooking, making it into a kind of stew. The individual pieces are removed, dipped into a beaten raw egg, and consumed. Sukiyaki was introduced to Japan in the 19th century when the Meiji emperor (r. 1868–1912) took up the Western custom of eating meat. Prior to that time, Japanese people followed the Buddhist custom of not eating the flesh of animals (fish, chicken and rabbit excepted).

A similar dish, called *shabu-shabu*, uses the same ingredients but cooks them in a pot of boiling water at the table. Noodles are cooked in the broth at the end of the meal. Two popular dipping sauces for the cooked ingredients are *ponzu*, consisting of soy sauce, rice vinegar and lemon juice, and *gomadare*, made with sesame seeds. See also COOKING; MEIJI, EMPEROR; NAMES OF INDIVIDUAL INGREDIENTS.

SUMIDA RIVER A large river that flows through the eastern section of Tokyo into Tokyo Bay. The Sumida River starts in the Kanto Mountains north of Tokyo and flows south for 14.6 miles. Many canals have been built along the river in Tokyo, and warehouses and factories line its banks. The river borders the old downtown merchant district known as Shitamachi, including the popular district of Asakusa, where boat rides can be taken. The Sumida River has been severely polluted by Tokyo's heavy industries, although recent efforts to clean up the river have been somewhat successful. In past times, it was a frequent subject of poems, songs and stories, and many pleasure boats sailed the river on summer evenings. Fireworks displays have been enjoyed along the banks of the Sumida River for several centuries. See also ASAKUSA; FIREWORKS; SHITAMACHI; TOKYO.

SUMI-E See BRUSHES; CALLIGRAPHY; HAKUIN EKAKU; INK PAINTING; JOSETSU; SENGAI GIBON.

SUMITOMO One of the six largest corporate groups in Japan, made up of 80 different firms. The initial activity of the House of Sumitomo, founded by Sumitomo Masatomo (1585–1652), was the refining of copper to extract silver. Sumitomo supplied copper to the Tokugawa Shogunate (1603–1867) and exported copper abroad. The company began diversifying in the Meiji Era (1868–1912), although mining and metallurgy remained its primary activities. It was reorganized as Sumitomo, Ltd. (Sumitomo Goshi Kaisha) in 1912 to serve as a holding company for its joint-stock subsidiaries. By the 1930s, Sumitomo was the third largest *zaibatsu* (business conglomerate) in Japan. In 1937 the holding company itself was reorganized as a joint-stock company, although nearly all the shares were held by the 16th-generation descendant who headed the Sumitomo family. The company expanded during World War II, but in 1948, the holding company was dissolved due to the dissolution of *zaibatsu* by the Allied Occupation of Japan. In the 1950s the Sumitomo group was again reorganized, this time as a *keiretsu* (enterprise grouping), with much less control by the Sumitomo family. Some of its major subsidiaries include Sumitomo Bank, Ltd. (Sumitomo Ginko), one of the three largest city banks (large urban commercial banks with numerous branches) in Japan; Sumitomo Corporation (Sumitomo Shoji), one of Japan's largest trading companies (*sogo shosha*); and chemical, cement, electrical, construction, heavy industries, metal industries and life insurance companies. The Sumitomo Group specializes in heavy industrial products such as steel, machinery, chemicals and electrical equipment, and imports iron and copper ore from Australia and Canada. Sumitomo has more than 100 overseas offices, branches and incorporated companies. Corporate headquarters are in Tokyo and Osaka. See also BANKING SYSTEM; CORPORATIONS; EXPORTS AND IMPORTS; TRADING COMPANY, GENERAL; ZAIBATSU.

SUMMER See BON FESTIVAL; CLIMATE OF JAPAN; FIREWORKS; GIFTS; RAIN; TYPHOONS.

SUMO An ancient form of wrestling that is now the national sport of Japan. Sumo has been historically associated with Shinto, the indigenous Japanese religion. The *Kojiki* and *Nihon Shoki*, official Japanese chronicles recorded in the eighth century A.D., describe a sumo-style wrestling match between the gods to determine which one would rule Japan. A match between human wrestlers in front of the legendary Emperor Suinin was also recorded. Sumo matches were held at Shinto shrines to entertain the *kami*

Sumo wrestlers trying to push each other out of the ring. Sumo is the national sport of Japan. The man on the left is Takamiyama, a Hawaiian whose real name is Jesse Kahualua, the first non-Japanese to become a sumo wrestler.

(divine spirits) at rice planting and harvesting festivals, and modern sumo matches still follow numerous ceremonial rituals that take up much more time than the actual contests. Each bout is fought by two heavy wrestlers (*rikishi*) inside an earthen ring (*dohyo*), which is 14.9 feet in diameter, marked out by a thick rope in the earth, and covered by a roof (*yakata*) resembling that on a Shinto shrine. Matches were formerly held outdoors, but are now held in indoor amphitheaters. Before a match, the wrestlers bow, touch the earth, clap their hands to summon the divine spirits (*kami*) and stamp their legs to chase evil spirits away. They also scatter salt to purify the ring and drink special water known as *chikara-mizu* to purify themselves. Tournaments begin with the "ring entrance of grand champions" (*yokozuna dohyoiri*). Sumo wrestlers wear distinctive loincloths (*mawashi*) and put their long hair up in a topknot (*mage*). For ceremonial purposes they also wear decorated ornamental aprons (*keshomawashi*) with strips of white paper known as *gohei*, which are important in Shinto rituals. The referee (*gyoji*) wears a 14th-century-style brocade kimono and a tall black hat, and holds a type of iron fan (*gumbai*) carried by feudal warriors. A match often takes less than a minute. When the referee gives the signal, the two wrestlers charge at each other with brute force. The first wrestler to make his opponent step or fall outside of the rope demarcating the ring or to touch the ground with any part of his body other than the soles of his feet is the winner.

Today there are fewer than 1,000 sumo wrestlers. They live and train in several dozen so-called stables (*heya*, "room"), each run by a "boss" (*oyakata*) who is a former sumo champion. The wrestlers eat huge quantities of food, especially a stew known as *chanko nabe,* which makes them grow to an average weight of 300 pounds. They are ranked by their ability. The top rank is *Yokozuna,* Grand Champion, designated by a heavy white rope worn around the waist. Other ranks in descending order are *Ozeki, Sekiwake, Komusubi, Maegashira* and *Juryo.* Teenage boys are recruited as apprentices and work hard to move up through the ranks. A Hawaiian named Jesse Kahualua was the first non-Japanese to become a sumo wrestler, under the name Takamiyama. *Sumo* became a professional sport during the Edo Era (1600–1868). Today it is regulated by the Japan Sumo Association (Nihon Sumo Kyokai), whose members include 105 former wrestlers plus representatives from groups connected with the operations of sumo matches. The association is led by a president *(rijicho)* and a 10-man elected board of directors. Offices are at the National Sport Arena (Kuramae Kokugikan) in Tokyo, which also houses an amphitheater with more than 10,000 seats, a Sumo Museum and a Sumo School (Sumo Kyoshujo) for new wrestlers. Six 15-day sumo tournaments *(basho)* are held each year and televised nationwide. The wrestlers meet in Tokyo in January, May and September, in Osaka in March, in Nagoya in July, and in Fukuoka in November. See also MARTIAL ARTS; SALT; SHINTO.

SUN See AMATERASU O MIKAMI; FLAGS AND BANNERS; NIPPON.

SUN GODDESS See AMATERASU O MIKAMI.

SUNTORY, LTD. See ALCOHOLIC BEVERAGES.

SUPREME COMMANDER FOR THE ALLIED POWERS

(SCAP) Commonly known as SCAP or General Headquarters (GHQ)-SCAP; the term for the chief administrator of the Allied Occupation of Japan (1945–1952) in Tokyo. SCAP-GHQ was housed in the Dai-Ichi Insurance Building near the Imperial Palace. This was the only time in history that Japan was occupied by any foreign power. U.S. General Douglas MacArthur (1880–1964) served as the Supreme Commander for the Allied Powers and as commander in chief, U.S. Far East Command, until President Harry S Truman replaced him in 1951 with General Matthew B. Ridgeway. SCAP was supervised by the Far Eastern Commission, located in Washington, D.C., composed of the 11 nations that had won the war. The Allied Council for Japan, located in Tokyo and consisting of the United States, Great Britain, China and the Soviet Union, advised SCAP on policy. However, in practice the United States almost completely controlled the Occupation of Japan and the concurrent reforms of the Japanese government and other institutions. Under the Supreme Commander were a chief of staff, the Allied Council for Japan and the International Military Tribunal for the Far East, which supervised the war crimes trials. In addition to the military staff, there were 17 nonmilitary sections that dealt with such issues as government, diplomacy, economy and science, and public health and welfare. SCAP did not serve as a military government, but worked with the Japanese bureaucracy, at first through SCAP's Central Liaison Office and then with the appropriate Japanese governing agencies. The U.S. 8th Army established military government teams around the country to carry out SCAP's orders and to work with local governing bodies. See also MACARTHUR, DOUGLAS; OCCUPATION OF JAPAN; SURRENDER OF JAPAN; WAR CRIMES TRIALS; WORLD WAR II.

SUPREME COURT (Saiko Saibansho) The highest judicial body in Japan. Prior to World War II, the highest court in civil and criminal cases was the Great Court of Cassation (Daishin'in); a special tribunal called the Administrative Court handled cases of administrative law. The Meiji Constitution of 1889 also provided for other special tribunals, but no Japanese court had been empowered to rule on constitutional law, and the Justice Department held the power of justice administration for issues of personnel, finances and so forth. The Japanese Constitution of 1947 states that there shall be a Supreme Court which is vested with the highest judicial power in cases of civil, criminal and administrative law. The Supreme Court has a chief justice and 14 associate justices. The Prime Minister's Cabinet nominates the chief justice, who is then formally appointed by the emperor; the cabinet appoints the other justices. Their names are then placed on the ballot of the first general election of the House of Representatives (lower house of the Japanese Diet, or Parliament) to be reviewed by the voters. Once appointed, the justices cannot be removed except by formal impeachment procedures or by popular vote. Justices retire at age 70.

Most legal cases brought before the Supreme Court are decided by one of its three petty benches of five judges each. A petty bench can refer a case to the grand bench, which includes all 15 justices. A full bench is required for decisions on cases involving constitutionality, on cases where there is no precedent in the Supreme Court, on those in which the decision of the petty bench ended in a draw, or on those that are otherwise of special importance. The constitution gives the Supreme Court the power of judicial review in order to defend individual rights of Japanese citizens. Although the Supreme Court is modeled on the American Supreme Court and can declare laws unconstitutional, it rarely exercises this power because it shies away from political issues and is reluctant to override political decisions made by the Diet. In fact, the Supreme Court usually overrides decisions of unconstitutionality made by lower courts.

The Supreme Court holds administrative powers formerly exercised by the Justice Department and thus administers the entire Japanese court system. The justices draw up lists of judges for appointment to lower courts, who are selected by the Prime Minister's Cabinet. Judges of lower courts can be removed only by formal impeachment procedures. The Supreme Court assigns judges to specific courts, appoints and removes court officials other than judges, prepares court budgets and establishes rules for the courts and for public prosecutors. See also CABINET, PRIME MINISTER'S; CONSTITUTION OF 1947; DIET; ELECTIONS; LEGAL SYSTEM.

SURIBACHI (grinding bowl) See SEASONING FOR FOOD.

SURIBACHI, MOUNT See IWO JIMA; WORLD WAR II.

SURRENDER OF JAPAN (August 15, 1945) The surrender of Japan to the Allied Powers, concluding World War II. Terms for the Japanese surrender had been set forth on July 26, 1945, in the Potsdam Declaration, issued by the Allied Powers at their last conference of the war, held July 17–August 2, 1945, in Potsdam, Germany. The declaration demanded that Japan surrender unconditionally and that the country rid itself of its militaristic government. Other terms stated that Japanese soldiers would have to lay down their arms but would be allowed to return to Japan; that Japan would be stripped of all territories it had seized since the Meiji Restoration of 1868; and that Allied troops would occupy Japan until the economic system that supported the military was dismantled and a new democratic government was established giving its citizens freedom of speech, religion, thought, and basic human rights.

After two atomic bombs were dropped on the Japanese cities of Hiroshima and Nagasaki on August 6th and 9th, and the Soviet Union declared war against Japan on August 8th, Japan formally accepted the terms of the Potsdam Declaration on August 14th. The Japanese people were informed of their country's surrender on August 15th, in a broadcast of a recorded announcement by Emperor Hirohito (1901–1989). The Japanese accepted Hirohito's request to "endure the unendurable." On September 2, 1945, the Instrument of Surrender (Nihon Kofuku Bunsho; the formal document of surrender) was signed on the battleship USS *Missouri* by Japanese Foreign Minister Shigemitsu Mamoru and Chief of Staff General Umezu Yoshijiro. The emperor was present, and U.S. General and Supreme Commander for the Allied Powers (SCAP) Douglas MacArthur (1880–1964) accepted the surrender. This document transferred all power for governing Japan to the Supreme Commander for the Allied Powers and thereby initiated the Occupation of Japan, which lasted until 1952. See also HIROHITO, EMPEROR; MACARTHUR, DOUGLAS; OCCUPATION OF JAPAN; SUPREME COMMANDER FOR THE ALLIED POWERS; WORLD WAR II.

SUSANOO NO MIKOTO A central character in Japanese mythology who is a composite of several figures. The Izumo people of western Japan, who were displaced by the Yamato clan, which came to rule the country, regarded Susanoo no Mikoto as their divine ancestor. Their legends portray him as a hero. His greatest act was to save a young woman by killing an eight-headed serpent, for which he received a famous sword. This sword, later termed *Kusanagi*, became one of the three imperial regalia that symbolized the rule of the Japanese emperors who originated with the Yamato clan. Yamato legends claim that Susanoo no Mikoto is the son of the Japanese creator god Izanagi and the brother of Sun Goddess Amaterasu o Mikami, the divine ancestor of the Yamato rulers. As the bad-tempered and violent god of storms, Susanoo no Mikoto destroyed Amaterasu's rice paddies and defiled her palace in heaven.

She became angry and withdrew into a cave, plunging the world into darkness until another goddess performed a dance that lured her out. All the gods demanded punishment of Susanoo no Mikoto for his misdeeds. They plucked his hair out and banished him to earth from heaven, the High Celestial Plain (*Takamagahara*), after which he went to the Izumo region and became god of the underworld. Susanoo no Mikoto has also been identified in Japan as god of agriculture, disease and bodies' of water. He was later associated with the deity Gozu Tenno, and is worshiped in this form at Yasaka Shrine in the old capital city of Kyoto. See also AMATERASU O MIKAMI; IMPERIAL REGALIA; IZANAGI AND IZANAMI; YAMATO.

SUSHI A popular food made of vinegared rice topped, rolled or mixed with raw seafood or other ingredients. Sushi originated with a traditional Japanese method of preserving fish by salting it and placing it on a bed of vinegared rice. To make sushi, rice vinegar is mixed into cooked white rice with a wooden paddle, and then the rice is spread out and fanned so it will become glossy. One type of sushi is *nigiri-zushi* (the "s" of *sushi* becomes a "z" in a second-position combination word), whereby small fingers of rice are formed by hand and topped with a thin layer of *wasabi* (Japanese horseradish) paste and a piece of raw or cooked fish or seafood. *Nigiri* means "clenching (with the hand)." Some favorite toppings are tuna (*maguro* or *toro*), sea urchin (*uni*), sea bream (*tai*), squid (*ika*), yellowtail (*hamachi* or *buri*, similar to tuna) salmon roe (*ikura*), grilled eel (*unagi*), shrimp (*ebi*), abalone (*awabi*), vinegared mackerel (*shime-saba*), and portions of egg omelet (*tamago-yaki*). The seafood must be perfectly fresh and in season. It takes many years for a professional sushi chef to become skilled in buying the freshest ingredients, slicing them properly, and forming the sushi. Japanese believe that the best way to enjoy *sushi* is sitting at the counter in a small sushi bar and discussing the ingredients with the chef. Sushi is dipped into soy sauce (*shoyu*) that has *wasabi* mixed

A plate of sushi, small portions of vinegared rice topped with seafood. Japanese cuisine emphasizes fresh, seasonal ingredients presented in artful arrangements.

into it, and served with slices of pickled ginger, which refresh the palate.

Another type of sushi is *maki-zushi*, or "rolled sushi," also known as *nori-maki* because rice and other ingredients are rolled up in a square of seaweed called *nori*. The rolls can be thick (*futomaki*) or thin (*hosomaki*) and eaten as is or cut into slices. Two popular ingredients are cucumber (*kappa-maki*) and raw tuna (*tekka-maki*). Other fish are also used, as well as fish roe, sea urchin, octopus and pickled daikon (Japanese radish). A new American combination is "California roll" with crab meat and avocado. A specialty of the Osaka area is *oshi-zushi*, in which rice is pressed into a mold and covered with fish to make a cake-like sushi that is cut into pieces. Many varieties of *chirashi-zushi*, or "scattered sushi," are prepared by mixing rice in a bowl with pieces of seafood, omelette and vegetables. *Inari-zushi* is a small bag of sweetened deep-fried tofu (soybean curd) stuffed with rice. In Japan many kinds of sushi are sold as take-out food in small boxes called *bento*, or *eki-ben* when they are sold at railroad stations (*eki*). Sushi restaurants can now be found in many cities in North America and Europe. See also ABALONE; BENTO; DAIKON; EEL; FISH AND FISHING INDUSTRY; GINGER; RESTAURANTS; RICE; SEA BREAM; SEAFOOD; SEAWEED; SOY SAUCE; TOFU, TUNA; WASABI.

SUTRA See SCRIPTURES, RELIGIOUS.

SUWA SHRINE A Shinto shrine located in Nagano Prefecture on central Honshu Island that has 10,000 branch shrines throughout Japan, the most of any Shinto shrine group. Suwa Shrine actually consists of two shrines, an Upper Shrine (Kami Sha) in Suwa City and a Lower Shrine (Shimo Sha) in the town of Shimo Suwa 6 miles away. The shrine's date of founding is not known, but ancient legends trace the gods of the shrine back to Okuninushi no Mikoto, who was believed to exist in this area prior to the time when the descendants of the Sun Goddess Amaterasu o Mikami came down to the earth. The Suwa clan claimed to be the direct descendants of his second son, Takeminakata no Kami, who is a god of Suwa Shrine, along with Yasakatome no Kami and Kotoshironushi no Kami. These divine spirits were originally worshipped as hunting deities, but later became agricultural deities, and finally, during the warrior era of medieval Japan, came to be worshiped as war deities. Every sixth year, during the year of the monkey and the year of the tiger in the traditional Japanese 12-year zodiac cycle, a festival is held, the Ombashira Matsuri, in which a thousand men carry large fir trees to the Upper and Lower Suwa Shrine to replace the *ombashira*, which are posts inhabited by the shrine's gods and which mark off the sacred areas of the shrine. See also KAMI; SHINTO; SHRINES, SHINTO; ZODIAC.

SUZUKI DAISETZ TEITARO (1870–1966) Known as Suzuki Daisetsu in Japan; a writer and philosopher who introduced Zen Buddhist thought to the Western world. Suzui was born in Kanazawa and educated at Tokyo University. He also studied Zen Buddhism with Shaku Soen, abbot of Engakuji Temple in Kamakura, and attained en-

lightenment (*satori*) at the age of 27. In 1897, Shaku Soen sent Suzuki to work with Paul Carus, who ran Open Court Publishing in LaSalle, Illinois. Suzuki, who was fluent in English, spent 11 years translating Buddhist texts into English for the first time and editing two magazines published by Carus, *Open Court* and *The Monist*. In 1907, Suzuki published the first major work in English on Buddhism, *Outlines of Mahayana Buddhism*. Suzuki returned to Japan in 1909, and two years later he married an American woman, Beatrice Lane, who worked with him until she died in 1939. He began publishing the journal, *Eastern Buddhist*, in 1921 when he was a professor of Buddhist philosophy at the Buddhist Otani University in the city of Kyoto. During the next two decades he also published a translation of and a commentary on the important Zen scripture the *Lankavatara Sutra*, a three-volume series, *Essays in Zen Buddhism*, and one of his major works, *Zen Buddhism and Its Influence on Japanese Culture*. In 1949, Suzuki was elected to the Japan Academy and awarded the Order of Culture by the Japanese government. He traveled frequently to the United States and Europe to lecture on Zen Buddhism, and spent several years as visiting professor at Columbia University. Suzuki wrote dozens of books in Japanese and in English, many of which are still in print. He was single-handedly responsible for creating a strong interest in Zen Buddhism among Western thinkers, and his influence continues today. *A Zen Life: D. T. Suzuki Remembered*, an anthology of essays by various scholars edited by Abe Masao, was published in 1986. See also BUDDHISM; KAMAKURA; SATORI; ZEN SECT OF BUDDHISM.

SUZUKI KANTARO (1867–1948) An admiral in the Japanese Navy who was the last prime minister of Japan before the end of World War II. Suzuki was born in Osaka and attended the Japanese Naval Academy and the Naval War College. After serving in the Sino-Japanese War of 1894–1895 and the Russo-Japanese War (1904–1905), he was appointed principal of the Naval Academy, then commander of the Kure Naval Station, and chief of the Naval General Staff. He became an admiral in 1923. In 1929 he was appointed grand chamberlain (*jijucho*), but was forced to resign in 1936 after being wounded during an attempted army coup (February 26th Incident). Suzuki became prime minister of Japan shortly before World War II ended, when General Koiso Kuniaki resigned on April 5, 1945, a few days after the American military landed on Okinawa Island. At this time the Soviet Union refused to extend the Soviet-Japanese Neutrality Pact and rejected Suzuki's secret request that Russia act as peace mediator. The atomic bombs dropped on Hiroshima on August 6th and Nagasaki on August 9th, and Russia's declaration of war against Japan on August 8th, pressed Suzuki to surrender to the Allied Forces on August 14th. His entire cabinet resigned the next day. See also ATOMIC BOMB; CABINET, PRIME MINISTER'S; FEBRUARY 26TH INCIDENT; IMPERIAL JAPANESE ARMY AND NAVY; OKINAWA, BATTLE OF; PRIME MINISTER; RUSSO-JAPANESE WAR; SINO-JAPANESE WAR OF 1894–1895; SURRENDER OF JAPAN; WORLD WAR II.

SUZUKI MOTOR CO., LTD. See MOTORCYCLE INDUSTRY.

SUZUKI VIOLIN METHOD   A method for developing musical talent in very young children through violin study, developed by Suzuki Shin'ichi (b. 1898). Suzuki, the son of a famous Japanese violin maker, studied with violin teachers in Japan and Germany and later initiated the so-called Talent Education Movement and founded the Suzuki Violin School in Matsumoto City, Nagano Prefecture. Using the motto, "Any person's talent can be developed through education," Suzuki claimed that all children have equal musical ability, which can be developed with proper training. The Suzuki method starts young children playing by rote on small violins, and requests that parents be involved in their children's study. Suzuki's school produced many virtuoso Japanese violinists and created worldwide interest in the Suzuki method. There are now about 100 Suzuki schools in Japan, with more than 10,000 students, and around 300,000 students in foreign countries.

SUZUKI ZENKO (1911–   )   Prime minister of Japan 1980–1982. Born in Iwate Prefecture, Suzuki was educated at the Fisheries Institute of the Ministry of Agriculture and Forestry (now Tokyo University of Fisheries) and held positions with fishing organizations and cooperative movements. As a member of the Japan Socialist Party (Nihon Shakaito; known as the JSP), Suzuki was elected in 1947 to the House of Representatives, the lower house of the Japanese Diet (Parliament). However, he left the JSP for the Socialist Reform Party (Shakai Kakushinto), and then joined another party that soon merged with another to form the Liberal Democratic Party (Jiyu Minshuto; known as the LDP), Japan's predominant political party. He served over a dozen terms in the House of Representatives as a member of the LDP and also held a number of cabinet posts. Under Prime Minister Ikeda Hayato, Suzuki was minister of posts and telecommunications in 1960 and chief cabinet secretary in 1964. He served as welfare minister 1965–1966 under Prime Minister Sato Eisaku. When Prime Minister Ohira Masayoshi died unexpectedly in 1980, Suzuki, then chairman of the Executive Board of the LDP, was appointed to succeed him. Not a strong leader, Suzuki resigned in 1982, and Nakasone Yasuhiro, (p.m. 1982–1987) took his place. See also DIET; FISH AND FISHING INDUSTRY; JAPAN SOCIALIST PARTY; LIBERAL DEMOCRATIC PARTY; NAKASONE YASUHIRO; OHIRA MASA-YOSHI; PRIME MINISTER; SATO EISAKU.

SUZURIBAKO   See BOXES; CALLIGRAPHY.

SWEET FLAG   See IRIS.

SWEET POTATO (satsuma-imo)   A root vegetable introduced into Japan from the Ryukyu Islands (Okinawa), through the old province of Satsuma (now southern Kyushu Island). It is similar to the sweet potato grown in North America but is firmer with a sweeter taste. Street merchants with carts sell hot baked sweet potatoes from the autumn through the spring. Sweet potatoes are also sliced and deep-fried in batter for tempura. Sweets made with sweet potatoes are also eaten. Kinton is a sweet prepared especially for the New Year Festival, for which sweet potatoes

are cooked, pureed and molded into chestnut shapes. An alcoholic beverage called shochu is distilled from sweet potatoes. It is drunk either cold with ice or hot mixed with boiling water. See also ALCOHOLIC BEVERAGES; NEW YEAR FESTIVAL; RYUKYU ISLANDS; SATSUMA PROVINCE; SWEETS; TEMPURA.

SWEETFISH   See CORMORANTS, FISHING WITH; FISH AND FISHING INDUSTRY.

SWEETS (kashi; wagashi)   Various types of confections and cakes that are served between meals with green tea (cha) or in a tea ceremony (chanoyu), and are thus also known as tea sweets (chagashi). The word for sweets, kashi, is usually preceded by the honorific prefix o-, as okashi. The word kashi comes from kajitsu, the word for fruit; shi in kashi means "seed." From ancient times, the Japanese ate fruit, either fresh or dried, between meals and in place of desserts. Dried persimmons are still popular in Japan. The first sweets were introduced into Japan from China during the Nara Era (710–794). Made of ground grain or soybean dough fried in oil, they were named "Chinese fruit" and provided the model for Japanese-style sweets (wagashi). Sugar was also introduced during this era, but until the Meiji Era (1868–1912) it was used only as a medicine by the aristocratic class. The Japanese began using sweets as offerings to Shinto and Buddhist deities, and special sweets are still made in the areas around many shrines and temples.

The development of the tea ceremony in the 16th century spread the custom of eating sweets with tea to all social classes in Japan. Japanese sweets differ from candies, pastries, cakes and other sweets eaten in the West. There are three basic types of Japanese sweets, "raw," "semi-raw," and "dry." Namagashi ("fresh") sweets do not keep very well, and are considered "wet" because they are filled with an, sweetened red bean paste. Namagashi are made with a dough of rice flour and water, or with mochi, glutinous rice cakes. The dough is steamed or left uncooked. Sweets of the second type, hanamagashi ("semi-raw"), keep longer. They include various kinds of firm bean-paste jelly called yokan, and Chinese-style steamed buns (manju) filled with an. The third type, higashi ("dry sweets"), includes a variety of colorful candy-like sweets as well as unsweetened rice crackers, known as sembei.

Japanese sweets are made in a variety of beautiful shapes and colors that reflect the season of the year. For example, cherry-blossom motifs are frequently used in the spring, and chrysanthemums and maple leaves in the autumn. Sweets are also given poetic seasonal names. A popular summer sweet is a pale-green jelly made with kanten (agar-agar, an edible seaweed thickener), which has the refreshing name kokeshimizu, "moss in a stream." Many department stores and tea shops in Japan sell sweets for eating on the premises or carrying home. Sweets are frequently given as gifts, especially when paying social calls. They are usually served individually on small plates and eaten with picks made of wood, ivory, metal or plastic. In a tea ceremony, each guest uses special chopsticks to take his or her sweet from a large serving bowl (hachi) or lidded lacquer box (*futamono.*). *See also* BEANS; CRACKERS, RICE; MOCHI; TEA; TEA CEREMONY.

SWORD, JAPANESE (*nihonto, katana*)

Straight swords (*jokoto* or *chokuto*) had been introduced into ancient Japan from China, before the eighth century A.D. but during the Kamakura Shogunate (1192–1333), curved swords were made because they were easier to handle by samurai who fought on horseback. Because of their high quality and beauty, swords produced in Japan during this era have remained the finest in the world. The first Japanese curved swords were the *tachi* type (worn on a waist sash with the cutting edge down), followed by the *katana* type (worn with the cutting edge up), which became standard. Both types are longer than 2 feet. The *katana* was paired with a 1–2-foot sword called a *wakizashi*, in a set known as *dai-sho* ("large and small"). A straight-bladed dagger shorter than 1 foot, called a *tanto*, was also used for close fighting.

Swords have been treasured in Japan as the "soul" of the samurai. Old swords handed down as heirlooms in samurai families have both historical and artistic value. They symbolize the samurai virtues of loyalty to one's feudal lord and honor, which requires death in battle or by suicide (*seppuku*) in case of defeat. A sword believed to have been presented by the Shinto deity Susanoo no Mikoto to his sister, Sun Goddess Amaterasu o Mikami, the divine ancestor of the Japanese imperial family, is one of the three imperial regalia that symbolize imperial rule in Japan.

Swords are made with remarkable technical skill. Swordsmiths traditionally have been priests of Shinto, who practice religious rules of abstinence when making a blade. Swordmakers still create swords according to the ancient rituals, which combine the elements of fire, water and earth. River sand rich in iron is heated at a low temperature to produce steel, which is then heated at a high temperature, hammered and folded many times to create a hard "skin steel" (*kawa-gane*). A layer of softer-core steel (*shin-gane*) is welded between two layers of skin steel so that the finished blade can cut well without breaking or bending. This "sandwich" is coated with a mixture of clay and straw ash (*yakiba-zuchi*) on which a pattern (*hamon*) is drawn, a process known as clay treatment (*tsuchi-dori*). It is then dried, heated in a furnace, hammered and folded back into shape. These steps are repeated 15 to 20 times, creating thousands of layers of steel. The hot blade is rapidly cooled in water to harden the portion of the blade not covered with the clay, which remains softer and more flexible although sharp. When the strip of metal is worked into the desired length, it is scraped by a two-handled curved knife (*sen*), and then filed with large metal files. The final step is polishing (*kenma*) the sword, to adjust its form and thickness and to bring out the color of the steel and the wavy pattern (*jihada*) on the face of the blade. The beauty of a sword is determined by its shape, the lie of the grain on the blade, the pattern and tiny dots (*nakano*) that comprise a design along the edge. Finally, beautifully crafted small metal fittings (*kodogu*) and braided silk cords are mounted on the sword. The most important fitting is the

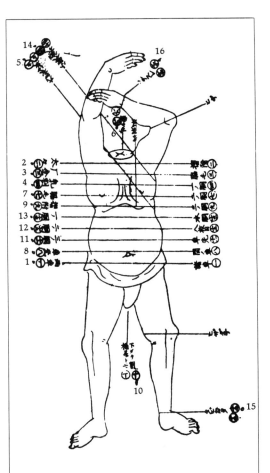

TESTS FOR NEW SWORDS

Before accepting a new sword, a samurai had its blade extensively tested—often on the body of a beheaded criminal (*above*). Cuts, which had exotic names, varied in difficulty from one across the hips (1), the hardest, to lopping off a hand (16).

1 ryo kuruma—"*pair of wheels*"
2 tai-tai—"*very big*"
3 karigane—"*wild goose*"
4 chiwari—"*splitting the breast*"
5 o-kesa—"*priest's robe*"
6 kami-tatewari—"*top vertical split*"
7 wakige—"*armpit*"
8 kurumasaki—"*end of the wheel*"
9 suritsuke—"*rubbing in*"
10 shimo-tatewari—"*bottom vertical split*"
11 san-no-do—"*third body cut*"
12 ni-no-do—"*second body cut*"
13 ichi-no-do—"*first body cut*"
14 ko-kesa—"*small priest's robe*"
15 tabigata—"*sock region*"
16 sodesuri—"*cutting the sleeve*"

A practice diagram for a samurai to test making different cuts with a new sword.

sword guard (*tsuba*), which separates the blade of a sword from the handle, or hilt (*tsuka*). A beautiful scabbard (*saya*) decorated with lacquer, sharkskin or other materials is used to protect the sword when not in use.

Although swords are still made for ceremonial and artistic purposes, the wearing of swords was prohibited in 1876 by the Meiji government (1868–1912). Swords were worn by Japanese military officers during World War II but confiscated by authorities during the postwar Occupation (1945–1952). Japanese were later permitted to retain swords proven to be antiques. In 1953 the Japanese government approved the making of swords once again. There is a Society for Conserving Swords of Beauty and its Museum of Japanese Swords in Tokyo. The Japanese government has designated several swordsmiths and sword polishers as Living National Treasures. Swords and sword guards have become valuable collector's items both in Japan and abroad. The art of drawing a sword from its scabbard (*iaido;* formerly, *iaijutsu*) and the art of cutting with a sword (*tameshi-giri*) are still practiced in association with *kendo,* the martial art of swordfighting. See also IMPERIAL REGALIA; KENDO; LACQUER WARE; LIVING NATIONAL TREASURES; METALWORK; SAMURAI; SHINTO; SUICIDE.

SWORD GUARD (*tsuba*)   A piece of steel or other metal fitted onto a sword to separate the blade from the handle, so as to protect the hand holding the sword in battle. A sword guard also adds weight to help the hand balance the sword in combat. About 3 inches across, it has a hole in the center (*nakagoana*) where it slides onto the sword blade, and may also have one or two smaller holes for the blades of a small dagger (*kozuka*) and an implement like a skewer (*kogai*), both of which can be carried in the scabbard along with the sword. Sword guards are beautifully crafted with a variety of designs, which often include the engraved family crests (*mon*) of the samurai who owned the swords, or the crests of their feudal lords. Religious symbols were also used, although the most frequent motifs were taken from nature, such as birds, animals or trees. Some were even delicately inlaid with gold, silver or other decorative metals. Cloisonne and lacquer were also applied to sword guards. Starting in the 15th century, the Goto family became the preeminent makers of sword guards and other small metal fittings that ornamented swords and scabbards. They excelled at making decorative ceremonial swords that were worn in the courts of the feudal lords, the shogun and the emperor. The art of decorating sword guards reached its high point in the 17th century, when Japan was enjoying peace and prosperity under the Tokugawa Shogunate (1603–1867), and swords became more decorative than functional. The art of designing and crafting sword guards came to an end in 1876 when the Meiji government outlawed carrying swords. Since that time, sword guards have become collector's items in their own right, in the West as well as in Japan. See also CLOISONNE; LACQUER WARE; SAMURAI; SHOGUN; SWORD; TOKUGAWA SHOGUNATE.

T

TABI See FOOTWEAR.

TACHIBANA CLAN See TAIRA CLAN.

TAIFU See TYPHOONS.

TAIHO CODE (Taiho Ritsuryo) "Great Treasure" Code; a code of law that remained the basis of the Japanese legal system from the eighth century A.D. until the Meiji Era (1868–1912). The Taiho Code of 701–702, compiled by a commission appointed by the Yamato court centered in Nara on Western Honshu Island, was the first formal legal code issued in Japan. The code comprised six volumes of penal laws (*ritsu*) and 11 volumes of administrative laws (*ryo*), all of which meticulously recorded case laws and commentaries. The Taiho Code was influenced by the legal code followed by the complex bureaucracy that governed China during the Tang (T'ang) dynasty (618–907). The Japanese court had begun adapting many aspects of Chinese government and culture in the sixth century A.D., and the *ritsuryo* system governed by the Taiho Code in Japan was an attempt to imitate the Chinese system of recruiting and promoting bureaucrats according to their ability. This went against the Japanese practice of assigning positions and ranks by heredity, so the Taiho Code was revised in A.D. 718 to accommodate Japanese customs. The specific laws were superseded by the Yoro Code of A.D. 757; however, the principles of the Taiho Code were incorporated into law codes promulgated by feudal rulers beginning with the Kamakura Shogunate (1192–1333) that overthrew the imperial court. See also CHINA AND JAPAN; LEGAL SYSTEM; NARA; RITSURYO SYSTEM; YAMATO.

TAIKA REFORM (Taika no Kaishin) The first legal measures carried out A.D. 645–649 by the Yamato court in the region of west Japan now known as Nara Prefecture to change the political organization of Japan, based on the independent power of various clans (*uji*), and replace it with a centralized bureaucracy. Prince Shotoku (574–622) had tried to institute central reforms based on the Chinese model of government, but the powerful Soga clan resisted these attempts. In A.D. 645 a faction of court leaders overthrew the Soga clan by force and began the Taika, or "Great Change," reform. That same year Emperor Kotoku took the throne, and the court proclaimed the doctrine that imperial power is absolute, making all citizens direct subjects of the emperor. In A.D. 646 the Reform Edict (Kaishin no Cho) was issued with four articles that centered the government in one capital city and instituted new systems for local government, taxation and allocation of land. This edict is recorded in the official chronicle *Nihon Shoki* (A.D.

720). The court claimed ownership of all farmlands, and sent officials to all provinces in the Nara region and in eastern Japan controlled by the Yamato court to make surveys of the population and the economy that would enable the central government to control both land and people. Peasants were assigned a standard portion of land to cultivate during their lifetime, and aristocrats were compensated by being given positions and stipends that corresponded to their former ranks. Although most of these reforms were not put into effect until the 690s, the Taika Reform enabled the court to enforce its principles of centralized power and state ownership. See also CHINA AND JAPAN; NIHON SHOKI; SHOTOKU, PRINCE; SOGA CLAN; TAIHO CODE; YAMATO.

TAIKO See DRUMS.

TAIRA CLAN One of the four great clans, along with the Fujiwara, Minamoto and Tachibana, that were powerful during the Heian Era (794–1185). The Taira came into conflict with the Minamoto clan, culminating in the Taira-Minamoto War (1180–1185), in which the Taira were decisively defeated and ruling power was transferred from the court to the military government known as the Kamakura Shogunate (1192–1333).

As a means of limiting the number of imperial descendants who would make a claim to the throne, and balancing the growing power of the Fujiwara clan, Emperor Kammu created the new family named Taira for his grandson Takamune in A.D. 825. Emperor Saga had similarly created the Minamoto family in A.D. 814. Many members of the royal family were thus removed from the imperial line and were known as "surname-receiving royalty" (*shisei kozoku*). Such persons from then on were named either Minamoto or Taira. The Chinese characters for *Taira* were also pronounced *Heishi* or *Heike*, the name by which the clan is commonly known.

Several branches of the Taira or Heike family descended from emperors who reigned after Kammu. The strongest line originated with Kammu's great-grandson, Prince Takamochi, who became a provincial official in eastern Japan, north of modern Tokyo. His descendants became warriors in that region, known as the "Eight Bands of Taira from the East" (*Bando Hachi Heishi*), and fought in the Taira-Minamoto War. Another Taira branch, which settled in Ise Province in east-central Japan, became the most powerful Taira family line. The Taira reached their greatest power under Taira no Kiyomori, who won the Hogen War of 1156 and the Heiji War of 1160, a rebellion led by Minamoto no Yoshitomo (1123–1160). His sons Minamoto no Yoritomo (1147–1199) and Minamoto no Yoshitsune (1159–1189) built up an army to oppose Kiyomori, grand minister of state (dajo daijin) whose infant grandson was put on the throne as Emperor Antaku in 1180. The Taira-Minamoto War brought the long-standing conflict between the two clans to a head. The Minamoto thoroughly defeated the Taira, killing Kiyomori, his young grandson the Emperor Antaku and other Taira leaders, and marking the end of the Taira (Heike) clan as a national power in Japan. The story of the Taira clan's brief rise and fall between 1156 and 1185 is told in the 13th-century historical saga, *The Tale of the Heike* (*Heike Monogatari*). See also CLANS; HEIAN ERA; HEIKE, THE TALE OF THE; KAMAKURA SHOGUNATE; MINAMOTO NO YORITOMO; MINAMOTO NO YOSHITSUNE; SAMURAI; TAIRA-MINAMOTO WAR.

TAIRA-MINAMOTO WAR (1180–1185) (*Gempei no Soran*) A decisive war fought between two factions, the Taira (or Heike) clan and the Minamoto (or Genji) clan, which were powerful rivals during the Heian Era (794–1185). The Minamoto defeat of the Taira resulted in the establishment of military government (*bakufu*) in Japan, which overrode the Heian imperial court. Japan was ruled by military governments for nearly seven centuries, until the Meiji Restoration of 1868. The Taira and Minamoto families were descended from members of the imperial family who had been prevented from making a claim to the throne in the ninth century A.D. Whereas the imperial family was centered in the city of Kyoto in western Japan, the Taira and Minamoto built power bases in eastern Japan. They originally settled there as provincial government officials but soon became military leaders. Conflicts increased between the rival Taira and Minamoto in the 12th century A.D. The warrior Taira no Kiyomori killed many leaders of the Sewa Genji family, the main branch of the Minamoto, in the Hogen War of 1156. In retaliation, Minamoto no Yoshitomo led an unsuccessful rebellion against Kiyomori (Heiji War of 1159–1160). Yoshimitsu was killed, but Kiyomori let his sons live, and sent them into exile. Members of the imperial court began plotting against the Taira because of Kiyomori's overbearing power, but a rebellion led by Prince Mochihito and Minamoto no Yorimasa was crushed by Kiyomori. Todaiji, a magnificent Buddhist temple built by the imperial court in the old capital city of Nara to represent its power and prestige, supported the rebellion and was burned down by the Taira. Yoshitomo's son Minamoto no Yoritomo (1147–1199) began gathering an army in eastern Japan to fight the Taira. After escaping defeat, he founded a military headquarters in Kamakura and acquired 200,000 warriors. Yoritomo won the Battle of Fujigawa in 1180 and then spent three years consolidating his power in the eastern provinces. He instituted a system of vassals (*gokenin*) that laid the foundation for feudalism in Japan. In 1183 his cousin, Minamoto no Yoshinaka, routed the Tairas from Kyoto. Yoritomo distrusted Yoshinaka and sent troops that defeated him in Kyoto in 1184. They were headed by Yoritomo's brother, Minamoto no Yoshitsune (1159–1189), who then led the Minamoto forces in successful battles against the Taira, who fled to Yashima on Shikoku Island in 1184. The following year, Yoshitsune defeated the Taira at Yashima. Once again they fled west.

The Taira and Minamoto met for their final, decisive battle at Dannoura in the Strait of Shimonoseki, which separates Honshu and Kyushu Islands. On April 25, 1185, the Minamoto fleet crushed the Taira. Their leaders were killed and the young Emperor Antoku was drowned. Yoritomo took control of Japan and established the military government known as the Kamakura Shogunate (1192–1333). See also BAKUFU; DANNOURA, BATTLE OF; FEUDALISM; HEIAN ERA; KAMAKURA SHOGUNATE; MINAMOTO NO YORITOMO; MINAMOTO NO YOSHITSUNE; SHIMONOSEKI; TAIRA CLAN; TODAIJI.

TAISHO ERA (1912–1926) A period of Japanese history taking its name from the reign of Emperor Taisho (personal name Yoshihito; 1879–1926), the son of Emperor Meiji (1852–1912; r. 1868–1912). Because Emperor Taisho was in poor health, his son, Crown Prince Hirohito (now known as Emperor Showa; 1901–1989), was made regent (*sessho*), in 1921. Yoshihito was the first emperor to receive a public, although elite, education, at the Peers' School (now Gakushuin University), studying Western as well as Japanese and Chinese subjects.

During the Taisho Era, Japan continued the process of Westernization and economic expansion that had begun with the Meiji Restoration of 1868. The Taisho Era started with the Taisho Political Crisis (Taisho Seihen) of 1912–1913, in which the military brought down Prime Minister Saionji Kimmochi's cabinet, and retired army general Katsura Taro was appointed to succeed him. However, members of the Friends of Constitutional Government Party (Seiyukai) in the Diet (Japanese Parliament) increasingly resented the interference of the military and the *genro* ("elder statesmen") in Japanese politics. The Japanese public also supported constitutional government in which the cabinets would answer to majorities in the Diet. As a result, the Seiyukai gained more representatives in the Diet and greater power in the Prime Minister's Cabinet. Katsura founded a political party as well that held power in the cabinet of Prime Minister Okuma Shigenobu (1914–1916). During the Taisho Era, the Diet took over leadership of the Japanese government from the *genro*, who had previously functioned as a so-called transcendental cabinet. The period from 1913 to 1932 was later termed the Taisho Democracy. In 1925 the right to vote was extended to all adult Japanese males. Japan entered World War I on August 8, 1914 to aid Great Britain, which had become an ally of Japan with the Anglo-Japanese Alliance of 1902. The Japanese defeated the Germans in Shandong (Shantung) Province, China, and on Pacific islands north of the equator. In 1915, Japan presented the so-called Twenty-One Demands to force China to give it greater political and economic concessions. The war enabled great expansion of the Japanese industry and military. Japan participated in the Paris Peace Conference in 1919, resulting in the Treaty of Versailles, which ended the war. In 1918, Hara (Kei) Takashi, the head of the Seiyukai, became prime minister of Japan. Hara accepted an invitation to participate in the Washington Naval Conference in the United States in 1921, where he agreed that Japan would limit naval expansion, return Shandong to China, and retreat from an expedition into

Siberia. After Hara was assassinated in 1921, cabinets were headed by men from outside the Seiyukai. In 1924, Kato Takaaki, head of the alternate political party (which took the name Minseito, or People's Government Party, in 1927), was appointed prime minister. For eight years, the heads of these two parties alternated in serving as prime minister. The Japan Communist Party was founded in 1922, when there was interest in radical ideas by intellectuals and a growing labor movement in Japan. The Japanese army and military budget were greatly reduced in 1924, and foreign trade was encouraged. See also DIET; FRIENDS OF CONSTITUTIONAL GOVERNMENT PARTY; GENRO; HIROHITO, EMPEROR; JAPAN COMMUNIST PARTY; MEIJI ERA; OKUMA SHIGENOBU; PEOPLE'S GOVERNMENT PARTY; POLITICAL PARTIES; PRIME MINISTER; SAIONJI KIMMOCHI; SHOWA ERA; TWENTY-ONE DEMANDS ON CHINA; WASHINGTON NAVAL CONFERENCE AND NAVAL TREATY OF 1922; WORLD WAR I.

TAIWAN AND JAPAN   Taiwan, formerly known as Formosa, is an island just southwest of Japan's southern Ryukyu chain (Okinawa Prefecture) and 80 miles southeast of China. It became a Japanese colony in 1895 and remained so until 1952.

Japanese merchants in the late 16th century used Taiwan as an intermediate base between Japan and China, in the so-called vermilion seal ship trade, named for the seals on licenses for ships authorized to trade by the Japanese government. Japan sent unsuccessful expeditions to acquire Taiwan in 1593, 1609 and 1616. The Dutch gained control of Taiwan in 1624 and used it as a trading base with Japan. Direct Japanese trade with Taiwan ended around 1633, and Qing (Ch'ing) dynasty (1644–1912) China brought Taiwan under its rule in 1683. After Japan was opened to Western trade in the mid-1800s, it resumed trading with Taiwan. The Japanese Meiji government (1868–1912) planned to expand into Taiwan and sent an unsuccessful military expedition to the island in 1874. Japan defeated China in the Sino-Japanese War of 1894–1895 and acquired Taiwan and the neighboring Pescadore Islands (Penghu or P'enghu) from China. Japan established military and political rule over Taiwan and made an enormous investment in its economic growth and modernization. Taiwan in turn provided much-needed agricultural products and raw materials for Japan. During World War II, Japan used Taiwan as a staging area for its coastal occupation of southeast China and its invasions of the Philippines and Southeast Asia, and mobilized the Taiwanese for military purposes. When the Communists took control of China in 1949, the nationalist Kuomintang (KMT) Party in China, led by Chiang Kai-shek (1887–1975), fled to Taiwan and established themselves as the ruling elite. Under the Peace Treaty of 1952, following Japan's defeat in World War II and Occupation by the Allied Powers, Japan gave up Taiwan and other territories it acquired after 1895. In 1952 Japan also signed a peace treaty with the Chinese Nationalist regime. In 1972, Japan established diplomatic relations with the People's Republic of China, but continued its economic and cultural ties with Taiwan. Most Taiwanese have had positive feelings toward Japan despite its earlier colonization of the island. Between 1950 and 1983, Japan made 4% of its direct

overseas investments in Taiwan, and Taiwan has been the fourth largest buyer of Japanese exports. See also CHINA AND JAPAN; KOREA AND JAPAN; MEIJI ERA; PEACE TREATY OF 1952; RYUKYU ISLANDS; SINO-JAPANESE WAR OF 1894–1895; SINO-JAPANESE WAR OF 1937–1945; VERMILION SEAL SHIP TRADE; WORLD WAR II.

TAKADA KENZO   See FASHION DESIGNERS.

TAKAMATSU   A city on Shikoku Island on the Inland Sea that grew up around a castle built in 1588 by Ikoma Chikamasa. During the Edo Era (1600–1868), the castle was taken over and restored by the Matsudaira clan. The few remains of the castle are preserved in Tamamo Park. Other local attractions are Ritsurin Koen, a beautiful park; the Folk Art Museum; Shikoku Mura, an open-air museum of traditional architecture; and Yashima, a battle site of the Taira-Minamoto War (1180–1185). Takamatsu is the largest city on Shikoku, with a population of more than 300,000, and is the capital of Kagawa Prefecture. The city became a center for transportation when a ferryboat service was begun in 1910 linking it with Uno in Okayama Prefecture on the main island of Honshu. Major products of Takamatsu include processed foods, noodles, machinery, lacquer ware and paper. Prawns were first cultivated by the Japanese in this area. See also CASTLE; FERRIES; HONSHU ISLAND; INLAND SEA; SHIKOKU ISLAND.

TAKARAZUKA OPERA COMPANY   Known prior to 1940 as the Takarazuka Girls Opera Company; a popular all-female theater troupe that performs Western musical revues and operettas as well as Japanese folk songs and dances. Actresses specialize in male, female or child roles. The Takarazuka Opera Company was founded in 1913 by Kobayashi Ichizo (1873–1957), the owner of a resort near Osaka City named Takarazuka. He sent several touring companies around Japan, opened a school to train performers, and built large theaters at Takarazuka in 1922 and in Tokyo in 1934. Since 1930, there have been four distinct Takarazuka troupes performing at the same time: Flower (Hana), Moon (Tsuki), Snow (Yuki), and Star (Hoshi). Many successful Japanese stage and movie actresses got their start in the Takarazuka Opera Company. The company, which performs in Takarazuka theater near the Ginza district in Tokyo, now has around 350 members. Teenage girls especially love their grand production numbers and their romantic shows about love and friendship. A rival Girls Opera Company was founded by the Shochiku Co., Ltd. in 1922. The Shochiku troupe still performs, and emphasizes larger production numbers and more dancing than singing.

TAKASHIMAYA CO., LTD.   See DEPARTMENT STORES.

TAKEGAWA BATH HOUSE   See BEPPU.

TAKESHITA NOBORU (1924–)   The prime minister of Japan from November 1987 until June 1989. Takeshita was born in 1924 in Shimane Prefecture on the southwest coast of Honshu Island. The Takeshita family had a sake brewing business. His father was a politician serving in the Shimane Prefectural Assembly. While attending Waseda University in Tokyo during World War II, Takeshita was drafted into the army and trained as a pilot. After the war he resumed his studies and graduated from the School of Commerce in 1947. He then returned to his hometown to teach school and work to rebuild Japan through the Youth Group Movement.

He was elected to the Shimane Prefectural Assembly in 1951, and in 1958 he was elected to the House of Representatives, the lower house of the Japanese Diet (Parliament). He served 11 consecutive terms in the Diet for a period of 29 years. He was a member of the powerful Tanaka faction of the Liberal Democratic Party (Jiyu Minshuto; abbreviated as LDP), the dominant political party in postwar Japan. In 1971, Prime Minister Sato Eisaku (p.m. 1964–1972) made Takeshita a secretary in his cabinet, and then construction minister. In 1979, Takeshita began the first of five terms as minister of finance. The LDP chose him to be its secretary-general from July, 1986 to October, 1987. By July, 1987 he was also leader of the LDP's largest faction, the Keiseikai. In November 1987, Takeshita was selected head of the LDP and thereby became prime minister of Japan.

Takeshita's political slogans were "trust and harmony" and *furusato*, the creation of a "homelike" atmosphere for the Japanese nation. His policies emphasized housing, education, and reform of the tax system and land holdings. He also had to address the economic issues of Japan's external trade imbalance and pressure by foreign countries for more open markets in Japan. The so-called Recruit Scandal, which erupted in 1988, implicated many leaders of the LDP in giving political and economic favors to the Recruit Company in return for large shares of stock and other gifts. Public outcry forced Takeshita to resign on June 2, 1989 to take responsibility for the Recruit Scandal. He was replaced as prime minister by Uno Sosuke, who also became involved in scandal and had to resign in less than two months, after the LDP lost many seats in the July 1989 elections for the House of Councillors (upper house of the Diet). See also DIET; EXPORTS AND IMPORTS; FACTIONS, POLITICAL; LIBERAL DEMOCRATIC PARTY; PRIME MINISTER; RECRUIT SCANDAL; SATO EISAKU; UNO SOSUKE.

TALES See BAMBOO CUTTER, THE TALE OF THE; HEIKE, THE TALE OF THE; ISE, TALES OF; KINTARO; MOMOTARO; MONOGATARI; STORYTELLING; YANAGI SOETSU.

TALISMANS (*omamori, ema*) Objects sold or given out at Shinto shrines and Buddhist temples to ward off evil and to bring good fortune. There are a great variety of talismans, made of such materials as paper, cloth, wood or even plastic. Small amulets or good-luck charms are frequently hung in windows of homes or cars. One type of amulet is the *gofu*, a small piece of paper inscribed with the name of a deity. The Japanese have traditionally believed that written words have spiritual power. Small bows and arrows (*hamaya* and *hamayumi*) are talismans that the

Japanese buy on their first visit to a Shinto shrine in the New Year. The word *hama* is written with characters that originally meant "target" but now mean "to repel evil spirits." *Yumi* and *ya* mean "bow" and "arrow." Today they have a purely symbolic function, but formerly, archery competitions were held at the New Year in some areas of Japan to predict the autumn harvest. *Kumade* are decorated bamboo rakes sold in November at Otori Shrine in Tokyo to bring good fortune. *Ema* are small wooden plaques or votive tablets that have a picture of a horse or other animal painted on them. The word *ema* is written with the Chinese characters for "picture" (*e*) and "horse" (*uma*). They are sold at shrines as modern substitutes for horses that were offered as supplications to the *kami* (sacred spirits) in former times. A black horse would be given to a shrine as a request for rain, and a white horse for good weather. Today the Japanese buy *ema* to pray for all sorts of wishes to be granted, such as a good marriage, recovery from illness or success in school examinations. They write their names, dates and prayers on the *ema,* and hang them on a special board in the shrine or temple, or in a special building known as an *emado*. Many students leave *ema* at shrines dedicated to Kitano Tenjin, the patron saint of scholarship. Large antique *ema* have been collected as folk art by museums in Japan and other countries. During the Edo Era (1600–1868), many artists also painted beautiful pictures on *ema* to advertise their talents. See also AMULETS; ARCHERY; HORSE; KITANO SHRINE; NEW YEAR FESTIVAL; SHINTO; SHRINES, SHINTO.

TAMARI See SOY SAUCE.

TAMBA WARE (*tamba-yaki*) A type of pottery made in Tamba Province (part of modern Hyogo Prefecture) on west-central Honshu Island. Pottery containers for use by farm households were first made at Tamba during the Kamakura Shogunate (1192–1333). Thick jars with broad shoulders and small mouths for storing food were made by building up coils of clay. During the firing process in *anagama* (underground wood-burning kilns), flames turned the pottery reddish-brown, and falling wood ash created spots of greenish glaze. By the 17th century, Tamba potters were using kick-wheels to construct the objects and Korean-style *noborigama* (kilns erected on hillsides) to fire them. Along with storage jars, Tamba potters produced rice bowls, tea bowls, *hibachi*, sake bottles and vases. The great Japanese potter Nonomura Ninsei (fl. mid-17th century) was originally a potter at Tamba. Tamba ware is simple, rough, strong in design and resembles Shigaraki ware. After a century of decline and industrialized mass-production, there has been a return to the traditional handcrafted Tamba style. Currently more than 50 small workshops produce Tamba ware in the towns of Kami- and Shimo-Tachikui. Tamba is considered one of the Six Old Kilns in Japan. *Tamba Pottery,* an English-language book by Daniel Rhodes, was published in 1970. See also HIBACHI; NONOMURA NINSEI; POTTERY; SHIGARAKI WARE.

TANABATA See STAR FESTIVAL.

TANAKA KAKUEI (1918–) Prime minister of Japan (1972–1974) and a central figure in the Lockheed aircraft company scandal, in 1976, the worst Japanese political scandal since World War II until the Recruit Scandal of 1988–1989. Tanaka was apprenticed to a building contractor before completing his education, and went on to become a successful businessman with his own construction company. He turned to politics after World War II, making large contributions to the Japan Progressive Party (Nihon Shimpoto) and then winning a seat in the House of Representatives (the Lower House of the Diet, or Japanese parliament) in 1947 as a member of the Democratic Party (Minshuto). In 1948 he switched to the new Democratic Liberal Party (Minshuto Jiyuto), which in 1955 became the Liberal Democratic Party (Jiyu Minshuto; known as the LDP), Japan's dominant political party. Tanaka held positions in the cabinets of several prime ministers, serving as minister of postal services and communications, finance, and international trade and industry. He also served two terms as secretary-general of the LDP. When Tanaka was named the LDP's president in 1972, as leader of the preeminent party, he automatically became prime minister of Japan. One of his important actions in office was to visit Beijing in 1974 and establish diplomatic relations between Japan and the People's Republic of China in place of relations with Taiwan. He also attempted to spread the distribution of industries throughout the Japanese islands. However, Tanaka is best known for his role in financial scandals that forced him to resign as prime minister in December 1974. In 1976 he was indicted, along with other leading Japanese politicians and businessmen, for taking large bribes from the Lockheed Corporation, a U.S. company that wanted to sell airplanes to Japan. Tanaka resigned from the LDP, as did other indicted members who held seats in the Diet. However, they all ran as independents in the December 1976 election and won their Diet seats back. Tanaka retained his political influence in Japan during the following decade, but his power declined after he had a stroke and his party faction was taken over by Takeshita Noboru (p.m. 1987–1989). See also DIET; ELECTIONS; LIBERAL DEMOCRATIC PARTY; POLITICAL PARTIES; PRIME MINISTER; TAKESHITA NOBORU.

TANAKA KINUYO (1910–1977) A famous movie actress for more than 50 years who also became one of the few Japanese women to direct movies. Tanaka began her career in musical theater and then joined the film studio Shochiku Co., Ltd., in 1924. She appeared in many silent films, starting with *Genroku onna* (*Woman of Genroku;* 1924). In 1931 she appeared in the first popular Japanese talking picture, *Madamu to nyobo* (*The Neighbor's Wife and Mine*) by Gosho Heinosuke. Tanaka remained a popular actress in the 1930s and 1940s. After World War II, she played major roles in critically acclaimed movies by the important Japanese director Mizoguchi Kenji (1898–1956), with whom she was long associated. In *Saikaku ichida onna* (1952; shown abroad as *The Life of Oharu*), Tanaka played the leading role of an aristocratic woman whose strong love for the wrong man causes her to fall to the lowest levels of society. Mizoguchi also featured her in *Ugetsu* (*Ugetsu Monogatari, Ghost Story;* 1953) and *Sansho-Dayu* (*Sansho the Bailiff;* 1954). In 1953 Tanaka directed her first movie, *Koibumi* (*Love Letter*) and went on to direct six movies altogether while still performing in movies and serial television dramas. She won the Kinema Jumpo Prize in Japan (comparable to an Academy Award in America) for her final movie role, an old prostitute who tells the tragic story of her life in *Sandakan hachiban shokan: Bokyo* (1974; shown abroad as *Sandakan No. 8*) by the Japanese director Kumai Kei (1930–). This movie was also nominated for an Academy Award in America. See also FILMS; MIZOGUCHI KENJI.

TANEGASHIMA See FIREARMS, INTRODUCTION OF; PORTUGUESE IN JAPAN.

TANIZAKI JUNICHIRO (1886–1965) A novelist especially known for writing about men's obsessive sexual desire for women. Tanizaki was born in the cosmopolitan heart of Tokyo and studied Japanese literature at Tokyo University. His first published work was a one-act play in 1909, followed by a highly praised short story, "Shisei," in 1910 (translated as "The Tattooer" in 1963). This story, and others written over the next few years, portray men's masochistic erotic desire for the beautiful yet demonic power that women seemed to embody for Tanizaki. During the 1920s, he wrote plays and novels that developed this theme. His work was interrupted by the destruction of Tokyo during the Great Kanto Earthquake of 1923, which led him to move to the Kyoto-Osaka region. The traditional culture of Kyoto, the former capital of Japan, created a transformation in Tanizaki. He turned away from the urban Westernization of his Tokyo days and toward classical Japanese literature, in particular *The Tale of Genji* (*Genji Monogatari*). Written in the early 11th century by a court lady named Murasaki Shikibu, this was Japan's first long work of fiction, and its lasting influence on the culture of Japan can be seen in Tanizaki's best-known novel, translated into English in 1957 as *The Makioka Sisters* (*Sasameyuki;* 1943–1948) and made into a film. Tanizaki drew this book's theme, the lives of four sisters in a once-wealthy family that is sadly declining, from the actual circumstances of his third wife, Matsuko. Tanizaki was awarded the Japanese Imperial Prize in Literature in 1949. He wrote many more stories and novels, some of which have been translated into English. "The Mother of Captain Shigemoto" (translated in 1956 from "Shosho Shigemoto no haha"; 1949–1950) is about the deep love between a mother and her son. *The Key* (translated in 1961 from *Kagi*, 1956) depicts sexual conflict between a husband and wife. "The Bridge of Dreams" (translated 1963 from "Yume no ukihashi," 1960) and *Diary of a Mad Old Man* (translated 1965 from *Futen rojin nikki*, 1961–1962) continue Tanizaki's sexual themes. The latter tells how an old man resolves his obsession with the feet of his daughter-in-law. Another famous work is *Some Prefer Nettles* (*Tade Kuu mushi*, 1928–1929; translated

1955). His memoir, *Childhood Years,* was published in 1988. See also GENJI, THE TALE OF; NOVELS.

TANKA "Short poem"; a form of classical Japanese poetry *(waka),* consisting of five lines with 31 syllables in a 5-7-5-7-7 pattern. The *tanka* dates back at least to the seventh century A.D. The majority of poems in the earliest Japanese poetry anthology, *Manyoshu* (eighth century A.D.), are *tanka.* They are differentiated from *choka* or *nagauta,* "long poems," which are composed of numerous pairs of 5- and 7-syllable lines, and which end with an extra 7-syllable line. *Tanka* soon replaced *choka* as the dominant poetic form in Japan, and has continued to be the major form of Japanese poetry. *Tanka* are written in the native Japanese syllabic system, or *kana.* Since early Japanese poets also wrote in the Chinese language using *kanji* or Chinese characters, *tanka* became synonymous with *waka,* or "Japanese poetry," as opposed to *kanshi,* "Chinese verse." In A.D. 905 the first official court anthology of *tanka,* known as the *Kokinshu,* was published.

The Japanese language lends itself to short forms of poetry because it is made up of a limited number of vowels and two-letter syllables. Many words with different meanings have the same pronunciation. Word games, puns, epigrams and aphorisms are basic elements of *tanka,* as are images which connote a complex meaning. During the Heian Era (794–1185), artists of the *Yamato-e* (indigenous Japanese) style wrote poems on their paintings that described the scenes and seasons of the year that they portrayed. Thus the three arts of poetry, painting and calligraphy *(shodo,* the "Way of Writing") became intertwined.

During the medieval era (12th-16th centuries), Japanese poets used the *tanka* form to sustain the past glories of Heian culture. The important *tanka* anthology, the *Shinkokinshu (New Kokinshu),* was compiled c. 1205 by the renowned poet and critic Fujiwara no Teika (1162–1241) and others. In the 14th century, the *tanka* form was adapted into *renga,* or "linked verse," which consists of two sections, one consisting of the first three *tanka* lines of 5, 7 and 5 syllables, and the other the final lines of 7 and 7 syllables. Two or more poets could alternately compose these two "linked" sections endlessly. However, the *tanka* form came to be considered too rigid. In the 17th century, a spontaneous and expressive short poetic form known as *haikai* or *haiku* developed from the first section of the *tanka* form, consisting of three lines with 5-7-5 syllables. In the late 19th century, there was renewed interest in the traditional *tanka* form of poetry by poets who wanted to revive Japanese culture in reaction to Western culture then being introduced into Japan. In the 20th century, the term *waka* has become associated with poets who wrote in the classical 31-syllable form prior to the 20th century, whereas *tanka* refers to 20th-century poets who use the *tanka* form in a more spontaneous and expressive manner. Every year in Japan there is a *tanka* contest on a set theme. Winners read their poems in the presence of the emperor, who also contributes a poem. See also FUJIWARA NO TEIKA; HAIKU; HEIAN ERA; KANA; KANJI; KOKINSHU; MANYOSHU; POETRY; RENGA; WAKA; YAMATO.

TANSU See CHEST; FURNITURE, TRADITIONAL.

TAPE RECORDER See ELECTRONICS INDUSTRY; SONY CORPORATION.

TATAMI Thick woven straw mats used as floor coverings in Japanese-style rooms. *Tatami* are about 6 feet long, 3 feet wide, and 2 inches thick. The activities of Japanese daily life traditionally take place on tatami-covered floors, and eating, working, socializing and sleeping can all be done in the same space. Originally, in the Heian Era (794–1185), *tatami* were individual mats that were brought out and placed on the wooden floors for sitting and sleeping. Since the noun *tatami* comes from the verb *tatamu* (to pile up or fold), the earliest *tatami* may have been thin mats that were piled up in many layers for use and folded when put away. The mats had seamed cloth binding or borders *(herinuno)* in colors that symbolized the owners' social rank. Some wealthy people were covering their entire floor space with *tatami* by the Muromachi Era (1333–1568). By this time *tatami* were made of a thick base *(toko)* of rice straw and a soft, tightly woven cover *(omote)* of a rush or grass called *igusa.* By the modern era the floors of all Japanese rooms were commonly covered by thick *tatami.* The size and floor plan of a Japanese-style room are measured by the number of *tatami* required to cover the floor. Eight, six and four-and-a-half mats are standard room sizes. However, *tatami* are slightly smaller in the Tokyo area because the great demand for housing has caused developers to build more apartments on a smaller scale.

Until the Taisho Era (1912–1926), *tatami* were made by hand, but since then the rice-straw bases have been made by machines. Today, the bases can even be made with fillings of artificial materials. A *tatami* maker cuts the base *(wara)* to the proper size, covers it with a woven mat *(goza),* and hand-sews the cover onto the base. He finishes the *tatami* by sewing on strips of cloth binding *(hedi)* in a dark color or green brocade. If the woven covering of a *tatami* wears out, it can be replaced. The Japanese take off their shoes indoors to protect the *tatami,* and they do not step on the cloth borders of the *tatami.* They also protect the *tatami* by using very little furniture. Only a low table is used for eating and writing, and cushions *(zabuton)* or legless chairs *(zaisu)* are used for sitting. Futon are put on the *tatami* at night for sleeping and are put away in the morning. See also FURNITURE; FUTON; HOMES AND HOUSING; PILLOWS; STRAW WARE.

TATEMAE AND HONNE See ETIQUETTE.

TATTOO *(irezumi* or *horimono)* Although Japanese tattooing reached its highest level during the Edo Era (1600–1868), tattooing was done throughout the islands' history, for a number of purposes. The *Wei Zhi* (or *Wei Chi),* a third-century A.D. Chinese chronicle, mentions tattoos on Japanese men of the time. The Japanese chronicle *Nihon Shoki (Chronicle of Japan;* A.D. 720) records the punishment of a criminal by facial tattooing, and tattoos were used as a method of punishment in Japan until the early 18th century. At that time, tattoos acquired a new social significance. Prostitutes in the licensed pleasure quarters of Edo (modern Tokyo) and Osaka often had the names of their lovers discreetly tattooed on their arms, thighs or hands. These tattoos were called "pledge marks" (kishi-bori). In the 1820s and 1830s, certain groups of men began displaying tattoos that covered much of their bodies: volunteer firemen and those who wore little clothing while doing their jobs, such as palanquin bearers, postal runners, gardeners and carpenters. Young sons of wealthy businessmen also had full tattoos to impress others in the pleasure quarters. A special guild of tattooers (horshi), many of whom were also street barbers or carvers of woodblocks for making prints (ukiyo-e), developed the technical and artistic skills to create elaborate multicolored patterns on clients' bodies. Using many steel needles, they worked outlines of designs in black ink that turned blue under the skin. Then they filled in the colors with quick movements of their hands, a technique called hane-bari, while holding the needles. Clients could examine pattern books for design ideas. Japanese police in the Meiji Era (1868–1912) shut down tattoo parlors out of fear that Westerners then coming into Japan would consider the Japanese barbaric. But the art of tattooing has survived to the present day. Now it is associated mainly with yakuza (gangsters), who wear fantastic full-body tattoos under their business suits. See also EDO ERA; WOODBLOCK PRINTS; YAKUZA; YOSHIWARA.

TAWARAYU SOTATSU See SOTATSU.

TAX SYSTEM The postwar Japanese tax system was established in 1949 by the Shoup Tax Mission during the Allied Occupation (1945–1952). In 1955 a Tax Advisory Commission was established to suggest annual modifications in the tax system and develop long-term tax policies. The Japanese pay national taxes (kokuzei) and local prefectural and municipal taxes (chihozei), which together total around 20% of their income, a relatively low figure by Western standards. The Japanese government derives approximately 70% of its revenues from taxes. The Japanese tax system is administered by the National Tax Administration Agency (Kokuzeicho), a semi-independent agency of the Ministry of Finance (MOF), which maintains 12 regional tax offices and 509 local tax offices throughout Japan. There is no general Japanese tax code, and the Tax Bureau of the MOF adjusts tax schedules and estimates revenues in accord with the annual national budget prepared by the MOF. Customs are handled by the Customs and Tariff Bureau of the MOF, which has nine regional customhouses. Local governments impose their own taxes under the guidance of the Tax Affairs Bureau of the Ministry of Home Affairs.

Income taxes are graduated so that people in higher brackets have higher tax rates and smaller deductions than those in lower brackets. Many types of individual savings are deductible, such as accounts in the postal savings system. Most wage-earners are not required to file tax returns because taxes are withheld from their paychecks. Business executives are given large tax-exempt expense accounts by their companies for entertaining business clients. One reason taxes in Japan have been comparatively low is the ceiling on defense spending for the Self-Defense Forces, which is restricted to no more than 1% of the country's annual budget. However, there is an increasing demand for social security programs, especially as the Japanese population ages.

The tax system was recently overhauled by the administration of Prime Minister Takeshita Noboru, with reforms taking effect on April 1, 1989. The tax-reform program had five major points: substantial reductions in the national individual income tax; a reduction of the corporate tax rate for ordinary corporations and small and medium-size companies; reduction of the inheritance tax; taxation of capital gains from securities transactions, which were previously tax exempt; and abolition of consumption taxes on such items as sugar, travel, playing cards, gas and local electricity. The government also reduced taxes on alcoholic beverages and automobiles. However, it introduced a 3% value-added consumption tax on all goods and services sold or provided by business entities, with a few exemptions. This was Japan's first national sales tax, and it proved extremely unpopular with the public. Voters expressed their disapproval of the tax by handing the dominant Liberal Democratic Party (LDP) a humiliating defeat in elections for the House of Councillors (upper house of the Diet, or parliament) on July 23, 1989. Widespread dissatisfaction with the current tax situation has been satirized by Japanese film director Itami Jugo in two films starring his wife, Miyamoto Nobuko, as a tax bureau investigator: A Taxing Woman (1987) and A Taxing Woman Returns (1989). See also EXPENSE ACCOUNTS; INCOME; MINISTRY OF FINANCE; POSTAL SYSTEM; SELF-DEFENSE FORCES.

TEA (cha) Japanese tea is known as green tea because the leaves of the tea plant (Camellia sinensis) are not fermented, as are those of black tea. The honorific o- is added to the name for Japanese green tea, ocha, while black or Western-style tea is called kocha. Japanese tea leaves are processed only by steaming for 35–50 seconds to prevent oxidation or fermentation, which would turn the leaves black. This process also enables the leaves to retain vitamins, potassium and phosphoric acid. Tea contains an astringent chemical called tannin; caffeine, which is a stimulant; and amino acids.

Half of all Japanese green tea is produced in Shizuoka Prefecture on the Pacific (eastern) coast side of central Honshu Island. Tea bushes are planted in rounded hedges, usually on hillsides, with 2–3 feet between each row. The bushes are trimmed so they grow no higher than 3–4 feet, which stimulates the growth of more leaves. Workers pick the new leaves by hand.

There are several different types of green tea. Sencha ("infused tea"), the most common type, is made by steaming the leaves, rolling and crushing them, and drying them with warm air. Gyokuro ("jewel dew" or "dewdrop") is the finest and most expensive grade of Japanese green tea. The plants are protected by bamboo coverings, and the youngest and most tender leaves are carefully picked at the exact moment of ripeness, then are processed with the same method as *sencha. Gyokuro* is delicate green in color but very aromatic. *Matcha* is powdered tea used for the Japanese tea ceremony. It is also made with the finest tea leaves, but they are ground into powder rather than crushed. The finest tea for *matcha* is grown in the Uji region near the old capital city of Kyoto. *Matcha* is made by pouring hot water over the powder in a large tea bowl (*chawan*) and then whipping it with a bamboo tea whisk (*chasen*). Thin and thick tea (*usucha* and *koicha*) are both made this way, depending on how much tea is mixed with water. The taste of dark green *matcha* is strong and bitter. It is accompanied by Japanese-style sweets, which are frequently made with red bean paste. *Bancha* is a lower grade of tea made the same way as *sencha* but from older leaves, which produce a brown, astringent liquid when steeped. It is commonly served in restaurants. *Bancha* can be roasted to make *hojicha,* a strong-tasting tea, or blended with toasted rice grains to make *genmaicha.* A refreshing beverage made with roasted barley, known as *mugicha,* is also drunk hot in winter and iced in summer.

Green tea other than *matcha* is steeped with hot water (around 175°–210°F) for a short time in a large porcelain pot and poured into cups without handles. It can also be steeped directly in handleless pottery mugs. Tea sets have three or five cups because the number four, which sounds the same as the word for death in Japanese, is generally avoided. There are also two-cup "husband and wife" teacup sets (*meoto-jawan*) with the larger cup for the husband. Around 3 grams of tea are used for every 7 ounces of water. Lemon, milk and sugar are never added to green tea.

Buddhist monks first brought seeds of the tea plant to Japan from China, where it was called *cha,* in the ninth century A.D. However, tea drinking did not become widespread in Japan until the 12th century, when Eisai (1141–1215), founder of the Rinzai sect of Zen Buddhism, introduced *matcha* from China. Zen monks promoted tea as a medicinal and stimulating beverage that helped them stay awake during meditation. They also laid the foundation for the development of the highly formalized Japanese tea ceremony. At first, only the higher social classes could afford to drink *matcha.* Commoners were not able to drink tea until the mid-18th century, when the process for producing *sencha* tea leaves became widespread in Japan. See also EISAI; O-; SWEETS; TEA BOWL; TEA CEREMONY; UJI; ZEN SECT OF BUDDHISM.

TEA BOWL (*chawan*) A large pottery bowl in which a special tea known as *matcha* is served during the Japanese tea ceremony. *Matcha* is made from tea leaves that have been ground into a powder. Thin informal tea (*usucha*) is made by spooning three bamboo scoops (*chashaku*) of *matcha* into a tea bowl, pouring in some hot water and whipping the tea into a froth with a specially made brush-like tea whisk (*chasen*). Thick tea (*koicha*), which is more formal, is made by scooping more tea into a tea bowl, adding hot water and kneading it with a whisk. In either case, a large tea bowl with a wide bottom is necessary to provide room for the tea whisk.

Ceremonial tea was first drunk in Japan from brown Chinese bowls known as *temmoku.* Sen no Rikyu (1522–1591), the renowned tea master who established the rules of the tea ceremony, worked with a Korean immigrant potter named Chojiro (1516–1592) to develop the straight-sided black Raku (*raku-yaki*) style of tea bowl. Black and red Raku are still considered the most appropriate tea bowls, particularly for thick tea. Hagi ware, Karatsu ware and Shino ware are also preferred forms of pottery. The rough hand-formed shapes of rice bowls made in Korea, such as the Ido and Irabo types, have also been highly valued as tea bowls. Rikyu in his choice of utensils emphasized an aesthetic principle known as *wabi,* which finds the highest beauty in things that are natural, spontaneous and asymmetrical. A tea bowl not only has to look beautiful and be the proper size for making tea, but it must also feel good in the hand while the tea is being drunk. Raku transmits heat slowly and thus feels warm and alive. Tea bowls for informal thin tea are generally more colorful and are often decorated with natural motifs that reflect the season of the year, such as an iris flower in May or a chrysanthemum or maple leaf in the autumn. The tea ceremony has had such a widespread influence on Japanese culture that tea bowls, and pottery of all types, are some of the most important collectible art objects in Japan. See also CHOJIRO; HAGI WARE; KARATSU WARE; KILN; POTTERY; RAKU WARE; SEN NO RIKYU; SHINO WARE; TEA; TEA CEREMONY; TEMMOKU; SABI AND WABI.

TEA CEREMONY (*chado, chanoyu*) A formal ritual for preparing and drinking a bitter green tea made with *matcha,* tea leaves that have been ground into a powder. This ritual is termed *chado* (or *sado*), the "Way of Tea," or *chanoyu,* literally "hot water for tea." The ceremony originated in Zen (Chan or Ch'an in Chinese) Buddhist monasteries in China, where monks shared a bowl of tea in front of an ink painting of Daruma (Bodhidharma), who is traditionally believed to have founded Zen in China in A.D. 520. Tea drinking was introduced to Japan in the 12th century and spread from the monasteries to the upper classes of society. Japanese tea masters such as Noami (1397–1471), Murata Shuko (1422–1502) and especially Sen no Rikyu (1522–1591) developed the tea ceremony into a comprehensive social and aesthetic experience. Rikyu favored the so-called *wabi* style of tea ceremony, which emphasizes austerity and naturalness over the ostentatious display of utensils. He developed the black Raku tea bowl as the most appropriate style for the tea ceremony. Rikyu was tea master to the national unifiers Oda Nobunaga (1534–1582) and Toyotomi Hideyoshi (1536–1598); military leaders found participating in the tea ceremony a useful means of enhancing their prestige. Rikyu's descendants established the major tea ceremony schools, which continue today. The Urasenke School is the largest and the only one that has established branch schools outside of Japan. The tea cere-

A woman in kimono performing a tea ceremony. She pours hot water onto powdered green tea in the tea bowl and whips the mixture with a bamboo whisk. The tea ceremony combines many elements of Japanese culture.

mony was originally a man's activity, but today many young Japanese women study tea, flower arranging and cooking as part of their "bridal training."

A complete, formal tea ceremony (chaji) takes several hours and includes the making of a charcoal fire; a special meal, known as kaiseki; the serving of "wet" sweets made with bean paste, followed by formal thick tea (koicha); an interlude for the guests to enjoy the garden outside the teahouse; and the serving of informal thin tea (usucha) and "dry" sweets, such as rice crackers or light confections. Most tea ceremonies are much less formal. The preferred number of guests ranges to three or five; the number four is avoided because the Japanese word for four is pronounced the same as that for death. The ceremony is held in a small, plain tearoom or teahouse (chashitsu) that has a tokonoma (alcove) in one wall where a scroll and simple flower arrangement are displayed. Host (teishu) and guests (okyakusama) kneel on tatami (straw floor mats). Water is boiled over charcoal (or an electric unit) in a large iron kettle (kama). The host spoons the tea with a bamboo scoop (chashaku) from a pottery or lacquer ware container (chaire

or natsume) into a large pottery bowl (chawan); pours in hot water with a bamboo ladle (hishaku); and kneads or whips the mixture with a split-tine bamboo whisk (chasen). Guests share a bowl of thick tea by rotating the drinking spot, but each guest drinks his or her own bowl of thin tea. They also admire the unique, handmade utensils, which have been carefully chosen by the host to reflect the occasion and the season of the year. The first guest speaks for the group and asks the host questions about the utensils. Everyone follows strictly prescribed rules of etiquette, which include a great deal of respectful bowing to each other and to the utensils, and the handling of each utensil in a specific way. Students of the tea ceremony must therefore learn how to be guests as well as hosts.

There are many variations in the tea ceremony, ranging from very formal to informal, which are performed to fit the occasion, the time of day, the social rank of the guests and the season of the year. A synthesis of Japanese social customs and crafts, the tea ceremony has had a widespread influence on Japanese culture. See also BAMBOO; BOWING; GARDENS; KETTLE; ODA NOBUNAGA; POTTERY; SABI AND WABI; SCROLLS;

SEN NO RIKYU; SWEETS; TATAMI; TEA; TEA BOWL; TEAHOUSE; TOKO-
NOMA; TOYOTOMI HIDEYOSHI; URASENKE SCHOOL OF THE TEA CERE-
MONY; ZEN SECT OF BUDDHISM.

TEACHER See APPRENTICE SYSTEM; DOJO; EDUCATION SYSTEM;
IEMOTO; SENSEI; UNIVERSITIES.

TEAHOUSE *(chashitsu, chaya, ryotei)* A small building in
a garden, or a special room, where a tea ceremony *(chado*
or *chanoyu)* is held. Known as a *chashitsu* or *chaya*, a teahouse is built with wooden posts and a raised floor, a
bamboo ceiling, and a roof covered with thatch, shingles
or tiles. The interior has a traditional atmosphere with
rough plaster walls, *tatami* (thick straw floor mats) on which
host and guests sit, sliding doors *(fusuma)*, and small
windows *(shoji)* covered with handmade paper *(washi)* to
filter bright sunlight. This setting creates a warm, intimate
feeling and allows the guests to focus on the specially
chosen utensils that the host brings out to make tea. Sen
no Rikyu (1522–1591), who formalized the tea ceremony,
preferred the *soan*, or "grass hut," style of teahouse based
on the aesthetic principle of *wabi*, or natural, unpretentious
beauty. The walls of a tearoom are no more than 6 feet
high. Floor size ranges from two to eight or more tatami
(about 3 feet × 6 feet each), with the preferred size being
four and a half *tatami*. There is a *tokonoma*, a special alcove
where a hanging scroll and a simple flower arrangement
are displayed. A small tea garden surrounds the teahouse
and is known as a *roji*, or "dewy path," through which
the guests walk on stepping stones separating them from
the hectic outside world and preparing them for the calm
world of the tea ceremony. The term teahouse is also used
in English for *ryotei* (formerly known as *machiai)*, the places
where parties are held at which geisha perform; *ryotei*
means an inn or place to eat. The rooms in these teahouses
also have plain walls and *tatami*. Geisha teahouses are
managed by older geisha, who are addressed as *okasan*
(mother). See also GARDENS; GEISHA; SEN NO RIKYU; SHOJI; TA-
TAMI; TEA CEREMONY; TOKONOMA; SABI AND WABI.

TEAPOTS *(dobin, kyusu)* Japanese teapots, made of porcelain or pottery, usually have a strainer built into the
spout to prevent tea leaves from being poured into the tea
cups. *Dobin* are large round teapots that have an attached
curved handle on top, usually made from bamboo. They
are used for steeping *bancha*, coarse green tea that is the
lowest grade but the most commonly drunk tea in Japan.
Bancha is served free in restaurants in large handleless
mugs *(yunomi)* and is also drunk by office and factory
workers during their breaks. *Kyusu* are small teapots that
have a handle, made from the same material as the pot,
which projects at a right angle to the spout. They are used
for brewing the highest grades of tea, *gyokuro* and *sencha*,
in small quantities, to be drunk from small handleless
porcelain or pottery cups. *Sencha* is offered to important
visitors in offices or factories and is served in exclusive
restaurants, especially ones that serve sushi. *Matcha*, the
powdered tea used in the tea ceremony *(chanoyu)*, is not
brewed in a teapot but is mixed with hot water in a large

tea bowl *(chawan)* with a bamboo whisk *(chasen)*. Water for
tea was traditionally heated over charcoal fires in large iron
kettles *(kama)*, which are still used in the tea ceremony.
Iron kettles with handles and spouts, resembling teapots,
are known as *tetsubin*. Japanese teapots have matching
cups in sets of five; the number four *(shi)* is avoided because
it is pronounced the same as the word for death. See also
BAMBOO; FOUR; KETTLE; PORCELAIN; POTTERY; TEA; TEA BOWL; TEA
CEREMONY; TEAHOUSE.

TECHNOLOGY, MODERN See AUTOMOBILE INDUSTRY;
CAMERAS AND PHOTOGRAPHY; COMPUTER INDUSTRY; ELECTRONICS
INDUSTRY; FIFTY-GENERATION ADVANCED COMPUTER SYSTEMS; JOINT-
VENTURE CORPORATION; RESEARCH AND DEVELOPMENT; ROBOTS AND
ROBOTICS; SCIENCE AND TECHNOLOGY AGENCY; SEMICONDUCTOR IN-
DUSTRY; TELECOMMUNICATIONS SYSTEM; TSUKUBA ACADEMIC NEW
TOWN.

TELECOMMUNICATIONS SYSTEM *(tsushin seido)*
Telephone and telegraph services were first established in
Japan by the Meiji government (1868–1912), utilizing Western technology and equipment. Public telegraph service
was begun between Tokyo and Yokohama in 1869 and
between Tokyo and Nagasaki in 1873; a national telegraph
network was in place by 1878. A submarine cable laid
between Nagasaki and Shanghai in 1871 enabled international telegraph service between Tokyo and Europe. Public
telephone service was established in Tokyo and Yokohama
in 1890. After the Great Earthquake of 1923 seriously damaged telephone and telegraph systems, the Japanese government reconstructed them with new automatic switching
equipment imported from the West. By the 1930s, Japan
was producing its own telephone sets and switching equipment and developing advanced new systems. Reorganization of the government under the postwar Occupation
(1945–1952) established the Ministry of Telecommunications in 1949 and the Nippon Telegraph and Telephone
Public Corporation (NTT; Nihon Denshin Denwa Kosha;
abbreviated Denden Kosha) in 1952. The following year,
international telecommunication services were separated
from NTT and assigned to the Kokusai Denshin Denwa
Co., Ltd. (KDD). KDD is responsible for telephone, telegraph, telex and television relay services between Japan
and foreign countries. NTT and KDD were made private
companies in the late 1980s. Private telecommunications
operations are also maintained by all Japanese police organizations, the Ministry of Construction, Japan Railways
and others.

NTT has been at the forefront of technological development for telephone sets, switching equipment and transmission systems, such as coaxial cable and microwave
systems. A trans-Pacific coaxial cable was laid in 1964, and
satellite circuits were initiated in 1967. Direct dialing is now
possible between Japan and more than 30 foreign countries.
By the early 1980s, there were more than 40 million telephone customers (about 35% of the population) in Japan.
Telephones are widely used for computer data and facsim-
ile (FAX) transmissions and television relay, as well as for
voice transmission. There are public telephones on railroad

cars of the new Tokaido-San'yo Line between Tokyo and Fukuoka.

Charges for telephone calls in Japan are relatively low; a three-minute local call costs 10 yen (about 15 cents). Public telephones are available in busy locations such as stations, shopping districts and restaurants. They are colored yellow, blue, green, pink or red based on their function (long distance, local, etc.) and the amount of money they accept. Magnetic prepaid telephone cards are very popular. Each time a card is inserted in a telephone, the balance is digitally displayed, and the cost of the call is automatically deducted from the balance. See also BROADCASTING SYSTEM; COMPUTER INDUSTRY; NIPPON TELEGRAPH AND TELEPHONE CORPORATION.

TELEPHONE SYSTEM See NIPPON TELEGRAPH AND TELEPHONE CORPORATION; TELECOMMUNICATIONS SYSTEM.

TELEVISION See BROADCASTING; ELECTRONICS INDUSTRY; JAPAN BROADCASTING CORPORATION; SONY CORPORATION.

TEMMOKU The Japanese name for a glossy, dark brown or purplish black pottery glaze; also, an object covered with this glaze. The name *temmoku* derives from T'ien Mu Shan, a mountain in Zhejiang (Chekiang), China, where Zen (Chan or Ch'an in Chinese) Buddhist temples held tea ceremonies using bowls with dark glazes. These bowls, often with light brown streaks or brown, reddish brown, or silver spots, were made during the Song (or Sung) dynasty (960–1279) at the Chien-yao pottery kilns in Fujian (Fukien) Province. Japanese Zen monks brought *temmoku* bowls to Japan along with the tea ceremony. During the Muromachi Era (1338–1568), potters at the important Seto pottery center in Owari Province (modern Aichi Prefecture) began copying the *temmoku* style. Iron oxide in the clay and the glaze they used gave Japanese *temmoku* its deep brown color. The glaze was applied thickly, and when the pieces were fired in woodburning kilns, it flowed downward and pooled at the bases, which were left unglazed. Streaks left where the glaze thinned during firing were called "wild rabbits' fur." Another effect was "oil-spot" *temmoku* (*yuteki temmoku*), which developed crystal spots if there was too much iron in the glaze. The *temmoku* style was used especially for tea bowls (*chawan*) and tea caddies (*chaire*). *Temmoku* was the forerunner of Shino ware, another major style of pottery highly valued by tea ceremony masters. See also SETO WARE; SHINO WARE; TEA BOWL; TEA CEREMONY; ZEN SECT OF BUDDHISM.

TEMPLES, BUDDHIST (*jiin* or *tera*) A sacred site of Buddhism, the religion introduced into Japan from China in the sixth century A.D. Temples house statues of Buddhist deities, contain residences for priests or nuns, and are the site of religious rituals. There are thousands of Buddhist temples of various sizes and historical significance in Japan. Their buildings are laid out and named in different ways, according to the historical eras when the temples were built and the Buddhist sects to which they belong. The main sects of Buddhism in Japan have been Nichiren, Pure Land, Shingon, Tendai and Zen.

The most prominent building at many temples is the pagoda (*to*), a multi-storied structure housing sacred relics and scriptures, which derives from the Indian *stupa*, which housed relics of the Buddha. Other important structures in a temple compound include the *sanmon*, or entrance gate; the *kondo* or *butsuden*, the building where statues of deities are enshrined; and the *hotto* or *kodo*, the building where Buddhist *sutras* (scriptures) are read. Additional buildings in the compound contain temple offices, kitchens and residence halls for priests or nuns, and lodgings for visitors. Temple buildings are made of wood and have sloping roofs covered with tiles (*onigawara*). They are elaborately decorated, in comparison to the plain architecture of traditional Shinto shrines. Buddhist worshippers stand in the outer chamber of the main hall facing the inner altar, where religious statues and various ritual items such as incense and flowers, are placed. Temples have hanging bells (*tsurigane* or *bonsho*) which are struck with large wooden posts, to ring the hours and on festive occasions.

The Japanese imperial court patronized Buddhism starting in the sixth century A.D. as a way of enhancing its authority. Prince Shotoku (Shotoku Taishi; 574–622) built the so-called Seven Great Temples in Nara, the capital from 710 to 794, where Horyuji remains an important historical site visited by many tourists. Emperor Shomu (r. 724–749) ordered temples and nunneries to be built in every province, and constructed Todaiji as the principal temple in Nara. Todaiji, another tourist attraction, is the largest wooden structure in the world and houses an enormous bronze statue of Buddha (*Daibutsu*), which was dedicated in 752 with a massive state ceremony. Buddhist temples became wealthy through state support and the acquisition of lands in the provinces. During the medieval era (12th–16th century), temples were powerful centers of cultural and economic activities. Large temples had their own bands of warrior-monks, and the national unifier Oda Nobunaga (1534–1582) destroyed many Buddhist temples to eliminate the military threat they posed. His successor, Toyotomi Hideyoshi (1536–1598), collected taxes from temples based on their land holdings. The Tokugawa Shogunate (1603–1867) closed Japan to Western influences, such as Christianity, and kept records on Japanese citizens by requiring that they register with a local Buddhist temple, both of which measures further enhanced Buddhism's importance. By the 19th century, Buddhist temples and Shinto shrines had become intertwined in Japan, but the Meiji government (1868–1912) established Shinto as the national religion (known as State Shinto), separated Buddhist elements from Shinto shrines, and strictly controlled Buddhist activities. The postwar Constitution of 1947 guarantees freedom of religion in Japan, and Buddhist temples have attempted to recover, many by opening their grounds to tourists. Major temples of many Buddhist sects may be visited, especially in the old capital city of Kyoto. Japanese usually do not attend temples except for special occasions, such as festivals and funerals. But families usually have small Buddhist altars (*butsudan*) in their homes where they keep memorial tablets (ihai) for deceased ancestors. See also ALTARS IN HOMES; BUDDHISM; DAIBUTSU; HORYUJI; HOSSO SECT OF BUDDHISM; KYOTO; NARA; PAGODA; PURE LAND SECT OF BUDDHISM; SHINGON SECT OF BUDDHISM; SHINTO; TODAIJI; TENDAI SECT OF BUDDHISM; ZEN SECT OF BUDDHISM.

TEMPURA Deep-fried seafood and vegetables. Fresh ingredients are dipped into a light batter and deep-fried in hot oil. These ingredients can include seafood, such as shrimp or prawns, squid, scallops and many types of fish, and seasonal vegetables such as eggplants, mushrooms, sweet potatoes, green peppers and slices of lotus root. Unlike many fried meals, tempura is light and delicate. The cooking batter, called koromo ("clothing"), consists of egg and flour mixed with ice water and is prepared just before use so it is still full of air bubbles. The oil is a blend of sesame and vegetable oils and must be kept at a temperature of 340°–360° F. Just before eating, cooked tempura is dipped into a sauce made with a fish-stock base (dashi) and soy sauce flavored with grated ginger and daikon (Japanese radish). Deep-fried foods were introduced into Japan by the Portuguese at the end of the 16th century. The name tempura may come from the Portuguese word for Lent, Tempora, since Portuguese Catholics ate fish during Lent and on Fridays. Tempura became very popular by the end of the 18th century and was available mainly at portable street food stalls (yatai). See also COOKING; FOOD STALLS; PORTUGUESE IN JAPAN; NAMES OF INDIVIDUAL FOODS.

TEMPYO ERA (729–749) A period during the Nara Era (710–794) that is especially significant in the history of Japanese art and culture. The Tempyo Era corresponds to the reign of Emperor Shomu (724–749), who made Buddhism, which had been introduced into Japan from China, the national religion of Japan. Shomu, who used Buddhism to strengthen the central rule of the imperial court, constructed Todaiji as the central Buddhist temple in the capital city of Nara, and established branch temples throughout the provinces. This stimulated the creation of impressive works of art for the temples, particularly large, realistic sculptures and paintings of Buddhist deities. The sculptures were made of wood, bronze and two materials new to Japanese sculptors, clay and dry lacquer. The Shosoin (imperial treasure house) was built to store a vast quantity of art works and other gifts donated to Todaiji, which are still preserved today. Japan sent embassies to China, then under rule of the Tang (T'ang) dynasty (608–907), and adopted the Chinese style of government known in Japan as the ritsuryo system. However, Emperor Shomu's monumental projects drained the financial resources of the Nara court and in fact weakened its administrative power. See also BUDDHISM; CHINA AND JAPAN; DAIBUTSU; NARA; NARA ERA; PAINTING; RITSURYO SYSTEM; SCULPTURE; SHOSOIN; TEMPLES, BUDDHIST; TODAIJI.

TENDAI SECT OF BUDDHISM A sect of Buddhism, introduced into Japan from India through China in the sixth century A.D., which was founded by the Japanese monk Saicho (767–822). Tendai Buddhism in Japan derives from the Tiantai (T'ien-t'ai) sect in China, named for its headquarters on Mount Tiantai. Saicho traveled to China in A.D. 804 and studied for nine months at Mount Taintai, where he became accredited as a master of Tiantai Buddhism. The Japanese Emperor Kammu had given Saicho permission to build a Buddhist temple on Mount Hiei, in the northeast sector of the capital city of Kyoto. When Saicho returned to Japan, he made this temple the Japanese headquarters of the Tendai sect. Emperor Kammu moved the capital from Nara to Kyoto, and supported Saicho and Tendai Buddhism because members of other Buddhist sects in Nara had interfered with the imperial government. Enryakuji, as Saicho's temple on Mount Hiei came to be known, grew into a huge complex of more than 3,000 buildings. Many great religious leaders studied Tendai Buddhism there and went on to found Pure Land and other popular Japanese Buddhist sects.

Tendai teachings are based on the Lotus Sutra (Hokke kyo), a scripture that proclaims that all human beings have the potential to become enlightened Buddhas. Tendai belongs to the Mahayana (Greater Vehicle) branch of Buddhism, which has a universal and non-monastic emphasis, enabling conversion of large numbers of people, while Buddhist sects in Nara such as the Hosso sect taught that only monks could become Buddhas. One practice of Tendai Buddhism that became central to Pure Land and other sects in Japan that worship the Buddhist deity Amida, was the nembutsu. Repetition of the phrase nembutsu, short for Namu Amida Butsu ("Save me, Amida Buddha"), enables one to be saved and reborn in Amida's Western Paradise. Saicho also emphasized the need to live a morally perfect life.

Tendai monks received 12 years of strict training in Buddhist scriptures and meditation at Mount Hiei. Tendai Buddhism was one of the two dominant Japanese Buddhist sects, along with Shingon (Esoteric) Buddhism, from the founding of Kyoto in the eighth century A.D. until the 13th century. The Tendai sect reached its height in the 10th and 11th centuries, when the Japanese emperors and powerful families such as the Fujiwara gave it their support. Tendai also incorporated the worship of kami (divine spirits) of Shinto, the native Japanese religion, into its practices. Because Tendai was associated with the aristocracy, it was later surpassed in popularity by the mass movements of the Pure Land and Nichiren sects of Buddhism, and by the Zen Sect, which was embraced by feudal military rulers, all of which had their origins in Tendai teachings but later became distinctive sects. See also AMIDA; BUDDHISM; ENRYAKUJI; HIEI, MOUNT; HOSSO SECT OF BUDDHISM; LOTUS SUTRA; NARA ERA; NEMBUTSU; NICHIREN SECT OF BUDDHISM; PURE LAND SECT OF BUDDHISM; SAICHO; ZEN SECT OF BUDDHISM.

TENGU See DEMONS AND GHOSTS.

TENJIN SHRINE See BRIDGES.

TENNO "Heavenly sovereign"; the title for the reigning emperor in Japan. The Japanese term kotei is used to refer to reigning monarchs of other countries. The title *tenno,* which is translated into English as "emperor," was originally used in either the sixth or seventh century A.D. by rulers of the Yamato court, from whom the Japanese imperial family claims to have descended in an unbroken line. *Tenno,* as applied to these rulers, reflects the influence of Chinese culture, which was introduced into ancient Japan. Emperors were called "Sons of Heaven" in China, and the Japanese adopted this concept of the central ruler as transcendent and divine. Japanese mythology, as recorded in the eighth-century chronicles *Kojiki* and *Nihon Shoki,* traced the ancestry of the emperors to Amaterasu o Mikami, the Sun Goddess who is the chief deity of Shinto, the native Japanese religion. In the legend, the reign of the Japanese emperor is legitimized by the three imperial regalia (sacred sword, mirror, and jewels), which Amaterasu gave to her grandson Ninigi no Mikoto. She sent her grandson Ninigi from heaven down to earth, and his descendants became the imperial family of Japan. The main function of the emperor, or *tenno,* has not been to wield political power but to intercede with the *kami* (sacred spirits) of Shinto. See also AMATERASU O MIKAMI; CHINA AND JAPAN; EMPEROR; IMPERIAL REGALIA; KOJIKI; NINIGI NO MIKOTO; NIHON SHOKI; SHINTO; YAMATO.

TENRIKYO "Religion of Divine Wisdom"; a so-called new religion in Japan that was founded in 1838 by Nakayama Miki (1798–1887). She was a farm woman who claimed to be possessed by a *kami,* or divine spirit, known as Tenri O no Mikoto, and spent her life preaching faith in his revelation of "divine wisdom" (*tenri*) through her. Nakayama's supposed faith healing attracted many followers, to whom she was a "living god" (*ikagami*). She taught that human beings could attain a joyful life by giving up selfishness and restoring harmony between themselves and "God the Parent" (*oyagami*), and her message gave believers hope that individual suffering and social injustice alike would soon come to an end. Despite severe persecution by the Japanese government, Nahakayama wrote down the divine revelations that form Tenrikyo's scriptures. She also taught a "salvation dance service" (*kagura-zutome*), which is the central ritual of the religion. Tenrikyo was the first of the new religions to attract a large number of followers. It built up a strong organization under the leadership of Nakayama's successor, a male disciple named Iburi Izo (1833–1907). In 1908 Tenrikyo was acknowledged by the Japanese government as an official Shinto sect (Kyoha Shinto). Many members make a pilgrimage to the place where the religion was founded, now the city of Tenri, in Nara prefecture on western Honshu Island. Nakayama Miki's spirit is believed to reside in the sacred spot, known as the *jiba,* in the temple at Tenri. By 1980, Tenrikyo had around 2.5 million followers in Japan and more than 16,000 member groups in Japan and foreign countries. Tenrikyo operates a library, museum, hospital and radio station. Tenri University (Tenri Daigaku) was founded in 1925 as the first private coeducational foreign-language institute in Japan. See also KAMI; MEIJI ERA; NEW RELIGIONS; SHAMANS AND SHAMANISM; SHINTO.

TENUGUI A small, lightweight towel that can be worn as a headband (*hachimaki*) and is a popular souvenir. A *tenugui* is about 1 foot wide. Its length depends on how the fabric is cut from a bolt of cloth, which is often dyed with traditional patterns. *Tenugui* can be draped on the head in many different styles, which in the traditional Japanese theater (Kabuki), reflects the social status of the wearer. Before the Edo Era (1600–1868), *tenugui* were made of undyed linen, but then cotton came into use. The cotton towels were decorated by various techniques for textiles such as tie-dyeing with red or indigo dyes. When Kabuki became a popular entertainment, famous actors had their crests printed on *tenugui* to be given out as souvenirs or advertisements. This practice was taken up by other schools of traditional Japanese arts. Today, shops and companies often give away *tenugui* when they open for business. Many tourist attractions also sell *tenugui* as souvenirs. See also CREST; HEADWEAR; INDIGO; KABUKI; TEXTILES.

TERIYAKI A popular method of cooking pieces of fish, seafood, chicken, beef or pork by glazing them with a sweet sauce before grilling or pan-frying. The sauce is a mixture of soy sauce, sake, *mirin* (sweetened rice wine), and sugar. *Teri* refers to the "luster" or "gloss" of the sauce, and *yaki* indicates grilling over a fire. Commercially bottled *teriyaki* sauce is available in many stores. See also COOKING; MIRIN; SAKE; SOY SAUCE.

TEXTILES The Japanese have developed the arts of weaving, dyeing and decorating fabrics to a very high level of skill and beauty. Textiles have always been highly valued by the Japanese, who have used them as tribute payments to feudal lords, offerings to the gods, covers for treasured gifts and wrappers for valuable objects, as well as for beautiful garments. Ancient Japanese wore clothing woven from natural fibers, such as hemp (*asa*) and mulberry (*kozo*), and colored with natural dyes such as indigo. Elaborate techniques for silk (*kinu*) cultivation, weaving and dyeing were introduced into Japan almost 2,000 years ago by immigrant groups from Korea and China, notably the Hata clan. Many textiles were used for banners and other ceremonial purposes by the imperial court and the Buddhist religion, which was introduced from China in the sixth century A.D. The Nara Era (710–794) was a high point in the history of Japanese textiles. Many fabrics made in Japan and other Asian countries have been preserved in the Shosoin, an eighth-century imperial storehouse. After the capital was moved from Nara to Heiankyo (later known as Kyoto) in 794 A.D., it remained the center of Japanese textile arts for a thousand years.

The kimono, the traditional Japanese garment worn by both men and women, is made from long, straight panels that are sewn together and wrapped around the body. The simplicity of the kimono functions like a blank canvas that can be decorated with an infinite variety of design motifs, patterns and colors. The Japanese especially admire designs of flowers and plants, birds and other motifs taken from nature and the four changing seasons. Plaids, stripes, small dots (*komon*), tortoise-shells, lozenges and other abstract or geometric designs have also been widely used. A design may be large or small, and it may decorate the entire kimono or just part of it, such as the bottom edge, shoulders or sleeves. Formal Kimono have circular family crests *(mon)* on the neck and shoulders. Kimono from the Azuchi-Momoyama Era (1568–1600), especially costumes for Noh drama, are highly valued works of art, and among the finest textiles in the world. During the Edo Era (1600–1868), *obi* (sashes worn around kimono) became very wide and stiff, and their decorative designs are as important as those of kimono. Some of the most famous Japanese textile techniques are brocade, *yuzen* dyeing, *kasuri* (tie-dye weaving, known abroad as ikat), and hand-painting. *Tsujigahana* is a technique perfected in the Muromachi (1333–1568) and Azuchi-Momoyama eras that combines tie-dye weaving and hand-painting to make beautiful designs. Brocade (*nishiki*, "beautiful combination of colors") is heavy, richly textured silk that often has woven gold or silver patterns. Such techniques were introduced to Japan by Chinese weavers in the 16th century. Weavers in the Nishijin district of Kyoto have made brocades for *obi*, Noh costumes, bindings for scrolls and many other purposes. Japanese brocades are often embellished with fine embroidery in colored silk threads and threads wrapped with gold and silver foil.

The southern Ryukyu Islands (Okinawa Prefecture) have had a distinct tradition of fine textiles, which were paid as tribute to the Shimazu clan of Satsuma in southern Japan, which controlled the islands from 1609 until they were made a prefecture of Japan in 1872. *Bingata* is a Ryukyu fabric dyed in multicolored patterns with stencils. This technique was adapted in mainland Japan as *yuzen* dyeing. *Katazome* is a technique for dyeing or printing textiles using stencils (*katagami*). *Bashofu* is fabric made from fibers of a type of banana tree. *Kasuri* is a complex technique for tie-dyeing and weaving threads to make a subtle pattern. This technique also become widespread in the main islands of Japan.

The cultivation of cotton was introduced in the 15th century. In the cold northern regions, peasant garments made of cotton that is quilted in layers, a technique known as *sashiko*, became popular. Weavers and dyers continue to produce beautiful handmade textiles using this great variety of techniques. The most skilled have been designated by the Japanese government as Living National Treasures. Apart from kimono and *obi*, patterned textiles have traditionally been used for *noren*, divided curtains hung over doorways of restaurants and shops; *furoshiki*, colorful squares of fabric used to wrap and carry objects; and *fukusa*, small squares of silk used for handling utensils in the tea ceremony. Dolls dressed in beautiful traditional kimono are collected and displayed. The Japanese have also become specialists in making synthetic textiles such as rayon and polyester, which can even resemble silk. Modern mills using jacquard looms produce beautiful textiles for domestic use and the export market. See also BROCADE; CLOTHING; CREST; DOLLS; FUROSHIKI; GEISHA; HAKAMA; HAORI; HATA CLAN; HEMP; INDIGO; KABUKI; KASURI; KIMONO; LIVING NATIONAL TREASURES; MULBERRY; NISHIJIN; NOH DRAMA; NOREN; OBI; QUILTING; RYUKYU ISLANDS; QUILTING; SHOSOIN; SILK; STENCILS; TEA CEREMONY; YUKATA; YUZEN DYEING.

THANK YOU See ARIGATO.

THEATER, MODERN *(shimpa, shingeki)* Modern Japanese theater that developed in reaction against the highly stylized traditional Kabuki theater and Noh drama, and emphasized realistic acting and contemporary themes. *Shimpa*, "new school," which evolved out of Kabuki, was the first modern theater movement in Japan. It began in 1888 when Sudo Sadanori (1867–1907) formed an amateur theatrical troupe to put on plays with political themes. A similar troupe was formed in 1891 by Kawakami Otojiro (1864–1911), a political activist who soon turned to sentimental contemporary melodrama, which became a standard feature of *shimpa* plays. A troupe named Saibikan formed in 1891 by Ii Yoho (1871–1932) and Yodo Gakkai (1833–1909), a Kabuki playwright, was the first theatrical group to have men and women act together on stage since mixed casts were banned by the Tokugawa Shogunate (1603–1867) in the early 1600s. Kabuki-style female impersonators, known as *onnagata*, still played major roles, however. *Shimpa* became an established theatrical style in the first decade of the 20th century, known as the "Golden Age of *Shimpa*" and also the "Hongoza Era," named for the theater in Tokyo where many *shimpa* plays were performed. The shimpa style, employing melodramatic pathos, female impersonators and contemporary settings, was adapted by the Japanese motion picture industry when it began in the second decade of the century. After World War II, *shimpa* actors, directors, and dramatists combined into one troupe that still performs today. The plays of Kawaguchi Matsutaro (1899–) are standards in the *shimpa* repertoire, such as *Life of a Meiji Era Woman* (*Meiji ichidai onna*, 1935). Today the female roles are played by strong actresses, notably Mizutani Yaeko, a leading 20th-century Japanese actress.

Shingeki, "new theater," was an early-20th-century movement inspired by modern Western theater. It was begun by Shoyo Tsubouchi (1859–1935), a professor at Waseda University, who translated the complete works of Shakespeare into Japanese and formed the Literary Society (Bungei Kyokai) in 1906. That same year, young Japanese writers formed a society to study the work of Henrik Ibsen, whose plays *A Doll's House* and *An Enemy of the People* had been translated into Japanese in 1901. In 1909, Osanai Kaoru (1881–1928) established the Free Theater (Jiyu Gekijo), which produced modern Western plays such as Ibsen's *John Gabriel Borkman*. After the great earthquake of 1923 destroyed most theaters in Tokyo, Osanai built the Tsukiji Little Theater as the home for the Free Theater, where many actors, directors and set designers trained by presenting modern Western dramas. The preeminent Japanese *shingeki* playwright was Kishida Kunio (1890–1954), who helped develop several theater companies. The most significant was the Literary Theater (Bungakuza), which began in 1938 and whose productions are still important. Between 1925 and 1940, troupes with radical political views and close ties to labor unions dominated *shingeki*. Since World War II, many *shingeki* troupes have been formed to produce experimental and avant-garde plays. Translations of dramas by Arthur Miller, Tennessee Williams, Jean Paul Sartre and works by other Western playwrights have been performed along with those by Japanese authors. Mishima Yukio (1925–1970), Abe Kobo (1924–   ), Minoru Betsuyaku and Yamazaki Masakazu (1934–   ) were some of the most important experimental playwrights during the 1970s and 1980s in Japan. In 1979 Abe took his play, *The Little Elephant Is Dead,* on tour in the United States.

Since the 1960s experimental theater troupes such as Kara Juro's Situation Theater, which performs in a red tent, have reintroduced the lively circus atmosphere of early Kabuki performances. The Shiki (Four Seasons) troupe founded in 1953 now produces popular Japanese productions of Broadway musicals. Revues by all-female troupes that perform sentimental plays about love and friendship, Western songs, and dance are also well-attended. The most famous troupe of this type is the Takarazuka Opera Company in Tokyo. See also ABE KOBO; KABUKI; MISHIMA YUKIO; NOH DRAMA; TAKARAZUKA OPERA COMPANY.

THEATER, TRADITIONAL   See BUNRAKU; KABUKI; KYOGEN; NOH DRAMA; STORYTELLING.

THOUSAND CRANES   See ATOMIC BOMB; CRANE; HIROSHIMA; KAWABATA YASUNARI; ORIGAMI.

THREE FAMOUS SIGHTS OF JAPAN   See AMANOHASHIDATE; MATSUSHIMA; MIYAJIMA.

THREE FRIENDS OF WINTER (*shochikubai*)   An auspicious design motif of pine (*matsu*), plum (*ume*) and bamboo (*take*), all of which remain green through the winter months. The three friends motif, which originated in China, symbolizes longevity and happiness. It became popular in Japanese painting and as a decorative motif for objects used by urban merchants (*chonin*, townspeople) during the Edo Era (1600–1868). An arrangement of the three friends is often displayed at the New Year. The plum is the first flower to bloom in the year. It is feminine but also represents bravery because it blooms while snow is still on the ground. The pine tree represents masculinity and longevity, and the bamboo strength and moral uprightness. Japanese brides wear wedding kimono decorated with the three friends of winter motif as emblems of good fortune and happiness. See also BAMBOO; NEW YEAR FESTIVAL; PINE TREE; PLUM TREE; WEDDINGS.

TIDAL WAVE   See WAVES.

TIE-DYE WEAVING   See KASURI.

TIGER (*tora*)   The tiger, not native to Japan, became known there through the introduction of Chinese painting. The tiger is often paired with the mythical dragon as the powerful rulers of the earth and the heavens. The tiger symbolizes the protection of human life and chases away the so-called "three disasters": thieves, fire and ghosts. Ink paintings (*sumi-e*) depicting strong tigers have been popular in Japan. A pair of scroll paintings of a tiger and dragon by the Chinese painter Mu-ch'i (Mokkei in Japanese; late 13th century) is greatly admired by the Zen Sect of the Buddhist religion, and tigers figure in many Zen stories.

The tiger is one of the animals in the traditional 12-year zodiac calendar. A person born in the Year of the Tiger is thought to be courageous, strong, aggresive, and temperamental but sympathetic. It is especially fortunate for a man to be born in the tiger year. Tiger women supposedly leave their husbands since the tiger is believed to run a thousand miles and back in one night. See also DRAGON; ZEN SECT OF BUDDHISM; ZODIAC.

TOA DOMESTIC AIRLINES CO., LTD.   See AIRLINES AND AIRPORTS.

TODAIJI   "Great Eastern Temple"; a Buddhist temple and monastery in the ancient capital city of Nara. Todaiji's main hall, the Daibutsuden, is claimed to be the largest wooden building in the world. The Daibutsuden measures 57 meters (188 ft.) wide, 50.4 meters (166 ft.) long, and 47.3 meters (156 ft.) high. It houses the 53 foot high Nara Daibutsu (Great Buddha of Nara), the world's largest bronze statue. Todaiji was erected by decree of Emperor Shomu (r. 724–749) for the worship of Roshana Buddha, the supreme and universal Buddha, the central deity of the Kegon sect of Buddhism. Todaiji was built on the site of an earlier Buddhist temple named Kinshoji, beginning in A.D. 747. The walled compound of Todaiji covered more than seven blocks of Nara City. The main entrance was the great south gate (*nandaimon*). Leading to the Daibutsuden were an inner gate and two seven-storied pagodas. The compound also contained a lecture hall, bell tower, scripture storeroom, monks' quarters and a refectory. When the Daibutsuden was completed in A.D. 752, a spectacular ceremony was held to consecrate the great statue of Buddha. In attendance were the retired Emperor Shomu and his consort, the reigning Empress Koken, and 10,000 Buddhist monks and dignitaries from foreign countries. The magnificent gifts and ritual objects used during the ceremony were placed in the Shosoin (imperial storehouse) on the temple grounds for safe keeping. Several thousand carpenters, metalworkers and laborers worked on Todaiji at enormous expense to the nation. It was completed in A.D. 798. Nearly all of its buildings were destroyed in 1180 by armies of the Taira clan, as punishment for the armed monks of Todaiji, who aided their rivals the Minamoto clan. After the Taira were defeated in 1185, Abbot Shunjobo Chogen (1121–1206) began reconstruction of Todaiji. The temple was burned again in 1567 by General Matsunaga Hisahide, after which Tokugawa Shogunate (1603–1867) undertook the restoration of the Daibutsu, completed in 1692, and the buildings of Todaiji. The current Daibutsuden, which is visited by more than a million tourists every year, dates from 1709. See also BUDDHISM; CHINA AND JAPAN; DAIBUTSU; EMPEROR; KEGON SECT OF BUDDHISM; NARA; PAGODA; SHOSOIN; TAIRA CLAN; TEMPLES, BUDDHIST.

TOEI CO., LTD.   See FILM; YAKUZA.

TOFU   Bean curd, a firm white food high in protein that is made from soybeans. Tofu is one of the most prominent foods in the Japanese diet because it is nutritious, inexpensive and can be prepared in many different ways. Tofu is made by soaking soybeans until they are soft and swollen, grinding them, boiling the mixture with water and straining it to remove the pulp, which is called *okara*. The liquid soy milk that remains is mixed with *nigari*, a coagulating agent that changes the milk into firm tofu. Bittern, made from sea salt and containing calcium or calcium chloride and magnesium, is the traditional coagulating agent, although calcium sulfate is used today. Two kinds of tofu are made in Japan and are named according to their texture. "Regular" or "cotton" tofu (*momengoshi-tofu*) is denser and has a rougher texture. Similar to the Chinese type of bean curd, cotton tofu is used in dishes that require cooking, such as soups and stews (*nabe*). It is made by pressing the mixture of soy milk and *nigari* to separate the curds from the whey, after which the curds are poured into molds. Smaller cakes are cut from these larger blocks of tofu. "Silk" tofu (*kinugoshi-dofu*) is smoother and softer. It is made by simply adding the *nigari* to the soy milk and pouring the entire mixture into molds without separating the curds and whey. When firm, it too is cut into small blocks. Silk tofu can be cooked for a short time but breaks apart easily. It can also be eaten uncooked with a sauce made of soy sauce, grated ginger, scallions and dried bonito flakes.

Tofu was brought to Japan from China by Buddhist priests and monks in the eighth century A.D. Because they were forbidden to eat meat, tofu took a central place in their diet as a source of protein. Buddhist temples have developed a type of vegetarian cuisine known as *shojin ryori*, which puts tofu to many uses, even disguising it as meat. The first written record of tofu in Japan states that it was served as an offering to the gods at Kasuga Shrine in Nara in A.D. 1183. By the 15th century, tofu was being eaten by members of all classes in Japan. A book published in 1782 in Osaka provided *One Hundred Rare Tofu Recipes* (*Tofu hyakuchin*), and its sequel was published the following year, *One Hundred More Rare Tofu Recipes*. Tofu has a mild flavor that mixes well with a great variety of ingredients. There are also many different tofu products that are served in Japan. *Yakidofu* is grilled tofu, a common ingredient in sukiyaki. Thick blocks of fried tofu (*atsu-age*) are used in stews. Thin slices of fried tofu (*aburage*) are filled with vinegared rice to make a type of sushi. *Yudofu* is a winter dish of tofu simmered in a broth. *Dengaku* is tofu that is grilled over charcoal with a coating of miso (soybean paste) mixed with sugar, sake and pepper-leaf buds (*sansho*) or sesame seeds. Tofu can be freeze-dried and kept for a long time. It must be soaked in water before using to soften it. This spongy-textured tofu is named *koyadofu* for the temple on Mount Koya where it was invented. Two by-products of tofu are also used in Japanese cooking. *Yuba* is the skin that forms on the surface of soy milk when it is heated. *Okara*, a fibrous pulp that is left when soy milk is strained, is very nutritious. However, it is now used primarily to feed livestock. Tofu must be eaten as fresh as possible. It will last up to a week if refrigerated, but it has to be kept in water that is changed daily. Although tofu is often made in large factories, in Japan there are still many small family-operated tofu shops that may deliver fresh tofu, which

usually has a better taste, to private homes. In the United States, tofu has also been manufactured for a century in Asian communities and has been accepted by the general population as a health food. See also BUDDHISM; COOKING; SOYBEANS; SUKIYAKI; SUSHI.

TOGO HEIHACHIRO (1848–1934)   A fleet admiral in the Imperial Japanese Navy who commanded naval operations during the Russo-Japanese War (1904–1905), in which the Japanese combined fleet destroyed the Russian Baltic fleet at the Battle of Tsushima on May 27–28, 1905. This victory, regarded by many as the greatest victory in naval history, brought Japan recognition as a leading world power. Togo was born in the southern province of Satsuma (modern Kagoshima Prefecture), the home of many leaders in the Boshin Civil War who overthrew the Tokugawa Shogunate (1603–1867) and restored power to the emperor with the Meiji Restoration of 1868. Togo served on the Satsuma warship *Kasuga* during the Boshin Civil War. He then studied naval science in Great Britain from 1871 to 1878, during which time he trained for three years on the British ship *Worcester*. In 1894, as captain of the Japanese cruiser *Naniwa*, Togo sparked the Sino-Japanese War of 1894–1895 by sinking a British ship carrying a Chinese regiment of soldiers to Korea. After the war he served as head of the Naval War College, commander of two naval stations and commander in chief of the standing Japanese fleet during the Boxer Rebellion (1900) in China. In 1903 Togo was appointed commander in chief of the combined fleet, and in 1904 he was made an admiral. Following the Russo-Japanese War, he served as chief of the Naval General Staff Office and war councillor to the emperor. In 1913 he was promoted to the rank of fleet admiral. From 1914 to 1924 Togo oversaw the education of Crown Prince Hirohito, who became regent in 1921 for his ailing father, Emperor Taisho (1879–1926; r. 1912–1926), and later reigned as emperor (1926–1989). Togo's experiences in Great Britain led Hirohito to visit that country in 1921, the first time an heir to the Japanese throne had traveled abroad. When Togo died in 1934, he was given a state funeral, and Togo Shrine was built in Tokyo to honor him. See also CROWN PRINCE; HIROHITO, EMPEROR; IMPERIAL JAPANESE ARMY AND NAVY; RUSSO-JAPANESE WAR; SINO-JAPANESE WAR OF 1894–95.

TOGU PALACE   See AKIHITO, EMPEROR.

TOHO CO., LTD.   See FILMS.

TOHOKU REGION   See GEOGRAPHIC REGIONS; SENDAI.

TOILET (*oteari, benjo*)   A Japanese-style toilet is made of porcelain and is embedded in a raised section in the floor. A person squats over the toilet facing a small hooded section at one end. No part of the body comes in contact with the toilet. The toilet, considered the dirtiest part of the home, is kept separate from the bath, the place of purification. Traditionally, a separate pair of sandals is kept at the door to the toilet for a person to wear just while using it. Modern Japanese toilets are flushed, but in rural areas, non-flushing pit toilets over septic tanks are frequently used. Western-style toilets are becoming more commonplace in Japan. The term *benjo* for toilet is used by men, and is considered impolite for women, who use the term *oteari*. See also BATH; HOMES AND HOUSING.

TOJO HIDEKI (1884–1948) An army general who became prime minister of Japan (1941–1944). Tojo was born in Tokyo and educated at the Japanese Imperial Military Academy and the Army Staff College. He taught at the college after serving as a military attache in Germany and Switzerland (1919–1922). He held several other army positions, and was promoted to major general in 1933. Two years later he was assigned to the Japanese Guandong (Kwantung) Army in Manchuria, which Japan had captured in 1931. In 1936, he arrested all military officers who sympathized with the Kodoha (Imperial Way) faction, which attempted a coup d'etat in the February 26th Incident. As Chief of Staff of the Guandong Army when the Sino-Japanese War broke out in July 1937, Tojo carried out his policy of all-out-war in China. He pressed for expansion of the war when he returned to Tokyo in 1938 and served in three cabinets of Prime Minister Konoe Fumimaro. Tojo strongly advocated the Tripartite Pact between Japan, Germany and Italy, the Japanese invasion of French Indochina and the supplanting of political parties by the Imperial Rule Assistance Association. Japan's relations with the United States worsened, and Tojo successfully opposed Konoe's wish for a rapprochement between the two countries.

Tojo was named prime minister in Konoe's place in October 1941. He appointed himself minister of the army as well, and placed members of his military faction in cabinet posts. Japan's attack on the American naval fleet at Pearl Harbor on December 7, 1941 increased Tojo's authority. Under his leadership, the Japanese invaded all of Southeast Asia and engaged in full-scale war throughout the Pacific. However, Japan began suffering reversals in the war, and Tojo was ousted in July 1944 by a faction led by Konoe Fumimaro and Admiral Okada Keisuke. The war crimes trials held by the Allies following World War II indicted Tojo as a Class A war criminal and hanged him on December 23, 1948. He was interred at Yasukuni Shrine, a Shinto shrine in Tokyo that honors Japanese war heroes. See also KONOE FUMIMARO; MANCHURIAN INCIDENT; OCCUPATION OF JAPAN; PRIME MINISTER; WAR CRIMES TRIALS; WORLD WAR II; YASUKUNI SHRINE.

TOKAIDO ROAD A major route between the cities of Edo (now Tokyo) and the former capital of Kyoto, with a spur to Osaka. Tokaido means "Eastern Sea Circuit." Much of the Tokaido road paralleled the Pacific Ocean along the east coast of central Honshu Island, skirting the mountains that cover much of inland Japan. The road between Edo and Kyoto was about 300 miles long and dated back to the Yamato Era (300–709) when the government of Japan was centralized in the Yamato region, today known as Nara, in western Honshu. The Yamato rulers sent military expeditions, civil bureaucrats and Buddhist priests on the Tokaido

Road to expand their domain eastward. Seven main highways were developed to the seven provincial regions established by the Yamato government. The importance of the Tokaido Road was increased in the 12th century when the warlord Minamoto no Yoritomo founded the Kamakura Shogunate (1192–1333). Heavy traffic flowed between the military capital of Kamakura on the east coast and the imperial capital of Kyoto to the west. The heaviest use of the Tokaido Road came during the Edo Era (1600–1868), when the Tokugawa Shogunate (1603–1867) moved the capital of Japan to the new city of Edo, north of Kamakura. The Tokugawa improved the road, which was made of crushed gravel covered with sand or stone and had an average width of 18 feet. Light cargo was carried on pack horses, and people were often carried in palanquins on the shoulders of porters. Heavier cargo was shipped by boat. The Tokugawa established 53 post stations on the Tokaido Road for security and traffic supervision. Towns grew up around the stations to provide food and lodging for travelers. Grand processions of *daimyo* (feudal lords) moved along the highway in obedience to the shogun demand that *daimyo* spend every other year or half-year in Edo, known as "alternate attendance". The road was also filled with couriers, government officials, merchants, priests and pilgrims, especially those traveling to Ise Shrine, the center of the Shinto religion. Famous artists such as Hiroshige and Hokusai made woodblock prints of the 53 Stages of the Tokaido Road. See also ALTERNATE ATTENDANCE; DAIMYO; EDO ERA; HIROSHIGE; HOKUSAI; ISE SHRINE; KAMAKURA SHOGUNATE; KYOTO; NARA; OSAKA; PACIFIC OCEAN; PILGRIMAGE; TOKUGAWA SHOGUNATE; WOODBLOCK PRINTS; YAMATO.

TOKONAME WARE (*tokoname-yaki*) A thick, reddish brown pottery that is one of the two preemineet native Japanese wares, along with Bizen ware (*bizen-yaki*). Tokoname ware is named for the pottery village of Tokoname on the Chita Peninsula, south of Nagoya City on central Honshu Island. Potters were most active there from the early 12th until the mid-16th century, although Tokoname ware is still produced today. Tokoname is the largest of the so-called Six Old Kilns in Japan. More than 600 old kiln sites have been discovered in the Tokoname region on the Chita Peninsula, the largest concentration in Japan, and more than 500 have been excavated. These kilns produced thick, heavy objects for daily use in local farm households, and also large jars, flower vases and bowls. The jars, used for burials as well for storing water and food, were made by building up coils of clay, and were originally fired in wood-fired underground kilns (*anagama*), until the climbing kiln (*noborigama*) was introduced into Japan by Korean potters around the 16th century. The mountains surrounding Tokoname have an abundance of malleable, fine-grained clay, which is excavated to make the pottery. Tokoname potters have been skillful in working the clay, which is sticky and shrinks more than 30% when it is fired. Most Tokoname ware is known as *shudei*, or "red mud" ware. It is made with clay that contains iron, but potters add more iron oxide to intensify the red color. The pieces are formed on a potter's wheel, dried to the hardness of leather, and trimmed. Then they are burnished with steel tools while being turned on the wheel, so that they will have a smooth surface. Finally, they are slowly fired in a climbing wood-fired kiln for eight days. After the kiln cools for 10 days, the pieces are taken out and polished with very fine sandpaper. A number of Tokoname pieces are beige in color and known as *hakudei*, or "white mud" ware. In Tokoname today there are individual pottery workshops that produce pieces in the traditional style, and also small factories that produce clay pipes and roof tiles. A museum exhibits ancient and contemporary Tokoname ware. See also BIZEN WARE; KILN; POTTERY.

TOKONOMA A recessed alcove built into the main room of a traditional Japanese home or a tea ceremony room for the display of art objects and flower arrangements. A *tokonoma* is usually about 6 feet wide and 3 feet deep, although it can be larger, and its floor is usually raised about 3 inches from the floor of the room. The base is usually covered with a *tatami* (thick straw mat), although it may be of wood. There is a post next to the *tokonoma*, called the *toko-bashira*, which is made of pine, chestnut or other varieties of wood. The wooden post can retain its natural bark or be planed smooth. *Tokonoma* developed in Japan during the Muromachi Era (1333–1568), from platforms placed in front of Buddhist scrolls in the sleeping rooms of the noble classes. The most important objects displayed in a *tokonoma* are hanging scrolls (*kakemono*) of either brush painting or calligraphy. One scroll is hung at a time, and scrolls can be easily changed to fit the season or the occasion for which they are hung. Flower arrangements, also created to reflect the season, are placed on the floor of the *tokonoma* or hung from the wooden post. The *tokonoma*, which developed out of the *shoin* style of architecture, allows the beauty of single art objects and simple flower arrangements to be appreciated by the viewer without distractions. See also CALLIGRAPHY; FLOWER ARRANGING; HOMES AND HOUSING; PAINTING; SCROLLS; SHOIN STYLE OF ARCHITECTURE; TATAMI; TEAHOUSE; WOODWORKING.

TOKUGAWA IEMITSU (1605–1651) The third shogun of the Tokugawa Shogunate (1603–1867), who ruled Japan 1623–1651. He was the grandson of Tokugawa Ieyasu (1543–1616), who founded the Tokugawa Shogunate. Iemitsu became shogun in 1623 when his father, the second shogun Tokugawa Hidetada (1579–1632), retired. Iemitsu's only rival for the shogunate was his younger brother, Tadanaga (1606–1633); but Iemitsu forced Tadanaga to commit suicide after their father died in 1632. Iemitsu enforced many policies that consolidated the shogunate's control and brought it to its greatest power in Japan. Under his rule, the government became a virtual police state that was run by several major bodies. The "great elders" (*tairo*) advised the shogun on policy matters. The "elder councillors" (*roju*), who served for one month at a time in a rotation system, administered the vast government bureaucracy. The Judicial Council (Hyojosho), composed of the *roju* and additional commissioners, performed numerous administrative and judicial functions; they oversaw national and municipal government departments, gathered secret intelligence about *daimyo* (feudal lords of Japanese provinces), and handled the finances of the Tokugawa estates. The shogunate appointed commissioners of Japanese cities from among its own vassals (*fudai daimyo*). To ensure their loyalty, Ieyasu demanded that all *daimyo* leave their provinces to reside in the capital city of Edo (modern Tokyo) in alternate years, a practice known as *sankin kotai* (alternate attendance). He persecuted Japanese Christians, of whom there were a large number on the southern Japanese island of Kyushu, and slaughtered more than 30,000 Christians in the Shimabara Uprising of 1637–1638. Iemitsu feared the independent power of *daimyo* on Kyushu, who had close relations with Christians and other foreigners. In response, he expelled all Western missionaries and traders from Japan, forbade Japanese to leave the country except in certain cases, and permitted trading privileges only to Chinese and Dutch Protestant merchants, who were strictly supervised in Nagasaki. By 1639, Japan was virtually isolated from all foreign influences. This so-called national seclusion (*sakoku*) lasted until Western nations forced Japan to open its ports to foreign trade in the mid-19th century. See also ALTERNATE ATTENDANCE; CHRISTIANITY IN JAPAN; DAIMYO; DUTCH IN JAPAN; KYUSHU; NAGASAKI; SECLUSION, NATIONAL; SHIMABARA UPRISING; TOKUGAWA SHOGUNATE.

TOKUGAWA IEYASU (1543–1616) A warlord who was one of three national unifiers of Japan, along with Oda Nobunaga (1534–1582) and Toyotomi Hideyoshi (1536–1598), and the founder of the Tokugawa Shogunate (1603–1867), the third of three military regimes (*bakufu*) that governed Japan for nearly seven centuries. Ieyasu was born Matsudaira Takechiyo in Okazaki in Mikawa Province (part of modern Aichi Prefecture). His father, a local warlord who claimed to be a descendant of the Minamoto clan that founded the Kamakura Shogunate (1192–1333), sent him to a neighboring warlord to cement a military and political alliance. Ieyasu was used as a hostage by several factions until 1560, when at age 18 he was freed by Oda Nobunaga.

Ieyasu allied himself with Nobunaga and constantly increased the amount of territory he controlled and the size of his army. He consolidated his power in central Japan when Nobunaga was assassinated in 1582. Ieyasu worked out a truce with Nobunaga's successor, Toyotomi Hideyoshi, in which Ieyasu sent his son to be adopted by Hideyoshi and Hideyoshi had his sister divorce and sent to marry Ieyasu. In 1590 Hideyoshi and Ieyasu joined forces at the Battle of Odawara to defeat Hojo Ujimasa (1538–1590), a powerful warlord in the Kanto region of eastern Honshu Island. Hideyoshi then forced Ieyasu to give up the land he already controlled in exchange for the Kanto region.

Ieyasu chose a small fishing town named Edo as the site of his new headquarters. He built a great castle there, drained the swamps and began developing what soon became Japan's largest city, now known as Tokyo. Meanwhile, Hideyoshi undertook two massive invasions of Korea, and died suddenly in 1598. Hideyoshi had made Ieyasu and other leading *daimyo* (feudal lords) promise to support his son Toyotomi Hideyori (1593–1615) as his successor. Ieyasu broke that promise, however, and forged an alliance with four other powerful *daimyo,* who were opposed by an alliance of *daimyo* in western Japan. The two sides clashed on October 21, 1600 at the Battle of Sekigahara, from which Ieyasu emerged the victor. He confiscated the lands of his defeated enemies and also took control of the capital city of Kyoto in western Japan, where Emperor Go-Yozei (1571–1617) resided. In 1603, in imitation of the founders of the Kamakura and Ashikaga Shogunates, Ieyasu forced the emperor to award him the title of *seii tai shogun* ("barbarian-subduing generalissimo" or commander in chief), abbreviated *shogun.* Ieyasu thereby accomplished his aim of unifying the whole of Japan under his control. He built Nijo Castle as the headquarters of his deputy in Kyoto. In 1605 Ieyasu handed the title of shogun over to his third son, Tokugawa Hidetada (1579–1632), but continued to be active in such matters as foreign trade and gold and silver mining, which made him very wealthy.

Ieyasu was an astute administrator. He also learned much about Western culture and technology from William Adams (1564–1620), a shipwrecked English navigator who remained in Japan. In 1614 Ieyasu eliminated any possibility of a challenge to Tokugawa rule by attacking Osaka Castle, headquarters of Toyotomi Hideyori. Hideyori committed suicide and his family was killed. In 1615 Ieyasu issued the Laws for Military Houses (*Buke Shohatto*) and Laws Governing the Imperial Court and Nobility (*Kinchu Narabi ni Kuge Shohatto*). Ieyasu died in 1616 (according to rumor, from eating too much *tempura,* or fried food). The next year his remains were enshrined at Toshogu Shrine in Nikko, and he was given the title Tosho Daigongen, meaning that he was a manifestation of the deity Buddha as Healer. Ieyasu thus became known in Japan as Gongen Sama, the protector of the Japanese people. See also ADAMS, WILLIAM; BAKUFU; DAIMYO; EDO; KANTO; NIJO CASTLE; NIKKO; ODA NOBUNAGA; OSAKA; SEKIGAHARA, BATTLE OF; SHOGUN; TEMPURA; TOKUGAWA SHOGUNATE; TOSHOGU SHRINE; TOYOTOMI HIDEYOSHI.

TOKUGAWA SHOGUNATE (1603–1867) The military government (*bakufu*) established by Tokugawa Ieyasu (1543–1616), who completed the unification of Japan with his victory at the Battle of Sekigahara (1600). The Tokugawa Shogunate outlasted the two previous military governments, the Kamakura Shogunate (1192–1333) and the Ashikaga Shogunate (1338–1573). Ieyasu located his capital in the village of Edo (modern Tokyo) on east-central Honshu Island. A city rapidly grew up around Edo Castle, and a dynamic popular culture flourished with the rise of the wealthy urban merchant class. The period from 1600 to 1868 is also known as the Edo Era. Ieyasu's government consolidated its rule over Japan by enacting the Laws for Military Houses (*Buke Shohatto*) and Laws Governing the Imperial Court and Nobility (*Kinchu Narabi ni Kuge Shohatto*). The third shogun, Tokugawa Iemitsu (1605–1651), consolidated the shogunate's power over *daimyo* (feudal lords) by issuing the Regulations for Vassals (*Shoshi Hatto*) and reinstating the Judicial Council (*Hyojosho*), the national tribunal of the Kamakura and Ashikaga Shogunates, which

made the shogunate the legal center of the nation. The eighth shogun, Tokugawa Yoshimune (1684–1751), compiled in 1742 a comprehensive legal code, the *Kujikata Osadamagaki.*

The Tokugawa Shogunate attempted to control all aspects of Japanese life. It enforced a system of four social classes, samurai, farmer, artisan and merchant (*shi-no-ko-sho*), with merchant being the lowest. The philosophy of Neo-Confucianism and the code of *Bushido* ("Way of the Warrior") provided the ideology for the strict ordering of society. The so-called *bakuhan* system placed the shogunate (*bakufu*) at the head of the government and required allegiance to the shogun by the *daimyo* (feudal lords) who ruled the Japanese provinces (*han*). All *daimyo* were required to spend every other year or half-year in Edo (alternate attendance, *sankin kotai*). Tokugawa vassals who had no domains of their own lived in Edo and served in the civil bureaucracy and the army. The highest vassals were the *hatamoto* (bannermen), below which were the *gokenin* (housemen), and then the retainers of the higher vassals. During the more than two centuries of peace under the Tokugawa shogunate, the samurai were transformed from warriors into civil servants. The shogunate persecuted the Christian religion, which had been introduced by Portuguese Jesuits in the 16th century, as a threat to its power. In 1639 Tokugawa Iemitsu banned foreigners from Japan, except for a few Dutch Protestant and Chinese traders in Nagasaki, and sealed off Japan from outside influences.

Altogether there were 15 Tokugawa shoguns. Gradually the shogunate became financially and politically weakened by the mid-19th century. Its capitulation to demands made by U.S. Commodore Matthew Perry (1794–1858) and American Consul-General Townsend Harris (1804–1878) to open some Japanese ports to Western trade in 1854 was an obvious sign of Tokugawa decline. Samurai who opposed the shogunate, especially those from the southern domains of Satsuma and Choshu, carried out a coup d'etat in 1867 in Kyoto, the imperial capital. Their forces defeated the Tokugawa Shogunate in the Boshin Civil War and brought about the Meiji Restoration of 1868. See also ALTERNATE ATTENDANCE; ANSEI COMMERCIAL TREATIES; BAKUFU; BOSHIN CIVIL WAR; BUSHIDO; CHRISTIANITY IN JAPAN; CONFUCIANISM; DAIMYO; DUTCH IN JAPAN; EDO ERA; HARRIS, TOWNSEND; MEIJI RESTORATION OF 1868; PERRY, MATTHEW CALBRAITH; PORTUGUESE IN JAPAN; SAMURAI; SEKIGAHARA, BATTLE OF; SHOGUN; TOKUGAWA IEMITSU; TOKUGAWA IEYASU.

TOKUGAWA YOSHINOBU See BOSHIN CIVIL WAR; MEIJI RESTORATION OF 1868; TOKUGAWA SHOGUNATE.

TOKYO The capital and largest city in Japan, and the country's political, economic and cultural center. Tokyo covers 828.32 square miles and has a population of around 12 million, making it one of the world's largest cities. Tokyo was originally known as Edo, "estuary," because three rivers, the Arakawa, Edogawa and Sumidagawa, flow through this region into Tokyo Bay. For strategic reasons, Tokugawa Ieyasu (1543–1616) chose the open Kanto Plain of Edo village on the east (Pacific) coast of Honshu Island

The Mitsubishi Exhibition Center in the neon-lit Ginza, the main shopping and entertainment district of Tokyo.

to be the new headquarters for his military government, known as the Tokugawa Shogunate (1603–1867), and Edo grew rapidly into a city around Ieyasu's castle. The shogunate required all *daimyo*, feudal lords who controlled the Japanese provinces, to spend every other year or half year in Edo, which centralized ruling power in the city. The growing service and merchant class, which provided goods for the *daimyo* and their large retinues, became wealthy and stimulated a lively popular culture, especially during the Genroku Era (1688–1704). This culture was associated with the licensed pleasure quarters of the city, such as the Yoshiwara. Although Edo was the locus of political power, Kyoto ("Western Capital") remained the official seat of the Japanese emperor until the Meiji Restoration of 1868, when rule by the emperor replaced the shogunate. Edo was made the capital of Japan as Tokyo ("Eastern Capital"), and Emperor Meiji (1852–1912) took up residence in Edo Castle, which is now known as the Imperial Palace. The Meiji government undertook a program of modernization that spurred Tokyo's growth. After the Great Kanto Earthquake of 1923 destroyed half of Tokyo and killed 100,000 people, Tokyo was rebuilt with modern steel and concrete buildings. The city grew, and in 1943 the surrounding districts

and towns were added to it to form one administrative district known as Metropolitan Tokyo (Tokyo To). Much of the city was destroyed by Allied bombing during World War II, and after the war the Allied Occupation of Japan (1945–1952) made its headquarters in Tokyo. During the economic recovery of the 1950s, many Japanese companies and financial institutions moved their headquarters to Tokyo. The city undertook a massive building program when it was chosen as the first Asian city to host the Olympic Games in 1964.

Some of Tokyo's traditional *shitamachi* (downtown) merchant and artisan districts have managed to survive, such as Asakusa and Ueno. There are many museums in Ueno Park. However, high-rise buildings now dominate the city, as in the new Shinjuku and Shibuya districts. Railroad lines from all parts of Japan connect to Tokyo, Shinjuku and Ueno stations. New Tokyo International Airport (now Narita Airport) is the principal airport in Japan. Tokyo International Airport (Haneda Airport) is the main terminal for domestic flights and some foreign ones. Tokyo has a large transportation network of subways, railroad and bus lines, and highways. Buildings housing the Diet (Parliament), National Diet Library, Supreme Court and other government buildings are located in the Akasaka district, close to the Imperial Palace. The Ginza is world famous as Tokyo's main shopping and entertainment district. Most of Japan's best universities are located in Tokyo, with Tokyo University at the top. Kanda district has many bookstores. Harajuku is a popular district for young people. Akihabara is known for discount electronic goods. Tokyo has 23 wards (ku) and many smaller administrative divisions. The Kanto region, which includes Tokyo, Chiba Prefecture and the port cities of Kawasaki and Yokohama, is the most highly industrialized region in Japan, also known as the Keihin Industrial Zone. One-quarter of all Japanese live in the Tokyo region. The Edo-Tokyo museum scheduled to open in 1992 will exhibit displays on the city's history and culture. See also AIRLINES AND AIRPORTS; CHIBA PREFECTURE; EDO; KANSAI AND KANTO; KAWASAKI; MUSEUMS IN JAPAN; TOKUGAWA SHOGUNATE; YOKOHAMA; NAMES OF INDIVIDUAL DISTRICTS, ERAS AND FIGURES.

TOKYO CENTRAL WHOLESALE MARKET The largest market in Japan for seafood and fresh produce. The Tokyo Central Wholesale Market is located on the Sumida River (Sumidagawa) in the Tsukiji district of Tokyo. It handles around 1 million tons of seafood and 2 million tons of fruits and vegetables annually. Seafood and produce are delivered to the market by ship, truck and train from the afternoon through late at night. Wholesalers sell these products to brokers, who are large-scale consumers and processors. The brokers inspect the quality of the products before they are sold at auction the next morning. Fish, mainly frozen tuna, are turned over with hook-like tools so that all sides can be examined, and small samples of meat are cut from them. From 5 A.M. to 6 A.M., auctioneers conduct the bidding between brokers and buying agents for fish retailers, restaurants and sushi chefs. From 6 A.M. to noon, brokers take their products to their shops inside the market, where they sell to retailers, who carry their purchases by truck or car to their own stores. Just outside the market are shops selling fresh and prepared food, especially sushi, to individual consumers. The Tokyo Central Wholesale Market is open every day except Sundays and national holidays. Other large Japanese cities also have central wholesale markets. In 1987 there were about 1,300 wholesale fish markets in Japan. See also COOKING; DISTRIBUTION SYSTEM; FISH AND FISHING INDUSTRY; RESTAURANTS; SASHIMI; SUMIDA RIVER; SUSHI; TOKYO; TUNA.

TOKYO METEOROLOGICAL OBSERVATORY See EARTHQUAKE.

TOKYO METROPOLITAN ART MUSEUM See MUSEUMS IN JAPAN; UENO.

TOKYO NATIONAL MUSEUM See AINU; MUSEUMS IN JAPAN; UENO.

TOKYO ROSE The American nickname given to female announcers on entertainment and propaganda programs broadcast by Radio Tokyo, the international section of the

Japan Broadcasting Corporation, to the Pacific region during World War II to demoralize foreign troops. After the war, a Japanese-American woman named Iva Toguri D'Aquino was accused by two Americans of being Tokyo Rose. She had been born and raised in California and, like many nisei (second-generation Japanese-Americans), was visiting relatives in Japan when war broke out between Japan and the United States in 1941. She worked as a typist at the Japan Broadcasting Corporation (Nippon Hoso Kyokai; abbreviated as NHK) and supposedly agreed to be the announcer on a radio program, "Zero Hour," that three Allied prisoners of war were forced to organize. American military authorities arrested her in 1945 but released her in 1946 after fully investigating her activities during the war. However, the U.S. Department of Justice prosecuted her for treason in 1948. The jury declared her guilty, and she was imprisoned for more than six years. But in 1976, witnesses for the prosecution in her trial admitted that the government had pressured them to present false testimony against her. President Gerald Ford pardoned her in 1977. *The Hunt for "Tokyo Rose"* by Russell Warren Howe, published in 1990, shows that there were actually 27 Japanese-American women who were forced to make English-language broadcasts during the war. See also BROADCASTING SYSTEM; JAPAN BROADCASTING CORPORATION; NISEI; WORLD WAR II.

TOKYO STOCK EXCHANGE See STOCK MARKET.

TOKYO TRIALS See WAR CRIMES TRIALS.

TOKYO UNIVERSITY The first and most prestigious national university in Japan, established when three institutions of higher learning sponsored by the Tokugawa Shogunate (1603–1867) were combined in 1877. Those schools were an academy for Confucian studies, a school of medicine and a school of Western learning. Renamed Tokyo Imperial University in 1886, this was the only university of its type until Kyoto Imperial University was founded in 1897. Many officials of the Japanese government were trained at Tokyo Imperial University. "Imperial" was dropped from the school's name after World War II, and today it is commonly referred to as Todai, the abbreviation of Tokyo Daigaku. The university has 10 faculties: agriculture, economics, education, engineering, law, letters, medicine, pharmacology, science and a college of general education. A number of cultural and scientific research institutes are also affiliated with Tokyo University. The university is now coeducational and has an enrollment of around 14,000. See also EDUCATION SYSTEM; UNIVERSITIES.

TOMB MOUND (kofun) A tumulus of mounded earth distinguishing the burial sites of aristocrats in Japan duriing the Kofun Era (A.D. 300–710). The smallest tomb mounds are about 50 feet in diameter, while the largest cover 80 acres. Their basic shapes are round (empun), square (hofun), front-square and rear-square (zempo koho fun), and front-square and rear-round (zempo koen fun). The latter two shapes resemble a keyhole. Prehistoric mounded graves dating from the Yayoi Era (c. 300 B.C.–c. A.D. 300) have been discovered in Japan. Large Kofun Era tomb mounds were first built at the end of the third century A.D. on western Honshu Island in the Kansai region of modern Kyoto, Nara and Osaka. In the fourth century, the practice of building tomb mounds spread south along the Inland Sea to Kyushu Island and then east and north on Honshu. Early tomb mounds were built on hillsides surrounded by rich farmland. The body was placed in a wooden coffin and buried in the top of the mound, sometimes surrounded by a stone-lined pit. *Haniwa*, unglazed pottery figures, were often placed on the mound. Objects buried with the body included ceremonial bronze mirrors from China, curved jade jewels known as *magatama* and other stone jewelry. A wealth of objects from Korea, such as gold earrings, pottery and horse trappings, were often buried with the body. Multiple burials in one mound became common when a type of burial chamber that could be entered by way of a corridor was also introduced from Korea. During the sixth and seventh centuries, tomb mounds became smaller as they came to be used by people outside the ruling class as well. *Haniwa* were no longer placed on tombs in western Japan, but became widespread in the Kanto region of eastern Japan, where the tombs continued to be built in keyhole shapes. The construction of tomb mounds declined in the late seventh century with the sumptuary laws against lavish burials as well as promulgation of the spread of the Buddhist religion, which was introduced from China in the sixth century A.D. Many aristocrats began to build Buddhist temples in place of tomb mounds. See also BUD-DHISM; CHINA AND JAPAN; HANIWA; KOREA AND JAPAN; TEMPLES, BUDDHIST.

TOOTH BLACKENING *(kane or ohaguro)* The custom of blackening women's teeth with a liquid made by soaking iron scraps or nails in a mixture of tea and sake or vinegar. Oxidation of the metal turned the liquid black, and it was painted onto the teeth every day. Until the 12th century A.D., Japanese girls ritually blackened their teeth to indicate their coming of age. Blackening the teeth was thought to help keep them healthy and to make women sexually attractive. From the 12th to the 18th centuries, men of the aristocratic and samurai classes also took up the custom of tooth blackening. Until it was forbidden during the Meiji Era (1868–1912), Japanese women continued to blacken their teeth. Teeth-blackening equipment *(ohaguro)* was included in the trousseau of wealthy brides, along with mirrors, stands and various cosmetic boxes and shelves. These sets were often made of decorated lacquer ware. See also COSMETICS; LACQUER WARE.

TORA-SAN The protagonist of the world's longest-running film series, known collectively as *It's Tough Being a Man (Otoko Wa Tsurai Yo)*. The first Tora-san movie, *Oto-kawa Tsuraiyo (Tora-San the Loveable Tramp)*, was made in Japan in 1969, and more than 40 have been released to date. Tora-san, played by Atsumi Kiyoshi, is a wandering souvenir peddler who is neither handsome nor heroic. In each movie he falls in love with a different woman, whom he helps out of some kind of trouble, but she is never

available for a relationship with him. Tora-san movies are comedies but have a bittersweet sentimental undertone. Their theme is the way a simple, small-town Japanese man tries to cope with the complexities of modern life. Tora-san's closest relationship is with his sister Sakura, who never denies him the help he needs. Tora-san spends most of his time on the road but he always comes back to visit his family in an old-fashioned district of Tokyo known as Shitamachi. Tora-san movies are written and directed by Yamada Yoji (b. 1931), who works for the Japanese movie studio Shochiku Co., Ltd. He films two Tora-san movies each year, to be released at the main holiday seasons, New Year in January and Bon in midsummer. The Tora-san series has gained an audience all over the world. The character goes abroad in the 41st movie, *Tora-san Goes to Vienna*. See also BON FESTIVAL; FILM; NEW YEAR FESTIVAL; SHI-TAMACHI.

TORII Large gates that stand at the entrances to Shinto shrines, marking the sacred precincts beyond. Worshippers are purified as they pass through the gates. A *torii* has two round upright columns and two crossbeams. The *kasagi* is the cross-beam across the top of the columns, and the *nuki* is a rail below the top beam that fits into or cuts through the vertical columns. *Torii* is written with two Chinese characters that represent "bird" and "dwelling." Some people believe that *torii* were originally used as perches for chickens that were sacrificed at Shinto shrines. Others believe that since *torii* at Ise, Kasuga and other shrines have doors, the original function of *torii* was to serve as a gateway to places of worship. From ancient times, *torii* have been built of wood. They can be plain or painted red. The purest and most primitive style of *torii* uses logs that have not had their bark removed and are called *kuroki*, or black-wood style. *Torii* made with smooth logs are constructed in a number of different styles. The more elaborate ones have a slightly curved top rail and a piece of wood connecting the two crossbeams on which is hung a tablet *(gaku)* inscribed with the name of the shrine. The *ryobu* style of *torii* has two shorter vertical posts and two cross-

The large *torii* gate at Heian Shrine in Kyoto. Whether large or small, a *torii* stands at the entrance to every Shinto shrine.

rails joined to the base of each of the two taller columns. The style of *torii* most commonly seen, the *myojin* style, has vertical columns that lean in slightly and are topped by a curved double crossbeam. From the time of the Kamakura Era (1192–1333), many *torii* have been made of stone. Concrete, copper and porcelain have also been used. The red *torii* rising out of the sea at Itsukushima Shrine on Miyajima Island is one of the most famous symbols of Japan. See also CHICKEN AND ROOSTER; MIYAJIMA; SHINTO; SHRINES, SHINTO.

TORTOISE *(kame)* Four families of tortoises and turtles are found throughout the Japanese islands. There are both land and marine species, some of which live in freshwater lakes and rivers, and others in the saltwater seas around Japan. The freshwater tortoise known as *ishigame* is a common pet, and the *suppon* tortoise is raised to be eaten. The shell of the *taimai* tortoise has long been used to make decorative objects such as combs. The tortoise, like the crane *(tsuru)*, represents old age and good fortune. There is a Japanese saying, "a crane lives a thousand years and a tortoise ten thousand years." The tortoise, crane and pine tree *(matsu)*, another symbol of old age, are often depicted together, especially on auspicious occasions such as weddings. The tortoise is often shown with Jurojin, the god of longevity. A marine tortoise with algae growing on its shell reminds the Japanese of a bearded old man, and was believed to be a messenger of the gods. There are also many Japanese folktales about tortoises. The Japanese traditionally believe that the six cardinal virtues are inscribed on the tortoise shell: wisdom, loyalty, sincerity, friendship, charity and contemplation. The tortoise is a common decorative motif. See also COMBS AND HAIR ORNAMENTS; CRANE; JUROJIN; PINE TREE; WEDDINGS.

TOSA DIARY *(Tosa nikki)* The first Japanese literary diary, which was written in A.D. 935 (translated into English in 1969) by the leading Heian Era (794–1185) poet Ki no Tsurayuki (872?–945). The diary form is one of the most important genres in Japanese literature. The *Tosa Diary* describes Tsurayuki's return to the capital city of Kyoto on western Honshu Island from Tosa on Shikoku Island, where he had served as governor. He wrote the diary in the vernacular syllabic script known as *kana*, which was used by almost exclusively by women (Japanese men of the time wrote in Chinese characters, or *kanji*), and made it seem as if the diary was written by a court lady who accompanied him. Tsurayuki's daughter died in Tosa, so he may have written the diary in commemoration of her. The diary also contains 57 classical poems, known as *waka*, which give expression to the most important events in the diary. Poetry has always been considered the greatest literary form in Japan, and poems abound in all classical Japanese literature. Tsurayuki was a court poet who helped compile the *Kokinshu*, the first anthology of Japanese poetry commissioned by the imperial court. He wrote a preface to the anthology in *kana* in which he emphasized the indigenous aspects of Japanese culture in contrast to Chinese culture, which had become dominant in ninth-century Japan. Tsu-

rayuki wrote prefaces to two other poetry anthologies as well. Around 500 of his poems have been included in imperial anthologies, including more than 100 in the *Kokinshu*. See also DIARIES; KANA; KANJI; KOKINSHU; POETRY; WAKA.

TOSA SCHOOL OF PAINTING A school of painting of the early 15th to the late 19th centuries that preserved the *Yamato-e*, or native Japanese style of painting that developed in the Heian Era (794–1185). This style uses bright colors to depict such themes as nature and the changing seasons. The Tosa school kept the *Yamato* style of painting alive when it was overshadowed in the early Muromachi Era (1333–1568) by Chinese-style monochromatic ink painting *(sumi-e)*. Members of the Tosa School held the position of official artists to the imperial court. The Tosa family claimed to have descended from an 11th-century painter named Fujiwara no Motomitsu and from several prominent 12th-century artists. Motomitsu originated the native Japanese style of painting known as the Kasuga school. The name Tosa was taken from Tosa Province (modern Kochi Prefecture) where, according to a document written in A.D. 1406, the painter Fujiwara no Yukihiro was governor. The position of superintendent of the Imperial Painting Bureau *(edokoro azukari)*, held by Yukihiro's father, Funiwara no Yukimitsu, was inherited by successive generations of the Tosa family. Tosa Mitsunobu (1434–1525) is regarded as the greatest painter in the Tosa school. His illustrated horizontal handscrolls *(emakimono)* are greatly admired. In 1469 the Ashikaga Shogunate (1338–1573) appointed Mitsunobu *edokoro*.

Artists of the Tosa school painted stylized compositions with precisely drawn simple outlines and colors that are rich but flat and opaque. They often depicted classical literary works such as the *Tale of Genji*. However, after Mitsunobu, the Tosa school was eclipsed by the Chinese-style Kano school. Many Tosa artists had to move to the provinces to earn money, or, if they stayed in Kyoto, make rough drafts for Kano artists who hired them. Kano Motonobu (1476–1559), son of the founder of the Kano school of painting, incorporated elements from the *Yamato* style of the Tosa school, such as bright colors, the use of gold and classical literary themes. The Tosa and Kano schools became so closely associated that Motonobu married the daughter of Tosa Mitsunobu. The Kano family assumed the post of *edokoro azukari* when Mitsunobu's grandson Mitsumoto was killed in 1569 and his successor Mitsuyoshi later had to leave Kyoto for the port of city of Sakai. The Tosa school revived when Mitsuyoshi's grandson Mitsuoki (1617–1691) returned to Kyoto in 1634 and was appointed *edokoro azukari* in 1654. He studied Chinese paintings of birds and flowers and specialized in painting these subjects. His successors continued to produce bird-and-flower and literary paintings for the imperial court during the Edo Era (1600–1868). The Sumiyoshi School broke off from the Tosa School in the 17th century and concentrated on genre scenes of daily life. The Tosa school had a formative influence on the style used by artists for book illustrations and, by extension, on the paintings and woodblock prints known as "pictures of the floating world," or *ukiyo-e*. See also

ASHIKAGA SHOGUNATE; FLOATING WORLD; INK PAINTING; KANO SCHOOL OF PAINTING; MUROMACHI ERA; PAINTING; SCROLLS; WOODBLOCK PRINTS; YAMATO.

TOSHIBA CORPORATION (Tokyo Shibaura Denki) A large electronics company that was criticized by the U.S. government when one of its units, Toshiba Machine Co., Ltd. (Toshiba Kikai), sold sophisticated defense-related machinery to the Soviet Union in 1987. By doing so, Toshiba violated the rules of the Coordinating Committee for East-West Trade policy (COCOM). Japan is a member of this committee, which controls exports of strategic high-technology.

The Toshiba Corporation developed out of the Shibaura Engineering Works, Co., Ltd., founded in 1904 to manufacture electric generators and communications equipment. In 1939 Shibaura merged with Tokyo Electric Co., Ltd. and changed its name to Toshiba Corporation. It manufactured a variety of electric products. Toshiba grew rapidly in the 1950s, especially in the area of home appliances. It also expanded into many other fields, such as computers and other electronics, and equipment to generate atomic, geothermal, hydroelectric and thermoelectric power. Toshiba is connected with Mitsui, a Japanese conglomerate, and has had a long association with the American company General Electric.

The head office of Toshiba was recently moved to Tokyo from Kawasaki City. Toshiba has dozens of overseas subsidiaries and sales outlets, and operates plants that manufacture color televisions, computers and semiconductors in the United States and Great Britain. At present, Toshiba produces semiconductors at a much higher rate than any other Japanese company. When the United States learned of Toshiba's illegal sales to the Soviet Union, Congress passed a trade bill that would have imposed a three-year ban on imports of Toshiba products and restricted its sales to the U.S. government, but President Reagan vetoed the bill. Toshiba has surmounted its negative publicity, expanded sales of its products and is engaging in joint ventures with Motorola Inc. and other companies. See also COMPUTER INDUSTRY; CORPORATIONS; ELECTRONICS INDUSTRY; EXPORTS AND IMPORTS; MITSUI.

TOSHOGU SHRINE A shrine of Shinto, the indigenous Japanese religion, built in Nikko to house the remains of the shogun Tokugawa Ieyasu (1543–1616), founder of the Tokugawa Shogunate (1603–1867). Nikko, a city 87 miles north of Tokyo, is the center of a heavily visited national park. It was chosen as the site of a mausoleum that would glorify the achievements of Ieyasu in unifying and controlling Japan so successfully that he and his heirs ruled the country for 250 years. Unlike the plain architecture of most Shinto shrines, Toshogu is decorated with vibrant colors and delicate carvings of animals and flowers. Shinto elements are mixed with those of Buddhism, the religion introduced into Japan from China in the sixth century A.D. A Shinto *torii* (entrance gate) and Buddhist pagoda stand together in front of the elaborate main entrance, adorned with gold leaf and black lacquer. The shrine, with many ornate buildings, including the mausoleum of Ieyasu, is a secular monument as much as a religious center. It is a major tourist attraction, especially during its annual festival held on May 17th, capped by a procession of hundreds of men authentically costumed as samurai. The year after Ieyasu died, the imperial court posthumously deified him as "The Great Incarnation Who Illuminates the East" *(Tosho Daigongen)*. Eventually, more than a hundred branch Toshogu shrines were built throughout Japan. In 1873 Toshogu Shrine was also dedicated to two other great warlords in Japanese history, Toyotomi Hideyoshi (1536–1598) and Minamoto no Yoritomo (1147–1199). See also BUDDHISM; MINAMOTO NO YORITOMO; NIKKO; SHINTO; SHRINES, SHIWTO; SHOGUN; TOKUGAWA IEYASU; TOKUGAWA SHOGUNATE; TOYOTOMI HIDEYOSHI; TEMPLES, BUDDHIST.

TOWELS See SHIBORI; TENUGUI.

TOWNSPEOPLE (TRADERS OR MERCHANTS) (chonin) A class of people that originated during the Heian Era (794–1185) in the old capital city of Kyoto, where they supplied the needs of the court aristocracy. The number of *chonin* remained small until the Edo Era (1600–1868), when Japan was unified and cities grew up rapidly around castles, especially Edo, Osaka and Nagoya. During the building of castles in the late 16th century, large numbers of merchants and artisans came to castle towns to supply the needs of the samurai who settled in them. *Chonin* were restricted to low-lying districts, which became known as *shitamachi* ("the area below"). *Chonin* fell into two general groups, artisans and merchants, who were at the bottom of the Confucian class system enforced by the Tokugawa Shogunate (1603–1867). Many *chonin* in Kyoto worked in traditional crafts such as textile weaving and dyeing, and pottery making. Osaka was a large port through which rice and other products from western Japan were distributed throughout the country, and hence became a city of merchants and financiers. In Edo, the first *chonin* were construction workers who built Edo Castle and the mansions of *daimyo* (feudal lords of the provinces), whom the shogunate required to spend half their time residing in the city. Edo's burgeoning population later spawned a growing class of wholesalers, retailers and peddlers. The shogunate organized the *chonin* into occupational guilds and administrative associations. Most *chonin* worked hard and lived in extremely crowded neighborhoods. However, wholesalers and other merchants often became quite wealthy, although the shogunate limited their display of wealth through sumptuary regulations. They patronized the numerous bars and restaurants, theaters and brothels of the pleasure quarters licensed by the shogunate for sex and entertainment, such as the Yoshiwara in Edo. The dominant culture of the Edo Era, including art, literature and music, developed in these pleasure quarters, known as the "floating world" *(ukiyo)*. *Chonin* children were taught reading, writing and use of the abacus for mathematical calculations in urban private schools known as *terakoya*. After the Meiji Restoration of 1868, the government attempted to spread samurai values to other social classes, and abolished the *chonin* as an administrative class. However, the *chonin* life-style and values have survived in *shitamachi* districts of modern Japanese cities. See also APPRENTICE SYSTEM; CASTLES; CITIES; CLASS STRUCTURE; EDO ERA; FLOATING WORLD; MEIJI RESTORATION OF 1868; TOKUGAWA SHOGUNATE; YOSHIWARA.

TOYO KOYGO CO., LTD. (MAZDA) See AUTOMOBILE INDUSTRY.

TOYOTA MOTOR CORPORATION (Toyota Jidosha) The largest automobile manufacturer in Japan and the third largest in the world, after General Motors and Ford. In addition to passenger cars, Toyota produces trucks, buses and prefabricated houses. Toyota Motor Corporation is the nucleus of the Toyota group, which includes auto assembly plants operated by Toyota Auto Body Co., Ltd., Daihatsu Motor Co, Ltd. and Kanto Auto Works, Ltd. The Toyota group also includes more than 200 suppliers of parts, who in turn hire more than 40,000 subcontractors. In the 1950s, Toyota invented the "just in time" (JIT) inventory delivery system, whereby parts are delivered to assembly lines just before they are needed, which enables the company to produce a variety of automobiles while keeping costs relatively low through maintaining low inventories of parts. This system was subsequently adopted by many manufacturers around the world.

Toyota Motor Corporation was founded in 1933 as the automobile division of Toyota Automatic Loom Works, Ltd. In 1937 it became an independent company, and by 1941 it was producing 2,000 passenger cars a month. After World War II, Toyota decided to remain independent of investments from foreign companies. In 1955 it began selling the Toyopet Crown in Japan, a popular model that stimulated the Japanese automobile industry. Recent Toyota models include the Publica, Corona, Corolla and Celica. In 1982 the Toyota Motor Co., Ltd. merged with Toyota Motor Sales Co., Ltd. to form Toyota Motor Corporation. The company has maintained a high profit ratio and high retained profits. Toyota operates several dozen assembly plants in foreign countries, including the United States, and is producing cars under different names through joint venture corporations. It also exports nearly half the vehicles it manufactures in Japan. Headquarters are in Toyota City, now part of Nagoya City, in Aichi Prefecture. See also AUTOMOBILE INDUSTRY; JOINT-VENTURE CORPORATION; "JUST IN TIME" INVENTORY DELIVERY SYSTEM.

TOYOTOMI HIDEYORI See TOYOTOMI HIDEYOSHI.

TOYOTOMI HIDEYOSHI (1536–1598) A warlord who was the second of three great national unifiers of Japan, with Oda Nobunaga (1534–1582) and Tokugawa Ieyasu (1543–1616). Hideyoshi was born in Nakamura in Owari Province (part of modern Aichi Prefecture). His father, Kinoshita Yaemon, formerly a peasant, was a foot soldier *(ashigaru)* in the service of Oda Nobuhide (1510–1551), the father of Oda Nobunaga. Hideyoshi was originally named Hiyoshimaru, but took several different names in the course of his life. He entered the service of Oda Nobunaga in 1558 and acquired the name Hideyoshi in 1562. Nobunaga gave him the nickname Saru, "Monkey," for his unattractive looks. Hideyoshi rose quickly from the rank of foot soldier to become one of Nobunaga's generals. When Nobunaga was assassinated in 1582, Hideyoshi became embroiled in warfare that erupted over Nobunaga's successor. The next year he won a battle at Mount Shizugatake on Lake Biwa, and gained control of Echizen, Kaga and Noto provinces. By 1590 he controlled northern Honshu, Shikoku and Kyushu islands. He allowed the powerful *daimyo* Tokugawa Ieyasu, who swore allegiance to Hideyoshi, to retain control of eastern Honshu (known as Kanto).

Hideyoshi established close relations with the emperor in order to enhance his prestige. He was appointed imperial regent in 1585; he could not be awarded the higher title of shogun because of his low social class. In 1586 he was awarded the family name Toyotomi when he was appointed grand minister of state *(dajo daijin)*. Hideyoshi is known in Japan by the honorary title *taiko,* which is given to a retired imperial regent *(kampaku)*. Hideyoshi built a palace in Kyoto, the Juraku no Tei (or Jurakudai), and forced all the *daimyo* (feudal lords) of Japan to gather there to swear allegiance to Emperor Go-Yozei (r. 1586–1611) and to himself as imperial regent. He also built a magnificent castle in Osaka, which had a room for the tea ceremony decorated with gold foil and golden tea utensils. Hideyoshi was a fervent practitioner of the tea ceremony and hosted a famous tea party in 1588 at Kitano Shrine in Kyoto that was open to everyone in Japan. He retained the great tea ceremony master Sen no Rikyu (1522–1591) in his personal service. Rikyu was from the wealthy merchant port of Sakai, and Hideyoshi benefited from commerce there in rice, guns and ammunition. Conflicts between the two men culminated in Hideyoshi ordering Rikyu to commit ritual suicide *(seppuku)* in 1591.

In 1587 Hideyoshi abruptly banned the Christian religion, which had been introduced to Japan by the Jesuit Francis Xavier (1506–1552) in 1549 and had become widespread on Kyushu Island. Hideyoshi feared that Christianity would enhance foreign influence and threaten political unity in Japan. He had the whole country surveyed and instituted a taxation system based on agricultural production. He disarmed the peasantry and created a sharp distinction between those who farmed the land and samurai, who clustered in the castle towns of their lords.

Hideyoshi became obsessed with conquering China. He launched two invasions of Korea in 1592 and 1597, but Chinese and Korean armies stopped his forces in northern Korea. Hideyoshi did not go to Korea himself but directed the military campaign from Nagoya City.

When Hideyoshi died in 1598, he had executed his adopted son Hidetsugu and had gotten the leading *daimyo* to pledge to support his son Hideyori (1593–1615) as his successor. But Hideyoshi's most powerful vassal, Tokugawa Ieyasu, defeated rival *daimyo* at the Battle of Sekigahara in 1600, became Hideyoshi's successor, and completed the unification of Japan, establishing the Tokugawa Shogunate (1603–1867). See also CASTLES; CHRISTIANITY IN JAPAN;

KITANO SHRINE; KOREA AND JAPAN; ODA NOBUNAGA; OSAKA CASTLE; SAMURAI; SEKIGAHARA, BATTLE OF; SEN NO RIKYU; TEA CEREMONY; TOKUGAWA IEYASU; TOKUGAWA SHOGUNATE; XAVIER, ST. FRANCIS.

TOYS, TRADITIONAL Small, colorful objects made of clay, paper, wood and straw that have been used not only as playthings for children but as religious objects to protect against evil spirits. Although the word *gangu* is a general term for toys, each Japanese toy has a specific name. The most popular word for toy is *omocha,* an abbreviation of *omocha asobi,* "honorable article to play with." Traditionally, Japanese toys were only sold at religious shrines during festivals and were believed to have the power of exorcism or of guaranteeing protection or a good harvest. Each kind of toy had its own prescribed shape or style that could not be changed without the toy losing its power. Many shrines still sell toy horses, Daruma dolls, lions and similar talismans to bring good fortune and prevent illness. Clay or papier-mache figures of dogs *(inu hariko* or *Azuma inu)* are sold at shrines to protect children. An important category of Japanese toys consists of various types of dolls. The Chinese characters for doll, *ningyo,* mean "human shape," but can be read as *hito gata,* meaning a piece of paper in the shape of a person that was thrown into a river to purge sin or pollution from a human being. *Hina,* another word for doll, has overtones of ancient beliefs and practices, when clay figures known as *haniwa* were placed on burial mounds. The Girl's Festival on March 3rd, when beautiful sets of dolls are displayed in homes, is also called the Doll Festival (Hina Matsuri). During the Edo Era (1600–1868), many types of toys, such as dolls, animal figures, spinning wooden tops, balls and miniature drums, were made by hand in different regions of Japan. Still made today, they are admired as children's playthings and also as *mingei,* or traditional folk-art objects. Restaurants often display a clay figure of a beckoning cat *(manekineko)* to attract customers. Flying colorfully decorated paper kites has also been a popular pastime in Japan. The game of *hanetsuki,* similar to badminton, is played at the New Year with beautifully decorated paddles or battledores *(hagoita)* and shuttlecocks. Toy balls *(temari),* made with paper and cloth and covered with colored silk threads, are another popular traditional toy. See also DARUMA; DOLL FESTIVAL; DOLLS; FESTIVALS; GAMES; HANIWA; KITE; MINGEI; SHINTO; TALISMANS; NAMES OF INDIVIDUAL ANIMALS.

TRADE See CORPORATIONS; EXPORTS AND IMPORTS; INVESTMENTS OVERSEAS, JAPANESE; JAPAN EXTERNAL TRADE ORGANIZATION; JOINT-VENTURE CORPORATION; MINISTRY OF INTERNATIONAL TRADE AND INDUSTRY; RYUKYU ISLANDS; TRADING COMPANY, GENERAL; VERMILION SEAL SHIP TRADE.

TRADING COMPANY, GENERAL *(sogo shosha)* The import-export arm of a large, diversified Japanese corporation. A general trading company belongs to a large corporate group that includes a bank, many manufacturers and other companies. The bank connected with a trading company finances its projects and provides credit for manufacturers and wholesales. Trading companies were organized after the Meiji Restoration of 1868 to function as wholesalers for Japanese manufacturers in domestic and foreign markets and to purchase raw materials for manufacturing plants. Large industrial and financial combines, known before World War II as *zaibatsu,* each had a trading company to manage its activities. *Zaibatsu* were dissolved during the postwar Allied Occupation of Japan (1945–1952), but large postwar corporate groups have retained similarities to their predecessors, including trading companies.

In 1981 more than 6,000 trading companies existed in Japan, but nine companies handled the majority of transactions, with gross sales totaling more than a quarter of the Japanese gross national product (GNP) and accounting for more than half Japan's imports and close to half its exports. The four largest trading companies are Mitsubishi, Mitsui, C. Itoh and Marubeni.

Trading companies serve as financial mediaries, absorb foreign exchange risks for their customers, provide technical advice to small firms wishing to export products and make overseas investments. An integrated trading company handles thousands of different products with many suppliers and has the resources, personnel, and business and technical expertise to undertake major projects in Japan and overseas. Japanese trading companies have made multinational operations a major priority, and locate senior managing directors in regional headquarters such as New York or Brussels. They frequently engage in third-party trade, such as selling an American chemical plant to another foreign country. Foreign companies wishing to do business in Japan associate themselves with trading companies, often through joint venture corporations, which act as their agents or distributors in the Japanese market. See also BANKING SYSTEM; CORPORATIONS; EXPORTS AND IMPORTS; INVESTMENTS OVERSEAS, JAPANESE; ITOH C.; JOINT VENTURE CORPORATION; MARUBENI; MITSUBISHI; MITSUI; SUMITOMO.

TRAINING HALL See DOJO; MARTIAL ARTS.

TRANSPORTATION See AIRLINES AND AIRPORTS; AUTOMOBILE INDUSTRY; BRIDGES; BULLET TRAIN; FERRIES; INLAND SEA; JAPAN AIR LINES; JAPAN RAILWAYS; MOTORCYCLE INDUSTRY; PALANQUIN; RAILROADS; RICKSHAW; SHIPPING AND SHIPBUILDING; SUBWAYS; TOKAIDO ROAD.

TRAYS *(bon)* Flat trays of various shapes and sizes have been used in Japan since ancient times. They are usually made of wood and are often decorated with lacquer. Trays may also be made of other materials such as pottery or woven bamboo. Plain wooden trays are used to offer food to *kami* (sacred spirits) in Shinto rituals. Tall, footed lacquer trays known as *takatsuki* were used to hold food offerings during Buddhist and Shinto religious services at least as early as the Heian Era (794–1185). During the Edo Era (1600–1868), they also became used for presenting food on ceremonial occasions. *Kakeban* are tablelike decorative lacquer trays used for special occasions. They may come in sets with matching lidded bowls, hot water ewers and rice containers. Each guest eats from an individual *kabekan.*

Small square, diamond-shaped, round or rectangular trays are used for many other functions, such as serving sweets in the tea ceremony or presenting formal gifts or documents. Plastic trays are commonly used today for handling money in restaurants, shops and banks. *Bonseki* are miniature gardens placed in trays that include sand, stones and moss. They are related to *bonsai,* miniature trees and plants cultivated in wide, flat containers. See also BAMBOO; BONSAI; BOXES; KAMI; LACQUER WARE; SHINTO; TEA CEREMONY; WOODWORKING.

TREASURE SHIP   See SEVEN GODS OF GOOD FORTUNE.

TREATY OF MUTUAL COOPERATION AND SECURITY   See SECURITY TREATY BETWEEN JAPAN AND THE U.S.

TREATY OF PEACE WITH JAPAN   See PEACE TREATY OF 1952.

TREATY PORTS   See ANSEI COMMERCIAL TREATIES; HARRIS, TOWNSEND; PERRY, MATTHEW CALBRAITH.

TREES   Trees have always been revered in Japan as dwelling places of *kami,* sacred spirits worshipped in Shinto, the native Japanese religion. Shinto shrines are traditionally located within groves of trees. In ancient Japan the word "forest" *(mori)* designated a shrine, and the word meaning "shelter of a *kami*" *(kannabi)* was used for the surrounding woods. Within a shrine's precincts there is often an old or irregularly shaped tree regarded as especially sacred *(shimboku),* with a straw rope hung with short paper strips placed around its trunk. A tree outside a shrine precinct that has a peculiar shape is also believed to have special qualities deriving from the kami that dwells in it. Often such a tree has a small gate and other Shinto symbols at its base. The *sakaki* is a sacred evergreen tree whose branches are used by Shinto priests in formal rituals. Pine trees are auspicious symbols in Japanese culture and are widely cultivated in Japanese gardens. Flowering trees such as cherry, plum and peach are much admired. The Japanese enjoy viewing cherry blossoms in the spring and maple trees in the autumn. Pines, maples and flowering trees are also cultivated in miniature arrangements known as *bonsai.* Wood plays an indispensable part in Japanese daily life, and handmade objects made of cypress, paulownia and other wood are appreciated for their natural beauty and simplicity. These include trays, boxes, chests and even chopsticks used for eating. Traditional homes, shrines and other buildings are constructed of wood. See also BONSAI; BOXES; CHEST; CHOPSTICKS; GARDENS; HOMES AND HOUSING; SHINTO; SHRINE, SHINTO; TORII; TRAYS; WOODWORKING; NAMES OF INDIVIDUAL TREES.

TRIPARTITE PACT (Nichidokui Sangoku Domei)   A military pact signed by Japan *(Nichi),* Germany *(Doku)* and Italy *(I)* on September 27, 1940 to strengthen the military alliance among these three countries, known as the Axis Powers, against the United States, England, France and Holland, known as the Allied Powers.

Japan had signed an Anti-Comintern Pact with Germany in November 1936, in order to oppose the spread of communism and to gain powerful allies in the West. Italy entered the pact in 1937 and Spain in 1939. Japan had been politically isolated since it left the League of Nations in 1933 after the League had condemned the Japanese military occupation of Manchuria and the creation of the puppet state of Manchukuo. The Anti-Comintern pact prevented the Soviet Union from advancing into Manchuria, allowing the Japanese army to move into China without the risk of fighting on two fronts.

Japan was humiliated when Germany signed a non-aggression pact with the Soviet Union in 1939. However, when Hitler invaded France and seemed about to defeat Britain, Japan negotiated the Tripartite Pact with Germany and Italy. Japan hoped that the pact would (1) improve its relations with the Soviet Union, (2) enable it to take control of Southeast Asian colonies previously owned by defeated Western countries, (3) help end the war in China by cutting off outside support for Chiang Kai-shek's government, and (4) isolate the United States, making it less likely to intervene in China. American opinion was hostile to Japanese aggression in China, and the Tripartite Pact intensified these feelings. The United States, confident that its defenses in the Pacific could withstand any Japanese attack, banned all American exports to Japan in July 1941, thus depriving Japan of oil and other necessary raw materials. Japanese Prime Minister Konoe Fumimaro was replaced by General Tojo Hideki in October 1941, and Japan attacked the American fleet at Pearl Harbor on December 7, 1941, thus drawing the United States into World War II. Germany and Italy also declared war against the United States shortly after. See also KONOE FUMIMARO; LEAGUE OF NATIONS AND JAPAN; MANCHURIAN INCIDENT; PEARL HARBOR, JAPANESE ATTACK ON; SOVIET UNION AND JAPAN; WORLD WAR II.

TRUE PURE LAND SECT OF BUDDHISM   See PURE LAND SECT OF BUDDHISM; SHINRAN.

TRUE WORD SECT OF BUDDHISM   See KUKAI; SHINGON SECT OF BUDDHISM.

TSUBA   See SWORD GUARD.

TSUNAMI   See WAVES.

TSUKUBA ACADEMIC NEW TOWN (Tsukuba Kenkyu Gakuen Toshi)   A planned "science city" consisting of six towns and villages with 45 universities and government and private research institutions. Completed in 1979, this community is located at the base of Mount Tsukuba in Ibaraku Prefecture on central Honshu Island, two hours northeast of Tokyo. Tsukuba was the first of several newly created university-science-industry complexes set up in Japan in recent years. It was founded as a national research center by the Japanese government under the jurisdiction of the Agency of Industrial Science and Technology (AIST). The agency, a branch of the Ministry of International Trade and Industry (MITI), located nine of its 16 research laboratories at Tsukuba, including Tsukuba Space Center. There are also housing developments, stores and schools to accommodate the needs of families who settle in Tsukuba Science City, as it is called. Tsukuba University (Tsukuba Daigaku) was created in 1973 as part of an attempt by the Japanese Ministry of Education to reform higher education. This university, which incorporated Tokyo University of Education in 1978, operates on a system similar to American universities and fosters interaction between different academic disciplines. However, this model has been opposed by the established Japanese academic community.

From March to September 1985 a world's fair known as Expo '85 was held at Tsukuba. The theme of the Expo was Science and Technology for Man at Home. Exhibits demonstrated the beauty and pleasure in modern technology as well as the relationship of science and technology to human life. See also MINISTRY OF INTERNATIONAL TRADE AND INDUSTRY; RESEARCH AND DEVELOPMENT; UNIVERSITIES.

TSUMUGI See AMAMI ISLANDS; SILK.

TSUSHIMA, BATTLE OF See RUSSO-JAPANESE WAR; TOGO HEIHACHIRO; TSUSHIMA ISLAND.

TSUSHIMA ISLAND An island in the Korea Strait between South Korea and northwest Kyushu, the southernmost main island of Japan. Only 31 miles southeast of Korea, Tsushima has been a stepping stone for the flow of people and culture from the Asian mainland into Japan. Tsushima Island has two regions, the Upper Island (Kamishima) to the north, covering 98.4 square miles, and the Lower Island (Shimoshima) to the south, occupying 174 square miles. The total population today is around 50,000. The island is administered by Nagasaki Prefecture, on Kyushu. The Tsushima Strait (Tsushima Kaikyo) lies between the islands of Tsushima and Iki, off the northwest coast of Kyushu Island. Connecting the Sea of Japan to the north and the East China Sea to the south, the Tsushima Strait is broadly considered to include the Korea Strait. The narrowest point of Tsushima Strait is 31 miles, and the deepest point is 426 feet. The Tsushima Current (Tsushima Kairyu) is a warm ocean current that flows up the Sea of Japan, on the western side of the Japanese islands. It is a small branch of the Kuroshio or Black Current, which flows north on Pacific side to Tokyo.

Mongols crossed the Tsushima Strait when they attempted to invade Japan in 1274 and 1281. Autumn weather is very changeable in the strait, and both Mongol fleets were stopped by typhoons, which helped save Japan from invasion; the storms are known as *kamikaze*, or "divine wind." The Russian warship *Posadnik* attempted to establish a base on Tsushima Island in 1861. The Tokugawa Shogunate (1603–1867) sent its foreign affairs commissioner Oguri Tadamasa to attempt peaceful settlement, but it was not until two British warships finally sailed to Tsushima that the Russian warship left after a stay of more than six months. On May 27–28, 1905, during the Russo-Japanese War (1904–1905), Japanese Admiral Togo Heihachiro de-

stroyed the Russian Baltic fleet in Tsushima Strait, when the fleet was sent to rescue Russian ships at Port Arthur. The Battle of Tsushima, which is known to Japanese as the Battle of the Sea of Japan (Nihonkai Kaisen), is considered by many naval historians as the greatest victory in the history of sea warfare. The Battle of Tsushima brought Japan recognition as a world power and gave it naval supremacy in northeast Asian waters.

Today most of Tsushima Island is covered with forests. Mushrooms, soybeans, millet and buckwheat are grown on the 4% of land that is arable, and squid and cultured pearls are principal marine products. The remains of the castle of the So clan, which ruled the northern part of the island for seven centuries, can be seen in Izuhara, the main port. Tsushima Island belongs to the Iki-Tsushima Quasi-National Park. See also GEOGRAPHY OF JAPAN; KOREA AND JAPAN; KYUSHU ISLAND; MONGOL INVASIONS OF JAPAN; SEA OF JAPAN; RUSSO-JAPANESE WAR; TYPHOONS.

TSUZUMI See DRUMS.

TUNA (*maguro*) A large saltwater fish that is a favorite Japanese food, in particular the species called the North Pacific bluefin, which grows 10 feet long and weighs over 650 pounds. Much of the tuna eaten in Japan is now caught in foreign waters, especially off the West Coast of the United States. The Japanese eat tuna raw in sushi and sashimi. Regular raw tuna meat is red in color. Meat cut from the side section of the fish, called *chu-toro*, is a marbled pink color. The best cut of tuna, known as *toro,* is from the area around the fins close to the head of the fish and is a pale color referred to as "white" by the Japanese. The yellowtail fish (called *hamachi* when young and *buri* when fully grown) is very similar to tuna and served in the same way. Tuna has always been a part of the Japanese diet. It is mentioned in the *Kojiki,* an official chronicle compiled in A.D. 712 (where it is called *shibi*) and in the *Manyoshu,* an important eighth-century collection of poetry. See also FISH AND FISHING INDUSTRY; SASHIMI; SUSHI.

TUTTLE, CHARLES E. See BOOKS AND BOOKSTORES.

TWENTY-ONE DEMANDS ON CHINA (Taika Nijuikkajo Yokyu; 1915) Strong demands intended to strengthen Japan's position in China that the Japanese government secretly presented to Yuan Shikai (Yuan Shih-k'ai), then president of the Republic of China, which had been proclaimed after the overthrow of the Qing (Ch'ing) dynasty in 1911. When Japan defeated China in the Sino-Japanese War (1894–1895) and Russia in the Russo-Japanese War (1904–1905), it gained Taiwan and part of Manchuria, including the Guandong (Kwantung) Territory on the Liaodong (Liaotung) Peninsula in southern Manchuria. In 1914 Japan entered World War I on the side of Great Britain, and Japanese troops took Shandong (Shantung) Peninsula in China, which had been controlled by Germany. Yuan Shikai asked Japan to withdraw all troops from the Shandong Peninsula in late 1914, and Japanese Foreign Minister

Kato Takaaki (1860–1926) responded by presenting the Twenty-one Demands to Yuan, with threats of retaliation if China did not comply. The demands fell into five groups. The first two groups sought to increase Japanese control of Shandong Province, South Manchuria and Inner Mongolia. The third group would make Japan an equal owner of the Hanyeping (Han-yeh-p'ing) mining and metallurgical company. The fourth group intended to prevent the United States from gaining a presence in Fujian (Fukien) Province, where Japan already had concessions. The fifth group demanded that China purchase half its military supplies from Japan, that Japanese military and financial advisers be accepted in China, and that Japan be granted railway rights in the Yangzi (Yangtze) region and other regions where the British were already established. The Chinese people reacted angrily to the demands and boycotted Japanese trade goods and shipping. After several months of negotiations, China rejected Japan's revised version of the Twenty-one Demands. In response, Japan dropped the fifth group of demands but doubled the number of Japanese soldiers in China. Yuan yielded to Japanese threats and signed the agreement on May 25, 1915. However, the Twenty-one Demands caused the United States, Great Britain and other nations to oppose Japanese aggression against China, and they also heightened the Chinese people's patriotic fervor and fear of Japan. In January 1922, Japanese ambassador to the U.S. Shidehara Kijuro (1872–1951) attempted to restore relations between Japan and China to what they had been before the Twenty-one Demands, advising the Japanese Diet (Parliament) that Japan should respect China's territory and not interfere in its internal affairs. Yamagata Aritomo (1838–1922), a leading statesman and architect of the modern Japanese army, also supported diplomacy with China rather than threats such as the Twenty-one Demands. However, Japanese opposition to Shidehara's China policy brought down the cabinet of Prime Minister Wakatsuki Reijiro in 1927. See also CHINA AND JAPAN; RUSSO-JAPANESE WAR; SHIDEHARA KIJURO; SINO-JAPANESE WAR; WORLD WAR I; YAMAGATA ARITOMO.

232ND ENGINEER COMBAT COMPANY See 442ND REGIMENTAL COMBAT TEAM.

TYPHOON (*taifu*) Tropical storms that develop in the southern and western regions of the Pacific Ocean. Comparatively small storms of extremely low pressure, typhoons usually form east of the Philippine Islands. Over the spring and summer, hot water vapor builds up in the atmosphere and eventually condenses into heavy rainfall. Typhoons travel northwest toward Japan and are generally strongest as they travel along the Ryukyu Island chain and Kyushu Island. Every year five or six storms pass over or near Japan in August and September, about nine or 10 days after they form far out in the Pacific. This is the time when the rice crops are ripening for harvest, so the heavy rain and winds brought by typhoons have been a major threat to Japanese agriculture since ancient times. Under the traditional Japanese lunar calendar, typhoons were referred to as the 210th and 220th days of the year. A traditional Japanese term for typhoons, used in *haiku* poetry to evoke the summer season, is *nowaki*, a "wind that levels the fields." The word *taifu* has been traced to two origins, either an Arabic word or a Chinese word meaning a strong wind off the Taiwan coast. Some typhoons have caused severe destruction and deaths. The most famous typhoons in Japanese history reportedly saved Japan from the Mongol Invasions of 1274 and 1281, the only premodern attempt by a foreign nation to conquer Japan, when the Mongol fleets were destroyed in the storms. This led the Japanese to believe that their country was protected by *kamikaze*, or "divine wind." A typhoon that struck Ise Bay on September 26, 1959 left more than 5,000 people dead or missing and over a million buildings damaged. The Japanese Meteorological Agency (Kishocho) collects data from weather observation stations all over the country, prepares forecasts and issues advisories about typhoons that are broadcast to the general public. See also CALENDAR; CLIMATE OF JAPAN; HAIKU; KAMIKAZE; KYUSHU ISLAND; MONGOL INVASIONS OF JAPAN; PACIFIC OCEAN; RAIN; RICE; RYUKYU ISLANDS.

U

UDON See NOODLES.

UENO A district in northern Tokyo centered around Japan's first public park, museum and zoo, and one of Tokyo's largest railroad stations. Department stores, bargain shopping centers, restaurants and bars are clustered around Ueno Station, from which trains depart for northern Japan.

Within Ueno Park can be found several important museums, Ueno Zoo and Shinobazu Pond. The Tokyo National Museum houses the world's greatest collection of Japanese art, including paintings, Buddhist sculptures, lacquer ware, swords and other metalwork, armor, ceramics, kimono and other textiles, and archaeological artifacts. Art from other Asian countries also forms part of the collection. The Horyuji Treasure House displays rare ancient objects. The Tokyo Metropolitan Art Museum exhibits modern Japanese art. Western works of art are displayed in the National Museum of Western Art, much of which came from the early 20th-century Japanese art collector Matsukata Kojiro. The National Science Museum houses a great variety of displays on science and technology, traditional Japanese crafts and nature. The daily life of people in Tokyo's old "downtown" (shitamachi) area can be seen in the Shitamachi Museum.

Shinobazu Pond was artifically created in the 17th century. In May 1868 the final battle between the last supporters of the Tokugawa Shogunate (1603–1867) and those who supported the restoration of the emperor was waged in the marshes around the pond. Saigo Takamuri, the great samurai and statesman of the Meiji Restoration of 1868, is honored by a statue at the entrance to Ueno Park. Today Shinobazu Pond is filled with lotus plants and serves as a bird sanctuary. An island in the center has a small temple dedicated to Benten, the goddess of the arts. Ueno Municipal Zoo dates back to 1882. Crowds flock here to see the two giant pandas that were a gift to Japan from the People's Republic of China. Toshogu Shrine was built in 1651 to honor Tokugawa Ieyasu, the founder of the Tokugawa Shogunate. Large stone lanterns line the pathway to the shrine. Kan'ei-ji Kiyomizudo Temple replicates the renowned Kiyomizudera Temple in Kyoto. Women leave dolls around an altar here to protect the health of their babies, and the dolls that accumulate during the year are ritually burned every September 25th. See also BENTEN; DEPARTMENT STORES; KIYOMIZUDERA TEMPLE; MEIJI RESTORATION OF 1868; MUSEUMS IN JAPAN; SAIGO TAKAMORI; SHITAMACHI; TOKUGAWA SHOGUNATE; TOKYO; ZOOLOGICAL GARDENS.

UJI A small city near the former capital, Kyoto, on central Honshu Island that is famous for the finest grades of green tea in Japan. Uji tea has been cultivated for seven centuries and is highly prized by the tea ceremony schools headquartered in Kyoto. Every June, new tea is offered to the gods at Agata Shrine. A bridge over the Uji River (Ujigawa) was originally constructed in A.D. 646 by Dosho (629–700), a priest who founded the Hosso sect of Buddhism. Located on the road connecting Kyoto with Nara, the ancient capital city, Uji Bridge was the site of several great battles in the 12th century between factions of the Minamoto clan and between the Minamoto and Taira clans. The great warlord Toyotomi Hideyoshi (1536–1598), who was a patron and practitioner of the tea ceremony, supposedly stood on the bridge to dip water for a tea ceremony he once performed, and a water-dipping ceremony is held on this spot every October 1st. Fujiwara no Michinaga (966–1028) built a villa in Uji, which his son Yorimichi (990–1074) converted into a Buddhist temple and monastery named Byodo-in ("Temple of Equality") in 1052. The main hall, which is the only original building that remains today, was built in the shape of a phoenix, the mythical bird that regenerates itself. The temple has a stone monument to Uji tea that was erected in 1887. In Uji there is also a Zen Buddhist temple, Mampukuji, built in the Ming Chinese style in the 17th century by the Chinese monk Ingen. See also BRIDGES; HOSSO SECT OF BUDDHISM; KYOTO; MINAMOTO CLAN; NARA; PHOENIX; TAIRA-MINAMOTO WAR; TEA CEREMONY; TOYOTOMI HIDEYOSHI; TEMPLES, BUDDHIST.

UKIYO-E See FLOATING WORLD; WOODBLOCK PRINTS.

UMBRELLA (kasa) Umbrellas covered with silk were introduced into Japan from Korea during the sixth century A.D. and served as sunshades for members of the aristocracy. Such umbrellas are called higasa. Amagasa, or rain umbrellas, came to be used by people of all classes during the Edo Era (1600–1868). Traditional Japanese paper umbrellas, known as karakasa, are made of bamboo frames and handles, with coverings of handmade paper painted with decorative designs and coated with tung oil. Ehigasa is the particular name for paper umbrellas decorated with paintings of birds and flowers. Another popular decorative motif is the janomegasa, or "snake-eye umbrella," which has a black, red or navy-blue paper covering with a white ring in the center that looks like the eye of a snake. A similar design often used in the countryside and at hot-spring resorts is a plain umbrella with two circles that make a bull's-eye. Very large umbrellas are used in parades and other special occasions such as outdoor tea ceremonies. They are usually red, but can also be yellow or green and have a gold or silver lining. Traditional paper umbrellas are beautiful but quite expensive today, and Western-style

A craftsman decorating a traditional paper umbrella. After being painted, the paper is waterproofed with oil.

cloth umbrellas are common in Japan for ordinary use. See also BAMBOO; PAPER, HANDMADE; RAIN; SILK; TEA CEREMONY.

UMEBOSHI See PICKLES; PLUM TREE.

UNEQUAL TREATIES See ANSEI COMMERICAL TREATIES.

UNIONS See LABOR UNIONS.

UNITED NATIONS AND JAPAN Japan became a member of the United Nations on December 18, 1956. It had belonged to the League of Nations, the precursor of the United Nations formed after World War I. Japan's entry into the UN was supported by the United States but had been blocked by the Soviet Union. Tensions between the two countries were due largely to Russian occupation of Kuril and other islands off the northern coast of Japan in 1945, which Japan had formerly claimed as its territory; Russian control of Japanese fishing grounds; and Russian mistreatment of Japanese prisoners of war during World War II. In October 1956 Japan and Russia reached a settlement over trade and diplomatic relations, and Japan was admitted to the United Nations one month later.

The Japanese government has maintained a policy of international cooperation through the UN, as well as other multilateral organizations, for the cause of world peace, nuclear disarmament, aid to developing countries, and educational and technical cooperation. As the only country to suffer nuclear attack, Japan has played an active role in nuclear test ban and nonproliferation treaties. In 1954 the UN Association of Japan expressed the desire of the Japanese people for world peace by donating a "Peace Bell," which is exhibited at UN Headquarters in New York City.

Japan is a member of nearly all UN committees, including the Economic and Social Council, the Environment Program Council, the Industrial Development Council, the World Food Council, the International Labor Organization, the International Monetary Fund and the Educational, Scientific, and Cultural Organization. Japan has also channeled resources to other countries through the UN Development Program and the Children's Fund. In 1980 Japan was elected to the UN Security Council, where it continues to play an important role as the most highly industrialized Asian country. Ten UN agencies also operate in Japan, the largest being the UN University, a network of research facilities established in Tokyo in 1974. There are also 12 nongovernmental organizations in Japan registered with the UN, such as the Japan Red Cross Society. Japan is now second only to the United States in the amount of money it contributes to the UN. See also KURIL ISLANDS; LEAGUE OF NATIONS; WORLD WAR II.

UNITED STATES AND JAPAN See EXPORTS AND IMPORTS; EXPOSITIONS, INTERNATIONAL; HARRIS, TOWNSEND; IMMIGRANTS, JAPANESE; INVESTMENTS OVERSEAS, JAPANESE; JAPANESE-AMERICAN CITIZENS LEAGUE; MACARTHUR, DOUGLAS; OCCUPATION OF JAPAN; OKINAWA ISLAND; PEACE TREATY OF 1952; PEARL HARBOR, JAPANESE ATTACK ON; PERRY, MATTHEW CALBRAITH; REISCHAUER, EDWIN OLDFATHER; SUPREME COMMANDER FOR THE ALLIED POWERS; WAR CRIMES TRIALS; WASHINGTON CONFERENCE AND NAVAL TREATY OF 1922; WORLD WAR II.

UNIVERSITIES (*daigaku*) In Japan, all institutions for higher education are termed "universities" (*daigaku*). Two- or three-year junior colleges are called "short-term universities" (*tanki daigaku*). In 1980 Japan was second to the United States in the number of institutions of higher learning, with more than 500 junior colleges, 450 colleges and universities, and 250 graduate schools, 155 of which offered doctoral studies. Most students go to work after they receive their degrees; only about 5% go on to graduate schools. Japanese universities are recruiting grounds for large corporations and the government, and the prestige of the school one attends is most important. Most prestigious is Tokyo National University, which was founded in 1877 to train students for service in the national government. Other national universities (formerly called Imperial Universities) were founded soon after, such as Kyoto, Tohoku (in Sendai), Kyushu (in Fukuoka) and Hokkaido (in Sapporo). Next in prestige are elite private universities, especially Keio and Waseda. Keio University was founded by Fukuzawa Yukichi (1835–1901) as the first private university in Japan. Other private universities, such as Chuo, Meiji and Nihon, were originally founded to teach law. There are also large private Christian institutions, such as Doshisha and International Christian University, and Buddhist universities, such as Ryukoku. About one-third of Japanese universities, particularly the most prestigious ones, are in the Tokyo area. Another third are in the large cities of Yokohama, Nagoya, Kyoto, Osaka and Kobe.

The Japanese educational system was revised during the Occupation following World War II, when universities were consolidated along American lines into four-year institutions and were democratized to provide higher education to all students who qualified, not just those from elite backgrounds. Two-year junior colleges were established in 1948 for training in the liberal arts, teaching and home economics. Their credits can be transferred toward a Bachelor of Arts degree at a four-year institution. In 1989, 36.9% of Japanese high school graduates entered college. Private institutions gain 75% of university students and 90% of junior college students. Women usually attend junior colleges, and only one-quarter of female university students attend the elite universities.

Universities are made up of various schools, which are in turn broken down into departments, and then chairs (koza) or subjects of specialization (gakkamoku). It is very difficult to transfer between departments or between schools. Students in bachelor of arts programs spend the first two years studying general subjects and the last two specializing in a major subject. Social sciences, engineering and the humanities are popular majors. The Ministry of Education, Science and Culture administers the national universities, nationally established junior and technical colleges, and research institutes. Universities develop their own curricula but must confrom to certain general standards set by the Ministry of Education. Starting in the mid-1970s, many private universities have been given financial assistance from the Japanese government.

Riots led by the Zengakuren and other radical student groups disrupted or closed many Japanese universities 1968–1969 but led to a few government reforms of the rigid Japanese educational system, such as government financial aid to private universities. However, students still suffer intense competition for entrance into universities, which is determined by difficult examinations nicknamed "examination hell" (nyushi jigoku). Preparation for these exams accelerates in high school, when many students attend "cram schools" (juku). Once admitted to universities, students generally do not have to work quite as hard. New-concept universities such as Tsukuba have recently been founded to overcome problems of centralized control in universities and lack of communication among faculty in various disciplines. Students of all ages can also attend the new University of the Air, a television correspondence course. See also EDUCATION SYSTEM; JUKU; MINISTRY OF EDUCATION, SCIENCE AND CULTURE; TOKYO UNIVERSITY; TSUKUBA ACADEMIC NEW TOWN; ZENGAKUREN.

UNO SOSUKE (1922–) A politician of the Liberal Democratic Party (LDP; Jiyu Minshuto) who was selected prime minister by the LDP-dominated Japanese Diet (Parliament) on June 1, 1989. Uno replaced Takeshita Noboru, who resigned as prime minister and president of the LDP in the wake of the so-called Recruit Scandal, the worst political scandal in postwar Japan. While Uno was neither the head of a party faction nor a popular choice, he was chosen—after the party's first choice, former Foreign Minister Ito Masayoshi, refused to accept the position without massive reforms—because he was not implicated in the Recruit Scandal and because he was Takeshita's foreign

minister. Uno was backed by Takeshita and by the LDP's number two leader, Secretary General Abe Shintaro. Nevertheless, many LDP party members protested the choice of Uno and the secretive method by which he was selected, especially since Uno was closely associated with former Prime Minister Nakasone Yasuhiro, who was himself implicated in the Recruit Scandal. Less than a month after he became prime minister, and just before national elections, on July 23, 1989, for half the members of the House of Councillors (upper house of the Diet), Uno became embroiled in a scandal when a former geisha and several other women charged him with paying them for sex. LDP members quickly distanced themselves from Uno, whose government had the lowest popularity rating for any new government in postwar Japan. In the election the LDP lost its majority in the House of Councillors to the opposition Japan Socialist Party (JSP; Nihon Shakaito), partially because of the LDP scandals and partially because of the nation's first sales tax, which the LDP-dominated Diet passed in April 1989. The loss was its worst political setback since its founding in 1955. Uno took the blame for his party's humiliating defeat and resigned after the election, less than two months after he took office, making his one of the shortest terms of any Japanese prime minister. He was replaced by Kaifu Toshiki.

Uno was born into a wealthy sake-brewing family in Moriyama, Shiga Prefecture. He was conscripted into the military from Kobe University in 1943, and spent two years in a Siberian internment camp after World War II. His first book, *Home to Tokyo*, about this experience, was made into a movie. The book's influence on Japanese government policies led him to enter politics. See also DIET; ELECTIONS; FACTIONS, POLITICAL; JAPAN SOCIALIST PARTY; KAIFU TOSHIKI; LIBERAL DEMOCRATIC PARTY; NAKASONE YASUHIRO; PRIME MINISTER; RECRUIT SCANDAL; TAKESHITA NOBORU.

URASENKE SCHOOL OF THE TEA CEREMONY   The largest school that teaches the traditional Japanese tea ceremony (chanoyu or chado), a highly formalized ritual for preparing and serving ground tea, known as matcha, in large pottery tea bowls (chawan). The iemoto, or head, of the Urasenke School is Sen Soshitsu (1923–), a 15th-generation direct descendant from Sen no Rikyu (1522–1591), who established the rituals of the tea ceremony. Rikyu's grandson and tea successor, Sen Sotan (1578–1658), divided the Sen family residence in Kyoto among three of his grandsons, who founded separate family lines and schools of tea named for the locations of their homes: Urasenke (back house), Omotesenke (front house), and Mushakojisenke (house on Mushakoji Street). These homes still serve as the Sen family residences and the headquarters for their tea schools. Sen Soshitsu traveled through the United States following World War II to acquaint foreigners with the Japanese tea ceremony and to promote world peace. Under his guidance, Urasenke is the only Japanese tea school that has opened branch schools in foreign countries, including the United States, Canada, Thailand and many other countries in Europe and Latin America. North American headquarters are in New York

City. Today millions of Japanese and foreign students belong to the Urasenke school. See also IEMOTO; SEN NO RIKYU; TEA; TEA BOWL; TEAHOUSE; TEA CEREMONY.

UTAMARO (1753–1806) Full name Kitagawa Utamaro; one of the greatest woodblock print artists and painters in the *ukiyo-e* ("pictures of the floating world") style of the Edo Era (1600–1868). Utamaro came of age just after a terrible fire destroyed much of Edo (modern Tokyo) in 1772. He studied with Toriyama Sekien (1712–1788), an independent artist connected with the Kano school. Utamaro's earliest known works are cover pictures for the libretto of a Kabuki play, *The Many Intricacies of Love (Shiju Hatte Koi no Showake)*. He created numerous broadsheets and picture books for other Kabuki plays, illustrations for popular novels, and erotic prints (*makura-e,* or "pillow pictures"). He also produced many beautiful albums of illustrations, such as *Insect Book (Ehon mushi erami;* 1788), *Silver World (Ginsekai;* 1790), and *Bird Book (Momo chidori kyoka awase;* 1790). In the 1790s Utamaro devoted his creative efforts to making single-sheet prints of human figures. His finest works depict beautiful women of the licensed pleasure quarters, known as the Yoshiwara in Edo City, in intimate poses and settings. Utamaro's women are typically mature, tall and sensual, and are portrayed with refined subtlety and a concern with their emotional life. Utamaro enjoyed the patronage of Tsutaya Juzaburo (1750–1797), the preeminent publisher in Edo, who advanced the careers of many of the most talented *ukiyo-e* artists and writers. Numerous artists studied with Utamaro and used his family name of Kitagawa. After 1800, Utamaro's work seemed to lose some of its originality, perhaps because his popularity made it necessary for him to create too many works on demand. He was jailed for a short time in 1804 because the Tokugawa Shogunate judged that he portrayed the great Japanese warlord Toyotomi Hideyoshi (1566–1598) in a disrespectful way. He died two years later. See also EDO ERA; FLOATING WORLD; TOKUGAWA SHOGUNATE; TOYOTOMI HIDEYOSHI; WOODBLOCK PRINTS; YOSHIWARA.

VALUE-CREATING SOCIETY See SOKA GAKKAI.

VASSALS See DAIMYO; FEUDALISM.

VCR See ELECTRONICS INDUSTRY.

VEGETABLES See COOKING; DAIKON; LOTUS; MUSHROOMS; PICKLES; SEAWEED; SWEET POTATO.

VENDING MACHINES (*jidohanbaiki*) Commonly found on many streets in Japanese cities and small towns, vending machines dispense a wide variety of items, including soft drinks, alcoholic beverages such as beer and sake, cigarettes, ice cream, cooked foods, batteries, comic books, pornographic magazines and frozen beef. Western-style vending machines were first seen in Japan in 1888, but only after World War II did they become common throughout the country, even in rural areas. Many Japanese vending machines are colorfully decorated with cartoons and twinkling lights. See also ALCOHOLIC BEVERAGES; COMIC BOOKS; MAGAZINES; SAKE; YEN.

VERMILION SEAL SHIP TRADE (*shuinsen boeki*) Foreign trade licensed by the national unifier Toyotomi Hideyoshi (1537–1598) and the early Tokugawa Shogunate (1603–1867), named for the shogun's vermilion seal (*shuin*) on licenses (*jo*) carried by authorized ships. One license was issued for each trading voyage made by a ship to one port. Hideyoshi and Tokugawa Ieyasu (1543–1616), who systematized the vermilion seal ship trade, wanted to control foreign trade to further their unification of Japan. The licenses also gave Japanese ships some protection on the high seas by limiting the activities of pirate-traders known as *wako*. Japan had long traded with China, but in 1547, when the Chinese Ming dynasty (1368–1644) prohibited exchange between China and Japan, Japanese merchants sent their ships to the Philippines, Indochina and Southeast Asia. In 1601, Ieyasu requested rulers of Southeast Asian countries to trade only with Japanese ships carrying vermilion seal licenses. Ieyasu asked rulers of foreign countries to trade only with Japanese ships bearing licenses, and threatened sanctions against those who interfered with licensed ships. The Tokugawa Shogunate issued more than 350 licenses until it ended the system in 1635. More than 200 of the licensed ships went to Siam (Thailand) or Indochina. These regions had communities of Japanese merchants, known as Nihommachi, and overseas Chinese merchants. Licensed Japanese ships exported copper, silver, iron, sulfur and craft items such as lacquer ware and decorative textiles and imported silk thread and cloth,

spices and medicines. The shogunate came to regard Portuguese and Spanish traders and Roman Catholic missionaries in Japan as a threat to its authority, and closed the country to foreigners in 1639. The vermilion seal ship trade was disbanded in 1635, and only specially licensed trading voyages to the southern Ryukyu Islands (Okinawa Prefecture) and Korea were permitted. Limited trade with a few Dutch and Chinese traders was also allowed in the Japanese city of Nagasaki. See also CHINA AND JAPAN; KOREA AND JAPAN; NAGASAKI; PORTUGUESE IN JAPAN; RYUKYU ISLANDS; SECLUSION, NATIONAL; SILK; TOKUGAWA SHOGUNATE; TOYOTOMI HIDEYOSHI.

VERY LARGE SCALE INTEGRATED CIRCUIT (VLSI) PROJECT See COMPUTER INDUSTRY; FIFTH–GENERATION ADVANCED COMPUTER SYSTEMS; RESEARCH AND DEVELOPMENT.

VINING, ELIZABETH GRAY (1902–) An American teacher chosen to be the private tutor from 1946 to 1950 for then Crown Prince Akihito (1933–), who became emperor of Japan in 1989 with the reign name Heisei ("Achieving Peace"). Vining was born and raised in Philadelphia and educated at Bryn Mawr College. She also received a master's degree in library science. Under her maiden name, Elizabeth Janet Gray, she wrote many children's books between 1929 and 1945, some of which have been reprinted. When Vining went to Japan in 1946, Crown Prince Akihito was 12 years old and was being groomed to succeed his father, Emperor Hirohito (1901–1989). After Japan surrendered in 1945, the Allied Powers made the emperor renounce his divinity. Vining was charged with the task of preparing Akihito for the emperor's new role in Japan and Japan's new role in the world. As a member of the Society of Friends (Quakers), she presented a curriculum intended to give the Crown Prince a comprehensive understanding of Japanese society and international affairs and to develop his moral character. Her pacifism, one of the major Quaker beliefs, strongly influenced the Japanese people. Vining also taught at Gakushuin University and Tsuda College in Japan. In 1950 she returned to the United States and wrote many more books. She described her experiences as Akihito's tutor in *Windows for the Crown Prince* (1952). After attending his wedding in 1959, she wrote *Return to Japan* (1960). She was interviewed extensively when Akihito became emperor in 1989. See also AKIHITO, EMPEROR; HIROHITO, EMPEROR; OCCUPATION OF JAPAN.

VLSI See COMPUTER INDUSTRY; FIFTH–GENERATION ADVANCED COMPUTER SYSTEMS; RESEARCH AND DEVELOPMENT.

VOLCANO *(kazan)* The mountainous Japanese islands lie in the volcanic zone that surrounds the Pacific Ocean, and one-tenth of the world's active volcanoes are located in Japan. Numerous fault lines in the earth's crust also run throughout Japan, causing frequent and sometimes destructive earthquakes. Volcanic eruptions have affected the lives of the Japanese people throughout the history, killing many yet creating fertile soil for agriculture, exposing ore deposits, and gracing the landscape with their natural beauty. Many Japanese volcanoes are shaped like a cone with a wide base, such as Mount Fuji *(Fuji-san)*, the largest volcano in Japan and the sacred symbol of the country. A conical volcano, or stratovolcano, is built up from layers of lava and other materials expelled from the crater and is usually about 3,000–6,000 feet high. More than 20 volcanoes in Japan have calderas, large basin-like depressions caused by the explosion of the crater. Some calderas have beautiful lakes and have been designated national parks. At present there are few active volcanoes in Japan. How-ever, Sakurajima, across the bay from Kagoshima on the island of Kyushu, exploded violently in 1914 and still sends out clouds of destructive ash. Mount Aso on Kyushu is the world's largest active volcano. During the time when Japan was ruled by the Yamato court (c. fourth century–c. mid-seventh century), volcanoes erupted frequently enough for them to be feared and given a high place in the pantheon of *kami* (divine spirits) of Shinto, the native Japanese religion. Attempts were even made by imperial envoys to appease them. In the late 19th century, Japanese scientists began using Western techniques to study volcanoes. Today the Japanese Meteorological Agency observes volcanic activity and forecasts dangers. See also EARTHQUAKES; FUJI, MOUNT; KAGOSHIMA; KAMI; MOUNTAINS; PACIFIC OCEAN; SHINTO; WAVES; YAMATO.

VOLCANO ISLANDS (IO ISLANDS) See BONIN ISLANDS.

VOTING See CONSTITUTION OF 1947; DIET; ELECTIONS.

W

WA- A term used as a prefix to identify things as typically Japanese, especially in contrast to Chinese or Western things. For example, classical forms of vernacular Japanese poetry have been termed *waka*, "Japanese" poems or songs, to distinguish them from *kanshi*, Chinese-style poetry. Similarly, Japanese-style clothing is termed *wafuku*, in distinction to Western-style clothing, termed *yofuku*. Japanese-style sweets enjoyed with green tea are called *wagashi*. The character used to write *wa*, which is pronounced *he* or *ho* in Chinese, also connotes peace or harmony. *Wa* is also the Japanese pronunciation of another character (*Wo* in Chinese) that was used in ancient China and Korea to refer to the land of Japan and the Japanese people. The oldest known references to *Wa* are notations regarding geography in two Chinese texts from the first century A.D. A more detailed mention of *Wa* is recorded in the Chinese text *Wei Zhi* (*Wei chih;* c. A.D 297), where it describes a region, apparently on the southern Japanese island of Kyushu, with several small kingdoms that were unified by a female ruler named Himiko. Since the Chinese usage of *Wa* had the perjorative meaning of "dwarf," in the seventh century A.D., Prince Shotoku, regent to Empress Suiko, decided to use *Nippon* or *Nihon*, meaning the land where the sun rises, rather than *Wa* as the official name for Japan.

WABI See SABI AND WABI; SEN NO RIKYU.

WAGES See EMPLOYMENT; EXPENSE ACCOUNTS; INCOME.

WAKA "Japanese poems or song"; classical forms of Japanese poetry written in the vernacular from the sixth century A.D., as distinct from *kanshi*, Chinese style poetry. Specifically, the term *waka* is applied to poetry written in the classical form known as *tanka*, or "short poem," which had become dominant in Japan by the ninth century A.D. A *tanka* consists of five lines with 31 syllables in a 5-7-5-7-7 pattern and is written in the native Japanese syllabic system known as *kana*. Since early Japanese poets also wrote Chinese-style poems in the Chinese language using *kanji*, or Chinese characters, *tanka* became synonymous with *waka*. The *tanka* form was adapted into *renga*, or "linked verse," in the 14th century. By the 17th century the *tanka* form was considered too rigid and a more expressive and spontaneous short poetic form with three lines and 17 syllables, known as *haikai* or *haiku*, became popular. In the broad sense, *waka* includes all of these poetic forms. Poets who aimed to revive traditional Japanese culture in the late 19th century spurred a renewed interest in the five-line, 31-syllable *tanka* form. In the 20th century, the term *waka* has become associated with poets who wrote in the classical 31-syllable *tanka* form prior to the 20th century, while the term *tanka* refers to 20th-century poets who attempt to use the *tanka* form in a more spontaneous and creative manner. See also CALLIGRAPHY; HAIKU; KANA; KANJI; LANGUAGE, JAPANESE; POETRY; RENGA; TANKA; WRITING SYSTEM, JAPANESE.

WALEY, ARTHUR DAVID (1889–1966) A British translator who introduced classical Japanese and Chinese literature to the West. Waley was born in England and educated at Rugby. He attended but never graduated from Cambridge University. He virtually taught himself to read the Japanese and Chinese languages, and began translating while holding a position at the British museum. Although the majority of his works were translations of Chinese writings, Waley is well remembered for his beautiful translation of the important Japanese novel *The Tale of Genji* (*Genji Monogatari*), written in the 11th century by Murasaki Shikibu; Waley published his translation in six volumes between 1925 and 1933. Other Japanese works that he translated are *The No Plays of Japan* (1921), *The Pillow Book of Sei Shonagon* (1928), and "The Lady Who Loved Insects" (1929), a story from the collection *Tsutsumi Chunagon Monogatari*. Waley's translations, which became popular with general readers, and were translated into other Western languages, have influenced many modern writers, such as Bertolt Brecht. However, scholars have criticized Waley for taking too many liberties with the original texts and have issued translations that are more accurate than Waley's but less beautiful. Waley also wrote many essays on Japanese Art and on Zen Buddhism. Concentrating solely on classical literature, Waley never taught in a university, traveled to Asia, or learned to speak Japanese. See also GENJI, THE TALE OF; MURASAKI SHIKIBU; SEI SHONAGON; ZEN SECT OF BUDDHISM.

WALKMAN See MORITA AKIO; SONY CORPORATION.

WAR CRIMES TRIALS Various trials and military tribunals held by the Allied powers during and after World War II to judge whether Japanese military and civilian leaders committed war crimes, which were defined as actions during the war that were illegal according to international standards of military conduct. The Potsdam Declaration, which listed the conditions for the surrender of Japan in 1945, had called for punishment of Japanese war criminals, and the victorious Allies held many local trials in Japan and other Asian countries to judge 6,000 Japanese for war crimes, of whom 927 were executed. A notorious example of these trials was held in the Philippine Islands in 1946, when General Yamashita Tomoyuki, leader of Japanese forces in the Philippines when the Allies won back those islands, was hastily sentenced to death.

On May 3, 1946, the International Military Tribunal for the Far East, commonly known as the Tokyo Trial, was convened to bring charges against 28 top Japanese political and military leaders, 25 of whom were ultimately convicted and sentenced to either imprisonment or death. The most prominent defendant was Tojo Hideki (1884–1948), Japanese prime minister during the war and also a general in the Imperial Japanese Army, who was among those who were executed. Eleven justices from countries that had suffered Japanese military aggression sat on the bench. Sir William Webb of Australia served as president of the Tokyo Trial, which met for two and a half years. The chief prosecutor was Joseph B. Keenan of the United States. The convicted defendants appealed unsuccessfully to General Douglas MacArthur, Supreme Commander for the Allied Powers (SCAP) during the Occupation, and the U.S. Supreme Court. Many on the Allied side thought that Emperor Hirohito (1901–1989; now known as Emperor Showa) should have been charged as a "Class A" war criminal. However, MacArthur feared that if the emperor were tried or removed from the throne Japan would fall into turmoil. Japanese suspects who had been imprisoned 1945–1948 without ever being indicted were released by Occupation authorities after the Tokyo Trial. More than two hundred thousand Japanese (half of whom belonged to the military) were barred from holding public office by Occupation authorities because of their involvement in Japan's military aggression. However, after the Occupation ended in 1952, the Japanese government in need of experienced public leaders reinstated those who had been purged. See also HIROHITO, EMPEROR; MACARTHUR, DOUGLAS; OCCUPATION OF JAPAN; SUPREME COMMANDER FOR THE ALLIED POWERS; SURRENDER OF JAPAN; TOJO HIDEKI; WORLD WAR II.

WARD *(ku)* An administrative division within Tokyo, Kyoto, Osaka and other large Japanese cities. A ward is further divided into precincts *(machi* or *cho)*. The capital city of Tokyo is divided into 23 wards, which are different in most cases from the 17 named regions of the city. Each ward *(ku)* has an administrative office *(yakusho)*, known as a *kuyakusho*, that handles official matters for citizens of that ward. The ward office also keeps official household registers *(koseki)* and issues certificates of alien registration to non-citizens living in the ward. An address within a large city always includes the name of the ward, for example, Chiyoda-ku (Chiyoda Ward in the center of Tokyo). See also HOUSEHOLD REGISTER; KYOTO; OSAKA; TOKYO.

WARRING STATES ERA See SENGOKU ERA.

WARRIORS See ARCHERY; ARMOR; BAKUFU; BUSHIDO; CASTLES; DAIMYO; FEUDALISM; HACHIMAN; HEIKE, THE TALE OF THE; HORSE-RIDER THEORY; KUSUNOKI MASASHIGE; MARTIAL ARTS; SAMURAI; SHOGUN; SWORD.

WASABI ("mountain hollyhock") Japanese horseradish; a plant whose root is grated to use as a condiment in dipping sauces for sushi and sashimi (raw fish). The *wasabi* plant grows in marshes at the edges of cold, clear mountain streams. *Wasabi* can be made using the fresh root, or using processed *wasabi* powder sold in cans that can be mixed with water to make a firm paste. When prepared for use, *wasabi* paste has a bright green color. The taste of *wasabi,* like horseradish, is so sharp that only a small amount is needed. The Japanese nickname for *wasabi* is *nami-da* ("tears") because of its strong effect. It is mixed with soy sauce to make a dipping sauce. For sushi, *wasabi* is also rubbed on small portions of vinegared rice, which are then topped with raw fish, vegetables or other foods. See SASHIMI; SOY SAUCE; SUSHI.

WASHI See MULBERRY BUSH; ORIGAMI; PAPER, HANDMADE; WRAPPING.

WASHINGTON CONFERENCE AND WASHINGTON NAVAL TREATY OF 1922 A meeting of representatives from Japan, France, Great Britain, Italy, and the United States, held in Washington, D.C. from November 1921 to February 1922. The conference was called to limit naval expansion in the Pacific region and resolve political problems in East Asia. Participants from the five nations signed the Washington Naval Treaty on February 6, 1922, which limited the size of war ships, their weapons and deployment. This treaty, which remained in effect for 15 years, replaced the Anglo-Alliance of 1902. The conference was deemed necessary because world leaders were concerned about the weakening of European strength in East Asia after World War I, and about the policies of both Japan and the United States to increase their naval fleets. Japanese Prime Minister Hara Takashi accepted U.S. President Warren G. Harding's invitation to attend the conference because he thought it would help reduce the cost of Japanese defense, improve relations with the United States and ensure his political alliance with the Japanese navy. Ambassador Shidehara Kijuro, Navy Minister Admiral Kato Tomosaburo, and Prince Tokugawa Iesato, Japan's delegates to the conference, agreed to a ratio of three Japanese capital ships (battleships) for every five American and every five British ships. In return, America and Great Britain were not to build naval bases beyond Hawaii and Singapore, which would ensure Japanese naval dominance in East Asia. These naval agreements were revised at the London Naval Conference of 1930. At the Washington Conference, Japan also agreed to return to China Shandong (Shantung) Province, which it had seized from Germany at the end of World War I. Nine nations at the conference signed a treaty intended to ensure China's political and territorial rights and to give all these powers an equal opportunity to conduct business in China. Member nations of the League of Nations criticized Japanese military activity in China during the 1930s as a violation of this treaty, and Japan withdrew from the League in 1933. See also ANGLO-JAPANESE ALLIANCE; IMPERIAL JAPANESE ARMY AND NAVY; LONDON NAVAL CONFERENCES; SHIDEHARA KIJURO; WORLD WAR I.

WATER See ATAMI; BATH; BEPPU; BIWA, LAKE; BRIDGES; FERRIES; FISH AND FISHING INDUSTRY; FUJI-HAKONE-IZU NATIONAL PARK; GEOGRAPHY OF JAPAN; HOT SPRING; INLAND SEA; KAMO RIVER; KEGON

WATERFALL; KETTLE; NARUTO STRAIT; PACIFIC OCEAN; PURIFICATION; RAIN; SEA OF JAPAN; SEAFOOD; SHIMONOSEKI; SHIPPING AND SHIP-BUILDING; SUMIDA RIVER; TEA CEREMONY; WAVES.

"WATER TRADE" (*mizu shobai*) A popular term for the nighttime world of bars, adult entertainment and sex in Japanese cities. Establishments catering to male pleasures are concentrated in certain districts, such as Akasaka and the Ginza in Tokyo. Japanese men generally do not entertain at home or go out with their wives but frequently go out together in groups after work to drink and socialize. *Karaoke* ("empty orchestra") bars, where people sing the words to recorded songs, are very popular. Thousands of women work in the "water trade" as hostesses who spend time with male customers in bars and nightclubs. Some hostesses also engage in prostitution, even though it was outlawed in Japan in 1957. Bar hostesses generally work shorter hours and make more money than women who work in offices; they are paid according to how many drinks they can persuade their clients to buy. Business executives have large tax-exempt expense accounts to entertain clients in expensive nightclubs. Wealthy businessmen and politicians often hold private parties for which they hire geisha, women entertainers trained in traditional arts such as singing and dancing. At the other end of the spectrum, the "water trade" includes cheaper bars for ordinary workers and students, and establishments such as striptease shows and massage parlors, now euphemistically called "soaplands." There are also thousands of "love hotels" where couples can rent rooms by the hour for sexual purposes.

The modern nighttime world of entertainment for males is a continuation of the "floating world" (*ukiyo*) of the Edo Era (1600–1868), districts licensed as pleasure quarters by the Tokugawa Shogunate (1603–1867). The best-known is the Yoshiwara in Edo (modern Tokyo). Men of the samurai and merchant classes frequented the teahouses, brothels, Kabuki and Bunraku (puppet) theaters, and public bathhouses, where a popular urban culture developed. The term *water trade* has been introduced into English by a best-selling novel by John D. Morley, *Pictures from the Water Trade: Adventures of a Westerner in Japan* (1985). See also AKASAKA; ALCOHOLIC BEVERAGES; BATH; COURTESAN; EXPENSE ACCOUNT; GEISHA; GINZA; KARAOKE; LOVE HOTEL; PROSTITUTION; SALARYMAN; YOSHIWARA.

WAVES (*nami*) Since Japan is an island nation and water plays a central role in Japanese culture, waves have been a popular design motif since ancient times. A common design motif from the Heian Era (794–1185) is wooden cartwheels being soaked in a stream to prevent their drying out. The lines of the waves and the upper halves of curved wheels above the waves make an elegant pattern, which was frequently used to decorate handmade paper (*washi*) used for writing poetry, for copying religious scriptures (*sutras*) and for making fans. It has also been used to decorate textiles for kimono, especially those for summer wear. Waves also appear on pottery, such as tea bowls (*chawan*), and on lacquer ware such as writing boxes. The

technique of *maki-e*, decorating lacquer with inlaid gold, creates particularly beautiful wave designs on black lacquered objects. A well-known woodblock print by Hokusai (1760–1849) of a great wave dwarfing Mount Fuji, from the series *Thirty-Six Views of Mount Fuji* (*Fugaku sanjurokkei*), has become a famous symbol of Japan.

Japan has been hit by many tidal waves (*tsunami*) caused by underwater earthquakes, especially on its eastern (Pacific Ocean) coast. In A.D. 1494 an enormous tidal wave swept over Kamakura, south of Tokyo, destroying every building, including Kotokuin Temple, which housed a 13th-century bronze Daibutsu (giant statue of the Buddha) more than 37 feet tall. The Daibutsu still sits in the open on the temple grounds and is a popular tourist attraction. See also CLIMATE OF JAPAN; DAIBUTSU; EARTHQUAKES; GEOGRAPHY OF JAPAN; HOKUSAI; ISLANDS; KAMAKURA; KIMONO; LACQUER WARE; TEXTILES.

WEATHER See CLIMATE OF JAPAN; RAIN; SNOW; TYPHOONS.

WEAVING See BROCADE; HEMP; KASURI; NISHIJIN; SILK; TEXTILES.

WEDDED ROCKS OF FUTAMIGAURA See FUTAMI-GAURA; ROCKS.

WEDDINGS Although the Japanese hold elaborate wedding ceremonies, a marriage is legalized only when the couple opens a new household register (*koseki*) at the local administrative office where they live. Couples have traditionally been brought together by a go-between (*nakodo*), usually a relative or family friend. In earlier times photographs were exchanged (*miai shashin*) and then a meeting between the couple, known as a *miai*, was arranged. Today, Japanese young people who fall in love on their own ("love matches"), about half of all married couples, still have a go-between for formality's sake. An engagement is celebrated with a toast of sake and the exchange of presents, a ritual known as *yuino*. Objects symbolizing happiness and good fortune are exchanged between the two families, such as money, kelp, dried bonito, a fan, abalone, linen thread and dried cuttlefish. The bride's family gives gifts that equal half the value of those given by the groom's family.

Japanese weddings have traditionally been family banquets held at the home of the groom, or of the bride if the groom is adopted into her family (known as *mukoirikon* marriage). In the 20th century, Japanese began holding Shinto, Buddhist or Christian wedding ceremonies. At a Shinto wedding, the most common type, the bride and groom sit before the altar of a shrine with their parents and the go-between and his or her spouse. After being purified by a priest, the bride and groom seal the wedding before the *kami* (sacred spirits) by each drinking from three cups of sake three times, a practice known as *san-san-kudo* ("three-three-nine"). The groom wears a *montsuki*, consisting of a formal kimono and formal *haori* (jacket) with five crests (*mon*), and *hakama* (a formal divided skirt). The bride wears a white kimono and *uchikake* (long decorated overgarment). White, the color of purity, symbolizes the death of her ties to her own family, and her readiness to be "dyed in the colors or customs" (kafu no somaru) of the groom's family. She also wears a special hat known as a "horn cover" (tsuno-kakushi) to cover her "horns of jealousy." Many couples now hold both the wedding ceremony and reception at a large hotel, restaurant or wedding hall. Male guests wear formal black suits and women wear dresses or formal kimono. Guests bring gifts of money wrapped in special white envelopes called shugibukuro, which are decorated with a fancy knot of red and white or silver and white paper strings, and with noshi, a folded paper symbolizing a dried strip of abalone. The characters for kotobuki, "congratulations," are also written on the envelope.

Auspicious symbols are displayed at the wedding, such as butterflies and pictures of pine, bamboo and plum tree branches. The go-between makes a speech, the main guests also make speeches and a sake toast is offered to the couple. While the guests eat and drink, the master of ceremonies (shikaisha) asks various friends of the bride or groom to make speeches or sing songs. The newlywed couple sits at the main table between the husband and wife go-betweens. The seating order of the guests depends on their age, social status and relationship with the bride and groom, with more important seats closer to the main table. Parents of the couple sit at the back of the reception hall. During the reception the couple changes clothes several times, a practice called ironaoshi. The bride usually changes from the uchikake to a furisode (colorful long-sleeved kimono) to a Western-style wedding gown, and the groom from montsuki to morning coat. These outfits are very expensive even though rented. Cutting the wedding cake is very important, and many couples create other rituals and special effects for their receptions. After the reception, the guests say goodbye to the couple at the door, and each guest is given a present, called hikidemono. The newlyweds take a brief honeymoon; Hawaii is a popular destination today. Some couples even marry there to avoid the great expense of a wedding in Japan. See also ABALONE; FAMILY; GIFTS; GO-BETWEEN; HAKAMA; HAORI; HOUSEHOLD REGISTER; KIMONO; SAKE; SHINTO; WHITE.

WHALING (hogei) Whales (kujira) have been an important source of animal protein for the Japanese since ancient times. Oil from baleen and sperm whales has also been an important product in Japan for making such products as lubricants and cosmetics. In the 17th century, whaling became an organized industry but was confined to coastal waters because of Japan's seclusion policy under the Tokugawa Shogunate (1603–1867). Western whaling ships appeared in Japanese waters in the 19th century and caused a decline in right whales, the main Japanese catch. In the 20th century, Japanese whalers began using modern whaling methods, including deep-sea factory ships that process whales as soon as they are caught. As catches declined, whalers moved into waters as distant as Antarctica. In 1976, the three largest whaling companies merged to become the Japan Joint Whaling Company, Ltd.

Japan is one of the few nations in the world that still permits the hunting of whales, which are endangered animals, and the nation has been the target of intense criticism for its policies. As a member of the International Whaling Commission, Japan pledged that its fleets would obey the agreed-upon international quotas for whale catches. Pressure on Japan led its whaling industry to reduce its operations to one factory ship and four large-scale whaling stations by 1977. However, in 1981 Japan was widely criticized for refusing to agree to a moratorium on sperm whaling. In 1984 Japan signed an agreement with the United States to stop commercial whaling if the United States allowed Japan to keep its fishing quota in territorial waters of the United States. Japan agreed in principle to abide by an international moratorium on commercial whaling that began in 1989, although Japanese officials sought an exemption by the International Whaling Commission from the ban for small whalers who operate along Japan's coasts.

Whale meat is sold in Japan in frozen, refrigerated and salted form. It is eaten both raw and cooked, and is also canned and processed into sausages. A popular whale dish is sarashikujira, tail flukes cut into thin slices and scalded with hot water. Whale organs and salted hide of baleen whale are also eaten. Every part of a whale is used to make some product, including gelatin, fertilizers, animal feed, cosmetics, lubricants and pharmaceuticals. Japan has long imported whale meat but cannot import enough today to meet its demands. See also FISH AND FISHING INDUSTRY; SEAFOOD.

WHISKEY See ALCOHOLIC BEVERAGES.

WHITE (shiro) An auspicious color in Japan. The color represents purity in Shinto, the native Japanese religion, because it is the color of the kami (sacred spirits). Shinto priests wear white kimono, over which are worn hakama (formal divided skirts) and formal outer robes, both in white or other colors. Young girl attendants (miko) who dance at Shinto shrines also wear white kimono, over which are worn red hakama. Within Shinto shrines, priests and miko wear white tabi on the feet for all ceremonial occasions. Tabi are special white socks with a division between the big toe and other toes, so they can be worn with thong sandals. All Japanese people wear white tabi whenever they dress in kimono. White handmade paper (washi) plays an important role in Shinto ceremonies. Sacred spaces where kami are believed to dwell are marked off with shimenawa (straw ropes) hung with white paper cut and folded into zig-zags. A gohei, a wand hung with strips of zig-zag paper, usually white, stands in front of the doors to the shrine's inner chamber, where the kami dwell. A haraigushi, a wand hung with long white paper streamers, is waved by a priest when performing an act of purification. A newborn baby is regarded as a kami and is clothed in white until 17 days old, when it is then considered a human being. A bride wears a white kimono during a Shinto wedding ceremony to symbolize that first she is a bride of the kami. After the ceremony, she changes into a brightly colored kimono as a bride of a human being.

When a person dies, the body is wrapped in white as preparation for his or her return to the *kami*. White rice-flour face and body powder, known as the "honorable white" (*oshiroi*), was used in Japan for more than a thousand years, and is still worn by geisha and actors in the traditional theater known as Kabuki; white skin is considered beautiful in Japan. Japanese traditionally wrap gifts of money and other objects in white paper. *Origami*, the art of folding paper, has a white crane as one of its most important shapes. White rice, the basic food of the Japanese diet, is considered sacred. In a traditional Japanese meal, white rice is served and eaten in its own bowl. See also FOOTWEAR; GEISHA; GIFTS; HAKAMA; KIMONO; MAKEUP; KABUKI; ORIGAMI; PAPER; PURIFICATION; RICE; SHINTO; SHRINES, SHINTO; TATAMI.

WHITE-COLLAR WORKERS See EMPLOYMENT; OFFICE LADY; SALARYMAN.

WHOLESALE BUSINESS See DISTRIBUTION SYSTEM.

WINE See ALCOHOLIC BEVERAGES; SAKE.

WINTER See CLIMATE OF JAPAN; HOKKAIDO ISLAND; JAPAN ALPS; NEW YEAR FESTIVAL; PLUM TREE; SAPPORO; SNOW; SNOW COUNTRY; SNOW FESTIVAL; THREE FRIENDS OF WINTER.

WINTER OLYMPICS, SAPPORO, 1972 See OLYMPIC GAMES; SAPPORO.

WISTERIA (*fuji*) A climbing shrub whose fragrant purple flowers, hanging in long clusters, bloom in the spring. The wisteria, also known as *nodafuji*, is a climbing shrub that grows by coiling around trees or other objects, such as a fence, in a clockwise direction. Its long, sturdy stem sends forth many branches. Wisteria grow wild in mountainous regions of Japan, and many varieties are also widely cultivated in gardens. The flower clusters of the *kushakufuji* variety grow as long as 80 inches. The *akebonofuji* has red flowers, the *shirobanafuji* has white flowers and the *yaefuji* has double flowers. A related species known as the *yamafuji* grows wild in the mountains of southwest Japan; coiling in a counterclockwise direction, it has larger flowers in shorter clusters. A popular variety of this species is the *shirafuji*, which has white flowers. One of the most famous Japanese classical dances is The Wisteria Maiden (Fuji Musume), in which the spirit of the wisteria appears as a young woman. The dancer wears a large hat and colorful long-sleeved kimono decorated with a wisteria motif, and carries a branch of purple wisteria blossoms over her shoulder. The Fujiwara clan, influential in the imperial court up to the modern era and originally called Nakatomi, changed its name when Naka no Oe (614–669) was awarded the name Fujiwara ("Wisteria Field") after he plotted the downfall of the rival Soga clan in a wisteria garden. See also FLOWERS; FUJIWARA CLAN; GARDENS.

WOLF See DOG.

WOMEN IN JAPAN See BLUESTOCKING SOCIETY; CLOTHING; COSMETICS; COURTESAN; DEPENDENCY; DIARIES; DOI TAKAKO; EMPLOYMENT; FAMILY; FASHION DESIGNERS, CONTEMPORARY; FEMINIST MOVEMENTS; GEISHA; HOSOKAWA GRACIA; ICHIKAWA FUSAE; IZUMI SHIKIBU; JINGU, EMPRESS; JITO, EMPRESS; KYO MACHIKO; LANGUAGE, JAPANESE; MONASTICISM, BUDDHIST; MORI HANAE; MOTHER; MURASAKI SHIKIBU; OFFICE LADY; OKUNI; PRIESTS AND PRIESTESSES, SHINTO; SARASHINA DIARY; SEI SHONAGON; SHAMANS AND SHAMANISM; SUIKO, EMPRESS; TANAKA KINUYO; TAKARAZUKA OPERA COMPANY; TOOTH BLACKENING; WATER TRADE; WEDDINGS; WOMEN'S ASSOCIATIONS; WRITING SYSTEM, JAPANESE.

WOMEN'S ASSOCIATIONS (*fujinkai*) Consumer's groups and other organizations through which women members, primarily housewives, are able to exert some political and economic influence. Women's associations are concerned with specific issues that affect the quality of life, such as health and social services, cost and safety of consumer goods, and environmental pollution, as well as political corruption. The largest associations are Shufuren (Housewives' Association, with about one million members), Chifuren (National Federation of Regional Women's Associations, with about six million members) and Seikyoren (National Association of Consumer Cooperatives). After the Basic Law for Consumer Protection was passed in 1968, the national women's associations organized successful boycotts against companies selling canned foods containing carcinogenic cyclamates and against companies selling color television sets at artificially high prices. In the 1970s, Chifuren organized a national boycott of Shiseido Co., Ltd., Japan's largest cosmetic maker, because of the exhorbitant cost of its products. Chifuren also produced its own inexpensive cosmetics, popularly known as "100 yen" cosmetics, which sold well for a few years and temporarily decreased Shiseido's sales. Women's associations were active in opposing the unpopular 3% national consumption tax in 1989, a factor in the stunning defeat for the dominant Liberal Democratic Party in national elections that year following the Recruit Scandal. See also ENVIRONMENTAL ISSUES; FAMILY; NEIGHBORHOOD ASSOCIATIONS; RECRUIT SCANDAL; SHISEIDO CO., LTD.

WOMEN'S SUFFRAGE See BLUESTOCKING SOCIETY; CONSTITUTION OF 1947; ICHIKAWA FUSAE; OCCUPATION OF JAPAN.

WOODBLOCK PRINTS (*hanga*) Pictures made by printing colors on handmade paper with blocks of wood carved with pictures or writing. Woodblock prints are known as *ukiyo-e*, "pictures of the floating world," because they most often portrayed the so-called "floating world" (*ukiyo*) of the government-licensed pleasure quarters in Japan during the Edo Era (1600–1868), such as the Yoshiwara. Most woodblock prints depict famous Kabuki actors, courtesans and the daily activities of their maids, geisha, famous landscapes, or erotic pictures, known as *shunga*. The term *ukiyo-e* also includes paintings, greeting cards and book illustrations of similar themes.

Woodblock prints became very popular because they were colorful and inexpensive, since many copies can be printed from one block of wood *(hanga)*. Each print requires from three to 15 blocks, a master block with black outlines of the picture and one block for each color. After an artist draws the picture to be printed, a woodblock carver uses various tools to carve the outlines of the picture on thin slabs of wild cherry or other hardwood. Finally, a printer applies water-based pigments to the blocks by hand and rubs them onto paper with a *baren,* a small disc made of bamboo skin fibers and covered with bamboo skin. Each block has to be applied in exactly the same place so that the colors are printed in the proper place. Paper *(washi)* used for woodblock prints is made by hand from the bark of mulberry *(kozo)* and other shrubs and trees. It is very durable, resists water, and does not tear while many different colors are rubbed on the prints. Multicolored woodblock prints are usually reproduced between 20 and 30 times, and occasionally nearly 100 times.

Techniques for printing from wooden blocks were introduced into Japan from China in ancient times, and were first used in Japan to mass-produce Buddhist charms and religious scriptures *(sutras).* During the Edo Era, Japanese artists became masters in the use of combining and applying colors, and in creating pictures with great details. *Ukiyo-e* were brought to Europe and the United States by traders and ship captains, and as wrappings for export porcelains. They became quite popular in 19th-century France and inspired many artists, such as Toulouse-Lautrec and Vincent van Gogh. *Ukiyo-e* from the Edo Era have become expensive collectors' items around the world. Some of the most famous Japanese *ukiyo-e* artists are Moronobu (?–1694), Harunobu (1725–1770), Utamaro Kitagawa (1753–1806), Hokusai (1760–1849) and Hiroshige (1797–1858). Japanese artists have continued to produce woodblock prints of landscapes and other subjects. One well-known modern printmaker is Munakata Shiko (1909–1975). See also COURTESAN; EDO ERA; FLOATING WORLD; GEISHA; KABUKI; PAPER, HANDMADE; SHUNGA; YOSHIWARA; NAMES OF INDIVIDUAL ARTISTS.

WOODWORKING Woodenware *(mokkohin)* and bamboo ware have been produced widely in Japan since ancient times. Japanese homes have relatively little furniture, except for chests of drawers and low tables, so woodworkers frequently concentrated on objects that are decorative as well as functional, such as bowls, boxes and trays. Early on, woodworking became intimately associated with decorative lacquer ware.

Engraved wooden food containers were used in prehistoric times in Japan. Advanced woodworking techniques were brought to Japan from the Asian mainland with the Buddhist religion, which was introduced in the sixth century A.D. Early examples of fine Buddhist woodworking include Tamamushi Shrine in the Horyuji in Nara, Lady Tachibana's shrine in Horyuji and a cabinet of red-lacquered zelkova wood in the Shosoin, an eighth-century imperial storehouse. The Tamamushi Shrine is decorated with lacquer, metal fittings and paintings. In the eighth century A.D. the government set up a woodworker's bureau. The Nara Era (710–794) was a high point in Japanese woodworking, but lacquer ware took precedence in the

Heian Era (794–1185), and woodworkers mainly supplied materials and core forms for lacquer makers to decorate. The tea ceremony, which flourished in the 16th century, stimulated the art of woodworking, because it required objects of subtle, natural beauty. A large demand for wooden ware was created by the rise of the urban merchant class in Edo Era (1600–1868). Not only household objects but ornamental hair combs, netsuke and other decorative items were also made of wood. Most Japanese farm tools have traditionally been made of wood, and members of farm households often carved their own objects. Woodworkers known as *kijiya, kijishi, kijihiki* or *rokuroshi,* traditionally traveled Japan in highly organized nomadic communities. Some settled in artisan areas of castle and temple towns, where they joined guilds and developed woodworking and lacquer ware techniques. The guild system lasted until the Meiji Era (1868–1912). The modern *mingei* (folk art) movement begun by Yanagi Soetsu (1889–1961) also valued the beauty of natural wood objects and encouraged wood craftsmen. Two woodworking artists have been designated by the Japanese government as Living National Treasures, Himi Kodo and Kuroda Tatsuaki. George Nakashima is a famous Japanese-American woodworker who specializes in furniture.

There are a variety of Japanese woodworking techniques. *Sashi-mono,* or joinery, is the method of constructing furniture and other household objects by combining boards, or boards and square bars of wood, usually cypress *(hinoki),* without iron nails. The pieces of wood are tightly joined so the object has a beautiful form and will not warp over long periods. This technique is also known as *ita-mono,* or "board work." *Hiki-mono* (lathe work) is the turning of wood on a lathe to form bowls, trays etc. Hardwoods such as horse chestnut *(tochi-no-ki)* and zelkova *(keyaki)* are commonly used. Other commonly used woods in Japan have included cypress, paulownia *(kiri),* zelkova *(keyaki),* cherry *(sakura),* cedar *(sugi),* boxwood *(tsuge),* oak *(nara),* persimmon *(kaki),* maple *(kaede),* camphor, red sandalwood *(shitan)* and camellia *(tsubaki).* Bamboo *(take)* is used for numerous objects, including flower vases, water ladles and baskets made from bamboo strips. *Kuri-mono* (scooping) is a method of hollowing out a piece of wood with an adze or other tools, then finishing it with a small plane; this technique is used for making containers. *Mage-mono* (bent work) is the bending of a thin strip of cypress or cedar *(sugi)* into a circle and sewing the overlapped ends with cherry-bark strips; it is used mainly to form covered containers, such as rice tubs, which are strong and durable. *Hon-mono* (carving) is used for making Buddhist statues, masks for *bugaku* (ancient ritual dance) and Noh drama, and for containers. *Mokuga* (marquetry, or "wood picture") is a method of inlaying small pieces of wood with other beautiful materials, such as ivory and deer horn, into wooden objects such as boxes to make designs of birds, flowers, geometric patterns and similar motifs. Other inlay techniques are used for lacquer ware. *Saie* (color painting) is the decorating of wooden objects with pigments mixed with *gofun,* a white paint made of calcium carbonate obtained from burning clam shells. See also BAMBOO; BASKETS; BOXES; CHEST; COMBS

AND HAIR ORNAMENTS; CYPRESS; FURNITURE, TRADITIONAL; LACQUER WARE; MASKS; MINGEI; NAKASHIMA, GEORGE; NETSUKE; PAULOWNIA; SCULPTURE; SHOSOIN; SHRINES, SHINTO; TEA CEREMONY; TEMPLES, BUDDHIST; TRAYS; TREES; YANAGI SOETSU.

WORKERS See CORPORATIONS; EMPLOYMENT; INCOME; LABOR UNIONS; LIFETIME EMPLOYMENT SYSTEM; OFFICE LADY; RETIREMENT; SALARYMAN; SENIORITY SYSTEM.

WORLD WAR I Japan became involved in World War I as an ally of Britain through the Anglo-Japanese Alliance of 1902. On August 1, 1914, Germany, which was allied with Austria and Italy, declared war on Russia, an ally of Great Britain and France. Germany declared war on France on August 3rd, and Britain declared war on Germany the following day. Britain, Germany and France all had political and economic interests in Asia. Germany held a concession in China in Qingdao (Tsingtao) on the Shandong (Shantung) Peninsula, as well as bases in the north Pacific Ocean in the Caroline, Mariana and Marshall islands. Britain had a concession at Weihaiwei in China and a military base and trading center at Hong Kong. On August 7th, Britain asked for Japanese naval assistance in destroying armed German merchant ships in China. The Anglo-Japanese Alliance did not require Japan to enter the war, but Japanese Foreign Minister Kato Takaaki (1860–1926) saw the conflict as an opportunity to gain territory at Germany's expense. Despite Britain's opposition, on August 8th Japan declared war on Germany. In three months Japan seized the German concession in Shandong and islands in the North Pacific where Germany had bases. Japan did not send its troops to the Western front, as Britain and France repeatedly requested, although it did send naval destroyers to escort merchant convoys in the Indian Ocean and Mediterranean Sea. In 1915 Japan issued the so-called Twenty-one Demands on China to force China to give Japan numerous trading rights, land and other privileges. After Russia had made peace with Germany in 1917, the Allies sent an expedition into Siberia to assist prisoners of war and an army of Czechoslovakian soldiers held in camps there. Japan sent five army divisions into Siberia, totalling 70,000 soldiers, who remained in Siberia until 1922.

At the Paris Peace Conference in 1919, which drew up the Treaty of Versailles concluding World War I, Japan had an equal place with Great Britain, France, Italy and the United States, thus becoming the first Asian nation to achieve political power equal to that of the great Western powers. Under the treaty, Japan was permitted to keep the territory in China and the Pacific that it had taken from Germany. Japan thus enlarged its empire, which already included sections of China and southern Manchuria, southern Sakhalin Island, Korea and Taiwan. Japan was also given a major place in the newly formed League of Nations. World War I boosted the Japanese economy because Japanese manufacturers sold a great deal of military equipment to its allies and, more important, Japan took over the markets in Asia that the European countries were forced to neglect during the war. See also ANGLO-JAPANESE ALLIANCE; LEAGUE OF NATIONS AND JAPAN; TWENTY-ONE DEMANDS ON CHINA.

WORLD WAR II Japan became increasingly militaristic during the 1920s and 1930s, as leaders of the Imperial Japanese Army and Navy exerted increasing control over the government and economy. Military leaders pursued a policy of expansion on the Asian continent, in order to secure supplies of raw materials such as oil and rubber. Korea and Taiwan had been colonies of Japan for several decades. Japan won former German concessions in Manchuria from China after World War I. After the so-called "Manchurian Incident" of 1931, Japan established a puppet state in Manchuria, known as Manchukuo, and began expanding into China. Full-scale war developed, termed by the Japanese the Sino-Japanese War of 1937–1945. Under Prime Minister Konoe Fumimaro, Japan signed the Anti-Comintern Pact with Nazi Germany in 1936, and with Fascist Italy in 1937. The three nations confirmed their military alliance by signing the Tripartite Pact in 1940. Because of the war raging in Europe at this time, the United States, an ally of Great Britain and a strong critic of Japanese aggression in China, was the only naval power in the Pacific that could prevent Japan from pursuing its expansionist policy. In 1940 the United States banned sales of fuel, iron and steel to Japan, and in 1941 it banned all exports to Japan and froze its assets in the United States, in response to Japanese aggression. Prime Minister Konoe, who had conceived of the Greater East Asia Coprosperity Sphere, a Japanese empire that would be self-sufficient in natural resources and not dependent on imports of oil from the United States, was forced to resign and was succeeded by General Tojo Hideki. As Japan planned its final move on Asia, it decided to attack the American fleet at Pearl Harbor, Hawaii, on December 7, 1941, to neutralize American naval power in the region. Immediately after Pearl Harbor, Japan also attacked the Philippine Islands, Guam, Wake, Midway and Hong Kong islands, and sank two British warships.

In response to the surprise attack, the United States declared war on all the Axis Powers and swung into full-scale wartime production. U.S. General Douglas MacArthur, based in the Philippines, became Supreme Commander for the Allied Powers in the Pacific. Japan quickly took control of French Indochina; the Philippines, a U.S. territory; the Dutch East Indies (now Indonesia); the British colonies of Malaya (now Malaysia and Singapore) and Burma; and several islands in the Pacific. Tojo's government suppressed all opposition, abrogated civil rights in Japan and treated people in occupied territories brutally.

The Battle of Midway, June 3–6, 1942 in which American bombers sank four Japanese aircraft carriers and put the Imperial Navy on the defensive, was the turning point in the war against Japan. The Allied victory at Guadalcanal in the Solomon Islands by February 7, 1943, began a general advance toward Japan. The Allied strategy was to "island hop" to take strategic bases from which air strikes could be staged. On April 18, 1943, the Allies shot down the plane of Admiral Yamamoto Isoroku, killing the Japanese fleet commander. As the Allied net tightened, most of Japan's merchant ships were sunk, cutting off military supplies and crucial raw materials. Japanese suicide air units known as *kamikaze* were formed in 1944, and although hundreds of *kamikaze* crash-dived into American ships, few caused serious damage. Japanese troops fought bitterly to hold on to the islands they had invaded and casualties were high on both sides. The Allied capture of Saipan on July 9, 1944 after the greatest naval air battle of the war, in which all but 35 of the 430 Japanese planes were destroyed, provided bases from which American bombers could attack the main Japanese islands. Tojo resigned as prime minister on July 18, 1944, and was replaced by General Koiso Kuniaki.

The U.S. invasion of Leyte Gulf in the Philippines on October 20, 1944, began the final phase of the war. MacArthur's forces invaded Luzon, the Philippines, on January 9, 1945. U.S. Marines landed on Iwo Jima on February 19, 1945, and took the island.

The Japanese people suffered terribly during the war from deprivation and bombing raids. Food, clothing, oil and other materials were in short supply, and many people died from tuberculosis and other diseases. American bombing raids destroyed Japanese cities (although Kyoto was spared for its cultural and historic importance) and damaged railroads and factories. The violent climax of the war was the Battle of Okinawa, April 1–July 2, 1945, when the United States invaded the largest island of the southern Ryukyu Islands of Japan. Almost the entire Japanese military force on Okinawa of 110,000 died, as did 150,000 Japanese civilians. More than 50,000 Americans were killed or wounded. Prime Minister Koiso was replaced by Admiral Suzuki Kantaro on April 5, 1945.

In July, 1945 the Allied Powers issued the Potsdam Declaration to the Japanese, demanding that they surrender unconditionally or face "prompt and utter destruction." Although some Japanese leaders advocated peace, Japan did not surrender, and the Allies feared they would have to invade the main Japanese islands, with casualties on an enormous scale. Faced with Japanese intransigence, new American President Harry Truman decided to drop an atomic bomb on Hiroshima on August 6, 1945, which destroyed most of the city and killed about 80,000 people. On August 9, the United States dropped a second atomic bomb on Nagasaki, the same day the Soviet Union had declared war on Japan. Japan accepted the terms of the Potsdam Declaration on August 14, 1945, and Emperor Hirohito's statement of surrender was broadcast to the Japanese people on August 15, 1945, beginning the occupation by the Allied Powers under General MacArthur, which would last until 1952.

The Japanese refer to the Pacific Theater of World War II as the Greater East Asia War. Thirty percent of the Japanese people were made homeless by the war, 2.3 million Japanese soldiers were killed between 1937 and 1945, and there were 800,000 civilian casualties. The economy was shattered, and cities, industries and transportation were destroyed. See also ATOMIC BOMB; GREATER EAST ASIA COPROSPERITY SPHERE; HIROHITO, EMPEROR; HIROSHIMA; IMPERIAL JAPANESE ARMY AND NAVY; IWO JIMA; KAMIKAZE; KONOE FUMIMARO; MACARTHUR, DOUGLAS; MANCHURIAN INCIDENT; NAGASAKI; OCCUPATION OF JAPAN; OKINAWA, BATTLE OF; PEARL HARBOR, JAPANESE ATTACK ON; SINO-JAPANESE WAR OF 1937–1945; SUPREME COMMANDER FOR ALLIED POWERS (SCAP); SURRENDER OF JAPAN; SUZUKI KANTARO; TOJO HIDEKI; TRIPARTITE PACT; WAR CRIMES TRIALS; WORLD WAR I; YAMAMOTO ISOROKU.

WRAPPING *(origata; tsutsumi)* A general term that includes both the wrapping of gifts and the covering or containment of objects for aesthetic or religious purposes. *Origata* is the traditional way of wrapping gifts, which follows strictly prescribed rules governing style and materials. These depend on the gift, the person who receives it, the season of the year and the occasion on which it is given. There are two main gift-giving seasons in Japan: *chugen* (late June to early July) and *seibo* (end of the year). Certain traditional gifts, such as money, calligraphy brushes and ink stones, chopsticks, kimono and *obi* (sashes), combs, and incense, each have their own rules for wrapping. The Japanese have always felt that it is rude to hand someone an object that is not wrapped. Objects were traditionally wrapped in white handmade paper *(washi)* to symbolize their purity, because a crease made in *washi* cannot be undone and thus it symbolically seals the object against impurity. White is also the color of purity in Japan. Gifts wrapped in *washi* are bound with special cords, called *mizuhiki*, made of starched and twisted *washi*. *Mizuhiki* are colored red and white or gold and silver for festive occasions such as weddings, and black and white, silver and white, or yellow and white for funerals and other sad occasions. The *mizuhiki* are tied in specific decorative knots according to the occasion. *Mizuhiki* are also used to make three-dimensional ornaments that symbolize good fortune, such as cranes, pine trees and turtles. These play an important part in weddings. A *noshi*, a specially folded piece of paper with a strip of dried abalone inside, is also glued on wrapped gifts for happy occasions, or printed on the wrapping paper. Some gifts may be wrapped in decorative squares of silk called *furoshiki*, which are also commonly used to carry objects.

Tsutsumi, the general concept of wrapping, derives from the verb *tsutsushimu*, (to refrain, to be discreet or moderate). Restraint or discreet concealment is the essence of refined elegance in Japanese culture. Many types of things are concealed, covered or enclosed. For example, statues of deities are enclosed in small household altars *(butsudan)* or portable shrines *(mikoshi)*. Gardens are surrounded by various types of fences, and food is served in covered lacquer containers. Even the traditional way of dressing in *kimono* and *obi* wraps the body in many layers of cloth. Department stores and shops always wrap purchases, even foods such as sweets or crackers, in beautifully decorated paper. Functional ways of wrapping objects for carrying or storing them also have an aesthetic dimension in Japan, as illustrated in the English-language book *How to Wrap Five More Eggs: Traditional Japanese Packaging*, by Oka Hideyuki (1975). See also ABALONE; FUNERALS; FUROSHIKI; GIFTS; PAPER, HANDMADE; WEDDINGS; WHITE.

WRESTLING See SUMO.

WRIGHT, FRANK LLOYD See GINZA; IMPERIAL HOTEL.

WRITING SYSTEM, JAPANESE *(kaku)* The system for writing the Japanese language combines Chinese characters, or ideographs *(kanji)*, and two phonetic or syllabic systems *(kana)*, *hiraguna* and *katakana*. The Japanese language is widely acknowledged as the most complex and difficult to write in the world. Writing is traditionally done with a brush and black ink *(sumi)*, although it can be easily written with a pen or pencil. Chinese characters were adopted by the Japanese for writing their own language starting in the fifth century A.D. In China, each character, represents one sound. In Japan, however, one character may have several different pronunciations. Japanese syllabic systems were developed from Chinese characters (and were perhaps also influenced by Sanskrit, the classical language of India) to write Japanese words that could not be written with *kanji*, and to add particles of grammar and inflectional endings to *kanji*. For many centuries, *kanji* was considered proper or "real" writing, and was used by men to write official documents, classical poetry and so forth. However, the use of *kana* during the Heian Era (794–1185), especially by women, contributed to the rise of vernacular Japanese literature, such as diaries, novels and poetry. The first and most influential Japanese novel, *The Tale of Genji (Genji Monogatari)*, was written in *kana* by a court lady named Murasaki Shikibu (fl. c. A.D. 1000).

The Japanese language is written from top to bottom and from the right side of the page to the left. Japanese students must memorize 1,945 required *kanji*. Each character is made up of a certain number of strokes that must be written in proper sequence. Students must also learn to write the 48 syllables in each of the two *kana* systems. Writing as an art form is called calligraphy or *shodo*, the "Way of Writing." The Japanese have always treasured calligraphy as the highest form of art, closely related to the arts of poetry and ink painting *(sumi-e)*. The Japanese language can also be written phonetically using the Roman alphabet *(romaji)*. See also CALLIGRAPHY; DIARIES; GENJI, THE TALE OF; HIRAGANA; INK PAINTING; KANA; KANJI; KATAKANA; NOVELS; POETRY.

X

XAVIER, ST. FRANCIS (1506–1552) A Spanish member of the Jesuit order (Society of Jesus) of the Roman Catholic Church who became the first Christian missionary in Japan. Francis Xavier is the Anglicized version of the name Francisco de Javier. He was born in the Basque country of northern Spain and educated at the University of Paris, then joined Ignatius Loyola in founding the Society of Jesus before the pope sent him to Asia as a missionary in 1541. Xavier first went to India and Malacca, where in 1547 he met a Japanese man named Anjiro, who interested him in Japan. Xavier, two other Jesuits, and Anjiro arrived in Kagoshima on the southern tip of Kyushu Island on August 15, 1549. With Anjiro assisting as interpreter, Xavier composed a basic catechism in Japanese and began converting the Japanese to Christianity. In 1550 Xavier went to the towns of Hirado and Yamaguchi. He then traveled to the capital city of Kyoto to meet with Emperor Go-Nara and to request permission to preach throughout Japan. However, he did not succeed in meeting the emperor because at the time Kyoto was wracked by military conflict. Otomo, the *daimyo* (feudal lord) of Bungo, invited Xavier to his territory on Kyushu, where Xavier was able to convert more Japanese. Otomo himself was baptized and took the Christian name Francisco. In 1551 Xavier left Japan for India on Jesuit business. Realizing that a great deal of Japanese culture had been adapted from China, he also intended to travel to China and convert the Chinese people. Xavier died on a small island in the Pearl River Delta before he was able to carry out his mission in China. His work in Japan was continued by other Jesuits for nearly a century until the Tokugawa Shogunate (1603–1867) banned Christianity as a threat to its authority. The Catholic Church later canonized Xavier. He is commemorated in the city of Kagoshima in Southern Kyushu by St. Francis Xavier Park, which has a bust of him under an archway resembling a church door. See also CHRISTIANITY IN JAPAN; KAGOSHIMA; PORTUGUESE IN JAPAN.

Y

YABUSAME See ARCHERY.

YAEYAMA ISLAND GROUP See RYUKYU ISLANDS.

YAKITORI Literally, "grilled chicken," which is popular as a quick snack or for a complete meal. Small pieces of chicken or chicken parts, such as the heart and liver, are threaded onto small bamboo skewers and grilled over a charcoal fire. The chicken is grilled with salt (*shioyaki*) or basted prior to cooking with a thick sweet sauce made of soy sauce, sake, *mirin* (sweet rice wine for cooking) and sugar. Chicken meat is also ground and formed into small meat balls, which are cooked the same way. *Yakitori* restaurants (*yakitori-ya*) are often identified by red paper lanterns hanging outside. The restaurants are generally inexpensive and informal, and the bill is counted up by how many skewers of food have been served. Street food stalls also serve *yakitori*. See also CHICKEN AND ROOSTER; FOOD STALLS; LANTERNS; MIRIN; RESTAURANTS; SOY SAUCE.

YAKUZA "Good for nothing"; a gangster belonging to an organized crime ring. The name *yakuza* derives from a "three-card game" (*sammai karuta*) similar to blackjack that was popular during the Tokugawa Shogunate (1603–1867), when the *yakuza* originated. The object of this game was to draw three cards, which totalled 19 points or came closest to that score without going above it. An 8 (*ya*), 9 (*ku*) and 3 (*sa* or *za*) equalled 20 points, which was "good for nothing" (*yakuza*). The gangsters take pride in their name, which flaunts Japanese social conventions of hard work and obedience to law.

The *yakuza* have controlled gambling operations in Japan since the end of the 18th century, as well as other underworld activities, including extortion, loan sharking, blackmail and prostitution. Gang members follow a strict code of honor among themselves based on the "parent-child" type of family relationship (*oyabun-kobun* or *oyakata-kokata*) that has determined many aspects of Japanese society since ancient times. The *oyabun* (parent or leader) guides and provides for the *kobun* (child or follower), who in turn is loyal and does what the *oyabun* requires. *Yamaguchi-Gumi* is the largest of the seven major groups into which *yakuza* gangs are organized. *Yakuza* have been feared in Japan, but also romanticized as larger-than-life characters in popular culture, such as Kabuki (traditional theater) plays and gangster movies made by Toei Co., Ltd. in the 1960s. Gang members enhance their notoriety by getting elaborate tattoos that cover most of their bodies. See also FILM; GAMBLING; KABUKI; PROSTITUTION; TATTOO; TOKUGAWA SHOGUNATE.

YAMABUSHI See DEMONS AND GHOSTS; SHAMANS AND SHAMANISM.

YAMAGATA ARITOMO (1838–1922) A leading political figure of the Meiji (1868–1912) and Taisho (1912–1926) eras who organized the modern Japanese army. Yamagata was born to a samurai family in Choshu Province (modern Yamaguchi Prefecture) on the southern tip of Honshu Island. He joined with other young samurai from Kyushu in the anti-foreign movement of the 1850s and 1860s that defeated the Tokugawa Shogunate (1603–1867) and returned power to the emperor in the Meiji Restoration of 1868. Yamagata became one of the "Big Three" oligarchs who guided the dissolution of the feudal system that had governed Japan for nearly seven centuries.

The Meiji government gave top priority to developing the Imperial Japanese Army and Navy; in the 1880s Japanese defense expenditures comprised one-third of the annual national budget. Yamagata went to Europe to study military systems of the great world powers, and in 1870 he was appointed assistant vice-minister of military affairs. Yamagata modeled the Japanese army of 73,000 soldiers on the Prussian system of military organization, with a general staff, a staff college and a divisional structure. He also played a major role in establishing, over the objection of the samurai, a system of universal conscription to build a modern Japanese army. The samurai, who as the ruling class had been the only Japanese permitted to bear arms, did not like sharing this privilege with the members of the peasant class now being brought into the army. Yamagata believed it good that all citizens of Japan would now live up to the ideals of discipline and loyalty embodied in the samurai code, known as *Bushido*. In 1877 Yamagata successfully commanded the new conscript army to defeat the Satsuma Rebellion, by disgruntled samurai under Saigo Takamori (1827–1877). During his career Yamagata held the high military positions of army minister, chief of the General Staff, and field marshal.

In 1882 Yamagata turned to the political sphere and became president of the Board of Legislation (Sanjiin), a branch of the civil bureaucracy. He also served twice as home minister, twice as premier, and three times as president of the Privy Council. In these positions he helped organize the civil bureaucracy and prepare the new Japanese Constitution. He also modernized the Japanese police system and supported a new system of local government that was instituted 1888–1890. Yamagata was responsible for the Imperial Rescript to Soldiers and Sailors of 1882, a code of conduct that also placed the military under the emperor's direct command and thus protected it from outside influence. When the first Japanese constitution (1889) was developed by Ito Hirobumi (1841–1909), the first prime minister of Japan, Yamagata also ensured that the military would be free of influence from political parties. Yamagata was named commander of the First Army in the Sino-Japanese War of 1894–1895, but illness forced him to leave the field and serve as army minister in Tokyo. During the Russo-Japanese War (1904–1905), Yamagata served as chief of the General Staff. He supported the Anglo-Japanese Alliance of 1902, as well as friendly relations with Russia, China and the United States, and opposed the Twenty-one Demands that Japan forced on China in 1915. In 1907 Yamagata was honored with the title of prince *(koshaku)*. Until his death in 1922, Yamagata was the preeminent member of the body of senior statesmen known as *genro*, and had great influence on government affairs, particularly in choosing prime ministers. See also ANGLO-JAPANESE ALLIANCE; CONSTITUTION, MEIJI (1889); GENRO; IMPERIAL JAPANESE ARMY AND NAVY; ITO HIROBUMI; MEIJI RESTORATION OF 1868; RUSSO-JAPANESE WAR; SAIGO TAKAMORI; SATSUMA REBELLION; SINO-JAPANESE WAR OF 1894–1895.

YAMAGUCHI PREFECTURE   See CHOSHU PROVINCE.

YAMAHA MOTOR CO., LTD.   See MOTORCYCLE INDUSTRY.

YAMAICHI SECURITIES CO., LTD.   See SECURITIES COMPANIES.

YAMAMOTO ISOROKU (1884–1943)   A naval officer who was commander in chief of the Japanese Combined Fleet during World War II. Yamamoto planned the surprise attack that destroyed much of the American naval fleet at Pearl Harbor on December 7, 1941.

Born into a family named Takano in Nagaoka, Niigata Prefecture, he was later adopted into the Yamamoto family. After attending the Japanese Naval Academy, he served in the Russo-Japanese War (1904–1905), receiving a wound during the Battle of Tsushima in which Japan destroyed the Russian Baltic fleet. Yamamoto spent some years at sea, then graduated from the Japanese Naval War College in 1916. He later commanded an aircraft carrier, which gave him an interest in naval aviation, and helped developed the long-range bomber known as the Zero fighter. He also studied at Harvard University and served as naval attache at the Japanese embassy in Washington, D.C. (1926–1928). In this post he became familiar with American naval power and foresaw that, while relations between the United States and Japan were at the breaking point over Japanese aggression in Asia, it would be a hopeless cause if Japan went to war with the United States. Despite Yamamoto's reservations, the navy minister appointed him commander of the Combined Fleet in 1940. Recognizing the inevitability of war between Japan and the United States, Yamamoto suggested the attack on Pearl Harbor, to give Japan an early, and hopefully decisive, advantage in the conflict. The Japanese navy won a series of victories in the Pacific theater, but the Japanese invasion of Midway Island in June 1942, planned by Yamamoto, ended in a stunning defeat for Japan that marked the turning point of the war. American forces began a counteroffensive in the Solomon Islands in August, 1942. Americans broke the Japanese military code and killed Yamamoto on April 18, 1943, by shooting down the plane that was taking him to inspect Japanese troops in the Solomons. The Japanese government honored Yamamoto with the posthumous title of fleet admiral. *Attack on Yamamoto* (New York: Crown/Orion) by Carroll V. Glines was published in 1990. See also IMPERIAL JAPANESE ARMY AND NAVY; PEARL HARBOR, JAPANESE ATTACK ON; RUSSO-JAPANESE WAR; WORLD WAR II; ZERO FIGHTER PLANE.

YAMANOTE LINE   See RAILROADS.

YAMATO   A general term applied to Japan as a nation and to things that are distinctly Japanese. Yamato is the ancient name of a province, known as Yamato no Kuni, on west-central Honshu Island that is now called Nara Prefecture. The name Yamato derives from the words *yama* (mountain) and *to* (place). It is also related to the name *Yamatai*, a region in western Japan. The Yamato Era is also referred to as the Kofun Era (c. 300–710) after the tomb mounds *(kofun)* that were built to bury members of the ruling class.

Japanese culture and a unified state governed by an imperial court developed in Yamato from the third through the eighth centuries. During the early Yamato era, a number of clans *(uji)* vied for power in western Japan. By the fifth century one clan, the Yamato, had gained ascendancy and began to establish a centralized power base known as the Yamato court *(Yamato chotei)*. This clan had migrated in the 1st century A.D. from the southern island of Kyushu up through the Inland Sea to the Yamato region. The Horse-Rider Theory held by many scholars maintains that the ruling clan came from Korea in the 4th century A.D. Clan legends claimed its divine descent from the Sun Goddess Amaterasu o Mikami through the first emperor Jimmu Tenno. The Yamato Court, particularly under Prince Shotoku (574–622), adopted many elements of Chinese culture and political organization to enhance its authority. This is known as the Taika Reform of 645–649. The term *Yamato* was used to distinguish Japanese things from Chinese. For example, *Yamato-e* means Japanese-style painting, as contrasted with *kara-e* or Chinese-style painting. Common *yamato-e* subjects include paintings of the four seasons *(shiki-e)*, scenes of famous places in Japan *(meisho-e)*, and activities of people in Heiankyo (later, Kyoto), the capital city starting in 794 A.D. *Yamato-e* were often visual representations of poems in the 31-syllable Japanese form known as *waka*, and were frequently painted on folding screens *(byobu)* or sliding door screens *(fusuma)*. Today, the term *Yamato-e* is also applied to painted handscrolls that are unrolled horizontally, known as *emakimono*, and to works of art in general that are an expression of Japanese aesthetics. The term *yamato-gokoro* or *yamato-da-mashii*, meaning "Japanese spirit," appeared in many texts during the Heian Era (794–1185), beginning with the novel *The Tale of Genji (Genji Monogatari;* 11th century). This term was revived in the late Edo Era (1600–1868) by scholars who opposed Japanese Neo-Confucianists who favored Chinese culture. Others, however, associated *yamato-da-mashii* with the phrase used by modern Japanese militarists and anti-Western nationalists, Revere the Emperor, Expel the Barbarians *(sonno joi)*.

The name Yamato was given to a battleship completed in 1941 by the Imperial Japanese Navy. It was 820 feet long and displaced 64,000 tons, the largest battleship ever built. The *Yamato* saw action in the Battles of Midway, the Philippine Sea and Leyte Gulf during World War II, and was sunk by Allied planes in April 1945. See also CLAN; CONFUCIANISM; GENJI, THE TALE OF; HEIAN ERA; HEIANKYO; IMPERIAL JAPANESE ARMY AND NAVY; JIMMU TENNO; KOFUN ERA; KOREA AND JAPAN; NARA; SCREENS; SCROLLS; SHOTOKU, PRINCE; WAKA; WORLD WAR II.

YAMATOTAKERU, PRINCE   See ATSUTA SHRINE.

YANAGI SOETSU (1889–1961)   Also known as Yanagi Muneyoshi; an art critic and founder of the Japanese folk crafts movement (*mingei undo*). Yanagi attended the Peer's School (Gakushuin) in Tokyo and graduated from Tokyo University in 1913. As a student he helped found the art magazine *Shirakaba*. In 1916 he made his first trip to Korea, where he was so impressed that in 1924 he founded the Museum of Korean Art in Seoul. He also supported the movement to free Korea from colonial rule by Japan. Yanagi admired simple everyday utensils created by craftsmen in both Korea and Japan and applied the term *mingei* (folk crafts) to such objects. Yanagi become a friend of Bernard Leach (1887–1979), an English potter who spent many years in Japan, and Hamada Shoji (1894–1978), a Japanese potter and friend of Leach. In 1926 the three men, along with Japanese craftsmen Tomimoto Kenkichi and Kawa Kanjiro, formally initiated the *mingei* (folk crafts) movement in Japan. They began collecting *mingei* objects and encouraging artists of the *mingeiha*, or folk crafts school, throughout the country. They also began publishing the magazine *Decorative Arts (Kogei)* in 1931. In 1936 Yanagi and his colleagues founded the Japan Folkcraft Museum (Nihon Mingeikan) in Tokyo. Yanagi made many trips to North America and Europe with Leach and Hamada, and also traveled frequently to other Asian countries. He presented a series of lectures on Asian art at Harvard University in 1929. Yanagi was a strong supporter of the culture and language of minorities in Japan, such the Ainu people on Hokkaido Island, and the Okinawan language in Okinawa Prefecture (Ryukyu Islands). Yanagi's collected writings were published in 10 volumes in 1954–1955. See also AINU; HAMADA SHOJI; KOREA AND JAPAN; LEACH, BERNARD; MINGEI; RYUKYU ISLANDS.

YANAGITA KUNIO (1875–1962)   The founder of Japanese folklore studies (*minzokugaku*). Yanagita was born in Hyogo Prefecture and educated in law at Tokyo University. His family name was Matsuoka, but he married into an important family and took his wife's family name, Yanagita. He wrote numerous literary articles in the early 1900s while also working in several government bureaucracies starting in 1900. In 1910 he published *The Legends of Tono (Tono Monogatari)*, a modern literary classic on folk beliefs. During the period 1910–1915 he became familiar with British folklore studies. Yanagita worked as a journalist for the newspaper *Asahi shimbun* between 1919 and 1930, after

which he decided to devote himself to developing the new field of folklore studies and began traveling throughout Japan to gather information about the country's folk traditions. He further attempted to systematize this information in order to determine exactly which customs found in the various regions of Japan are shared by all Japanese people. Yanagita's appreciation for Japanese folk traditions inspired later folklore scholars in Japan. He also influenced Yanagi Soetsu (1889–1961), who helped to found the Japanese folk craft (*mingei*) movement. Selected works from Yanagita's vast body of publications have been compiled in a 36-volume anthology, *Teihon Yanagita Kunio shu (Collected Works of Yanagita Kunio)*. *The Yanagita Kunio Guide to the Japanese Folktale* was edited and translated in 1986 by Fanny Hagin Mayer. See also FOLKLORE; MINGEI; YANAGI SOETSU.

YASAKA SHRINE   See SUSANOO NO MIKOTO.

YASHICA CO., LTD.   See CAMERAS AND PHOTOGRAPHY

YASUKUNI SHRINE   "Shrine of National Peace"; an important and sometimes controversial Shinto shrine in Tokyo dedicated to the spirits of Japanese soldiers and civilians who have died in wars at home and abroad since 1853. The shrine is situated on Kudan Hill on the north side of the Imperial Palace. Large *torii* (gateways) lead to its extensive grounds and fine buildings, including a Treasure House of war memorabilia. Yasukuni Shrine was built at the request of Emperor Meiji (1852–1912; r. 1867–1912) to honor Japanese who died in the struggle to reinstate imperial authority in the Meiji Restoration of 1868. Built in 1869, the shrine was originally named Shokonsha ("Shrine for Inviting the Spirits"), and was given its present name in 1879. Throughout its history, Yasukuni Shrine has been closely associated with Japanese emperors. The emperor sends his personal emissary (*chokushi*) to attend spring and autumn memorial services and rituals held when new groups of war dead are enshrined. Yasukuni Shrine functions as a national monument in Japan. It is the central shrine of State Shinto (Kokka Shinto), an institution created by Meiji leaders to promote reverence for the emperor and patriotic nationalism. The military leaders who seized control of Japan in the 1930s and brought the country into World War II used Yasukuni to heighten Japanese nationalism and militarism. Authorities of the Allied Occupation following the defeat of Japan in 1945 attempted to sever the ties between State Shinto and the Yasukuni Shrine. The 1947 constitution of Japan separating religion and the state also ended official government support for the shrine. During the past several decades, Yasukuni Shrine has been the center of political controversy. Against the opposition of Socialists, Communists, Buddhists and Christians, conservative factions led by the predominant Liberal Democratic Party (LDP) have attempted to restore government support for the shrine. In 1979, General Tojo Hideki (1884–1948) and six other World War II leaders who had been convicted and hanged by the war crimes trials were enshrined at Yasukuni. The visit to the shrine shortly afterward by Prime Minister Ohira Masayoshi (p.m. 1978–1980) and several cabinet members created a public outcry, because it seemed to sanction war criminals and violate the separation of religion and state. Controversy erupted again when Prime Minister Nakasone Yasuhiro (p.m. 1982–1987) also visited Yasukuni Shrine. See also EMPEROR; IMPERIAL PALACE; MEIJI RESTORATION OF 1868; NAKASONE YASUHIRO; OCCUPATION OF JAPAN; OHIRA MASAYOSHI; STATE SHINTO; TOJO HIDEKI; WAR CRIMES TRIALS; WORLD WAR II.

YAYOI ERA (c. 300 B.C.–c. A.D. 300) A prehistoric period in Japan when wet-rice agriculture was begun; people started turning from a nomadic life to a settled existence as farmers; bronze and iron weapons and utensils were first made, including mirrors and bells; and society became stratified into social classes. All these developments represented the introduction of Chinese and Korean influences into Japan. The name Yayoi comes from a district in the modern city of Tokyo where pottery from this era was first unearthed in 1884. Yayoi pottery differed from pottery of the previous hunting-gathering period, the Jomon Era (c. 10,000 B.C.– 300 B.C.), in having less decoration but more delicate and controlled forms. Typical Yayoi pottery is not glazed but smoothly finished inside and out, and often incised with lines around the middle of the pot. Yayoi pottery, along with knowledge of wet-rice cultivation brought by immigrants from China and Korea on the Asian mainland, originated on northern Kyushu Island, from where migrants spread these developments through western Japan. Yayoi culture eventually reached as far as the northern tip of Honshu, the main Japanese island. Chinese historical documents of the time record that a kingdom known as Yamatai ruled over 30 other regions in Japan, each of which was led by a local chieftain. This kingdom was controlled by the Empress Himiko in the second century A.D. The Yayoi Era was followed by the Kofun Era (c. 300–710), during which great tomb mounds (kofun) were built. See also AGRICULTURE; CHINA AND JAPAN; HIMIKO, EMPRESS; HONSHU ISLAND; IMPERIAL REGALIA; JOMON ERA; KYUSHU ISLAND; POTTERY; RICE; TOMB MOUND; YAMATO.

YELLOWTAIL FISH See TUNA; SASHIMI; SUSHI.

YEN The currency of Japan, now pronounced "en" in standard Japanese. En, meaning "circular" or "round," refers to the shape of the coins. Prior to the Meiji Era (1868–1912), many different monetary systems had been used in Japan. In ancient times, objects such as rice and cloth rather than coins were used as currency, in a barter system of trade. Some coins were minted in Japan as far back as the eighth century A.D., and for many centuries, Japanese rulers imported coins from countries such as China and Korea for use in Japan, but their values fluctuated. The warlord Toyotomi Hideyoshi, who unified most of Japan in the late 16th century A.D., minted large gold and copper coins. The Tokugawa Shogunate (1603–1867) standardized the Japanese monetary system and founded a gold mint (kinza), silver mints (ginza), and mints for copper, iron, and brass (zeniza), to make coins with set values. In 1636 the Tokugawa declared coins of the Kan'ei

Era (Kan'ei tsuho) as the official currency of the country, but they could not enforce this system. Many coins lost their face value, a number of regions in Japan began to print their own paper currency and Mexican silver dollars flooded into Japan after it was opened to the West in 1854.

The Meiji government (1868–1912) passed the New Currency Regulation of 1871 to stabilize the Japanese economy by making the yen the official monetary unit. It introduced a decimal system, denoting coins of 1, 5, 10 and 100 yen and notes of 500, 1,000, 5,000 and 10,000 yen. One yen was equal to one ryo, a traditional Japanese unit of weight for valuables such as gold, which became a standard unit of currency in the late 16th century. The law also put the yen on the gold standard, with 1 yen equivalent to 1.5 grams of gold, the same as one Mexican dollar, which was then the standard for trade throughout East Asia. In 1882 the Bank of Japan was founded to replace the former paper currencies, which no longer had value. Japan dropped the gold standard from 1917 to 1930, then used it for one year, and abandoned it again due to the worldwide economic depression. In April 1949, during the Occupation of Japan following World War II, the yen was fixed at the exchange rate of 360 yen to one U.S. dollar. In 1953 the International Monetary Fund (IMF) accepted this rate and declared the yen to be equal to 2.5 milligrams of gold. Japan began playing a larger role in international trade, and in 1964, it lifted restrictions on foreign exchange transactions. Japanese foreign trade grew so rapidly and the yen became so strong that in 1971–1973 the U.S. dollar was devalued against the yen. During the 1980s the yen continued to grow in strength (endaka, rise of the yen) against other currencies, becoming a major international currency for financial transactions. However, it became weaker in 1990, falling by more than 10% against the U.S. dollar in three months, along with the 25% decline in the Japanese stock market. See also MEIJI ERA; STOCK MARKET; TOKUGAWA SHOGUNATE.

YOKAN See BEANS; SWEETS.

YOKO ONO See ONO, YOKO.

YOKOHAMA An industrial and shipping center for Tokyo, the Japanese capital and largest city. Yokohama, Japan's second largest city, faces Tokyo Bay on central Honshu Island and is the largest port in Japan. The capital of Kanagawa Prefecture, Yokohama has a population of 3 million and covers 163 square miles. It was a fishing village until 1858 when the Harris Treaty was signed between Japan and the United States, opening Yokohama and several other Japanese cities to foreign trade. Communities of Western and Chinese merchants quickly grew there, and Yokohama now has Japan's largest Chinatown (Chukagai). In 1872 Japan's first railroad was opened, between Yokohama and Tokyo 17.4 miles away. Factories were built on land reclaimed from the Tsurumi River (Tsurumigawa) beginning in 1913. Although Yokohama was destroyed during the Great Kanto Earthquake of 1923 and again during World War II, it is completely rebuilt today. The cities of Yokohama and Kawasaki are known as the Keihin Industrial Zone. Some major industries there are automobiles, chemicals, electronics, food processing, petroleum, steel and shipbuilding. Many tourists come to Yokohama to see Chinatown, the Soto Zen Buddhist temple Sojoji, and Sankeien, a large landscape garden with traditional Japanese homes and teahouses. Yokohama is undergoing an ambitious urban redevelopment program under the Yokohama 21st Century Plan. See also EXPORTS AND IMPORTS; HARRIS, TOWNSEND; INDUSTRIAL ZONES; KAWASAKI; MINORITIES IN JAPAN; RAILROADS; NAMES OF INDIVIDUAL INDUSTRIES.

YOMIURI SHIMBUN See NEWSPAPERS.

YOSHIDA SHIGERU (1878–1967) The prime minister of Japan for five terms totalling seven years between May 1946 and December 1954; five of the seven years were under the Occupation of Japan following World War II. Yoshida was born in Yokohama, adopted into a wealthy family, and educated at Peers' School (Gakushuin) and Tokyo University. As a career diplomat, he served in various foreign-service positions, including ambassador to Italy and Great Britain. He gained access to high political circles through his wife, Makino Yukiko, a granddaughter of the important Meiji statesman Okubo Toshimichi (1830–1878), and a daughter of a close advisor to the emperor. Yoshida helped draft Japan's final offer to the United States in negotiations just before the two countries entered war. In September 1945 Yoshida became the Japanese foreign minister, and thus served as a link between the Japanese government and authorities of the postwar Occupation. He helped set up the meeting between General Douglas MacArthur and Japanese Emperor Hirohito (1901–1989), which convinced MacArthur not to abolish the imperial system. In 1946 Yoshida became president of the dominant Liberal Party (Jiyuto; now called the Liberal Democratic Party) and hence prime minister of Japan. His cabinets had to deal with such Occupation issues as land reform, purges of Japanese militarists and ultranationalists, labor laws, and the San Francisco peace treaty in 1952 that returned independence to Japan. The rearmament of Japan also began during his administration, but he resisted American pressure to increase the numbers and activities of the Self-Defense Forces. The United States did succeed in forcing Yoshida to recognize the Nationalist government on Taiwan, against the opposition of other political parties and the majority of the Japanese people. In 1952 political opposition began mounting against Yoshida, while he became more aloof and autocratic, gaining him the nickname, "One Man" (Wamman). During his fourth and fifth cabinets, starting in October 1952, Yoshida oversaw the revision of certain Occupation policies in Japan regarding the education and police systems, autonomy of local governments and economic measures against monopolies. The Mutual Security Agreement was signed between Japan and the United States in March 1954. That same year, Yoshida traveled to America on a failed mission to request economic aid for Asia. When he returned to Japan, he was removed as president of the Liberal Party and prime minister. See

also CABINET, PRIME MINISTER'S; EMPEROR; LIBERAL DEMOCRATIC PARTY; MACARTHUR, DOUGLAS; OCCUPATION OF JAPAN; POLITICAL PARTIES; PRIME MINISTER; SELF-DEFENSE FORCES.

YOSHIDA SHRINE See BEAN-THROWING FESTIVAL.

YOSHINO SAKUZO (1878–1933) A scholar and politician who was the main spokesman for liberal democracy in Japan during the Taisho Era (1912–1926). Yoshino was born to a merchant family in Miyagi Prefecture on the main Japanese island of Honshu and was educated in the city of Sendai. He converted to Christianity in 1898. From 1900 to 1904, he studied law at Tokyo University. Yoshino visited China in 1906 and studied in Europe from 1910 to 1913. When he returned to Japan, he joined the Law Faculty of Tokyo University and taught political thought there until he died in 1933. Yoshino wrote a series of articles on democracy for the Japanese magazine *Central Review (Chuo Koron)*. In a famous article written in 1916, "On the Meaning of Constitutional Government and the Methods to Perfect It," Yoshino advocated a form of representative government relying on the Meiji Constitution. By this he meant that the Japanese government is responsible for the welfare of the people, who can use elections to pass judgment on the government. Yoshino's notion that the people are the foundation of the state was criticized by right-wing politicians, who argued that popular democracy was incompatible with *kokutai*, the notion that the emperor is the source and ultimate authority for government in Japan.

Yoshino also concerned himself with practical reforms, such as universal suffrage for men, which was adopted in 1925. He attempted to increase the power of the House of Representatives, the lower house of the Japanese Diet (Parliament) whose members are elected, by calling for reform of the House of Peers, the upper house of the Diet, whose members were then appointed. Moreover, he called for restriction of the powers of the military high command, the Privy Council, the Prime Minister's Cabinet, and the *genro* (elder statesmen). Yoshino favored legalization and government regulation of labor unions and policies for social welfare, but he criticized left-wing politicians and labor leaders. In 1925 he supported the budding Socialist People's Party (Shakai Minshuto). Yoshino's greatest scholarly achievement was a 24-volume collection of historical documents from the Meiji Era (1868–1912), published 1927–1930 as *Meiji bunka zenshu (Complete Collection on the Meiji Era)*. See also CONSTITUTION, MEIJI (1889); DIET; GENRO; MEIJI RESTORATION OF 1868; POLITICAL PARTIES; TAISHO ERA; TOKYO UNIVERSITY.

YOSHIHITO, EMPEROR See HIROHITO, EMPEROR; TAISHO ERA.

YOSHIWARA A district of the city of Edo (modern Tokyo) licensed in 1617 by the Tokugawa Shogunate (1603–1867) for prostitution. The Tokugawa created the Yoshiwara as part of their plan to control all aspects of Japanese society. Most cities in Japan soon had licensed pleasure quarters, the largest of which were Yoshiwara, Shimabara in Kyoto and Shimmachi in Osaka. The name Yoshiwara, or "Reed Plain," refers to the swampy area that was filled in to build the district. Some other names applied to Yoshiwara were "love town," "play quarter" and the "nightless city" (fuyajo). The district was surrounded by walls and a moat, and customers entered through a "great gate" (omon) that prevented them from leaving without paying their bills and that prohibited the several thousand prostitutes from escaping their bondage to the brothel owners. Many of the women came from poor families and were indentured by their parents, for a price, to owners who kept most of them in debt their whole lives. A prostitute had the slim hope of miuke, or being bought out of her contract by an admirer. Arrangements between customers and brothels for prostitutes were handled by teahouses (hikitejaya). Yoshiwara became a lively entertainment center where the latest trends in fashion and the arts sprang up to please the tastes of wealthy urban merchants (chonin) who frequented the pleasure quarters. Although Yoshiwara remained the center of prostitution in Japan until the practice was outlawed in 1958, the district had lost its glamour by the turn of the century. See also COURTESAN; EDO ERA, GEISHA; KABUKI; PROSTITUTION; SAMISEN; TOKUGAWA SHOGUNATE; TOWNSPEOPLE; WOODBLOCK PRINTS.

YOYOGI PARK See HARAJUKU.

YUGEN The central aesthetic concept in Japanese arts from the 12th through the 17th centuries, such as poetry, painting, Noh drama, and even the tea ceremony and the design of gardens. Often translated as "mystery," yugen has to do with that which is mysterious, profound and not easily grasped or expressed in words. Some examples are mist on red maple leaves in autumn or a thin cloud veiling the moon. The origin of yugen was the Chinese term you xuan or yu hsuan meaning something that is too deep to see or understand. The concept was influenced by the Buddhist notion of absolute truth that cannot be grasped by the intellect. The 10th-century scholar Ki no Yoshimochi was the first to use the term yugen in Japanese literary criticism. In the 12th century, yugen became associated with another aesthetic concept, yojo, or "overtones." The most admired poetry of the time did not state things directly but made subtle and evocative associations. During the 13th and 14th centuries, the quality of elegant beauty was also added to the concept of yugen. Zeami (1363–1443), the greatest playwright of Noh drama, regarded yugen as the fundamental principle of the Noh theater. Actors and dancers having this quality are serene and elegant, and their beautiful form suggests rather than overtly expresses the meaning of the play. Noh drama is largely symbolic, with its central character frequently a ghost from the spirit world that can only be suggested or intimated, not directly represented. Sabi, another Japanese aesthetic concept became linked with yugen by the 13th century. Something that has the quality of sabi is aged, lonely, faded, imperfect. The philosophy of Zen Buddhism has had a great influence in developing these concepts, especially in the objects used in the tea ceremony. Although yugen and sabi were developed during the medieval age, they have continued to influence artistic activity in modern Japan. See also NOH DRAMA; PAINTING; POETRY; SABI AND WABI; TEA CEREMONY; ZEAMI; ZEN SECT OF BUDDHISM.

YUISHIKI SECT OF BUDDHISM. See HOSSO SECT OF BUDDHISM.

YUKATA A light, informal robe made of white cotton with blue, black or red dyed patterns. A yukata is similar to a kimono and has the same shape and is worn in the same way. The left side is crossed over the right and an obi, or sash, neatly tied at the back, holds the overlapping front sections together. Patterns on women's yukata are different from those for men and often have flowers or leaves. Men wear yukata with more abstract, geometric patterns. Ryokan (traditional Japanese inns) provide yukata for their guests to wear while staying there. Yukata are also worn at home to relax. A nemaki is a thin robe similar to a yukata that is worn for sleeping. Yukata can be worn outdoors in the summer. This type is of better quality and is worn with shoelike sandals (zori) or geta (sandals with two pieces of wood under the foot that elevate the feet off the ground). A flat fan (uchiwa) can be tucked into the sash to keep it handy on a hot summer day. See also FANS; FOOTWEAR; KIMONO; RYOKAN.

YUZEN DYEING A starch-resist method of dyeing textiles to create detailed colorful designs. This method, known as yuzen-zome, was invented by Miyazaki Yuzen, a fan painter in Genroku Era (1688–1704) Kyoto. Yuzen dyeing could be done on linen and cotton as well as silk, and so the method became very popular throughout the Edo Era (1600–1868), especially since members of the merchant class were prohibited by law from wearing silk. Yuzen was probably inspired by a paste-resist technique, known as bingata, used in the southern Ryukyu Islands which came under Japanese control in 1609. The traditional hand-drawn yuzen method (tegaki yuzen) begins with the drawing of a pictorial or graphic outline design with ink made from the spiderwort (tsuyukusa) plant on plain white fabric. The outline of the design is next covered with paste made from glutinous rice to protect it from absorbing the colored dyes that are to be applied. Soybean milk is then brushed on the fabric to prevent the design from blurring when colored dyes are brushed on. After the soybean milk dries, designs are painted in the outlined areas with a brush and colored dyes. The dyes are set by steaming the fabric. Next, the parts of the fabric that have been colored are covered with rice paste. Then dye is brushed on the fabric to color the base or background. The fabric is steamed again to fix the base dye, and then rinsed in running water to remove the rice paste. Panels of yuzen-dyed fabric were traditionally rinsed in Kyoto in the Kamo River (Kamogawa), so yuzen dyeing is also known as kamogawa-zome, and as Kyo yuzen. Today the fabrics are washed in large tubs of running water. Hand-drawn yuzen enables the subtle and delicate depiction of natural motifs beloved in Japan, such as flowers, maple leaves and birds. Because it is a very laborious and expensive process, some designers have begun to use a more economical method of *yuzen* dyeing that uses stencils *(kata yuzen)* to create the designs. A design is cut into specially treated paper to make a stencil *(katagami)*, the stencil is attached to the fabric, and then rice paste colored with dyes is brushed over the stencil. The paste goes through the stencil holes and dyes the fabric. Then the same steps are followed for rinsing, steaming and dyeing the background color. Ten to 50 stencils are usually required for a kimono design, although as many as 300 stencils have been used. A stencil-made design is not as clear as a hand-drawn one, but it enables *yuzen*-dyed textiles to be produced in large quantities. *Yuzen* designs may also be embellished with embroidery or gold leaf. The *yuzen* method is still practiced by some artisans in Kyoto and Kanazawa. Some contemporary *yuzen* dyers have been designated Living National Treasures by the Japanese government. See also GENROKU ERA; KIMONO; LIVING NATIONAL TREASURES; RYUKYU ISLANDS; STENCILS; TEXTILES.

YUZU   See CITRUS FRUIT.

Z

ZABUTON See PILLOWS.

ZAIBATSU A large industrial and financial combine in the period from the Meiji Era (1868–1912) to the end of World War II, in 1945. *Zaibatsu* is a combination of two terms meaning "wealth" or "finance" *(zai)* and "group" or "clique" *(batsu)*. The term *zaibatsu* was applied to these economic combines beginning in the 1920s, when they grew to enormous size. A great deal of Japanese wealth and political power was concentrated in fewer than a dozen *zaibatsu*, the top four of which were Mitsui, Mitsubishi, Sumitomo and Yasuda. By World War II, Mitsubishi was made up of around 250 corporations, and Mitsui some 300 corporations. Every *zaibatsu* was built around a central holding company owned and controlled by one family. The holding company directed the activities of the member companies and subsidiaries of the *zaibatsu*. Each *zaibatsu* had its own bank, which provided the financing for its member companies and subsidiaries, which were active in such fields as chemicals, manufacturing, mining, shipping and shipbuilding, and foreign trade. Each *zaibatsu* also had a trading company *(sogo shosha)* to handle exports and imports, and thus exercised considerable control over the domestic economy. The Allied Powers that occupied Japan after World War II felt that the *zaibatsu* were largely responsible for the Japanese militarism that had caused the war, and economic directives were issued in 1945 and 1946 ordering the dissolution of the *zaibatsu*; further regulatory laws were passed in 1947, to decentralize the Japanese economy. Under the new regulations, 2,000 high-level officers and 40 major stockholders of the largest *zaibatsu* were forced to give up their stocks and controlling power. Following the Occupation, many Japanese companies that formerly belonged to *zaibatsu*, such as Mitsubishi, Mitsui and Sumitomo, came together again for the purpose of increasing Japan's foreign trade. These new corporate groups, known as *keiretsu*, differ from *zaibatsu* in that although private they are not controlled by single families, and each corporation in the group functions with greater autonomy. See also CORPORATIONS; MITSUBISHI; MITSUI; OCCUPATION OF JAPAN; SUMITOMO; TRADING COMPANY, GENERAL.

ZAZEN See MEDITATION; ZEN SECT OF BUDDHISM.

ZEAMI (1363–1443) The greatest actor and playwright of the classical Japanese theatrical form known as Noh drama. Zeami's father, Kan'ami Kiyotsugu (1333–1384), led the famous Kanze troupe that traveled throughout western Japan performing *sarugaku*, a form of entertainment that Kanami developed into Noh. When the Kanze were invited to perform in the capital city of Kyoto in 1374, the shogun Ashikaga Yoshimitsu (ruled 1369–1395), a connoisseur of the arts, was so taken with Zeami that he brought him into his court. Zeami assumed the leadership of the Kanze troupe when his father died. In 1402 Yoshimitsu awarded him the name Zeami (also spelled Seami) as one of his "Companions of Art," replacing his theatrical name Kanze Motokiyo. During his career Zeami wrote dozens of Noh plays (which include music, singing and dancing) and adapted all previously written Noh plays according to his own philosophy. He also wrote 21 critical works in which he explained his theories of Noh. Zeami spoke of the "flower" *(hana)* that a great actor displays when he makes a well-known role seem fresh and new. He valued an aesthetic concept called *yugen*, which combines subtle beauty, mystery and graceful elegance. Zeami was influenced by the teachings of the Zen sect of Buddhism, which had been introduced into Japan from China and stimulated all of the Japanese arts. For him, Noh was a way of life that engaged the total being of the actor. Regarding what Zen terms "doing nothing" or "non-action" as the highest form of acting, Zeami transformed Noh from a theater of representation to one of symbolic suggestion. The main character in many of his plays is a spirit from the world beyond who expresses suffering that was endured in life and who resolves the pain in the dance that climaxes the drama.

In 1422 Zeami became a Zen Buddhist monk and passed the leadership of his troupe to his talented son Kanze Motomasa. However, the new shogun, Ashikaga Yoshinori, favored Zeami's nephew and rival On'ami. Motomasa died in 1432, two years after Zeami's second son, Motoyoshi, rejected Noh to become a Zen monk. Yoshinori exiled Zeami to the northern island of Sado in 1434, but he was allowed to return to Kyoto some years later. His son-in-law Komparu Zenchiku was the only one to succeed Zeami in his form of Noh drama. Zeami's plays and critical works have been translated into English by a number of scholars. See also ASHIKAGA SHOGUNATE; ASHIKAGA YOSHIMITSU; NOH DRAMA; YUGEN; ZEN SECT OF BUDDHISM.

ZEN SECT OF BUDDHISM *(Zazen)* A sect of Buddhism named for its emphasis on the practice of sitting in meditation *(zazen)*. Zen *(dhyana* in Sanskrit, *Chan* or *Ch'an* in Chinese) originated in India and was brought to China by the legendary monk Daruma (Bodhidharma), a popular figure in Japan. Zen was introduced into Japan from China in the 12th century A.D. There are two main branches of the Zen sect established by Japanese monks who studied Zen in China: Rinzai Zen, founded by Eisai (1141–1215), and Soto Zen, founded by Dogen (1200–1253). In contrast to other Buddhist sects, which offer salvation through faith in a deity, esoteric rituals, or knowledge of written scriptures, Zen emphasizes that *satori* (enlightenment) can be attained only by a person's own efforts, mainly through the practice of meditation. Zen Buddhism has had an enormous influence on Japanese culture. Traditional arts associated with Zen include Noh drama, ink painting and the tea ceremony, as well as the martial arts. Because Zen, which required discipline and strength of will, appealed to the military leaders who governed Japan during the Ashikaga Shogunate (1338–1573), they built many Zen temples throughout the country and patronized the Zen arts. In addition to Eisai and Dogen, some of the greatest Zen figures in Japanese history are Ikkyu Sojun (1394–1481), an iconoclastic monk, and the ink painters Sengai Gibon (1750–1837) and Hakuin Ekaku (1686–1769). Zen is the best-known Japanese religion outside Japan, due largely to Suzuki Daisetz Teitaro (1870–1966), a lay scholar who published extensively in English as well as Japanese and introduced Zen to the Western world. Numerous Zen scriptures and books by Zen thinkers, including Hisamatsu Shin'ichi (1889–1980), have been translated into English. Zen meditation centers have been established in many countries. See also ASHIKAGA SHOGUNATE; BUDDHISM; DARUMA; DOGEN; EISAI; HISAMATSU SHIN'ICHI; IKKYU; INK PAINTING; MARTIAL ARTS; MEDITATION; NOH DRAMA; SATORI; SUZUKI DAISETZ TEITARO; TEA CEREMONY.

ZENGAKUREN (Zen Nihon Gakusei Jichikai Sorengo) All Japan Federation of Student Self-Governing Associations; the national organization of the radical left-wing student movement in Japan. The Zengakuren formed as a national federation of individual self-governing associations (*jichikai*). These student governments operate in each department of a university, all students of which are automatically enrolled in its *jichikai*. Membership fees are paid out of the students' university tuition. Although the Zengakuren controls most of the *jichikai*, the hundreds of thousands of student members are not politically active.

The Zengakuren was founded in 1948 by student members of the Japan Communist Party (Nihon Kyosanto; abbreviated JCP). In 1958 the Communist League (Kyosan Shugisha Domei; known as the Bunto), which opposed the JCP, took control of the Zengakuren. After the turmoil in Japan in 1960 regarding the revised Security Treaty with the United States, the Zengakuren splintered into a number of rival federations. The faction favoring the JCP founded a new Zengakuren, which since 1964 has called itself the Minsei Zengakuren. Factions opposing the JCP were controlled mainly by the Kakumaru faction and an alliance known as the Three (Sampa) faction. Since this latter alliance dissolved in 1968, several other rival Zengakuren groups have vied for power, although the Minsei Zengakuren continues to be dominant. Some factions became violent ideological groups, such as the Red Army (Sekigun) and Revolutionary Marxist (Kakumaru) factions. Zengakuren factions played a major role in the student riots over the Vietnam War and American military bases in Okinawa that disrupted or closed many Japanese universities 1968–1969. Today they are relatively inactive and play virtually no role in campus life in Japan. See also JAPAN COMMUNIST

PARTY; RED ARMY FACTION; SECURITY TREATY BETWEEN JAPAN AND THE UNITED STATES; UNIVERSITIES.

ZERO DEFECTS   See QUALITY CONTROL CIRCLE.

ZERO FIGHTER PLANE (*Zerosen*)   The fighter plane used most frequently by the Imperial Japanese Navy in World War II. The plane was designed and built of a new light aluminum alloy by Mitsubishi Heavy Industries in 1937 to be used on aircraft carriers. This company was a branch of Mitsubishi, the largest Japanese *zaibatsu*, or industrial and financial combine. The plane's engine was built by the Nakajima Aircraft Co. More than 10,000 Zero fighters were produced altogether during World War II. The Japanese government accepted the Mitsubishi plane in July 1940 and named it the *Zeroshiki Kanjo Sentoki*, abbreviated as *Zerosen*. Its official name was Mitsubishi A6M2 "Zero-Sen" Navy Type O Carrier Fighter Model 21. Zeroes were first used to attack the headquarters of Chiang Kaishek in the Chinese city of Chongqing (Chungking) in August 1940. Modified versions of the Zero had 7.9-inch machine guns and a cruising range as long as 6 to 8 hours, which gave Japan an advantage in the Pacific during the first year after it attacked the U.S. base at Pearl Harbor, Hawaii, on December 7, 1941. However, America soon developed fighter planes superior to the Zero: they were studier and more heavily armed and could fly faster. By the end of the war, the Zero fighter was used for dive-bombing and suicide missions by the Kamikaze ("divine wind") Special Attack Force. See also KAMIKAZE; MITSUBISHI; PEARL HARBOR, JAPANESE ATTACK ON; WORLD WAR II; ZAIBATSU.

ZEROSEN   See ZERO FIGHTER PLANE.

ZITHER   See KOTO.

ZODIAC (*junishi*)   A calendrical system, introduced into Japan from China in the late sixth century A.D., that arranges the years in a repeating cycle of 12, with each year in the cycle being symbolized by a different animal. The Japanese traditionally believe that a person has the traits of the animal representing the year in which he or she is born. The animal signs originated in a legend about the Buddha, in which he asked all the animals to pay homage to him on New Year's Day, promising that he would give a gift to all who came and would name a year after them. Only 12 animals came; these were, in the order of their appearance before the Buddha, the rat (*ne*), ox (*ushi*), tiger (*tora*), rabbit (*u*), dragon (*tatsu*), snake (*mi*), horse (*uma*), sheep (*hitsuji*), monkey (*saru*), rooster (*tori*), dog (*inu*) and boar (*i*). The system of 12 animals was also traditionally used to indicate compass directions, to name days and to divide days into two-hour segments. The two hours before and after midnight (12 on a clock face and north on a compass) were the time period of the rat. Each cycle of 12 years was further associated with one of the five elements—wood, fire, earth, metal and water—to create a 60-year cycle. When the calendar has run through all five sets of 12 animals, for a total of 60 years, it starts at the beginning again. A person who has lived through an entire 60-year cycle is thought to be like a child once more and is given a special birthday party. See also CALENDAR; CHINA AND JAPAN; NAMES OF INDIVIDUAL ANIMALS.

ZOOLOGICAL GARDENS (*dobutsuen*) There are about 70 zoological gardens in Japan, around 30 of which are large enough to house more than 100 varieties of animals. The Ueno Zoological Garden, located in Ueno Park in Tokyo City, is the oldest and largest facility in Japan, with close to 1,000 species. Ueno Zoo was founded in 1882 as a research facility but soon attracted large crowds of sight-seers. The zoo's most popular attraction is its pandas, which were gifts to Japan from the People's Republic of China. Zoos were opened in the cities of Kyoto in 1903 and Osaka in 1915. Tama Zoo outside Tokyo features animals exhibited in a natural setting. This was the first Japanese zoo where lions were permitted to roam freely. Some zoos are modeled on safari parks in which the animals roam wild and visitors view them from buses or cars. The first Japanese safari park was opened in 1971 in Miyazaki Prefecture. See also UENO.

ZORI See FOOTWEAR.

BIBLIOGRAPHY

Abe, Masao, ed. *A Zen Life: D.T. Suzuki Remembered.* Tokyo: John Weatherhill, Inc., 1986.

Abegglen, James C., and George Stalk, Jr. *Kaisha: The Japanese Corporation.* New York: Basic Books, 1985.

Adachi, Barbara. *The Living Treasures of Japan.* Photographs by Peccinotti, drawings by Michael Foreman, foreword by Jo Okada, introduction by Bernard Leach, edited and designed by Derek Birdsall. Tokyo: Kodansha International, Ltd., 1973.

————. *The Voices and Hands of Bunraku.* Tokyo: Kodansha International, Ltd., 1978.

Agency for Cultural Affairs, Japan. *Japanese Religion.* Trans. Yoshiya Abe and David Reid. Tokyo: Kodansha International, Ltd., 1981.

Ames, Walter L. *Police and Community in Japan.* Berkeley: University of California Press, 1981.

Barrett, Timothy. *Japanese Papermaking: Traditions, Tools, and Techniques.* Tokyo: John Weatherhill, Inc., 1983.

Barron, R. and Iwao Tomita. *Financial Behavior of Japanese Corporations.* Tokyo: Kodansha International, Ltd., 1988.

Basho Matsuo. *A Haiku Journey: Basho's Narrow Road to a Far Province.* Trans. Dorothy Britten. Tokyo: Kodansha International, Ltd., 1981.

Bestor, Theodore C. *Neighborhood Tokyo.* Stanford: Stanford University Press, 1989.

Beauchamp, Edward R. and Richard Rubinger. *Education in Japan: A Sourcebook.* Reference Books in International Education 5. New York: Garland Publishing, 1989.

Bock, Audie. *Japanese Film Directors.* New York: Kodansha International, Ltd., 1978.

Bolitho, H. *Meiji Japan.* New York: Cambridge University Press, 1977.

Bowers, Faubion. *Japanese Theatre.* Westport, CT: Greenwood Press, 1976.

Brandon, James R., William P. Malm, and Donald H. Shively. *Studies in Kabuki: Its Acting, Music, and Historical Context.* Honolulu: University of Hawaii Press, 1978.

Britton, Dorothy, and Mary Sutherland. *National Parks of Japan.* Tokyo: Kodansha International, Ltd., 1981.

Bushell, Raymond. *The Inro Handbook: Studies of Netsuke, Inro, and Lacquer.* Tokyo: John Weatherhill, Inc., 1979.

Butow, Robert J.C. *Tojo and the Coming of the War.* Stanford: Stanford University Press, 1961.

Castile, Rand. *The Way of Tea.* Tokyo: John Weatherhill, Inc., 1979.

Cherry, Kittredge. *Womansword: What Japanese Words Say about Women.* Tokyo: Kodansha International, Ltd., 1987.

Coaldrake, W.H. *The Way of the Carpenter: Tools and Japanese Architecture.* Tokyo: John Weatherhill, Inc., 1990.

Cohen, Theodore. *Remaking Japan: The American Occupation as New Deal.* Ed. Herbert Passin. New York: The Free Press, 1987.

Collcutt, Martin, Jansen, Marius, and Kumakura, Isao. *Cultural Atlas of Japan.* New York: Facts On File, 1988.

Cooper, Michael, ed. *The Southern Barbarians: The First Europeans in Japan.* Tokyo: Kodansha International, Ltd., 1971.

Cort, Louise Allison. *Shigaraki: Potters' Valley.* Tokyo: Kodansha International, Ltd., 1980.

Costello, John. *The Pacific War.* New York: Rawson, Wade, 1982.

Curtis, Gerald L. *The Japanese Way of Politics.* New York: Columbia University Press, 1988.

Dalby, Liza. *Geisha.* Berkeley, CA: University of California Press, 1983.

A Day in the Life of Japan: Photographed by 100 of the World's Leading Photojournalists on One Day, June 7, 1985. Project directed by Rick Smolan, David Cohen. New York: Collins, 1985.

Doi, Takeo. *The Anatomy of Dependence.* Trans. John Bester. Tokyo: Kodansha International, Ltd., 1973.

———. *The Anatomy of Self.* Trans. M.A. Harbison. Tokyo: Kodansha International, Ltd., 1986.

Dower, J.W. *The Elements of Japanese Design: A Handbook of Family Crests, Heraldry and Symbolism.* Tokyo: John Weatherhill, Inc., 1971.

Draeger, Don. *The Martial Arts and Ways of Japan.* 3 Volumes. Tokyo: John Weatherhill, Inc., 1973–74.

Dumoulin, Heinrich. *Zen Enlightenment: Origins and Meaning.* Tokyo: John Weatherhill, Inc., 1979.

Duus, Peter. *Feudalism in Japan.* New York: Alfred A. Knopf, 1969.

Duus, Peter, Ramon H. Myers and Mark R. Peattie, eds. *The Japanese Informal Empire in China, 1895–1937.* Princeton: Princeton University Press, 1989.

Elison, George and Bardwell L. Smith, eds. *Warlords, Artists, and Commoners: Japan in the Sixteenth Century.* Honolulu: University Press of Hawaii, 1981.

Ernst, Earle. *The Kabuki Theatre.* Honolulu: University of Hawaii Press, 1974.

Famous Ceramics of Japan Series. 12 Volumes. Tokyo: Kodansha International, Ltd., 1981–1983.

Frederic, Louis. *Daily Life in Japan at the Time of the Samurai, 1185–1603.* Trans. E.M. Lowe. Tokyo: Charles E. Tuttle, 1972.

From the Country of Eight Islands. [Anthology of ancient and modern Japanese poetry.] Trans. Hiroaki Sato and Burton Watson. Seattle: University of Washington Press, 1981.

Glines, Carroll V. *Attack on Yamamoto.* New York: Crown/Orion, 1990.

Gluck, Carol. *Japan's Modern Myths: Ideology in the Late Meiji Period.* Princeton: Princeton University Press, 1985.

Great Japanese Art Series. 3 Volumes. Tokyo: Kodansha International, Ltd., 1982.

Grilli, Peter, ed. *Japan in Film: A Comprehensive Annotated Catalogue of Documentary and Theatrical Films on Japan Available in the United States.* New York: Japan Society, 1984.

Grilli, Peter, and Dana Levy. *Furo: The Japanese Bath.* Tokyo: Kodansha International, Ltd., 1985.

Gunji, Masakatsu. *Kabuki.* Rev. ed. Photographs by Chiaki Yoshida. Tokyo: Kodansha International, Ltd., 1985.

Hall, John. *Government and Local Power in Japan, 500 to 1700.* Princeton: Princeton University Press, 1966.

———. *Japan from Prehistory to Modern Times.* New York: Delacorte Press, 1970.

Hall, John, Nagahara Keiji, and Kozo Yamamura, eds. *Japan before Tokugawa: Political Consolidation and Economic Growth, 1500–1650.* Princeton: Princeton University Press, 1980.

Hall, John W. and Jeffrey P. Mass, eds. *Medieval Japan: Essays in Institutional History.* Stanford: Stanford University Press, 1974.

Hamabata, Matthews Masayuki. *Crested Kimono: Power and Love in the Japanese Business Family.* Ithaca: Cornell University Press, 1990.

Hardacre, Helen. *Shinto and the State, 1868–1988.* Princeton: Princeton University Press, 1989.

Hasegawa, Keitaro. *Japanese-Style Management.* Trans. R.D. Williams. Tokyo: Kodansha International, Ltd., 1986.

Heibonsha Survey of Japanese Art, The. 31 Volumes. Tokyo: Heibonsha; New York: John Weatherhill, Inc., 1972–1981.

Heine, William, *With Perry to Japan: A Memoir by William Heine.* Frederic Trautman, translator and annotator. Honolulu: University of Hawaii Press, 1990.

Heineken, Ty and Kiyoko. *Tansu: Traditional Japanese Cabinetry*. Tokyo: John Weatherhill, Inc., 1981.

Hendry, Joy. *Becoming Japanese: The World of the Pre-School Child*. Honolulu: University of Hawaii Press, 1987.

Hickman, Money, and Peter Fetchko. *Japan Day by Day*. An Exhibition Honoring Edward Sylvester Morse and Commemorating the Hundredth Anniversary of His Arrival in Japan in 1977. Salem, MA: Peabody Museum of Salem, 1977.

Hisamatsu, Shin'ichi. *Zen and the Fine Arts*. Trans. Gishin Tokiwa. Tokyo: Kodansha International, Ltd., 1974.

Hori, Ichiro. *Folk Religion in Japan: Continuity and Change*. Ed. Joseph M. Kitagawa and Alan L. Miller. Chicago: University of Chicago Press, 1974.

Hosoya, Chihirol, Nisuke Ando et al., eds. *The Tokyo War Crime Trial: An International Symposium*. Tokyo: Kodansha International, Ltd., 1986.

Huber, Thomas M. *The Revolutionary Origins of Modern Japan*. Stanford: Stanford University Press, 1981.

Hughes, Sukey. *Washi: The World of Japanese Paper*. Tokyo: Kodansha International, Ltd., 1978.

Ikegami, Kojiro. *Japanese Bookbinding: Instruction from a Master Craftsman*. Adapted by B. Stephan. Tokyo: John Weatherhill, Inc., 1979.

Imamura, Anne E. *Urban Japanese Housewives: At Home and in the Community*. Honolulu: University of Hawaii Press, 1987.

Iriye, Akira. *Pacific Estrangement: Japanese and American Expansion, 1897–1911*. Cambridge: Harvard University Press, 1972.

———. *Power and Culture: The Japanese-American War, 1941–1945*. Princeton: Princeton University Press, 1981.

Iriye, Akira and Warren I. Cohen, eds. *The United States and Japan in the Postwar World*. Lexington: University of Kentucky Press, 1989.

Ishinomori, Shotaro. *Japan Inc. (The Comic Book): An Introduction to Japanese Economics*. Trans. B. Scheiner. Tokyo: Nihon Keizai Shimbun, Inc., 1988.

Itoh, Teiji, ed. *The Elegant Japanese House*. New York: Photographs by Futagawa, Yukio. Tokyo: John Weatherhill, Inc., 1969.

———. *The Gardens of Japan*. Trans. R. Gage. Tokyo: Kodansha International, Ltd., 1984.

———. *Space and Illusion in the Japanese Garden*. Tokyo: John Weatherhill, Inc., 1973.

———. *Traditional Japanese Houses*. New York: Rizzoli, 1983.

Japan Bonsai Association. *The Masters' Book of Bonsai*. Tokyo: Kodansha International, Ltd., 1969.

Japan Economic Journal. International Weekly Edition, published by Nihon Keizai Shimbun, New York.

Japan Textile Design Center. *Textile Designs of Japan*. Tokyo: Kodansha International, Ltd., 1980.

Japanese Arts Library Series. 15 Volumes. Tokyo: Kodansha International, Ltd., 1977–1987.

Jeremy, Michael and M.E. Robinson. *Ceremony and Symbolism in the Japanese Home*. Honolulu: University of Hawaii Press, 1989.

Johnson, Chalmers. *MITI and the Japanese Miracle: The Growth of Industrial Policy, 1925–1975*. Stanford: Stanford University Press, 1982.

Kanada, Margaret M. *Color Woodblock Printmaking: The Traditional Method of Ukiyo-e*. Tokyo: Shufunotomo, 1989.

Kawabata, Yasunari. *The Master of Go*. Trans. Edward G. Seidensticker. New York: Putnam Perigee, 1981.

———. *Snow Country*. Trans. Edward G. Seidensticker. New York: Putnam Perigee, 1981.

———. *Thousand Cranes*. Trans. Edward G. Seidensticker. New York: Putnam Perigee, 1981.

Kawahara, Toshiaki. *Hirohito and His Times.* Tokyo: Kodansha International, Ltd., 1990.

Kawakita, Michiaki, Seiko Hokama, Yoshinobu Tokugawa, Hirokazu Arakawa, and Yoshitaro Kamakura. *Craft Treasures of Okinawa.* The National Museum of Modern Art, Kyoto. Trans. and adapted by Erika Kaneko. Tokyo: Kodansha International, Ltd., 1978.

Kawashima, Chuji. *Minka: Traditional Houses of Rural Japan.* Trans. L. Riggs. Tokyo: Kodansha International, Ltd., 1986.

Keene, Donald. *Appreciations of Japanese Culture.* Tokyo: Kodansha International, Ltd., 1981.

———. *Japanese Literature: An Introduction for Western Readers.* Tokyo: Charles E. Tuttle, 1977.

———. *Landscapes and Portraits: Appreciations of Japanese Culture.* Tokyo: Kodansha International, Ltd., 1971.

———. *No: The Classical Theatre of Japan.* Tokyo: Kodansha International, Ltd., 1966.

Keene, Donald, comp. and ed. *Anthology of Japanese Literature. From the Earliest Era to the Mid-Nineteenth Century, Volume I. Modern Japanese Literature: An Anthology, Volume II.* New York: Grove Press, 1955 and 1956.

Kerr, George H. *Okinawa: The History of an Island People.* Tokyo: Charles E. Tuttle, 1960.

Kinoshita, June, and Nicholas Palevsky. *Gateway to Japan.* Tokyo: Kodansha International, Ltd., 1990.

Kitagawa, Joseph. *Religion in Japanese History.* New York: Columbia University Press, 1966.

Kodansha Encyclopedia of Japan. 8 Volumes and Index. Tokyo: Kodansha International, Ltd., 1983. Supplement, 1986.

Koizumi, Kazuko. *Traditional Japanese Furniture.* Trans. A. Birnbaum. Tokyo: Kodansha International, Ltd., 1986.

Kokinshu: A Collection of Poems Ancient and Modern. Trans. L.R. Rodd. Tokyo: University of Tokyo Press, 1984.

Komparu, Kunio. *The Noh Theater: Principles and Perspectives.* New York: John Weatherhill, Inc., 1983.

Kondo, Hiroshi. *Sake: A Drinker's Guide.* Tokyo: Kodansha International, Ltd., 1984.

Kuck, Lorraine. *The World of the Japanese Garden.* Tokyo: John Weatherhill, Inc., 1968.

Kuiseko, Ryokushu. *Brush Writing.* Tokyo: Kodansha International, Ltd., 1988.

Kurosawa, Akira. *Something Like an Autobiography.* Trans. Audie E. Bock. New York: Alfred A. Knopf, 1982.

Lane, Richard. *Images from the Floating World: The Japanese Print.* New York: Putnam, 1979.

Leach, Bernard. *Hamada, Potter.* Tokyo: Kodansha International, 1975.

Lebra, Takie S. *Japanese Women: Constraint and Fulfillment.* Honolulu: University of Hawaii Press, 1985.

Lebra, Takie S., and William P. Lebra, eds. *Japanese Culture and Behavior: Selected Readings.* Rev. ed. Honolulu: University of Hawaii Press, 1986.

Lee, Sherman E. *The Genius of Japanese Design.* Tokyo: Kodansha International, Ltd., 1981.

Lehmann, Jean-Pierre. *The Image of Japan: From Feudal Isolation to World Power, 1850–1905.* London: Allen & Unwin, 1978.

Lidell, Jill. *The Story of the Kimono.* New York: E.P. Dutton, 1989.

Mass, Jeffrey P. and William B. Hauser, eds. *The Bakufu in Japanese History.* Stanford: Stanford University Press, 1985.

McCullough, Helen, ed. *Classical Japanese Prose.* Stanford: Stanford University Press, 1990.

McFarland, H.N. *Daruma: The Founder of Zen in Japanese Art and Popular Culture.* Tokyo: Kodansha International, Ltd., 1987.

Minear, Richard H., ed. and trans. *Hiroshima: Three Witnesses*. Princeton: Princeton University Press, 1990.

Miner, Earl. *An Introduction to Japanese Court Poetry*. Stanford: Stanford University Press, 1968.

Miner, Earl, Hiroko Odagiri, and Robert E. Morrell. *The Princeton Companion to Classical Japanese Literature*. Princeton: Princeton University Press, 1988.

Mishima, Yukio. *The Temple of the Golden Pavilion*. Trans. Ivan Morris. New York: Putnam Perigee, 1980.

Morita, Akio, E.M. Reingold and Mitsuko Shimomura. *Made in Japan: Akio Morita and Sony*. Tokyo: John Weatherhill, Inc., 1987.

Morris, Ivan. *The World of the Shining Prince: Court Life in Ancient Japan*. Middlesex: Penguin, 1964.

Morse, Ronald A., ed. *United States-Japan Relations: An Agenda for the Future*. Lanham, MD: University Press of America, 1989.

Mosher, Gouvernor. *Kyoto, A Contemplative Guide*. Tokyo: Charles E. Tuttle, 1982.

Munsterberg, Hugo. *The Japanese Print: A Historical Guide*. Tokyo: John Weatherhill, Inc., 1982.

Murasaki, Lady. *The Tale of Genji*. Trans. Edward Seidensticker. Tokyo: Charles E. Tuttle, 1984.

———. *The Tale of Genji*. Trans. Arthur Waley. New York: The Modern Library, 1960.

Nakamura, Kyoko. *Miraculous Stories from the Japanese Buddhist Tradition*. Cambridge: Harvard University Press, 1973.

Nakane, Chie. *Japanese Society*. Berkeley: University of California Press, 1970.

Nakano, Eisha and B.B. Stephan. *Japanese Stencil Dyeing: Paste-resist Techniques*. Tokyo: John Weatherhill, Inc., 1982.

Nakano, Mei. *Japanese American Women Three Generations, 1890–1990*. The National Japanese Historical Society. Sebastopol, CA: Mina Press, 1990.

Ogawa, Dennis M. *Kodomo no Tame Ni—For the Sake of the Children: The Japanese American Experience in Hawaii*. Honolulu: University of Hawaii Press, 1978.

Oh, Sadaharu and D. Faulkner. *Sadaharu Oh*. Tokyo: Kodansha International, Ltd., 1984.

Oka, Hideyuki. *How to Wrap Five More Eggs: Traditional Japanese Packaging*. Tokyo: John Weatherhill, Inc., 1974.

Okakura, Kakuzo. *The Book of Tea*. (Reprint of 1906 edition.) Tokyo: Charles E. Tuttle, 1956.

Okimoto, Daniel. *Between MITI and the Market: Japanese Industrial Policy for High Technology*. Stanford: Stanford University Press, 1989.

Okimoto, Daniel and Thomas P. Rohlen, eds. *Inside the Japanese System: Readings on Contemporary Society and Political Economy*. Stanford: Stanford University Press, 1988.

Omae, Kinjiro and Yuzuru Tachibana. *The Book of Sushi*. Trans. R.L. Gage. Tokyo: Kodansha International, Ltd., 1982.

Ono, Sokyo and W.P. Woodard. *Shinto: The Kami Way*. Tokyo: Charles E. Tuttle, 1962.

Pacific War Research Society, The. *The Day Man Lost: Hiroshima, 6 August 1945*. Tokyo: Kodansha International, Ltd., 1981.

Picken, Stuart D.B. *Shinto: Japan's Spiritual Roots*. Tokyo: Kodansha International, Ltd., 1980.

Reed, William. *Shodo: The Art of Coordinating Mind, Body and Brush*. New York: Japan Publications, 1990.

Reischauer, Edwin O. *Japan: The Story of a Nation*. New York: Alfred A. Knopf, 1974.

———. *My Life between Japan and America*. Tokyo: John Weatherhill, Inc., 1986.

———. *The Japanese Today: Change and Continuity*. Cambridge, MA: Belknap Press of Harvard University Press, 1988.

————. *The United States and Japan.* 3rd ed. New York: Alfred A. Knopf, 1981.

Reischauer, Haru M. *Samurai and Silk: A Japanese and American Heritage.* Cambridge: Belknap Press of Harvard University Press, 1986.

Richie, Donald. *The Films of Akira Kurosawa.* Berkeley and Los Angeles: University of California Press, 1970.

————. *The Japanese Movie.* Rev. and expanded ed. Tokyo: Kodansha International, Ltd., 1982.

————. *A Taste of Japan: Customs and Etiquette.* Tokyo: Kodansha International, Ltd., 1985.

Roberts, Laurance O. *Roberts' Guide to Japanese Museums.* Tokyo: Kodansha International, Ltd., 1978.

Ryokan. *One Robe, One Bowl: The Zen Poetry of Ryokan.* Trans. John Stevens. New York: John Weatherhill, Inc., 1977.

Sadler, A.L. *The Maker of Modern Japan: The Life of Shogun Tokugawa Ieyasu.* Tokyo: Charles E. Tuttle, 1983.

Sansom, George. *Japan: A Short Cultural History.* Stanford: Stanford University Press, 1978.

————. *A History of Japan.* 3 Vols. Stanford: Stanford University Press, 1963.

Saunders, E.D. *Buddhism in Japan: With an Outline of Its Origins in India.* (Reprint of 1964 edition.) Tokyo: Charles E. Tuttle, 1972.

Schodt, F.L. *Inside the Robot Kingdom: Japan, Mechatronics and the Coming Robotopia.* Tokyo: Kodansha International, Ltd., 1988.

————. *Manga Manga: The World of Japanese Comics.* Tokyo: Kodansha International, Ltd., 1983.

Seidensticker, Edward. *Low City, High City: Tokyo from Edo to the Earthquake.* New York: Alfred A. Knopf, 1983.

————. *Tokyo Rising: The City Since the Great Earthquake.* New York: Alfred A. Knopf, 1990.

Sei Shonagon. *The Pillow Book of Sei Shonagon.* Trans. Ivan Morris. Middlesex: Penguin, 1981.

Seike, Kiyosi. *The Art of Japanese Joinery.* Trans. Yuriko Yobuko and Rebecca M. Davis. New York: Weatherhill, Inc., 1977.

Sen, Soshitsu. *Chado: The Japanese Way of Tea.* Tokyo: John Weatherhill, Inc., 1979.

Sharnoff, L. *Grand Sumo: The Living Sport and Tradition.* Tokyo: John Weatherhill, Inc., 1989.

Shimizu, Yoshiaki, ed. *Japan: The Shaping of Daimyo Culture, 1185–1868.* New York: George Braziller, Inc., 1989.

Shulman, Frank Joseph. *Japan.* World Bibliographical Series, Volume 103. Oxford: Clio Press, 1990.

Sievers, Sharon L. *Flowers in Salt: The Beginnings of Feminist Consciousness in Modern Japan.* Stanford: Stanford University Press, 1983.

Simpson, P. and Kanji Sodeoka. *The Japanese Pottery Handbook.* Tokyo: Kodansha International, Ltd., 1979.

Singer, Kurt. *Mirror, Sword and Jewel: The Geometry of Japanese Life.* Tokyo: Kodansha International, Ltd., 1981.

Slackman, Michael. *Target: Pearl Harbor.* Published in association with the Arizona Memorial Museum. Honolulu: University of Hawaii Press, 1990.

Smith, Henry, ed. *Learning from Shogun: Japanese History and Western Fantasy.* Santa Barbara: Program in Asian Studies, University of California, 1980.

Smith, Robert. *Ancestor Worship in Contemporary Japan.* Stanford: Stanford University Press, 1974.

Soho, Takuan. *The Unfettered Mind: Writings of the Zen Master to the Sword Master.* Trans. W.S. Wilson. Tokyo: Kodansha International, Ltd., 1986.

Sparke, Penny. *Modern Japanese Design.* New York: E.P. Dutton, 1987.

Spry-Leverton, Peter, and Peter Kornicki; Photographs by Joel Sackett. *Japan.* New York: Facts On File, 1988.

Statler, Oliver. *Japanese Pilgrimage.* New York: Morrow, 1973.

Statistical Handbook of Japan 1989. Tokyo: Japan Statistical Association, 1989.

Steiner, Kurt. *Local Government in Japan.* Stanford: Stanford University Press, 1990.

Storry, Richard. *A History of Modern Japan.* Baltimore: Penguin Books, 1960.

———. *The Way of the Samurai.* New York: Putnam, 1978.

Suzuki, Daisetz T. *Zen and Japanese Culture.* Princeton, NJ: Princeton University Press, 1970.

Suzuki, Takao. *Japanese and the Japanese: Words in Culture.* Tokyo: Kodansha International, Ltd., 1978.

Swann, Peter C. *A Concise History of Japanese Art.* Rev. ed. Tokyo: Kodansha International, Ltd., 1979.

Tanabe, George G. Jr. and Willa Jane Tanabe. *The Lotus Sutra in Japanese Culture.* Honolulu: University of Hawaii Press, 1989.

Tanaka, Ikko. *Japan Style.* Tokyo: Kodansha International, Ltd., 1980.

Tanizaki, Junichiro. *The Makioka Sisters.* Trans. Edward Seidensticker. New York: Putnam Perigee, 1981.

Ten Thousand Leaves: A Translation of Manyoshu, Japan's Premier Anthology. [planned in 4 vols.] Trans. Ian Hideo Levy. Princeton: Princeton University Press, 1981 [vol. I].

Totman, Conrad. *The Collapse of the Tokugawa Bakufu, 1862–1868.* Honolulu: University of Hawaii Press, 1980.

———. *Japan before Perry: A Short History.* Berkeley: University of California Press, 1981.

Tsuji, Kaichi. *Kaiseki: Zen Tastes in Japanese Cooking.* Foreword by Yasunari Kawabata, introductions by Soshitsu Sen, Seizo Hayashiya, photographs by Muneori Kuzunishi, Yoshihiro Matsuda, adapted by Akiko Sugawara. Kyoto: Tankosha; Tokyo: Kodansha International, Ltd., 1972.

Tsuji, Shizuo, with Mary Sutherland. *Japanese Cooking: A Simple Art.* Introduction by M.F.K. Fisher. Tokyo: Kodansha International, Ltd., 1980.

Tsunoda, Ryusaku, Wm. Theodore de Bary and Donald Keene, compilers. *Sources of Japanese Tradition.* 2 Volumes. Introduction to Oriental Civilizations series, Wm. Theodore de Bary, ed. New York: Columbia University Press, 1958.

Tsurumi, Kenichi, ed. *Collection of Traditional Japanese Folklore.* Bilingual Edition. Tokyo: Nihon Minwa Aiko Kai, 1988.

Turnbull, S.R. *The Samurai: A Military History.* New York: Macmillan, 1977.

Varley, H. Paul. *Japanese Culture.* 3rd ed., revised. Honolulu: University of Hawaii Press, 1984.

———. *A Syllabus of Japanese Civilization.* Rev. ed. New York: Columbia University Press, 1972.

Varley, Paul, and Kumakura Isao, eds. *Tea in Japan: Essays on the History of Chanoyu.* Honolulu: University of Hawaii Press, 1990.

Veith, Ilza. *Englishman or Samurai: The Story of Will Adams.* Lawrence, Kansas: Coronado Press, 1981.

Vogel, Ezra F. *Japan as Number One: Lessons for America.* New York: Harper and Row, 1979.

———. *Modern Japanese Organization and Decision-Making.* Berkeley: University of California Press, 1975.

Waley, P. *Tokyo Now and Then: An Explorer's Guide.* Tokyo: John Weatherhill, Inc., 1984.

Waley, Arthur. *The No Plays of Japan.* Tokyo: Charles E. Tuttle, 1976.

Warner, G. and D.F. Draeger. *Japanese Swordsmanship: Technique and Practice.* Tokyo: John Weatherhill, Inc., 1982.

Watson, William, ed. *The Great Japan Exhibition: Art of the Edo Period, 1600–1868.* London: Royal Academy of Arts, 1981.

Wilson, Robert A. and Bill Hosokawa. *East to America: A History of the Japanese in the United States.* New York: William Morrow, 1980.

Yamanaka, Norio. *The Book of Kimono.* Tokyo: Kodansha International, Ltd., 1982.

Yanagi, Soetsu. *The Unknown Craftsman.* Tokyo: Kodansha International, Ltd., 1972.

Yasuda, Kenneth. *Masterworks of the No Theater.* Bloomington: Indiana University Press, 1990.

Yokoi, Yuho and Daizen Victoria. *Zen Master Dogen: An Introduction with Selected Writings.* Tokyo: John Weatherhill, Inc., 1977.

Yonemura, Ann. *Japanese Lacquer.* Washington, DC: The Freer Gallery of Art, Smithsonian Institution, 1979.

Yoshida, Mitsukuni. *Forms, Textures, Images: Traditional Japanese Craftsmanship in Everyday Life.* Tokyo: Weatherhill/Tankosha, 1979.

Yoshino, M.Y. *Japan's Multinational Enterprises.* Cambridge: Harvard University Press, 1976.

Yuasa, Nobuyuki. *The Zen Poems of Ryokan.* Princeton: Princeton University Press, 1981.

Videocassettes and Color Slides

Faces of Japan. Series 1: Volumes 1–13; Series 2: Volumes 14–16. Documentary video packages (VHS/Beta). Ed. Telejapan/Linguaphone.

Japan Today. Video Library, 20 volumes. Telejapan/Linguaphone.

The Japan of Today Series. Color slides. Numbers 4–18. International Society for Educational Information.